3ds max™ 5 Bible

3ds max™ 5 Bible

Kelly L. Murdock

Wiley Publishing, Inc.

3ds max™ 5 Bible

Published by
Wiley Publishing, Inc.
909 Third Avenue
New York, NY 10022
www.wiley.com

Copyright © 2003 by Wiley Publishing, Inc., Indianapolis, Indiana

Library of Congress Control Number: 2002111136

ISBN: 0-7645-3703-2

Manufactured in the United States of America

10 9 8 7 6 5 4 3 2 1

1B/QT/RS/QS/IN

Published by Wiley Publishing, Inc., Indianapolis, Indiana
Published simultaneously in Canada

For general information on our other products and services or to obtain technical support, please contact our Customer Care Department within the U.S. at 800-762-2974, outside the U.S. at 317-572-3993 or fax 317-572-4002.

Wiley also publishes its books in a variety of electronic formats. Some content that appears in print may not be available in electronic books.

About the Author

Kelly Murdock has been involved with more computer books than he cares to count — to the point that he avoids the computer book section of the bookstore, except for the graphics section, which still remains an obsession. His book credits include various Web, graphics, and multimedia titles, including two previous editions of this book, *3ds max 5 Bible.* Other major accomplishments include *Master VISUALLY HTML and XHTML, JavaScript Visual Blueprint, Adobe Atmosphere Bible*, and co-authoring duties on two editions of the *Illustrator Bible* (for versions 9 and 10).

With a background in engineering and computer graphics, Kelly has been all over the 3D industry and still finds it fascinating. He's used high-level CAD workstations for product design and analysis, completed several large-scale visualization projects, created 3D models for feature films, worked as a freelance 3D artist, and even done some 3D programming. Kelly's been using 3D Studio since version 3 for DOS.

In his spare time, Kelly coaches Little League baseball, competes in sports, and is learning how to rock climb.

Credits

Acquisitions Editor
Tom Heine

Project Editor
Martin V. Minner

Technical Editor
Chris Murdock

Copy Editor
Paula Lowell

Editorial Manager
Rev Mengle

Vice President and Executive Group Publisher
Richard Swadley

Vice President and Executive Publisher
Bob Ipsen

Executive Editorial Director
Mary Bednarek

Project Coordinators
Jennifer Bingham
Ryan Steffen

Graphics and Production Specialists
Beth Brooks, Melanie DesJardins,
Brian Drumm, Joyce Haughey,
Heather Pope, Ron Terry

Quality Control Technicians
John Bitter, Tyler Connoley,
Susan Moritz

Senior Permissions Editor
Carmen Krikorian

Media Development Specialist
Megan Decraene

Proofreading and Indexing
TECHBOOKS Production Services

Cover Image
Anthony Stuart
Character image by Kelly L. Murdock
Model by Zygote Media

An empty canvas. A silent screen.

A loaded brush, a material palette.

A swish of the wrist, a click of the mouse.

A lump of clay, a panel of primitives.

There are many ways to create perfection, we just choose to use different tools.

To Angie, 2002

Preface

Whenever I withdrew to the computer room, my wife would say that I was off to my "fun and games." I would flatly deny this accusation, saying that it was serious work that I was involved in. But later, when I emerged with a twinkle in my eye and excitedly asked her to take a look at my latest rendering, I knew that she was right. Working with 3D graphics is pure "fun and games."

My goal in writing this book was to take all my fun years of playing in 3D and boil them down into something that's worthwhile for you — the reader. This goal was compounded by the fact that all you Max-heads out there are at different levels. Luckily, I was given enough leeway that I could include a little something for everyone.

The audience level for the book ranges from beginning to intermediate, with a smattering of advanced topics for the seasoned user. If you're new to Max, then you'll want to start at the beginning and move methodically through the book. If you're relatively comfortable making your way around Max, then review the table of contents for sections that can enhance your fundamental base. If you're a seasoned pro, then you'll want to watch for coverage of the features new to Release 5.

If you're so excited to be working with Max that you can't decide where to start, then head straight for the Quick Start. The Quick Start is a single chapter-long tutorial that takes you through the creation of an entire scene and animation. This Quick Start was included in response to some feedback from readers of the first edition who complained that they didn't know where to start. For those of you who were too anxious to wade through a mountain of material before you could create something, this Quick Start is for you.

Another goal of this book is to make it a complete reference for Max. To achieve this goal, I've gone into painstaking detail to cover almost every feature in Max, including coverage of every primitive, material and map type, modifier, and controller.

As this book has come together, I've tried to write the type of book that I'd like to read. I've tried to include a variety of scenes that are infused with creativity. It is my hope that these examples will not only teach you how to use the software, but provide a creative springboard for you in your own projects. After all, that's what turns 3D graphics from work into "fun and games."

Who Is Max?

Max is coming of age. Now with the number 5 attached to its name, it is starting to show some maturity. I'd say that version numbers are akin to dog years, which would place Max in its mid-30s.

Before we go any further, I should explain my naming convention. The official name of the product in this release is 3ds max 5 with a lowercase *m*, but rather than writing this name to refer to the product, I simply refer to it as Max with a capital *M*. This reference is a nickname given to a piece of software that has become more familiar to me than the family pets (whose names are Fuzzy and Curious, by the way). Note: I have not been successful in training Max to come when I call or to sit on command, but it will on occasion play dead.

One way we humans develop our personalities is to incorporate desirable personality traits from those around us. Max's personality is developing as well — every new release has incorporated a plethora of desirable new features. Many of these features come from the many additional plug-ins being developed to enhance Max. With Release 5, many features that were available as plug-ins for previous releases have been adopted by Max. Several new features have been magically assimilated into the core product. These additions make Max's personality much more likable, like a human developing a sense of humor.

Other personality traits are gained by stretching in new directions. Max and its developers have accomplished this feat as well. Many of the new features are completely new, not only to Max, but to the industry. As Max grows up, it will continue to mature by adopting new features and inventing others. I just hope Max doesn't experience a mid-life crisis in the next edition or two.

The Different Flavors of Max

Now that Max is starting to grow up, it is finding itself with something new running around the house — two kid brothers. These kid brothers have many of the same features and they kind of look the same, but they are unique in their own ways. These two kid brothers are gmax and Plasma, and both are subsets of Max designed for a specific market. gmax was created for game content creators, and Plasma was created for Web graphic professionals.

If you own Max, you have almost all the features that these other two products have (plus a whole lot more); and what you don't have, you can obtain and install as plug-ins. However, if you have one of these tools instead of Max and you're trying to learn some tricks from big brother, then you'll need to know where the boundaries are between the various products.

 Note   You could consider the older versions of Max as siblings as well, but I'd like to think of them as the school pictures from years gone by that really belong in a photo album, so they will not be included here.

3ds max 5

3ds max 5 is the featured product that this book covers and the base set of code that the other products are based on. It is the professional-level standard that includes the broadest set of features covering all markets.

Plasma

There is no arguing that 3D images and animations are very compelling, and more and more of them are finding their way to the Web; but the process of getting 3d images from a package like Max to a Web page has been difficult. Enter Plasma. Plasma makes it easy to create and deploy 3d images to the Web. It offers tight integration with Macromedia's Flash and Shockwave and makes pushing 3d content to the Web easy.

gmax

gmax is a version of Max that is easily available for download. It enables game-content creators to build custom worlds, characters, and weapons using the same tool that was used to create the game. gmax works with games that ship with a Game Pack. Game Packs allow players to modify their games and share them with other players. Because rendering is accomplished using the game engine, gmax doesn't include any rendering options.

About This Book

Let me paint a picture of the writing process. It starts with years of experience, which is followed by months of painstaking research. There were system crashes and personal catastrophes and the always-present, ever-looming deadlines. I wrote into the early hours of the morning and during the late hours of the night — burning the candle at both ends and in the middle all at the same time. It was grueling and difficult, and spending all this time staring at the Max interface made me feel like . . . well . . . like an animator.

Sound familiar? This process actually isn't much different from what 3D artists, modelers, and animators do on a daily basis, and, like you, I find satisfaction in the finished product.

Tutorials aplenty

I've always been a very visual learner — the easiest way for me to gain knowledge is by doing things for myself while exploring at the same time. Other people learn by reading and comprehending ideas. In this book, I've tried to present information in a number of ways to make the information useable for all types of learners. That is why you'll see detailed discussions of the various features along with tutorials that show these concepts in action.

The tutorials appear throughout the book and are clearly marked with the "Tutorial" label in front of the section title. They always include a series of logical steps, typically ending with a figure for you to study and compare. These tutorial examples are provided on the book's CD-ROM to give you a firsthand look and a chance to get some hands-on experience.

I've attempted to "laser focus" all the tutorials down to one or two key concepts. This means that you probably will not want to place the results in your portfolio. For example, many of the early tutorials don't have any materials applied because I felt that using materials before they've been explained would only confuse you.

I've attempted to think of and use examples that are diverse, unique, and interesting, while striving to make them simple, light, and easy to follow. I'm happy to report that every example in the book is included on the CD-ROM along with the models and textures required to complete the tutorial.

The tutorials often don't start from scratch, but instead give you a starting point. This approach lets me "laser focus" the tutorials even more; and with fewer, more relevant steps, you can learn and experience the concepts without the complexity. On the book's CD-ROM, you will find the Max files that are referenced in Step 1 of most tutorials.

I've put a lot of effort into this book, and I hope it helps you in your efforts. I present this book as a starting point. In each tutorial, I've purposely left most of the creative spice out, leaving room for you to put it in — you're the one with the vision.

Third time's a charm

This book is now in its third edition and, like aged cheddar cheese, is getting better with time. This edition posed an interesting dilemma. The last edition clocked in at 1,246 pages, which was the largest number of pages that can be bound into a paperback book. So, for this edition, I needed to rework and tighten the current content to make room for pages where the new features could be covered (this would have been easier if Discreet simply deleted a number of features, but for some reason, they didn't do that).

In tightening the current material, I looked for places where I could compile information into a succinct table placing all the information in one centrally located place. Another common element change was to streamline the figures by replacing a single figure that showed the entire Max interface with four side-by-side smaller images without all the clutter. I'm rather pleased with the results as it makes it easier to compare similar features or to visually interpret what changing a parameter does.

How this book is organized

Many different aspects of 3D graphics exist, and in some larger production houses, you might be focused on only one specific area. However, for smaller organizations or the general hobbyist, you end up wearing all the hats — from modeler and lighting director to animator and post-production compositor. This book is organized to cover all the various aspects of 3D graphics, regardless of the hat on your head.

The book is divided into the following parts:

✦ **Quick Start** — This single chapter (which is actually a chapter in Part I) is an entire animation project presented in several focused tutorials. It is designed to whet your appetite and get you up to speed and producing animations immediately.

✦ **Part I: Getting Started with 3ds max 5** — Whether it's understanding the interface, working with the viewports, dealing with files, or customizing the interface, the chapters in this part get you comfortable with the interface so you won't get lost moving about this mammoth package.

✦ **Part II: Working with Objects** — Max objects can include meshes, cameras, lights, Space Warps, and anything that can be viewed in a viewport. This part includes chapters on how to reference, select, clone, group, link, transform, and modify these various objects.

✦ **Part III: Modeling** — Max includes several different ways to model objects. This part includes chapters on working with spline shapes, meshes, polys, patches, NURBS, compound objects like Lofts and Morphs, and particle systems.

✦ **Part IV: Materials and Maps** — With all the various materials, maps, and parameters, understanding how to create just what you want can be difficult. These chapters explain all the various types and how to use them.

✦ **Part V: Cameras and Lights** — This part describes how to control cameras and lights, and also includes a chapter on advanced lighting.

✦ **Part VI: Animation** — To animate your scenes, you'll want to learn about keyframing, the Track Views, constraints, and controllers. I also cover Space Warps, expressions, and dynamic simulations in this part.

✦ **Part VII: Character Animation** — I cover creating and working with characters, bone systems, and skinning, and give complete coverage of the various Inverse Kinematics methods in this part.

✦ **Part VIII: Rendering and Post-Production** — To produce the final output, you can render the scene or composite it in the Video Post dialog box, as described in this part. In addition, this part discusses environments, Render Elements, Render Effects, network rendering, and raytracing.

✦ **Part IX: Adding Functionality with MAXScript and Plug-Ins** — This part provides details on using Max's scripting language, MAXScript, and on using plug-ins.

✦ **Part X: Appendixes** — At the very end of this book, you'll also find four appendixes that cover installation and system configuration, Max keyboard shortcuts, plug-ins exclusive to this book, and the contents of the book's CD-ROM.

Using the book's icons

The following margin icons are used to help you get the most out of this book:

Note boxes highlight useful information that you should take into consideration.

Tips provide an additional bit of advice that will make a particular feature quicker or easier to use.

Cautions warn you of a potential problem before you make a mistake.

The New Feature icon highlights features that are new to Release 5.

Watch for this icon to learn where in another chapter you can go to find more information on a particular feature.

This icon points you toward related materials that are included on the book's CD-ROM.

The book's CD-ROM and exclusive plug-ins

Computer book CD-ROMs are sometimes just an afterthought that includes a handful of examples and product demos. This book's CD-ROM, however, includes a full, working trial version of 3ds max 5. Max is an expensive piece of software to just play around with, but the trial version gives you 30 days to try out the software and gain some valuable experience. Appendix D, "What's on the CD-ROM," supplies the details of the content on the CD-ROM.

The CD-ROM includes a selection of 3D models that you can use in your projects if you choose. Many of these models are used in the tutorials. The CD-ROM also includes the Max files for every tutorial.

As a special bonus, the CD-ROM also includes several custom-built, exclusive plug-ins developed by Furious Research and Dave Brueck, one of this book's contributing authors. To find out more about these plug-ins, see Appendix C, "Exclusive Bible Plug-Ins."

Color insert pages

The possibilities of Max are endless, but there are many individuals and groups who have pushed the software a long way. As a sampling of the type of finished work that can be created, I've included a set of color insert pages that showcase some amazing work done with Max. The 3D artists represented in these pages give you some idea of what is possible.

Acknowledgments

I have a host of people to thank for their involvement in this major work. The order in which they are mentioned doesn't necessarily represent the amount of work they did.

Thanks to my family, Angela, Eric, and Thomas, without whose support I wouldn't get very far. I was recently playing a game with Eric and Thomas where we needed to guess the word on a card given some synonyms. Eric gave the hint that this is what Dad likes to do, and Thomas immediately blurted out, "Work on the computer!" so I guess I haven't hidden my work from my boys. The funny part of the story was that the word on the card was "groove." The moral of this story is that working long hours on the computer is okay as long as you know how to groove.

In the first edition, the task at hand was too big for just me, so I shared the pain with two co-authors. But for subsequent editions, I've decided to do all the updates solo (actually Dave was busy with a book of his own, so he also had better learn how to groove). I would still like to thank my former two co-authors, Dave Brueck and Sanford Kennedy, whose work, although overhauled, still maintains their spirits.

Another thanks goes to Kelvin Lau, who took over the work that Dave did on the exclusive plug-ins and managed to create some plug-ins of his own. These exclusive plug-ins by themselves make this book worth having.

Major thanks and choruses of gratitude go out to the editors at Wiley: to Tom Heine for steering the ship during a few corporate tidal waves; to Marty Minner, who project-managed this fastball, curveball, and screwball all at once; to Paula Lowell for her excellent copy editing input, and to Chris Murdock for taking on the technical editing of this monster while slaying some computer demons of his own. What a great virtual team we have here. Additional thanks go out to Carmen Krikorian and her co-workers in the media department for chasing down the required permissions and for compiling the resources for the CD-ROM, and finally, to the entire staff at Wiley who helped me on this journey.

The various people who work in the graphics industry are amazing in their willingness to help and support. I'd like to thank first of all David Marks and the entire Discreet beta team for getting me the product when I needed it and to Peter Nguyen for getting the product in my hands with hours to spare. I'd also like to thank Hou Soon Ming and the talented people at Zygote Media, Curious Labs, and Viewpoint Digital Media for many of their models, which make the examples much more interesting (you can only do so much with the teapot after all).

Finally, I'd like to thank the many artists that contributed images for the color insert pages for sharing their talent, knowledge, and vision with us. They are an inspiration to me.

Contents at a Glance

Contents

• •

Part II: Working with Objects   157

Chapter 5: Using Primitive Objects 159

Chapter 6: Selecting Objects and Setting Object Properties 183

Part IX: Adding Functionality with MAXScript and Plug-Ins   975

Part X: Appendixes   1019

Getting Started
with 3ds max 5

Quick Start: Animating a Space Shuttle Re-Entry

When you first got your hands on 3ds max, you were probably focused on one goal — to create cool 3D images and animations. I know many of you bought Max to make money, claim a tax write-off, earn a way to Hollywood, or impress your girl or boyfriend, but I'll just ignore those reasons for now. The goal is to create something cool.

If you've perused this book's Table of Contents or thumbed through its many pages, you've seen sections on modeling, NURBS, dynamics, and other topics. But if you're like me, you don't want to wade through tons of material before you have something to show off to Mom (actually, if you're like me, then you've opened straight to the special effects section, in which case you won't be reading this).

The purpose of this Quick Start is to give you a taste of what Max can do. This soaring view of the software from 20,000 feet is intended to show you the big picture before you delve into the details. It exposes you to the most common features and whets your appetite for the more in-depth chapters to follow.

This part of the book is intended for those new to the software. If you're an experienced user, then your mom is no doubt already impressed with your work, so you can happily advance to whichever chapter appeals to you. (Forgive me for catering to the "newbie," but we were all beginners once.)

The Fascination with Space

Space seems to be a major category for 3D artists and almost every artist's portfolio includes some sort of space scene. Whether it's a laser battle in the Gamma quadrant or a warp jump to the far reaches of the universe, there is something inspirational about the great unknown that captivates the realms of imagination.

Animating in Max isn't bound by reality. You can animate anything you can imagine, and I'll get to the unbelievable soon enough, but for this Quick Start I've elected to work with an example that is based loosely in reality. This example lets you play with a space shuttle. The tasks to be completed include the following:

✦ Import a digital model of the space shuttle into Max.

✦ Apply materials to all the different parts of the shuttle.

✦ Create a scene or environment to fly the shuttle around.

✦ Include a prop of the distance moon.

✦ Animate some jitter motion as the shuttle re-enters the atmosphere.

✦ Add a glow Render Effect to the underside of the shuttle.

✦ Render the final animation.

This Quick Start is divided into separate tutorials, with each tutorial containing a series of easy-to-follow steps. These steps are intended to show you the results of performing certain Max operations, but feel free to deviate from these steps to create your own results. Being creative and exploring the software is the best way to learn.

After each of the following tutorials, I saved the scene file. You can find these files on the book's CD along with the examples in the Quickstart directory.

Tutorial: Importing the shuttle model

Accurately modeling an object such as the space shuttle can take many months of skilled work, which brings me to my first tip of modeling—don't build it when it's already been done for you. You can find many repositories of digital models—from Web sites to software dealers, to the CD in the back of this book. An untold number of models exist, covering almost any possible subject matter you could think of. The difficult part is wading through all the available models to find the exact model you need, and if it doesn't fit your exact needs, you can always modify an existing model to fit your needs.

The space shuttle model was created and provided by Viewpoint Datalabs.

Follow these steps to learn the easiest method for modeling:

1. Reset the Max interface by choosing File ⇨ Reset, and click Yes in the alert box that appears, asking whether you really want to reset.

2. Insert the CD-ROM from the back of the book, then choose File ⇨ Import.

   The Select File to Import dialog box appears.

3. In the Files of Type drop-down list, select 3DStudio Mesh. Locate the Quickstart directory on the CD-ROM, and select the file named shuttle.3ds. Click OK.

   The 3DS Import dialog box appears.

4. Select the Merge Objects with Current Scene option, check the Convert Units check box, and click OK.

The shuttle model appears at the center of each viewport. The *viewports* are the sections of the interface that provide a view into the scene. The default viewports include Top, Front, Left, and Perspective.

5. Save the file by choosing File ➪ Save As (or press the Ctrl+S key) to open the Save File As dialog box. Select a directory in the Save in field where you want to save the file, type **Imported shuttle** in the File Name field, and click the Save button.

The name of the current file appears in the title bar of the Max window.

The imported shuttle appears as shown in Figure QS-1.

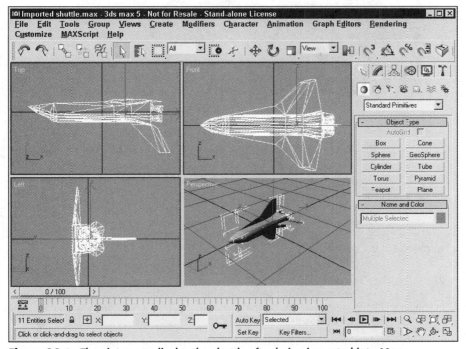

Figure QS-1: The viewports display the shuttle after being imported into Max.

Tutorial: Applying materials to the shuttle

Nice shuttle, huh? Try a quick smooth rendering in the ActiveShade window by choosing Rendering ➪ ActiveShade Floater to open the ActiveShade Floater and render the active viewport. Rendering the scene computes the effects of the lights, material, and environment into a single image. This process could take some time, depending on the complexity of the scene, but the ActiveShade window is a quick rendering window that lets you see the results of materials and lights. The results of the ActiveShade rendering show the shuttle model with simple tan-colored materials on a black background, which doesn't look very accurate. Well, don't worry; you're just getting started. You can close the ActiveShade window by clicking the close icon in the upper-right corner of the window.

The next step is to choose individual parts of the plane and apply different materials to each. So, the windows will be glass, the wings will be white, and the underneath tiles will be black.

To apply materials to the model parts, follow these steps:

1. To assign materials, you must first select the model parts. Open the Select Objects dialog box, shown in Figure QS-2, by choosing Edit ➪ Select By ➪ Name (or press the H key).

   Notice that the pane on the left displays all the various parts that make up this model.

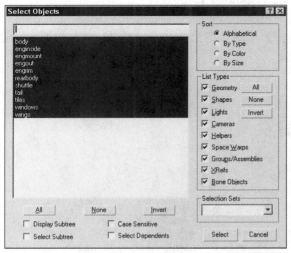

Figure QS-2: The Select Objects dialog box lists all the objects in the scene.

2. Double-click the part called "body" in the left pane. Doing so selects the part and causes you to exit the dialog box at the same time. Alternatively, click its name, then click the Select button at the bottom of the dialog box. (You can clear any selections by clicking the None button.)

   The shuttle fuselage will be highlighted white in the viewports.

3. Open the Material Editor by choosing Rendering ➪ Material Editor (or pressing the M key).

   The Material Editor, shown in Figure QS-3, allows you to create, edit, and apply materials to objects in the scene.

4. In the Material Editor, click the Get Material button (the small, leftmost icon button with an arrow pointing to a sphere).

   The Material/Map Browser dialog box, shown in Figure QS-4, opens. In it, you can load a library of preset materials.

Sample shots

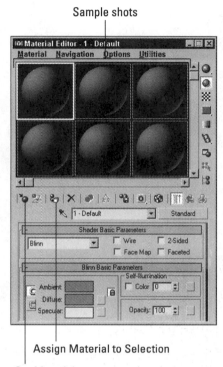

Assign Material to Selection

Get Material

Figure QS-3: With the Material Editor, you can create a vast assortment of materials.

5. In the Browse From section, select the Mtl Library radio button.

   Several File buttons appear at the bottom of the left side.

6. Click the Open button to access the Open Material Library dialog box. Using this dialog box, locate and select the quickstart.mat file from the Quickstart directory on the CD-ROM. Press the X button in the upper-right corner to close the Material/Map Browser.

7. For the selected fuselage object, select the white body material found in the second sample slot and apply it to the selected object by clicking on the Assign Material to Selection button (the third small button from the left that has an icon with an arrow pointing from a sphere to a cube).

8. Open the Select Objects dialog box (by pressing the H key) and select a different object, then select the appropriate material, as listed in Table QS-1 and apply it to the object.

9. Save the file by choosing File ⇨ Save As to open the Save File As dialog box. Type **Shuttle with materials** in the File Name field and click the Save button.

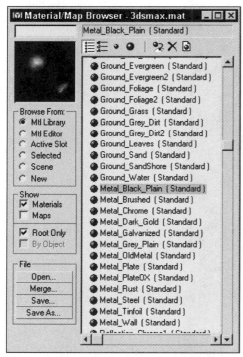

Figure QS-4: Use the Material/Map Browser dialog box to manage materials.

Table QS-1: Shuttle Material Assignments

Model Part	Preset Material
body	white body
enginside	engine fire
engmount	black tiles
engout	black tiles
engrim	white body
rearbody	black tiles
tail	white body
tiles	black tiles
windows	window glass
wings	white body

Figure QS-5 shows the shuttle model with all materials that you applied to it rendered in the Virtual Frame Buffer. This image was created using the Render Scene dialog box, which you access by choosing Rendering ➪ Render (or pressing F10).

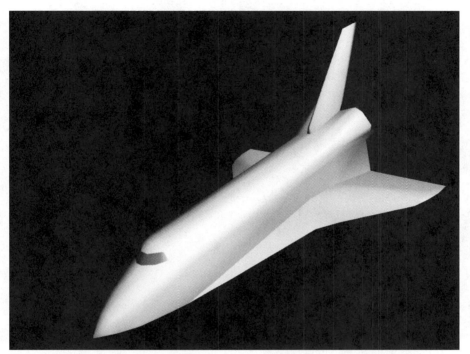

Figure QS-5: This rendered image shows how the shuttle looks with the materials applied.

Tutorial: Positioning the background environment

Okay, I have a confession to make. Earlier I mentioned that almost every 3D artist's portfolio has a space scene because space is such an inspiration. Well, the real reason that you usually see space scenes is that they are set in space, and space is a very easy backdrop to work with. You don't need to match up the object with the ground plane, and you don't need to worry about the perspective size of the objects in the scene. All you need are some stars and planets and a lot of dark black—no buildings, no trees, and no people. The same applies to sky and ocean scenes.

So, all you need to create a realistic space environment is a starry background. Now you could use Max to create an original image, but the easier method is to find a bitmap image of a space backdrop. Plenty of these types of images are available. After you locate a perfect space background image, then you need to include it as the background image in the current project.

You can use two separate commands for dealing with background images:

✦ **Views ▷ Viewport Background (Alt+B):** Displays an image as a viewport background. Be aware that you mainly use this background image just for aligning the objects to the background, and it is not included as part of the rendered image.

✦ **Rendering ▷ Environment (8):** Assigns a rendered background image called an *environment map*.

To add a background to a scene, follow these steps:

1. Open the Environment dialog box, shown in Figure QS-6, by choosing Rendering ▷ Environment (or press the 8 key). Enable the Use Map check box, and click the Environment Map button labeled "None."

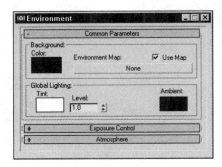

Figure QS-6: Use the Environment dialog box to set environment properties, such as a background image.

The Material/Map Browser dialog box appears.

2. In the right pane of the Material/Map Browser is a list of materials and maps. Double-click on the Bitmap item.

The Select Bitmap Image File dialog box opens.

3. Locate the background image named Space.tif in the Quickstart directory on the CD-ROM, and click it to select it. You will need to select the TIF image format in the File Type drop-down list for the image filename to appear.

When selected, the image will be shown in the Preview pane, as shown in Figure QS-7.

4. Click Open to load the background image.

5. Click the close icon in the upper-right corner of the Environment dialog box to close it.

6. Although a background image was specified, it doesn't show up in the viewport background. To make the environment map appear in the viewport, you need to open the Viewport Background dialog box, shown in Figure QS-8, by choosing Views ▷ Viewport Background (or pressing Alt+B).

7. Check the Use Environment Background and the Display Background check boxes and click OK.

The background appears in the viewport.

8. Save the file by choosing File ▷ Save As to open the Save File As dialog box. Save the file with the name **Shuttle with a space background** and click the Save button.

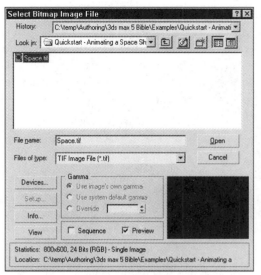

Figure QS-7: The Select Image File dialog box includes a preview pane to view images before opening them.

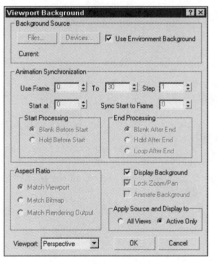

Figure QS-8: Use the Viewport Background dialog box to make background images viewable in the viewport.

Figure QS-9 shows the environment background in the active viewport. You can re-align the shuttle with the Rotate Arc tool found in the Viewport Navigation Controls in the lower-right corner of the interface and maximize the active viewport by clicking the Min/Max toggle (or by pressing Alt+W).

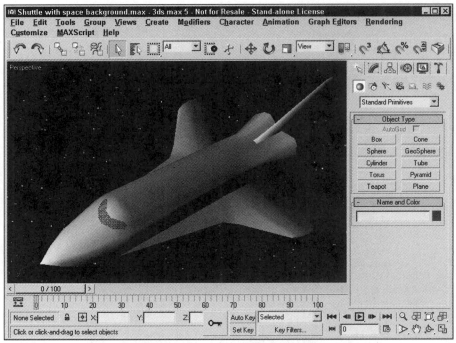

Figure QS-9: This maximized viewport displays the background image.

Tutorial: Grouping the shuttle objects

Before we add any more objects to the scene, we need to group all the shuttle objects together so we can move them as a unit instead of as separate objects. Right now if you were to click on the shuttle object and move it (which you may have already done; just choose Edit ➪ Undo or Ctrl+Z if this happens), you would only select and move a single part. And I hear that the shuttle doesn't fly too well without wings.

To group the shuttle objects together, follow these steps:

1. Select all the parts for the shuttle by choosing Edit ➪ Select All (or press Ctrl+A). Then group all the parts into one by choosing Group ➪ Group.

2. In the Group dialog box that opens, shown in Figure QS-10, give the group the name **shuttle** and click OK.

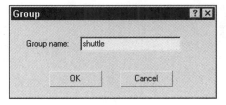

Figure QS-10: Use the Group command to group several objects together.

You'll be able to tell when objects are grouped because the white selection brackets will encompass the entire object set. In the Select Objects dialog box, grouped objects have brackets around them.

Tutorial: Adding a Moon Prop

The space background works to a small degree, but to really show off the motion of your shuttle, you need another background element in the scene. The moon model has been created (using a simple sphere primitive) and mapped with one of the default materials and saved as a separate file.

To load and position the moon prop, follow these steps:

1. Select the File ➪ Merge menu command. This opens a file dialog box. Locate and open the Moon.max file in the Quickstart directory on the CD-ROM.

2. In the Merge dialog box that opens, shown in Figure QS-11, select the Sphere01 object and click the OK button.

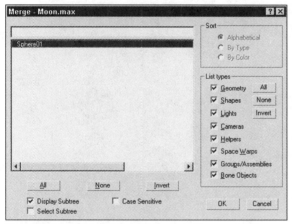

Figure QS-11: The Merge dialog box lets you add objects saved in other files to the current scene.

3. Save the file by choosing File ➪ Save As to open the Save File As dialog box. Save the file with the name **Shuttle and moon** and click the Save button.

Tutorial: Adding a Camera and Positioning Objects

With the shuttle and moon included, you've got all the pieces that you need, but you still need a camera to control the scene view. The Perspective viewport can be used to render the scene, but a camera will give you more control.

To add a camera to the scene and position the scene objects, follow these steps:

1. In the Create panel, select on the Camera category and click the Target button.

2. In the Front viewport, click on the lower-left corner and drag to the shuttle to create a camera in the scene.

3. Right-click on the Perspective viewport to make it the active viewport and right-click on the viewport title (in the upper left corner of the viewport) and select Views ➪ Camera01 (or press the C key) to make the viewport a camera view.

4. Using the Select and Move button (or press the W key) on the main toolbar and position the moon and camera objects relative to the shuttle as displayed in Figure QS-12.

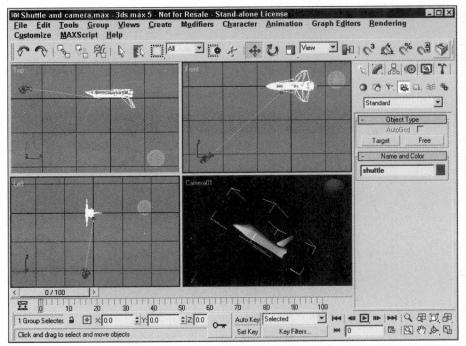

Figure QS-12: The Select and Move button can be used to place all the objects in their correct positions.

5. With the objects in the correct position, you may need to roll the camera about its axis. You can do this by selecting the camera viewport and dragging in the viewport with the Roll Camera button found in the Viewport Navigation Controls in the lower-right corner.

6. Save the file by choosing File ➪ Save As to open the Save File As dialog box. Save the file with the name **Shuttle and camera** and click the Save button.

With all the objects in their correct positions and a camera in place, you're ready to begin the animation phase of the project. There is typically another phase before you animate, which is to add lights to the scene. Space scenes such as this typically get their light from other sources like laser blasts or nearby suns, which is another reason why space scenes are so popular. For this Quick Start, the default lights are sufficient as a little bit of light will come from the glow effect.

Animating the Shuttle

Within a Max scene, you can animate many things besides the models, such as materials, lights, and cameras. Many ways exist to animate, as well. For this example, you won't create a lot of moving action, but you'll want to animate the shuttle to show the effect of falling through the atmosphere. Part of this motion is to cause the shuttle to vibrate as the animation progresses and the easiest way to do this is with a controller.

Tutorial: Creating random vibrating motion

To create the necessary motion with a controller, you'll need to apply and configure the controller to the shuttle object. You can then increase the impact of the controller over time.

To animate a vibrating motion using a controller, follow these steps:

1. Click on the shuttle object to select it and open the Motion panel. In the Assign Controller rollout, select the Position track and click the Assign Controller button (at the top of the rollout) and double-click on the Noise Controller to assign it. This opens the Noise Controller dialog box, shown in Figure QS-13.

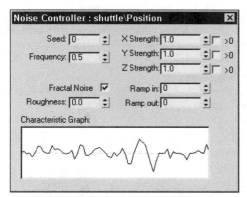

Figure QS-13: The Noise Controller dialog box lets you select the intensity of the jittering motion.

2. Click on the Auto Key button (at the bottom of the Max interface or press the N key) to enable auto-key creation mode (the red button and Time Slider reminds you that you're in this mode).

3. In the Noise Controller dialog box, set the X, Y, and Z Strength to 0.5. Drag the Time Slider to frame 100 (or press the End key) and set the X, Y, and Z Strength values in the Noise Controller dialog box to 2.0. This automatically sets keys that gradually increase the intensity of the vibrating motion as the animation progresses.

4. Click the Auto Key button again (or press the N key) to exit Auto Key animation mode.

5. Save the file by choosing File ⇨ Save As to open the Save File As dialog box. Save the file with the name **Vibrating shuttle** and click the Save button.

Tutorial: Adding a glow Atmospheric Effect

As the space shuttle careens through the atmosphere, the tiles on its underside begin to heat up as it impacts with the atmosphere. This causes a fiery glow to slowly appear. You can simulate this effect with an atmospheric effect. The intensity of this effect can then be animated over time.

To add a fiery atmospheric effect to the shuttle, follow these steps:

1. Open the Create panel and select the Helper category and the Atmospheric Apparatus subcategory. Click the SphereGizmo button and drag in the Top viewport to create two spherical gizmos.

2. Use the Select and Move (W) button to move and position the gizmos underneath the shuttle object. Then use the Select and Non-Uniform Scale (R) button to squash the gizmos along all three axes until it looks like a rounded pancake.

3. Since the shuttle will be vibrating around, you'll want to have these gizmos move with the shuttle's motions, so you need to link them to the shuttle. Click the Link button on the main toolbar and drag from each gizmo to the shuttle.

4. Select the Rendering ⇨ Environment menu command (or press the 8 key) to open the Environment panel. In the Atmosphere rollout, click on the Add button and select the Fire Effect item. In the Fire Effect Parameters rollout, click the Pick Gizmo button and select one of the gizmos. Then repeat this step for the second gizmo object, so two Fire Effects appear in the list.

5. Click on the Auto Key button (at the bottom of the Max interface or press the N key) to enable auto-key creation mode. Drag the Time Slider to frame 100 (or press the End key).

6. In the Fire Effect Parameters dialog box, set the Flame Size to 3500, the Density to 150, and the Flame Detail to 10. This automatically sets keys for these parameter changes. Repeat these changes for the second gizmo.

7. Click the Auto Key button again (or press the N key) to exit Auto Key animation mode.

8. Save the file by choosing File ⇨ Save As to open the Save File As dialog box. Save the file with the name **Re-Entry shuttle - final** and click the Save button.

Figure QS-14 shows the final frame of the re-entry shuttle including the fiery atmosphere effect.

Figure QS-14: The underside of the shuttle begins to glow red as it re-enters the atmosphere.

Rendering the Final Animation

Rendering the final animation can take a lot of time, depending on the output resolution and the power of your computer. The final output is started through the Render Scene dialog box, which you can open with the Rendering ⇨ Render command (or by pressing the F10 key). The Render Scene dialog box offers several options for customizing the output, but before we render the final output, let's create a preview animation to make sure that everything looks okay.

Tutorial: Creating a preview animation

Before we render the final scene, it is a good idea to produce a Preview animation. Doing so helps to eliminate some problems before the time is spent rendering the entire animation. The Preview is simply the viewport scene stitched together into an animation. The shading options are the same as those available for the viewports.

To create a Preview animation, follow these steps:

1. With the Camera01 viewport active, choose Animation ⇨ Make Preview.

   The Make Preview dialog box appears, as shown in Figure QS-15.

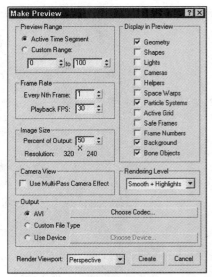

Figure QS-15: The Make Preview
dialog box can produce a quick look
at your animation sequence.

2. In the Make Preview dialog box, you can select the Active Time Segment, which will
include all frames in the animation. Set the Image Size to **50** percent and select the AVI
Output option. In the Display in Preview section, make sure to check the Geometry,
Lights, and Background check boxes.

3. Click the Create button.

Max begins the rendering, opens the default Media Player when finished, and plays the
preview.

4. Choose Animation ➪ View Preview to view the preview again, if desired. Figure QS-16
shows the preview playing in the Media Player window.

As you look at the preview, notice that the material maps and atmospheric effects aren't
included in the preview, but you can watch for the following types of errors:

✦ Objects moving through one another

✦ Insufficient lighting

✦ Erratic object (non-smooth) motion

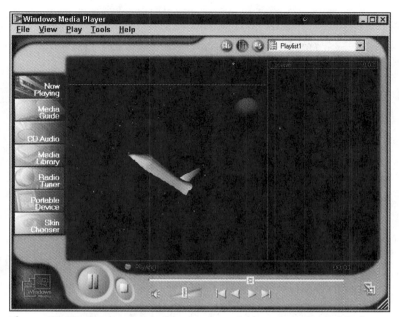

Figure QS-16: Preview animations render quickly and are viewed in the default Media Player window.

Tutorial: Rendering the final animation

After you've fixed all the errors and you're comfortable with the Preview animation, you can open the Render Scene dialog box and prepare your final animation for rendering.

To view the final animation rendering settings, follow these steps:

1. Open the Render Scene dialog box, shown in Figure QS-17, by choosing Rendering ➪ Render (or by pressing F10).

2. In the Time Output section, select Active Time Segment. In the Output Size section, select 320×240 as the resolution.

3. Next, we'll save the rendered scene to a file. In the Render Output section, click the Files button to open the Render Output File dialog box. Select the location to save the file, enter the name **Re-entry shuttle**, and from the Save as type drop-down list, select .AVI as the format. Click Save.

Tip   If you don't want to save the file, you can render the scene to the Virtual Frame Buffer. After the rendering is complete, you can save the animation by clicking the Save Bitmap button. The Virtual Frame Buffer can save animation and bitmap formats.

The Video Compression dialog box appears.

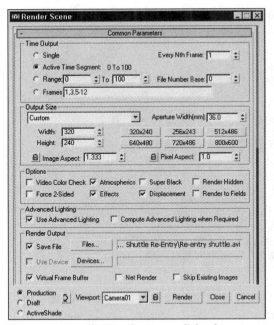

Figure QS-17: The Render Scene dialog box includes many diverse rendering settings.

4. Select the Cinepak Codec by Radius Compressor with a Quality setting of 100 and a Key Frame every 15 frames. Click OK to continue.

5. Back in the Render Scene dialog box, check the viewport setting at the bottom of the dialog box and make sure Perspective is selected. Then click the Render button to start the rendering process.

6. Save the file by choosing File ➪ Save As to open the Save File As dialog box. Save the file with the name **Final render** and click the Save button.

Figure QS-18 shows some frames from the final animation.

We could do much more to this animation, such as using lens effects or adding a motion blur, but I wanted to save some effects for the rest of the book. Feel free to load and modify this simple animation as you desire.

With the Quick Start completed, you're ready to dive into the features of Max, beginning with Chapter 1, "Exploring the Max Interface."

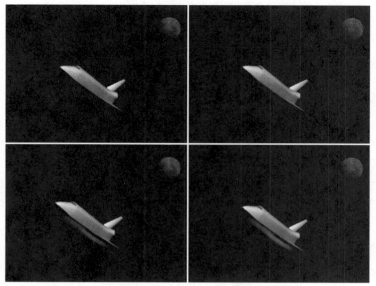

Figure QS-18: Four frames from the final animation of our shuttle fly-by

Summary

I hope you're happy with your first footsteps into Max. This chapter exposed you to a number of important aspects of Max including

✦ Opening a scene file and importing an object

✦ Selecting and applying materials to scene objects

✦ Loading a background image for the scene

✦ Grouping objects and merging a simple scene prop

✦ Adding a camera to the scene

✦ Animating the shuttle with a controller

✦ Using an Atmosphere Effect to create a fiery effect

✦ Rendering a preview and the final animation

But hold onto your seats because so much of the software lies ahead. In the first chapter, you'll start easily with an in-depth look at the Max interface. If you feel ready for more advanced challenges, review the Table of Contents and dive into any topic that looks good.

✦　　✦　　✦

Exploring the Max Interface

Well, here we are with a new version of Max, and the first question on the minds of existing users is "Did the interface change?" The answer is a gleeful "not much." Most serious users would rather go through plastic surgery than have their UI change, and although Discreet has learned and respected this valued opinion, there are some minor changes.

As you look around the new interface, you'll see that everything is still there. Some menu commands have been moved, some keyboard shortcuts have been altered, and a small collection of new icons and controls seem to have sprouted up, but for the most part it is all still there intact.

So, why is the software interface so important? Well, consider this: The interface is the set of controls that enables you to access the program's features. Without a good interface, you may never use many of the best features of the software or spend a frustrating bit of time locating it. A piece of software can have all the greatest features, but if the user can't find or access them, then the software won't be used to its full potential. Max is a powerful piece of software with some amazing features and, luckily, the interface makes these amazing features easy to find and use.

The interface is all about making the features accessible, and in Max you have many different ways to access the same command. Some of these access methods are faster than others. This feature is on purpose because it gives beginning users an intuitive command and an advanced user direct access. For example, to undo a command, you can choose Edit ⇨ Undo (requiring two mouse clicks) but as you gain more experience, you can simply click the Undo icon on the toolbar (only one click); an expert with his hands on the keyboard will press Ctrl+Z without having to reach for the mouse at all. All three of these methods have the same result, but you can use the one that is easiest for you.

Has the Max interface succeeded? Yes, to a degree, but like most interfaces, room always exists for improvement and each new version will hopefully take us closer to the perfect interface (but I'm still looking for the "balance your checkbook" feature). Discreet has built a loophole into the program to cover anyone who complains about the interface — customization. If you don't like the current interface, you can change it to be exactly what you want.

Cross-Reference   Customizing the Max interface is covered in Chapter 4, "Customizing the Max Interface."

This chapter examines the latest incarnation of the Max interface and presents some tips that will make the interface feel comfortable, not cumbersome.

Tip   If you are an existing user, I've made liberal use of the New Feature icon to highlight exactly what has changed, so you can quickly scan this chapter looking for the new stuff and then move on to the new, interesting, and powerful behind-the-interface features.

The Interface Elements

If you're new to the Max interface, then the first order of business is to take a stroll around the block and meet your new neighbors. The Max interface has a number of interface elements that neatly group all the similar commands together. For example, all the commands for controlling the viewports are grouped together in the Viewport Navigation Controls found in the lower right-hand corner of the interface.

Note   If all the details of every interface command were covered in this chapter, it would be an awfully long chapter. So, most commands will include simply a cross-reference on where to find more information.

The entire interface can be broken down into five easy elements. Each of these interface elements, in turn, will have groupings of sub-elements. The five main interface elements are listed here and shown in Figure 1-1:

✦ **Menus:** The default source for most commands, but also one of the most time-consuming interface elements. The menus are found along the top edge of the Max window.

✦ **Main Toolbar:** A toolbar of icons at the top of the Max window just under the menus, enabling one-click access to the most commonly used features.

✦ **Viewports:** Four separate windows into the scene showing the Top, Front, Left, and Perspective views.

✦ **Command Panel:** The major control panel located to the right of the four viewports. It has six tabbed icons at the top that you can click to open the various panels. Each panel includes rollouts containing parameters and settings. These rollouts change depending on the object and tab that is selected.

✦ **Lower Interface Bar:** Along the bottom edge of the interface window is a collection of many different miscellaneous controls.

Menus   Main Toolbar

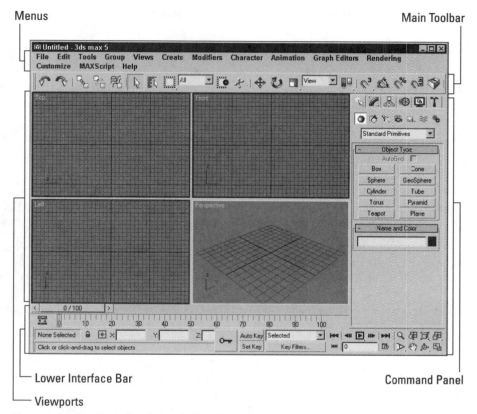

Lower Interface Bar   Command Panel

Viewports

Figure 1-1: Max includes five main interface elements.

In addition to these, available by default, controls are several additional interface elements that you will find useful. These controls aren't initially visible when Max is first loaded, but can be accessed by working with the interface. These additional interface elements include

✦ **Tab Panel:** An expanded toolbar divided into many tabs containing icons for every major feature. You can open the Tab Panel by using the Customize ➪ Show UI ➪ Show Tab Panel or by pressing the Y keyboard shortcut.

✦ **Floating Toolbars:** Two toolbars are available as floating toolbars — Axis Constraints and Layers. You access them by choosing Customize ➪ Show UI ➪ Show Floating Toolbars.

✦ **Quadmenus:** Right-clicking on the active viewport will make these pop-up menus appear. They offer context-sensitive commands based on the object or location being clicked.

✦ **Dialog Boxes and Editors:** Some commands will open a separate window of controls. These dialog boxes may contain their own menus, toolbars, and interface elements.

Cross-Reference

The additional interface controls are covered in more detail later in the section titled "Using the Additional Interface Elements."

Using the Menus

The pull-down menus at the top of the Max interface include most of the features available in Max and are a great place for beginners to start. Several of the menu commands have corresponding toolbar buttons and keyboard shortcuts. To execute a menu command, you can choose it from the menu where it resides, click its corresponding toolbar button if it has one, or press its keyboard shortcut.

The main menu includes the following options: File, Edit, Tools, Group, Views, Create, Modifiers, Character, Animation, Graph Editors, Rendering, Customize, MAXScript, and Help.

 New Feature   The Character menu is new in 3ds max 5.

If a keyboard command is available for a menu command, then it will be shown to the right of the menu item. If an ellipsis (three dots) appears after a menu item, then that menu command causes a dialog box to be opened. A small black arrow to the right of a menu item indicates that a submenu for this item exists. Clicking the menu item or holding the mouse over the top of a menu item makes the submenu appear. Toggle menu options (such as Views ⇨ Show Ghosting) change state every time they are executed. If a toggle menu option is enabled, a small check mark appears to its left and if disabled, no check mark appears.

You can also navigate the menus using the keyboard by pressing the Alt key by itself. Doing so selects the File menu, and then you can use the arrow keys to move up and down and between menus. With a menu selected, you can press the keyboard letter that is underlined to select and execute a menu command or you can navigate to a menu command and press Enter to execute that command. For example, pressing Alt, then F (for File) and N (for New) will execute the File ⇨ New command; or you could press Alt and then use the down arrow to select the New command and press the Enter key.

Not all menu commands are available at all times. If a menu command is unavailable, then it is grayed out and you will not be able to select it. For example, the Clone command is only available when an object is selected, so if no objects are selected, the Clone command is grayed out and unavailable. After you select an object, this command becomes available.

The File menu

The File menu includes commands for working with Max files. These commands enable you to create a new scene, open and save scene files, and work with externally referenced (XRefs) objects and scenes. You can also reset the scene, merge scenes, merge animation sequences, and replace objects in the current scene. The File menu also includes commands to import and export objects.

 Cross-Reference   Because most of the commands found in the File menu affect files, you can find information about these commands in Chapter 3, "Working with Files."

The Archive command copies all files used in the scene to an easily portable archive file format. The Summary Info and File Properties commands open dialog boxes where you can get information about the current scene file. The View Image File command opens a dialog box where you can view an image before loading it, and the Exit command exits the application.

The Edit menu

The Edit menu wins an award for having the most listed keyboard shortcuts per menu item of any other menu. It includes commands for recovering from mistakes (Undo and Redo), preparing for catastrophe (Hold and Fetch), and the ubiquitous Delete. The Hold command (Alt+Ctrl+H) saves the current scene in a buffer. This scene can be recalled at any time using the Fetch (Alt+Ctrl+F) command. The Edit menu also includes a Clone command for making copies of an object.

The Edit menu also includes several commands for selecting objects — Select All, Select None, Select Invert, and Select By Color and/or Name. You can also specify the type of selection region and whether objects are selected by dragging the cursor across the object (Crossing) or by enclosing the entire object in the dragged region (Window). The Named Selection Sets command opens a dialog box where you can name a selected set of objects for easy recalling. Finally, the Object Properties command opens a dialog box where you can find all the properties for the selected object.

To learn about the Undo/Redo and Delete commands, see Chapter 5, "Using Primitive Objects." The Hold and Fetch commands are covered in Chapter 10, "Using Modifiers." The Clone command is covered in (no surprise) Chapter 7, "Cloning Objects," and the remainder of the Edit menu commands are covered in Chapter 6, "Selecting Objects and Setting Object Properties."

The Tools menu

The Tools menu can be considered dialog box heaven because almost every menu command opens a dialog box. The Transform Type-In (F12) command opens a dialog box that lets you enter precise values for moving, rotating, and scaling objects. The Display Floater opens a dialog box where you can hide, freeze, and set the object display options. The Selection Floater opens a dialog box that lets you select objects by several different criteria. The Light Lister command opens a dialog box with details on all the lights in the scene.

A floater is a unique type of dialog box. It can stay open and active while you work in the background viewports. Other dialog boxes do not allow this and must be closed before you can continue.

The Mirror command uses the Mirror dialog box to create a symmetrical copy of an object across a designated axis. The Array command opens an Array dialog box where you can create multiple instances of an object with each instance offset from the others. The Snapshot command clones objects over time using the Snapshot dialog box. The Spacing Tool command (Shift+I) opens the Spacing Tool dialog box, which creates and spaces objects along a path.

The Tools menu also includes several ways to align objects. The Align command (Alt+A) opens an Align dialog box where you can line up objects by axis, edges, or centers. The Normal Align command (Alt+N) enables you to align the face normals of two objects. The Align Camera moves the selected camera in order to be directly in front of the point you select, and the Align to View command aligns the object to one of the axes. Place Highlight (Ctrl+H) moves the selected light in order to reproduce a highlight in the location you specify.

The Isolate Selection (Alt+Q) command hides all objects except for the selected object. It also opens a simple dialog box with an Exit Isolation button in it. Clicking this button or selecting the Isolate command again exits isolation mode and displays all the objects again. The Rename Objects command opens the Rename Objects dialog box where you can rename several objects at once.

The details on the Tools menu commands are spread across the rest of the book. For information about the Transform Type-In and the alignment commands, see Chapter 9, "Transforming Objects." The Display and Selection Floater dialog boxes and the Isolate Selection command are covered in Chapter 6, "Selecting Objects and Setting Object Properties." I discuss the Mirror, Array, Snapshot, and Spacing Tool commands in Chapter 7, "Cloning Objects"; the Light Lister and Place Highlight commands in Chapter 22, "Working with Lights"; the Align Camera command in Chapter 21, "Controlling Cameras"; and the Rename Objects dialog box in Chapter 5, "Using Primitive Objects."

The Group menu

The Group menu commands let you control how objects are grouped together. Selecting several objects and using the Group command opens a simple dialog box where you can type a name for the group. The Ungroup command disassembles the group and is only active if a group is selected. You can nest groups one inside another. You can also open groups, which enables individual group objects to be transformed or deleted. You can attach or detach objects from a group; the Explode command ungroups all nested group objects.

For a more complete examination of groups and grouping, check out Chapter 8, "Grouping and Linking Objects."

The Views menu

The Views menu includes commands for controlling the viewports. The Undo View Change (Shift+Z) and Redo View Change (Shift+Y) commands give you control over viewport changes, enabling you to undo and redo any changes made with the Viewport Navigation Controls. You can also save and restore each viewport's active view with the Save Active View and Restore Active View commands.

Keep in mind that Undo View Change (Shift+Z) is distinct from undoing changes made to the current object accomplished with the Edit ➪ Undo (Ctrl+Z) command.

Grids are helpful in establishing your bearings in 3D space. The Grids command opens a submenu with the following options: Show Home Grid, Activate Home Grid, Activate Grid Object, and Align Grid to View. The Viewport Background command (Alt+B) opens a dialog box in which you can select an image or animation to appear as a background behind a viewport. If the background image changes, you can update the viewport using the Update Background Image command (Alt+Shift+Ctrl+B). The Reset Background Transform command automatically rescales and recenters the background image to fit the viewport.

Next on the Views menu are several commands that control what is displayed in the viewport. If these commands are enabled, a check mark appears to the left of the command. The Show Transform Gizmo command displays axes and special handles to move, rotate, and scale the object in different directions. The Show Ghosting command displays the position of the selected object in the previous several frames, the next several frames, or both. The Show Key Times command displays frame numbers along the trajectory path where every animation key is located. The Shade Selected command turns on shading for the selected object in all viewports, and the Show Dependencies command shows any objects that are linked or instanced from a parent object.

The Match Camera to View command (Ctrl+C) repositions a selected camera to match the current scene (you first need to have a camera in the scene and selected). The Add Default Lights to Scene command converts the default lights to actual light objects in the scene. This feature lets you start with the default lights and modify them as needed.

Caution   The keyboard shortcut for the Match Camera to View command is Ctrl+C, which is the same as the commonly used Copy command in most other Windows programs. The concept of Cut, Copy, and Paste doesn't really work in Max and you might find yourself using this keyboard shortcut on accident occasionally. If you find that you've used this command incorrectly, you can use the Undo View Change (Shift+Z) to undo the change.

The Redraw All Views (keyboard shortcut, \) command refreshes each viewport and makes everything visible again (as objects get moved around, they often mask one another and lines will disappear). Activate All Maps turns on all maps, and Deactivate All Maps turns off all maps. Material maps can take up a lot of memory and can slow down the viewport rendering. Update During Spinner Drag causes a viewport to interactively show the results of a parameter value change set with spinner controls. Spinners are controls with up and down arrows to their right and can be changed by clicking and dragging on the control. The Adaptive Degradation Toggle (O) is an option that enables the animation to degrade the image resolution (by downgrading the rendering method) in order to maintain a consistent frame rate. This can help when you're trying to perfect the timing of an animation sequence and you don't need the prettiest looking images in the viewports.

New Feature   Although adaptive degradation isn't new, it is new as a menu command in 3ds max 5.

The Expert Mode command (Ctrl+X) maximizes viewport space by removing the menus, Main Toolbar, Command Panel, Viewport Navigation buttons, status bar, and prompt line from the interface.

Cross-Reference   Most of the Views menu commands are covered in detail in Chapter 2, "Working with the Viewports," except for the grid commands and the Transform Gizmo, which are covered in Chapter 9, "Transforming Objects"; and Ghosting and Key Times, which are covered in Chapter 24, "Animation Basics." Dependencies are covered in Chapter 8, "Grouping and Linking Objects"; Match Camera to View is covered in Chapter 21, "Controlling Cameras"; Adding Default Lights to Scene is covered in Chapter 22, "Working with Lights"; and activating and deactivating maps are covered in Chapter 20, "Using Material Maps."

The Create menu

The Create menu includes an easy way to create objects without your having to access the Create tab in the Command Panel. Selecting an object from the Create menu automatically opens the Create panel and selects the correct category, subcategory, and button needed to create the object. After selecting the menu option, you simply need to click in one of the viewports to create the object.

The Create menu includes several categories, and you can find a corresponding button for each submenu item in the Command Panel. Table 1-1 lists the Create menu and submenus.

Table 1-1: Create Menu Items

Menu	Submenu Items
Standard Primitives	Box, Cone, Sphere, GeoSphere, Cylinder, Tube, Torus, Pyramid, Plane, Teapot
Extended Primitives	Hedra, Torus Knot, Chamfer Box, Chamfer Cylinder, Oil Tank, Capsule, Spindle, L-Extrusion, Gengon, E-Extrusion, RingWave, Hose, Prism
Shapes	Line, Text, Arc, Circle, Donut, Ellipse, Helix, NGon, Rectangle, Section, Star
Lights	Target Spotlight, Free Spotlight, Target Directional Light, Directional Light, Omni Light, Skylight, Target Point, Free Point, Target Linear, Free Linear, Target Area, Free Area, IES Sky, IES Sun, Sunlight System, Daylight
Cameras	Free Camera, Target Camera
Particles	Blizzard, PArray, PCloud, Snow, Spray, Super Spray

Cross-Reference   You can learn about primitives in Chapter 5, "Using Primitive Objects"l shapes in Chapter 12, "Drawing and Using 2D Splines and Shapes"; lights in Chapter 22, "Working with Lights"; and particles in Chapter 17, "Creating and Controlling Particle Systems."

The Modifiers menu

The Modifiers menu offers a way to apply modifiers without your having to go to the Modify panel. Before you can apply a modifier, you must select an object. Only the modifiers that you can apply to the selected object will be enabled.

Selecting a modifier from the Modifiers menu automatically opens the Modify panel, in which you can adjust the Parameters for the applied modifier. The modifiers in the Modifiers menu are grouped into several categories listed in Table 1-2.

Cross-Reference   Menu items that include an asterisk (*) are World Space Modifiers. These unique modifiers and a general discussion of modifiers can be found in Chapter 10, " Using Modifiers."

Table 1-2: Modifiers Menu Items

Menu	Submenu Items
Selection Modifiers	Mesh Select, Poly Select, Patch Select, Spline Select, Volume Select, FFD Select, NURBS Surface Select
Patch/Spline Editing	Edit Patch, Edit Spline, Cross Section, Surface, Delete Patch, Delete Spline, Lathe, Normalize Spline, Fillet/Chamfer, Trim/Extend
Mesh Editing	Cap Holes, Delete Mesh, Edit Mesh, Edit Normals, Extrude, Face Extrude, Normal Modifier, Optimize, Smooth, STL Check, Symmetry, Tessellate, Vertex Paint, Vertex Weld

Menu	Submenu Items
Animation Modifiers	Skin, Morpher, Flex, Melt, Linked XForm, PatchDeform, PathDeform, SurfDeform, * SurfDeform
UV Coordinates	UVW Map, UVW XForm, Unwrap UVW, * Camera Map, Camera Map
Cache Tools	Point Cache
Subdivision Surfaces	MeshSmooth, HSDS Modifier
Free Form Deformers	FFD 2x2x2, FFD 3x3x3, FFD 4x4x4, FFD Box, FFD Cylinder
Parametric Deformers	Bend, Taper, Twist, Noise, Stretch, Squeeze, Push, Relas, Ripple, Wave, Skew, Slice, Spherify, Affect Region, Lattice, Mirror, Displace, XForm, Preserve
Surface	Material, Material By Element, Disp Approx
NURBS Editing	NURBS Surface Select, SurfDeform, Disp Approx
Radiosity Modifiers	Subdivide, *Subdivide

The Character menu

The Character menu lets you create and work with characters as separate entities. The Create and Destroy Character commands will add or delete characters to the scene. Characters can be locked or unlocked to allow free movement. Characters can also be saved as a separate entity and inserted into another scene.

New Feature The Character menu is new to 3ds max 5.

The Bone Tools command opens a dialog box where you can edit the underlying bone system. Characters also have skin, and the Character menu includes commands for setting and assuming a skin pose.

Cross-Reference To learn about characters in more detail, see Chapter 32, "Working with Characters." For information about the Bone Tools and Skin Poses, see Chapter 31, "Working with Bones and Skin."

The Animation menu

The Animation menu contains many commands that help in producing animation sequences such as IK Solvers, Constraints, and Controllers. The IK Solvers menu command lets you select from a submenu of Inverse Kinematics (IK) Solvers. The options include HI Solver, HD Solver, IK Limb Solver, and SplineIK Solver.

New Feature The SplineIK Solver is new to 3ds max 5.

The Constraints menu includes options that limit the motion of an object during an animation sequence. This feature is helpful for keeping the movement of objects within certain boundaries. Controllers, like Constraints, are parameter-driven options for animating objects. Table 1-3 lists the available Constraints and Controllers.

Table 1-3: Constraints and Controllers Menu Items

Menu	Submenu Items
Constraints	Attachment Constraint, Surface Constraint, Path Constraint, Position Constraint, Link Constraint, Look-At Constraint, Orientation Constraint
Transform Controllers	Link Constraint, Position/Rotation/Scale, Script
Position Controllers	Audio, Bézier, Expression, Linear, Motion Capture, Noise, Quaternion (TCB), Reactor, Spring, Script, XYZ, Attachment Constraint, Path Constraint, Position Constraint, Surface Constraint
Rotation Controllers	Audio, Euler XYZ, Linear, Motion Capture, Noise Rotation, Quaternion (TCB), Reactor, Script, Smooth, Look-At Constraint, Orientation Constraint
Scale Controllers	Audio, Bézier, Expression, Linear, Motion Capture, Noise, Quaternion (TCB), Reactor, Script, XYZ

The Add Custom Attribute command opens the Add Parameter dialog box. Using this dialog box, you can add new parameters to an object. These new parameters, once defined, show up in the Custom Attributes rollout of the Command Panel. You can use the Wire Parameters menu command and Parameter Wire dialog box to make objects respond to the changes of another object. For example, you can specify that the radius of one sphere increase as another sphere is moved.

Previews give you a chance to see your animation (rendered in the active viewport) before you spend time rendering it. Preview commands include Make Preview, View Preview, and Rename Preview. Previews are saved to a temporary buffer.

For information about the basics of animation, wiring parameters, and previews, see Chapter 24, "Animation Basics." You can learn about IK Solvers in Chapter 33, "Creating and Using Inverse Kinematics"; constraints in Chapter 27, "Restricting Movement with Constraints"; Controllers in Chapter 28, "Animating with Controllers"; and finally, custom attributes in Chapter 24, "Animation Basics."

The Graph Editors menu

The Graph Editors menu includes commands for opening the Curve Editor, the Dope Sheet, and the Schematic View windows, along with several menus of commands for creating, opening, and deleting saved views. The Track View editors provide a detailed way to examine the object parameters as graphs and bars.

The features of the bulky Track View window from previous versions have been reworked into two different layouts called the Function Curves Editor and the Dope Sheet Editor, both of which are new to 3ds max 5.

The Schematic View is a high-level, node-based view of the scene. It can be used to link and select objects and clearly represents the relationships between different objects.

All the graph editors, including the Function Curves Editor, the Dope Sheet Editor, and the Schematic View, are covered in detail in Chapter 25, "Working with the Track View."

The Rendering menu

The Rendering menu is the doorway to the final output. The Render command (F10) opens the Render Scene dialog box where you can set output options such as which frames to render and final image size. The Environment command opens the Environment dialog box where you can specify the environment settings such as a background color or image, global lighting settings, and atmospheric effects such as Combustion, Fog, and Volume Lights.

The Effects command opens the Rendering Effects dialog box. You use the Rendering Effects dialog box to add rendered effects to an image without having to use the Video Post dialog box. The Effects categories include options such as Lens Effects, Blur, and Color Balance. The Advanced Lighting command opens a control panel where the settings for Light Tracing and Radiosity are located.

New Feature The Rendering menu holds many new features to 3ds max 5 including Advanced Lighting, Render to Texture, and Network Render Region.

The Render to Texture command allows you to render the current scene as an image to be used as a texture. Network rendering is made possible using a manager application that resides alongside 3ds max, but within Max, you can access a manager to render specified regions via a network. The Network Render Region command opens a dialog box where you can manage different rendering jobs.

The Raytracer Settings command opens a dialog box for enabling raytracing options, and the Raytrace Global Include/Exclude command opens a dialog box where you can specify which objects are rendered using raytracing and which are not.

The ActiveShade Floater opens the ActiveShade window, where you can get immediate rendered results. The ActiveShade Viewport command displays the immediate rendered results in the active viewport. The Material Editor (keyboard shortcut, M) and Material/Map Browser commands open their respective dialog boxes for creating, defining, and applying materials.

The Video Post command opens a dialog box for scheduling and controlling any post-processing work. The dialog box manages events for compositing images and including special effects such as glows, lens effects, and blurs. Near the bottom of the Rendering menu is the Show Last Rendering command. This command immediately recalls the last rendered image produced by the Render command. The RAM Player can display images and animations in memory and includes two channels for overlaying images and comparing animations side by side.

Cross-Reference The basics of rendering, along with the ActiveShade views and the RAM Player, are covered in Chapter 34, "Rendering Basics." To learn about environments, see Chapter 35, "Working with Environments and Atmospheric Effects." See Chapter 36, "Using Render Elements and Render Effects," for information on Rendering Effects. You can learn about advanced lighting in Chapter 23, "Advanced Lighting and Radiosity"; Render to Texture in Chapter 20, "Using Material Maps"; and network region render in Chapter 38, "Network Rendering." Raytracing is covered in Chapter 37, "Raytracing"; the Material Editor is covered in Chapter 18, "Exploring the Material Editor"; and the Video Post dialog box is covered in Chapter 39, "Post-Processing with the Video Post Interface."

The Customize menu

The Customize menu provides commands for controlling and customizing the Max interface. The Customize User Interface command opens the Customize User Interface dialog box. This dialog box includes panels for customizing the keyboard shortcuts, the toolbars, quadmenus, menus, and colors. The Load Custom UI and Save Custom UI As commands let you load and save different custom interfaces. If your customization gets confusing, you can reset the layout with the Revert to Startup Layout command.

The Show UI menu contains a submenu of interface elements that you can toggle on or off. Elements that you can toggle include the Command Panel, Floating Toolbars, the Main Toolbar (Alt+6), the Tab Panel (Y), and the Track Bar.

A random click and drag can really mess up your interface. To prevent this from happening, you can lock the interface. The Lock UI Layout prevents an interface from being changed. This feature is helpful if you accidentally keep dragging toolbars out of place. The Configure Paths command opens the Configure Paths dialog box where you can define all the default paths. These paths let Max know where it can go find things like plug-ins, scenes, materials, and so on.

The Units Setup command opens the Units Setup dialog box for establishing system units. The Grid and Snap Settings command opens the Grid and Snap Settings dialog box for controlling grid objects and determining which points to snap to.

The Viewport Configuration command lets you configure the viewport using the Viewport Configuration dialog box. The Plug-in Manager command opens the Plug-in Manager dialog box, which contains a detailed list of all the loaded plug-ins. This dialog box includes the plug-in name, description, status, size, and its full path. The Preferences command opens the Preference Settings dialog box for controlling many aspects of Max.

You can learn about most of the commands found in the Customize menu in Chapter 4, "Customizing the Max Interface," except units setup and Viewport Configuration, which are covered in Chapter 2, "Working with the Viewports." Grids and snap settings are covered in Chapter 9, "Transforming Objects," and the Plug-in Manager is covered in Chapter 42, "Using Third-Party Plug-ins."

The MAXScript menu

From the MAXScript menu, you can create, open, and run scripts. You can also open the MAXScript Listener (F11) and enable the Macro Recorder. The MAXScript menu also includes a command for loading the Visual MAXScript Editor, which simplifies the process of building scripts.

Chapter 40, "Using MAXScript," covers the basics of MAXScript, and Chapter 41, "Using the Visual MAXScript Editor" covers the Visual MAXScript Editor.

The Help menu

The Help menu is a valuable resource that provides access to reference materials and tutorials. The User Reference and the MAXScript Reference are comprehensive help systems that work like a Web browser. The Tutorial command loads the tutorials, which offer a chance to gain valuable experience.

The Hotkey Map displays an interactive interface for learning all the keyboard shortcuts. Additional Help presents help systems for any external plug-ins that are loaded. The 3ds max on the Web options (Online Support and Updates) will automatically open a Web browser and load the Discreet Support Web pages or look for updates. The Plug-in Information command loads a Web browser with a page of active plug-ins for Max.

The Authorize 3ds max command lets you enter an authorization number to authorize the software. The About 3ds max command opens the About dialog box. This dialog box displays the serial number and current display driver.

All the commands found in the Help menu are covered at the end of this chapter in the section titled "Getting Help."

Using the Main Toolbar

Now that you've learned the menu two-step, it is time for the toolbar one-step. The Main Toolbar appears by default directly under the menus at the top of the Max window. It is one of the most convenient ways to execute commands because most commands require only a single click.

In addition to the main toolbar, Max includes two default floating toolbars, and you can add more floating toolbars as needed (see Chapter 4, "Customizing the Max Interface"). These floating toolbars are covered later in the "Using the Additional Interface Elements" section.

You can make the main toolbar a floating panel by clicking and dragging the two vertical lines on the left end of the toolbar away from the interface edge. After you separate it from the window, you can resize the floating toolbar by dragging on its edges or corners. You can then drag and dock it to any of the window edges or double-click on the toolbar title to automatically dock the toolbar to its latest location. Figure 1-2 shows the Main Toolbar as a floating panel.

You can make the Main Toolbar disappear with Customize ⇨ Show UI ⇨ Show Main Toolbar menu command, by pressing the Alt+6 keyboard shortcut, or by clicking the close button in its upper-right corner if it is a floating toolbar.

Figure 1-2: The Main Toolbar includes buttons for controlling many of the most popular Max functions.

On smaller resolution screens, the toolbar is too long to be entirely visible. To view the hidden end of the toolbar, position the cursor on the toolbar away from the buttons (the cursor will change to a hand). Then click and drag the toolbar in either direction. Using the hand cursor to scroll also works in the Command Panel, Material Editor, and any other place where the panel exceeds the given space.

Tip   To see the entire Main Toolbar, you will need to set your monitor to 1280 by 1024 pixels.

All toolbar buttons include tooltips, which are identifying text labels. Hold the cursor over the icon to display the tooltip label. This feature is useful for identifying buttons.

Note   The General panel in the Preference Settings dialog box includes an option for using Large Toolbar Buttons or the small buttons from the previous versions. If you select a different button size, you will need to restart Max in order to use it.

The toolbar buttons with a small triangle in the lower right-hand corner are flyouts. A flyout is a button that expands to reveal additional buttons. Click and hold on the flyout to reveal the additional icons and drag to select one.

Table 1-4 lists the controls found in the Main Toolbar. Buttons with flyouts are separated with commas.

Table 1-4: Main Toolbar Buttons

Toolbar Button	Name	Description
	Undo (Ctrl+Z)	Removes the last performed command. You can set the levels of Undo in the Preferences dialog box.
	Redo (Ctrl+Y)	Brings back the last command that was undone.
	Select and Link	Establishes links between objects.
	Unlink Selection	Breaks links between objects.
	Bind to Space Warp	Assigns objects to be modified by a space warp.
	Select Object (Q)	Chooses an object.
	Select by Name (H)	Opens a dialog box for selecting objects by name.
	Rectangular Selection Region, Circular Selection Region, Fence Selection Region, Lasso Selection Region (Q or Ctrl+F to cycle)	Determines the shape used for selecting objects.
All ▼	Selection Filter drop-down list	Limits the type of objects that can be selected.
	Window/Crossing Toggle	Specifies whether an object must be crossed or windowed to be selected.
	Select and Manipulate	Selects an object and allows parameter manipulation via a manipulator.

Toolbar Button	Name	Description
	Select and Move (W)	Selects an object and allows positional transforms.
	Select and Rotate (E)	Selects an object and allows rotational transforms.
	Select and Uniform Scale, Select and Non-Uniform Scale, Select and Squash (R to cycle)	Selects an object and allows scaling transforms using different methods.
	Reference Coordinate System drop-down list	Specifies the coordinate system used for transforms.
	Use Pivot Point Center, Use Selection Center, Use Transform Coordinate Center	Specifies the center about which rotations are completed.
	Snap Toggle 2D, Snap Toggle 2.5D, Snap Toggle 3D (S)	Specifies the snap mode. 2D snaps only to the active construction grid, 2.5 snaps to the construction grid or to geometry projected from the grid, and 3D snaps to anywhere in 3D space.
	Angle Snap Toggle (A)	Causes rotations to snap to specified angles.
	Percent Snap (Shift+Ctrl+P)	Causes scaling to snap to specified percentages.
	Spinner Snap Toggle	Determines the amount a spinner value changes with each click.
	Keyboard Shortcut Override Toggle	Enables keyboard shortcuts specified by plug-ins instead of Max's defaults.
	Named Selection Sets	Opens a dialog box for creating and managing selection sets
	Named Selection Sets drop-down list	Selects a set of named objects.
	Mirror Selected Objects	Creates a mirrored copy of the selected object.
	Align (Alt+A), Normal Align (Alt+N), Place Highlight (Ctrl+H), Align to Camera, Align to View	Opens the alignment dialog box for positioning objects, allows objects to be aligned by their normals, determines the location of highlights, or aligns object to a camera or view.
	Open Function Curve Editor	Opens the Function Curves Editor.

Continued

Table 1-4 (continued)

Toolbar Button	Name	Description
	Open Schematic View	Opens the Schematic View window.
	Material Editor (M)	Opens the Material Editor window.
	Render Scene (F10)	Opens the Render Scene dialog box for setting rendering options.
View ▼	Render Type drop-down list	Selects the area to render.
	Quick Render (Production), Quick Render (Draft), Quick Render (ActiveShade)	Produces a quick test rendering of the current viewport without opening the Render Scene dialog box.

New Feature   The Main Toolbar includes several new additions in 3ds max 5. These new additions include the Keyboard Shortcut Override toggle, and the four Snap toggle buttons. Another change is that the Axis Constraint buttons along with the Array flyout button have been moved to a separate floating toolbar.

Using the Viewports

The four viewports make up the largest area of the entire interface and provide a way of viewing the objects within the scene. Each of the viewports is configurable and can be unique from the others.

Cross-Reference   Understanding how to work with the viewports is vital to accomplishing tasks with Max, so viewports have an entire chapter dedicated just to them — Chapter 2, "Working with the Viewports."

Using the Command Panel

If the Max interface had a heart, it would be the Command Panel. The Command Panel is located to the right of the viewports along the right edge of the interface. This is where most of the object parameters and settings are located. The features are split into six panels, each accessed via a tab icon located at the top of the Command Panel. These six tabs are Create, Modify, Hierarchy, Motion, Display, and Utilities.

You can pull away the Command Panel from the right window edge as a floating dialog box, as shown in Figure 1-3, by clicking on the open space to the right of the tabbed icons at the top of the Command Panel and dragging away from the interface edge. You can also dock it to the left window edge.

You can re-dock the Command Panel to its last position by double-clicking on its title bar. You can also right-click on the title bar to access a pop-up menu that includes options to dock (either left or right), customize, or hide the Command Panel.

Create panel

Modify panel

Hierarchy panel

Motion panel

Display panel

Utilities panel

Figure 1-3: The Command Panel includes six separate panels accessed via tab icons.

Most of the controls, buttons, and parameters in the Command Panel are contained within sections called rollouts. A *rollout* is a grouping of controls positioned under a gray, boxed title, as shown in Figure 1-4. Each rollout includes a title bar with a plus or minus sign (a minus sign indicates that the rollout is expanded and a plus sign shows retracted rollouts). Clicking the rollout title displays or retracts the rollout. You can also reposition the order of the rollouts by dragging the rollout title and dropping it above or below the other rollouts.

Note You cannot reposition some of the rollouts, such as the Object Type and Name and Color rollouts found in the Create panel.

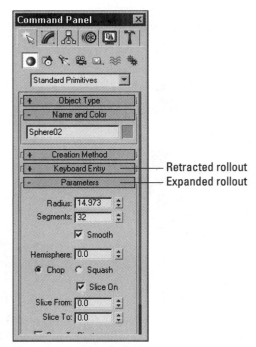

Retracted rollout
Expanded rollout

Figure 1-4: Expand or retract panel rollouts by clicking on the rollout title.

Expanding all the rollouts often exceeds the screen space allotted to the Command Panel. If the rollouts exceed the given space, then a small vertical scroll bar will appear at the right edge of the Command Panel. You can drag this scroll bar to access the rollouts at the bottom of the Command Panel, or you can move the cursor around the Command Panel until a hand cursor appears. With the hand cursor, click and drag in either direction to scroll the Command Panel. Right-clicking within a rollout displays a pop-up menu that enables you to open or close any or all rollouts or reset the rollout order.

 Cross-Reference You can customize the Command Panel like the other toolbars. I cover customizing the Command Panel in Chapter 4, "Customizing the Max Interface."

The Command Panel can also be doubled or tripled in width by dragging its left edge toward the center of the interface. The width of the Command Panel is increased at the expense of the viewports. Figure 1-5 shows the Command Panel double its normal size.

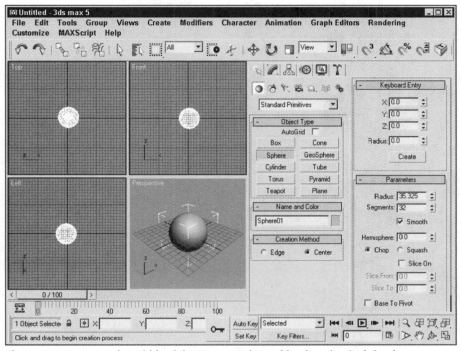

Figure 1-5: Increase the width of the Command Panel by dragging its left edge.

Create panel

The Create panel is the place you go to create objects for the scene. These objects could be geometric objects like spheres, cones, and boxes or other objects like lights, cameras, or Space Warps. There is quite a variety of objects contained in the Create panel. To create an object, you simply need to find the button for the object you want to create, click it, click in one of the viewports, and voilá — instant object.

Cross-Reference

Creating objects is covered in detail in chapters throughout the rest of the book, but the first chapter that really gets into creating objects is Chapter 5, "Using Primitive Objects." You can buzz over to that chapter, if you are anxious to start creating things.

The Create panel includes several categories and subcategories of objects. The categories, shown in Figure 1-6, are displayed as icons directly under the Command Panel tabs. Subcategories are displayed in the drop-down list under the category icons. Each subcategory will display a different set of buttons in the Object Type rollout when selected.

Note

Selecting an object from the Create menu automatically opens the Create panel and selects the requested object type. Not all objects found in the Create panel categories are found in the Create menu.

Figure 1-6: The Create panel includes seven different categories of objects.

Below the Object Type rollout is the Name and Color rollout. Every object created with the Create panel is given a default name and color. Using this rollout, you can change the object name and color. The color is used to display the object in the viewports if no material is applied.

Note   The selected object's name and color will appear at the top of all the other Command Panel panels.

Table 1-5 lists all the available Create panel buttons for each subcategory.

Table 1-5: Command Panel Buttons per Subcategory

Category (icon)	Subcategory (drop-down list)	Available Buttons
Geometry		
	Standard Primitives	Box, Sphere, Cylinder, Torus, Teapot, Cone, GeoSphere, Tube, Pyramid, Plane
	Extended Primitives	Hedra, ChamferBox, OilTank, Spindle, Gengon, RingWave, Hose, Torus Knot, ChamferCyl, Capsule, L-Ext, C-Ext, Prism
	Compound Objects	Morph, Conform, ShapeMerge, Terrain, Mesher, Scatter, Connect, Boolean, Loft
	Particle Systems	Spray, Super Spray, PArray, Snow, Blizzard, PCloud
	Patch Grids	Quad Patch, Tri Patch
	NURBS Surfaces	Point Surf, CV Surf
	Dynamics Objects	Spring, Damper
Shapes		
	Splines	Line, Circle, Arc, NGon, Text, Section, Rectangle, Ellipse, Donut, Star, Helix
	NURBS Curves	Point Curve, CV Curve
Lights		
	Standard	Skylight, Free Spot, Free Direct, Target Spot, Target Direct, Omni
	Photometric	IES Sky, Free Point, Free Linear, Free Area, Target Point, Target Linear, Target Area, IES Sun
Cameras		
	Standard	Target, Free
Helpers		
	Standard	Dummy, Grid, Tape, Compass, Character, Point, Protractor
	Atmospheric Apparatus	BoxGizmo, CylGizmo, SphereGizmo
	Camera Match	CamPoint
	Manipulators	Cone Angle, Slider, Plane Angle
	VRML97	Anchor, ProxSensor, NavInfo, Fog, Sound, LOD, TouchSensor, TimeSensor, Background, AudioClip, Billboard, Inline

Continued

Table 1-5 *(continued)*

Category (icon)	Subcategory (drop-down list)	Available Buttons
Space Warps		
	Forces	Push, Vortex, PBomb, Gravity, Displace, Motor, Drag, Path Follow, Wind
	Deflectors	POmniFlect, SOmniFlect, UOmniFlect, SDeflector, Deflector, PDynaFlect, SDynaFlect, UDynaFlect, UDeflector
	Geometric/Deformable	FFD (Box), Wave, Displace, Bomb, FFD (Cyl), Ripple, Conform
	Modifier-Based	Bend, Taper, Noise, Twist, Skew, Stretch
Systems		
	Standard	Bones, Sunlight, Ring Array, Daylight

After you select a button, several additional rollouts magically appear. These new rollouts hold the parameters for the selected object and are displayed in the Create panel below the Name and Color rollout. Altering these parameters changes the object.

Modify panel

The parameters found in the Create panel are great for changing an object, but they are only available while you're creating the object. If you select another object and then return to the Create panel with the first object selected, all its parameters will be gone. It's not that the parameters are gone, but just that they've migrated to the Modify panel. The Modify panel is the permanent location of object parameters.

In addition to modifying object parameters, you can use the Modify panel to apply modifiers to the selected object. Modifiers are parameter-driven functions for modifying an object. You can see a complete list of modifiers in the Modifier List drop-down list (there are currently 79 available modifiers).

Once applied, you can control the modifiers via parameters displayed in the Modify panel. All modifiers that are applied to an object are displayed in the Modifier Stack (like the Twist modifier applied to a sphere object in Figure 1-7), which appears at the top of the Modify panel (directly under the Modifier List drop-down list). You can also apply modifiers using the Modifiers menu.

The Modifier Stack displays all modifiers that have been applied to the current selected object. This stack lets you revisit any modifier and change its parameters, reorder it in the stack, or delete it.

Cross-Reference Look for more information on modifiers in Chapter 10, "Using Modifiers." You can find coverage of other modifiers sprinkled throughout the rest of the chapters. For example, see Chapter 15, "Working with NURBS" for more on the NURBS Editing modifiers.

Modifier List drop-down list

Modifier Stack

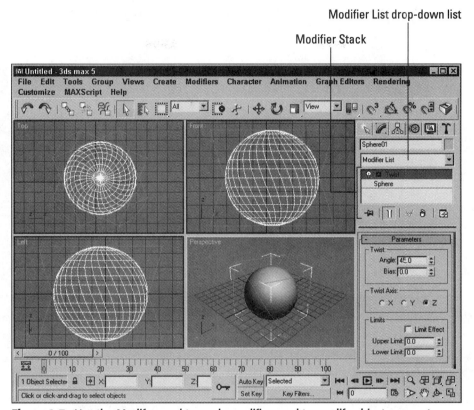

Figure 1-7: Use the Modify panel to apply modifiers and to modify object parameters.

Hierarchy panel

The Hierarchy panel, shown in Figure 1-8, includes three different sets of controls. You access them by using the three buttons located at the top of the panel. These sets are Pivot, Inverse Kinematics (IK), and Link Info. Each of these buttons when selected will present several different rollouts of parameters. The button for the selected set of controls is white.

The Pivot button opens rollouts that let you move and reorient an object's pivot point. A pivot point is the point about which transformations are applied. The IK button opens rollouts that let you set up an inverse kinematics structure and to define how the joints of such a structure can move. Finally, the Link Info button opens rollouts for setting locks, which prevent an object from moving, rotating, or scaling along certain axes.

Note   Check out the details on pivots in Chapter 9, "Transforming Objects," Inverse Kinematics in Chapter 33, "Creating and Using Inverse Kinematics," and links in Chapter 8, "Grouping and Linking Objects."

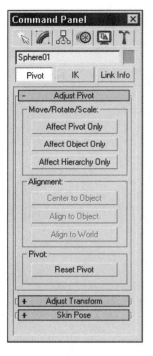

Figure 1-8: The Hierarchy panel offers controls for adjusting pivot points among other things.

Motion panel

Similar to the Hierarchy panel, the Motion panel has a dual personality. There are two buttons at the top of the Motion panel, shown in Figure 1-9, including Parameters and Trajectories. One common way of modifying object motion is to apply Controllers and Constraints. The Parameters button opens several rollouts that enable you to apply animation Controllers and Constraints. Controllers affect the position, rotation, and scaling of objects in preset ways, and Constraints limit the motion of an object. You can access a list of Controllers by clicking the Assign Controller button positioned at the top of the Assign Controller rollout or by choosing one from the Animation menu.

The Trajectories button opens a single rollout that displays the motion path of an object as a spline.

 Cross-Reference Constraints and Controllers are the subjects of Chapter 27, "Restricting Movement with Constraints" and Chapter 28, "Animating with Controllers." Trajectories are covered in Chapter 24, "Animation Basics."

Assign Controller button

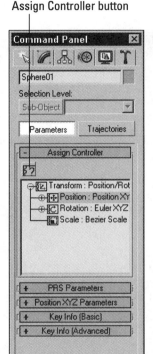

Figure 1-9: The Motion panel offers an interface for assigning animation Controllers to an object.

Display panel

The Display panel, shown in Figure 1-10, controls how objects are seen within the viewports. You can set display parameters for individual objects. Using this panel, you can hide or freeze objects and modify all display parameters. Many of these same commands are found in the Display Floater and in the Object Properties dialog box.

Cross-Reference I cover the Display panel in Chapter 6, "Selecting Objects and Setting Object Properties."

Utilities panel

You can find an assortment of miscellaneous tools in the Utilities panel, shown in Figure 1-11. The default utilities include the Asset Browser, Camera Match, Collapse, Color Clipboard, Measure, Motion Capture, Reset XForm, and MAXScript. Click the More button at the top of the Utilities panels to open an additional list of utilities. To execute a utility, simply click its button or select it from the list. Some utilities will open dialog boxes and others will present rollouts in the bottom of the panel. The button for the selected utility will be highlighted in white.

Cross-Reference This panel also includes the Configure Button Sets button for customizing which buttons appear in the default Utilities rollout. See Chapter 4, "Customizing the Max Interface," for more information.

Figure 1-10: The Display panel includes settings for the color of the object.

Figure 1-11: The Measure utility is one of the default utilities found in the Utilities panel.

Using the Lower Interface Bar Controls

The last major interface element isn't really an interface element, but just a collection of several different controls located along the bottom edge of the window. These controls cannot be pulled away from the interface like the Main Toolbar, but you can hide them using Expert Mode (Ctrl+X). These controls, shown in Figure 1-12, include the following from left to right:

✦ **Time Slider and Track Bar:** The Time Slider, located under the viewports, enables you to quickly locate a specific frame. The Track Bar displays all animation keys on a scale of frames.

✦ **Status Bar and Prompt Line:** Text located at the bottom left of the window offers information about the scene and describes what Max is expecting you to do next. The Status Bar also includes the Transform Type-In fields.

Note   If the interface opens with pink and white text fields located at the bottom-left corner of the interface, this is a mini MAXScript Listener. You can close this control by dragging its left edge to the left. I cover this control in detail in Chapter 40, "Using MAXScript."

✦ **Time Controls:** Resembling the controls on a VCR, the Time Controls offer an easy way to move through the various animation frames and keys.

✦ **Key Controls:** These controls are for creating animation keys and include two different modes — Auto Key and Set Key.

✦ **Viewport Navigation Controls:** In the lower-right corner of the interface are the controls for manipulating the viewports.

Accessing frames and keys with the Time Slider and the Track Bar

Directly beneath the viewports is a slider control known as the Time Slider. It spans the number of frames included in the current animation. Dragging the Time Slider can move you quickly between frames. The arrows surrounding the slider will select the previous or next frame.

The Track Bar, positioned under the Time Slider, displays animation keys as black rectangles. You can hide it with the Customize ➪ Show UI ➪ Hide Track Bar menu command. Using the Track Bar, you can select, move, and delete keys.

Cross-Reference   See Chapter 24, "Animation Basics," for more information on the Track Bar.

At the left end of the Track Bar is the Show Curves button that you can use to expand the Track Bar to show function curves.

New Feature   The Function Curve Editor that is part of the Track Bar is new in 3ds max 5. Note that this interface is separate from the full-featured Function Curves Editor accessed via the Graph Editors menu. More information on the Function Curve Editor can be found in Chapter 25, "Working with the Track View."

Track Bar

Time Slider

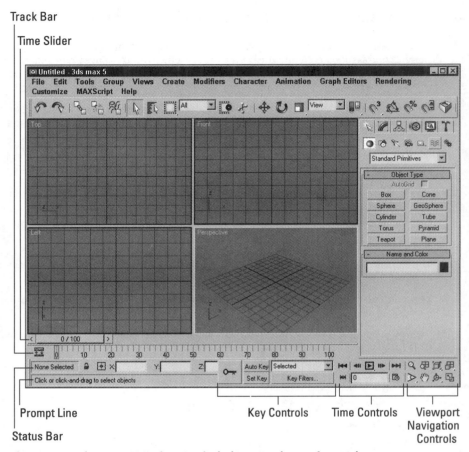

Prompt Line

Status Bar

Key Controls   Time Controls   Viewport Navigation Controls

Figure 1-12: The Lower Interface Bar includes several sets of controls.

Learning from the Status Bar and the Prompt Line

As you work, the Status Bar provides valuable information, such as the number and type of objects selected, transformation values, and grid size. There are also two buttons on the Status Bar — the Selection Lock Toggle button (keyboard shortcut = space) and the Absolute/Offset Mode Transform Type-In toggle button. Clicking the Selection Lock Toggle button prevents the selection of any additional objects. The button is yellow when selected.

Note   The Grid Size and Time Tags fields aren't visible in Figure 1-12 due to the resolution of the figure, but will be available if the interface size is increased.

The Transform Type-In fields display the world coordinates of the cursor in the active viewport, unless an object is selected. For the selected object, these fields show the absolute world coordinate values if the Absolute Mode Transform Type-In toggle button is selected. If the Offset mode is selected, then the fields show the offset values as the object is transformed.

The values that are displayed depend on the type of transformation that is taking place (units for moves, degrees for rotation, and percentages for scaling). You can also enter values into these fields to transform the object.

New Feature The Absolute/Offset Mode Transform Type-In button and Time Tags are both new to 3ds max 5.

The Prompt Line is directly below the Status Bar. If you're stuck as to what to do next, look at the Prompt Line for information on what Max is expecting. To the right of the Prompt Line is a field marked Add Time Tag. Click this field to pop up a menu with options to Add or Edit a Time Tag. You can set Time Tags for each frame in the scene. Once set, the Time Tags will be visible in the Time Tag field whenever you select that time.

Cross-Reference I cover the Selection Lock Toggle in Chapter 6, "Selecting Objects and Setting Object Properties." I cover the Transform Type-In fields in more detail in Chapter 9, "Transforming Objects," and Time Tags in Chapter 24, "Animation Basics."

Using the Time Controls

Although the Time Controls sound like an interface to a time machine, you use them to control animation sequences.

Based on the selected mode (keys or frames), the Time Controls can move between the first, previous, next, or last frames or keys. You can also reset the number of frames and the frame rate using the Time Configuration dialog box.

Cross-Reference Chapter 24, "Animation Basics" covers both the Key Controls and the Time Controls in detail.

Using the Key Controls

You can use the Key Controls to set animation keyframes for objects in the scene. Setting keys can be done in two modes — Auto Key (N) or Set Key ('). Auto Key mode sets keys for any changes made to the scene objects. Set Key mode gives you more precise control and only sets keys for the selected filters when you click the Set Keys button (K). You can set keys for the selected object or for a specified character.

New Feature The Key Controls are new to the 3ds max 5 interface.

Viewport Navigation Controls

The Viewport Navigation Controls are the eight buttons located in the lower-right corner of the interface. They enable you to zoom, pan, and rotate the active viewport's view. You can undo any viewport changes with the Views ➪ Undo Viewport Change (Shift+Z) menu command.

Cross-Reference I cover the Viewport Navigation Controls in detail in Chapter 2, "Working with Viewports."

Using the Additional Interface Elements

Max includes some other interface elements, but you need to work to see them. These aren't visible elements by default but can be made visible using different menu and mouse actions.

Using the Tab Panel

The Tab Panel, shown in Figure 1-13, is like a super toolbar with tabs across the top that let you switch between many different toolbars. This toolbar is an efficient use of space if you want toolbar access to all commands. You can make the Tab Panel appear by choosing Customize ➪ Show UI ➪ Show Tab Panel, by right-clicking any toolbar (away from the buttons) and choosing Tab Panel from the pop-up menu, or by pressing the Y keyboard shortcut.

Tab Panel

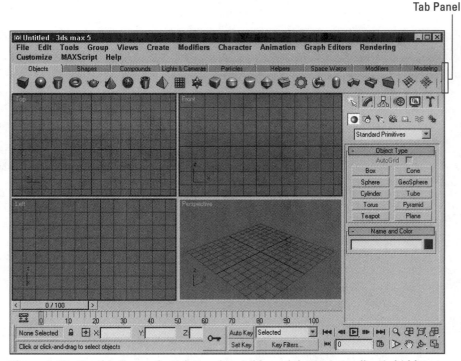

Figure 1-13: For this figure, the Tab Panel is visible and the Main Toolbar is hidden.

The toolbars included in the default Tab Panel include the following (although they are all not visible in Figure 1-13): Objects, Shapes, Compounds, Lights & Cameras, Particles, Helpers, Space Warps, Modifiers, Modeling, and Rendering. You can remove any of these individual toolbars from the Tab Panel and reposition it by dragging its tab away from the Tab Panel; however, you cannot remove the Tab Panel itself from the top of the window. Detached panels can be returned to the Tab Panel using the right-click pop-up menu.

Cross-Reference Chapter 4, "Customizing the Max Interface," provides more information on customizing the Tab Panel.

Viewing the default floating toolbars

If you right-click on the Main Toolbar you may notice that two other toolbars are available. These are floating toolbars. You can display them using the Customize ⇨ Show UI ⇨ Show Floating Toolbars menu command. These two floating toolbars are Axis Constraints and Layers, as shown in Figure 1-14.

New Feature Layers and the Layers toolbar are new to 3ds max 5.

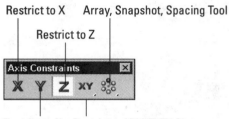

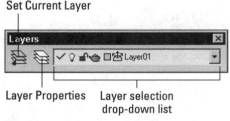

Figure 1-14: The Axis Constraints and Layers toolbars are available as floating toolbars.

The Axis Constraints toolbar includes buttons for restricting transformations to the X (F5), Y (F6), or Z (F7) axes or to restrict transformations to a single plane: XY, YZ, or ZX (F8 to cycle). It also includes a flyout button for the Array, Snapshot, and Spacing Tool (Shift+I) dialog boxes.

The Layers toolbar includes several buttons creating, enabling, locking, and selecting layers. You can also set the properties for each layer.

Cross-Reference I cover constraining transformations to a single axis or plane in Chapter 9, "Transforming Objects." I cover the Array, Snapshot, and Spacing Tools in Chapter 7, "Cloning Objects," and layers in Chapter 6, "Selecting Objects and Setting Object Properties."

Quick access with the Right-click quadmenus

Quadmenus are pop-up menus with up to four separate sections that surround the cursor, as shown in Figure 1-15. Right-clicking in the active viewport opens these quadmenus. The contents of the menus depend on the object selected.

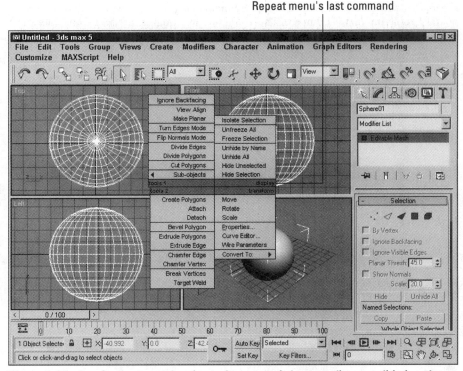

Figure 1-15: Quadmenus contain a host of commands in an easily accessible location.

Clicking with the left mouse button away from the quadmenu closes the quadmenu. For each menu, the last menu item selected will be displayed in blue. To quickly access the blue menu item again, simply click the blue-shaded bar. Using Customize ➪ Customize User Interface, you can specify which commands appear on the quadmenus.

Interacting with the Interface

Knowing where all the interface elements are located is only the start. Max includes several interactive features that make the interface work. Learning these features will make a difference between an interface that works for you and one that doesn't.

Tutorial: Moving the Command Panel for lefties

I used to work for a company that required that all computers have the mouse to the left of the keyboard. We swapped computers a lot and the boss felt that this would enable us to work the mouse and the keypad at the same time (and you thought your work environment was weird). The reality is that some people like it on the left and others on the right and Max can accommodate both.

With the Command Panel on the right side of the interface, the default Max interface obviously favors right-handers, but with the docking panels, you can quickly change it to be friendly to lefties.

To move the Command Panel to the left side of the interface, follow these steps:

1. Click the Command Panel on the empty space to the right of the Utilities tab and drag toward the center of the interface. As you drag the Command Panel away from the right edge, the cursor will change.

2. Continue to drag the Command Panel to the left edge and the cursor will change again to indicate that it will be docked when released. Release the mouse button and the Command Panel will be docked to the left side.

3. If the Command Panel is floating, you can right click on its title bar and select Dock ⇨ Left from the pop-up menu. If the Command Panel is closed by clicking on the close button in the upper-right corner when floating, then you can make it reappear by selecting Customize ⇨ Show UI ⇨ Show Command Panel.

Figure 1-16 shows the Command Panel docked to the left side of the interface.

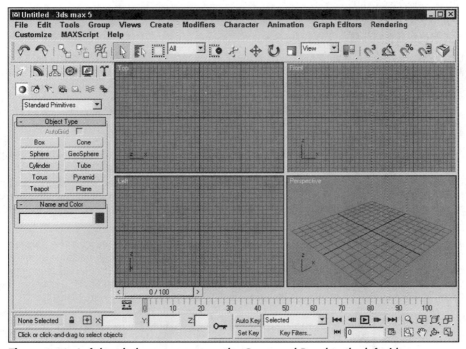

Figure 1-16: Left-handed users can move the Command Panel to the left side.

Understanding the button color cues

Max's interface uses color cues to help remind you of the current mode. When a button is yellow, it warns that it has control of the interface. For example, if one of the select buttons is selected, it will turn yellow, and any dragging in the viewport will affect the object; however, if one of the Viewport Navigation Control buttons is selected, it will turn yellow and dragging the viewport will change the view. Knowing what the current mode is at all times can keep you out of trouble.

Tip   Right-clicking in the active viewport exits any mode that has control and returns control to the Select Object mode.

Another common color is red. When the Auto Keys or Set Keys buttons are depressed, they turn red. The edge of the active viewport being animated also turns red. This reminds you that any modifications will be saved as a key.

Toggle buttons are buttons that can be turned on or off. Example toggle buttons include the Snap buttons. When a toggle button is enabled, it turns white. Toggle buttons highlighted in blue are non-exclusive, but notify you of a mode that is enabled, such as the Key Mode Toggle.

Cross-Reference   All interface colors can be customized using the Customize User Interface dialog box that is discussed in Chapter 4, "Customizing the Max Interface."

Drag-and-drop features

Dialog boxes that work with files benefit greatly from Max's drag-and-drop features. The Material Editor, Background Image, View File, and Environmental Settings dialog boxes all use drag and drop. These dialog boxes let you select a file or a material and drag it on top of where you want to apply it.

Controlling spinners

Spinners are those little controls throughout the interface with a value field and two small arrows to its right. As you would expect, clicking the up arrow increases the value and clicking the down arrow decreases the value. The amount of the increase or decrease depends on the setting in the General tab of the Preference Settings dialog box. Another way to control the spinner value is to click the arrows and drag with the mouse. Dragging up increases the value and down decreases it.

The effect of the spinner drag will be shown in the viewport if the Update During Spinner Drag menu option is enabled in the Views menu. If the cursor is located within a spinner, you can press Ctrl+N to open the Numeric Expression Evaluator, which lets you set the value using an expression. For example, you can set a spinner value by adding numbers together like you would using a calculator. An expression of 30+40+35 sets the value to 105.

Cross-Reference   Chapter 29, "Using Expressions," covers the Numeric Expression Evaluator in more detail.

Keyboard shortcuts

Many features include keyboard shortcuts. These shortcuts can give you direct access to a command without moving the mouse. The default shortcuts for the menu commands are listed to the right of the command. You can use the Keyboard panel of the Customize User Interface dialog box to view and change the keyboard shortcuts for any feature.

Appendix B, "Max Keyboard Shortcuts," lists all the default keyboard shortcuts.

Using strokes

Strokes are similar to the keyboard shortcuts, except they allow you to draw a pre-defined shape using the middle mouse button as a shortcut to a command. For example, you can set up a stroke that will undo the last action using a shape that looks like the letter U. Then undoing the last action can be done by clicking the middle button and dragging in the shape of the letter U. Strokes are convenient because they use the mouse, and you don't need to reach for the keyboard.

Setting up and using strokes is covered in more detail in Chapter 4, "Customizing the Max Interface."

Modeless and persistent dialog boxes

Many dialog boxes in Max are *modeless,* which means that the dialog box doesn't need to be closed before you can work with objects in the background viewports. The Material Editor is an example of a modeless dialog box. With the Material Editor open, you can create, select, and transform objects in the background. Other modeless dialog boxes include the Material/Map Browser, the Render Scene dialog box, the Video Post dialog box, the Transform Type-In dialog box, the Display and Selection Floaters, and the various graph editors.

Another feature of many, but not all, dialog boxes is *persistence,* which means that values added to a dialog box remain set when the dialog box is reopened. This feature only applies within a given Max session. Choosing the File ➪ Reset command button or exiting and restarting Max will reset all the dialog boxes.

Getting Help

If you get stuck, Max won't leave you stranded. You can turn to several places in Max to get help. The Help menu is a valuable resource that provides access to reference materials and tutorials.

Browser-based reference guides

The User Reference, MAXScript Reference, and Tutorials are Web browser-based help interfaces. An organized list of topics is available in the left navigation pane, as shown in Figure 1-17, and the right includes a pane where the details on the selected topic are displayed. Across the top are five toolbar buttons used to control the interface. The Hide button hides the left navigation pane, the Back and Forward buttons move between visited pages, the Print button prints the information in the right pane, and the Options button displays a pop-up menu of options.

Figure 1-17: The User Reference includes panels for viewing the index of commands and searching the reference.

Above the left navigation pane are five tabs that open separate panels when selected. The Contents panel displays a list of topics; the Index panel lists all topics alphabetically; the Search panel includes a text field where you can search for specific keywords; the Favorites panel keeps a list of bookmarks to topics you add to the list; and the Query panel lets you type in a question and query for answers.

Throughout the textual descriptions, keywords that are linked to other related topics are highlighted in blue and underlined.

Online help

The Web offers many sites that can help, and Max links to the Online Support, Updates, and Resources pages on the Discreet site from the Help ➪ 3ds max on the Web menu. Selecting either of these menu commands automatically opens a Web browser and loads the Discreet Web pages.

The Help ➪ Plug-in Information menu command opens a Web browser and loads the page found at www.maxusers.com where all the available plug-ins are listed.

Summary

You should now be familiar with the interface elements for Max. Understanding the interface is one of the keys to success in using 3ds max. Max includes a variety of different interface elements. Among the menus, toolbars, and keyboard shortcuts, several ways to perform the same command exist. Discover the method that works best for you.

This chapter covered the following topics:

- ✦ The interface elements
- ✦ Viewing and using the pull-down menus
- ✦ Working with the Main Toolbar
- ✦ Using the Command Panel
- ✦ Learning the lower interface controls
- ✦ Interfacing with the Max interface
- ✦ Getting additional help

In this chapter, we've skirted about the viewports covering all the other interface elements, but in the next chapter, we're going to hit the viewports head-on.

✦　　✦　　✦

Working with the Viewports

Although Max consists of many different interface elements such as panels, dialog boxes, and menus, the main areas that will attract the attention of your eyes are the viewports. The four main viewports make up the bulk of the interface and are the one place where scene objects are visible. You can think of it as looking at the television screen instead of the remote. Learning to control and use the viewports can make a huge difference with your comfort level with Max.

The viewports are powerful and have numerous settings that you can use to provide thousands of different ways to look at your scene and beginners can feel frustrated in not being able to control what they see. This chapter includes all the details you'll need to make the viewports reveal their secrets.

Understanding 3D Space

It seems silly to be talking about 3D space because we live and move in 3D space. If we stop and think about it, 3D space is natural to us. For example, consider a filing cabinet with four drawers. Within each drawer, you can stuff papers in the front, back, or sides, as well as in the drawers above or below. These positions represent three unique directions.

When I ask my wife where our passports are (don't ask why I'm looking for my passport) and she says, "They're in the top drawer toward the back on the left side," I know exactly where they are and can find them immediately (unless, of course, my kids have been in the cabinet). The concept of three dimensions is comfortable and familiar.

Now consider the computer screen, which is inherently 2D. If I have many windows open, including a scanned image of my passport, and I ask my wife where the scanned image is, she would reply, "It's somewhere behind the large window where you're writing that book." And

I would look and search before locating it. In 2D space, I understand top and bottom and left and right and have a little notion of above and below.

This conundrum is what 3D computer artists face—how do you represent 3D objects on a 2D device? The answer that 3ds max provides is to present several views, called *viewports,* of the scene. A viewport is a small window that displays the scene from one perspective. These viewports are the windows into Max's 3D world. They are probably called viewports instead of windows because the word, *Windows,* has a different meaning in the computer world and it is copyrighted. Each viewport has numerous settings and viewing options.

Orthographic views

Orthographic views are displayed from the perspective of looking straight down an axis at an object. This reveals a view in only one plane. Because orthographic viewports are constrained to one plane, they show the actual height and width of the object. Available orthographic viewports in Max include Front, Back, Top, Bottom, Left, and Right. Max starts up with the Top, Front, and Left orthographic viewports visible. The top-left corner of the viewport displays the viewport name.

Perspective view

The fourth viewport is a Perspective view. Although not as precise when manipulating objects, this view is the closest to what we see in reality and gives a more intuitive definition of the relationship between objects.

Tip   Max includes several keyboard shortcuts for quickly changing the view in the active viewport including T (Top View), B (Bottom View), F (Front View), L (Left View), C (Camera View), $ (Spotlight View), P (Perspective View), U (User View), D (Enable/Disable viewport), and G (Enable/Disable Grid). Pressing the V key will open a quadmenu that lets you select a new view.

Figure 2-1 shows the viewports with the model of a dog imported from Poser. You can see this fine dog (we'll call him Fido) from several directions in each of the viewports. If you want to measure Fido's length from nose to tail, you could get an accurate measurement using the Top or Left viewports, whereas you can use the Front and Left viewports to measure his precise height. So, using these different viewports, you can accurately work with all object dimensions.

Note   Poser is an external application created by Curious Labs that is particularly good at working with characters.

Top viewport   Front viewport

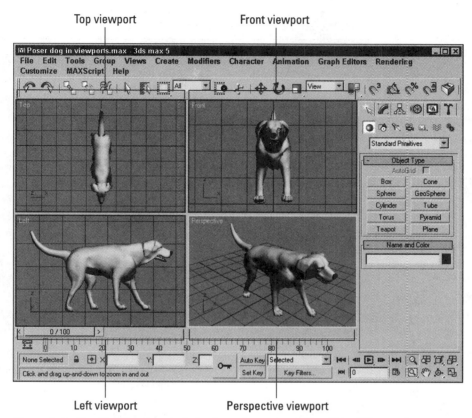

Left viewport   Perspective viewport

Figure 2-1: The Max interface includes four viewports, each with a different view.

Using the Viewport Navigation Controls

The standard viewports will show you several different views of your current project, but the default views aren't necessarily the ones you want. To alter these default views you'll need to use the Viewport Navigation Control buttons. These eight buttons are located at the bottom-right corner of the window. With these buttons you can Zoom, Pan, and Rotate the active view. In Table 2-1, the keyboard shortcut for each button is listed in parentheses next to its name.

Tip　　　The active viewport is always marked with a yellow border.

Table 2-1: Viewport Navigation Controls

Toolbar Button	Name	Description
	Zoom (Alt+Z or [or])	Moves closer or farther from the objects in the active viewport by dragging the mouse with the Alt+Z key or zooming by steps with the bracket keys.
	Zoom All	Zooms in or out of all the viewports simultaneously by dragging the mouse.
	Zoom Extents (Ctrl+Alt+Z), Zoom Extents Selected	Zooms in on the objects or the selected object until it fills the current viewport.
	Zoom Extents All (Ctrl+Shift+Z), Zoom Extents All Selected (Z)	Zooms in on the objects or the selected object until it fills all the viewports.
	Field of View, Region Zoom (Ctrl+W)	The Field of View button (only available in the Perspective view) controls the width of the view. The Region Zoom button zooms into the region selected by dragging the mouse.
	Pan (Ctrl+P or I)	Moves the view to the left, right, up, or down by dragging the mouse or by moving the mouse while holding the I key down.
	Arc Rotate, Arc Rotate Selected, Arc Rotate SubObject	Rotates the view around the global axis, selected object, or subobject by dragging the mouse.
	Min/Max Toggle (Alt+W)	Makes the current viewport fill the screen. Clicking this button a second time shows all four viewports again.

Caution When one of the Viewport Navigation buttons is selected, it will be highlighted yellow. You cannot select, create, or transform objects while one of these buttons is highlighted.

Zooming a view

There are several ways to zoom in and out of the scene. Clicking the Zoom (Alt+Z) button enters zoom mode where you can zoom in and out of a viewport by dragging the mouse. This works in whichever viewport you drag in. To the right of the Zoom button is the Zoom All button, which does the same thing as the Zoom button, only to all four viewports at once. The Zoom Extents (Ctrl+Alt+Z) button zooms the active viewport so all objects (or the selected objects with the Zoom Extents Selected button) are visible in the viewport. There is also a Zoom Extents All (Ctrl+Shift+Z) button for zooming in all viewports to the object's extents.

In previous versions of Max, the Z key entered zoom mode, but it now is used to Zoom Extents Selected All, which gives you a single key press to center the viewports on the current selection.

You can use the brackets keys to zoom in ([) and out (]) by steps. Each key press will zoom in (or out) another step. There is also a Region Zoom (Ctrl+W) button that lets you drag over the region that you want to zoom in on. If you select a non-orthogonal view, such as the Perspective view, the Region Zoom button has a fly-out called the Field of View. Using this button, you can control how wide or narrow the view is. This is like using a wide angle or telephoto lens on your camera. This feature is different from zoom in that the perspective is distorted as the Field of View is increased.

If your mouse has a scroll wheel, you can use it to zoom in and out of the active viewport.

Panning a view

The Viewport Navigation Controls also offer two ways to pan in a viewport. In Pan mode (Ctrl+P), dragging in a viewport will pan the view. Note that this doesn't move the objects, only the view. The second way to pan is to hold down the I key while moving the mouse. This is known as an interactive pan.

Pressing the middle mouse button (or the scroll wheel) will also let you pan by moving the mouse.

Rotating a view

Rotating the view can be the most revealing of all the view changes. When the Arc Rotate button is selected, a rotation guide appears in the active viewport, as shown in Figure 2-2. This rotation guide is a circle with a square located at each quadrant. Clicking and dragging the left and right squares rotates the view side to side, and the top and bottom squares rotates the view up and down. Clicking within the circle and dragging rotates within a single plane, and clicking and dragging outside of the circle rotates the view about the circle's center either clockwise or counterclockwise. If you get confused, look at the cursor, which will change depending on the type of rotation.

Holding down the Alt key while pressing the middle mouse button (or the scroll wheel) will let you arc rotate the active viewport by moving the mouse.

If you rotate an orthogonal view, it automatically becomes a User view.

Rotation guide

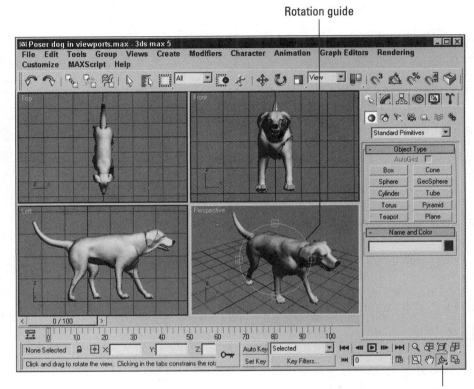

Arc Rotate button

Figure 2-2: The rotation guide appears whenever the Arc Rotate button is selected.

You can set any viewport to be a camera view (C) or a spotlight view ($) if a camera or a spotlight exist in the scene. When either of these views is active, the Viewport Navigation Control buttons will change. In camera view, controls for dolly, roll, truck, pan, orbit, and field of view become active. A light view includes controls for falloff and hotspots.

Chapter 21, "Controlling Cameras," and Chapter 22, "Working with Lights," cover these changes in more detail.

Grids are helpful in establishing your bearings in 3D space. For the active viewport, the G key will turn the grids on and off. The Views menu also includes several options for working with grids.

Chapter 9, "Transforming Objects," covers grids in more detail.

Undoing and saving changes made with the Viewport Navigation Controls

If you get lost in your view, you can undo and redo viewport changes with Views ➪ Undo View Change (Shift+Z) and Views ➪ Redo View Change (Shift+Y). These commands are different from the Edit ➪ Undo and Edit ➪ Redo commands, which can undo or redo geometry changes.

You can save changes made to a viewport by using the Views ➪ Save Active Viewport menu command. This command saves the Viewport Navigation settings for recall. To restore these settings, use Views ➪ Restore Active Viewport.

Note   The Save and Restore Active Viewport commands do not save any viewport configuration settings, just the navigated view. Saving an active view uses a buffer, so it only remembers one view for each viewport.

Maximizing the active viewport

Sooner or later, the viewports will feel too small. When this happens, you have several different ways to increase the size of your viewports. The first trick to try is to change the viewport sizes by clicking and dragging any of the viewport borders. Dragging on the intersection of the viewports will resize all the viewports. Figure 2-3 shows the viewports after being dynamically resized.

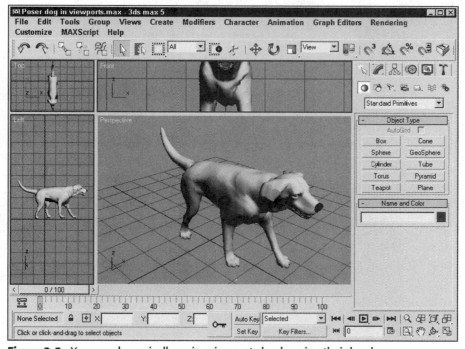

Figure 2-3: You can dynamically resize viewports by dragging their borders.

The second trick to try is to use the Min/Max Toggle (Alt+W) to expand the active viewport to fill the space reserved for all four viewports, as shown in Figure 2-4. Clicking the Min/Max Toggle (or pressing Alt+W) a second time returns to four viewports.

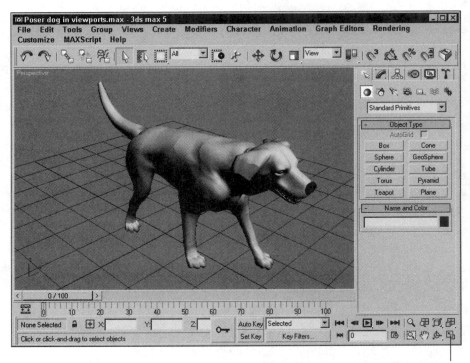

Min/Max Toggle button

Figure 2-4: Use the Min/Max Toggle to maximize the size of the active viewport.

Maximizing the viewport will help temporarily, but there is still another step to take before you need to convince your boss that you need a larger monitor. You can enter Expert Mode by choosing Views ➪ Expert Mode (Ctrl+X). It maximizes the viewport space by removing the toolbars, the Command Panel, and most of the lower interface bar.

With most of the interface elements gone, you'll need to rely on the menus, keyboard shortcuts, and the quadmenus to execute commands. To re-enable the default interface, click the Cancel Expert Mode button in the lower right of the Max window (or press Ctrl+X again). Figure 2-5 shows the interface in Expert Mode.

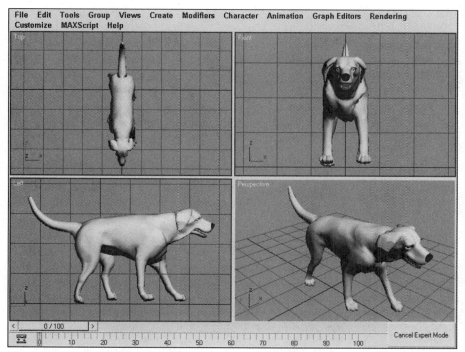

Figure 2-5: Expert Mode maximizes the viewports by eliminating most of the interface elements.

Tutorial: Navigating the active viewport

Over time, working with the Viewport Navigation controls will become second nature to you, but you'll need to practice to get to that point. In this tutorial, you'll get a chance to take the viewports for a spin—literally.

To practice navigating a viewport, follow these steps:

1. Open Poser dog in viewports.max from the Chap 02 directory on the CD-ROM.

   This file includes a model of a dog imported from Poser (affectionately named Fido). It will provide a reference as we navigate the viewport. The active viewport is the Perspective viewport.

2. Click the Min/Max Toggle button (or press Alt+W) to make the Perspective viewport fill the space of all four viewports.

3. Click the Pan button (or press Ctrl+P) and drag the window until Fido's head is centered in the viewport. Then click the Zoom button (or press Alt+Z) and drag in the Perspective viewport until Fido's head fills the viewport, as shown in Figure 2-6.

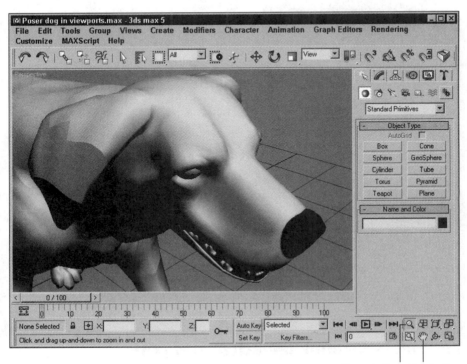

Zoom button Pan button

Figure 2-6: The Perspective viewport zoomed in on the dog's head using the Zoom and Pan controls

4. Choose Views ➪ Save Active Perspective View to save the current view of the dog's head.

5. Click the Zoom Extents button (or press Ctrl+Alt+Z) to size the entire dog body in the current viewport.

6. Click the Arc Rotate button and drag from the right square on the rotation guide to the left. This will rotate Fido to make his front side more visible, as shown in Figure 2-7.

Figure 2-7: The Perspective viewport after a slight rotation shows Fido's good side.

Configuring the Viewports

If the Viewport Navigation Controls help define what you see, then the Viewport Configuration dialog box helps define how you see objects in the viewports. You can configure each viewport using this dialog box. To open this dialog box, choose the Customize ⇨ Viewport Configuration menu command. You can also open this dialog box by right-clicking the viewport's name located in the upper-left corner of each viewport and choosing Configure from the pop-up menu. The pop-up menu itself includes many of the settings found in the Viewport Configuration dialog box, but the dialog box will let you alter several settings at once. You can also make this dialog box appear for the active viewport by right-clicking any of the Viewport Navigation buttons in the lower-right corner.

The Viewport Configuration dialog box contains several panels, including Rendering Method, Layout, Safe Frames, Adaptive Degradation, and Regions. I cover each of these panels in the sections that follow. The Preference Settings dialog box also includes many settings for controlling the behavior and look of the viewports.

Cross-Reference   See Chapter 4, "Customizing the Max Interface" for more on the Preference Settings dialog box and all of its options.

Setting the viewport rendering method

Complex scenes take longer to display and render. If every viewport is set to display the highest-quality view, then updating each viewport can slow the program to a crawl even on a fast machine. The Viewport Configuration dialog box's Rendering Method panel, shown in Figure 2-8, lets you set the rendering settings for the Active Viewport, All Viewports, or All but Active viewport.

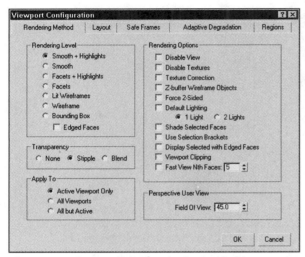

Figure 2-8: The Rendering Method panel holds controls for specifying the Rendering Level and several other rendering options.

 Note   These settings have no effect on the final output rendering specified using the Rendering menu. They only affect the display in the viewport.

Rendering Levels

The Rendering Level options, from slowest to fastest include the following:

✦ **Smooth+Highlights:** Shows smooth surfaces with lighting highlights. This rendering type is the slowest.

✦ **Smooth:** Shows smooth surfaces without any lighting effects.

✦ **Facets+Highlights:** Shows individual polygon faces and lighting highlights.

✦ **Facets:** Shows individual polygon faces with any lighting effects.

✦ **Lit Wireframes:** Shows polygon edges with lighting effects.

✦ **Wireframe:** Shows polygon edges.

✦ **Bounding Box:** Shows a box that encloses the object. This rendering type is the quickest.

Note Although it really isn't a rendering method, the Edged Faces option shows the edges for each face when a shaded rendering method is selected. You can enable and disable this option with the F4 keyboard shortcut.

Figure 2-9 shows all the various viewport rendering methods applied to a simple sphere side by side.

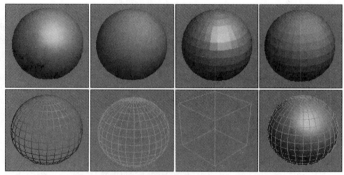

Figure 2-9: The viewport rendering methods from left to right are
First Row: Smooth+Highlights, Smooth, Facets+Highlights, Facets.
Second Row: Lit Wireframes, Wireframe, Bounding Box, and
Edged Faces applied to Smooth+Highlights.

The most common rendering setting is Wireframe. Faceted rendering displays every face as a flat plane, but it shows the object as a solid model and is good for checking whether objects overlap. The Smooth rendering level shows a rough approximation of the final rendering. Setting the rendering level to include highlights shows the effect of the lights in the scene.

Note Many effects, such as bump maps, transparent maps, and shadows, cannot be seen in the viewport and only show up in the final render.

Viewing transparency

In addition to these shading types, you can set the viewport to display objects that contain transparency (which is set in the Object Properties dialog box). The three Transparency options are None, which doesn't display any transparency; Stipple, which cross-hatches the transparent object; and Blend, which includes a transparency effect for a smooth look. Figure 2-10 shows these three transparency options with the help of a Pacman-like creature and his ghostly rival.

Note In the viewport pop-up menu, these transparency options are called None, Simple, and Best.

Figure 2-10: The viewport transparency options include None, Stipple, and Blend.

Rendering Options

The Rendering Options section within the Rendering Method panel includes several other options, such as Disable View (D) and Disable Textures. These options can help speed up viewport updates or increase the visual detail of the objects in the viewport. At any time, you can also choose Views ⇨ Redraw All Views (or press the ` key) to force all viewports to be immediately redrawn (as objects get moved around, they will often mask one another and lines will disappear).

Tip   At any time during a viewport update, you can click the mouse or press a key to cancel the redraw. Max doesn't make you wait for a screen redraw to be able to execute commands with the mouse or keyboard shortcuts.

The Disable View (D) option causes a viewport not to be updated when changes are made unless the viewport is active. Setting this option increases the speed with which the other viewports update. To reactivate the viewport, simply select Disable View again (or press the D key). When a viewport is disabled, the word *Disabled* is placed next to the viewport name.

Disable Textures turns off texture rendering for quick viewport updates. Texture Correction speeds rendering updates by interpolating the current texture rather than re-rendering. Texture Correction (along with Disable View) is one of the options available in the pop-up menu by right-clicking the viewport name.

A Z-Buffer is used to keep track of each object's distance from the camera. Enabling Z-Buffer Wireframe Objects takes advantage of this buffer for quicker updates.

Force 2-Sided makes both sides of all faces visible. For example, suppose you have a sphere with a hole in it. This setting would enable you to see the interior surface of the sphere through the hole.

The Default Lighting toggle deactivates your current lights and uses the default lights. This option can be helpful when you're trying to view objects in a dark setting. You can also specify whether default lighting uses one light or two. Scenes with one light update quicker than scenes with two.

You use Shade Selected Faces (F2) to shade selected faces in a red, semitransparent look, which enables you to see the faces shaded but still see what is behind them.

Note   The Shade Selected Faces (F2) option, which shades selected subobject faces is different from the Views ⇨ Shade Selected menu command, which turns on shading for the selected object in all viewports.

The Use Selection Brackets option displays white corners around the current selection. Selection brackets are useful for helping you see the entire size of a grouped object but can be annoying if left on with many objects selected. Uncheck this option to make these brackets disappear.

The option to Display Selected with Edged Faces helps to highlight the selected object. If this option is enabled, then the edges of the current selection are displayed regardless of whether the Edged Faces check box is enabled. Figure 2-11 shows Fido with his upper torso selected with the Display Selected with Edged Faces option and the Use Selection Brackets enabled. These options make the current selection easy to see.

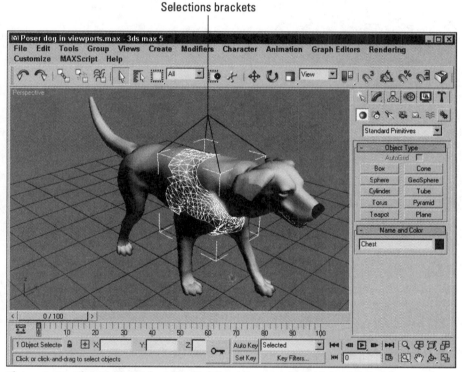

Figure 2-11: The Display Selected with Edged Faces and Use Selection Brackets options make identifying the current selection easy.

Clipping planes defines an invisible barrier beyond which all objects are invisible. For example, if you have a scene with many detailed mountain objects in the background, working with an object in the front of the scene can be difficult. By setting the clipping plane between the two, you can work on the front objects without having to update the mountain objects every time you update the scene.

Viewport Clipping places a yellow line with two arrows on the right side of the viewport, as shown in Figure 2-12. The top arrow represents the back clipping plane, and the bottom arrow is the front clipping plane. Drag the arrows to set the clipping planes. You can quickly turn viewport clipping on or off by right-clicking the viewport name and choosing Viewport Clipping from the pop-up menu.

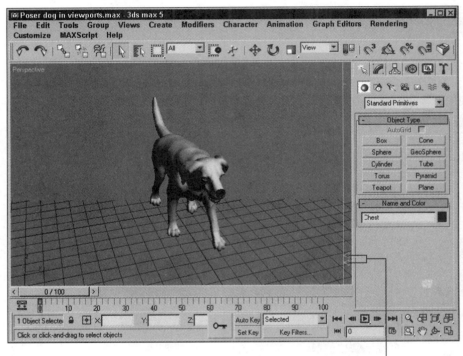

Clipping Plane markers

Figure 2-12: The Clipping Plane is hiding the grid plane directly behind Fido. Run, boy, run!

Fast View speeds viewport updates by only drawing a limited number of faces. The spinner value determines how often faces are drawn. For example, a setting of 5 would only draw every fifth face. Fast View will render viewport updates much quicker and give you an idea of the objects without displaying the entire object.

Tutorial: Creating interesting patterns with the Fast View setting

You can use the Fast View setting in the Viewport Configuration dialog box to create some interesting patterns.

To create patterned spheres, follow these steps:

1. Open the Patterned sphere.max file from the Chap 02 directory on the CD-ROM.

   This file has a simple smooth sphere.

2. Click in the Top view and choose Customize ➪ Viewport Configuration to open the Viewport Configuration dialog box. Select the Smooth Rendering Level and the Fast View Nth Faces options. Set the Fast View Nth Faces value to 2.

3. Repeat Step 2 for the Front, Left, and Perspective viewports, setting the Fast View Nth Faces values to 3, 4, and 5, respectively.

Figure 2-13 shows a sphere rendered using the Fast View option. Notice how the settings for each viewport can be different.

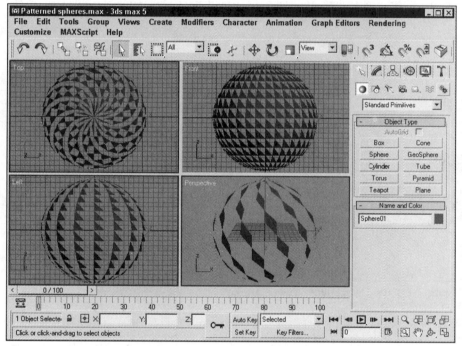

Figure 2-13: Cool patterns created with the Fast View setting in the Viewport Configuration dialog box

Note If any of these spheres were rendered using the Rendering menu, the entire sphere would be visible. The Fast View option only affects the viewport display.

Setting the Field of View

You can also alter the Field of View for the Perspective view in the Viewport Configuration dialog box. To create a fish-eye view, increase the FOV setting to 10 or less. The maximum FOV value is 180 and the default value is 45. You can also change the Field of View using the button in the Viewport Navigation Controls. The Viewport Configuration dialog box, however, lets you enter precise values.

Cross-Reference See Chapter 21, "Controlling Cameras," for more coverage on Field of View.

Altering the Viewport layout

Now that you've started to figure out the viewports, you might want to change the number and size of viewports that are displayed. The Layout panel, shown in Figure 2-14, in the Viewpoint Configuration dialog box offers several layouts as alternatives to the default layout (not that there is anything wrong with the default and its four equally sized viewports).

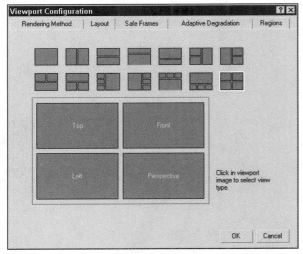

Figure 2-14: The Layout panel offers many layout options.

After selecting a layout from the options at the top of the panel, you can assign each individual viewport a different view by clicking the viewport and choosing a view from the pop-up menu. The view options include Perspective, User, Front, Back, Top, Bottom, Left, Right, ActiveShade, Track, Schematic, Grid, Extended, and Shape.

Views can also be set to Camera and Spotlight if they exist in the scene. Each camera and light that exists will be listed by name at the top of the pop-up menu.

Using Safe Frames

Completing an animation and converting it to some broadcast medium, only to see that the whole left side of the animation is being cut off in the final screening, can be discouraging. Using the Safe Frames feature, you can display some guides within the viewport that will show where these clipping edges are.

The Safe Frames panel of the Viewport Configuration dialog box lets you define several different safe frame options, as shown in Figure 2-15, including

✦ **Live Area:** Renders the full screen, marked with yellow lines.

✦ **Action Safe:** The area ensured to be visible in the final rendered file, marked with light blue lines.

✦ **Title Safe:** The area where the title can safely appear without distortion, marked with orange lines.

✦ **User Safe:** The output area defined by the user, marked with magenta lines.

✦ **12-Field Grid:** Displays a grid in the viewport, marked with a pink grid.

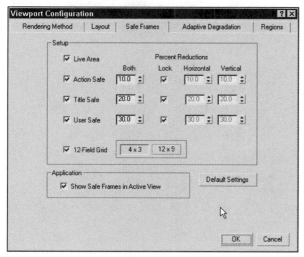

Figure 2-15: The Safe Frames panel lets you specify areas to render.

For each type of safe frame, you can set the percent reduction by entering values in the Horizontal, Vertical, or Both fields. The 12-Field Grid option offers 4 × 3 and 12 × 9 aspect ratios.

The Show Safe Frames in Active View option will display the Safe Frame borders in the active viewport. You can quickly enable or disable Safe Frames by right-clicking the viewport name and choosing Show Safe Frame in the pop-up menu (or you can use the Shift+F keyboard shortcut).

Figure 2-16 shows the Perspective viewport with all the safe frame guides enabled. Fido should feel pretty safe.

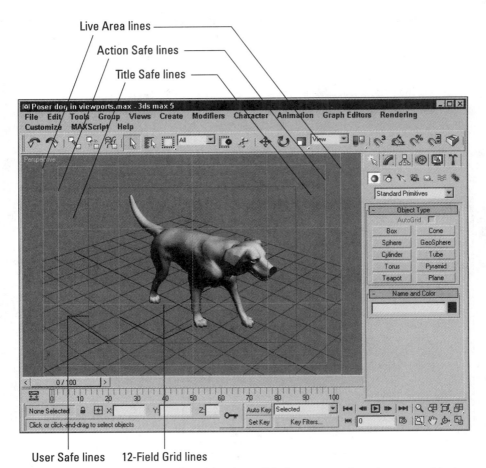

Figure 2-16: Safe frames provide guides that will help you see when the scene objects are out of bounds.

Understanding Adaptive Degradation

When you are previewing a complex animation sequence in a viewport, slow updates can affect the timing of the animation. This can make proofing your work difficult and would require many additional, fully rendered tasks. The feature in Max that addresses this issue is called Adaptive Degradation. It enables you to force a viewport to display at a prespecified number of frames per second. If the display update takes too long to maintain this rate, then it automatically degrades the rendering level in order to maintain the frame rate. This option is very helpful because when you're testing an animation, you are not as concerned about the model details or textures.

The Adaptive Degradation panel is available in the Viewport Configuration dialog box, as shown in Figure 2-17.

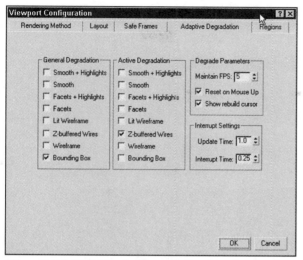

Figure 2-17: The Adaptive Degradation panel maintains a defined frame rate by degrading the rendering level.

You can enable Adaptive Degradation by using the Views ➪ Adaptive Degradation menu command (or by pressing the O key). Adaptive Degradation, when enabled, will only be used for animation sequences where the objects are updated within the viewport quickly. If the animation isn't progressing, then enabling and disabling Adaptive Degradation will have no effect.

Cross-Reference

You can learn to animate objects in Chapter 24, "Animation Basics."

You enter the frame rate that you want to maintain into the Maintain FPS box in the Degrade Parameters section. The General Degradation selection specifies the render level used by all inactive viewports; the Active Degradation selection is used by the active viewport. You can select several rendering levels in each section.

Tip

Another way to speed the frame rate in the active viewport is to disable (D) the inactive viewports.

The Reset on Mouse Up option forces Max to render at the specified rendering levels when the mouse is released. The Show Rebuild Cursor option makes the cursor visible as the viewports are rendered. The Update Time is the amount of time between rendering updates. At a setting of 0, each frame must be completely rendered before the next frame is attempted. The Interrupt Time value is how long Max waits before checking to see whether the mouse has moved.

Defining regions

Regions, the final panel in the Viewport Configuration dialog box, enables you to define regions and focus your rendering energies on a smaller area. Complex scenes can take considerable time and machine power to render. Sometimes you'll want to test render only a portion of a viewport to check material assignment, texture map placement, or lighting.

You can define the size of the various Regions in the Regions panel of the Viewport Configuration dialog box, shown in Figure 2-18.

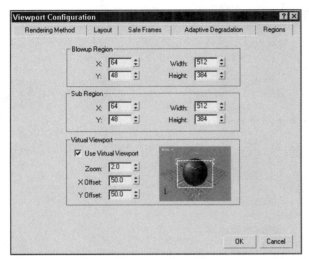

Figure 2-18: The Regions panel enables you to work with smaller regions within your scene.

 After you've specified a Blowup Region or a Sub Region, you can select to render using these regions by selecting Region or Blowup from the Render Type drop-down list on the far right end of the main toolbar, and clicking the Quick Render button. The difference between these two regions is that the Sub Region displays the Virtual Frame Buffer in black except for the specified subregion. The Blowup region fills the entire Virtual Frame Buffer.

Cross-Reference You can learn more about Render Types and the Virtual Frame Buffer in Chapter 24, "Animation Basics."

The Virtual Viewport is a feature that lets you zoom in and pan within the viewport image using the number pad keys. This feature is only available if you are using the OpenGL display driver. You can check to see which display driver you are using by selecting Help ➪ About 3ds max. This will open a credits screen that lists the current driver. You can change the current display driver in the Viewport panel of the Preference Settings dialog box.

If you have OpenGL set up as the current display driver, then you can select Use Virtual Viewport to display the viewport in the area to the right. Using the Zoom, X, and Y Offset values, you can specify where the Virtual Viewport looks or you can drag the rectangular outline in the visible screen to the right.

Once enabled, you can use the divide key (/) on the numeric keypad to turn the virtual viewport on and off. Use the plus (+) and minus (-) numeric keypad keys to zoom in and out, and use the 2, 4, 6, and 8 keys on the numeric keypad to pan within the virtual viewport.

Caution The Virtual Viewport feature is only available if you are using the OpenGL driver. If you've specified either the Software Z-Buffer or the Direct X driver, then this option isn't available.

Working with Viewport Backgrounds

Remember in grade school when you realized that you could immediately draw really well using tracing paper (where all you needed to do was follow the lines)? Well, it's not quite tracing paper, but you can load background images into a viewport that can help as you create and position your objects.

Loading viewport background images

The Views ➪ Viewport Background menu command (Alt+B) opens a dialog box, shown in Figure 2-19, in which you can select an image or animation to appear behind a viewport. The displayed background image is helpful for aligning objects in a scene, but it is for display purposes only and will not be rendered. To create a background image to be rendered, use the Environment command in the Rendering menu.

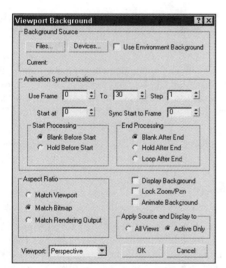

Figure 2-19: The Viewport Background dialog box lets you select a background source image or animation.

If the background image changes, you can update the viewport using the Views ➪ Update Background Image menu command (Alt+Shift+Ctrl+B). The Views ➪ Reset Background Transform menu command automatically rescales and recenters the background image to fit the viewport.

Each viewport can have a different background image. To load and configure a viewport background image, choose Views ➪ Viewport Background (or press the Alt+B keyboard shortcut). This opens the Viewport Background dialog box, shown previously.

The Files button opens the Select Background Image dialog box, where you can select the image to load. The Devices button lets you obtain a background from a device such as a Video Recorder. If an environment map is already loaded into the Environment dialog box, you can simply click the Use Environment Background option. Keep in mind that the background image will not be rendered unless it is made into an Environment map.

Cross-Reference   I cover environment maps in Chapter 35, "Working with Environments and Atmospheric Effects."

Loading viewport background animations

The Animation Synchronization section lets you set which frames of a background animation sequence are displayed. The Use Frame and To values determine which frames of the loaded animation are used. The Step value trims the number of frames that are to be used by selecting every Nth frame. For example, a Step value of 4 would use every fourth frame.

Tip   Loading an animation sequence as a viewport background can really help as you begin to animate complex motions like a running horse. By stepping through the frames of the animation, you can line up your model with the background image for realistic animations.

The Start At value is the frame in the current scene where this background animation would first appear. The Sync Start to Frame value is the frame of the background animation that should appear first. The Start and End Processing options let you determine what appears before the Start and End frames. Options include displaying a blank, holding the current frame, and looping.

If you select an animation as the background, make sure the Animate Background option is selected. Also note that the viewport background will not be visible if the Display Background option is not selected.

The Aspect Ratio section offers options for setting the size of the background image. You can select to Match Viewport, Match Bitmap, or Match Rendering Output.

The Lock Zoom/Pan option is available if either the Match Bitmap or Match Rendering Output options are selected. This option will lock the background image to the geometry so that when the objects in the scene are zoomed or panned, the background image follows. If the background gets out of line, you can reset its position with the Views ➪ Reset Background Transform command.

Caution   When the Lock Zoom/Pan option is selected, the background image is resized when you zoom in on an object. Resizing the background image will fill the virtual memory, and if you zoom in too far the background image could exceed your virtual memory. If this happens a dialog box will appear that informs you of the problem and gives you the option of not displaying the background image.

You can set the Apply Source and Display to option to display the background in All Views or in the Active Only.

Tutorial: Loading reference images for modeling

When modeling a physical object, you can get a jump on the project by taking pictures with a digital camera of the front, top and left views of the object, then load them as background images in the respective viewports. The background images can then be a reference for your work. This is especially helpful with models that need to be precise. You could even work from CAD drawings.

To load the background images of a brass swan sculpture, follow these steps:

1. Choose File ➪ New (or press Ctrl+N) to open a blank scene file.

2. Right-click on the Front viewport to make it the active viewport and choose Views ➪ Viewport Background (or press Alt+B). The Viewport Background dialog box opens.

3. Click on the Files button and in the file dialog box that opens, select the Brass swan-front view.jpg image from the Chap 02 directory on the CD-ROM.

4. Select the Match Bitmap, Display Background, Lock Zoom/Pan, and Active Only options and click OK to close the dialog box. The image now appears in the background of the Front viewport.

5. Repeat Steps 2 through 4 for the Top and Left viewports.

Figure 2-20 shows the Max interface with background images loaded in the Front, Top, and Left viewports.

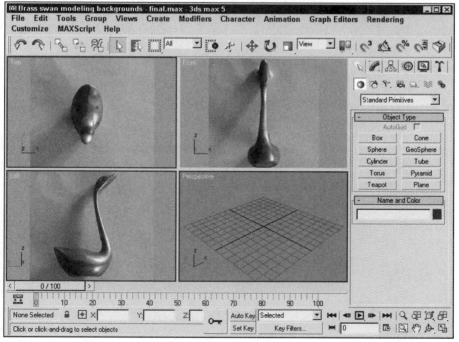

Figure 2-20: Adding a background image to a viewport can help as you begin to model objects.

Summary

Viewports are the window into the Max world. Remember that if you can't see it, you can't work with it, so you'll need to learn to use the viewports. You can also configure viewports to display just the way you desire.

In this chapter, you

- ✦ Learned about the various viewport types
- ✦ Covered the various Viewport Navigation buttons
- ✦ Set the Rendering Level and Display options in the Viewport Configuration dialog box
- ✦ Used the other panels of the Viewport Configuration dialog box to change the layout, safe frames, and regions
- ✦ Learned how you can use Adaptive Degradation to maintain a constant frame rate for viewport animation sequences
- ✦ Loaded a viewport background image

In the next chapter, you find out all the details about working with files, including loading, saving, and merging scene files. You also learn about External References (XRefs) and how to use them to manage scene creation in a workgroup. The next chapter also covers import and export options for interfacing with other software packages.

✦   ✦   ✦

Working with Files

Complex scenes can end up being a collection of hundreds of files, and misplacing any of them will affect the final output, so learning to work with files is critical. This chapter focuses on working with files whether they be object files, texture images, or backgrounds. Files enable you to move scene pieces into and out of Max. You can also export and import files to and from other packages.

Max scenes can also be composed from several different objects that have been created by a team. Using external references (XRefs), you can pull all the different pieces together into a single scene.

Working with Max Scene Files

Of all the different file types and formats, there is one file type that you will probably work with more than any other—the max format. Max has its own proprietary format for its scene files. These files have the .max extension and allow you to save your work as a file and return to it at a later time.

When Max starts, a new scene opens. You can start a new scene at any time with the File ⇨ New (Ctrl+N) command, but Max can have only one scene open at a time. Starting a new scene deletes the current scene, but Max asks you whether you want to keep the objects and hierarchy, keep the objects, or make everything new, as shown in Figure 3-1. Starting a new scene with the File ⇨ New command maintains all the current interface settings, including the viewports and Command Panel. To reset the interface, choose File ⇨ Reset. When reset, all interface settings return to their default states, but interface changes aren't affected.

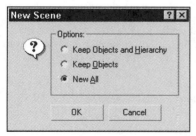

Figure 3-1: When creating a new scene, you can keep the current objects.

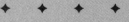

Saving files

After you start up Max, the first thing you should learn is how to save your work. After a scene has changed, you can save it as a file. Choose File ➪ Save (Ctrl+S) to save the scene to the current name. If the scene hasn't been saved yet, then a Save File As dialog box appears, as shown in Figure 3-2. You can also make this dialog box appear using the File ➪ Save As command. Pretty simple—just don't forget to do it often.

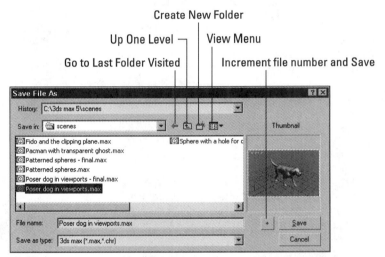

Figure 3-2: Use the Save File As dialog box to save a scene as a file.

The Save File As dialog box keeps a history list of the last five directories that you've opened. You can select these directories from the History drop-down list at the top of the dialog box. The buttons in this dialog box are the standard Windows file dialog box buttons used to go to the last folder visited, go up one directory, create a new folder, and to view a pop-up menu of file view options. The options include Large Icons, Small Icons, List, Details, and Thumbnails. The thumbnail displays an image of the active viewport of the scene.

Note   If you try to save a scene over the top of an existing scene, then Max presents a dialog box confirming this action.

Clicking the button with a plus sign to the right of the Save button automatically appends a number onto the end of the current filename and saves the file. For example, if you select the myScene.max file and click the plus button, then a file named myScene01.max will be saved.

Tip   Use the auto increment file number and Save button to save progressive versions of a scene. This is an easy version control system. If you ever need to backtrack to an earlier version, you will be able to.

The File menu also includes an option to Save Selected. This option saves the current selected objects to a separate scene file.

Another useful feature for saving files is to enable the Auto Backup feature in the File panel of the Preference Settings dialog box. This dialog box can be accessed with the Customize ➪ Preferences menu command.

Cross-Reference I talk about the Auto Backup feature in Chapter 4, "Customizing the Max Interface."

Opening files

After you've saved a file, it might be important to know how to open it again. Choosing File ➪ Open (Ctrl+O) opens a file dialog box that is the same as the one used to save files, shown in Figure 3-2. Selecting a file and clicking on the plus button opens a copy of the selected file with a new version number appended to its name.

Note If Max cannot locate resources used within a scene (such as maps) when you open a Max file, then a dialog box appears enabling you to locate or skip the missing files.

If you open a file that includes features that have changed since the previous version, then Max presents a warning statement like the one shown in Figure 3-3. Resaving the file can fix this problem.

Tip You can disable the Obsolete File Message in the Files panel of the Preference Settings dialog box.

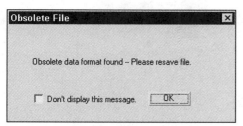

Figure 3-3: This warning appears when you open a scene file with obsolete data.

The most recently opened scenes will all be listed at the bottom of the File menu. Selecting these scenes from the list will open the scene file.

Caution If you save a file created with a previous version of Max as a Max 5 scene file, then you will not be able to open the file again in the previous versions of Max.

Merging and replacing objects

If you happen to create the perfect prop in one scene that you want to integrate with another scene, you can use the Merge menu command. Choose File ➪ Merge to load objects from another scene into the current scene. Using this command opens a file dialog box that is exactly like the Save As dialog box, but after you select a scene and click the Open button, the Merge dialog box, shown in Figure 3-4, appears. This dialog box displays all the objects found in the selected scene file. It also has options for sorting the objects and filtering certain types of objects. Selecting an object and clicking the OK button loads the object into the current scene.

Note   The Merge dialog box is very similar to the Select Objects dialog box.

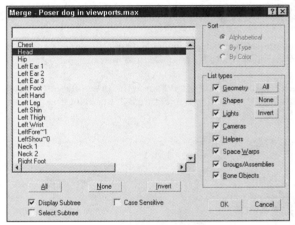

Figure 3-4: The Merge dialog box lists all the objects from a merging scene.

If you ever get involved in a modeling duel, then you'll probably be using the replace command at some time. A modeling duel is when two modelers work on the same rough model of named objects and the animator (or boss) gets to choose which object parts to use. With the File ➪ Replace command, you can replace a named object with an object of the same name in a different scene. The objects are selected using the same dialog box shown in Figure 3-4, but only the objects with identical names in both scene files display. If no objects with the same name appear in both scene files, a warning box will be displayed.

Cross-Reference   The File menu also includes a Merge Animation menu command. I cover this command in Chapter 24, "Animation Basics."

Archiving files

By archiving a Max scene along with its reference bitmaps, you can ensure that it includes all the necessary files. This is especially useful if you need to send the project to your cousin to show off or to your boss and you don't want to miss any ancillary files. Choose File ➪ Archive to save scene files as a compressed archive. The default archive format is .zip (but you can change it in the Preference Settings dialog box to use whatever archive format you want). Saving an archive as a .zip file compiles all external files, such as bitmaps, into a single compressed file. The File Type drop-down list of the File Archive dialog box also includes an option to create a List of Files. When you select this file type, a text file is created that lists all relevant files and their paths.

Getting out

As you can probably guess, you use the File ➪ Exit command to exit the program, but only after it gives you a chance to save your work. Clicking on the window icon with an X on it in the upper right has the same affect (but I'm sure you knew that).

Importing and Exporting

If you haven't noticed, Max isn't the only game in town. A number of different 3D packages exist, and exchanging files between them is where the importing and exporting menu commands come in. You can find both of these commands in the File menu.

On the CD-ROM in the Chap 03 directory, you can find samples of many of these formats.

Importing geometric objects

Choose File ➪ Import to open the Import dialog box. This dialog box looks like a typical Windows file dialog box. The real power comes with the various Import Settings dialog boxes that are available for each format. For example, let's say that you want to import an old 3DS file into a current Max session. After you select the file to import, a small dialog box titled 3DS Import appears with options to merge the imported objects with the current scene or completely replace the current scene (you'll also have the option to convert units on the imported file). The settings in the Import Settings dialog box will be different for the various format types.

In addition to importing, there will be times when you'll want to export Max objects for use in other programs. You access the Export command by choosing File ➪ Export. You also have the option to Export Selected (available only if an object is selected).

Max can import and export several different formats. Files that Max can import include

✦ 3D Studio Mesh, Projects, and Shapes (3DS, PRJ, SHP)

✦ Adobe Illustrator (AI)

✦ AutoCAD (DWG, DXF)

✦ FiLMBOX (FBX)

✦ IGES (IGE, IGS, IGES)

✦ Lightscape (LS, VW, LP)

✦ StereoLithography (STL)

✦ VRML97 (WRL, WRZ)

Note   The AutoCAD (DWG), StereoLithography (STL), and VRML (WRL) formats are scene formats that cannot save individual objects.

In addition to these formats, Max can also export a scene using the ASCII Scene Export (ASE) option. The Lightscape export options also include support for several different types of formats.

Note   You can set Max to reorient all the viewports by automatically zooming to the extents of the imported object by setting the Zoom Extents on Import option in the Files panel of the Preference Settings dialog box.

Importing and exporting 3D Studio files (3DS, PRJ, SHP)

It shouldn't be a surprise that Max can import 3D Studio (3DS) files without much headache—after all, 3D Studio was the predecessor to Max.

Everything in a 3DS file is imported into Max except for Morph Keys, Keyframer Instances, .CUB cubic maps, and decal transparency defined by the upper-left pixel. Imported SHP files convert 2D polygons created with 3D Studio's Shaper tool into Bézier splines. The shapes can be imported as a single object or as multiple objects. PRJ files are simply 3DS files that include shapes. Or, you can select to not import shapes.

Importing a 3D Studio file opens a simple dialog box, shown in Figure 3-5. The dialog box offers options to merge or replace the current scene. It also includes an option to Convert Units. With the Convert Units option selected, Max assumes that the 3DS file is based in inches and converts it to the currently defined units.

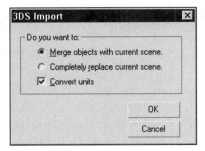

Figure 3-5: The 3DS Import dialog box enables you to merge objects into or completely replace the current scene.

Before loading the file, Max asks whether you want to set the animation length of the current scene to match the animation length in the 3DS file.

Max can only export to the 3DS format and not the PRJ and SHP formats. After you select Export, the Export Scene to .3DS File dialog box appears with only one option—to Preserve Max's Texture Coordinates. When you are exporting to the 3DS format, all mesh characteristics are exported except for any composite or procedural maps, UV mapping coordinates, any transformations applied to a group, and global shadow parameters.

Any objects that aren't represented by meshes, such as NURBS and procedural primitives, are converted to meshes.

Importing and exporting Illustrator files (AI)

You can import files created using Adobe Illustrator into Max. After you have selected an Illustrator file, the AI Import dialog box offers the same options of merging the objects into the current scene or replacing the current scene. Following the AI Import dialog box, the Shape Import dialog box appears with options to import the shapes as a single object or as multiple objects. During the import process, the 2D polygons are all converted to Bézier curves. Max can only import curves and paths from Illustrator. All effects such as fills, gradients, and filter effects will be lost in the translation.

Note   Max cannot import text created in Illustrator unless it has been converted to outlines. In Illustrator, you perform this task by selecting the text and choosing Type ➪ Outlines.

Many different Illustrator versions exist. When saving a file in Illustrator, you can specify to use version 3.0, 4.0, 5.0/5.5, 6.0, 7.0, 8.0, 9.0, and now 10.0. The AI88 refers to the format used prior to Illustrator version 3.0. Max can import all these different formats.

Only shapes and splines can be exported to the AI format. If you try to export a Max file containing any objects except for shapes to the AI format, you get an AIEXP error message. You can export shapes from within a scene using the Export Selected command.

Importing and exporting AutoCAD files (DWG, DXF)

AutoCAD is a sister product to Max, aimed at the Computer-Aided Design market. It was produced by the same parent company and for that reason interacts very well with Max. AutoCAD uses two main formats — DWG (which stands for Drawing files) and the older DXF (which stands for Drawing Exchange Format).

Importing DWG files

Objects in AutoCAD are named differently from Max objects. For example, AutoCAD includes a 3D Face object, a Polyline Mesh object, a Polyface Mesh object, and an ACIS object. During the import process, all these objects are converted to corresponding mesh objects in Max, because Max doesn't distinguish among these types.

Note   AutoSurf and AutoCAD Designer use the 3DSOUT command to export models to Max.

The Import AutoCAD DWG File dialog box, shown in Figure 3-6, includes many options that help define the translation process. Distinct objects in an AutoCAD file can be identified by layer, color, or type. The Import AutoCAD DWG dialog box can specify how to interpret these separate objects through the Layer, Color, and Entity options in the Derive Objects By section.

In AutoCAD, objects are grouped together as blocks. In the Import AutoCAD DWG File dialog box, these blocks can be converted to single objects or to groups. You can also select to skip layers that are turned off or frozen, and to ignore hatch patterns and point objects.

When DWG files are saved, extra vertices are often saved with the model. The Weld option automatically combines vertices that are closer than the Threshold value. This option can quickly reduce the complexity of the model.

The Smooth-angle setting defines whether adjacent polygons are rendered smoothly or with a sharp edge. The angle is calculated by comparing the normals of the adjacent polygons (a *normal* is a vector that is perpendicular to the polygon face). Polygons that are coplanar (existing in the same plane) have normals that point in the same direction, so their angle would be zero. On the other hand, two polygons that are at right angles would have an angle of 90 degrees and would appear as a sharp edge if the smooth angle were less than 90.

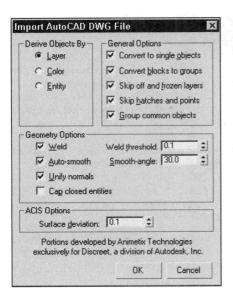

Figure 3-6: The Import AutoCAD DWG File dialog box determines how the file is imported.

The single ACIS option lets you specify a Surface deviation value. Small values produce more faces for greater detail, and larger values do the opposite.

Importing DXF files

After the initial merge/replace dialog box, the Import DXF File dialog box, shown in Figure 3-7, opens. This dialog box also includes settings for extracting different objects within the DXF file. You can also separate DXF models into different parts with the Layers, Colors, and Entities options. The most common way of separating various parts is by Layer. If your object appears as one solid mass, try importing again and changing this setting.

The Arc Subdivision section specifies degree values between successive vertices required to begin a new mesh or spline on imported polygon meshes and splines. A setting of 90 for splines means that if the difference between this node and the next node is less than 90 degrees, then the node will be part of the existing spline.

The Miscellaneous options can fix common problems with DXF files such as duplicate faces, noncapped meshes being mistaken for splines, and normals that point toward the center of the object, producing a hole when rendered.

Other options include a Weld Threshold, Auto Smoothing of angles, and Unify Normals.

Exporting AutoCAD files (DWG, DXF)

Exporting to the DXF format opens the Export DXF File dialog box, which contains the Save To Layers options of By Objects, By Materials, and 1 Layer. The Export AutoCAD DWG File dialog box is more complicated than other export options, as shown in Figure 3-8. The Convert Groups To option enables you to choose Groups or Layers. The General Options enable you to save the file in the AutoCAD R14 format. The default is to save it as an AutoCAD 2000 file. Additional General Options include Convert Instances to Blocks, Skip Hidden Objects, Ignore Extrude Capping, and Export Selected Objects Only.

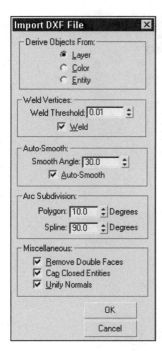

Figure 3-7: The Import DXF File dialog box offers settings for making the file import correctly.

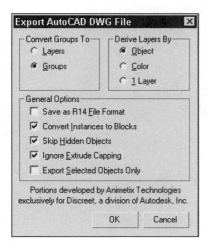

Figure 3-8: The Export AutoCAD DWG File dialog box can export groups as well as layers.

Importing and exporting FilmBox files (FBX)

Another common 3D format was created by a company named Kaydara for their FilmBox product. FilmBox is used to work with motion capture data. Files saved in this format have the .fbx extension.

New Feature

Importing and exporting to the FilmBox format is new in 3ds max 5.

The Import FBX File dialog box, shown in Figure 3-9, lets you import any animation sequences listed in the top list box. These animation sequences can be merged, exclusive merged, or added to the current scene or a new scene. You can also specify to import a Hierarchy, Bones, Geometries, Cameras, Lights, Markers, Shapes, and Animations. You also have the options to Rescale scene root nodes to unit size and rotate the root nodes with Y-up to Z-up.

Tip   Both SoftImage and Maya support the FilmBox file format, so this format can be used to move scenes between these systems.

The export options include the same set of objects with the addition of Skin objects. You can also set the Resampling rate and enable options to Show Warnings and to embed textures. The Export FBX File dialog box is also shown in Figure 3-9.

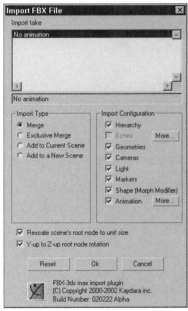 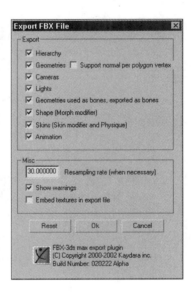

Figure 3-9: The Import and Export FBX File dialog boxes allow you to import and export animation sequences.

Importing and exporting IGES files (IGES)

IGES stands for Initial Graphics Exchange Standard. The IGES format supports NURBS and provides a standard way to import and export NURBS objects. With IGES import and export features, Max files can share objects with packages such as Mechanical Desktop, Maya, Pro/ENGINEER, SoftImage, and CATIA, among others.

When you import an IGES file, the only dialog box to appear is the Merge/Replace dialog box shown in earlier sections.

In the IGES format, all entities have an entity number and name. The Max Online Reference includes a table that correlates the conversion of the various IGES entities to Max objects. For example, an IGES element labeled 100 is a Circular Arc that will be converted to a Max Arc Shape.

IGES conversion can be tricky, so a log file of the process is saved with the .XLI extension. An IGES file with several meshes is converted to a single NURBS surface in Max with each original mesh being a separate subobject surface. To work with these subobject surfaces, you need to make them independent from the NURBS object.

Cross-Reference   Chapter 15, "Working with NURBS," covers NURBS in more detail.

Exporting objects to the IGES format presents a single simple dialog box with options to Export Hidden Objects and to Export Selected Objects Only.

Importing and exporting Lightscape files (LS, VW, LP)

Lightscape is an architectural rendering system that can generate scenes with an advanced lighting method known as radiosity. Radiosity simulates real lighting effects by taking into account how light bounces off objects.

Cross-Reference   Many of the features from the Lightscape product have been included in Max. You can find information on these features in Chapter 23, "Advanced Lighting and Radiosity."

Files saved in Lightscape with the LS, VW, or LP extensions can be imported into Max. These represent older Lightscape files, Lightscape Views, and Lightscape Preparation files. Importing a Lightscape Preparation file opens the dialog box shown in Figure 3-10. This dialog box lets you group entities by layers, materials, or materials within layers. You can also select to skip any layers that are off and replace the current scene.

New Feature   Importing and exporting to the Lightscape format is new in 3ds max 5.

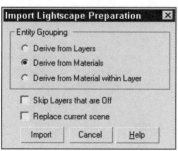

Figure 3-10: The Import Lightscape Preparation dialog box can specify how entity grouping is derived.

Exporting Lightscape files offers many more options. Max files can be exported to Lightscape as Lightscape Materials (ATR), Blocks (BLK), Parameters (DF), Layers (LAY), Preparation (LP), and Views (VW). Each of these formats will have its own unique export options.

The Lightscape format with the most options is the Preparation files. The other Lightscape formats have many of the same options. Figure 3-11 shows two panels (General and Lights) on the Export Lightscape Preparation File dialog box.

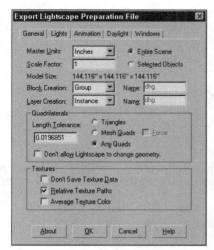 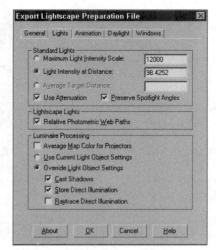

Figure 3-11: The Export Lightscape Preparation dialog box includes multiple panels of options.

Importing and exporting StereoLithography files (STL)

StereoLithography is a file format used by various manufacturing machines for rapid prototyping of products. Importing an STL file opens the Import STL File dialog box, shown in Figure 3-12. Available options include Weld Vertices (including a Quick Weld feature), which you use to combine vertices closer than the Weld Threshold value; Auto-Smooth, which defines whether adjacent polygon faces should be smoothed; Unify Normals, which causes all normals to point the same direction; and Remove Double Faces, which simplifies the geometry.

The Export STL File dialog box offers options for choosing whether to export the STL file as a Binary or ASCII file. Be aware that StereoLithography objects must be closed surfaces. Max includes the STL-Check modifier that verifies this. Using this modifier can save you some headaches when exporting.

Cross-Reference   I discuss modifiers such as the STL-Check modifier in Chapter 10, "Using Modifiers."

Importing and exporting VRML files (WRL, WRZ)

VRML stands for Virtual Reality Modeling Language and like HTML, defines scenes that can be interpreted by VRML browsers embedded within a Web browser. Max can import VRML files with the WRL and WRZ (which are compressed VRML files), but only export to the VRML97 standard with the WRL extension.

Importing VRML files

The VRML Import dialog box includes options to Reset Scene, Turn to 3DS Coordinates, and Create Primitives. The Reset Scene option deletes the existing scene. Once deselected, the imported file merges into the current scene. The Turn to 3DS Coordinates option switches the Y and Z coordinates. In VRML scenes, the Y-axis points up, but in Max the Z-axis points up. The Create Primitives option converts VRML primitives to their Max equivalents.

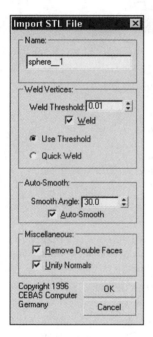

Figure 3-12: The Import STL File dialog box enables you to name the STL file and set other options.

Exporting VRML97

VRML97 is the only VRML format that Max can export to. The VRML97 Exporter dialog box, shown in Figure 3-13, includes many options, including generating Normals, Primitives, Color per Vertex, Coordinate Interpolators, and a Flip-Book.

The Initial View drop-down list lets you select a camera to display when the file first loads into a browser. Many VRML browsers support multiple viewpoints. Each camera in the scene will become a different viewpoint when the VRML file is viewed in a browser. You can select Export Hidden Objects, but by default they are not exported. The Show Progress Bar is only visible while the file is being exported.

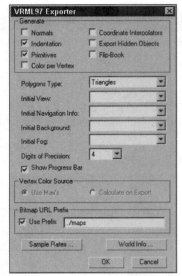

Figure 3-13: The VRML97 Exporter dialog box includes options set by the VRML97 Helper. The Animation Sample Rates dialog box lets you define the frames per second.

The Normals option aids the browser in rendering smooth objects. The Indentation option aligns the actual code to make it more readable in a text editor.

Primitives supported by the VRML browser are much more efficient than polygonal meshes. The Primitives option converts objects to primitive objects when possible.

The Color per Vertex option exports any vertex colors that are defined in the scene. You can also select Use Max's Settings or Calculate on Export, which will calculate vertex colors based on scene lighting. The Digits of Precision can also be defined.

By default, all texture maps must reside in the same directory as the WRL file. The Use Prefix option lets you define a subdirectory for holding any texture maps.

The Coordinate Interpolators option exports animation effects caused by Modifiers and Space Warps. The Flip-Book option exports VRML scenes as multiple files. Clicking the Sample Rates button opens the Animation Sample Rates dialog box, also shown in Figure 3-13, which enables you to specify custom frame rates for the Flip-Book, for the Transform Controllers, and for the Coordinate Interpolators.

Note   Exporting animation effects using the Coordinate Interpolators can produce huge VRML files.

The Polygons Type section of the VRML97 Exporter dialog box lets you specify how individual faces are exported — options include Ngons, Quads, Triangles, and Visible Edges. The Initial View drop-down list is still available, and below it are drop-down lists for Initial Navigation Info, Initial Background, and Initial Fog. All three are set by the VRML97 helper and are found as subcategories under the Helpers category in the Create panel.

The World Info button opens the World Info dialog box, in which you can give the VRML file a Title and file description.

The VRML97 Helper objects

To aid in the creation of VRML worlds, Max includes several additional helper objects. The VRML97 helper objects provide a way to add features such as anchors and sensors to scene objects in preparation for exporting a scene to the VRML97 format. You can find these tools as a subcategory under the Helpers category in the Create panel.

The VRML97 subcategory from the Helper category in the Create panel includes buttons for the following VRML97 features: Anchor, TouchSensor, ProxSensor, TimeSensor, NavInfo, Background, Fog, AudioClip, Sound, Billboard, LOD, and Inline, shown in Figure 3-14. Each of these buttons opens a rollout containing its parameters. Many of these features are beyond the scope of this book but are covered in detail in the many VRML references that are available.

The Anchor rollout lets you pick a Trigger object that will hyperlink the user to a separate URL. The TouchSensor rollout lets you select objects to animate when a Trigger object is touched. The ProxSensor rollout lets you set a trigger when a user gets within a certain defined proximity to an object. The TimeSensor rollout sets regular time intervals.

Figure 3-14: Use the VRML97 Helper objects to define export options for VRML files.

The NavInfo rollout tells the VRML Browser how the user can navigate about the VRML Scene. The Background rollout specifies the sky and ground colors and any images to use for the background. The Fog rollout lets you define how fog appears in the scene.

The AudioClip rollout is used in conjunction with the Sound rollout. The Sound rollout defines the sound characteristics, and the AudioClip rollout specifies where the sound clips are located. The Billboard rollout creates images that always face the user.

LOD stands for Level of Detail. This button opens a rollout containing a Pick Object button, a Distance value, and a list of objects. To add an object to the list, click the Pick Object button and then specify a Distance value for that object. When the VRML Browser gets closer than the specified distance, the object will appear. You can use this procedure to display both a scaled-down version of an object when far away and a more detailed version up close.

The Inline button opens a rollout where you can add a Web URL link to the selected object. VRML browsers will recognize this link when the object is clicked on.

Exporting ASCII scene files (ASC, ASE)

To see all the gritty detail of a Max file, try exporting the file as an ASCII Scene file. The ASCII Export dialog box, shown in Figure 3-15, includes Output Options and Mesh Options. With this dialog box, you can also select which object types to export as well as specify an individual frame to export.

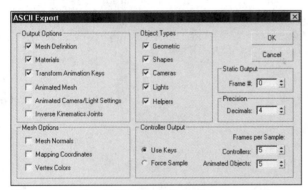

Figure 3-15: The ASCII Export dialog box exports the Max scene to a file that a text editor can read.

Importing from external applications

Even if Max could import several times the current number of import formats, new formats are being created for new products all the time, many of which Max wouldn't support. This situation does not mean that Max cannot use objects created in these new products. The trick is to find a common format that both products support.

Tutorial: Importing vector drawings from Illustrator

In most companies, a professional creative team will use an advanced vector drawing tool such as Illustrator to design the company logo. If you need to work with such a logo, learning how to import the externally created file will give you a jumpstart on your project.

Note When importing vector-based files into Max, only the lines are imported. Max cannot import fills, blends, or other specialized vector effects. All imported lines are automatically converted to Bézier splines in Max.

Although Max can draw and work with splines, this feature takes a backseat to the vector functions available in Adobe Illustrator. If you have an Illustrator file, you can save it as an AI file and import it into Max. To import Adobe Illustrator files into Max, follow these steps:

1. Within Illustrator, save your file as an AI file by choosing File ⇨ Save As.

   Figure 3-16 shows a logo created using Illustrator.

2. Open Max and choose File ⇨ Import.

   A file dialog box opens.

3. Select Abode Illustrator (AI) as the File Type. Locate the file to import and click OK.

   The AI Import dialog box asks whether you want to merge the objects with the current scene or replace the current scene.

4. For our purposes, select the replace the current scene option and click OK.

5. The Shape Import dialog box asks whether you want to import the shapes as single or multiple objects. Select multiple and click OK.

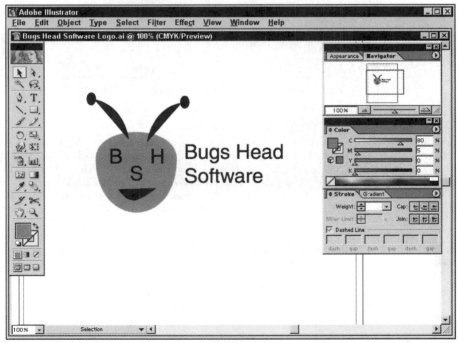

Figure 3-16: A company logo created in Illustrator and ready to save and import into Max

Figure 3-17 shows the logo after it has been imported into Max. Notice that all the fills are missing.

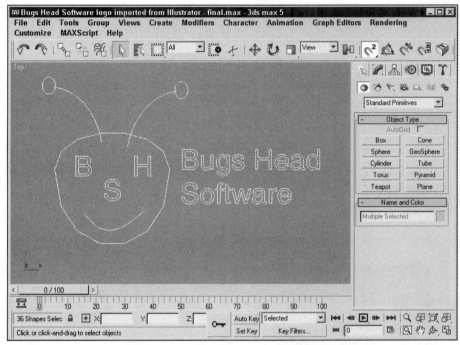

Figure 3-17: A company logo created in Illustrator and imported into Max

Importing human figures from Poser

Many animation projects require human figures. Modeling a human figure from scratch can require the same patience and artistic skill that Michelangelo exercised when painting the ceiling of the Sistine Chapel. Luckily (for those of us facing deadlines), this level of commitment isn't necessary. Curious Labs offers a tool devoted to modeling the human body. It is named Poser, and the current version is 4. Its features include posing and animating lifelike characters. Importing Poser models into Max can save you from some major modeling headaches.

A full working evaluation copy of Poser 4 is included on the book's CD-ROM.

With Poser, you can choose from a variety of male and female human figures, both unclothed and clothed in all sorts of attire. Even animal models are available. You can easily position these figures to any pose. Figure 3-18 shows the Business Man model posed as if hailing a taxi.

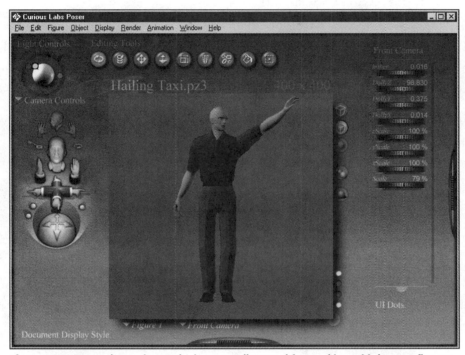

Figure 3-18: Poser by Curious Labs is an excellent tool for working with human figures.

Poser can animate characters. To change the pose, simply click and drag a body part to its desired location. Poser also includes modules for controlling basic facial expressions and hand gestures.

Tutorial: Using Poser models in Max

Poser makes modeling and positioning human figures easy, but to get the figures into Max, you need to export them from Poser and import them into Max. Poser can export several formats, but only two coincide with Max—3DS and DXF.

To use Poser models in Max, follow these steps:

1. Position your figure in Poser and export it by choosing Poser's File ➪ Export command.

2. In the Export dialog box, select the 3DS file type and save the file.

3. In Max, import the file by choosing File ➪ Import.

4. Select the Completely Replace Current Scene and Convert Units options and click OK. The figure appears in the viewports.

5. Save the scene as a Max file by choosing File ➪ Save.

Figure 3-19 shows the imported figure.

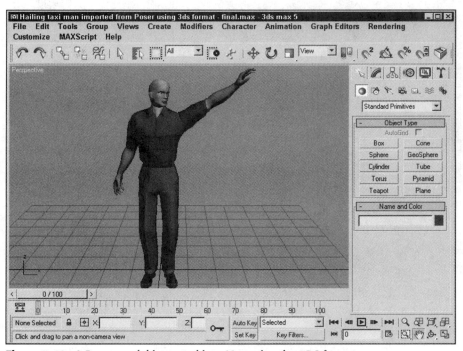

Figure 3-19: A Poser model imported into Max using the 3DS format

If you repeat the preceding steps using the DXF format, you can see the results in Figure 3-20. Notice how the details of the face have disappeared.

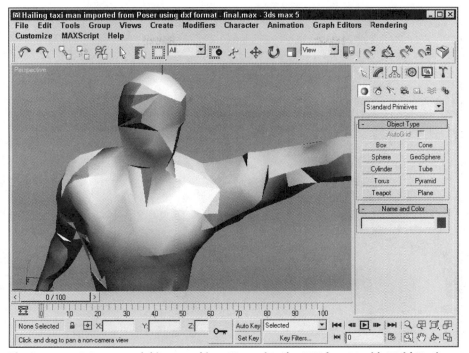

Figure 3-20: A Poser model imported into Max using the DXF format with Weld Vertices set to 0.01

You can fix the face problems by turning off the Weld Vertices option in the Import DXF File dialog box. Turning off this option results in the model in Figure 3-21.

The 3DS format is clearly a better choice for importing models from Poser, but for some software products the DXF format might be the only choice. To see all the problems that your imported model has, apply the STL Check modifier. This modifier can help identify abnormal geometry.

Cross-Reference You can find out more about modifiers in Chapter 10, "Using Modifiers."

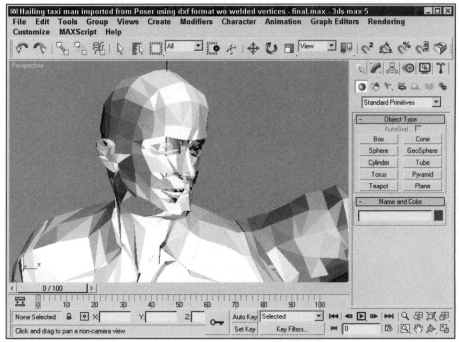

Figure 3-21: A Poser model imported into Max using the DXF format with Weld Vertices turned off

Referencing External Objects

No man is an island, and if Discreet has its way, no Max user will be an island either. XRefs (which stands for eXternal Reference) make it easy for creative teams to collaborate on a project without having to wait for one or the other group member to finish his or her respective production tasks. External references are objects and scenes contained in separate Max files and made available for reference during a Max session. This arrangement enables several artists on a team to work on separate sections of a project without interfering with one another or altering each other's work.

Max includes two different types of XRefs—XRef Scenes and XRef Objects.

Using XRef Scenes

An externally referenced scene is one that will appear in the current Max session, but that will not be accessible for editing or changing. The scene can be positioned and transformed when linked to a parent object and can be set to update automatically as changes are made to the source file.

As an example of how XRef Scenes facilitate a project, let's say a design team is in the midst of creating an environment for a project while the animator is animating a character model. The animator can access the in-production environment as an XRef Scene in order to help him move the character correctly about the environment. The design team will be happy because the animator didn't modify any of their lights, terrain models, maps, and props. The animator will be happy because he won't have to wait for the design team to finish all their tweaking before he can get started. The end result is one large, happy production team (if they can meet their deadlines).

Choose File ⇨ XRef Scenes to open the XRef Scenes dialog box (shown in Figure 3-22), which you use to load XRef Scenes into a file.

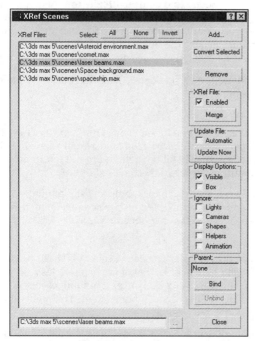

Figure 3-22: The XRef Scenes dialog box lets you specify which scenes to load as external references.

XRef Scene options

In the XRef Scenes dialog box are several options for controlling the appearance of the scene objects, how often the scene is updated, and which object the scene is bound to. This dialog box is modeless, and you can open and change the options in this dialog box at any time.

The pane on the left lists all XRef Scenes in the current scene. To the right are the settings, which can be different for each XRef Scene in the list. To view or apply a setting, you first need to select the scene from the list. You can remove any scene by selecting it from the list and clicking the Remove button.

Caution   If an XRef Scene in the list is displayed in red, then the scene could not be loaded. If the path or name is incorrect, you can change it in the Path field at the bottom of the list.

The Convert Selected button converts any selected objects in the current scene to XRef objects by saving them as a separate file. This button opens a dialog box to let you name and save the new file. If no objects are selected in the current scene, then this option is disabled.

Use the Enabled option to enable or disable all XRef Scenes. Disabled scenes are displayed in gray. The Merge button lets you insert the current XRef Scene into the current scene. This button removes the scene from the list and acts the same way as the File ⇨ Merge command.

Updating an external scene

Automatic is a key option that can set any XRef Scene to be automatically updated. Enable this option by selecting a scene from the list and checking the Automatic option box; thereafter, the scene is updated any time the source file is updated. This option can slow down the system if the external scene is updated frequently, but the benefit is that you can work with the latest update.

The Update Now button is for manually updating the XRef Scene. Click this button to update the external scene to the latest saved version.

External scene appearance

Other options let you decide how the scene is displayed in the viewports. You can choose to make the external scene invisible or to display it as a box. Making an external scene invisible only removes it from the viewports, but the scene will still be included in the rendered output. To remove a scene from the rendered output, deselect the Enabled option.

The Ignore section lists objects such as lights, cameras, shapes, helpers, and animation; selecting them causes them to be ignored and to have no effect in the scene. If an external scene's animation is ignored, then the scene will appear as it does in frame 0.

Positioning an external scene

Positioning an external scene is accomplished by binding the scene to an object in the current scene (a dummy object, for example). The XRef Scenes dialog box is modeless, so you can select the object to bind to without closing the dialog box. After a binding object is selected, the external scene transforms to the binding object's pivot point. The name of the parent object is also displayed in the XRef Scene dialog box.

Transforming the object that the scene is bound to can control how the external scene is repositioned. To unbind an object, click the Unbind button in the XRef Scenes dialog box. Unbound scenes are positioned at the World origin for the current scene.

Working with XRef Scenes

You can't edit XRef Scenes in the current scene. Their objects are not visible in the Select by Name dialog box or the Track and Schematic Views. You also cannot access the Modifier Stack of external scenes' objects. However, you can make use of external scene objects in other ways. For example, you can change a viewport to show the view from any camera or light in the external scene. External scene objects are included in the Summary Info dialog box.

Tip Another way to use XRef Scenes is to create a scene with lights and/or cameras positioned at regular intervals around the scene. You can then use the XRef Scenes dialog box to turn these lights on and off or to select from a number of different views without creating new cameras.

You can also nest XRef Scenes within each other, so you can have one XRef Scene for the distant mountains that includes another XRef for a castle.

Note If a Max file is loaded with XRef files that cannot be located, a warning dialog box will appear, enabling you to browse to the file's new location. If you click OK or Cancel, the scene will still load, but the external scenes will be missing.

Tutorial: Adding an XRef Scene

As an example of a project that would benefit from XRefs, I've created a maze environment. I will open a new Max file and animate a diamond moving through this maze that will be opened as an XRef Scene.

To set up an XRef Scene, follow these steps:

1. Create a new Max file by choosing File ➪ New.

2. Choose File ➪ XRef Scenes to open the XRef Scenes dialog box.

3. Click the Add button, locate the Maze.max file from the Chap 03 directory on the CD-ROM, and click Open to add it to the XRef Scene dialog box list.

Tip You can add several XRef Scenes by clicking the Add button again. You can also add a scene to the XRef Scene dialog box by dragging a .max file from Windows Explorer or from the Asset Manager window.

4. In the new scene, open the Create panel, select the Helpers category, and click the Dummy Object button. Then create a simple dummy object in the scene.

5. In the XRef Scenes dialog box, click the Bind button and select the dummy object.

   This will enable you to reposition the XRef Scene as needed.

6. Select the Automatic update option, and then click the Close button to exit the dialog box.

7. Now animate objects moving through the maze.

Figure 3-23 shows the Maze.max scene included in the current Max file as an XRef.

Tip With the diamond animated, you can replace it at a later time with a detailed model of a mouse using the File ➪ Replace command.

Figure 3-23: The maze.max file loaded into the current file as an XRef Scene

Using XRef Objects

XRef Objects are slightly different from XRef Scenes. They are objects that appear in a scene that you can transform and animate, but the original object's structure and Modifier Stack cannot be changed.

An innovative way to use this feature would be to create a library of objects that you could load on the fly as needed. For example, if you had a furniture library, you could load several different styles until you got just the look you wanted.

You can also use XRef Objects to load low-resolution proxies of complex models in order to lighten the system load during a Max session. This method will increase the viewport refresh rate.

Many of the options in the XRef Objects dialog box, shown in Figure 3-24, are the same as in the XRef Scenes dialog box.

The left side of the XRef Objects dialog box is divided into two sections. The top section displays the externally referenced files, and the lower section displays the objects selected from that file. A file needs to be selected in order for you to see its objects.

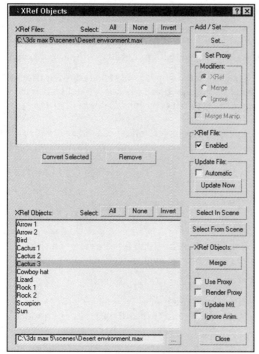

Figure 3-24: The XRef Objects dialog box lets you choose which files to look in for external objects.

You have several options for controlling how the XRef Objects are displayed:

✦ **Use Proxy:** Lets you choose between displaying the proxy and displaying the actual object.

✦ **Render Proxy:** Forces the proxy object to be rendered instead of the actual referenced object. If this option is not selected, then the referenced object will be rendered regardless of the object displayed in the viewports.

✦ **Update Materials:** Enables the object's materials to update as the source gets updated.

✦ **Ignore Animation:** Turns off any Modifier Stack animations associated with the object.

The Convert Selected button works the same as in the XRef Scenes dialog box. It enables you to save the selected objects in the current scene to a separate file just like the File ⇨ Save Selected command.

In the XRef Objects dialog box, you can choose to automatically update the external referenced objects or use the Update Now button. You can also Enable and Disable all objects in a file.

The Select In Scene and Select From Scene buttons are useful for seeing which objects in the scene are related to which items in the XRef Objects dialog box list.

Using proxies

The Add as Proxy button opens a low-resolution proxy object in place of a more complex object. This feature saves memory by not requiring the more complex object to be kept in memory. You can also select to render the proxy, update its materials, or ignore its animation.

If an object in the lower section of the XRefs Objects dialog box is selected, then the Add button changes to a Set button. The Set button lets you choose a file and object to use as a proxy. The proxy will be displayed in place of the actual referenced object.

Tip

The real benefit of using proxies is to replace complex referenced objects with simpler objects that update quickly. When creating a complex object, remember to also create a low-resolution version to use as a proxy.

Tutorial: Using an XRef proxy

To set up an XRef proxy, follow these steps:

1. Open the Post Box with XRef Tree.max file from the Chap 03 directory on the CD-ROM. This file includes the post box model produced by Zygote Media.

2. Open the XRef Objects dialog box by choosing File ⇨ XRef Objects.

3. Click the Add button and locate the Park Bench under a Tree.max file from the Chap 03 directory on the CD-ROM. This file includes the old tree and park bench models made by Zygote Media.

   The XRef Merge dialog box, shown in Figure 3-25, automatically opens and displays a list of all the objects in the file just added.

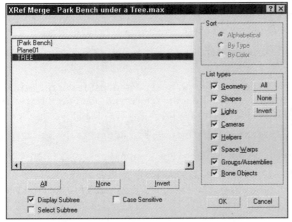

Figure 3-25: The XRef Merge dialog box lets you choose specific objects from a scene.

4. Select the Tree object to add to the current scene and click OK. (Hold down the Ctrl key to select several objects.) Use the Filter and Sort options to locate specific objects.

Note If an object you've selected has the same name as an object that is currently in the scene, the Duplicate Name dialog box will appear to let you rename the object, merge it anyway, skip the new object, or delete the old version.

5. Select the Tree object in the lower pane and click the Set button with the Set Proxy option selected.

   The Open File dialog box appears.

6. Select the Tree Lo-Res.max file from the Chap 03 directory on the CD-ROM.

   The Merge dialog box opens.

7. Select the Cylinder01 object, and click OK.

Caution If the proxy object has a different offset than the original object, a warning dialog box will appear instructing you to use the Reset XForm utility to reset the transform of the objects.

8. With the Tree object selected in the lower pane, select the Use Proxy option to see the proxy object, and deselect it to see the actual object.

XRef Objects that you add to a scene instantly appear in the current scene as you add them. Figure 3-26 shows the Post Box with the actual tree object. The XRef Objects dialog box will let you switch to the proxy object at any time.

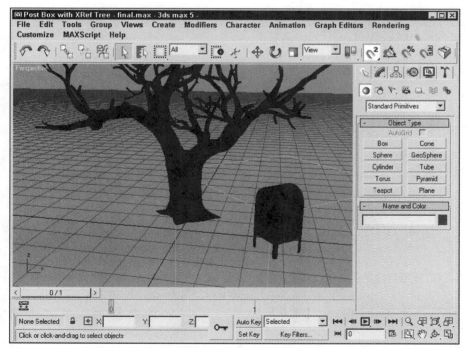

Figure 3-26: The tree object is an XRef from another scene. Its proxy is a simple cylinder.

XRef Objects in the Modifier Stack

XRef Objects will appear and act like any other object in the scene. About the only difference you'll see will be if you open the Modifier Stack. The Stack displays "XRef Object" as its only entry.

When you select the XRef Object item in the Modifier Stack, a rollout, shown in Figure 3-27, appears. The rollout includes many of the same controls displayed in the XRef Objects dialog box discussed earlier. These controls include the XRef File Name, Object Name, Proxy File Name, and Proxy Object Name.

Figure 3-27: The XRef Object rollout in the Modify panel lets you choose which objects from which files to include as external references.

Configuring XRef paths

The Configure Paths dialog box includes an XRefs tab for setting the paths for XRef Scenes and Objects, shown in Figure 3-28. Choose Customize ➪ Configure Paths to open the XRefs panel.

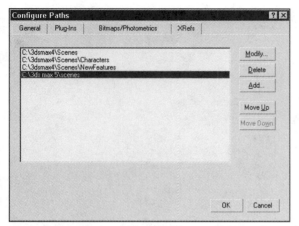

Figure 3-28: The XRefs panel in the Configure Paths dialog box lets you specify paths to be searched when an XRef cannot be located.

Max keeps track of the path of any XRefs used in a scene, but if it cannot find them, it will look at the paths designated in the XRefs panel of the Configure Paths dialog box. For projects that use a lot of XRefs, populating this list with potential paths is a good idea. Paths will be scanned in the order they are listed, so place the most likely paths at the top of the list.

To add a new path to the panel, click the Add button. You can also modify or delete paths in this panel with the Modify and Delete buttons.

Using the File Utilities

With all these various files floating around, Max has included several utilities that makes it easier to work with them. The Utilities panel of the Command Panel includes several useful utilities for working with files. You can access these utilities by opening the Utilities panel and clicking the More button to see a list of available utilities.

Using the Asset Browser utility

The Asset Browser utility is the first default button in the Utility panel. Clicking this button opens the Asset Browser window. The Asset Browser resembles Windows Explorer, except that it displays thumbnail images of all the supported formats contained within the current directory. Using this window, shown in Figure 3-29, you can browse through directory files and see thumbnails of images and scenes.

The supported file types include AVI, BMP, CIN, CEL, GIF, IFL, IPP, JPEG, PNG, PSD, MOV, RGB, RLA, RPF, VST, TIF, and YUV. These types are the same ones that the File ➪ View File command can open. All files with these extensions are viewable within the Asset Browser. You can select to view only a certain type of file using the Filter menu.

Tip　　Open and display the Asset Manager within a viewport by right-clicking the viewport title and choosing Views ➪ Extended ➪ Asset Manager from the pop-up menu.

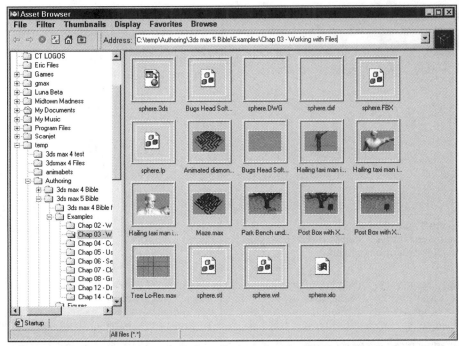

Figure 3-29: The Asset Browser window displays thumbnails of the files in the current directory.

You can also drag and drop files from the Asset Browser window to Max. Drag a scene file and drop it on Max's title bar to open the scene file within Max. You can drop image files onto the map buttons in the Material Editor window or drop an image file onto a viewport to make a dialog box appear, which will let you apply the image as an Environment Map or as a Viewport Background, respectively.

The Asset Browser window is modeless, so you can work with the Max interface while the Asset Browser window is open. Double-clicking an image opens it full size in the Virtual Frame Buffer window.

The Asset Browser can also act as a Web browser to look at content online. When the Asset Browser first opens, a dialog box reminds you that online content may be copyrighted and cannot be used without consent from the owner.

The Display menu includes three panes that you can select. The Thumbnail pane shows the files as thumbnails. You can change the size of these thumbnails using the Thumbnails menu. The Explorer pane displays the files as icons the same as you would see in Windows Explorer. The Web pane displays the Web page for the site listed in the Address field.

To view Web sites, you need to be connected to the Internet. The Asset Browser can remember your favorite Web sites using the Favorites menu. The Asset Browser window also includes the standard Web browser navigation buttons, such as Back, Forward, Home, Refresh, and Stop. You can also find these commands in the Browse menu.

Max keeps thumbnails of all the images you access in its cache. The cache is a directory that holds thumbnails of all the recently accessed images. Each thumbnail image points to the actual directory where the image is located. Choose File ➪ Preferences to open the Preference dialog box, in which you can specify where you want the cache directory to be located. Its default location is the abcache directory located where Max is installed. To view the cached files, choose Filter ➪ All in Cache.

Choose File ➪ Print to print the selected image.

Finding files with the Max File Finder utility

Another useful utility for locating files is the Max File Finder utility, which you get to by using the More button in the Utilities panel. When you select this utility, a rollout with a Start button appears in the Utility panel. Clicking this button opens the MAXFinder dialog box. Using MAXFinder, you can search for scene files by any of the information listed in the File Properties dialog box.

You can use the Browse button to specify the root directory to search. You can select to have the search also examine any subfolders. Figure 3-30 shows the MAXFinder dialog box locating all the scene files that include the word *blue*.

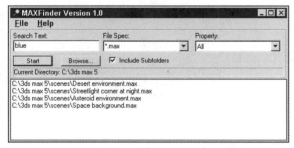

Figure 3-30: You can use the MAXFinder utility to search for scene files by property.

Collecting files with the Resource Collector utility

When a scene is created, image and object files can be pulled from several different locations. The Resource Collector utility helps you consolidate all these files into one location. The settings for this utility appear in the Parameters rollout in the Utility panel, as shown in Figure 3-31. The Output Path is the location where the files are collected. You can change this location using the Browse button.

The utility includes options to Collect Bitmaps, to include the Max scene file, and to Compress the files into a compressed WinZip file. The Copy option makes copies of the files, and the Move option moves the actual file into the directory specified in the Output Path field. The Update Materials option updates all material paths in the Material Editor. When you're comfortable with the settings, click the Begin button to start the collecting.

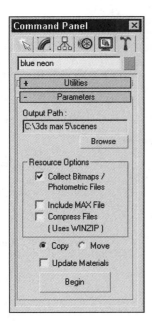

Figure 3-31: The Resource Collector utility can compile all referenced files into a single location.

Accessing File Information

As you work with files, several dialog boxes in Max supply you with extra information about your scene. Using this information to your advantage can help you keep track of files and record valuable statistics about a scene.

Displaying scene Information

If you like to keep statistics on your files (to see whether you've broken the company record for the model with the greatest number of faces), you'll find the Summary Info dialog box useful. Use the File ⇨ Summary Info menu command to open a dialog box that displays all the relevant details about the current scene, such as the number of objects, lights, and cameras; the total number of vertices and faces; and various model settings, as well as a Description field where you can describe the scene. Figure 3-32 shows the Summary Info dialog box.

The Plug-In Info button on the Summary Info dialog box displays a list of all the plug-ins currently installed on your system. Even without any external plug-ins installed, the list will be fairly long because many of the core features in Max are implemented as plug-ins. The Summary Info dialog box also includes a Save to File button for saving the scene summary information as a text file.

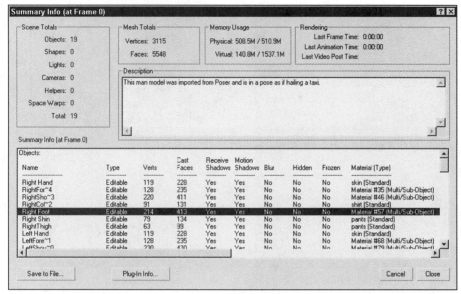

Figure 3-32: The Summary Info dialog box shows all the basic information about the current scene.

Viewing file properties

As the number of files that you have on your system increases, you'll be wishing you had a card catalog to keep track of them all. Max has an interface that you can use to attach keywords and other descriptive information about the scene to the file. The File ➪ File Properties menu command opens the File Properties dialog box. This dialog box, shown in Figure 3-33, includes three panels: Summary, Contents, and Custom. The Summary panel holds information such as the Title, Subject, and Author of the Max file and can be useful for managing a collaborative project. The Contents panel holds information about the scene such as the total number of objects and much more. Much of this information is also found in the Summary Info dialog box. The Custom panel, also shown in Figure 3-33, includes a way to enter a custom list of properties such as client information, language, and so on.

Note   You can also view the Properties dialog box information while working in Windows Explorer by right-clicking the file and selecting Properties. Two unique tabs are visible — Summary and Statistics. The Summary tab holds the file identification information, including the Author, Keywords, Comments, Title, Subject, and Template. The Statistics tab displays the creation and modification dates, the name of the user who last saved the file, a revision number, and any descriptive information.

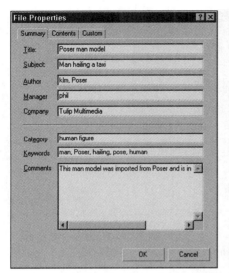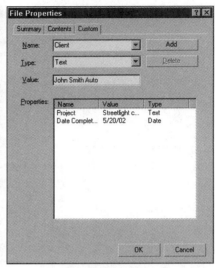

Figure 3-33: The File Properties dialog box contains workflow information such as the scene author, comments, and revision dates.

Viewing files

Sometimes looking at the thumbnail of an image isn't enough to help you decide whether you have the right image. For these cases, you can quickly load the image in question into a viewer to look at it closely. The File ➪ View Image File menu command opens the View File dialog box shown in Figure 3-34. This dialog box lets you load and view graphic and animation files using the Virtual Frame Buffer or the default Media Player for your system.

Figure 3-34: The View File dialog box can open an assortment of image and animation formats.

I discuss the Virtual Frame Buffer window in more detail in Chapter 34, "Rendering Basics."

The View File dialog box includes several controls for viewing files. The Devices and Setup buttons let you set up and view a file using external devices such as Video Recorders. The Info button lets you view detailed information about the selected file. The View button opens the file for viewing while leaving the View File dialog box open. The Open button closes the dialog box. At the bottom of the View File dialog box, the statistics and path of the current file are displayed.

The View File dialog box can open many types of files, including Microsoft videos (AVI), Bitmap images (BMP), Kodak Cineon (CIN), Autodesk Flic images (CEL), Graphics Image Format (GIF), IFL images, Paint* by Discreet Logic (IPP), JPEG images (JPG), PNG images, Adobe Photoshop images (PSD), QuickTime movies (MOV), SGI images (RGB), RLA images, RPF images, Targa images (VST), Tagged image file format images (TIF), and YUV images.

You use the Gamma area on the View File dialog box to specify whether an image uses its own gamma settings or the system's default setting, or whether an override value should be used.

Summary

Working with files will let you save your work, share it with others, and collaborate across teams. This chapter covered these basics, including

✦ Creating, saving, opening, merging, and archiving files

✦ Understanding the various import and export types

✦ Importing models from other programs, such as Illustrator and Poser

✦ Using externally referenced scenes and objects to work on the same project at the same time as your fellow team members without interfering with their work (or they with yours)

✦ Configuring XRef paths to help Max track your XRef Scenes and Objects

✦ Working with the file utilities, such as the Asset Browser

✦ Using the Summary Info and File Properties dialog box to keep track of scene files

By now you should be becoming more comfortable with the user interface, but if you're not, the next chapter covers how to customize the user interface.

✦   ✦   ✦

Customizing the Max Interface

When you get into a new car, one of the first things you do is to rearrange the seat and mirrors. You do this to make yourself comfortable. The same principle can apply to software packages — arranging or customizing an interface makes it more comfortable to work with.

Early versions of Max allowed only minimal changes to the interface, but later versions enable significant customization. The Max interface can be customized to show only the icons and tools that you want to see. There is also a rather bulky set of preferences that you can use to set almost every aspect of Max. This chapter covers various ways to make the Max interface more comfortable for you (now if we could only get cars that could save a custom setup).

Using the Customize User Interface Window

The key to customizing the interface is the Customize ⇨ Customize User Interface menu command. This command opens the Customize User Interface dialog box. This dialog box includes five panels including Keyboard, Toolbars, Quads, Menus, and Colors. You can also access this dialog box by right-clicking any toolbar away from the buttons and selecting Customize from the pop-up menu.

Customizing keyboard shortcuts

If used properly, keyboard shortcuts can increase your efficiency dramatically. Figure 4-1 shows the Keyboard panel of the Customize User Interface dialog box. In this panel, you can assign shortcuts to any command and define sets of shortcuts. You can assign keyboard shortcuts for any of the interfaces listed in the Group drop-down list. When an interface is selected from the Group drop-down list, all of its commands are listed below along with their current keyboard shortcut. You can disable the keyboard shortcuts for any of these interfaces using the Active option located next to the drop-down list.

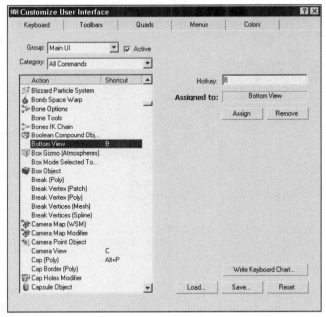

Figure 4-1: The Keyboard panel enables you to create keyboard shortcuts for any command.

Groups that have a large number of commands will be split into categories. You can use the Category drop-down list to filter only select types of commands. This helps you to quickly locate a specific type of commands such as controllers, modifiers, or Space Warps. Entering a keyboard shortcut into the Hotkey field will show in the Assigned To field if that key is currently assigned to a command. You can Assign the hotkey to the selected command or Remove the hotkey from its current assignment.

Note   Assigned hotkeys for menu commands will be displayed to the right of the menu.

You can use the Write Keyboard Chart button to output all the keyboard commands to a text file. Using this feature, you can print and post a chart of keyboard shortcuts next to your computer monitor. You can also Load, Save, and Reset selected keyboard shortcut sets. The default installation includes 3dsmax-3, 3dsmax-4, DefaultUI, and MaxKeys sets that can be loaded. Keyboard shortcut sets are saved as .kbd files in the UI directory where Max is installed.

Cross-Reference   You can find a reference of the available default keyboard shortcuts in Appendix B.

Tutorial: Assigning keyboard shortcuts

Do you use both hands to control the mouse? If not, then you have one hand that is idle most of the time. If you can train this hand to control features using the keyboard, then you will be much more efficient.

To assign a new keyboard shortcut to create a Sphere object, follow these steps:

1. Open the Customize User Interface dialog box by choosing Customize ➪ Customize User Interface.

2. Open the Keyboard panel and select Main UI in the Group drop-down list. Scroll through the list and select the Sphere Object command.

Tip With a list of objects available, you can quickly jump close to a desired item by typing the first letter of the item. For example, pressing the S key will jump to the first item that begins with an *S*.

3. Place the cursor in the Hotkey field and press Alt+Shift+Ctrl+S keys together. This will enter the hotkey into the field. In the default interface, this key isn't assigned to any command. Click the Assign button to assign the hotkey to the command.

4. Click the Save button to save the keyboard shortcut set as myShortcuts.kbd. You can load the resulting set from the Chap 04 directory on the CD-ROM.

Figure 4-2 shows the Keyboard panel of the Customize User Interface dialog box before you've assigned the hotkey.

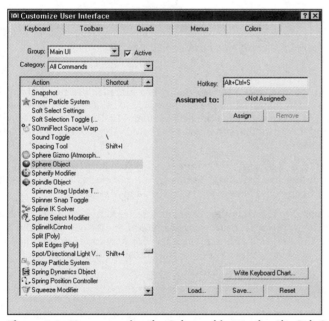

Figure 4-2: You can assign the Sphere object to the Alt+Ctrl+S keyboard shortcut.

Customizing toolbars

You can use the Customize User Interface dialog box's Toolbar panel to create custom toolbars. Figure 4-3 shows this panel.

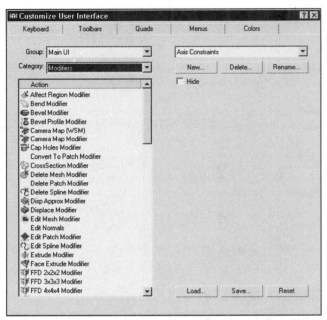

Figure 4-3: The Customize User Interface dialog box enables you to create new toolbars.

The Toolbars panel of the Customize User Interface dialog box includes the same Group and Category drop-down lists and command list as the Keyboard panel. Clicking the New button opens a simple dialog box where you can name the new toolbar. The Delete button lets you delete toolbars. You can only delete toolbars that you've created. The Rename button lets you rename the current toolbar.

Use the Load and Save buttons to load and save your newly created interface, including the new toolbar, to a custom interface file. Saved toolbars have the .cui extension; the default installation includes toolbars named 3dsmax-4.cui, DefaultUI, and MaxStart.

After you create a new toolbar, you can drag the commands in the Action list to either a new blank toolbar created with the New button or to an existing toolbar. Holding down the Alt key, you can drag a button from another toolbar and move it to your new toolbar. Holding down the Ctrl key and dragging a button will retain a copy of the button on the first toolbar.

If you drag a command that has an icon associated with it, the icon will appear on the new toolbar. If the command doesn't have an icon, then the text for the command will appear on the new toolbar.

Tutorial: Creating a custom toolbar

If you've been using Max for a while, you probably have several favorite commands that you use extensively.

To create a custom toolbar with your favorite commands, follow these steps:

1. Open the Customize User Interface dialog box by choosing Customize ➪ Custom User Interface.

2. Open the Toolbars panel and click the New button. A New Toolbar dialog box appears where you can name the new toolbar. After you type a name and click OK, a new blank toolbar appears.

3. From the Action list on the left, select and drag the commands to place on your toolbar to the new blank toolbar.

4. Continue to drag commands to the toolbar until you have all the commands you need.

5. Click the Save button to save the changes to the customized interface file.

Figure 4-4 shows the new toolbar. With the new toolbar created, you can float, dock, or add this toolbar to the Tab panel just like the other toolbars.

Figure 4-4: A new toolbar created using the Customize User Interface dialog box

You can right-click on any of the buttons on the new custom toolbar (which is outside the Customize User Interface dialog box) to access a pop-up menu. This menu enables you to change the button's appearance, delete the button, edit the button's macro script, or open the Customize User Interface dialog box.

Cross-Reference

To learn more about editing macro scripts, see Chapter 40, "Using MAXScript."

Changing a button's appearance

Selecting the Edit Button Appearance command from the pop-up menu opens the Edit Macro Button dialog box, shown in Figure 4-5. This dialog box enables you to quickly change the button's icon, tooltip, or text label. Each icon group will show both the standard icon and the grayed-out disabled version of the icon. Default buttons can also be changed. The Odd Only check box shows only the standard icons.

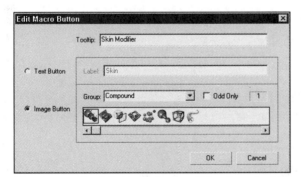

Figure 4-5: The Edit Macro Button dialog box provides a quick way to change an icon, tooltip, or text label.

Note

If a text label doesn't fit within the toolbar button, you can increase the button width using the Fixed Width Text Buttons spinner in the General tab of the Preference Settings dialog box.

Tutorial: Adding custom icons

The Max interface uses two different sizes of icons. Large icons are 24 × 24 pixels and small icons are 16 × 15 pixels. Large icons can be 24-bit color, and small ones must be only 16-bit. The easiest way to create some custom toolbars is to copy an existing set of icons into an image-editing program, make the modifications, and save them under a different name. You can find all the icons saved as BMP and used by Max in the UI/Icons directory where Max is installed.

To create a new group of icons, follow these steps:

1. Select a group of current icons to edit from the UI directory and open them in Photoshop. I've selected the Cameras group, which includes all the files that start with the word *Cameras*. This group includes only two icons. To edit icons used for both large and small icon settings and both active and inactive states, open the following four files: Cameras_16a.bmp, Cameras_16i.bmp, Cameras_24a.bmp, and Cameras_24i.bmp.

2. In each file, the icons are all included side by side in the same file, so the first two files are 32 × 15 and the second two are 48 × 24. Edit the files, being sure to keep each icon within its required dimensions.

3. When you've finished editing or creating the icons, save each file with the name of the icon group in front of the underscore character. My files were saved as Kels_16a.bmp, Kels_16i.bmp, Kels_24a.bmp, and Kels_24i.bmp, so they will show up in Kels group in the Edit Macro Button dialog box. Make sure the files are placed in the UI\Icons directory.

4. After the files are saved, you'll need to restart Max. The icon group will then be available within the Customize User Interface dialog box when assigned to a command.

Figure 4-6 shows the Edit Macro Button dialog box with my custom icon group named "Kels" open.

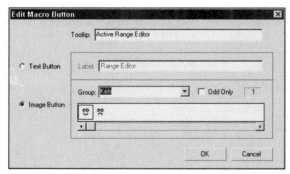

Figure 4-6: The Edit Macro Button dialog box with a custom icon group selected

Customizing quadmenus

The third panel in the Customize User Interface dialog box allows you to customize the quadmenus. You can open quadmenus by right-clicking on one of the viewports or in certain interfaces. Figure 4-7 shows this panel.

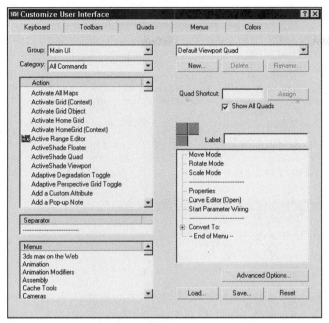

Figure 4-7: The Quads panel of the Customize User Interface dialog box lets you modify pop-up quadmenus.

To the left of the panel are the Group and Category drop-down lists and a list of actions that are the same as the Keyboard and Toolbars panels, but the Quads panel also includes a Separator and a list of Menu commands. Quadmenus can include separators to divide the commands into different sections and menus that appear at the top of the standard interface.

The drop-down list at the top right of the Quads panel includes many different Quadmenu sets. These different quadmenus will appear in different locations, such as with the ActiveShade window. Not only can you customize the default viewport quadmenus, but you can also create your own named custom quadmenus with the New button or Rename an existing quadmenu. The Quad Shortcut field lets you assign a keyboard shortcut to a custom quadmenu.

Tip   Several quadmenus have keyboard shortcuts applied to them. Right-clicking with the Shift key held down will open the Snap quadmenu. Other shortcuts include Alt+right-click for the Animation quadmenu, Ctrl+right-click for the Modeling quadmenu, and Ctrl+Alt+right-click for the Lighting/Rendering quadmenu.

If the Show All Quads option is disabled, it causes only a single quadmenu to be shown at a time when unchecked. Although only one quadmenu is shown at a time, the corner of each menu is shown, and you can switch between the different menus by moving the mouse over the corner of the menu.

The four quadrants of the current quadmenu are shown as four boxes. The currently selected quadmenu is highlighted yellow, and its label and commands are shown in the adjacent fields. Click on the gray boxes to select one of the different quadmenus.

To add a command to the selected quadmenu, drag an action, separator, or menu from the panes on the left to quadmenu commands pane on the right. You can reorder the commands in the quadmenu commands pane by dragging the commands and dropping them in their new location. To delete a command, just select it and press the Delete key or select Delete Menu Item from the right-click pop-up menu.

The right-click pop-up menu also lets you edit the command name or flatten a submenu, which will display all submenu commands on the top level with the other commands.

Custom quadmenus can be loaded and saved as menu files (with the .mnu extension).

The Quads panel also includes an Advanced Options button. Clicking this button opens the Advanced Quad Menu Options dialog box, shown in Figure 4-8. Using this dialog box, you can set options such as the colors used in the quadmenus.

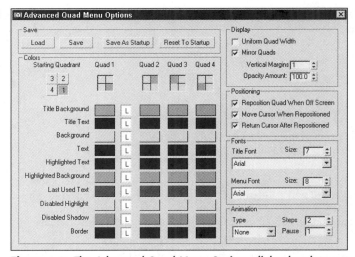

Figure 4-8: The Advanced Quad Menu Options dialog box lets you change quadmenu fonts and colors.

Changes to the Advanced Quad Menu Options dialog box affect all quadmenus. You can load and save these settings to files (with the .qop extension). The Starting Quadrant determines which quadrant is first to appear when the quadmenu is accessed. You can select to change the colors for each quadmenu independent of the others. The column with the L locks the colors so they are consistent for all quadmenus if enabled.

The remainder of the Advanced Quad Menu Options dialog box includes settings for controlling how the quadmenus are displayed and positioned, as well as the fonts that are used.

The Animation section lets you define the animation style that is used when the quadmenus appear. The animation types include None, Stretch, and Fade. The Stretch style will slowly stretch the quadmenus out until they are full size over the designated number of steps and the Fade style slowly makes the quadmenus appear.

Tip   I personally don't like to wait for the quadmenus to appear and like to keep the Animation setting set to None.

Customizing menus

The Menus panel of the Customize User Interface dialog box allows you to customize the menus used at the top of the Max window. Figure 4-9 shows this panel.

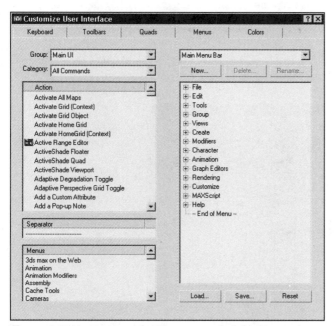

Figure 4-9: You can use the Menus panel of the Customize User Interface dialog box to modify menus.

This panel includes the same Group and Category drop-down lists and the Action, Separator, and Menus panes found in the Quads panel. You can drag and drop these commands on the menu pane to the right. Menus can be saved as files (with the .mnu extension). In the menu pane on the right, you can delete menu items with the Delete key or by right-clicking and selecting Delete Item from the pop-up menu.

Tutorial: Adding a new menu

Adding a new menu is easy to do with the Customize User Interface dialog box. For this example, you'll tack another menu on the end of the current default menu.

To add another menu item, follow these steps:

1. Choose Customize ➪ Customize User Interface to open the Customize User Interface dialog box.

2. Click the Menus tab to open the Menus panel.

3. In the top-right drop-down list, select Main Menu Bar. The current main menu bar opens in the right pane. Click the New button. A New Menu dialog box opens. Type the name of the new menu, myMenu. This name will be added to the Menus pane on the right.

4. Drag the myMenu menu item from the Menus pane on the left to the command pane on the right and drop it right after the Help menu item. Click the plus sign to the left of the new menu item to expand it. As you drag, a blue line will indicate where the menu will be located.

5. Select several commands from the Action pane on the left and drag and drop them under the myMenu item in the right pane.

6. Click the Save button to save the menu as a file.

Figure 4-10 shows the menu before it is saved. You can reset the default UI by choosing Customize ➪ Revert to Startup Layout.

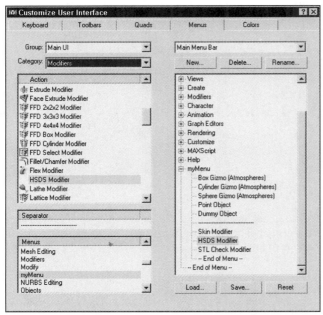

Figure 4-10: A custom menu added to the default menu, compliments of the Customize User Interface dialog box.

Customizing colors

Within Max, the colors often indicate the mode that you're working in. For example, red marks animation mode. Using the Colors panel of the Customize User Interface dialog box, you can set custom colors for all Max interface elements. This panel, shown in Figure 4-11, includes two panes. The upper pane displays the available items for the interface selected in the Elements drop-down list. Selecting an item in the list displays its color in the color swatch to the right.

The lower pane displays a list of the custom colors that can be changed that will affect the appearance of the interface. For example, Highlight Text isn't an element, but an interface appearance. The Scheme drop-down list can alter the color scheme between custom colors and the Windows Default Colors.

You can save custom color settings as files with the .clr extension. You can use the Apply Colors Now button to immediately update the interface colors.

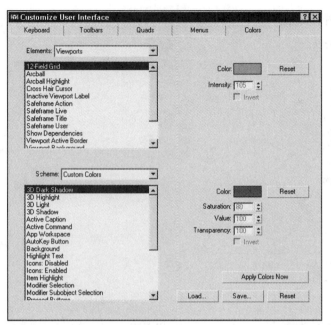

Figure 4-11: You can use the Colors panel of the Customize User Interface dialog box to set the colors used in the interface.

Customizing the Tab Panel

The Tab Panel (keyboard shortcut Y or 2) makes all possible toolbars available. When you click a tab, its toolbar appears. The default toolbars include the following: Objects, Shapes, Compounds, Lights & Cameras, Particles, Helpers, Space Warps, Modifiers, Modeling, and Rendering.

By right-clicking any tab, you can modify the Tab panel. From the pop-up menu, you can choose to add a tab, delete a tab, or rename a tab. There are also options to move tabs to the left or the right.

You can convert tabs on the Tab panel to floating toolbars by selecting Convert to Toolbar from the tab's right-click menu, or simply by dragging the tab away from the Tab panel.

You can add an existing toolbar to the Tab panel by dragging it onto the Tab panel, right-clicking on the toolbar's title bar, and selecting Move to Tab Panel. It will be added to the right end of the Tab panel.

Customizing Command Panel Buttons

The Modify and the Utilities panels in the Command Panel both include a button called Configure Button Sets that allows you to configure how the modifiers are grouped and which utility buttons appear in the Utilities panel.

In the Modify panel, the Configure Modifier Sets button is the right-most button directly under the Modifier Stack. This button opens the Configure Modifier Sets dialog box, shown in Figure 4-12, where you can control which modifiers are grouped with which sets.

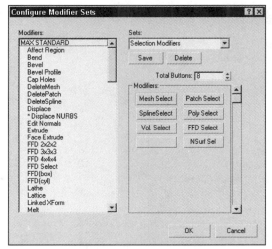

Figure 4-12: The Configure Modifier Sets dialog box lets you group the modifiers as you want.

To add a modifier to a set, select the set from the Sets drop-down list and drag the modifier from the list of Modifiers on the left to the button set on the right. To create a new set, simply type a new name into the Sets field. After a set has changed, you will need to save it with the Save button.

You can find the same Configure Button Sets button on the Utilities panel. Clicking this button opens a similar dialog box where you can drag from a list of Utilities onto a list of buttons on the right. These buttons will then be displayed in the Utilities panel.

Working with Custom Interfaces

If you've changed your interface, you'll be happy to know that the Customize menu includes a way for you to save and then reload your custom setup. This feature is especially helpful for users who share a copy of Max.

Tip   Any custom .ui file can be loaded as the default interface from the command line by adding a **–c** and the .ui filename after the 3dsmax.exe file (for example, **3dsmax.exe –c my_ interface.ui**).

Saving and loading a custom interface

Custom interface schemes are saved with the .ui extension using the Customize ⇨ Save Custom UI Scheme menu command. When you save a custom scheme, Max will open a Custom Scheme dialog box, shown in Figure 4-13. This dialog box lets you choose which customizations to include in the custom scheme. It also lets you select the icon type to use. The options are Classic and 2D Black and White.

Figure 4-13: The Custom Scheme dialog box appears when you're saving a custom interface and lets you select which items to include.

You can load saved user interface schemes with Customize ➪ Load Custom UI. The default Max install includes several predefined interface setups that are located in the UI directory. The standard available interfaces include

✦ **DefaultUI:** Default interface that opens when Max is first installed.

✦ **Discreet-dark:** Displays the standard interface with black windows, backgrounds, and viewports. All the icons and menus are light gray and many of the icons are different.

✦ **Discreet-light:** Same as the Discreet-dark layout, except the icons and menus are black and the backgrounds are all light gray. Many icons are different here, too.

✦ **MaxStart:** This is the interface that Max loads when it starts and includes any changes you've made to the interface.

You can use both the load and save menu commands to save and load any of the custom user interface files types including:

✦ Interface Scheme files (.ui)

✦ UI files (.cui)

✦ Menu files (.mnu)

✦ Color files (.clr)

✦ Keyboard Shortcut files (.kbd)

✦ Quadmenu Options files (.qop)

Tutorial: Saving a custom interface

You can save personalized interfaces for later recall in the UI directory where Max is installed. To do so, choose Customize ➪ Save Custom UI. If you save your custom settings to the MaxStart.ui file, then your custom file will be loaded when Max starts.

To have Max start with your custom interface, follow these steps:

1. Customize your interface by making any desired changes.

2. Choose Customize ➪ Save Custom UI Scheme.

   The Save Custom UI Scheme dialog box opens.

3. Open the UI subdirectory (if you are not already there), select the MaxStart.ui file, and click OK.

4. Click OK to replace the existing file.

Note You can set Max to automatically save your interface changes when exiting. Select the Save UI Configuration on Exit option in the General tab of the Preference Settings dialog box.

Locking the interface

After you're comfortable with your interface changes, locking the interface to prevent accidental changes is a good idea. To lock the current interface, choose Customize ➪ Lock UI Layout (or press the Alt+0 keyboard shortcut).

Reverting to the startup interface

When you're first playing around with Max's customization features, really messing things up can be easy. If you get in a bind, you can reload the default startup interface (MaxStart.ui) with the Customize ➪ Revert to Startup UI Layout command. Using the File ➪ Reset menu command will not reset changes to the layout.

Note If your MaxStart.ui file gets messed up, you can reinstate the original default interface setup by deleting the MaxStart.ui file before starting Max.

Configuring Paths

When strolling through a park, you can be assured that any paths you encounter lead somewhere. One might take you to the lake and another to the playground. Knowing where the various paths lead can help you as you navigate around the park. Paths in Max lead, or point to, various resources, either locally or across the network.

All paths can be configured using the Configure Paths dialog box, shown in Figure 4-14. Choose Customize ➪ Configure Paths to open this dialog box. The dialog box includes four panels: General, Plug-Ins, Bitmaps/Photometrics, and XRefs.

When Max is installed, all the paths are set to point to the default subdirectories where Max was installed. To modify a path, select the path and click the Modify button. A file dialog box will let you locate the new directory.

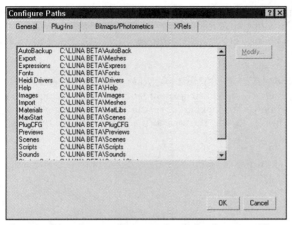

Figure 4-14: The Configure Paths dialog box specifies where to look for various resources.

The General tab includes paths for the following:

✦ **AutoBackup:** Directory where backups are saved

✦ **Export:** Directory where exported files are saved

✦ **Expressions:** Directory containing expression files

✦ **Fonts:** Directory containing fonts

✦ **Heidi Drivers:** Directory containing the Heidi Drivers

✦ **Help:** Directory containing help files

✦ **Images:** Directory to open when loading images

✦ **Import:** Directory to open when importing geometry

✦ **Materials:** Directory containing material files

✦ **MaxStart:** Directory containing programs to execute when Max is started

✦ **PlugCFG:** Directory containing plug-in configuration files

✦ **Previews:** Directory where previews are saved

✦ **Scenes:** Directory where saved scene files are stored

✦ **Scripts:** Directory where scripts are stored

✦ **Sounds:** Directory to open when sound files are loaded

✦ **Startup Scripts:** Directory containing scripts that load when Max is started

✦ **VideoPost:** Directory where Video Post output is saved

Tip
Personally, I like to keep all my content in a separate directory from where the application is installed. That way new installs or upgrades won't risk overwriting my files. To do this, I typically change the paths to AutoBackup, Export, Images, Import, Materials, Previews, Scenes, Scripts, and Video Post.

Under the Plug-Ins, Bitmaps/Photometrics, and XRefs tabs, you can add and delete additional paths. The XRefs panel specifies where to look for external resources and can include several paths. All paths will be searched when you're looking for resources such as plug-ins, but file dialog boxes will open only to the first path. Use the Move Up and Move Down buttons to realign path entries.

Caution
Using the Customize ➪ Revert to Startup UI Layout command does not reset path configuration changes.

Setting Preferences

The Preference Settings dialog box lets you configure Max so it works in a way that is most comfortable for you. You open it by choosing Customize ➪ Preferences. The dialog box includes ten different panels: General, Files, Viewports, Gamma, Rendering, Advanced Lighting, Animation, Inverse Kinematics, Gizmos, and MAXScript.

New Feature
The Preference Settings dialog box includes two new panels in 3ds max 5 — Advanced Lighting and Gizmos.

General preferences

The first panel in the Preference Settings dialog box is for General settings. Figure 4-15 shows the dialog box with the General panel selected.

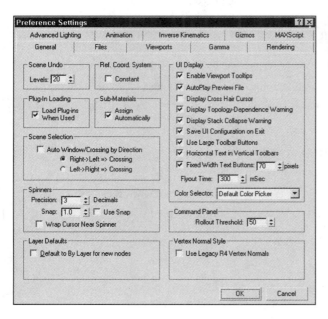

Figure 4-15: The General panel enables you to change the unit scale, among other options.

The General panel includes many global settings that affect the entire interface.

Tip   The quickest way I've found to open the Preference Settings dialog box is to right-click on the Spinner Snap Toggle.

Undo Levels and Loading Plug-Ins

The Scene Undo spinner sets the number of commands that can be kept in a buffer for undoing. A smaller number will free up memory, but will not let you backtrack through your work. The default Undo Levels is 20.

The Load Plug-Ins When Used option keeps plug-ins out of memory until they are accessed. This saves valuable memory and still makes the plug-ins accessible.

Reference Coordinate System and Sub-Material settings

The Reference Coordinate System setting will make all transform tools use the same coordinate system when the Constant option is enabled. If disabled, each transform will use the coordinate system last selected.

The Automatic Sub-Material Assignment option, when enabled, enables materials to be dragged and dropped directly onto a subobject selection.

Scene Selection settings

The Auto Window/Crossing by Direction option lets you select scene objects using the windowing method (the entire object must be within the selected windowed area to be selected) and the crossing method (which selects objects if their borders are crossed with the mouse) at the same time depending on the direction that the mouse is dragged. If you select the first option, then the Crossing method will be used when the mouse is dragged from right to left and the Window method will be used when the mouse is dragged from left to right.

Spinner and Layer settings

Spinners are interface controls that enable you to enter values or interactively increase or decrease the value by clicking the arrows on the right. The Preferences Settings dialog box includes settings for changing the number of decimals displayed in spinners and the increment or decrement value for clicking an arrow. The Use Spinner Snap option enables the snap mode.

 You can also enable the snap mode using the Spinner Snap button on the main toolbar.

You can also change the values in the spinner by clicking on the spinner and dragging up to increase the value or down to decrease it. The Wrap Cursor Near Spinner option keeps the cursor close to the spinner when you change values by dragging with the mouse, so you can drag the mouse continuously without worrying about hitting the top or bottom of the screen.

Note   A quick way to access these spinner settings is to right-click the Spinner Snap Toggle button on the main toolbar.

For Layers, you can set the default to use a new layer for each new node that is added to the scene. This will enable rendering, motion blur, and display properties in the Layers dialog box for all new objects.

New Feature   Layers are new to 3ds max 5.

Interface Display settings

Finally, toggle switches in the UI Display section control additional aspects of the interface. Enable Viewport Tooltips can toggle tooltips on or off. Tooltips are helpful when you're first learning the Max interface, but they quickly become annoying and you'll want to turn them off.

The AutoPlay Preview File setting automatically plays Preview Files in the default media player when they are finished rendering. If this option is disabled, you'll need to play the previews with the Animation ➪ View Preview menu command. The Display Cross Hair Cursor option changes the cursor from the Windows default arrow to a crosshair cursor similar to the one used in AutoCAD.

For some actions, such as nonuniform scaling, Max displays a warning dialog box asking whether you are sure of the action. To disable these warnings, uncheck this option (or you could check the Disable this Warning box in the dialog box). Actions with warnings include nonuniform scaling, topology-dependence, and collapsing the Modifier Stack.

The Save UI Configuration on Exit switch automatically saves any interface configuration changes. You can de-select Use Large Toolbar Buttons option, enabling the use of smaller toolbar buttons and icons that will reclaim valuable screen real estate.

The Horizontal Text in Vertical Toolbars options will fix the problem of text buttons that take up too much space, especially when printed horizontally on a vertical toolbar. You can also specify a width for text buttons. Any text larger than this value will be clipped off at the edges of the button.

The Flyout Time spinner adjusts the time the system waits before displaying flyout buttons. The Color Selection drop-down list will let you choose which color selector interface Max uses.

The Rollup Threshold value sets how many pixels can be scrolled before the rollup is shifted to another column. This is only used if you've made the Command Panel wider.

The Use Legacy R5 Vertex Normals option will compute vertex normals based on the Max version 4 instead of the new method used in Max 5.

 New Feature   The method for computing normals is new in 3ds max 5, resulting in smoother objects.

Files panel preferences

The Files panel holds the controls for backing up, archiving, and logging Max files. You can set files to be backed up, saved incrementally, or compressed when saved. Figure 4-16 shows this panel.

Handling files and archives

The Files panel includes several options that define how to handle files. You can enable an option to Backup on Save. This causes the existing copy of a file to be saved as a backup (with the .bak extension) before saving the new file. This option always retains two copies of the file.

The Increment on Save option adds an incremented number onto the end of the existing file every time it is saved. This retains multiple copies of the file and is an easy way to version-control your scene files. This way you can always go back to an earlier file when the client changes their mind.

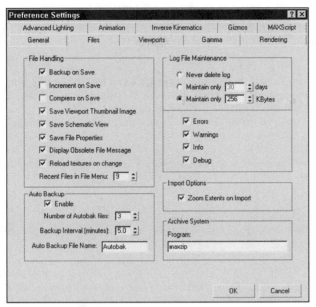

Figure 4-16: The Files panel includes an Auto Backup feature.

The Compress on Save option compresses the file automatically when it is saved. Compressed files require less file space but take longer to load. If you're running low on hard drive space, then you'll want to enable this option.

The Save Viewport Thumbnail Image option saves a 64 × 64 pixel thumbnail of the active viewport along with the file. This thumbnail is displayed in the Open dialog box.

Tip The Save Viewport Thumbnail Image option is another good option to keep enabled. Thumbnails make it easier to find scene files later, and nothing is more frustrating than seeing a scene without a thumbnail.

In addition to a thumbnail, Max also offers an option to save the Schematic View with the file. Although Max can generate a new Schematic View from an existing file, saving the Schematic View with the file is quicker if you work a lot with this view. File Properties are another set of data that is helpful to save with the file, but be warned that saving this extra info with the file will increase its file size.

When a Max file created in a previous version of Max is opened, a warning dialog box appears that says, "Obsolete data format found – Please resave file." To eliminate this warning, disable the Display Obsolete File Message option.

When textures are updated, the Reload Textures on Change options will force the textures to be reloaded when they are altered. This will slow down your system while Max waits for the textures to reload, but offers the latest look immediately.

New Feature The Save Schematic View, Save File Properties, and Reload Textures on Change options are all new in 3ds max 5.

The Recent Files in File Menu option determines the number of recently opened files that appear at the bottom of the File menu.

Tip   I like to set the Recent Files in File Menu option at its highest value because I find that this is the easiest way to open up the latest scenes.

Backing up files

The Auto Backup feature in Max can save you from the nightmare of losing all your work due to a system crash. With Auto Backup enabled, you can select the number of Autobak Files and how often the files are backed up. The backup files are saved to the directory specified by the Configure Paths dialog box. The default is to save these backups to the AutoBack directory.

Tip   I highly recommend that you keep the Auto Backup option enabled. This feature has saved my bacon more than once.

Tutorial: Setting Auto Backup

Now that it has been stressed that setting up Auto Backup is an important step to do, let's run through exactly how to set it up.

To set up this feature, follow these steps:

1. Open the Preferences Settings dialog box by choosing Customize ➪ Preferences, and click the Files panel.

2. Turn on Auto Backup by selecting the Enable option in the Auto Backup section.

3. Set the number of Autobak files to 3.

Note   To maintain version control of your Max scenes, use the Increment on Save feature instead of increasing the Number of Autobak Files.

4. Set the Backup Interval to the amount of time to wait between backups.

   The Backup Interval should be set to the maximum amount of work that you are willing to redo. (I keep my settings at 15 minutes.) You can also give the Auto Backup file a name.

5. Auto Backup will save the files in the directory specified by the Auto Backup path. To view where this path is located, choose Customize ➪ Configure Paths.

Maintaining log files

You can also use the Files panel to control log files. Log files keep track of any errors, general command info, and any debugging information. You can set log files to never be deleted, expire after so many days, or keep a specified file size with the latest information. If your system is having trouble, checking the error log will give you some idea as to what the problem is. Logs are essential if you plan on developing any custom scripts or plug-ins. You can select that the log contain all Errors, Warnings, Info, and Debug statements.

The name of the log file is Max.log. It is saved in the "network" subdirectory.

Import options

The Import Options group has only a single option: Zoom Extents on Import. When this option is enabled, it automatically zooms all viewports to their extents. Imported objects can often be scaled so small that they aren't even visible. This option helps you to locate an object when imported.

Note If you are importing an object into a scene with several objects, then this option will not necessarily make the imported object visible.

The Archive System lets you specify which archive program Max will use to archive your files. Maxzip is the default, but you can change it to whichever program you want to use.

Viewport preferences

The viewports are your window into the scene. The Viewports panel, shown in Figure 4-17, contains many options for controlling these viewports.

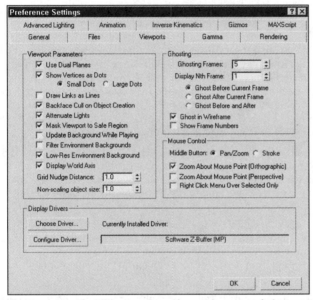

Figure 4-17: The Viewports panel contains several viewport parameter settings.

 Cross-Reference Although the viewports were the major topic in Chapter 2, "Working with the Viewports," the viewport preference settings are covered here.

Viewport Parameter options

In the Viewport Parameters group are several options specific to viewports. The Use Dual Planes option enables a method designed to speed up viewport redraws. Objects close to the scene are included in a front plane and objects farther back are included in a back plane. When this option is enabled only the objects on the front plane are redrawn.

In subobject mode, the default is to display vertices as small plus signs. The Show Vertices as Dots option displays vertices as either Small or Large dots. The Draw Links as Lines option shows all displayed links as lines that connect the two linked objects.

Caution   I've found that keeping the Draw Links as Lines option can make it confusing to clearly see objects and tend to keep it turned off.

The Backface Cull on Object Creation option shows the backfaces of objects when viewed in wireframe mode. The Attenuate Lights option causes objects farther back in a viewport to appear darker. Attenuation is the property that causes lights to diminish over distance.

Note   There is also a Backface Cull display option in the Object Properties dialog box.

In the Viewport Configuration dialog box, you can set Safe Regions, which are borders that the renderer will include. The Mask Viewport to Safe Region causes the objects beyond the Safe Region border to be invisible.

The Update Background While Playing option causes viewport background bitmaps to be updated while an animation sequence plays. Viewport backgrounds can be filtered if the Filter Environment Background option is enabled, but this slows the update time. If this option is disabled, the background image appears aliased and pixelated. For quicker refresh times, enable the Low-Res Environment Background option. This reduces the resolution of the background image by half and resizes it to fill the viewport. Enabling this option results in a blocky appearance, but the viewport updates much more quickly.

The Display World Axis option displays the axes in the lower-left corner of each viewport. You can use the arrow keys to nudge objects into position. The Grid Nudge Distance is the distance that an object moves when an arrow key is pressed. Objects without scale, such as lights and cameras, appear in the scene according to the Non-Scaling Object Size value.

Enabling ghosting

Ghosting is similar to the use of "onion-skins" in traditional animation, making an object's prior position and next position to be displayed. When producing animation, knowing where you're going and where you've come from is helpful. Enabling ghosting will enable you to produce better animations.

Max offers several ghosting options. You can set whether a ghost appears before the current frame, after the current frame, or both before and after the current frame. You can set the total number of ghosting frames and how often they should appear. You can also set an option to show the frame numbers.

Cross-Reference   For a more detailed discussion of ghosting, see Chapter 24, "Animation Basics."

Using the middle mouse button

If you're using a mouse that includes a middle button (this includes a mouse with a scrolling wheel), then you can define how the middle button is used. The two options are Pan/Zoom and Stroke. The Pan/Zoom option will pan the active viewport if the middle button is held down, will zoom in and out if you move the scrolling wheel and will rotate the view if you hold down the Alt key while dragging. You can select options to zoom about the mouse point in the orthographic and perspective viewports.

The Stroke option enables another interface that lets you execute commands by dragging a pre-defined stroke in a viewport. With the Stroke option selected, close the Preference

Settings dialog box and drag with the middle mouse button held down in one of the viewports. A simple dialog box will identify the stroke and execute the command associated with it. If no command is associated, then a simple dialog box appears that lets you Continue (do nothing) or Define the stroke.

Another way to work with strokes is to enable the Strokes Utility. This is done by selecting on the Utility panel, clicking the More button, and selecting Strokes from the pop-up list of utilities. This utility will make a Draw Strokes button active. When the button is enabled, it will turn yellow and you will be able to draw strokes with the left or middle mouse buttons.

If you select to define the stroke, the Define Stroke dialog box, shown in Figure 4-18, is opened. You can also open this dialog box directly by holding down the Ctrl key while dragging a stroke with the middle mouse button. In the upper-left corner of this dialog box is a grid. Strokes are identified by the lines they cross on this grid as they are drawn. For example, an "HK" stroke would be a horizontal line that is dragged from the top of the viewport straight down to the bottom.

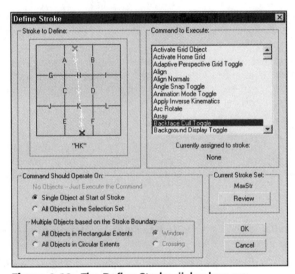

Figure 4-18: The Define Stroke dialog box can associate strokes dragged with the middle mouse button with a command.

With a stroke identified, you can select a command in the upper-right pane. This is the command that executes when you drag the stroke with the middle mouse button in the viewport. For each command you can set the options found below the stroke grid. These options define what the command is executed on.

All defined strokes are saved in a set and you can review the current set of defined strokes with the Review button. Clicking this button opens the Review Strokes dialog box where all defined strokes and their commands are displayed. The only default defined stroke is to open this dialog box, as shown in Figure 4-19.

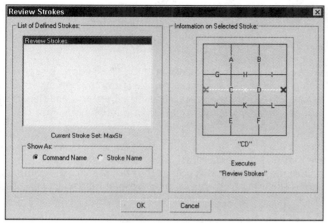

Figure 4-19: The Review Strokes dialog box lists all defined strokes and their respective commands.

One of the commands available in the list of commands is Stroke Preferences. Using this command will open the Stroke Preferences dialog box where you can save and delete different stroke sets, specify to list commands or strokes in the Review Strokes dialog, set the time that the stroke grid and extents appear and set the Stroke Point Size.

Tutorial: Defining a stroke

As you get some experience with the Max interface, you'll find that for some commands you'll always use keyboard shortcuts, for others you'll use the main toolbar, and for others the menus. Strokes offer another way to quickly execute commands without the pain of searching the menus for a given command.

To assign a stroke to a command, follow these steps:

1. Open the Preference Settings dialog box with the Customize ➪ Preferences menu command.

2. Select the Viewports panel and in the Mouse Control section, select the Stroke option. Then close the Preference Settings dialog box.

3. With the middle mouse button, drag a "U"-shaped stroke in the active viewport. A dialog box will identify the stroke as not found. Click the Define button to open the Define Stroke dialog box.

4. The stroke (as you drew it) will be displayed in the upper-left grid and if you drew it correctly should be identified as 'GJEFLI.' In the Command list, select the Unhide All command and click the OK button to close the dialog box.

5. Use the Tools ➪ Display Floater to hide some objects in the current scene, then drag a "U"-shaped stroke with the middle mouse button and all the hidden objects will become visible.

Choosing and configuring display drivers

When Max was first launched, a simple dialog box asked you which display driver to use (see Figure 4-20). If you were anxious to get a look at Max, you probably didn't pay much attention to this dialog box. However, weeks later when you happen to be looking through your video card information, you realize that your card supports other drivers like OpenGL and Direct 3D.

Caution   The Graphics Driver Setup dialog box only displays the options for the drivers that it finds on your system, but just because an option exists doesn't mean it will work correctly. If a driver hangs your system, you can restart it from a command line with the –h flag after 3dsmax.exe to force Max to present the Graphics Driver Setup dialog box again.

Figure 4-20: You use the Graphics Driver Setup dialog box to select the display drivers.

If you want to try out or configure the different display drivers, you can use the Viewports panel of the Preference Settings dialog box. The Viewports panel includes a field that displays the currently installed driver along with two buttons to Choose Driver and Configure Driver. The Choose Driver button opens the Graphics Driver Setup dialog box again. If you change the display driver, you will need to restart Max.

Note   The driver you use really depends on the video card that you have in your system. Check with the documentation that came with your video card to see what drivers it supports. If you're unsure, use the default Heidi drivers.

The Configure Driver opens a dialog box of configurations for the driver that is currently installed. The various configuration dialog boxes include options such as specifying the Texture Size, which is the size of the bitmap used to texture map object. Larger maps have better image quality, but can slow down your display.

All the display driver configuration settings present trade-offs between image quality and speed of display. By tweaking the configuration settings, you can optimize these settings to suite your needs. In general, the more memory available on your video card, the better the results.

Gamma preferences

The Gamma panel, shown in Figure 4-21, controls the gamma correction for the display and for bitmap files.

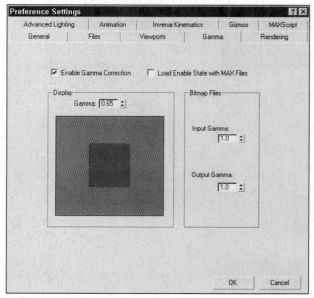

Figure 4-21: Enabling gamma correction makes colors consistent regardless of the monitor.

Setting screen gamma

Have you ever noticed in an electronics store that television screen displays vary in color? Colors on monitor screens may be fairly consistent for related models, but may vary across brands. Gamma settings are a means by which colors can be consistently represented regardless of the monitor that is being used.

Gamma value is a numerical offset required by an individual monitor in order to be consistent with a standard. To enable gamma correction for Max, open the Gamma panel in the Preferences Settings dialog box, and click the Enable Gamma Correction option. To determine the gamma value, use the spinner or adjust the Gamma value until the gray square blends in unnoticeably with the background.

Setting bitmap gamma

Many bitmap formats, such as TGA, contain their own gamma settings. The Input Gamma setting for Bitmap files sets the gamma for bitmaps that don't have a gamma setting. The Output Gamma setting is the value set for bitmaps being output from Max.

Note　　Match the Input Gamma value to the Display Gamma value so that bitmaps loaded for textures will be displayed correctly.

Rendering preferences

Figure 4-22 shows the Preference Settings dialog box with the Rendering panel selected. These settings affect the rendering output.

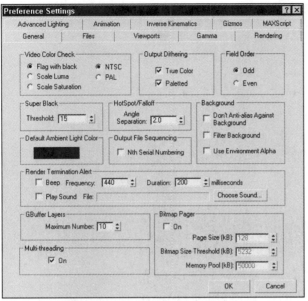

Figure 4-22: The Rendering panel includes settings such as the ambient light color and the current renderer.

The details of the Rendering Preferences panel are covered in Chapter 34, "Rendering Basics."

The Rendering panel includes controls for setting the Video Color Check, Output Dithering, and Field Order. In addition, you can set the Super Black Threshold, Hotspot Falloff, Background Anti-Aliasing, Default Ambient Light Color, and Output File Sequencing in this panel. There are also controls for playing an alert sound when a rendering is finished, and settings you can use to determine the number of Gbuffers and to enable multithreading and a way to break up bitmaps into pages.

Advanced Lighting preferences

The Advanced Lighting panel, shown in Figure 4-23, includes settings that determine how radiosity is processed, whether advanced lighting options are saved with the scene file, or whether Reflectance and Transmittance is displayed in the Material Editor. You can also specify whether radiosity is displayed in the viewports. You can also disable advanced lighting warnings.

Check out Chapter 23, "Advanced Lighting and Radiosity," for greater detail on Advanced Lighting preferences.

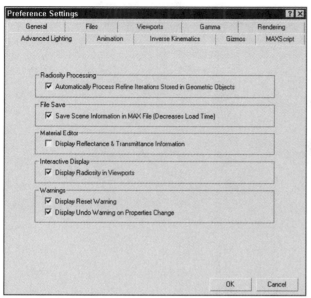

Figure 4-23: The Advanced Lighting panel of the Preference Settings dialog box includes several settings for controlling how radiosity is used.

Animation preferences

The Animation panel, shown in Figure 4-24, contains options dealing with animations. When a specific frame is selected, all objects with keys for that frame are surrounded with white brackets. The Animation panel offers options that specify which objects get these brackets. Options include All Objects, Selected Objects, and None. You can also limit the brackets to only those objects with certain transform keys.

The Local Center During Animate option causes all objects to be animated about their local centers. Turning this option off enables animations about other centers (such as screen and world).

The MIDI Time Slider Controls include an On option and a Setup button. The Setup button opens the MIDI Time Slider Control Setup dialog box shown in Figure 4-25. When this control is set up, you can control an animation using a MIDI device.

You can use the Animation panel to assign a new Sound Plug-In to use, as well as to set the default values of all animation controllers. Clicking the Set Defaults button opens the Set Controller Defaults dialog box. This dialog box includes a list of all the controllers and a Set button. When you select a controller and click the Set button, another dialog box appears with all the values for that controller.

Cross-Reference   You can learn more about specific controllers in Chapter 28, "Animating with Controllers."

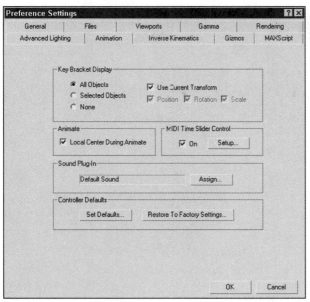

Figure 4-24: The Animation panel includes settings for displaying Key Brackets.

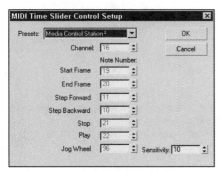

Figure 4-25: The MIDI Time Slider Control Setup dialog box lets you set up specific notes to start, stop, and step through an animation.

Inverse Kinematics preferences

The Inverse Kinematics panel, shown in Figure 4-26, includes Positional, Rotational, and Iteration thresholds for both Applied IK and Interactive IK.

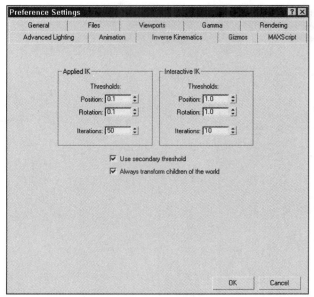

Figure 4-26: The Inverse Kinematics panel of the Preference Settings dialog box includes threshold values for Inverse Kinematics systems.

Cross-Reference   To learn more about Applied IK and Interactive IK, see Chapter 33, "Creating and Using Inverse Kinematics."

Gizmo preferences

Gizmos are controllers that show up in the viewports that provide an interactive way to transform objects. The Gizmos panel of the Preference Settings dialog box is shown in Figure 4-27. This panel includes settings for turning the Transform Gizmos on and off. You can also set the size of the Move, Rotate, and Scale gizmos.

Cross-Reference   See Chapter 9, "Transforming Objects" for more detail on Transform Gizmo preferences.

MAXScript preferences

Settings for working with MAXScript are included in the MAXScript panel, shown in Figure 4-28. These commands include options for loading Startup scripts, controlling the Macro Recorder, the font used in the MAXScript window, and the amount of Memory to use.

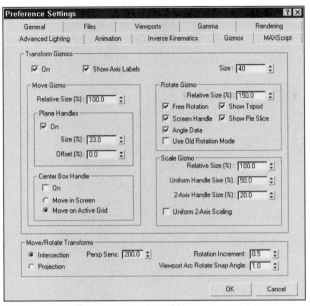

Figure 4-27: The Gizmos panel includes options for controlling the various Transform gizmos.

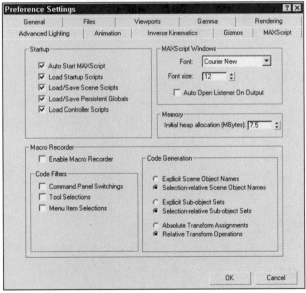

Figure 4-28: The MAXScript panel includes options for controlling MAXScript.

Check out Chapter 40, "Using MAXScript" for more on MAXScript commands and preferences.

Summary

There are many ways to customize the Max interface. Most of these customization options are included under the Customize menu. In this chapter, you learned how to use this menu and its commands to customize many aspects of the Max interface. Customizing the Max interface will make the interface more efficient and comfortable for you.

Specifically, this chapter covered the following topics:

✦ Using the Customize User Interface dialog box to customize keyboard shortcuts, toolbars, quadmenus, menus, and colors

✦ Customizing the Tab panel and the Command Panel buttons

✦ Saving and loading custom interfaces

✦ Configuring paths

✦ Setting preferences

The next chapter is the first chapter in Part II, "Working with Objects." The first chapter covers the primitive objects and actually gets some objects in a scene for you to work with.

✦　　✦　　✦

Working with Objects

Using Primitive Objects

CHAPTER

5

So what exactly did the Romans use to build their civilization? The answer is lots and lots of basic blocks. The basic building blocks in Max are primitives. You can use these basic primitives to start any modeling job. I cover bending, stretching, smashing, and cutting these primitives to create new objects in later chapters, but primitives have many uses in their default shape.

This chapter covers the basics of primitive object types and introduces you to all the various primitive objects, including how to accurately create and control them. They will also be base objects that you can use to learn about selecting, cloning, grouping, and transforming in the coming chapters.

Modeling is covered in depth in Part III, but first, you need to learn how to create some basic blocks and move them around. Later, you can work on building a civilization. I'm sure Rome would be jealous.

Creating Primitive Objects

Max is all about creating objects and scenes, so it fits that one of the first things to learn is how to create objects. Although you can create complex models and objects, Max includes many simple, default geometric objects called *primitives* that you can use as a starting point. Creating these primitive objects can be as easy as clicking and dragging in a viewport.

Using the Create panel

The creation of all default Max objects, such as primitive spheres, shapes, lights, and cameras, starts with the Create panel. This panel is the first panel in the Command Panel with an icon of an arrow pointing to a star.

Of all the panels in the Command Panel, only the Create panel (see Figure 5-1) includes both categories and subcategories. After you click the Create tab in the Command Panel, seven category icons are displayed. From left to right, they are Geometry, Shapes, Lights, Cameras, Helpers, Space Warps, and Systems.

✦   ✦   ✦   ✦

In This Chapter

Creating primitive
objects

Naming objects and
setting object colors

Using different creation
methods

Setting object
parameters

Exploring the various
primitive types

✦   ✦   ✦   ✦

When you select the Geometry button (which has an icon of a sphere on it), a drop-down list with several subcategories appears directly below the category icons. The first available subcategory is Standard Primitives. When you select this subcategory, several buttons appear that enable you to create some simple primitive objects.

Note The second subcategory is called Extended Primitives. It also includes primitive objects.

Create panel icon

Category icons

Subcategory drop-down list

Figure 5-1: The Create panel includes categories and subcategories.

As an example, click the button labeled Sphere (not to be confused with the Geometry category, which has a sphere icon). Several rollouts appear at the bottom of the Command Panel — these rollouts for the Sphere primitive object include Name and Color, Creation Method, Keyboard Entry, and Parameters. The rollouts for each primitive will be slightly different, as well as the parameters within each rollout.

If you want to ignore these rollouts and just create a sphere, simply click and drag within one of the viewports, and a sphere object appears. Figure 5-2 shows the new sphere and its parameters.

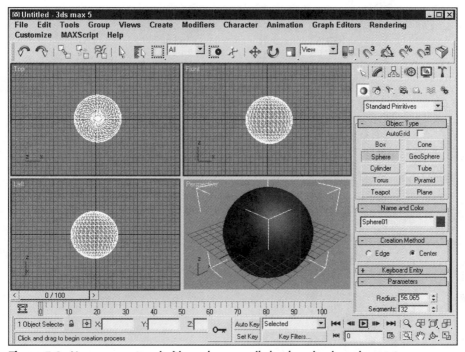

Figure 5-2: You can create primitive spheres easily by dragging in a viewport.

When an object button, such as the Sphere button, is selected, it turns dark yellow. This color change reminds you that you are in creation mode. Clicking within any viewport window creates an additional sphere. While in creation mode, you can create many spheres by clicking and dragging several times in one of the viewports. To get out of creation mode, click the Select Object button or one of the transform buttons on the main toolbar.

Using the Create menu

The Create menu offers quick access to the buttons in the Create panel. Most of the objects that you can create using the Create panel (including both Standard and Extended Primitives, Shapes, Lights, Cameras, and Particles) you can access using the Create menu. Selecting an object from the Create menu opens the Create panel and automatically selects the matching button. You still need to click and drag in the viewport to create the object.

Naming objects, renaming objects, and assigning colors

Every object in the scene can have both a name and color assigned to it. Each object is given a default name and random color when first created. The default name is the type of object followed by a number. For example, when you create a sphere object, Max labels it "Sphere01." These default names aren't very exciting and can be confusing if you have many objects. You can change the object's name at any time by modifying the Name field in the Name and Color rollout of the Command Panel.

Cross-Reference   Names and colors are useful for locating and selecting objects, as you find out in Chapter 6, "Selecting Objects and Setting Object Properties."

The Tools ➪ Rename menu command will open a dialog box that will let you change the object name of several objects at once. The Rename Objects dialog box, shown in Figure 5-3, will let you set the Base Name along with a Prefix, Suffix, or a number. These new names can be applied to the selected objects or to the specific objects that you pick from the Select Objects dialog box.

New Feature   The Rename Objects dialog box is new to 3ds max 5.

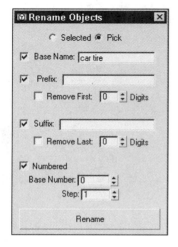

Figure 5-3: The Rename Objects dialog box can rename several objects at once.

The object color is shown in the color swatch to the right of the object name. This color is the color that is used to display the object within the viewports. To change an object's color, just click the color swatch next to the Name field to make the Object Color dialog box appear. This dialog box, shown in Figure 5-4, lets you select a different color or pick a custom color.

Select by Color button

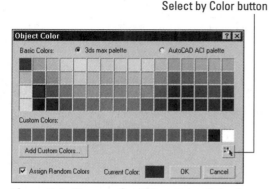

Figure 5-4: You use the Object Color dialog box to define the color of objects displayed in the viewports.

The Object Color dialog box includes the standard 3ds max palette and the AutoCAD ACI palette. The AutoCAD palette has many more colors than the Max palette, but the Max palette allows a row of custom colors. Above the Cancel button is the Select by Color button. Click this button to open the Select Objects dialog box where you can select all the objects that have a certain color.

With the Object Color dialog box, if the Assign Random Colors option is selected, then a random color from the palette is chosen every time a new object is created. If this option is not selected, the color of all new objects is the same until you choose a different object color. Making objects different colors makes distinguishing between the two objects easier for selection and transformation.

You can select custom colors by clicking the Add Custom Colors button. This button opens a Color Selector: Add Color dialog box, shown in Figure 5-5.

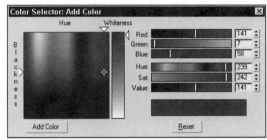

Figure 5-5: The Color Selector: Add Color dialog box lets you choose new custom colors.

The Color Selector: Add Color dialog box defines colors using the RGB (red, green, and blue) and HSV (hue, saturation, and value) color systems. Another way to select colors is to drag the cursor around the rainbow palette to the left. After you find the perfect custom color to add to the Object Color dialog box, click the Add Color button. This custom color will then be available wherever the Object Color dialog box is opened.

Note If no material has been applied to an object, then the object will be rendered using the object color.

Object colors are also important because you can use them to select and filter objects. For example, the Selection Floater (open by choosing Tools ⇨ Selection Floater) includes a Sort by Color setting. You can also choose Edit ⇨ Select by ⇨ Color menu (or click the Select by Color button) to select only objects that match a selected color.

Note You can set objects to display an object's default color or its Material Color. These options are in the Display Color rollout under the Display panel (the fifth tab from the left in the Command Panel with an icon of a monitor). You can set them differently for Wireframe and Shaded views.

Using the Color Clipboard

The object color is one of the first places where colors are encountered, but it certainly won't be the last. If you find a specific color that you like and want to use elsewhere, you can use the Color Clipboard utility to carry colors to other interfaces. You can find this utility in the Utilities panel, as shown in Figure 5-6.

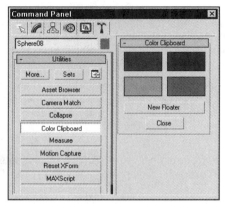

Figure 5-6: The Color Clipboard utility offers a way to transport colors.

When selected, the Color Clipboard appears as a rollout in the Utilities panel and includes four color swatches. These color swatches can be dragged to other interfaces like the Material Editor. Clicking on any of these swatches launches the Color Selector. The New Floater button opens a floatable Color Clipboard that holds 12 colors, shown in Figure 5-7. Using this clipboard, you can open and save color configurations. The files are saved as Color Clipboard Files with the .ccb extension.

Figure 5-7: The Color Clipboard floating palette can hold 12 colors.

Using different creation methods

You actually have a couple of ways to create primitive objects by dragging in a viewport. With the first method, the first place you click sets the object's initial position. You then need to drag the mouse to define the object's first dimension and then click again to set each additional dimension, if needed. Primitive objects with a different number of dimensions require a different number of clicks and drags.

For example, a sphere is one of the simplest objects to create. To create a sphere, click in a viewport to set the location of the sphere's center, then drag the mouse to the desired radius and release the mouse button to complete. A Box object, on the other hand, requires a click and drag move to define the base (width and depth), then another drag and click again to set the height. If you ever get lost when defining these dimensions, check the Prompt Line to see what dimension the interface is expecting next.

When you click a primitive object button, the Creation Method rollout appears and offers different methods for creating the primitives. For example, click the Sphere button, and the Creation Method rollout displays two options: Edge and Center. When you choose the Edge method, the first viewport click will set one edge of the sphere, and dragging and clicking again will set the diameter of the sphere. The default Center creation method defines the sphere's center location; dragging sets the sphere's radius. The creation method for each primitive can be different. For example, the Box primitive object has a creation method for creating perfect cubes. Table 5-1 shows the number of clicks required to create an object and the creation methods for each primitive object.

Table 5-1: Primitive Object Creation Methods

	Primitive Object	Number of Viewport Clicks to Create	Default Creation Method	Other Creation Method
	Box	2	Box	Cube
	Sphere	1	Center	Edge
	Cylinder	2	Center	Edge
	Torus	2	Center	Edge
	Teapot	1	Center	Edge
	Cone	3	Center	Edge
	GeoSphere	1	Center	Diameter
	Tube	3	Center	Edge
	Pyramid	2	Base/Apex	Center
	Plane	1	Rectangular	Square
	Hedra	1	-	-
	ChamferBox	3	Box	Cube
	OilTank	3	Center	Edge
	Spindle	3	Center	Edge
	Gengon	3	Center	Edge

Continued

Table 5-1 *(continued)*

Primitive Object		Number of Viewport Clicks to Create	Default Creation Method	Other Creation Method
	RingWave	2	-	-
Hose		2	-	-
	Torus Knot	2	Radius	Diameter
	ChamferCyl	3	Center	Edge
	Capsule	2	Center	Edge
	L-Ext	3	Corners	Center
	C-Ext	3	Corners	Center
	Prism	3	Base/Apex	Isosceles

Some primitive objects, such as the Hedra, RingWave, and Hose, don't have any creation methods.

Using the Keyboard Entry rollout for precise dimensions

When creating a primitive object, you can define its location and dimensions by clicking in a viewport and dragging, or you can enter precise values in the Keyboard Entry rollout, located in the Create panel. Within this rollout, you can enter the offset XYZ values for positioning the origin of the primitive and the dimensions of the object. The offset values are defined relative to the active construction plane that is usually the Home Grid.

When all the dimension fields are set, click the Create button to create the actual primitive. You can create multiple objects by clicking the Create button several times. After a primitive is created, altering the fields in the Keyboard Entry rollout has no effect on the current object, but you can always use the Undo feature to try again.

Altering object parameters

The final rollout for all primitive objects is the Parameters rollout. This rollout holds all the various settings for the object. Compared to the Keyboard Entry rollout, which you can use only when creating the primitive, you can use the Parameters rollout to alter the primitive's parameters before or after the creation of the object. For example, increasing the Radius value after creating an object will make an existing sphere larger.

The parameters are different for each primitive object, but you can generally use them to control the dimensions, the number of segments that make up the object, and whether the object is sliced into sections. You can also select the Generate Mapping Coordinates option (which automatically creates material mapping coordinates that are used to position maps).

Note After you de-select an object, the Parameters rollout disappears from the Create tab and moves to the Modify tab. You can make future parameter adjustments by selecting an object and clicking the Modify tab.

Recovering from mistakes and deleting objects

Before going any further, you need to learn how to undo the last action with the Undo menu command. The Undo (Ctrl+Z) menu command will undo the last action whether it's creating an object or changing a parameter. The Redo (Ctrl+Y) menu command lets you redo an action that was undone.

Caution Many operations such as applying or deleting modifiers and changing parameters cannot be undone.

You can set the levels of undo in the Preference Settings dialog box. If you right-click on either the Undo or Redo buttons on the main toolbar, a list of recent actions is displayed. You can select any action from this list to be undone.

The Edit ➪ Delete menu command removes the selected object (or objects) from the scene. (The keyboard shortcut for this command is, luckily, the Delete key, as anything else would be confusing.)

Tutorial: Exploring the Platonic solids

Among the many discoveries of Plato, an ancient Greek mathematician and philosopher, were the mathematical formulas that defined perfect geometric solids. A perfect geometric solid is one that is made up of polygon faces that are consistent throughout the object. The five solids that meet these criteria have come to be known as the Platonic solids.

Using Max, you can create and explore these interesting geometric shapes. Each of these shapes is available as a primitive object using the Hedra primitive object. The Hedra primitive object is one of the Extended Primitives.

To create the five Platonic solids as primitive objects, follow these steps:

1. Open the Create panel, click the Geometry category button, and select Extended Primitives from the subcategory drop-down list. Click the Hedra button to enter Hedra creation mode.

2. Click in the Top viewport and drag to the left to create a simple Tetrahedron object.

   After the object is created, you can adjust its settings by altering the settings in the Parameters rollout.

3. Select the Tetra option in the Parameters rollout, set the P value in the Family Parameters section to **1.0**, and enter a value of **50** for the Radius. Be sure to press the Enter key after entering a value to update the object. Enter the name **Tetrahedron** in the Object Name field.

4. Click and drag again in the Top viewport to create another object. In the Parameters rollout, select the Cube/Octa option, and enter a value of **1.0** in the Family Parameter's P field and a value of **50** in the Radius field. Name this object **Octagon**.

5. Drag in the Top viewport to create another object. The Cube/Octa option is still selected. Enter a value of **1.0** in the Family Parameter's Q field this time and set the Radius to **50**. Name this object **Cube**.

6. Drag in the Top viewport again to create the fourth scene object. In the Parameters rollout, select the Dodec/Icos option, enter a value of **1.0** in the P field, and set the Radius value to **50**. Name the object **Icosahedron**.

7. Drag in the Top viewport to create the final object. With the Dodec/Icos option set, enter **1.0** for the Q value, and set the Radius to **50**. Name this object **Dodecahedron**.

8. To get a good look at the objects, click the Perspective viewport and maximize the viewport by clicking the Min/Max Toggle (or press Alt+W) in the lower right-hand corner of the window.

Figure 5-8 shows the five perfect solid primitive objects. Using the Modify panel, you can return to these objects and change their parameters to learn the relationships between them. Later in this chapter, I discuss the Hedra primitive in greater detail.

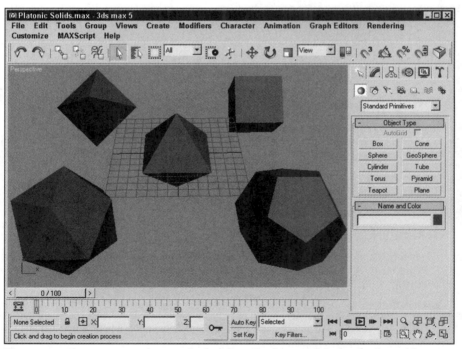

Figure 5-8: The octagon, cube, tetrahedron, icosahedron, and dodecahedron objects; Plato would be amazed.

Primitive Object Types

In the Create panel are actually two different subcategories of primitives — Standard Primitives and Extended Primitives. These primitives include several diverse objects from simple boxes and spheres to complex torus knots. You can create all of these primitives from the Create panel.

Standard Primitives

The Standard Primitives include many of the most basic and most used objects, including boxes, spheres, and cylinders. Figure 5-9 shows all the Standard Primitives.

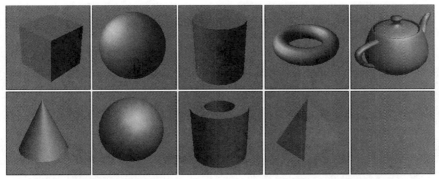

Figure 5-9: The Standard Primitives: Box, Sphere, Cylinder, Torus, Teapot, Cone, GeoSphere, Tube, Pyramid, and Plane

Box

You can use the Box primitive to create regular cubes and boxes of any width, length, and height. Holding down the Ctrl key while dragging the box base creates a perfect square for the base. To create a cube, select the Cube option in the Creation Method rollout. A single click and drag completes the cube.

The Length, Width, and Height Segment values indicate how many polygons make up each dimension. The default is only one segment.

Sphere

Spheres appear everywhere from sports balls to planets in space. Spheres are also among the easiest primitives to create. After clicking the Sphere button, simply click and drag in a viewport.

In the Parameters rollout, the Segments value specifies the number of polygons that make up the sphere. The higher the number of segments, the smoother the sphere will be. The default value of 32 produces a smooth sphere, and a value of 4 actually produces a diamond-shaped object. The Smooth option lets you make the sphere smooth or faceted. Faceted spheres are useful for identifying faces for modifications. Figure 5-10 shows five spheres. The one on the left has 32 Segments and the Smooth option turned on. The remaining spheres have the Smooth option disabled with Segment values of 32, 16, 8, and 4.

Figure 5-10: Sphere primitives of various Segment values with the Smooth option on and off

The Parameters rollout also lets you create hemispheres. The hemisphere shape is set by the Hemisphere value, which can range from 0.0 to 1.0, with 0 being a full sphere and 1 being nothing at all. (A value of 0.5 would be a perfect hemisphere.) With the Hemisphere value specified, you now have two options with which to deal with the unused polygons that make up the originating sphere: the Chop option, which removes the unused polygons, and the Squash option, which retains the polygons but "squashes" them to fit in the hemisphere shape.

Figure 5-11 shows two hemispheres with Hemisphere values of 0.5. The Edged Faces option was enabled in the Viewport Configuration dialog box so you could see the polygon faces. The left hemisphere was created using the Chop option and the right hemisphere was created with the Squash option. Notice how many extra polygons are included in the right hemisphere.

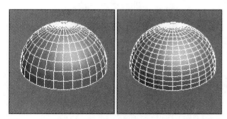

Figure 5-11: Creating hemispheres with the Chop and Squash options

The Slice option enables you to dissect the sphere into slices (like segmenting an orange). The Slice From and Slice To fields accept values ranging from 0 to 360 degrees. Figure 5-12 shows three spheres that have been sliced. Notice how because the Segments value hasn't changed, all slices have the same number of faces.

Note   You can use the Slice feature on several primitives, including the sphere, cylinder, torus, cone, tube, oiltank, spindle, chamfercyl, and capsule.

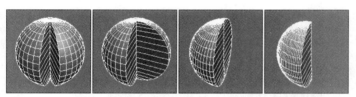

Figure 5-12: Using the Slice option to create sphere slices

The Base to Pivot parameter determines whether the position of the pivot point will be at the bottom of the sphere or at the center. The default (with the Base to Pivot setting not enabled) will set the pivot point for the sphere at the center of the sphere.

Cylinder

You can use a cylinder in many places; for example, as a pillar in front of a home or as a car driveshaft. To create one, first specify a base circle and then a height. The default number of sides is 18, which produces a smooth cylinder. Height and Cap Segments values define the number of polygons that make up the cylinder sides and caps. The Smooth and Slice options work the same as they do with a sphere (see preceding section).

Tip   If you don't plan on modifying the ends of the cylinder, make the Cap Segments equal to 1 to keep the model complexity down.

Torus

A Torus (which is the mathematical name for a "doughnut") is a ring with a circular cross section. To create a Torus, you need to specify two radii values. The first is the value from the center of the Torus to the center of the ring; the second is the radius of the circular cross section. The default settings create a Torus with 24 segments and 12 sides. The Rotation and Twist options cause the sides to twist a specified value as the ring is circumnavigated.

Figure 5-13 shows some sample Toruses with a Smooth setting of None. The first three have Segments values of 24, 12, and 6. The last two have Twist values of 90 and 360. The higher the number of segments, the rounder the Torus looks when viewed from above. The default of 24 is sufficient to create a smooth Torus. The number of sides defines the circular smoothness of the cross section.

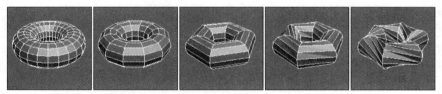

Figure 5-13: Using the Segments and Twist options on a Torus

The Parameters rollout includes settings for four different Smooth options. The All option smoothes all edges, and the None option displays all polygons as faceted. The Sides option smoothes edges between sides, resulting in a Torus with banded sides. The Segment option smoothes between segment edges, resulting in separate smooth sections around the Torus.

The Slice options work with a Torus the same way as they do with the sphere and cylinder objects (see the section "Sphere" earlier in this chapter).

Teapot

Okay, let's all sing together, "I'm a little teapot, short and stout . . ." The teapot is another object that, like the sphere, is easy to create. Within the Parameters rollout, you can specify the number of Segments, whether the surface is smooth or faceted, and which parts to display, including Body, Handle, Spout, and Lid.

Note You may recognize most of these primitives as standard shapes, with the exception of the teapot. The teapot has a special place in computer graphics. In early computer graphics development labs, the teapot was chosen as the test model for many early algorithms. It is still included as a valuable benchmark for computer graphics programmers.

Cone

The Cone object, whether used to create ice cream cones or megaphones, is created exactly like the cylinder object except that the second cap can have a radius different from that of the first. You create it by clicking and dragging to specify the base circle, dragging to specify the cone's height, and then dragging again for the second cap to create a Cone.

In addition to the two cap radii and the Height, parameter options include the number of Height and Cap Segments, the number of Sides, and the Smooth and Slice options.

GeoSphere

The GeoSphere object is a sphere that is created using fewer polygon faces than the standard Sphere object. This type of sphere spreads the polygon faces, which are all equal in size around the object, instead of concentrating them on either end like the normal Sphere object. This makes the GeoSphere object easier to model while using less memory. One reason for this is that a GeoSphere uses triangle faces instead of square faces.

In the Parameters rollout are several Geodesic Base Type options, including Tetra, Octa, and Icosa. The Tetra type is based on a four-sided tetrahedron, the Octa type is based on an eight-sided Octahedron, and the Icosa type is based on the 20-sided Icosahedron. Setting the Segment value to 1 produces each of these Hedron shapes. Each type aligns the triangle faces differently.

GeoSpheres also have the same Smooth, Hemisphere, and Base to Pivot options as the Sphere primitive. Selecting the Hemisphere option changes the GeoSphere into a hemisphere, but there are no additional options like Chop and Squash. GeoSpheres also cannot be sliced.

Tutorial: Comparing Spheres and GeoSpheres

To prove that GeoSpheres are more efficient than Sphere objects, follow these steps:

1. Create a normal Sphere and set its Segment value to 4.

2. Next to the Sphere object, create a GeoSphere object with a Tetra Base Type and the number of Segments set to 4.

3. Create another GeoSphere object with the Octa Base Type and 4 Segments.

4. Finally, create a GeoSphere with the Icosa Base Type and 4 Segments.

Figure 5-14 shows these spheres as a comparison. The normal sphere, shown to the left, looks like a diamond, but the GeoSpheres still resemble spheres. Notice how the Icosa type GeoSphere, shown in the lower right, produces the smoothest sphere.

Tube

The Tube primitive is useful for any time you need a pipe object. You can also use it to create ring-shaped objects that have rectangular cross sections. Creating a Tube object is very similar to the Cylinder and Cone objects. Tube parameters include two radii for the inner and outer tube wall. Tubes also have the Smooth and Slice options.

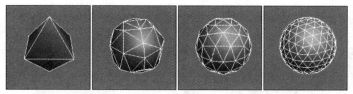

Figure 5-14: Even with a similar number of segments, GeoSpheres are much more spherical.

Pyramid

Pyramid primitives are constructed with a rectangular base and triangles at each edge that rise to meet at the top, just like they made in Egypt. Two different creation methods are used to create the base rectangle. With the Base/Apex method, you create the base by dragging corner to corner, and with the Center method, you drag from the base center to a corner.

The Width and Depth parameters define the base dimensions, and the Height value determines how tall the pyramid is. You can also specify the number of segments for each dimension.

Plane

The Plane object enables you to model the Great Plains (good pun, eh?). The Plane primitive creates a simple plane that looks like a rectangle, but it includes Multiplier parameters that let you specify the size of the plane at render time. This feature makes working in a viewport convenient because you don't have to worry about its actual dimensions.

The Plane primitive includes two creation methods: Rectangle and Square. The Square method creates a perfect square in the viewport when dragged. You can also define the Length and Width Segments, but the real benefits of the Plane object are derived from the use of the Render Multipliers.

The Scale Multiplier value determines how many times larger the plane should be at render time. Both Length and Width are multiplied by equal values. The Density Multiplier specifies the number of segments to produce at render time.

Extended Primitives

Access the Extended Primitives by selecting Extended Primitives in the subcategory drop-down list in the Create panel. These primitives aren't as generic as the Standard Primitives but are equally useful (see Figure 5-15).

Hedra

Hedras, or Polyhedra, form the basis for a class of geometry defined by fundamental mathematical principles. In addition to Plato, Johannes Kepler used these Polyhedra as the basis for his famous "Harmony of the Spheres" theory. The Hedra primitives (shown in the first tutorial of this chapter) available in Max are Tetrahedron, Cube/Octahedron, Dodecahedron/Icosahedron, and two Star types called Star1 and Star2. From these basic Polyhedra, you can create many different variations.

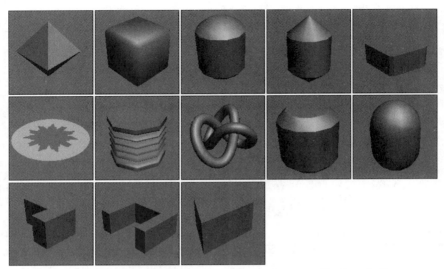

Figure 5-15: The Extended Primitives: Hedra, ChamferBox, OilTank, Spindle, Gengon, RingWave, Hose, Torus Knot, ChamferCyl, Capsule, L-Ext, C-Ext, and Prism

The Family section options determine the shape of the Hedra. Each member of a Hedra pair is mathematically related to the other member. The Family Parameters include P and Q values. These values change the Hedra between the two shapes that make up the pair. For example, if the family option is set to Cube/Octa, then a P value of 1 will display an Octagon, and a Q value of 1 will display a Cube. When both P and Q values are set to 0, the shape becomes an intermediate shape somewhere between a Cube and an Octagon. Because both values are interrelated, only one shape of the pair can have a value at 1 at the same time. Both P and Q cannot be set to 1 at the same time.

Figure 5-16 shows each of the basic Hedra Families in columns from left to right: Tetra, Cube/Octa, Dodec/Icos, Star1, and Star2. The top row has a P value of 1 and a Q value of 0, the middle row has both P and Q set to 0, and the bottom row sets P to 0 and Q to 1. Notice how the middle row shapes are a combination of the top and bottom rows.

The relationship between P and Q can be described in this manner: When the P value is set to 1 and the Q value is set to 0, one shape of the pair is displayed. As the P value decreases, each vertex will become a separate face. The edges of these new faces will increase as the value is decreased down to 0. The same holds true for the Q value.

Tip   Altering the P and Q parameters can create many unique shapes. For each Hedra, try the following combinations: P = 0, Q = 0; P = 1, Q = 0; P = 0, Q = 1; P = 0.5, Q = 0.5; P = 0.5, Q = 0; P = 0, Q = 0.5. These represent the main intermediate objects.

As the geometry of the objects changes, the Hedra can have as many as three different types of polygons comprising the faces. These polygons are represented by the P, Q, and R Axis Scaling values. Each type of face can be scaled, creating sharp points extending from each face. If only one unique polygon is used for the faces, then only one Axis Scaling parameter will be active. The Reset button simply returns the Axis Scaling value back to its default at 100. For example, using the R Axis Scaling value, pyramid shapes can be extended from each face of a cube.

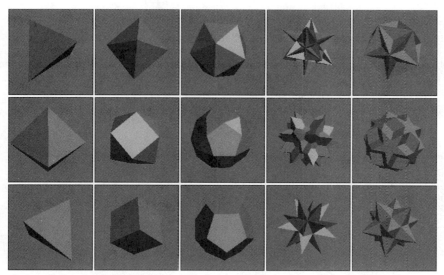

Figure 5-16: The Hedra Families with the standard shapes in the top and bottom rows and the intermediate shapes in the middle row

Figure 5-17 shows some results of using the Axis Scaling options. One of each family type has been created and displayed in the top row for reference. The bottom row has had an axis scaled to a value of 170. This setting causes one type of polygon face to be extended, thereby producing a new shape.

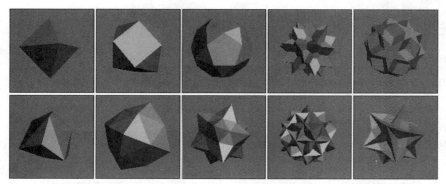

Figure 5-17: Hedras with extended faces, compliments of the Axis Scaling option

The Vertices parameter options add additional vertices and edges to the center of each extended polygon. The three options are Basic, which is the default and doesn't add any new information to the Hedra; Center, which adds vertices to the center of each extended polygon; and Center and Sides, which add both center vertices and connecting edges for each face that is extended using the Axis Scaling options. With these options set, you can extend the polygon faces at your own discretion.

Way at the bottom of the Parameters rollout is the Radius value.

ChamferBox

A chamfered object is an object whose edges have been smoothed out, so a ChamferBox primitive is a box with beveled edges. The parameter that determines the amount of roundness applied to an edge is Fillet. In many ways, this object is just a simple extension of the Box primitive.

The only additions in the Parameters rollout are two fields for controlling the Fillet dimension and the Fillet Segments. Figure 5-18 shows a ChamferBox with Fillet values of 0, 5, 10, 20, and 30 and the Smooth option turned on.

Figure 5-18: A ChamferBox with progressively increasing Fillet values

Cylindrical extended primitives

The Extended Primitives include several objects based on the Cylinder primitive that are very similar. The only real differences are the shape of the caps at either end. These four similar objects include the OilTank, Spindle, ChamferCyl, and Capsule. Figure 5-19 shows these similar objects side by side.

Figure 5-19: Several different cylindrical extended primitive objects exist, including Oil Tank, Spindle, ChamferCyl, and Capsule.

OilTank

OilTank seems like a strange name for a primitive. This object is essentially the Cylinder primitive with dome caps like you would see on a diesel truck transporting oil. The Parameters rollout includes an additional option for specifying the Cap Height. The Height value can be set to indicate the entire height of the object with the Overall option, or the height to the edge of the domes using the Centers option. The only other new option is Blend, which smoothes the edges between the cylinder and the caps. All cylindrical primitives can also be sliced just like the sphere object.

Spindle

The Spindle primitive is the same as the OilTank primitive, except that the dome caps are replaced with conical caps. All other options in the Parameters rollout are identical to the OilTank primitive.

ChamferCyl

The ChamferCyl primitive is very similar to the ChamferBox primitive, only applied to a cylinder instead of a box. The Parameters rollout includes some additional fields for handling the Fillet values.

Capsule

The Capsule primitive is a yet another primitive based on the cylinder, only this time with hemispherical caps. This object resembles the OilTank primitive very closely. The only real noticeable difference is in the border between the cylinder and caps.

Gengon

The Gengon primitive creates and extrudes regular polygons such as triangles, squares, and pentagons. There is even an option to Fillet (or smooth) the edges. To specify which polygon to use, enter a value in the No. of Sides field.

Figure 5-20 shows five simple Gengons with different numbers of edges.

Figure 5-20: Gengon primitives are actually just extruded regular polygons.

RingWave

The RingWave primitive is a specialized primitive that you can use to create a simple gear or a sparkling sun. It consists of two circles that make up a ring. You can set the circle edges to be wavy and even fluctuate over time. You can also use RingWaves to simulate rapidly expanding gases that would result from a planetary explosion. If you're considering a Shockwave effect, then you should look into using a RingWave primitive.

The Radius setting and the inner edge define the outer edge by the Ring Width. This ring can also have a Height. The Radial and Height Segments and the number of Sides determine the complexity of the object.

The RingWave Timing controls set the expansion values. The Start Time is the frame where the ring begins at zero, the Grow Time is the number of frames required to reach its full size, and the End Time is the frame where the RingWave object stops expanding. The No Growth option prevents the object from expanding, and it remains the same size from the Start frame to the End frame. The Grow and Stay option causes the RingWave to expand from the Start Time until the Grow Time frame is reached, and then remain full-grown until the End Time. The Cyclic Growth begins expanding the objects until the Grow Time is reached. It then starts again from zero and expands repeatedly until the End Time is reached.

Cross-Reference   An example of the RingWave primitive is included in Chapter 19, "Creating and Applying Materials."

The last two sections of the Parameters rollout define how the inner and outer edges look and are animated. If the Edge Breakup option is on, then the rest of the settings are enabled. These additional settings control the number of Major and Minor Cycles, the Width Flux for these cycles, and the Crawl Time, which is the number of frames to animate.

The Surface Parameters section includes an option for creating Texture Coordinates, which are the same as mapping coordinates for applying textures. There is also an option to Smooth the surface of the object.

Figure 5-21 shows four animated frames of a RingWave object with both Inner and Outer Edge Breakup settings. Notice how the edges change over the different frames.

Figure 5-21: Four frames of a rapidly expanding and turbulent RingWave object

Torus Knot

A Torus Knot is similar to the Torus covered earlier, except that the circular cross-section follows a 3D curve instead of a simple circle. The method for creating the Torus Knot primitive is the same as that for creating the Torus. The Parameters rollout even lets you specify the base curve to be a circle instead of a knot. A knot is a standard, mathematically defined 3D curve.

Below the Radius and Segment parameters are the P and Q values. These values can be used to create wildly variant Torus Knots. The P value is a mathematical factor for computing how the knot winds about its vertical axis. The maximum value is 25, which makes the knot resemble a tightly wound spool. The Q value causes the knot to wind horizontally. It also has a maximum value of 25. Setting both values to the same number results in a simple circular ring.

Figure 5-22 shows some of the beautiful shapes that are possible by altering the P and Q values of a Torus Knot. These Torus Knots have these values: P = 3, Q = 2; the second has P = 1, Q = 3; the third has P = 10, Q = 15; the fourth has P = 15, Q = 20; and the fifth has P = 25, Q = 25.

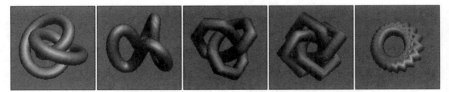

Figure 5-22: Various Torus Knots display the beauty of mathematics.

When the Base Curve is set to Circle, like those in Figure 5-22, the P and Q values become disabled, and the Warp Count and Warp Height fields become active. These fields control the number of ripples in the ring and their height. Figure 5-23 shows several possibilities. From left to right, the settings are Warp Count = 5, Warp Height = 0.5; Warp Count = 10, Warp Height = 0.5; Warp Count = 20, Warp Height = 0.5; Warp Count = 50, Warp Height = 0.5; and Warp Count = 100, Warp Height = 0.75.

Figure 5-23: Torus Knots with a Circle Base Curve are useful for creating impressive rings.

In addition to the Base Curve settings, you can also control several settings for the Cross Section. The Radius and Sides values determine the size of the circular cross section and the number of segments used to create the cross section. The Eccentricity value will make the circular cross section elliptical by stretching it along one of its axes. The Twist value will rotate each successive cross section relative to the previous one creating a twisting look along the object. The Lumps value sets the number of lumps that appear in the Torus Knot and the Lump Height and Offset values set the height and starting point of these lumps.

The Smooth options work just like the Torus object by smoothing the entire object, just the sides, or none. You can also set the U and V axis Offset and Tiling values for the mapping coordinates.

L-Ext

The L-Ext primitive stands for L-Extension. You can think of it as two rectangular boxes that are connected at right angles to each other. To create an L-Ext object, you need to first drag to create a rectangle that defines the overall area of the object. Next you drag to define the Height of the object, and, finally, you drag to define the width of each leg.

The Parameters rollout includes dimensions for Side and Front Lengths, Side and Front Widths, and the Height. You can also define the number of Segments for each dimension.

C-Ext

The C-Ext primitive is the same as the L-Ext primitive with an extra rectangular box. The C shape connects three rectangular boxes at right angles to each other.

The Parameters rollout includes dimensions for Side, Front, and Back Lengths and Widths, and the Height. You can also define the number of Segments for each dimension. These primitives are great if your name is Clive Logan or Carrie Lincoln.

Prism

The Prism primitive is essentially an extruded triangle. If you select the Base/Apex creation method, then each of the sides of the base triangle can have a different length. With this creation method, the first click in the viewport sets one edge of the base triangle, the second click sets the opposite corner of the triangle that affects the other two edges, and the final click sets the height of the object.

The other creation method is Isosceles, which doesn't let you skew the triangle before setting the height.

Hose

The Hose primitive is a flexible connector that can be positioned between two other objects. It acts much like a spring but has no dynamic properties. In the Hose Parameters rollout, you can specify the Hose as a Free Hose or Bound to Object Pivots. If the Free Hose option is selected, you can set the Hose Height. If the Bound to Object Pivots option is selected, then two Pick Object buttons appear for the Top and Bottom objects. Once bound to two objects, the hose will stretch between the two objects as either one is moved. You can also set the Tension for each bound object.

For either the Bound or Free Hose, you can set the number of Segments that make up the hose, whether the flexible section is enabled, to smooth along the Sides, Segments, neither or all, whether the hose is Renderable, and to Generate Mapping Coordinates for applying texture maps. If the flexible section is enabled, then you can set where the flexible section Starts and Ends, the number of Cycles, and its Diameter.

You can also set the Hose Shape to Round, Rectangular, or D-Section. Figure 5-24 shows a flexible hose object bound to two sphere objects.

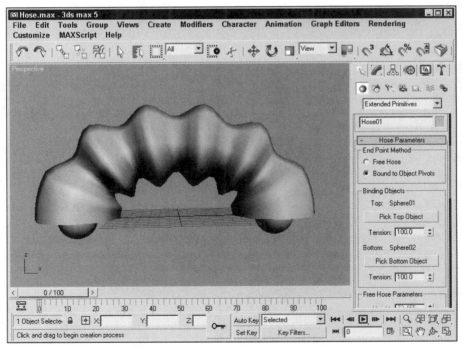

Figure 5-24: The Hose object flexes between its two bound objects.

Modifying object parameters

Primitive objects provide a good starting point for many of the other modeling types. They also provide a good way to show off parameter-based modeling.

All objects have parameters. These parameters help define how the object looks. For example, consider the primitive objects. The primitive objects contained in Max are parametric. Parametric objects are mathematically defined, and you can change them by modifying their parameters. The easiest object modifications to make are simply changing these parameters. For example, a sphere with a radius of 4 can be made into a sphere with a radius of 10 by simply typing a 10 in the Radius field. The viewports display these changes automatically when you press the Enter key.

When an object is first created, its parameters are displayed in the Parameters rollout of the Create panel. As long as the object remains the current object, you can modify its parameters using this rollout. After you select a different tool or object, the Parameters rollout is no longer accessible from the Create panel. It can be found from then on under the Modify panel.

Tutorial: Filling a treasure chest with gems

I haven't found too many treasure chests lately, but if I remember right, they are normally filled with bright, sparkling gems. In this tutorial, we'll fill the chest with a number of Hedra primitives and alter the object properties in the Modify panel to create a diverse offering of gems.

To create a treasure chest with many unique gems, follow these steps:

1. Open the Treasure chest of gems.max file from the Chap 5 directory on the CD-ROM.

   This file includes a simple treasure chest model.

2. Click the Create panel and select the Extended Primitives subcategory. Then click the Hedra button.

3. Create several Hedra objects. The size of the objects won't matter at this time. Move all the Hedra objects to the top of the chest.

4. Open the Modify panel and select one of the Hedra objects.

5. Alter the values in the Parameters rollout to produce a nice gem.

6. Repeat Step 5 for all Hedra objects in the chest.

Figure 5-25 shows the resulting chest with a variety of gems.

Every modeling type, whether it is an Editable Spline, a Compound Conform object, or a NURBS Point curve, has parameters. These parameters, which you can modify, appear in rollouts using the Modify panel.

Figure 5-25: A treasure chest full of gems quickly created by altering object parameters

Summary

Primitives are the most basic shapes and often provide a starting point for more ambitious modeling projects. The two classes of primitives—Standard and Extended—provide a host of possible objects. In this chapter, you

✦ Learned about the basics of creating primitives by both dragging and entering keyboard values

✦ Discovered how to name objects and set and change the object color

✦ Learned the various creation methods for all the primitive objects

✦ Explored all the various primitives in both the Standard and Extended subcategories

✦ Covered the possible parameters for each of the primitive objects

Now that you know how to create objects, you can focus on selecting them once they're created, which is what the next chapter covers. There are numerous different ways to select objects.

✦   ✦   ✦

Selecting Objects and Setting Object Properties

Now that you've learned how to create objects and had some practice, you've probably created more than you really need. To eliminate, move, or change the look of any objects, you first have to know how to select the object. Doing so can be tricky if the viewports are all full of objects lying on top of one another. Luckily, Max offers several selection features that make looking for a needle in a haystack easier.

Max offers many different ways to select objects. You can select by name, color, type, and even material. You can also use selection filters to make only certain types of objects selectable. And after you've found all the objects you need, you can make a selection set, which will allow you to quickly select a set of objects by name. Now where is that needle?

All objects have properties that define their physical characteristics, such as shape, radius, and smoothness, but objects also have properties that control where they are located in the scene, how they are displayed and rendered, and what their parent objects are. These properties have a major impact on how you work with objects; understanding them can make objects in a scene easier to work with.

Selecting Objects

Max includes several methods for selecting objects — the easiest being simply clicking on the object in one of the viewports. Selected objects turn white and are enclosed in brackets called *selection brackets*.

In addition to turning white and displaying selection brackets, there are several options you can use to mark selected objects. You can find these options in the Viewport Configuration dialog box (which you access with the Customize ➪ Viewport Configuration menu command) and they include selection brackets (keyboard shortcut, J), and edged faces (F4). Either or both of these options can be enabled, as shown in Figure 6-1. Another way to detect the selected object is that the object's axes appear at the object's pivot point.

Caution   The Viewport Configuration dialog box also includes an option to Shade Selected Faces (F2), but this option will only shade selected subobject faces.

Figure 6-1: Selected objects can be highlighted with selection brackets (left), edged faces (middle), or both (right).

With many objects in a scene, clicking directly on a single object, free from the others, can be difficult, but persistence can pay off. If you continue to click an object that is already selected, then the object directly behind the object you clicked on will be selected. For example, if you have a row of spheres lined up, you can select the third sphere by clicking three times on the first object.

Tip   In complicated scenes, finding objects is often much easier if they have a relevant name. Be sure to name your new objects using the Name and Color rollout.

Selection filters

Before examining the selection commands in the Edit menu, I need to tell you about Selection Filters. With a complex scene that includes geometry, lights, cameras, shapes, and so on, selecting the exact object that you want can be difficult. Selection filters can simplify this task.

A selection filter specifies which types of objects can be selected. The Selection Filter drop-down list is located on the main toolbar. Selecting Shapes, for example, makes only shape objects available for selection. Clicking a geometry object with the Shape Selection Filter enabled does nothing.

The available filters include All, Geometry, Shapes, Lights, Cameras, Helpers, and Warps. If you're using Inverse Kinematics, you can also filter by Bone, IK Chain Object, and Point.

The Combos option opens the Filter Combinations dialog box, shown in Figure 6-2. From this dialog box, you can select combinations of objects to filter. These new filter combinations will be added to the drop-down list. For example, to create a filter combination for lights and cameras, open the Filter Combinations dialog box, select Lights and Cameras, and click Add. The combination is listed as LC in the Current Combinations section, and the LC option is added to the drop-down list.

The Filter Combinations dialog box also includes a list of Class IDs. Using these IDs, you can filter very specific object types, such as a Boolean object or a Box primitive. In fact, the Bone IK Chain Object and Point filters are Class IDs.

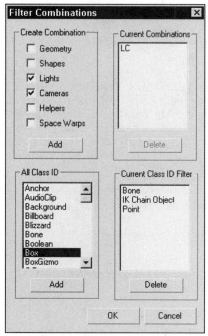

Figure 6-2: The Filter Combinations dialog box enables you to create a custom selection filter.

Select buttons

On the main toolbar are five buttons used to select objects, shown in the following table. The button looks like the arrow cursor. The other three buttons select and transform objects. They are Select and Rotate (E), and Select and Scale (R). You can also select objects with the Select and Manipulate button. You can use any of these buttons to select objects.

Button	Description
	Select Object (Q)
	Select and Move (W)
	Select and Rotate (E)
	Select and Scale (R)
	Select and Manipulate

Cross-Reference   See Chapter 9, "Transforming Objects" for more details on the Select and Transform buttons.

Selecting with the Edit menu

The Edit menu includes several convenient selection commands. The Edit ⇨ Select All (Ctrl+A) menu command does just what you would think it does. It selects all objects in the current scene of the type defined by the selection filter. The Edit ⇨ Select None (Ctrl+D) menu command deselects all objects. You can also simulate this command by clicking in any viewport away from all objects. The Edit ⇨ Select Invert (Ctrl+I) menu command selects all objects defined by the selection filter that are currently not selected and de-selects all currently selected objects.

Choosing Edit ⇨ Select by ⇨ Color lets you click a single object in any of the viewports. All objects with the same color as the one you selected will be selected.

Note   Even if you already have an object of that color selected, you still must select an object of the desired color.

This command, of course, will not work on any objects without an associated color, such as Space Warps.

Select by Name

Choosing Edit ⇨ Select by ⇨ Name (H) opens the Select Objects dialog box, as shown in Figure 6-3. Clicking the Select by Name button on the main toolbar, positioned to the right of the Selection Filter drop-down list, or pressing the keyboard shortcut, H, can also open this dialog box.

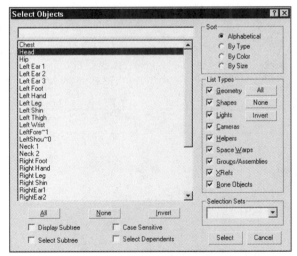

Figure 6-3: The Select Objects dialog box displays all objects in the current scene by name.

You select objects by clicking their names in the list and then clicking the Select button. To pick and choose several objects, hold down the Ctrl key while selecting. Holding down the Shift key selects a range of objects.

Note   An identical version of the Select Objects dialog box works in a modeless state and enables you to interact with the viewports behind the dialog box. This dialog box is called the Selection Floater, and you can access it by choosing Tools ⇨ Selection Floater.

You can also type an object name in the field above the name list. All objects that match the typed characters will be selected. The Sort options affect how the list is displayed. Selecting the Sort by Size option sorts the objects by the number of faces. This is an easy way to find the most complicated object in the scene.

Tip   Within the Select by Name text field, you can use wildcards to locate objects. Acceptable wildcards include an asterisk (*) for multiple characters in a row and a question mark (?) for single characters. For example, an entry of **hedra*** will select all objects beginning with "hedra" regardless of the ending.

The Display Subtree option includes all child objects in the list. By enabling the Select Subtree option, you select all child objects along with their parent objects. The Select Dependents option automatically selects all instances and references. The Case Sensitive option checks the case of the letters typed in the name search field. If this option is not selected, then capital letters are the same as their lowercase counterparts.

The Select Object dialog box isn't subject to the selection filter because the object types can be selected in the dialog box. Selection sets are also accessible from the Select Objects dialog box.

Select by Region

The Edit ⇨ Region command lets you select from one of two different methods for selecting objects in the viewport using the mouse. First, make sure you're in select mode, click away from any of the objects, and drag over the objects to select. The first method for selecting objects is Window Selection. This method selects all objects that are contained completely within the dragged outline. The Crossing Selection method selects any objects that are inside or overlapping the dragged outline. You can also access these two selection methods via the Window Selection buttons on the main toolbar—Window and Crossing, shown in the following table.

Button	*Description*
▦	Window
▦	Crossing

You can also change the shape of the selection outline. The Selection Region button on the main toolbar to the left of the Selection Filter drop-down list includes flyout buttons for Rectangular, Circular, Fence, and Lasso Selection Regions, shown in the following table.

Button	Description
	Rectangular
	Circular
	Fence
	Lasso

The Rectangular selection method lets you select objects by dragging a rectangular section (from corner to corner) over a viewport. The Circular selection method selects objects within a circle that grows from the center outward. The Fence method lets you draw a polygon-shaped selection area by clicking at each corner. Simply double-click to finish the fenced selection. The Lasso method lets you draw by freehand the selection area.

Pressing the Q keyboard shortcut selects the Select Object mode in the main toolbar, but repeated pressing of the Q keyboard shortcut will cycle through the selection methods. Figure 6-4 shows each of the selection methods.

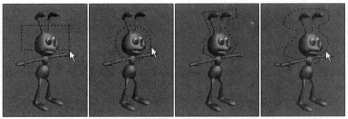

Figure 6-4: The ant's head is selected using the Rectangular, Circular, Fence, and Lasso selection methods.

Selecting multiple objects

As you work with objects in Max, there will be times when you'll want to apply a modification or transform to several objects at once. You can select multiple objects in several ways. With the Select by Name dialog box open, you can choose several objects from the list using the standard Ctrl and Shift keys. Holding down the Ctrl key selects or deselects multiple list items, but holding down the Shift key selects all consecutive list items between the first selected and the second selected items.

The Ctrl key also works when selecting objects in the viewport using one of the main toolbar Select buttons. You can tell whether you're in select mode by looking for a button that's highlighted dark yellow. If you hold down the Ctrl key and click an object, then the object is added to the current selection set. If you click an item that is already selected, then it is de-selected. If you drag over multiple objects while holding down the Ctrl key, then all items in the dragged selection are added to the current selection set.

The Alt key de-selects objects from the current selection set, which is opposite of what the Ctrl key does.

If you drag over several objects while holding down the Shift key, then the selection set will be inverted. Each item that is selected will be de-selected and vice versa.

Object hierarchies are established using the Link button on the main toolbar. You can select an entire hierarchy of objects by double-clicking on its parent object. You can also select multiple objects within the hierarchy. When you double-click an object, then any children of that object will also be selected. When an object with a hierarchy is selected, the Page Up and Page Down keys select the next object up or down the hierarchy.

Grouping and linking the Deer parts together will make working with the entire character easier. Another way to organize the model is to link all the various body parts to the body object. Then the parts will move along with the body.

You can learn more about linking objects and creating hierarchies in Chapter 8, "Grouping and Linking Objects."

Another way to select multiple objects is by dragging within the viewport using the Window and Crossing Selection methods discussed previously in the "Select by Region" section.

Tutorial: Selecting objects

Every Saturday morning, a regular activity for most children is deciding which cartoons to watch on TV. Now that you've learned all about selecting objects, you can try this activity also (and it doesn't need to be on Saturday morning). Hou Soon Ming is a modeler based in Singapore who creates some fun cartoon-like characters. We'll use these characters to practice our selection skills.

The models used in this example have been included on the CD-ROM, compliments of Hou Soon Ming. You can find more of Ming's work at the 3D Toon Shop Web site at www.its-ming.com.

To select objects, follow these steps:

1. Open the 3D Toon Shop's Deer.3ds scene. You can find it with the chapter examples on the CD-ROM in the Chap 06 directory.

2. Click the Select Object button (or press the Q key) and click the deer's body in one of the viewports.

   In the Command Panel, the name for this object, "headbody," will be displayed in the Name and Color rollout.

3. Click the Select and Move button, and then click the Deer's body and drag in the Perspective viewport to the right.

   As you can see, the deer's head and body form an object independent of the other parts of the Deer object. Moving it separates it from the rest of the model's parts.

4. Choose Edit ➪ Undo Move (or press Ctrl+Z) to piece the Deer back together again.

5. With the Select and Move tool still selected, drag an outline around the entire Deer in the Top view to select all the Deer parts, and then click and drag the entire Deer again.

   This time, the entire Deer moves as one entity and the name field displays "Multiple Selected."

6. Open the Select Objects dialog box by clicking the Select by Name button on the main toolbar (or by pressing the H key).

All the individual parts that make up this model are listed.

7. Double-click the "Nose" object listed in the dialog box.

The dialog box automatically closes, and the Nose object becomes selected in the viewports. Figure 6-5 shows our cartoon friend with just its nose object selected. Notice how the name of the selected object in the Name and Color rollout says "nose."

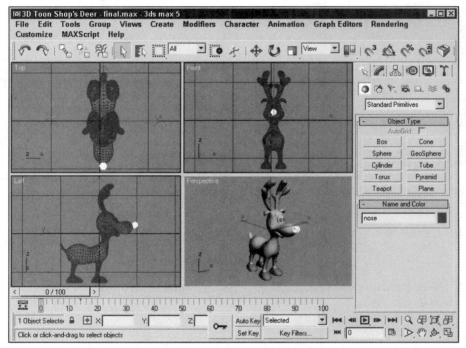

Figure 6-5: A deer cartoon character with its white selected nose. Sorry, Rudolph.

Locking selection sets

If you've finally selected the exact objects that you want to work with, you can disable any other selections using the Selection Lock Toggle button on the Status Bar (it looks like a lock). When this button is enabled, it is colored yellow, and clicking objects in the viewports won't have any effect on the current selection. The keyboard shortcut toggle for this command is the spacebar.

Using named selection sets

With a group of selected objects, you can establish a selection set. Once established as a selection set, you can recall this group of selected objects at any time by selecting its name from the Named Selection Set drop-down list on the main toolbar, or by opening the Named Selection Sets dialog box, shown in Figure 6-6.

You can access this dialog box using the Named Selection Sets button on the main toolbar or by selecting the Edit ⇨ Named Selection Sets menu command. To establish a selection set, type a name in the Named Selection Set drop-down list toward the right end of the main toolbar or use the dialog box.

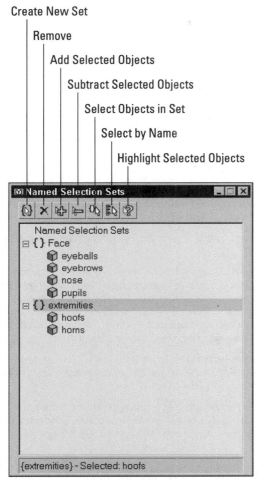

Figure 6-6: The Edit Named Selection Sets dialog box lets you view and manage selection sets.

New Feature The Named Selection Sets dialog box is new for 3ds max 5.

You can also set named selection sets for subobject selections. Be aware that these subobject selection sets are only available when you're in subobject edit mode and only for the currently selected object.

Editing named selections

After you've created several named selection sets, you can use the Named Selections Sets dialog box to manage the selection sets. The buttons at the top let you create and delete sets, add or remove objects from a set, and select and highlight set objects. You can also move an object between sets by dragging its name to the set name that you want to add it to. Dragging one set name onto another set name combines all the objects from both sets under the second set name. Double-clicking on a set name selects all the objects in the set.

Isolating the current selection

The Tools ➪ Isolate Selection (Alt+Q) menu command hides all objects except for the selected object. It also zooms to extents on the object in the active viewport. It also opens a simple dialog box with an Exit Isolation button in it. Clicking this button or selecting the Isolate command again exits isolation mode and displays all the objects again.

Selecting objects in other interfaces

In addition to selecting objects in the viewports, you can use many of the other interfaces and dialog boxes to select objects. For example, the Material Editor includes a button that selects all objects in a scene with the same material applied.

 The Select by Material button opens the Select Object dialog box with all objects that use the selected material highlighted.

Another way to select objects is in the Curve Editor and Dope Sheet. To view all the objects, click the + sign that precedes the Objects track. You can identify the Objects track by a small yellow cube. A hierarchy of all the objects in a scene will be displayed. At the bottom left of the Curve Editor and Dope Sheet windows is the Select by Name text field. Typing an object name in this field automatically selects the object's track in the editor's window, but not in the viewport. Clicking the yellow cube icon selects the object in the viewport.

A third interface that you can use to select objects is the Schematic View. It offers a hierarchical look at your scene and displays all links and relationships between objects. Each object in the Schematic View is displayed as a rectangular node.

To select an object in the viewport, find its rectangular representation in the Schematic View and simply double-click it. To select multiple objects in the Schematic View, click the Synchronize Selection button and then drag an outline over all the rectangular nodes that you want to select.

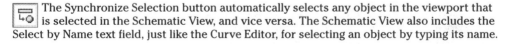 The Synchronize Selection button automatically selects any object in the viewport that is selected in the Schematic View, and vice versa. The Schematic View also includes the Select by Name text field, just like the Curve Editor, for selecting an object by typing its name.

 Cross-Reference The Material Editor is covered in detail in Chapter 18, "Exploring the Material Editor," and the Curve Editor, Dope Sheet, and Schematic View interfaces are covered in Chapter 25, "Working with the Track View."

Setting Object Properties

After you select an object or multiple objects, you can view their object properties by choosing Edit ➪ Object Properties. Alternatively, you can right-click the object and select Properties from the pop-up menu. Figure 6-7 shows the Object Properties dialog box. This dialog box includes four panels — General, Advanced Lighting, Mental Ray, and User Defined.

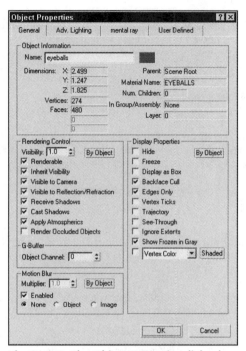

Figure 6-7: The Object Properties dialog box displays valuable information about a selected object.

Viewing object information

For a single object, the General panel of the Object Properties dialog box lists details about the object in the Object Information section. These details include the object's name, color, origin dimensions, and number of vertices and faces, as well as who the object's parent is, its Material Name, the number of children attached to the object, the object's group name if it's part of a group, and the layer it can be found on. All of this information (except for its name and color) is for display only and cannot be changed.

Note   The two fields underneath the Vertices and Faces are used only when the properties for a Shape are being displayed. These fields show the number of Shape Vertices and Shape Curves.

If the properties for multiple objects are to be displayed, the Object Properties dialog box places the text, "Multiple Selected," in the Name field. The properties that are in common between all these objects are displayed. With multiple objects selected, you can set their properties all at once.

The Object Properties dialog box can be displayed for all geometric objects and shapes, as well as for lights, cameras, helpers, and Space Warps. Not all properties are available for all objects.

Setting rendering controls

In the Object Properties dialog box, the Rendering Controls section includes options that affect how an object is rendered. In this section along with the Motion Blur and Display Properties sections are three By Object/By Layer toggle buttons. If the By Object button is displayed, then the By Layer option is enabled and setting changes will affect all objects on the same layer. If By Object is selected, then the settings apply only to the selected object or objects.

New Feature   Applying settings by object or by layer is a new feature in 3ds max 5.

The Visibility spinner defines a value for how opaque (nontransparent) an object is. A value of 1 makes the object completely visible. A setting of 0.1 makes the object almost transparent. The Inherit Visibility option causes an object to adopt the same visibility setting as its parent.

Tip   The Visibility option can also be animated for making objects slowly disappear.

The Renderable option determines whether or not the object is rendered. If this option isn't selected, then the rest of the options are disabled because they don't have any effect if the object isn't rendered.

Tip   The Renderable option is useful if you have a complex object that takes a while to render. You can disable the renderability of the single object to quickly render the other objects in the scene.

You can use the Visible to Camera and Visible to Reflection/Refraction options to make objects invisible to the camera or to any reflections or refractions. This feature can be useful when you are test rendering scene elements and raytraced objects.

The Receive Shadows and Cast Shadows options control how shadows are rendered for the selected object. The Apply Atmospherics options enable or disable rendering atmospherics. Atmospheric effects can increase the rendering time by a factor of 10 in some cases.

Cross-Reference   Atmospheric effects are covered in Chapter 35, "Working with Environments and Atmospheric Effects."

The Render Occluded Objects option causes the rendering engine to render any objects hidden by the selected object. The hidden or occluded objects can have glows or other effects applied to them that would show up if rendered.

You use the G-Buffer Object Channel value to apply Render or Video Post effects to an object. By matching the Object Channel value to an effect ID, you can make an object receive an effect.

Cross-Reference   I cover render effects in Chapter 36, "Using Render Elements and Render Effects," and the Video Post interface in Chapter 39, "Post Processing with the Video Post Interface."

Enabling Motion Blur

You can also set Motion Blur from within the Object Properties dialog box. The Motion Blur effect causes objects that move fast (such as the Road Runner) to be blurred (which is useful in portraying speed). The render engine accomplishes this effect by rendering multiple copies of the object or image.

More information on these blur options is in Chapter 34, "Rendering Basics."

The Object Properties dialog box can set two different types of Motion Blur: Object and Image. Object motion blur only affects the object and is not affected by the camera movement. Image motion blur applies the effect to the entire image and is applied after rendering.

A third type of Motion Blur is called Scene Motion Blur and is available in the Video Post interface. See Chapter 39, "Post-Processing with the Video Post Interface," for information on using Scene Motion Blur.

You can turn the Enabled option on and off as an animation progresses, allowing you to motion blur select sections of your animation sequence. The Multiplier value is only enabled for the Image Motion Blur type. It is used to set the length of the blur effect. The higher the Multiplier value, the longer the blurring streaks. The Motion Blur settings found in the Object Properties dialog box can be overridden by the settings in the Max Default Scanline A-Buffer rollout of the Render Scene dialog box (this dialog box is opened with the Rendering ➪ Render Scene menu command).

Setting Display properties

Display properties don't affect how an object is rendered, only how it is displayed in the viewports. These options can speed up or slow down the viewport refresh rates. For example, Display as Box increases the viewport update rate dramatically for complex scenes, but at the expense of any detail. This setting can be useful to see how the objects generally fit in comparison to one another. The Hide and Freeze options are covered later in this chapter.

You can also find and set the same Display properties that are listed in the Object Properties dialog box in the Display Properties rollout of the Display panel in the Command Panel.

The Backface Cull option causes the faces on the backside of the object to not be displayed when turned on. Max considers the direction that each normal is pointing and doesn't display a face whose normal is pointing away from the view.

The Edges Only option displays only the edges of each face when the viewport is set to Wireframe mode. When Edges Only is not selected, a dashed line indicates polygon faces. The Vertex Ticks option displays all object vertices as blue plus signs.

The Trajectory option displays any animated motions as paths.

To learn more about using animated motion paths, see Chapter 24, "Animation Basics."

The See-Through option causes shaded objects to appear transparent. This option is similar to the Visibility setting in the Rendering Control section, except it doesn't affect the rendered image. It is only for displaying objects in the viewports. This option really doesn't help in Wireframe mode.

The Ignore Extents option causes an object to be ignored when you are using the Zoom Extents button in the Viewport Navigation controls. For example, if you have a camera or light that is positioned at a distance from the objects in the scene, then anytime you use the Zoom Extents All button, the objects would be so small that you would not be able to see them. If you set the Ignore Extent option for the camera or light, then the Zoom Extents All button would zoom in on just the geometry objects.

When objects are frozen, they appear dark gray, but if the Show Frozen in Gray option is disabled, then the object appears as it normally does in the viewport.

The Vertex Color option displays the colors of any Editable Mesh vertices that have been assigned colors. You can select to use Vertex Color, Vertex Illumination, or Vertex Alpha. The Shaded button causes the meshes to be shaded by the vertex colors. You can only assign vertex colors to editable meshes.

For more information about vertex colors, check out Chapter 19, "Creating and Applying Materials."

Advanced Lighting and Mental Ray panels

The second and third panels in the Object Properties dialog box contain object settings for working with Advanced Lighting and for configuring the Mental Ray renderer. Using the settings in the Advanced Lighting panel, you can exclude an object from any Advanced Lighting calculations, set an object to cast shadows and receive illumination, and set the number of refine iterations to complete.

The Mental Ray panel includes options for making an object generate and/or receive caustics and global illumination. These options are only available if the Mental Ray plug-in has been installed.

Advanced Lighting is covered in Chapter 23, "Advanced Lighting and Radiosity."

Using the User-Defined panel

The User-Defined panel contains a simple text window. In this window, you can type any type of information. This information will be saved with the scene and can be referred to as notes about an object.

Hiding and freezing objects

You can hide or freeze objects in a scene by selecting the Hide or Freeze option at the top of the Display Properties section of the General panel. You can also hide and freeze objects using the Display Floater dialog box, which you access by choosing Tools ➪ Display Floater.

Tip   There are also several keyboard shortcuts used to hide specific objects. These shortcuts are toggles, so one press will make the objects disappear and another press will make them reappear. Object types that can be hidden with these shortcuts include cameras (Shift+C), geometry (Shift+G), grids (G), helpers (Shift+H), lights (Shift+L), particle systems (Shift+P), and Space Warps (Shift+W).

The Hide option makes the selected object in the scene invisible, and the Freeze option turns the selected object dark gray and doesn't enable it to be transformed or selected. You cannot select hidden objects by clicking in the viewport. These controls are useful if you want to make sure that an object doesn't move.

Note   When you use the Zoom Extents button to resize the viewports around the current objects, hidden objects aren't included.

Using the Display Floater dialog box

The Display Floater dialog box includes two tabs: Hide/Freeze and Object Level. The Hide/Freeze tab splits the dialog box into two columns, one for Hide and one for Freeze. Both columns have similar buttons that let you hide or freeze Selected or Unselected objects, By Name or By Hit. The By Name button opens the Select Objects dialog box (which is labeled Hide or Freeze Objects). The By Hit option lets you click in one of the viewports to select an object to hide or freeze. Each column also has additional buttons to unhide or unfreeze All objects, By Name, or in the case of Freeze, By Hit. You can also select an option to Hide Frozen Objects.

Note   Other places to find the same buttons found in the Display Floater are the Hide and Freeze rollouts of the Display panel of the Command Panel.

The Object Level panel of the Display Floater lets you hide objects by category such as All Lights or Cameras. You can also view and change many of the Display Properties that are listed in the Object Properties dialog box.

Figure 6-8 shows the Hide/Freeze and Object Level panels of the Display Floater dialog box.

Figure 6-8: The Display Floater dialog box includes two panels — Hide/Freeze and Object Level.

Using the Display panel

If you were to take many of the features of the Display Floater and the Object Properties dialog box and mix them together with some new features, the result would be the Display panel. You access this panel by clicking the fifth icon from the left in the Command Panel (the icon that looks like monitor screen).

The first rollout in the Display panel, shown in Figure 6-9, is the Display Color rollout. This rollout includes options for setting whether Wireframe and Shaded objects in the viewports are displayed using the Object Color or the Material Color.

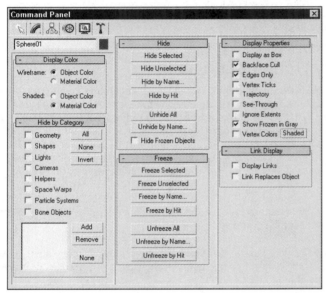

Figure 6-9: The Display panel includes many of the same features of the Display Floater and Object Properties dialog box.

The panel also includes a Hide by Category rollout. Using this rollout, you can add new categories that will appear in the Object Level panel of the Display Floater. To add a new category, click the Add button of the Hide by Category rollout. The Add Display Filter list appears, as shown in Figure 6-10. From this list, you can choose specific object categories to add to the Hide by Category list.

The Display panel also includes Hide and Freeze rollouts that include the same buttons and features as the Hide/Freeze panel of the Display Floater. There is also a Display Properties rollout that is the same as the list found in the Display Floater's Object Level panel and the Object Properties dialog box.

The Link Display rollout at the bottom of the Display panel includes options for displaying links in the viewports. Links are displayed as lines that extend from the child to its parent object. Using the Link Replaces Object option, you can hide the objects in the viewport and see only the links.

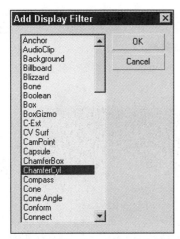

Figure 6-10: From this dialog box, you can add new categories to the Hide by Category list.

Tutorial: Playing hide and seek

Children often learn by playing games, so I have a game for you to try. It's the classic game of hide and seek with a new twist. The twist is that I've hidden two objects in this scene, and you need to find them.

To play hide and seek, follow these steps:

1. Open the Hide and Seek.max scene file. You can find it with the chapter examples on the CD-ROM in the Chap 06 directory.

2. Locate the hidden object in the scene by opening the Display Floater (choose Tools ➪ Display Floater).

3. In the Display Floater, select the Hide/Freeze tab, and in the Unhide section click the Name button.

   The Unhide Objects dialog box appears, which lists all the hidden objects in the scene.

4. Select the Ant Body object from the list and click the Unhide button.

   The Unhide Objects dialog box closes, and the hidden objects become visible once again.

Note   Notice that the Display Floater is still open. That's because it's modeless. You don't need to close it in order for you to keep working.

   The Deer and Moon objects are grayed out, which means that they are frozen and you cannot select and move them.

5. To unfreeze these objects, you use the Freeze column in the Display Floater. In the Unfreeze section, click the By Hit button, then unfreeze the Deer and Moon by clicking each.

Figure 6-11 shows the Hide and Seek scene before starting the game. Notice how hidden objects aren't visible and frozen objects are grayed out.

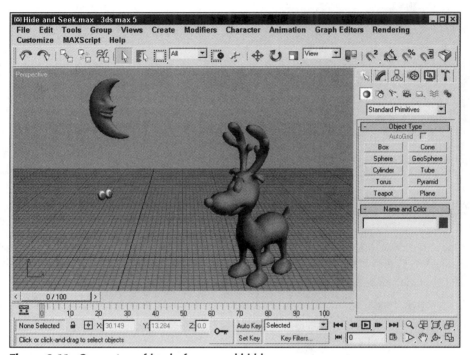

Figure 6-11: Our cartoon friends, frozen and hidden

Using Layers

So what does 3ds max have in common with a wedding cake? The answer is layers. Layers provide a way to separate scene objects into easy-to-select and easy-to-work-with groupings. These individuals layers have properties that can then be turned on and off.

New Feature Layers are new to 3ds max 5.

You create, access, and manage layers through the Layers toolbar, shown in Figure 6-12. You can access this toolbar by right-clicking on the main toolbar away from the buttons and selecting Layers toolbar from the pop-up menu or by selecting the Customize ➪ Show UI ➪ Floating Toolbars menu command. Table 6-1 shows the Layers toolbar buttons.

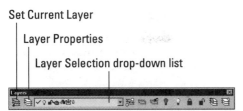

Set Current Layer

Layer Properties

Layer Selection drop-down list

Figure 6-12: Use the Layers toolbar to set the active layer.

Table 6-1: Layers Toolbar Buttons

Button Icon	Name	Description
	Set Current Layer	Makes layer for the selected object current.
	Layer Properties	Opens the Layer Properties dialog box where you can set the layer properties.
✓ ♀ ⬏ ⬥ ⬥ ⬠ 0 ▾	Layer Selection drop-down list	Displays all available layers and their properties.
	Match Object's Layer	Click to select the object whose layer you wish to move the selected objects to.
	Isolate Object's Layer	Turns off all layers except for the layer of the selected object.
	Undo Last Isolate Layer	Reverts the last isolate Object's Layer command.
	Turn Object's Layer Off	Turns off the layer of the selected object.
	Turn All Layers On	Turns all layers on for the entire scene.
	Lock Object's Layer	Locks the layer of the selected object so it cannot be moved or edited.
	Unlock Object's Layer	Unlocks the layer of the selected object so it can be moved or edited.
	Select Layer	Selects all objects that belong to the same layer as the selected object.
	Set Properties By Layer	Sets the properties of the selected object as defined by the layer.

Using the Layer Properties dialog box

Clicking on the Layer Properties button in the Layers toolbar opens a dialog box, shown in Figure 6-13, where you can create and delete layers. Clicking the New button will create a new layer with the default name of Layer01. You can give the layer a name by typing its name in the Name column.

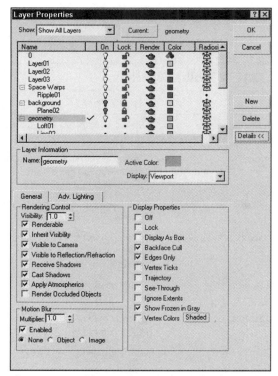

Figure 6-13: The Layer Properties dialog box with the Details panel expanded.

The Show drop-down list at the top of the Layer Properties dialog box gives the option to view All Layers, All Used Layers, and All Unused Layers. Only a single layer can be selected at a time. This current layer is marked with the check mark in the first column, and the layer's name is listed to the right of the Current button. To make a different layer current, select the layer and click the Current button.

All new objects added to the scene are added to the current layer. Layer 0 is the default layer that all objects are added to if other layers don't exist. Layer 0 cannot be renamed.

Each layer can have the following properties: On, Lock, Render, Color, and Radiosity. You can turn these properties on and off by clicking on them. You can also set these properties in the Layers toolbar. The On/Off toggle determines whether the layer's objects are visible in the viewports. The Lock toggle makes objects on a layer so they can't be selected. The Render toggle will enable the layer's objects to be rendered. The Color will color all objects in the layer the same designated color. Layer 0 is set to assign random colors and cannot be changed. The Radiosity toggle will include the layer's objects in the radiosity calculations.

Clicking on the plus sign to the left of the layer name displays all the objects that are part of this layer. The Details button expands the Layer Properties dialog box to include a Layer Information section and the General and Advanced Lighting panels. The General and Advanced Lighting panels include the same options as the Object Properties dialog box.

Tutorial: Dividing a scene into layers

As a scene begins to come together, you'll start to find that it is difficult to keep track of all the different pieces. This is where the layers interface can really help. In this example, we'll take a simple scene and divide it into several layers.

To divide a scene into layers, follow these steps:

1. Open the Deer on hill layers.max scene file. You can find it with the chapter examples on the CD-ROM in the Chap 06 directory.

2. Right click on the toolbar away from the buttons and select Layers from the pop-up menu to open the Layers toolbar.

3. Click on the Layer Properties button in the Layers toolbar. Click the New button and name the layer, Hill and Trees. Click the New button again and name this layer Deer. Click the New button again and create a layer named Moon and background. Then click the OK button to exit the Layer Properties dialog box.

4. Select the hill object along with all the tree objects in the scene. Select the Hill and trees layer from the layer list drop-down list in the Layers toolbar and click the Match Object's Layer button.

5. Repeat Step 4 to add the remaining parts for the moon, background plane, and deer parts to their respective layers.

You can now switch between the different layers depending on which one you want to add objects to or work on. Figure 6-14 shows the various layers and the objects in each layer.

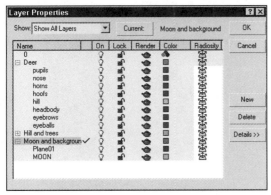

Figure 6-14: All objects assigned to a layer can be viewed in the Layer Properties dialog box.

Summary

Selecting objects enables you to work with them, and Max includes many different ways to select objects. In this chapter you've done the following:

- ✦ Learned how to use selection filters

- ✦ Selected objects with the Edit menu by Name, Color, and Region

- ✦ Selected multiple objects and used a named selection set to find the set easily

- ✦ Selected objects using other interfaces

- ✦ Accessed the Object Properties dialog box to set Rendering and Display settings for an object

- ✦ Learned how to hide and freeze objects

- ✦ Separated objects using layers

In the next chapter, you work more with multiple objects by learning how to clone objects. Using these techniques, you could very quickly have too many objects (and you were worried that there weren't enough objects).

✦   ✦   ✦

Cloning Objects

CHAPTER 7

The only thing better than one perfect object is two perfect objects. Cloning objects is the process of creating copies of objects. These copies can maintain an internal connection (called an Instance or a Reference) to the original object that allows them to be modified along with the original object. For example, if you create a school desk from a Box primitive and modify its parameters, the same resulting effect will be applied to all instances of the original.

An *array* is a discrete set of objects that are regularly ordered. So, creating an array of objects involves cloning several copies of an object in a pattern, such as in rows and columns or in a circle.

I'm sure you have the concept for that perfect object in your little bag of tricks, and this chapter will let you copy it over and over after you get it out.

Cloning Objects

You can clone objects in Max in a couple of ways (and it luckily has nothing to do with DNA or gene splices). One method is to use the Edit ➪ Clone (Ctrl+V) menu command, and another method is to transform an object while holding down the Shift key. And you won't need to worry about these clones attacking anyone (unlike *Star Wars: Episode II*).

Using the Clone command

You can create a duplicate object by choosing the Edit ➪ Clone (Ctrl+V) menu command. You must select an object before the Clone command becomes active. Selecting this command opens the Clone Options dialog box, shown in Figure 7-1, where you can give the clone a name and specify it as a Copy, Instance, or Reference. You can also copy any controllers associated with the object as a Copy or an Instance.

Caution   The Edit menu doesn't include the common cut, copy, and paste commands because many objects and subobjects cannot be easily cut and pasted into a different place. However, you will find a Clone (Ctrl+V) command, which can duplicate a selected object.

Figure 7-1: The Clone Options dialog box defines the new object as a Copy, Instance, or Reference.

A copy has the same geometry as the original, but all links to the original are cut. An instance maintains a link to the original and mirrors the changes of the original object as the original is modified. A reference lies somewhere between a copy and an instance, in that only some of the modifications applied to the original affect the reference. I cover more on copies, instances, and references later in this chapter.

When a clone is created with the Clone menu, it is positioned directly on top of the original, making distinguishing it from the original difficult. To verify that it has been created, open the Select by Name dialog box by pressing H and look for the cloned object (it will have the same name but an incremented number). To see both objects, click the Select and Move button on the main toolbar and move one of the objects away from the other.

Using the Shift-clone method

Another, and easier, way to create clones is with the Shift key. You can use the Shift key when objects are transformed using the Select and Move, Select and Rotate, and Select and Scale commands. Holding down the Shift key while you use any of these commands on an object clones the object and opens the Clone Options dialog box. This Clone Options dialog box is identical to the dialog box previously shown, except it includes a spinner to specify the number of copies.

Performing a transformation with the Shift key held down defines an offset that is applied repeatedly to each copy. For example, holding down the Shift key while moving an object five units to the left (with the Number of Copies set to 5) will place the first cloned object five units away from the original, the second cloned object ten units away from the original object, and so on.

Tutorial: Cloning cows

The scientific world has been in an uproar lately with the successful cloning of various animals. It started with a sheep named "Dolly," but I think they just cloned a rabbit (at least they're cloning furry animals instead of less desirable creatures like earwigs or slugs). With Max, we can perform similar experiments on our own, but we'll be using a cow named "Rolly." Viewpoint Datalabs created this cow model.

To investigate cloning objects, follow these steps:

1. Open the Rolly Cow.max file found in the Chap 07 directory of the CD-ROM.

2. Select the cow group by clicking it in one of the viewports.

3. With the cow model selected, choose Edit ➪ Clone (or press Ctrl+V).

   The Clone Options dialog box appears.

4. Name the clone Polly, select the Copy option, and click OK.

5. Click the Select and Move button (or press the W key) on the main toolbar. Then in the Left viewport, click and drag the cow model to the right.

As you move the model, the original model beneath it is revealed.

6. Select each model in turn and notice the name change in the Create panel's Name field. Notice that the clone is even the same color as the original.

7. With the Select and Move button still active, hold down the Shift key, click the cloned cow in the Left viewport, and move it to the right again. In the Clone Options dialog box that appears, select the Copy option, set the Number of Copies to 3, and click OK.

8. Click the Zoom Extents All button (or press Shift+Ctrl+Z) in the lower right-hand corner to view all the new cows.

Three additional cows have appeared, equally spaced from each other. The spacing was determined by the distance that you moved the second clone before releasing the mouse. Figure 7-2 shows the results of our cow cloning experiment. (It's starting to feel like a dairy.)

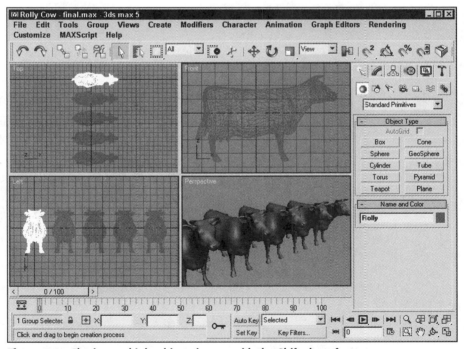

Figure 7-2: Cloning multiple objects is easy with the Shift-clone feature.

Understanding Cloning Options

When cloning in Max, you'll be offered the option to create the copy as a copy, an instance, or a reference. This is true not only for objects, but for materials, modifiers, and controllers as well.

Working with copies, instances, and references

When an object is cloned, the Clone Options dialog box appears. This dialog box enables you to select to make a copy, an instance, or a reference of the original object. Each of these clone types is unique and offers different capabilities.

A copy is just what it sounds like—an exact replica of the original object. The new copy maintains no ties to the original object and will be a unique object in its own right. Any changes to the copy will not affect the original object or vice versa.

Instances are different from copies in that they maintain strong ties to the original object. All instances of an object are interconnected, so that any geometry modifications (done with modifiers) to any single instance changes all other instances. For example, if you create several instances of a sphere and then use a modifier on one of the spheres, all instances will also be modified. Note that transformations (moving, rotating, or scaling) of an instance will not affect the other instances.

 References are objects that inherit modifier changes from their parent objects but do not affect the parent when modified. At any time, you can break the tie between objects with the Make Unique button in the Modifier Stack.

Note   Instances and references can have different object colors and materials.

When an object is selected, all its instances and references will be surrounded with an orange-colored bounding box.

Tutorial: Copied, instanced, and referenced teddy bears

Learning how the different clone options work will save you lots of future modifications. To investigate these options, let's leave the farm and visit the children's room where teddy bear is feeling lonely. To clone some friends for the teddy bear, follow these steps:

1. Open the Teddy Bear.max file from the Chap 07 directory on the CD-ROM.

2. Click on the bear object to select it.

3. With the bear model selected, click the Select and Move button (or press the W key). Hold down the Shift key, and in the Front viewport move the bear to the right. In the Clone Options dialog box, select the Copy option, set the Number of Copies to 1, name the new bear **Teddy's Copy**, and click OK. Click the Zoom Extents All button to widen your view.

4. Select the original bear again and repeat Step 3, but this time select the Instance option from the Clone Options dialog box and name the newly cloned bear **Teddy's Instance**.

5. Select the original bear again and repeat Step 3 again, but this time select the Reference option from the Clone Options dialog box and name the new cloned bear **Teddy's Reference**. You should now see four bears.

Note   Be sure to select the original bear each time you make a clone or you'll accidentally make a reference of an instance.

6. Select the original bear again. From the main menu, choose Modifiers ➪ Parametric Deformers ➪ Squeeze. Then in the Parameters rollout of the Command Panel, enter **1.0** in the Amount field, and press the Enter key on the keyboard to apply the value. This will elongate the bear.

Note   If you have trouble locating the original bear, click the Select by Name button on the main toolbar to open the Select Objects dialog box, select Teddy Bear from the objects listed, and click the Select button.

7. Notice how the instanced and referenced objects (but not the copy) were modified along with the original, as shown in Figure 7-3.

Cross-Reference   You can use modifiers to alter geometry. You can learn about using modifiers in Chapter 10, "Using Modifiers."

If you were to return to this file and apply another modifier to Teddy's Reference, then only the reference would be changed and the original would not. Understanding how these various copy types work will enable you to create duplicates of objects and modify them without taking the time to change each one individually.

Original object   Instanced object

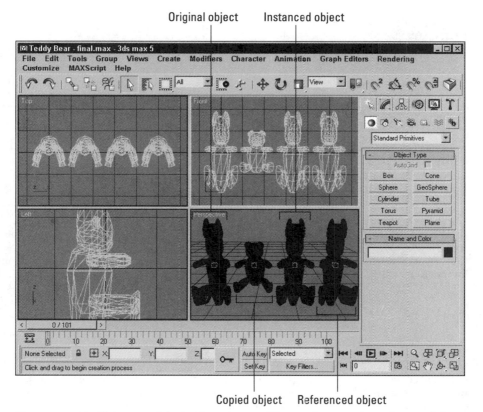

Copied object   Referenced object

Figure 7-3: Modifying an original object also modifies any instanced or referenced clones.

Mirroring Objects

Have you ever held the edge of a mirror up to your face to see half your head in the mirror? Many objects have a natural symmetry that you can exploit to require that only half an object be modeled. The human face is a good example. You can clone symmetrical parts using the Mirror command.

Using the Mirror command

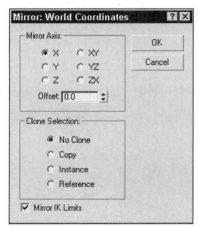 The Mirror command creates a clone (or No Clone if you so choose) of the selected object about the current coordinate system. To open the Mirror dialog box, shown in Figure 7-4, choose Tools ➪ Mirror, or click the Mirror button located on the main toolbar. You can access the Mirror dialog box only if an object is selected.

Figure 7-4: The Mirror dialog box can create an inverted clone of an object.

Within the Mirror dialog box, you can specify an axis or plane about which to mirror the selected object. You can also define an offset value. As with the other clone commands, you can specify whether the clone is to be a Copy, an Instance, or a Reference, or you can choose No Clone, which will flip the object around the axis you specify. The dialog box also lets you mirror Inverse Kinematics Limits, which reduces the number of IK parameters that need to be set.

 Cross-Reference   I talk about Inverse Kinematics in Chapter 33, "Creating and Using Inverse Kinematics."

Tutorial: Mirroring an ant character

Creating a decent human-like character is one of the tougher, more time-consuming modeling tasks that confront today's modelers. Luckily, the human body is one of the best examples of symmetry (as long as you're looking at only the external parts). Using the Mirror command, you can save time and effort by having to create only one half of a human figure.

After you model or import a human figure, work on details like eyes, ears, and arms on only one half of the figure. You can then cut off the unneeded half with the Slice modifier, and mirror the remaining half to create a perfectly symmetrical human figure.

To mirror an ant character, follow these steps:

1. Open the Half an Ant.max file from the Chap 07 directory on the CD-ROM.

   The Perspective viewport is maximized. For this example, the ant character was sliced in half using the Slice modifier.

2. With the half ant selected, choose Tools ➪ Mirror to open the Mirror: World Coordinates dialog box or click the Mirror button on the main toolbar.

3. In the Mirror: World Coordinates dialog box, select X as the Mirror Axis and Instance as the Clone Selection. Set the Offset value to **–20.0**.

   Any changes made to the dialog box are immediately shown in the viewports.

4. Click OK to close the dialog box.

> **Note**
>
> By making the clone selection an instance, you can ensure that any future modifications to the right half of the figure will be automatically applied to the left half.

Figure 7-5 shows the resulting figure — our ant character with his split personalities combined.

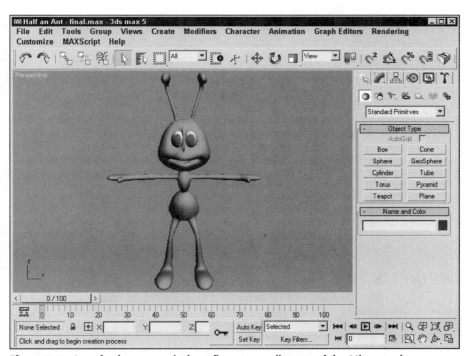

Figure 7-5: A perfectly symmetrical ant figure, compliments of the Mirror tool

Cloning over Time

Another useful way to create multiple copies of an object is to have them appear at different times in an animation. This cloning over time is accomplished with the Snapshot feature.

Using the Snapshot command

The Snapshot command creates copies, instances, references, or even meshes of a selected object as it is transformed over time. For example, you could create a series of stairs by positioning the bottom stair at frame 1 and the top stair at frame 100, and then choose Tools ➪ Snapshot and enter the number of steps to appear between these two in the Snapshot dialog box. Be aware that the Snapshot command only works with objects that have an animation path defined.

 You can open the Snapshot dialog box by choosing Tools ➪ Snapshot or by clicking the Snapshot button (under the Array flyout on the Axis Constraints toolbar). Snapshot is the second button in the flyout. In the Snapshot dialog box, shown in Figure 7-6, you can choose to produce a single clone or a range of clones over a given number of frames. Selecting Single creates a single clone at the current frame.

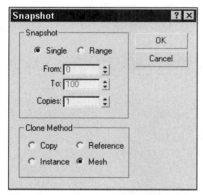

Figure 7-6: The Snapshot dialog box lets you clone a Copy, Instance, Reference, or Mesh.

> **Tip**   Use the Snapshot command with the Snow Particle System to make snow pile up.

Tutorial: Following a mouse through a maze

A fine example of the Snapshot tool is to trace an object as it moves through the scene. For this example, you'll use the Snapshot tool to follow a mouse as it moves through a maze.

To use the Snapshot tool to create clones at individual frames, follow these steps:

1. Open the Mouse in a Maze.max file from the Chap 07 directory on the CD-ROM.

   The Perspective viewport is maximized. This file has an animation sequence defined that moves the mouse through the maze.

2. To take a snapshots of the mouse as it moves through the maze, select the mouse object and then choose Tools ➪ Snapshot or select the Snapshot flyout button from the Axis Constraints toolbar.

3. In the Snapshot dialog box, select the Range option from frame 0 to frame 100 and specify 30 copies. Then click the OK button.

Figure 7-7 shows the maze after the Snapshot tool cloned the mouse during his journey.

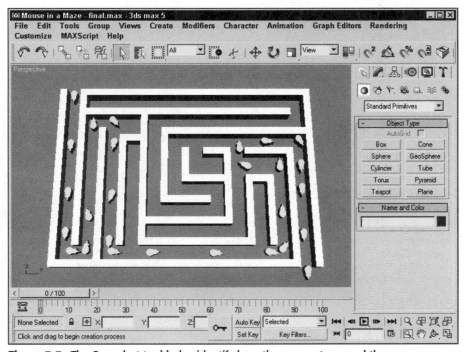

Figure 7-7: The Snapshot tool helps identify how the mouse traversed the maze.

Spacing Cloned Objects

The Snapshot tool offers a convenient way to clone objects along an animation path, but what if you want to clone objects along a path that isn't animated? The answer is the Spacing tool. The Spacing tool can position clones at regular intervals along a path by either selecting a path and the number of cloned objects or by picking points along the path.

Using the Spacing tool

You access the Spacing tool by clicking the last button in the flyout under the Array button on the Axis Constraints toolbar. You can also access it using the Tools ➪ Spacing Tool (Shift+I) menu command. When accessed, it opens the Spacing Tool dialog box, shown in Figure 7-8. At the top of this dialog box are two buttons — Pick Path and Pick Points.

Enabled Lock icon   Disabled Lock icon

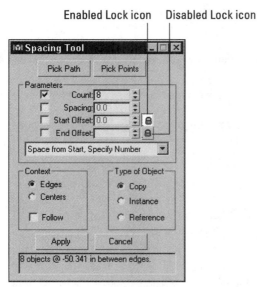

Figure 7-8: The Spacing Tool dialog box lets you
select how to position clones along a path.

You can also specify Count, Spacing, Start Offset, and End Offset values. The drop-down list offers several preset options, including Divide Evenly, Centered, End Offset, and more. These values and preset options are used to define the number and spacing of the objects. The Lock icons next to the Start and End Offset values will not require that an object be placed at the end of the path or point if enabled (the background of the Lock icon is white when enabled).

Before you can use either the Pick Path or Pick Points buttons, you must select the object to be cloned. Using the Pick Path button, you can select a spline path in the scene, and cloned objects will be regularly spaced according to the values you selected. The Pick Points method lets you click in the viewport where the start and end points are, and the cloned objects will be spaced in a straight line between the two points.

The two options for determining the spacing width are Edges and Centers. The Edges option spaces objects from the edge of its bounding box to the edge of the adjacent bounding box, and the Centers option spaces objects based on their centers. The Follow option aligns the object with the path if the path is selected. Each object can be a copy, instance, or reference of the original. The text field at the bottom of the dialog box specifies the number of objects and the spacing value between each.

You can continue to modify the Spacing Tool dialog box's values while the dialog box is open, but the objects will not be added to the scene until you click the Apply button.

Tutorial: Building a roller coaster

To create a roller coaster, we'll need a path and a single cart. Then we can use the Spacing tool to clone this cart along the path.

To create a line of roller coaster carts by using the Spacing tool, follow these steps:

1. Open the Roller Coaster.max file from the Chap 07 directory on the CD-ROM.

   The Perspective viewport is maximized. This file includes a path and a single roller coaster cart.

2. Select the roller coaster cart and open the Spacing tool by selecting the flyout button under the Array button on the Axis Constraints toolbar (or by pressing Shift+I).

3. In the Spacing Tool dialog box, click the Pick Path button and select the wavy roller coaster path.

   The path name appears on the Pick Path button.

4. From the drop-down list in the Parameters section of the Spacing Tool dialog box, choose Start Offset, Divide Evenly. Enter a Count value of **10** and a Start Offset of **100**.

5. Select the Edges context option, check the Follow check box, and make all clones Instances. Click Apply when the result looks right and close the Spacing Tool dialog box.

Figure 7-9 shows the simple results. The Spacing Tool dialog box remains open until you click the Close button.

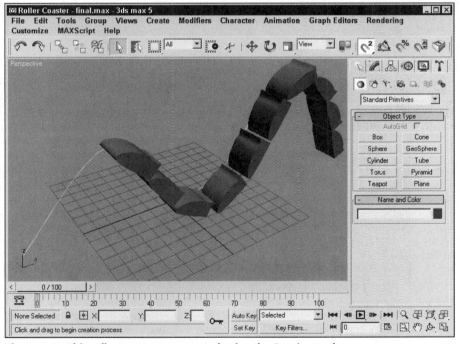

Figure 7-9: This roller coaster was created using the Spacing tool.

Creating Arrays of Objects

After you've figured out how to create objects, the Array command multiplies the fun by making it easy to create many copies instantaneously. The Array dialog box lets you specify the array dimensions, offsets, type of object, and transformation values. These parameters enable you to create an array of objects easily.

Access the Array dialog box by selecting an object and choosing Tools ⇨ Array, or by clicking the Array button on the Axis Constraints toolbar. Figure 7-10 shows the Array dialog box. The top of the Array dialog box displays the coordinate system and the center about which the transformations are performed.

The Array dialog box is persistent, meaning that, after being applied, the settings remain until they are changed. You can reset all the values at once by clicking the Reset All Parameters button.

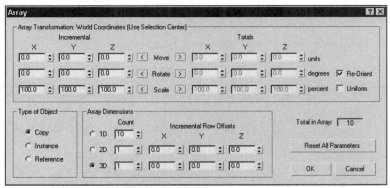

Figure 7-10: The Array dialog box defines the number of elements and transformation offsets in an array.

Linear arrays

Linear arrays are arrays where the objects form straight lines, such as rows and columns. Using the Array dialog box, you can specify an offset along the X, Y, and Z axes at the top of the dialog box and define this offset as an incremental amount or as a total amount. To change between incremental values and total values, click the arrows to the left and right of the Move, Rotate, and Scale labels. For example, an array with ten elements and an incremental value of 5 would position each successive object a distance of five units from the previous one. An array with five elements and a total value of 100 would position each element a distance of 20 units from the previous one.

The Move row values represent units as specified in the Units Setup dialog box. The Rotate row values represent degrees, and the Scale row values are a percentage of the selected object. All values can be either positive or negative values.

Clicking the Re-Orient check box causes the coordinate system to be reoriented after each rotation is made. If this check box isn't enabled, then the objects in the array will not successively rotate. Clicking the Uniform check box to the right of the Scale row values disables the Y and Z Scale value columns and forces the scaling transformations to be uniform. To perform non-uniform scaling, simply de-select the Uniform check box.

The Type of Object section lets you define whether the new objects are copies, instances, or references. If you plan on modeling all the objects in a similar manner, then you will want to select the Instance option.

In the Array Dimensions section, you can specify the number of objects to copy along three different dimensions. You can also define incremental offsets for each individual row.

Caution   You can use the Array dialog box to create a large number of objects. If your array of objects is too large, your system may crash.

Tutorial: Building a white picket fence

To start with a simple example, we'll create a white picket fence. Because a fence repeats, we only need to create a single slat and use the Array command to duplicate it consistently.

To create a picket fence, follow these steps:

1. Open the White Picket Fence.max file from the Chap 07 directory on the CD-ROM.

2. With the single fence board selected, choose Tools ➪ Array or click on the Array button on the Axis Constraints toolbar to open the Array dialog box.

3. In the Array dialog box, click the Reset All Parameters button to start with a clean slate. Then enter a value of **50** in the X column's Move row under the Incremental section. (This is the incremental value for spacing each successive picket.) Next, enter **20** in the Array Dimensions section next to the 1D radio button. (This is the number of objects to include in the array.) Click OK to create the objects.

Note   Don't worry if you don't get the values right the first time. The most recent values you entered into the Array dialog box will stay around until you exit Max.

4. Click the Zoom Extents All button (or press Shift+Ctrl+Z) in the lower-right corner of the Max window to see the entire fence in the viewports.

Figure 7-11 shows the completed fence.

Circular arrays

You can use the Array dialog box for creating more than just linear arrays. For the last example, all transformations were done around the pivot point center. Notice that in the previous figure World Coordinates (Use Pivot Point Center) are listed at the top of the Array dialog box. In the next tutorial, you'll see how changing the transform center can create circular arrays.

 All transformations are done relative to a center point. You can change the center point about which transformations are performed using the Use Selection Center button on the main toolbar. The three flyout options are Use Pivot Point Center, Use Selection Center, and Use Transform Coordinate Center.

Cross-Reference   For more about how these settings affect transformations, see Chapter 9, "Transforming Objects."

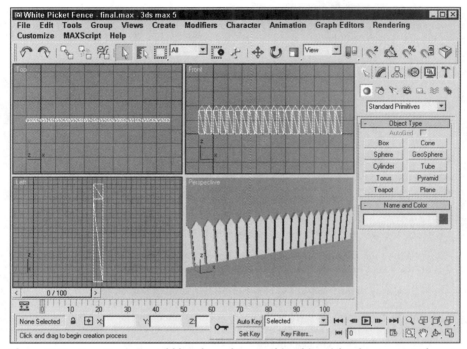

Figure 7-11: Tom Sawyer would be pleased to see this white picket fence, created easily with the Array dialog box.

Tutorial: Building a Ferris wheel

Ferris wheels, like most of the rides at the fair, entertain by going around and around, with the riders seated in chairs spaced around the Ferris wheel's central point. The Array dialog box can also create objects around a central point.

 In this example, you use the Rotate transformation along with the Use Transform Coordinate Center button to create a circular array.

To create a circular array, follow these steps:

1. Open the Ferris Wheel.max file from the Chap 07 directory on the CD-ROM.

   This file has the Front viewport maximized to show the profile of the Ferris wheel.

2. Click on the Use Selection Center button on the main toolbar and drag down to the last icon, which is the Use Transform Coordinate Center button.

   The Use Transform Coordinate Center button becomes active. This button causes all transformations to take place about the axes in the center of the screen.

3. Select the light blue chair object and open the Array dialog box by choosing Tools ➪ Array or by clicking the Array button on the Axis Constraint toolbar. Before entering any values into the Array dialog box, click the Reset All Parameters button.

4. In-between the Incremental and Totals sections are the labels Move, Rotate, and Scale. Click the arrow button to the right of the Rotate label. Set the Z column value of the Rotate row to **360** degrees and make sure the Re-Orient option is disabled.

A value of 360 degrees defines one complete revolution. Disabling the Re-Orient option will keep each chair object from gradually turning upside down.

5. In the Array Dimensions section, set the 1D spinner Count value to **8** and click the OK button to create the array.

6. Next select the green strut and open the Array dialog box again with the Tools ⇨ Array command. Select the Re-Orient option and leave the rest of the settings as they are. Click the OK button to create the array.

Figure 7-12 shows the resulting Ferris wheel. You can click the Min/Max toggle in the lower-right corner to view all four viewports again.

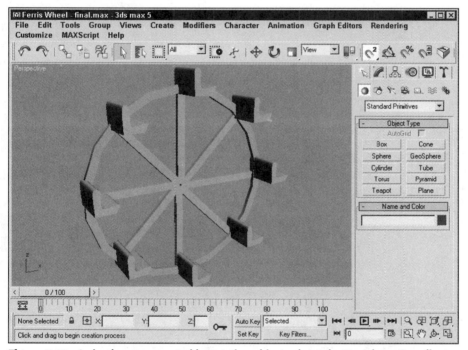

Figure 7-12: A circular array created by rotating objects about the Transform Coordinate Center.

Spiral arrays

Before leaving arrays, there is one more special case to examine: spiral arrays. A spiral array results from moving and rotating objects along the same axis. Combinations of transforms in the Array dialog box can produce many interesting modeling possibilities.

Tutorial: Building a spiral staircase

To create a spiral staircase, we will first need to create a simple rectangular box that can be used for the steps. Because a spiral staircase winds about a center pole, we will need our transform's center to be located at one end of the stair object.

To create a spiral staircase, follow these steps:

1. Open the Spiral Staircase.max file from the Chap 07 directory on the CD-ROM.

   This file has the Top viewport maximized, which is the easiest view to use to create the spiral staircase.

2. Select the Use Transform Coordinate Center flyout from the Use Center button on the main toolbar.

   This setting transforms the selected object about the center of the active viewport. You should notice the axes will be relocated to the center of the viewport.

3. Select the single stair and open the Array dialog box by choosing Tools ➪ Array, or by clicking the Array button on the Axis Constraint toolbar. Before entering any values into the Array dialog box, click the Reset All Parameters button.

4. In the Incremental section, enter the value of **50** in the Z column of the Move row, and **45** in the Z column of the Rotate row.

5. Set the 1D Count spinner to 20 and click the OK button to create the array.

Figure 7-13 shows the results of the spiral array in the Perspective viewport.

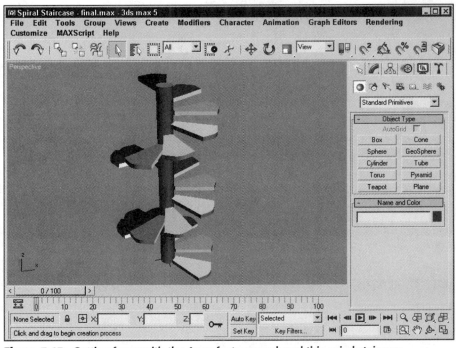

Figure 7-13: Getting fancy with the Array feature produced this spiral staircase.

Working with a ring array

You can find the Ring Array system by opening the Create panel and selecting the Systems category. Doing so makes four buttons appear for Bones, Sunlight, Daylight, and Ring Array. Clicking the Ring Array button opens a Parameters rollout, shown in Figure 7-14. In this rollout are parameters for the ring's Radius, Amplitude, Cycles, Phase, and the Number of elements to include.

You create the actual array by clicking and dragging in one of the viewports. Initially, all elements are simple box objects surrounding a green dummy object.

Figure 7-14: The Parameters rollout of the Ring Array system can create an oscillating circular array of objects.

Cross-Reference

You can change the boxes that appear as part of the ring array to another object using the Dope Sheet. To do so, you need to locate the copy object's track and paste it where the ring array's boxes are. Chapter 25, "Working with the Track View," shows how to do this.

The Amplitude, Cycles, and Phase values define the sinusoidal nature of the circle. The Amplitude is the maximum distance that you can position the objects from the center axis. If the Amplitude is set to 0, then all objects lie in the same plane. The Cycles value is the number of waves that occur around the entire circle. The Phase determines which position along the circle starts in the up position.

For example, Figure 7-15 shows a ring array with 20 elements, a Radius of 100, an Amplitude of 25, a Cycles value of 2, and a Phase of 0. The Dummy object in the middle lets you control the entire ring's position and orientation.

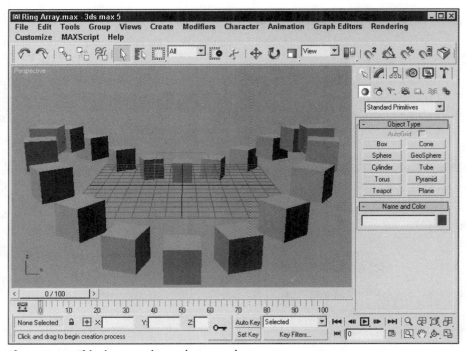

Figure 7-15: This ring array has only two cycles.

Tutorial: Using Ring Array to create a carousel

Continuing with the theme park attractions motif, this example will create a carousel. The horse model comes from Poser, but was simplified using the MultiRes modifier.

To use a Ring Array system to create a carousel, follow these steps.

1. Open the Carousel.max file from the Chap 07 directory on the CD-ROM. This file includes a carousel structure made from primitives along with a carousel horse

2. Open the Create panel, select the Systems category, and click on the Ring Array button. Drag in the Top viewport from the center of the carousel to create a ring array. Then enter a Radius value of 300, an Amplitude of 20, a Cycles value of 3 and a Number value of 6.

3. Select the Dummy object in the Left viewport and drag it upward with the Select and Move tool until all the box objects are positioned between the carousel base and the top cone.

4. Select the Track View ➪ Track View – Dope Sheet. Click on the plus sign to the left of the Object track. Click on the plus sign next to the Horse object and locate the 'Object (Editable Mesh)' object and select it. Then right-click and select Copy from the pop-up menu.

5. Locate the Box01 track under the Objects ⇨ Dummy01. Select the 'Object (Editable Mesh)' track and right-click and select the Paste command from the pop-up menu. This will open the Paste dialog, shown in Figure 7-16. Select Instance and the Replace all Instances option and click Ok. Then close the Track View.

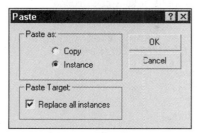

Figure 7-16: This Paste dialog box lets you replace all instances.

Figure 7-17 shows the finished carousel. Notice how each horse is at a different height.

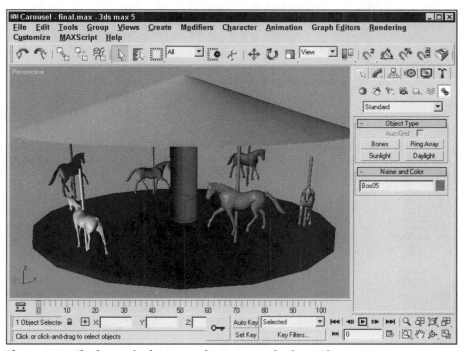

Figure 7-17: The horses in the carousel were created using a Ring Array system.

Summary

Many ways exist to clone an object. You could use the Clone command under the Edit menu or the Shift-cione feature for quickly creating numerous clones. Clones can be copies, instances, or references. Each differs in how it retains links to the original object. You can also clone using the Mirror, Snapshot, and Spacing tools.

Arrays are another means of cloning. You can use the Array dialog box to produce clones in three different dimensions, and you can specify the offset transformations.

This chapter covered the following cloning topics:

✦ Cloning objects and Shift-cloning

✦ Understanding copies, instances, and references

✦ Using the Mirror, Snapshot, and Spacing tools

✦ Building linear, circular, and spiral arrays of objects

✦ Using the Ring Array system

In the next chapter, you learn to group objects and link them into hierarchies. Then you'll be able to organize all the objects that you've learned to create.

✦   ✦   ✦

Grouping and Linking Objects

Now that you've learned how to select and clone objects, you will want to learn how to group objects together in an easily accessible form, especially as a scene becomes more complex. Max's grouping features enable you to organize all the objects that you're dealing with, thereby making your workflow more efficient.

Another way of organizing objects is to build a linked hierarchy. A linked hierarchy attaches, or links, one object to another and makes it possible to transform the attached object by moving the one it is linked to. For example, the arm is a classic example of a linked hierarchy—when the shoulder rotates, so do the elbow, wrist, and fingers. Establishing linked hierarchies can make moving, positioning, and animating many objects easy.

Another valuable tool for selecting, linking, and organizing scene objects is the Schematic View window. This window offers a 1,000-foot view of the objects in your scene. From this whole scene perspective, you can find the exact item you seek.

Working with Groups

Grouping objects organizes them and makes them easier to select and transform. Groups are different from selection sets in that groups exist like one object. Selecting any object in the group selects the entire group, whereas selecting an object in a selection set selects only that object and not the selection set. You can open groups to add, delete, or reposition objects within the group. Groups can also contain other groups. This is called nesting groups.

Creating groups

The Group command enables you to create a group. To do so, simply select the desired objects and choose Group ➪ Group. A simple Name Group dialog box opens and enables you to give the group a name. The newly created group displays a new bounding box that encompasses all the objects in the group. You can also create or nest groups within groups.

Tip   You can always identify groups in the Select by Name dialog box because they are surrounded by square brackets.

Ungrouping objects

The Ungroup command enables you to break up a group (kind of like a poor music album). To do so, simply select the desired group and choose Group ➪ Ungroup. This menu command dissolves the group, and all the objects within the group revert to separate objects. The Ungroup command only breaks up the currently selected group. All nested groups within a group stay intact.

The easiest way to dissolve an entire group, including any nested groups, is with the Explode command. This command eliminates the group and the groups within the group and makes each object separate.

Opening and closing groups

The Open command enables you to access the objects within a group. Grouped objects move, scale, and rotate as a unit when transformed, but individual objects within a group can be transformed independently after you open a group with the Open command.

To move an individual object in a group, select the group and choose Group ➪ Open. The white bounding box changes to dark red. Then select an object within the group and move it with the Select and Move button (W). Choose Group ➪ Close to reinstate the group.

Attaching and detaching objects

The Attach and Detach commands enable you to insert or remove objects from an opened group without dissolving the group. To do so, select an object in the opened group and choose Group ➪ Attach or Detach. Remember to close the group when finished.

Tutorial: Grouping the deer parts together

Positioning objects relative to one another takes careful and precise work. After spending the time to place the eyes, ears, and nose of a face exactly where they need to be, transforming these objects can spell disaster (unless your name is Picasso). By grouping all the objects together, you can move all the objects at once.

For this tutorial, you can get some practice grouping all the parts of the deer character together. Follow these steps:

1. Open the Cartoon deer.max file from the Chap 08 directory on the CD-ROM. This file includes a cartoon deer model created by Hou Soon Ming.

2. Click the Select by Name button on the main toolbar (or press the H key) to open the Select by Name dialog box. In this dialog box, notice all the different deer character parts. Click the All button to select all the separate objects and click the Select button to close the dialog box.

3. With all the objects selected, choose Group ➪ Group to open the Group dialog box. Give the group the name **Deer**, and click OK.

4. Click the Select and Move button (or press W) and click and drag the deer. The entire group now moves together.

Figure 8-1 shows the deer grouped as one unit. Notice how only one set of brackets is around the deer in the Perspective viewport. The group name is displayed in the Name field of the Command Panel instead of saying Multiple Selected.

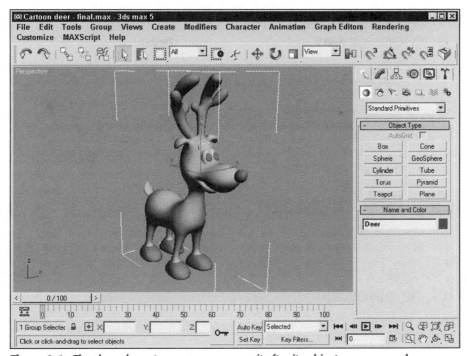

Figure 8-1: The deer character moves as one unit after its objects are grouped.

Understanding Parent, Child, and Root Relationships

Max uses several terms to describe the relationships between objects. A parent object is an object that controls any secondary, or child, objects linked to it. A child object is an object that is linked to and controlled by a parent. A parent object can have many children, but a child can have only one parent. Additionally, an object can be both a parent and a child at the same time.

A hierarchy is the complete set of linked objects that includes these types of relationships. Ancestors are all the parents above a child object. Descendants are all the children below a parent object. The root object is the top parent object that has no parent and controls the entire hierarchy.

Each hierarchy can have several branches or subtrees. Any parent with two or more children represents the start of a new branch.

Cross-Reference

The default hierarchies established using the Link tool are referred to as forward-kinematics systems, in which control moves forward down the hierarchy from parent to child. In forward-kinematics systems, the child has no control over the parent. An inverse kinematics system (covered in Chapter 33, "Creating and Using Inverse Kinematics") enables child objects to control their parents.

All objects in a scene, whether linked or not, belong to a hierarchy. Objects that aren't linked to any other objects are, by default, a child of the world object, which is an imaginary object that holds all objects.

Note   You can view the world object, labeled Objects, in the Track View. Individual objects are listed under the Objects track by their object name.

You have several ways to establish hierarchies using Max. The simplest method is to use the Link and Unlink buttons found on the main toolbar. You can also find these buttons in the Schematic View window. The Hierarchy panel in the Command Panel provides access to valuable controls and information about established hierarchies. When creating complex hierarchies, the bones system can help.

Building Links between Objects

The main toolbar includes two buttons that you can use to build a hierarchy: Link and Unlink. The order of selection defines which object becomes the parent and which becomes the child.

Linking objects

The Link button always links children to the parents. To remind you of this order, remember that a parent can have many children but a child can't have more than one parent.

To link two objects, click the Link button. This places you in Link mode, which continues until you turn it off by selecting another button, such as the Select button or one of the Transform buttons. When you're in Link mode, the Link button is highlighted dark yellow.

With the Link button highlighted, click an object, which will be the child, and drag a line to the target parent object. The cursor arrow changes to the link icon when it is over a potential parent. When you release the mouse button, the parent object flashes once, and the link is established. If you drag the same child object to a different parent, the link to the previous parent is replaced by the link to the new parent.

Once linked, all transformations applied to the parent are applied equally to its children about the parent's pivot point. A *pivot point* is the center about which the object rotates.

Unlinking objects

The Unlink button is used to destroy links, but only to the parent. For example, if a selected object has both children and a parent, clicking the Unlink button destroys the link to the parent of the selected object, but not the links to its children.

To eliminate all links for an entire hierarchy, double-click an object to select its entire hierarchy and click the Unlink button.

Tutorial: Creating a solar system

Because the planets in the solar system all rotate about the sun, a solar system is a good model to show the benefits of linking. After you link all the planets to the sun, you can reposition the entire system simply by moving the sun.

To create a solar system of spheres that are linked together, follow these steps:

1. Open the Linked Solar System.max file from the Chap 08 directory on the CD-ROM. This file includes spheres that represent all the planets in the solar system.

2. Click the Link button in the main toolbar, and drag a line from each planet to the sun object.

3. Click the Select and Rotate button (or press the E key) and rotate the sun. Notice how all the planets rotate with the sun.

Figure 8-2 shows the planets as they orbit about the sun. The Link button made it possible to rotate all the planets simply by rotating their parent.

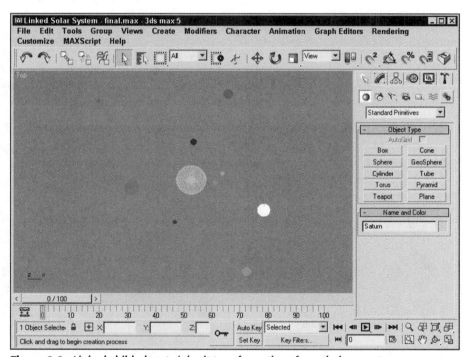

Figure 8-2: Linked child planets inherit transformations from their parent sun.

Displaying Links and Hierarchies

The Display panel includes a rollout that lets you display all the links in the viewports.

After links have been established, there are several places where you can see linked objects listed as a hierarchy. The Select Objects dialog box, opened with the Select by Name button (or with the H key) can display objects in this manner, as well as the Schematic and Track Views.

Displaying links in the viewport

You can see links between objects in the viewports by selecting the Display Links option in the Link Display rollout of the Display panel. The Display Links option shows links as lines that run between the pivot points of the objects with a diamond-shaped marker at the end of each line; these lines and markers are the same color as the object.

The Link Display rollout also offers the Link Replaces Object option, which removes the objects and displays only the link structure. This feature removes the complexity of the objects from the viewports and lets you work with the links directly. Although the objects disappear, you can still transform the objects using the link markers.

Figure 8-3 shows the solar system we created in the previous tutorial with the Display Links option enabled for all links.

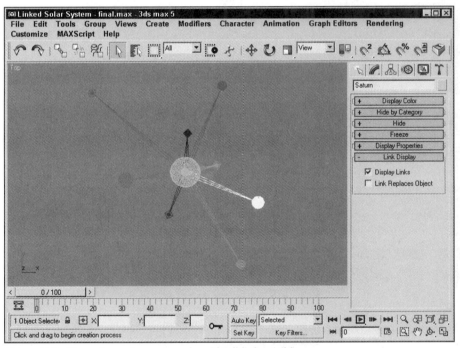

Figure 8-3: The solar system example with all links visible.

Viewing hierarchies

The Select Objects dialog box and the Schematic and Track Views can display the hierarchy of objects in a scene as an ordered list, with child objects indented under parent objects.

Clicking the Select by Name button (H) on the main toolbar opens the Select Objects dialog box; click the Display Subtree option to see all the children under the selected object. Figure 8-4 shows the Select Objects dialog box with the Display Subtree option selected.

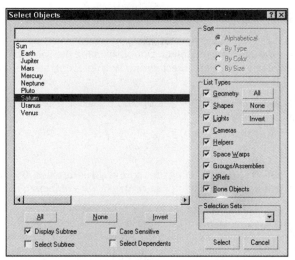

Figure 8-4: The Select Objects dialog box indents all child objects under their parent.

The Schematic View (opened with the Graph Editors ⇨ New Schematic View menu command) presents a graph in which objects are represented by rectangles with their hierarchical links drawn as lines running between them. I cover the Schematic View window later in the chapter.

The Track View (opened with the Graph Editors ⇨ New Track View menu command) displays a lot of scene details in addition to the object hierarchy. In the Track View, you can easily expand and contract the hierarchy to focus on just the section you want to see or select.

Cross-Reference For more information on using the Track View, see Chapter 25, "Working with the Track View."

Working with Linked Objects

If you link some objects together, set some animation keys, and the magical Play button starts sending objects hurtling off into space, chances are that you have a linked object that you didn't know about. Understanding object hierarchies and being able to transform those hierarchies are the keys to efficient animation sequences.

All transformations are done about an object's pivot point. You can move and reorient these pivot points as needed by clicking the Pivot button under the Hierarchy panel.

Several additional settings for controlling links are available under the Hierarchy panel of the Command Panel (the Hierarchy panel tab looks like a mini-org chart). Just click the Link Info button. This button opens two rollouts if a linked object is selected. You can use the Locks and Inherit rollouts to limit an object's transformations and specify the transformations it inherits.

Cross-Reference I present more information on object transformations in Chapter 9, "Transforming Objects."

Selecting hierarchies

You need to select a hierarchy before you can transform it, and you have several ways to do so. The easiest method is simply to double-click an object. Double-clicking the root object selects the entire hierarchy, and double-clicking an object within the hierarchy selects it and all of its children.

After you select an object in a hierarchy, pressing the Page Up and Page Down keyboard shortcuts selects its parent or child objects.

Linking to dummies

Dummy objects are useful as root objects for controlling the motion of hierarchies. By linking the parent object of a hierarchy to a dummy object, you can control all the objects by moving the dummy.

To create a dummy object, open the Create panel and click the Helpers category button (this button looks like a small tape measure). Within the Object Type rollout is the Dummy button; click it, and then click in the viewport where you want the dummy object to be positioned. Dummy objects look like wireframe box objects in the viewports, but dummy objects are not rendered.

Tutorial: Creating the two-cars-in-a-sphere stunt

Have you ever seen the circus act where two motorcycles race around the inside of a wire sphere without colliding? Well, we're going to do that stunt one better — we're going to do it with cars.

To perform this stunt, we'll create two dummy objects in the center of the sphere, link a car model to each, and rotate the dummy objects. The car we'll be using is the '57 Chevy model created by Viewpoint Datalabs. This tutorial involves transforming and animating objects, which I cover in later chapters.

 Translating objects is covered in chapter 9, "Transforming Objects," and the basics of animation are covered in chapter 24, "Animation Basics."

To link and transform objects using a dummy object, follow these steps:

1. Open the Two cars in a sphere stunt.max file found in the Chap 08 directory on the CD-ROM.

   This file includes a transparent wireframe sphere with two grouped car objects inside of it.

2. Open the Create panel, click the Helpers category button, and click the Dummy button. Then create two dummy objects in the center of the sphere; make them different sizes so that they are easier to select.

3. To make the cars move consistently around the sphere, you need to align the center of the sphere with the centers of the two dummy objects. To do so, select the two dummy objects, and choose Tools ➪ Align (or press Alt+A). Select the sphere object to open the Align Selection dialog box. Select the X, Y, and Z Position options and the Center options for both the Current and Target Objects, and then click OK.

4. Because both the cars and the dummy objects are inside the sphere, creating the link between them can be difficult. To simplify this process, select and right-click the sphere object, select Properties from the pop-up menu, and select the Hide option in the Object Properties dialog box. This hides the sphere so that you can create the links between the cars and the dummy objects.

5. Click the Link button on the main toolbar, and drag a line from one of the cars to one of the dummy objects. Then drag a line from the second car to the second dummy object.

6. Click the Select and Rotate button on the main toolbar (or press E) and select one of the dummy objects. Then rotate the dummy object and notice how the linked car also rotates along the inner surface of the sphere.

7. Open the Display Floater with the Tools ⇨ Display Floater menu command and click on the Unhide All button to make the sphere visible again.

By linking the cars to dummy objects, you don't have to worry about moving the individual cars' pivot points. Figure 8-5 shows a frame from the final scene.

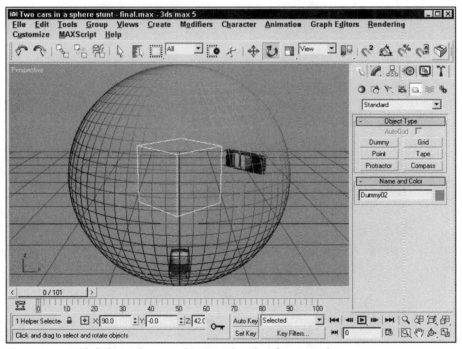

Figure 8-5: With links to dummy objects, animating these cars is easy.

Using the Schematic View Window

Another great way to organize and select objects is by using the Schematic View window. Every object in the Schematic View is displayed as a rectangular box. These boxes, or nodes, are connected to show the relationships among them. You can rearrange them and save the customized views for later access.

You access the Schematic View window via the Graph Editors menu command or by clicking its button on the main toolbar. When the window opens, it floats on top of the Max interface and can be moved by dragging its title bar. You can also resize the window by dragging on its borders. The window is modeless and lets you access the viewports and buttons in the interface beneath it.

The Schematic View menu

The Schematic View menu options enable you to manage several different views. The Graph Editors ➪ Schematic View ➪ New Schematic View command opens the Schematic View window, shown in Figure 8-6. Enter a name in the View Name Entry field at the top of the window to name and save the current view.

The Schematic View ➪ Open Schematic View command opens the current Schematic View window. If several named views exist, a dialog box appears, enabling you to select the view you want to open.

Tip   You can open the Schematic View window within a viewport by right-clicking the viewport title and choosing Views ➪ Schematic ➪ New from the pop-up menu.

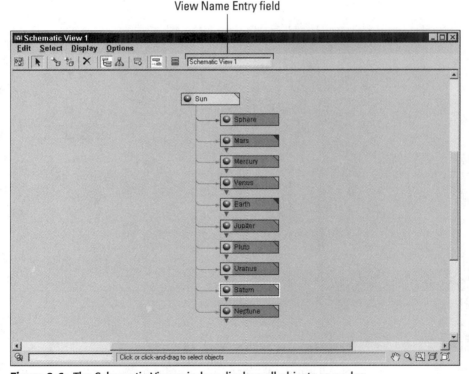

Figure 8-6: The Schematic View window displays all objects as nodes.

The Graph Editors ➪ Schematic View ➪ Delete Schematic View command opens a Schematic View dialog box that displays all the saved views. Select the view you want to delete, and then click the Delete button.

The Schematic View interface

The Schematic View window includes four menus at the top of its interface—Edit, Select, Display, and Options. You can also select most of these same commands from the toolbar. The Edit menu includes commands for accessing the Link and Unlink tools and the Object Properties dialog box. The Select menu includes commands for accessing the Select tool; selecting all, none, and invert; selecting and de-selecting children; and commands to synch the selected nodes in the Schematic View with the scene (Get From Scene) and vice versa (Put to Scene). The Display menu includes commands for panning, zooming, hiding, and unhiding objects. It also includes a command for accessing the Schematic View Settings (Filters) dialog box. The Options menu lets you select from Hierarchy and Reference modes.

The Schematic View window also includes a toolbar of buttons across its top under the menus. There are also some buttons along the bottom of the window. These buttons are shown in Table 8-1 and are described in the following sections.

Table 8-1: Schematic View Buttons

Toolbar Button	Name	Description
	Filters	Opens the Schematic View Settings dialog box, where you can toggle which items are displayed or hidden.
	Select	Used to select object nodes.
	Link	Enables you to create links between objects in the Schematic View window. It is also used to copy modifiers and materials between objects.
	Unlink Selection	Destroys the link between the selected object and its parent.
	Delete Objects	Deletes the selected object in both the Schematic View and in the viewports.
	Hierarchy Mode	Displays all child objects indented under their parents.
	References Mode	Displays all object references and instances. This mode displays all materials and modifiers associated with the objects.
	Synchronize Selection	Synchronizes the selected objects in the Schematic View window with the corresponding object viewports, and vice versa.

Continued

Table 8-1 *(continued)*

Toolbar Button	Name	Description
	Auto-Arrange Graph Nodes	Automatically rearranges the object nodes into a sensible display to ensure that all objects are visible.
	Toggle Visibility Downstream	Causes all child nodes of the current selection to be hidden. Clicking this button again displays all nodes.
Schematic View 1	View Name Entry Field	Enter a name into this field to name the current display. Named displays show up underneath the Schematic View menu.
	Zoom Selected Viewport Object	Zooms in on the nodes that correspond to the selected viewport objects.
Saturn	Search Name Entry Field	Locate an object node by typing its name.
	Pan	Move the node view by dragging in the window.
	Zoom	Zoom by dragging the mouse in the window.
	Region Zoom	Zoom to an area selected by dragging an outline.
	Zoom Extents	Increases the window view until all nodes are visible.
	Zoom Extents Selected	Increases the window view until all selected nodes are visible.

Note   Most of the menu and toolbar buttons commands are available in a pop-up menu that you can access by right-clicking in the Schematic View window.

Schematic View settings

The Filters button opens the Schematic View Settings dialog box, shown in Figure 8-7, where you can set which items are displayed or hidden. Object categories that can be displayed or hidden include Base Objects, Modifiers, Materials, Maps, Assigned Controllers, and Bone Objects. You can also specify to show only the selected, visible, or animated objects. The Hide by Category section works just like the interface in the Display Floater dialog box.

Cross-Reference   I discuss the Display Floater dialog box in Chapter 6, "Selecting Objects and Setting Object Properties."

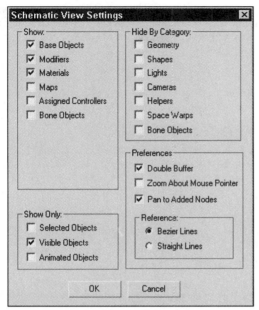

Figure 8-7: The Schematic View Settings dialog box lets you display or hide various categories of objects.

The Schematic View Settings dialog box also includes several preference settings. These preference settings include Double Buffer, which enables a double-buffer display and helps improve the viewport update performance. The Zoom About Mouse Pointer preference enables zooming by using the scroll wheel on your mouse or by pressing the middle mouse button while holding down the Ctrl key. The Pan to Added Nodes preference automatically resizes and moves the nodes to enable you to view any additional nodes that have been added.

The Reference options let you specify reference lines as curved Bézier lines or straight lines.

Selecting nodes

The Select button enters select mode, which lets you select objects within the window and in the viewports by double-clicking the object node. You can select multiple objects by dragging an outline over them. Holding down the Ctrl key while clicking an object node selects or deselects it.

You can select different objects in the viewports and in the Schematic View at the same time. The node of an object selected in the Schematic View turns yellow, whereas the nodes of objects selected in the viewports are outlined in white. You can select in the Schematic View but not select in the viewports, and vice versa. The Synchronize Selection button synchronizes selections in the Schematic View and the viewports.

Working with Schematic View nodes

Every object displayed in the scene (as determined by the Filter dialog box) has a *node* — a simple rectangular box that represents the object. Each node contains an icon representing the type of object, the object name, and the object color or material, which is shown in the upper-right corner of the rectangular box.

Figure 8-8 shows two object nodes close up. The arrow to the right of the bottom two Sphere nodes specifies that the object is an instance of another object. Click the arrow to select and highlight all instances and references. These arrows can appear for any instances, including objects, materials, modifiers, and more.

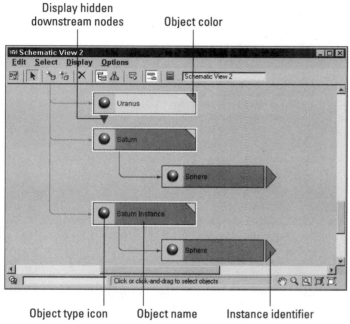

Figure 8-8: Schematic View nodes contain object information, including type, name, color, hierarchy, and references.

Hierarchical relationships are shown as lines that connect the nodes. Other hierarchical elements can include materials, modifiers, controllers, and more. Using the Toggle Visibility Downstream button, you can display or hide these subnodes. When all downstream nodes are hidden, a red arrow (shown off the Uranus node in Figure 8-7) appears underneath the node. Clicking this red arrow displays the subnodes.

Rearranging nodes

You can move nodes and rearrange them in any order. To move a node, simply click and drag it to a new location. When a node is dragged, all selected nodes move together, and any links follow the node movement.

Node colors

Nodes have a color scheme to help identify them. Selected nodes are yellow. Material nodes are brown, modifier nodes and Space Warps are dark yellow, geometry objects are light blue, camera nodes are dark green, helper nodes are light green, shapes are cyan, controllers are salmon colored, and light object nodes are orange. You can set the colors used in the Schematic View using the Colors panel of the Customize User Interface dialog box.

Renaming objects

In the Schematic View window, you can rename objects quickly and conveniently. To rename an object, click a selected node and click again to highlight the text. When the text is highlighted, you can type the new name for the object.

Changing the object color

The upper-right corner of the node rectangle shows the object color or the material color if one has been assigned. Because the Schematic View window is modeless, you can click the color swatch in the Command Panel to change the object color or access the Material Editor to change the material color. Another method to change the object color is to right-click the node to open the pop-up menu, select Properties, and change the color in the Object Properties dialog box.

Deleting nodes

To delete a node, select the node and click the Delete Objects button on the Schematic View toolbar or press the Delete key. If several nodes are selected, they are all deleted.

Creating a hierarchy

To create a hierarchy, use the Link button on the Schematic View toolbar. The Link button works the same way here as it does on the main toolbar — selecting the child node and dragging a line from the child node to its parent makes a link.

The Unlink button destroys the link between any object and its immediate parent. Remember that every child object can have only one parent.

Copying materials between objects

In the Schematic View, materials can only be copied between objects — you cannot apply new materials from the Material Editor to Schematic View nodes. To copy a material, select the material node for one object, click the Link button, and drag the material to the other object.

Note   Materials and modifiers show up only if they are selected in the Schematic View Settings dialog box. You can access this dialog box by clicking the Filters button.

Copying and reordering modifiers

To view the modifiers that are associated with an object, click the arrow at the bottom of the node rectangle. You can copy a modifier to other objects by selecting it from the list, clicking the Link button, and then dragging the modifier to its destination and releasing the mouse. A dialog box appears, asking whether you want to Copy, Move, or Instance the modifier.

Tutorial: Linking a cartoon deer with Schematic View

Perhaps one of the greatest benefits of the Schematic View is its ability to link objects. Before you can do this, you'll need to name all the parts that make up the model; then it becomes as easy as connecting the dots.

To link a cartoon deer model using the Schematic View, follow these steps:

1. Open the Linked cartoon deer.max file from the Chap 08 directory on the CD-ROM. This file includes a simple cartoon deer model created by Hou Soon Ming. All of the deer's parts have been named.

2. Select Graph Editors ➪ New Schematic View and the Schematic View window will open. Drag in the lower-right corner of the Schematic View window to increase its size and click on the Zoom Extents button (or press Alt+Ctrl+Z).

3. Click on the Link button in the toolbar and drag from the pupils node to the eyeballs node. Then drag each of the remaining nodes one by one to the headbody node. This will link all the deer parts to the headbody part.

4. With all the parts linked, each child node displays an Editable Mesh and a material node. You can make these nodes hidden by selecting the child nodes and selecting Display ➪ Hide Downstream, but this will also hide the pupils node.

5. To make the pupils node visible, select the Select button in the toolbar, click the red arrow under the eyeballs node to display the downstream nodes. Then select and right click on the Editable Mesh and material nodes and select Show/Hide ➪ Hide Selected from the pop-up menu.

Figure 8-9 shows the final geometry object nodes of the linked deer. If you move the headbody part in the viewports, all the parts will move together.

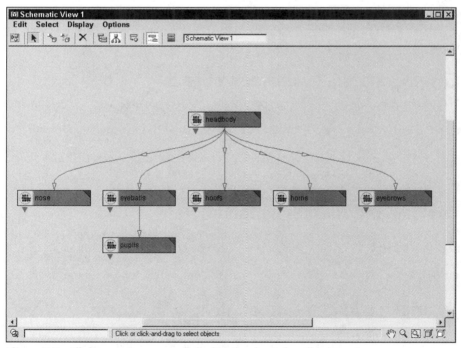

Figure 8-9: All deer parts are now linked to the deer's headbody part.

Summary

As scenes become more complex, the name of the game is organization. There are several ways to organize objects within the scene, including grouping, linking, and using the Schematic View window.

In this chapter you've done the following:

✦ Grouped objects using the Group menu and learned to work with groups

✦ Learned about parent, child, and root relationships

✦ Created a hierarchy of objects using the Link and Unlink features

✦ Viewed links in the viewport

✦ Learned how to create dummy objects

✦ Viewed all objects as nodes using the Schematic View window

✦ Used the Schematic View window to select, delete, and copy objects, materials, and modifiers

In the next chapter, you'll learn how to transform objects using the move, rotate, and scale features — finally, some motion for our static scenes.

✦ ✦ ✦

Transforming Objects

Although a transformation sounds like something that would happen during the climax of a superhero film, transformation is simply the process of "repositioning" or changing an object's position, rotation, and scale. So, moving an object from here to there is a transformation. Superman would be so jealous.

Transformations occur when you select an object or objects, click one of the transformation buttons located on the main toolbar, and then drag in the viewport to apply the transformation. Max includes various tools to help in the transformation of objects, including the Transform Gizmos, the Transform Type-In dialog box, and the Transform Managers.

This chapter covers each of these tools and several others that make transformations more automatic, such as the alignment, grid, and snap features.

Moving, Rotating, and Scaling Objects

So you have an object created and it's just sitting there—sitting and waiting. Waiting for what? Waiting to be transformed. To be moved a little to the left or to be rotated around to show its good side or to be scaled down a little smaller. These actions are called *transformations* because they transform the object to a different state. Transformations are different from modifications. Modifications change the object's geometry, but transformations do not affect the object's geometry at all.

The three different types of transformations are translation (which is a fancy word for moving objects), rotation, and scaling.

Moving objects

The first transformation type is *translation* or moving objects. You can move objects in any of the three axes. You can move objects to an absolute coordinate location or move them to a certain offset distance from their current location.

To move objects, click the Select and Move button on the main toolbar (or press the W key), select the object to move, and drag the object in the viewport to the desired location. Translations are measured in the defined system units for the scene, which may be inches, centimeters, meters, and so on.

Rotating objects

↻ *Rotation* is the process of spinning the object about its Transform Center point. To rotate objects, click the Select and Rotate button on the main toolbar (or press the E key), select an object to rotate, and drag it in a viewport. Rotations are measured in degrees where 360 degrees is a full rotation.

Scaling objects

Scaling increases or decreases the overall size of an object. Most scaling operations are uniform, or equal in all directions. All Scaling is done about the Transform Center point.

▭ To scale objects uniformly, click the Select and Uniform Scale button on the main tool bar (or press the R key), select an object to scale, and drag it in a viewport. Scalings are measured as a percentage of the original. For example, a cube that is scaled to a value of 200 percent will be twice as big as the original.

Non-uniform scaling

The Select and Scale button includes two flyout buttons for scaling objects non-uniformly, allowing objects to be scaled unequally in different dimensions. The two additional tools are Select and Non-Uniform Scale, and Select and Squash, shown in the following table. With Select and Non-Uniform Scale, resizing a basketball using this tool could result in a ball that is taller than it is wide. Scaling is done about the axis or axes that have been constrained (or limited) using the Restrict Axes buttons on the Axis Constraints toolbar.

Button	Description
▭	Select and Non-Uniform Scale
▭	Select and Squash

Squashing objects

The Squash option is a specialized type of non-uniform scaling. This scaling causes the constrained axis to be scaled at the same time the opposite axes are scaled in the opposite direction. For example, if you push down on the basketball by scaling the Z-axis, the sides, or the X- and Y-axes, it will bulge outward. This simulates the actual results of such materials as rubber and plastic.

Figure 9-1 shows a basketball that has been scaled using uniform scaling, non-uniform scaling, and squash mode.

Using the transform buttons

The three transform buttons located on the main toolbar are Select and Move, Select and Rotate, and Select and Uniform Scale, as shown in Table 9-1. Using these buttons, you can select objects and transform them by dragging in one of the viewports with the mouse. You can access these buttons using three of the big four keyboard shortcuts — Q for Select Objects, W for Select and Move, E for Select and Rotate, and R for Select and Scale.

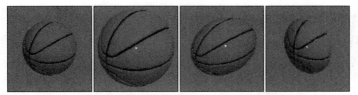

Figure 9-1: These basketballs have been scaled using uniform, non-uniform, and squash modes.

New Feature The Q, W, E, and R shortcut keys are new in 3ds max 5.

Table 9-1: Transform Buttons

Toolbar Button	Name	Description
	Select and Move	Enters move mode where clicking and dragging an object moves it.
	Select and Rotate	Enters rotate mode where clicking and dragging an object rotates it.
	Select and Uniform Scale	Enters scale mode where clicking and dragging an object scales it.
	Select and Non-Uniform Scale	
	Select and Squash	

Transformation Tools

To help you in your transformations, you can use several tools to transform objects (and you don't even need a phone booth). These tools include the Transform Gizmos, the Transform Type-In dialog box (F12), Status Bar fields, and the Transform Managers.

Working with the Transform Gizmos

The Transform Gizmos appear at the center of the selected object (actually at the object's pivot point) when you click one of the transform buttons. The type of gizmo that appears depends on the transformation mode that is selected. There are actually three different gizmos, one for each transformation type. Each gizmo includes three color-coded arrows, circles, and lines representing the X-, Y-, and Z-axes. The X-axis is colored red, the Y-axis is colored green, and the Z-axis is colored blue. Figure 9-2 shows the gizmos for each of the transformation types — move, rotate, and scale.

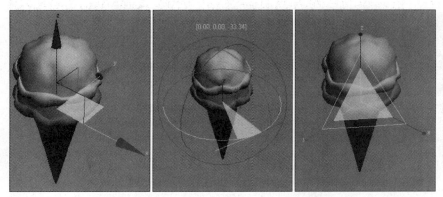

Figure 9-2: The Transform Gizmos lets you constrain a transformation to a single axis or a plane.

If the Transform Gizmo is not visible, you can enable it by choosing Views ➪ Show Transform Gizmo or by pressing the X key to toggle it on and off. You can use the – (minus) and = (equals) keys to decrease or increase the gizmo's size.

Using the interactive gizmos

Moving the cursor over the top of one of the Transform Gizmo's axes in the active viewport selects the axis, which changes to yellow. Dragging the selected axis restricts the transformation to that axis only. For example, selecting the red X axis on the Move Gizmo and dragging will move the selected object along only the X axis.

The Move Gizmo

In addition to the arrows for each axis, in each corner of the Move Gizmo are two perpendicular lines for each plane. These lines let you transform along two axes simultaneously. The colors of these lines match the various colors used for the axes. For example, in the Perspective view, dragging on a red and blue corner would constrain the movement to the XZ plane. Selecting one of these planes highlights it. At the center of the Move Gizmo is a Center Box that marks the pivot point's origin.

The Rotate Gizmo

The Rotate Gizmo surrounds the selected object in a sphere. A colored line for each axis circles the surrounding sphere. As you select an axis and drag, an arc is highlighted that shows the distance of the rotation along that axis and the offset value is displayed in text above the object. Clicking on the space between the axes lets you rotate the selected object in all directions.

The Scale Gizmo

The Scale Gizmo consists of two triangles and a line for each axis. Selecting and dragging the center triangle uniformly scales the entire object. Selecting a slice of the outer triangle scales the object along the adjacent two axes, and dragging on the axis lines scales the object in a non-uniform manner along a single axis. Selecting the triangle or a portion of the outer triangle highlights it.

Setting Gizmo preferences

For each of these gizmos, you can set the preferences using the Gizmos panel in the Preference Settings dialog box, shown in Figure 9-3. In this panel for all gizmos, you can turn the gizmos on or off, set to Show Axis Labels, Allow Multiple Gizmos, and set the Size of the gizmo's axes. The Allow Multiple Gizmos option will enable a separate gizmo for each selection set object. The Labels option labels each axis with an X, Y, or Z.

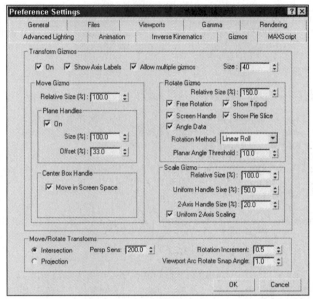

Figure 9-3: The Gizmos panel in the Preference Settings dialog box lets you control how the transform gizmos look.

For the Move Gizmo section, you can set the Relative Size of the gizmo relative to the top Size value. You can also select to turn the plane handles on or off and set their size and offset values, which determine how large the highlighted planes will be and where they are located relative to the center of the gizmo. You can also enable the Center Box Handle for moving in all three axes.

The Rotate Gizmo preferences also include a Relative Size value. The Free Rotation option enables you to click and drag between the axes to rotate the object freely along all axes. The Show Tripod option displays an axes tripod at the center of the object. The Screen Handle option displays an additional gray circle that surrounds all the axes. Dragging on this handle spins the object about the viewport's center. The Show Pie Slide highlights a slice along the selected axis that is as big as the offset distance. The Angle Data option displays the rotation value above the gizmo.

The Gizmos panel offers three different Rotation Methods—Linear Roll, Circular Crank, and Legacy R4. The Linear Roll method displays a tangent line at the source point where the rotation starts. The Circular Cranks method rotates using the gizmo axes that surround the object. The Legacy R4 method uses the Move gizmo that was available in the previous Max version. The Planar Angle Threshold value determines the minimum value to rotate within a plane.

The Scale Gizmo section can also set a Relative Size of the entire gizmo. The Uniform Handle Size value sets the size of the inner triangle and the 2-Axis Handle Size value sets the size of the outer triangle. The Uniform 2-Axis Scaling option makes scaling with the outer triangle uniform along both axes.

For the Move/Rotate Transforms section has some additional settings that control how objects move in the Perspective viewport. The Intersection and Projection options are for two different modes. The Intersection mode, moves objects faster the farther they get from the center. In Projection mode, the Perspective Sensitivity value is used to set the mouse movements to the distance of the transformation. Small values result in small transformation for a large mouse drag. The Rotation Increment value sets the amount of rotation that occurs for a given mouse drag distance and the Viewport Arc Rotate Snap Angle sets where the arc snaps to.

Using the Transform Type-In dialog box

The Transform Type-In dialog box (F12) lets you input precise values for moving, rotating, and scaling objects. This command provides more exact control over the placement of objects than dragging with the mouse.

The Transform Type-In dialog box allows you to enter numerical coordinates or offsets that can be used for precise transformations. Open this dialog box by choosing Tools ➪ Transform Type-In, or by pressing the F12 key.

Tip   Right-clicking any of the transform buttons opens the Transform Type-In dialog box, but the dialog box will open for whichever button is enabled, regardless of which button you right-click.

The Transform Type-In dialog box is modeless and allows you to select new objects as needed, or switch between the various transforms. When the dialog box appears, it displays the coordinate locations for the current selection in the Absolute: World column.

Within the Transform Type-In dialog box are two columns. The first column displays the current Absolute coordinates. Updating these coordinates will transform the selected object in the viewport. The second column displays the Offset values. These values are all set to 0.0 when the dialog box is first opened, but changing these values will transform the object. Figure 9-4 shows the Transform Type-In dialog box for the Move Transform.

Note   The name of this dialog box changes depending on the type of transformation taking place and the coordinate system. If the Select and Move button is selected along with the world coordinate system, the Transform Type-In dialog box is labeled Move Transform Type-In and the column titles will indicate the coordinate system.

Figure 9-4: The Transform Type-In dialog box displays the current Absolute coordinates and Offset values.

Using the status bar Type-In fields

The status bar includes three fields labeled X, Y, and Z for displaying transformation coordinates. When you move, rotate, or scale an object, the X, Y, and Z offset values appear in these fields. The values depend on the type of transformation taking place. Translation shows the unit distances, rotation displays the angle in degrees, and scaling shows a percentage value of the original size.

When you click the Select Objects button, these fields show the absolute position of the cursor in world coordinates based on the active viewport.

You can also use these fields to enter values, like with the Transform Type-In dialog box. The type of transform depends on which transform button you select. The values that you enter can be either absolute coordinates or offset values, depending on the setting of the Transform Type-In toggle button that appears to the left of the transform fields. This toggle button lets you switch between Absolute and Offset modes, shown in the following table.

Button	Description
	Absolute
	Offset

Understanding the various Transform Managers

The Transform Managers are three different types of controls that help you define the system about which objects are transformed. These controls, found on the main toolbar and the Axis Constraints toolbar, directly affect your transformations. They include the following:

 ✦ **Reference Coordinate System:** Defines the coordinate system about which the transformations take place.

 ✦ **Transform Center settings:** The Pivot Point Center, the Selection Center, and the Transform Coordinate Center. These settings specify the center about which the transformations take place.

 ✦ **Axis Constraint settings:** Allow the transformation to happen using only one axis or plane. These buttons are on the Axis Constraints toolbar.

Understanding coordinate systems

Max supports several different coordinate systems, and knowing which coordinate system you are working with as you transform an object is important. Using the wrong coordinate system can produce unexpected transformations.

To understand the concept of coordinate systems, imagine you're visiting the Grand Canyon and are standing precariously on the edge of a lookout. To nervous onlookers calling the park rangers, the description of your position would vary from viewpoint to viewpoint. A person standing by you would say you are next to him. A person on the other side of the canyon would say that you're across from her. A person at the floor of the canyon would say you're above him. And a person in an airplane would describe you as being on the east side of the canyon. Each person would have a different viewpoint of you (the object), even though you have not moved.

The coordinate systems that Max recognizes include the following:

✦ **View Coordinate System:** A coordinate system based on the viewports; X points right, Y points up, and Z points out of the screen (toward you). The views are fixed, making this perhaps the most intuitive coordinate system to work with.

✦ **Screen Coordinate System:** Identical to the View Coordinate System, except the active viewport determines the coordinate system axes whereas the inactive viewports show the axes as defined by the active viewport.

✦ **World Coordinate System:** Specifies X pointing to the right, Z pointing up, and Y pointing into the screen (away from you). The coordinate axes remain fixed regardless of any transformations applied to an object.

✦ **Parent Coordinate System:** Uses the coordinate system applied to a linked object's parent and maintains consistency between hierarchical transformations. If an object doesn't have a parent, then the world is its parent and the system is set to the World Coordinate System.

✦ **Local Coordinate System:** Sets the coordinate system based on the selected object. The axes are located at the pivot point for the object. You can reorient and move the pivot point using the Pivot button in the Hierarchy panel.

✦ **Gimbal Coordinate System:** Provides interactive feedback for objects using the Euler XYZ controller. If the object doesn't use the Euler XYZ controller, then this coordinate system works just like the World coordinate system.

✦ **Grid Coordinate System:** Uses the coordinate system for the active grid.

✦ **Pick Coordinate System:** Lets you select an object about which to transform. The Coordinate System list keeps the last four picked objects as coordinate system options.

New Feature   The Gimbal coordinate system is new in 3ds max 5.

All transforms occur relative to the current coordinate system as selected in the Referenced Coordinate System drop-down list found on the main toolbar.

Each of the three basic transforms can have a different coordinate system specified, or you can set it to change uniformly when a new coordinate system is selected. To do this, open the General panel in the Preference Settings dialog box, and select the Constant option in the Reference Coordinate System section.

Using a transform center

All transforms are done about a center point. When transforming an object, you must understand what the object's current center point is, as well as the coordinate system that you're working in.

The Transform Center flyout consists of three buttons: Use Pivot Point Center, Use Selection Center, and Use Transform Coordinate Center, shown in the following table. Each of these buttons alters how the transformations are done. The origin of the Transform Gizmo is always positioned at the center point specified by these buttons.

Button	Description
	Use Pivot Point Center
	Use Selection Center
	Use Transform Coordinate Center

Pivot Point Center

Pivot points are typically set to the center of an object when the object is first created, but they can be relocated anywhere within the scene including outside of the object. Relocating the pivot point allows you to change the point about which objects are rotated. For example, if you have a car model that you want to position along an incline, moving the pivot point to the bottom of one of the tires will allow you to easily line up the car with the incline.

 Cross-Reference   I discuss pivot points in detail in the next section.

Selection Center

The Use Selection Center button sets the transform center to the center of the selected object or objects regardless of the individual object's pivot point. If multiple objects are selected, then the center will be computed to be in the middle of a bounding box that surrounds all the objects.

Transform Coordinate Center

The Transform Coordinate Center button uses the center of the Local Coordinate System. If View Coordinate System is selected, then all objects are transformed about the center of the viewport. If an object is selected as the coordinate system using the Pick option, then all transformations will be transformed about that object's center.

When you select the Local Coordinate System, the Use Transform Center button is ignored, and objects are transformed about their local axes. If you select multiple objects, then they all transform individually about their local axes. Grouped objects transform about the group axes.

Figure 9-5 shows the ice cream cone and firecracker object using the different transform center modes. The left image shows the Pivot Point Center mode, the middle image shows the Selection Center mode with both objects selected, and the right image shows the Transform Coordinate Center mode. For each mode, notice that the Move Gizmo is in a different location.

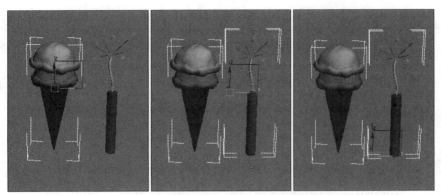

Figure 9-5: The Move Gizmo is located in different places depending on the selected Transform Center mode.

Selecting Axis Constraints

Three-dimensional space consists of three basic directions defined by three axes: X, Y, and Z. If you were to stand on each axis and look at a scene, you would see three separate planes: the XY plane, the YZ plane, and the ZX plane. These planes show only two dimensions at a time and restrict any transformations to the two axes.

By default, the Top, Side, and Front viewports show only a single plane and thereby restrict transformations to that single plane. The Top view constrains movement to the XY plane, the Left or Right side view constrains movement to the YZ plane, and the Front view constrains movement to the ZX plane. This setting is adequate for most modeling purposes, but sometimes you might need to limit the transformations in all the viewports to a single plane. In Max, you can restrict movement to specific transform axes using the Restrict Axes buttons in the Axis Constraints toolbar. You access this toolbar, shown in Figure 9-6, by right-clicking on the main toolbar (away from the buttons) and selecting Axis Constraints options from the pop-up menu.

Figure 9-6: The Axis Constraints toolbar includes buttons for restricting transformations to a single axis or plane.

The four Restrict axes buttons are Restrict to X (F5), Restrict to Y (F6), Restrict to Z (F7), and the flyout buttons, Restrict to XY, YZ, and ZX Plane (F8). The effect of selecting one of the Restrict axes buttons will be based on the coordinate system selected. For example, if you click the Restrict to X button and the coordinate system is set to View, then the object will always be transformed to the right because, in the View coordinate system, the X-axis is always to the right. If you click the Restrict to X button and the coordinate system is set to Local, the axes will be attached to the object, so transformations along the X-axis will be consistent in all viewports (with this setting, the object will not move in the Left view because it only shows the YZ plane).

Caution   If the axis constraints don't seem to be working, check the Preference Settings dialog box and look at the General panel to make sure that the Reference Coordinate System option is set to Constant.

Additionally, you can restrict movement to a single plane with the Restrict to Plane flyouts consisting of Restrict to XY, Restrict to YZ, and Restrict to ZX. (Use the F8 key to quickly cycle through the various planes.) If the Transform Gizmo is enabled, then the axis or axes that are available will be displayed in yellow.

Locking axes and inheriting transformations

To lock an object's transformation axes on a more permanent basis, go to the Command Panel and select the Hierarchy tab. Click the Link Info button to open the Locks rollout, shown in Figure 9-7. The rollout displays each axis for the three types of transformations: Move, Rotate, and Scale. Make sure the object is selected, then click the transformation axes you want to lock. Be aware that if all Move axes are selected, you won't be able to move the object until you de-select the axes.

Locking axes is helpful if you want to prevent accidental scaling of an object or restrict a vehicle's movement to a plane that makes up a road.

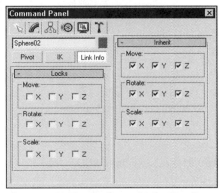

Figure 9-7: The Locks and Inherit rollouts can prevent any transforms along an axis and specify which transformations are inherited.

The Locks rollout displays unselected X, Y, and Z check boxes for the Move, Rotate, and Scale transformations. By selecting the check boxes, you limit the axes about which the object can be transformed. For example, if you check the X and Y boxes under the Move transformation, the object can move only in the Z direction of the Local Coordinate System.

Note   These locks work regardless of the axis constraint settings in the main toolbar.

The Inherit rollout, like the Locks rollout, includes check boxes for each axis and each transformation, except here, all the transformations are selected by default. By de-selecting a check box, you specify which transformations an object does not inherit from its parent. The Inherit rollout will only appear if the selected object is part of a hierarchy.

For example, suppose a child object is created and linked to a parent and the X Move Inherit check box is de-selected. As the parent is moved in the Y or Z directions, the child follows, but if the parent is moved in the X direction, the child does not follow. If a parent doesn't inherit a transformation, then its children don't either.

Using the Link Inheritance utility

The Link Inheritance utility works in the same way as the Inherit rollout of the Hierarchy panel, except that you can apply it to multiple objects at the same time. To use this utility, open the Utility panel, and click the More button. In the Utilities dialog box, select the Link Inheritance utility, and click OK. The rollout for this utility is identical to the Inherit rollout discussed in the previous section.

Tutorial: Re-creating a chess game

Chess is a great game, and every time I get a book to help me become a better player, I am presented with example after example of the great matches throughout history that have been re-created using this strange notation that is completely foreign and difficult to follow — obviously a case where 3D graphics, which is all about visualization, would help.

To re-create a chess game for this tutorial, I could model a chess set and a board, or I could borrow a model from my friends at Viewpoint Datalabs. The tutorial deals with transforming objects and not with modeling, so I chose the latter option.

On the CD-ROM   The chess set is included on the CD-ROM, compliments of Viewpoint Datalabs.

With the pieces in place, I can re-create the game by moving the pieces. (Now all I need is help understanding chess game notation.)

To re-create a chess game, follow these steps:

1. Open the Chess game.max file from the Chap 09 directory on the CD-ROM.

2. To prevent any extraneous movements, restrict any movement of the board itself by locking the transformation axes. Select the board by clicking it (be sure to get the border also). Open the Hierarchy panel and click the Link Info button. Then in the Locks rollout, select all nine boxes to restrict all transformations.

3. Back in the Top viewport, click the Select and Move button (or press W) and try to drag the board in the viewport.

   It won't move because all of its transformations are now locked.

Note   Another way to keep the chessboard from moving is to use the Freeze option. To freeze an object, open the Display panel and in the Freeze rollout, select Freeze Selected. You can also choose Edit ➪ Properties to open the Object Properties dialog box. In the Object Information section, click the Freeze option.

4. The next step is to restrict all pieces to move only in the XY plane. For this to happen, the coordinate system needs to change. Select the World Coordinate System from the Reference Coordinate System drop-down list on the main toolbar.

5. Open the Axis Constraints toolbar (by right clicking on the main toolbar away from the buttons and selecting it from the pop-up menu) and click the Restrict to XY Plane button (or you can cycle through the constrain planes using the F8 key). Select and move an object in the scene and notice how its movements stay within the XY plane.

   You can also restrict movement to the XY Plane by moving only objects in the Top viewport.

6. Before you make your first move, click the Set Key button in the Lower Interface Bar (or press the ' key) and go to the next animation frame by clicking the Next Frame button in the Time Controls (or press the . key).

7. Select and Move a chess piece, repositioning the object in the Top view. Then click the large Set Keys button (or press the K key) to record the transformation.

8. Continue clicking the Next Frame button and moving the pieces frame by frame until the game is finished.

9. After you finish the game, click the Go to Start button in the Time Controls (or press the Home key) and click repeatedly on the Next Frame button to see the game unfold.

Figure 9-8 shows the chess game in progress.

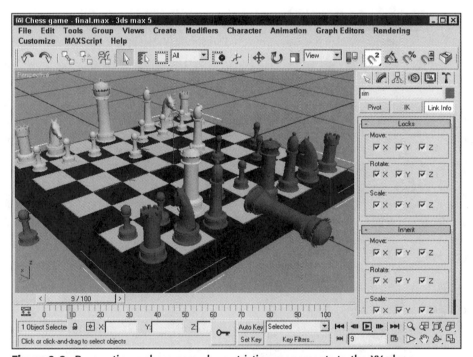

Figure 9-8: Re-creating a chess game by restricting movements to the XY plane.

Tutorial: Setting the dining room table

Using Max, the age-old chore of setting the table for dinner becomes easy (still not fun, but easy). Now, you could just move the dishes into place, but learning to rotate them will make it easier for the diners. In this tutorial, you'll start with a dining room table model provided by Zygote Media from their Sampler CD-ROM.

To set the table, follow these steps:

1. Open the Dining Room.max file from the Chap 09 directory on the CD-ROM.

2. Clone the set of dishes by selecting the Dishes group and choosing Edit ➪ Clone (or by pressing Ctrl+V).

3. Select the World Coordinate System and Restrict to XY Plane (F8) to ensure that the dishes stay on the table plane.

4. Select and Move the cloned dishes across the table.

5. With the cloned dishes still selected, click the Select and Rotate button (E). Then right-click the Select and Rotate button to open the Rotate Transform Type-In dialog box.

6. In the Rotate Transform Type-In dialog box (F12), enter **180** degrees for the Z-axis and press the Enter key; then close the dialog box.

   This step reorients the dishes correctly.

7. Hold down the Ctrl key while selecting both sets of dishes. Select the Use Selection Center flyout. Then choose Edit ➪ Clone (Ctrl+V) to create the last two sets of dishes.

8. With the second set of cloned dishes still selected, right-click the Select and Rotate button to open the Rotate Transform Type-In dialog box again. This time, enter **90** in the Z offset field and press the Enter key; then close the dialog box.

9. Select and Move each individual place setting to its final place. Figure 9-9 shows the table all set and ready for dinner.

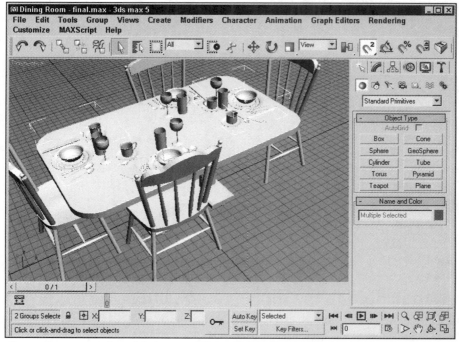

Figure 9-9: Setting the table is accomplished by moving and rotating cloned copies of the dishes.

Now you've done some translation and some rotation. In the next example, you'll scale some sphere objects to build a snowman.

Tutorial: Building a snowman

A snowman is a fine example of symmetrical body parts. First, you start with a base, then duplicate the base, only smaller, and finally create the head, which is even smaller. This sounds like a good place to use the Scale transformation.

To build a snowman, follow these steps:

1. Open the Create panel in the Command Panel and click the Sphere button.

2. Create a sphere object by dragging in the Top viewport.

   This will be the base of your snowman.

3. Snowman parts are never perfectly round, so let's squash the sphere by clicking the Select and Squash flyout button under the Select and Scale button (or press R to cycle through the scale tools). When the non-uniform scaling warning dialog box appears, click Yes.

   We won't be applying any modifiers to these squashed spheres so clicking Yes to close the warning dialog box isn't a problem.

4. Set the coordinate system to Local and click the Restrict to Z-Axis button (or press F7). Now, drag the sphere downward in the Front viewport to squash it slightly.

5. Select the Select and Uniform Scale (R) flyout, and clone the sphere by holding down the Shift key while dragging on the sphere. Enter **2** in the Clone Options dialog box to create two clones at the same time (one for the upper torso and one for the head).

   Each successive clone will be scaled by the same offset between the original and first cloned spheres.

6. Click the Select and Move (W) button and position the new cloned spheres on top of the original sphere.

Note   If you have any problems moving the spheres, check your coordinate system setting. It should be set to Local.

7. To complete the snowman, add some primitive objects for coal eyes, a mouth, a carrot nose, and a top hat.

Figure 9-10 shows the finished snowman produced by scaling spheres.

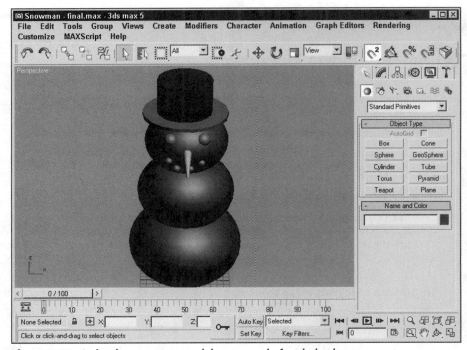

Figure 9-10: A simple snowman model composed of scaled spheres

Using Pivot Points

An object's pivot point is the center about which the object is rotated and scaled and about which most modifiers are applied. Pivot points are created by default when an object is created and are usually created at the center or base of an object. You can move and orient a pivot point in any direction, but repositioning the pivot cannot be animated. Pivot points exist for all objects, whether they are part of a hierarchy or not.

Caution   Try to set your pivot points before animating any objects in your scene. If you relocate the pivot point after animation keys have been placed, all transformations are modified to use the new pivot point.

Positioning pivot points

To move and orient a pivot point, open the Hierarchy panel in the Command Panel and click the Pivot button, shown in Figure 9-11. At the top of the Adjust Pivot rollout are three buttons; each button represents a different mode. The Affect Pivot Only mode makes the transformation buttons affect only the pivot point of the current selection. The object will not move. The Affect Object Only mode causes the object to be transformed, but not the pivot point; and the Affect Hierarchy Only mode allows an object's links to be moved.

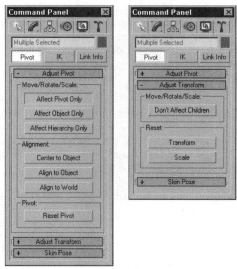

Figure 9-11: The Pivot button under the
Hierarchy panel includes controls for affecting
the pivot point.

 Note　Using the Scale transformation while one of these modes is selected alters the selected
object but has no effect on the pivot point or the link.

Aligning pivot points

Below the mode buttons are three more buttons that are used to align the pivot points. These
buttons are only active when a mode is selected. These buttons are Center to Object/Pivot,
Align to Object/Pivot, and Align to World. The first two buttons switch between Object and
Pivot, depending on the mode that is selected. You may select only one mode at a time. The
button turns light blue when selected.

The Center to Object/Pivot button moves the object or the pivot point so that its centers are
aligned. The Align to Object/Pivot button rotates the object or pivot point until the object's
Local Coordinate System and the pivot point are aligned. The Align to World button rotates
either to the World Coordinate system. For example, if the Affect Object Only mode is
selected and the object is separated from the pivot point, clicking the Center to Pivot button
will move the object so that its center is on the pivot point.

Under these three alignment buttons is another button labeled Reset Pivot, which you use to
reset the pivot point to its original location.

Transform adjustments

The Hierarchy panel of the Command Panel includes another useful rollout labeled Adjust
Transform. This rollout, also shown in Figure 9-11, includes another mode that you can use
with hierarchies of objects. Clicking the Don't Affect Children button places you in a mode
where any transformations of a linked hierarchy will not affect the children. Typically, transformations are applied to all linked children of a hierarchy, but this mode disables this.

The Adjust Transform rollout also includes two buttons that allow you to reset the Local Coordinate System and scale percentage. These buttons set the current orientation of an object as the World coordinate or as the 100 percent standard. For example, if you select an object and move it 30 units to the left and scale it to 200 percent, these values will be displayed in the coordinate fields on the status bar. Clicking the Reset Transform and Reset Scale buttons resets these values to 0 and 100 percent.

You use the Reset: Scale button to reset the scale values for an object that has been scaled using non-uniform scaling. Non-uniform scaling can cause problems for child objects that inherit this type of scaling such as shortening the links, and the Reset: Scale button can remedy these problems by resetting the parents scaling values. When the scale is reset, there is no visible change to the object, but if you open the Scale Transform Type-In dialog box while the scale is being reset, you see the absolute local values being set back to 100 each.

Tip   If you are using an object that has been non-uniformly scaled, using Reset: Scale before the item is linked will save you some headaches if you plan on using modifiers.

Using the Reset XForm utility

You can also reset transform values using the Reset XForm utility. To use this utility, open the Utility panel and click the Reset XForm button, which is one of the default buttons. The benefit of this utility is that you can reset the transform values for multiple objects simultaneously. The rollout for this utility includes only a single button labeled Reset Selected.

Using the Align Commands

The Align commands are an easy way to automatically transform objects. You can use these commands to line up object centers or edges, align normals and highlights, align to views and grids, and even line up cameras.

Aligning objects

Any object that you can transform, you can align, including lights, cameras, and Space Warps. After selecting the object to be aligned, click the Align flyout button on the main toolbar or choose Tools ➪ Align (or press Alt+A). The cursor changes to the Align icon; now click a target object with which you want to align all the selected objects. Clicking the target object opens the Align Selection dialog box with the target object's name displayed in the dialog box's title, as shown in Figure 9-12.

The Align Selection dialog box includes settings for the X, Y, and Z positions to line up the Minimum, Center, Pivot Point, or Maximum dimensions for the selected or target object's Bounding Box. As you change the settings in the dialog box, the objects reposition themselves, but the actual transformations don't take place until you click the Apply button or the OK button.

Aligning normals

You can use the Normal Align command to line up points of the surface of two objects. A Normal vector is a projected line that extends from the center of a polygon face exactly perpendicular to the surface. When two Normal vectors are aligned, the objects are perfectly adjacent to one another. If the two objects are spheres, then they will touch at only one point.

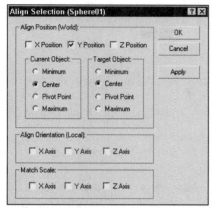

Figure 9-12: The Align Selection dialog box can align objects along any axes by their Minimum, Center, Pivot, or Maximum points.

To align normals, you need to first select the object to move (this is the source object). Then choose Tools ➪ Normal Align or click the Normal Align flyout button under the Align button on the main toolbar (or press Alt+N). The cursor will change to the Normal Align icon. Drag the cursor across the surface of the source object, and a blue arrow pointing out from the face center will appear. Release the mouse when you've correctly pinpointed the position to align.

Next click the target object and drag the mouse to locate the target object's align point. This is displayed as a green arrow. When you release the mouse, the source object moves to align the two points and the Normal Align dialog box appears, as shown in Figure 9-13.

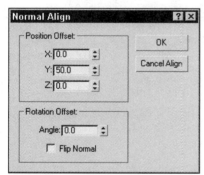

Figure 9-13: The Normal Align dialog box allows you to define offset values when aligning normals.

When the objects are aligned, the two points match up exactly. The Normal Align dialog box lets you specify offset values that you can use to keep a distance between the two objects. You can also specify an Angle Offset, which is used to deviate the parallelism of the normals. The Flip Normal option aligns the objects so that their selected normals point in the same direction.

Objects without any faces, like Point Helper objects and Space Warps, use a vector between the origin and the Z-axis for normal alignment.

Tutorial: Aligning a kissing couple

Aligning normals positions two faces directly opposite one another, so what better way to practice this tool than to align two faces.

To connect the kissing couple using the Normal Align command, follow these steps:

1. Open the Kissing couple.max file from the Chap 09 directory on the CD-ROM. This file includes two extruded shapes of a boy and a girl. The extruded shapes give us a flat face that is easy to align.

2. Select the girl shape and choose the Tools ➪ Align Normals menu command (or press Alt+N). Then drag the cursor over the extruded shape until the blue vector points out from the front of the lips, as shown Figure 9-14.

3. Then drag the cursor over the boy shape until the green vector points out from the front of the lips. Release the mouse and the Normal Align dialog box appears. Enter a value of **5** in the Z-Axis Offset field and click OK.

Figure 9-14 shows the resulting couple with normal aligned faces.

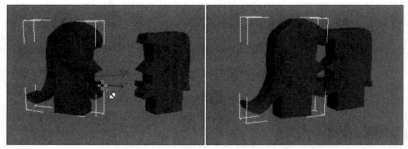

Figure 9-14: Using the Normal Align feature, you can align object faces.

Cross-Reference   In the Align button flyout are two other common ways to align objects—Align Camera and Place Highlight (Ctrl+H). I talk about these features in Chapter 21, "Controlling Cameras," and Chapter 22, "Working with Lights," respectively.

Aligning to a view

The Align to View command provides an easy and quick way to reposition objects to one of the axes. To use this command, select an object and then choose Tools ➪ Align to View. The Align to View dialog box appears, as shown in Figure 9-15. Changing the settings in this dialog box displays the results in the viewports. You can use the Flip command for altering the direction of the object points. If no object is selected, then the Align to View command cannot be used.

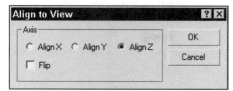

Figure 9-15: The Align to View dialog box
is a quick way to line up objects with the axes.

The Align to View command is especially useful for fixing the orientation of objects when you create them in the wrong view. All alignments are completed relative to the object's Local Coordinate System. If several objects are selected, each object is reoriented according to its Local Coordinate System.

Note   Using the Align to View command on symmetrical objects like spheres doesn't produce any noticeable difference in the viewports.

Using Grids

When Max is started, the one element that is visible is the Home Grid. This grid is there to give you a reference point for creating objects in 3D space. At the center of each grid are two darker lines. These lines meet at the origin point for the World Coordinate System where the coordinates for X, Y, and Z are all 0.0. This point is where all objects are placed by default.

In addition to the Home Grid, you can create and place new grids in the scene. These grids are not rendered, but you can use them to help you locate and align objects in 3D space.

The Home Grid

You can turn the Home Grid on or off by choosing Views ⇨ Grid ⇨ Show Home Grid (you can also turn the Home Grid on and off for the selected viewport using the G key). If the Home Grid is the only grid in the scene, then by default it is also the construction grid where new objects are positioned when created.

You can access the Home Grid parameters (shown in Figure 9-16) by choosing Customize ⇨ Grid and Snap Settings. You can also access this dialog box by right-clicking the Snap, Angle Snap, or Percent Snap Toggle buttons located on the main toolbar.

In the Home Grid panel of the Grid and Snap Settings dialog box, you can set how often Major Lines appear, as well as Grid Spacing. (The Spacing value for the active grid is displayed on the status bar.) You can also specify to dynamically update the grid view in all viewports or just in the active one.

The User Grids panel lets you activate any new grids when created.

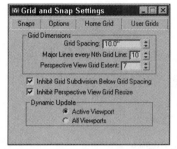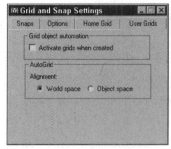

Figure 9-16: The Home Grid and User Grids panels of the Grid and Snap Settings dialog box let you define the grid spacing.

Creating and activating new grids

In addition to the Home Grid, you can create new grids. To create a new Grid object, open the Create panel, select the Helpers category, and click the Grid button. In the Parameters rollout are settings for specifying the new grid object's dimensions, spacing, and color, as well as which coordinate plane to display (XY, YZ, or ZX).

You can designate any newly created grid as the default active grid. To activate a grid, make sure it is selected and choose Views ➪ Grids ➪ Activate Grid Object. Keep in mind that only one grid may be active at a time, and the default Home Grid cannot be selected. You can also activate a grid by right-clicking the grid object and selecting Activate Grid from the pop-up menu. To deactivate the new grid and reactivate the Home Grid, choose Views ➪ Grids ➪ Activate Home Grid, or right-click the grid object and choose Activate Grid ➪ Home Grid from the pop-up quadmenu.

You can find further grid settings for new grids in the Grid and Snap Settings dialog box on the User Grids panel. The settings include automatically activating the grid when created, and an option for aligning an AutoGrid using World space or Object space coordinates.

Using AutoGrid

You can use the AutoGrid feature to create a new construction plane perpendicular to a face normal. This feature provides an easy way to create and align objects directly next to one another without manually lining them up or using the Align features.

The AutoGrid feature shows up as a check box at the top of the Object Type rollout for every category in the Create panel. It only becomes active when you're in Create Object mode.

To use AutoGrid, click the AutoGrid option after selecting an object type to create. If no objects are in the scene, then the object is created as usual. If an object is in the scene, then the cursor will move around on the surface of the object with its coordinate axes perpendicular to the surface that the cursor is over. Clicking and dragging will create the new object based on the precise location of the object under the mouse.

The AutoGrid option stays active for all new objects you create until you turn off the AutoGrid option by unchecking the box. Holding down the Alt key before creating the object makes the AutoGrid stay around after the object is created.

Using Snap Options

Often when an object is being transformed, you know exactly where you want to put it. The Snap feature can be the means whereby objects get to the precise place they should be. For example, if you are constructing a set of stairs from box primitives, you could enable the edge snap feature to make each adjacent step be aligned precisely along the edge of the previous step. With the snap feature enabled, an object automatically moves (or snaps) to the specified snap position when you place it close enough. If you enable the Snap features, they will affect any transformations that you make in a scene.

Snap points are defined in the Grid and Snap Settings dialog box that you can open by choosing Customize ➪ Grid and Snap Settings or by right-clicking any of the first three Snap buttons on the main toolbar (these Snap buttons have a small magnet icon in them). Figure 9-17 shows the Snaps panel of the Grid and Snap Settings dialog box for Standard and NURBS objects. NURBS stands for Non-Uniform Rational B-Splines. They are a special type of object that is created from spline curves.

Cross-Reference

In addition to the snap points for standard objects, the Snaps panel also includes a list of snap points for NURBS objects. For more information on NURBS, see Chapter 15, "Working with NURBS."

Figure 9-17: The Snaps panel includes many different points to snap to depending on the object type.

After snap points have been defined, the Snap buttons on the main toolbar activate the Snaps feature. The first Snaps button consists of a flyout with three buttons: 3D Snap Toggle, 2.5D Snap Toggle, and 2D Snap Toggle. The 2D Snap Toggle button limits all snaps to the active construction grid. The 2.5D Snap Toggle button snaps to points on the construction grid as well as projected points from objects in the scene. The 3D Snap Toggle button can snap to any points in 3D space.

Tip

Right-clicking the snap toggles opens the Grid and Snap Settings dialog box, except for the Spinner Snap Toggle, which opens the Preference Settings dialog box.

These Snap buttons control the snapping for translations. To the right are two other buttons: Angle Snap Toggle and Percent Snap. These buttons control the snapping of rotations and scalings.

Note   The keyboard shortcut for turning the Snaps feature on and off is the S key.

With the Snaps feature enabled, the cursor becomes blue crosshairs wherever a snap point is located.

Setting snap points

The Snap tab in the Grid and Snap Settings dialog box has many different points that can be snapped to in two different categories: Standard and NURBS. The Standard snap points (previously shown in Figure 9-17) include the following:

- ✦ **Grid Points:** Snaps to the Grid intersection points
- ✦ **Grid Lines:** Snaps only to positions located on the Grid lines
- ✦ **Pivot:** Snaps to an object's pivot point
- ✦ **Bounding Box:** Snaps to one of the corners of a bounding box
- ✦ **Perpendicular:** Snaps to a spline's next perpendicular point
- ✦ **Tangent:** Snaps to a spline's next tangent point
- ✦ **Vertex:** Snaps to polygon vertices
- ✦ **Endpoint:** Snaps to a spline's end point or the end of a polygon edge
- ✦ **Edge:** Snaps to positions only on an edge
- ✦ **Midpoint:** Snaps to a spline's midpoint or the middle of a polygon edge
- ✦ **Face:** Snaps to any point on the surface of a face
- ✦ **Center Face:** Snaps to the center of a face

Several snap points are specific to NURBS objects such as NURBS points and curves, also shown in Figure 9-17. These points include

- ✦ **CV:** Snaps to any NURBS Control Vertex subobject
- ✦ **Point:** Snaps to a NURBS point
- ✦ **Curve Center:** Snaps to the center of the NURBS curve
- ✦ **Curve Normal:** Snaps to a point that is normal to a NURBS curve
- ✦ **Curve Tangent:** Snaps to a point that is tangent to a NURBS curve
- ✦ **Curve Edge:** Snaps to the edge of a NURBS curve
- ✦ **Curve End:** Snaps to the end of a NURBS curve
- ✦ **Surf Center:** Snaps to the center of a NURBS surface
- ✦ **Surf Normal:** Snaps to a point that is normal to a NURBS surface
- ✦ **Surf Edge:** Snaps to the edge of a NURBS surface

Setting snap options

The Grid and Snap Settings dialog box holds a panel of Options, shown in Figure 9-18, in which you can set whether markers display or not, the size of the markers, and their color. If you click on the color swatch, a Color Selector dialog box opens and enables you to select a new color. The Snap Strength setting determines how close the cursor must be to a snap point before it snaps to it. The Angle and Percent values are the strengths for any rotate and scale transformations, respectively. You can also cause translations to be affected by the designated axis constraints with the Use Axis Constraints option.

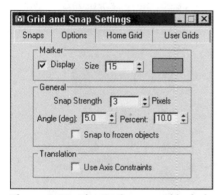

Figure 9-18: The Options panel includes settings for marker size and color and the Snap Strength value.

Within any viewpoint, holding down the Shift key and right-clicking in the viewport can access a pop-up menu of grid points and options. This pop-up quadmenu lets you quickly add or reset all the current snap points and change snap options, such as Transformed Constraints and Snap to Frozen.

Tutorial: Creating a lattice for a methane molecule

Many molecules are represented by a lattice of spheres. Trying to line up the exact positions of the spheres by hand could be extremely frustrating, but using the Snap feature makes this challenge, well . . . a snap.

One of the simpler molecules is methane, which is composed of one carbon atom surrounded by four smaller hydrogen atoms. To reproduce this molecule as a lattice, we will first create a tetrahedron primitive and snap spheres to each of its corners.

To create a lattice of the methane molecule, follow these steps:

1. Open the Methane Molecule.max file from the Chap 09 directory on the CD-ROM.

   This file includes a simple tetrahedron object created with the Hedra Extended Primitive surrounded by a sphere.

2. Open the Grid and Snap Settings dialog box by right-clicking the 3D Snap Toggle button on the main toolbar. In the Snaps panel, click the Clear All button to de-select any previous selections, then select the Vertex option. Close the dialog box.

3. Enable the Snap feature by clicking the 3D Snap Toggle button (or press the S key).

4. In the Create panel drop-down list, select the Standard Primitives category, and then click the Sphere button.

5. Now create our four hydrogen atoms. In the Top viewport, move the cursor over the tetrahedron. Now move the cursor over each of the four corners of the tetrahedron until a blue vertex appears. Click and drag to create a sphere; then in the Parameters rollout, enter a Radius value of **30**. Do this procedure for each of the spheres placed at a vertex.

6. When you've completed the molecule, you can delete the tetrahedron by selecting it from the Select by Name dialog box (the name is Hedra01).

Figure 9-19 shows the finished methane molecule.

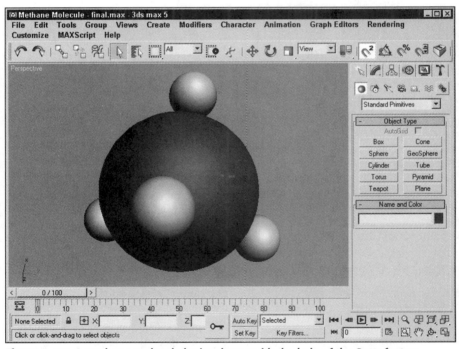

Figure 9-19: A methane molecule lattice drawn with the help of the Snap feature

Summary

Transforming objects in Max is one of the fundamental actions. The three basic ways to transform objects are moving, rotating, and scaling. Max includes many helpful features to enable these transformations to take place quickly and easily. In this chapter we covered many of these features, including

✦ Using the Move, Rotate, and Scale buttons and the Transform Gizmos

✦ Transforming objects precisely with the Transform Type-In dialog box and status bar fields

✦ Using Transform Managers to change coordinate systems and lock axes

✦ Aligning objects with the Align dialog box, aligning normals, and aligning to views

✦ Manipulating pivot points

✦ Working with grids

✦ Setting up snap points

✦ Snapping objects to snap points

In the next chapter, we'll investigate the features in the Modify panel that enable you to modify objects with modifiers.

✦　　✦　　✦

Using Modifiers

hink for a moment of a wood shop with all its various (and expensive) tools and machines. Some tools are simple like a screwdriver or a sander and others like a planer or router are more complex, but they all change the wood (or model) in different ways. In some ways, you can think of modifiers as these tools and machines that work on 3D objects.

Each woodshop tool has different parameters that control how it works, such as how hard you turn the screwdriver or the coarseness of the sandpaper. Likewise, each modifier has parameters that you can set that determine how it affects the 3D object.

Modifiers can be used to reshape objects, apply material mappings, deform an object's surface, and perform many other actions. Many different types of modifiers exist. This chapter introduces you to many different modifiers and more importantly, teaches you how to use them.

Exploring the Modifier Stack

All modifiers that are applied to an object are listed together in a single location known as the Modifier Stack. This Stack is the manager for all modifiers applied to an object and can be found at the top of the Modify panel in the Command Panel. You can also use the Stack to apply and delete modifiers; cut, copy, and paste modifiers between objects; and reorder them.

Applying modifiers

An object can have several modifiers applied to it. Modifiers can be applied using the Modifiers menu or by selecting the modifier from the Modifier List drop-down list located at the top of the Modify panel directly under the object name. Selecting a modifier in the Modifiers menu or from the Modifier List applies the modifier to the current selected object. Modifiers can be applied to multiple objects if several objects are selected.

Note   Some modifiers aren't available for some types of objects. For example, the Extrude and Lathe modifiers are enabled only when a spline shape is selected.

Using the Modifier Stack

After a modifier is applied, its parameters appear in rollouts within the Command Panel. The Modifier Stack rollout, shown in Figure 10-1, lists the base object and all the modifiers that have been applied to an object. Any new modifiers applied to an object are placed at the top of the stack. By selecting a modifier from the list in the Modifier Stack, all the parameters for that specific modifier are displayed in rollouts.

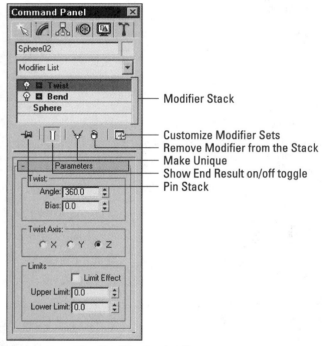

— Modifier Stack

— Customize Modifier Sets
— Remove Modifier from the Stack
— Make Unique
— Show End Result on/off toggle
— Pin Stack

Figure 10-1: The Modifier Stack rollout displays all modifiers applied to an object.

Tip   You can increase or decrease the size of the Modifier Stack by dragging the horizontal bar that is beneath the Modifier Stack buttons.

Beneath the Modifier Stack are five buttons that affect the selected modifier. They are as follows:

✦ **Pin Stack button:** Makes the parameters for the selected modifier available for editing even if another object is selected (like taking a physical pin and sticking it into the screen so it won't move).

✦ **Show End Result on/off toggle button:** Shows the results of all the modifiers in the entire Stack when enabled and only the modifiers up to the current selected modifier if disabled.

✦ **Make Unique button:** Used to break any instance or reference links to the selected object. After you click this button, an object will no longer be modified along with the other objects that it was an instance or reference for.

✦ **Remove Modifier from the Stack button:** Used to delete a modifier from the Stack or unbind a Space Warp if one is selected. Deleting a modifier will restore it to its same state that it was in before the modifier was applied.

✦ **Customize Modifier Sets button:** Opens a pop-up menu where you can select to show a set of modifiers as buttons above the Modifier Stack. You can also select which modifier set appears at the top of the list of modifiers. The pop-up menu also includes an option to configure and define the various sets of modifiers.

 For more information on configuring modifier sets, see Chapter 4, "Customizing the Max Interface."

If you right-click on a modifier, a pop-up menu will appear. This pop-up menu includes commands to rename the selected modifier, which you might want to do if the same modifier is applied to the same object multiple times. This pop-up menu also includes an option to delete the selected modifier.

Copying and pasting modifiers

The pop-up menu also includes options to Cut, Copy, Paste, and Paste Instance modifiers. The Cut command deletes the modifier from the current object but makes it available for pasting onto other objects. The Copy command retains the modifier for the current object and makes it available to paste onto another object. After you use the Cut or Copy command, you can use the Paste command to apply the modifier to another object. The Paste Instance command retains a link between the original modifier and the instanced modifier, so that any changes to either modifier affect the other instances.

 The format of the modifier name indicates whether it is an instance or reference. Instanced objects appear in bold in the Modifier Stack, and instanced modifiers appear in italic. Referenced objects have a black bar above them.

You can also apply modifiers for the current object onto other objects by dragging the modifier from the Modifier Stack and dropping it on the other object (like the Copy and Paste commands). Holding down the Ctrl key while dropping a modifier onto an object applies the modifier as an instance (like the Paste Instance command). Holding down the Shift key removes the modifier from the current modifier and applies it to the object that it is dropped on (like the Cut and Paste commands).

 You can also cut, copy, and paste modifiers using the Schematic View window. See Chapter 8, "Grouping and Linking Objects," for more details.

Using instanced modifiers

When you apply a single modifier to several objects at the same time, the modifier will show up in the Modifier Stack for each object. These are instanced modifiers that maintain a connection to each other. If any of these instanced modifiers are changed, the change is propagated to all other instances. This feature is very helpful for modifying large groups of objects.

When a modifier is copied between different objects, you can select to make the copy an instance.

To see all the objects that are linked to a particular modifier, choose Views ➪ Show Dependencies. All objects with instanced modifiers that are connected to the current selection appear in bright pink. At any time, you can break the link between a particular instanced modifier and the rest of the objects using the Make Unique button in the Modifier Stack rollout.

Disabling modifiers

Clicking the light bulb icon to the left of the modifier name toggles the modifier on and off. The right-click pop-up menu also offers options to turn the modifier off in the viewport or off for the renderer.

Reordering the Stack

The Stack order is important and can change the appearance of the object. Max applies the modifiers starting with the lowest one in the Stack first and the topmost modifier last. You can change the order of the modifiers in the Stack by selecting a modifier and dragging it above or below the other modifiers. You cannot drag it below the object type.

Tutorial: Learning the effect of Stack order

To see the effect of the Stack order, you'll apply some simple modifiers to a cylinder object and then copy those modifiers to another object and reorient their order.

To learn how the Stack order can affect the resulting geometry, follow these steps:

1. Open the Cylinders showing modifier stack order.max file from the Chap 10 directory on the CD-ROM. This file includes two simple cylinders.

2. Select the cylinder on the left and open the Modify panel. In the Modifier List drop-down list, select the Bend modifier, and in the Parameters rollout set the Angle value to 60 and the Bend Axis to Z.

3. Next select the Skew modifier from the Modifier List drop-down list in the Modify panel. Set the Skew Amount to 30 and Skew Axis to Z in the Parameters rollout. These settings cause the cylinder to curve to the right.

4. In the Modifier Stack, select and drag the Bend modifier to the cylinder on the right. Then select and drag the Skew modifier also onto the right cylinder. Notice how the right cylinder now bends to the right just like the other cylinder.

5. Select the cylinder on the right, and in the Modify panel select the Skew modifier in the Modifier Stack and drag it below the Bend modifier to reorder the modifiers. With the modifiers reordered, the cylinder on the right looks different from the one on the left.

Figure 10-2 shows the original cylinder (left), the cylinder with the Bend and Skew modifiers applied (middle), and the same cylinder with the order of the two modifiers reversed (right). The box surrounding the modified cylinders is the modifier gizmo that will be covered in the next section.

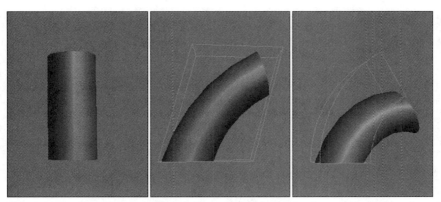

Figure 10-2: Changing the order of the modifiers in the Stack can affect the end result.

Collapsing the Stack

Collapsing the Stack removes its history and resets the modification history back to a baseline. All the individual modifiers in the Stack are combined into one single modification. This feature eliminates the ability to change any modifier parameters, but it simplifies the object and conserves memory. The right-click pop-up menu also offers options to Collapse To and Collapse All. You can collapse the entire Stack with the Collapse All command, or you can collapse to the current selected modifier with the Collapse To command.

When you apply a collapse command, a warning dialog box appears, notifying you that this action will delete all the creation parameters. Click Yes to continue with the collapse.

Note   In addition to the Yes and No buttons, the warning dialog box includes a Hold/Yes button. This button saves the current state of the object to the Hold buffer and then applies the Collapse All function. If you have any problems, you can retrieve the object's previous state before the collapse was applied by choosing Edit ➪ Fetch (Alt+Ctrl+F).

Using the Collapse utility

You can also use the Collapse utility found on the Utility panel. This utility enables you to collapse an object or several objects to a Modifier Stack Result or to a Mesh object. Collapsing to a Modifier Stack Result doesn't necessarily produce a mesh but collapses the object to its base object state, which is displayed at the bottom of the Stack hierarchy. Depending on the Stack, this could result in a patch, spline, or other object. You can also collapse to a Single Object or to Multiple Objects. The Boolean operations are available if you are collapsing several overlapping objects into one. Figure 10-3 shows the rollout for the Collapse utility.

Cross-Reference   Boolean operations can also be performed using the Boolean compound object. See Chapter 16, "Building Compound Objects" for details on this object type.

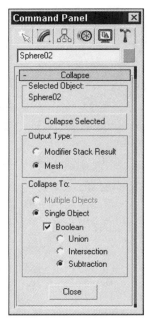

Figure 10-3: The Collapse utility can collapse several objects at once.

Caution Collapsing the Modifier Stack is not an action that you can undo. Before proceeding with the collapse, choose Edit ➪ Hold to provide a way to recover before the collapse.

Using gizmo subobjects

As you've worked with modifiers, you've probably noticed the orange wireframe box that surrounds the object in the viewports when you apply the modifier. These boxes are called modifier gizmos, and they provide a visual control for how the modifier changes the geometry. If you want you can work directly with these gizmos.

Clicking the plus sign to the left of the modifier name reveals any subobjects associated with the modifier. To select the modifier subobjects, simply click the subobject name. Many modifiers create gizmo subobjects. Gizmos have a center and can be transformed and controlled like regular objects using the transformation buttons on the main toolbar. Another common modifier subobject is Center, which controls the point about which the gizmo is transformed.

Modifying subobjects

In addition to being applied to complete objects, modifiers can also be applied and used to modify subobjects. Subobjects are defined as portions of an object. Subobjects can be vertices, edges, faces, or combinations of object parts.

To learn more about applying modifiers to subobject selections, see Chapter 11, "Modeling Basics."

To work in subobject selection mode, click the plus sign to the left of the object name to see the subobjects. Several modifiers, including Mesh Select, Spline Select, and Volume Select, can select subobject areas for passing these selections up to the next modifier in the Stack. For example, you can use the Mesh Select modifier to select several faces on the front of a sphere and then apply the Face Extrude modifier to extrude just those faces.

Topology dependency

When you attempt to modify the parameters of a base object that has a modifier applied, you will often get a warning dialog box, shown in Figure 10-4, that tells you that the modifier depends on topology that may change. You can disable the warning by selecting the "Do not show this message again" option on the dialog box or by opening the Preference Settings dialog box and turning off the Display Topology-Dependence Warning option in the General panel of the Preference Settings dialog box. Disabling the warning will not make the potential problem go away; it only prevents the warning dialog box from appearing.

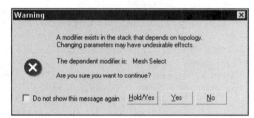

Figure 10-4: You can disable the Topology Dependence warning dialog box.

Holding and fetching a scene

Before going any farther, you need to know about an important feature in Max that allows you to set a stopping point for the current scene. The Hold command saves the scene into a temporary buffer for easy recovery. After a scene is set with the Hold command (Alt+Ctrl+H), you can bring it back instantly with the Fetch command (Alt+Ctrl+F). These commands provide a quick way to backtrack on modifications to a scene or project without your having to save and reload the project. If you use these commands before applying or deleting modifiers, you can save some potential headaches.

It is a good idea, along with saving your file often, to use the Hold command before applying any complex modifier to an object.

Exploring Modifier Types

To keep all the various modifiers straight, they have been grouped into several distinct modifier sets. The default modifier sets (as defined by right-clicking on the Modifier List in the Modify panel) include the following: Selection Modifiers, Patch/Spline Editing, Mesh Editing, Animation Modifiers, UV Coordinates, Cache Tools, Subdivision Surfaces, Free Form Deformations, Parametric Modifiers, Surface Modifiers, and Conversion Modifiers. These modifier sets are roughly the same as the submenus found in the Modifiers menu, except for some name changes and the addition of the NURBS Editing and Radiosity Modifiers in the menu.

Covering all the modifiers in a single chapter would result in a very long chapter. Instead, I decided to cover most of the modifiers in their respective chapters. For example, you can learn about the Mesh Editing modifiers in Chapter 13, "Modeling with Meshes and Polys"; animation modifiers in Chapter 24, "Animation Basics"; and the UV Coordinates modifiers in Chapter 20, "Using Material Maps"; and so on. This chapter covers the Selection Modifiers, Parametric Deformers, and FFD modifiers.

Object-Space vs. World Space modifiers

If you view the modifiers listed in the Modifier List, they are broken into two categories — Object-Space and World-Space modifiers. Object-Space modifiers are modifiers that are applied to individual objects and that use the object's Local coordinate system. World-Space modifiers are based on World-Space coordinates instead of on an object's Local coordinate system. Object-Space modifiers are more numerous than World-Space modifiers. World-Space modifiers are all identified with an asterisk that appears in front of the modifier name, but they often function the same as their Object-Space counterpart.

All Space Warps are also applied using World-Space coordinates, so they also have an asterisk preceding them in the Modifier Stack. You can get more information on Space Warps in Chapter 26, "Using Space Warps."

Selection modifiers

The first set of modifiers available in the Modifiers menu is the Selection modifiers. You can use these modifiers to select subobject sections for the various object types. You can then apply other modifiers to these subobject selections by selecting the Selection modifier and applying a new modifier.

You can see an example of how a Select modifier can be used to select and apply a modifier to a subobject selection in Chapter 11, "Modeling Basics."

Selection modifiers are available for every modeling type, including Mesh Select, Poly Select, Patch Select, Spline Select, Volume Select, FFD Select, and NURBS Surface Select. You can apply the Mesh Select, Poly Select, Patch Select, and Volume Select modifiers to any 3D object, but you can apply the Spline Select modifier only to spline and shape objects, the FFD Select modifier only to the FFD Space Warps objects, and the NURBS Surface Select modifier only to NURBS objects. Any modifiers that appear above one of these Selection modifiers in the Modifier Stack will only be applied to the selected subobjects.

Cross-Reference You can learn about the Selection modifiers for the various modeling types in their respective chapters.

Volume Select modifier

Among the Selection modifiers, the Volume Select modifier is unique. It selects subobjects based on the area defined by the modifier's gizmo. In the Parameters rollout for the Volume Select modifier, shown in Figure 10-5, you can specify whether subobjects selected within a given volume should be Object, Vertex, or Face subobjects. Any new selection can Replace, be Added to, or be Subtracted from the current selection. There is also an Invert option, which you can use to select the subobjects outside of the current volume. You can also choose either a Window or Crossing Selection Type.

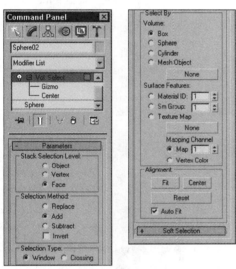

Figure 10-5: The Volume Select parameters let you select using different shaped volumes.

The actual shape of the gizmo can be a Box, a Sphere, a Cylinder, or a Mesh Object. To use a Mesh Object, click the button beneath the Mesh Object option and then click the object to use in a viewport. In addition to selecting by a gizmo-defined volume, you can select by Material IDs, Smoothing Groups, or a Texture Map.

The Alignment options can Fit or Center the volume on the current subobject selection. The Reset button moves the gizmo to its original position and orientation, which typically is the bounding box of the object.

Tutorial: Melting half an ice cream cone

Applying modifiers to a subobject selection is accomplished by passing the subobject selection up the Stack. This means that the select modifier needs to come below the other modifier in the Modifier Stack. To give you some practice, this example shows how to use the Volume Select and Melt modifiers to melt only half of an ice cream cone.

To apply the Volume Select and Melt modifiers to a subobject selection, follow these steps:

1. Open the Melting ice cream cone.max file from the Chap 10 directory on the CD-ROM. This file includes an ice cream cone model created by Zygote Media.

2. With the top scoop object selected, choose the Modifiers ➪ Selection Modifiers ➪ Volume Select menu command. This command applies the Volume Select modifier to the top cone object.

3. In the Parameters rollout, select the Vertex option. Then click on the Volume Select modifier in the Modifier Stack to select the gizmo subobject mode. With the Select and Move button on the main toolbar selected, drag in the Top viewport over the right half of the top scoop.

4. With the subobject still selected, choose the Modifiers ➪ Animation Modifiers ➪ Melt menu command to apply the Melt modifier to the subobject selection. In the Parameters rollout, set the Melt Amount to 30 and the Spread value to 20.

Tip   If you drag the Melt modifier in the Modifier Stack and drop it below the Mesh Select modifier, then the Melt modifier will be applied to the entire scoop instead of just the subobject selection.

Figure 10-6 shows the resulting ice cream cone with half of the top scoop starting to melt.

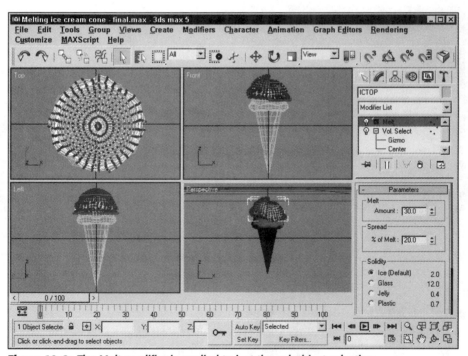

Figure 10-6: The Melt modifier is applied to just the subobject selection.

FFD Select modifier

The FFD Select modifier is another unique selection modifier. It enables you to select a group of control point subobjects for the FFD (Box) or the FFD (Cyl) Space Warps and apply additional modifiers to the selection. When an FFD Space Warp is applied to an object, you can select the Control Points subobjects and apply modifiers to the selection. The FFD Select modifier lets you select a different set of control points for a different modifier.

Parametric Deformer modifiers

Perhaps the most representative group of modifiers is the Parametric Deformers. These modifiers affect the geometry of objects by pulling, pushing, and stretching them. They all can be applied to any of the modeling types, including primitive objects.

 You might start to get sick of seeing the hammer model used over and over again, but using the same model will enable you to more easily compare the effects of the various modifiers.

Bend modifier

The Bend modifier can bend an object along any axis. Bend parameters include the Bend Angle and Direction, the Bend Axis, and the Limits. The hammer in Figure 10-7 shows several bending options. Limit settings are the boundaries beyond which the modifier has no effect. You can set Upper and Lower Limits. The left hammer shows a bend value of 75 degrees around the Z-axis, the middle hammer also has a Direction value of 60, and the right hammer has an Upper Limit of 8. Limits are useful if you want the modifier applied to only one half of the object.

 Several modifiers have the option to impose limits on the modifier including upper and lower limit values.

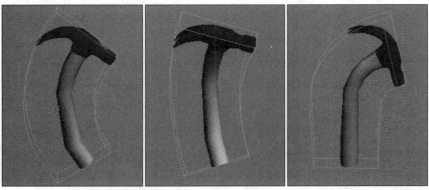

Figure 10-7: The Bend modifier can bend objects about any axis.

Taper modifier

The Taper modifier scales only one end of an object. Taper parameters include the Amount and Curve, Primary and Effect Axes, and Limits. The Curve value tapes the object along a curve. You can also select a Symmetry option to taper both ends equally. The left hammer in Figure 10-8 shows a taper of 1.0 about the Z-axis, the middle hammer also has a Curve value of –2, and the right hammer has the Symmetry option selected.

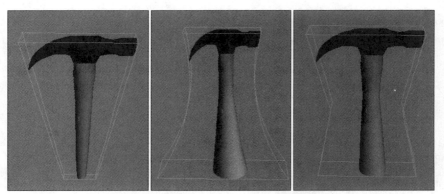

Figure 10-8: The Taper modifier can proportionally scale one end of an object.

Twist modifier

The Twist modifier deforms an object by rotating one end of an axis in one direction and the other end in the opposite direction. Twist parameters include Angle and Bias values, a Twist Axis, and Limits. The Bias value determines how much of the twist is completed; a value of 0 is the full twist, and 100 keeps the object in its original state. The Bias value makes it easy to animate the twisting of the object. The left hammer in Figure 10-9 shows a twist angle of 120 about the Z-axis, the middle hammer shows a Bias value of 20, and the right hammer has an Upper Limit value of 8.

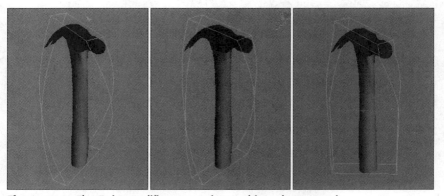

Figure 10-9: The Twist modifiers can twist an object about an axis.

Tutorial: Twisting a bridge

Do you remember back in science class seeing the short film on the collapse of the Tacoma Narrows Bridge caused by resonate winds through a canyon? We can re-create this scenario using the Twist modifier.

To use the Twist modifier on a bridge model, follow these steps:

1. Open the Twisting bridge.max file from the Chap 10 directory on the CD-ROM.

   This file includes a simple bridge spanning a canyon.

2. Select the bridge object and apply the Twist modifier by choosing Modifiers ➪ Parametric Deformers ➪ Twist.

3. Click the Auto Key button and drag the Time Slider to frame 30. Enter an Angle value of **–15** in the Parameters rollout and select the Y Twist Axis option. Drag the Time Slider to frame 60 and enter an Angle value of **0**. Drag the slider to frame 90 and enter **15**. At frame 100 enter a value of **0** again.

4. Click the Play Animation button to see the brief animation.

This example shows how all modifiers can be animated. Figure 10-10 includes a frame from this simple animation.

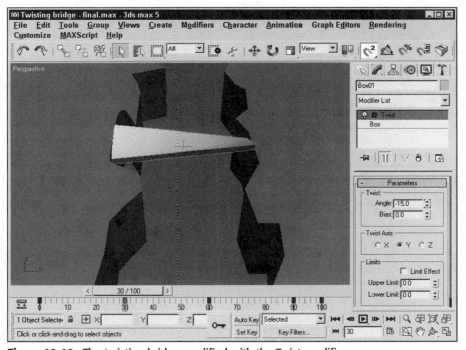

Figure 10-10: The twisting bridge modified with the Twist modifier.

Noise modifier

The Noise modifier randomly varies the position of object vertices. Noise parameters include Seed and Scale values, a Fractal option with Roughness and Iterations settings, Strength about each axis, and Animation settings. The Seed value sets the randomness of the noise. Two objects with similar settings will have the effect if the Seed values are the same. The Scale value determines the size of the position changes, so larger Scale values result in a smoother, less rough shape. For the Animation settings, the Frequency controls how quickly the object's noise changes and the Phase setting determines where the noise wave starts and will set keys when changed.

Figure 10-11 shows the Noise modifier applied to several sphere objects. These spheres make the Noise modifier easier to see than on the hammer object. The left sphere has Seed, Scale, and Strength values along all three axes set to 1.0, the middle sphere has increased the Strength values to 2.0, and the right sphere has enabled the Fractal option with a Roughness value of 1.0 and an Iterations value of 6.0.

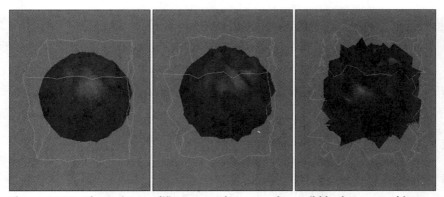

Figure 10-11: The Noise modifier can apply a smooth or wild look to your objects.

Tutorial: Creating a terrain

As a simple example of applying a modifier to a patch grid, we'll create a terrain. Using a patch grid and the Noise modifier, we can quickly create a hilly or jagged terrain.

To create a terrain, follow these steps:

1. In the Create panel, click the Geometry category button and select the Patch Grids sub-category from the subcategory drop-down list.

2. Click the Quad Patch button and create a patch in the Top view. In the Parameters rollout, change the Length and Width Segments to 20 each.

   These settings supply ample resolution for the terrain.

3. Choose Modifiers ➪ Parametric Deformations ➪ Noise to apply the Noise modifier. In the Parameters rollout, enter a Z Strength value of **200** for smooth, rolling hills, or click the Fractal option for more rough and jagged peaks.

Figure 10-12 shows a sample terrain with gently rolling hills.

Cross-Reference   Check out the new Terrain compound object covered in Chapter 16, "Building Compound Objects," for an alternative way to create terrains.

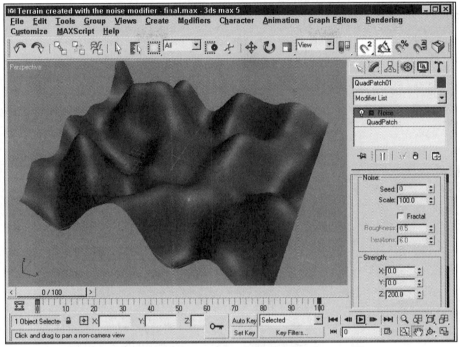

Figure 10-12: A terrain created from a patch grid and the Noise modifier.

Stretch modifier

The Stretch modifier pulls one axis while pushing the other axes in the opposite direction, like pulling a piece of taffy. Stretch parameters include Stretch and Amplify values, a Stretch Axis, and Limits. The Stretch value equates the distance the object is pulled, and the Amplify value determines how great the stretch curve is. Figure 10-13 shows a Stretch value of 0.2 about the Z-axis applied to the hammer, the middle hammer has also an Amplify value of 2.0, and the right hammer has an Upper Limit value of 8.

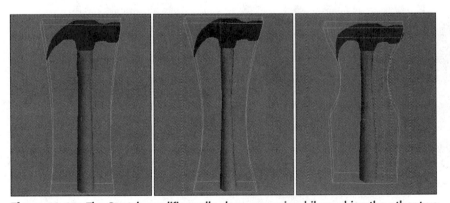

Figure 10-13: The Stretch modifier pulls along one axis while pushing the other two.

Squeeze modifier

The Squeeze modifier takes the points close to one axis and moves them away from the center of the object while it moves other points toward the center to create a bulging effect. Squeeze parameters include Amount and Curve values for Axial Bulge and Radial Squeeze, and Limits and Effect Balance settings. The Effect Balance settings include a Bias value, which changes the object between the maximum Axial Bulge or the maximum Radial Squeeze. The Volume setting will increase or decrease the volume of the object within the modifier's gizmo. Axial Bulge is enabled with an Amount value of 0.2 and a Curve value of 2.0 in the left hammer in Figure 10-14, the middle hammer has also added Radial Squeeze values of 0.4 and 2.0, and the right hammer has an Upper Limit value of 8.

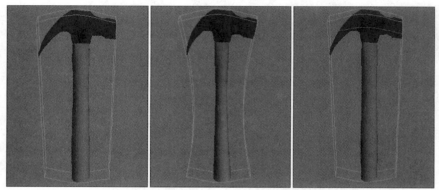

Figure 10-14: The Squeeze modifier can bulge or squeeze along two different axes.

Push modifier

The Push modifier pushes an object's vertices inward or outward as if they were being filled with air. The Push modifier also has one parameter: the Push Value. This value is the distance to move with respect to the object's center. Figure 10-15 shows the hammer pushed with 0.05, 0.1, and 0.15 values.

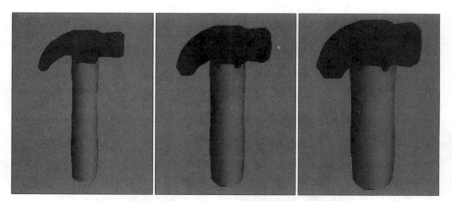

Figure 10-15: The Push modifier can increase the volume of an object.

Relax modifier

The Relax modifier tends to smooth the overall geometry by separating vertices that lie closer than an average distance. Parameters include a Relax Value that is the percentage of the distance that the vertices move. Values can range between 1.0 and –1.0. A value of 0 has no effect on the object. Negative values have the opposite effect, causing an object to become tighter and more distorted.

The Iterations value determines how many times this calculation is computed. The Keep Boundary Points Fixed option removes any points that are next to an open hole. Save Outer Corners maintains the vertex position of corners of an object. The left and middle hammers of Figure 10-16 have Relax values of 1.0 and Iteration values of 1 and 3. The right hammer has a Relax value of –1.0 and an Iteration value of 1.

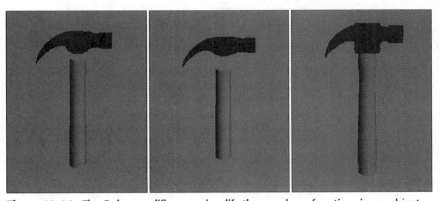

Figure 10-16: The Relax modifier can simplify the number of vertices in an object.

Ripple modifier

The Ripple modifier creates ripples across the surface of an object. This modifier is best used on a single object; if several objects need a ripple effect, use the Ripple Space Warp. The ripple is applied via a gizmo that you can control. Parameters for this modifier include two Amplitude values, and values for the Wave Length, Phase, and Decay of the ripple. The two amplitude values cause an increase in the height of the ripples opposite one another. Figure 10-17 shows the Ripple modifier applied to a simple Quad Patch with values of 10 for Amplitude 1 and a Wave Length value of 50. The right Quad Patch also has an Amplitude 2 value of 20.

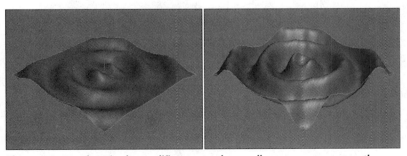

Figure 10-17: The Ripple modifier can make small waves appear over the surface of an object.

Wave modifier

The Wave modifier produces a wave-like effect across the surface of the object. All the parameters of the Wave Parameter are identical to the Ripple modifier parameters. The difference is that the waves produced by the Wave modifier are parallel, and they propagate in a straight line. Figure 10-18 shows the Wave modifier applied to a simple Quad Patch with values of 5 for Amplitude 1 and a Wave Length value of 50. The right Quad Patch also has an Amplitude 2 value of 20.

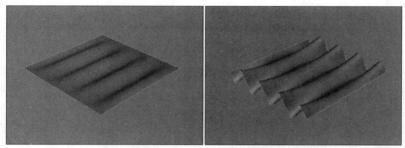

Figure 10-18: The Wave modifier produces parallel waves across the surface of an object.

Skew modifier

The Skew modifier changes the tilt of an object by moving its top portion while keeping the bottom half fixed. Skew parameters include Amount and Direction values, a Skew Axis, and Limits. Figure 10-19 shows the hammer with a Skew value of 2.0, the middle hammer has a Skew value of 5, and the right hammer has an Upper Limit of 8.

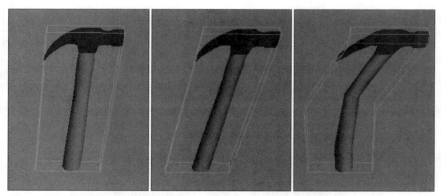

Figure 10-19: You can use the Skew modifier to tilt objects.

Slice modifier

You can use the Slice modifier to divide an object into two separate objects. Applying the Slice modifier creates a Slice gizmo. This gizmo looks like a simple plane and can be transformed and positioned to define the slice location. To transform the gizmo, you need to select it from the Stack hierarchy.

Note You can use the Slice modifier to make objects slowly disappear a layer at a time.

The Slice parameters include four slice type options. Refine Mesh simply adds new vertices and edges where the gizmo intersects the object. The Split Mesh option creates two separate objects. The Remove Top and Remove Bottom options delete all faces and vertices above or below the gizmo intersection plane.

Using Triangular or Polygonal faces, you can also specify whether the faces are divided. Figure 10-20 shows the top and bottom halves of a hammer object. The right hammer is sliced at an angle.

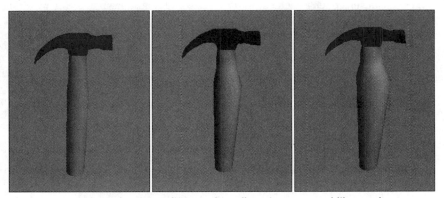

Figure 10-20: The Slice modifier can cut objects into two separate pieces.

Note Editable Meshes also have a Slice tool that can produce similar results. The difference is that the Slice modifier can work on any type of object, not only on meshes.

Spherify modifier

The Spherify modifier distorts an object into a spherical shape. The single Spherify parameter is the percent of the effect to apply. Figure 10-21 shows the hammer with Spherify values of 10, 20, and 30 percent.

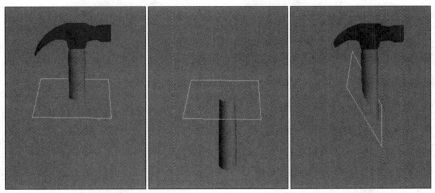

Figure 10-21: The Spherify modifier pushes all vertices outward like a sphere.

Affect Region modifier

The Affect Region modifier can cause a local surface region to bubble up or be indented. Affect Region parameters include Falloff, Pinch, and Bubble values. The Falloff value sets the size of the area that is affected. The Pinch value makes the region tall and thin, and the Bubble value rounds the affected region. You can also select the Ignore Back Facing option. Figure 10-22 shows the Affect Region modifier applied to a Quad Patch with a Falloff value of 80 on the left, and on the right with a Bubble value of 1.0. The height and direction of the region is determined by the position of the modifier gizmo, which is a line connected by two points.

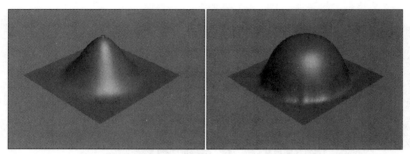

Figure 10-22: The Affect Region modifier can raise or lower the surface region of an object.

Lattice modifier

The Lattice modifier changes an object into a lattice by creating struts where all the edges are located or by replacing each joint with an object. The Lattice modifier considers all edges as struts and all vertices as joints.

The parameters for this modifier include several options to determine how to apply the effect. These options include the Entire Object, to Joint Only, to Struts Only, or Both (Struts and Joints). If the Apply to Entire Object option isn't selected, then the modifier is applied to the current subobject.

For struts, you can specify Radius, Segments, Sides, and Material ID values. You can also specify to Ignore Hidden Edges, to create End Caps, and to Smooth the Struts.

For joints, you can select Tetra, Octa, or Icosa types with Radius, Segments, and Material ID values. There are also controls for Mapping Coordinates.

Note   Although the joints settings enable you to select only one of three different types, you can use the Scatter compound object to place any type of object instead of the three defaults. To do this, apply the Lattice modifier and then select the Distribute Using All Vertices option in the Scatter Objects rollout.

Figure 10-23 shows the effect of the Lattice modifier. The left hammer has only joints applied, the middle hammer has only struts applied, and the right hammer has both applied.

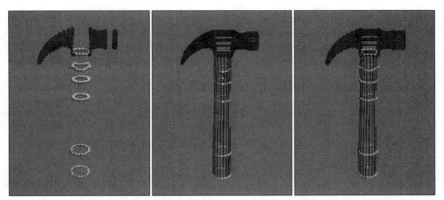

Figure 10-23: The Lattice modifier divides an object into struts, joints, or both.

Mirror modifier

You can use the Mirror modifier to create a mirrored copy of an object or subobject. The Parameters rollout lets you pick a mirror axis or plane and an Offset value. The Copy option creates a copy of the mirrored object and retains the original selection.

> **Cross-Reference** The Displace modifier can alter an object's geometry using a grayscale bitmap image. For more information about this modifier, see Chapter 20, "Using Material Maps."

Displace modifier

The Displace modifier offers two unique sets of features. It can alter an object's geometry by displacing elements using a gizmo or it can change the object's surface using a grayscale bitmap image. The Displace gizmo can have one of four different shapes: Planar, Cylindrical, Spherical, or Shrink Wrap. This gizmo can be placed exterior to an object or inside an object to push it from the inside.

The Displace modifier parameters include Strength and Decay values. You can also specify the dimensions of the gizmo. A cylindrical-shaped gizmo can be capped or uncapped. The alignment parameters let you align the gizmo to the X, Y, or Z axes or you can align it to the current view. The rest of the parameters deal with displacing the surface using a bitmap image. Figure 10-24 shows a Quad Patch with the Plane-shaped gizmo applied with a Strength value of 25. To the right is a Quad Patch with the Sphere-shaped gizmo.

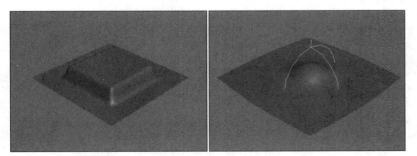

Figure 10-24: You can use the Displace modifier's gizmo as a modeling tool to change the surface of an object.

The Displace modifier can also alter an object's geometry using a grayscale bitmap image. This aspect of the modifier is covered in Chapter 20, "Using Material Maps." In many ways, the Displace gizmo works like the Conform compound object. You can learn about the Conform compound object in Chapter 16, "Building Compound Objects."

XForm modifier

The XForm modifier enables you to apply transforms such as Move, Rotate, and Scale to objects and/or subobjects. This modifier is applied by means of a gizmo that can be transformed using the transform buttons on the main toolbar. The XForm modifier has no parameters.

XForm is short for the word *transform*.

Preserve modifier

The Preserve modifier works to maintain Edge Lengths, Face Angles, and Volume as an object is deformed and edited. Before an object is modified, make an additional copy. Then, edit one of the copies. To apply the Preserve modifier, click the Pick Original button, then click the unmodified object, and finally, click the modified object. The object will be modified to preserve the Edge Lengths, Face Angles, and Volume as defined in the Weight values. This helps prevent the topology of the modified object becoming too irregular.

The Iterations option determines the number of times the process is applied. You can also specify to apply to the Whole Mesh, to Selected Vertices Only, or to an Inverted Selection.

Free Form Deformer modifiers

The Free Form Deformers category of modifiers causes a lattice to appear around an object. This lattice is bound to the object, and you can alter the object's surface by moving the lattice control points. Modifiers include FFD (Free Form Deformation) and FFD (Box/Cyl).

FFD (Free Form Deformation) modifier

The Free Form Deformation modifiers create a lattice of control points around the object. The object's surface can deform the object when you move the control points. The object will only be deformed if the object is within the volume of the FFD lattice. The three different resolutions of FFDs are 2×2, 3×3, and 4×4. The Set Number of Points button enables you to specify the number of points to be included in the FFD lattice.

You can also select to display the lattice or the source volume, or both. If the Lattice option is disabled, only the control points are visible. The Source Volume option shows the original lattice before any vertices were moved.

The two deform options are Only In Volume and All Vertices. The Only In Volume option limits the vertices that can be moved to the interior vertices only. If the All Vertices option is selected, the Falloff value determines the point at which vertices are no longer affected by the FFD. Falloff values can range between 0 and 1. The Tension and Continuity values control how tight the lines of the lattice are when moved.

The three buttons at the bottom of the FFD Parameters rollout help in the selection of control points. If the All X button is selected, then when a single control point is selected, all the adjacent control points along the X-axis are also selected. This feature makes selecting an entire line of control points easier. The All Y and All Z buttons work in a similar manner in the other dimensions.

Use the Reset button to return the volume to its original shape if you make a mistake. The Conform to Shape button sets the offset of the Control Points with Inside Points, Outside Points, and Offset options.

To move the control points, select the Control Points subobject. This enables you to alter the control points individually.

FFD (Box/Cyl) modifier

The FFD (Box) and FFD (Cyl) modifiers can create a box- or cylinder-shaped lattice of control points for deforming objects. Figure 10-25 shows how you can use the FFD modifier to distort the hammer by selecting the Control Point's subobjects. The left hammer is distorted using a 2×2×2 FFD, the middle hammer has a 4×4×4 FFD, and the right hammer is surrounded with an FFD (Cyl) modifier.

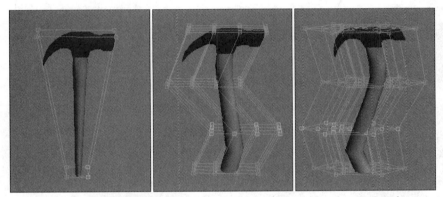

Figure 10-25: The FFD modifier changes the shape of an object by moving the lattice of Control Points that surround it.

The FFD (Box) and FFD (Cyl) lattices are also available as Space Warps. To learn more about Space Warps, see Chapter 26, "Using Space Warps."

Tutorial: Modeling hyperspace deformation

Why is it that whenever a person or object travels through a hyperspace portal, they deform before disappearing? It must have something to do with compressing the molecules. (Anyway, it looks like it hurts. I prefer the *Star Trek* method where you just twinkle and you're gone.) In this tutorial, we'll re-create this hyperspace deformation using an FFD modifier. The object I'm transporting is a television created by Zygote Media. (Perhaps the *Enterprise* crew wants to watch some old episodes.)

To simulate the hyperspace deformation effect, follow these steps:

1. Open the TV – hyperspace deformation.max file from the Chap 10 directory on the CD-ROM.

   This file includes a television object and a set of semi-transparent rings to represent the hyperspace portal.

2. With the television selected, choose Modifiers ➪ Free Form Deformers ➪ FFD 3×3×3 menu option.

A lattice gizmo appears around the television.

3. Click the FFD name in the Modifier Stack and select the Control Points subobject from the hierarchy list. Then select the corner Control Points individually and move them up and outward.

Figure 10-26 shows our television being deformed as it travels through the hyperspace transporter.

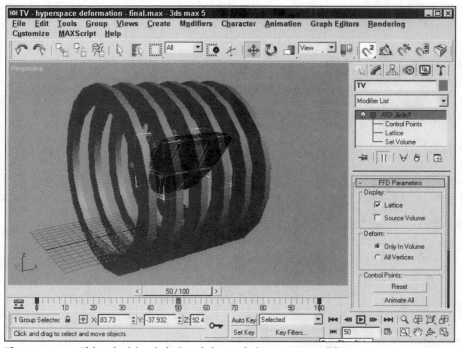

Figure 10-26: This television is being deformed via an FFD modifier.

Point Cache modifier

The Point Cache modifier is the only modifier available for the Cache Tools set. This modifier is uniquely different from the other modifiers and really belongs in its own set.

The Point Cache modifier saves the changes in each vertex to a file. The files are saved using the .pts extension. In the Parameters rollout are settings for specifying the Start and End times and a Record button that opens a File dialog box in which you can specify a filename.

Using Instanced Modifiers

When a single modifier is applied to several objects at the same time, the modifier shows up in the Modifier Stack for each object. These are instanced modifiers that maintain a connection to each other. If you change any of these instanced modifiers, the change is propagated to all other instances. This feature is very helpful for modifying large groups of objects.

When a modifier is copied between different objects, you can select to make the copy an instance.

To see all the objects that are linked to a particular modifier, choose Views ⇨ Show Dependencies. All objects with instanced modifiers that are connected to the current selection appear as bright pink.

At any time, you can break the link between a particular instanced modifier and the rest of the objects using the Make Unique button in the Modifier Stack rollout. After clicking this button, a dialog box appears that asks whether you are sure about this action. Click Yes to complete the action.

Summary

With the modifiers contained in the Modify panel, you can alter objects in a vast number of ways. Modifiers can work with every aspect of an object, including geometric deformations, materials, and general object maintenance. In this chapter, we've taken a look at the Modifier Stack and how modifiers are applied, and examined several useful modifier sets. The topics covered in this chapter included

✦ Working with the Modifier Stack to apply, reorder, and collapse modifiers

✦ Exploring the Select modifiers

✦ Using the Parametric Deformer and FFD modifiers

This chapter concludes Part II, "Working with Objects." You're now ready to learn about the individual modeling object types. In the next chapter, I cover the basics of modeling.

✦　　✦　　✦

Modeling

Modeling Basics

Modeling is the process of pure creation. Whether it is sculpting, building with blocks, construction work, carving, architecture, or advanced injection molding, many different ways exist for creating objects. Max includes many different model types and even more ways to work with these model types.

This chapter gives you the scoop on modeling and introduces you to many utilities and helpers that, well, help as you begin to model objects.

Exploring the Modeling Types

There are many ways to climb a mountain, and there are many ways to model one. You could make a mountain model out of primitive objects like blocks, cubes, and spheres, or you could create one as a polygon mesh. As your experience grows, you'll discover that some objects are easier to model using one method and some are easier using another. Max offers several different modeling types to handle various modeling situations.

Max includes the following modeling types:

+ **Primitives:** Basic parametric shapes such as cubes, spheres, and pyramids.

+ **Shapes and splines:** Simple vector shapes such as circles, stars, arcs and text, and splines such as a Helix. These objects are fully renderable.

+ **Meshes:** Complex models created from many polygon faces that are smoothed together when the object is rendered.

+ **Polys:** Objects composed of polygon faces, similar to mesh objects with unique features.

+ **Patches:** Based on spline curves; patches can be modified using control points.

+ **NURBS:** Stands for Non-Uniform Rational B-Splines. NURBS are similar to loft objects in that they also have control points that can control how a surface spreads over curves.

+ **Compound objects:** A miscellaneous group of modeling types, including objects such as Booleans, loft, and scatter objects. Other compound objects are good at modeling one specialized type of object such as Terrain or Morph objects.

+ **Particle systems:** Systems of small objects that work together as a single group. They are useful for creating effects such as rain, snow, and sparks.

See Chapter 5, "Using Primitive Objects," for more on primitive objects. Shapes and splines are covered in Chapter 12, "Drawing and Using 2D Splines and Shapes," and mesh and poly objects are covered in Chapter 13, "Modeling with Meshes and Polys." Patches are the topic of Chapter 14, "Creating Patches." Chapter 15, "Working with NURBS," covers NURBS objects. I cover compound objects in Chapter 16, "Building Compound Objects" and particle systems in Chapter 17, "Creating and Controlling Particle Systems."

Converting objects

Although the Create panel includes subcategories and buttons to create primitives, shapes and splines, compound objects, and particle systems, you won't find any subcategories for creating mesh, poly, patch, or NURBS objects.

To create one of these object types, you'll need to convert it from another object type. You can convert objects by right-clicking on the object in the viewport and selecting the Convert To submenu from the pop-up quadmenu, or by right-clicking on the object in the Modifier Stack and selecting the object type to convert to in the pop-up menu. Once converted, all the editing features of the selected type will be available in the Modify panel, but the object will no longer be parametric.

Parametric vs. Non-Parametric

All geometric primitives in Max are parametric. *Parametric* means that the geometry of the object is controlled by variables called parameters. Modifying these parameters modifies the geometry of the object. This powerful concept gives parametric objects unlimited flexibility. For example, the sphere object has a parameter called Radius. Changing this parameter changes the size of the sphere.

Non-parametric objects do not have this flexibility. After you've created a non-parametric object, you cannot modify it by changing parameters. The editable objects (Editable Spline, Mesh, Poly, Patch, or NURBS) in Max are non-parametric and don't have parameters; they rely on modifiers or subobject edits to change their geometry.

When a primitive object is converted to a different object type like an Editable Mesh or a NURBS object, it loses its parametric nature and can no longer be changed by altering its parameters. Editable objects do have their advantages, though. You can edit subobjects such as vertices, edges, and faces of meshes — all things that you cannot edit for a parametric object. Each editable object type has a host of functions that are specific to its type. I discuss these functions in the coming chapters.

Several modifiers enable you to edit subobjects while maintaining the parametric nature of an object. These include Edit Patch, Edit Mesh, and Edit Spline.

Working with Subobjects

Most of the editable modeling types offer the ability to work with subobjects. Subobjects are the elements that make up the model and can include vertices, edges, polygons, and elements. These individual subobjects can be selected and transformed just like normal objects using the transformation tools located on the main toolbar. But, before you can transform these subobjects, you'll need to select them. You can only select subobjects when you're in a particular subobject mode.

If you expand the object's hierarchy in the Modifier Stack (by clicking on the small plus sign to the left of the object's name), all subobjects for an object are displayed, as shown in Figure 11-1. Selecting a subobject in the Modifier Stack will place you in subobject mode for that subobject type. You can also enter subobject mode by clicking on the subobject icons located at the top of the Selection rollout or by pressing the 1 through 5 keys on the keyboard. When you're in subobject mode, the subobject title and the icon in the Selection rollout are highlighted yellow. You can only work with the selected subobjects while in subobject mode. To transform the entire object again, you'll need to exit subobject mode, which you can do by clicking either the subobject title, the subobject icon, or by pressing one of the keyboard shortcuts, 1–5.

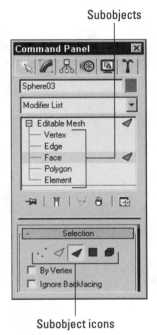

Figure 11-1: Expanding an editable object in the Modifier Stack reveals its subobjects.

Using Soft Selection

When working with mesh, poly, patches, or splines, the Soft Selection rollout, shown in Figure 11-2, becomes available in subobject mode. Soft Selection selects all the subobjects surrounding the current selection and applies transformations to them to a lesser extent. For example, if a face is selected and moved a distance of 2, then with linear Soft Selection, the neighboring faces within the soft selection range will move a distance of 1. The overall effect is a smoother transition.

Soft Selection curve

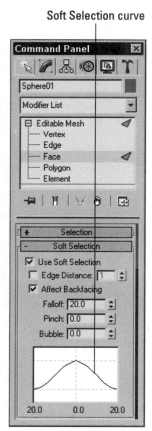

Figure 11-2: The Soft Selection rollout is only available in subobject mode.

The Use Soft Selection parameter enables or disables the Soft Selection feature. The Edge Distance option sets the range (the number of edges from the current selection) that Soft Selection will affect. The Affect Backfacing option applies the Soft Selection to selected subobjects on the backside of an object.

The Soft Selection Curve shows a graphical representation of how the Soft Selection is applied. The Falloff value defines the spherical region where the Soft Selection has an effect. The Pinch button sharpens the point at the top of the curve. The Bubble button has an opposite effect and widens the curve. Figure 11-3 shows several sample values and the resulting curve.

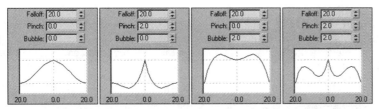

Figure 11-3: The Soft Selection curve is affected by the Falloff, Pinch, and Bubble values.

Tutorial: Soft selecting a heart from a plane

Soft Selection enables a smooth transition between subobjects, but sometimes you'll want the abrupt edge. This tutorial looks at moving some subobject vertices in a plane object with and without soft selection enabled.

To move subobject vertices with and without Soft Selection, follow these steps:

1. Open the Soft Selection heart.max file from the Chap 11 directory on the CD-ROM. This file contains two simple plane objects that have been converted to Editable Meshes. Several vertices in the shape of a heart are selected.

2. The vertices on the first plane object are already selected; in Vertex subobject mode, click the Select and Move button (or press the W key) and move the cursor over the selected vertices and drag upward in the Left viewport away from the plane.

3. Exit subobject mode, select the second plane object, and enter Vertex subobject mode. The same vertices will again be selected. Open the Soft Selection rollout, enable the Use Soft Selection option, and set the Falloff value to 40.

4. Click the Select and Move button (or press the W key) and move the selected vertices upward. Notice the difference that Soft Selection makes.

Figure 11-4 shows the two resulting plane objects with the heart selections.

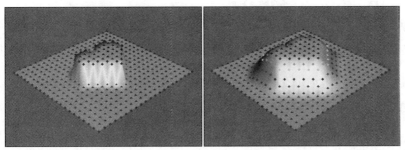

Figure 11-4: Soft Selection makes a smooth transition between the subobjects that are moved and those that are not.

When you select subobjects, they turn red. Non-selected subobjects are blue, and soft selected subobjects are colored a gradient from orange to yellow depending on their distance from the selected subobjects. This visual clue provides valuable feedback on how the Soft Selection will impact the subobjects. Figure 11-5 shows the selected vertices from the previous tutorial with Falloff values of 0, 20, 40, 60, and 80.

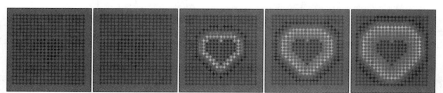

Figure 11-5: A gradient of colors shows the transition zone for soft selected subobjects.

Applying modifiers to subobject selections

Although the last chapter presented modifiers in detail, all the examples applied modifiers to entire objects. But, you can also apply modifiers to subobjects. If the modifier isn't available for subobjects, it will be excluded from the Modifier List or disabled in the Modifiers menu.

If your object isn't an editable object with available subobjects, then you can still apply a modifier using one of the specialized Select modifiers. These modifiers let you select a subobject and apply a modifier to it without having to convert it to a non-parametric object. These Select modifiers include Mesh Select, Poly Select, Patch Select, Spline Select, Volume Select, FFD Select, and NURBS Surface Select. You can find all these modifiers in the Modifiers ⇨ Selection Modifiers submenu.

After you apply a Select modifier to an object, you can select subobjects in the normal manner using the hierarchy in the Modifier Stack or the subobject icons in the Parameters rollout. Any modifiers that you apply after the Select modifier (they will appear above the Select modifier in the Modifier Stack) will affect only the subobject selection.

Tutorial: Building a superman logo

Applying modifiers to a subobject selection is accomplished by passing the subobject selection up the Stack. This means that the Select modifier needs to come below the other modifier in the Modifier Stack. To give you some practice, this example uses the Extrude modifier to build a superman logo.

To apply the Extrude modifier to a subobject selection, follow these steps:

1. Open the Superman logo.max file from the Chap 11 directory on the CD-ROM. This file includes a simple extruded shape with the shape of a letter *S* in it.

2. With the S shape selected, top scoop object selected, choose the Modifiers ⇨ Selection Modifiers ⇨ Spline Select menu command. This command applies the Spline Select modifier to the top cone object.

3. In the Modifier Stack, expand the Spline Select title and select the Spline subobject icon to enter spline subobject selection mode. Click on the S shape to select it.

4. With the spline subobject still selected, choose the Modifiers ⇨ Mesh Editing ⇨ Extrude menu command to apply the Extrude modifier to the subobject selection. In the Parameters rollout, set the Amount to 10.

Figure 11-6 shows the resulting extruded S shape. Now the power of this example is that you can select the Text object in the Modifier Stack and change the letter S to a B (for batman) or an A (for aquaman) and the same modifier is applied to the new letter.

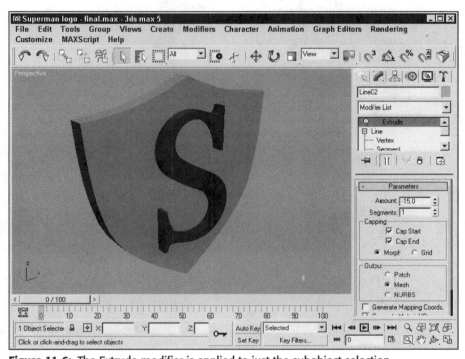

Figure 11-6: The Extrude modifier is applied to just the subobject selection.

Low-Res Modeling

Many 3D games require fast real-time scene updates. For these types of games, low-resolution models are necessary. Another common use of 3D models that is growing quickly is on the Web. The bandwidth for objects on the Web also requires that objects are small and simple. Max includes several tools that aid in developing low-res versions of complex models.

Enabling a polygon count

Another way to count the number of polygons used in a single object is with the Polygon Count feature. This feature can be enabled for the active viewport using the keyboard short-cut, 7. The number of faces is displayed directly under the viewport name in the upper-left corner. Pressing the 7 key again will make this count disappear.

The Polygon Counter utility

For game worlds and models intended for the Web, the polygon count is important when fig-uring out how quickly a scene will load. For example, a model with 2000 polygons will take roughly twice the amount of time to download and display as a model with 1000 polygons.

To accurately determine the number of polygons in a scene, use the Polygon Counter utility. This simple utility, displayed in Figure 11-7, enables you to set a Budget value for the Selected Objects and for All Objects. It also displays the number of polygons and a graph for each. This utility is located in the Utilities panel, and you can open it by clicking the More button and selecting the Polygon Counter utility.

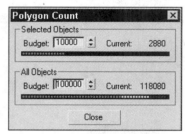

Figure 11-7: The Polygon Counter utility helps you understand how complex an object or scene is.

The Level of Detail utility

As a scene is animated, some objects will be close to the camera and others will be far from it. It doesn't make much sense to render a complex object that is far from the camera. Using the Level of Detail (LOD) utility, you can have Max render a simpler version of a model when it is farther from the camera and a more complex version when it is close to the camera.

Cross-Reference The MultiRes modifier can also create real-time level of detail updates. You can also create characters with low- and high-res versions. I cover both these features in Chapter 32, "Working with Characters."

To open the utility, click the More button in the Utility panel and select the Level of Detail utility. A single rollout is loaded into the Utility panel, as shown in Figure 11-8. To use this utility, you'll need to create several versions of an object and group them together. The Create New Set button will let you pick an object group from the viewports. The objects within the group are individually listed in the rollout pane.

If you select a listed object, you can specify the Thresholds in Pixels or as a percentage of the target image. For each listed item, you can specify a minimum and maximum threshold. The Image Output Size values are used to specify the size of the output image, and the different models that will be used are based on the size of the object in the final image. The Display in Viewpoints option causes the appropriate LOD model to appear in the viewport.

Using the MultiRes Modifier

You can use the MultiRes modifier to create lower resolution versions of a mesh object. This modifier is especially useful for creating real-time updated meshes for the gaming market. Once applied to a mesh object using the Modifier List in the Modify panel, you can set the desired options in the Generation Parameters section of the MultiRes Parameters rollout and click the Generate button to apply the MultiRes solution to the selected object.

Figure 11-8: The Level of Detail utility (split into two parts) can specify how objects are viewed based on given thresholds.

Caution The MultiRes modifier isn't found in any of the Modifiers submenus.

The Vertex Merging option maintains continuity between vertices within the mesh. When enabled, vertices within the Threshold value are welded as the mesh is reduced. The Within Mesh option collapses the boundaries of adjacent elements. The Boundary Metric option looks for boundaries where different materials are applied and tries to maintain these boundaries.

Cross-Reference The MultiRes modifier is similar in function to the Optimize modifier, covered in Chapter 13, "Modeling with Meshs and Polys."

The MultiRes modifier includes a single subobject — Vertex. Using this subobject mode, you can select vertices that you don't wish to change. These selected subobject vertices will not be altered if the Maintain Base Vertices option is enabled. The Crease Angle value can be used to maintain sharp edges. If any of the options are changed, you can update the solution by clicking on the Generation button again.

Once generated, you can use the Vertex Percent and Vertex Count spinners to control the mesh complexity. The viewport will display the updated mesh as you change its complexity. The rollout will display the number of vertices and faces. The Max Vertex and Max Face fields are the number of vertices and faces in the original mesh; the Face Count is the current number of faces.

Tutorial: Creating a MultiRes turtle

You can use the Optimize modifier to quickly create the lower resolution models, but the MultiRes modifier offers more functionality and enables you to dynamically dial down the resolution to exactly what you want. In this example, we use the MultiRes modifier on a turtle model created by Zygote Media.

To create a MultiRes turtle, follow these steps:

1. Open the MultiRes turtle.max file from the Chap 11 directory on the CD-ROM.

   This file contains a simple turtle model.

2. With the cloned turtle selected, choose MultiRes from the Modifier List to apply the modifier to the turtle model.

3. In the MultiRes Parameters rollout, enable the Vertex Merging option and set the Threshold to 0.05. Also enable the Boundary Metric and Multiple Vertex Normals options and set the Crease Angle to 75. Then click the Generate button.

4. Create a copy of the turtle by holding down the Shift key and dragging the turtle to the right. In the Clone Options dialog box that appears, select Copy, name the clone, Turtle – Lo and click OK.

5. With the cloned turtle selected, set the Vert Percent to 15 and notice how the number of faces has dropped from over 13,000 to 2,305.

Figure 11-9 shows the results of the MultiRes modifier. If you look close, you can see that the turtle on the right isn't as smooth in the legs, neck, and nose, but it still looks pretty good.

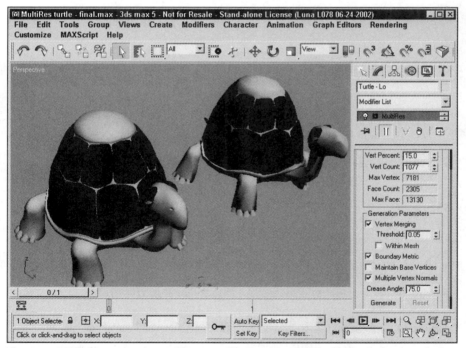

Figure 11-9: You can use the MultiRes modifier to dynamically dial back the complexity of a mesh.

Selecting System Units

One of the first tasks you need to complete before you can begin modeling is to set the system units. The system units have a direct impact on modeling and define the units that are represented by the coordinate values. Units directly relate to parameters entered with the keyboard. For example, with the units set to meters, a sphere created with the radius parameter of 2 would be 4 meters across.

Max supports several different measurement systems, including Metric and U.S. Standard units. You can also define a Custom units system (I suggest parsecs if you're working on a space scene). Working with a units system enables you to work with precision and accuracy using realistic values.

To specify a unit system, choose Customize ⇨ Units Setup to display the Units Setup dialog box, shown in Figure 11-10. For the Metric system, options include Millimeters, Centimeters, Meters, and Kilometers. The U.S. standard units system can be set to the default units of Feet or Inches. You can also select to work with fractional inches or decimal inches from the drop-down list. Fractional values can be divided from 1/1 to 1/100 increments.

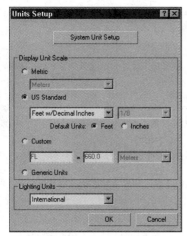

Figure 11-10: The Units Setup dialog box lets you choose which units system to use. Options include Metric, U.S. Standard, Custom, and Generic.

To define a Custom units system, modify the fields under the Custom option, including a units label and its equivalence to known units. The final option is to use the default Generic units. Generic units relate distances to each other, but the numbers themselves are irrelevant. You can also set lighting units to use American or International standards.

New Feature   Lighting units are new to 3ds max 5.

At the top of the Units Setup dialog box is the System Unit Setup button. This button opens the System Unit Scale dialog box, also shown in Figure 11-10. This dialog box enables you to define the measurement system used by Max. Options include Inches, Feet, Miles, Millimeters, Centimeters, Meters, and Kilometers.

There is also a multiplier field that you can use to alter the value of each unit. The Respect System Units in Files toggle presents a dialog box whenever a file with a different system units setting is encountered. If this option is disabled, all new objects will be automatically converted to the current unit system.

The Origin control helps you determine the accuracy of an object as it is moved away from the scene origin. If you know how far objects will be located from the origin, then entering that value will tell you the Resulting Accuracy. You can use this feature to determine the accuracy of your parameters. Objects farther from the origin will have a lower accuracy.

Modeling Helpers

In the Create panel is a category of miscellaneous objects called Helpers (the icon looks like a tape measure). These objects are useful in positioning objects and measuring dimensions. The buttons in the Helper category include Dummy, Point, Protractor, Grid, Tape, and Compass.

Using Dummy and Point objects

The Dummy object is a useful object for controlling complex object hierarchies. This object is a simple cube with a pivot point at its center that doesn't render and has no parameters. It is only used as an object about which to transform objects. For example, you could create a Dummy object that the camera could follow through an animation sequence. Dummy objects will be used in many examples throughout the remainder of the book.

The Point object is very similar to the Dummy object in that it is not rendered either and has only two modifiable parameters. A Point object defines a point in space and is identified by an axis tripod. This tripod and its length are the only parameters that you can alter under the Parameters rollout in the Command Panel. The main purpose for the Point object is to mark positions within the scene.

Caution Point objects are difficult to see and easy to lose. If you use a point object, but sure to name it so it is easy to find in the Select by Name dialog box.

Measuring coordinate distances

The Helpers category also includes several handy utilities for measuring dimensions and directions. These are the Tape, Protractor, and Compass objects. The units are all based on the current selected system units.

Using the Tape helper

You use the Tape object to measure distances. To use it, simply drag the distance that you would like to measure and view the resulting dimension in the Parameters rollout. You can also set the length of the Tape object using the Specify Length option. You can move and reposition the endpoints of the Tape object with the Select and Move button, but the Rotate and Scale buttons have no effect.

Using the Protractor helper

The Protractor object works in a manner similar to the Tape object, but it measures the angle between two objects. To use the Protractor object, click in a viewport to position the Protractor object. (The Protractor object will look like two pyramids aligned point to point and represents the origin of the angle.) Then click the Pick Object 1 button and select an object in the scene. A line will be drawn from the Protractor object to the selected object. Next, click the Pick Object 2 button. The angle-formed objects and the Protractor object will be displayed in the Parameters rollout. The value will change as either of the selected objects or the Protractor is moved.

Note   All measurement values are presented in gray fields within the Parameters rollout. This gray field indicates that the value cannot be modified.

Using the Compass helper

The Compass object identifies North, East, West, and South positions on a planar star-shaped object.

Cross-Reference   The Compass object is mainly used in conjunction with the Sunlight System, which I talk about in Chapter 22, "Working with Lights."

Using the Measure utility

In the Utilities panel is another useful tool for getting the scoop on the current selected object. You can open the Measure utility as a floater dialog box, shown in Figure 11-11. This dialog box displays the object's name along with its Surface Area, Volume, Center of Mass, Length (for shapes), and Dimensions. It also includes an option to Lock the current Selection.

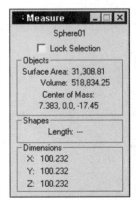

Figure 11-11: The Measure utility dialog box displays some useful information.

Tutorial: Testing the Pythagorean Theorem

I always trusted my teachers in school to tell me the truth, but maybe they were just making it all up, especially my math teacher. (He did have shifty eyes, after all.) For my peace of mind, I would like to test one of the mathematical principles he taught us, the Pythagorean Theorem. (What kind of name is that anyway?)

If I remember the theorem correctly, it says that the sum of squares of the sides of a right triangle equals the sum of the hypotenuse squared. So, according to my calculations, a right triangle with a side of 3 and a side of 4 would have a hypotenuse of 5. Because Max is proficient at drawing shapes such as this one, we'll test the theorem by creating a box with a width of 40 and a height of 30 and then measuring the diagonal.

To test the Pythagorean Theorem, follow these steps:

1. Open the Testing Pythagoras.max file from the Chap 11 directory on the CD-ROM.

   This file includes a simple box with the dimensions: $40 \times 30 \times 10$.

2. Right-click on any of the Snap buttons on the main toolbar to open the Snap and Grid Settings dialog box, select the Snaps panel, and set the Snap feature to snap to vertices by selecting the Vertex option. Close the Grid and Snap Settings dialog box and enable the 3D Snap feature.

3. Open the Create panel and select the Helper category. Click the Tape object.

4. In the viewport, move the cursor over the upper-left corner of the object and click on the blue vertex that appears. Then drag down to the lower-right corner and click the next blue vertex that appears. Note the measurement in the Parameters rollout.

Well, I guess my math teacher didn't lie about this theorem, but I wonder whether he was correct about all those multiplication tables. Figure 11-12 shows the resulting box and measurement value.

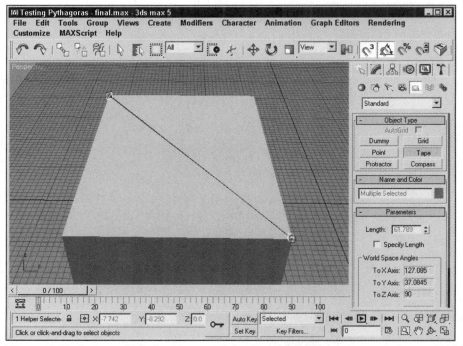

Figure 11-12: I guess old Pythagoras was right. (Good thing I have Max to help me check.)

Summary

Understanding the basics of modeling will help you as you build scenes. In this chapter, you've seen several different object types that are available in Max. Many of these types will have similar features such as Soft Selection and low-res modeling. There are also several helper objects that can assist as well. This chapter covered

✦ Understanding parametric objects and the various modeling types

✦ Using subobjects and soft selections

✦ Working with low-res models

✦ Setting system units

✦ Using Helper objects

Now that you have the basics covered, you're ready to dive into the various modeling types, and the first modeling type on the list is splines and shapes, which I cover next.

✦　　✦　　✦

Drawing and Using 2D Splines and Shapes

✦ ✦ ✦ ✦

In This Chapter

Working with shape primitives

Editing splines and shapes

Using spline modifiers

✦ ✦ ✦ ✦

Many modeling projects start from the ground up, and you can't get much lower to the ground than 2D. But this book is on 3D you say? What place is there for 2D shapes? Within the 3D world, you frequently encounter flat surfaces — the side of a building, the top of a table, a billboard, and so on. All these objects have flat 2D surfaces. Understanding how objects are composed of 2D surfaces will help as you start to build objects in 3D. This chapter examines the 2D elements of 3D objects and covers the tools needed to work with them.

Working in 2D in Max, you'll work with two general objects — splines and shapes. A *spline* is a special type of line that curves according to mathematical principles. In Max, splines are used to create all sorts of shapes such as circles, ellipses, and rectangles.

You can create splines and shapes using the Shapes category on the Create panel, and, just as with the other categories, there are several spline-based shape primitives. Spline shapes can be rendered, but they are normally used to create more advanced 3D geometric objects by extruding or lathing the spline. You can use splines to create animation paths as well as Loft and NURBS objects, and you will find that splines and shapes are used frequently in Max.

Drawing in 2D

Shapes in Max are unique from other objects because they are drawn in 2D, which confines them to a single plane. That plane is defined by the viewport used to create the shape. For example, drawing a shape in the Top view constrains the shape to the XY plane, whereas drawing the shape in the Front view constrains it to the ZX plane. Even shapes drawn in the Perspective view are constrained to a plane such as the Home Grid.

You usually produce 2D shapes in a drawing package like Adobe Illustrator or CorelDRAW. Max supports importing line drawings using the AI format.

 Cross-Reference See Chapter 3, "Working with Files," to learn about importing AI files.

Whereas newly created or imported shapes are 2D and are confined to a single plane, splines can exist in 3D space. The Helix shape, for example, exists in 3D, having height as well as width values. Animation paths in particular need to move into 3D space.

Working with shape primitives

The shape primitives that are displayed in the Object Type rollout of the Create panel when the Shapes category is selected include many basic shapes, including Line, Circle, Arc, NGon (a polygon where you can set the number of sides), Text, Section, Rectangle, Ellipse, Donut, Star, and Helix, as shown in Figure 12-1. Clicking any of these shape buttons lets you create the shape by dragging in one of the viewports. You can also use the Create ➪ Shapes menu to select a shape to create. After a shape is created, several new rollouts appear.

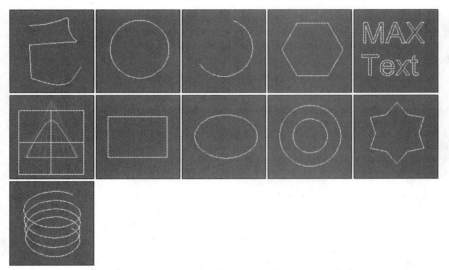

Figure 12-1: These shape primitives in all their 2D glory: Line, Circle, Arc, NGon, Text, Section, Rectangle, Ellipse, Donut, Star, and Helix.

Above the Shape buttons are two check boxes: AutoGrid and Start New Shape. AutoGrid creates a temporary grid, which you can use to align the shape with the surface of the nearest object under the mouse at the time of creation. This feature is helpful for starting a new spline on the surface of an object.

Cross-Reference   I discuss AutoGrid in more detail in Chapter 9, "Transforming Objects."

The Start New Shape option creates a new object with every new shape drawn in a viewport. Leaving this option unchecked lets you create compound shapes, which consist of several shapes used to create one object. Because compound shapes consist of several shapes, you cannot edit them using the Parameters rollout. For example, if you want to write out your name using splines, keep the Start New Shape option unselected to make all the letters part of the same object.

Just as with the Geometric primitives, every shape that is created is given a name and a color. You can change either of these in the Name and Color rollout.

Most of the shape primitives have several common rollouts—Rendering, Interpolation, Creation Method, Keyboard Entry, and Parameters, as shown in Figure 12-2. I cover these rollouts initially and then present the individual shape primitives.

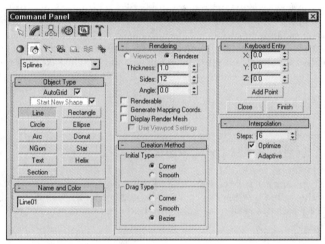

Figure 12-2: These rollouts are common for most of the shape primitives.

Rendering rollout

The Rendering rollout includes options for making a spline a renderable object. Making a spline a renderable object converts the spline into a 3D object that you can view in the viewport or renderer. For renderable objects, you can specify a Thickness, the number of Sides, and the Angle values. The Thickness is the diameter of the renderable spline. The number of Sides sets the number of sides that make up the cross-section of the renderable spline. The lowest value that is possible is 3, which would create a triangle cross-section. The Angle value determines where the corners of the cross-section sides start, so you could set a three-sided spline to have a corner pointing up or an edge.

Note By default, a renderable spline has a 12-sided circle as its cross-section.

The Rendering rollout also includes the Generate Mapping Coordinates option. These coordinates are automatically generated when this option is selected and are used to mark where a material map is placed.

Cross-Reference I talk about mapping coordinates in Chapter 20, "Using Material Maps."

Renderable splines appear as normal splines in the viewport unless the Display Render Mesh option is selected. If this option is selected, the Use Viewport Settings option is enabled, which will let you specify separate Thickness, Sides, and Angle values for the viewport. To view the renderable spline in the viewport, select the Display Render Mesh and Use Viewport Settings options and then click the Viewport radio button.

Interpolation rollout

In the Interpolation rollout, you can define the number of interpolation steps or segments that make up the shape. The Interpolation Steps value determines how many segments to include between vertices. For example, a circle shape with a Steps value of 0 will have only 4 segments and look like a diamond. Increasing the Steps value to 1 will make a circle out of eight segments. For shapes composed of straight lines (like the Rectangle and simple NGons), the Steps value isn't an issue, but for a shape with many sides (like a Circle, Ellipse, or Helix), it can have a big effect. Larger step values result in smoother curves. The Adaptive option automatically sets the number of steps to produce a smooth curve and sets the number of steps for straight segments to 0. The Optimize option attempts to reduce the number of steps to produce a simpler spline by eliminating all the extra vertices and segments associated with the shape.

Note   The Section and Helix shape primitives have no Interpolation rollout.

Creation Method and Keyboard Entry rollouts

Most shape primitives also include Creation Method and Keyboard Entry rollouts (Text, Section, and Star are the exceptions). The Creation Method rollout offers options for specifying different ways to create the spline by dragging in a viewport, such as from edge to edge or from the center out. Table 12-1 lists the various creation method options for each of the shapes.

Table 12-1: Shape Primitive Creation Methods

Primitive Object	Number of Viewport Clicks to Create	Default Creation Method	Other Creation Method
🌀 Line	2 to Infinite	Corner Initial, Bézier Drag	Smooth, Initial, Corner, or Smooth Drag
⬡ Circle	1	Center	Edge
⌒ Arc	2	End-End-Middle	Center-End-End
⬡ NGon	1	Center	Edge
A≋ Text	1	none	none
△ Section	1	none	none
▢ Rectangle	1	Edge	Center
⬡ Ellipse	1	Edge	Center

Primitive Object		Number of Viewport Clicks to Create	Default Creation Method	Other Creation Method
⊚	Donut	2	Center	Edge
✪	Star	2	none	none
⬓	Helix	3	Center	Edge

Some shape primitives such as Star, Text, and Section don't have any creation methods because Max only offers a single way to create these shapes.

The Keyboard Entry rollout offers a way to enter exact position and dimension values. After you enter the values, click the Create button to create the spline or shape in the active viewport. The settings are different for each shape.

The Parameters rollout includes such basic settings for the primitive as Radius, Length, and Width. You can alter these settings immediately after an object is created. However, after you deselect an object, the Parameters rollout moves to the Modify panel, and you must do any alterations to the shape there.

Line

The Line primitive includes several creation method settings, enabling you to create hard, sharp corners or smooth corners. You can set the Initial Type option to either Corner or Smooth to create a sharp or smooth corner for the first point created.

After clicking where the initial point is located, you can add additional points by clicking in the viewport. Dragging while creating a new point can make a point either a Corner, Smooth, or Bézier based on the Drag Type option selected in the Creation Method rollout. The curvature created by the Smooth option is determined by the distance between adjacent vertices, whereas you can control the curvature created by the Bézier option by dragging with the mouse a desired distance after the point is created. Bézier corners have control handles associated with them, enabling you to change their curvature.

Tip   Holding down the Shift key while clicking creates points that are vertically or horizontally in line with the previous point. Holding down the Ctrl key snaps new points at an angle from the last segment, as determined by the Angle Snap setting.

After creating all the points, you exit line mode by clicking the right mouse button. If the last point is on top of the first point, then a dialog box asks whether you want to close the spline. Click Yes to create a closed spline, or No to continue adding points. Even after creating a closed spline, you can add additional points to the current selection to create a compound shape if the Start New Shape option isn't selected. If the first and last points don't correspond, then an open spline will be created.

Figure 12-3 shows several splines created using the various creation method settings. The left spline was created with all the options set to Corner, and the second spline with all the options set to Smooth. The third spline uses the Corner Initial type and shows where dragging has smoothed many of the points. The last spline was created using the Bézier option.

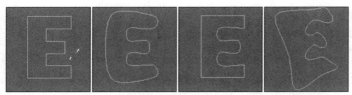

Figure 12-3: The Line shape can create various combinations of shapes with smooth and sharp corners.

In the Keyboard Entry rollout, you can add points by entering their X, Y, and Z dimensions and clicking the Add Point button. You can close the spline at any time by clicking the Close button or keep it open by clicking the Finish button.

Circle

The Circle button creates — you guessed it — circles. The only adjustable parameter in the Parameters rollout is the Radius. All other rollouts are the same, as explained earlier.

Arc

The Arc primitive has two creation methods. Use the End-End-Middle method to create an arc shape by clicking and dragging to specify the two end points and then dragging to complete the shape. Use the Center-End-End method to create an arc shape by clicking and dragging from the center to one of the end points and then dragging the arc length to the second end point.

Other parameters include the Radius and the From and To settings where you can enter the value in degrees for the start and end of the arc. The Pie Slice option connects the end points of the arc to its center to create a pie-sliced shape, as shown in Figure 12-4. The Reverse option lets you reverse the arc's direction.

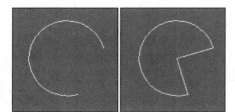

Figure 12-4: Enabling the Pie Slice option connects the arc ends with the center of the circle.

NGon

The NGon shape lets you create regular polygons by specifying the Number of Sides and the Corner Radius. You can also specify whether the NGon is Inscribed or Circumscribed, as shown in Figure 12-5. Inscribed polygons are positioned within a circle that touches all the polygon's vertices. Circumscribed polygons are positioned outside of a circle that touches the midpoint of each polygon edge. The Circular option changes the polygon to a circle that inscribes the polygon.

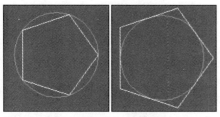

Figure 12-5: An inscribed pentagon and a circumscribed pentagon

Text

You can use the Text primitive to add outlined text to the scene. In the Parameters rollout, you can specify a Font by choosing one from the drop-down list at the top of the Parameters rollout. Under the Font drop-down list are six icons, shown in the following table. The left two icons are for the Italics and Underline styles. Selecting either of these styles applies the style to all the text. The right four icons are for aligning the text to the left, centered, right, or justified.

Icon	Description
I	Italics
U	Underline
≣	Left
≣	Centered
≣	Right
≣	Justified

Note The list of available fonts includes only the Windows TrueType fonts and Type 1 PostScript fonts installed on your system and any extra fonts located in the font path listed in the Configure Paths dialog box.

The size of the text is determined by the Size value. The Kerning (which is the space between adjacent characters) and Leading (which is the space between adjacent lines of text) values can actually be negative. Setting the Kerning value to a large negative number actually displays the text backwards.

There is also a text area where you can type the text to be created. You can cut, copy, and paste text into this text area from an external application. After setting the parameters and typing the text, the text will appear as soon as you click in one of the viewports. The Text will be automatically updated when any of the parameters (including the text) is changed. To turn off automatic updating, select the Manual Update toggle. You can then update with the Update button.

Figure 12-6 shows an example of some text and an example of kerning values in the Max interface.

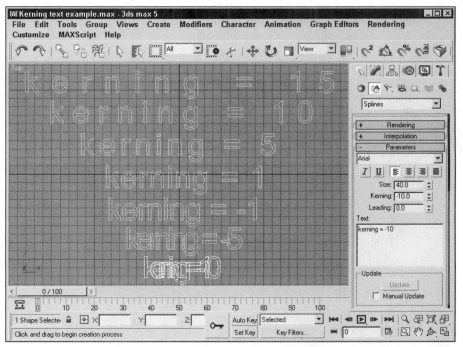

Figure 12-6: The Text shape can create text with several settings such as font, justification, and style.

Section

Section stands for cross-section. The Section shape is a cross-section of the edges of any 3D object that the Section's cutting plane passes through. The process consists of dragging in the viewport to create a cross-sectioning plane. You can then move, rotate, or scale the cross-sectioning plane to obtain the desired cross-section. In the Section Parameters rollout is a Create Shape button. Clicking this button opens a dialog box where you can name the new shape. Additionally, you can use one Section object to create multiple shapes.

Note
You can only make sections from intersecting a 3D object. If the cross-sectioning plane doesn't intersect the 3D object, then it won't create a shape. You cannot use the Section primitive on shapes.

The Parameters rollout includes settings for updating the Section shape. You can update it when the Section plane moves, when the Section is selected, or Manually (using the Update Section button). You can also set the Section Extents to Infinite, Section Boundary, or Off. The Infinite setting creates the cross-section spline as if the cross-sectioning plane were of infinite size, whereas the Section Boundary limits the plane's extents to the boundaries of the visible plane.

To give you an idea of what the Section shape can produce, Figure 12-7 shows the shapes resulting from sectioning two Cone objects, including a circle, an ellipse, a parabola, and a hyperbole. The shapes have been moved to the sides to be more visible.

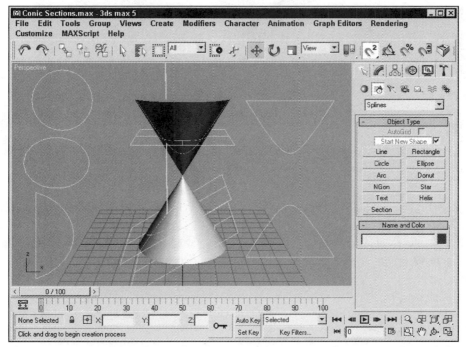

Figure 12-7: You can use the Section shape primitive to create the conic sections (circle, ellipse, parabola, hyperbola) from a set of 3D cones.

Rectangle

The Rectangle shape produces simple rectangles. In the Parameters rollout, you can specify the Length and Width and also a Corner Radius.

Ellipse

Ellipses are simple variations of the Circle shape. You define them by Length and Width values.

Donut

As another variation of the Circle shape, the Donut shape consists of two concentric circles; you can create it by dragging once to specify the outer circle and again to specify the inner circle. The parameters for this object are simply two radii.

Star

The Star shape also includes two radii values — the larger Radius value defines the distance of the outer points of the Star shape from its center, and the smaller Radius value is the distance from the center of the star to the inner points. The Point setting indicates the number of points. This value can range from 3 to 100. The Distortion value causes the inner points to rotate relative to the outer points and can be used to create some interesting new star types. The Fillet Radius 1 and Fillet Radius 2 values adjust the Fillet for the inner and outer points. Figure 12-8 shows a sampling of what is possible with the Star shapes.

Figure 12-8: The Star primitive can be changed to create some amazing shapes.

Helix

A Helix is like a spring coil shape, and it is the one shape of all the Shape primitives that exists in 3D. Helix parameters include two radii for specifying the inner and outer radius. These two values can be equal to create a coil or unequal to create a spiral. Parameters also exist for the Height and number of Turns. The Bias parameter causes the Helix turns to be gathered all together at the top or bottom of the shape. The CW and CCW options let you specify whether the Helix turns clockwise or counterclockwise. Figure 12-9 shows a sampling of Helix shapes: The first Helix has equal radii values, the second one has a smaller second radius, the third Helix spirals to a second radius value of 0, and the last two Helix objects have Bias values of 0.8 and –0.8.

Figure 12-9: The Helix shape can be straight or spiral shaped.

Tutorial: Drawing a company logo

One of the early uses for 3D graphics was to animate corporate logos, and although Max can still do this without any problems, it now has capabilities far beyond those available in the early days. One can even use the Shape tools to help design the logo. In this example, we'll design and create a simple logo using the Shape tools for the fictitious company named "Expeditions South."

To use the Shape tools to design and create a company logo, follow these steps:

1. Start by creating a four-pointed star. Click the Star button and drag in the Top view to create a shape. Change the parameters for this star as follows: Radius1 = 60, Radius2 = 20, and Points = 4.

2. Select and move the star shape to the left side of the viewport.

3. Now, click the Text button. Change the font to Impact and the Size to 50. In the Text area, type Expeditions South and include a line return and several spaces between the two words so they are offset. Click in the Top viewport to place the text.

4. Use the Select and Move button (W) to reposition the text next to the Star shape.

5. Click the Line button and create several short highlighting lines around the bottom point of the star.

The finished logo is now ready to extrude and animate. Figure 12-10 shows the results.

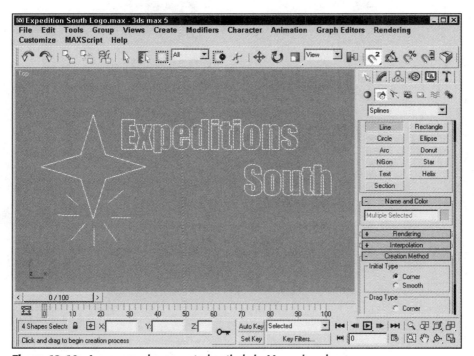

Figure 12-10: A company logo created entirely in Max using shapes

Tutorial: Viewing the interior of a heart

As an example of the Section primitive, let's explore a section of a Heart model. The model was created by Viewpoint Datalabs and is very realistic — so realistic in fact, it could be used to teach medical students the inner workings of the heart.

To create a spline from the cross-section of the heart, follow these steps:

1. Open the Heart Section.max file from the Chap 12 directory on the CD-ROM.

2. Open the Create panel, select the Shapes category, and click the Section button. Drag a plane in the Top viewport that is large enough to cover the heart.

   This plane is your cross-sectioning plane.

3. Select the Select and Rotate button on the main toolbar (or press the E key) and rotate the cross-sectioning plane to cross the heart at the desired angle.

4. In the Parameters rollout, click the Create Shape button and give the new shape the name Heart Section.

5. From the Select by Name dialog box (opened with the H key), select the section by name, separate it from the model, and reposition it to be visible.

Figure 12-11 shows the resulting model and section.

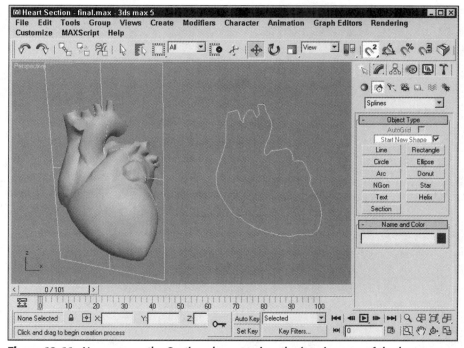

Figure 12-11: You can use the Section shape to view the interior area of the heart.

Editing Splines

After you create a shape primitive, you can edit it by modifying its parameters, but the parameters for shapes are fairly limited. For example, the only parameter for the Circle shape is Radius. All shapes can be converted to Editable Splines or could have the Edit Spline modifier applied to them. Doing either will enable a host of editing features. Before you can use these editing features, you must convert the shape primitive to an Editable Spline (except for the Line shape). You can do so by right-clicking the spline shape and choosing Convert to ⇨ Convert to Editable Spline from the pop-up quadmenu. Another way to enable these features is to apply the Edit Spline modifier.

Editable Splines versus the Edit Spline modifier

After you convert the spline to an Editable Spline, you can edit individual subobjects within the spline, including Vertices, Segments, and Splines. There is a subtle difference in applying the Edit Spline modifier and converting the shape to an Editable Spline. Applying the Edit Spline modifier maintains the shape parameters and enables the editing features found in the Geometry rollout. However, an Editable Spline loses the ability to be able to change the base parameters associated with the spline shape.

Note   When you create an object that contains two or more splines (such as when you create splines with the Start New Shape option disabled), all the splines in the object are automatically converted into Editable Splines.

Another difference is that the shape primitive name will be listed along with the Edit Spline modifier in the Modifier Stack. Selecting the shape primitive name will make the Rendering, Interpolation, and Parameters rollouts visible and the Selection, Soft Selection, and Geometry rollouts are made visible by selecting the Edit Spline modifier in the Modifier Stack. For Editable Splines, only a single name is visible in the Modifier Stack and all rollouts are accessible under it.

Making splines renderable

Splines normally will not show up in a rendered image, but using the Renderable option in the Rendering rollout and assigning a thickness to the splines will make them appear in the rendered image. Figure 12-12 shows a rendered image of the Expeditions South logo after all shapes have been made renderable and assigned a Thickness of 3.0.

Cross-Reference   The settings in the Rendering and Interpolation rollouts are the same as those used for newly created shapes, which were covered earlier in the chapter.

Selecting spline subobjects

When editing splines, you must choose the subobject level to work on. For example, when editing splines, you can work with Vertex (1), Segment (2), or Spline (3) subobjects. Before you can edit spline subobjects, you must select them. To select the subobject type, click the small plus sign icon to the left of the Editable Spline object in the Modifier Stack. This will list all the subobjects available for this object. Click the subobject in the Modifier Stack to select it. Alternatively, you can click the red-colored icons under the Selection rollout, shown in Figure 12-13. When you select a subobject, the selection in the Modifier Stack and the associated icon in the Selection rollout turn yellow.

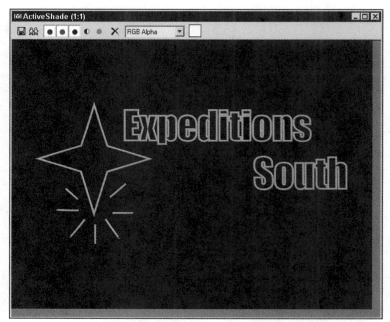

Figure 12-12: Using renderable splines with a Thickness of 3.0, the logo can be rendered.

Note   The Sub-Object button turns yellow when selected to remind you that you are in subobject edit mode. Remember, you must exit this mode before you can select another object.

You can select many subobjects at once by dragging an outline over them in the viewports. You can also select and de-select vertices by holding down the Ctrl key while clicking them. Holding down the Alt key removes any selected vertices from the selection set.

After selecting several vertices, you can create a named selection set by typing a name in the Name Selection Sets drop-down list in the main toolbar. You can then copy and paste these selection sets onto other shapes using the buttons in the Selection rollout. The Lock Handles option causes the angle between the Bézier handles of the selected vertices to be locked and move together. The Alike option will cause all handles on one side to move together. The Area Selection option selects all the vertices within a defined radius.

The Segment End option, when enabled, allows you to select a vertex by clicking the segment. The closest vertex to the segment that you clicked is selected. This feature is useful when you are trying to select a vertex that lies near other vertices. The Select By button opens a dialog box with Segment and Spline buttons on it. These buttons allow you to select all the vertices on either a spline or segment that you choose.

The Selection rollout also has the Show Vertex Numbers option to display all the vertex numbers of a spline or to show the numbers of only the selected vertices. This can be convenient for understanding how a spline is put together and to help you find noncritical vertices.

Vertex subobject mode

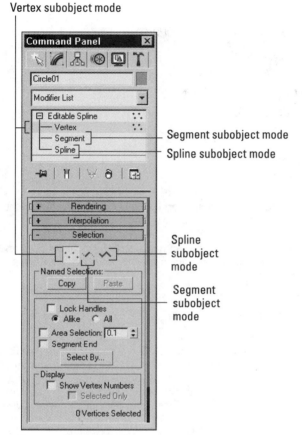

Segment subobject mode

Spline subobject mode

Spline subobject mode

Segment subobject mode

Figure 12-13: The Selection rollout provides icons for entering the various subobject modes.

Figure 12-14 shows a simple star shape that was converted to an Editable Spline. The left image shows the spline in Vertex subobject mode. All the vertices are marked with a small plus signs and the end point is marked with a small square. The middle image has the Show Vertex Numbers option enabled. For the right image, the vertex numbers are shown after the Reverse button was used (in Spline subobject mode).

Spline end point

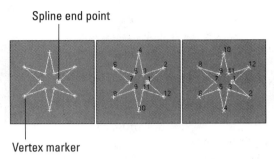

Vertex marker

Figure 12-14: Several spline shapes displayed with vertex numbering turned on.

At the bottom of the Selection rollout, the Selection Information is displayed. This information tells you the number of selected items and whether a spline is closed or not.

 Note The Soft Selection rollout allows you to alter adjacent non-selected subobjects (to a lesser extent) when selected subobjects are moved, creating a smooth transition. See Chapter 11, "Modeling Basics" for the details on this rollout.

Controlling spline geometry

Much of the power of editing splines is contained within the Geometry rollout, shown in Figure 12-15, including the ability to add new splines, attach objects to the spline, weld vertices, use Boolean operations such as Trim and Extend, and many more. Some Geometry buttons may be disabled, depending on the subobject type that you've selected. Many of the features in the Geometry rollout can be used in all subobject modes. Some of these features do not even require that you be in a subobject mode. These features will be covered first.

Create line

While editing splines, you can add new lines to a spline by clicking the Create Line button and then clicking in the one of the viewports. You can add several lines at the same time. Right-click in the viewport to exit this mode. Any new lines will be their own spline, but you can weld them to the existing splines.

Break

Clicking the Break button and then clicking a vertex breaks the segment at that location by creating two separate end points. You can use the Break button in the Geometry rollout to add another vertex along a segment, thereby breaking the segment into two. You can exit Break mode by right-clicking in the viewport or by clicking the Break button again. You can use the Break button in Vertex and Segment subobject modes.

Attach and Attach Mult.

The Attach button lets you attach any existing splines to the currently selected spline. The cursor changes when you're over the top of a spline that can be attached. Clicking an unselected object will make it part of the current object. The Reorient option aligns the coordinate system of the spline being attached with the selected spline's coordinate system.

For example, using the Boolean button requires that objects be part of the same object. You can use the Attach button to attach several splines into the same object.

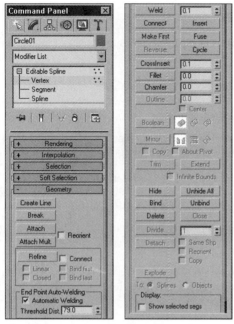

Figure 12-15: For Editable Splines, the Geometry rollout holds most of the features.

The Attach Mult. button enables several splines to be attached at once. When you click the Attach Mult. button, the Attach Multiple dialog box (which looks a lot like the Select by Name dialog box) opens. Use this dialog box to select the objects you want to attach to the current selection. Click the Attach button in the dialog box when you're finished. A right-click in the viewport or another click of the Attach Mult. button exits Attach mode. You can use both the Attach and Attach Mult. buttons in all three subobject modes.

Insert

Insert adds vertices to a selected spline. Click the Insert button, then click the spline to place the new vertex. At this point you can reposition the new vertex and its attached segments — click again to set it in place. A single click adds a Corner type vertex, and a click-and-drag adds a Bézier type vertex.

After positioning the new vertex, you can add another vertex next to the first vertex by dragging the mouse and clicking. To add vertices to a different segment, right-click to release the currently selected segment but stay in Insert mode. To exit Insert mode, right-click in the viewport or click the Insert button to de-select it.

Refine

The Refine button adds vertices to a spline without changing the curvature, giving you more control over the details of the spline. The Connect option makes a new spline out of the added vertices. When the Connect option is enabled, then the Linear, Closed, Bind First, and Bind Last options become enabled. The Linear option creates Corner type vertices resulting in linear segments. The Closed option closes the spline by connecting the first and last vertices. The Bind First and Bind Last options bind the first and last vertices to the center of the selected segment. Refine is only available for Vertex and Segment subobject modes.

Hide/Unhide All

The Hide and Unhide All buttons hide spline subobjects. They can be used in any subobject mode. To hide a subobject, select the subobject and click the Hide button. To Unhide the hidden subobjects, click the Unhide All button.

Delete and Detach

The Delete button deletes the selected subobject. You can use it to delete vertices, segments, or splines. This button is available in all subobject modes.

The Detach button separates the selected subobjects from the rest of the object (opposite of the Attach button). When you click this button, the Detach dialog box opens, enabling you to name the new detached subobject. When segments are detached, you can select the Same Shape option to keep them part of the original object. The Reorient option realigns the new detached subobject to match the position and orientation of the current active grid. The Copy option creates a new copy of the detached subobject.

You can use Detach on either selected Spline or Segment subobjects.

Show Selected Segs

The Show Selected Segs option causes any selected segments to continue to be highlighted in Vertex subobject mode as well as Segment subobject mode. This feature helps you keep track of the segments that you are working on when moving vertices.

Editing vertices

To edit a vertex, click the Vertex subobject in the Modifier Stack or select the vertex icon from the Selection rollout. After the Vertex subobject type is selected, you can use the Select and Move button on the main toolbar to move vertices. Moving a vertex around causes the associated spline segments to follow.

With a vertex selected, you can change its type from Corner, Smooth, Bézier, or Corner Bézier by right-clicking and selecting the type from the pop-up quadmenu. Clicking the Bézier type vertex reveals two green-colored handles on either side of the vertex. Dragging these handles away from the vertex alters the curvature of the segment. Bézier type vertices have both handles in the same line, but Corner Bézier type vertices do not. This allows them to create sharp angles.

Note   Holding down the Shift key while clicking and dragging on a handle causes it to move independently of the other handle, turning it into a Bézier Corner type vertex instead of a plain Bézier. You can use it to create sharp corner points.

Weld and Fuse

When two vertices are selected and are within the specified Weld Threshold, they can be welded into one vertex using the Weld button. Several vertices can be welded simultaneously. Another way to weld vertices is to move one vertex on top of another. If they are within the threshold distance, a dialog box asks whether you want them to be welded. Click the Yes button to weld them. The Fuse button is similar to the Weld command, except it doesn't delete any vertices.

To work with surfaces, you'll typically need a closed spline. By enabling the Automatic Welding option in the End Point Auto-Welding section and specifying a threshold, all end points that are within the threshold value will be welded together, thus making a closed spline.

The End Point Auto-Welding feature is new in 3ds max 5.

In Figure 12-16, the left image shows a star shape with all its lower vertices selected. The middle image is the same star shape after the selected vertices have been welded together, and the right image shows the star shape with the selected vertices fused. The Selection rollout shows five selected vertices for the fused version.

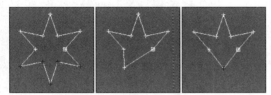

Figure 12-16: Using the Fuse and Weld buttons, several vertices in our star shape have been combined.

You can use the Fuse button to move the selected vertices to a single location. This is accomplished by selecting all the vertices to relocate and clicking the Fuse button. The average point between all the selected vertices becomes the new location. You can combine these vertices into one after they've been fused by clicking the Weld button.

Connect

The Connect button lets you connect end vertices to each other to create a new line. This will only work on end vertices and not on connected points within a spline. To connect the ends, click the Connect button and drag the cursor from one end point to another (the cursor will change to a plus sign when it is over a valid end point) and release. To exit Connect mode, click the Connect button again or right-click anywhere in the viewport. Figure 12-17 shows an incomplete star drawn with the Line primitive, the middle image shows a line being drawn between the end points (notice the cursor), and the third image is the resulting star.

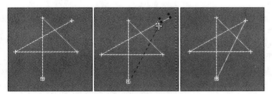

Figure 12-17: You can use the Connect button to connect end points of shapes.

Make First

The Show Vertex Numbers option displays the number of each vertex. The first vertex is identified with a square around it. The Make First button lets you change which vertex you want to be the first vertex in the spline. To do this, select a single vertex and click the Make First button. If more than one vertex is selected, Max will ignore the command. If the selected spline is an open spline, an end point must be selected.

Note   The vertex number is important because it determines the first key for path animations and where Loft objects start.

Cycle

If a single vertex is selected, the Cycle button causes the next vertex in the Vertex Number order to be selected. The Cycle button can be used on open and closed splines and can be repeated around the spline. The exact vertex number is shown at the bottom of the Selection rollout. This is very useful to locate individual vertices in groups that are close together, such as groups that have been fused.

CrossInsert

If two splines that are part of the same object overlap, you can use the CrossInsert button to create a vertex on each spline at the location where they intersect. The distance between the two splines must be closer than the Threshold value for this to work. Note that this button does not join the two splines; it only creates a vertex on each spline. Use the Weld button to join the splines. To exit this mode, right-click in the viewport or click the CrossInsert button again. Figure 12-18 shows how you can use the CrossInsert button to add vertices at the intersection points of two elliptical splines. Notice how each ellipse now has eight vertices.

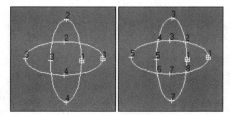

Figure 12-18: The CrossInsert button can add vertices to any overlapping splines of the same object.

Fillet

The Fillet button is used to round the corners of a spline where two edges meet. To use the Fillet command, click the Fillet button and then drag on a corner vertex in the viewport. The more you drag, the larger the Fillet. You can also enter a Fillet value in the Fillet spinner for the vertices that are selected. The Fillet has a maximum value based on the geometry of the spline. To exit Fillet mode, right-click in the viewport or click the Fillet button again. Figure 12-19 shows the Fillet command applied to an eight-pointed star with values of 10, 15, and 20. Notice how each selected vertex has split into two.

Note   You can fillet several vertices at once by selecting them and then clicking the Fillet button and dragging the Fillet distance.

Chamfer

The Chamfer button works much like the Fillet button, except the corners are replaced with straight-line segments instead of smooth curves. This keeps the resulting shape simpler and maintains hard corners. To use the Chamfer command, click the Chamfer button and drag on a vertex to create the Chamfer. You can also enter a Chamfer value in the rollout. To exit Chamfer mode, right-click in the viewport or click the Chamfer button again. Figure 12-20 shows chamfers applied to the same eight-pointed shape with the same values of 10, 15, and 20.

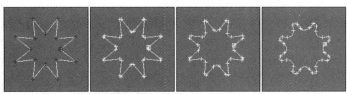

Figure 12-19: The Fillet button can round the corners of a shape.

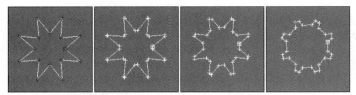

Figure 12-20: Chamfers alter the look of spline corners.

Bind/Unbind

The Bind button attaches an end vertex to a segment. The bound vertex then cannot be moved independently, but only as part of the bound segment. The Unbind button removes the binding on the vertex and lets it move independently once again. To bind a vertex, click the Bind button and then drag from the vertex to the segment to bind to. To exit Bind mode, right-click in the viewport or click the Bind button again.

For Figure 12-21, a circle shape is created and converted to an Editable Spline object. The right vertex is selected and then separated from the circle with the Break button. Then by clicking the Bind button and dragging the vertex to the opposite line segment, the vertex is bound to the segment. Any movement of the spline keeps this vertex bound to the segment.

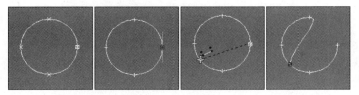

Figure 12-21: The Bind button attached one end of the circle shape to a segment.

Tutorial: Making a ninja star

If you're involved with fighting games, either creating or playing them, then chances are that when you look at the Star primitive, you think, "wow, this is perfect for creating a ninja star weapon." If not, then just pretend.

To create a ninja star using splines, follow these steps:

1. Open the Ninja star.max file from the Chap 12 directory on the CD-ROM. This file includes a ten-pointed star shape with a circle in its center. Both of these shapes have already been converted to Editable Splines.

2. Select the circle shape, click the Modify tab in the Command Panel and click the Vertex icon in the Selection rollout (or press 1) to enter Vertex subobject mode.

3. Click the Create Line button in the Geometry rollout, then click the circle's top vertex and the circle's bottom vertex, then right-click to end the line and right-click again to exit Create Line mode.

4. Select the top vertex of the line that you just created (be careful not to select the circle's top vertex; you can use the Cycle button to find the correct vertex). Right-click the vertex and select the Bézier vertex type from the quadmenu. Then drag its lower handle until it is on top of the circle's left vertex. Repeat this step for the bottom vertex and drag its handle to the circle's right vertex to create a ying-yang symbol in the center of the ninja star.

5. While holding down the Ctrl key, click on all the inner vertices of the star shape. Click the Chamfer button and enter the value of **15** in the Chamfer field and press the Enter key.

Figure 12-22 shows the resulting ninja star.

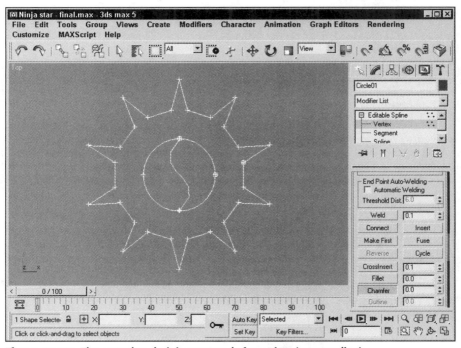

Figure 12-22: The completed ninja star, ready for action (or extruding)

Editing segments

To edit a segment, click the Segment subobject in the Modifier Stack or select the segment icon from the Selection rollout to enter segment subobject mode. Clicking again on either will exit this mode. Segments are the lines or edges that run between two vertices. Many of the editing options work in the same way as when editing Vertex subobjects. You can select multiple segments by holding down the Ctrl key while clicking the segments, or you can hold down the Alt key to remove selected segments from the selection set. You can also copy segments when they're being transformed by holding down the Shift key. The cloned segments break away from the original spline while still remaining attached to it.

You can change segments from straight lines to curves by right-clicking the segment and selecting Line or Curve from the pop-up quadmenu. Line segments created with the Corner type vertex option cannot be changed to Curves, but lines created with Smooth and Bézier type vertex options can be switched back and forth.

Several Geometry rollout buttons work on more than one subobject type.

When you select a segment, the Divide button becomes active. This button adds the number of vertices specified to the selected segment or segments. Figure 12-23 shows the diamond shape (second row, second from right) after all four segments were selected, a value of 1 was entered into the spinner, and the Divide button was clicked.

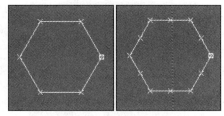

Figure 12-23: The Divide button adds segments to the spline.

Editing Spline subobjects

To edit a spline, click Spline subobject in the Modifier Stack or select the spline icon from the Selection rollout. Transforming a spline object containing only one spline works the same way in subobject mode as it does in a normal transformation. Working in spline subobject mode on a spline object containing several splines lets you transform individual splines. Right-clicking a spline in subobject mode opens a pop-up quadmenu that lets you convert it between Curve and Line types. The Curve type option changes all vertices to Bézier type, and the Line type option makes all vertices Corner type. Spline subobject mode includes many of the buttons previously discussed as well as some new ones in the Geometry rollout.

Reverse

The Reverse button is only available for Spline subobjects. It reverses the order of the vertex numbers. For example, a circle that is numbered clockwise from 1 to 4 would be numbered counterclockwise after using the Reverse button. The vertex order is important for splines that are used for animation paths or loft compound objects.

Outline

The Outline button creates a spline identical to the one selected, and that is offset based upon an amount specified by dragging or specified in the Offset value. The Center option creates an outline on either side of the selected spline, centered on the original spline. When the Center option is not selected, then an outline is created by offsetting a duplicate of the spline on only one side of the original spline. To exit Outline mode, click the Outline button again or right-click in the viewport. Figure 12-24 shows an arc that has had the Outline feature applied. The right image is with the Center option enabled.

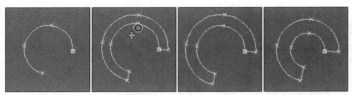

Figure 12-24: The Outline button creates a duplicate copy of the original spline and offsets it.

Boolean

Boolean operations work with two or more splines that overlap one another. There are three different operations that can happen—you could combine the splines to create a single spline (union), you could subtract the overlapping area from one of the splines (subtract), or you could throw away everything except the overlapping area (intersection).

Cross-Reference   You can also use Booleans to combine or subtract 3D volumes, which are covered in Chapter 16, "Building Compound Objects."

The Boolean button works on overlapping closed splines and has three different options: Union, Subtraction, and Intersection, shown in the following table. The splines must all be part of the same object. The Union option combines the areas of both splines, the Subtraction option removes the second spline's area from the first, and the Intersection option only keeps the areas that overlap.

Button	Description
⧉	Union
⧉	Subtraction
⧉	Intersection

To use the Boolean feature, select one of the splines and select one of the Boolean operation options. Then click the Boolean button and select the second spline. Depending on which Boolean operation you chose, the overlapping area will be deleted, the second spline will act to cut away the overlapping area on the first, or only the overlapping area will remain. To exit Boolean mode, right-click in the viewport.

Note   Boolean operations can only be performed on closed splines.

Figure 12-25 shows the results of applying the Spline Boolean operators on a circle and star shape. The second image is the Union feature, the third (circle selected first) and fourth (star selected first) are the Subtraction feature, and the fifth image is the Intersection feature.

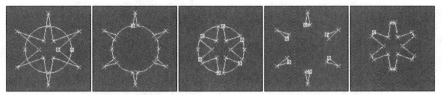

Figure 12-25: Using the Boolean operations on two overlapping shapes

Mirror

You can use the Mirror button to mirror a spline object horizontally, vertically, or along both axes. To use this feature, select a spline object to mirror, then locate the Mirror button. To the right of the Mirror button are three smaller buttons, each of which indicates a direction: Mirror Horizontally, Mirror Vertically, and Mirror Both, shown in the following table. Select a direction and then click the Mirror button. If the Copy option is selected, a new spline is created and mirrored. The About Pivot option causes the mirroring to be completed about the pivot point axes.

Button	Description
	Mirror Horizontally
	Mirror Vertically
	Mirror Both

Figure 12-26 shows a little pacman critter that has been mirrored horizontally, vertically, and both. The right image was horizontally mirrored with the About Pivot option disabled. Notice how the eye spline was mirrored about its own pivot.

Figure 12-26: Mirroring a shape is as simple as selecting a direction and clicking the Mirror button.

Trim and Extend

The Trim button cuts off any extending portion between two overlapping splines. The splines must be part of the same object. To use the Trim feature, select the spline that you want to keep and click the Trim button, then click the segment to trim. The spline you click will be trimmed back to the nearest intersecting point of the selected object. To exit Trim mode, right-click in the viewport or click the Trim button again. This button only works in Spline subobject mode.

Figure 12-27 shows a circle intersected by two ellipse shapes. The Trim button was used to cut the center sections of the ellipse shapes away.

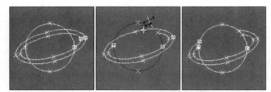

Figure 12-27: You can use the Trim button to cut away the excess of a spline.

The Extend button works in the reverse manner compared to the Trim button. The Extend button lengthens the end of a spline until it encounters an intersection. (There must be a spline segment to intersect.) To use the Extend command, click the Extend button, then click the segment to extend. The spline you click will be extended. To exit Extend mode, right-click in the viewport or click the Extend button again.

The Infinite Bounds option works for both the Trim and Extend buttons. When enabled, it treats all open splines as if they were infinite for the purpose of locating an intersecting point.

Close

The Close button completes an open spline and creates a closed spline by attaching a segment between the first and last vertices. You can check which vertex is first by enabling the Show Vertex Numbers in the Selection rollout. This is similar to the Connect feature (accessible in Vertex subobject mode), but the Connect feature can connect the end point of one spline to the end point of another as long as they are part of the same Editable Spline object. The Close feature will only work in Spline subobject mode and will only connect the end points of each given spline.

Explode

The Explode button performs the Detach command on all subobject splines at once. It separates each segment into a separate spline.

Cross-Reference   The final rollout available for Editable Splines is the Surface Properties rollout. This rollout lets you assign a Material ID to a spline. You can find information on Material IDs in Chapter 19, "Creating and Applying Materials."

Tutorial: Spinning a spider's web

Now that you're familiar with the many aspects of editing splines, let's try to mimic one of the best spline producers in the world — the spider. The spider is an expert at connecting lines together to create an intricate pattern. (Luckily, unlike the spider who depends on its web for food, we won't go hungry if this example fails.)

To create a spider web from splines, follow these steps:

1. Open the Spider web.max file from the Chap 12 directory on the CD-ROM. This file includes a circle shape that represents the edges of the web (we'll pretend that the spider is building this web inside a tire swing). The circle shape has already been converted to an Editable Spline.

2. Open the Modify panel and select the Spline subobject in the Modifier Stack (or press the 3 key) to enter Spline subobject mode.

3. Click the Create Line button in the Geometry rollout and click in the center of the circle and again outside the circle to create a line. Then right-click to end the line. Repeat this step until there are 12 or so radial lines that extend from the center of the circle outward.

4. While you're still in Create Line mode, click on the circle's center and in a spiral pattern create lines by clicking on each radial line that you intersect. Right-click to end the line when you finally reach the edge of the circle. Then right-click again to exit Create Line mode.

5. Select the circle shape and click the Trim button. Then click on each line segment on the portion that extends beyond the circle. This will trim the radial lines to the edge of the circle.

6. Change to Vertex subobject mode by clicking Vertex in the Modifier Stack (or by pressing 1). Then select all the vertices in the center of the circle and click the Fuse and Weld buttons.

Figure 12-28 shows the finished spider web. (I have a new respect for spiders.)

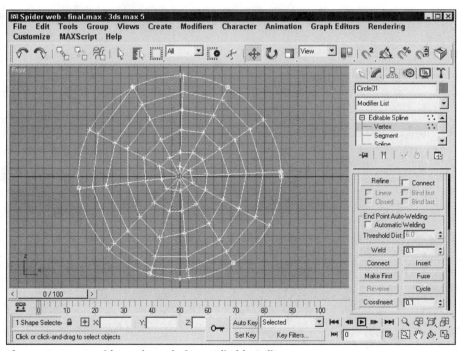

Figure 12-28: A spider web made from Editable Splines

Using Spline Modifiers

Modifiers are used to change the geometry of objects, but they can also be used on splines. In fact, there are several modifiers that can only be used on splines. You can find these modifiers in the Modifiers ⇨ Patch/Spline Editing menu.

Spline-specific modifiers

Of the modifiers that work only on splines, several of these duplicate functionality that is available for Editable Splines, such as the Fillet/Chamfer modifier. Applying these features as modifiers gives you better control over the results because you can remove them using the Modifier Stack at any time.

Edit Spline modifier

The Edit Spline modifier (mentioned at the start of the chapter) makes spline objects so they can be edited. It has all the same features as the Editable Spline object. The Edit Spline modifier isn't really a modifier, but an Object type. It shows up in the Modifier Stack above the base object. The key benefit of the Edit Spline modifier is that it enables you to edit spline subobjects while maintaining the parametric nature of the primitive object.

Spline Select modifier

This modifier enables you to select spline subobjects, including Vertex, Segment, and Spline. You can copy and paste named selection sets. The selection can then be passed up the Stack to the next modifier. The Spline Select modifier provides a way to apply a modifier to a subobject selection.

Delete Spline modifier

You can use the Delete Spline modifier to delete spline subobjects. Another good use of this modifier is to hide splines that are used for other purposes. For example, when creating an animation path, you could apply this modifier to the path to hide it, but by removing this modifier, you can get back to the base spline at any time.

Normalize Spline modifier

The Normalize Spline modifier adds new points to the spline. These points will be spaced regularly based on the Segment Length value. This provides a quick way to optimize a spline. Figure 12-29 shows a simple flower shape with the Spline Select modifier applied so you can see the vertices. The Normalize Spline modifier was then applied with Segment Length values of 1, 5, 10, and 15. Notice how the shape is changing with less vertices.

Figure 12-29: The Normalize Spline modifier relaxes the shape by removing vertices.

Fillet/Chamfer modifier

You can use the Fillet/Chamfer modifier to Fillet or Chamfer the corners of shapes. Fillets create a smooth corner, and a Chamfer adds another segment where two edges meet.

Parameters include the Fillet Radius and the Chamfer Distance. Both include an Apply button. The results of this modifier are the same as if you were to use the Fillet or Chamfer features of an Editable Spline.

Trim/Extend modifier

The Trim/Extend modifier lets you trim the extending end of a spline or extend a spline until it meets another spline at a vertex. The Pick Locations button turns on Pick mode, where the cursor changes when it is over a valid point. Operations include Auto, Trim Only, and Extend Only with an option to compute Infinite Boundaries. You can also set the Intersection Projection to View, Construction Plane, or None.

Using the Shape Check utility

The Shape Check utility is helpful in verifying that a shape doesn't intersect itself. Shapes that have this problem cannot be extruded, lofted, or lathed without problems. To use this utility, open the Utilities panel (the icon for the Utilities panel looks like a hammer) and click the More button. Select Shape Check from the Utilities dialog box list and click OK.

The Shape Check rollout includes only two buttons: Pick Object and Close. Click the Pick Object button and click the shape you want to check. Any intersection points will be displayed as red squares, as shown in Figure 12-30, and the response field will display "Shape Self-Intersects." If the shape doesn't have any intersections, then the response field reports, "Shape OK."

Note   You can use the Shape Check utility on normal splines and on NURBS splines.

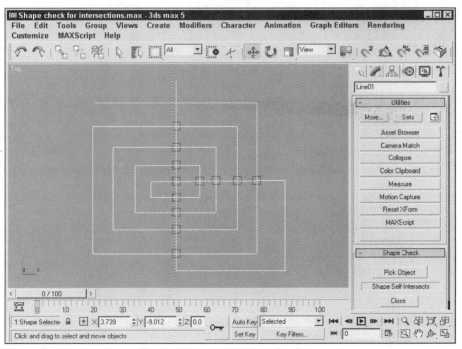

Figure 12-30: The Shape Check utility can identify spline intersections.

Moving Splines to 3D

Although splines can be rendered, the real benefit of splines in Max is to use them to create 3D objects and for animation paths. There are several ways to use splines as you model 3D objects including Loft objects and modifiers. One way to use splines to make 3D objects is with modifiers.

Using splines to create an animation path is covered in Chapter 24, "Animation Basics," and Loft objects are covered in Chapter 16, "Building Compound Objects." General information on working with modifiers is covered in Chapter 10, "Using Modifiers."

Extruding splines

Because splines are drawn in a 2D plane, they already include two of the three dimensions. By adding a Height value to the shape, we can create a simple 3D object. The process of adding Height to a shape is called extruding.

To extrude a shape, you'll need to apply the Extrude modifier. To do so, select a spline object and choose Modifiers ⇨ Mesh Editing ⇨ Extrude, or select the Extrude modifier from the Modifier Stack drop-down list. In the Parameters rollout, you can specify an Amount, which is the height value of the extrusion; the number of Segments; and the Capping options (caps fill in the surface at each end of the Extruded shape). You can also specify the final Output to be a Patch, Mesh, or NURBS object. Figure 12-31 shows our capital Es that modeled the various vertex types extruded to a depth of 10.0.

Figure 12-31: Extruding simple shapes adds depth to the spline.

Tutorial: Routing a custom shelf

In Woodshop 101, you use a router to add a designer edge to doorframes, window frames, and shelving of all sorts. In Woodshop 3D, the Boolean tools will work nicely as we customize a bookshelf.

To create a custom bookshelf using spline Boolean operations, follow these steps:

1. Open the Bookshelf.max file from the Chap 12 directory on the CD-ROM. This file includes a triangle shape drawn with the Line primitive that is overlapped by three circles. All these shapes have been converted to Editable Splines.

2. With the triangle shape selected, open the Modify panel and select the Spline subobject mode (or press the 3 key).

3. Select the Subtraction Boolean operation (the middle icon) in the Geometry rollout and click the Boolean button. Then select each of the circles.

4. Click the Subtraction button next to the Boolean button (it's the middle one). Then select the triangle shape and click the Boolean button. Right-click in the viewport to exit Boolean mode and click Spline in the Modifier Stack again to exit subobject mode.

5. Back in the Modify panel, select the Extrude modifier from the Modifier drop-down list and enter an Amount of **1000**. Select Zoom Extents All to resize your viewports and view your bookshelf.

Figure 12-32 shows the finished bookshelf in the Perspective viewport ready to hang on the wall.

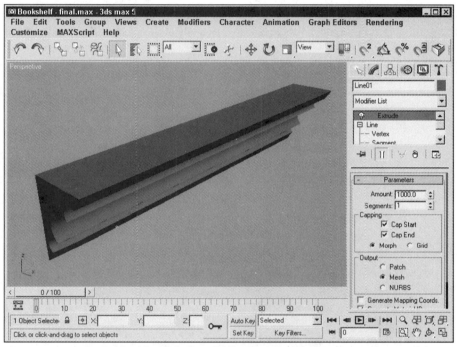

Figure 12-32: The finished bookshelf created with spline Boolean operations and the Extrude modifier.

Lathing splines

Another useful modifier for 2D splines is the Lathe. This modifier rotates the spline about an axis to create an object with a circular cross-section (such as a baseball bat). In the Parameters rollout, you can specify the Degrees to rotate (a value of 360 will make a full rotation) and Cappings, which add ends to the resulting mesh. Additional options include Weld Core, which causes all vertices at the center of the lathe to be welded together, and Flip Normals, which realigns all the normals.

The Direction option determines the axis about which the rotation takes place. The rotation will take place about the object's pivot point.

Caution   If your shape is created in the Top view, then lathing about the screen Z-axis will produce a thin disc without any depth.

Tutorial: Lathing a crucible

As an example of the Lathe modifier, we'll create a simple crucible, although we could produce any object that has a circular cross-section. A crucible is a thick porcelain cup used to melt chemicals. I chose this as an example because it is simple (and saying "crucible" sounds much more scientific than "cup").

To create a crucible using the Lathe modifier, follow these steps:

1. Open the Crucible.max file from the Chap 12 directory on the CD-ROM. This file includes a rough profile cross-section line of the crucible that has been converted to an Editable Spline.

2. Select the line and select Modifiers ➪ Patch/Spline Editing ➪ Lathe menu command. Set the Degrees value in the Parameters rollout to 360. Because you'll lathe a full revolution, you don't need to check the Cap options. In the Direction section, select the Y button (the Y-axis), and you're done.

Figure 12-33 shows the finished product. You can easily make this into a coffee mug by adding a handle. To make a handle, simply loft an ellipse along a curved path.

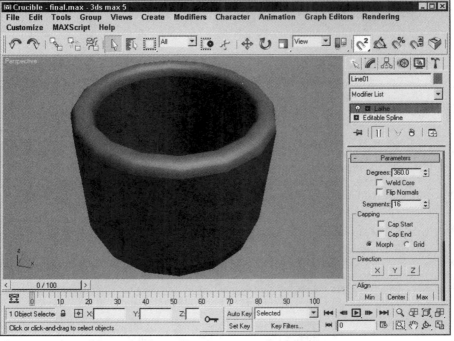

Figure 12-33: Lathing a simple profile can create a circular object.

CrossSection modifier

The CrossSection modifier is one of two modifiers that collectively are referred to as the surface tools. The surface tools provide a way to cover a series of connected cross-sections with a surface. It connects the vertices of several cross-sectional splines together with additional splines in preparation for the Surface modifier. These cross-sectional splines can have different numbers of vertices. Parameters include different spline types such as Linear, Smooth, Bézier, and Bézier Corner.

 Cross-Reference The second half of the surface tools is the Surface modifier. You can find this modifier and an example in Chapter 14, "Creating Patches." The surface tools are similar in many ways to the Loft compound object, which I cover in Chapter 16, "Building Compound Objects."

Summary

As this chapter has shown, there is much more to splines than just points, lines, and control handles. Splines in Max are one of the fundamental building blocks and the pathway to advanced modeling skills using NURBS.

This chapter covered the following spline topics:

✦ Understanding the various shape primitives

✦ Editing splines

✦ Working with the various spline subobjects

✦ Applying modifiers to splines

The next chapter continues our voyage down the modeling pathway with perhaps the most common modeling types — meshes and polys.

✦   ✦   ✦

Working with Meshes and Polys

Meshes, or — more specifically — polygon meshes, are perhaps the most popular and the default model type for most 3D programs. You create them by placing polygonal faces next to one another so the edges are joined. The polygons can then be smoothed from face to face during the rendering process. Using meshes, you can create almost any 3D object including simple primitives such as a cube converted to a mesh or a realistic dinosaur.

Meshes have a lot of advantages. They are common, intuitive to work with, and supported by a large number of 3D software packages. In this chapter, you'll learn how to create and edit mesh and poly objects, and you'll also get experience using some mesh object modifiers.

Creating Editable Mesh and Poly Objects

There is no method in the Create panel for making mesh objects — mesh objects need to be converted from another object type or produced as the result of a modifier. Object types that you can convert include shapes, primitives, Booleans, patches, and NURBS. Many models that are imported will appear as mesh objects. Most 3D formats, including 3DS and DXF, import as mesh objects.

Note   You can even convert spline shapes to editable meshes, whether they are open or closed. Closed splines are filled with a polygon, whereas open splines are only a single edge and can be hard to see.

Before you can use many of the mesh editing functions discussed in this chapter, you'll need to convert the object to an Editable Mesh or an Editable Poly object, collapse an object with modifiers applied, or apply the Edit Mesh modifier.

Converting objects

To convert an object into an Editable Mesh or an Editable Poly object, right-click on the object and choose Convert To ⇨ Convert to Editable Mesh or Convert to Editable Poly from the pop-up quadmenu. You can also convert an object by right-clicking on the object within the Modifier Stack and selecting one of the convert options from the pop-up menu.

Collapsing to a mesh object

When an object is collapsed, it loses its parametric nature and the parameters associated with any applied modifiers. Only objects that have had modifiers applied to them can be collapsed. Objects are made into an Editable Mesh object when you use the Collapse To option available from the right-click pop-up menu in the Modifier Stack or when you use the Collapse utility.

Most objects will collapse to an Editable Mesh object, but objects with the Select Poly modifier applied will collapse to an Editable Poly object.

Applying the Edit Mesh modifier

Another way to enable the mesh editing features is to apply the Edit Mesh modifier to an object. You apply this modifier by selecting the object and choosing Modifiers ➪ Mesh Editing ➪ Edit Mesh, or selecting Edit Mesh from the Modifier drop-down list in the Modify panel.

The Edit Mesh modifier is different from the Editable Mesh object in that as an applied modifier, it maintains the parametric nature of the original object. For example, you cannot change the Radius value of a sphere object that has been converted to an Editable Mesh, but you could if the Edit Mesh modifier were applied.

Note   There is no Edit Poly modifier.

Editable Mesh verses Editable Poly objects

Editable Mesh objects split all polygons up into triangular faces, but the Editable Poly object maintains four-sided polygon faces. Another key difference is found in the subobjects. Editable Meshes can work with Vertex, Edge, Face, Polygon, and Element subobjects; and Editable Poly objects can work with Vertex, Edge, Border, Polygon, and Element subobjects.

The majority of features are the same for both Editable Mesh and Editable Poly objects, but some features are only available for one of these. These differences will be pointed out in the sections to follow.

New Feature   Most of the new modeling enhancements found in 3ds max 5 are found in the Editable Poly objects. For serious modelers, Editable Polys is clearly the preferred modeling type.

Editing Mesh Objects

After an object has been converted to an Editable Mesh or an Editable Poly, you can alter its shape by applying modifiers, or you can work with the mesh subobjects. In the Modify panel are many tools for controlling meshes and working with their individual subobjects.

Note   Open spline objects that have been converted to an Editable Mesh have only the Vertex subobject mode available because they don't have any edges or faces.

Editable Mesh subobjects modes

Before you can edit Mesh subobjects, you must select them. To select a Subobject mode, select Editable Mesh in the Modifier Stack and click the small plus sign to its left to display a hierarchy of subobjects, then click the subobject type that you want to work with. Another way to select a subobject type is to click on the appropriate subobject button in the Selection rollout. The subobject button in the Selection rollout and the subobject listed in the Modifier Stack both turn bright yellow when selected. You can also type a number 1–5 to enter subobject mode with 1 for Vertex and 5 for Element.

To exit subobject edit mode, click the subobject button (displayed in yellow) again. Remember, you must exit this mode before you can select another object.

Note   Selected subobject edges appear in the viewports in red to distinguish them from edges of the selected object, which appear white when displayed as wireframes.

After you're in a subobject mode, you can click an object (or drag over an area to select multiple subobjects) to select it and edit the subobject using the transformation buttons on the main toolbar. You can transform subobjects just like other objects.

Cross-Reference   For more information on transforming objects, see Chapter 9, "Transforming Objects."

You can select multiple subobjects at the same time by dragging an outline over them. You can also select multiple subobjects by holding down the Ctrl key while clicking them. The Ctrl key can also de-select selected subobjects while maintaining the rest of the selection. Holding down the Alt key removes any selected vertices from the current selection set.

With the Select and Move button selected, hold down the Shift key while clicking and dragging on a subobject to clone it. During cloning, the Clone Part of Mesh dialog box appears that enables you to Clone to Object or Clone to Element. Using the Clone to Object option makes the selection an entirely new object, and you will be able to give the new object a name. If the Clone to Element option is selected, the clone remains part of the existing object but will be a new element within that object.

Selection rollout

The Selection rollout includes options for selecting subobjects. The By Vertex option is available in all but the Vertex subobject mode. It requires that you click a vertex in order to select an edge, face, polygon, or element. It selects all edges and faces that are connected to a vertex when the vertex is selected. The Ignore Backfacing option selects only those subobjects with normals pointing toward the current viewport. For example, if you are trying to select some faces on a sphere, only the faces on the side closest to you will be selected. If this option is off, then faces on both sides of the sphere are selected. This option is helpful if many subobjects are on top of one another in the viewport.

The Ignore Visible Edges option is only active in Polygon subobject mode. This button enables you to select all the polygons within a plane, as determined by the Planar Threshold value. If the Ignore Visible Edges option is not selected, the selection is limited to the edges of the polygon that is clicked. For example, if you click a sphere toward one end with a Planar Threshold of 10, all the polygons within a single ring around the sphere will be selected.

In all subobject modes except for Edge, you can select to Show Normals and set a Scale value. Normals are vectors that extend outward perpendicular to the surface of an object. Using this option, you can determine which way a subobject is facing, which could affect how the object is smoothed. Figure 13-1 shows a sphere object that has been converted to an Editable Mesh with all faces selected in Face subobject mode with the Show Normals option selected.

The Hide button hides the selected subobjects. You can make hidden objects visible again with the Unhide All button.

After selecting several subobjects, you can create a named selection set by typing a name in the Name Selection Sets drop-down list in the main toolbar. You can then copy and paste these selection sets onto other shapes.

At the bottom of the Selection rollout is the Selection Information, which is a text line that automatically displays the number and type of selected items.

Cross-Reference   The Soft Selection rollout allows you to alter adjacent non-selected subobjects when selected subobjects are moved, creating a smooth transition. For the details on this rollout, see Chapter 11, "Modeling Basics."

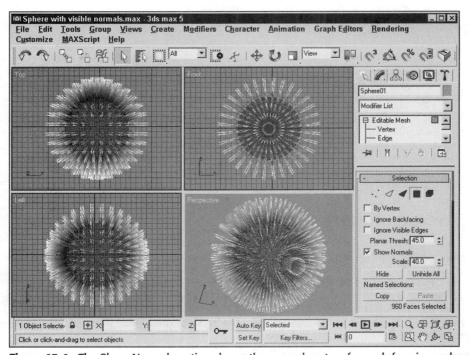

Figure 13-1: The Show Normals option shows the normal vectors for each face in a sphere.

Edit Geometry rollout

Much of the power of editing meshes is contained within the Edit Geometry rollout. Features contained here include, among many others, the ability to create new subobjects, attach sub-objects to the mesh, weld vertices, chamfer vertices, slice, explode, and align. Some Edit Geometry buttons will be disabled depending on the subobject mode that you've selected. The following buttons will be enabled before you enter a subobject mode.

Attach

The Attach button is available with all subobject modes and even when you are not in subobject mode. When no subobject mode is selected, the Detach button (to the right) changes to an Attach List button for mesh objects. Clicking the Attach List button opens the Attach List dialog box (or you can click the settings dialog box icon for poly objects) where you can select from a list of all the objects to attach. The list contains only objects that you can attach.

Use the Attach button to add objects to the current Editable Mesh objects. You can add primitives, splines, patch objects, and other mesh objects. Any object that is attached to a mesh object is automatically converted into an editable mesh. Any objects that are added to a mesh object can be selected using the Element subobject mode.

To use this feature, select the main object and click the Attach button. Move the mouse over the object to be attached — the cursor will change over acceptable objects. Click the object to select it. Click the Attach button again or right-click in the viewport to exit Attach mode.

Explode

The Explode button can also be used outside of all subobject modes and with the Face, Polygon and Element subobject modes. It is the opposite of the Attach button and can be used to separate all selected faces or polygons into individual objects or elements. The spinner to the right sets the angle value of the faces to include in this operation. If the Objects option is selected, the Explode to Objects dialog box appears, enabling you to name the object.

Remove Isolated Vertices

The Remove Isolated Vertices button can be used at anytime and in any subobject mode. It automatically deletes all isolated vertices associated with a mesh object, selected or not. Isolated vertices can result from deleting a face, or they could be inserted with the Create button and never connected. This helpful feature cleans up a mesh before applying any modifiers. Some modifiers cannot be applied if isolated vertices are part of the mesh.

View and Grid Align

The View and Grid Align buttons move and orient all selected vertices to the current active viewport or to the current construction grid. These buttons can also be used in all subobject modes.

Editing vertices

When working with Editable Mesh and Poly objects, after you select Vertex subobject mode (1) and select vertices, you can transform them using the transform buttons on the main toolbar. When you move the vertices around, the mesh edges will follow.

Create

The Create button lets you add new vertices to a mesh object. To create a new vertex, click the Create button to enter Create mode. You can then click where you want the new vertex to be located. Click the Create button again or right-click in the viewport to exit Create mode.

Create mode works for all mesh subobject types except edges. Be aware that creating a vertex doesn't add it to any of the edges, but the Create button in Edge subobject mode can connect edges to these isolated vertices.

Delete

The Delete button lets you delete the selected vertices. To use this button, select a vertex or vertices to delete and click the Delete button. This button works for all the subobject types.

Caution   Deleting a vertex also deletes all faces and their edges connected to that vertex. This deletion can cause holes in the geometry and cause problems with many modifiers.

Figure 13-2 shows an Editable Mesh sphere object with several deleted vertices. The deleted vertices have created a hole in the geometry. You can see the back inside of the sphere because the Force 2-Sided option was enabled in the Viewport Configuration dialog box.

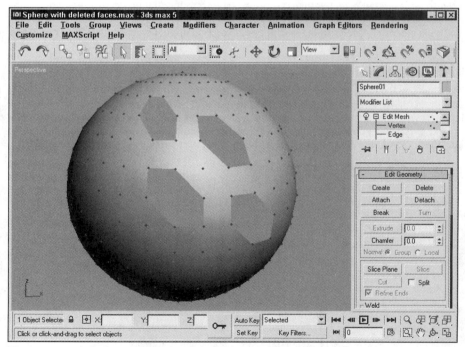

Figure 13-2: Deleting vertices also deletes the adjoining faces and edges.

Detach

Use the Detach button to separate the selected subobjects from the rest of the object. To use this button, select the subobject and click the Detach button. The Detach dialog box opens, enabling you to name the new detached subobject. You also have the options to Detach to Element or to Detach as Clone. All subobject modes except Edge have a Detach option. This button will appear in place of the Attach List button in all subobject modes.

Break

You use the Break button to create a separate vertex for adjoining faces that are connected by a single vertex.

In a normal mesh, faces are all connected by vertices—moving one vertex changes the position of all adjoining faces. The Break button enables you to move the vertex associated with each face independent of the others. The button is only available in Vertex subobject mode.

Figure 13-3 shows a hexagon shape with polygon faces that were joined at the center. The Break button was used to separate the center vertex into separate vertices for each face. The faces can be manipulated independently, as the figure shows.

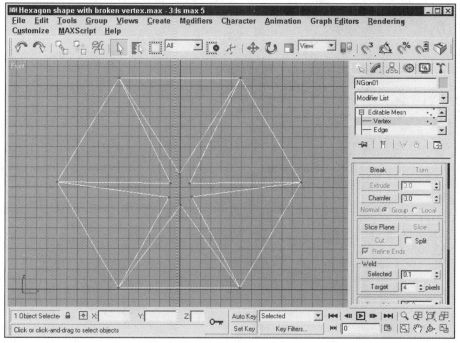

Figure 13-3: You can use the Break button to give each face its own vertex.

Chamfer

The Chamfer button, which is enabled in Vertex, Edge, and Border subobject modes, lets you cut the edge off a corner and replace it with a face. This existing corner vertex is deleted and automatically replaced with a face as well as vertices for each edge that was connected to the original corner vertex. The Chamfer amount is the distance the new face vertices move along the edge away from the original vertex position.

To use this feature, click the Chamfer button, then click and drag the vertex to be chamfered or select a vertex and enter a value in the Chamfer spinner. If multiple vertices are selected, they all are chamfered equal amounts. If you click and drag on an unselected vertex, then the current selection is dropped and the new selection is chamfered.

Figure 13-4 shows the results of chamfering all the vertices of a cube at the same time.

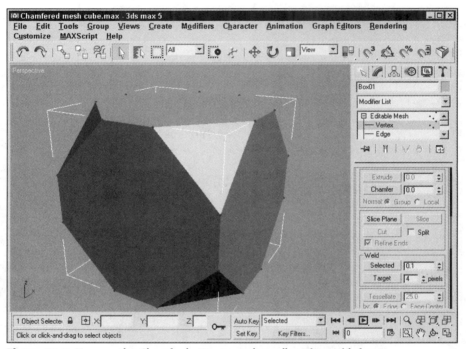

Figure 13-4: You use the Chamfer button to replace all vertices with faces.

Slice

The Slice Plane button lets you split the mesh object along a plane. When you click the Slice Plane button, a yellow slice plane gizmo appears on the selected object. You can move, rotate, and scale this gizmo using the transform buttons. After you properly position the plane and set all options, click the Slice button to finish slicing the mesh. All intersected faces split in two and new vertices and edges are added to the mesh where the Slice Plane intersects the original mesh.

The Slice Plane mode stays active until you de-select the Slice Plane button or until you right-click in the viewport; this feature enables you to make several slices in one session. The Slice Plane button is enabled for all subobject modes. For the Editable Poly object, a Reset Plane button is located next to the Slice Plane button. Use this button to reset the slice plane to its original location.

You use the Split option to double the number of vertices along the Slice Plane. Choosing the Refine Ends option causes open ends on adjacent faces to be connected to avoid discontinuities in the surface.

Weld Selected and Weld Target

The Weld Selected button works like the Weld function for splines. To use this feature, select two or more vertices and click the Weld button. If the vertices are within the threshold value specified by the spinner to the right of the button, they are welded into one vertex. If no vertices are within the threshold, an alert box opens and notifies you of this situation.

Tip   If you run into trouble with the Weld button and its Threshold value, then try using the Collapse button.

The Weld Target button lets you select a vertex and drag and drop it on top of another vertex. If the target vertex is within the number of pixels specified by the Target value, the vertices are welded into one vertex. To exit Weld Target mode, click the Target button again or right-click in the viewport.

Both of these buttons are available only in Vertex subobject mode.

Make Planar

A single vertex or two vertices don't define a plane, but three or more vertices do. If three or more vertices are selected, you can use the Make Planar button to make these vertices copla-nar (which means that all vertices are on the same plane). Doing so positions the selected vertices so they lie in the same plane. This is helpful if you want to build a new polygon face. Polygonal faces need to be coplanar. This button works in all subobject modes.

Collapse

The Collapse button is used to collapse all the selected subobjects to a single subobject located at the averaged center of the selection. This button is similar to the Weld button, except that the selected vertices don't need to be within a Threshold value to be combined. This button works in all subobject modes.

Vertex Surface properties

The Surface Properties rollout in Vertex subobject mode lets you define the Weight, Color, and Illumination of object vertices. In Vertex mode, this rollout lets you give selected vertices a Weight. Vertices with higher weight have a greater pull, like the gravity of a larger planet. Several modifiers (such as MeshSmooth) use this weight setting.

Also within this rollout are several color swatches, which enable you to select Color and Illumination colors for the selected vertices. The Alpha value sets the amount of trans-parency for the vertices. After you assign colors, you can then recall vertices with the same color by selecting a color (or illumination color) in the Select Vertices By section and clicking the Select button. The RGB values match all colors within the Range defined by these values. For example, if the RGB Range values are all set to 255, then every vertex will be selected.

Cross-Reference   You can find more information on vertex colors in Chapter 20, "Using Material Maps."

Editing edges

Edges are the lines that run between two vertices. Edges can be closed, which means that each side of the edge is connected to a face; or open, which means that only one face connects to the edge. Mesh edges, such as in the interior of a shape that has been converted to a mesh, can also be invisible.

You can select multiple edges by holding down either the Ctrl key while clicking the edges, or the Alt key to remove selected edges from the selection set. You can also copy edges using the Shift key while transforming the edge. The cloned edge maintains connections to its vertices by creating new edges.

Many of the Edge subobject options work in the same way as the Vertex subobject options.

Divide

The Divide button adds a new vertex at the middle of the edge and splits the edge into two equal sections. When in Edge, Face, Border, Polygon, or Element subobject mode, the Divide button replaces the Break button. To exit Divide mode, click the Divide button again or right-click in the viewport.

This button works in all subobject modes except Vertex.

Turn

The Turn button rotates the hidden edges that break up the polygon into triangles (all polygonal faces include these hidden edges). For example, if a quadrilateral (four-sided) face has a hidden edge, which runs between vertices 1 and 3, then the Turn button would change this hidden edge to run between 2 and 4. This affects how the surface is smoothed when the polygon is not coplanar. To exit Turn mode, click the Turn button again or right-click in the viewport.

This button is available only in Edge subobject mode for the Editable Mesh object.

Extrude

The Extrude button adds depth to an edge by extending it and creating a new face behind the extruded edge. For example, a square extruded from a patch grid would form a box with no lid. To use this feature, select an edge or edges and click the Extrude button; then drag in a viewport. The edges interactively show the extrude depth. Release the button when you've reached the desired distance.

Alternatively, you can set an extrude depth in the Extrusion spinner. The Normal Group option extrudes all selected edges along the normal for the group (the normal runs perpendicular to the face) and the Normal Local option moves each individual edge along its local normal. To exit Extrude mode, click the Extrude button again or right-click in the viewport.

The Extrude button is enabled for Face, Polygon, and Element subobject modes for the Editable Mesh object.

Cut

The Cut button enables you to split an edge into two by cutting an existing edge. To use this feature, click the Cut button and then click and drag across the edges you want to cut. If you drag across several faces, a new vertex and edge will be created at each intersection. You can also create a single vertex at any point along an edge by double-clicking. To exit this mode, right-click. Then right-click again to disable the Cut button.

The Split option creates two vertices at every junction, enabling these faces to be easily separated. The Refine Edges option maintains the continuous surface of the mesh by adding additional vertices to all adjacent faces to the cut. The Cut button is available for Editable Mesh objects in all subobject modes except Vertex.

Select Open Edges and Create Shape from Edges options

The Select Open Edges button locates and selects all open edges. Using this button is a good way to find any holes in the geometry. This feature is another one that helps eliminate potential problems with a mesh object. The Create Shape from Edges button creates a new spline shape from selected edges. The Create Shape dialog box appears, enabling you to give the new shape a name. You can also select options for Smooth or Linear shape types and to Ignore Hidden Edges.

Edge Surface properties

The Surface Properties rollout for the Editable Mesh object in the Edge subobject mode includes Visible and Invisible buttons that you can use to make invisible edges between polygons visible. The Auto Edge button automatically makes all selected edges less than the Threshold value invisible if the Set and Clear Edge Vis option is selected. The Set option only makes invisible edges visible, and the Clear option only makes visible edges invisible.

Editing Face, Border, Polygon, and Element subobjects

Editable Mesh objects include two different types of faces: Face and Polygon subobjects. Face subobjects have only three edges. This polygon is the simplest possible, and all other polygons can be broken down into this type of face. Polygon subobjects are any faces with more than three vertices. A Polygon subobject includes two or more faces. A dashed line contained within the polygon designates these faces.

Editable Poly objects do not need the Face subobject because they support polygon faces. Instead, they have a Border subobject. The Border subobject is polygons without any face and edges on all sides that are actually holes within the geometry.

Transforming a face or polygon object works the same way in subobject mode as in normal transformations. The Edit Geometry rollout includes many of the same buttons previously covered in the "Editing vertices" and "Editing edges" sections, but includes some additional features that only apply to Face, Border, and Polygon subobjects.

A mesh object can also contain several elements. The Element subobject mode includes all the same commands as the Face, Border, and Polygon subobject modes.

Create

You can use the Create button to create new faces and/or polygons based on new or existing vertices. To create a new face, click the Create button — all vertices in the selected mesh will be highlighted. Next, click a vertex to start the face — after clicking two more vertices, a new face is created. You can also create a new vertex not based on any existing vertices by holding down the Shift key while clicking.

Polygons aren't limited to three vertices. You can click as many times as you want to add additional vertices to the polygon. Click the first vertex, or double-click to complete the polygon. Figure 13-5 shows a simple shape that has been supplemented with additional polygon faces.

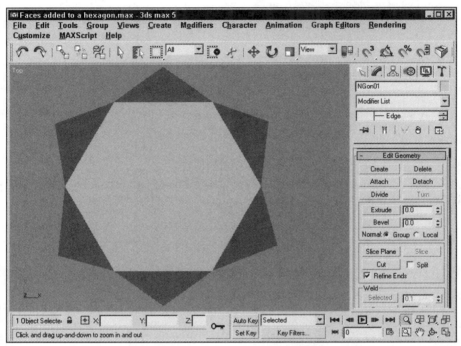

Figure 13-5: All the triangles exterior to the center hexagon were added using the Create button in Face subobject mode.

Bevel

The Bevel button appears in place of the Chamfer button for Face, Polygon, and Element subobject modes. It extrudes the Face or Polygon subobject selection and then lets you bevel the edges. To use this feature, select a face or polygon and click the Bevel button; then drag up or down in a viewport to the Extrusion depth and release the button. Drag again to specify the Bevel amount. The Bevel amount determines the relative size of the extruded face.

The Normal Group option extrudes all selected faces or polygons along the normal for the group, and the Normal Local option moves each individual face or polygon along its local normal. For Editable Poly objects, you can also use the bevel by polygon option. To exit Bevel mode, click the Bevel button again or right-click in the viewport. The Bevel button is enabled for all subobject modes except Vertex, Edge, and Border.

Figure 13-6 displays a poly dodecahedron. Each face has been locally extruded with a value of 20 and then locally beveled with a value of –10.

Tessellate

You can use the Tessellate button to increase the resolution of a mesh by splitting a face or polygon into several faces or polygons. You have two options to do this: Edge and Face-Center.

The Edge method splits each edge at its midpoint. For example, a triangular face would be split into three smaller triangles. The Tension spinner to the right of the Tessellate button specifies a value that is used to make the tessellated face concave or convex.

The Face-Center option creates a vertex in the center of the face and also creates three new edges, which extend from the center vertex to each original vertex. For a square polygon, this option would create six new triangular faces. (Remember, a square polygon is actually composed of two triangular faces.)

Figure 13-7 shows the faces of a cube that has been tessellated once using the Edge option and then again using the Face-Center option.

Face, Polygon, and Element Surface properties

For Face, Polygon, and Element subobjects, the Surface Properties rollout includes Flip, Unify, and Flip Normal Mode buttons to control the direction of the normal vectors. Flip reverses the direction of the normals of each selected face; Unify makes all normals face in the same direction based on the majority. The Flip Normal Mode button activates a mode where you can click individual faces and flip their normals. This mode stays active until you click the Flip Normal Mode button again or right-click in the viewport. These buttons are only available for the Editable Mesh object.

The Surface Properties rollout also includes Material IDs and Smoothing Groups options.

The Material IDs option settings are used by the Multi/Sub-Object material type to apply different materials to faces or polygons within an object. By selecting a polygon subobject, you can use these option settings to apply a unique material to the selected polygon. The Select By ID button opens a simple dialog box where you can enter a Material ID. Clicking OK selects all subobjects that have the specific material ID applied.

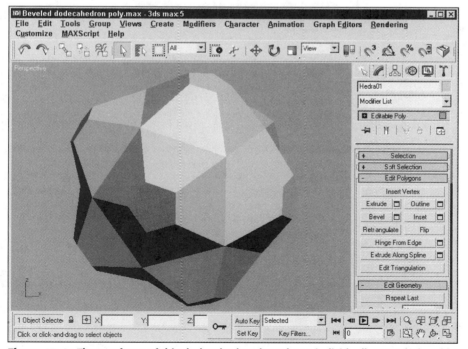

Figure 13-6: The top faces of this dodecahedron have been individually extruded and beveled.

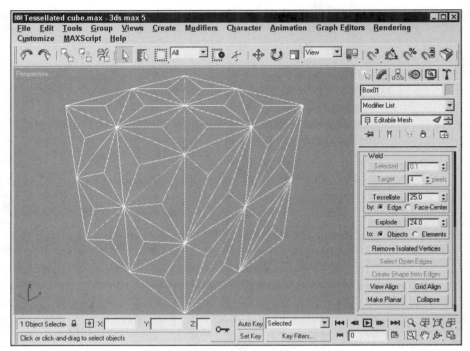

Figure 13-7: A cube tessellated twice using each option

Cross-Reference
You can find more information on the Multi/Sub-Object material type in Chapter 19, "Creating and Applying Materials."

You use the Smoothing Group option to assign a subobject to a unique smoothing group. To do this, select a subobject and click a Smoothing Group number. The Select By SG button, like the Select By ID button, opens a dialog box where you can enter a smoothing group number, and all subobjects with that number are selected. The Clear All button clears all smoothing group number assignments, and the Auto Smooth button automatically assigns smoothing group numbers based on the angle between faces as set by the value to the right of the Auto Smooth button.

Tutorial: Modeling a clown head

Now that all the editable mesh features have been covered, let's use them to actually get some work done. In this example, you'll quickly deform a mesh sphere to create a clown face, by selecting, moving, and working with some vertices.

To create a clown head by moving vertices, follow these steps:

1. Open the Mesh clown head.max file from the Chap 13 directory on the CD-ROM.

   This file includes a simple sphere that has been converted to an Editable Mesh object.

2. Open the Modify panel. Now, make a long, pointy nose by pulling a vertex outward from the sphere object. Click the small plus sign to the left of the Editable Mesh object in the Modifier Stack and select Vertex in the hierarchy (or press the 1 key). This activates the Vertex subobject mode. Then select the single vertex at the top of the sphere. Make sure the Select and Move button is selected, and in the Top viewport, drag the vertex along the Y-axis until it projects from the sphere.

3. Next, create the mouth by selecting and indenting a row of vertices. For this selection, open the Soft Selection rollout, and click the Use Soft Selection option. Underneath the nose, select several vertices in a circular arc that make a smile and press the spacebar to lock the selection. Then move the selected vertices along the negative Y-axis.

4. Unlock the mouth selection. For the eyes, select two sets of three vertices above the nose and lock the selection once again. With the Soft Selection still enabled, move the eye vertices in the Y-axis, but not as far as the nose.

5. Unlock the eyes selection. Select each eye set of vertices independently and click the Weld Selected button. (If the vertices aren't within the threshold, increase the threshold and try again.)

6. Select both sets of eye vertices and click the Chamfer button. Then drag in the viewport an intermediate distance back to the surface of the sphere.

This clown head is just a simple example of what is possible by editing subobjects. Figure 13-8 shows the clown head in a shaded view.

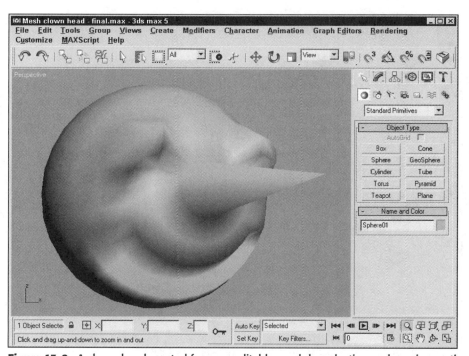

Figure 13-8: A clown head created from an editable mesh by selecting and moving vertices

Tutorial: Cleaning up imported meshes

Almost all 3D formats are mesh formats, and importing mesh objects can sometimes create problems. By collapsing an imported model to an editable mesh, you can take advantage of several of the editable mesh features to clean up these problems.

Figure 13-9 shows a model that was exported from Poser using the 3ds format. Notice that the model's waist is black. It only appears this way because I've turned off the Backface Cull option in the Viewport Configuration dialog box. If it were turned on, his waist would be invisible. The problem here is that the normals for this object are pointing the wrong direction. This problem is common for imported meshes, and we'll fix it in this tutorial.

To fix the normals on an imported mesh model, follow these steps:

1. Open the Hailing taxi man with incorrect normals.max file from the Chap 13 directory on the CD-ROM.

2. Select the problem object — the waist. Open the object hierarchy by clicking the plus sign to the left of the Editable Mesh object in the Modifier Stack and select Element subobject mode.

3. In the Selection rollout, select the Show Normals option and set the Scale value to a small number such as 0.1.

   The normals will be visible. Notice how some of them point outward and some of them point inward.

4. With the element subobject still selected, click the Unify button in the Surface Properties rollout and then click the Flip button until all normals are pointing outward.

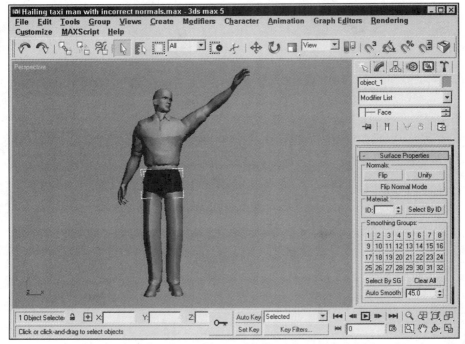

Figure 13-9: This mesh suffers from objects with flipped normals, which makes them invisible.

This problem is now fixed, and the waist object is now a visible part of the mesh. The fixed mesh will look just like the original mesh without the ugly black shorts.

Editing Poly Objects

Editable Poly objects are created just like Editable Mesh objects, by converting, collapsing, or importing them. After an object has been converted to an Editable Poly object, you can work with its subobjects just like its meshy brother. Many of the buttons found in the Editable Mesh rollouts work exactly the same for Editable Poly objects. Only the differences will be noted.

Editable Poly subobject modes

The subobject modes for the Editable Poly are a little different though. They include Vertex, Edge, Border, Polygon, and Element. The Border subobject mode will select all the edges around a polygon face, which may be more than three. The various subobject modes can be selected in the same manner as the Editable Mesh.

Before you can edit Mesh or Poly subobjects, you must select them. To select a Subobject mode, select the hierarchy element under the Editable Poly object, click one of the subobject buttons in the Selection rollout, or use the keyboard shortcuts (1-5).

Many of the buttons for the Editable Poly include a small icon to the right of the button that opens a settings dialog box. These settings dialog boxes allow you to change the settings and see immediately in the viewports the results. The OK button applies the settings and closes the dialog box and the Apply button will apply the settings and leave the dialog box open. These settings dialog boxes are included next to the Attach, MSmooth, Tessellate buttons for all subobject modes and next to many of the subobject specific buttons such as Extrude, Bevel, Outline, and Inset.

Selection rollout

For Editable Poly objects, the Selection rollout includes the Subobject buttons, the By Vertex and Ignore Backfacing options, and four buttons. These buttons include Shrink, Grow, Ring, and Loop. Use the Grow button to increase the current selection around the perimeter of the current selection, as shown in Figure 13-10. Click the Shrink button to do the opposite.

The Ring and Loop buttons are only available in Edge and Border subobject modes. Use Ring and Loop to select all adjacent subobjects horizontally and vertically around the entire object. Ring selection looks for parallel edges and Loop selection looks for all edges around an object that are aligned the same as the initial selection.

Note For Editable Poly objects, the Hide Selected, Unhide All, Copy, and Paste buttons are located at the bottom of the Edit Geometry rollout.

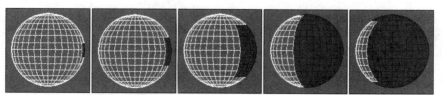

Figure 13-10: Using the Grow button, you can increase the subobject selection.

Edit Geometry rollout

For the Editable Poly object, each subobject mode has a separate rollout. For example, when you enter Vertex subobject mode, the Edit Vertex rollout appears. This rollout holds all the buttons that relate to the Vertex subobject mode. The general functions that apply to several subobject modes (and that can be used with no subobject mode selected) are found in the Edit Geometry rollout.

Repeat Last

The first button in the Edit Geometry rollout is the Repeat Last button. This button will repeat the last subobject command. This button will not work on all features but is very convenient for certain actions.

Enabling constraints

The Constraints drop-down list will limit the movement of subobjects to a specified subobject. The available constraints are None, Edge, and Face. For example, if you select and move a vertex with the Edges constraint enabled, then the movement will be constrained to the adjacent edges.

QuickSlice

The QuickSlice button lets you click anywhere on an Editable Poly object where you want a slicing line to be located. You can then move the mouse and the QuickSlice line will rotate about the point you clicked on. When you click the mouse again, a new vertex will be added at every place where the QuickSlice line intersects an object edge.

Cut

For Editable Poly objects, the Cut button is interactive. If you click on a polygon corner, the cut edge will snap to the corner and a new edge will extend from the corner to a nearby corner. As you move the mouse around, the edge will move until you click where the edge should end. If you click in the middle of an edge or face, then new edges will appear to the nearest corner. This interactive cut method is much easier to use than the Editable Mesh object method.

MSmooth and Tessellate

Both the MSmooth and Tessellate buttons include new settings dialog boxes, as shown in Figure 13-11. The MSmooth setting for Smoothness will round all the sharp edges of an object. Tessellation can be done using Edges or Faces, and the Tension setting controls how tight the adjacent faces are.

The MSmooth button can be used to apply the MeshSmooth modifier to the selected subobjects. This button can be used several times. The Smoothness value determines which vertices are used to smooth the object. The higher the value, the more vertices are included and the smoother the result. You can also select that the smoothing is separated by Smoothing Groups or by Materials.

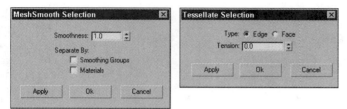

Figure 13-11: The settings dialog boxes for the MSmooth and Tessellate buttons let you interactively set the Smoothness and Tension values.

Editing vertices

When working with the Editable Poly objects, after you select a Vertex subobject mode (1) and select vertices, you can transform them using the transform buttons on the main toolbar. All vertex commands are found within the Edit Vertices rollout.

Remove

The Delete button for Editable Mesh objects lets you delete the selected vertices. However, the Remove button is similar to the Delete button, except a hole isn't left after the vertex is removed. The Remove button will automatically adjust the surrounding subobjects to maintain the mesh integrity.

Figure 13-12 shows a sphere object with several vertex subobjects selected. The middle image is an Editable Mesh that used the Delete feature and the right image is an Editable Poly that used the Remove feature.

Figure 13-12: Deleting vertices also deletes the adjoining faces and edges, but Remove maintains the mesh.

Extrude, Weld, and Chamfer

The Extrude, Weld, and Chamfer buttons all include a settings dialog box that lets you interactively see the results of different settings. The Extrude settings dialog box includes options for setting the Extrusion Height and the Extrusion Base Width. The Weld settings dialog box includes a weld Threshold value and it also displays the number of vertices before and after the welding process. The Chamfer button, which is enabled in Vertex, Edge, and Border subobject modes, lets you cut the edge off a corner and replace it with a face. Using the settings dialog box, you can interactively specify a Chamfer Amount.

Connect

The Connect button can be used to add new edges to subobjects. In Vertex subobject mode, the button will connect vertices on the opposite side of a face. In Edge and Border subobject mode, they make a settings dialog box available, which includes a setting to Connect Edge Segments. This value is the number of edge segments to use to add between the selected edges or borders.

Remove Unused Map Vertices

The Remove Unused Map Vertices button will remove any left-over mapping vertices from the object.

Tutorial: Building a beveled pyramid

The Egyptians were pyramid masters, but modeling a pyramid is too easy because it is one of the primitives. Instead, we'll look to the Aztec civilization for a pyramid example that has several flat terraces on the way to the top. This will give you a chance to practice working with an Editable Poly object.

To create a multi-stage pyramid from an Editable Poly object, follow these steps:

1. Open the Aztec pyramid.max file from the Chap 13 directory on the CD-ROM.

   This file includes a simple box primitive that has been converted to an Editable Poly.

2. Open the Modify panel. In the Selection rollout, click the Polygon subobject button and enable the Ignore Backfacing option. Select the Select Objects button on the main toolbar and click on the box object in the Top viewport to select the topmost polygon.

   Notice at the bottom of the Selection rollout that only one polygon is mentioned as being selected.

3. In the Edit Polygon rollout, click the Bevel button and enter a value of –5 in the Outline field. This makes the top polygon smaller than the bottom polygon. Click again on the Select Objects button on the main toolbar to exit this mode.

4. In the Edit Geometry rollout, select the Edge option and click the Tessellate button three times.

   This divides the top polygon into 64 separate polygons.

5. While still in Polygon subobject mode, drag over all the internal polygons to select them.

   The bottom of the Selection rollout lists 36 polygons selected.

6. Click on the Bevel button in the Edit Geometry rollout again and enter a value of **20** for the Extrusion value and **–5** for the Outline value.

7. Repeat Steps 5 and 6 two more times to complete the pyramid.

Figure 13-13 shows the completed pyramid.

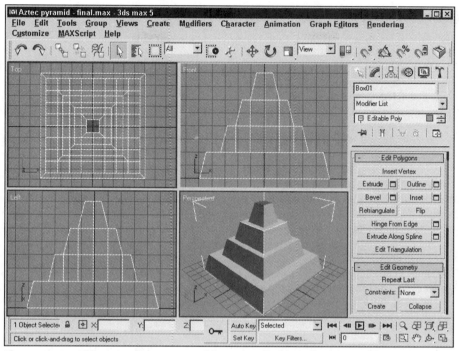

Figure 13-13: This pyramid was created from an Editable Poly object.

Editing edges and borders

Edges are the lines that run between two vertices. All buttons that work with edges are located in the Edit Edges rollout. Most include the same functionality as those covered in the Editable Mesh object.

Editable Poly objects do not need the Face subobject because they support polygon faces. Instead, they have a Border subobject. The Border subobject is polygons without any face and edges on all sides that are actually holes within the geometry.

Insert Vertex

The Insert Vertex button adds a new vertex at the middle of the edge and splits the edge into two equal sections. When in Edge, Border, Polygon, or Element subobject mode, this button also makes vertices visible.

Edit Triangulation

For the Editable Poly object, the Edge, Border, Polygon, and Element subobjects include the Edit Triangulation button. The Edit Triangulation button lets you change the internal edges of the polygon by dragging from one vertex to another.

Editing Polygon and Element subobjects

Like the other subobject modes, Editable Polys can be edited at the polygon and element subobject level. The buttons for these modes are found in the Edit Polygons and Edit Elements rollouts.

Outline and Inset

The Outline button will offset the selected polygon a specified amount. This will increase the size of the selected polygon or element. The Inset button will create another polygon set within the selected polygon and their edges will be connected. For both these buttons, a settings dialog box is available that includes the Outline or Inset Amount values.

Retriangulate and Flip

The Retriangulate button automatically computes all the internal edges for you, and Flip Normals flips the normal vectors for the selected subobjects. The Flip button is only available in Polygon and Element subobject modes.

Hinge From Edge

The Hinge From Edge button will rotate a selected polygon as if one of its edges were a hinge. The angle of the hinge depends on the distance that you drag with the mouse, or you could use the available settings dialog box. In the settings dialog box, shown in Figure 13-14, you can specify an Angle value and the number of segments to use for the hinged section.

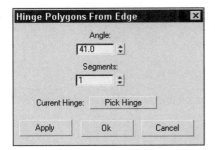

Figure 13-14: The Hinge Polygons From Edge dialog box lets you select a hinge.

By default, one of the polygon's edges will be used as the hinge about which the section rotates, but in the settings dialog box, you can click the Pick Hinge button and select an edge (which doesn't need to be attached to the polygon). Figure 13-15 shows a sphere primitive with four polygon faces that have been hinged around an edge at the sphere's center.

Extrude Along Spline

The Extrude Along Spline button can be used to extrude a selected polygon along the spline path. The settings dialog box includes a Pick Spline button that you can use to select the spline to use. You can also specify the number of segments, the Taper Amount and Curve, and a Twist value. There is also an option to Align the extrusion to the face normal or to rotate about the normal.

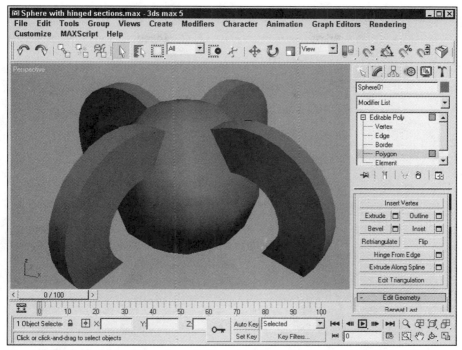

Figure 13-15: Several polygon faces in the sphere have been extruded along a hinge.

Tutorial: Building an octopus

The one thing about the octopus that makes it unique is the eight legs that it has (actually spiders also have eight legs, but work with me here). Creating these legs can be easily accomplished with the Extrude Along Spline feature.

To create an octopus using the Extrude Along Spline feature, follow these steps:

1. Open the Octopus.max file from the Chap 13 directory on the CD-ROM.

   This file includes the base of an octopus created from a squashed sphere primitive that has been converted to an Editable Poly. There are also eight splines that surround the object.

2. Open the Modify panel. In the Selection rollout, click the Face subobject button and enable the Ignore Backfacing option.

3. Select the Select Objects button on the main toolbar and click on a single face object at the base of the sphere object, click the Extrude Along Spline settings dialog box button to open the Extrude Polygons Along Spline dialog box, shown in Figure 13-16.

4. Click the Pick Spline button and select the spline to the side of the face. Set the Taper Amount to –1.0 and click the OK button. Then repeat the last two steps for each spline surrounding the octopus.

Figure 13-17 shows the resulting octopus.

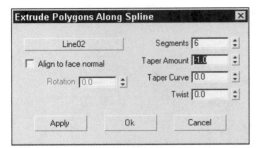

Figure 13-16: The Extrude Polygons Along Spline settings dialog box

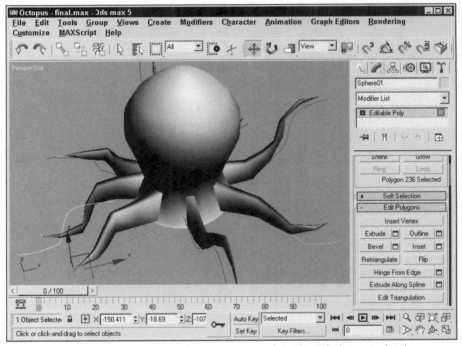

Figure 13-17: The arms of this octopus were created easily with the Extrude Along Spline feature.

Using Mesh Editing Modifiers

The Editable Mesh and Editable Poly objects can have modifiers applied to them. The Modifiers menu includes a submenu of modifiers that are specific to mesh objects. These modifiers are found in the Mesh Editing submenu and can be used to enhance the features available for Editable Mesh objects.

You can find a more general explanation of modifiers in Chapter 10, "Using Modifiers."

Edit Mesh modifier

All mesh objects are by default Editable Mesh objects. This modifier enables objects to be modified using the Editable Mesh feature while maintaining their basic creation parameters.

 Modifying an object's parameters after applying the Edit Mesh modifier or any modifier that alters the geometric topology of an object can cause erratic results.

When an object is converted to an Editable Mesh, its parametric nature is eliminated. However, if you use the Edit Mesh modifier, you can still retain the same object type and its parametric nature while having access to all the Editable Mesh features. For example, if you create a sphere and apply the Edit Mesh modifier and then extrude several faces, you can still change the radius of the sphere by selecting the Sphere object in the Modifier Stack and changing the Radius value in the Parameters rollout.

There is not an Edit Poly modifier.

Cap Holes modifier

The Cap Holes modifier patches any holes found in a geometry object. Sometimes when objects are imported, they are missing faces. This modifier can detect and eliminate these holes by creating a face along open edges.

For example, if a spline is extruded and you don't specify Caps, the Cap Holes modifier will detect these holes and create a Cap. Cap Holes parameters include Smooth New Faces, Smooth with Old Faces, and Triangulate Cap. Smooth with Old Faces applies the same smoothing group used on the bordering faces.

Delete Mesh modifier

You can use the Delete Mesh modifier to delete mesh subobjects. Subobjects that you can delete include Vertices, Edges, Faces, and Objects.

The Delete Mesh modifier deletes the current selection as defined by the Mesh Select (or Poly Select) modifier. It can be used to delete a selection of Vertices, Edges, Faces, Polygons, or even the entire mesh if there is no subobject selection. The Delete Mesh modifier has no parameters.

 Even if the entire mesh is deleted using the Delete Mesh modifier, the object still remains. To completely delete an object, use the Delete key.

Edit Normals

The Edit Normals modifier enables you to select and move normal directions. It includes a Normals subobject that you can select and change its direction. You can select to Select normals by Normal, Edge, Vertex, or Face. There are also options to Ignore Backfacing and to

Show Handles. If your viewport has shading enabled, you can see the effect of moving the normals. Figure 13-18 shows the parameters for this modifier.

The modifier also includes buttons to Unify, Break, Specify, Reset, and Make Explicit. For a selection, you can copy and paste normal selections between objects. The Display Length value defines the length of the normals displayed in the viewports.

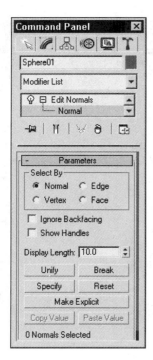

Figure 13-18: The Edit Normals Parameters let you work with normals.

Extrude modifier

The Extrude modifier copies the spline, moves it a given distance, and connects the two splines to form a 3D shape. Parameters for this modifier include an Amount value, which is the distance to extrude, and the number of segments to use to define the height. The Capping options let you specify a Start Cap and/or an End Cap. The Cap fills the spline area and can be made as a Patch, Mesh, or NURBS object. Only closed splines that are extruded can be capped. You can also have mapping coordinates and Material IDs generated automatically.

Face Extrude modifier

The Face Extrude modifier extrudes the selected faces in the same direction as their normals. Face Extrude parameters include Amount and Scale values and an option to Extrude From Center. Figure 13-19 shows a mesh object with several extruded faces. The Mesh Select modifier was used to select the faces, and the extrude Amount was set to 30.

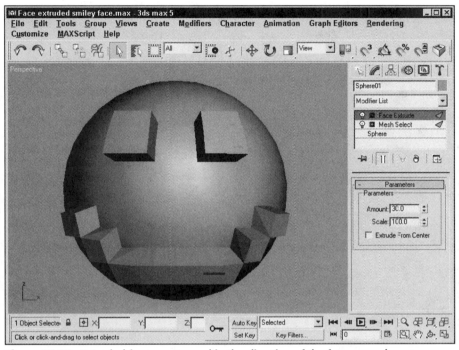

Figure 13-19: Extruded faces are moved in the direction of the face normal.

Normal modifier

The Normal modifier enables object normals to be flipped or unified. When some objects are imported, their normals can become erratic, producing holes in the geometry. By unifying and flipping the normals, you can restore an object's consistency. This modifier includes two options: Unify Normals and Flip Normals.

Optimize modifier

The Optimize modifier does the opposite of the Tessellation modifier. It simplifies models by reducing the number of faces, edges, and vertices. The Level of Detail can be set differently for the Renderer and the Viewports. Face and Edge Thresholds determine whether elements should be collapsed. Other options include Bias and Maximum Edge Length. Parameters can also be set to Preserve Material and Smoothing Boundaries. The Update button enables manual updating of the object, and the text field at the bottom of the rollout displays the number of vertices and faces for the current optimization.

Figure 13-20 shows a cow model that has been optimized. Notice the dramatic reduction in the number of faces from the left to the right. Viewpoint Datalabs, known for producing high-resolution models, created this model. At the bottom of the Modify panel, the number of faces has been reduced from 4,326 to 670 faces by setting the Face Threshold to 20. (I guess that would be considered "lean beef.")

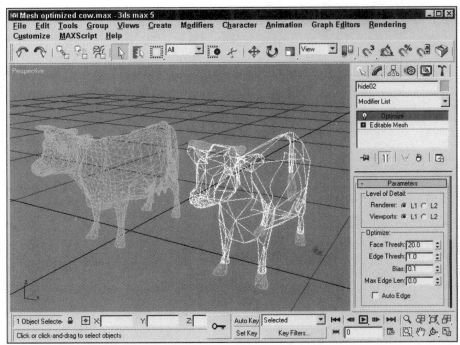

Figure 13-20: You can use the Optimize modifier to reduce the complexity of the cow model.

 Caution Applying the Optimize modifier reduces the overall number of polygons, but it also reduces the detail of the model. Be careful when using this modifier repeatedly because it could increase the number of polygons to an unwieldy number.

Smooth modifier

You can use the Smooth modifier to auto-smooth an object. Smooth parameters include options for Auto Smooth and Prevent Indirect Smoothing along with a Threshold value. The Parameters rollout also includes a set of 32 Smoothing Groups buttons labeled 1 through 32.

STL Check modifier

The STL Check modifier checks a model in preparation for exporting it to the StereoLithography (STL) format. StereoLithography files require a closed surface—geometry with holes or gaps can cause problems. Any problems are reported in the Status area of the Parameters rollout.

This modifier can check for several common errors, including Open Edge, Double Face, Spike, or Multiple Edge. Spikes are island faces with only one connected edge. You can select any or all of these options. If found, you can have the modifier select the problem Edges or Faces, or neither, or you can change the Material ID of the problem area.

Symmetry modifier

The Symmetry modifier allows you to mirror a mesh object across a single axis. You can also select to Slice Along Mirror and weld along the seam with a defined Threshold. The gizmo for this modifier is a plane, which matches the selected axis and the arrow vector that extend from the plane.

New Feature   This modifier is new to 3ds max 5.

Tessellate modifier

You use the Tessellate modifier to subdivide the selected faces for higher-resolution models. You can apply tessellation to either Triangle or Polygonal faces. The Edge option creates new faces by dividing the face from the face center to the middle of the edges. The Face-Center option divides each face from the face center to the corners of the face. The Tension setting determines whether the faces are convex or concave. The Iterations setting is the number of times the modifier is applied.

Caution   Applying the Tessellate modifier to an object with a high Iterations value produces objects with many times the original number of faces.

Vertex Weld modifier

The Vertex Weld modifier is a simple modifier that welds all vertices within a certain Threshold value. This is a convenient modifier for cleaning up mesh objects.

Subdivision Surface modifiers

The Modifiers menu also includes a submenu of modifiers for subdividing surfaces. These include the MeshSmooth and HSDS Modifiers. You can use these modifiers to smooth and subdivide the surface of an object. Subdividing a surface increases the resolution of the object, allowing for more detailed modeling.

MeshSmooth modifier

The MeshSmooth modifier smoothes the entire surface of an object by applying a chamfer function to both vertices and edges at the same time. This modifier has the greatest effect on sharp corners and edges. With this modifier, you can create a NURMS object. NURMS stands for Non-Uniform Rational MeshSmooth. NURMS can weight each control point. The Parameters rollout includes three MeshSmooth types: Classic, NURMS, and Quad Output. You can set it to operate on triangular or polygonal faces. Smoothing parameters include Strength and Relax values.

There are also settings for the number of Subdivision Iterations to run and controls for weighting selected control points. Update Options can be set to Always, When Rendering, and Manually using the Update button. You can also select and work with either Vertex or Edge subobjects. These subobjects give you local control over the MeshSmooth object. Included within the Local Control rollout is a Crease value, which is available in Edge subobject mode. Selecting an Edge subobject and applying a 1.0 value causes a hard edge to be retained while the rest of the object is smoothed. The MeshSmooth modifier also makes the Soft Selection rollout available. The Reset rollout is included to quickly reset any crease and weight values.

Tutorial: Creating a heart-shaped NURMS

Here's an example just for Valentine's Day. Create a spline heart, extrude it, and then convert it to a NURMS object using the MeshSmooth modifier.

To create a heart-shaped NURMS object, follow these steps:

1. Open the Heart Shaped NURMS.max file from the Chap 13 directory on the CD-ROM.

   This file includes a simple extruded heart shape.

2. With the heart shape selected, choose Modifiers ➪ Subdivision Surfaces ➪ MeshSmooth to apply the MeshSmooth modifier. In the Parameters rollout, select the NURMS option in the Subdivision Method drop-down list (if it isn't already selected).

3. In the Local Control rollout, select the Edge subobject icon and click in the Front viewport on the single edge at the center of the heart shape. Then set the Crease value to 1.0. Click again on the Edge subobject to exit subobject mode.

4. To apply the smoothing option to the entire object, select an Iterations value of 1 in the Subdivision Amount rollout. The entire heart will be smoothed with the exception of the crease located at the center of the heart. If you click the vertex icon in the Local Control rollout, you can use the transform buttons on the main toolbar to edit selected vertices. Changing the weight of its vertices also alters a NURMS object. In the Parameters rollout, select the Display Control Mesh option, select the two vertices at the heart's top (the bottom of the crease), and increase the Weight value to 100.

   The faces gravitate toward the selected vertices.

Figure 13-21 shows the NURMS heart.

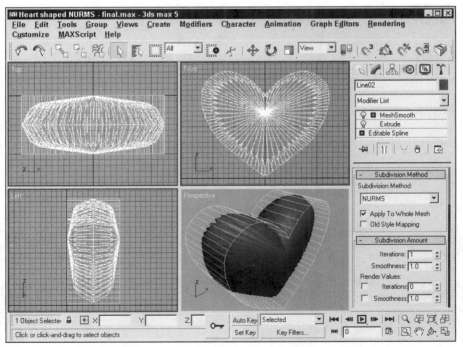

Figure 13-21: A NURMS heart created with the MeshSmooth modifier

HSDS modifier

You use the HSDS (Hierarchical SubDivision Surfaces) modifier to increase the resolution and smoothing of a localized area. It works like the Tessellate modifier except that it can work with small subobject sections instead of the entire object surface. The HSDS modifier lets you work with Vertex, Edge, Polygon, and Element subobjects. After a subobject area is selected, you can click the Subdivide button to subdivide the area.

The Level of Detail spinner lets you move back and forth between the various subdivision hierarchy levels. When polygon subobjects are selected, you can also Delete or Hide them. The Adaptive Subdivision button opens the Adaptive Subdivision dialog box in which you can specify the detail parameters. This modifier also includes a Soft Selection rollout and an Edge rollout where you can specify a Crease value to maintain sharp edges.

Summary

Meshes are probably the most common 3D modeling types. You can create them by converting objects to Editable Meshes or Editable Poly objects or by collapsing the Stack. Editable Meshes and Editable Poly objects in Max have a host of features for editing meshes, as you learned in this chapter.

More specifically, in this chapter you've

✦ Created Editable Mesh and Editable Poly objects by converting other objects or applying the Edit Mesh modifier

✦ Discovered the features of the Editable Mesh and Editable Poly objects

✦ Learned to select and use the various mesh subobject modes

✦ Discovered the various modifiers that you can use with mesh objects

In the next chapter, you'll learn about modeling and working with patch objects.

✦   ✦   ✦

Creating Patches

Patches are a modeling type that exists somewhere between polygon meshes and NURBS. They are essentially polygon surfaces stretched along a closed spline. Modifying the spline alters the surface of the patch.

In many ways, patches have advantages over the more common mesh objects. They take less memory to store, they are easier to edit at the edges, and they are easy to join to one another.

Introducing Patch Grids

Because patches have splines along their edges, a patch can be deformed in ways that a normal polygon cannot. For example, a polygon always needs to be coplanar, meaning that if you look at it on edge it appears as a line. A patch doesn't have this requirement and can actually bend, which permits greater control over the surface and makes it better for modeling things like clothes and natural objects like leaves.

Another key advantage of Patch objects is that they efficiently represent the object geometry. If you examine a mesh object, you will notice that they contain a discrete vertex at the intersection of every edge at the corner of every face. Patch grids, on the other hand, only have a vertex at the corner of every patch. Each patch can consist of several faces. This reduction of vertices makes patches much cleaner and less cumbersome objects to work with.

Creating a patch grid

Patches are named according to the number of vertices at their edges; for example, a Tri Patch has three vertices, a Quad Patch has four vertices, and so on. The default Quad Patch is made up of 36 visible rectangular faces, and the default Tri Patch has 72 triangular faces, as shown in Figure 14-1.

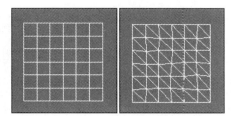

Figure 14-1: A Quad Patch and a Tri Patch

To create patches, open the Create panel and select the Geometry category. In the Object-Type drop-down list, select Patch Grids. Under the Object Type rollout, two buttons will appear: Quad Patch and Tri Patch. To create a patch grid, click a button, click in a viewport, and drag to specify the dimensions of the grid.

You can also use the Keyboard Entry rollout to create patch grids with precise dimensions. To use this rollout, enter the grid's position coordinates and its dimensions and click the Create button. The X, Y, and Z coordinates define the location of the center of the grid.

The Patch Grid Parameters rollout includes Length and Width values and values for the number of Segments for each dimension (but only for the Quad Patch). A Segment value of 1 creates six rows or columns of segments, so the total number of polygons for a Quad Patch will never drop below 36. Tri Patches do not have a Segments parameter. You can also select to automatically Generate Mapping Coordinates.

Newly created patches are always flat.

Tutorial: Creating a checkerboard

In this tutorial, we'll create a simple checkerboard. To keep the white squares separate from the black squares, we'll use Quad and Tri Patches.

To create a checkerboard from patch surfaces, follow these steps:

1. Open the Create panel and click the Geometry category. Select Patch Grids from the subcategory drop-down list.

2. Click the Quad Patch button in the Command Panel and, in the Top view, create a perfect square using the grid. Click the color swatch in the Name and Color rollout and select the color black.

3. In the Command Panel, click the Tri Patch button and drag in the Top view to create an equally sized patch to the right of the first object. Select the Tri Patch, click its color swatch, and change its object color to white.

Caution   With the Tri Patch's object color set to white, telling when it is selected can be difficult.

4. Repeat Steps 2 and 3, alternating which color comes first until the complete 8×8 checkerboard is complete.

Tip   An easier way to accomplish the checkerboard would be to create the first two squares and then to use the Array dialog box to create the rest. Find out more about the Array dialog box in Chapter 7, "Cloning Objects."

Figure 14-2 shows the completed checkerboard.

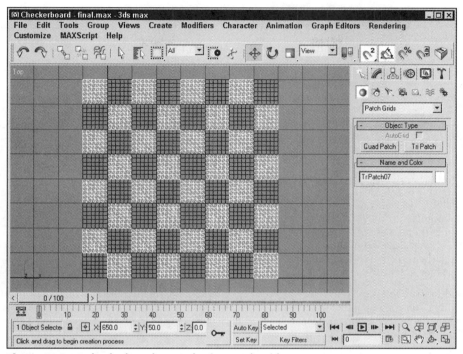

Figure 14-2: A checkerboard created using patch grids

Editing Patches

Creating and working with patches is easy, but because they are always flat, they have limited functionality. The key to making patches really useful is to convert the object into an Editable Patch object. Any type of geometric object can be converted to an Editable Patch object. Even patch grids created with the Quad Patch and Tri Patch buttons described earlier need to be converted before they can be edited at the subobject level.

You have several ways to convert an object to an Editable Patch. One way is to right-click a selected object and choose Convert To ➪ Convert to Editable Patch from the pop-up quad-menu. Another way is to apply the Edit Patch modifier by selecting it from the Modifier List in the Modifier Stack, or by choosing Modifiers ➪ Patch/Spline Editing ➪ Edit Patch. These two methods create slightly different Editable Patches.

Editable patches versus the Edit Patch modifier

The differences between Editable Patches and objects with the Edit Patch modifier applied are subtle. The main difference between these two appears in the Modifier Stack. Editable Patch objects have the type Editable Patch displayed in the Stack. Patch grids with the Edit

Patch modifier applied maintain their creation parameters, and the Edit Patch modifier is displayed in the Stack above the object type, where you can move or remove it at any time.

The other big difference is that the transformation of an Editable Patch subobject can be animated, whereas patch grids with the Edit Patch modifier cannot.

Editable patches and patch grids with the Edit Patch modifier applied both access subobjects and their parameters in the same way. These are covered in the next section.

Note   The Editable Patch object actually requires less memory than using the Edit Patch modifier and is the recommended method.

Selecting patch subobjects

Editable patches and the Edit Patch modifier both make patch subobjects accessible. The subobjects for patches include Vertex (1), Edge (2), Patch (3), and Element (4). Before you can edit patch subobjects, you must select them. To select a subobject type, click the small plus sign to the left of the Editable Patch object in the Modifier Stack. Alternatively, you can click the red-colored icons under the Selection rollout. When selected, the subobject button and hierarchy turn yellow.

A third way to enter subobject edit mode is to right-click the Editable Patch and select Sub-Object and the subobject type to edit from the pop-up quadmenu. You can also select the different subobject modes using the 1–5 keyboard shortcuts — 1 enters Vertex mode, 2 enters Edge mode, and so on.

Clicking either the subobject button or the hierarchy object again exits subobject mode. Remember, you must exit this mode before you can select another object. This is called Top Level in the quadmenu.

To select many subobjects at once, drag an outline over them. You can also select and deselect many subobjects by holding down the Ctrl key while clicking them. Hold down the Alt key to remove any selected vertices from the current selection set.

With subobjects selected, the options in the Selection rollout become enabled. Using these controls will enable you to more easily select the desired subobjects. Figure 14-3 shows the Selection and Soft Selection rollouts.

After selecting several subobjects, you can create a named selection set by typing a name in the Name Selection Sets drop-down list on the main toolbar. You can then copy and paste these selection sets onto other patch objects using the Copy and Paste buttons in the Selection rollout. In Vertex subobject mode, the Selection rollout will let you see, when selected, just Vertices or just Vectors or both. The Lock Handles option causes all selected Bézier handles to move together when one handle is moved.

The By Vertex option is available in all but the Vertex subobject mode. It requires that you click a vertex in order to select an Edge, Face, Polygon, or Element. It selects all edges and faces that are connected to a vertex when the vertex is selected. This is handy because selecting a vertex is often easier than selecting numerous faces or edges.

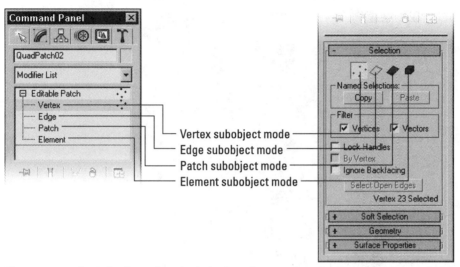

Figure 14-3: The Selection rollout includes icon buttons for selecting the various subobject modes.

The Ignore Backfacing option selects only those subobjects with normals pointing toward the current viewport. This option is helpful if many subobjects are on top of one another in the viewport. For example, if a sphere object were converted into an Editable Patch, you could enable the Ignore Backfacing option, and then selecting subobjects on the front of the sphere would not select the subobjects on the back of the sphere at the same time.

The Select Open Edges option is only active in Edge subobject mode. This button lets you select all the edges in the patch that are only connected to one face. This provides an easy way to quickly locate all the holes in your current model.

At the bottom of the Selection rollout is some information on the current selection. This lists the current subobject type and number selected.

 Cross-Reference The Soft Selection rollout allows you to alter (to a lesser extent) adjacent non-selected subobjects when selected subobjects are moved, creating a smooth transition. Check out the details of this rollout in Chapter 11, "Modeling Basics."

Working with Patch Geometry

Much of the power of editing patches is contained within the Geometry rollout, shown in Figure 14-4. You can use this rollout to attach new patches, weld and delete vertices, and bind and hide elements. Some Geometry rollout buttons may be disabled in the various subobject modes but will be enabled in one of the other subobject editing modes.

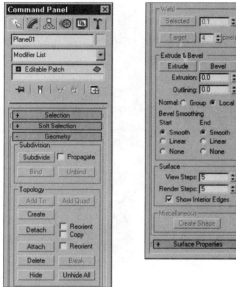

Figure 14-4: The Geometry rollout (shown in two parts) includes controls for editing patches.

Editing vertices

After you select Vertex subobject mode, you can transform selected vertices using the transform buttons on the main toolbar, or you can also distort the faces around the selected vertex by transforming the handles, shown as small green squares. Dragging these handles changes the surface of the patch as shown in Figure 14-5. The first patch shows the handles before being moved, the second patch shows the effect of moving the handles with the Lock Handles option enabled, the third patch has moved a single handle, and the fourth patch shows where both handles have been moved.

Selected vertex

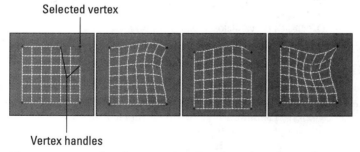

Vertex handles

Figure 14-5: Moving the Vertex handles alters the adjacent faces.

Patch vertices can be either of two types: Coplanar or Corner. Coplanar vertices maintain a smooth transition from vertex to vertex because their handles are locked. This causes the handles to always move so as to prevent any surface discontinuities. You can drag the handles of corner vertices to create gaps and seams in the surface.

You can switch between these different vertex types by right-clicking a vertex while in vertex subobject mode and selecting the desired type from the pop-up quadmenu.

Note   Holding down the Shift key while clicking and dragging on a handle unlocks the handles and automatically changes the vertex type to Corner.

Bind and Unbind

You can use the Bind button to connect edge vertices of one patch to an edge of another patch, which is useful for connecting edges with a different number of vertices. Be aware that the two patches must be part of the same object (you can make them part of the same object using the Attach button) and that the corner vertices must be welded together first. If you try to bind a vertex before welding the corner vertices, then the Bind action won't work. To use the Bind feature, click the Bind button, then drag a line from a vertex to the edge where it should join.

The Bind button attaches vertices to edges; to attach vertices to vertices, use one of the Weld buttons. When binding vertices, the point of contact between the two patches will be seamless and the vertex will become part of the interior. To exit Bind mode, click the Bind button again or right-click in a viewport.

You use the Unbind button to detach vertices that have been connected using the Bind button.

Create

You can use the Create button in the Vertex subobject mode to create patch vertices by clicking in the viewport. Use the Create button in Patch or Element subobject mode to connect the created vertices into three- or four-sided patches. Right-click in the viewport or click again on the Create button to exit Create mode.

The order in which you click on the vertices determines the direction of the normal vector, which determines the visibility of the patch in the viewports (unless the Force 2-Sided display option is enabled). If you click on the vertices in a clockwise direction, then the normal vector will point away from the current viewport. The counterclockwise order will point the normal vector out toward the user (which will make it visible).

Tip   An easy way to determine the direction of the normal vector is to curl the fingers on your right hand in the direction that the vertices were clicked. Your thumb will point toward the direction of the normal vector. This is called the right-hand rule.

Attach

The Attach button is available in all subobject modes and even when you're not in subobject mode. You use it to add objects to the current Editable Patch object, such as primitives, mesh objects, and other patch objects. However, be aware that you cannot attach a spline. Objects that are attached to an Editable Patch also become Editable Patches. Most Editable Patch features only work if all the involved patch pieces are attached as part of the same patch object.

To use this feature, select an object, click the Attach button, and move the mouse over the object to attach. The cursor changes over acceptable objects. Click the object to be attached. Click the Attach button again or right-click in the viewport to exit Attach mode. The Reorient option aligns the attached object's local coordinate system with the local coordinate system of the patch that it is being attached to.

Caution   Converting mesh objects to patch objects results in objects with many vertices.

Delete

The Delete button (or pressing the Delete key) deletes the selected vertices. This button works for all the subobject types.

Note   Deleting a vertex also deletes all faces and edges connected to that vertex. For example, deleting a single (top) vertex from a sphere that has been converted to an Editable Patch object leaves only a hemisphere.

Break

Click the Break button to create a separate vertex for adjoining faces that are connected by a single vertex.

Patches are all connected by vertices — moving one vertex changes the position of all adjoining patches. The Break button enables you to move the vertex associated with each patch independent of the others. The button is only available in Vertex subobject mode.

Hide and Unhide All

The Hide and Unhide All buttons hide and unhide selected vertices. They can be used in any subobject mode. To hide a subobject, select the subobject and click the Hide button. To Unhide the hidden subobjects, click the Unhide All button. Clicking the Unhide All button makes all subobjects, regardless of type, visible.

Weld Selected and Weld Target

The Weld button enables you to take two or more vertices and weld them into one vertex. To use this feature, move the vertices close to one another, drag an outline over them to select them, and then click the Weld button. You can tell whether the weld has been successful by looking at the number of vertices selected at the bottom of the Selection rollout. If the Weld was unsuccessful, increase the Weld Threshold specified by the spinner and try again.

The Weld Target button lets you select a vertex and drag and drop it on top of another vertex. If the target vertex is within the number of pixels specified by the Target value, the vertices are welded into one vertex. To exit Weld Target mode, click the Target button again or right-click in the viewport.

Figure 14-6 shows two inverted sloping patches that have been combined. The resolution of the patch on the right is twice that of the patch on the left. The Bind button was used to attach the center vertex to the edge of the other patch. Notice how the seam between the two patches is smooth.

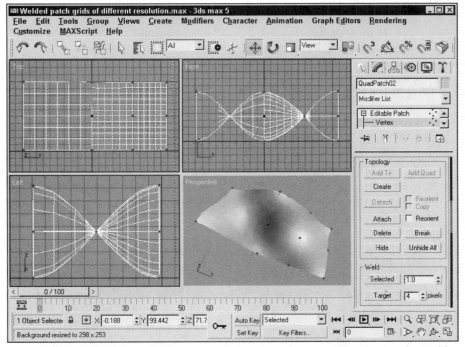

Figure 14-6: Two patches of different resolutions have been combined using the Weld and Bind buttons.

Surface settings

The View Steps value determines the resolution of the patch grid that is displayed in the viewport. You can change this resolution for rendering using the Render Steps value. You can turn off the Interior Edges altogether using the Show Interior Edges option.

A Quad Patch with a View Steps value of 0 is a simple square. Figure 14-7 shows four spheres that have all been cloned from one, converted to Editable Patches, and set with different View Steps. From left to right, the View Steps values are 0, 2, 4, 6, and 10.

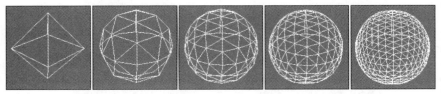

Figure 14-7: The only differences in these patch spheres are the View Steps values.

Vertex surface properties

In Vertex subobject mode, the Surface Properties rollout appears that lets you color the object by assigning colors to its vertices. For each vertex, you can also specify an Illumination color and an Alpha value, which sets the transparency. You can also specify vertex colors in Patch and Element subobject modes.

You can find more information on vertex colors in Chapter 19, "Creating and Applying Materials."

After you assign colors, you can then recall vertices with the same color by selecting a color (or illumination color) in the Select Vertices By section and clicking the Select button. The RGB values match all colors within the Range defined by these values. For example, if the RGB Range values are all set to 255, then every vertex will be selected.

Editing edges

Edges are the lines that run between two vertices. You can select multiple edges by holding down the Ctrl key while clicking the edges or by holding down the Alt key to remove selected edges from the current selection set.

Many of the features in the Geometry rollout work in the same way as the Vertex subobjects, but the Geometry rollout also includes some features that are enabled in Edge subobject mode, like the ones in the following sections.

Subdivide

You use the Subdivide button to increase the resolution of a patch. This is done by splitting an edge into two separate edges divided at the original edge's center. To use this feature, select an edge or edges and click the Subdivide button. The Propagate option causes the edges or neighboring patches to also be subdivided. Using Subdivide without the Propagate option enabled can cause cracks to appear in the patch. The Subdivide button also works in Patch subobject mode.

In Figure 14-8, I've subdivided a Quad Patch edge three times after selecting the upper-right corner edges.

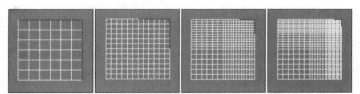

Figure 14-8: By subdividing edge subobjects, you can control where the greatest resolution is located.

Add Tri and Add Quad

You can add Quad and Tri Patches to any open edge of a patch. To do this, select the open edge or edges and click the Add Tri or Add Quad button. You can locate all open edges using the Select Open Edges button in the Selection rollout. The new patch extends along the current curvature of the patch. To add a patch to a closed surface, like a box, you'll first need to detach one of the patches to create an open edge. This feature provides a way to extend the current patch.

Figure 14-9 shows a simple quad patch that was subdivided and then added to using the Add Quad button. This provides an easy way to very quickly create a rough outline of an object that you want to model.

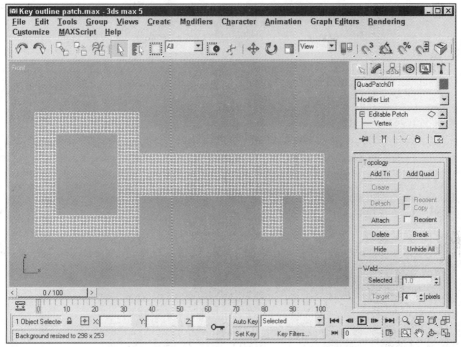

Figure 14-9: A quick outline of a key was created by selecting edge subobjects and adding Quad patches.

Create Shape

You can use the Create Shape button that appears at the bottom of the Geometry rollout in Edge subobject mode to create spline shapes from all the selected edges. To use this button, select several edge subobjects and click the button. A dialog box appears that allows you to name the new shape. You can then use the Select by Name dialog box (keyboard shortcut, H) to select the newly created shape.

Editing Patch and Element subobjects

Transforming a patch object containing only one patch works the same way in subobject mode as it works for normal transformations. Working with the Patch subobject on an object that contains several patches lets you transform individual patches. A key advantage of working with the patch subobjects is controlling their Geometry using the buttons in the Geometry rollout. The following sections discuss the additional features available in Patch subobject mode.

Detach

The Detach button separates the selected patch or element subobjects from the rest of the object. Using this button opens the Detach dialog box, which enables you to name the detached subobject. The Reorient option realigns the detached subobject patch to match the position and orientation of the current active patch. The Copy option creates a new copy of the detached subobject.

Note This feature is different from Delete. Detach maintains the subobject and gives it a separate name, but the Delete function eliminates the subobject.

Extrude

The Extrude button adds depth to a patch by replicating a patch surface and creating sides to connect the new patch surface to the original. For example, a square patch grid that is extruded forms a cube. To use this feature, select a patch, click the Extrude button, and then drag in a viewport — the patch will interactively show the extrude depth. Release the button when you've reached the desired distance.

Alternatively, you can specify an extrude depth in the Extrusion spinner. The Outlining value lets you resize the extruded patch. Positive outlining values cause the extrusion to get larger, whereas negative values reduce its size. The Normal Group option extrudes all selected patches along the normal for the group, and the Normal Local option moves each individual patch along its local normal. To exit extrude mode, click the Extrude button again or right-click in the viewport.

Tip One place to use this function is to add arms to the torso of a character. If you've created a torso model out of patches, you can add arms by detaching a patch and extruding the area where the arms will go.

Figure 14-10 shows the key-shaped patch that has been extruded using the Extrude button.

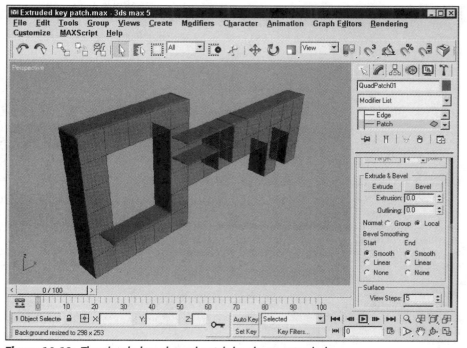

Figure 14-10: The simple key-shaped patch has been extruded.

Bevel

The Bevel button extrudes a patch and then lets you bevel the edges. To use this feature, select a patch, click the Bevel button, and then drag in a viewport to the Extrusion depth and release the button. Then drag again to specify the Outlining amount.

You can use the same options for the Bevel button as for the Extrude button described previously. In addition, the Bevel button includes Smoothing options for the bevel. Set the Start and End Smoothing options to Smooth, Linear, or None.

Figure 14-11 displays a sphere that has been converted to an Editable Patch object. Each corner of the sphere object was selected and beveled with an Extrusion value of 25 and an Outline value of –5.

Patch and element surface properties

If either the patch or element subobject modes are selected, the Surface Properties rollout appears. You can use this rollout to control Normal vectors and assign Material IDs and Smoothing groups.

The Surface Properties rollout includes Flip and Unify buttons to control the direction of the normal vectors. Flip reverses the direction of the normals of each selected face; Unify makes all normals face in the same direction based on the majority. The Flip Normal Mode button activates a mode where you can click individual faces and flip their normals. This mode stays active until you click the Flip Normal Mode button again or right-click in the viewport.

Material IDs are used by the Multi/Sub-Object material type to apply different materials to different patches within an object. By selecting a patch subobject, you can use this control to apply a unique material to each patch.

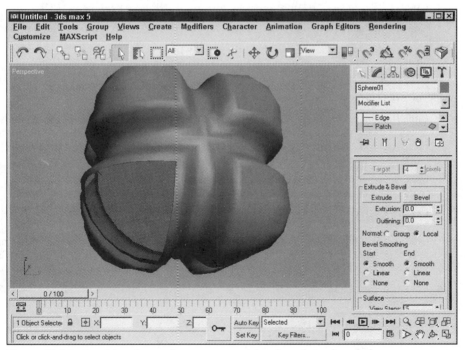

Figure 14-11: A patch sphere whose corner patches have been beveled

Cross-Reference You can find more information on the Multi/Sub-Object material type in Chapter 19, "Creating and Applying Materials."

You can also assign a patch to a unique Smoothing group. To do this, select a patch and click a Smoothing Group number.

Relaxing a patch

When the Editable Patch object is selected without any subobject modes, the Surface Properties rollout includes an option to Relax the patch. Enabling this option moves vertices too close to neighboring vertices slightly apart. The net result is to smooth the areas of tension, making the entire patch more continuous and less abrupt.

With the Relax option enabled, the other options in the rollout become available. The Relax Viewports option displays the results of the Relax option in the viewports. The Relax Value determines how far the vertices will move. The Iterations value sets how many times the relax function is performed. The Keep Boundary Points Fixed and Save Outer Corners options can be used to maintain the exterior profile of the patch and prevent edges and corners from being relaxed.

Tutorial: Modeling a shell

Now that you've seen all the various tools, let's try some of them out. A Patch object can be used to create a common beach shell, as we'll do in this tutorial.

To model a shell using a patch, follow these steps:

1. Open the Patch seashell.max file from the Chap 14 directory on the CD-ROM.

   This file includes a simple disk that has been converted to an Editable Patch object.

2. Select the extruded circle and open the Modify panel. Click the small plus icon to the left of the Editable Patch object in the Modifier Stack and select Vertex from the hierarchy (or press the 1 key).

   You are now in Vertex subobject mode.

3. Click the Select and Move button on the main toolbar (or press the W key). Then while holding down the Ctrl key, select all the vertices in the lower half of the circle in the Front viewport and move them close to the main vertex to form a fan-shaped patch.

4. After the neighboring vertices have been positioned, select them all (including the main vertices that all the edges are connected to) and click the Weld button. If the vertices fail to be welded, increase the Weld Threshold and try again.

5. Click Edge in the Modifier Stack hierarchy to enter Edge subobject mode (or press the 2 key). Then select every other interior set of edges in the Front viewport along the top of the circle while holding down the Ctrl key. Make sure that you select both the front and back edges. The Info line at the bottom of the Selection rollout tells you what is selected. When you have the edges selected, press the spacebar to lock the selection.

6. Click the Select and Move button (or press the W key) and move the edges upward in the Top view.

   A zigzag pattern appears on the surface of the patch.

Figure 14-12 shows the completed shell.

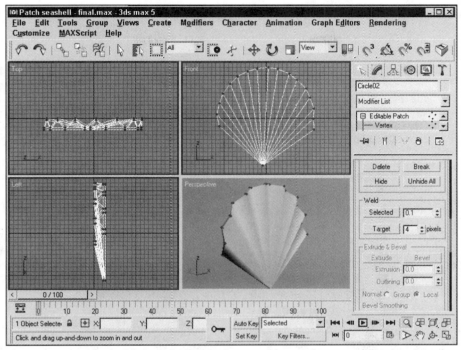

Figure 14-12: This shell is an Editable Patch created by moving every other interior edge.

Tutorial: Creating a maple leaf from patches

Because patches are a good modeling type for organic objects, let's put it to the test by trying to create a maple leaf. Because of the symmetry of the leaf, we really only need to create half of the leaf. We can then use the Mirror tool to create the other half.

To model a maple leaf using patches, follow these steps:

1. Open the Maple leaf.max file from the Chap 14 directory on the CD-ROM.

   This file includes a background image of a real maple leaf loaded into the Front viewport.

2. Open the Create panel and select the Patch Grids subcategory. Click on the Tri Patch button and drag in the Front viewport to create a square patch grid from the base where the stem is to the upper-left interior area of the leaf. The right edge of the patch should run about halfway up along the midline of the leaf.

3. In the Modify panel, right-click on the Tri Patch name and select Convert to Editable Patch from the pop-up menu.

4. In the Modifier Stack, select the Element subobject mode (or press the 4 key), then select the patch element, and with the Propagate option selected, click the Subdivision button.

5. Select the Edge subobject mode (or press the 2 key) and select one of the edges that is completely within the interior area of the background leaf image. Then press the Add Tri button to extend the patch. Repeat this step until you have added a patch for each point around the outer perimeter of the leaf.

6. Select Vertex subobject mode (or press the 1 key) and with the Select and Move button on the main toolbar, select and drag the edge vertices so they align with the corners of the background leaf. Move all internal vertices so they lie within the leaf area. Select each vertex that lies along the outer edge of the leaf and move its handles so the patch edge aligns with the background leaf's border. If the handles move together, hold down the Shift key to move them individually.

7. De-select the Vertex subobject mode, and in the Surface Properties rollout, enable all the options, and set the Relax Value to 1.0 and the Iterations to 50. This smoothes out the wrinkles in the patch.

Figure 14-13 shows the completed maple leaf patch (half of it, anyway). To complete this leaf, use the Mirror tool and add a spline object for the stem.

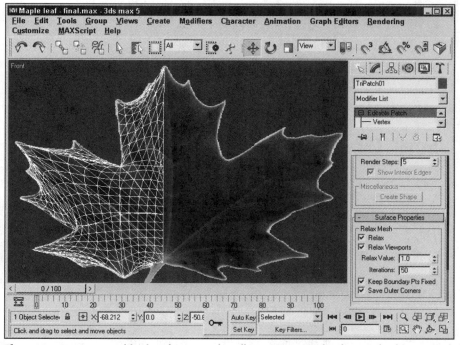

Figure 14-13: By repositioning the vertex handles, you can make the patch object match the leaf's edges precisely.

Using Modifiers on Patch Objects

Several modifiers work specifically on patch objects. The Modifiers ⇨ Patch/Spline Editing submenu contains most of these modifiers.

Tip

Many other modifiers work on patch objects. To see which modifiers work on patch objects, select the patch object and check the Modifiers menu to see which modifiers are enabled.

Patch Select modifier

The Patch Select modifier enables you to select patch subobjects, including Vertex, Edge, Patch, and Element. You can copy and paste named selection sets. The selection can then be passed up the Stack to the next modifier. The Patch Select modifier provides a way to apply a separate modifier to a subobject selection.

Edit Patch modifier

This modifier includes tools for editing patch objects. The features of this modifier are the same as those of the Editable Patch object. If you want to animate the features of an Editable Patch, use the Edit Patch modifier. You can even apply the Edit Patch modifier to an Editable Patch. The key benefit of the Edit Patch modifier is that it enables you to edit patch subobjects while maintaining the parametric nature of the object.

Delete Patch modifier

You can use the Delete Patch modifier to delete a patch subobject from a patch object. You use the Patch Select modifier to select the patch subobjects to delete, and you apply the Delete Patch modifier to the Patch Select modifier.

Using the Surface tools

The surface tools, which include the CrossSection and Surface modifiers, provide a way to model that is similar to lofting. The CrossSection modifier takes several cross-section shapes and connects their vertices with additional splines to create a spline framework. You can then use the Surface modifier to cover this framework with a skin.

Cross-Reference

Lofting is accomplished with the Loft compound object. For more information on it, see Chapter 16, "Using Compound Objects."

CrossSection modifier

The CrossSection modifier is the first modifier that is used to create surfaces based on cross-sectional splines. This modifier and the Surface modifier are the key reason why the spline and patch modifiers have been combined into a single submenu.

The CrossSection modifier works only on spline objects, but without the Surface modifier it isn't very useful. This modifier connects the vertices of several cross-sectional splines together with another spline that runs along their edges like a backbone. The various cross-sectional splines can have different numbers of vertices. Parameters include different spline types such as Linear, Smooth, Bézier, and Bézier Corner.

To apply this modifier, all the cross-section splines need to belong to the same Editable Spline object. You can connect them using the Attach button. The cross-section splines are attached in the order they exist. Figure 14-14 shows a spline network that has been created with the CrossSection modifier.

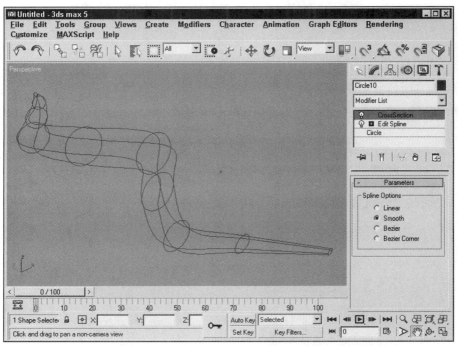

Figure 14-14: The CrossSection modifier joins several cross-section splines into a network of splines ready for a surface.

Surface modifier

The Surface modifier is the other part of the surface tools. It creates a surface from several combined splines. It can use any spline network but works best with structures created with the CrossSection modifier. The surface created with this modifier is a patch surface.

Parameters for this modifier include a Spline Threshold value and options to Flip Normals, Remove Interior Patches, and to Use Only Selected Segments. You can also specify the steps used to create the patch topology. After the surface is created, you can apply the Edit Patch modifier to further edit and refine the patch surface.

Figure 14-15 shows the spline structure illustrated in the previous figure with the Surface modifier applied.

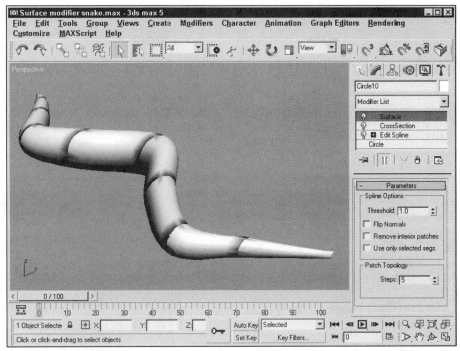

Figure 14-15: The Surface modifier applies a surface to the cross-section spline network.

Tutorial: Modeling the Mercury space capsule

One of the early space capsules used in the space race was the Mercury space capsule. Although a lot of advanced technology was contained within the capsule, the exterior shape was relatively simple. Primitive shapes could be used to create the capsule, but in this tutorial, we'll create it using the surface tools.

To create a space capsule, follow these steps:

1. Open the Mercury space capsule.max file from the Chap 14 directory on the CD-ROM.

   This file includes all the cross-section splines needed to create the space capsule.

2. Select the top circle, open the Modify panel, click the Attach button, and then click each individual circle in order (the order is important for the CrossSection modifier).

   This step attaches all the circles together into one Editable Spline object.

Note   You can check the spline order by entering Spline subobject mode and selecting each spline. The spline number appears at the bottom of the Selection rollout.

3. With the entire spline selected, choose Modifiers ➪ Patch/Spline Editing ➪ CrossSection to apply the CrossSection modifier to the spline object. Select the Linear option in the Parameters rollout.

   This command automatically connects all the splines in order by connecting their vertices.

4. Choose Modifiers ➪ Patch/Spline Editing ➪ Surface to apply the Surface modifier.

This command creates a surface that covers the spline framework. The surface that is created is a patch object.

Figure 14-16 shows the completed Mercury space capsule. Using the surface tools to create patch objects results in objects that are easy to modify. You can change any patch subobject by applying the Edit Patch modifier and using the rollouts in the Modify panel.

Another common modifier that is used with patch objects is the PatchDeform modifier. Learn more about this modifier in Chapter 24, "Animation Basics."

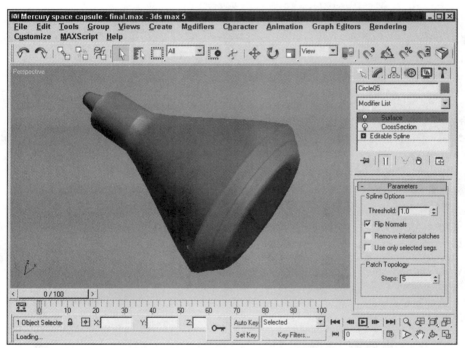

Figure 14-16: The Mercury space capsule, created using the CrossSection and Surface modifiers.

Summary

Patches don't have the overhead of NURBS objects and are better optimized than mesh objects. Editable Patch objects include a huge list of tools that you can use to edit and modify them. In this chapter, you learned how to create and edit patches.

More specifically, in this chapter, you've

✦ Learned to create Quad and Tri Patch grids

✦ Discovered the features of an Editable Patch object

✦ Worked with the Editable Patch subobjects

✦ Worked with patch-specific modifiers such as the surface tools

Now that splines, meshes, and patches have been covered, we'll take the escalator to the next floor, which covers NURBS in all their nurby glory.

✦　　✦　　✦

Working with NURBS

NURBS is an acronym for Non-Uniform Rational B-Splines. They are the ideal modeling tool for creating organic characters because they are easy to work with, they give you good interactive control, they blend together seamlessly, and the surfaces remain smooth even when distorted. NURBS are superior to polygonal modeling methods for building models with smooth flowing contours such as plants, flowers, animals, and skin.

In this chapter we explore different methods of NURBS model construction and then look at some advanced NURBS tutorials.

Creating NURBS Curves and Surfaces

If you boil down any complex NURBS object, you'll find a collection of fundamental building pieces. These fundamental pieces consist of curves and surfaces. From these simple pieces, you can form complex models. You can create both of these fundamental pieces using the Create panel.

From the Create panel, you can create two types of NURBS curves and two types of NURBS surfaces. For both curves and surfaces, one type works with points and the other type works with control vertices (referred to as CVs). The point type includes lines that always run through the points that make up the curves or surfaces. The CV type is different. It has a lattice of points that control how the lines run. The lines do not run through the CVs, but are affected by their distance, much like how Bézier curves work.

NURBS curves

The two kinds of NURBS curves are CV curves and point curves. CV curves are the most commonly used NURBS curves. You can create both of these curves by opening the Create panel, selecting the Shapes category, and selecting the NURBS Curves subcategory. Then click and drag in the viewport to set the first point and begin drawing the curve. After each click, drag the mouse to a new location and click again to continue extending the curve, and then right-click to end the curve.

Figure 15-1 shows a NURBS point curve on the left and a NURBS CV curve on the right.

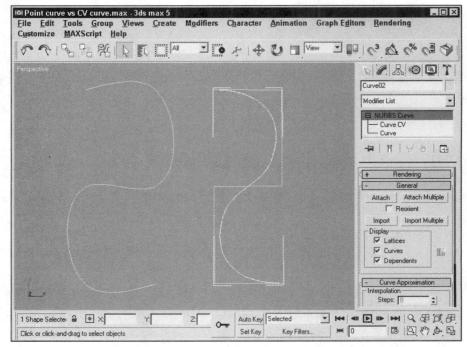

Figure 15-1: NURBS curves come in two different types: point and CV curves.

 Note   You can also create NURBS curves and surfaces using the NURBS Creation Toolbox, which you find out more about later in this chapter.

CV curves have a CV control lattice with points that let you control the shape of an individual curve or the entire surface. The point curve is similar to a CV curve except that the NURBS curve passes through the points. Point curves give you more intuitive control over the shape of a curve or surface, but they are not as stable as CV curves, and point surfaces do not have as many modification options. Notice that NURBS curves are automatically smoothed, but, unlike splines, they do not have Bézier control handles to adjust their shape. You can adjust the shape of a NURBS curve by moving the control vertices or by adjusting the weights (strengths of attraction) of individual CVs.

The Rendering rollout includes many of the same rendering options that apply for splines. You can make the curves renderable and give them a Thickness value. You can also make the curves appear in the renderer and/or the viewports and have Max generate mapping coordinates.

Using the Create CV Curve rollout, which becomes available when you choose the CV Curve option, you can set the Interpolation Steps value. The Optimize and Adaptive options automatically reduce the number of points required for the curve. The Automatic Reparameterization options include None, Chord Length, and Uniform. The Chord Length and Uniform options use different algorithms to determine the spacing of the CVs.

The Create Point Curve rollout has the same parameters as the Create CV Curve rollout, except that there are no Reparameterization options.

NURBS surfaces

You can create NURBS point surfaces and CV surfaces by opening the Create panel, selecting the Geometry category, and selecting the NURBS Surfaces subcategory. Then, to create the surface, you simply click and drag to make a rectangular shape in any viewport; when you release the mouse button, the surface is built. These rectangles, also referred to as NURBS patches, are easy to form into shapes by moving, scaling, and rotating the CVs. You can build a large model by assembling a group of these NURBS patches and attaching them with various NURBS surface tools.

The Create Parameters rollout includes settings to specify the Length and Width of the surface. You can also specify the number of points or CVs the surface will have. This rollout also includes options to Generate Mapping Coordinates and Flip Normals. For CV surfaces, you can set Automatic Reparameterization to None, Chord Length, or Uniform.

You can modify CV surfaces by selecting the Surface CV subobject in the Modifier Stack and moving the control vertices that surround the surface or by adjusting the weight of the individual CVs in the CV rollout. Point surfaces have no lattice, but you can shape them directly by selecting the Point subobject and moving the points on the surface.

Tip

When building some models such as a human head, using point surfaces is often easier because you can adjust the surface interactively, and you avoid the confusion of having a complex control vertex lattice floating on top of your model, obscuring the area you are working on.

Figure 15-2 shows a NURBS point surface on the left and a NURBS CV surface on the right.

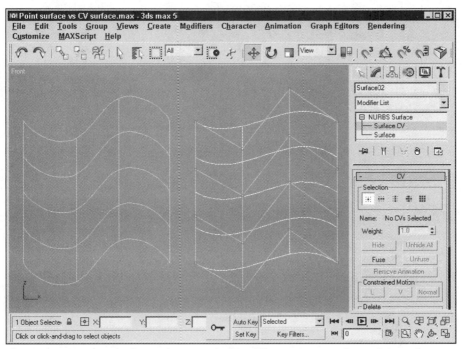

Figure 15-2: NURBS surfaces also come in two different types: point and CV surfaces.

You can create different types of NURBS surfaces from NURBS curves and patches using the various buttons found in the Create Surfaces rollout in the Modify panel. You learn more about these buttons in the sections that follow.

When a surface is created from two or more NURBS curves using the buttons in the Create Surfaces rollout, the surface is displayed in the form of U and V isoparms. *Isoparms* are lines that span the distance from one curve to the next and establish the NURBS surface. Isoparms are displayed in the viewport as green lines when a NURBS surface is selected.

Converting objects to NURBS

To convert a standard primitive object to a NURBS object, select the primitive object, right-click in the viewport and choose Convert To ➪ Convert to NURBS in the pop-up quadmenu. Another option for converting primitives is to right-click the object title in the Modifier Stack and select the Convert to NURBS option from the pop-up menu.

Figure 15-3 shows two spheres. The one on the left is a normal primitive sphere, and the one on the right has been converted to a NURBS surface.

Another method to convert a standard primitive to a NURBS object is to attach it to a NURBS object. To do this, select the NURBS object, open the Modify panel, and under the General rollout click the Attach button and select the polygon object to attach. Any object that is attached to a NURBS object is automatically converted to a NURBS object.

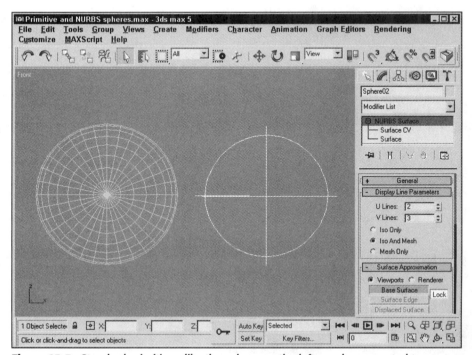

Figure 15-3: Standard primitives, like the sphere on the left, can be converted to NURBS surfaces.

Some modifiers, such as the Lathe modifier, give you the option of creating a patch, mesh, or NURBS as the output type. However, after a lathed object has been output as a polygonal mesh or a patch object, it can no longer be converted to a NURBS object.

You can also convert splines to NURBS curves, but not all types of splines will convert to one-piece NURBS curves. For example, a line created using the Corner Initial type and Drag type options will convert to a series of separate NURBS curves. If you want the spline to convert to a single curve, you must set the Drag type option to Smooth or Bézier. Of the many types of splines available in the Shapes category, only the Helix cannot be converted to a NURBS curve. The Rectangle, NGon, and Text shapes yield segmented NURBS curves, and closed shapes such as the Circle, Star, Ellipse, and Donut yield one-piece NURBS curves when converted.

Note

If you plan to use multiple-piece curve shapes as cross sections in a one- or two-rail sweep (discussed later in the chapter) or as NURBS Extrusion curves, considering whether a curve is closed or not is important. To function properly, multiple-piece curve shapes need to be welded into a single NURBS curve after conversion.

Editing NURBS

You can edit and model NURBS curves and surfaces into desired shapes using the rollouts in the Modify panel, using the tools in the NURBS Creation Toolbox, or by working with the NURBS subobjects.

NURBS rollouts

When a NURBS curve is selected, several rollouts are available in the Modify panel. The first two of these are the Rendering and General rollouts, shown in Figure 15-4. The Rendering rollout works the same as explained in the "NURBS curves" section earlier. The General rollout includes buttons to attach and import NURBS. The Attach Multiple and Import Multiple buttons let you select from a dialog box several objects to attach or import. When attaching NURBS, you have the option of reorienting the attached object.

The General rollout also includes a Display section where you can select which elements get displayed. For curves, the options include Lattices, Curves, and Dependents. For surfaces, the options include Surfaces, Surface Trims, and Transform Degrade, and you can also choose the surface display to be a Tessellated Mesh or a Shaded Lattice. Next to the Display section is the NURBS Creation Toolbox button. This button opens a floating window of buttons that make working with NURBS easy. You find out more about the NURBS Creation Toolbox buttons in the next section.

For NURBS surfaces, the Display Line Parameters rollout, shown along with the General rollout for NURBS surfaces in Figure 15-5, lets you specify the number of U and V isoparms to use to display the NURBS surface. These isoparms are the lines that make the NURBS object visible in the viewport.

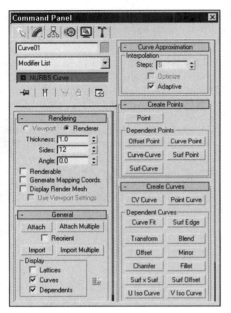

Figure 15-4: The NURBS rollouts for curves enable you to set many options.

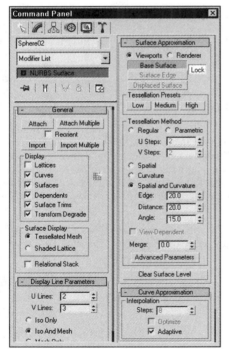

Figure 15-5: The rollouts for NURBS surfaces also control many settings.

When you're working with NURBS surfaces, the Surface Approximation rollout lets you control the surface details for both the viewport and the renderer. For Base Surface, Surface Edge, and Displaced Surface, you can set the Tessellation Method. The three Tessellation Presets are Low, Medium, and High. These presets set the parameters for the various tessellation methods, with Low representing the values that produce the lowest-quality surface. You can also select which tessellation method to use — Regular, Parametric, Spatial, Curvature, or Spatial and Curvature. Each of these methods uses a different algorithm to compute the surface.

The Merge value determines the space between surfaces that should be combined to eliminate gaps when the surface is rendered. In most cases, the default value is acceptable for eliminating surface gaps. The Advanced Parameters button opens an additional dialog box of parameters, shown in Figure 15-6, that are used by the Spatial, Curvature, and Spatial and Curvature tessellation methods. Use the Clear Surface Level button to eliminate all Surface Approximation settings.

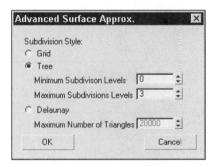

Figure 15-6: The Advanced Surface Approximation dialog box lets you specify subdivision levels.

The Curve Approximation rollout lets you select the number of interpolation steps to use. You can also select the Optimize or Adaptive option. These options define the number of segments that are used to represent the curve.

The final three rollouts for NURBS objects are Create Points, Create Curves, and Create Surfaces. The buttons included in these rollouts work in the same fashion as the icon buttons found in the NURBS Creation Toolbox, which is covered next.

The NURBS Creation Toolbox

Clicking the NURBS Creation Toolbox button in the General rollout opens the toolbox shown in Figure 15-7. Clicking the button a second time closes the toolbox. This toolbox has three sections: Points, Curves, and Surfaces.

Note   You can also open the NURBS Creation Toolbox by using the Ctrl+T keyboard shortcut.

Each of these sections includes buttons that create dependent subobjects. Dependent subobjects are objects that depend on other points, curves, or surfaces. When the parent object is changed, the dependent subobjects are changed also.

Figure 15-7: The NURBS Creation Toolbox lets you work with NURBS points, curves, and surfaces.

The Points section includes buttons for creating dependent NURBS points. Table 15-1 describes these point types and their respective buttons.

Table 15-1: Points NURBS Creation Toolbox Buttons

Toolbar Button	Name	Description
	Create Point	Creates a free independent point.
	Create Offset Point	Creates a point that is offset from another point.
	Create Curve Point	Creates a point that is on a curve.
	Create Curve-Curve Point	Creates a point that intersects two curves.
	Create Surf Point	Creates a point that is on a surface.
	Create Surface Curve Point	Creates a point that intersects a curve and a surface.

Creating freestanding or dependent NURBS points gives you another way to build curves. When one of these buttons is selected, the cursor changes when it is positioned over a place where the point can be created. For example, clicking the Create Surf Point button causes the cursor in the viewport to change when it is over a NURBS surface.

The Curves section includes many more buttons than the Points section. You can use these buttons to create dependent NURBS curves. Table 15-2 describes each of these buttons.

You can create dependent curve subobjects from points, curves, or surfaces. The cursor indicates when these can be created. Some dependent curves require two objects. For example, the Create Blend Curve button can attach two curves together. Selecting the first and then selecting the second does this. Each curve is highlighted blue as it is selected. The curves must be part of the same object.

Table 15-2: Curves NURBS Creation Toolbox Buttons

Toolbar Button	Name	Description
	Create CV Curve	Creates a CV curve.
	Create Point Curve	Creates a point curve.
	Create Fit Curve	Creates a point curve that fits the selected points.
	Create Transform Curve	Creates a copy of a curve that is transformed.
	Create Offset Curve	Creates copy of the original curve that is larger or smaller and moved to one side according to the distance setting.
	Create Blend Curve	Blends or smoothly connects the ends of two NURBS curves.
	Create Mirror Curve	Creates a mirrored copy of the original curve in the selected axis at a user-set distance.
	Create Chamfer Curve	Creates a bevel where two curves meet.
	Create Fillet Curve	Creates a radius line to make a smooth transition between two curves that cross each other.
	Create Surface-Surface Intersection Curve	Creates a curve along the edge created when two NURBS surfaces intersect each other.
	Create U Iso Curve	Creates a dependent curve from the U isoparm that make up the NURBS surface.
	Create V Iso Curve	Creates a dependent curve from the V isoparm that makes up the NURBS surface.
	Create Normal Projected Curve	Projects a curve on a NURBS surface by projecting along a surface normal.
	Create Vector Projected Curve	Projects a curve on a NURBS surface by projecting along a vector.
	Create CV Curve on Surface	Enables the user to create a CV curve directly on a NURBS surface.
	Create Point Curve on Surface	Enables the user to create a point curve directly on a NURBS surface.
	Create Surface Offset Curve	Creates a curve that is offset from a surface curve.
	Create Surface Edge Curve	Creates a curve that lies on the surface edge.

The Surfaces section includes buttons for creating dependent NURBS surfaces. Table 15-3 describes each of these buttons.

Table 15-3: Surfaces NURBS Creation Toolbox Buttons

Toolbar Button	Name	Description
	Create CV Surface	Creates a CV surface.
	Create Point Surface	Creates a point surface.
	Create Transform Surface	Creates a copy of a surface that is transformed.
	Create Blend Surface	Connects one surface to another with a smooth surface between them.
	Create Offset Surface	Creates a copy of the original curve that is moved to one side according to the distance setting.
	Create Mirror Surface	Creates a mirrored copy of the original surface in the selected axis at a user set distance.
	Create Extrude Surface	Creates a NURBS surface at right angles to the construction plane.
	Create Lathed Surface	Creates a NURBS surface by rotating a curve about an axis.
	Create Ruled Surface	Creates a straight surface that joins the edges of two separate surfaces; one edge can be curved and the other straight.
	Create Capped Surface	Creates a surface that closes the edges of a closed surface.
	Create U Loft Surface	Creates a surface by linking multiple closed curved contours along the U axis.
	Create UV Loft Surface	Creates a surface by linking multiple closed curved contours along the U and V axes.
	Create 1-Rail Sweep	Creates a surface using an edge defined by one curve with a cross section defined by another.
	Create 2-Rail Sweep	Creates a surface using an edge defined by two curves with a cross section defined by another.
	Create a Multisided Blend Surface	Creates a surface by blending several curves and surfaces.
	Create a Multicurved Trimmed Surface	Creates a surface that is trimmed by several curves that form a loop.
	Create Fillet Surface	Creates a surface with rounded corners where the surfaces meet.

The buttons included in the NURBS Creation Toolbox give you a wide variety of possible NURBS objects to work with. We use many of these NURBS objects in the tutorials later in this chapter.

Using NURBS subobject editing tools

Max provides you with many tools that you can use to edit the various NURBS points, curves, and surfaces. To access these tools, select a NURBS object, open the Modify panel, select the object name in the Modifier Stack, and click the small plus sign icon to its left. A hierarchical list of subobjects appears in the Modifier Stack. The rollouts present the available editing tools. For example, if you select CV Surface in the Modifier Stack list, you can then adjust the position of the control vertices (or points on a point surface), using Max's standard transform buttons to change the shape of any NURBS surface.

The rollouts change depending on the type of NURBS object and subobject selected. The tools in these rollouts let you select and name specific areas, as well as hide, delete, break, and detach NURBS elements, and even work with a Soft Selection.

Many details of these various subobject tools are demonstrated in the tutorials that follow.

Working with NURBS

You'll learn many of the details of working with NURBS as you dive in and start building NURBS objects. This section includes several tutorials that can help as you try to grasp the power and flexibility of modeling with NURBS.

Lofting a NURBS surface

U Loft is one of the most versatile NURBS surface tools — you can use it to create simple or very complex surfaces. In the following tutorial, we create a spoon by U Lofting a NURBS surface over a series of point curve cross sections.

Tutorial: Creating a U-Loft NURBS spoon

Lofting a skin over a series of cross-section curves can create NURBS surfaces. In this tutorial, we create the point curves necessary for modeling a NURBS spoon. Then we use the U Loft tool to skin the surface and create the finished spoon.

To create a NURBS spoon using the U Loft feature, follow these steps:

1. Open the U-Loft spoon.max file from the Chap 15 directory on the CD-ROM.

   This file includes ten cross-section NURBS point curves that are correctly positioned to form a spoon.

2. Select one of the curves and open the Modify panel. In the General rollout, click the Attach Multiple button to open the Attach Multiple dialog box, click the All button to select all the curves, and then click the Attach button to attach all the curves to the first curve you selected.

3. You are now ready to U Loft the spoon's surface. In the General rollout, click the NURBS Creation Toolbox icon (or press Ctrl+T) to open the NURBS Toolbox window. In the Surfaces section, select the Create U Loft Surface icon.

   The cursor changes to a pointer accompanied by the U Loft Surface icon. (Notice that when you place the cursor over a cross section, it changes to a cross and the curve turns blue.)

Note   You can also create this surface using the U Loft button found in the Create Surfaces rollout.

4. Click the smallest cross section at the tip of the spoon and then drag to the next adjacent curve and click again.

   The first section of the U Lofted NURBS surface is then generated as indicated by the green isoparm lines displayed in the viewport.

5. Continue clicking each curve in sequential order until you have lofted the entire spoon. After you've clicked the final section, right-click to exit this mode.

6. Now cap the ends by returning to the NURBS Toolbox window, selecting the Create Cap Surface tool, and clicking each small end curve.

Figure 15-8 shows the completed NURBS spoon.

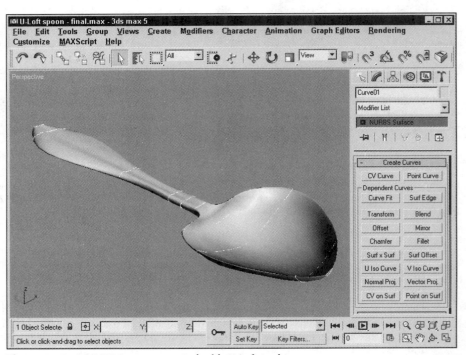

Figure 15-8: A NURBS spoon created with U Loft tool

Creating a UV Loft surface

A UV Loft surface can have more complex contours than a U Loft surface. UV Lofts are created from several curves spanning two dimensions. To use this tool, select the cross-section curves in the order that they will be skinned along the U dimension, right-click in the viewport, and click the cross-sectional curves for the V dimension. The resulting surface will be made up of cross-sectional curves for both dimensions to create a complex NURBS surface. Just like the U Loft surface, all curves need to be attached to the same NURBS object.

As an example, Figure 15-9 shows a chair seat that has been UV Lofted using three curves in the U direction and five curves in the V direction, thus enabling the surface to be contoured to fit a human being without our having to go back later and modify it by moving control vertices.

This technique is very useful for building mechanical shapes, automobiles, and spaceships, and for modeling product designs.

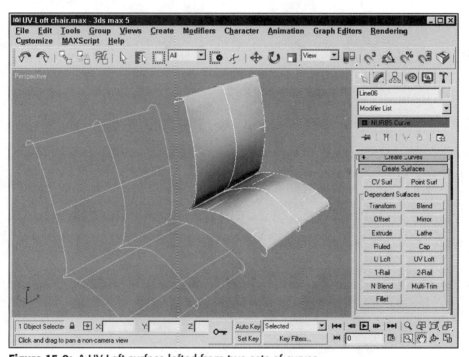

Figure 15-9: A UV Loft surface lofted from two sets of curves

Lathing a NURBS surface

Lathing a NURBS curve works the same way as lathing a spline. You simply need to select a curve, click the Lathe button in the Create Surface rollout (or click the Create Lathe Surface button in the NURBS Creation Toolbox), and then click the curve. You can change the Degrees value and the axis of rotation in the Lathe Surface rollout that appears under the Create Surfaces rollout in the Modify panel.

Tutorial: Lathing a NURBS CV curve to create a vase

In this tutorial we create a NURBS CV curve profile shape. We then use this curve with the Lathe modifier to create a vase.

To create a Lathed NURBS surface, follow these steps:

1. Open the Lathed NURBS vase.max file from the Chap 15 directory on the CD-ROM.

   This file includes two CV curves that you can lathe to create a vase.

2. Open the Modify panel and click the Lathe button in the Create Surfaces rollout (or click the Create Lathe Surface button in the NURBS Creation Toolbox). The Lathe Surface rollout appears at the bottom of the Modify panel. Enter a value of **360** in the Degrees field and click the Y-axis button. Then click on both CV curves to complete the lathe. Click the Lathe button again to exit Lathe mode.

Figure 15-10 shows the completed vase produced using the Lathe tool.

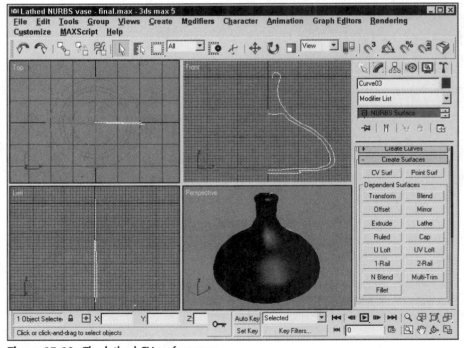

Figure 15-10: The lathed CV surface vase

Creating a 1- and 2-rail sweep surface

The 1-rail sweep surface tool lets you create a NURBS surface by using one NURBS curve to act as a side rail, and one or more profile shape curves to sweep along the rail to generate the surface. A 2-rail sweep surface is similar, except that it uses two NURBS curves as side rails.

Tutorial: Creating a flower stem

Now that we have carefully constructed a flower vase, we need to create some flowers to place in the vase. We start with the flower stem.

To create a NURBS point surface using a 1-rail sweep, follow these steps:

1. Open the Flower stem.max file from the Chap 15 directory on the CD-ROM.

   This file includes three cross sections and a curve correctly positioned that you can sweep to form a flower stem.

2. Select the long stem curve. Open the Modify panel and click the Attach button and click the three cross-section shapes. Then click the Attach button again to exit attach mode.

3. Open the Create Surfaces rollout and click the 1-Rail (Sweep) button (or click the Create 1-Rail Sweep button in the NURBS Creation Toolbox). Click the long stem curve, then click the cross-section shapes in order from the bottom to the top. Right-click to end the creation of the 1-rail sweep.

The NURBS skin is generated on the stem as shown in Figure 15-11.

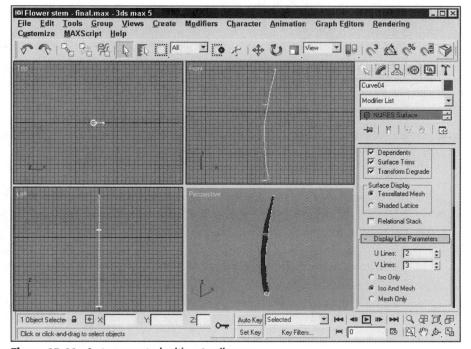

Figure 15-11: A stem created with a 1-rail sweep

Sculpting a rectangular NURBS surface

NURBS patches are a quick way to create a surface that can be sculpted using the subobject elements, such as a control lattice. For each subobject type, you can use many different tools to form the patch.

Tutorial: Creating a NURBS leaf

In this tutorial we create a NURBS CV surface plane that is sculpted into a leaf for the NURBS flower. To do this, we work in the Surface CV subobject level and use the Select and Move transform tool to move CVs and sculpt the NURBS rectangle into a leaf shape.

To create a rectangular NURBS CV surface, follow these steps:

1. In the Create panel, click the Geometry category button and select NURBS Surfaces from the subcategory drop-down list. Click the CV Surf button and in the Create Parameters rollout, increase the Length CVs to 6 and Width CVs to 6. Click the Generate Mapping Coords check box.

2. In the Top viewport, click and drag to create the NURBS surface. In the Create Parameters rollout, set both the Length and Width to 180. Still in the Top viewport, rotate the NURBS surface 45 degrees along the Z-axis using the Select and Rotate tool so that it looks like a diamond shape.

3. With the NURBS surface selected, open the Modify panel and click the plus sign to the left of the NURBS Surface object to gain access to the subobjects. Select the Surface CV subobject.

   The CV lattice is displayed in the Top viewport.

4. Select the Non-Uniform Scale tool (R), constrain it to the X-axis (F5), and then drag-select the middle horizontal row of CVs. Scale them down (narrower) to 85 percent.

5. Select the middle three horizontal rows of CVs (including the one just scaled) and scale them down to 90 percent. Then select the middle five horizontal rows and scale them down to 90 percent.

   This step gently rounds the outside contours of the NURBS surface.

6. In the Front viewport, you should see the edge of the NURBS surface. Maximize the viewport, and then select the Rotate tool, constrain it to the Z-axis, and select the right half of the CVs but do not select the CVs at the very center. Rotate the CVs upward –60 degrees.

7. Repeat the select-and-rotate process with the CV on the left half of the center, but do not alter the CVs at the very center.

   The leaf should now be U-shaped.

8. Click the Move tool (W), constrain it to the Y-axis (F6), and then select the center row of CVs and move them downward –40 units to make a deep V shape.

Figure 15-12 shows the NURBS leaf with the control lattice visible.

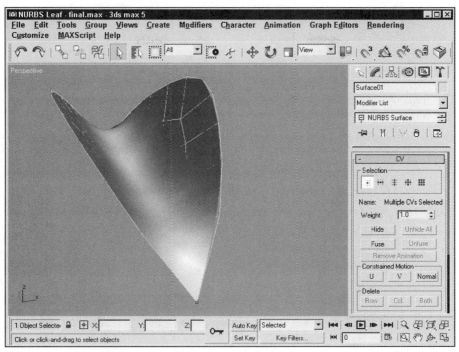

Figure 15-12: Translating CVs to sculpt a NURBS leaf

Tutorial: Sculpting a flower petal

Continuing to build our flower, we now sculpt a second rectangular NURBS surface into the shape of a flower petal. In this case the center CVs of the surface are raised to create a soft, rounded shape. We then sculpt one end of the NURBS rectangle into a blossom petal shape, and then scale and clone it to create three more petals.

To sculpt the flower petal shape, follow these steps:

1. In the Create panel, click the Geometry category button and select NURBS Surfaces from the subcategory drop-down list. Click the CV Surf button, and in the Keyboard Entry rollout create a NURBS rectangular surface 80 units long and 80 units wide, with 6 Length CVs and 6 Width CVs.

2. Select the Rotate tool (or press the E key), and in the Top view rotate the surface 45 degrees. Open the Modify panel, click the plus sign to the left of the NURBS Surface object, and select the Surface CV subobject.

3. Select the Non-Uniform Scale tool (R), constrain to the X-axis (F5), and then select the center horizontal row of CVs and scale it down (narrower) to 86 percent.

   This step rounds the outside corners of the petal.

4. Drag-select the six CVs that make up the upper tip of the petal. Non-uniform-scale the triangle of CVs in the Y-axis down to 35 percent to blunt the point at the top of the petal.

5. Click and drag a selection box around all the CVs in the center of the petal (don't select any CVs on the edges). You can use the Ctrl key to add CVs to the selection and the Alt key to remove CVs from the selection. In the Front viewport, select the Move tool and move the CVs upward 6 units in the Y-axis to round the top of the petal.

6. In the Top viewport, select the lower half of the center vertical row of CVs, click the Lock Selection icon (or press the spacebar), and then in the Front viewport use the Move tool to move the CVs 7 units downward in the Y-axis. A groove appears halfway down the center of the petal. Unlock the selection set.

7. To clone the petal, turn off subobject mode, and then activate the Top viewport. Select World from the Reference Coordinate System drop-down list. Click the Mirror icon to open the Mirror: Screen Coordinates dialog box, and then clone the petal by selecting the Y-axis and Copy options. Move the new petal downward in the Y-axis so that the points of the petals touch.

8. Now clone the petals again, but smaller. Select the Uniform Scale button (or press the R key), select both petals in the Top viewport, and then press the Shift key and scale the petals down to 40 percent to create smaller cloned versions of the petals. Lock the selection set (spacebar), click Rotate (E), and then rotate the small petals 90 degrees to finish the blossom.

Figure 15-13 shows the completed flower.

Figure 15-13: Flower petals that were sculpted using NURBS

To finish the flower and vase model, you need to merge all the parts of the flower vase project into one scene. Clone and position the leaves next to the stem. Position the stem in the throat of the vase at a slight angle. Position the leaves midway up the stem, and then place the flower at the top of the stem, at right angles to the leaves. Finally, texture-map all objects, applying a glass material to the vase, dark green to the leaves and stem, and a pink and white radial gradient to each petal of the blossom. The finished flower is shown in Figure 15-14.

Figure 15-14: A vase and flower built completely from NURBS

NURBS modifiers

The Modifiers ➪ NURBS Editing menu includes a set of modifiers unique to NURBS objects. This set includes the following modifiers: NURBS Surface Select, Surf Deform, and Disp Approx. There is also a World-Space modifier called Displace NURBS.

The NURBS Surface Select modifier (known in the Modifier List at NSurfSel) lets you make a subobject selection for the selected NURBS object. This selection is then passed up the modifier stack to the next modifier. The two subobjects for this modifier are Surface CV and Surface.

The Surf Deform modifier works on NURBS surfaces just like the PatchDeform and PathDeform modifiers. After applying this modifier, you can select another NURBS object with the Pick Object button to deform the selected NURBS object. There is also a World-Space version of this modifier.

The Displacement Approximation (or Disp Approx) modifier makes displacement mapping (which is applied using materials) available in the modifier stack. This modifier alters the surface of an object based on displacement mapping. This modifier can work with any object that can be converted to an Editable Mesh, including primitives, NURBS, and Patches. Parameters for this modifier include Subdivision Preset settings of Low, Medium, and High.

The Displace NURBS World-Space modifier is similar to the Disp Approx modifier. It can convert a NURBS object into a mesh object and will include the effect of a displacement map. In the Displace NURBS rollout, you can select the Tessellation method to be Regular, Parametric, Curvature, Spatial, or both.

Summary

NURBS are an ideal method for modeling if you require free-flowing models. In this chapter you've

- ✦ Created CV and point curves
- ✦ Discovered how to convert primitives to NURBS objects
- ✦ Created NURBS surfaces from curves
- ✦ Learned to edit NURBS curves and surfaces
- ✦ Used NURBS subobject tools
- ✦ Lofted surfaces from point and CV curves
- ✦ Created NURBS surfaces by lathing and sweeping

The next chapter focuses on working with a miscellaneous group of mutant objects called compound objects. These objects are unique and used for special purposes.

✦   ✦   ✦

Building Compound Objects

So far, we have covered a variety of different modeling types, including shapes, meshes, polys, patches and NURBS. The Compound Objects subcategory includes several additional modeling types that don't seem to fit anywhere else. As you will see in this chapter, these modeling types provide several new and unique ways to model objects such as working with Boolean objects, scattering objects across the surface of another object, or lofting a cross section along a spline path.

Understanding Compound Object Types

The Compound Objects subcategory includes several unique object types. You can access these object types by clicking the Geometry category button in the Create panel and by selecting Compound Objects in the subcategory drop-down list. All the object types included in the Compound Object subcategory are displayed as buttons at the top of the Create panel. They include the following:

✦ **Morph:** Consists of two or more objects with the same number of vertices. The vertices are interpolated from one object to the other over several frames.

✦ **Conform:** Wraps the vertices of one object onto another. You can use this option to simulate a morph between objects with different numbers of vertices.

✦ **ShapeMerge:** Lets you embed a spline into a mesh object or subtract the area of a spline from a mesh object.

✦ **Terrain:** Creates terrains from the elevation contour lines like those found on topographical maps.

✦ **Mesher:** Creates an object that converts particle systems into mesh objects as the frames progress. This makes assigning modifiers to particle systems possible.

✦ **Scatter:** Randomly scatters a source object about the scene. You can also select a Distribution object that defines the volume or surface where the objects scatter.

✦ **Connect:** Connects two objects with open faces by joining the holes with additional faces.

✦ **Boolean:** Created by performing Boolean operations on two or more overlapping objects. The operations include Union, Subtraction, Intersection, and Cut.

✦ **Loft:** Sweeps a cross-section shape along a spline path.

Morphing Objects

Morph objects are used to create a Morph animation by interpolating the vertices in one object to the vertex positions of a second object. The original object is called the Base object, and the second object is called the Target object. The Base and Target objects must have the same number of vertices. One Base object can be morphed into several targets.

Caution　To ensure that the Base and Target objects have the same number of vertices, create a copy of one object and modify it to be a target. Be sure to avoid such modifiers as Tessellate and Optimize, which change the number of vertices.

To morph a Base object into a Target, select the Base object and open the Create panel. Select the Compound Objects subcategory and click the Morph button. Then click the Pick Target button in the Pick Targets rollout, shown in Figure 16-1, and select a Target object in the viewport. The cursor will change to a plus sign when it is over an acceptable object. Unavailable objects (that have a different number of vertices) cannot be selected. Pick Target options include Copy, Instance, Reference, and Move. (The Move option deletes the original object that is selected.) The Target object appears under the Current Targets rollout in the Morph Targets list.

Each Morph object can have several Target objects. You can use the Pick Target button to select several targets, and the order in which these targets appear in the list is the order in which they are morphed. To delete a Target object, select it from the list and click the Delete Morph Target button. Beneath the list is a Name field where you can change the name of the selected Target object.

Creating Morph keys

With a Target object name selected in the Morph Targets list, you can drag the Time Slider to a frame and set a Morph key by clicking the Create Morph Key button found at the bottom of the rollout. This option sets the number of frames used to interpolate among the different morph states.

Note　If the Morph object changes dramatically, set the Morph Keys to include enough frames to interpolate smoothly.

If a frame other than 0 is selected when a Target object is picked, a Morph Key is automatically created.

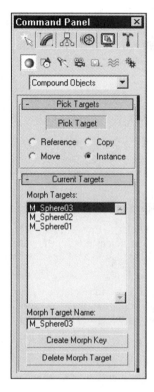

Figure 16-1: A Morph rollout lets you pick targets and create morph keys.

Morph objects versus the Morph modifier

Max includes two different ways to morph an object. You can create a Morph object or apply the Morph modifier to an existing object. The Morph object is different from the Morph modifier, but the results are the same; however, some subtle differences exist between these two.

A Morph object can include multiple Morph targets, but it can only be created once. Each target can have several Morph keys, which makes it easy to control. For example, you could set an object to morph to a different shape and return to its original form with only two Morph keys.

The Morph modifier, on the other hand, can be applied multiple times and works well with other modifiers, but the control for each modifier is buried in the Stack. The Parameters rollout options available for the Morph modifier are much more extensive than for the Morph object, and they include channels and support for a Morph material.

Cross-Reference You can find more information on the Morph modifier in Chapter 24, "Animation Basics."

For the best of both worlds, apply the Morph modifier to a Morph object.

Tutorial: Morphing an alien head

In my virtual intergalactic travels, I've encountered many different types of aliens. One interesting alien had a head that would change when it got angry. Using the Morph compound object, I can show what it looked like.

To morph an alien head, follow these steps:

1. Open the Morphing alien head.max file from the Chap 16 directory on the CD-ROM.

   This file includes a simple alien head created using primitives. The eyes and mouth have been animated with keys.

2. Open the Create panel, click the Geometry category button, and select Compound Objects from the subcategory drop-down list.

3. With the Alien helmet start object selected, click the Morph button.

4. In the Pick Targets rollout, select the Move option and click the Pick Target button. Then click the 'Alien helmet' object or press the H key and select it from the Select Objects dialog box (actually it is the only object that you can select). Click the Pick Target button again to disable pick mode.

5. In the Morph Targets list, select the Alien helmet start object and click the Create Morph Target button. Then, drag the Time Slider (below the viewports) to frame 100, select the Alien helmet object, and press the Morph Target button again.

6. Click the Play button (in the Time Controls section at the bottom of the Max window) to see the morph.

   The Alien helmet object morphs. Figure 16-2 shows different stages of the morph object.

Figure 16-2: A simple alien head being morphed

Creating Conform Objects

Conform compound objects mold one object over the surface of another. This compound object is useful for adding geometric details to objects, such as stitches to a baseball or a quilt.

The object that is modified is called the Wrapper object. The other object is the Wrap-To object. These objects need to be either mesh objects or objects that you can convert to mesh objects.

Cross-Reference Another way to mold one object over the surface of another is with the Conform Space Warp. Find out more about this Space Warp in Chapter 26, "Using Space Warps."

To create a Conform object, select an object to be the Wrapper object, open the Create panel, and select the Compound Objects subcategory. Then click the Conform button. To select the Wrap-To object, click the Pick Wrap-To Object button in the Pick Wrap-To Object rollout and choose one of the options below the button (Reference, Move, Copy, or Instance).

Caution   Shapes and splines cannot be used as either the Wrapper or Wrap-To objects.

In the Parameters rollout, shown in Figure 16-3, the Objects section lists both the Wrapper and Wrap-To objects. Name fields are also available for changing the names of both objects.

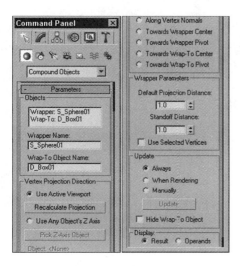

Figure 16-3: The Parameters rollout of the Conform object lets you define how the object is wrapped.

The Wrapper Parameters section includes two adjustable values: Default Projection Distance, which is the distance that the Wrapper moves if it doesn't intersect with the Wrap-To object, and Standoff Distance, which is the distance between the Wrapper and the Wrap-To object. The Use Selected Vertices option causes only the selected vertices passed up the Stack to be moved.

Setting a vertex projection direction

The Parameters rollout also includes controls for specifying the Vertex Projection Direction settings. You can select to project the vertices based on the current active viewport with the Use Active Viewport option. If the view changes, you can use the Recalculate Projection button to compute the new projection direction.

You can also use the local Z-axis of any object in the scene as the projection direction. The Pick Z-Axis Object button lets you select the object to use. After you have selected it, rotating this object can alter the projection direction. The name of the object is displayed below the Pick Z-Axis Object button.

Other projection options include Along Vertex Normals, Towards Wrapper Center, Towards Wrapper Pivot, Towards Wrap-To Center, and Towards Wrap-To Pivot. The Along Vertex Normals option sets the projection direction opposite the Wrapper's normals. The other options set the direction toward the center or pivot of the Wrapper or Wrap-To objects. Figure 16-4 shows the projection resulting from the Along Vertex Normals option.

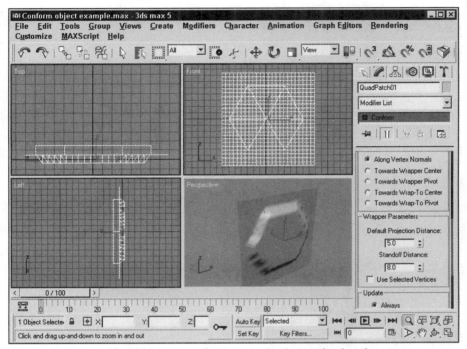

Figure 16-4: A Conform object created using a projection set by the Along Vertex Normals option

Tutorial: Placing a facial scar

As an example of the Conform object, let's add a gruesome scar to the face of our General character. Using the Conform compound object, details like this scar can be a mesh object and still perfectly match the contour of the face object.

To create a facial scar using the Conform object, follow these steps:

1. Open the General's scar.max file from the Chap 16 directory on the CD-ROM.

   This file includes a face mesh of a General with a mesh scar placed to its side. The General mesh was created by Viewpoint Datalabs.

2. Click the Select and Move button on the main toolbar and select and move the scar to position it over the top and in front of the face mesh.

3. Open the Create panel and select the Geometry category. Select the Compound Object subcategory from the drop-down list, and click the Conform button with the scar mesh selected.

4. Click the Pick Wrap-To Object button and click the face mesh. Select the Move option.

5. Under the Parameters rollout, select the Use Active Viewport option and make sure that the Front viewport is active. In the Wrapper Parameters section, set the Standoff Distance value to 0.03.

Figure 16-5 shows a close-up of our surgery in the maximized Perspective view.

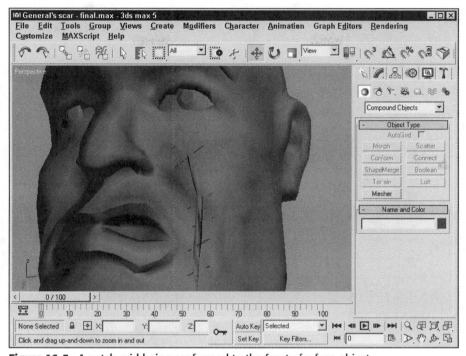

Figure 16-5: A patch grid being conformed to the front of a face object

Creating a ShapeMerge Object

The ShapeMerge compound object enables you to use a spline shape as a cookie cutter to extract a portion of a mesh object. This button is only enabled if a mesh object and a spline exist in the scene. To use this object, select a mesh object and click the Pick Shape button in the Pick Operand rollout, and then select a spline shape. The shape can be a Reference, Move, Instance, or a Copy.

The spline shape is always projected toward its negative Z-axis. By rotating and positioning the spline before selecting it, you can apply it to different sides of an object. You can apply multiple shapes to the same mesh object.

The Parameters rollout, shown in Figure 16-6, displays each mesh and shape object in a list. You can also rename either object using the Name field. The Extract Operand button lets you separate either object as an Instance or a Copy.

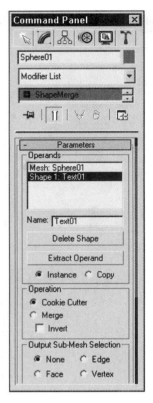

Figure 16-6: Use the Parameters rollout for the ShapeMerge compound object to cookie-cutter or merge a shape.

Cookie Cutter and Merge options

The Operations group includes options for cutting the mesh, including Cookie Cutter and Merge. The Cookie Cutter option cuts the shape out of the mesh surface, and the Merge option combines the spline with the mesh. You can also Invert the operation to remove the inside or outside of the selected area.

Like the Boolean Subtraction operations, the Cookie Cutter option can remove sections of the mesh, but it uses the area defined by a spline instead of a volume defined by a mesh object. The Merge option is useful for marking an area for selection. Figure 16-7 shows a ShapeMerge object with the Cookie Cutter option selected.

Note   You can use the Merge option to create a precise face object that can be used with the Connect object.

The Output Sub-Mesh Selection option lets you pass the selection up the Stack for additional modifiers. Options include None, Face, Edge, and Vertex.

Note   To see the backsides of the faces, right-click the object, select Properties from the pop-up menu, and disable the Backface Cull option.

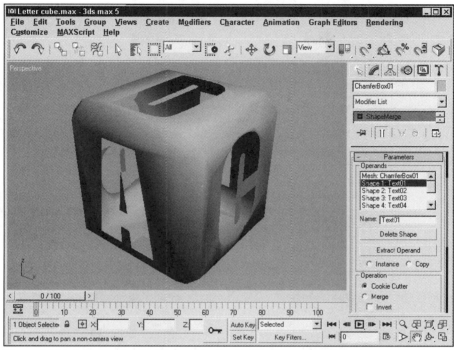

Figure 16-7: A ShapeMerge object using the Cookie Cutter option

Tutorial: Using the ShapeMerge compound object

When outlined text is imported into Max, it typically contains letters that have shapes within shapes. For example, the letter *p*, when outlined, includes the outline of the letter *p* and a circle shape to denote the interior section of the letter. When outline text like this is converted to a mesh object, both the letter outline and its interior section will be covered, making the text illegible. You can use the ShapeMerge compound object to remedy this tricky situation.

In Chapter 3, "Working with Files," you encounter an example where the logo for the fictional Bugs Head Software company was imported from Illustrator. Before this logo can be extruded, you'll need to do some work involving the ShapeMerge object.

To use the ShapeMerge object to remove the center area from an extrusion, follow these steps:

1. Open the Bugs Head Software logo.max file from the Chap 16 directory on the CD-ROM.

   This file is slightly different from the file found in Chapter 3. One difference is that the bug's mouth has been made into a closed spline and all the shapes have been extruded.

2. Click away from the objects to de-select all the objects and select (while holding down the Ctrl key) the two interior splines of the letter *B* that make up the bug's left eye. Open the Display Floater by choosing Tools ➪ Display Floater and click the Selected button under the Hide column to hide the interior portions of this letter.

3. Select the bug's head shape again. Then open the Create panel, select the Compound Objects subcategory, and click the ShapeMerge button.

4. Set the Operation to Cookie Cutter and click the Pick Shape button in the Pick Operand rollout. Select the mouth and the letters used for the eyes and nose. Click the Pick Shape button again to exit pick mode. Click away from the objects in the viewport to de-select the bug's head.

5. Now, select the letter B in the logo name and click the ShapeMerge button again. Use the Pick Shape button and the Cookie Cutter operation option to remove the centers of this letter. Click the Select Object button on the main toolbar to exit ShapeMerge mode. Repeat this step for each of the letters that has an interior portion including the g, e, a, d, o, a, and e letters.

6. Open the Display panel again and, in the Hide rollout, click Unhide All to redisplay the interior splines of the letter *B* that make up the bug's left eye. Hold down the Ctrl key and select the two splines and choose Modifiers ➪ Mesh Editing ➪ Extrude and enter an Amount value of **0.2**.

Figure 16-8 shows the finished logo. Notice that the letters have the interior sections removed.

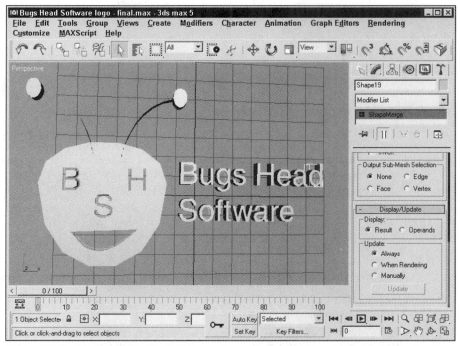

Figure 16-8: The logo with the interior centers removed from extruded letters using the ShapeMerge object

Creating a Terrain Object

The Terrain object is a great object that enables you to create terrains from splines representing elevation contours. These contour splines can be created in Max or imported using a format like AutoCAD's DWG. If the splines are created in Max, make sure that they are attached to each other as one object, in the order in which they will eventually be attached. The splines all need to be closed splines.

To create a terrain, create splines at varying elevations, select all the splines, and click the Terrain button. You can use the Pick Operand button in the Pick Operand rollout to select additional splines to add to the Terrain object. All splines in the object become operands and are displayed in the Operands list.

The Form group includes three options that determine how the terrain is formed: Graded Surface, Graded Solid, and Layered Solid. The Graded Surface option displays a surface grid over the contour splines; the Graded Solid adds a bottom to the object; and the Layered Solid displays each contour as a flat, terraced area.

The Display group includes options to display the Terrain mesh, the Contour lines, or Both. You can also specify how you want to update the terrain.

The Simplification rollout lets you alter the resolution of the terrain by selecting how many vertical and horizontal vertices to use. Options include using all vertices, half of the vertices, or a quarter of the vertices.

Coloring elevations

The Color by Elevation rollout, shown in Figure 16-9, displays as reference the Maximum and Minimum Elevations. In between these is a Reference Elevation value, which is the location where the landmass meets the water. Entering a Reference Elevation and clicking the Create Defaults button automatically creates several separate color zones. You can add, modify, or delete New zones using the Add, Modify, or Delete Zone buttons.

You can access each color zone from a list. To change a zone's color, select it and click the color swatch. You can set colors to Blend to the Color Above or to be Solid to Top of Zone.

Tutorial: Creating an island with the Terrain compound object

In this tutorial, we'll create a simple island. The Color by Elevation rollout makes distinguishing the water from the land easy.

To create an island using the Terrain object, follow these steps:

1. In the Create panel, click the Shapes category button and then click the Ellipse button. Drag in the Top view to create several ellipses of various sizes representing the contours of the island. The first ellipse you create should be the largest, and they should get progressively smaller.

2. In the Left view, select and move the ellipses up and down so that the largest one is on the bottom and the smallest one is on top. You can create two smaller hills by including two ellipses at the same level.

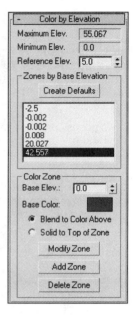

Figure 16-9: The Color by Elevation rollout

3. Return to the Create panel, click the Geometry category button, and then select the Compound Objects subcategory. Use the Edit ⇨ Select All (Ctrl+A) menu command to select all the ellipses and click the Terrain button.

   The ellipses automatically join together. Joining all the ellipses forms the island.

4. In the Color by Elevation rollout, select a Reference Elevation of 5 and click the Create Defaults button. This automatically creates color zones for the island. The elevation values for each zone are displayed in a list within the Color by Elevation rollout. Selecting an elevation value in the list displays its color in the color swatch. Select each elevation value individually and set all Zones to Blend to the Color Above option for all zones, except for the Zone with the lightest blue. This creates a distinct break between the sea and the land of the island.

Figure 16-10 shows the final terrain. In an example later in this chapter, we'll use the Scatter compound object to add trees to the small terrain island.

Using the Mesher Object

You can use the Mesher compound object to convert objects to mesh objects on the fly as an animation progresses. This feature is useful for objects such as particle systems. After you convert the object to a mesh object, you can apply modifiers that weren't possible before, such as Optimize, UVW Map, and others.

Another benefit of the Mesher object is that you could apply several complex modifiers to a single Mesher object and tie it to a particle system rather than applying the modifiers to all the pieces that make up a particle system.

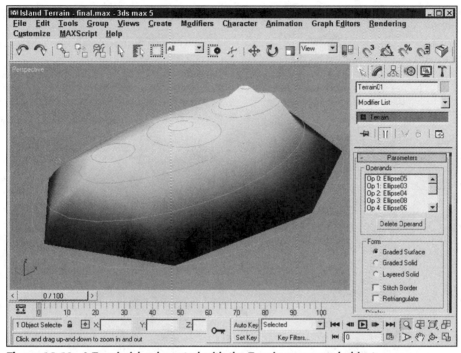

Figure 16-10: A Terrain island created with the Terrain compound object

The Parameters rollout of the Mesher object includes a Pick Object button. Click this button and select an object in the viewport to make the selected object an instance of the Mesher object. This action does not delete the original object, and the Mesher instance will be oriented to the Mesher object's coordinate system. The object name will then appear on the button. You can change the object by clicking the button again and selecting a new object.

Caution   Do not delete the original object or the Mesher instance will also disappear. If you want to render only the Mesher instance, then select the original object and hide it using the Tools ⇨ Display Floater command.

The Time Offset is the number of the frames ahead (values can be negative) or behind the original object the animation should progress. If the Build Only at Render Time option is set, then the Mesher instance will not be visible in the viewports but will show up in the final rendered image. You can use the Update button to manually force an update of the Mesher instance after the settings for the original object have been modified.

When you use the Mesher object to create an instance of a particle system, the bounding box of the particle system as it streams the particles will, over time, become long and thin. This long and thin bounding box can potentially cause problems with certain modifiers. You can prevent these problems by selecting an alternative bounding box that doesn't change over time. To select a new bounding box, select the Custom Bounding Box option, click the Pick Bounding Box button, and click an object in the viewport. You can select the original object as the new bounding box. With the Mesher object selected, the bounding box will be shown in orange wherever it is located. The corner coordinates of the custom bounding box are displayed under the Pick Bounding Box button.

Figure 16-11 shows a Super Spray particle system on the right and its Mesher instance with the Bend modifier applied on the left.

Cross-Reference   Chapter 17, "Creating and Controlling Particle Systems," has more information on working with particle systems.

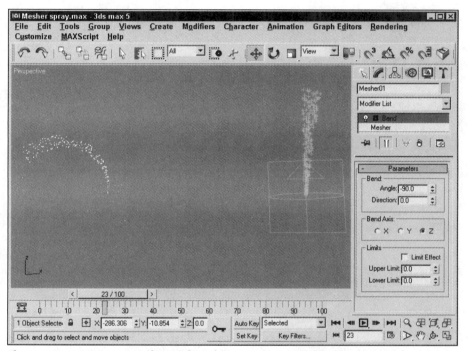

Figure 16-11: You can use the Mesher object to create an instance of a particle system with modifiers applied.

Creating a Scatter Object

A Scatter object spreads multiple copies of the object about the scene or within a defined area. The object that is scattered is called the Source object, and the area where the scatter objects can be placed is defined by a Distribution object.

Cross-Reference   Particle systems, discussed in Chapter 17, "Creating and Controlling Particle Systems," can also create many duplicate objects, but you have more control over the placement of objects with a Scatter object.

To create a Scatter object, open the Create panel, select the Compound Objects subcategory, and click the Scatter button. The selected object becomes the Source object. A rollout then opens, in which you can select the Distribution object or use defined transforms.

Under the Scatter Objects rollout, the Objects section lists the Source and Distribution objects. Name fields are also available for changing the names of either object. The Extract Operand button is only available in the Modify panel — it lets you select an operand from the list and make a copy or instance of it.

Working with Source objects

The Source object is the object that is to be duplicated. Figure 16-12 shows a Cylinder primitive scattered over a spherical Distribution object with 500 duplicates. The Perpendicular and Distribute Using Even options are set.

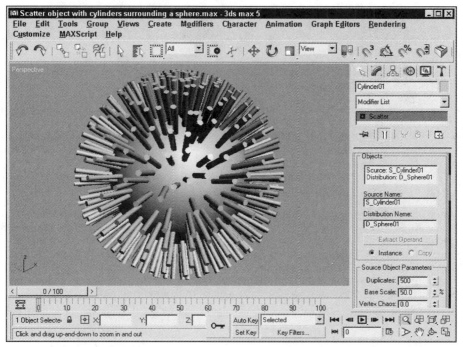

Figure 16-12: A Scatter object made of a Cylinder spread over an area defined by a sphere.

In the Scatter Objects rollout are several parameters for controlling the Source object. In the Source Object Parameters rollout, the Duplicates value specifies how many objects to scatter. You can also specify a Base Scale and the Vertex Chaos values. The Base Scale is the value that the object is scaled to before being scattered. All new objects are scaled equally to this value. The Vertex Chaos button randomly distributes the object vertices.

The Animation Offset defines the number of frames between a new duplicate and the previous one.

Note   If you look closely at a Scatter object, you'll notice that both the Source and Distribution objects have the same object color. To color them differently, use the Multi/Sub-Object Material.

Working with Distribution objects

To select a Distribution object, click the Pick Distribution Object button and select an object in the viewport (make sure the Use Distribution Object option is selected in the Scatter Objects rollout). You can specify the Distribution object as a Copy, an Instance, a Reference, or a Move.

Under the Distribution Object Parameters rollout are several options for controlling the Distribution object. The Perpendicular option causes the Source objects to be aligned perpendicular to the Distribution object. If the Perpendicular option is disabled, the orientation will remain the same as that of the default Source object. Figure 16-13 shows the same Scatter object as in the previous figure, but with several different options.

Figure 16-13: A Scatter object with different options: Base Scale at 20%, Vertex Chaos at 2.0, Perpendicular option disabled, and Duplicates at 100

The Use Selected Faces Only option enables you to select the faces over which the duplicates are positioned. The Selected Faces are those passed up the Stack by the Mesh Select modifier.

Other Distribution object parameter options include Area, Even, Skip N, Random Faces, Along Edges, All Vertices, All Edge Midpoints, All Face Centers, and Volume. The Area option evenly distributes the objects over the surface area, and the Even option places duplicates over every other face. The Skip N option lets you specify how many faces to skip before placing an object. The Random Faces and Along Edges options randomly distribute the duplicates around the Distribution object. The All Vertices, All Edge Midpoints, and All Face Centers options ignore the Duplicates value (that specifies the number of duplicates) and place a duplicate at every vertex, edge midpoint, and face. Figure 16-14 shows several of these options.

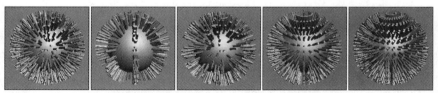

Figure 16-14: A Scatter object with different distribution options: Area, Skip N where N=7, Random Faces, All Vertices, and All Face Centers

All the options described thus far place the duplicates on the surface of the object, but the Volume option scatters the duplicates inside the Distribution object's volume.

Setting Transforms

The Transforms rollout is used to specify the individual transformation limits of the duplicate objects. For example, if the Z-axis value is set to 90, then each new duplicate will be randomly rotated about its local Z-axis at a distance somewhere between –90 and 90.

You can use these transformations with a Distribution object or by themselves if the Use Transforms Only option is selected under the Scatter Objects rollout. The Use Maximum Range option causes all three axes to adopt the same value. The Lock Aspect Ratio option maintains the relative dimensions of the Source object to ensure uniform scaling.

Speeding updates with a proxy

Working with a large number of duplicates can slow the viewport updates down to a crawl. To speed up these updates, select the Proxy option in the Display rollout. This option replaces each duplicate with a wedge-shaped object. For example, if you used the Scatter object to place people on a sidewalk, you could use the Proxy option to display simple cylinders in the viewports instead of the details of the person mesh.

Another way to speed the viewport updates is to use the Display spinner. Using this spinner, you can select a percentage of the total number of duplicates to display in the viewport. The rendered image will still use the actual number specified.

The Hide Distribution Object option lets you make the Distribution object visible or invisible. The Seed value is used to determine the randomness of the objects.

Loading and saving presets

With all the various parameters, the Load/Save Presets rollout enables you to Save, Load, or Delete various presets. You can use saved presets with another Source object.

Tutorial: Filling a box with spiders

When I was a kid, my brothers and I always had a terrarium full of snakes, lizards, or spiders. Mom was okay with this as long as we remembered the one key rule — keep the lid on. Well, kids will be kids, and at times we forgot. Then it was spiders everywhere (and you thought this effect was only good for horror flicks — it also works well on little sisters).

To scatter spiders across the surface of a box, follow these steps:

1. Open the Scatter box of spiders.max file from the Chap 16 directory on the CD-ROM.

   This file includes a simple box mesh and a spider mesh.

2. With the spider object selected, open the Create panel, select the Compound Objects subcategory, and click the Scatter button.

3. In the Pick Distribution Object rollout, click the Pick Distribution Object button and click the box object. Select the Move option.

4. In the Source Object Parameters section of the Scatter Objects rollout, enter a value of 60 in the Duplicates field.

5. Select the Perpendicular and Even options in the Distribution Object Parameters section.

   The spiders spread across the surface of the box.

Figure 16-15 shows the spiders creeping about. Notice how the box and spiders are all part of the same object and have the same object color.

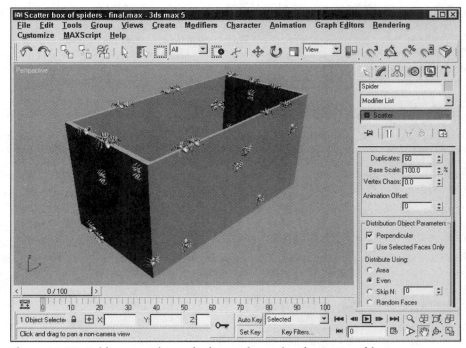

Figure 16-15: Spiders spread over the box surface using the Scatter object

Tutorial: Creating jungle vines

You can use the Vertex Chaos setting to randomly order the vertices of an object. You can use this randomness to simulate random natural patterns like foliage growing on a pillar. Using the Vertex Chaos value, you can simulate the effect of jungle vines growing thick upon the surface of an object.

To cover an object with jungle vines, follow these steps:

1. Open the Jungle vine.max file from the Chap 16 directory on the CD-ROM.

   This file includes a simple cylinder and a small sphere with its object color set to dark green.

2. With the sphere object selected, open the Create panel, select the Compound Objects subcategory, and click the Scatter button.

3. Click the Pick Distribution Object button and select the cylinder with the Move option selected.

4. In the Scatter Objects rollout, set the number of Duplicates to 500 and the Vertex Chaos value to 5 (lower the number of Duplicates if necessary).

Figure 16-16 shows the resulting overgrowth.

Figure 16-16: You can use the Scatter object and the Vertex Chaos option to create the look of jungle vines growing on a pillar.

Tutorial: Covering the island with trees

You can combine several different types of compound objects to create interesting effects. In this next tutorial, we'll add trees to the Terrain object island created earlier in this chapter using the Scatter object.

To add trees to the island with the Scatter object, follow these steps:

1. Open the Island terrain with trees.max file from the Chap16 directory on the CD-ROM.

   This file is the same island terrain example that you completed earlier in this chapter, but it also has a simple tree added to it.

2. With the tree object selected, select the Compound Object subcategory from the Create panel and click the Scatter button.

3. Click the Pick Distribution Object button and select the island terrain. Set the number of Duplicates to 100 and disable the Perpendicular option.

   All the trees now stand upright.

4. Select the Random Faces option.

   The trees become denser around the hills where there are more faces.

Figure 16-17 shows the island with the trees.

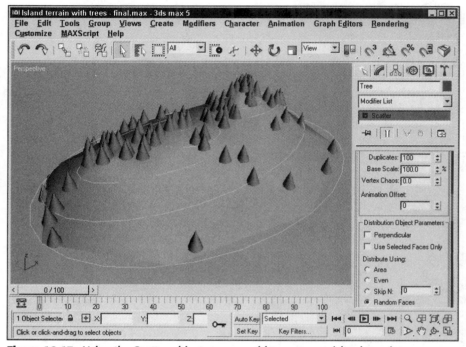

Figure 16-17: Using the Scatter object, we can add trees to our island terrain.

Creating Connect Objects

A Connect object is useful for building a connecting bridge between two separate objects. Each object must have an open face or hole that specifies where the two objects are to be connected.

To use this object, delete a face on two Editable Mesh objects and then position the holes across from each other. Select one of the objects. In the Create panel, select the Compound Objects subcategory from the drop-down list. Click the Connect button, click the Pick Operand button, and select the second object. The Connect object will build the additional faces required to connect the two holes.

Filling object holes

If multiple holes exist between the objects, the Connect object will attempt to patch them all. You can also use the button several times to connect a single object to multiple objects.

The Connect object doesn't work well with NURBS objects.

Figure 16-18 shows a normal Connect object without any smoothing options.

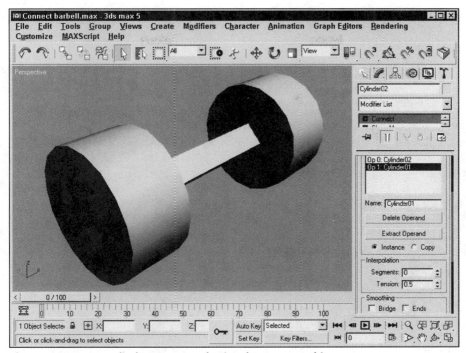

Figure 16-18: Two cylinders connected using the Connect object

The Parameters rollout includes a list of all the operands or objects involved in the connection. You can delete any of these with the Delete Operand button. The Extract Operand button lets you separate the Operand object from the Connect object.

In the Interpolation section, the Segments value is the number of segments used to create the bridge section, and the Tension value is the amount of curvature to use in an attempt to smooth the connected bridge.

The Bridge Smoothing option smoothes the faces of the bridge, and the Ends option smoothes where the bridge and the original objects connect.

Tutorial: Creating a park bench

The Connect object is best used between two symmetrical copies of an object that need to be attached, as with a table or bridge. For this tutorial, we'll use the Connect object to create a park bench between two end pieces.

To connect two ends of a park bench, follow these steps:

1. Open the Park bench.max file from the Chap 16 directory on the CD-ROM.

   This file includes symmetrical ends of the park bench. Each end was created by extruding a spline shape and using the ShapeMerge tool to cut the holes. The Mirror tool was then used to create and rotate the symmetrical clone.

2. Select one end of the park bench, open the Create panel, select the Compound Objects subcategory, and click the Connect button.

3. In the Pick Operand rollout, click the Pick Operand button, select the Move option, and click on the opposite side of the park bench.

   The two end pieces connect.

4. In the Parameters rollout, select the Smoothing: Bridge option to smooth the seat of the bench.

Figure 16-19 shows the resulting park bench.

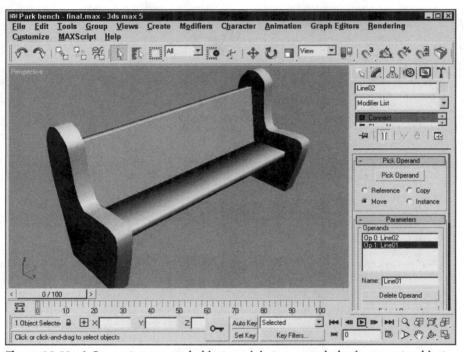

Figure 16-19: A Connect compound object can join two open holes in separate objects.

Modeling with Boolean Objects

When two objects overlap, you can perform different Boolean operations on them to create a unique object. The Boolean operations include Union, Subtraction, Intersection, and Cut. The Union operation combines two objects into one. The Subtraction operation subtracts the overlapping portions of one object from another. The Intersection operation retains only the overlapping sections of two objects, and the Cut operation can cut an object like the Subtraction operator does, while letting the cut piece remain. Figure 16-20 shows each of the possible Boolean operators.

Note   Unlike many CAD packages that deal with solid objects, Max's Booleans are applied to surfaces, so if the surfaces of the two objects don't overlap, the Boolean operation has no effect.

Figure 16-20: Boolean operations: Union, Intersection, Subtraction (A-B), Subtraction (B-A), and Cut: Remove Inside

All Boolean operations are layered in the Stack. You can revisit an operation at any time and make changes to it.

Cross-Reference   You can also apply Boolean operations to shapes using the Boolean operators available for Editable Meshes in the Geometry rollout. Chapter 12, "Drawing and Using 2D Splines and Shapes," covers these 2D Boolean operators.

Union

The Union operation combines two objects into one. To Union two objects, select an object and click the Boolean button. Under the Parameters rollout, the selected object will be referred to as Operand A. In the Pick Operand rollout, click the Pick Operand B button and select a second object in the viewport. (Operand B can be a Copy, Instance, Reference, or Move object.) To apply the Boolean operation, click the Union option.

Intersection

The Intersection operation creates an object from the overlapping sections of two objects. For this operation, like the Union operator, which object is A and which is B isn't important.

Subtraction

The Subtraction operation subtracts the overlapping portions of one object from the other. For this operation, the order in which the objects are selected is important. Subtracting object A from object B gives you a different object from what you get when you subtract object B from object A.

Cut

The Cut operation is similar to the Slice modifier except it uses another object instead of a slice plane gizmo, and only Operand A is modified in the process. The Cut operation has several options, including Refine, Split, Remove Inside, and Remove Outside.

The Refine option marks the selected object with new edges where it intersects Operand B. The Split option actually divides the mesh object into separate elements.

The Remove Inside and Remove Outside options are variations of the Split option. They remove the inner or outer portion of the object. These options work like the Subtraction and Intersection options, except the Cut operation leaves holes in the base geometry.

Tips for working with Booleans

Working with Boolean objects can be difficult. If you try to perform a Boolean operation on an ill-suited object, the results could end up being erratic. As you prepare objects for Boolean operations, keep the following points in mind:

✦ Avoid meshes with long, skinny polygon faces. All faces should have roughly equal lengths and widths. The ratio of edge length to width should be less than 4 to 1.

✦ Avoid curved lines where possible. Curved lines have the potential of folding back on themselves, which will cause problems. If you need to use a curve, try not to intersect it with another curve; keep the curvature to a minimum.

✦ Unlink any objects not involved in the Boolean operation. Linked objects, even if they don't intersect, can cause problems.

✦ If you're having difficulty getting a Boolean operation to work, try applying the XForm modifier (found in the Modifiers List) to combine all the transformations into one. Then collapse the Stack and convert the objects to Editable Mesh objects. This technique removes any modifier dependencies.

✦ Make sure that your objects are completely closed surfaces with no holes, overlapping faces, or unwelded vertices. You can check these criteria by applying the STL-Check modifier or by looking at all sides of the objects in a viewport with Smooth Shading enabled.

✦ Make sure that all surface normals are consistent — inconsistent normals will cause unexpected results. You can use the Normal modifier to unify and flip all normals on an object. The Show Normals option in the viewport can also help.

✦ Collapsing the Stack after all Boolean operations have been performed eliminates dependencies on the previous object types.

Tutorial: Creating a Lincoln Log set

In the household where I grew up, we had sets of Legos and a lesser-known construction set known as Lincoln Logs that let you to create buildings using notched logs that fit together. Using a Subtraction operation, you can create your own virtual set of Lincoln Logs.

Cross-Reference   This tutorial transforms objects and uses the Array dialog box. You can find information about transforming objects in Chapter 9, "Transforming Objects."

To use Boolean objects to create a log cabin, follow these steps:

1. Open the Lincoln logs booleans.max from the Chap 16 directory on the CD-ROM.

   This file contains some simple primitives.

2. Clone the Box object three times and position two of the objects at each end of the log at a distance of 10 from the end, top, and bottom.

3. Select the Cylinder object, select the Compound Objects subcategory from the drop-down list in the Create panel, and click the Boolean button. In the Operation section, select the Subtraction (A–B) option. Then in the Pick Boolean rollout, click the Pick Operand B button and select one of the Box objects.

4. Repeat the Subtraction operation on the other three boxes by clicking the Select button and performing Step 3 again.

   When finished, you should have a cylinder with four notches.

Note

If you simply click the Pick Operand B button again, the first notch will be replaced by the second operation.

5. Clone the single log by choosing Edit ➪ Clone and then selecting the Copy option. Move the cloned log along the negative Y-axis a distance of 160. The easiest way to do so is to select the Select and Move button and right-click it to open the Move Transform Type-In dialog box. In the Absolute World field, enter **–160** as the Y-axis value.

   This step positions two logs next to one another to form the bottom layer of the house.

6. Select both logs and open the Array dialog box by choosing Tools ➪ Array. In the Incremental Move row, enter 10 for the Z-axis. In the Incremental Rotate row, enter **90** for the Z-axis. In the Array Dimensions section, enter a Count value of **16**. Click the OK button.

   This step stacks several layers of logs.

7. Select one log and use the right-click pop-up menu to convert that log to an Editable Mesh. Open the Modify panel and click the Attach button, and then select every log to combine them all into a single object. Click the Attach button again to exit attach mode when you're done.

8. In the Create panel, click the Geometry category button, select the Box button, and create a Box object with the following dimensions: Length of 40, Width of 40, and Height of 80. Then position the Box where the front door should be.

9. Return to the Compound Objects subcategory, select the logs, and click the Boolean button. Then click the Pick Operand B button again and select the Box.

   The rollout will remember and retain the last options selected, including the Subtract (A–B) operation.

10. To add a roof, select the Extended Primitives subcategory and click the Prism button. Drag in the Left view to create a prism object that covers the logs.

Figure 16-21 shows our Boolean log cabin — ready for the virtual pioneers.

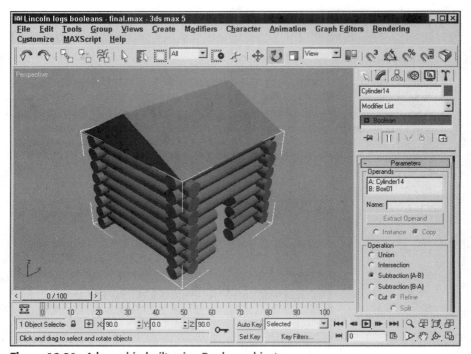

Figure 16-21: A log cabin built using Boolean objects

Creating a Loft Object

Lofting is a term that comes from the shipbuilding industry. It describes a method for building ships that creates and positions the cross sections and then attaches a surface or skin along the length of the cross sections.

To create a Loft object, you need to have at least two spline shapes: one shape that defines the path of the Loft and a second shape that defines its cross section. After the shapes are created, open the Create panel, click the Geometry category button, and select Compound Objects from the subcategory drop-down list. A Loft button will be enabled if two or more splines are present in the viewport.

Using the Get Shape and Get Path buttons

After you click the Loft button, the Creation Method rollout displays the Get Path and Get Shape buttons, which you use to specify which spline will be the path and which spline will be the cross section. Select a spline and then click either the Get Path button or the Get Shape button. If you click the Get Shape button, the selected spline will be the path and the next spline shape you select will be the cross section. If you click the Get Path button, the selected spline will be the shape and the next spline shape you select will be the path.

After you click the Get Path or Get Spline button, although the cursor changes when you're over a valid spline, not all spline shapes can be used to create Loft objects. For example, you cannot use a spline created with the Donut button as a path.

When creating a Loft object with the Get Shape and Get Path buttons, you can specify either to Move the spline shape, or to create a Copy or an Instance of it. The Move option replaces both splines with a Loft object. The Copy option leaves both splines in the viewport and creates a new Loft object. The Instance maintains a link between the spline and the Loft object. This link enables you to modify the original spline. The Loft object will be updated automatically.

The vertex order of the path spline is important. The Loft object will be created starting at the vertex numbered 1.

You can tell which vertex is the first by enabling Vertex Numbering in the Selection rollout of an editable spline.

Controlling surface parameters

All Loft objects include the Surface Parameters rollout. Using this rollout, you can set the smoothing of the Loft object with two different options: Smooth Length and Smooth Width. You can use the Mapping options to control the mapping of textures by setting values for the number of times the map repeats over the Length or Width of the Loft. The Normalize option applies the map to the surface evenly or proportionately according to the shape's vertex spacing. You can set the Loft object to automatically generate Material and Shape IDs, and you can specify the output of the Loft to be either a Patch or Mesh.

Changing path parameters

The Path Parameters rollout, shown in Figure 16-22, lets you position several different cross-sectional shapes at different positions along the Loft path. The Path value indicates either the Distance or Percentage along the path where this new shape should be located. The Snap option, if turned on, enables you to snap to consistent distances along the path. The Path Steps option enables you to place new shapes at steps along the path where the vertices are located. Each path will have a different number of steps depending on its complexity.

The viewport displays a small yellow X at the location where the new cross-sectional shape will be inserted. At the bottom of the rollout are three buttons, which are illustrated and described in Table 16-1.

Table 16-1: Path Rollout Buttons

Toolbar Button	Name	Description
	Pick Shape	Selects a new cross-section spline to be inserted at the specified location.
	Previous Shape	Moves to the previous cross-section shape along the Loft path.
	Next Shape	Moves to the next cross-section shape along the Loft path.

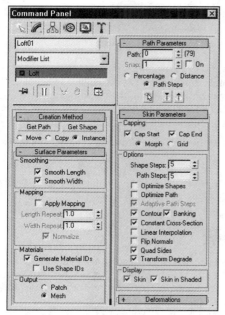

Figure 16-22: The Loft compound object rollouts

Setting skin parameters

The Skin Parameters rollout includes many options for determining the complexity of the Loft skin. You can specify whether to cap either end of the Loft using the Cap Start and/or Cap End options. The caps can be either Morph or Grid type.

This rollout also includes many options for controlling the look of the skin. These include the following:

✦ **Shape and Path Steps:** Sets the number of segments that appear in each vertex's cross-sectional shape and between each division along the path. The straight segments are ignored if the Optimize Path option is selected.

✦ **Optimize Shapes and Paths:** Reduces the Loft's complexity by deleting any unneeded edges or vertices.

✦ **Adaptive Path Steps:** Automatically determines the number of steps to use for the path.

✦ **Contour:** Determines how the cross-sectional shapes line up with the path. If this option is enabled, the cross section is aligned to be perpendicular to the path at all times. If disabled, this option causes the cross-sectional shapes to maintain their orientation as the path is traversed.

✦ **Banking:** Causes the cross-section shape to rotate as the path bends.

✦ **Constant Cross-Section:** Scales the cross-sectional shapes in order to maintain a uniform width along the path. Turning off this option causes the cross-sections to pinch at any sharp angles along the path.

✦ **Linear Interpolation:** Causes straight linear edges to appear between different cross-sectional shapes. Turning off this option causes smooth curves to connect various shapes.

✦ **Flip Normals:** Used to correct difficulties that would appear with the normals. Often the normals will be flipped accidentally when the Loft is created.

✦ **Quad Sides:** Creates four-sided polygons to connect to adjacent cross-section shapes with the same number of sides.

✦ **Transform Degrade:** Makes the Loft skin disappear when subobjects are transformed. This feature can help you better visualize the cross-sectional area while it is being moved.

The Display options at the bottom of the Skin Parameters rollout give you the choice of displaying the skin in all viewports or displaying the Loft skin only in the viewports with shading turned on.

Tutorial: Designing a slip-proof hanger

As an example of creating a Loft object with different cross-sectional shapes, we'll design a new hanger that includes some rough edges along its bottom section to keep slacks from sliding off.

To design a hanger Loft object with different cross sections, follow these steps:

1. Open the Lofted slip-proof hanger.max from the Chap 16 directory on the CD-ROM.

   This file includes a spline outline of a hanger and two simple shapes.

2. Click the Geometry category button in the Create panel, select the Compound Objects subcategory from the drop-down list, and select the hanger spline. Click the Loft button.

3. In the Creation Method rollout, click the Get Shape button and then click the small circle shape (make sure the Copy option is selected).

   This lofts the entire hanger with a circular cross section.

4. In the Path Parameters rollout, select the Path Steps option. A dialog box appears warning that this may change the relocate shapes. Click OK to continue. Increment the Path value until the yellow X marker in the viewport is positioned at the beginning of the hanger's bottom bar (at Step 53 for this tutorial). Click the Get Shape button again and click the small circular shape again. This extends the circular cross section from the start at Step 0 to Step 53.

5. Increment the Path value by 1 to Step 54, click the Get Shape button, and select the star shape. This makes the remainder of the hanger use a star-shaped cross section. Increment the Path value again to the end of the hanger's bottom bar (at Step 60), click the Get Shape button, and select the star shape again to end the star cross section.

   Note If you forget to start and end a section with the same cross section, the loft will blend between the two different cross sections.

6. Increment the Path value a final time to Step 61, click the Get Shape button, and click the circular shape. Click the Get Shape button at the bottom of the Path Parameters dialog box to change the cross section of the hanger to the end of the path. Right-click in the viewport to exit Get Shape mode.

   Figure 16-23 shows the finished designer hanger.

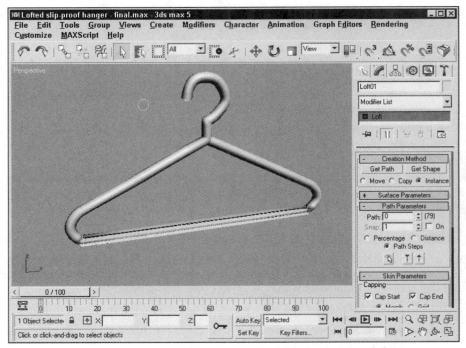

Figure 16-23: A lofted hanger created with two different cross-sectional shapes

Deforming Loft objects

When you select a Loft object and open the Modify panel, the Deformation rollout appears. This rollout includes five buttons that let you Scale, Twist, Teeter, Bevel, and Fit the cross-section shapes along the path. All five buttons open similar graph windows that include control points and a line that represents the amount of the effect to apply. Next to each button is a toggle button with a light switch on it. This button enables or disables the respective effect.

The Deformation window interface

All five deformation options use the same basic window and controls. The lines within the window represent the length of the path. As an example of the Deformation window interface, Figure 16-24 shows the Scale Deformation window.

Dragging the curve directly can modify the deformation curve. You can also insert control points at any location along the curve. These control points can be one of three different types: Corner, Bézier Corner, or Bézier Smooth. Bézier type points have handles for controlling the curvature at the point. To change the point type, select the point and right-click. Then make your selection from the pop-up menu. The end points must always be either Corner or Bézier Corner type.

To move a control point, select and drag it or enter a horizontal and/or vertical value in the fields at the bottom of the window.

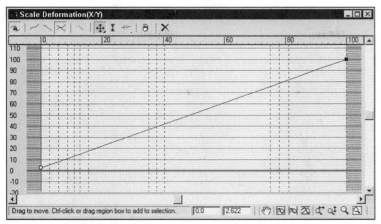

Figure 16-24: The Deformation dialog box interface lets you control the cross section over the length of the path.

Table 16-2 describes the buttons at the top of the Deformation window.

Table 16-2: Deformation Dialog Box Buttons

Toolbar Button	Name	Description
	Make Symmetrical	Links the two curves so that changes made to one curve are also made to the other.
	Display X-Axis	Makes the line controlling the X-axis visible.
	Display Y-Axis	Makes the line controlling the Y-axis visible.
	Display XY axes	Makes both lines visible.
	Swap Deform Curves	Switches the lines.
	Move Control Point	Enables you to move control points and includes flyouts for horizontal and vertical movements.
	Scale Control Point	Scales the selected control point.
	Insert Corner Point, Insert Bézier Point	Inserts new points on a deformation curve.
	Delete Control Point	Deletes the current control point.
	Reset Curve	Returns the original curve.

Continued

Table 16-2 *(continued)*

Toolbar Button	Name	Description
	Pan	Pans the curve as the mouse is dragged.
	Zoom Extents	Zooms to display the entire curve.
	Zoom Extents Horizontal	Zooms to display the entire horizontal curve range.
	Zoom Extents Vertical	Zooms to display the entire vertical curve range.
	Zoom Horizontal	Zooms on the horizontal curve range.
	Zoom Vertical	Zooms on the vertical curve range.
	Zoom	Zooms in and out as the mouse is dragged.
	Zoom Region	Zooms to the region specified by the mouse.

Note   Several buttons are disabled on the Twist and Bevel Deformation windows because these dialog boxes have only one deformation curve.

At the bottom of the Deformation dialog boxes are two value fields. The value fields display the X and Y coordinate values for the currently selected point. The navigation buttons enable you to pan and zoom within the dialog box.

Figure 16-25 and Figure 16-26 show each of the various deformation options applied to a lofted column.

Figure 16-25: The Loft compound object deformation options: Scale, Twist, and Teeter

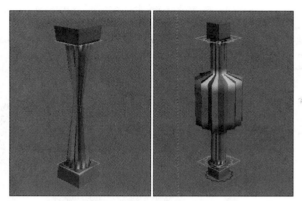

Figure 16-26: The Loft compound object deformation options: Bevel and Fit

Scale Deformation

The Scale Deformation window can alter the relative scale of the Loft object at any point along its path. This window includes two lines — one red and one green. The red line displays the X-axis scale, and the green line displays the Y-axis scale. By default, both lines are positioned equally at the 100 percent value. Specifying a value that is greater than 100 percent increases the scale, and specifying a value that is less than 100 percent has the opposite effect.

Twist Deformation

The Twist Deformation rotates one cross section relative to the others and can be used to create an object that spirals along its path. This option is similar to the Banking option, which can also produce rotations about the path.

Twist Deformation window includes only one red line representing the rotation value. By default, this line is set to a 0-degree rotation value. Positive values result in counterclockwise rotations, and negative values have the opposite effect.

Teeter Deformation

Teeter Deformation rotates a cross section so that its outer edges move closer to the path. This is done by rotating the cross section about its local X- or Y-axis. The result is similar to that produced by the Contour option.

The Teeter Deformation window includes two lines — one red and one green. The red line displays the X-axis rotation, and the green line displays the Y-axis rotation. By default, both lines are positioned equally at the 0 degree value. Positive values result in counterclockwise rotations, and negative values have the opposite effect.

Bevel Deformation

Bevel Deformation bevels the cross-section shapes. The Bevel Deformation window includes only one red line representing the amount of bevel that is applied. By default, this line is set to a 0 value. Positive values increase the bevel amount, which equals a reduction in the shape area, and negative values have the opposite effect.

You can also use the Bevel Deformation window to select three different types of beveling: Normal, Adaptive Linear, and Adaptive Cubic. Table 16-3 shows and describes the buttons for these three beveling types. You can select them from a flyout at the right end of the window.

Table 16-3: Bevel Deformation Buttons

Toolbar Button	Name	Description
	Normal Bevel	Produces a normal bevel with parallel edges, regardless of the path angle.
	Adaptive (Linear)	Alters the bevel linearly, based on the path angle.
	Adaptive (Cubic)	Alters the bevel using a cubic spline based on the path angle.

Fit Deformation

The Fit Deformation window, shown in Figure 16-27, lets you specify a profile for the outer edges of the cross-section shapes to follow. This window includes two lines — one red and one green. The red line displays the X-axis scale, and the green line displays the Y-axis scale. By default, both lines are positioned equally at the 100 percent value. Specifying a value that is greater than 100 percent increases the scale, and specifying a value that is less than 100 percent has the opposite effect.

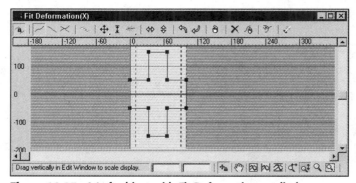

Figure 16-27: A Loft object with Fit Deformation applied

The Fit Deformation window includes ten buttons unique to it that are used to control the profile curves. These buttons are illustrated and described in Table 16-4.

Table 16-4: Fit Deformation Dialog Box Buttons

Toolbar Button	Name	Description
	Mirror Horizontally	Mirrors the selection horizontally.
	Mirror Vertically	Mirrors the selection vertically.
	Rotate 90 degrees CCW	Rotates the selection 90 degrees counterclockwise.
	Rotate 90 degrees CW	Rotates the selection 90 degrees clockwise.
	Delete Control Point	Deletes the selected control point.
	Reset Curve	Returns the curve to its original form.
	Delete Curve	Deletes the selected curve.
	Get Shape	Selects a separate spline to use as a profile.
	Generate Path	Replaces the current path with a straight line.
	Lock Aspect	Maintains the relationship between height and width.

Modifying Loft subobjects

When you select a Loft object, you can work with its subobjects in the Modify panel. The subobjects for a Loft include Path and Shape. The Path subobject opens the Path Commands rollout. This rollout has only a single button — Put — for creating a copy of the Loft path. If you click this button, the Put To Scene dialog box appears, enabling you to give the path a name and select to create it as a Copy or an Instance.

If your path is created as an Instance, you can edit the instance to control the Loft path.

The Shape subobject opens the Shape Commands rollout. This rollout also includes a Put button along with some additional controls. The Path Level value adjusts the shape's position on the path. The Compare button opens the Compare dialog box, which is discussed in the following section. The Reset button returns the shape to its former state before any rotation or scaling has taken place, and the Delete button deletes the shape entirely.

Note   You cannot delete a shape if it is the only shape in the Loft object.

The Shape Commands rollout also includes six Align buttons for aligning the shape to the Center, Default, Left, Right, Top, and Bottom. For the Loft object local coordinates, Left and Right move the shape along the X-axis, and Top and Bottom move it along the Y-axis.

Comparing shapes

The Compare dialog box superimposes selected cross-sectional shapes included in a Loft object on top of one another to check their center alignment. The button in the upper-left corner is the Pick Shape button. This button lets you select which shapes to display in the dialog box. The button to its right is the Delete Shape button, for removing a shape from the dialog box. Figure 16-28 shows the Compare dialog box with the two shapes from the pillar example selected. Notice how the first vertices on these two shapes are in different locations. This causes the strange twisting at both the top and bottom of the pillar.

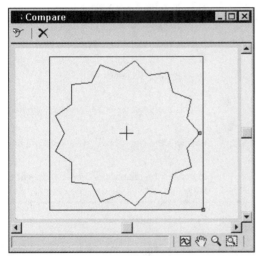

Figure 16-28: You can use the Compare dialog box to align shapes included in a Loft.

 Note   You can align these two vertices by subdividing the square shape in Edit Spline mode and selecting a new first vertex with the Make First button.

While the Compare dialog box is open, the Align buttons in the Shape Commands rollout are still active and can be used to move and position the shapes. The first vertex on each shape is shown as a small square. If these vertices aren't correctly aligned on top of one another, then the resulting Loft object will have skewed edges. The lower-right corner of the dialog box includes buttons to View Extents, Pan, Zoom, and Zoom Region.

Editing Loft paths

The original shapes that were used to create the Loft object can be edited at any time. These updates will also modify the Loft object. The shapes, if not visible, can be selected using the Select by Name button. The shapes maintain their base parameters or they can be converted to an Editable Spline.

Tutorial: Creating drapes

Modeling home interiors is a task commonly performed by professional architects and interior designers, but creating the drapes can be tricky. In this tutorial, we'll create some simple drapes using a Loft object.

To create drapes using a Loft object, follow these steps:

1. Open the Lofted drapes.max file from the Chap 16 directory on the CD-ROM.

   This file contains two splines that can be used to create the loft.

2. Click the Geometry category button in the Create panel and select the Compound Objects subcategory from the drop-down list. Select the straight line spline and click the Loft button. In the Creation Method rollout, click the Get Shape button, and then click the cross-section spline.

3. Open the Modify panel, and under the Skin Parameters rollout, turn off the Contour and Banking options.

4. Use the Deformation functions to add more control to the drapes, such as tying them together as shown in Figure 16-29.

Loft objects versus Surface tools

You can create compound loft objects completely from 2D shape splines — one open spline is typically used as the Loft path and other, closed splines are used as the cross sections. You can have several different cross sections, and these can change as you travel the path. Loft cross sections aren't required to have the same number of vertices, and you can modify the scale and rotation of the cross sections with the Deformation options.

Cross-Reference   See Chapter 14, "Creating Patches," for more detail on the surface tools.

The surface tools, which include the CrossSection and Surface modifiers, provide another way to model that is similar to lofting. The CrossSection modifier takes several cross-section shapes and connects their vertices with additional splines to create a spline framework. You can then use the Surface modifier to cover this framework with a skin.

Although similar in nature, Loft objects and the surface tools have different subtleties and strengths.

One difference is that the CrossSection modifier connects spline cross sections according to their order. This can cause strange results if the order is incorrect. A Loft always follows a path, so the cross-section order isn't a problem.

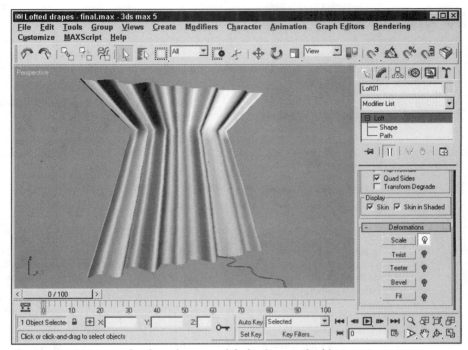

Figure 16-29: Drapes that have been modeled using a Loft object

Another difference is that surface tools give you more control over the surface of a created object. Because the underlying structure is a series of splines, you can add new branches and objects without much difficulty. This can be hard to do with Loft objects.

As a general guideline, Loft objects are better suited to modeling rigid objects with relatively uniform cross sections, whereas the surface tools are better for modeling more organic model types.

Tutorial: Modeling a vacuum hose

To get a better understanding of the differences between Loft objects and surface tools, let's model the end of a vacuum hose using these two methods. Both will use the same cross-section shapes, but the results will be a little different.

To model a vacuum hose using a Loft object and surface tools, follow these steps:

1. Open the Vacuum hose attachment.max file from the Chap 16 directory on the CD-ROM. This file includes two sets of circle and rectangle shapes that define the cross sections of a vacuum cleaner extension.

2. Let's create the Loft version first. Select the vertical path for the set of the shapes on the left. Then in the Create panel, click the Geometry category button and select Compound Objects from the subcategory drop-down list.

3. Click the Loft button, and in the Creation Method rollout click the Get Shape button and click the top circle.

4. In the Path Parameters rollout, enable the Snaps option with the Snap value of 10.0. Set the Path value to 60, click on the Get Shape button, and select the second circle shape. Then set the Path value to 80, click the Get Shape button, and select the smaller rectangle. Finally, set the Path value to 100, click the Get Shape button, and select the bottom rectangular shape.

This bunches all the shapes, and you'll need to straight them.

5. Open the Modify panel, and in the Modifier Stack expand the Loft object and select the Shape subobject. In the viewport, click on a shape, and in the Shape Command rollout click on the Center button. Repeat this for each shape.

6. For the surface tools version, we'll work on the shapes on the right. Select the shapes (they are all attached into a single Editable Spline object) and select Modifiers ➪ Patch/Spline Editing ➪ CrossSection to apply the CrossSection modifier to the shapes.

This connects all the shapes together.

7. Next select the Modifiers ➪ Patch/Spline Editing ➪ Surface modifier to cover the connected shapes with a surface.

Figure 16-30 shows the resulting models with the Loft object on the right and the surface tools model on the left. Notice how the Loft object is twisted. This is because the Loft object automatically aligned the vertices of the different shapes. You can fix this twist using the Loft Deformation options.

The surface tools model has a small bump at the neck of the extension. This is caused by the mesh being rotated to line up the vertices between the circle and the rectangles. From this example, you can see that each method has its advantages and disadvantages.

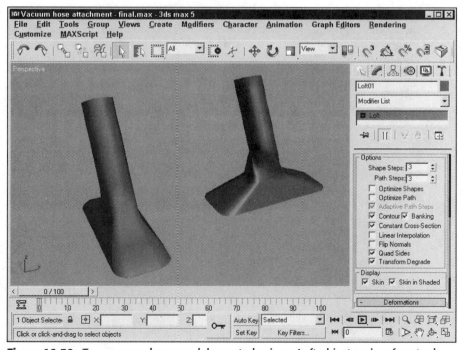

Figure 16-30: Two vacuum hose models created using a Loft object and surface tools

Summary

Compound objects provide several additional modeling types to our bulging modeling toolkit. From morph objects to complex deformed lofts, you can use these special-purpose types to model many different objects. In this chapter, you

✦ Learned about the various compound object types

✦ Morphed objects with the same number of vertices

✦ Created a Conform object with differing number of vertices

✦ Used splines and mesh objects to create a ShapeMerge object

✦ Created a Terrain object using splines

✦ Learned about the Mesher object

✦ Created a Scatter object

✦ Created a Connect object to join two objects

✦ Modeled with Boolean objects

✦ Created a Loft object

✦ Discovered how to control Loft parameters

✦ Learned to use Loft deformations

✦ Modified Loft subobjects

✦ Compared the strengths of loft objects versus surface tools

With all these different modeling types, you've probably started to create a lot of different objects, but get ready to really start creating a lot with particle systems.

✦   ✦   ✦

Creating and Controlling Particle Systems

Every object that you add to the scene slows down Max to a small degree, because Max needs to keep track of every object. If you add thousands of objects to a scene, not only will Max slow down noticeably, but the objects will also become difficult to identify. For example, if you had to create thousands of simple snowflakes for a snowstorm scene, the system would become unwieldy, and the number wouldn't get very high before you ran out of memory.

Particle systems are specialized groups of objects that are managed as a single entity. By grouping all the particle objects into a single controllable system, you can easily make modifications to all the objects with a single parameter. This chapter discusses using these special systems to produce rain and snow effects, fireworks sparks, sparkling butterfly wings, and even fire-breathing dragons.

Understanding the Various Particle Systems

A particle is a small, simple object that is duplicated en masse, like snow, rain, or dust. Just as in real life, Max includes many different types of particles that can vary in size, shape, texture, color, and motion. These different particle types are included in various particle systems.

When a particle system is created, all you can see in the viewport is a single gizmo known as an emitter icon. An emitter icon is the object (typically a gizmo, but it can be a scene object) where the particles originate. Selecting a particle system gizmo will make the parameters for the particle system appear in the Modify panel.

Max includes the following particle systems:

+ **Spray:** Simulates drops of water. These drops can be Drops, Dots, or Ticks. The particles travel in a straight line from the emitter's surface after they are created.

+ **Snow:** Similar to the Spray system, with the addition of some fields to make the particles Tumble as they fall. You can also render the particles as a Six Pointed shape that looks like a snowflake.

✦ **Super Spray:** An advanced version of the Spray system that can use different mesh objects, closely packed particles called MetaParticles, or an instanced object as its particles. Super Spray is useful for rain and fountains. Binding it to the Path Follow Space Warp can create waterfalls.

✦ **Blizzard:** An advanced version of the Snow system that can use the same mesh object types as the Super Spray system. Binding the system to the Wind Space Warp can create storms.

✦ **PArray:** Can use a separate Distribution Object as the source for the particles. For this system, you can set the particle type to Fragment and bind it to the PBomb Space Warp to create explosions.

✦ **PCloud:** Confines all generated particles to a certain volume. A good use of this system is to reproduce bubbles in a glass or cars on the road.

Creating a Particle System

You can find all the various particle systems under the Create panel. To access these systems, click the Geometry category and select the Particle Systems subcategory from the drop-down list. All the particle systems will then appear as buttons.

With the Particle Systems subcategory selected, click the button for the type of particle system you want to use, and then click in a viewport to create the particle system emitter icon. The emitter icon is a gizmo that looks like a plane or a sphere and that defines the location in the system where the particles all originate. Attached to the icon is a single line that indicates the direction in which the particles move when generated. This line points by default toward the construction grid's negative Z-axis when first created. Figure 17-1 shows the emitter icons for each particle system type including, from left to right, Spray and Snow (which have the same icon), Super Spray, Blizzard, PArray, and PCloud.

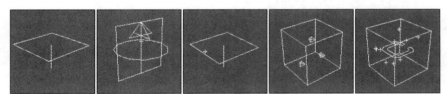

Figure 17-1: The emitter icons for each particle system type

You can transform these icons using the standard transform buttons on the main toolbar. Rotating an emitter changes the direction in which the particles initially move.

After an icon is created, you can set the number, shape, and size of the particles and define their motion in the Parameter rollouts. To apply a material to the particles, simply apply the material to the system's icon. This material will be applied to all particles included in the system.

Note   Be aware that the particles are displayed as simple objects such as ticks or dots in the viewports. To see the actual resulting particles, you need to render the scene file.

You can set the parameters for the Max particle systems in the Create panel when they are first created or in the Modify panel at any time. The simpler systems, Spray and Snow, have a single Parameters rollout, but the advanced systems, Super Spray and Blizzard, include multiple Parameters rollouts. The PArray and PCloud systems have similar multiple rollouts, with a few subtle differences. The following sections describe how to use these rollouts to set the parameters for each of the six particle systems.

Using the Spray and Snow Particle Systems

All I can say about the Spray and Snow particle systems is that "when it rains, it pours." The Spray Parameters rollout, shown in Figure 17-2, includes values for the number of particles to be included in the system. These values can be different for the viewport and renderer. By limiting the number of particles displayed in the viewport, you can make the viewport updates quicker. You can also specify the drop size, initial speed, and variation. The Variation value will alter the spread of the particle's initial speed and direction. A Variation value of 0 will make the particles travel in a straight line away from the emitter.

Figure 17-2: The Spray Parameters rollout holds the parameters for the Spray particle system.

Spray particles can be Drops, Dots, or Ticks, which affect how the particles look only in the viewport. Drops appear as streaks, Dots are simple points, and Ticks are small plus signs. You can also set how the particles are rendered — as Tetrahedron objects or as Facing objects (square faces that always face the viewer).

Note   The Facing option is visible only in the Perspective view.

The Timing values determine when the particles appear and how long the particles stay around. The Start Frame is the first frame where particles begin to appear, and the Life value determines the number of frames in which the particles are visible. When a particle's lifetime is up, it disappears. The Birth Rate value lets you set how many new particles appear in each frame; you can use this setting or select the Constant option. The Constant option determines the Birth Rate value by dividing the total number of particles by the number of frames.

The emitter dimensions specify the width and height of the emitter gizmo. You can also hide the emitter with the Hide option.

Note   The Hide option hides the emitter only in the viewports. Emitters are never rendered.

The parameters for the Snow particle system are similar to the Spray particle system, except for a few unique settings. Snow can be set with a Tumble and Tumble Rate. The Tumble value can range from 0 to 1, with 1 causing a maximum amount of rotation. The Tumble Rate determines the speed of the rotation.

The Render options are also different for the Snow particle system. The three options are Six Point, Triangle, and Facing. The Six Point option renders the particle as a six-pointed star. Triangles and Facing objects are single faces.

Tutorial: Creating rain showers

One of the simplest uses for particle systems is to simulate rain or snow. In this tutorial, you'll use the Spray system to create rain and then learn how to use the Snow system to create snow.

To create a scene with rain using the Spray particle system, follow these steps:

1. Open the Simple rain.max file from the Chap 17 directory on the CD-ROM. This file includes an umbrella model created by Zygote Media.

2. Open the Create panel, click the Geometry category button, and then select the Particle Systems subcategory. Click the Spray button, and drag the icon in the Top viewport to cover the entire scene. Position the icon above the objects, and make sure the vector is pointing down toward the scene objects.

3. Open the Modify panel, and in the Parameters rollout set the Render Count to 1000 and the Drop Size to 2. Keep the default speed of 10, and select the Drops option; these settings make the particles appear as streaks. Select the Tetrahedron Render method, and set the Start and Life values to 0 and 100, respectively.

Note   To cover the entire scene with an average downpour, set the number of particles to 1000 for a 100-frame animation.

4. Open the Material Editor (by pressing the M key) and drag a light-blue-colored material to the particle system icon. Figure 17-3 shows the results.

Figure 17-3: Rain created with the Spray particle system

Tutorial: Creating a snow storm

Creating a snowstorm is very similar. To create a snowstorm, use the Snow particle system with the same number of particles and apply a white material to the particle system. Figure 17-4 shows a scene with these settings.

To create a scene with rain using the Spray particle system, follow these steps:

1. Open the Snowman in snowstorm.max file from the Chap 17 directory on the CD-ROM. This file includes a snowman created using primitive objects.

2. Open the Create panel, click the Geometry category button, and then select the Particle Systems subcategory. Click the Snow button, and drag the icon in the Top viewport to cover the entire scene. Position the icon above the objects, and make sure the vector is pointing down toward the scene objects.

3. Open the Modify panel, and in the Parameters rollout, set the Render Count to 1000, the Flake Size to 6, and use the Six Point Render option. Select the Start and Life values to 0 and 100, respectively.

4. Open the Material Editor (by pressing the M key) and drag a white-colored material with some self-illumination added to the particle system gizmo. Figure 17-4 shows the results.

Figure 17-4: A simple snowstorm created with the Snow particle system

Using the Super Spray Particle System

If you think of the Spray particle system as a light summer rain shower, then the Super Spray particle system is like a fire hose. The Super Spray particle system is considerably more complex than its Spray and Snow counterparts. With this complexity comes a host of features that make this one of the most robust effects creation tools in Max.

Unlike the Spray and Snow particle systems, the Super Spray particle system includes several rollouts.

Super Spray Basic Parameters rollout

The Super Spray particle system emits all particles from the center of the emitter icon. The emitter icon is a simple cylinder and an arrow that points in the direction in which the particles will travel. In the Basic Parameters rollout, shown in Figure 17-5, the Off Axis value sets how far away from the icon's arrow the stream of particles will travel. A value of 0 will line the particle stream with the icon's arrow and a value of 180 will emit particles in the opposite direction. The Spread value can also range from 0 to 180 degrees and fans the particles equally about the specified axis. The Off Plane value spins the particles about its center axis and the Spread value sets the distance from this center axis that particles can be created. If all these values are left at 0, then the particle system emits a single, straight stream of particles and if all values are 180, then particles will go in all directions from the center of the emitter icon.

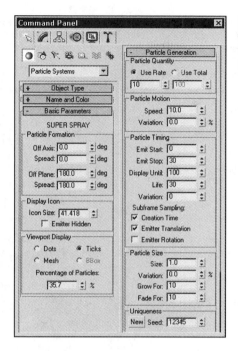

Figure 17-5: The Basic Parameters and Particle Generation rollouts let you specify where and how the particles appear in the viewports.

The icon size can be set or the icon can be hidden in the viewport. You can also set the particles to be displayed in the viewport as Dots, Ticks, Meshes, or Bounding Boxes. The Percentage value is the number of the total particles that are visible in the viewport and should be kept low to ensure rapid viewport updates.

Particle Generation rollout

The Particle Generation rollout, also shown in Figure 17-5, is where you set the number of particles to include in a system as either a Rate or Total value. The Rate value is the number of particles per frame that are generated. The Total value is the number of particles generated over the total number of frames. Use the Rate value if you want the animation to have a steady stream of particles throughout the animation and the Total value if you want to set the total number of particles that will appear throughout the entire range of frames.

In the Particle Motion group, the Speed value determines the initial speed and direction of particles. The Variation value alters this initial speed as a percentage of the Speed value. A high Variation value will result in particles with all sorts of different speeds.

In the Particle Timing group, you can set when the emitting process starts and stops. Using the Display Until value, you can also cause the particles to continue displaying after the emitting has stopped. The Life value is how long particles stay around, which can vary based on another Variation setting.

When an emitter is animated (such as moving back and forth), the particles can clump together where the system changes direction. This clumping effect is called puffing. The Subframe Sampling options help reduce this effect. The three options are Creation Time (which controls emitting particles over time), Emitter Translation (which controls emitting particles as the emitter is moved), and Emitter Rotation (which controls emitting particles as the emitter is rotated. All three options can be enabled, but each one that is enabled will add the computation time required to the render.

Note   The Subframe Sampling options increase the rendering time and should be used only if necessary.

You can specify the particle size along with a Variation value. You can also cause the particles to grow and fade for a certain number of frames.

The Seed value helps determine the randomness of the particles. Clicking the New button automatically generates a new Seed value.

Particle Type rollout

The Particle Type rollout, shown in Figure 17-6, lets you define the look of the particles. At the top of the rollout are three Particle Type options: Standard Particles, MetaParticles, and Instanced Geometry.

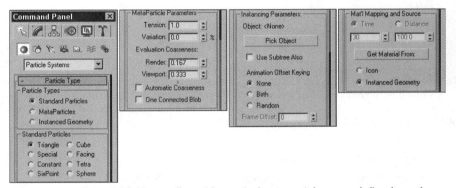

Figure 17-6: The Particle Type rollout (shown in four parts) lets you define how the particles look.

If you select Standard Particles as the particle type, you can select which geometric shape you want to use from the Standard Particles section. The options are Triangle, Special, Constant, Six Point, Cube, Facing, Tetra, and Sphere.

The Special type consists of three intersecting planes, which are useful if you apply maps to them. The Facing type is also useful with maps; it creates a simple, square face that always faces the view. The Constant type maintains the same pixel size regardless of the distance from the camera or view. Six Point renders each particle as a 2D six-pointed star. All other types are common geometric objects.

Tutorial: Creating a fireworks fountain

As an example of the Super Spray particle system, you'll create a firework fountain. Fireworks are essentially just lots of particles with a short life span and a high amount of self-illumination. (Tell yourself that next time you watch a fireworks display.)

This ready-made material for this example uses the Glow Render effect to make the particles glow. You can learn more about render effects in Chapter 36, "Using Render Elements and Render Effects."

To create a fireworks fountain using a particle system, follow these steps:

1. Open the Fireworks fountain.max file from the Chap 17 directory on the CD-ROM. This file includes a simple fountain base and the Gravity space warp to cause the particles to curve back toward the ground.

Some of the most amazing special effects are made possible by combining particle systems with Space Warps.

2. From the Create panel, select the Particle Systems subcategory and click the Super Spray button. Drag in the Top view and position the system at the top of the cylinder with the direction arrow pointing toward the sky.

3. Open the Modify panel and set the Off Axis Spread to 45 and the Off Plane Spread to 90. In the Particle Generation rollout, set the number of Particles to 2000 with a Speed of 20 and a Variation of 100. Set the Emit Start to 0 and the Emit Stop to 100. Set the Display Until to 100 and the Life to 25 with a Variation of 20. The Size of the particles should be 5.

4. Open the Material Editor (by pressing the M key) and select the first sample slot. This slot includes a material named Spark. Drag the material from the Material Editor to the particle system's icon.

5. Select the Super Spray icon and right-click it to open the pop-up menu, then select the Properties menu option. In the Object Properties dialog box, select the Object Motion Blur option.

When viewing the animation, maximize a single viewport. If Max tries to update all four viewports at once with this many particle objects, the update will be slow.

Figure 17-7 shows sparks emitting from the fireworks fountain.

Figure 17-7: The Super Spray particle system is used to create firework sparks.

Tutorial: Adding spray to a spray can

The Super Spray particle system is complex enough that another example is worth looking at. What good is a spray can without any spray? In this tutorial, we'll create a spray can model and then use the Super Spray particle system to create the spray coming from it.

To create a stream of spray for a spray can, follow these steps:

1. Open the Spray can.max file from the Chap 17 directory on the CD-ROM.

   This file includes a simple spray can object created using a cylinder for the can base and the nozzle and a lathed spline for the top of the can.

2. Select the Particle Systems subcategory button and click the Super Spray button. Drag in the Top viewport to create the Super Spray icon and position it at the mouth of the nozzle.

3. Set the Off Axis Spread to 20 and the Off Plane Spread to 90. In the Particle Generation rollout, set the Emit Rate to 1000, the Speed to 20, and the Life to 30. Set the Size of the particles to 5.

4. Open the Material Editor (by pressing M) and select the material named Spray Mist. Then drag this material onto the Super Spray icon to apply this material to the Super Spray particle system.

Figure 17-8 shows the fine spray from an aerosol can.

Figure 17-8: Using a mostly transparent material, you can create a fine mist spray.

Using the MetaParticles option

The MetaParticles option in the Particle Type rollout makes the particle system release Metaball objects. Metaballs are viscous spheres that, like mercury, flow into each other when close. These particles take a little longer to render but are effective for simulating water and liquids. The MetaParticles type is available for the Super Spray, Blizzard, PArray, and PCloud particle systems.

Selecting the MetaParticles option in the Particle Types section enables the MetaParticle Parameters group. In this group are options for controlling how the MetaParticles behave. The Tension value determines how easily objects blend together. MetaParticles with a high tension resist merging with other particles. You can vary the amount of tension with the Variation value.

Because MetaParticles can take a long time to render, the Evaluation Coarseness settings enable you to set how computationally intensive the rendering process is. This can be set differently for the viewport and the renderer _ the higher the value, the quicker the results. You can also set this to Automatic Coarseness, which automatically controls the coarseness settings based on the speed and ability of the renderer. The One Connected Blob option speeds the rendering process by ignoring all particles that aren't connected.

Tutorial: Spilling soda from a can

MetaParticles are a good option to use to create drops of liquid, like those from a soda can.

To create liquid flowing from a can, follow these steps:

1. Open the MetaParticles from a soda can.max file from the Chap 17 directory on the CD-ROM.

   This file includes a soda can model created by Zygote Media positioned so the can is on its side.

2. Open the Create panel, click the Geometry category button, and select the Particle Systems subcategory from the drop-down list. Then click the Super Spray button, and drag the icon in the Front viewport. Position the icon so its origin is at the opening of the can and the directional vector is pointing outward.

3. With the Super Spray icon selected, open the Modify panel, and in the Basic Parameters rollout set the Off Axis and Off Plane Spread values to 40.

4. In the Particle Generation rollout, keep the default Rate and Speed values, but set the Speed Variation to 50 to alter the speed of the various particles. Set the Particle Size to 20.

5. In the Particle Type rollout, select the MetaParticles option, set the Tension value to 1, and make sure the Automatic Coarseness option is selected.

6. Open the Material Editor (by pressing the M key), and drag the Purple Soda material to the particle system icon.

Figure 17-9 shows a rendered image of the MetaParticles spilling from a soda can at frame 25.

Figure 17-9: MetaParticles emitting from the opening of a soda can

Instanced Geometry

Using the Particle Type rollout, you can select an object to use as the particle. If the Instanced Geometry option is selected as the particle type, you can select an object to use as the particle. To choose an object to use as a particle, click the Pick Object button, and then select an object from the viewport. If the Use Subtree Also option is selected, then all child objects are also included.

Caution Using complicated objects as particles can slow down a system and increase the rendering time.

The Animation Offset Keying determines how an animated object that is selected as the particle is animated. The None option animates all objects the same, regardless of when they are born. The Birth option starts the animation for each object when it is created, and the Random option offsets the timing randomly based on the Frame Offset value. For example, if you have selected an animated bee that flaps its wings as the particle, and you select None as the Animation Offset Keying option, all the bees flap their wings in concert. Selecting the Birth option instead starts them flapping their wings once they are born, and selecting Random offsets each instance differently.

For materials, the Time and Distance values determine the number of frames or the distance traveled before a particle is completely mapped. You can apply materials to the icon that appears when the particle system is created. The Get Material From button lets you select the object from which to get the material. The options include the icon and the Instanced Geometry.

Rotation and Collision rollout

In the Rotation and Collision rollout is an option to enable interparticle collisions. This option causes objects to bounce away from one another when their object boundaries overlap.

The Rotation and Collision rollout, shown in Figure 17-10, contains several controls to alter the rotation of individual particles. The Spin Time is the number of frames required to rotate a full revolution. The Phase value is the initial rotation of the particle. You can vary both of these values with Variation values.

Note The Rotation and Collision rollout options can also increase the rendering time of a scene.

You can also set the axis about which the particles rotate. Options include Random, Direction of Travel/MBlur, and User Defined. The Stretch value under the Direction of Travel option causes the object to elongate in the direction of travel. The User Defined option lets you specify the degrees of rotation about each axis.

Interparticle collisions are computationally intensive and can easily be enabled or disabled with the Enable option. You can also set how often the collisions are calculated. The Bounce value determines the speed of particles after collisions as a percentage of their collision speed. You can vary the amount of Bounce with the Variation value.

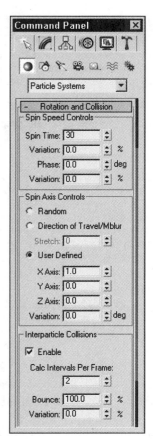

Figure 17-10: The Rotation and Collision rollout options can control how objects collide with one another.

Tutorial: Basketball shooting practice

When an entire team is warming up before a basketball game, the space around the basketball hoop is quite chaotic — with basketballs flying in all directions. In this tutorial, we use a basketball object as a particle and spread it around a hoop. (Watch out for flying basketballs!)

To use a basketball object as a particle, follow these steps:

1. Open the Basketballs at a hoop.max file from the Chap 17 directory on the CD-ROM.

   This file includes basketball and basketball hoop models created by Zygote Media.

2. Open the Create panel, and select the Particle Systems subcategory. Then click the Super Spray button, and drag the icon in the viewport. Position the icon in the Front view so that its origin is above and slightly in front of the hoop and the directional vector is pointing down (you'll need to rotate the Space Warp).

3. Open the Modify panel, and in the Basic Parameters rollout, set the Off Axis Spread value to 90 and the Off Plane Spread value to 40; this randomly spreads the basketballs around the hoop. In the Viewport Display group of the Basic Parameters rollout, select the Mesh option. Set the Percentage of Particles to 100 percent to see the position of each basketball object in the viewport.

Caution Because the basketball is a fairly complex model, using the Mesh option severely slows down the viewport update. You can speed the viewport display using the Bbox option, but you'll need to choose it after selecting the Instanced Geometry option.

4. In the Particle Generation rollout, select the Use Total option, and enter **30** for the value. (This number is reasonable and not uncommon during warm-ups.) Set the Speed value to 0.2, the Life value to 100 because we don't want basketballs to disappear. Because of the low number of particles, you can disable the Subframe Sampling options. Set the Grow For and Fade For values to 0.

5. In the Particle Type rollout, select the Instanced Geometry option, and click the Pick Object button. Make sure the Use Subtree Also option is selected to get the entire group, and then select the basketball group in the viewport. At the bottom of this roll-out, select the Instanced Geometry option, and click the Get Material From button to give all the particles the same material as the original object.

6. In the Rotation and Collision rollout, set the Spin Time to 100 to make the basketballs spin as they move about the scene. Set the Spin Axis Control to Random. Also enable the Interparticle Collisions option, and set the Calculation Interval to 1 and the Bounce value to 100. With the Collisions option enabled, the basketballs will be prevented from overlapping one another.

7. At the floor of the basketball hoop is a Deflector Space Warp. Click the Bind to Space Warp button in the main toolbar and drag from this floor deflector to the Super Spray icon. This will make the basketballs bounce off the floor.

Figure 17-11 shows a rendered image of the scene at frame 30 with several basketballs bouncing chaotically around a hoop.

Figure 17-11: Multiple basketball particles flying around a hoop

Object Motion Inheritance rollout

The settings on the Object Motion Inheritance rollout, shown in Figure 17-12, determine how the particles move when the emitter is moving. The Influence value defines how closely the particles follow the emitter's motion; a value of 100 has particles follow exactly, and a value of 0 means they don't follow at all.

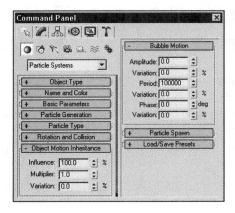

Figure 17-12: The Object Motion Inheritance rollout sets how the particles inherit the motion of their emitter.

The Multiplier value can exaggerate or diminish the effect of the emitter's motion. Particles with a high multiplier can actually precede the emitter.

Bubble Motion rollout

The Bubble Motion rollout, also shown in Figure 17-12, simulates the wobbling motion of bubbles as they rise in a liquid. Three values define this motion, each with variation values. Amplitude is the distance that the particle moves from side to side. Period is the time that it takes to complete one side-to-side motion cycle. The Phase value defines where the particle starts along the amplitude curve.

Particle Spawn rollout

The Particle Spawn rollout, shown in Figure 17-13, sets options for spawning new particles when a particle dies or collides with another particle. If the setting is None, colliding particles bounce off one another, and dying particles simply disappear. The Die After Collision option causes a particle to disappear after it collides. The Persist value sets how long the particle stays around before disappearing. The Variation value causes the Persist value to vary by a defined percentage.

The Spawn on Collision, Spawn on Death, and Spawn Trails options all enable the spawn controls and define when particles spawn new particles. The Spawns value is the number of times a particle can spawn other particles. The Affects value is the percentage of particles that can spawn new particles; lowering this value creates some duds that do not spawn. The Multiplier value determines the number of new particles created.

Note   The Spawn Trails option causes every particle to spawn a new particle at every frame. This option can very quickly create an enormous number of particles and should be used with caution.

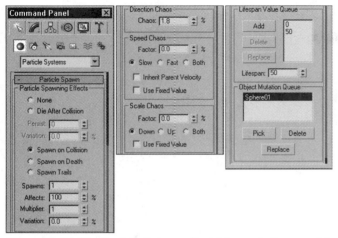

Figure 17-13: The Particle Spawn rollout (shown in three parts) can cause particles to spawn new particles.

The Chaos settings define the direction and speed of the spawned particles. A Direction Chaos value of 100 gives the spawned particles the freedom to travel in any direction, whereas a setting of 0 moves them in the same direction as their originator.

The Chaos Speed Factor is the difference in speed between the spawned particle and its originator. This factor can be faster or slower than the original. Selecting the Both option speeds up some particles and slows others randomly. You can also choose to have spawned particles use their parent's velocity or use the factor value as a fixed value.

The Scale Chaos Factor works similarly to the Chaos Speed Factor, except that it scales particles to be larger or smaller than their originator.

The Lifespan Value Queue lets you define different lifespan levels. Original particles have a lifespan equal to the first entry in the queue. The particles that are spawned from those spawned particles last as long as the second value, and so on. To add a value to the list, enter the value in the Lifespan spinner and click the Add button. The Delete button removes values from the list, and the Replace button switches value positions.

If Instanced Geometry is the selected particle type, you can fill the Object Mutation Queue with additional objects to use at each spawn level. These objects appear once a particle is spawned. To pick a new object to add to the queue, use the Pick button. You can select several objects, and they are used in the order in which they are listed.

Load/Save Presets rollout

You can save and load each particle configuration using the Load/Save Presets rollout, shown in Figure 17-14. To save a configuration, type a name in the Preset Name field, and click the Save button. All saved presets are displayed in the list. To use one of these preset configurations, select it, and click the Load button.

Note   A saved preset is valid only for the type of particle system used to save it. For example, you cannot save a Super Spray preset and load it for a Blizzard system.

Figure 17-14: The Load/Save Presets rollout enables you to save different parameter settings.

Max includes several default presets that can be used as you get started. These presets include Bubbles, Fireworks, Hose, Shockwave, Trail, Welding Sparks, and Default (which produces a straight line of particles).

Using the Blizzard Particle System

The Blizzard particle system uses the same rollouts as the Super Spray system, with some slightly different options. The Blizzard emitter icon is a plane with a line pointing in the direction of the particles (similar to the Spray and Snow particle systems). Particles are emitted across the entire plane surface.

The differences between the Blizzard and Super Spray parameters include dimensions for the Blizzard icon. In the Particle Generation rollout, you'll find values for Tumble and Tumble Rate. Another difference is the Emitter Fit Planar option under the Material Mapping group of the Particle Type rollout. This option sets particles to be mapped at birth, depending on where they appear on the emitter. The other big difference is that the Blizzard particle system has no Bubble Motion rollout, because snowflakes don't make very good bubbles. Finally, you'll find a different set of presets in the Load/Save Presets rollout including Blizzard, Rain, Mist, and Snowfall.

Using the PArray Particle System

The PArray particle system is a unique particle system. It will emit particles from the surface of a selected object. These particles can be emitted from the object's surface, edges, or vertices. The particles are emitted from an object separate from the emitter icon.

The PArray particle system includes many of the same rollouts as the Super Spray particle system. The PArray particle system's emitter icon is a cube with three tetrahedron objects inside it. There are some interesting parameter differences with this system, starting with the Basic Parameters rollout, shown in Figure 17-15.

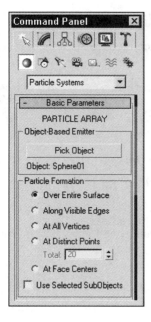

Figure 17-15: The Basic Parameters rollout for the PArray particle system lets you select the location where the particles form.

In the PArray system, you can select separate objects as emitters with the Pick Object button. You can also select the location on the object where the particles are formed. Options include Over Entire Surface, Along Visible Edges, At All Vertices, At Distinct Points, and At Face Centers. For the At Distinct Points option, you can select the number of points to use.

The Use Selected Sub-Object option forms particles in the locations selected with the Pick Object button, but only within the subobject selection passed up the Stack. This is useful if you want to emit particles only from a certain selection of a mesh, such as a dragon's mouth or the end of a fire hose. The other options in the PArray system's Basic Parameters rollout are the same as in the other systems.

The Particle Generation rollout includes a Divergence value. This value is the angular variation of the velocity of each particle from the emitter's normal.

Splitting an object into fragments

The Particle Type rollout for the PArray system contains a unique particle type: Object Fragments. This type breaks the selected object into several fragments. Object Fragment settings include a Thickness value. This value gives each fragment a depth. If the value is set to 0, the fragments are all single-sided polygons.

Also in the Particle Type rollout, the All Faces option separates each individual triangular face into a separate fragment. An alternative to this option is to use the Number of Chunks option, which enables you to divide the object into chunks and define how many chunks to use. A third option splits an object up based on the smoothing angle, which can be specified.

In the Material section of the Particle Type rollout, you can select material IDs to use for the fragment's inside, outside, and backside.

The Load/Save Presets rollout includes a host of interesting presets including the likes of Blast, Disintegrate, Geyser, and Comet.

Tutorial: Magic butterfly wings

In this tutorial, we create the effect of sparkling magic dust floating from butterfly wings using the PArray particle system with the butterfly wings as emitters.

Cross-Reference This ready-made material used in this example uses the Lens Effects render effect to make the particles sparkle. You can learn more about render effects in Chapter 36, "Using Render Elements and Render Effects."

To emit particles from butterfly wings, follow these steps:

1. Open the Magic butterfly.max file from the Chap 17 directory on the CD-ROM.

   This file includes butterfly and flower models created by Zygote Media.

2. Open the Create panel, and select the Particle Systems subcategory. Click the PArray button, and drag in the Top view to create the system.

3. In the Basic Parameters rollout, click the Pick Object button, and select the butterfly wings.

4. In the Particle Generation rollout, set the Emit Stop value to 100.

5. In the Particle Type rollout, select the Standard Particles and the Sphere options.

6. Open the Material Editor (by selecting the M key), and drag the Magic Dust material in the first sample slot to the PArray icon.

Figure 17-16 shows the butterfly at frame 30 with sparkling magic particles being emitted from its wings.

Figure 17-16: The wings of this magic butterfly are the emitters for the particle system.

Using the PCloud Particle System

The PCloud particle system keeps all emitted particles within a selected volume. This volume can be a box, sphere, cylinder, or a selected object. The emitter icon will be shaped as the selected volume. This particle system includes the same rollouts as the Super Spray system with some subtle differences.

The options on the Basic Parameters rollout are unique to this system. This system can use a separate mesh object as an emitter. To select this emitter object, click the Pick Object button, and select the object to use. This button is active only if the Object-based Emitter option is selected. If it is selected, the button icon displays the word "Fill" until an object is selected using the Pick Object button. Other options include Box, Sphere, and Cylinder Emitter. For these emitters, the Rad/Len, Width, and Height values are active for defining its dimensions.

In addition to these differences in the Basic Parameters rollout, several Particle Motion options in the Particle Generation rollout are different for the PCloud system as well. Particle Motion can be set to either a random direction, a specified vector, or in the direction of a reference object's Z-axis.

The only two presets for this particle system in the Load/Save Presets rollout are Cloud/Smoke and Default.

Using Particle System Maps

Using material maps on particles is another way to add detail to a particle system without increasing its geometric complexity. You can apply all materials and maps available in the Material Editor to particle systems. To apply them, select the particle system icon, and click the Assign Material to Selection button in the Material Editor.

Cross-Reference

For more details on using maps, see Chapter 20, "Using Material Maps."

Two map types are specifically designed to work with particle systems: Particle Age and Particle MBlur. You can find these maps in the Material/Map Browser. You can access the Material/Map Browser using the Rendering ⇨ Material Map Browser menu command or from the Material Editor by clicking on the Get Material button.

Using the Particle Age map

The Particle Age map parameters include three different colors that can be applied at different times, depending on the Life value of the particles. Each color includes a color swatch, a map button, an Enable check box, and an Age value for when this color should appear.

This map typically is applied as a Diffuse map because it affects the color.

Using the Particle MBlur map

The Particle MBlur map changes the opacity of the front and back of a particle, depending on the color values and sharpness specified in its parameters rollout. This results in an effect of blurred motion if applied as an Opacity map.

Note   MBlur does not work with the Constant, Facing, MetaParticles, or PArray object fragments.

Tutorial: Creating a fire-breathing dragon

The Particle Age and MBlur maps work well for adding opacity and colors that change over time, such as hot jets of flames, to a particle system. A good example of this is the breath from a fire-breathing dragon.

To create a fire-breathing dragon, follow these steps:

1. Open the Fire breathing dragon.max file from the Chap 17 directory on the CD-ROM.

   This file includes a dragon model created by Viewpoint Datalabs.

2. Open the Create panel, and select the Particle Systems subcategory. Click the Super Spray button, and drag the icon in the viewport. Position the icon so that its origin is right in the dragon's mouth and the directional vector is pointing outward and down.

3. Open the Modify panel, and in the Basic Parameters rollout set the Off Axis Spread value to 20 and the Off Plane Spread value to 90; these settings focus the flames shooting from the dragon's mouth.

4. In the Particle Generation rollout, use the default values, except for the Particle Size, which you should set to 50.

5. In the Particle Type rollout, select the Standard Particles option and select the Sphere type.

6. Open the Material Editor by pressing the M key, and select the first sample slot. Name this material **Dragon's Breath**, and click the map button to the right of the Diffuse color.

7. From the Material/Map Browser that opens, select the Particle Age map. In the Particle Age Parameters rollout, select red, orange, and yellow colors for the ages 0, 50, and 100.

8. Select the Dragon's Breath material from the drop-down list, and click the map button to the right of the Opacity setting. Select the Particle MBlur map.

9. In the Particle MBlur Parameters rollout, make Color #1 white and Color #2 black with a Sharpness value of 2.0. Then drag this material from the first sample slot onto the particle system's icon.

Figure 17-17 shows the dragon at frame 30 with its fiery breath.

Figure 17-17: A fire-breathing dragon created using the Particle Age and MBlur maps.

Summary

This chapter presented particle systems and showed how you can use them. The chapter also took a close look at each system, including Spray, Snow, Super Spray, Blizzard, PArray, and PCloud. In this chapter, you

✦ Learned about the various particle systems

✦ Created a particle system for producing rain and snow

✦ Used the Super Spray particle system

✦ Worked with MetaParticles

✦ Specified an object to use as a particle and an object to use as an emitter

✦ Learned to use the PArray and PCloud particle systems

✦ Used the Particle Age and Particle MBlur maps on particles

In the next chapter, you start learning about materials and how to apply them using the Material Editor.

✦　　✦　　✦

Materials and Maps

Exploring the Material Editor

Materials are used to dress color, and paint objects. Just as materials in real life can be described as scaly, soft, smooth, opaque, or blue, materials applied to 3D objects can mimic properties such as color, texture, transparency, shininess, and so on. In this chapter, you'll learn the basics of working with materials and all the features of the Material Editor.

Understanding Material Properties

Before jumping into the Material Editor, let's take a close look at the type of material properties that you can deal with. Understanding these properties will help you as you begin to create new materials, which I cover in detail in Chapter 19.

Up until now, the only material property that has been applied to an object has been the default object color, randomly assigned by Max. The Material Editor can add a whole new level of realism using materials that simulate many different types of physical properties, such as the ones discussed in the following sections.

Note   Many of these material properties will not be visible until the scene is rendered.

Colors

Color is probably the simplest material property and the easiest to identify. However, unlike the object color defined in the Create and Modify panels, there isn't a single color swatch that controls an object's color.

Consider a basket of shiny red apples. When you shine a bright blue spotlight on them, all the apples turn purple. So, even if the apples are assigned a red material, the final color in the image might be very different.

Within the Material Editor are several different color swatches that control different aspects of the object's color. The following list describes the types of color swatches that are available:

✦ **Ambient:** Defines an overall background lighting that affects all objects in the scene, including the color of the object when it is in the shadows. This color can often be locked to the Diffuse color so that they are changed together.

✦ **Diffuse:** The surface color of the object surface in normal, full light. The normal color of an object is typically defined by its Diffuse color.

✦ **Specular:** The color of the highlights where the light is focused on the surface of a shiny material.

✦ **Self-Illumination:** The color that the object glows from within. This color takes over any shadows on the object.

✦ **Filter:** The transmitted color caused by light shining through a transparent object.

✦ **Reflect:** The color that is reflected by a raytrace material to other objects in the scene.

✦ **Luminosity:** Causes an object to glow with the defined color. It is similar to Self-Illumination color, but can be independent of the Diffuse color.

If you ask someone the color of an object, he or she would respond by identifying the Diffuse color, but all these properties play an important part in bringing a sense of realism to the material. Try applying very different, bright materials to each of these color swatches and notice the results. The object will look unique, but not very realistic.

Tip   For realistic materials, your choice of colors depends on the scene lights. Indoor lights have a result different from an outdoor light like the sun. You can simulate objects in direct sunlight by giving their Specular color a yellow tint and their Ambient color a complementary, dark, almost black or purple color. For indoor objects, make the Specular color bright white and use an Ambient color that is the same as the Diffuse color, only much darker.

Opacity and transparency

Opaque objects are objects that you cannot see through, such as rocks and trees. Transparent objects, on the other hand, are objects that you can see through, like glass and clear plastic. Max's materials include several controls for adjusting these properties, including Opacity and several Transparency controls.

Opacity is the amount that an object refuses to allow light to pass through it. It is the opposite of transparency and is typically measured as a percentage. An object with 0 percent opacity is completely transparent, and an object with an opacity of 100 percent doesn't let any light through.

Transparency is the amount of light that is allowed to pass through an object. Because this is the opposite of opacity, transparency can be defined by the opacity value. Several options enable you to control the transparency including Falloff, Amount, and Type. I discuss each of these options later in this chapter.

Reflection and refraction

A reflection is what you see when you look in the mirror. Shiny objects reflect their surroundings. By defining a material's reflection values, you can control how much it reflects its surroundings. A mirror, for example, reflects everything, but a rock won't reflect at all.

Refraction is the bending of light as it moves through a transparent material. The amount of refraction a material produces is expressed as a value called the Index of Refraction. The Index of Refraction is the amount that light bends as it goes through a transparent object. For example, thick glasses bend light farther than thin ones and therefore have a higher Index of Refraction value. The default Index of Refraction value is 1.0. Water has a value of 1.3, glass a value of around 1.5, and solid crystal a value of around 2.0.

Reflection Dimming controls how much of the original reflection is lost as the surroundings are reflected within the scene.

 Note   In the Advanced Lighting panel of the Preference Settings dialog box is an option to Display Reflectance & Transmittance Information. If this option is enabled, this information (average and maximum percent values) will appear directly below the sample slots.

Shininess and specular highlights

Shiny objects, such as polished metal or a clean windows, include highlights where the lights reflect off their surfaces. These highlights are called specular highlights and are determined by the Specular settings. These settings include Specular Level, Glossiness, and Soften values.

The Specular Level is a setting for the intensity of the highlight. The Glossiness determines the size of the highlight — higher values result in a smaller highlight. The Soften value thins the highlight by lowering its intensity and increasing its size.

A rough material has the opposite properties of a shiny material and almost no highlights. The Roughness property sets how quickly the Diffuse color blends with the Ambient color. Cloth and fabric materials have a high Roughness value, and plastic and metal Roughness values will be small.

Other properties

Max uses several miscellaneous properties to help define standard materials, including properties such as Diffuse Level and Metalness.

The Diffuse Level property controls the brightness of the Diffuse color. Decreasing this value darkens the material without affecting the specular highlights. The Metalness property controls the metallic look of the material.

Some properties are only available for certain material types. For example, several properties are unique to raytrace materials, including Extra Lighting, Translucency, and Fluorescence.

 Cross-Reference   I talk about raytracing in more detail in Chapter 37, "Raytracing."

You can apply Extra Lighting to raytrace materials to increase the effect of Ambient light on a particular material. You can use this option to simulate radiosity, which is the effect of increasing light in an environment by simulating the light bouncing off other objects.

Translucency is similar to transparency in that it lets light pass through an object, but it also scatters the light so that other objects cannot be seen through the translucent object; an example of such a translucent object is frosted glass.

Raytrace materials can also simulate Fluorescence, which is the ability to reflect light in fluorescent colors under a black light.

Working with the Material Editor

The Material Editor is the interface with which you define, create, and apply materials. You can access the Material Editor by choosing Rendering ⇨ Material Editor, clicking the Material Editor button on the main toolbar (it has four small rendered spheres on the icon), or by using the M keyboard shortcut.

Using the Material Editor controls

At the top of the default Material Editor window is a menu of options including Material, Navigation, Options, and Utilities. The menu commands found in these menus offer the same functionality as the toolbar buttons, but the menus are often easier to find than the buttons you are unfamiliar with.

 New Feature   The Material Editor menus are new to 3ds max 5.

Below the menus are six sample slots that display a preview of some available materials. Surrounding these slots are button icons for controlling the appearance of these sample slots and interacting with materials. Figure 18-1 shows the Material Editor with all rollouts contracted.

Sample slots   Vertical buttons

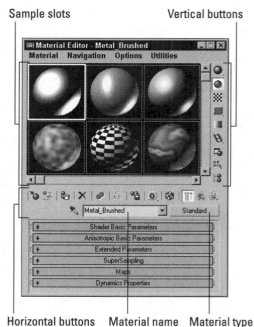

Horizontal buttons   Material name   Material type

Figure 18-1: Use the Material Editor window to create, store, and work with materials.

Note

Before proceeding, you need to understand the difference between a material and a map. A *material* is an effect that permeates the 3D object, but most *maps* are 2D images (although procedural 3D maps also exist) that can be wrapped on top of the object. Materials can contain maps, and maps can be made up of several materials. In the Material Editor, materials appear shaded in the sample slots and maps appear as 2D images. You usually can tell whether you're working with a material or a map by looking at the default name. Maps show up in the name drop-down list as Map and a number (Map #1) and materials are named a number and Default (7- Default).

The button icons to the right and below the sample slots control how the materials appear in the editor. These buttons are defined in Tables 18-1 and 18-2.

Table 18-1: Material Editor Buttons — Vertical

Toolbar Button	Name	Description
	Sample Type (Sphere, Cylinder, Box, Custom)	Controls the type of object displayed in the sample slot. The default object is a sphere. Other options available as flyouts include a Cylinder and a Cube. You can also select a custom object to use as the preview object.
	Backlight (L)	Turns backlighting in the selected sample slot on or off.
	Background (B)	Displays a checkered background image (or a custom background) behind the material, helpful when displaying a transparent material.
	Sample UV Tiling (1×1, 2×2, 3×3, 4×4)	Sets UV tiling for the map in the sample slot. The default is 1×1. Additional options available as flyouts are 2×2, 3×3, and 4×4. This setting only affects maps.
	Video Color Check	Checks the current material for colors that are unsupported by the NTSC and PAL formats.
	Make Preview (P), Play Preview, Save Preview	Used to generate, view, and save material preview renderings. These animated material previews enable you to see the effect of an animated material before rendering.
	Options (O)	Opens the Material Editor Options dialog box. This dialog box includes settings for enabling material animation, loading a custom background, defining the light intensity and color, and number of sample slots.
	Select by Material	Selects all objects using the current material. This button opens the Select Objects dialog box with those objects selected.
	Material/Map Navigator	Opens the Material/Map Navigator dialog box. This dialog box displays a tree of all the levels for the current material.

Table 18-2: Material Editor Buttons — Horizontal

Toolbar Button	Name	Description
	Get Material (G)	Opens the Material/Map Browser for selecting materials.
	Put Material in Scene	Updates the materials applied to objects in the viewport after materials have been edited.
	Assign Material to Selection	Paints the selected object with the selected material.
	Reset Map/ Mtl to Default Settings	Removes any modified properties and resets the material properties to their defaults.
	Make Material Copy	Creates a copy of the current material in the selected sample slot.
	Make Unique	Makes instanced materials into a new standalone material.
	Put to Library	Opens a simple dialog box that lets you rename the material and saves it into the current open library.
	Material Effects Channel	Sets a unique channel ID for applying post-processing effects. This button includes channels 1–15 as flyouts. A material with channel 0 means no effect will be applied.
	Show Map in Viewport	Displays 2D material maps on objects in the viewports.
	Show End Result	Displays the material in the sample slot with all levels applied. If this button is disabled, you will see only the level that is currently selected.
	Go to Parent	Moves up one level for the current material. This applies only to compound objects with several levels.
	Go Forward to Sibling	Selects the next maps or material at the same level.
	Pick Material From Object	Enables you to select a material from an object in the scene and load the material into the selected sample slot.
Metal_Brushed	Material drop-down list	Lists the elements in the current material. You can change the material or map name by typing a new name in this field.
Standard	Type button	Displays the current material or map type that is being used. Clicking this button opens the Material/Map Browser where you can select a new material or map type.

Below the material name and type button is where the rollouts for the current material are opened. These rollouts will change depending on the material type.

Cross-Reference

The Material Effects Channel IDs are used with the Rendering Effects dialog box to apply specific effects such as glow and blur to a material. To learn more about these effects, see Chapter 36, "Using Rendering Elements and Render Effects."

Using the sample slots

The Material Editor includes twenty-four sample slots that display materials and map examples. Each of these sample slots contains one material or map. The materials are rendered using the Scanline renderer, but you can specify a different renderer in the Options dialog box. Only one sample slot can be selected at a time — the selected slot is outlined with a white border. Click one of the material slots to select it.

Note

Sample slots cannot be empty — they always contain a material of some kind.

Sample slots are temporary placeholders for materials and maps. An actual scene can have hundreds of materials. By loading a material into a sample slot, you can change its parameters, apply it to other materials, or save it to a library for use in other scenes.

Twenty-four slots are available, but the default layout displays only six. You can access the other eighteen slots using the scroll bars. You can also change the number of displayed slots. To change the number of slots, choose Options ➪ Cycle Sample Slots (or press the X key), or right-click any of the material slots and select 2×3, 3×5, or 4×6 from the pop-up menu. These options are also available in the Options dialog box (keyboard shortcut, O). Figure 18-2 shows the Material Editor with twenty-four sample slots displayed.

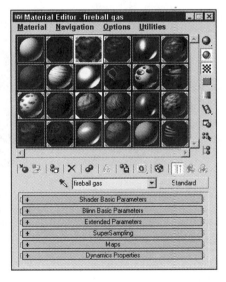

Figure 18-2: You can set the number of sample slots in the Material Editor to display 6, 15, or 24 slots.

Note The 24 default sample slots that are available when the Material Editor is opened are loaded from the medit.mat file in the \matlibs subdirectory. To load your own default materials, save them into this file.

Magnifying a sample slot

The Material ➪ Launch Magnify Window menu command (also found in the right click pop-up menu) opens the material in a magnified window. You can also open this window by double-clicking the sample slot. You can resize the window to view the material at any size, and you can set it to automatically update when changes are made. If the Auto option is disabled, you can update the material by clicking the Update button. Figure 18-3 shows the magnified window. This window is great for seeing the intricate details of a material.

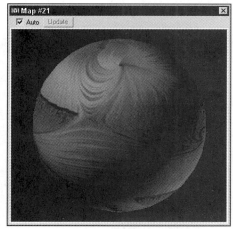

Figure 18-3: You can open materials in a magnified window by double-clicking them.

Using different sample objects

You can change the Sample Type object displayed in the sample slots to be a sphere, cylinder, or box using the Sample Type button at the top right of the Material Editor window.

The Options button (the seventh button from the top in the vertical column of buttons at the right) opens the Material Editor Options dialog box (also opened with the keyboard shortcut, O) where you can designate a custom sample object. The sample object must be contained in a .max or .chr file. To create a sample object, create and save a Max scene with a single object that fits inside a 100-unit cube.

The scene can also include custom lights and cameras. The object must have Mapping Coordinates enabled. You can enable them by selecting the Generate Mapping Coordinates option for objects like primitives or by applying the UVW Map modifier. To make the object available, click the File Name button and select the option to Load Camera and/or Lights. After the object loads, its name will appear on the button. You can then select the custom object from the Object Type flyout button. Figure 18-4 shows the Material Editor with several different object types loaded including a custom object.

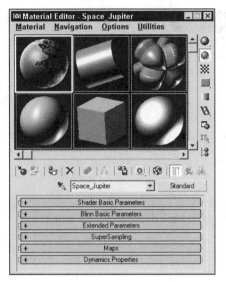

Figure 18-4: You can load a custom sample object to be displayed in the sample slots.

Dragging materials

When you right-click the active sample slot, a pop-up menu appears. From this menu you can select several commands. The Drag/Copy command is a toggle setting. This option also lets you drag and drop materials between the various sample slots. When the Drag/Copy option is enabled, it leaves a copy of the material when it's dragged to another slot. This option also allows you to drag a material to an object in the viewports. Dropping a material onto an object automatically assigns the material to that object.

The Drag/Rotate pop-up menu command (also found in the Options menu) lets you rotate the material object in the sample slot when you drag with the mouse. Dragging on the object rotates it about its X- and Y-axes, and dragging from the corner of the sample slot rotates it about its Z-axis. This feature is useful for looking at how maps are applied. Holding down the Shift key constrains the rotation about a single axis. The Material ➪ Reset Sample Slot Rotation menu command resets the material object to its original orientation.

You can also drag materials from the sample slots back and forth among the Material/Map Browser, the Asset Manager Utility, and any rollouts where you can specify maps, such as the Environment Map button (found in the Environment dialog box accessed via Rendering ➪ Environment), and the Projector and Shadow Map buttons (found in the rollouts for a selected light).

Naming materials

Every material has a name that appears underneath the sample slots in a drop-down list. This same name will appear in the Material Editor's title bar. You can rename a material by typing a new name in the material name drop-down list. This name will appear in the Material/Map Navigator dialog box and in the Track View. When a material is saved to a Library with the Put to Library button, a dialog box opens that enables you to rename the material. You can see the name of any of the materials in the sample slots by moving the mouse over the top of the sample slot; the material name will appear as a tooltip.

Note If you drag a material from one sample slot to another, a copy is made with the same name as the original. If one of these materials is changed and then applied to the scene, a warning dialog box will appear stating that a material with the same name already exists in the scene. It also gives you the option of replacing or renaming the material.

Getting new materials

You load new materials into the sample slots by clicking the Get Material button (leftmost button on the horizontal toolbar), choosing the Material ⇨ Get Material menu command, or pressing the G key. This opens the Material/Map Browser where you can select a new material by double-clicking on it. The new material loads into the selected sample slot. The Material/Map Browser is covered later in this chapter.

Caution The Material/Map Browser holds materials and maps. If you select a material map, a 2D map is loaded into the sample slot. 2D maps cannot be applied directly to an object in the viewport. You can tell the difference between a map and material because maps are flat 2D bitmaps and materials are shown on an object like a sphere.

Assigning materials to objects

When you select a material, you can apply it to the selected object in the viewports with the Assign Material to Selection button (this button is the third from the left on the horizontal toolbar under the sample slots) or with the Material ⇨ Assign to Selection menu command. Alternatively, you could drag a material from its sample slot and drop it on an object.

When you assign a material to an object in the scene, the material becomes "Hot." A *Hot material* is automatically updated in the scene when the material parameters change. Hot materials have white corner brackets displayed around their sample slots. You can "cool" a material by clicking on the Copy Material button (fifth from the left) or choosing Material ⇨ Make Material Copy menu command. This detaches the sample slot from the material in the scene that it is applied to, so that any changes to the material aren't applied to the object.

Whenever a material is applied to an object in the scene, the material is added to a special library of materials that get saved with the scene. Materials do not need to be loaded in one of the sample slots to be in the scene library. You can also load materials into the scene library that aren't applied to an object using the Put Material to Scene button (second button from the left) or the Material ⇨ Put to Scene menu command. You can see all the materials included in the scene library in the Material/Map Browser by selecting the Scene radio button.

In addition to the scene library, you can also put materials into a separate material library. The Put to Library button (seventh from the left) or the Material ⇨ Put to Library menu command places the current selected material into the default library. Clicking the Get Material button opens the Material/Map Browser where you can see the current library by clicking the Material Library radio button.

Picking materials from a scene

Another useful option is obtaining a material from an object in the scene. Clicking the eyedropper button to the left of the Material Name or with the Material ⇨ Pick from Object menu command changes the cursor to an eyedropper. You can then click an object in one of the viewports and the object's material will be loaded into the current sample slot.

Selecting objects by material

If you want to select all the objects in your scene with a specific material applied (like the shiny gold material), then select the material in the sample slots and click on the Select by Material button in the vertical set of buttons, or choose the Utilities ➪ Select Objects by Material menu command. This command opens the Select Objects dialog box with all the objects that have the selected material applied. Clicking the Select button selects these objects in the viewport.

Previewing materials and rendering maps

The Material ➪ Make Preview menu command, along with the Make Preview button and the P keyboard shortcut, opens the Create Material Preview dialog box, shown in Figure 18-5. Using this dialog box, you can create a preview of an animated material. The dialog box lets you specify the Preview Range and Frame Rate, as well as the Image Size, which is a percentage of the default resolution.

Cross-Reference
Animated materials are covered in Chapter 19, "Creating and Applying Materials."

After you create a material preview, you can view the preview with the Material ➪ View Preview menu command. This opens the default media player and plays the animated preview. To save the preview as a file, use the Material ➪ Save Preview menu command.

The Utilities ➪ Render Map menu command (also found in the right-click pop-up menu) opens the Render Map dialog box, shown in Figure 18-5. This option is only available if the selected material has a map applied. The Render Map dialog box lets you select the Range of frames to include and the Dimensions of the rendered image. You can click the Files button to open a file dialog box where you can name the render map and specify the file type. The Render button renders the current map as a bitmap or an animation to the Virtual Frame Buffer and to the file (if selected).

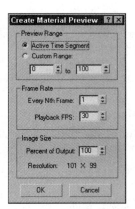
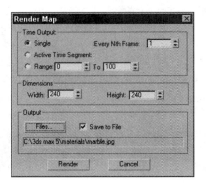

Figure 18-5: The Render Map dialog box lets you render and save a map applied to a material.

Note
You can save render maps as AVI, BMP, Kodak Cineon, EPS, FLC, JPEG, PNG, MOV, SGI, RGB, RLA, RPF, TGA, and TIF files.

Setting Material Editor options

You open the Material Editor Options dialog box by clicking the Options button to the right of the sample slots, selecting Options from the Options menu, right-clicking the pop-up menu, or by just pressing the O key. Figure 18-6 shows this dialog box.

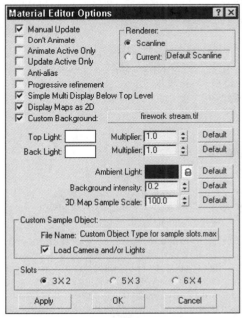

Figure 18-6: The Material Editor Options dialog box offers many options for controlling the Material Editor window.

The Material Editor Options dialog box includes options that control how the materials are displayed in the sample slots. These options are as follows:

✦ **Manual Update:** Doesn't update any changes in the sample slot until the slot is clicked on.

✦ **Don't Animate:** Causes materials not to animate when an animation is played or the Time Slider is dragged. It does, however, update these materials to the current frame.

✦ **Animate Active Only:** Animates only the active sample slot if it contains an animated material. This option isn't available when the Don't Animate option is selected.

✦ **Update Active Only:** Updates only the active sample slot when changes are made to the material.

✦ **Anti-alias:** Enables anti-aliasing for all sample slots. Aliasing is a negative staircase-type effect that occurs for pixel-based images when adjacent pixels along the edges of an image are different colors. Anti-aliasing is a process for eliminating this distracting effect and smoothing the edges.

✦ **Progressive refinement:** Causes materials to be rendered progressively. This causes the material to appear quickly as blocky sections and then slowly in more detail. This gives you a rough idea of how the material looks before the rendering is finished.

✦ **Simple Multi Display Below Top Level:** Displays several different areas for only the top level when a Multi/Sub-Object material is applied.

✦ **Display Maps as 2D:** Displays standalone maps in 2D and not on the sample object. This feature helps you to know when you're looking at a map versus a material.

✦ **Custom Background:** Enables you to use a custom background behind the sample slots. You can load the background using the button to the right of the option. Once changed, the new background is used in all sample slots where the background is enabled.

Also, within the Material Editor Options dialog box, you can select the renderer you want to use to render the materials in the sample slots. The Scanline option is the default option. The Current option lets you select to use the renderer that is specified in the Preference Settings dialog box. The Scanline renderer is always an option, regardless of the current renderer.

This dialog box also offers options to adjust the color and intensity of the Top- and Backlights used to render the materials in the sample slots. The intensity of these lights is determined by the Multiplier values. You use the Ambient Light Intensity value to control the brightness of the Ambient light in the sample slots, and the lock icon to set the color to the same as the Diffuse color. The Background Intensity value sets the brightness of the background — a value of 0 produces a black background and 1 produces a white background. The 3D Map Sample Scale option scales the maps applied to the sample object for all slots. By scaling the map, you can match it up with the scale of an object in the scene. You can reset all these options to their default values using the Default buttons on the right.

The Custom Sample Object button is for loading a Custom Sample Object (as discussed earlier) as well as options for specifying the number of sample slots.

Resetting materials

The Reset Material/Maps to Default Settings button (fourth from the left) lets you reset the selected material to its default settings. If you apply the selected material to a material in the scene, then a dialog box appears that lets you reset just the sample slots or both the sample slots and the material applied to objects in the scene.

Removing materials and maps

If you accidentally apply an unwanted material to an object, you can replace the material with another material by dragging the new material onto the object. If you want to view the object color within the viewport, then open the Display panel and in the Display Color rollout, select the Object color option for Wireframe and Shaded. The Material Color options display the material color in the viewports.

If you apply a material or map to an object that doesn't look just right and tweaking it won't help, you can always return to square one by removing the material or any mappings that have been applied to the object. The tool to remove materials and maps is the UVW Remove utility. You can access this utility by clicking the More button in the Utility panel and selecting UVW Remove from the list of Utilities.

This utility includes a single rollout that lists the number of objects selected. It also includes two buttons. The UVW button removes any mapping coordinates from the selected objects, and the Materials button removes any materials from the selected objects. This button restores the original object color to the selected objects. Alternatively, you can select the Set Gray option, which makes the selected object gray when the materials are removed.

Tutorial: Coloring Easter eggs

Everyone loves spring with its bright colors and newness of life. One of the highlights of the season is the tradition of coloring Easter eggs. In this tutorial, we'll use virtual eggs — no messy dyes and no "egg salad" sandwiches for the next two weeks.

To create our virtual Easter eggs and apply different colors to them, follow these steps:

1. Open the Easter eggs.max file from the Chap 18 directory on the CD-ROM.

   This file contains several egg-shaped objects.

2. Open the Material Editor by choosing Rendering ⇨ Material Editor (or press the M key).

3. Increase the number of sample slots by right-clicking the active material and selecting 5×3 Sample Windows from the pop-up menu.

4. Select the first sample slot and click the Diffuse color swatch in the rollout below it. From the Color Selector that appears, drag the cursor around the color palette until you find the color you want, then click Close.

5. In any viewport, select an egg and then click the Assign Material to Selection button in the Material Editor or you could simply drag the material from its sample slot to the viewport object.

6. Repeat Steps 4 and 5 for all the eggs. Figure 18-7 shows the assortment of eggs we just created.

Figure 18-7: These eggs have been assigned materials with different Diffuse colors.

Using the Material/Map Browser

The Material/Map Browser, shown in Figure 18-8, is the place where all your materials are stored. They are stored in sets called libraries. These libraries are saved along with the scene file or they can be saved as a separate file. The Material/Map Browser opens whenever you change material types (by clicking on the material type button), choose a new map, or click the Get Material button. Materials are indicated with a blue sphere icon, and material maps have a green parallelogram next to them.

Figure 18-8: The Material/Map Browser lets you select new materials from a library of materials.

The Material/Map Browser includes several browse options accessible as radio buttons on the left of the dialog box. The browse options include Material Library, Material Editor, Active Slot, Selected, Scene, and New. The Material Library options list all the materials available in the open material library. The current library set is listed in the title bar of the Material/Map Browser. The Material Editor options lists the 24 materials found in the current sample slots.

The Active Slot option lists the single material sound in the selected sample slot. The Selected and Scene options list the materials applied to the selected viewport objects or all the materials found in the current scene. The New option is the default and lists all the available material types and maps.

Cross-Reference   I discuss the various material types in Chapter 19, "Creating and Applying Materials," and the available maps in Chapter 20, "Using Material Maps."

You can also limit the material list to show only materials, only maps, or both, and you can specify to see all the pieces that make up a material or only the base material with the Root Only option.

The view options buttons above the material list enable you to display the materials and maps in different ways including List, List + Icons, Small Icons, and Large Icons, shown in the following table. Figure 18-9 shows two different display methods.

Button	Description
≣	List
⅀≣	List + Icons
•	Small Icons
●	Large Icons

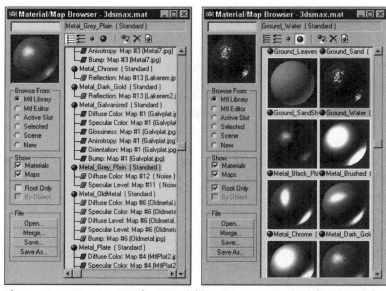

Figure 18-9: You can use the Material/Map Browser to view the materials in many different ways, such as List and Large Icons.

Working with libraries

The text field directly above the material sample slot in the Material/Map Browser is a selection field. Typing a name in this field will search and select materials. Above the material list, three additional buttons become enabled when you open a material library. These buttons let you update the scene, delete the selected material from the library, and clear the entire library.

Any time you adjust a material or a map parameter, a new material is created, and the material's sample slot is updated. Although newly created materials are saved along with the scene file, you can make them available for reuse by including them in a library.

Note Max ships with several different material libraries, including Backgrounds, Bricks, Concrete, Fabric, Ground, Metal, RayTraced, ReflectionMaps, Skys, Space, Stones, and Wood. You can find all these libraries in the matlibs directory.

You can save materials to a new library or to the default library. Select the material's sample slot and click the Put in Library button to open a simple dialog box in which you can name the material and add it to the current library.

To see which library is current, open the Material/Map Browser by clicking the Get Material button. Select the Mtl Library option in the Browse From section — the library name will be shown in the title bar. The File section includes four buttons for opening, merging, and saving material libraries. Once you've created all the materials you want to keep to a library, the Save button lets you save the library as a file. Material libraries are saved with the .mat extension.

Tutorial: Loading a custom material library

To practice loading a material library, I've created a custom library of materials using various textures created with Kai's Power Tools.

To load a custom material library, follow these steps:

1. Choose Rendering ⇨ Material Editor (or press the M key) to open the Material Editor. Then click the Get Material button, which is the leftmost button on the horizontal toolbar (or press the G key) to open the Material/Map Browser.

2. In the Browse From section, select the Mtl Library option and click the Open button.

3. Select and open the KPT.mat file from the Chap 18 directory on the CD-ROM.

   The library loads into the Material/Map Browser.

4. In the selection field (above the sample slot), type **Bug** to locate and select the bug eyes material.

Figure 18-10 shows the Material/Map Browser with the custom material library open.

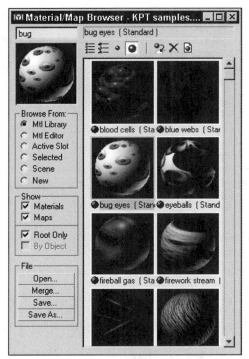

Figure 18-10: The Material/Map Browser also lets you work with saved custom material libraries.

Using the Material/Map Navigator

Each material can consist of several submaterials. For example, anytime a map is added to a material, it becomes a submaterial. A single material can consist of many submaterials, which may be maps or materials. You can edit each submaterial by accessing the rollouts associated with it. The trick is being able to locate the various submaterials. This is where the Material/Map Navigator comes in handy.

The Material/Map Navigator, shown in Figure 18-11, shows all the submaterials that make up a material in a hierarchy list. Double-clicking a submaterial opens the submaterial and all of its associated rollouts in the Material Editor.

The Material/Map Navigator, like the Material/Map Browser, offers several viewing methods for the submaterials including View List, View List + Icons, View Small Icons, and View Large Icons.

When you select a submaterial, its object type is displayed on the Object Type button. Directly above this button are three buttons that become active when you select a submaterial. These buttons, shown in the following table, enable you to navigate the submaterial hierarchy. The rightmost button is Go Forward to Sibling. This moves to the next adjacent submaterial on the same level. The Go to Parent button (second from the right) selects the submaterial's parent. The Show End Result button is a toggle button that shows the selected submaterial or the resulting material with all submaterials included. These options are also available from the Navigation menu. The keyboard shortcuts for these buttons are the arrow keys — Up arrow for Go to Parent, Right arrow for Go Forward to Sibling and Left arrow for Go Backward to Sibling.

Figure 18-11: The Material/Map Navigator shows the layered material as a hierarchy.

Button	Description
	Go Forward to Sibling
	Go to Parent
	Show End Result

If the submaterial is itself a material, such as one of the submaterials for the Multi/Sub-object material, then you can separate the submaterial from the base material using the Make Unique button.

Summary

Materials can add much to the realism of your models. Learning to use the Material Editor, the Material/Map Browser, and the Material/Map Navigator enables you to work with materials. In this chapter, you've

✦ Learned about various material properties

✦ Worked with the Material Editor buttons and sample slots

✦ Used the Material/Map Browser and material libraries

✦ Used the Material/Map Navigator to view submaterials

The next chapter delves more into the topic of material, including all the various material types, including standard, raytrace, matte/shadow, and compound materials.

✦   ✦   ✦

Creating and Applying Materials

Now that you've learned the basic material properties and acquainted yourself with the Material Editor, you get a chance to see the variety of materials that you can create in Max. You can select all the various Max materials from the Material/Map Browser. Open this browser automatically by clicking on the Material Type button beneath the sample slots.

At this point, you should have no difficulty relating to the familiar adage about teaching a man to fish versus giving him a fish, because after you've learned the basics of materials, you'll be able to create an unlimited number of materials.

Using the Standard Material

Standard materials are the default Max material type. They provide a single, uniform color determined by the Ambient, Diffuse, Specular, and Filter color swatches. Standard materials can use any one of several different shaders. *Shaders* are algorithms used to compute how the material should look, given its parameters.

Standard materials also have parameters for controlling highlights, opacity, and self-illumination. These materials include the following rollouts: Shader Basic Parameters, Basic Parameters (based on the shader type), Extended Parameters, SuperSampling, Maps, Dynamic Properties, and Viewport Manager. By modifying these parameters, you can create really unique materials. With all the various rollouts, even a standard material has an infinite number of possibilities.

Using shading types

Max includes several different shader types. These shaders are all available in a drop-down list in the Shader Basic Parameters rollout. Each shader type displays different options in its respective Basic Parameters rollout. Figure 19-1 shows the basic parameters for the Blinn shader. Other available shaders include Anisotropic, Metal, Mutli-Layer, Oren-Nayar-Blinn, Phong, Strauss, and Translucent Shader.

The Shader Basic Parameters rollout also includes several options for shading the material, including Wire, 2-Sided, Face Map, and Faceted, as shown in Figure 19-1. Wire mode causes the model to appear as a wireframe model. The 2-Sided option makes the material appear on both sides of the face and is typically used in conjunction with the Wire option or with transparent materials. The Face Map mode applies maps to each single face on the object. Faceted ignores the smoothing between faces.

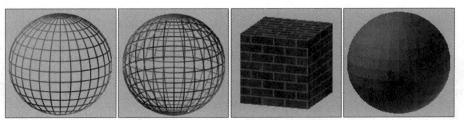

Figure 19-1: Basic parameter options include Wire, 2-Sided, Face Map, and Faceted.

Blinn shader

This shader is the default. It renders simple circular highlights and smoothes adjacent faces.

The Blinn shader includes color swatches for setting Ambient, Diffuse, Specular, and Self-Illumination colors. To change the color, click the color swatch and select a new color in the Color Selector dialog box.

Note   You can drag colors among the various color swatches. When you do so, the Copy or Swap Colors dialog box appears that enables you to copy or swap the colors.

You can use the Lock buttons to the left of the color swatches to lock the colors together so that a change to one automatically changes the other. You can lock Ambient to Diffuse, and Diffuse to Specular.

The small square buttons to the right of the Ambient, Diffuse, Specular, Self-Illumination, Opacity, Specular Level, and Glossiness controls are shortcut buttons for adding a map in place of the respective parameter. Clicking these buttons opens the Material/Map Browser where you can select the map type. You can also lock the Ambient and Diffuse maps together with the lock icon to the right of the map buttons.

When a map is loaded and active, it will appear in the Maps rollout, and an uppercase letter *M* will appear on its button. When a map is loaded but inactive, a lowercase *m* appears. After you apply a map, these buttons will open to make the map the active level and display its parameters in the rollouts. Figure 19-2 shows these map buttons.

Cross-Reference   For more on Maps and the various map types, see in Chapter 20, "Using Material Maps."

Self-Illumination can use a color if the Color option is enabled. If this option is disabled, a spinner appears that enables you to adjust the amount of default color used for illumination. Materials with a Self-Illumination value of 100 or a bright color like white will lose all shadows and highlights and appear to glow from within. To remove the effect of Self-Illumination, set the spinner to 0 or the color to black. Figure 19-3 shows a sphere with Self-Illumination values from left to right of 0, 25, 50, 75, and 100.

Locked colors   Locked maps icon

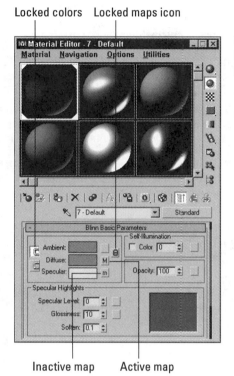

Figure 19-2: The Blinn Basic Parameters rollouts let you select and control properties for the Blinn shader.

Inactive map   Active map

Figure 19-3: Increasing the Self-Illumination value reduces the shadows in an object.

The Opacity spinner sets the level of transparency of an object. A value of 100 makes a material completely opaque, while a value of 0 makes the material completely transparent. Use the Background button to enable a patterned background image to make it easier to view the effects of the Opacity setting. Figure 19-4 shows materials with Opacity values of 10, 25, 50, 75, and 90.

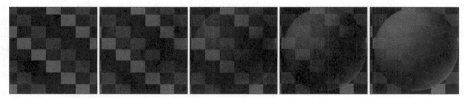

Figure 19-4: The Opacity value sets how transparent a material is.

Specular Highlights are the bright points on the surface where the light is reflected at a maximum value. The Specular Level value determines how bright the highlight is. Its values can range from 0, where there is no highlight, to 100, where the highlight is at a maximum. The graph to the right of the values displays the intensity per distance for a cross section of the highlight. The Specular Level defines the height of the curve or the value at the center of the highlight where it is the brightest. This value can be overloaded to accept numbers greater than 100. Overloaded values create a larger, wider highlight.

The Glossiness value determines the size of the highlight. A value of 100 produces a pinpoint highlight, and a value of 0 increases the highlight to the edges of the graph. The Soften value doesn't affect the graph, but it spreads the highlight across the area defined by the Glossiness value. It can range between 0 (wider) to 1 (thinner). Figure 19-5 shows a sampling of materials with Specular Highlights. The left image has a Specular Level of 20 and a Glossiness of 10, the second image has the Specular Level increased to 80, the third image has the Specular Level overloaded with a value of 150, and the last two images have the Glossiness value increased to 50 and 80.

Figure 19-5: Control Specular Highlights by altering brightness and size.

Phong shader

The Phong shader creates smooth surfaces like Blinn without the quality highlights, but it renders more quickly than the Blinn shader does. The parameters for the Phong shader are identical to those for the Blinn shader. The differences between Blinn and Phong are very subtle, but Blinn can produce highlights for lights at low angles to the surface, and its highlights are generally softer.

Anisotropic shader

The Anisotropic shader is characterized by non-circular highlights. The Anisotropy value is the difference between the two axes that make up the highlight. A value of 0 is circular, but higher values increase the difference between the axes, and the highlights are more elliptical.

Most of the parameters for this shader are the same as those for the Blinn shader, but several parameters of the Anisotropic type are unique. The Diffuse Level value determines how bright the Diffuse color appears. This is similar to Self-Illumination, but it doesn't affect the specular highlights or the shadows. Values can range from 0 to 400.

Compared with the Blinn shader, the specular highlight graph looks very different. That is because it is displaying two highlight components that intersect at the middle. The Specular Level value still controls the height of the curve, and the Glossiness still controls the width, but the Anisotropy value changes the width of one axis relative to the other, creating elliptical highlights. The Orientation value rotates the highlight. Figure 19-6 compares the specular highlight graphs for the Blinn and Anisotropic shaders.

Figure 19-6: The Specular highlight graph for the Blinn and Anisotropic shaders.

Figure 19-7 shows several materials with the Anisotropic shader applied. The first three images have Anisotropic values of 30, 60, and 90 and the last two images have Orientation values of 30 and 60.

Figure 19-7: Materials with the Anisotropic shader applied have elliptical highlights.

Multi-Layer shader

The Multi-Layer shader includes two Anisotropic highlights. Each of these highlights can have a different color. All parameters for this shader are the same as the Anisotropic shader described previously, except that there are two Specular Layers and one additional parameter — Roughness. The Roughness parameter defines how well the Diffuse color blends into the Ambient color. When Roughness is set to a value of 0, an object appears the same as with the Blinn shader, but with higher values, up to 100, the material grows darker.

Figure 19-8 shows several materials with a Multi-Layer shader applied. The first two images have two specular highlights each with an Orientation value of 60 and Anisotropy values of 60 and 90. The third image has an increased Specular Level of 110 and a decrease in the Glossiness to 10. The fourth image has a change in the Orientation value for one of the highlights to 20 and the final image has a drop in the Anisotrophy value to 10.

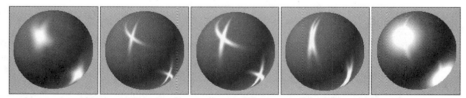

Figure 19-8: Materials with a Multi-Layer shader applied can have two crossing highlights.

Oren-Nayar-Blinn shader

The Oren-Nayar-Blinn shader is useful for creating materials for matte surfaces such as cloth and fabric. The parameters are identical to the Blinn shader, with the addition of the Diffuse Level and Roughness values.

Metal shader

The Metal shader simulates the luster of metallic surfaces. The Highlight curve has a shape that is different from that of the other shaders. It is rounder at the top and doesn't include a Soften value. It can also accept a much higher Specular Level value (up to 999) than the other shaders. You also cannot specify a Specular color. All other parameters are similar to those of the Blinn shader. Figure 19-9 shows the several materials with the Metal shader applied. These materials differ in Specular Level values, which are 50, 100, 200, 400, 800.

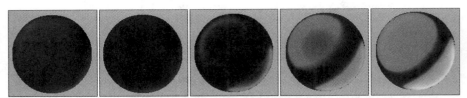

Figure 19-9: A material with a Metal shader applied generates its own highlights.

Strauss shader

The Strauss shader provides another alternative for creating metal materials. There are only four parameters for this shader: Color, Glossiness, Metalness, and Opacity. The Glossiness controls the entire highlight shape. The Metalness value makes the material appear more metal-like by affecting the primary and secondary highlights. Both of these values can range between 0 and 100.

Translucent shader

The Translucent shader allows light to easily pass through an object. It is intended to be used on thin, flat plane objects, such as a bed sheet used for displaying shadow puppets. Most of the settings for this shader are the same as the others, except it includes a Translucent color. This color is the color that the light becomes as it passes through an object with this material applied. This shader also includes a Filter color and an option for disabling the specular highlights on the backside of the object.

New Feature   The Translucent shader is new to 3ds max 5.

Tutorial: Making a butterfly's wings translucent

The translucent shader can be used to create an interesting effect. Not only will light shine through an object with this shader applied, but shadows are also visible.

To make a butterfly's wings translucent, follow these steps:

1. Open the Translucent butterfly wings.max file from the Chap 19 directory on the CD-ROM.

   This file contains a butterfly and flower mesh created by Zygote Media.

2. Open the Material Editor by choosing Rendering ➪ Material Editor, clicking the Material Editor button on the main toolbar, or by pressing the M key.

3. In the Material Editor, select the first sample slot, and in the Name field, name the material Butterfly wings. Select the Translucent Shader from the Shader Basic Parameters rollout. Click the Diffuse color swatch and select a light blue color. Click the Close button to exit the Color Selector.

4. Click on the Translucent Color swatch and change its color to a light gray and set the Opacity to 75.

5. Drag the "Butterfly wings" material onto the wings object in the Front viewport.

Figure 19-10 shows the resulting image. Notice how the flower's shadow is being cast on the butterfly wing.

Figure 19-10: A butterfly with translucent wings

Extended Parameters rollout

In addition to the Basic Parameters, the Material Editor includes several more settings, which are common for most shaders. The Extended Parameters rollout, shown in Figure 19-11, includes Advanced Transparency, Reflection Dimming, and Wire controls. It is the same for all shaders.

You can use the Advanced Transparency controls to set the Falloff to be In, Out, or a specified Amount. The In option increases the transparency as you get farther inside the object, and the Out option does the opposite. The Amount value sets the transparency for the inner or outer edge. Figure 19-12 shows two materials that use the Transparency Falloff options on a gray background and on a patterned background. The two materials on the left use the In option, and the two on the right use the Out option. Both are set at Amount values of 100.

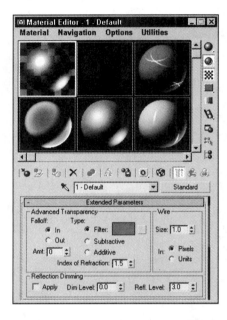

Figure 19-11: The Extended Parameters rollout includes Advanced Transparency, Reflection Dimming, and Wire settings.

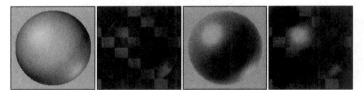

Figure 19-12: Materials with the In and Out Falloff options applied

The three transparency types are Filter, Subtractive, and Additive. The Filter type multiples the Filter color with any color surface that appears behind the transparent object. With this option, you can select a Filter color to use. The Subtractive and Additive types subtract from or add to the color behind the transparent object.

The Index of Refraction is a measure of the amount of distortion caused by light passing through a transparent object. Different physical materials have different Index of Refraction values. The amount of distortion also depends on the thickness of the transparent object. The Index of Refraction for water is 1.33 and for glass is 1.5. The default of 1.0 has no effect.

The Wire section lets you specify a wire size or thickness. Use this setting if the Wire mode is enabled in the Shaders rollout. The size can be measured in either Pixels or Units. Figure 19-13 shows materials with different Wire values from 1–5 pixels.

Reflection Dimming controls how intense a reflection is. You enable it by using the Apply option. The Dim Level setting controls the intensity of the reflection within a shadow, and the Refl Level sets the intensity for all reflections not in the shadow.

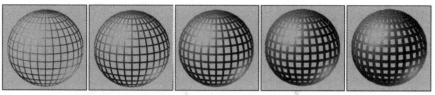

Figure 19-13: Three materials with Wire values of 1, 2, 3, 4, and 5 pixels

SuperSampling rollout

Pixels are small square dots that collectively make up the entire screen. At the edges of objects where the material color changes from the object to the background, these square pixels can cause jagged edges to appear. These edges are called *artifacts* and can ruin an image. Anti-aliasing is the process through which these artifacts are removed by softening the transition between colors.

Max includes anti-aliasing filters as part of the rendering process. SuperSampling is an additional anti-aliasing pass that can improve image quality that is applied at the material level. You have several SuperSampling methods to choose from.

Cross-Reference For more about the various anti-aliasing filters, see Chapter 34, "Rendering Basics."

SuperSampling is only calculated if the Anti-Aliasing option in the Render Scene dialog box is enabled. The raytrace material type has its own SuperSampling pass and doesn't need SuperSampling enabled.

Note Using SuperSampling can greatly increase the time it takes to render an image.

In a SuperSampling pass, the colors at different points around the center of a pixel are sampled. These samples are then used to compute the final color of each pixel. The four available SuperSampling methods are

✦ **Adaptive Halton:** Takes semi-random samples along both the pixel's X-axis and Y-axis. It can take from 4 to 40 samples.

✦ **Adaptive Uniform:** Takes samples at regular intervals around the pixel's center. It takes from 4 to 26 samples.

✦ **Hammersley:** Takes samples at regular intervals along the X-axis, but takes random samples along the Y-axis. It takes from 4 to 40 samples.

✦ **Max 2.5 Star:** Takes four samples along each axis.

The first three methods enable you to select a Quality setting. This setting specifies the number of samples to be taken. The more samples taken, the higher the resolution, but the longer it takes to render. The two Adaptive methods (Adaptive Halton and Adaptive Uniform) offer an Adaptive option with a Threshold spinner. This option takes more samples if the change in color is within the Threshold value. The SuperSample Texture option includes maps in the SuperSampling process along with materials.

Maps rollout

A *map* is a bitmap image that is pasted on an image. The Maps rollout includes a list of the maps that you can apply to an object. Using this rollout, you can enable or disable maps, specify the intensity of the map in the Amount field, and load maps. Clicking the Map buttons opens the Material/Map Browser where you can select the map type.

Find out more about maps in Chapter 20, "Using Material Maps."

Dynamic Properties rollout

The properties in the Dynamic Properties rollout are used along with the Dynamics utility in simulations. These properties define how the object is animated during collisions. If these properties are not specified for an object, then the default material settings, which are similar to steel, are used.

The Dynamic Properties rollout includes only the following three values:

✦ **Bounce Coefficient:** Determines how high an object will bounce after a collision. The default of 1.0 is equal to a normal elastic collision. A ball with a value greater than 1, for example, will continue to bounce higher with each impact.

✦ **Static Friction:** Determines how difficult it is to start an object moving when pushed across a surface. Objects with high Static Friction values will require a lot of force to move.

✦ **Sliding Friction:** Determines how difficult it is to keep an object in motion across a surface. Ice, for example, would have a low Sliding Friction value, because after it starts moving, it will continue easily.

For more information on dynamic simulations, check out Chapter 30, "Creating a Dynamic Simulation."

Viewport Manager rollout

The Viewport Manager rollout includes a single drop-down list with options for None, Light Map, and Metal Bump and an Enable check box. Using the options in the drop-down list, you can enable Light Maps and Metal Bump maps in the viewport.

Tutorial: Coloring a dolphin

As a quick example of applying materials, we'll take a dolphin model created by Zygote Media and position it over a watery plane. We'll then apply custom materials to both objects.

To add materials to a dolphin, follow these steps:

1. Open the Dolphin.max file from the Chap 19 directory on the CD-ROM.

   This file contains a simple plane object and a dolphin mesh.

2. Open the Material Editor by choosing Rendering ➪ Material Editor, clicking the Material Editor button on the main toolbar, or by pressing the M key.

3. In the Material Editor, select the first sample slot, and in the Name field (to the right of the Pick Material from Object button), rename the material Dolphin Skin. Click the Diffuse color swatch and select a light gray color. Then click the Specular color swatch and select a light yellow color. Click the Close button to exit the Color Selector. In the Specular Highlights section, increase the Specular Level to 45.

4. Drag the "Dolphin Skin" material from the first sample slot to the second sample slot and name it Ocean Surface. Click the Diffuse color swatch and select a light blue color. Set the Specular Level and Opacity values to 80. In the Maps rollout, click the None button to the right of the Bump selection. The Material/Map Browser opens. Then double-click the Noise selection.

5. Drag the "Ocean Surface" material onto the plane object in the Top viewport. Then drag the "Dolphin Skin" material onto the dolphin model.

Note This model also includes separate objects for the eyes, mouth, and tongue. These objects could have different materials applied to them, but they are so small in this image that we won't worry about them.

6. Choose Rendering ➪ Environment and then click the Background Color swatch and change it to a light sky blue.

Figure 19-14 shows the resulting image.

Figure 19-14: A dolphin over the water with applied materials

Using Compound Materials

Compound materials combine several different materials into one. You select a compound object type by clicking the Type button in the Material Editor and then selecting the material type from the Material/Map Browser. The Type button is the button to the right of the material name. It lists the current material on the button such as Standard, which is the default material. Most of the entries in the Material/Map Browser are compound objects.

Whenever compound materials are selected, the Replace Material dialog box appears, asking whether you want to discard the current material or make the old material a submaterial. This feature enables you to change a normal material into a compound material while retaining the current material.

Compound materials usually include several different levels. For example, a Top/Bottom material includes a separate material for both the top and bottom. Each of these submaterials could then include another Top/Bottom material and so on. The Material/Map Navigator dialog box (accessed by clicking the Material/Map Navigator button) displays the material as a hierarchical list. This list lets you easily choose the level you want to work with.

Cross-Reference Chapter 18, "Exploring the Material Editor," covers the Material/Map Navigator in more detail.

Each compound material will include a customized rollout for specifying the submaterials associated with the compound material.

Blend

The Blend material blends two separate materials on a surface. The Blend Basic Parameters rollout, shown in Figure 19-15, includes buttons for loading the two submaterials. The check boxes to the right of these buttons enable or disable each submaterial. The Interactive option enables you to select one of the submaterials to be viewed in the viewports.

The Mask button (which is listed below the two submaterial buttons) lets you load a map to specify how the submaterials are mixed. White areas on the map are well blended, and black areas don't blend at all. As an alternative to a mask, the Mix Amount determines how much of each submaterial to display. A value of 0 displays only Material 1, and a value of 100 displays only Material 2.

The Mixing Curve defines the transition between edges of the two materials. The Upper and Lower spinners help you control the curve.

Composite

The Composite material mixes up to ten different materials by adding, subtracting, or mixing the opacity. The Composite Basic Parameters rollout, shown in Figure 19-16, includes buttons for the base material and ten additional materials that can be composited on top of the base material. The materials are applied from top to bottom.

You enable or disable each material using the check box to its left. The buttons labeled with an A, S, and M specify the opacity type: Additive, Subtractive, or Mix. The Additive option brightens the material by adding the background colors to the current material. The Subtractive option has the opposite effect and subtracts the background colors from the current material. The Mix option blends the materials based on their Amount values.

To the right of the A, S, and M buttons is the Mix amount. This value can range from 0 to 200. At 0, none of the materials below it will be visible. At 100, full compositing occurs. Values greater than 100 cause transparent regions to become more opaque.

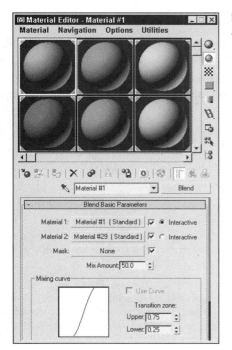

Figure 19-15: The Blend material can include a mask to define the areas that are blended.

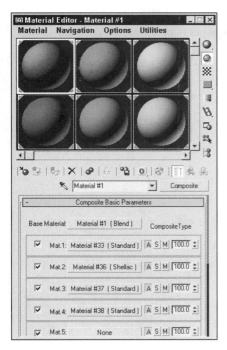

Figure 19-16: Composite materials are applied from top to bottom with the last layer being placed on top of the rest.

Double Sided

The Double Sided material specifies different materials for the front and back of object faces. There is also an option to make the material translucent.

The Double Sided Basic Parameters rollout includes two buttons for both the Facing and Back materials. The Translucency value sets how much of one material shows through the other.

Shellac

The Shellac material is added on top of the Base material. The Shellac Basic Parameters rollout includes only two buttons for each material along with a Color Blend value. There is no upper limit for the Blend value.

Multi/Sub-Object

You can use the Multi/Sub-Object material to assign several different materials to a single object via the material IDs. You can use the Mesh Select modifier to select each subobject area to receive the different materials.

At the top of the Multi/Sub-Object Basic Parameters rollout, shown in Figure 19-17, is a Set Number button that lets you select the number of subobject materials to include. This number is displayed in a text field to the right of the button. Each submaterial is displayed as a separate area on the sample object in the sample slots. Using the Add and Delete buttons, you can selectively add or delete submaterials from the list.

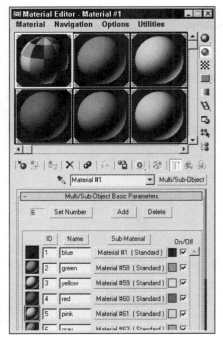

Figure 19-17: The Multi/Sub-Object material defines materials according to material IDs.

Each submaterial includes a sample preview of the submaterial and an index number listed to the left, a Name field where you can type the name of the submaterial, a button for selecting the material, a color swatch for creating solid color materials, and a check box for enabling or disabling the submaterial. You can sort the submaterials by clicking on the ID, Name, or Sub-Material buttons at the top of each column.

After you apply a Multi/Sub-Object material to an object, use the Mesh Select modifier to make a subobject selection. In the Material rollout for this subobject selection, choose a material ID to associate with a submaterial ID.

Tutorial: Creating a patchwork quilt

When I think of patches, I think of a 3D Max object type, but for many people, "patches" would instead bring to mind small scraps of cloth used to make a quilt. Because they share the same name, maybe we can use Max patches to create a quilt. We can then use the Multi/Sub-Object material to appropriately color the various patches.

You can learn more about modeling with patches in Chapter 14, "Creating Patches."

To create a quilt using patches, follow these steps:

1. Open the Patch quilt.max file from the Chap 19 directory on the CD-ROM.

   This file contains a quilt made of patch objects that have been combined into one object.

2. Open the Material Editor by choosing Rendering ⇨ Material Editor (or press M) and click the first sample slot. Then click the Type button. The Material/Map Browser opens. In the list of materials, locate and double-click the Multi/Sub-Object material.

   The Multi/Sub-Object material loads into the selected sample slot, and the Multi/Sub-Object Basic Parameters rollout displays in the Material Editor.

3. In the Multi/Sub-Object Basic Parameters rollout, click the color swatches to the right of the Material button to open the Color Selector. Select different colors for each of the first ten material ID slots.

4. Drag the Multi/Sub-Object material from its sample slot in the Material Editor and onto the patch object. Close the Material/Map Browser and the Material Editor.

5. In the Modify panel, select the Patch subobject and scroll to the bottom of the Modify panel to the Surface Properties rollout.

6. Assign each patch a separate material ID by clicking a patch and changing the ID number in the rollout field.

Figure 19-18 shows the finished quilt. Because it's a patch, you'll be able to drape it over objects easily.

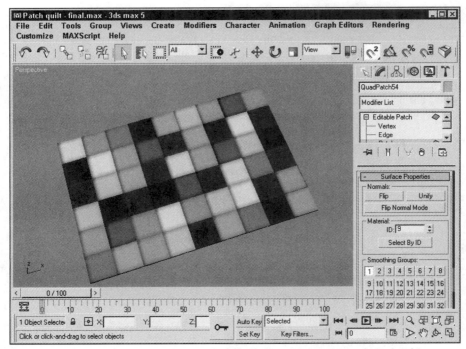

Figure 19-18: A quilt composed of patches and colored using the Multi/Sub-Object material

Morpher

The Morpher material type works with the Morpher modifier to change materials as an object morphs. For example, you can associate a blushing effect with light red applied to the cheeks of a facial expression to show embarrassment. You can only use this material on an object that has the Morpher modifier in its Stack. The Morpher modifier includes a button called Assign New Material for loading the Material Editor with the Morpher material type.

Cross-Reference   Discover more about the Morpher modifier in Chapter 24, "Animation Basics."

For the Morpher material, the Choose Morph Object button in the Morpher Basic Parameters rollout lets you pick a morpher object in the viewports and then opens a dialog box that is used to bind the Morpher material to an object with the Morpher modifier applied. The Refresh button updates all the channels. The base material is the material used before any channel effects are used.

The Morpher material includes 100 channels that correlate to the channels included in the Morpher modifier. Each channel can be turned on and off. At the bottom of the parameters rollout are three Mixing Calculation options that can be used to determine how often the blending is calculated. The Always setting can consume a lot of memory and can slow down the system. Other options are When Rendering and Never Calculate.

Shell

The Shell material consists of an original material and a baked material. For each of these materials, you can specify which appear in the Viewport and which are rendered.

Top/Bottom

The Top/Bottom material assigns different materials to the top and bottom of an object. The Top and Bottom areas are determined by the direction that the face normals point. These normals can be according to the World or Local coordinate system. You can also blend the two materials.

The Top/Bottom Basic Parameters rollout includes two buttons for loading the Top and Bottom materials. You can use the Swap button to switch the two materials. Using World coordinates enables you to rotate the object without changing the material positions. Local coordinates tie the material to the object.

The Blend value can range from 0 to 100, with 0 being a hard edge and 100 being a smooth transition. The Position value sets the location where the two materials meet. A value of 0 represents the bottom of the object and displays only the top material. A value of 100 represents the top of the object, and only the Bottom material is displayed.

Tutorial: Surfing the waves

There's nothing like hitting the surf early in the morning, unless you consider hitting the virtual surf early in the morning. As an example of a compound material, we'll apply the Top/Bottom material to a surfboard. Viewpoint Datalabs created the Surfboard model used in this tutorial.

To apply a Top/Bottom compound material to a surfboard, follow these steps:

1. Open the Surfboard.max file from the Chap 19 directory on the CD-ROM.

   This file contains a surfboard model and an infinite plane to represent the ocean.

2. Apply the "Ocean Surface" material from the earlier tutorial to the plane object by dragging the material from the Material Editor to the object.

3. In the Material Editor, select the second sample slot and click the Type button. From the Material/Map Browser, select the Browse From New option and double-click the Top/Bottom material.

4. When the Replace Material dialog box appears, select the Discard Old Material option. Type the name **Surfboard** for the new material. Then click the Top Material button, name the material **Surfboard Top**, and change the Diffuse color to White. In the material drop-down list, select Surfboard and then click the Bottom Material button. Give this material the name **Surfboard Bottom** and change the Diffuse color to Black.

5. Click the Material/Map Navigator button to view the hierarchy of the material. Then drag this material to the surfboard object.

Figure 19-19 shows the resulting image.

Figure 19-19: A rendered image of a surfboard with the Top/Bottom compound material applied

Using Raytrace Materials

Raytracing is a rendering method that calculates image colors by following imaginary light rays as they move through a scene. These rays can travel through transparent objects and reflect realistically off shiny materials. The results are stunning realistic images, but the draw-back is the amount of time it takes to render using raytrace materials. Scenes with lots of lights and reflecting materials will take even longer.

Chapter 37, "Raytracing," covers the raytracing material settings in detail.

Using the Matte/Shadow Material

You can apply matte/shadow materials to objects to make portions of the model invisible. This lets any objects behind the object or in the background show through. Objects with matte/shadow materials applied can also cast and receive shadows. The effect of these mate-rials is only visible when the object is rendered.

Matte/Shadow Basic Parameters rollout

You can apply a matte/shadow material by clicking the Type button and selecting Matte/Shadow from the Material/Map Browser. Matte/shadow materials only include a single rollout: the Matte/Shadow Basic Parameters.

The Opaque Alpha option causes the matte material to appear in an alpha channel. This essentially is a switch for turning Matte objects on and off.

You can apply atmospheric effects such as fog and volume light to Matte materials. The At Background Depth option applies the fog to the background image. The At Object Depth option applies the fog as if the object were rendered.

Cross-Reference Find out about Atmospheric effects in Chapter 35, "Working with Environments and Atmospheric Effects."

The Receive Shadows section enables shadows to be cast on a Matte object. You can also specify the Shadow Brightness and color. Increasing Shadow Brightness values makes the shadow more transparent. The Affect Alpha option makes the shadows part of the alpha channel.

Matte objects can also have Reflections. The Amount spinner controls how much reflection is used, and the Map button opens the Material/Map Browser.

Tutorial: Ballooning in New York

Touring New York City can be exhilarating and exasperating at the same time, but the real way to tour New York City is by balloon (or by virtual balloon). This way, you won't have to worry about the crowds or bustle, but taking the subway might be a little difficult. In this tutorial, we'll visit the Statue of Liberty in a balloon and use a Shadow/Matte material to fly the balloon behind the statue.

To use a matte/shadow material to hide geometry, follow these steps:

1. Open the Balloon over the Statue of Liberty.max file from the Chap 19 directory on the CD-ROM.

   This file contains a simple balloon mesh and a background image of the Statue of Liberty. I've also created in Adobe Photoshop a simple image with four horizontally striped colors to apply as a map to the balloon. Another preparation step was to create a mask for the Statue of Liberty. To do so, I loaded the Statue of Liberty image into a drawing program like Adobe Illustrator and used the Auto-Trace tool to convert the outline of the statue to splines. I saved the traced image as an AI file called Statue of Liberty Mask and imported the AI file into Max where I created an extruded spline with the same shape as the background statue.

2. Open the Material Editor by pressing the M keyboard shortcut. Select the first sample slot and name the material **Balloon Fabric**. Then click the map button to the right of the Diffuse color swatch. In the Material/Map Browser, double-click the Bitmap selection. A File dialog box loads. Locate the image named Balloon Stripes.tif and click the Open button. After loading the bitmap, enter **75** as the W Angle in the Coordinates rollout to apply the map at an angle. Drag the sample slot to the balloon to apply the map. Use the Show Map in Viewport button to see the applied results.

3. Use the Zoom and Pan tools to align the mask object on top of the background image so it covers the statue.

4. With the mask object in place, open the Material Editor and select the second sample slot. Name the slot **Statue of Liberty Matte** and click the Type button. Select the matte/shadow material by double-clicking it. Then apply it to the mask object.

5. Position the balloon in the viewport so it covers the Statue of Liberty in the Perspective view. Make sure that the balloon is behind the mask object.

6. To see the final result, you will need to render the image. To do this, select Rendering ➪ Render (or press F10) to open the Render Scene dialog box. Click the Render button at the bottom of the dialog box and the image will be rendered in the Virtual Frame Buffer.

Figure 19-20 shows the resulting rendered image.

Figure 19-20: A rendered balloon object behind an object with a matte/shadow material applied

Using the Ink 'n' Paint Material

Although it may seem silly, many different production houses use Max to create 2D line-drawn cartoons. This is accomplished using the Ink 'n' Paint material. Traditionally, cartoons have been drawn by hand using a paper and pen. Then animation houses found that using computers you can fill in a cartoon feature easily, but using a 3D program like Max with its ability to animate using keyframes simplifies the animation task even further. The difference is in how the objects are rendered; the Ink 'n' Paint material controls this.

With the Ink 'n' Paint material selected, several rollouts appear including the Basic Material Extensions. This rollout includes options for making the material 2-Sided, enabling a Face

Map and Faceted. There are also options to cause the background to be foggy when not painting and an option to make the alpha channel opaque. There are also maps for Bump and Displacement.

Controlling paint and ink

The Paint Controls rollout includes settings for how the paint (or colors inside the ink outline) is applied. You can specify colors for the Lighted, Shaded, and Highlight colors. The Lighted color is used for sections of the material that face the scene lights, the Shaded color is used for sections that are in the shadows and the Highlight color is for the specular highlights. For each color you can also select a map with an amount value. The Paint Levels value sets the number of colors that are used to color the material. The Glossiness value determines the size of the highlight. Figure 19-21 shows materials with Paint Level values of 2-6.

Figure 19-21: Use the Paint Level value to set the number of colors used in the material.

The Ink Controls rollout includes an Ink option that you can use to turn off the outlining ink completely. You can also set the Ink Quality to values between 1 and 3. The higher quality values trace the edges better, but require more time to complete. The width of the ink strokes can be set to Variable Width or a Clamped width. For each option, you can select a Minimum ink width and if the Variable Width is enabled, you can choose a Maximum ink width. For the Variable Width option, the stroke will change so that the minimum setting is used in lighted areas and the maximum width is used in shaded areas. This helps to accentuate the lighting. You can also the ink width as a map. Figure 19-22 shows the Ink 'n' Paint material applied to a cube. The first image shows a standard material, the second image has the Ink option disabled. The last three images have Width values of 1, 10, and 30.

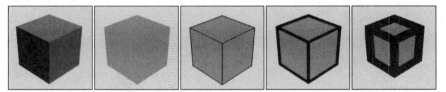

Figure 19-22: The Paint Level value sets the number of colors used in the material.

The rest of the options in the Ink Controls rollout are enabled to control where the ink is applied to the object. Options include Outline, Overlap, Underlap, Smoothing Group, and Material ID. For each of these options (except for Smoothing Group), you can alter a Bias value that can adjust intersecting edges. Each of these options can be applied as a map.

Tutorial: Cartooning a turtle

As an example of the Ink 'n' Paint material, we'll render a cartoonish turtle model created by Zygote Media as a cartoon that is fit for the Sunday papers.

To apply the Ink 'n' Paint material to a turtle model, follow these steps:

1. Open the Cartoon turtle.max file from the Chap 19 directory on the CD-ROM.

   This file includes a simple turtle model.

2. With the turtle model selected, open the Material Editor by choosing the Rendering ➪ Material Editor menu command (or by pressing the M key).

   The turtle's current materials are displayed.

3. In the Utility panel, select the Color Clipboard button and in the Color Clipboard roll-out, click the New Floater button. A palette of colors opens. Drag the Diffuse colors from each current material to the Color Clipboard for each of the five materials.

4. Select the first sample slot and click on the Material Type button to open the Material/Map Browser. Double-click on the Ink 'n' Paint material type from the list. Then drag the corresponding color from the Color Clipboard and copy it in the Lighted color swatch of the Paint Controls rollout. Repeat this for each of the five materials.

5. Open and render the Perspective viewport using the Render Scene dialog box.

Figure 19-23 shows the resulting cartoon.

Figure 19-23: Cartooning made easy with the Ink 'n' Paint material

Two more materials are available in the Material/Map Browser—Advanced Lighting Override and Lightscape material. Find out more about both these materials in Chapter 23, "Advanced Lighting and Radiosity."

Applying Multiple Materials

Most complex models are broken down into multiple parts, each distinguished by the material type that is applied to it. For example, a car model would be separated into windows, tires, and the body, so that each part could have a unique material applied to it.

Using material IDs

There may be times when you'll want to apply multiple materials to a single part. Selecting subobject areas and using material IDs can help you accomplish this task.

Many of the standard primitives have material IDs automatically assigned—spheres get a single material ID, whereas boxes get six (one for each side) and cylinders get three (one for the cylinder and one for each end cap). In addition to the standard primitives, you can assign material IDs to Editable Mesh objects. You can also assign these material IDs to any object or subobject using the Material modifier. These material IDs correspond to the various materials specified in the Multi/Sub-Object material.

Don't confuse these material IDs with the material effect IDs, which are selected using the Material Effect flyout buttons under the sample slots. Material IDs are used only with the Multi/Sub-Object material type, whereas the effect IDs are used with the Render Effects and Video Post dialog boxes for adding effects such as glows to a material.

Tutorial: Mapping die faces

As an example of mapping multiple materials to a single object, consider a die. Splitting the cube object that makes up the die into several different parts wouldn't make sense, so we'll use the Multi/Sub-Object material instead.

To create a die model, follow these steps:

1. Open the Pair of dice.max file from the Chap 19 directory on the CD-ROM.

   This file contains two simple cube primitives that will represent a pair of dice. I also used Adobe Photoshop and created six images with the dots of a die on them. All of these images are the same size.

2. Open the Material Editor and select the first sample slot. Name the material **Die Faces** and click the Type button. Select the Multi/Sub-Object material from the Material/Map Browser. In the dialog box that opens, select to discard the current map and click OK.

3. In the Multi/Sub-Object Basic Parameters rollout, click the Set Number button and enter a value of **6**.

4. Name the first material **face 1** and click the material button to open the parameter rollouts for the first material. Then click the map button to the right of the Diffuse color swatch to open the Material/Map Browser and double-click the Bitmap map. In the Select Bitmap Image File dialog box, choose the dieface1.tif image from the Chap 19 directory on the CD-ROM and click Open.

5. Back in the Material Editor, click the Go to Parent button twice to return to the Multi Sub-Object Basic Parameters rollout and repeat Step 4 for each of the die faces.

6. When the Multi/Sub-Object material is defined, select the cube object and click the Assign Material to Selection button.

Note   Because the cube object used in this example is a box primitive, we didn't need to assign the material IDs to different subobject selections. The box primitive automatically assigned a different material ID to each face of the cube. When material IDs do need to be assigned, you can specify them in the Surface Properties rollout for editable meshes.

Figure 19-24 shows a rendered image of two dice being rolled.

Caution   The Multi/Sub-Object material will not be visible in the viewport and can only be seen in the rendered image. You can use the ActiveShade window to view the results before rendering the final image.

Figure 19-24: These dice have different bitmaps applied to each face.

Material Modifiers

Of the many available modifiers, most modifiers will change the geometry of an object, but several work specifically with materials and maps, including the Material, Material By Element, UVW Map, UVW XForm, Unwrap UVW, and Vertex Paint modifiers. In this section, you'll get a chance to use several material-specific modifiers in a variety of tutorials. The Surface modifiers set includes several modifiers for working with materials. The Vertex Paint modifier is found in the Mesh Editing submenu.

Cross-Reference   Find out more about the modifiers that apply to maps in Chapter 20, "Using Material Maps."

Material modifier

The Material modifier lets you change the material ID of an object. The only parameter for this modifier is the Material ID. When you select a subobject and apply this modifier, the material ID will be applied to only the subobject selection. This modifier is used in conjunction with the Multi/Sub-Object Material type to create a single object with multiple materials.

Material By Element modifier

The Material By Element modifier enables you to change material IDs randomly. You can apply this modifier to an object with several elements, such as a group of spheres attached as a single mesh object. The object needs to have the Multi/Sub-Object material applied to it.

The parameters for this modifier can be set to assign material IDs randomly with the Random Distribution option, or according to a desired Frequency. The ID Count is the minimum number of material IDs to use. You can specify the percentage of each ID to use in the fields under the List Frequency option. The Seed option alters the randomness of the materials.

Tutorial: Creating random marquee lights with the Material By Element modifier

The Material By Element modifier enables you to change material IDs randomly. In this tutorial, we'll reproduce the effect of lights randomly turning on and off on a marquee by using the Multi/Sub-Object material together with the Material By Element modifier.

To create a randomly lighted marquee, follow these steps:

1. Open the Marquee Lights.max file from the Chap 19 directory on the CD-ROM.

   This file includes some text displayed on a rectangular object surrounded by spheres that represent lights.

2. Open the Material Editor and select the first sample slot. Then click the Type button and select the Multi/Sub-Object material from the Material/Map Browser. Select to discard the current material and click OK. Give the material the name **Random Lights**.

3. In the Multi/Sub-Object Basic Parameters rollout, click the Set Number button and change its value to 2. Then click the Material 1 button, and, in the Material name field, give the material the name **Light On**. Set the Diffuse color to yellow and Self Illumination to yellow. Then click the Go Forward to Sibling button to access the second material.

4. Name the second material **Light Off** and select a gray Diffuse color. Then click the Go to Parent button to return to the Multi/Sub-Object material.

5. Select all the spheres and click the Assign Material to Selection button to assign the material to the spheres.

6. With all the spheres selected, open the Modify panel and select the Material By Element modifier from the Modifier List drop-down list. In the Parameters rollout, select the Random Distribution option and set the ID Count to 2.

Figure 19-25 shows the marquee with its random lights. (I've always wanted to see my name in lights!)

Figure 19-25: This marquee is randomly lighted thanks to the Material By Element modifier.

Painting vertices with the Vertex Paint modifier

A unique way to color objects is with the Vertex Paint modifier. This modifier lets you paint on an object by specifying a color for each vertex. If adjacent vertices have different colors assigned, then a gradient is created across the face. The benefit of this coloring option is that it is very efficient and requires almost no memory.

Note   The Assign Vertex Color utility works a little differently. It converts any existing material colors to vertex colors. To use this utility, select an object, choose a Light Model (Scene Lights or Diffuse lighting), and click the Assign to Selected button.

The Vertex Paint modifier lets you specify a color and paint directly on the surface of an object by painting the vertices. The color is applied with a paintbrush-shaped cursor. If several vertices of one face have different colors, then the color is applied as a gradient across the face.

The parameters for this modifier include a Paint button, an Opacity toggle, and a color swatch for selecting the color to paint with. VertCol and Shaded toggles turn Vertex Shading and normal Shading on and off, and you can use a 16-color palette for quick color selection.

Figure 19-26 shows an umbrella with the Vertex Paint modifier applied.

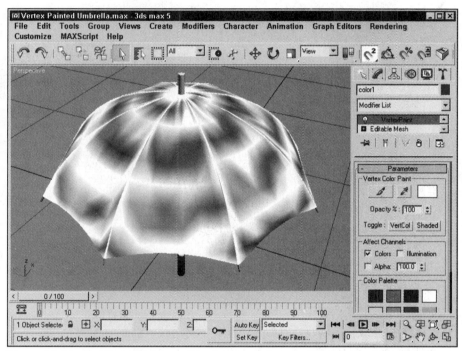

Figure 19-26: The Vertex Paint modifier lets you paint on object surfaces by coloring vertices.

Tutorial: Marking heart tension

As an example of using the Vertex Paint modifier, imagine a doctor who has a 3D model of the human heart. While discussing the results of the latest test with a patient, the doctor can color parts of the heart model to illustrate the various points.

To color on a human heart using the Vertex Paint modifier, follow these steps:

1. Open the Vertex Paint on Heart.max file from the Chap 19 directory on the CD-ROM.

   This file includes a heart mesh created by Viewpoint Datalabs.

2. Select a portion of the heart model and open the Modify panel. Select the Vertex Paint modifier from the Modifier List.

3. In the Parameters rollout, select the red color, select both the VertCol and Shaded button, and click the Paint button. Then drag the mouse over the surface of the Perspective view.

Figure 19-27 shows the resulting color.

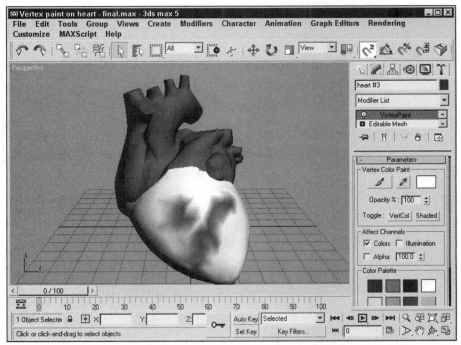

Figure 19-27: The Vertex Paint modifier can apply color to an object by assigning a color to its vertices.

Animating Materials

Materials can be animated if their properties are altered while the Auto Key button is active. Max will interpolate between the values as the animation progresses. The material must be consistent for the entire animation — you cannot change materials at different keys, you can only alter the existing materials parameters.

If you want to change materials as the animation progresses, you can use one of the materials that combines multiple materials, such as the Blend material. This material includes a Mix Amount value that can change at different keyframes. The next tutorial shows how to use the Blend material in this manner.

Several maps include a Phase value, including all maps that have a Noise rollout. This value provides the means to animate the map. For example, using a Noise map and changing the Phase value over many keys will animate the noise effect.

A useful way to view animated materials is to click the Make Preview button (sixth button from the top) to open the Create Material Preview dialog box, shown in Figure 19-28. Select the Active Time Segment option and click OK. The material will render every frame and automatically open and play the material preview.

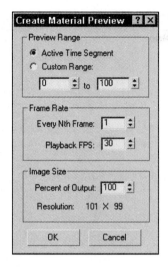

Figure 19-28: The Create Material Preview dialog box can render the entire range of frames or a select number of frames.

Tutorial: Dimming lights

Occasionally you'll want to change materials in a scene to gradually alter it in some way, such as dimming a light. You can easily accomplish this task with the Blend material.

To create a light that dims with time, follow these steps:

1. Open the Dimming light.max file from the Chap 19 directory on the CD-ROM.

   This file contains simple lamp object with a sphere to represent a light bulb.

2. Open the Material Editor by pressing the M key and select the first sample slot. Then click the Type button and select the Blend material from the Material/Map Browser. Give the material the name **Dimming Light**.

When using composite materials, a dialog box will appear asking whether you want to discard the old material or keep it as a submaterial. If you choose to keep it, the current material in the sample slot will become one of the maps for the composite material.

3. Click the Material 1 button and give the material the name **Light On**. Set the Diffuse color to yellow and the Self Illumination to yellow. Then click the Go Forward to Sibling button.

Composite materials such as Blend include several submaterials. When one of these submaterials is selected, you can move quickly to the other submaterials by clicking the Go Forward to Sibling button. To access the root material, click the Go to Parent button.

4. Name the second material **Light Off** and select a gray Diffuse color. Then click the Go to Parent button to return to the Blend material.

5. With the Time Slider at frame 0, click the Auto Key button (or press the N key). Then drag the Time Slider to frame 100 and change the Mix Amount to 100. Click the Auto Key button again to deactivate it. The material changes gradually from the "Light On" material to the "Light Off" material. By dragging the Time Slider, you'll be able to see the material in the sample slot change.

6. Select the light bulb object and click the Assign Material to Selection button to assign the material to the bulb object.

Figure 19-29 shows a simple lamp object with a dimming sphere in its center. The actual dimming effect isn't visible in the viewport, but only when the image is rendered.

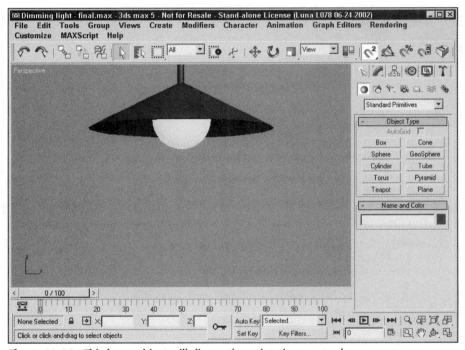

Figure 19-29: This lamp object will dim as the animation proceeds.

Using IFL files

Anyplace where you can load a bitmap map, you can also load an animation file such as an AVI or a FLC file. Another way to create animated material is with IFL files.

IFL files are text files that list which images should appear and for which frames. You save them with the .IFL extension and load them using the Bitmap map. To create an IFL file, open a text editor and type the name of the image followed by the number of frames that it should appear for. Be sure to include a space between the name and the number of frames. The images will be displayed in the order they are listed and repeated until all frames have been displayed. Once applied, the IFL file will be visible in the sample slot if you drag the Time slider, or you could create a material preview.

Note You can also use the * and ? wildcard characters within an IFL file. For example, **flyby*** will include any image file that begins with "flyby," and **flyby?** will include any image file that begins with "flyby" and has one additional character.

Generating IFL files with the IFL Manager Utility

If you don't want to create text files by yourself, you can use the IFL Manager Utility to generate IFL files for you. To use this utility, open the Utilities panel and click the More button. Then select the IFL Manager utility and click OK.

In the IFL Manager rollout, the Select button opens a File dialog box where you can select a sequential list of images to include in an IFL file. After you select a list of images, you can specify the Start and End images. You can cause the images to be displayed in reverse by placing a greater number in the Start field than is in the End field. The Every Nth field can specify to use every Nth image. You use the Multiplier field to specify in how many frames each image should appear.

The Create button opens a File dialog box where you can save the IFL file. The Edit button opens an IFL text file in the system's default text editor for editing.

Tutorial: What's on TV?

Animated files such as AVI and FLC can be opened and mapped to an object to animate the texture, but you can also use IFL files.

To create an IFL file that will be mapped on the front of a television model, follow these steps:

1. Open the Windows standard Notepad text editor and type the following:

```
; these frames will be positioned on a television screen.
static.tif 20
Exploding planet - frame 10.tif 2
Exploding planet - frame 15.tif 2
Exploding planet - frame 20.tif 2
Exploding planet - frame 25.tif 2
Exploding planet - frame 30.tif 2
Exploding planet - frame 35.tif 2
Exploding planet - frame 40.tif 2
Exploding planet - frame 45.tif 2
Exploding planet - frame 50.tif 2
Exploding planet - frame 55.tif 2
static.tif 60
```

Note The first line of text is referred to as a *comment line*. You enter comments into the IFL file by starting the line with a semicolon (;) character.

2. Save the file as **tv.ifl**. Make sure that your text editor doesn't add the extension ".TXT" on the end of the file. You can check your file with the one I created, which you can find in the Chap 19 directory on the CD-ROM.

Note The IFL file as described earlier will look for the image files in the same directory as the IFL file. Make sure that the images are included in this directory.

3. Open the Television – IFL File.max file from the Chap 19 directory on the CD-ROM.

   This file includes a television model (created by Zygote Media).

4. Select the television front screen object, open the Material Editor, and select the first sample slot. Name the material Television Screen. Click the map button to the right of the Diffuse color swatch. Double-click the Bitmap map. In the File dialog box, locate the tv.ifl file and click OK. Then click the Assign Material to Selection button to apply the material to the screen.

Tip To see the map in the viewport, click the Show Map in Viewport button. This button makes the frames of the IFL file visible in the viewport.

5. Because the screen object is a mesh object, you'll need to use the UVW Map modifier to create some mapping coordinates for the map. Open the Modify panel and click the UVW Map button. Set the mapping option to Planar. Then click the Sub-Object button and transform the planar gizmo until it covers the screen. Figure 19-30 shows one rendered frame of the television with the IFL file applied.

Figure 19-30: You can use IFL files to animate materials via a list of images.

Summary

This chapter concludes the materials and maps part of the book. In the previous two chapters, I introduced several features and showed you examples that we were able to explore more fully in this chapter. Along the way, I hope you've learned some tricks that will help you unravel the complexities of working with materials and maps. Materials can add a lot to the realism of your models. This chapter presented the various material types, including standard, compound, raytrace, matte/shadow, and Ink 'n' Paint materials.

In this chapter you

> ✦ Learned about various material types
>
> ✦ Discovered and learned to use the various material parameters
>
> ✦ Discovered the basics of using standard materials
>
> ✦ Learned how to use the various shaders
>
> ✦ Learned about raytrace, matte/shadow, Ink 'n' Paint, and compound materials
>
> ✦ Applied multiple materials to an object with material IDs
>
> ✦ Explored several material modifiers, including the Material, Material By Element, and Vertex Paint modifiers
>
> ✦ Learned to animate materials and use IFL files

The one big rollout that was skipped as we investigated materials dealt with maps. The next chapter delves into the topic of material maps.

✦　　✦　　✦

Using Material Maps

In addition to using materials, another way to enhance an object is to use a map — but not a roadmap; these maps are closer to bitmaps, with patterns that can be applied to the surface of an object. Some maps wrap an image onto objects, but others, such as displacement and bump maps, modify the surface based on the map's intensity. For example, you can use a diffuse map to add a label to a soup can or a bump map to add some texture to the surface of an orange.

Understanding Maps

To understand a material map, think of this example. Cut the label off of a soup can, scan it into the computer, and save the image as a bitmap. You could then create a cylinder with roughly the same dimensions as the can, load the scanned label image as a material map, and apply it to the cylinder object to simulate the original soup can.

Different types of maps exist. Some maps wrap images about objects, while others define areas to be modified by comparing the intensity of the pixels in the map. An example of this is a bump map. A standard bump map would be a grayscale image — when mapped onto an object, lighter color sections would be raised to a maximum of pure white and darker sections would be indented to a minimum of black. This enables you to easily create surface textures, such as an orange rind, without having to model them.

Still other uses for maps include background images called environment maps and projection maps that are used with lights.

Cross-Reference   For information on environment maps, see Chapter 35, "Working with Environments and Atmospheric Effects." Chapter 22, "Working with Lights," covers projection maps.

Maps that are used to create materials are all applied using the Material Editor. The Material/Map Browser lists all the available maps in several different categories. These maps have many common features.

Tip   To see applied maps in the viewports, select the Views ⇨ Activate All Maps menu command. But, this can slow the display, so the Views ⇨ Deactivate All Maps menu command can be used to speed the display.

Understanding Material Map Types

Maps are typically used along with materials. You can open most material maps from the Material/Map Browser. To open the Material/Map Browser, click on any of the map buttons found throughout the Material Editor including those found in the Maps rollout. Figure 20-1 shows this browser filtered to display the available maps.

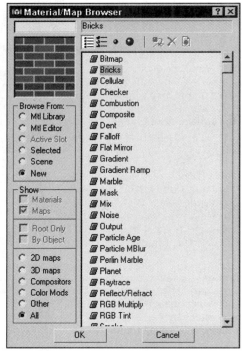

Figure 20-1: Use the Material/Map Browser to list all the maps available for assigning to materials.

In the Material/Map Browser, you can use the options in the Show group to filter the types of maps (of which there are several) to be displayed. Options include to show Maps, Materials, Root Only, and By Object. The additional options of 2D Maps, 3D Maps, Compositors, Color Mods, Other, and All are available if the New option is selected in the Browse From section. To load a material into the Material Editor, simply either double-click it or select it and click OK.

2D maps

A two-dimensional map can be wrapped onto the surface of an object or used as an environment map for a scene's background image. Because they have no depth, 2D maps only appear on the surface. The Bitmap map is perhaps the most common 2D map. It enables you to load any image, which can be wrapped around an object's surface in a number of different ways.

Many maps have several rollouts in common. These include Coordinates, Noise, and Time. In addition to these rollouts, each individual map type has its own parameters rollout.

The Coordinates rollout

Every map that is applied to an object needs to have mapping coordinates that define how the map lines up with the object. For example, with the soup can label example mentioned earlier, you'll probably want to align the top edge of the label with the top edge of the can, but you could position the top edge at the middle of the can. Mapping coordinates define where the map's upper-right corner is located on the object.

All map coordinates are based on a UVW coordinate system that equates to the familiar XYZ coordinate system, except that it is named uniquely so as not to be confused with transformation coordinates. These coordinates are required for every object that a map is applied to. In most cases, you can generate these coordinates automatically when you create an object by selecting the Generate Mapping Coordinates option in the object's Parameter rollout.

Note   Editable meshes don't have any default mapping coordinates, but you can generate mapping coordinates using the UVW Map modifier.

In the Coordinates rollout for 2D Maps, shown in Figure 20-2, you can specify whether the map will be a texture map or an environment map. The Texture option applies the map to the surface of an object as a texture. This texture will move with the object as the object moves. The Environ option creates an environment map. Environment maps are locked to the world and not to an object. Moving an object with an environment map applied to it will scroll the map across the surface of the object.

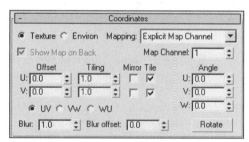

Figure 20-2: The Coordinates rollout lets you offset and tile a map.

Different mapping types are available for both the Texture and Environ options. Mapping types for the Texture option include Explicit Map Channel, Vertex Color Channel, Planar from Object XYZ, and Planar from World XYZ. The Explicit Map Channel option is the default. It applies the map using the designated Map Channel. The Vertex Color Channel uses specified vertex colors as its channel. The two planar mapping types will place the map in a plane based on the Local or World coordinate systems.

The Environ option includes Spherical Environment, Cylindrical Environment, Shrink-Wrap Environment, and Screen mapping types. The Spherical Environment mapping type is applied as if the entire scene were contained within a giant sphere. The same applies for the Cylindrical Environment mapping type except the shape is a cylinder. The Shrink-Wrap Environment plasters the map directly on the scene as if it were covering it like a blanket. The Screen mapping type just projects the map flatly on the background.

The Show Map on Back option causes planar maps to project through the object and be rendered on the object's back.

The U and V coordinates define the X and Y positions for the map. For each coordinate, you can specify an Offset value, which is the distance from the origin. The Tiling value is the number of times to repeat the image and is only used if the Tile option is selected. The Mirror option inverts the map. The UV, VW, and WU options apply the map onto different planes.

Tiling is the process of placing a copy of the applied map next to the current one and so on until the entire surface is covered with the map placed edge to edge. You will often want to use tiled images that are seamless, or that repeat from edge to edge.

Figure 20-3 shows an image tile that is seamless. The horizontal and vertical seams line up. Below the tile, three more tiles have been positioned next to each another. This tile was created using Fractal Design Painter 3D. Notice how the image repeats itself over and over.

Figure 20-3: Seamless image tiles are a useful way to cover an entire surface with a small map.

The Material Editor includes a button that you can use to check the Tiling and Mirror settings. The Sample UV Tiling button (fourth from the top) is a flyout button that you can switch to 2×2, 3×3, or 4×4.

You can also rotate the map about each of the U, V, and W axes by entering values in the respective fields, or by clicking the Rotate button, which opens the Rotate Mapping Coordinates dialog box, shown in Figure 20-4. Using this dialog box, you can drag the mouse to rotate the mapping coordinates. Dragging within the circle rotates about all three coordinates, and dragging outside the circle rotates the mapping coordinates about their center point.

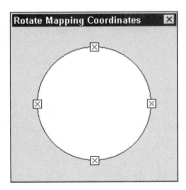

Figure 20-4: The Rotate Mapping Coordinates dialog box appears when you click the Rotate button in the Coordinates rollout.

The Blur and Blur Offset values affect the blurriness of the image. The Blur value blurs the image based on its distance from the view, whereas the Blur Offset value blurs the image regardless of its distance.

Tip   You can use the Blur setting to help make tile seams less noticeable.

The Noise rollout

The Noise rollout adds noise to the map. Noise can be thought of as static that you see on the television added to a bitmap. This feature is helpful for making textures more grainy, which is useful for certain materials.

The Amount value is the strength of the noise function that is applied; the value ranges from 0 for no noise through 100 for maximum noise. You can disable this noise function at any time, using the On option.

The Levels value defines the number of times the noise function is applied. The Size value determines the extent of the noise function based on the geometry. You can also Animate the noise. The Phase value controls how quickly the noise changes over time.

The Time rollout

Maps, such as bitmaps, that can load animations also include a Time rollout for controlling animation files. In this rollout, you can choose a Start Frame and the Playback Rate. The default Playback Rate is 1.0 — higher values run the animation faster, and lower values run it slower. You can also set the animation to Loop, Ping-Pong, or Hold the last frame.

The Output rollout

The Output rollout includes settings for controlling the final look of the map. The Invert option creates a negative version of the image. The Clamp option prevents any colors from exceeding a value of 1.0 and prevents maps from becoming self-illuminating if the brightness is increased.

The Alpha From RGB Intensity option generates an alpha channel based on the Intensity of the map. Black areas will become transparent and white areas opaque.

Note   For materials that don't include an Output rollout, you can apply an Output map, which accepts a submaterial.

The Output Amount value controls how much of the map should be mixed when it is part of a composite material. You use the RGB Offset value to increase or decrease the map's tonal values. Use the RGB Level value to increase or decrease the saturation level of the map. The Bump Amount value is only used if the map is being used as a bump map — it determines the height of the bumps.

The Enable Color Map option enables the Color Map graph at the bottom of the Output rollout. This graph displays the tonal range of the map. Adjusting this graph affects the highlights, midtones, and shadows of the map. Figure 20-5 shows a Color Map graph.

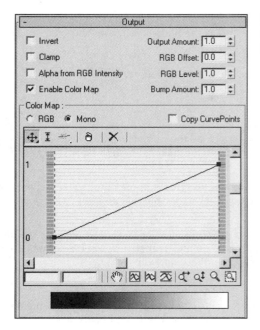

Figure 20-5: The Color Map graph enables you to adjust the highlights, midtones, and shadows of a map.

The left end of the graph equates to the shadows, and the right end is for the highlights. The RGB and Mono options let you display the graphs as independent red, green, and blue curves or as a single monocolor curve. The Copy CurvePoints option will copy any existing points from Mono mode over to RGB mode and vice versa. The buttons across the top of the graph are used to manage the graph points.

The buttons above the graph include Move (with flyout buttons for Move Horizontally and Move Vertically), Scale Point, Add Point (with a flyout button for adding a point with handles), Delete Point, and Reset Curves. Along the bottom of the graph are buttons for managing the graph view. The two fields on the left contain the horizontal and vertical values for the current selected point. The other buttons are to Pan and Zoom the graph.

Bitmap map

Selecting the Bitmap map from the Material/Map Browser opens the Select Bitmap Image File dialog box, shown in Figure 20-6, where you can locate an image file. Various image and animation formats are supported; these include AVI, BMP, CIN, GIF, IFL, IPP, FLC, JPEG, MOV, PNG, PSD, RGB, RLA, TGA, TIF, and YUV.

The name of the current bitmap file is displayed on the button in the Bitmap Parameters rollout, shown in Figure 20-7. If you need to change the bitmap file, click the Bitmap button and select the new file. Use the Reload button to update the bitmap if you've made changes to the bitmap image by an external program.

The Bitmap Parameters rollout includes three different Filtering options: Pyramidal, Summed Area, and None. These methods perform a pixel averaging operation to anti-alias the image. The Summed Area option requires more memory but produces better results.

You can also specify the output for a mono channel or for an RGB channel. For maps that only use the monochrome information in the image (such as an opacity map), the Mono Channel as RGB Intensity or Alpha option can be used. For maps that use color information (for example, a diffuse map), the RGB Channel can be RGB (full color) or Alpha as Gray.

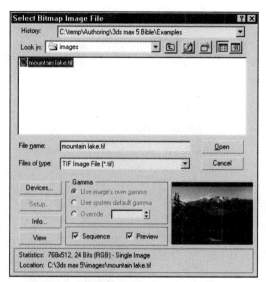

Figure 20-6: The Select Bitmap Image File dialog box lets you preview images before opening them.

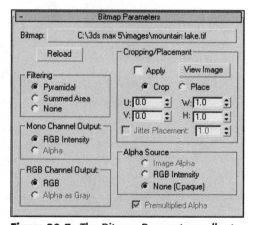

Figure 20-7: The Bitmap Parameters rollout offers several settings for controlling a bitmap map.

The Cropping/Placement controls enable you to crop or place the image. Cropping is the process of cutting out a portion of the image, and Placing is resizing the image while maintaining the entire image. The View Image button opens the image in a Cropping/Placement dialog box, shown in Figure 20-8. The rectangle is available within the image when Crop mode is selected. You can move the handles of this rectangle to specify the crop region.

Note

When the Crop option is selected, a UV button is displayed in the upper right of the Cropping/Placement dialog box. Clicking this button changes the U and V values to X and Y pixels.

Figure 20-8: Viewing an image in the Cropping/Placement dialog box enables you to set the crop marks.

You can also adjust the U and V parameters, which define the upper-left corner of the cropping rectangle, and the W and H parameters, which define the crop or placement width and height. The Jitter Placement option works with the Place option to randomly place and size the image.

Note   The U and V values are a percentage of the total image. For example, a U value of 0.25 will position the image's left edge at a location that is 25 percent of the distance of the total width from the left edge of the original image.

If the bitmap has an alpha channel, you can specify whether it is to be used with the Image Alpha option, or you can define the alpha values as RGB Intensity or as None. You can also select to use Premultiplied Alphas. Premultiplied Alphas are alpha channels that have already been multiplied by each separate RGB channel. By premultiplying, you won't need to multiply the channels when compositing the image.

Bricks map

The Bricks map creates brick patterns. The Standard Controls rollout contains a Preset Type drop-down list with a list of preset brick patterns. These patterns are popular brick patterns including Common Flemish, English, Stack, Fine Stack, Running, Fine Running, and Half Running. A Custom option also lets you define your own brick pattern.

In the Advanced Controls rollout under both the Bricks and Mortar Setup sections, you can use a custom texture map and color. You can specify the Horizontal and Vertical Count of the Bricks and the Mortar's Horizontal and Vertical Gaps as well as Color and Fade Variance values for both. The Mortar's Horizontal and Vertical Gaps can be locked to always be equal. For Mortar, you can also define the Percentage of Holes. Holes are where bricks have been left out. A Rough value controls the roughness of the mortar.

The Random Seed value controls the randomness of the patterns, and the Swap Texture Entries exchange the brick texture with the mortar texture.

In the Stacking Layout section, the Line Shift and the Random Shift values are used to move each row of bricks a defined or random distance.

The Row and Column Editing section offers options that let you change the number of bricks Per Row or Column and the Change in each row or column.

Figure 20-9 shows three different Brick map styles.

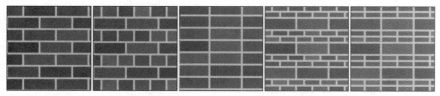

Figure 20-9: From the Standard Controls rollout, you can select from several preset Brick styles, including Running Bond, English Bond, and Fine Running Bond.

Checker map

The Checker map creates a checkerboard image with two colors. The Checker Parameters rollout includes two color swatches for changing the checker colors. You can also load maps in place of each color. Use the Swap button to switch the position of the two colors and the Soften value to blur the edges between the two colors.

Figure 20-10 shows three Checker maps with Tiling values of 2 for the U and V directions and Soften values of 0, 0.2, and 0.5.

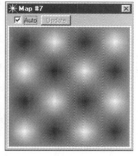

Figure 20-10: The Checker map can be softened as these three maps are with Soften values of 0, 0.2, and 0.5.

Combustion map

This map works with Discreet's Combustion package, which is used for post-processing compositing. The Combustion map enables you to include Combustion-produced effects as a material map.

The Project button lets you load a file to paint on. These files are limited to the types that Combustion supports. Use the Edit button to load the Combustion interface.

In the Live Edit section, the Unwrap Selected button places marking on the bitmap image to show where the mapping coordinates are located. The UV button lets you change from among UV, VW, and UW coordinate systems. The Track Time button lets you change the current frame, which enables you to paint materials that change over time. The Paint button changes the viewport cursor to enable you to interactively paint in the viewport.

The Combustion map also includes information about current project settings for specifying a custom resolution. You can also control the Start Frame and Duration of an animation sequence. The Filtering options are Pyramidal, Summed Area, or None, and the End Conditions can be set to Loop, Ping Pong (which moves back and forth between the start and end positions), or Hold.

Caution   To use this map type, you must have the Combustion program made by Discreet Logic installed. If the plug-in isn't installed, the text, "Error: Combustion Engine DLL Not Found" displays at the top of the Combustion Parameters rollout.

Gradient map

The Gradient map creates a gradient image using three colors. The Gradient Parameters rollout includes a color swatch and map button for each color. You can position the center color at any location between the two ends using the Color 2 Position value spinner. The value can range from 0 through 1. The rollout lets you choose between Linear and Radial gradient types.

The Noise Amount adds noise to the gradient if its value is nonzero. The Size value scales the noise effect, and the Phase controls how quickly the noise changes over time. The three types of noise that you can select are Regular, Fractal, and Turbulence. The Levels value determines how many times the noise function is applied. The High and Low Threshold and Smooth values set the limits of the noise function to eliminate discontinuities.

Figure 20-11 shows linear and radial Gradient maps.

Figure 20-11: A Gradient map can be linear or radial.

Gradient Ramp map

This advanced version of the Gradient map can use many different colors. The Gradient Ramp Parameters rollout includes a color bar with several flags along its bottom edge. You can add flags by simply clicking along the bottom edge. You can also drag or delete flags.

To define the color for each flag, right-click the flag and then select Edit Properties from the pop-up menu. The Flag Properties dialog box opens, shown in Figure 20-12, where you can select a color to use.

Figure 20-12: The Flag Properties dialog box enables you to specify a color and its position to use in the Gradient Ramp.

The Gradient Type drop-down in the Gradient Ramp Parameters rollout offers various Gradient Types, including 4 Corner, Box, Diagonal, Lighting, Linear, Mapped, Normal, Pong, Radial, Spiral, Sweep, and Tartan. You can also select from several different Interpolation Types including Custom, Ease In, Ease In Out, Ease Out, Linear, and Solid.

Figure 20-13 shows several of the gradient types available for the Gradient Ramp map.

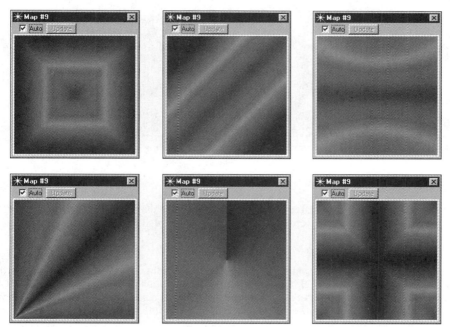

Figure 20-13: The Gradient Ramp map offers several different gradient types including (from top left to bottom right) Box, Diagonal, Normal, Pong, Spiral, and Tartan.

Swirl map

The Swirl map creates a swirled image of two colors — Base and Swirl. The Swirl Parameters rollout includes two color swatches and map buttons to specify these colors. The Swap button switches the two colors. Other options include Color Contrast, which controls the contrast between the two colors; Swirl Intensity, which defines the strength of the swirl color; and Swirl Amount, which is how much of the Swirl color gets mixed into the Base color.

Note   All maps that use two colors include a Swap button for switching between the colors.

The Twist value sets the number of swirls. Negative values cause the swirl to change direction. The Constant Detail value determines how much detail is included in the swirl.

With the Swirl Location X and Y values, you can move the center of the swirl. As the center is moved far from the materials center, the swirl rings become tighter. The Lock button causes both values to change equally. If the lock is disabled, then the values can be changed independently.

The Random Seed sets the randomness of the swirl effect.

Figure 20-14 shows the Swirl map with three different Twist values. From left to right, the Swirl values are 1, 5, and 10.

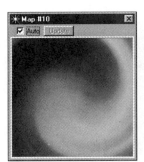 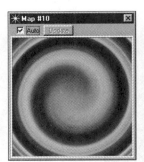 

Figure 20-14: The Swirl map combines two colors in a swirling pattern.

3D maps

3D maps are procedurally created, which means that these maps are more than just a grouping of pixels; they are actually created using a mathematical algorithm. This algorithm defines the map in three dimensions, so that if a portion of the object were to be cut away, the map would line up along each edge.

The Coordinates rollout for 3D maps is similar to the Coordinates rollout for 2D maps with a few exceptions; differences include Coordinate Source options of Object XYZ, World XYZ, Explicit Map Channel, and Vertex Color Channel. There are also Offset, Tiling, and Angle values for the X, Y, and Z axes as well as Blur and Blur offset options.

Cellular map

The Cellular 3D map creates patterns of small objects referred to as cells. In the Cell Color section of the Cellular Parameters rollout, you can specify the color for the individual cells or apply a map. Setting the Variation value can vary the cell color.

In the Division Colors section, two color swatches are used to define the colors that appear in between the cells. This space will be a gradient between the two colors.

In the Cell Characteristics section, you can control the shape of the cells by selecting Circular or Chips, a Size, and how the cells are Spread. The Bump Smoothing value smoothes the jaggedness of the cells. The Fractal option causes the cells to be generated using a fractal algorithm. The Iterations value determines the number of times that the algorithm is applied. The Adaptive option determines automatically the number of iterations to complete. The Roughness setting determines how rough the surfaces of the cells are.

The Size value affects the overall scale of the map, while the Threshold values specify the specific size of the individual cells. Settings include Low, Mid, and High.

Figure 20-15 shows three Cellular maps: the first with Circular cells and a Size value of 20, the second with Chips cells, and the final one with the Fractal option enabled.

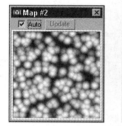  

Figure 20-15: The Cellular map creates small, regular-shaped cells.

Dent map

The Dent 3D map works as a bump map to create indentations across the surface of an object. In the Dent Parameters rollout, the Size value sets the overall size of the dents. The Strength value determines how deep the dents are, and the Iterations value sets how many times the algorithm is to be computed. You can also specify the colors for the Dent map. The default colors are black and white. Black defines the areas that are indented.

Figure 20-16 shows three spheres with the Dent map applied as bump mapping. The three spheres have Size values of 500, 1000, and 2000.

  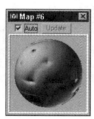

Figure 20-16: The Dent map causes dents in the object when applied as bump mapping.

Falloff map

The Falloff 3D map creates a grayscale image based on the direction of the surface normals. Areas with normals that are parallel to the view are black, and areas whose normals are perpendicular to the view are white. This map is usually applied as an opacity map, giving you greater control over the opacity of the object.

The Falloff Parameters rollout includes two color swatches, a Strength value of each, and an optional map. There are also drop-down lists for setting the Falloff Type and the Falloff Direction. Falloff Types include Perpendicular/Parallel, Towards/Away, Fresnel, Shadow/Light, and Distance Blend. The Falloff Direction options include Viewing Direction (Camera Z-axis); Camera X-Axis; Camera Y Axis; Object; Local X, Y, and Z Axis; and World X, Y, and Z Axis.

In the Mode Specific Parameters section, several parameters are based on the Falloff Type and Direction. If Object is selected as the Falloff Direction, then a button that lets you select the object becomes active. The Fresnel Falloff Type is based on the Index of Refraction and provides an option to override the material's Index of Refraction value. The Distance Blend Falloff Type offers values for Near and Far distances.

The Falloff map also includes a Mix Curve graph and rollout that give you precise control over the falloff gradient. The graph controls include icon buttons for adding new points to the curve, moving, scaling and deleting points, and resetting the curve. Points at the top of the graph have a value of 1 and represent the white areas of falloff. Points at the bottom of the graph have a value of 0 and are black.

The Output rollout is also included as part of the Falloff map.

Marble map

The Marble 3D map creates a marbled material with random colored veins. The Marble Parameters rollout includes two color swatches: Color #1 is the vein color and Color #2 is the base color. You also have the option of loading maps for each color. The Swap button switches the two colors. The Size value determines how far each vein is from each other, and the Vein Width defines the vein thickness.

Figure 20-17 shows three Marble maps with Vein Width values of 0.01, 0.025, and 0.05.

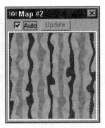

Figure 20-17: The Marble map creates a marbled surface.

Noise map

The Noise 3D map randomly alters the surface of an object using two colors. The Noise Parameters rollout offers three different Noise types: Regular, Fractal, and Turbulence. Each type uses a different algorithm for computing noise. The two color swatches let you alter the colors used to represent the noise. You also have the option of loading maps for each color. The Swap button switches the two colors, and the Size value scales the noise effect. To prevent discontinuities, the High and Low Noise Threshold can be used to set noise limits.

Figure 20-18 shows Noise maps with the Regular, Fractal, and Turbulence options enabled.

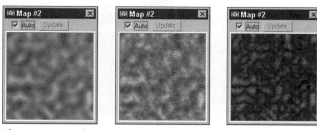

Figure 20-18: The Noise map produces a random noise pattern on the surface of the object.

Particle Age map

The Particle Age map is used with particle systems to change the color of particles over their lifetime. The Particle Age Parameters rollout includes three different color swatches and age values.

Particle MBlur map

The Particle MBlur map is also used with particle systems. This map is used to blur particles as they increase in velocity. The Particle Motion Blur Parameters rollout includes two colors — the first color is the one used for the slower portions of the particle, and the second color is used for the fast portions. When you apply this map as an opacity map, the particles are blurred. The Sharpness value determines the amount of blur.

Cross-Reference For more on both the Particle Age and Particle MBlur maps, see Chapter 17, "Creating and Controlling Particle Systems."

Perlin Marble map

This map creates marble textures using a different algorithm. Perlin Marble is more chaotic and random than the Marble map. The Perlin Marble Parameters rollout includes a Size parameter, which adjusts the size of the marble pattern, and a Levels parameter, which determines how many times the algorithm is applied. The two color swatches determine the base and vein colors, or you can assign a map. There are also values for the Saturation of the colors, and the Swap button switches the colors.

Figure 20-19 shows the Perlin Marble map Size value of 50, 100, and 200.

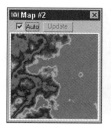

Figure 20-19: The Perlin Marble map creates a marble pattern with random veins.

Planet map

The Planet map is especially designed to create random areas of land and water. The Planet Parameters rollout includes three color swatches for the water areas and five color swatches for the land areas. These colors are displayed successively to simulate the elevation of the map. Other options include the Continent Size, the Island Factor (which determines the number of islands), an Ocean percentage, and a Random Seed. There is also an option to Blend Water and Land.

Figure 20-20 shows Planet map with Island Factor values of 0, 10, and 30.

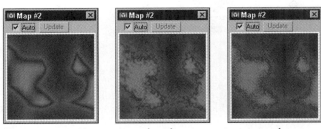

Figure 20-20: You can use the Planet map to create planets with landmasses and oceans.

Smoke map

The Smoke map can create random fractal-based patterns such as those you would see in smoke. In the Smoke Parameters rollout, you can set the Size of the smoke areas and the number of Iterations (how many times the fractal algorithm is computed). The Phase value shifts the smoke about, and the Exponent value produces thin, wispy lines of smoke. The rollout also includes two colors for the smoke particles and the area in between the smoke particles, or you could load maps instead.

Figure 20-21 shows the Smoke map with Size values of 40, 80, and 200.

Figure 20-21: The Smoke map simulates the look of smoke when applied as opacity mapping.

Speckle map

The Speckle map produces small randomly positioned specks. The Speckle Parameters rollout lets you control the Size and color of the specks. Two color swatches are for the base and speck colors.

Figure 20-22 shows the Speckle map with Size values of 100, 200, and 400.

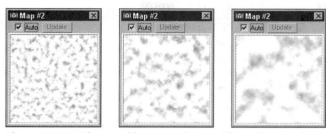

Figure 20-22: The Speckle map paints small random specks on the surface of an object.

Splat map

The Splat map can create the look of covering an object with splattered paint. In the Splat Parameters rollout, you can set the Size of the splattered areas and the number of Iterations, which is how many times the fractal algorithm is computed. For each additional Iteration, a smaller set of spatters will appear. The Threshold value determines how much of each color to mix. The rollout also includes two colors for the splattered sections, or you could load maps instead.

Figure 20-23 shows the Splat map with a Size value of 60, 6 Iterations, and Threshold values of 0.2, 0.3, and 0.4.

Figure 20-23: The Splat map splatters paint randomly across the surface of an object.

Stucco map

The Stucco map generates random patches of gradients that create the look of a stucco surface if applied as a bump map. In the Stucco Parameters rollout, the Size value determines the size of these areas. The Thickness value determines how blurry the patches are, which changes the sharpness of the bumps for a bump map. The Threshold value determines how much of each color to mix. The rollout also includes two colors for the patchy sections, or you could load maps instead.

Figure 20-24 shows the Stucco map with Size values of 10, 20, and 40.

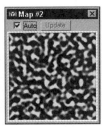 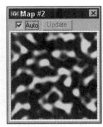 

Figure 20-24: The Stucco map creates soft indentations when applied as bump mapping.

Water map

This map creates wavy, watery-looking maps and can be used as both a diffuse and a bump map to create a water surface. You can use several values to set the wave characteristics in the Water Parameters rollout, including the number of Wave Sets, the Wave Radius, the minimum and maximum Wave Length, the Amplitude, and the Phase. There is also an option to Distribute the waves as 2D or 3D, and there is a Random Seed value.

Figure 20-25 shows the Water map with the Num Wave Sets value set to 1, 3, and 9.

Figure 20-25: You can use the Water map to create watery surfaces.

Wood map

The Wood map produces a two-color wood grain. The Wood Parameters rollout options include Grain Thickness, Radial, and Axial Noise. You can select the two colors to use for the wood grain.

Figure 20-26 shows the Wood map with Grain Thickness values of 8, 16, and 30.

 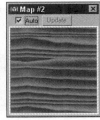 

Figure 20-26: The Wood map creates a map with a wood grain.

Compositor maps

Compositor maps are made from combining several maps into one. Compositor map types include Composite, Mask, Mix, and RGB Multiply.

Composite map

Composite maps combine a specified number of maps into a single map using the alpha channel. The Composite Parameters rollout enables you to specify the number of maps and has buttons for loading each.

In order for the maps to be specified, at least one of them must contain an alpha channel. If the submaterials contain an Output rollout, then you can select the Alpha from RGB Intensity option. If the submaterial doesn't have an Output rollout, then you can apply the Output map and keep the submaterial as a sub-map. This will enable the same options found in the Output rollout.

Figure 20-27 shows three different uses for the Composite map. The left image combines a Brick map with a Gradient map. The Gradient map includes an Output rollout with the Alpha from RGB Intensity option enabled. The last two images combine a Bricks map with Checker and Splat maps. To enable the alpha channel for these last two, the Output map was used.

Figure 20-27: The Composite map can use multiple maps.

Mask map

In the Mask Parameters rollout, you can select one map to use as a Mask and another one to display through the holes in the mask simply called Map. There is also an option to Invert the Mask. The black areas of the masking map are the areas that hide the underlying map. The white areas allow the underlying map to show through.

Mix map

You can use the Mix map to combine two maps or colors. It is similar to the Composite map, except that it uses a Mix Amount value to combine the two colors or maps instead of using the alpha channel. In the Mix Parameters rollout, the Mix Amount value of 0 includes only Color #1, and a value of 100 includes only Color #2. You can also use a Mixing Curve to define how the colors are mixed. The curve shape is controlled by altering its Upper and Lower values.

Figure 20-28 shows the Mix map with Bricks and Checker maps applied as sub-maps and a Mix value of 25, 50, and 75.

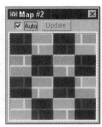

Figure 20-28: The Mix map lets you combine two maps and define the Mix Amount.

RGB Multiply map

The RGB Multiply map multiplies the RGB values for two separate maps and combines them to create a single map. Did you notice in the previous figure how the Mix map fades both maps? The RGB Multiply map keeps the saturation of the individual maps by using each map's alpha channel to combine the maps.

The RGB Multiply Parameters rollout includes an option to use the Alpha from either Map #1 or Map #2 or to Multiply the Alphas.

Figure 20-29 shows three samples of the RGB Multiply map. Each of these images combines a Bricks map with a Checker map, a Gradient map, and a Stucco map. Notice how the colors aren't faded for this map type.

Figure 20-29: The RGB Multiply map combines maps at full saturation using alpha channels.

Color modifier maps

You can use this group of maps to change the color of different materials. Color Modifier map types include Output, RGB Tint, and Vertex Color.

Output map

The Output map provides a way to add the functions of the Output rollout to maps that don't include an output rollout. Details on this map type are presented in the earlier section that covers the Output rollout.

RGB Tint map

The RGB Tint map includes color swatches for the red, green, and blue channel values. Adjusting these colors alters the amount of tint in the map. For example, setting the red color swatch in the RGB Tint Parameters rollout to white and the green and blue color swatches to black would create a map with a heavy red tint. You can also load maps in place of the colors.

Vertex Color map

The Vertex Color map makes the vertex colors assigned to an editable mesh, Poly, or Patch object visible when the object is rendered. When an Editable Mesh, Poly, or Patch object is in Vertex subobject mode, you can assign the selected vertices a Color, an Illumination color, and an Alpha value. These settings are in the Surface Properties rollout. You can also assign vertex colors using the Assign Vertex Colors utility. Use this utility to assign the current object color or assigned material colors to the object's vertices using the given lights. A third way to assign vertex colors is with the Vertex Paint modifier, which you access using the Modifiers ➪ Mesh Editing ➪ Vertex Paint menu command. This modifier lets you color vertices by painting directly on an object.

For more detail on the Vertex Paint modifier, see Chapter 19, "Creating and Applying Materials."

Once vertex colors are assigned, you need to apply the Vertex Color map to the diffuse color in the Material Editor and apply it to the object for the object to render the vertex colors. This map doesn't have any settings.

Reflection and refraction maps

These maps are actually grouped into a category called Other, but they all deal with reflection and refraction effects. Maps in this category include Flat Mirror, Raytrace, Reflect/Refract, and Thin Wall Refraction.

Flat Mirror map

The Flat Mirror map reflects the surroundings using a coplanar group of faces. In the Flat Mirror Parameters rollout, you can select a Blur amount to apply. You can specify whether to Render the First Frame Only or Every Nth Frame. There is also an option to Use the Environment Map or to apply to Faces with a given ID.

Flat Mirror maps are applied to selected coplanar faces only using the material ID.

The Distortion options include None, Use Bump Map, and Use Built-In Noise. If the Bump Map option is selected, you can define a Distortion Amount. If the Noise option is selected, you can choose Regular, Fractal, or Turbulence noise types with Phase, Size, and Levels values.

Tutorial: Creating a mirrored surface

Mirror, mirror on the wall, who's the best modeler of them all? Using the Flat Mirror map, you can create, believe it or not, mirrors. To create and configure a flat mirror map, follow these steps.

1. Open the Reflection in mirror.max file from the Chap 20 directory on the CD-ROM.

   This file includes a mesh of a man standing in front of a mirror. The mirror subobject faces have been selected and applied a material ID of 1.

2. Choose Rendering ➪ Material Editor (or press the M key) to open the Material Editor.

3. Select the second sample slot, name the material **Mirror,** and open the Maps rollout. Click the mapping button for the Reflection map. The Material/Map Browser opens. Double-click the Flat Mirror map to select it.

Note   If the Flat Mirror map isn't available, select the Map radio button in the Show section.

   4. In the Flat Mirror Parameters rollout, de-select the Apply Blur and User Environment Map options and select the Apply to Faces with ID option. Then set the ID value to 1.

   5. Drag the sample slot to the mirror object in the viewport to apply the material to the mirror.

Figure 20-30 shows a model being reflected off a simple patch object with a Flat Mirror map applied to it. The reflection will only be visible in the final rendered image.

Figure 20-30: A Flat Mirror map causes the object to reflect its surroundings.

Raytrace map

The Raytrace map is an alternative to the raytrace material discussed in the previous chapter and, as a map, can be used in places where the raytrace material cannot.

Cross-Reference   Check out Chapter 37, "Raytracing" for more on the Raytrace map.

Reflect/Refract map

Reflect/Refract maps are yet another way to create reflections and refractions on objects. These maps work by producing a rendering from each axis of the object, like one for each face of a cube. These rendered images, called cubic maps, are then projected onto the object.

These rendered images can be created automatically or loaded from prerendered images using the Reflect/Refract Parameters rollout. Using automatic cubic maps is easier, but they take considerably more time. If you select the Automatic option, you can select to render the First Frame Only or Every Nth Frame. If you select the From File option, then you are offered six buttons that can load cubic maps for each of the different directions.

In the Reflect/Refract Parameters rollout, you can also specify the Blur settings and the Atmospheric Ranges.

Thin Wall Refraction map

The Thin Wall Refraction map simulates the refraction caused by a piece of glass, such as a magnifying glass. The same result is possible with the Reflect/Refract map, but the Thin Wall Refraction map achieves this result in a fraction of the time.

The Thin Wall Refraction Parameters rollout includes options for setting the Blur, the frames to render, and Refraction values. The Thickness Offset determines the amount of offset and can range from 0 through 10. The Bump Map Effect value changes the refraction based on the presence of a bump map.

Tutorial: Creating a magnifying glass effect

Another common property of glass besides reflection is refraction. Refraction can enlarge items when the glass is thick, such as when you look at the other side of the room through a glass of water. Using the Thin Wall Refraction map, you can simulate the effects of a magnifying glass.

To create a magnifying glass effect, follow these steps.

1. Open the Magnifying glass.max file from the Chap 20 directory on the CD-ROM.

   This file includes a simple sphere with a Perlin Marble map applied to it and a magnifying glass modeled from primitive objects.

2. Choose Rendering ⇨ Material Editor (or press the M key) to open the Material Editor.

3. Select the fourth sample slot, name the material **Magnifying Glass**, and open the Maps rollout. Click the map button for the Refraction map. In the Material/Map Browser that opens, double-click the Thin Wall Refraction map.

4. In the Raytracer Parameters rollout, select the Refraction Trace Mode option and select the Black color swatch option in the Background section.

5. Drag the Magnifying Glass material to the magnifying glass object in the viewport to apply the material to the object.

Figure 20-31 shows the resulting rendered image. Notice how the texture in the magnifying glass appears magnified.

Figure 20-31: The Thin Wall Refraction map is applied to a magnifying glass.

Using the Maps Rollout

Now that you've seen all the different types of maps that are available, we'll revisit the Maps rollout (introduced in Chapter 19), shown in Figure 20-32, and cover it in more detail.

The Maps rollout is where you apply maps to the various materials. To use a map, click the Map button — this opens the Material/Map Browser where you can select the map to use. The Amount spinner sets the intensity of the map, and there is an option to enable or disable the map. For example, a white material with a red Diffuse map set at 50 percent Intensity will result in a pink material.

The available maps in the Maps rollout depend on the type of material and the Shader that you are using. Raytrace materials have many more available maps than the standard material. Some of the common mapping types found in the Maps rollout will be discussed in this section.

Ambient mapping

Ambient mapping replaces the ambient color component of the base material. You can use this feature to make an object's shadow appear as a map. Diffuse mapping (discussed next) also affects the Ambient color. A lock button in the Maps rollout enables you to lock these two mappings together.

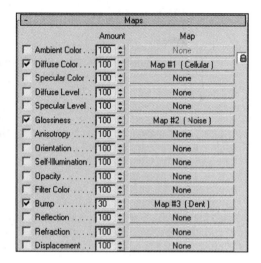

Figure 20-32: The Maps rollout can turn maps on or off.

Diffuse mapping

Diffuse mapping replaces the diffuse color component of the base material. This is the main color used for the object. When you select a map such as Wood, the object appears to be created out of wood. As mentioned previously, diffuse mapping can also affect the Ambient color if the lock button is selected.

Diffuse Level mapping

Diffuse Level mapping changes the diffuse color level from 0, where the map is black, to a maximum, where the map is white. This mapping is only available with the Anisotropic, Oren-Nayar-Blinn, and Multi-Level Shaders.

Diffuse Roughness mapping

Roughness mapping sets the roughness value of the material from 0, where the map is black, to a maximum, where the map is white. This mapping is only available with the Oren-Nayar-Blinn and Multi-Layer Shaders.

Specular mapping

Specular mapping replaces the specular color component of the base material. This option enables you to include a different color or image in place of the specular color. It is different from the Specular Level and Glossiness mappings, which also affect the specular highlights.

Specular Level mapping

Specular Level mapping controls the intensity of the specular highlights from 0, where the map is black, to 1, where the map is white. For the best effect, apply this mapping along with the Glossiness mapping.

Glossiness mapping

Glossiness mapping defines where the specular highlights will appear. You can use this option to make an object appear older by diminishing certain areas. Black areas on the map show the non-glossy areas, and white areas are where the glossiness is at a maximum.

Self-Illumination mapping

Self-Illumination mapping makes certain areas of an object glow, and, because they glow, they won't receive any lighting effects, such as highlights or shadows. Black areas represent areas that have no self-illumination, and white areas receive full self-illumination.

Opacity mapping

Opacity mapping determines which areas are visible and which are transparent. Black areas for this map will be transparent, and white areas will be opaque. This mapping works in conjunction with the Opacity value in the Basic Parameters rollout. Transparent areas, even if perfectly transparent, still receive specular highlights.

Filter color mapping

Filter color mapping is used to color transparent areas for creating materials such as colored glass. White light that is cast through an object using filter color mapping will be colored with the filter color.

Anisotropy mapping

Anisotropy mapping can control the shape of an anisotropy highlight. This mapping is only available with the Anisotropic and Multi-Layer Shaders.

Orientation mapping

Orientation mapping controls an anisotropic highlight's position. Anisotropic highlights are elliptical, and this mapping can position them at a different angle. Orientation mapping is only available with the Anisotropic and Multi-Layer Shaders.

Metalness mapping

Metalness mapping controls how metallic an area looks. It specifies metalness values from 0, where the map is black, to a maximum, where the map is white. This mapping is only available with the Strauss Shader.

Bump mapping

Bump mapping uses the intensity of the bitmap to raise or indent the surface of an object. The white areas of the map are raised, and darker areas are lowered. Although bump mapping appears to alter the geometry, it actually doesn't affect the surface geometry.

Reflection mapping

Reflection mapping reflects images off the surface as a mirror does. The three different types of Reflection mapping are Basic, Automatic, and Flat Mirror. Basic reflection mapping simulates the reflection of an object's surroundings. Automatic reflection mapping projects the map outward from the center of the object. Flat-Mirror reflection mapping reflects a mirror image off a series of coplanar faces.

Reflection mapping doesn't need mapping coordinates because the coordinates are based on world coordinates and not on object coordinates. Therefore, the map will appear different if the object is moved — which is how reflections work in the real world.

Refraction mapping

Refraction mapping bends light and displays images through a transparent object, in the same way a room appears through a glass of water. The amount of this effect is controlled by a value called the Index of Refraction. This value is set in the parent material's Extended Parameters rollout.

Displacement mapping

You can use displacement mapping, unlike bump mapping, to change the geometry of an object. The white areas of the map are pushed outward, and the dark areas are pushed in. The amount of the surface that is displaced is based on a percentage of the diagonal that makes up the bounding box of the object. Displacement mapping can only be applied to patches, Editable Meshes, and NURBS objects. For other object types, you can use displacement mapping only after the Disp Approx modifier has been applied.

Displacement mapping isn't visible in the viewports unless the Displace NURBS (for NURBS objects) or the Displace Mesh (for Editable Meshes) modifiers have been applied.

Tutorial: Creating space textures

"Space . . . the final frontier." Space is a great place to start creating and using new materials. With objects floating in space, you don't need to worry about lining things up, and modeling planets is easy because they are made from simple spheres — the materials are what make the planet spheres look good. So, as an example of creating new materials, let's create several new "space" materials.

In this tutorial, you'll learn how to make textures for the sun, a moon, and several different planets. To create several planetary textures, follow these steps:

1. Open the Space textures.max file from the Chap 20 directory on the CD-ROM.

   This file contains five simple spheres that represent some space planets.

2. Press the M key to open the Material Editor, select the first sample slot, and name the material **Sun**. Click the map button to the right of the Diffuse color swatch to open the Material/Map Browser, and double-click the Noise map. In the Noise Parameters rollout, select the Fractal option and set the Size to 20 and the Levels to 10. Choose an orange

color for Color #1 and black for Color #2. Next, open the Maps rollout and drag the Noise map from the Diffuse mapping to the Self Illumination mapping. A small dialog box opens, enabling you to Copy the map as an Instance or a Copy or Swap the maps. Select the Copy option and click OK. Drag the material to one of the spheres in the scene. Click the Go to Parent button to return to the base Sun material.

> **Tip**   Double-click the sample slot to open a magnified view of the material. This will let you see the details up close.

3. Select the second sample slot and name it **Planet 1**. Then click the map button to the right of the Diffuse color swatch to open the Material/Map Browser again and double-click the Planet map type. In the Planet Parameters rollout, select three shades of blue for the Water Colors and five shades of green for the Land Colors. Set the Continent Size to 20 and enable the Blend Water/Land option. Drag the material to another one of the spheres in the scene.

4. Select the third sample slot and name it **Planet 2**. Then click the map button to the right of the Diffuse color swatch to open the Material/Map Browser and double-click the Planet map type again. In the Planet Parameters rollout, select shades of orange and brown for both the water and landmass of this planet. Set the Continent Size to 40 and enable the Blend Water/Land option. Drag the material to one of the spheres in the scene.

5. Select the forth sample slot and name it **Planet 3**. Then click the map button to the right of the Diffuse color swatch and double-click the Planet map type once again. For this planet, select different shades of red. Set the Continent Size to 80, the Island Factor to 40, and the Ocean Percent to 20, and disable the Blend Water/Land option. Drag the material to one of the spheres in the scene.

6. Select the fifth sample slot and name it **Planet 4.** Then click the map button to the right of the Diffuse color swatch and double-click on the Swirl map type from the Material/Map Browser. In the Swirl Parameters rollout, select two colors for the Swirl and set the Swirl Intensity to 5.0. For the Swirl color, click the map button and select the Noise map. For the Noise map, set the Size value to 30 and select the Turbulence option. Drag the material to one of the spheres in the scene.

7. Select the sixth sample slot and name it **Moon**. Then click the Diffuse color map button and select Smoke from the Material/Map Browser. Set the Size value to 20 and click the map button for Color #1. Select the Noise map. Set the Size value to 25 and select the Turbulence option. Drag the material to one of the spheres in the scene.

8. Select the seventh sample slot (you'll need to drag the scroll bar to the right of the sample slots down to access the next row of sample slots) and name it **Star Background**. Then click the map button to the right of the Diffuse color swatch and select Noise. In the Noise Parameters rollout, select the Fractal option, set the Size value to 2.0, the High value to 0.5, and the Levels to 2.0. Click the Swap button until Color #2 is black. In the Output rollout, set the Output Amount to 2.0. Choose the Rendering ➪ Environment menu command (or press the 8 key) to open the Environment dialog box. Drag the Noise map from the Material Type button to the Environment Map button at the top of the dialog box and select the Use Map option.

Figure 20-33 shows the planets in space as a rendered image.

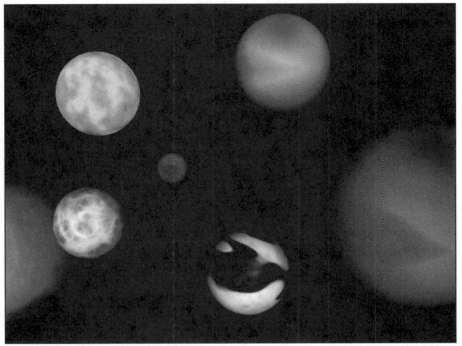

Figure 20-33: Using a variety of techniques, you can create an assortment of different space textures.

Tutorial: Aging objects for realism

I don't know whether your toolbox is well-worn like mine—it must be the hostile environment that it is always in (or all the things I keep dropping in and on it). To render a toolbox with nice specular highlights just doesn't feel right. This tutorial shows a few ways to age an object so that it looks older.

To add maps to make an object look old, follow these steps:

1. Open the Toolbox.max file from the Chap 20 directory on the CD-ROM.

   This file contains a simple toolbox mesh created using extruded splines.

2. Press the M key to open the Material Editor and select the first sample slot. Select the Metal shader from the drop-down list in the Shader Basic Parameters rollout. In the Metal Basic Parameters rollout, set the Diffuse color to a nice, shiny red and increase the Specular Level to 97 and Glossiness value to 59. Name the material **Toolbox**.

3. In the Maps rollout, click the button for the Glossiness mapping and double-click on the Splat map from the Material/Map Browser. In the Splat Parameters rollout, set the Size value to 100 and change Color #1 to a rust color and Color #2 to white.

4. Click on the Go to Parent button (which is located above the material Type button) to get back the Maps rollout for the base material. In the Maps rollout, click the Bump mapping button and double-click the Dent map from the Material/Map Browser. In the Dent Parameters rollout, set the Size value to 200 and Color #1 to black and Color #2 to white.

5. At the top of the Material Editor, select the second sample slot and name it **Hinge**. Select the Metal shader from the Shader Basic Parameters rollout for this material also and increase the Specular Level in the Metal Basic Parameters rollout to 26 and the Glossiness value to 71. Also change the Diffuse color to a light gray. Click the map button next to the Glossiness value and double-click the Noise map in the Material/Map Browser. In the Noise Parameters rollout, set the Noise map to Fractal with a Size of 10.

6. Drag the "Toolbox" material to the toolbox object and the "Hinge" material to the hinge and the handle.

Note   Bump and glossiness mappings will not be visible until the scene is rendered. To see the material's results, choose Rendering ➪ Render and click the Render button.

Figure 20-34 shows the well-used toolbox.

Figure 20-34: This toolbox shows its age with Glossiness and Bump mappings.

Using the Map Path Utility

After you have all your maps in place, losing them can really make life troublesome. However, Max includes a utility that helps you determine which maps are missing and lets you edit the path to them to quickly and easily locate them. The Bitmap/Photometric Path Editor utility is available in the Utility panel. To find it, click on the More button and select Bitmap/Photometric Path Editor from the list of utilities.

This utility is used for bitmaps as well as photometric lights. You can learn about photometric lights in Chapter 22, "Working with Lights."

When opened, the Path Editor rollout includes the Edit Resources button that opens the Bitmap/Photometric Path Editor window, shown in Figure 20-35. The rollout also includes two options for displaying the Materials Editor and Material Library bitmap paths. The Close button closes the rollout.

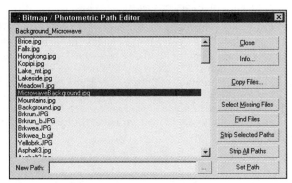

Figure 20-35: The Bitmap Path Editor window lets you alter map paths.

The Info button in the Bitmap/Photometric Path Editor dialog box lists all the nodes that use the selected map. The Copy Files button opens a File dialog where you can select to copy the selected map to. The Select Missing Files selects any maps in the list that can't be located. The Find Files button lists the maps in the current selection that can be located and the number that are missing. Striping paths remove the path information and leave only the map name. The New Path field lets you enter the path information to apply to the selected maps. The button with three dots to the right of the New Path field lets you browse for a path and the Set Path button applies the path designated in the New Path field to the selected maps.

Mapping Modifiers

Within the many modifiers found in the Modifiers menu are several that are specific to material maps. These modifiers are mainly found in the UV Coordinates submenu and are used to define the coordinates for positioning material maps. These modifiers include the UVW Map, UVW XForm, Unwrap UVW, Camera Map, and Displace modifiers.

UVW Map modifier

The UVW Map modifier lets you specify the mapping coordinates for an object. Primitives, Loft Objects, and NURBS can generate their own mapping coordinates, but you need to use this modifier to apply mapping coordinates to mesh objects and patches.

Note   Objects that create their own mapping coordinates apply them to Map Channel 1. If you apply the UVW Map modifier to Map Channel 1 of an object that already has mapping coordinates, then the applied coordinates overwrite the existing ones.

You can apply the UVW Map modifier to different map channels. Applying this modifier places a map gizmo on the object. You can move, scale, or rotate this gizmo. To transform a UVW Map gizmo, you must select it from the subobject list. Gizmos that are scaled smaller than the object can be tiled.

There are many different types of mappings, and the parameter rollout for this modifier lets you select which one to use. The Length, Width, and Height values are the dimensions for the UVW Map gizmo. You can also set tiling values in all directions.

The Alignment section offers eight buttons for controlling the alignment of the gizmo. The Fit button fits the gizmo to the edges of the object. The Center button aligns the gizmo center with the object's center. The Bitmap Fit button opens a File dialog box where you can align the gizmo to the resolution of the selected bitmaps. The Normal Align button lets you drag on the surface of the object, and when you release the mouse button, the gizmo origin will be aligned with the normal. The View Align button aligns the gizmo to match the current viewport. The Region Fit button lets you drag a region in the viewport and match the gizmo to this region. The Reset button moves the gizmo to its original location. The Acquire button aligns the gizmo with the same coordinates as another object.

Figure 20-36 displays a brick map applied to an umbrella using spherical mapping.

Tutorial: Using the UVW Map modifier to apply decals

We already used the UVW Map modifier in the television example earlier in this chapter, but it's worth exploring further. After mapping coordinates have been applied either automatically or with the UVW Map modifier, you can use the UVW XForm modifier to move, rotate, and scale the mapping coordinates.

Most objects can automatically generate mapping coordinates — with the exception of meshes. For meshes, you need to use the UVW Map modifier. The UVW Map modifier includes seven different mapping options. Each mapping option wraps the map in a different way. The options include Planar, Cylindrical, Spherical, Shrink Wrap, Box, Face, and XYZ to UVW.

In this tutorial, we use the UVW Map modifier to apply a decal to a rocket model. Zygote Media created the rocket model.

To use the UVW Map modifier, follow these steps:

1. Open the Nasa decal on rocket.max file from the Chap 20 directory on the CD-ROM.

   This file includes a model of a rocket with the appropriate materials applied. The Chap 20 directory on the CD-ROM also includes a 300 × 600 image of the word NASA in black capital letters on a white background. The background color of this image has been set to be transparent, and the image was saved as a .GIF file.

Figure 20-36: The UVW Map modifier lets you specify various mapping coordinates for material maps.

Note

The GIF file format, typically used for Web pages, can easily make areas of the image transparent. These transparent areas become the alpha channel when loaded into Max.

2. Open the Material Editor (or press the M key) and select the first sample slot. Name the material **NASA Logo**. Click the Diffuse color swatch and select a white color. Then click the map button to the right of the Diffuse color swatch, and from the Material/Map Browser, double-click the Bitmap map. Locate the NASA image from the Chap 20 directory on the CD-ROM and click Open. The bitmap image loads, and the Bitmap parameters display in the rollouts. In the Coordinates rollout, enter a value of **–90** in the W Angle field. The letters rotate vertically. Then, in the Bitmap Parameters rollout, select the Image Alpha option.

3. Select the lower white section of the rocket in the viewport and open the Modify panel. At the top of the Modify panel, click the Modifier List and select the UVW Map modifier. Select the Cylindrical Mapping option, but don't select the Cap option in the Parameters rollout.

4. With the cylinder section selected, open the Material Editor again, select the first sample slot, and click the Assign Material to Selection button.

Tip   When a bitmap is applied to an object using the UVW Map modifier, you can change the length, width, and tiling of the bitmap using the UVW Map manipulator. Enable the Select and Manipulate button on the main toolbar, and the manipulator appears as green lines. When you move the mouse over the top of these green lines, they turn red, and you can drag them to alter the map dimensions. Use the small green circles at the edges of the map to change the tiling values. As you use the manipulator, the map is updated in real time within the viewports if you have enabled the Show Map in Viewport option in the Material Editor.

Figure 20-37 shows the resulting rendered image.

Figure 20-37: You can use the UVW Map modifier to apply decals to objects.

UVW XForm modifier

The UVW XForm modifier enables you to adjust mapping coordinates. It can be applied to mapping coordinates that are automatically created or to mapping coordinates created with the UVW Map modifier. The parameter rollout includes values for the UVW Tile and UVW Offsets. You can also select the Map Channel to use.

Unwrap UVW modifier

The Unwrap UVW modifier lets you control how a map is applied to a subobject selection. It can also be used to unwrap the existing mapping coordinates of an object. You can then edit these coordinates as needed. You can also use the Unwrap UVW modifier to apply multiple planar maps to an object. You accomplish this task by creating planar maps for various sides of an object and then editing the mapping coordinates in the Edit UVWs interface.

The Unwrap UVW modifier has been overhauled in 3ds max 5.

The Unwrap UVW modifier lets you control precisely how a map is applied to an object. The Unwrap UVW modifier has a single subobject mode named Select Face. In this subobject mode, you can select face subobjects and the same face selection will be displayed in the Edit UVWs interface and vice versa. In the Modify panel, you'll find two rollouts — Selection Parameters and Parameters. The Selection Parameters rollout includes a button with a plus sign and one with a minus sign. These buttons grow or shrink the current selected subobject selection. You can also select to Ignore Backfacing, Select by Element (instead of faces), set the Planar Angle, or select by Material ID or Smoothing Group.

The Edit UVWs interface

The Parameters rollout includes a button named Edit. This button opens the Edit UVWs interface, shown in Figure 20-38 for a postbox model. You can also load and save the edited mapping coordinates using the Save and Load buttons in the Parameters rollout and the Reset UVWs button will reset all the mapped coordinates. Saved mapping coordinate files have the .UVW extension.

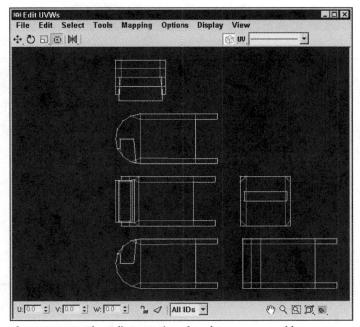

Figure 20-38: The Edit UVWs interface lets you control how different planar maps line up with the model.

Table 20-1 shows and describes the buttons in the Edit UVWs dialog box.

Table 20-1: Edit UVW Interface Buttons

Buttons	Name	Description
	Move, Move Horizontal, Move Vertical	Moves the selected vertices when dragged.
	Rotate	Rotates the selected vertices when dragged.
	Scale, Scale Horizontal, Scale Vertical	Scales the selected vertices when dragged.
	Freeform Mode	Displays a gizmo that you can use to transform the subobject selection.
	Mirror Horizontal, Mirror Vertical, Flip Horizontal, Flip Vertical	Mirrors or flips the selected vertices about the center of the selection.
	Show Map	Toggles the display of the map in the dialog box.
	Coordinates	Displays the vertices for the UV, UW, and WU axes.
	Pick Texture drop-down list	Displays a drop-down list of all the maps applied to this object. You can display new maps by using the Pick Texture option.
U: 0.0 V: 0.0 W: 0.0	U, V, W values	Displays the coordinates of the selected vertex. You can use these values to move a vertex.
	Lock Selected Vertices	Locks the selected vertices and prevents additional vertices from being selected.
	Filter Selected Faces	Displays vertices for only the selected faces.
All IDs ▾	All IDs drop-down list	Filters selected material IDs.

The buttons in the lower-right corner of the Edit UVWs dialog box work just like the Viewport Navigation buttons described in earlier chapters.

Many of the commands found in the menus can also be found in the pop-up options interface, shown in Figure 20-39. You can enable Soft Selection using this dialog box. In the Bitmap Options section, you can specify the resolution of the bitmap.

The File menu can also be used to load (Alt+Shift+Ctrl+L), save, and reset UV coordinates. The Edit menu lets you specify the mode to use to transform subobject selections. These modes include Move (Q), Rotate (Ctrl+R), Scale, and Freeform, which lets you use the gizmo to transform subobjects. The Edit menu also includes Copy, Paste, and a Paste Weld command. The Copy and Paste commands let you copy a mapping and paste it to another set of faces. The Paste Weld will weld vertices as it pastes the mapping.

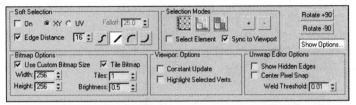

Figure 20-39: The Options pop-up interface includes many of the same features as the menus.

The gizmo is simply a rectangle gizmo that surrounds the current selection. Move the selection by clicking in the gizmo and dragging; a Shift-drag will constrain the selection to move horizontally or vertically. The plus sign in the center marks the rotation and scale center point. Scale the selection by dragging on one of its handles. A Ctrl-drag on a handle will maintain the aspect ratio of the selection. Click and drag the middle handles to rotate the selection. A Ctrl+drag will snap to 5-degree positions and an Alt+drag will snap to 1-degree positions.

Within the Edit UVWs interface, you can select vertices, edges, or faces. The Select ➪ Get Selection From Viewport (Alt+Shift+Ctrl+P) menu command lets you select and transfer the selection from the viewports, or you could convert selections between vertices, edges, and faces. Subobjects that are selected in one planar map will be also highlighted in the other planar maps. This makes it easy to stitch elements together.

The Tools menu includes commands for flipping, mirroring, welding, breaking, and detaching subobjects. The Tools ➪ Stitch Selected menu command lets you stitch mapped segments together into a single cluster and the Pack UVs menu command lets you combine UVs into a smaller space. Packed UVs are easy to move and work with because they use a smaller resolution bitmap. Within the Pack dialog box, the Spacing value sets the amount of space between each segment, and the Normalize Clusters option fits all clusters into the given space. The Rotate Clusters option allows segments to be rotated to fit better and the Fill Holes option places smaller segments within open larger segments.

The Tools ➪ Sketch Vertices command will let you select vertices by dragging over them. The vertices can then be aligned to a shape including Line, Circle, Box, or Freeform. You can also set the cursor size used to select vertices.

The Mapping menu includes three auto mapping options—Flatten, Normal, and Unfold Mapping. The Flatten Mapping option breaks the mesh into segments based on the angle between adjacent faces. This option is good for objects that have sharp angles like a robot or a machine. Figure 20-40 shows a television with the Flatten Mapping applied.

The Normal Mapping option lets you select to map a mesh using only specific views including: Top/Bottom, Front/Back, Left/Right, Box, Box No Top, and Diamond. These views are based on the direction of the normals from the faces of the mesh. This is the mapping that was used on the postbox model shown in the earlier figure. It is helpful for thin models like butterfly wings or a coin.

The Unfold Mapping option is unique because it starts at one face and slowly unwraps all the adjacent faces into a single segment if possible. Figure 20-41 shows a simple pyramid primitive that has been unwrapped using this method. The advantage of this mapping is that it results in a map with no distortions. It includes two options—Walk to Closest Face and Walk to Farthest Face. You'll almost always want to use the Walk to Closest Face option.

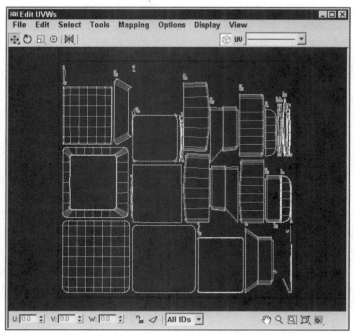

Figure 20-40: The Flatten Mapping option displays every part of a model as a separate segment.

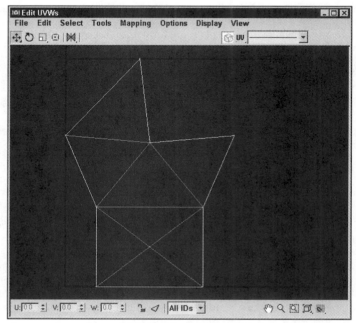

Figure 20-41: The Unfold Mapping option splits the model and unfolds it by adjacent faces into a single segment.

The Options ➪ Advanced Options (Ctrl+O) menu command opens the Unwrap Options dialog box, shown in Figure 20-42, and lets you set the Line and Selection Colors as well as the preferences for the Edit UVWs dialog box. You can load and tile background images at a specified map resolution or use the Use Bitmap Resolution option. There is also a setting for the Weld Threshold and options to constantly update, show selected vertices in the viewport, and snap to the middle pixel.

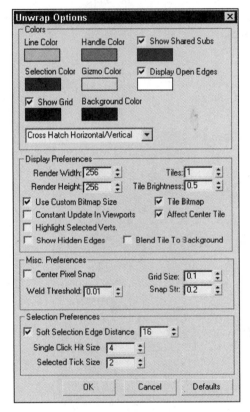

Figure 20-42: In the Unwrap Options dialog box you can set the preferences for the Edit UVWs dialog box.

Tutorial: Controlling the mapping of teddy bear's head

The teddy bear model created by Viewpoint Datalabs is fairly simplistic, but you can add details to it using planar maps. In this tutorial, we'll add and edit the mapping coordinates for the teddy bear's eyes using the Unwrap UVW modifier.

To control how planar maps are applied to the head of a teddy bear, follow these steps:

1. Open the Mapped teddy bear.max file from the Chap 20 directory on the CD-ROM.

   This file includes the teddy bear mesh. The Unwrap UVW modifier has already been applied to the teddy bear. The Chap 20 directory also includes a 600 × 400 image of the teddy bear details created in Photoshop. The file is saved as Teddy bear map.tif.

2. With the Teddy Bear selected, choose Modifiers ➪ UV Coordinates ➪ Unwrap UVW. In the Parameters rollout, click the Edit button.

   The Edit UVWs interface opens.

3. In the Edit UVWs interface, choose Mapping ➪ Normal Mapping. In the Normal Mapping dialog box, select the Back/Front Mapping option from the drop-down list and click OK. The front and back views of the teddy bear are displayed vertically in the Edit UVWs interface.

4. In the Edit UVWs dialog box, drag the mouse over all the vertices and click the Rotate –90 button in the options panel (located at the bottom of the dialog) to make the mapping appear side by side, and then click the Zoom Extents button to fill the interface.

5. From the drop-down list at the top of the interface, select the Pick Texture option. The Material/Map Browser opens. Double-click on the Bitmap option and select the Teddy bear map.tif image from the Chap 20 directory on the CD-ROM.

6. Drag over all the vertices for the front segment to select them all. Then, using the Freeform mode gizmo, line up the map details with the UVW segment. Figure 20-43 shows the teddy bear with the mapped bitmap.

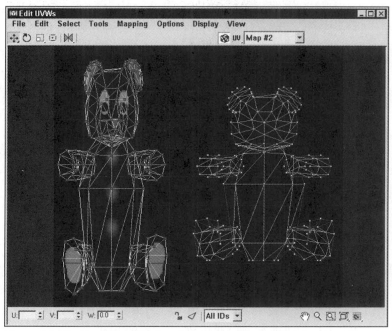

Figure 20-43: The Edit UVWs interface lets you transform the mapping coordinates by moving vertices.

7. Open the Material Editor by pressing the M key and then select the first sample slot. Name the material **Teddy bear** and click on the map button to the right of the Diffuse color button. Double-click on the Bitmap option from the Material/Map Browser that opens and select the Teddy bear map.tif file from the Chap 20 directory on the CD-ROM. Then drag this material to the teddy bear and click the Show Map in Viewport button (the small checkboard cube icon) to see the map on the teddy bear.

Figure 20-44 shows the results of the new mapping coordinates.

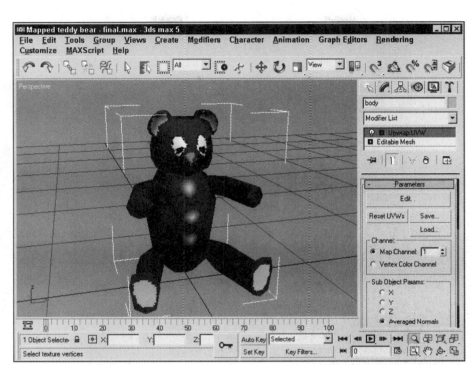

Figure 20-44: The position of this teddy bear's details has been set using the Unwrap UVW modifier.

Camera Map modifier

This modifier creates planar mapping coordinates based on the camera's position. The single parameter for this modifier is Pick Camera. To use this modifier, click the Pick Camera button and select a camera. The mapping coordinates will be applied to the selected object.

Displace modifier

The Displace modifier can alter an object's geometry by displacing elements using a Displace gizmo or a grayscale bitmap image (to create terrains, for example). The Displace gizmo can have one of four different shapes: Planar, Cylindrical, Spherical, or Shrink Wrap. Gizmos can be placed exterior to an object or inside an object to push it from the inside.

The Displace modifier parameters include Strength and Decay values. The Luminance Center value defines the center point for a grayscale bitmap. There are also buttons for Loading and Removing bitmaps and maps, and you can blur these objects with the Blur value. If a map is loaded, you can select and control its mapping coordinates. The final set of parameters lets you control the alignment of the bitmap or map. Figure 20-45 shows the effect of the Displace modifier on one side of a die.

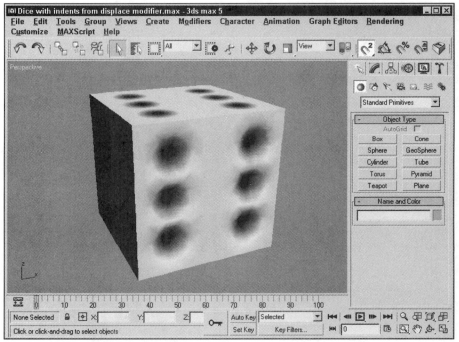

Figure 20-45: You can use the Displace modifier as a modeling tool to change the surface of an object.

Summary

We've covered a lot of ground in this chapter because there are a lot of different maps. Learning to use these maps will make a big difference in the realism of your materials.

In this chapter you've learned about

- ✦ The basics of mapping coordinates and tiling
- ✦ All the different map types in several different categories, including 2D, 3D, Compositors, Color Mods, and Reflection/Refraction
- ✦ The various mapping possibilities provided in the Maps rollout
- ✦ How to use the Bitmap Path Editor to change map paths
- ✦ Using mapping modifiers
- ✦ Controlling mapping coordinates with the Unwrap UVW modifier

In the next chapter, you'll gain some experience using the various materials and maps.

Cameras and Lights

Controlling Cameras

Do you remember as a kid when you first got your own camera? After taking the usual pictures of your dog and the neighbor's fence, you quickly learned how much fun you could have with camera placement such as a picture of a flagpole from the top of the flagpole or your mom's timeless expression when she found you inside the washing machine. Cameras in Max can also offer all kinds of amusing views of your scene.

The benefit of cameras is that you can position them anywhere within a scene to offer a custom view. You can open camera views in a viewport, and you can also use them to render images or animated sequences. Cameras in Max can also be animated (without damaging the camera, even if your mischievous older brother turns on the dryer).

Working with Cameras

If you're a photography hobbyist or like to take your video camera out and shoot your own footage, then many of the terms in this section will be familiar to you. The cameras used in Max to get custom views of a scene behave in many respects just like real-world cameras.

Max and real-world cameras both work with different lens settings, which are measured and defined in millimeters. You can select from a variety of preset stock lenses, including 35mm, 80mm, and even 200mm. Max cameras also offer complete control over the camera's focal length, field of view, and perspective for wide-angle or telephoto shots. The big difference is that you never have to worry about focusing a lens, setting flashes, or loading film.

Light coming into a camera is bent through the camera lens and focused on the film, where the image is captured. The distance between the film and the lens is known as the focal length. This distance is measured in millimeters, and you can change it by switching to a different lens. On a camera that shoots 35mm film, a lens with a focal length of 50mm produces a view similar to what your eyes would see. A lens with a focal length less than 50mm is known as a wide-angle lens because it displays a wider view of the scene. A lens longer than 50mm is called a telephoto lens because it has the ability to give a closer view of objects for more detail, as a telescope does.

Field of view is directly related to focal length and is a measurement of how much of the scene is visible. It is measured in degrees. The shorter the focal length, the wider the field of view.

When we look at a scene, objects appear larger if they are up close than they would lying at a farther distance. This effect is referred to as *perspective* and helps us to interpret distances. As mentioned, a 50mm lens gives a perspective similar to what our eyes give. Images taken with a wide field of view look distorted because the effect of perspective is increased.

Creating a Camera Object

To create a camera object, you'll need to open the familiar Create panel and click the Cameras category button. The two different types of cameras that you can create are a Free camera and a Target camera.

Camera objects are visible as icons in the viewports, but they aren't rendered. The camera icon looks like a box with a smaller box in front of it, which represents the lens or front end of the camera. Both the Free and Target camera types can include a cone that shows where the camera is pointing.

Free camera

The Free camera object offers a view of the area that is directly in front of the camera and is the better choice if the camera will be animated. When a Free camera is initially created, it points at the negative Z-axis of the active viewport. The single parameter for Free cameras defines a Target Distance — the distance to an invisible target about which the camera can orbit.

Target camera

A Target camera always points at a controllable target point some distance in front of the camera. Target cameras are easy to aim and are useful for situations where the camera won't move. To create this type of camera, click a viewport to position the camera and drag to the location of its target. The target can be named along with the camera. When a target is created, Max will automatically name the target by attaching ".target" on the end of the camera name. You can change this default name by typing a different name in the Name field.

Creating a Camera View

You can change any viewport to show a camera's viewpoint. To do so, right-click the viewport's title, and select View and the camera's name from the pop-up menu. Any movements done to the camera are reflected immediately in the viewport.

Another way to select a camera for a viewport is to press the C key. This keyboard shortcut makes the active viewport into a camera view. If several cameras exist in a scene, then the Select Camera dialog box appears, from which you can select a camera to use. Figure 21-1 shows two Target cameras pointing at a '57 Chevy. The two viewports on the right are the views from these cameras.

You can turn off the camera object icons using the Display panel. In the Display panel, under the Hide by Category rollout, select the Cameras option. When selected, the camera icons will not be visible in the viewports.

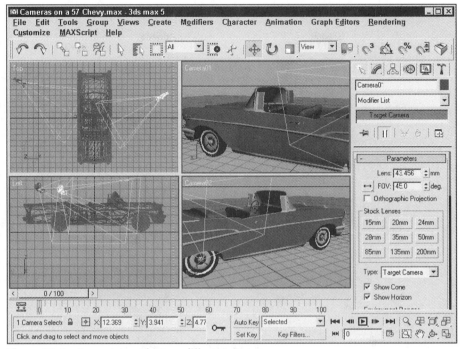

Figure 21-1: A car as seen by two different cameras

Note   Cameras are usually positioned at some distance away from the rest of the scene. Their distant position can make scene objects appear very small when the Zoom Extents button is used. If the visibility of the camera icons is turned off, the Zoom Extents will not include them in the zoom. You could also enable the Ignore Extents option in the camera's Object Properties dialog box.

Tutorial: Setting up an opponent's view

There is no limit to the number of cameras that you can place in a scene. Chapter 9, "Transforming Objects," shows an example of re-creating a chess game, in which one camera shows the board from one player's perspective. Creating another camera and moving the camera target will enable us to create a similar view from the opponent's perspective.

To create a new aligned view from the opponent's perspective, follow these steps:

1. Open the Chess game – Opponents View.max file from the Chapter 21 directory on the CD-ROM.

2. Open the Create panel, select the Cameras category, and click the Target Camera button. Drag in the Top viewport to create the camera. Then give the new camera the name **Black Camera**.

3. Position the new target camera behind the opponent's pieces roughly symmetrical to the other camera.

4. With the new camera selected, drag the target point and position it on top of the other camera's target point somewhere below the center of the board.

To see the new camera view, right-click the Perspective viewport title and choose View ➪ Black Camera (or select the camera and the Perspective viewport and press the C key). Figure 21-2 shows the view from this camera.

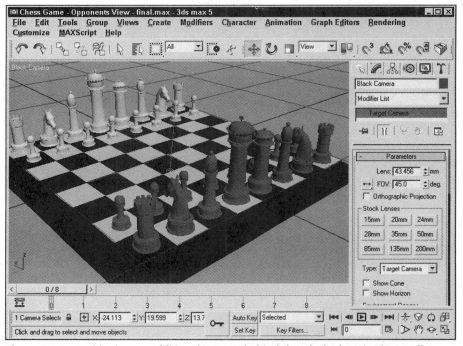

Figure 21-2: Positioning an additional camera behind the Black player's pieces offers the opponent's view.

Controlling a camera

I was once on a ride at Disneyland when a person behind me decided to blatantly disregard the signs not to take photographs. As he leaned over to snap another picture, I heard a fumbling noise, a faint, "Oh no," and then the distinct sound of his camera falling into the depths of the ride. (That was actually more enjoyable than the ride. It served him right.) As this example shows, controlling a camera can be difficult. This chapter offers many tips and tricks for dealing with the cameras in Max, and you won't have to worry about dropping them.

You control the camera view in a viewport by means of the Camera Navigation controls located in the lower-right corner of the screen. These controls replace the viewport controls when a camera view is selected and are different from the normal Viewport Navigation controls. The Camera Navigation controls are identified and defined in Table 21-1.

Note Many of these controls are identical to the controls for lights.

You can constrain the movements to a single axis by holding down the Shift key. The Ctrl key causes the movements to increase rapidly. For example, holding down the Ctrl key while dragging the Perspective tool magnifies the amount of perspective applied to the viewport.

You can undo changes in the normal viewports using the Views ⇨ Undo command, but you undo camera viewport changes with the regular Edit ⇨ Undo command.

Table 21-1: Camera Navigation Control Buttons

Control Button	Name	Description
	Dolly Camera, Dolly Target, Dolly Camera + Target	Moves the camera, its target, or both the camera and its target closer to or farther away from the scene in the direction it is pointing.
	Perspective	Increases or decreases the viewport's perspective by dollying the camera and altering its field of view.
	Roll Camera	Spins the camera about its local Z-axis.
	Zoom Extents All, Zoom Extents All Selected	Zooms in on all objects or the selected objects by reducing the field of view until they fill the viewport.
	Field of View	Changes the width of the view, similar to changing the camera lens or zooming without moving the camera.
	Truck Camera	Moves the camera perpendicular to the line of sight.
	Orbit, Pan Camera	The Orbit button rotates the camera around the target, and the Pan button rotates the target around the camera.
	Min/Max Toggle	Makes the current viewport fill the screen. Clicking this button a second time returns the display to several viewports.

Aiming a camera

In addition to the Camera Navigation buttons, you can use the Transformation buttons on the main toolbar to reposition the camera object. To move a camera, select the camera object, and click the Select and Move button (W). Then drag in the viewports to move the camera.

Using the Select and Rotate (E) button changes the direction in which a camera points, but only Free cameras will rotate in all directions. When applied to a Target camera, the rotate transformation only spins the camera about the axis pointing to the target. You aim Target cameras by moving their targets.

Note Don't try to rotate a Target camera so that it is pointing directly up or down, or the camera will flip.

Select the target for a Target camera by selecting its camera object, right-clicking to open the pop-up menu, and selecting Select Target.

Tutorial: Watching a rocket

Because cameras can be transformed like any other geometry, they can also be set to watch the movements of any other geometry. In this tutorial, we'll aim a camera at a distant rocket and watch it as it flies past us and on into the sky. Zygote Media created the rocket model used in this tutorial.

To aim a camera at a rocket as it hurtles into the sky, follow these steps:

1. Open the Following a rocket.max file from the Chap 21 directory on the CD-ROM.

   This file includes a rocket mesh and a camera.

2. Position the Target camera's target in the Left view about two-thirds of the way up along the rocket's path and to the right a distance. Set the Field of View value to 2.0 degrees. The corresponding Lens value is around 1031mm.

3. Click the Auto Key button (or press the N key) and position the camera's target on the rocket at its starting location. Then drag the Time slider to frame 100 and position the camera's target once again on top of the rocket at the top of the screen. Then, turn the Auto Key button off.

4. To view the scene from the camera's viewpoint, right-click the Perspective viewport title and choose Views ➪ Camera01 from the pop-up menu (or press the C button). Then click the Play Animation button to see how well the camera follows the target. If you need to, position the target on the rocket halfway through its motion at frame 50.

Figure 21-3 shows some frames from this animation.

Aligning cameras

 Another way to aim a camera is with the Tools ➪ Align Camera menu command or click on the Align Camera button on the main toolbar (under the Align flyout). After selecting this command, click an object face and hold down the mouse button; the normal to the object face that is currently under the cursor icon will be displayed as a blue arrow. When you've located the point at which you want the camera to point, release the mouse button. The camera will be repositioned to point directly at the selected point on the selected face along the normal.

 Cross-Reference The Align Camera command does the same thing for cameras that the Place Highlight command does for lights. I discuss the Place Highlight command in Chapter 22, "Working with Lights."

Cameras can be automatically positioned to match any view that a viewport can display, including lights and the Perspective view. To do this, select a camera, then activate the viewport with the view that you want to match, and choose Views ➪ Match Camera to View (Ctrl+C). The camera will be moved to display this view.

Caution If you use the Match Camera to View command while a camera view is the active viewport, the two cameras will be positioned on top of each other.

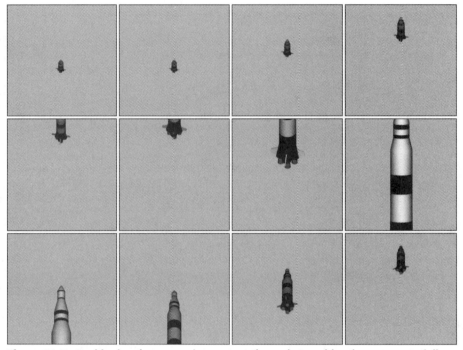

Figure 21-3: Positioning the camera's target on the rocket enables the camera to follow the rocket's ascent.

Tutorial: Seeing the snowman's good side

Using the Align Camera tool, you can place a camera so that it points directly at an item or the face of an object, such as the snowman's good side. To align a camera with an object point, follow these steps:

1. Open the Snowman.max from the Chap 21 directory on the CD-ROM.

    This file includes a snowman modeled from primitive objects.

2. Open the Create panel, select the Cameras category, and then click the Free button. Click in any viewport to create a new Free camera in the scene.

3. With the camera selected, choose Tools ➪ Align Camera, or click the Align Camera fly-out button on the main toolbar.

    The cursor changes to a small camera icon.

4. Click the cursor on the snowman's face just under its right eye.

    This point is where the camera will point.

5. To see the new camera view, right-click the viewport title and choose Views ➪ Camera01. Although the camera is pointing at the selected point, you may need to change the field of view to correct the zoom ratios.

Figure 21-4 shows our snowman from the newly aligned camera.

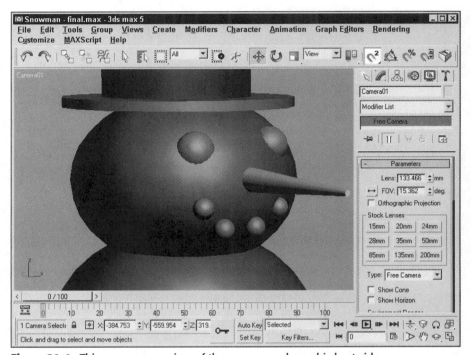

Figure 21-4: This new camera view of the snowman shows his best side.

The Align Camera command only points a camera at an object for the current frame. It will not follow an object if it moves during an animation. To have a camera follow an object, you need to use the Look At Controller, which I cover later in this chapter.

Setting Camera Parameters

When a camera is first created, you can modify the camera parameters directly in the Create panel as long as the new camera is selected. After the camera object has been deselected, you can make modifications in the Modify panel's Parameters rollout for the camera, shown in Figure 21-5.

Lens settings and field of view

The first parameter in the Parameters rollout sets the Lens value or more simply, the camera's focal length in millimeters.

The second parameter, FOV (which stands for field of view), sets the width of the area that the camera displays. The value is specified in degrees and can be set to represent a Horizontal, Vertical, or Diagonal distance using the flyout button to its left, as shown in the following table.

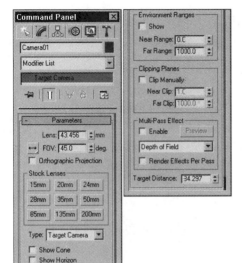

Figure 21-5: The Parameters rollout (shown in two parts) lets you specify Lens values or choose from a selection of stock lenses.

Button	Description
↔	Horizontal distance
↕	Vertical distance
↗	Diagonal distance

The Orthographic Projection option displays the camera view in a manner similar to any of the orthographic viewports such as Top, Left, or Front. This eliminates any perspective distortion of objects farther back in the scene and displays true dimensions for all edges in the scene.

Professional photographers and film crews use standard stock lenses in the course of their work. These lenses can be simulated in Max by clicking one of the Stock Lens buttons. Preset stock lenses include 15, 20, 24, 28, 35, 50, 85, 135, and 200mm lengths. The Lens and FOV fields will be automatically updated on stock lens selection.

Camera type and display options

The Type option enables you to change a Free camera to a Target camera and back at any time.

The Show Cone option enables you to display the camera's cone, showing the boundaries of the camera view when the camera isn't selected (the camera cone is always visible when a camera is selected). The Show Horizon option sets a horizon line within the camera view, which is a dark gray line where the horizon is located.

Environment ranges and clipping planes

You use the Near and Far Range values to specify the volume within which atmospheric effects like fog and volume lights are to be contained. The Show option causes these limits to be displayed as yellow rectangles within the camera's cone.

You use clipping planes to designate the closest and farthest object that the camera can see. In Max, they are displayed as red rectangles with crossing diagonals in the camera cone. The Clip Manually option lets you specify the Near Clip Plane to be something less than three units. Figure 21-6 shows a camera with Clipping Planes specified. The front Clipping Plane intersects the car and chops off its front end. The far Clipping Plane intersects the middle of the car and clips the back-end of the car as well as the construction grid.

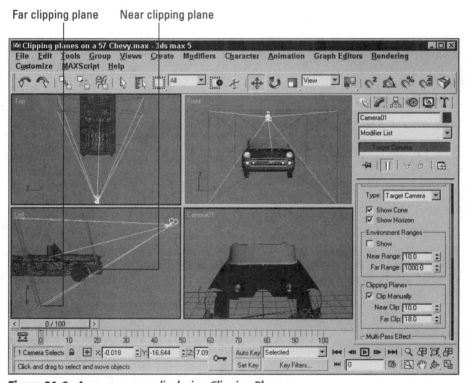

Figure 21-6: A camera cone displaying Clipping Planes

Multi-Pass effect

To create a depth of field or motion blur effect, you can use the Multi-Pass Effect settings in the Parameters rollout. These settings include an Enable switch for turning the effect on and off. Turning on this switch will create the effect by rendering the scene several times. Once enabled, the Preview button will become enabled.

Tip   The Preview button is worth its weight in render speed. Using this button, you can preview the effect without having to render the entire sequence.

You can also specify from a drop-down list either Depth of Field or Motion Blur. For each, an associated rollout of parameters opens. The Preview button makes the effect visible in the viewports. This feature can save you a significant amount of time that would normally be spent test-rendering the scene. The Render Effect Per Pass option causes any applied Render Effects to be applied at each pass. If disabled, then any applied Render Effects will be applied after the passes are completed.

Cross-Reference   You can also apply these multi-pass effects as Render Effects. See Chapter 36, "Using Render Elements and Render Effects."

The Depth of Field Parameters rollout, shown in Figure 21-7, includes settings for controlling the Depth of Field multi-pass effect. You can select to use the Target Distance or you can specify a separate Focal Depth distance.

Figure 21-7: Use the Depth of Field and Motion Blur parameters rollouts to set the number of passes.

Within this rollout, you also have the option to display each separate pass in the Virtual Frame Buffer with the Display Passes option and to use the camera's original location for the first rendering pass by enabling the Use Original Location option. The Total Passes is the number of times the scene is rendered to produce the effect, and the Sample Radius is the potential distance that the scene can move during the passes. By moving the scene about the radius value and re-rendering a pass, the object becomes blurred more away from the focal distance.

The Normalize Weights option allows you to control the dithering settings. This feature is helpful for avoiding streaking at the object edges. You can also disable filtering and anti-aliasing for quicker rendering times.

The Motion Blur rollout, also shown in Figure 21-7, also lets you specify the total number of passes to use to compute the motion blur effect. These passes can each have a specified Duration (measured in frames) and a Bias value, which weights the blurring toward the next frames (for higher values).

The Motion Blur rollout also includes options to Normalize Weights and to disable filtering and anti-aliasing.

Tutorial: Using a multi-pass effect camera

The motion blur effect only works on objects that are moving. Applying this effect to a stationary 2D shape will not produce any noticeable results. For this tutorial, you'll apply this effect to a speeding '57 Chevy model created by Viewpoint Datalabs.

To apply a motion blur multi-pass effect to the camera looking at a car mesh, follow these steps:

1. Open the motion blur on a 57 Chevy.max file from the Chap 21 directory on the CD-ROM.

   This file includes a car mesh, a camera, and a simple stop sign made of primitives. The car is animated.

2. Click the Select by Name button on the main toolbar to open the Select by Name dialog box (or press the H key). Double-click the Camera01 object to select it.

3. With the camera object selected, open the Modify panel. In the Multi-Pass Effect section of the Parameters rollout, click the Enable check box and select the Motion Blur effect from the drop-down list.

4. In the Motion Blur Parameters rollout, set the Total Passes to 10, the Sample Radius to 1.0, and the Sample Bias to 0.5. With the Perspective viewport active, click the Preview button in the Parameters rollout.

Figure 21-8 shows the results of the Motion Blur effect. This effect has been exaggerated to show its result. Notice how the stop sign isn't blurred. The only problem with this example is that with the Motion Blur effect enabled, you can't make out the license plate number, so you can't send this speeder a ticket.

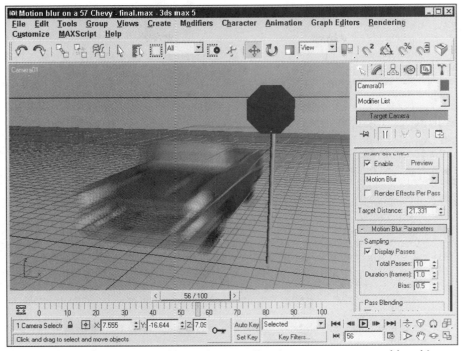

Figure 21-8: Using the motion blur multi-pass effect for a camera, you can blur objects moving in the scene.

Using the Camera Match and Camera Tracker Utilities

At times you'll want to integrate your rendered images with an existing background image or a background animation sequence. To do this, Max includes two unique utilities — Camera Match and Camera Tracker. The Camera Match utility can fit rendered scenes into an existing background image by matching the camera's position to the perspective of the image. The Camera Tracker utility can reproduce a camera's motion using an animated background.

Matching a camera to a background image

You use the Camera Match tool to align a camera's position to the background image. After you align the camera to the position that was used to take the image, you can place 3D objects within your scene and be assured that they will line up correctly with the objects within the image. For example, if you take a picture of a street scene and align the camera with the background image, then any cars or buildings that you digitally add to the scene will be correctly aligned.

You can find the Camera Match tool in the Utilities panel. Before you can use this tool, you need to load a bitmap image as a background. To do so, open the Environment dialog box by choosing Rendering ➪ Environment.

Chapter 35, "Working with Environments and Atmospheric Effects," provides more details on loading and working with environment maps.

After a bitmap image loads as an environment map, make the background visible in the viewport by choosing Views ⇨ Viewport Background (Alt+B) to open the Viewport Background dialog box. Here, you can specify a background source image or use the environment map you just loaded.

Setting Camera Match points

After a background image loads and is visible in the viewport, you need to create CamPoints in the scene. These CamPoints identify specific locations within the bitmap and help match them to scene dimensions. To create the CamPoints, open the Create panel, click the Helpers category button, and select the Camera Match subcategory.

The Camera Match utility needs to have at least five CamPoints defined before it can create a camera. You should position these CamPoints in the scene at precise coordinates that match the background image. For example, if the distance between two points is four feet, then create the CamPoints such that their distance is four units from each other. In the Keyboard Entry rollout, you can create new CamPoints by entering exact XYZ values.

To help keep the CamPoints straight, you can name each CamPoint by typing a name in the Name field. This helps when you try to identify each point in the Camera Match utility.

After positioning the CamPoints, open the Utility panel and click the Camera Match button. The CamPoint Info rollout, shown in Figure 21-9, includes a list of CamPoints. Each CamPoint needs to be assigned an XY position that matches its 3D location to a 2D position on the background bitmap. To assign these positions, click the Assign Position button, select a CamPoint from the list, and click the location in the viewport where this point should be positioned. You can also enter the X and Y coordinate values for the selected position in the X and Y fields in the CamPoint Info rollout.

As you line up the CamPoint positions, the bottom of the Camera Match rollout shows the current camera error. If the error value is greater than 5, the camera can't be created. The Use This Point option can disable a CamPoint without deleting it, which can help you pinpoint the CamPoint that is misaligned.

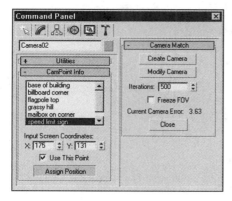

Figure 21-9: After the position of each CamPoint is identified, you can create a camera.

The Create Camera button creates a camera after all the CamPoints have been correctly positioned. The Modify Camera button lets you realign CamPoints and change the current camera position. The Iterations value determines the number of calculations required to position the camera; if your error values are too high, try reducing this number and creating the camera again. The Freeze FOV option prevents the FOV from changing as a camera is created.

Tutorial: Driving in Rome

The streets of Rome are narrow and intricate—maybe because they need to wind around all the ancient structures. In this tutorial, they provide a perfect opportunity to practice using the Camera Match utility.

To match a camera view to a background image, follow these steps:

1. Open the Rome – matched camera.max file from the Chap 21 directory on the CD-ROM.

   This file has the background image already loaded and visible in the viewport. This file also has the Porsche model created by Viewpoint Datalabs imported.

2. Now assign CamPoints throughout the scene. Open the Create panel, click the Helper category button, and then select the Camera Match subcategory. Click the CamPoint button, and click in the Perspective view six times to create six CamPoints. Then select the first CamPoint, and click the Select and Move button (W). Then open the Move Transform Type-In dialog box by choosing Tools ⇨ Transform Type-In (or by pressing the F12 key). Give the CamPoints the names and dimensions in the following list. Enter the dimensions in the Absolute column on the left.

   - Left base of pillar: X = 0, Y = 0, Z = 0
   - Right base of pillar: X = 10, Y = 0, Z = 0
   - Left edge of wall: X = –10, Y = 0, Z = 0
   - Right edge of wall: X = 20, Y = 0, Z = 0
   - Right end of structure: X = 0, Y = 20, Z = 0
   - Top of pillar: X = 0, Y = 0, Z = 30

Note   Although accurate measurements are better, these dimensions are relative approximations (because I didn't have time to fly to Rome with a tape measure).

3. After you position the six CamPoints, click the Camera Match button in the Utilities panel. In the CamPoint rollout is a list of the CamPoints that you've created. For each CamPoint in the list, click the Assign Position button, select the point, and click the background image where it is located. The following list has the exact dimensions that you can use to check your placement. When you're finished, click the Assign Position button again to exit position selection mode.

   - Left base of pillar: X = 279, Y = 324
   - Right base of pillar: X = 322, Y = 346
   - Left edge of wall: X = 236, Y = 306
   - Right edge of wall: X = 372, Y = 370
   - Right end of structure: X = 358, Y = 305
   - Top of pillar: X = 278, Y = 144

4. After you've positioned all CamPoints, click the Create Camera button. If the current camera error value is less than 5, a camera appears in the scene. You can update the CamPoint positions by clicking the Assign Position button, selecting a CamPoint from the list, and clicking the new location, or by changing the X and Y values. Click the Modify Camera button after moving the CamPoint's position to realign the camera.

Caution

If you get an error, the camera will not be created. The most likely error is that you have assigned a position to the wrong CamPoint. Check the positions of each CamPoint and try again.

5. With the camera positioned to match the background, you can position the car so that it is correctly aligned with the other cars in the image. Select the Porsche model, scale it down, and position it in the Camera viewport on the road. Turn off the construction grid by pressing the G key on the keyboard.

Figure 21-10 shows our current scene from the matched camera perspective.

Figure 21-10: The matched camera view with a car inserted into the scene

Using the Camera Tracker utility

The Camera Tracker utility recreates the movements of a camera that was used to create an animated background. As with the Camera Match utility, you access the Camera Tracker utility from the Utilities panel. Click the More button to open the Utilities dialog box and select it from the list of additional utilities.

Loading a movie file

One of the first tasks is to load a movie file to track. You can do so using the Movie File button (initially labeled "none") found in the Movie rollout, shown in Figure 21-11. This button opens the Browse Image for Input dialog box, where you can select a movie file to load. Usable formats include AVI, MOV, FLC, and IFL. After you select a movie file, the button's label changes to the name of the movie file. The Movie rollout also includes a Display Movie button to view a single frame of the movie. The Show Frame value lets you display a specific frame of the movie.

You can set the Deinterlace option to off, odd, or even and, if enabled, it de-interlaces a video file using odd or even lines. This feature enables you to view interlaced video segments whose individual frames include only odd or even lines. The Fade Display option fades the movie by 50 percent so you can clearly see the tracker gizmos. (See the next section for more about tracker gizmos.)

Figure 21-11: The Movie rollout lets you load and view a movie file.

The Movie rollout also includes buttons to Save, Save As, and Load camera tracker setting files, which are saved with the .MOT extension. The Auto Load/Save Setting option automatically saves these files in the same directory as the movie file; they are automatically updated anytime any of the settings change.

Working with trackers

The Camera Tracker utility uses CamPoints, just as the Camera Match utility does. CamPoints can be set up in the same manner discussed in the previous section. The Camera Tracker utility requires a minimum of six CamPoints and at least two that are in separate planes.

These CamPoints become the motion trackers for the utility. Motion trackers are points that are followed throughout the animation. These points are used to compute the camera's path. You display and control these trackers using the Motion Trackers rollout, shown in Figure 21-12. To add a tracker to the list, click the New Tracker button. This places the tracker gizmo in the list. You can change the parameters for the gizmo and move the gizmo as needed.

The Scene Object button lets you select a CamPoint or some other object as the object to track. You can also specify values for Match Weights and Max Move per Frame. The higher the Match Weights value, the more consistent the track points will be in the scene.

The Set Start and Set Stop buttons let you set the frames at which the tracking starts and stops. If a tracking object moves out of the scene, click the Set Stop button at the frame where it disappears.

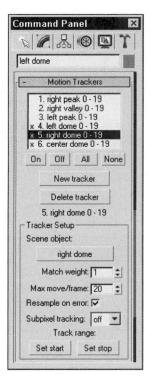

Figure 21-12: The Motion Trackers rollout lets you add trackers to the scene.

Using the tracker gizmo

The tracker gizmo looks like a box within a box. The crosshairs mark the center of the tracking object, the inner box (called the Feature Selection box) marks the edges of the tracking object, and the outer box (called the Motion Search box) determines the search area in which the tracker gizmo looks for the object in each frame. Figure 21-13 shows the tracker gizmo.

Stepping through frames

You use the Movie Stepper rollout, shown in Figure 21-14, to step through the animation frames. This feature is useful for ensuring that the tracking objects are visible throughout the entire animation. You can also use this rollout to manually set the tracking.

The Movie Frame spinner displays the current frame. The buttons under the frame number let you move forward or backward through the frames. These buttons can move to the beginning frame, back 10 frames, back one frame, forward one frame, forward 10 frames, or to the last frame.

The Feature tracking button, when enabled, computes the tracking locations; the tracker gizmos move to their tracked positions if the positions have already been tracked. The Step Keyframes option lets you move between keyframes instead of frames using the stepping buttons. The Show Track option displays the path traveled by each tracker as a line.

Motion Search box

Feature Selection box

Center of gizmo

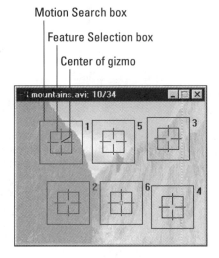

Figure 21-13: You use the tracker gizmo to track objects through several frames.

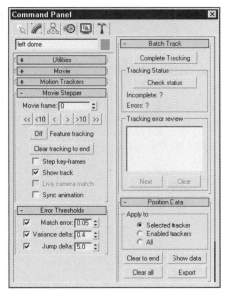

Figure 21-14: The Movie Stepper rollout lets you step through the movie frames, and the Batch Track rollout lets you initiate the tracking process.

Note   Red track lines indicate that the tracker has been tracked. White track lines are trackers that haven't been tracked.

The Live Camera Match option moves the camera as you reposition the tracker gizmos. The Sync Animation option causes the Time slider and the viewports to update along with the Movie Stepper buttons.

Caution   Be aware that updating the viewports with the Sync Animation option can slow down the system substantially.

The Error Threshold rollout, also shown in Figure 21-14, lets you set the maximum allowable error values for Match Error, Variance Delta, and Jump Delta. Match Error measures the differences in the current frame to the best match. The Variance Delta is a measure of the difference in color between the target and the match, and the Jump Delta will look at the distance the tracker has moved in the current frame compared to the last five frames. If the tracking exceeds these values, an error appears in the Tracking Error Review list in the Batch Track rollout.

Automating the tracking process

After the parameters have been set up, you can use the Complete Tracking button in the Batch Track rollout, also shown in Figure 21-14, to start the tracking process. As tracking proceeds, any errors are captured and displayed in the Tracking Error Review list. After reviewing the errors, go to the Movie Stepper rollout to correct them, and run the tracking process again. This iterative process produces the best results.

The Complete Tracking button initiates the tracking process. This process tracks only those frames that haven't been tracked yet. The Check Status button checks for errors and for any frames that haven't been tracked. Any errors are displayed in the Tracking Error Review list, and the tracks that haven't been completed are displayed next to the Incomplete label.

Note   Each error listed displays the tracker number, the frame number, an error code, and the threshold value. Possible error codes include "me" for match error, "vd" for color variance error, and "jd" for jump error.

The Next button moves to the next error in the list, and the Clear button removes an error from the list.

The Position Data rollout, also shown in Figure 21-14, lets you clear, show, or export the tracking data for the selected tracker, the enabled trackers, or all trackers. The Show Data button opens the data in a text window, shown in Figure 21-15. You can save exported data as an Excel spreadsheet in the .CSV format or as text with the .DAT extension.

```
Untitled - MAXScript                                    _ □ ×
File   Edit   Search   Help

Tracker 5
Tracking object $'right dome'
Frame, Position x, y, Key Feature left, top, right, bot, Search l, t, r, b
0, 133.0, 100.0, 118.0, 85.0, 148.0, 115.0, 103.0, 70.0, 163.0, 130.0
1, 133.0, 100.0
2, 131.0, 101.0
3, 131.0, 101.0
4, 131.0, 101.0
5, 131.0, 101.0
6, 130.0, 102.0
7, 130.0, 102.0
8, 129.0, 102.0
9, 127.0, 103.0
10, 127.0, 103.0
11, 127.0, 103.0
```

Figure 21-15: The Show Data button in the Position Data rollout displays the tracking data in a text window.

Matching the camera

After all the tracking positions have been established, you need to select a camera to match the tracking data. In the Match Move rollout, shown in Figure 21-16, is a Camera button (initially labeled "none"). Click this button to select the camera to use.

Note   The camera specified in the Match Move rollout must be a Free camera.

While matching the camera, you can specify which camera parameters to include in the process. Options include FOV, Pan, Tilt, Roll, Dolly, Truck H (horizontal), and Truck V (vertical). You can also specify the Movie Start and Animation Start frames, as well as the Frame Count. The Reset Ranges button resets the Movie Start, Animation Start, and Frame Count values to their defaults.

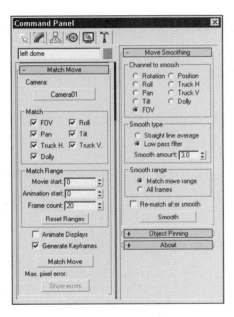

Figure 21-16: The Match Move and Move Smoothing rollouts let you select a camera to match to the tracking data and smooth the camera's motion.

The Animate Displays option updates the viewport frame by frame with the camera match. The Generate Keyframes option creates keys for each frame of the match. When you're all ready, the Match Move button starts the Match Move process. The Maximum Pixel Error displays the tracking error for each frame. To view all the error values in a text window, click the Show Errors button.

Smoothing the camera motion

After the camera is matched to the tracking data, its motion might be a little erratic and bumpy. You can smooth its motion using the Move Smoothing rollout, also shown in Figure 21-16. This rollout lets you select which options to include in the smoothing calculations: Rotation, Position, Roll, Pan, Tilt, FOV, Dolly, Truck Horizontal, or Truck Vertical.

The two smooth types that you can choose from are Straight Line Average and Low Pass Filter with a Smooth Amount. You can also smooth just the Match Move Range or All Frames. With the options set, click the Smooth button to initiate the smoothing calculations.

Pinning objects

After the tracked data is captured, you can select an object to follow the path that is positioned in front of the camera. This technique is called *pinning*. In the Object Pinning rollout, shown in Figure 21-17, select a tracker from the drop-down list and click the Object to Pin button. Then select the object to pin in the viewport. You can also set a Pin Range, the Pin Space (Screen or Grid), and Pin Mode (Absolute or Relative). To complete the pinning, click the Pin button.

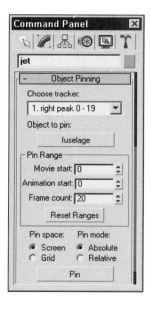

Figure 21-17: Use the Object Pinning rollout to position an object in front of the camera path.

Summary

Cameras can offer a unique look at your scene. You can position and move them anywhere. In this chapter, you discovered how cameras work and how to control and aim them at objects.

The Camera Match and Camera Tracker utilities enable you to match your scene's position and motion to a background image or animation. These features can be very helpful in creating realistic images and animations.

In this chapter, you've

✦ Learned the basics of cameras

✦ Created a camera object and view

✦ Discovered how to control a camera

✦ Aimed a camera at objects

✦ Changed camera parameters and used multi-pass camera effects

✦ Learned to use the Camera Match utility to match a camera to a background image

✦ Controlled a camera's position using the Camera Tracker utility

Although the director will typically say, "Lights, camera, action," we've switched the order to be cameras and then lights (action comes with animation later in the book) and we just finished cameras, so next we'll be moving on to lights.

Working with Lights

Lights play an important part in the visual process. Have you ever looked at a blank page and been told it was a picture of a polar bear in a snow blizzard or looked at a completely black image and been told it was a rendering of a black spider crawling down a chimney covered in soot? The point of these two examples is that with too much or too little light, you really can't see anything.

Light in the 3D world figures into every rendering calculation, and 3D artists often struggle with the same problem of too much or too little light. This chapter covers creating and controlling lights in your scene.

Understanding the Basics of Lighting

Lighting plays a critical part of any Max scene. Understanding the basics of lighting can make a big difference in the overall feeling and mood of your rendered scenes. Most Max scenes typically use one of two types of lighting: natural light or artificial light. Natural light is used for outside scenes and uses the sun and moon for its light source. Artificial light is usually reserved for indoor scenes where light bulbs provide the light. However, when working with lights, there will be cases where natural light is used indoors, such as sunlight streaming through a window, or where artificial light is used outdoors, such as a streetlight.

Natural and artificial light

Natural light is best created using lights that have parallel light rays coming from a single direction — you can create this type of light using a Direct Light. The intensity of natural light is also dependent on the time, date, and location of the sun — you can control this intensity precisely using Max's Sunlight or Daylight systems.

The weather can also make a difference in the light color. In clear weather, the color of sunlight is pale yellow; in clouds, sunlight has a blue tint; and in dark, stormy weather, sunlight is dark gray. The colors of light at sunrise and sunset are more orange and red. Moonlight is typically white.

Artificial light is typically produced with multiple lights of lower intensity. The Omni light is usually a good choice for indoor lighting because it casts light rays in all directions from a single source. Standard white fluorescent lights usually have a light green or light blue tint.

A standard lighting method

When lighting a scene, not relying on a single light is best. A good lighting method includes one key light and several secondary lights.

A spotlight is good to use for the main key light. It should be positioned in front of and slightly above the subject, and it should usually be set to cast shadows, because it will be the main shadow-casting light in the scene.

The secondary lights fill in the lighting gaps and holes. You can position these at floor level on either side of the subject, with the intensity set at considerably less than the key light, and set to cast no shadows. You can place one additional light behind the scene to backlight the subjects. This light should be very dim and also cast no shadows. From the user's perspective, all the objects in the scene will be illuminated, but the casual user will identify only the main spotlight as the light source, because it casts shadows.

Figure 22-1 shows the position of the lights that are included in the standard lighting model using a key light, two secondary lights, and a backlight. This model works for most standard scenes, but if you want to highlight a specific object, additional lights will be needed.

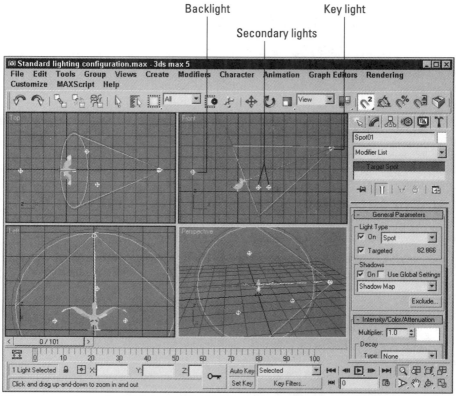

Figure 22-1: A standard lighting model includes a key light, two secondary lights, and a backlight.

Figure 22-2 shows a pelican model that is rendered using different levels of the standard lighting model. The left image uses the default lighting with no lights, the second image uses only the key light, the third image adds a backlight, and the final two images add the two secondary lights.

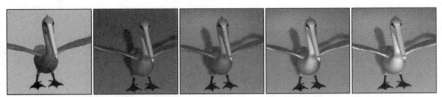

Figure 22-2: An image rendered using (from left to right) the default lights, a single key light, plus a backlight, plus one and then two secondary lights

The final type of light to keep in mind is ambient light. Ambient light is not from a direct source but is created by light that is deflected off walls and objects. It provides overall lighting to the entire scene and keeps shadows from becoming completely black. Global Lighting (including Ambient light) is set in the Environment panel.

Shadows

Shadows are the areas behind an object where the light is obscured. Max supports two types of shadows: shadow maps and raytraced shadows. Shadow maps are actual bitmaps that the renderer produces and combines with the finished scene to produce an image. These maps can have different resolutions, but higher resolutions require more memory. Shadow maps typically create more realistic, softer shadows.

Max calculates raytraced shadows by following the path of every light ray striking a scene. This process takes a significant amount of processing cycles but can produce very accurate, hard-edged shadows. Raytracing enables you to create shadows for objects that shadow maps can't, such as transparent glass.

Cross-Reference   You can learn more about raytracing in Chapter 37, "Raytracing."

Figure 22-3 shows several images rendered with the different shadow types. The image in the upper left includes no shadows. The upper-right image uses a shadow map set to a Size of 512. The lower-left image uses a shadow map set to a Size of 4096, and the lower-right image uses raytraced shadows. The last two images took considerably longer to create. Viewpoint Datalabs created the pelican model shown in this figure.

Figure 22-3: Images rendered with different shadow types, including no shadow (upper left), a 512 shadow map (upper right), a 4096 shadow map (lower left), and raytraced shadows (lower right)

Getting to Know the Light Types

Max includes several different types of lights. The main difference in these types is how the light rays are cast into the scene. Light can come from the default lights that are present when no other lights have been added to the scene. Light can also come from ambient light, which is light that bounces off other objects. Max also includes Omni, Direct, Spot, and sky-lights, each having its own characteristics. Understanding these sources of light will help you to know where to look to control the lighting.

Default lighting

So, you get Max installed, and you eagerly start the application, throw some objects in a scene, and render it . . . and you'll be disappointed in the output, because you forgot to put lights in the scene. Right? Wrong! Max is smart enough to place default lighting in the scene that does not have any light.

The default lighting disappears as soon as a light is created in a scene (even if the light is turned off). When all the lights in a scene are deleted, default lighting magically reappears. So you can always be sure that your objects will be rendered using some sort of lighting. Default lighting actually consists of two lights — the first light is positioned above and to the left, and the bottom light is positioned below and to the right.

The Viewport Configuration dialog box has an option to enable default lighting for any viewport or set the default lighting to use only one light. You can open this dialog box by choosing Customize ➪ Viewport Configuration or by right-clicking the viewport title and selecting Configuration from the pop-up menu.

If you want to access the default lights in your scene, you can use the Views ➪ Add Default Lights to Scene command to convert the default lights into actual light objects that you can control and reposition.

Ambient light

Ambient light is general lighting that uniformly illuminates the entire scene. It is caused by light that bounces off other objects. Using the Environment dialog box, you can set the ambient light color. You can also set the default ambient light color in the Rendering panel of the Preference Settings dialog box. This color is the darkest color that can appear in the scene, generally in the shadows.

In addition to these global ambient settings, each material can have an ambient color selected in the Material Editor.

Caution

Don't rely on ambient light to fill in unlit sections of your scene. If you use a heavy dose of ambient light instead of placing secondary lights, your scene objects will appear flat, and you won't get the needed contrast to make your objects stand out.

Omni light

The Omni light is like a light bulb—it casts light rays in all directions. The two default lights are Omni lights.

Spot light

Spot lights are directional—they can be pointed and sized. The two different spot lights available in Max are a Target Spot and a Free Spot. A Target Spot light consists of a light object and a target marker at which the spot light points. A Free Spot light has no target, which enables it to be rotated in any direction using the Select and Rotate transform button. Spot lights always are displayed in the viewport as a cone with the light positioned at the cone apex.

Cross-Reference

Both Target Spot and Target Direct lights are very similar in functionality to the Target Camera object, which you learn about in Chapter 21, "Controlling Cameras."

Direct light

Direct lights cast parallel light rays in a single direction, like the sun. Just like spotlights, direct lights come in two types: a Target Direct light and a Free Direct light. The position of the Target Direct light always points toward the target, which you can move within the scene using the Select and Move button. A Free Direct light can be rotated to determine where it points. Direct lights are always displayed in the viewport as cylinders.

Skylight

The Skylight light is like a controllable ambient light. You can move it about the scene just like the other lights and you can select to use the Scene Environment settings or select a Sky Color.

Cross-Reference Max also includes a separate class of lights called Photometric lights. For more on these lights, see in Chapter 23, "Advanced Lighting and Radiosity."

Creating and Positioning Light Objects

Max, in its default setup, can create many different types of light. Each of them has different properties and features. To create a light, just open the Create panel and click the Lights category button. Then click the button for the type of light you want to create and drag in a viewport to create it. The six standard light types are Target Spot, Target Direct, Omni, Free Spot, Free Direct, and Skylight. Omni, Skylight, and Free lights are created with a single click, but you create Target lights by clicking at the light's position and dragging to the position of the target. Spot lights are identified by a cone and direct lights are identified by a cylinder shape.

Transforming lights

Lights can be transformed just like other geometric objects; however, not all transformations are available for all the light types. An Omni light, for example, cannot be scaled, and rotating an Omni light has no effect on the scene. To transform a light, click one of the transformation buttons and select and drag the light.

Target lights can have the light and the target transformed independently, or you can select both the light and target by clicking the line that connects them. Target lights can be rotated and scaled only if the light and target are selected together. Scaling a Target light increases its cone or cylinder. Scaling a Target Direct light with only the light selected increases the diameter of the light's beam, but if the light and target are selected, then the diameter and distance are scaled.

An easy way to select or de-select the target is to right-click the light and select Select Target from the pop-up menu. All transformations work on free lights.

Listing lights

The Tools ➪ Light Lister menu command opens the Light Lister dialog box, shown in Figure 22-4, where you can see at a quick glance all the details for all the lights in the scene. This dialog box also lets you change the light settings. It includes two rollouts — Configuration, which lets you select to see All Lights, the Selected Lights, or the General Settings that apply to all lights.

If the General Settings option is selected, then a separate rollout opens with all the typical settings including Multiplier, Color, Shadows, Map Size, and so on. You can apply these changes to all the Selected Lights or to All Lights. The Light Lister provides an easy way to change the parameters of many lights at once.

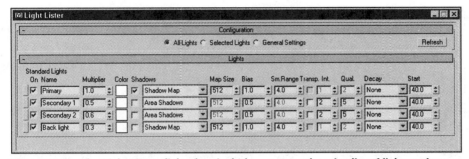

Figure 22-4: The Light Lister dialog box includes a comprehensive list of light settings in one place.

If the All Lights or the Selected Lights options are selected, then the parameters are listed in the Lights rollout. Using this rollout, you can change the settings for any of the listed lights that affect all lights, and Lights, which holds details on each individual light. The Refresh button updates the Light Lister dialog box if a new light has been added to the scene or if any parameters have been altered in the Modify panel.

Placing highlights

The Place Highlight (Ctrl+H) feature enables you to control the position and orientation of a light in order to achieve a highlight in a precise location. To use this feature, you must select a light object in the scene and then choose Tools ➪ Place Highlight or click the Place Highlight flyout button on the toolbar. The cursor will change to the Place Highlight icon. Click a point on the object in the scene where you want the highlight to be positioned, and the selected light will reposition itself to create a specular highlight at the exact location where you clicked. The light's position is determined by the Angle of Incidence between the highlight point and the light.

Tutorial: Lighting the snowman's face

You can use the Place Highlight feature to position a light for our snowman. To place a highlight, follow these steps:

1. Open the Snowman.max file from the Chap 22 directory on the CD-ROM.

   This file contains a simple snowman created using primitive objects.

2. Open the Create panel and select the Lights category; then click the Omni button and position it below and to the left of the Snowman model.

3. To place the highlight so it shows the Snowman's face, select the Omni light and then choose Tools ➪ Place Highlight (or press Ctrl+H). Then click the Snowman's face where the highlight should be located, right above his right eye.

Figure 22-5 shows the results.

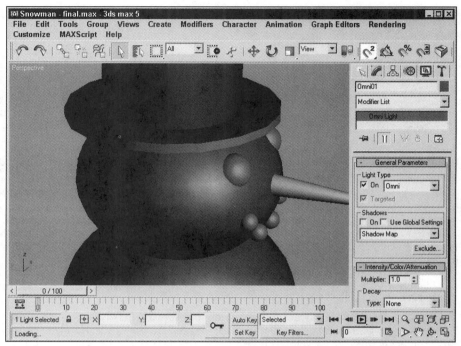

Figure 22-5: The snowman, after the lights have been automatically repositioned using the Place Highlights command

The effect of lights cannot be fully seen in the viewport. To see the rendered result of a light, render the scene or view the scene in the ActiveShade window. You can open the ActiveShade window with the Rendering ⟿ ActiveShade Floater menu command.

Viewing a Scene from a Light

You can configure viewports to display the view from any light, with the exception of an Omni light. To do so, right-click the viewport title and select Views and the light name at the top of the pop-up menu.

The keyboard shortcut for making the active viewport a Light view is the $ (the dollar sign that appears above the 4) key. If more than one light exists, then the Select Light dialog box appears and lets you select which light to use. This can only be used on spot and direct lights.

Light viewport controls

When a viewport is changed to show a light view, the Viewport Navigation buttons in the lower-right corner of the screen change into Light Navigation controls. Table 22-1 describes these controls.

Note   Many of these controls are identical for viewports displaying lights or cameras.

Table 22-1: Light Navigation Control Buttons

Toolbar Button	Name	Description
	Dolly, Target, Both	Moves the light, its target, or both the light and its target closer to or farther away from the scene in the direction it is pointing.
	Light Hotspot	Adjusts the angle of the light's hotspot, which is displayed as a blue cone.
	Roll Light	Spins the light about its local Z-axis.
	Zoom Extents All, Zoom Extents All Selected	Zooms in on all objects or the selected objects until they fill the viewport.
	Light Falloff	Changes the angle of the light's falloff cone.
	Truck Light	Moves the light perpendicular to the line of sight.
	Orbit, Pan Light	The Orbit button rotates the light around the target, whereas the Pan Light button rotates the target around the light.
	Full Screen Toggle	Makes the current viewport fill the screen. Clicking this button a second time returns the display to several viewports.

If you hold down the Ctrl key while using the Light Hotspot or Falloff buttons, Max maintains the distance between the hotspot and falloff cones. The Hotspot cone cannot grow any larger than the Falloff cone.

You can constrain any light movements to a single axis by holding down the Shift key. The Ctrl key causes the movements to increase rapidly.

For Free lights, an invisible target is determined by the distance computed from the other light properties. You can use the Shift key to constrain rotations to be vertical or horizontal.

Note   You can undo changes in the normal viewports using the Views ➪ Undo command, but you undo light viewport changes with the regular Edit ➪ Undo command.

Tutorial: Lighting a lamp

To practice using lights, let's try to get a lamp model to work as it should.

To add a light to a lamp model, follow these steps:

1. Open the Lamp.max from the Chap 22 directory on the CD-ROM.

   This file includes a lamp mesh surrounded by some plane objects used to create the walls and floor. The lamp model was created by Zygote Media. It looks like a standard living room lamp that you could buy in any department store.

2. Create an Omni light by opening the Create panel and clicking the Lights category. Click the Omni button and click again in any viewport.

3. Use the Select and Move transform button (W) to position the light object inside the lamp's light bulb.

The resulting image is shown in Figure 22-6. Notice how the light intensity is greater at places closer to the light.

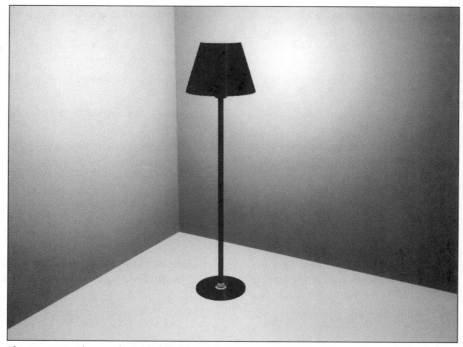

Figure 22-6: The rendered lighted-lamp image

Altering Light Parameters

Lights affect every object in a scene and can really make or break a rendered image, so it shouldn't be surprising that each light comes with many controls and parameters. Several different rollouts work with lights, as shown in Figure 22-7.

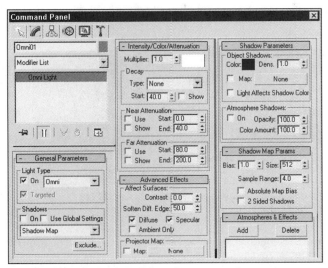

Figure 22-7: The various light rollouts control parameters and shadows.

General parameters

If you're looking for a light switch to turn lights on and off, look no further than the Modify panel. When a light is selected, the General Parameters rollout appears. The options contained in this rollout enable you to turn the lights on and off, select a light color and intensity, and determine how a light affects object surfaces.

The Type drop-down list lets you change the type of light instantly, so that you can switch from Omni light to Spot light without a lot of work. You can also switch between targeted and untargeted lights. To the right of the Targeted option is the distance in scene units between the light and the target. This feature provides an easy way to look at the results of using a different type of light. When you change the type of light, you lose the settings for the previous light.

The General Parameters rollout also includes some settings for shadows. Shadows can be easily turned on or off. In this rollout, you can defer to the global settings by selecting the Use Global Settings option. This option helps to maintain consistent settings across several lights. It applies the same settings to all lights, so that changing the value for one light changes that same value for all lights that have this option selected.

You can also select from a drop-down list whether the shadows are created using Area Shadows, a Shadow Map, regular, or advanced raytraced shadows. A new rollout will appear depending on the selection that you make. Figure 22-8 shows each of the available shadow types. On the left is an Area Shadow, which has the lowest resolution; the middle image shows a Shadow Map, which is better, but still fuzzy. The right image uses a raytraced shadow and has the highest resolution.

 The Area Shadows and advanced raytraced shadows are both new with 3ds max 5.

Figure 22-8: The Exclude/Include dialog box lets you set which objects are excluded or included from being illuminated.

The Exclude button opens the Exclude/Include dialog box, where you can select objects to be included or excluded from illumination and/or shadows. The pane on the left includes a list of all the current objects in the scene. To exclude objects from being lit, select the Exclude option, select the objects to be excluded from the pane on the left, and click the double arrow icon pointing to the right to move the objects to the pane on the right.

Figure 22-9 shows the Exclude/Include dialog box. This dialog box also recognizes any Selection Sets you've previously defined. You select them from the Selection Sets drop-down list.

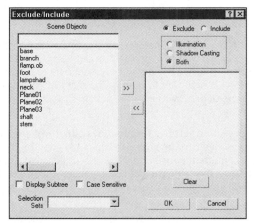

Figure 22-9: The Exclude/Include dialog box lets you set which objects are excluded or included from being illuminated.

The Intensity/Color/Attenuation rollout

In the Intensity/Color/Attenuation rollout, the Multiplier value controls the light intensity. A light with a Multiplier set to 2 will be twice as bright as a light with its Multiplier set to 1.

Note   Higher Multiplier values make a light appear white regardless of the light color.

To the right of the Multiplier value is a color swatch. Clicking the color swatch opens a color selector where you can choose a new light color.

Attenuation is a property that determines how light fades over distance. An example of this is a candle set in a room. The farther you get from the candle, the less the light shines.

You use three basic parameters to simulate realistic attenuation. Near Attenuation sets the distance at which the light begins to fade, and Far Attenuation sets the distance at which the light falls to 0. Both these properties are ranges that include Start and End values. The third parameter sets the Decay value—which simulates attenuation using a mathematical formula to compute the drop in light intensity over time.

Selecting the Use option enables the Near and Far Attenuation values—each has a Start and End value that sets the range for this attenuation type. The Show option makes the attenuation distances and decay values visible in the viewports. The three types of decay from which you can choose are None, Inverse, and Inverse Square. The Inverse type decays linearly with the distance away from the light. The Inverse Square type decays exponentially with distance.

Note   The Inverse Square type approximates real lights the best, but it is often too dim for computer graphic images. You can compensate for this by increasing the Multiplier value.

Spot and directional light parameters

The Spotlight Parameters rollout includes values to set the angular distance of both the Hot Spot and Falloff cones. The Show Cone option makes the Hotspot and Falloff cones visible in the viewport when the light is not selected. The Overshoot option makes the light shine in all directions like an Omni light, but projections and shadows only occur within the Falloff cone. You can also set the light shape to be circular or rectangular. For a rectangular-shaped spotlight, you can control the aspect ratio. You can use the Bitmap Fit button to make the aspect ratio match a particular bitmap.

The Directional Light Parameters rollout, which appears for Direct light types, is identical to the Spotlight Parameters rollout and also includes settings for the Hot Spot and Falloff values.

Advanced Effects

Options in the Affect Surface section of the Advanced Effects rollout control how light interacts with an object's surface. The Contrast value alters the contrast between the diffuse and the ambient surface areas. The Soften Diffuse Edge value blurs the edges between the diffuse and ambient areas of a surface. The Diffuse and Specular options let you disable these properties of an object's surface. When the Ambient Only option is turned on, the light affects only the ambient properties of the surface.

Cross-Reference   Find more detail on the Diffuse, Specular, and Ambient properties in Chapter 18, "Exploring the Material Editor."

You can use any light as a projector; you find this option in the Advance Effects rollouts. Selecting the Map option enables you to use the light as a projector. You can select a map to project by clicking the button to the right of the map option. You can drag a material map directly from the Material/Map Browser onto the Projector Map button.

Shadow parameters

All light types have a Shadow Parameters rollout that you can use to select a shadow color by clicking the color swatch. The default color is black. The Dens setting stands for "Density" and controls how dark the shadow appears. Lower values produce light shadows, and higher values produce dark shadows. This value can also be negative.

The Map option, like the Projection Map, can be used to project a map along with the shadow color. The Light Affects Shadow Color option alters the Shadow Color by blending it with the light color if selected.

In the Atmosphere Shadows section, the On button lets you determine whether atmospheric effects, such as fog, can cast shadows. You can also control the Opacity and the degree to which atmospheric colors blend with the Shadow Color.

When you select a light and open the Modify panel, one additional rollout is available — the Atmospheres and Effects rollout. This rollout is a shortcut to the Environment dialog box, where you can specify atmospheric effects such as fog and volume lights.

Chapter 35, "Working with Environments and Atmospheric Effects," covers atmospheric effects.

If the Area Shadows option is selected in the General Parameters rollout, then the Area Shadows rollout will appear, which includes several settings for controlling this shadow type. In the drop-down list at the top of the rollout, you can select from several Basic Options including Simple, Rectangle Light, Disc Light, Box Light, and Sphere Light. You can select dimensions depending on which option is selected. You can also set the Integrity, Quality, Spread, Bias, and Jitter amounts.

For the Shadow Map option, the Shadow Map rollout includes values for the Bias, Size, and Sample Range. You can also select to use an Absolute Map Bias and 2 Sided Shadows.

If the Ray Traced Shadows option is selected in the Shadow Parameters rollout, the Ray Traced Shadows Parameters rollout appears below it. This simple rollout includes only two values: Bias and Max Quadtree Depth. The Bias settings cause the shadow to move toward or away from the object that casts the shadow. The Max Quadtree Depth determines the accuracy of the shadows by controlling how long the ray paths are followed. There is also an option to enable 2 Sided Shadows.

For the Advanced Raytraced Shadows options, the rollout includes many more options including Simple, 1-Pass, or 2-Pass Anti-aliasing. This rollout also includes the same quality values found in the Area Shadows rollout.

Depending on the number of objects in your scene, shadows can take a long time to render. Enabling raytraced shadows for a complex scene can greatly increase the render time.

Optimizing lights

If you select either the Area Shadows or the Advanced Raytracing Shadows types, then a separate Optimizations rollout appears. This rollout includes settings that help speed up the shadow rendering process. Using this rollout, you can enable Transparent Shadows. You can also specify a color that is used at the Anti-aliasing Threshold. You can also turn off anti-aliasing for materials that have SuperSampling or Reflection/Refraction enabled. Or you can have the shadow renderer skip coplanar faces with a given threshold.

Manipulating Hotspot and Falloff cones

When the Select and Manipulate mode is enabled in the main toolbar, the end of the Hotspot and Falloff cones appear green for a selected spot light. When you move the mouse over these lines, the lines turn red, allowing you to drag the lines and make the Hotspot and/or Falloff angle values greater. These manipulators provide visual feedback as you resize the spot light cone.

Tutorial: Creating twinkling stars

Surely there is some poetry somewhere that speaks of dotting the sky with stars. In this tutorial, I'll be showing you how to do just that using a view full of Omni lights positioned close to a Plane object.

You can also create star fields using the Video Post dialog box, as shown in Chapter 39, "Post-Processing with the Video Post Interface."

To create a background of controllable stars, follow these steps:

1. Open the Create panel and select the Lights category. Then click the Omni button and click in the Top viewport to create about 30 to 50 lights.

   Each light will be a separate star.

2. Next, click the Geometry category and click the Plane button. Then drag in the Top view to create a simple plane object. The size of the plane doesn't matter, but the Scale Multiplier should be set to 50. Change the Object Color swatch for the plane object to dark blue.

3. With the Select and Move button, select the Plane object and right-click the Select and Move button to access the Move Transform Type-In dialog box (F12). In this dialog box, enter **–1.0** in the Z-axis field.

   This step moves the Plane object barely underneath all the Omni lights.

4. Click the Select by Name button on the main toolbar (or press the H key), and in the Select Objects dialog box, select all the Omni lights. Then open the Modify panel and click the Noise button. This applies the Noise Modifier to all the lights. In the Strength field for the Z-axis, enter **5** and select the Animate Noise option with a Frequency of 1.0.

5. When you render the animation, set the render viewport to the Top view.

Although a black-and-white figure doesn't really do the rendered image justice, Figure 22-10 shows the scene set up in Max.

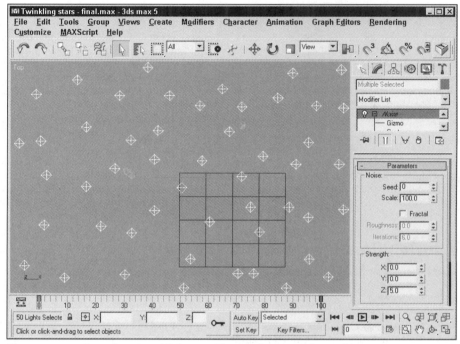

Figure 22-10: Countless Omni lights positioned close to a Plane object can create a realistic star field with animated twinkling stars.

Using the Sunlight and Daylight Systems

The Sunlight and Daylight systems, accessed through the Systems category of the Create panel, create a light that simulates the sun for a specific geographic location, date, time, and compass direction.

To create either of these systems, open the Create panel and click the Systems category button. Then click the Sunlight (or Daylight) button and drag the mouse in a viewport. A Compass helper object appears. Click again to create a Direct (or Skylight) light representing the sun. Figure 22-11 shows the Compass helper created as part of the Sunlight system. The main difference between these two systems is that the Sunlight system uses a Directional light and the Daylight system uses a Skylight.

Using the Compass helper

The Compass helper is useful when working with a Sunlight system. It can be used to define the map directions of North, East, South, and West. The Sunlight system uses these directions to orient the system light. This helper is not renderable and is created automatically when you define a sunlight object.

After you create a Sunlight system, you can alter the sun's position by transforming the Compass helper. Doing so causes the direct light object to move appropriately. You cannot transform the Direct light by itself.

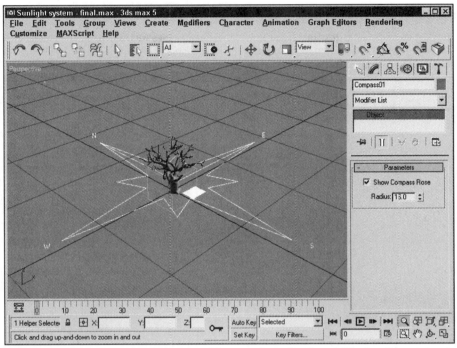

Figure 22-11: The Compass helper provides an orientation for positioning the sun in a Sunlight system.

Note You can change the settings for the light that is the sun by selecting the light from the Select by Name dialog box and opening the Modify panel. The sun light object uses raytraced shadows by default.

Understanding Azimuth and Altitude

Azimuth and Altitude are two values that help define the location of the sun in the sky. Both are measured in degrees. Azimuth refers to the compass direction and can range from 0 to 360, with 0 degrees being North, 90 degrees being East, 180 degrees being South, and 270 degrees being West. Altitude is the angle in degrees between the sun and the horizon. This value ranges typically between 0 and 90, with 0 degrees being either sunrise or sunset and 90 when the sun is directly overhead.

Specifying date and time

The Time section of the Control Parameters rollout lets you define a time and date. The Time Zone value is the number of offset hours for your current time zone. You can also set the time to be converted for Daylight Saving Time.

Specifying location

Clicking the Get Location button in the Control Parameters rollout opens the Geographic Location dialog box, shown in Figure 22-12, which displays a map or a list of cities. Selecting a location using this dialog box automatically updates the Latitude and Longitude values. In addition to the Get Location button, you can enter Latitude and Longitude values directly in the Control Parameters rollout.

The Daylight system also includes an option to set the Sky value from Clear, Partly Cloudy, to Cloudy.

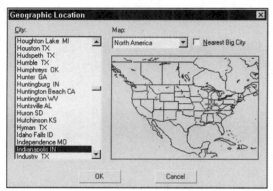

Figure 22-12: The Geographic Location dialog box lets you specify where you want to use the Sunlight system. You have many different cities to choose from.

Tutorial: Animating a day in 20 seconds

You can animate the Sunlight system to show an entire day from sunrise to sundown in a short number of frames. In this tutorial, we'll focus on an old tree positioned somewhere in Phoenix, Arizona, on Christmas. The tree certainly won't move, but watch its shadows.

To use the Sunlight system to animate shadows, follow these steps.

1. Open the Sunlight system.max file from the Chap 22 directory on the CD-ROM.

   This file includes a tree mesh created by Zygote.

2. Add a Sunlight System by selecting the Systems category in the Create panel and click-ing the Sunlight button. Then drag in the Top view to create the Compass helper and click again to create the light. In the Control Parameters, enter **12/25/2000** for the Date and an early morning hour for the Time.

3. Click the Get Location button, locate Phoenix in the Cities list, and click OK. Rotate the compass helper in the Top view so that north is pointing toward the top of the viewport.

4. Click the Auto Key button (or press the N key) and move the Time slider to frame 100.

5. In the Control Parameters rollout, change the Time value to an evening hour. Then click the Auto Key button (N) again to disable animation mode.

Note   You can tell when the sun comes up and goes down by looking at the Altitude value for each hour. A negative Altitude value indicates that the sun is below the horizon.

Figure 22-13 shows a snapshot of this quick day. The upper-left image shows the animation at frame 20, the upper-right image shows it at frame 40, the lower-left image shows it at frame 60, and the final image shows it at frame 80.

Figure 22-13: Several frames of an animation showing a tree scene from sunrise to sunset

Using Volume Lights

When light shines through fog, smoke, or dust, the beam of the light becomes visible. The effect is known as a Volume Light. To add a Volume Light to a scene, choose Rendering ⇨ Environment to open the Environment dialog box. Then click the Add button in the Atmosphere rollout to open the Add Atmospheric Effect dialog box and select Volume Light. The parameters for the volume light will be presented in the Volume Light Parameters rollout.

You can also access the Volume Light effect from the Atmospheres and Effects rollout in the Modify panel when a light is selected.

 Cross-Reference   Chapter 35, "Working with Environments and Atmospheric Effects," covers the other atmospheric effects.

Volume light parameters

At the top of the Volume Light Parameters rollout, shown in Figure 22-14, is a Pick Light button, which enables you to select a light to apply the effect to. You can select several lights, and they will be shown in a drop-down list. You can remove lights from this list with the Remove Light button.

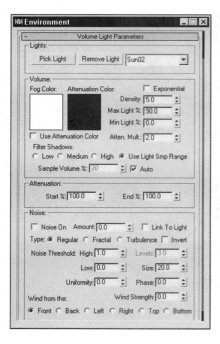

Figure 22-14: The Volume Light Parameters rollout in the Environment dialog box lets you choose which lights to include in the effect.

In the Volume section, the Fog Color swatch lets you select a color for the fog that is seen within the light. This color is combined with the color of the light. The Attenuation Color is the color the fog appears to have at a distance far from the light source. This color also combines with the Fog Color and is best set to a dark color.

The Density value determines the thickness of the fog. The Exponential option causes the density to increase exponentially with the distance. The Max and Min Light Percentage values determine the amount of glow that the volume light causes, and the Attenuation Multiplier controls the strength of the attenuation color.

You have four options for filtering shadows: Low, Medium, High, and Use Light Smp Range. The Low option renders shadows quickly but isn't very accurate. The High option takes a while but produces the best quality. The Use Light Smp Range option bases the filtering on the Sample Volume value and can be set to Auto. The Sample Volume can range from 1 to 10,000. The Low option has a Sample Volume value of 8; Medium, 25; and High, 50.

The Start and End Attenuation values are percentages of the Start and End range values for the light's attenuation. These values have an impact only if attenuation is turned on for the light.

The Noise settings help determine the randomness of Volume Light. Noise effects can be turned on and given an Amount. You can also Link the noise to the light instead of using world coordinates. Noise types include Regular, Fractal, Turbulence, and Invert. The Noise Threshold limits the effect of noise. Wind settings affect how the light moves as determined by the wind's direction, Wind Strength, and Phase.

Figure 22-15 shows several volume light possibilities. The left image includes the Volume Light effect, the middle image enables shadows, and the right image includes some Turbulent Noise.

Figure 22-15: The Volume Light effect makes the light visible.

Tutorial: Showing car headlights

One popular way to use volume lights is to display the headlights of cars. For this tutorial, we're going to once again use the '57 Chevy model created by Viewpoint Datalabs.

To display the headlights of a car, follow these steps:

1. Open the Headlights on a 57 Chevy.max file from the Chap 22 directory on the CD-ROM.

   This file includes a model of a '57 Chevy.

2. In the Create panel, click the Lights category, and then click the Target Spot button and drag in the Left viewport to create a spotlight object. Select and move the spotlight and the target to be positioned to look as if a light is shining out from the left headlight.

3. Open the Modify panel and, in the Spotlight Parameters rollout, set the Hotspot value to 20 and the Falloff to 25. In the Atmospheres and Effects rollout, click the Add button, select Volume Light from the Add Atmosphere or Effect dialog box that appears, and click OK.

Note   When a light is added to the scene, the default lights are automatically turned off. To provide any additional lighting, add some Omni lights above the car.

4. Select the Volume Light effect in the list within the Atmospheres and Effects rollout and click the Setup button. The Environment dialog box opens, in which you can edit the Volume Light parameters for the newly created light. Set the Density value to 100.

5. Now, create the second headlight. To do this, select both the first spotlight object and its target, and create a cloned copy by holding down the Shift key while moving it toward the right headlight. Position the second spotlight so that it shines outward from the right headlight.

Figure 22-16 shows the resulting car with its two headlights illuminated.

Figure 22-16: The car now has headlights, thanks to spotlights and the Volume Light effect.

Tutorial: Creating laser beams

Laser beams are extremely useful lights. From your CD-ROM drive to your laser printer, lasers are found throughout a modern-day office. They are also great to use in fantasy and science fiction images. You can easily create laser beams using direct lights and the Volume Light effect. In this tutorial, we'll add some lasers to the laser truck model created by Viewpoint Datalabs.

To add some laser beams to a scene, follow these steps:

1. Open the Laser truck.max file from the Chap 22 directory on the CD-ROM.

   This file includes a fantasy laser truck model.

2. Open the Create panel, select the Lights category, and add a Free Direct light to the end of one of the laser guns. Scale the light down until the cylinder is the size of the desired laser beam.

3. With the light selected, open the Modify panel and, in the Atmospheres and Effects rollout, click the Add button and double-click the Volume Light selection. Then select the Volume Light option in the list, and click the Setup button to open the Environment dialog box. Change the Fog Color to red, and make sure the Use Attenuation Color is disabled.

4. In the Top view, clone the direct light three times and move the cloned lights in front of the other guns.

5. With the direct lights added to the scene, the default lights will be deactivated, so you'll need to add some Omni lights above the truck model to illuminate it. To do this, open the Create panel, select the Lights category, and click the Omni button. Then click above the car in the Front view three times to create three lights. Set the Multiplier on the first light to 1.0, and position it directly above the model. Set the other two lights to 0.5, and position them on either side of the truck and lower than the first light.

Figure 22-17 shows the resulting laser beams shooting forth from the laser truck.

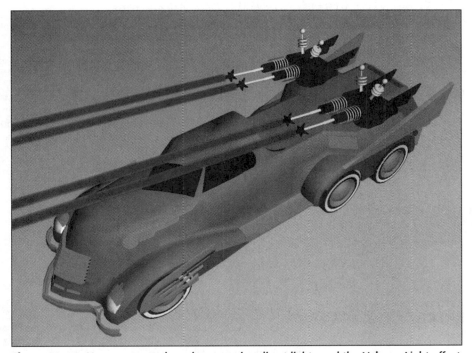

Figure 22-17: You can create laser beams using direct lights and the Volume Light effect.

Using projector maps and raytraced shadows

If a map is added to a light in the Parameters rollout, the light becomes a projector. Projector maps can be simple images, animated images, or black-and-white masks to cast shadows. To load a projector map, select a light, open the Modify panel, and under the Spotlight Parameters rollout click the Projector Map button and select the map to use from the Material/Map Browser.

Raytraced shadows take longer to render than the Shadow Maps or Area Shadows option, but the shadows will always have a hard edge and be an accurate representation of the object.

Note You can create shadows for wire-frame objects only by using raytraced shadows.

In the Shadow Parameters rollout, you can select whether shadows are computed using shadow maps or raytraced shadows. Using the latter selection lets you project a transparent object's color onto the shadow.

Tutorial: Projecting a trumpet image on a scene

As an example of a projector light, we'll create a musical scene with several musical notes and project the image of a trumpet on them.

To project an image onto a rendered scene, follow these steps:

1. Open the Trumpet mask.max file from the Chap 22 directory on the CD-ROM.

   This file includes a trumpet model created by Viewpoint Datalabs shown in the maximized Left viewport. This file will be used to generate a project map.

2. Choose Rendering ⇨ Render (or press the F10 key) to open the Render dialog box, set the resolution to 640 × 480, and select the Left viewport. Then click the Render button. The side view of the trumpet in the Virtual Frame Buffer renders. When the rendering completes, click the Save File button in the Virtual Frame Buffer, and save the file as **trumpet.tif**.

3. Open the trumpet image in Adobe Photoshop and select all black areas. Then invert the selection and color the selection white. Save this file as **Trumpet Mask.tif**.

 On the CD-ROM You can find a copy of the rendered trumpet.tif and the Trumpet Mask.tif images in the Chap 22 directory of the CD-ROM.

4. Back in Max, open the Musical notes.max file from the Chap 22 directory on the CD-ROM.

   This file contains several musical notes created from primitive objects.

5. Open the Create panel and select the Lights category. Click the Target Spot button and drag to create two lights in the Top viewport. Position the first spotlight to be perpendicular to the scene and to shine down on it from above.

6. Open the Modify panel and, in the Advanced Effects rollout, click the Projector Map button and double-click Bitmap from the Material/Map Browser. Locate and select the Trumpet Mask.tif file and click Open. This projects a silhouette of a trumpet onto the scene. Use the second spotlight to light the music notes.

Figure 22-18 shows the musical notes with the trumpet projection map.

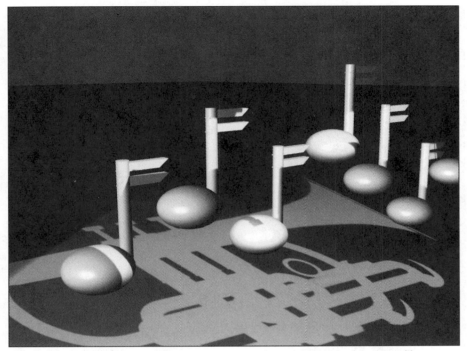

Figure 22-18: You can use Projection maps to project an image in the scene, like this trumpet.

Tutorial: Creating a stained-glass window

When a light that uses raytraced shadows shines through an object with transparent materials, the Filter color of the material is projected onto objects behind. In this tutorial, we will create a stained-glass window and shine a light through it using raytraced shadows.

To create a stained-glass window, follow these steps:

1. Open the Stained glass window.max file from the Chap 22 directory on the CD-ROM.

   This file includes a stained-glass window for a fish market (don't ask me why a fish market has stained-glass window).

2. In the Create panel, select the Lights category and click the Target Spot button. Then drag in the Left view from a position to the right and above the window to the window — this creates a target spotlight that shines through the stained-glass window onto the floor behind it.

3. In the General Parameters rollout, make sure the Cast Shadows option is selected and select Ray Traced Shadows from the drop-down list. In the Shadow Parameters rollout, enable the On option.

Figure 22-19 shows the stained-glass window with the colored shadow cast on the scene floor.

Figure 22-19: A stained-glass window effect created with raytraced shadows

Summary

I hope you have found this chapter enlightening. (Sorry about the bad pun, but I need to work them in where I can.) There are many different lights in Max, each with plenty of controls. Learning to master these controls can take you a long way toward increasing the realism of the scene. In this chapter, you've

✦ Learned the basics of lighting

✦ Discovered Max's light types

✦ Created and positioned light objects

✦ Learned to change the viewport view to a light

✦ Used the Sunlight and Daylight systems

✦ Used the Volume Light atmospheric effect

✦ Added projection maps to lights

✦ Used raytraced shadows to create a stained-glass window

In the next chapter, we'll cover photometric lights, advanced lighting, and radiosity.

✦   ✦   ✦

Advanced Lighting and Radiosity

If you were to walk into a dark room and reach for the light switch, you would be confused if there were a separate switch that controlled the advanced lighting. But, in Max the advanced lighting controls are worth the trouble. They enable you to take rendering to the next level.

The advanced lighting controls in Max enable you to light scenes using two separate global illumination techniques known as light tracing and radiosity. When natural light strikes a surface, some of it is absorbed and some of it is reflected. The reflected light will then travel until it hits another surface, which will also be affected by the light. This process continues adding a lot of subtle lighting throughout the scene.

Working with Photometric Lights

The standard Max lights rely on parameters like Multiplier, Decay, and Attenuation, but the last time I was in the hardware store looking for a light bulb with a 2.5 Multiplier value, I was disappointed. Lights in the real world have their own set of measurements that define the type of light that is produced. Photometric lights are lights that are based on real-world light measurement values such as Intensity in Lumens and temperatures in degrees Kelvin.

 New Feature Photometric lights are new to 3ds max 5.

If you select the Lights category in the Create panel, you'll notice a subcategory called Standard, which accesses the basic standard lights covered in Chapter 22, "Working with Lights." But, there is also a subcategory of lights called Photometric. Photometric lights are based on photometric values, which are the values of light energy.

The lights found in this subcategory include Target Point, Target Linear, Target Area, Free Point, Free Linear, Free Area, IES Sun, and IES Sky.

Target and Free photometric lights

Target photometric lights come in three shapes — Point, Linear, and Area. Selecting a different shaped light causes the light to be spread over a wider area, so in most cases, the Point light results in the brightest intensity. Figure 23-1 shows the three different shapes. The General Parameters rollout includes a drop-down list that you can use to change the light shape and whether it is targeted or not.

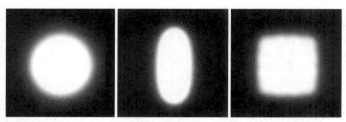

Figure 23-1: Photometric lights can be Point, Linear, or Area.

The gizmo for a point photometric lights is a simple sphere and linear and area lights are a simple sphere and a line and a sphere and a rectangle. For targeted lights, the target extends from the gizmo to the target. The dimensions for the light are in the Linear (Area) Light Parameters rollout.

Most of the light rollouts are the same as those for the standard lights, but the Intensity/Color/Distribution rollout, as shown in Figure 23-2, is unique.

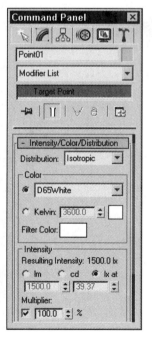

Figure 23-2: The Intensity/Color/Distribution rollout for photometric lights uses real-world intensity values.

Distribution options

The Distribution options are listed in the drop-down list at the top of the rollout. The options include Isotropic, Spotlight, and Web for the Point lights and Diffuse and Web for the Linear and Area lights.

The Isotropic and Diffuse options are the same, but work for different light shapes. They provide even light in all directions from the light. The light gradually becomes weaker as the distance from the light increases.

The Spotlight option is only available for Point lights. It concentrates the light energy into a cone that emits from the light. This cone of light energy is directional and can be controlled with the Hotspot and Falloff values.

The Web option is a custom option that lets you open a separate file that describes the emission pattern of the light. These files have the .ies, .cibse, or .ltli extensions. Light manufacturers have this data for the various real-world lights that they sell. You load these files using the Web File button found in the Web Parameters rollout. You can also specify the X-, Y-, and Z-axis rotation values.

Color options

The Color section of the Intensity/Color/Distribution rollout includes two different ways to specify a light's color. The first is a drop-down list of options. The options found in the list include standard real-world light types such as Cool White, Mercury, and Halogen. Each of these types and their approximate color are listed in Table 23-1.

Table 23-1: Photometric Light Colors

Light Type	Color
Cool White	Yellow-white
Custom	Any color
D65White	White
Daylight Fluorescent	Mostly white with a slight gray tint
Fluorescent	Yellow-white
Halogen	Beige-white
High Pressure Sodium	Tan
Incandescent	Beige-white
Low Pressure Sodium	Light orange
Mercury	Green-white
Metal Halide	Yellow-white
Phosphor Mercury	Light green
Quartz	Yellow-white
White Fluorescent	Yellow-white
Xenon	White

In addition to a list of available light types, you can specify a color based on temperature based in degrees Kelvin. Temperature-based colors run from a cool 1,000 degrees, which is a mauve-pink color, through light yellow and white (at 6,000 degrees Kelvin) to a hot light blue at 20,000 degrees Kelvin.

You can also set a Filter Color using the color swatch found in this section. The Filter Color simulates the color caused by some colored cellophane that is placed in front of the light.

Intensity options

The Intensity options can be specified in Lumens, Candelas, or Lux at a given distance. Light manufacturers have this information available. You can also specify a Multiplier value, which determines how effective the light is.

IES photometric lights

The Photometric light subcategory also includes two additional lights — IES Sky and IES Sun. The IES Sky light simulates ambient light. In the Sky Parameters rollout, you can specify the sky as Clear, Partly Cloudy, or Cloudy. These same parameters are also found in the Daylight system.

The IES Sun light simulates the bright outdoor light of the sun. It is a single light with a lot of power. It can be targeted and can have an Intensity value of 50 billion lux. This type of light is very valuable in architecture renderings.

Setting Advanced Lighting

You control the advanced lighting settings for the scene in the Advanced Lighting panel. You open this panel using the Rendering ⇨ Advanced Lighting menu command (or by pressing the 9 key). When first opened, it shows only a single drop-down list. From this drop-down list, you can select one of two options — Light Tracer and Radiosity.

New Feature   Advanced lighting is new to 3ds max 5.

These two options are two different techniques for applying advanced lighting to a scene. Although they are fundamentally different, they both simulate a critical piece of the lighting puzzle that adds dramatically to the realism of the lights in the scene — light bouncing. When light strikes a surface in real life, a portion of the light bounces off the surface and illuminates other surfaces. Traditionally, Max hasn't worried about this, which required that users add more lights to the scene to account for this additional lighting. Both the Light Tracer and the Radiosity solutions include light bouncing in their calculations.

Using a Light Tracer

The Light Tracer is a Global Illumination (GI) system that is similar to raytracing, but it focuses more on calculating how light bounces off surfaces in the scene. The results are fairly realistic without being computationally expensive and its solutions are rendered much quicker than a radiosity solution.

Cross-Reference   The Light Tracer is similar in many ways to raytracing. Chapter 37, "Raytracing," presents more information on raytracing.

It works by dividing the scene into sample points. These sample points are more heavily concentrated along the edges of objects in the scene. An imaginary light ray is then shot at each sample point and the light intensity at the location of contact is recorded; and then it is computed where the light ray would bounce to, and a reduced intensity value is recorded. One of the settings is how many times the light rays will bounce within the scene, and this value will increase the amount of time required to compute the solution. When all the rays and light bounces have been computed, the total light intensity value for each sample point is totaled and averaged.

Caution   Transparent objects will split each ray in two. One ray will bounce and the second ray will be projected through the transparent object. Transparent objects in the scene will quickly double the amount of time required to compute a solution.

To enable light tracing in a scene, open the Advanced Lighting panel and select Light Tracer from the drop-down list. This opens a Parameters rollout, as shown in Figure 23-3, full of settings for controlling the light.

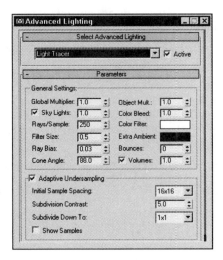

Figure 23-3: The Light Tracer Parameters rollout sets values for GI lighting.

The Global Multiplier value will increase the overall effect of the Light Tracer, much like increasing the multiplier of a light. The net result is to brighten the scene. You can also increase the multiplier of skylights and objects with the Sky Lights and Object Multiplier values.

Another characteristic of global illumination is color bleeding. As a light ray strikes the surface of an object and bounces, it carries the color of the object that is struck with it to the next object. The result of this is that colors from one object will bleed onto adjacent objects. You can control this effect using the Color Bleed setting. You can also select colors to use for a color filter and for extra ambient light.

The big trade-off of global illumination is between quality and render time. The more rays per sample that you specify, the better the quality and the longer the render time. This is controlled with the Rays/Sample setting. The Rays/Sample setting along with the number of Bounces dramatically increase the rendering time. The Ray Bias setting will bias rays toward object edges verses flat areas.

If you don't include enough rays in the scene, then noise patterns will appear within the scene. The Filter Size can help control the amount of noise that appears in the scene.

The number of Bounces will specify the number of times the ray bounces before being dropped from the solution. A setting of 0 is the same as disabling the Light Tracer, and the maximum value of 10 will require a long time to compute. The Cone Angle defines the cone region within which the rays are projected. The Volumes option is a multiplier for atmosphere effects.

With the Adaptive Undersampling option enabled, you can specify the spacing of the samples, and how finely the samples get subdivided. The Initial Sample Spacing options range from 1×1 to a very dense 32×32. The Subdivision Contrast affects the density for contrast edges between objects and shadows. These high contrast areas use the Subdivide Down To setting. The Show Samples option will display each sample as a red dot on the rendered image.

Tutorial: Viewing color bleeding

One of the easiest effects of the light tracer to see is color bleeding. Although this is often undesirable, it is a telltale sign of global illumination.

To compare the differences between a regular rendering and the light tracer, follow these steps:

1. Open the Bleeding spheres.max file from the Chap 23 directory on the CD-ROM. This file includes four spheres of different colors that overlap.

2. Open the Advanced Lighting panel by selecting Rendering ⇨ Advanced Lighting (or press the 9 key). In the drop-down list, select the Light Tracer option. In the Parameters rollout, set the Bounces to 3 and the Color Bleed value to 25.

3. Open the Render Scene panel by selecting the Rendering ⇨ Render menu command (or by pressing the F10 key). In the Common Parameters rollout, make sure the Use Advanced Lighting option is selected and click the Render button. This will render the scene in the Virtual Frame Buffer.

Figure 23-4 shows the scene rendered with and without advanced lighting. If you look closely, you can detect the color bleeding along the edges of the spheres where they overlap.

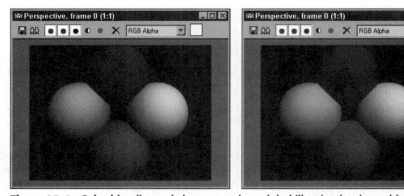

Figure 23-4: Color bleeding only happens when global illumination is enabled.

Lighting for Radiosity

The other option in the Advanced Lighting panel is Radiosity. Radiosity is a method for calculating light as it bounces around an environment. It can take some time to render, but the results are generally very good.

After a Radiosity solution is calculated, the results are saved as light maps. These maps are easy to apply to a scene and can be viewed within the viewports. However, when the geometry or lights of the scene change, you need to recalculate the lighting solution.

The Radiosity Processing Parameters rollout, shown in Figure 23-5, lets you set the quality of the Radiosity solution. You can also specify the number of iterations to use for the scene and for the selected objects. The Interactive Tools section lets you specify a Filtering value, includes a button to access the Exposure Control rollout in the Environment panel, and turns Radiosity off in the viewports. This rollout also includes the Start, Stop, and Reset buttons for enabling the Radiosity solution.

Cross-Reference   Chapter 34, "Rendering Basics," includes coverage of the Exposure Control rollout.

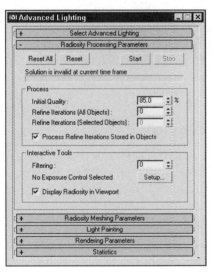

Figure 23-5: The Radiosity Processing parameters include buttons for computing a solution.

Subdividing a mesh for radiosity

As you begin to play with radiosity, you'll quickly find that to get accurate results, you need to have good, clean models. If any models have long, thin faces, then the results will be unpredictable.

The Radiosity Meshing Parameters rollout includes an option to enable meshing and a Meshing Size value. This setting is the same as the Size value parameter for the Subdivide modifier, except it is applied globally.

The Modifiers menu includes a submenu for Radiosity modifiers. This submenu only includes the Subdivide modifier and a World-Space version of the Subdivide modifier. This modifier accomplishes a simple task—to create a mesh that has regular equally shaped triangular faces that work well when computing a radiosity solution.

Tip Although this modifier was created to help with radiosity solutions, it also will help with other commands that require regular mesh faces such as the Boolean and Terrain compound objects.

The Parameters rollout includes a Size value that determines the density of the mesh. The lower the value the denser the mesh and the better resulting radiosity solution, but the longer the solution will take. This same Subdivision Size setting can also be found (and set globally) in the Radiosity Meshing Parameters rollout of the Advanced Lighting panel. It is also found in the Advanced Lighting panel of the Object Properties dialog box. Figure 23-6 shows a simple cube with the Subdivide modifier applied and the Size value set to 50, 30, 25, 20, and 12.

Tip If you drag the Size value, you'll probably want to set the Update option to Manual or you'll find yourself waiting while Max computes some seriously dense mesh, or just disable the Display Subdivision option.

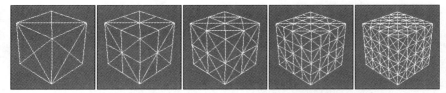

Figure 23-6: The Subdivide modifier changes all mesh faces into regularly shaped triangular faces.

Tutorial: Preparing a mesh for radiosity

When it comes to meshes that have long, thin and irregular faces, you don't have to look any further than Boolean compound objects. These objects typically will be divided along strange angles producing ugly meshes. The good news is that these meshes are easy to subdivide.

To subdivide an irregular mesh in preparation for a radiosity solution, follow these steps:

1. Open the Boolean object.max file from the Chap 23 directory on the CD-ROM. This file includes two copies of a Box object with an arch shape Boolean subtracted from it.

2. Select the top object and choose the Modifiers ➪ Radiosity Modifiers ➪ Subdivide menu command. This will apply the Subdivide modifier to the object.

3. In the Parameters rollout, select the Manual update option, set the Size value to 5.0 and click the Update Now. If the Display Subdivision option is enabled, then the changes will be visible in the viewport.

4. Open the Advanced Lighting panel with the Rendering ➪ Advanced Lighting menu command (or press the 9 key). Select Radiosity from the drop-down menu.

Figure 23-7 shows the two objects with and without the Subdivide modifier applied. The top object is ready for a radiosity solution.

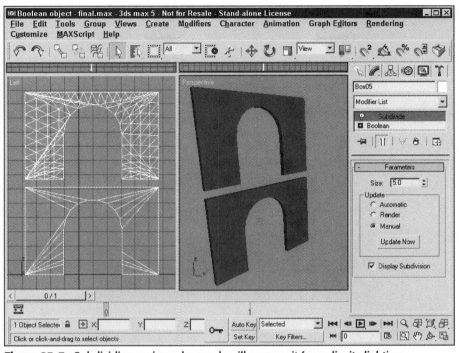

Figure 23-7: Subdividing an irregular mesh will prepare it for radiosity lighting.

Painting with light

The Light Painting rollout, shown in Figure 23-8, includes buttons for Adding Illumination, Subtracting Illumination, and Picking an Illumination value from the scene. Using these tools, you can paint lighting on the objects in the scene. This gives you a lot of control over the lighting.

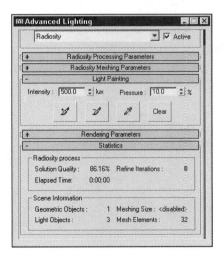

Figure 23-8: Because lighting is saved as a light map, you can add or subtract light from the scene using a brush tool.

Rendering parameters and statistics

Settings in the Rendering Parameters rollout (shown in Figure 23-9) are used during the rendering process. The Re-Use and Use Direct Illumination options give you the chance to re-use the existing radiosity solution when rendering or to re-calculate it as part of the rendering process. This can save some time during rendering.

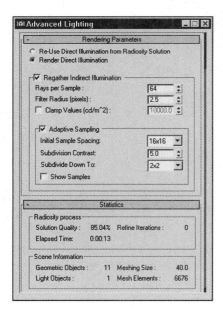

Figure 23-9: The Rendering Parameters and Statistics rollouts offer rendering options and statistics for radiosity solutions.

The Regather Indirect Illumination option enables a Light Tracer-like step along with the radiosity solution and produces an image that has the best of both solutions. The regathering options are the same as those defined for the light tracer.

The Statistics rollout includes information about the Radiosity process. Using this information, you can judge whether the settings are too high or too low.

Tutorial: Lighting an archway with radiosity

Radiosity works best in indoor scenes or scenes that are mostly interior, so I've created a simple walkway with several archways. The only light source for this scene is an IES Sun light streaming in from the left.

To light an archway with Radiosity, follow these steps.

1. Open the Arch walkway.max file from the Chap 23 directory on the CD-ROM. This file includes a simple walkway made from primitives.

2. Open the Advanced Lighting panel with the Rendering ➪ Advanced Lighting menu command (or by pressing the 9 key). Select Radiosity from the drop-down list in the Select Advanced Lighting rollout.

3. In the Radiosity Processing Parameters rollout, click the Start button to have Max compute the Radiosity solution.

4. In the Rendering Parameters rollout, enable the Render Direct Illumination, the Regather Indirect Illumination, and the Adaptive Sampling options.

Figure 23-10 shows the finished rendered walkway. Notice how all surfaces are well lit even though there is only a single light in the scene.

Figure 23-10: The Radiosity solution for this scene adds to the lighting levels for the entire room.

Using Local and Global Advanced Lighting Settings

You can set advanced lighting settings locally for specific objects using the Object Properties dialog box, as shown in Figure 23-11. This dialog box lets you specify whether this object should be excluded from the advanced lighting calculations. If included, you can select whether the object casts shadows, receives illumination, and how it handles Radiosity. You can also selectively enable Diffuse and Specular light or exclude the object from the regathering process.

The Preference Settings dialog box also includes a panel for Advanced Lighting. Using this panel, shown in Figure 23-12, you can set the advanced lighting settings that apply to all objects globally.

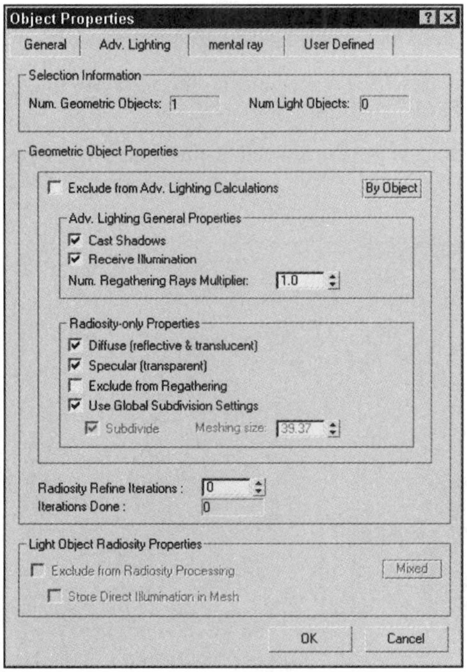

Figure 23-11: Use the Advanced Lighting panel in the Object Properties dialog box to disable advanced lighting.

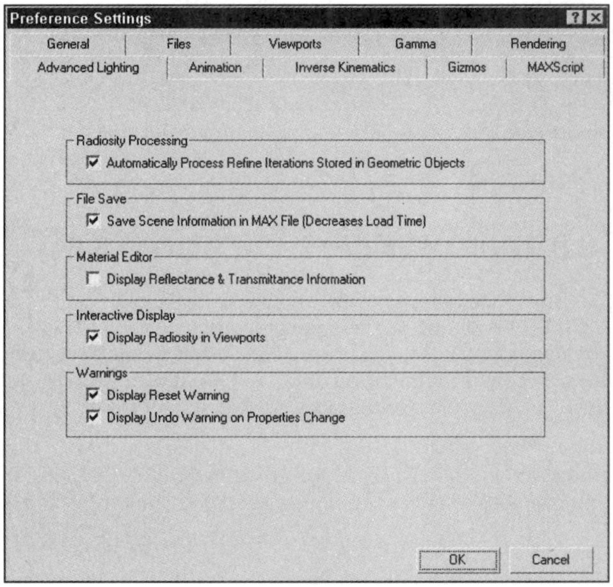

Figure 23-12: Use the Advanced Lighting panel of the Preference Settings dialog box to set global parameters.

In the Advanced Lighting panel of the Preference Settings dialog box is an option to Display Reflectance & Transmittance Information. If this option is enabled, this information (average and maximum percent values) will appear directly below the sample slots.

Working with Advanced Lighting Materials

Applying an advanced lighting solution can have a direct impact on the materials in the scene. The Material Editor includes two materials that are useful for working with advanced lighting.

Advanced Lighting Override

The Advanced Lighting Override material type includes material parameters that override the Advanced Lighting solution. These parameters, shown in Figure 23-13, let you set the amount of Reflectance, Color Bleed, Transmittance, Luminance, and Bump Map Scale that the material uses.

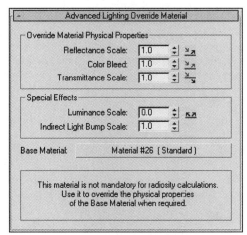

Figure 23-13: The Advanced Lighting Override Material rollout defines how light interacts with the material.

Lightscape Material

The Lightscape material type lets you control how the radiosity is mapped to objects. The Basic Parameters rollout includes values for Brightness, Contrast, Ambient Light, and Bump Amount. These values are applied in addition to the base material.

Summary

Advanced lighting offers a new way to shine lights on your scenes. With these features, many new lighting options are available. Advanced lighting enables two lighting methods — Global Illumination and Radiosity. In this chapter, you

✦ Learned about the various photometric lights

✦ Enabled advanced lighting

✦ Discovered light tracing and radiosity

✦ Using the Subdivide modifier

✦ Set local and global advanced lighting settings

✦ Used advanced lighting materials.

In the next chapter, you'll the basics of animation and working with keys.

✦   ✦   ✦

Animation

Animation Basics

Max can be used to create some really amazing images, but I bet more of you go to the movies than to see images in a museum. The difference is in seeing moving images versus static images.

In this chapter, we'll start discussing what is probably one of the main reasons that you decided to learn 3ds max in the first place — animation. Max includes many different tools to create animations. This chapter covers the easiest and most basic of these tools.

Using the Time Controls

Before jumping into animation, you need to understand the controls that make it possible. These controls collectively are called the Time Controls and can be found in the lower interface bar between the key controls and the Viewport Navigation Controls. The Time Controls also include the Time Slider found directly under the viewports.

The Time Slider provides an easy way to move through the frames of an animation. To do this, just drag the Time Slider button in either direction. The Time Slider button is labeled with the current frame number and the total number of frames. The arrow buttons on either side of this button work the same as the Previous and Next Frame (Key) buttons.

The Time Control buttons include buttons for jumping to the Start or End of the animation, or to step forward or back by a single frame. You can also jump to an exact frame by entering the frame number in the frame number field. The Time Controls are presented in Table 24-1.

The default scene starts with 100 frames, but this is seldom what you actually need. You can change the number of frames at any time by clicking the Time Configuration button, which is to the right of the frame number field. Clicking this button opens the Time Configuration dialog box, shown in Figure 24-1. You can also access this dialog box by right-clicking any of the Time Control buttons.

Table 24-1: Time Controls

Toolbar Button	Name	Description
![Go to Start]	Go to Start	Sets the time to frame 1.
![Previous Frame/Key]	Previous Frame/Key	Decreases the time by one frame or selects the previous key.
![Play Animation]	Play Animation, Play Selected	Cycles through the frames. This button becomes a Stop button when an animation is playing.
![Next Frame/Key]	Next Frame/Key	Advances the time by one frame or selects the next key.
![Go to End]	Go to End	Sets the time to the final frame.
![Key Mode Toggle]	Key Mode Toggle	Toggles between key and frame modes. With Key Mode on, the icon turns light blue and the Previous Frame and Next Frame buttons change to Previous Key and Next Key.
![Current Frame field]	Current Frame field	Indicates the current frame. A frame number can be typed in this field for more exact control than the Time Slider.
![Time Configuration]	Time Configuration	Opens the Time Configuration dialog box where settings like frame rate, time display, and animation length can be set.

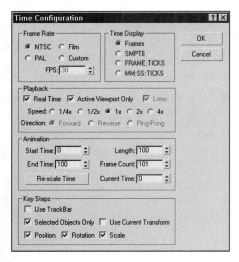

Figure 24-1: The Time Configuration dialog box lets you set the number of frames to include in a scene.

Setting frame rate

Within this dialog box, you can set several options, including the Frame Rate. Frame rate provides the connection between the number of frames and time. It is measured in frames per second. The options include standard frame rates such as NTSC (National Television Standards Committee, around 30 frames per second), Film (around 24 frames per second), and PAL (Phase Alternate Line, used by European countries, around 25 frames per second), or you can select Custom and enter your own frame rate.

The Time Display section lets you set how time is displayed on the Time Slider. The options include Frames, SMPTE (Society of Motion Picture Technical Engineers), Frame:Ticks or MM:SS:Ticks (Minute and Seconds). SMPTE is a standard time measurement used in video and television. A Tick is $1/4800$ of a second.

Setting speed and direction

The Playback section sets options for how the animation sequence is played back. The Real Time option skips frames to maintain the specified frame rate. The Active Viewport Only causes the animation to only play in a single viewport, which speeds up the animation. The Loop option repeats the animation over and over. The Loop option is only available if the Real Time option is disabled. If the Loop option is set, then you can specify the Direction as Forward, Reverse, or Ping Pong (which will repeat playing forward and then reverse). The Speed setting can be ¼, ½, 1, 2, or 4 times normal.

The Time Configuration dialog box also lets you specify the Start Time, End Time, Length, and Current Time values. These values are all interrelated, so setting the Length and the Start Time, for example, automatically changes the End Time. These values can be changed at any time without destroying any keys. For example, if you have an animation of 500 frames and you set the Start and End Time to 30 and 50, the Time Slider will control only those 21 frames. Keys before or after this time are still available and can be accessed by resetting the Start and End Time values to 0 and 500.

The Re-scale Time button fits all the keys into the active time segment by stretching or shrinking the number of frames between keys. You can use this feature to resize the animation to the number of frames defined by Start and End Time values.

The Key Steps group lets you set which key objects are navigated using key mode. If you select Use Track Bar, key mode only moves through the keys on the Track Bar. If you select the Selected Objects Only option, key mode only jumps to the keys for the currently selected object. You can also filter to move between Position, Rotation, and Scale keys. The Use Current Transform option locates only those keys that are the same as the current selected transform button.

Using Time Tags

To the right of the Prompt Line is a field marked Add Time Tag. Clicking this field pops up a menu with options to Add or Edit a Time Tag. Time Tags can be set for each frame in the scene. Once set, the Time Tags will be visible in the Time Tag field whenever that time is selected.

Working with Keys

It isn't just a coincidence that the largest button in the entire Max interface has a key on it. Creating and working with keys is how animations are accomplished. Keys define a particular state of an object at a particular time. Animations are created as the object moves or changes between two different key states. Complex animations can be generated with only a handful of keys.

There are numerous ways to create keys, but the easiest is with the Key Controls found in the lower interface bar. These controls are located to the left of the Time Controls. Table 24-2 displays and explains all these controls. Closely related to the Key Controls is the Track Bar, which is located under the Time Slider.

Table 24-2: Key Controls

Toolbar Button	Name	Description
⊶	Set Keys (K)	Creates animation keys in Set Key mode.
Auto Key	Toggle AutoKey Mode (N)	Sets keys automatically for the selected object when enabled.
Set Key	Toggle Set Key Mode (')	Sets keys as specified by the key filters for the selected object when enabled.
Selected ▼	Selection Set drop-down list	Specifies a selection set to use for the given keys.
Key Filters...	Open Filters Dialog box	Pop-up options for the filtering keys.

Max includes two different animation modes — Auto Key (N) and Set Key ('). You can select either of these modes by clicking on the respective buttons at the bottom of the interface. When active, the button turns bright red, and the border around the active viewport also turns red to remind you that you are in animate mode.

 Tip   You can set the Time slider bar to be red as well by adding the following to the 3dsmax.ini file:

```
[RedSliderWhenAnimating]
Enabled=1
```

Auto Key mode

With the Auto Key button enabled, every transformation or parameter change creates a key that defines where and how an object should look at that specific frame.

To create a key, drag the Time Slider to a frame where you want to create a key and then move the selected object or change the parameter and a key is automatically created. When the first key is created, Max automatically goes back and creates a key for frame 0 that holds the object's original position or parameter. Upon setting the key, Max then interpolates all the positions and changes between the keys. The key will be displayed in the Track Bar.

Each frame can hold several different keys, but only one for each type of transform and each parameter. For example, if you move, rotate, scale, and change the Radius parameter for a sphere object with the Auto Key mode enabled, then a key will be created for position, rotation, scaling, and a parameter change.

Set Key mode

The Set Key button (') offers more control over the key creation and only sets keys when you click the large Set Keys button (K). It also only creates keys for the key types enabled in the Key Filters dialog box. You can open the Key Filters dialog box, shown in Figure 24-2, by clicking on the Key Filters button. Available key types include Position, Rotation, Scale, IK Parameters, Object Parameters, Custom Attributes, Modifiers, and Materials.

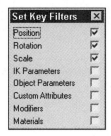

Figure 24-2: Use the Set Key Filters dialog box to specify the types of keys to create.

Tutorial: Rotating a changing hedra

The best way to learn is to practice, and there is no better time to practice than now. For this quick example, you'll create a Hedra object and animate it rotating about itself.

To animate a Hedra object rotating and changing parameters, follow these steps:

1. Open the Rotating and shape changing hedra.max file from the Chap 24 directory on the CD-ROM. This file includes a simple hedra primitive.

2. Click the Auto Key button (or press the N key) at the bottom of the Max window and drag the Time Slider to frame 50. Then click the Select and Rotate button on the main toolbar (or press E key) and rotate the Hedra object.

3. With the Hedra object selected, open the Modify panel and select the Star2 option in the Parameters rollout.

4. Click the Auto Key button (or press the N key) again to disable animation mode. Select the key in the Track Bar located at frame 1, hold down the Shift key, and drag the key to frame 100 (or press the End key).

   This step copies the key from frame 1 to frame 100. Doing so ensures a smooth looping animation.

5. Click the Play Animation button in the Time Controls to see the animation.

Figure 24-3 shows frame 50 of this simple animation.

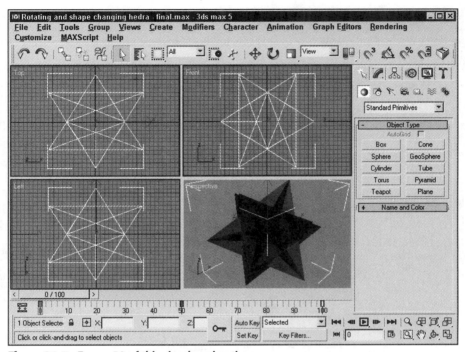

Figure 24-3: Frame 50 of this simple animation

Creating keys with the Time Slider

Another way to create keys is to select the object to be animated and right-click the Time Slider button. This opens the Create Key dialog box, shown in Figure 24-4, where you can set Position, Rotation, and Scale keys for the currently selected object. You can use this method only to create transform keys.

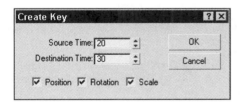

Figure 24-4: The Create Key dialog boxes enable you to create a Position, Rotation, or Scale key quickly.

If a key already exists, you can clone it by dragging the selected key with the Shift key held down. Dragging the track bar with the Ctrl and Alt keys held down will change the active time segment.

Copying parameter animation keys

If a parameter is changed while the Auto Key mode is enabled, then keys will be set for that parameter. You can tell when a parameter has a key set because the arrows to the right of its spinner will be outlined in red when the Time Slider is on the frame where the key is set. If you change the parameter value when the spinner is highlighted red, then the key value will be changed (and the Auto Key mode doesn't need to be enabled).

If you right click on the spinner, then a pop-up menu of options will appear. Using this pop-up menu, you can Cut, Copy, Paste, and Delete the parameter value. You can also select Copy Animation, which will copy all the keys associated with this parameter and let you paste them to another parameter. Pasting the animation keys can be done as a Copy, an Instance, or as a Wire. A Copy will be independent, an Instance will tie the animation keys to the original copy, so that they will both be changed when either changes, and a Wire lets one parameter control some other parameter.

The right-click pop-up menu also includes commands to let you Edit a wired parameter, show the parameter in the Track View, or show the parameter in the Parameter Wire Dialog.

Parameter wiring and the Parameter Wire Dialog box are discussed in more detail in the "Parameter Wiring" section later in this chapter.

Using the Track Bar

The Max interface includes a simple way to work with keys: the Track Bar, which is situated directly under the Time Slider. The Track Bar displays a rectangular marker for every key for the selected object. These markers are color-coded depending on the type of key. Position keys are red, rotation keys are green, scale keys are yellow, and parameter keys are blue.

In the Track View – Dope Sheet interface, position and rotation keys are red and green, but scale keys are blue and parameter keys are yellow.

The current frame is also shown in the Track Bar as a light blue transparent rectangle, as shown in Figure 24-5. The icon at the left end of the Track Bar opens a Track View.

For more on the Track View interface, see Chapter 25, "Working with the Track View."

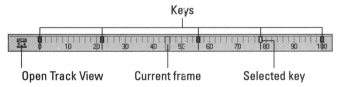

Figure 24-5: The Track Bar displays all keys for the selected object.

Using the Track Bar, you can move, copy, and delete keys. The Track Bar only shows key markers for the currently selected object or objects and each marker can represent several different keys. When the mouse is moved over the top of these markers, the cursor changes to a plus sign, and you can select it by clicking—selected markers will turn white. Using the Ctrl key, you can select multiple keys at the same time. You can also select multiple key markers by clicking an area of the Track Bar that contains no keys and then dragging an outline over all the keys you want to select. If you move the cursor over the top of a selected key, the cursor will be displayed as a set of arrows enabling you to drag the selected key to the left or right. Holding down the Shift key while dragging a key creates a copy of the key. Pressing the Delete key deletes the selected key.

Tip   If you drag a key off the end of the Track Bar, the frame number will be displayed on the Prompt Line at the bottom of the interface and the key will not be included in the current time range. If you ever want to remove a key without deleting it, you can drag it off the end of the Track Bar and recover it by resetting the time in the Time Configuration dialog box.

Because each marker can represent several keys, you can view all the keys associated with the marker in a pop-up menu by right-clicking on the marker.

Note   In the pop-up menu, a check mark next to a key indicates that the key is shared with another instance.

The marker pop-up menu also offers options for deleting selected keys or filtering the keys. In addition, there is a Goto Time command, which automatically moves the Time Slider to the key's location when selected.

To delete a key marker with all of its keys, right-click to open the pop-up menu and choose Delete Key ➪ All, or select the key marker and press the Delete key.

Viewing and Editing Key Values

At the top of the marker's right-click pop-up menu is a list of current keys for the selected object (or if there are too many keys for a marker, they will be placed under the Key Properties menu). When you select one of these keys, a key information dialog box opens. This dialog box displays different controls depending on the type of key that is selected. Figure 24-6 shows the dialog box for the Position key. There will be slight variations in this dialog box depending on the key type.

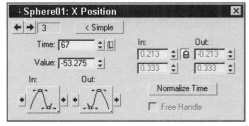

Figure 24-6: Key dialog boxes enable you to change the key parameters.

Note   You can also access key-specific dialog boxes in the Motion panel for a selected object by clicking the Parameters button.

Within each of these key dialog boxes is a Time value that shows the current frame. Next to the Time value are two arrows that enable you to move easily to the other keys in the scene. The dialog box also includes several text fields, where you can change the key parameters.

Most of the key dialog boxes also include flyout buttons for selecting Key Tangents. Key Tangents determine how the animation moves into and out of the key. For example, if the In Key Tangent is set to Slow and the Out Key Tangent is set to Fast, the object will approach the key position in a slow manner but accelerate as it leaves the key position. The arrow buttons on either side of the Key Tangent buttons can copy the current Key Tangent selection to the previous or next key.

The six different types of Tangents are detailed in Table 24-3.

Table 24-3: Key Tangents

Toolbar Button	Name	Description
	Smooth	The default type that produces straight, smooth motion.
	Linear	Moves at a constant rate between keys.
	Step	Causes discontinuous motion between keys. It occurs only between matching In-Out pairs.
	Slow	Decelerates as you approach the key.
	Fast	Accelerates as you approach the key.
	Custom	Lets you control the Tangent handles in function curves mode.
	Custom – Locked Handles	Lets you control the Tangent handles in function curves mode with the handles locked.

Using the Motion Panel

And yet, there is another way to create keys using the Motion panel. The Motion panel in the Command Panel includes settings and controls for animating objects. At the top of the Motion panel are two buttons: Parameters and Trajectories.

Setting parameters

The Parameters button on the Motion panel lets you assign controllers and create and delete keys. Controllers are custom key-creating algorithms that can be defined through the Parameters rollout, shown in Figure 24-7. These controllers are assigned by selecting the position, rotation, or scaling track and clicking the Assign Controller button to open a list of applicable controllers that you can select.

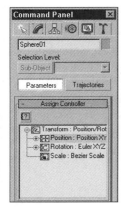

Figure 24-7: The Parameters section of the Motion panel lets you assign controllers and create keys.

Cross-Reference For more information on controllers, see Chapter 28, "Animating with Controllers."

Below the Assign Controllers rollout is the PRS Parameters rollout, where you can create and delete Position, Rotation, and Scale keys. You can use this rollout to create keys whether or not the Auto Key or Set Key buttons are enabled. For Position and Rotation keys, you can also select the Axis to use.

Below the PRS Parameters rollout are two Key Info rollouts: Basic and Advanced. These rollouts include the same key-specific information that you can access using the right-click pop-up menu found in the Track Bar.

Using trajectories

A trajectory is the actual path that the animation follows. When you click the Trajectories button in the Motion panel, the animation trajectory is shown as a spline with each key displayed as a node and each frame shown as a white dot. You can then edit the trajectory and its nodes by clicking the Sub-Object button at the top of the Motion panel, shown in Figure 24-8. The only subobject available is Keys. With the subobject button enabled, you can use the transform buttons to move and reposition the trajectory nodes. You can also add and delete keys with the Add Key and Delete Key buttons.

For more control over the trajectory path, you can convert the trajectory path to a normal editable spline with the Convert To button. You can also convert an existing spline into a trajectory with the Convert From button.

To use the Convert From button, select an object, click the Convert From button, and then click a spline path in the scene. This creates a new trajectory path for the selected object. The first key of this path is the selected object's original position, and the second key is located at the spline's first vertex position. Additional keys are added as determined by the Samples value listed in the Sample Range group. All these new keys will be equally spaced between the Start and End times. The selected spline will be traversed from its initial vertex around the spline in order to the last vertex.

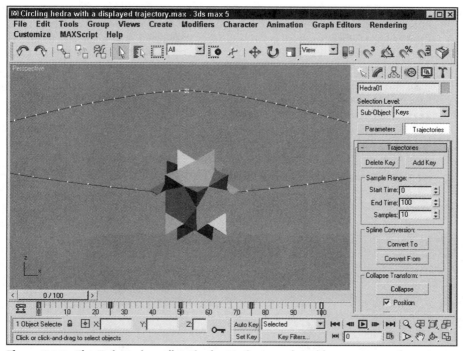

Figure 24-8: The Trajectories rollout in the Motion panel enables you to see the animation path as a spline.

Click the Collapse button at the bottom of the Trajectories rollout to reduce all transform keys into a single editable path. You can select which transformations to collapse including Position, Rotation, and Scale using the options under the Collapse button. For example, an object with several Controllers assigned can be collapsed, thereby reducing the complexity of all the keys.

Note If you collapse all keys, you will not be able to alter their parameters via the controller rollouts.

The Views menu includes an option to Show Key Times. Enabling this option causes the display of the frame numbers next to any key along a trajectory path.

Tutorial: Making an airplane follow a looping path

Airplanes that perform aerobatic stunts often follow paths that are smooth. You can see this clearly when watching a sky writer. In this example, I've created a simple looping path using the Line spline primitive, and we'll use this path to make a plane complete a loop.

To make an airplane follow a looping path, follow these steps:

1. Open the Looping airplane.max file from the Chap 24 directory on the CD-ROM. This file includes a simple looping spline path and an airplane created by Viewpoint Datalabs.

2. With the airplane selected, open the Motion panel and click on the Trajectories button. Then click on the Convert From button in the Trajectories rollout and select the path in the Front viewport.

3. If you drag the Time Slider, you'll notice that the plane moves along the path, but it doesn't rotate with the path. To fix this, Click the Key Mode Toggle button in the Time Controls to easily move from key to key. Click the Key Filters button and select only Rotation, then click the Set Key button (or press the ' key) to enter Set Key mode.

4. Select the Select and Rotate button, rotate the plane in the Front viewport to match the path and click the large Set Keys button (or press the K key) to create a rotation key. Click the Next Key button to move to the next key and repeat this step until rotation keys have been set for the entire path.

5. Drag the Time Slider and watch the airplane circle about the loop.

Cross-Reference   There is an easier way to make the plane follow the path using the Path constraint. To learn more about constraints, see Chapter 27, "Restricting Movement with Constraints."

Figure 24-9 shows the plane's trajectory.

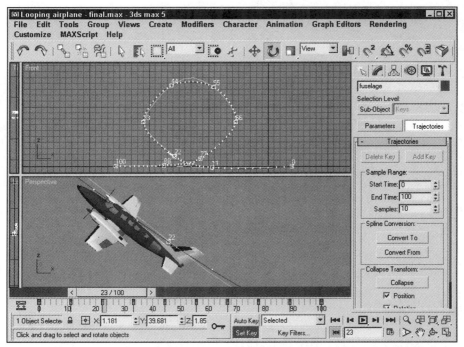

Figure 24-9: Using a spline path, the position keys are automatically set for this plane.

Using Ghosting

As you're trying to animate objects, using the ghosting feature can be very helpful. This feature displays a copy of the object being animated before and after its current position. To enable ghosting, choose Views ➪ Show Ghosting. This command uses the options set in the Preference Settings dialog box. Access this dialog box by choosing Customize ➪ Preferences. In the Viewports panel of this dialog box is a Ghosting section.

You use this Ghosting section to set how many ghosted objects are to appear, whether the ghosted objects appear before, after, or both before and after the current frame, and whether frame numbers should be shown. You can also specify every Nth frame to be displayed. There is also an option to display the ghost object in wireframe (they are displayed as shaded if this option is not enabled) and an option to Show Frame Numbers. Objects before the current frame are colored yellow and objects after are colored light blue.

Figure 24-10 shows a Hedra object that is animated to travel in a simple circle with ghosting enabled. The Preference settings are set to show three ghosting frames at every five frames before and after the current frame. The Trajectory path has also been enabled.

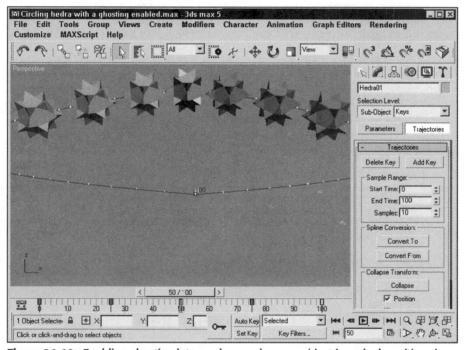

Figure 24-10: Enabling ghosting lets you know where an object is and where it's going.

Animating Objects

Many different objects in Max can be animated, including geometric objects, cameras, lights, and materials. In this section, we'll look at several different types of objects and parameters that can be animated.

Animating cameras

You can animate cameras using the standard transform buttons found on the main toolbar. When animating a camera that actually moves in the scene, using a Free camera is best. A Target camera can be pointed by moving its target, but you risk its being flipped over if the target is ever directly above the camera. If you want to use a Target camera, attach both the camera and its target to a Dummy object using the Link button and move the Dummy object.

Two useful constraints when animating cameras are the Path constraint and the Look At constraint. You can find both of these in the Animation ➪ Constraints menu. Path constraint can make a camera follow a spline path, and the Look At constraint can direct the focus of a camera to follow an object as the camera or the object moves through the scene.

 Cross-Reference   For more on constraints, including these two, see Chapter 27, "Restricting Movement with Constraints."

Animating lights

The process for animating lights includes many of the same techniques as that for animating cameras. For moving lights, use a Free spotlight or attach a Target spotlight to a Dummy object. You can also use the Look At and Path Controllers with lights.

 Cross-Reference   If you need to animate the sun at different times in the day, use the Sunlight system, which I discuss in Chapter 22, "Working with Lights."

To flash lights on and off, enable and disable the On parameter at different frames and assign a Step Tangent. To dim lights, just alter the Multiplier value over several frames.

Animating materials

You can animate materials by changing an object's parameters at different frames with the Auto Key button enabled. You can also control maps and their mapping coordinate systems in this manner.

You can also animate materials by applying an animated bitmap as a material. You can do so using an AVI, FLC, or IFL file.

 Cross-Reference   For more detail on these material types, see Chapter 19, "Creating and Applying Materials."

Tutorial: Animating darts hitting a dartboard

As a simple example of animating objects using the Auto Key button, we'll animate several darts hitting a dartboard.

To animate several darts hitting a dartboard, follow these steps:

   1. Open the Dart and Dartboard.max file from the Chap 24 directory on the CD-ROM.

   This file includes a dart and dartboard objects created by Zygote Media.

   2. Click the Auto Key button (or press the N key) to enable animation mode. Drag the Time Slider to frame 25 and click the Select and Move button on the main toolbar.

   3. Select the first dart in the Left viewport and drag it to the left until its tip just touches the dartboard.

   This step creates a key in the Track Bar for frames 0 and 25.

4. Click the Select and Rotate button on the main toolbar, set the reference coordinate system to Local, and constrain the rotation to the Y-axis. Then drag the selected dart in the Front viewport to rotate it about its local Y-axis.

   This step also sets a key in the Track Bar.

5. Select the second dart and click the Select and Move button again. Right-click the Time Slider to make the Create Key dialog box appear. Make sure that the check boxes for Position and Rotation are selected and click OK.

   This step creates a key that will keep the second dart from moving before it's ready.

6. With the second dart still selected, drag the Time Slider to frame 50 and move the dart to the dartboard as shown in Step 3. Then repeat Step 4 to set the rotation key for the second dart.

7. Repeat Steps 3, 4, and 5 for the last two darts.

8. Click the Auto Key button (or press the N key) again to disable animation mode, maximize the Perspective viewport, and click the Play Animation button to see the animation. Figure 24-11 shows the darts as they're flying toward the dartboard.

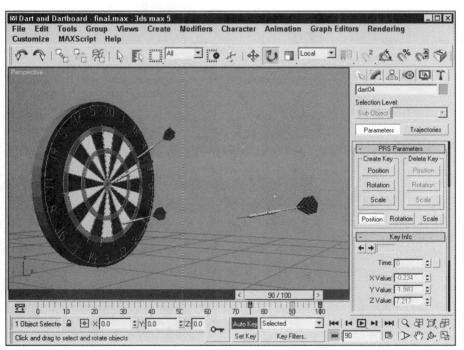

Figure 24-11: One frame of the dart animation

Working with Previews

More than likely, your final output will be rendered using the highest quality settings with all effects enabled, and you can count on this taking a fair amount of time. After waiting several days for a sequence to render is a terrible time to find out that your animation keys are off. Even viewing animation sequences in the viewports with the Play Animation button cannot catch all problems.

One way to catch potential problems is to create a sample preview animation. Previews are test animation sequences that render quickly to give you an idea of the final output. The Animation menu includes several commands for creating, renaming, and viewing previews. The rendering options available for previews are the same as the shading options that are available in the viewports.

Creating previews

You create previews by choosing Animation ➪ Make Preview to open the Make Preview dialog box, shown in Figure 24-12.

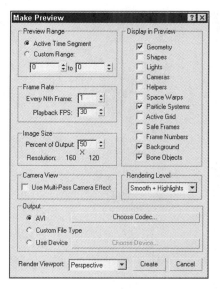

Figure 24-12: The Make Preview dialog box lets you specify the range, size, and output of a preview file.

In the Make Preview dialog box, you can specify what frames to include using the Active Time Segment or Custom Range options. You can also choose Every Nth Frame or select a specific frame rate in the Playback FPS field. The image size is determined by the Percent of Output value, which is a percentage of the final output size. The resolution is also displayed.

The Display in Preview section offers a variety of options to include in the preview. These options include Geometry, Shapes, Lights, Cameras, Helpers, Space Warps, Particle Systems, Active Grid, Safe Frames, Frame Numbers, Background, and Bone Objects. Because the preview output is rendered like the viewports, certain selected objects such as Lights and Cameras actually display their icons as part of the file. The Frame Numbers option prints the frame number in the upper-left corner of each frame.

The Rendering Level drop-down list includes the same shading options used to display objects in the viewports, including Smooth, Smooth + Highlights, Facets, Facets + Highlights, Lit Wireframes, Wireframe, and Bounding Box.

Output options include the default AVI option; a Custom File Type option, which enables you to choose your own format; and the Use Device option, which you can use to render the preview to a different device. For the AVI option, you can select a Codec, which is used to compress the resulting file. Options include Cinepak Code by Radius, Microsoft Video 1, and Full Frames (uncompressed), depending on the Codecs that are installed on your system. When the Use Device option is selected, the Choose Device button becomes active. Clicking this button opens the Select Output Image Device dialog box, where you can select and configure output devices such as a Digital Recorder.

At the bottom of the dialog box is a Render Viewport drop-down list where you can select which viewport to use to create your preview file. The Create button starts the rendering process. When a preview is being rendered, the viewports are replaced with a single image of the current render frame, and the Status Bar is replaced by a Progress Bar and a Cancel button. Figure 24-13 shows a preview file being created.

Tip   You can also use the Esc key on your keyboard to cancel a rendering job.

If you cancel the rendering, the Make Preview alert box offers the options Stop and Play, Stop and Don't Play, and Don't Stop.

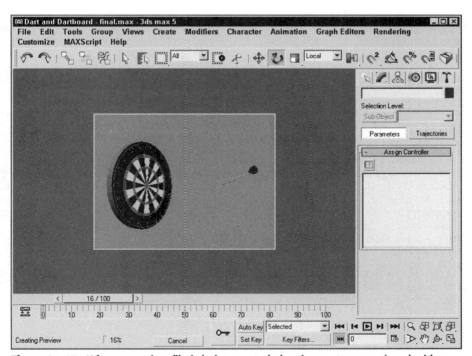

Figure 24-13: When a preview file is being created, the viewports are replaced with a single view of the current frame.

Viewing previews

When a preview file is finished rendering, the default Media Player for your system loads and displays the preview file. You can disable this autoplay feature using the Autoplay Preview File option in the General panel of the Preference Settings dialog box.

At any time, you can replay the preview file using the Animation ⇨ View Preview command. This command loads the latest preview file and displays it in the Media Player.

Renaming previews

The preview file is actually saved as a file named scene.avi and is saved by default in the previews subdirectory. Be aware that this file is automatically overwritten when a new preview is created. You can save a preview file by renaming it by choosing Animation ⇨ Rename Preview File. This command opens the Save Preview As dialog box, where you can give the preview file a name.

Wiring Parameters

Another useful way to expand the number of parameters is to create custom parameters. These custom parameters can define some aspect of the scene that makes sense to you. For example, if you create a model of the bicycle, you could define a custom parameter for the pedal rotation.

These custom parameters can then be wired to other objects using the Wiring Parameters feature. By wiring parameters, you can make the parameter of one object control the parameter of another object. For example, you can wire the On/Off parameter of a light to the movement of a switch. All parameters that can be animated can be wired.

Adding custom parameters

As if the standard parameters for the various modeling types weren't enough, you can also add your own custom parameters using the Add Parameter panel, shown in Figure 24-14. You can open this modeless panel by choosing Animation ⇨ Add Custom Attributes.

The Parameter Type drop-down list lets you choose the parameter format. Possibilities include float (a decimal-point number), integer, Boolean (true or false), array, node, color, and texture map. The UI Type drop-down list defines how the parameter is displayed in the rollout. How the parameter looks depends on the type of parameter. Float and integer values can be spinners or sliders, Boolean values can be check box or radio buttons, array values are drop-down lists, nodes are pick buttons (which allow you to select an object in the viewports), color values are color pickers, and texture maps are map buttons. You can also name the parameter.

The Options rollout changes depending on which parameter type was selected. These rollouts contain settings for the interface's Width, value ranges, default values, Alignment (left, right, or center), and list items.

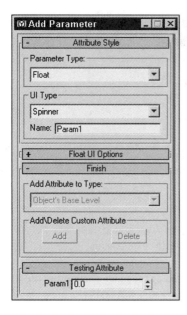

Figure 24-14: You can use the Add Parameter dialog box to create custom parameters.

The Finish rollout is used to tell which rollout to add the custom attribute to. From the Add Attribute to Type drop-down list, you can choose to add the attribute to the object's base level, to the selected modifier, or to the object material. The Add and Delete buttons can make the custom parameter appear or disappear in the rollout you specified. The Testing Attribute rollout shows what the interface element will look like.

The value of custom attributes becomes apparent when you start wiring parameters.

Using the Parameter Wiring dialog box

You can access the Parameter Wiring dialog box in several places. The Animation ➪ Wire Parameters ➪ Wire Parameters menu makes a pop-up menu of parameters appear. Selecting a parameter from the menu changes the cursor to a dotted line (like the one used when linking objects). Click the object that you want to wire to, and another pop-up menu lets you choose the parameter to wire to. The Parameter Wiring dialog box appears with the parameter for each object selected from a hierarchy tree.

You can also wire parameters using the right-click quadmenu and selecting Wire Parameters. The Wire Parameters option is disabled if multiple objects are selected.

The Parameter Wiring dialog box, shown in Figure 24-15, displays two tree lists containing all the available parameters. This tree list looks very similar to the Track View and lets you connect parameters in either direction or to each other. If you used the Wire Parameters feature to open the Parameter Wiring dialog box, then the parameter for each object will already be selected and highlighted in yellow.

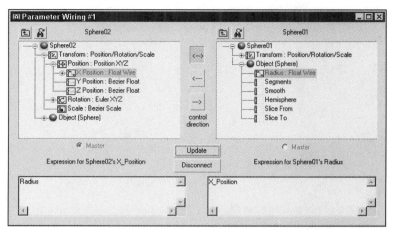

Figure 24-15: The Parameter Wiring dialog box can work with expressions.

The three arrow buttons between the two tree lists let you specify the connection direction. These buttons connect the parameter in one pane to the selected parameter in the opposite pane. The direction determines whether the parameter in the left pane controls the parameter in the right pane or vice versa. You can also select the top bidirectional button to make the parameters mutually affect each other. Below each tree list is a text area where you can enter an expression. An *expression* is a mathematical statement that follows a specific syntax for defining how one parameter controls the other. These expressions can be any valid expression that is accepted in the Animation Controller dialog box or in MAXScript.

You can learn more about creating and using expressions in Chapter 29, "Using Expressions."

After an expression is entered, click the Connect button to complete the wiring. Based on the connection direction, the Master radio button will indicate which object will control the other. You can also use this dialog box to disconnect existing wired parameters. You can use the two icon buttons at the top of the dialog box, shown in the following table, to Show All Tracks and to find the next wired parameter.

Button	Description
![icon]	Show All Tracks
![icon]	Next Wired Parameter

After the wiring is completed, the Parameter Wiring dialog box remains open. You can try out the wiring by moving the master object. If the results aren't what you wanted, you can edit the expression and click the Update button (the Connect button will change to an Update button).

If the expression contains an error, the track title will be displayed in red and an error dialog box appears, telling you what the error is. You need to correct the error and click the Update button before the wiring will be in effect. If the wiring is successful, then the track title is displayed in green.

Manipulator helpers

To create general use controls that can be wired to control various properties, Max includes three Manipulator Helpers. These helpers are Cone Angle, Plane Angle, and Slider. They are available as a subcategory under the Helpers category of the Create panel.

For the Cone Angle helper, you can set the Angle, Distance, and Aspect settings. The default cone is a circle, but you can make it a square. The Plane Angle helper includes settings for Angle, Distance, and Size.

You can name the Slider helper. This name will appear in the viewports above the slider object. You can also set a default value along with maximum and minimum values. To position the object, you can set the X Position, Y Position, and Width settings. You can also set a snap value for the slider.

Once created, you can use these manipulator helpers when the Select and Manipulate button on the main toolbar is enabled (this button must be disabled before the manipulator helpers can be created). The advantage of these helpers is in wiring parameters to be controlled using the helpers.

Tutorial: Controlling a crocodile's bite

One way to use manipulator helpers and wired parameters is to control within limits certain parameters that can be animated. This gives your animation team controls they can use to quickly build animation sequences. In this example, you'll use a slider to control a crocodile's jaw movement.

To create a slider to control a crocodile's bite, follow these steps:

1. Open the Biting crocodile.max file from the Chap 24 directory on the CD-ROM.

   This file includes a crocodile model created by Viewpoint Datalabs. For this model, the head, eyes, and upper teeth have been joined into a single object, and the pivot point for this object has been moved to where the jaw hinges.

2. Open the Create panel, select the Helpers category, and select the Manipulators subcategory from the drop-down list. Click the Slider button and drag in the Perspective view above the crocodile. Name the slider **Croc Bite** and set the Maximum value to 60.

3. With the Slider selected, choose Animation ➪ Wire Parameter ➪ Wire Parameter to access the pop-up menu. Choose Object (Slider) ➪ value option and drag the dotted line to the crocodile's head object and click. Choose Transform ➪ Rotation.

   The Parameter Wiring dialog box appears.

4. In the Parameter Wiring dialog box, click the direction arrow that points from the Slider to the head. In the expression text area under the head object, enter the expression **angleaxis value [0,1,0]** and click the Connect button.

5. Click the Select and Manipulate button on the main toolbar and drag the slider to the right.

   The crocodile's mouth opens.

Figure 24-16 shows the crocodile biting using the slider control.

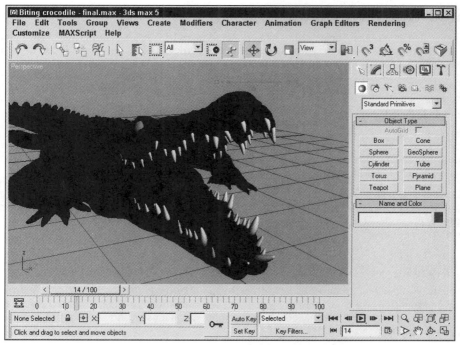

Figure 24-16: A slider control is wired to open the crocodile's mouth.

Animation Modifiers

Modifiers are used to deform and otherwise alter the geometry of objects in an automatic way. These alterations can include animated changes. The Modifiers menu includes a submenu that contains many such modifiers. These modifiers are unique in that each of them changes with time. They can be useful as an alternate to controllers, but their resulting effects are very specific.

Cross-Reference   Some of the modifiers contained in this submenu are covered elsewhere. I cover the Skin modifier in Chapter 31, "Working with Bones and Skin," and the Flex modifier in Chapter 30, "Creating a Dynamic Simulation."

Morpher modifier

The Morpher modifier lets you change a shape from one form into another. You can only apply this modifier to objects with the same number of vertices.

Cross-Reference   In many ways, the Morph modifier is similar to the Morph compound object, which is covered in Chapter 16, "Building Compound Objects."

The Morpher modifier can be very useful for creating facial expressions and character lip-synching. You can also use it to morph materials. There are 100 separate channels available for morph targets, and channels can be mixed. You can use the Morpher modifier in conjunction with the Morpher material. For example, you could use the Morpher material to blush a character for an embarrassed expression.

Tip   When it comes to making facial expressions, a mirror and your own face can be the biggest help. Coworkers will look at you funny, but your facial expressions will benefit from the exercise.

The first task before using this modifier is to create all the different morph targets. Since the morph targets need to contain the same number of vertices as the base object, make a copy of the base object for each morph target that you are going to create. As you create these targets, be careful not to add or delete any vertices from the object.

Once all your morph targets are created, select a channel in the Channel Parameters rollout, shown in Figure 24-17, and use the Pick Object from Scene button to select the morph target for that channel. Another option to picking is to Capture Current State. Once a morph target has been added to a channel, you can view it in the Channel List rollout.

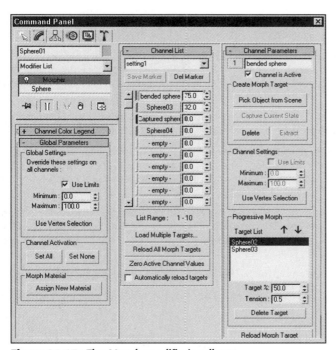

Figure 24-17: The Morph modifier's rollouts

As you animate, you can specify the amount of each morph target to include in the frame using the value to the right of the channel name in the Channel List rollout. The slim color bar to the left of the channel name designates the status of the channel. You can find information on what each color represents in the Channel Color Legend rollout.

The Channel Parameters rollout also includes a Progressive Morph section. This feature lets you define an intermediate step for how the morph is to progress with the final step being the morph target. Using these intermediate steps, you can control how the object morphs.

New Feature   The Progressive Morph feature is new to 3ds max 5.

Tutorial: Morphing facial expressions

The Morph modifier is very helpful when you're trying to morph facial expressions such as those to make a character talk. With the various sounds added to the different channels, you can quickly morph between them. In this example, we'll use the Morph modifier to change the facial expressions of the general character.

Tip   When creating facial expressions, be sure to enable the Soft Selection features, which makes modifying the face meshes much easier.

To change facial expressions using the Morph modifier, follow these steps:

1. Open the Morphing facial expressions.max file from the Chap 24 directory on the CD-ROM. This file includes the General's head model created by Viewpoint Datalabs. The model has been copied twice and the morph targets have already been created by modifying the subobjects around the mouth.

2. Select the face on the left where the General is snarling and select the Modifiers ⇨ Animation Modifiers ⇨ Morpher to apply the Morpher modifier.

3. In the Channel Parameters rollout, select channel 1, click the Pick Object from Scene button, select the middle face object, and name it Closed lips. Then repeat this step for smiling face and name it Smile. If you look in the Channel List rollout, you'll see Closed lips in Channel 1 and Smile in Channel 2.

4. Click the Auto Key button (or press the N key), drag the Time Slider to frame 50 and then increase the Closed lips channel in the Channel List rollout to 100. Drag the Time Slider to frame 100 and increase the Smile channel to 100 and the Closed lips channel to 0.

5. Click on the Play Animation button in the Time Controls to see the resulting animation.

Figure 24-18 shows the three facial expressions. The Morpher modifier is applied to the left face.

Tip   Be sure to keep the morph target objects around. You can hide them in the scene or select them and save them to a separate file with the File ⇨ Save Selected menu command.

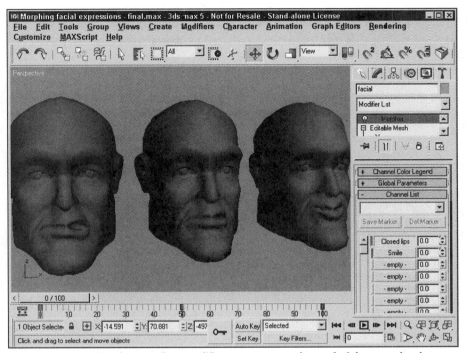

Figure 24-18: Using the Morpher modifier, you can morph one facial expression into another.

Melt modifier

The Melt modifier simulates an object melting by sagging and spreading edges over time. Melt parameters include Amount and Spread values, Solidity (which can be Ice, Glass, Jelly, or Plastic), and a Melt Axis.

Figure 24-19 shows the Melt modifier applied to the snowman model (it was inevitable).

Linked XForm modifier

The Linked XForm modifier passes all transformations of one object onto another, but not vice versa. The object that controls the transformation is designated as the Control Object and is selected via the Pick Control Object button (which is the only control in the Parameters rollout for this modifier). After the Control object is selected, the Control Object controls the selected object's transforms, but the object that is being controlled can move independent of the control object without affecting the control object.

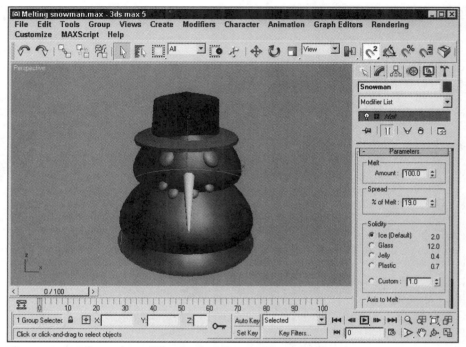

Figure 24-19: The Melt modifier slowly deforms objects to a flat plane.

PatchDeform and SurfDeform modifiers

Among the animation modifiers are several modifers that are similar in function, but that work on different types of objects. The PatchDeform modifier uses patches, and the SurfDeform modifier deforms an object according to a NURBS surface.

In the Parameters rollout for each of these modifiers is a Pick Patch (or Surface) button that lets you select an object to use in the deformation process. After the object is selected, you can enter the Percent and Stretch values for the U and V directions, along with a Rotation value.

Note   The PatchDeform modifier is also available as a World Space Modifier (WSM). WSM modifiers are similar to the normal Object Space Modifiers (OSM), except that they use World Space coordinates instead of Object Space coordinates. The most noticeable difference is that WSMs don't use gizmos.

Tutorial: Deforming a car going over a hill

Have you seen those commercials that use rubber cars to follow the curvature of the road as they drive? In this tutorial, we'll use the PatchDeform modifier to bend a car over a hill made from a patch.

To deform a car according to a patch surface, follow these steps:

1. Open the 57 Chevy bending over a hill.max file from the Chap 09 directory on the CD-ROM.

   This file contains a simple hill made from patch objects and a '57 Chevy model created by Viewpoint Datalabs.

2. Select the car model and choose the *PatchDeform modifier from the Modifier List drop-down list in the Modifier Stack of the Modify panel.

This applies the World Space PatchDeform modifier (WSM) to the car object.

3. In the Parameters rollout, click the Pick Patch button and select the hill object.

This makes the car deform around the patch hill object.

4. Set the U Percent value to 50, the V Percent value to 90, and the U and V Stretch values to 1.0. I've set the Deform Plane to the XY plane.

Figure 24-20 shows the results of this tutorial.

Figure 24-20: Our '57 Chevy hugs the road thanks to the PatchDeform modifier.

PathDeform modifier

The PathDeform modifier uses a spline path to deform an object. The Pick Path button lets you select a spline to use in the deformation process. You can select either an open or closed spline. The Parameters rollout also includes spinners for controlling the Percent, Stretch, Rotation, and Twist of the object. The Percent value is the distance the object moves along the path.

Figure 24-21 shows some text wrapped around a spline path.

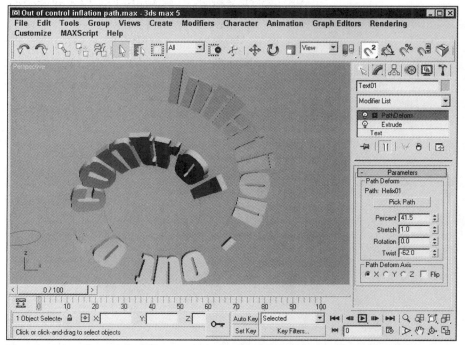

Figure 24-21: The text in this example has been deformed around a spline path using the PathDeform modifier.

Summary

This chapter covered the basics of animating objects in Max including working with time and keys. You've also learned about the two key creation modes and editing keys. There are a number of animation helps such as trajectories and ghosting. Also several ways to automatically create keys like wiring parameters and animation modifiers. In this chapter you've learned how to

✦ Control time and work with keys

✦ Use the two key creation modes

✦ Work with the Track Bar and the Motion panel

✦ View and edit key values

✦ Use trajectories and ghosting

✦ Create custom parameters, wire parameters, and use manipulator helpers

✦ Use the various animation modifiers

After this brief introduction to animation, you're ready to move on to the Track View, which offers the ability to control every aspect of an animation.

"The Golden Age of Battleships" (top image) won first prize for 3dluvr.com's Ship and Sea contest, and "on the station in 1902" won second prize in the 3dluvr.com's Iron Horse contest. Both images were created by Balazs Kiss (ward@3dluvr.com).

Alexander Beim created these images titled "Susy" and "Snake." In these images, Alex makes great use of detailed textures. You can find more of Alexander's work at his Web site at www.lotusart.de.

Enchanted Forest

www.pedramk.com | Pedram.K 2002

This image, titled "Enchanted Forest," was created by Pedram Karimfazli. It uses procedural textures and was rendered with the Brazil rendering system. Pedram's Web site is www.pedramk.com.

"Pixman's Dream," created by Victor Rodriguez (indi@3dluvr.com), was the winning entry in an internal contest for testers of the Arnold plug-in rendering system.

The image to the right titled "3 Heads" is a good example of the character-creation capabilities of Max. Created by Daniel Martinez Lara, these characters are infused with life and expression. These three characters are named Anibal, Pepe, and Leo. You can meet these characters at Daniel's Web site at www.Pepeland.com.

The image to the left, titled "Little Warriors," was created by Daniel Martinez Lara and rendered using the Arnold rendering system. The small marine soldier was modeled by Kike Oliva. Daniel's Web site shows some great character animation techniques and is worth checking out.

This image, titled "Tribirian Oasis," was created by Sue Blackman. It shows amazing attention to detail, such as the rings in the animal's ear and the various insects climbing the trees.

This image, titled "Chevy Shed," was created by Chris Pember (gunnah@3dluvr.com) using the new advanced lighting features of version 5.

This image of Ganesha, the Indian God of wisdom, prudence, and salvation, was created by Matt Clark (acme@3dluvr.com) and shows the amazing modeling capabilities of Max.

These vehicles, "'57 Chevy Sport Coupe" and "Messerschmidt KR-200," were created by Joaquin Alvarez (joaq@bigfoot.com).

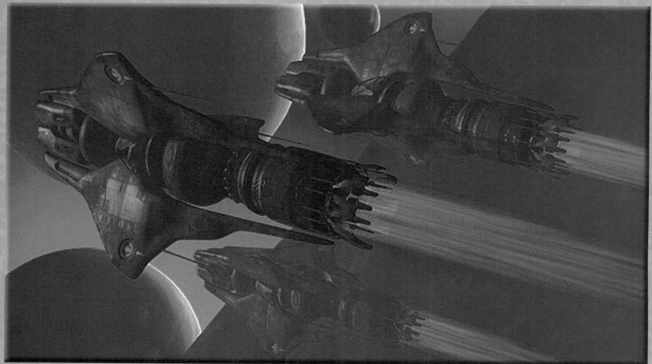

These vibrant space scenes, titled "Mars Civilization" and "Near Pegasus," were created by Stéphane Chasseloup (dsigna@3dluvr.com).

Joel LeLievre (intrinsia@3dluvr.com) created these images titled "Mountain Villa" and "Swamp Villa." Notice the use of projection lights on the lower image.

These images, titled "Smart Car" and "Mediterranean Window" were created by Jonatan Catalan (sytron@3dluvr.com).

This image, titled "Can't Rain All the Time," was created by Torbjorn Olsson (toby@3dluvr.com).

JUSTIN R. DURBAN - "EDGEN"

JUSTIN R. DURBAN - "EDGEN"

These two images, "Forest" and "Wildcat Eye," were taken from an animation created by Justin Durban. Justin's work is featured on his Web site at www.edgen.com.

The table set image was created by Syzmon Masiak and is a good example of the realism possible with Max. The lower image, titled "Space Lab," was created by Molly Barr. Molly's Web site, www.dragontree.com, features fantasy images created with Max.

Ayman Kamel (mgallery@idsc.net.eg) created these images, titled "Akhnaton @ Zero" and "Horus Release."

Working with the Track View

As you move objects around in a viewport, you'll often find yourself eyeballing the precise location of an object in the scene. If you've ever found yourself wishing that you could precisely see all the values behind the scene, then you need to find the Track View. The Track View can be viewed using three different layouts — Curve Editor, Dope Sheet, and Track Bar. Each of these interfaces offers a unique view into the details of the scene.

All of these Track View layouts can display all the details of the current scene, including all the parameters and keys. This view lets you manage and control all these parameters and keys without having to look in several different places.

Track Views also includes additional features that enable you to edit key ranges, add and synchronize sound to your scene, and work with animation controllers using function curves.

Learning the Track View Interface

Although the Track View can be viewed using different layouts, the basic interface elements are the same. They all have menus, toolbars, a Controller pane, a Key pane, and a Time Ruler. Figure 25-1 shows these interface elements. You can hide any of these interface elements using the Show UI Elements option in the right-click pop-up menu.

The Track View layouts

The Track View includes three different layouts — a Curve Editor, a Dope Sheet, and the Track Bar. The Curve Editor layout displays all parameter and motion changes as graphs that change over time. You manipulate these curves just like normal splines. You can use the Dope Sheet layout to coordinate key ranges between the different parameter tracks. And the Track Bar layout offers a way to quickly view the Track View within the viewports.

You can open the Curve Editor and Dope Sheet layouts using the Graph Editors menu command. You can open the Curve Editor window by choosing Graph Editors ⇨ Track View – Curve Editor or by clicking the Curve Editor button on the main toolbar. You open the Dope Sheet interface in a similar manner by choosing Graph Editors ⇨ Track View – Dope Sheet.

Menus   Controller pane   Key pane

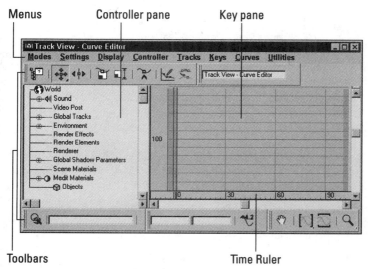

Toolbars   Time Ruler

Figure 25-1: The Track View interface offers a complete hierarchical look at your scene.

You also use the Graph Editors menu to access the Schematic View interface. For more on the Schematic View interface, see Chapter 8, "Grouping and Linking Objects."

After the Track View opens, you can give it a unique name using the field found in the Name: Track View toolbar. If the Name toolbar isn't visible, right-click on the title bar and select Show Toolbars ➪ Name: Track View from the pop-up menu. These named views are then listed in the Graph Editors ➪ Saved Track Views menu. Any saved Track Views that are named are saved along with the scene file.

To open the Track Bar layout in the viewports, expand the Track Bar using the small icon at the left end of the Track Bar. Close the Track Bar layout by clicking on the Close button on the toolbar. Figure 25-2 shows this Track View.

After you open a Track View, you can switch between the Curve Editor and the Dope Sheet using the Modes menu or by right-clicking on the menu bar or toolbar (away from the buttons) and selecting a new layout from the Load Layout menu. You can also save customized layouts using the Save Layout or Save Layout As menu commands.

Track View menus and toolbars

In many cases, the menus and the toolbars provide access to the same functionality. One difference is the Modes menu, which lets you switch the current interface between the Curve Editor and the Dope Sheet layouts. The Curve Editor menus include Modes, Settings, Display, Controller, Tracks, Keys, Curves, and Utilities. The Dope Sheet menu loses the Display and Curves menus and adds a Time menu. The Track Bar menus are the same as the Curve Editor except for the Modes menu.

The Track View now includes menus new to 3ds max 5.

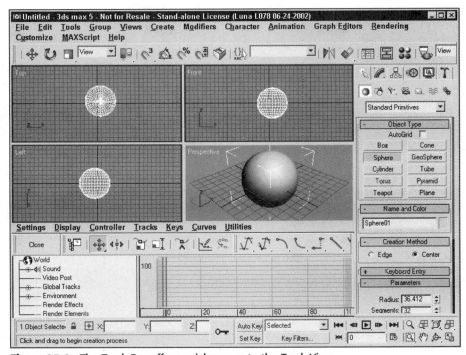

Figure 25-2: The Track Bar offers quick access to the Track View.

The Track View consists of several toolbars. You can open these toolbars by right-clicking on the toolbar (away from the buttons) and selecting the Show Toolbars submenu. The available toolbars depend on the layout, but they can include Name, Navigation, Key Stats, Key Tangents, Controllers, Track Selection, Keys, Time, Ranges, Display, Extras, Curves, and Tools, as shown in Figure 25-3. All of these toolbars can be docked, floated, and hidden. You can also add and delete new toolbars using the right-click pop-up menu.

You can learn more about docking and floating toolbars in Chapter 1, "Exploring the Max Interface."

For the Track View – Curve Editor layout, four toolbars appear by default at the top of the interface. These toolbars includes the Keys, Curves, Key Tangents, and Name toolbars. For the Track View – Dope Sheet, the default toolbars at the top of the interface include the Keys: Dope Sheet, Time, Display, and Name toolbars.

Depending on the size of the Track View window, you may need to drag the toolbar to the left to see the buttons at the right end of the toolbar.

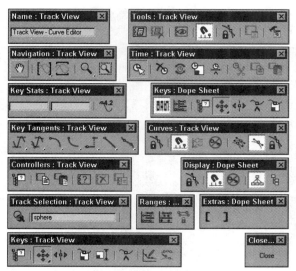

Figure 25-3: The Track View toolbars

Keys toolbar

The Keys toolbar is one of the default toolbars for the Curve Editor and for the Dope Sheet. The toolbar is slightly different in each layout. Table 25-1 describes these buttons.

Table 25-1: Keys Toolbar Buttons

Toolbar Button	Name	Description
	Filters	Opens the Filter dialog box, where you can specify which tracks will appear.
	Move Keys, Move Keys Horizontal, Move Keys Vertical	Enables you to move the selected keys or limit their movement to horizontal or vertical.
	Slide Keys	Enables you to slide the selected keys.
	Scale Keys	Enables you to scale the selected keys.
	Scale Values	Scales the selected keys' values vertically. Curve Editor layout only.
	Add Keys	Enables you to add new keys to a track.
	Draw Curves	Create a function curve by dragging the mouse. Curve Editor layout only.

Toolbar Button	Name	Description
	Reduce Keys	Optimizes the current time selection by eliminating unnecessary keys. Curve Editor layout only.
	Edit Keys	Enables edit keys mode. Dope Sheet layout only.
	Edit Ranges	Enables edit ranges mode. Dope Sheet layout only.

Curves toolbar

The Curves toolbar is another one of the default toolbars for the Curve Editor. This toolbar shares some of the same buttons with the Display toolbar, which is a default toolbar in the Dope Sheet layout. Table 25-2 describes these buttons.

Table 25-2: Curves and Display Toolbar Buttons

Toolbar Button	Name	Description
	Lock Selection	Prevents any changes to the current selection.
	Snap Frames	Causes moved tracks to snap to the nearest frame.
	Parameter Curve Out-of-Range Types	Opens the Parameter Curve Out-of-Range Types dialog box, where you can make tracks loop and cycle. Curve Editor layout only.
	Show Keyable Icons	Displays a key icon next to all tracks that can be animated.
	Show All Tangents	Displays the Bézier curve handles for all keys. Curve Editor layout only.
	Show Tangents	Displays the Bézier curve handles for the selected keys. Curve Editor layout only.
	Lock Tangents	Prevents the curve handles from moving. Curve Editor layout only.
	Modify Subtree	Causes changes to a parent to affect its children. Dope Sheet layout only.
	Modify Child Keys	Causes changes to child keys when parent keys are changed. Dope Sheet layout only.

Key Tangents toolbar

The Key Tangents toolbar is another one of the default toolbars for the Curve Editor. It is used to set the In and Out curve types. This toolbar is also available in the Dope Sheet layout. Table 25-3 describes these buttons.

Table 25-3: Key Tangents Toolbar Buttons

Toolbar Button	Name	Description
	Set Tangents to Auto, Set In Tangents to Auto, Set Out Tangents to Auto	Sets curve to approach and leave the key in an automatic manner.
	Set Tangents to Custom, Set In Tangents to Custom, Set Out Tangents to Custom	Sets curve to approach and leave the key in a custom manner defined by the handle positions.
	Set Tangents to Fast, Set In Tangents to Fast, Set Out Tangents to Fast	Sets curve to approach and leave the key in an ascending manner.
	Set Tangents to Slow, Set In Tangents to Slow, Set Out Tangents to Slow	Sets curve to approach and leave the key in a descending manner.
	Set Tangents to Step, Set In Tangents to Step, Set Out Tangents to Step	Sets curve to approach and leave the key in a stepping manner.
	Set Tangents to Linear, Set In Tangents to Linear, Set Out Tangents to Linear	Sets curve to approach and leave the key in a linear manner.
	Set Tangents to Smooth, Set In Tangents to Smooth, Set Out Tangents to Smooth	Sets curve to approach and leave the key in a smooth manner.

Time toolbar

The Time toolbar is one of the default toolbars for the Dope Sheet. It is used to work with time ranges. Table 25-4 describes these buttons.

Table 25-4: Time Toolbar Buttons

Toolbar Button	Name	Description
	Select Time	Enables you to select a block of time by clicking and dragging.
	Delete Time	Deletes the selected block of time.

Toolbar Button	Name	Description
	Reverse Time	Reverses the order of the selected time block.
	Scale Time	Scales the current time block.
	Insert Time	Inserts an additional amount of time.
	Cut Time	Deletes the selected block of time and places it on the clipboard for pasting.
	Copy Time	Makes a copy of the selected block of time on the clipboard for pasting.
	Paste Time	Inserts the current clipboard time selection.

Controller toolbar

The Controller toolbar is available in both the Curve Editor and the Dope Sheet. It is used to assign controllers to tracks. Table 25-5 describes these buttons.

Table 25-5: Controller Toolbar Buttons

Toolbar Button	Name	Description
	Filters	Opens the Filter dialog box, where you can specify which tracks will appear. Same button is found in the Keys toolbar.
	Copy Controller	Copies the selected track for pasting elsewhere.
	Paste Controller	Pastes the last copied track.
	Assign Controller	Enables you to assign a controller to the selected track.
	Delete Controller	Removes the current controller.
	Make Controller Unique	Changes an instanced track to one that is unique.

Tools toolbar

The Tools toolbar is available in the Curve Editor and includes buttons to add some additional tracks such as the Notes and Visibility. Table 25-6 describe these buttons.

Table 25-6: Tools Toolbar Buttons

Toolbar Button	Name	Description
	Add Note Track	Adds a note track to the current track for recording information.
	Delete Note Track	Deletes an associated note track.
	Add Visibility Track	Adds a track to an object for controlling its visibility.
	Snap Frames	Causes moved tracks to snap to the nearest frame. Also found in the Curves toolbar.
	Lock Selection	Locks the current selection of keys so that no other keys can be selected.
	Properties	Displays a dialog box of properties associated with the track.
	Track View Utilities	Opens a dialog box of available Track View utilities.

Other toolbars

The Dope Sheet layout includes two additional toolbars—Ranges and Extras. Table 25-7 describes these buttons.

Table 25-7: Ranges and Extras Toolbar Buttons

Toolbar Button	Name	Description
	Edit Ranges	Enables edit ranges mode. Same button is found in the Keys toolbar.
	Position Ranges	Enables position ranges mode.
	Recouple Ranges	Used to line up the keys with the range.
	Exclude Left End Point	Leaves the left end point out of the current time block.
	Exclude Right End Point	Leaves the right end point out of the current time block.

Controller and Key panes

Below the menus (and below the topped docked toolbars) are two panes. The left pane, called the Controller pane, presents a hierarchical list of all the tracks. The right pane is called the Key pane, and it displays the time range, keys, or function curves, depending on the layout. You can pan the Controller pane by clicking and dragging on a blank section of the pane: The cursor changes to a hand to indicate when you can pan the pane.

New Feature Each track with a controller applied has an icon that represents the controller appearing on its left side. These controller icons are new to 3ds max 5.

Each track can include several subtracks. To display these subtracks, click the plus sign (+) to the left of the track name. To collapse a track, click the minus sign (–). You can also use the Settings menu to Auto Expand select hierarchy. Under the Settings ➪ Auto Expand menu are options for Selected Objects Only, Transforms, XYZ Components, Base Objects, Modifiers, Materials, and Children. For example, if the Auto Expand ➪ Transforms options is enabled, then the Transform tracks for all objects will be automatically expanded in the Track View. Using these settings can enable you to quickly find the track you're looking for.

The Settings ➪ Auto Select ➪ Animated toggle will automatically select all tracks that are animated. You can also auto select Position, Rotation, and/or Scale tracks. The Settings ➪ Auto Scroll menu command can be set for Selected and/or Objects tracks. This command will automatically move either the Selected tracks or the Objects track to the top of the Controller pane.

Note You can also select, expand, and collapse tracks using the right-click pop-up quadmenu.

The Controller pane includes many different types of tracks. By default, every scene includes the following tracks: World, Sound, Video Post, Global Tracks, Raytrace Engine Globals, Environment, Render Effects, Render Elements, Renderer, Global Shadow Parameters, Scene Materials, Medit Materials (for materials in the Material Editor), and Objects, as shown in Figure 25-4.

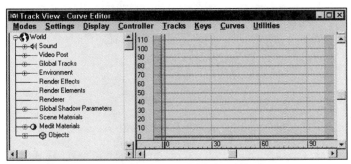

Figure 25-4: Several tracks are available by default.

The Shift, Ctrl, and Alt keys make selecting and de-selecting multiple tracks possible. To select a contiguous range of tracks, select a single track, then select another track while holding down the Shift key. This selects the two tracks and all tracks in between. Hold down the Ctrl key while selecting tracks to select multiple tracks that are not contiguous. The Alt key removes selected items from the selection set.

Below the right pane is the Time Ruler, which displays the current time as specified in the Time Configuration dialog box. The current frame is marked with a light blue time bar. This time bar is linked to the Time Slider, and moving one updates the other automatically.

At the top right of the Key pane (above the vertical scroll bar) is a split tab that you can use to split the Controller and Key pane into two separate views, as shown in Figure 25-5. Using this feature, you can look at two different sections of the tree at the same time. This makes it easy to copy and paste keys between different tracks.

Tip   You can drag the Time Ruler vertically in the right pane.

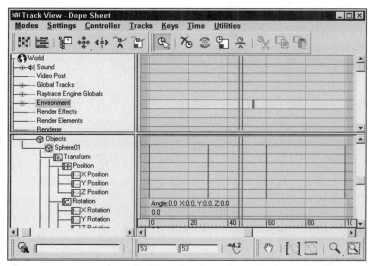

Figure 25-5: Drag the tab above the vertical scroll tab to split the Track View into two views.

Lower interface toolbars

At the bottom edge of the Track View window are three toolbars that appear by default. These toolbars include the Track Selection, Key Stats, and Navigation. Using these toolbars, you can locate specific tracks, see information on the various keys, and navigate the interface.

In the Track Selection toolbar is the Zoom Selected Object button and the Select by Name field, in which you can type a name to locate any tracks with that name.

Note   In the Select by Name field you can also use wildcard characters such as * (asterisk) and ? (question mark) to find several tracks.

The Key Stats toolbar includes Key Time and Value Display fields that display the current time and value. You can enter values in these fields to change the value for the current time. You can also enter an expression in these fields in which the variable n equals the key time or value. For example, to specify a key value that is 20 frames from the current frame, enter $n + 20$ (where you supply the current value in place of n). You can also include any function valid for the Expression controller, such as sin( ) or log( ). Click the Show Selected Key Stats button to display the key value in the Key pane.

Cross-Reference Chapter 29, "Using Expressions" presents the functions that are part of the Expression controller.

Table 25-8 describes the buttons found in the lower interface toolbars consisting of the Track Selection, Key Stats, and Navigation toolbars.

Table 25-8: Track Selection, Key Stats and Navigation Toolbar Buttons

Status Bar Button	Name	Description
	Zoom Selected Object	Places current selection at the top of the hierarchy.
	Show Selected Key Statistics	Displays the frame number and values next to each key.
	Pan	Pans the view.
	Zoom Horizontal Extents, Zoom Horizontal Extents Keys	Displays the entire horizontal track or keys.
	Zoom Value Extents	Displays the entire vertical track.
	Zoom, Zoom Time, Zoom Values	Zooms in and out of the view.
	Zoom Region	Zooms within a region selected by dragging the mouse.

Working with Keys

Keys define the main animation points in an animation. Max interpolates all the positions and values between the key points to generate the animation. Using the Track View, you can edit these animation keys with precision. Keys can be edited in either layout, but are probably easiest to edit in the Dope Sheet layout with the Edit Keys button enabled.

Cross-Reference Chapter 24, "Animation Basics," covers key creation in more detail.

In the Curve Editor, keys are shown as small squares positioned along the curve. In the Dope Sheet, keys are shown as colored lines that extend across the applicable tracks, as shown in Figure 25-6. The keys for the Position track are red, the Rotation track keys are green, the Scale track keys are blue, and the parameter tracks are yellow. Parent tracks (such as an object's name) will be colored gray. Selecting a parent key will select all its children keys. Any selected keys will appear white. The track title for any key that includes a key is highlighted yellow.

Caution   If the Key pane is not wide enough, then the keys will be shown as a thick, black line.

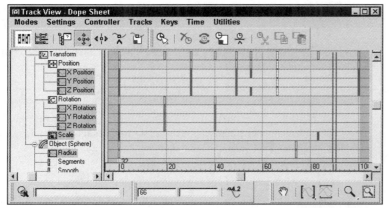

Figure 25-6: In the Dope Sheet, position keys are red, rotation keys are green, scale keys are blue, and parameter keys are yellow.

Selecting keys

Before you can move and edit keys, you need to be able to select them. Just like selecting keys on the Track Bar, you select keys by clicking on them. Selected keys will turn white. To select multiple keys hold down the Ctrl key while clicking on several keys, or drag an outline over several keys to select them. Click away from the keys to de-select all the selected keys.

With a key or multiple keys selected, you can lock the selection with the Lock Selection button. The Space key is the keyboard shortcut for this button. With the selection locked, you cannot select any new keys.

Tip   If you want to access a specific parameter in the Track View, you can right-click on the parameter and select the Show in Track View command from the pop-up menu, and the Track View will load with the parameter visible.

Using soft selection

The Keys menu also includes a Use Soft Select option. This feature is similar to the soft selection found in the Modify panel when working on subobject, except it works with keys. The Keys ⇨ Use Soft Select menu command will open a simple toolbar where you can enable soft selection and set the Range and Falloff values.

New Feature   Soft selection with the Curve Editor is new to 3ds max 5.

When enabled, all keys within a specified range are also selected and moved to a lesser degree than the selected key. When enabled, the function curve is displayed with a gradient for the Curve Editor layout and as a gradient across the key markers in the Dope Sheet layout. This shows the range and falloff for the curve.

Adding and deleting keys

You can add a key by clicking the Add Keys button (or pressing the A key) and clicking the location where the new key should appear. Each new key is set with the interpolated value between the existing keys.

To delete keys, select the keys, and click the Delete Keys button or press the Delete key on the keyboard. By selecting the track name and pressing the Delete key, you can delete all keys in a track.

Moving, sliding, and scaling keys

The Move Keys button (keyboard shortcut, M) lets you select and move a key to a new location. You can clone keys by holding down the Shift key while moving a key. Using the flyout buttons, you can select to restrict the movement horizontally or vertically. You can also move the selected key to the cursor's location with the Keys ⇨ Align to Cursor menu command.

The Slide Keys button lets you select a key and move all adjacent keys in unison to the left or right. If the selected key is moved to the right, all keys from that key to the end of the animation slide to the right. If the key is moved to the left, then all keys to the beginning of the animation slide to the left.

The Scale Keys button lets you move a group of keys closer together or farther apart. The scale center is the current frame. You can use the Shift key to clone keys while dragging.

If the Snap Frames (keyboard shortcut, S) button is enabled, then the selected key will snap to the nearest key as it is moved. This makes it easy to align keys to the same frame.

Editing keys

To edit the key parameters for any controller, click the Properties button; this opens the Key Info dialog box for most controllers. You can also access this dialog box by right-clicking a key and selecting Properties from the pop-up menu. These commands can also be used when multiple keys on the same or on different tracks are selected.

Using the Randomize Keys utility

The Randomize Keys utility lets you generate random time or key positions with an offset value. To access this utility, choose Utilities ⇨ Track View Utilities to open the Track View Utilities dialog box. From this dialog box, select Randomize Keys from the list of utilities and click OK; the Randomize Keys utility dialog box opens, as shown in Figure 25-7.

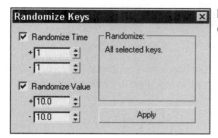

Figure 25-7: Use the Randomize Keys utility to create random key positions and values.

In this dialog box, you can specify positive and negative shift values for both Time and Value. Click the Apply button to apply the randomization process.

Displaying keyable icons

Sometimes it can be confusing to know what can be animated and what cannot. In the Curve Editor, you can identify which tracks can have keys set with the Display ➪ Keyable Icons menu command. This will display a red key icon to the left of each track that can hold a key.

These keys can also be disabled by clicking on the key icon. This will gray out the key and make the track so keys cannot be set for it. Figure 25-8 shows the Curve Editor with this feature enabled.

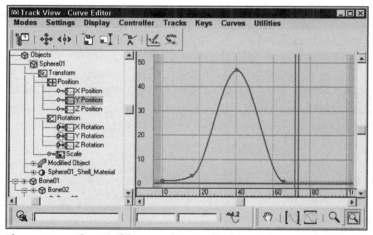

Figure 25-8: The Keyable Icons feature displays an icon next to all tracks that can be keyed.

Editing Time

In some cases, directly working with keys isn't what you want to do. For example, if you need to change the animation length from six seconds to five seconds, you'll want to work in Dope Sheet's Edit Ranges mode. To switch to this mode, click the Edit Ranges button on the Keys toolbar. In this mode, the key ranges are displayed as black lines with a square marker on either end, as shown in Figure 25-9.

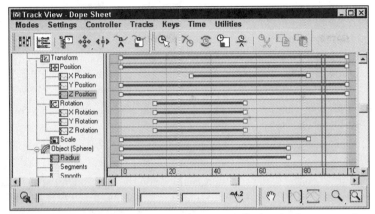

Figure 25-9: Click the Edit Ranges button to display the key ranges in the Key pane.

Selecting time and the Select Keys by Time utility

Before you can scale, cut, copy, or paste time, you need to select a track and then select a time block. To select a section of time, click the Select Time button and drag the mouse over the time block.

The Select Keys by Time utility lets you select all the keys within a given time block by entering the frame or time values. To use this utility, click the Track View Utilities button to open the Track View Utilities dialog box, and select the Select Keys by Time utility from the list. Then in the Select Keys by Time dialog box, enter the Start and End values to complete the selection.

Deleting, cutting, copying, and pasting time

After you select a block of time, you can delete it by clicking the Delete Time button. Another way to delete a block of time is to use the Cut Time button, which removes the selected time block but places a copy of it on the clipboard for pasting. The Copy Time button also adds the time block to the clipboard for pasting, but it leaves the selected time in the track.

After you copy a time block to the clipboard, you can paste it to a different location within the Track View. The track where you paste it must be of the same type as the one from which you copied it.

All keys within the time block are also pasted, and you can select whether they are pasted relatively or absolutely. *Absolute* pasting adds keys with the exact values as the ones on the clipboard. *Relative* pasting adds the key value to the current initial value at the place where the key is pasted.

You can enable the Exclude Left End Point and Exclude Right End Point buttons on the Extras toolbar when pasting multiple sections next to each other. By excluding either end point, the time block loops seamlessly.

Reversing, inserting, and scaling time

The Reverse Time button flips the keys within the selected time block.

The Insert Time button lets you insert a section of time anywhere within the current track. To insert time, click and drag to specify the amount of time to insert; all keys beyond the current insertion point slide to accommodate the inserted time.

The Scale Time button scales the selected time block. This feature causes all keys to be pushed closer together or farther apart.

Setting ranges

The Position Ranges button on the Ranges toolbar enables you to move ranges without moving keys. In this mode, you can move and scale a range bar independently of its keys, ignoring any keys that are out of range. For example, this button, when enabled, lets you remove the first several frames of an animation without moving the keys. The Recouple Ranges button can be used to line up the keys with the range again. The left end of the range aligns with the first key, and the right end aligns with the last key.

Editing Curves

When an object is moving through the scene, estimating the exact point where its position changes direction can sometimes be difficult. Function curves provide this information by presenting a controller's value as a function of time. Each key is a vertex in the curve. Function curves are only visible in the Curve Editor and the Track Bar layout.

Function curves mode lets you edit and work with these curves for complete control over the animation parameters. Figure 25-10 shows the Position curves for a sphere that moves about the scene.

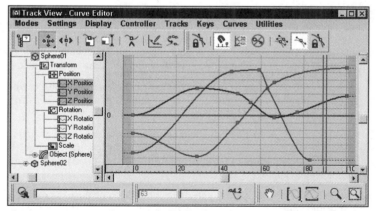

Figure 25-10: Function curves display keys as square markers along the curve.

Inserting new keys and moving keys

Function curves with only two keys are always linear. You can add some curvature to the line with the addition of another key. To add another key, click the Add Keys button, and then click the curve where you want to place the key.

If the curve contains multiple curves, such as a curve for the Position or RGB color values, then a point is added to each curve. The Move Keys button enables you to move individual keys by dragging them. It also includes flyouts for constraining the key movement to a horizontal or vertical direction.

Click the Scale Keys button to move the selected keys toward or away from the current time. The keys move only horizontally. Click the Scale Values button to move the selected keys toward or away from the zero value. The keys move only vertically.

Drawing curves

If you know what the curve you want is supposed to look like, you can actually draw the curve in the Key pane with the Draw Curves button enabled. This mode will add a key for every change in the curve. You'll probably want to use the Reduce Keys optimization after drawing a curve.

Tip

If you make a mistake, you can just draw over the top of the existing curve to make corrections.

Figure 25-11 shows a curve that was created with the Draw Curves feature.

New Feature

The Draw Curves mode is new to 3ds max 5.

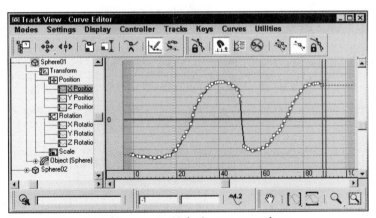

Figure 25-11: Drawing curves results in numerous keys.

Reducing keys

The Reduce Keys button enables you to optimize the number of keys used in an animation. Certain IK methods and the Dynamics utility calculate keys for every frame in the scene, which can increase your file size greatly. By optimizing with the Reduce Keys button, you can reduce the file size and complexity of your animations.

Clicking the Reduce Keys button opens the Reduce Keys dialog box. The threshold value determines how close to the actual position the solution must be to eliminate the key. Figure 25-12 shows the same curve created with the Draw Curves feature after it has been optimized with a Threshold value of 5 using the Reduce Keys button.

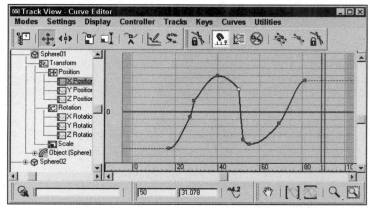

Figure 25-12: The Reduce Keys button optimizes the curve by reducing keys.

Working with tangents

Function curves for the Bézier controller have tangents associated with every key. To view and edit these tangents, click the Show All Tangents or the Show Tangents button. These tangents are lines that extend from the key point with a handle on each end. By moving these handles, you can alter the curvature of the curve around the key.

You can select the type of tangent from the Key Tangents toolbar. These can be different for the In and Out portion of the curve. You can also select them using the Key dialog box.

New Feature   The default key tangent type is the auto tangent type, which prevents the motion of objects overshooting by accident. This is a significant new feature found in 3ds max 5.

You open the Key dialog box, shown in Figure 25-13, by selecting a key and clicking the Properties button or by right-clicking the key. It lets you specify two different types of tangent points: Continuous and Discontinuous. *Continuous* tangents are points with two handles that are on the same line. The curvature for continuous tangents is always smooth. *Discontinuous* tangents have any angle between the two handle lines. These tangents form a sharp point.

Tip   Holding down the Shift key while dragging a handle lets you drag the handle independently of the other handle.

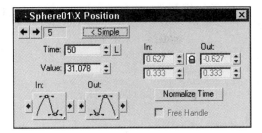

Figure 25-13: The Key dialog box lets you change the key's Time, Value, or In and Out tangent curves.

The Lock Tangents button lets you change the handles of several keys at the same time. If this button is disabled, adjusting a tangent handle affects only the key of that handle.

Applying ease and multiplier curves

You can apply ease curves (choose Curves ➪ Apply Ease Curve or press Ctrl+E) to smooth the timing of a function curve. You can apply multiplier curves (Curves ➪ Apply Multiplier Curve, Ctrl+M) to alter the scaling of a function curve. You can use ease and multiplier curves to automatically smooth or scale an animation's motion. Each of these buttons adds a new track and function curve to the selected controller track.

Note Not all controllers can have an ease or multiplier curve applied.

You can delete these tracks and curves using the Delete Ease/Multiplier Curve button. You can also enable or disable these curves with the Enable Ease/Multiplier Curve Toggle button.

After you apply an ease or multiplier curve, you can assign the type of curve to use with the Ease Curve Out-of-Range Types button. This button opens the Ease Curve Out-of-Range Types dialog box, shown in Figure 25-14. The dialog box includes seven different ease curves. By clicking the buttons below the types, you can specify an ease curve for the beginning and end of the curve. The seven ease types include Constant, Cycle, Loop, Ping Pong, Linear, Relative, and Identity.

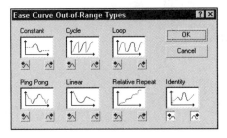

Figure 25-14: The Ease Curve Out-of-Range Types dialog box lets you select the type of ease curve to use.

Note In the Ease Curve Out-of-Range Types dialog box is an option that isn't present in the Parameter Curve Out-of-Range Types dialog box. The Identity option begins or ends the curve with a linear slope that produces a gradual, constant rate increase.

When editing ranges, you can make the range of a selected track smaller than the range of the whole animation. These tracks then go out of range at some point during the animation. The Ease/Multiplier Curve Out-of-Range Types buttons are used to tell the track how to handle its out-of-range time.

Note   You can also apply an out-of-range curve to a select range of frames using the Create Out-of-Range Keys utility. This utility is available via the Track View Utilities button.

This Out-of-Range dialog box includes six different options:

✦ **Constant:** Holds the value constant for all out-of-range frames

✦ **Cycle:** Repeats the track values as soon as the range ends

✦ **Loop:** Repeats the range values, like the Cycle option, except the beginning and end points are interpolated to provide a smooth transition

✦ **Ping Pong:** Repeats the range values in reverse order after the range end is reached

✦ **Linear:** Projects the range values in a linear manner when out of range

✦ **Relative Repeat:** Repeats the range values offset by the distance between the start and end values

Filtering Tracks

With all the information included in the Track View, finding what you need can be difficult. The Filters button on the Keys toolbar can help. Clicking this button opens the Filters dialog box, shown in Figure 25-15.

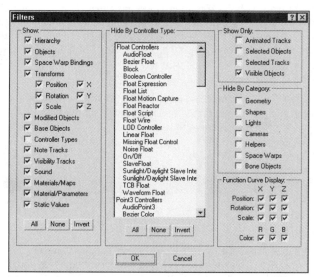

Figure 25-15: The Filters dialog box lets you focus on the specific tracks.

Tip   Right-clicking the Filters button reveals a quick list of filter items.

Using this dialog box, you can limit the number of tracks that are displayed in the Track View. The Show section contains many different display options. The Hide by Controller Type pane lists all the available controllers. Any controller types selected from this list do not show up in the Track View. You can also elect to not display objects by selecting Hide Object by Category.

The Show Only group includes options for displaying only the Animated Tracks, Selected Objects, Selected Tracks, Visible Objects, or any combination of these. For example, if you wanted to see the animation track for a selected object, select the Animated Tracks option and click the OK button, then open the Filters dialog box again, select Selected Objects, and click OK.

You can also specify whether the function curve display includes the Position, Rotation, and Scale components for each axis or the RGB color components.

Working with Controllers

Controllers offer an alternative to manually positioning keys. Each controller can automatically control a key's position or a parameter's value. The Controller toolbar includes several buttons for working with controllers. The Copy Controller and Paste Controller buttons let you move existing controllers between different tracks, and the Assign Controller button lets you add a new controller to a track.

Cross-Reference   Chapter 28, "Animating with Controllers," covers all the various controllers used to automate animated sequences.

Although the buttons are labeled Copy Controller and Paste Controller, they can be used to copy different tracks. Tracks can only be copied and pasted if they are of the same type. You can copy only one track at a time, but that single controller can be pasted to multiple tracks. A pasted track can be a copy or an instance, and you have the option to replace all instances. For example, if you have several objects that move together, using the Replace All Instances option when modifying the track for one object modifies the tracks for all objects that share the same motion.

All instanced copies of a track change when any instance of that track is modified. To break the linking between instances, you can use the Make Controller Unique button.

Clicking the Assign Controller button opens the Assign Controller dialog box, where you can select the controller to apply. If the controller types are similar, the keys are maintained, but a completely different controller replaces any existing keys in the track.

Using visibility tracks

When an object track is selected, you can add a visibility track using the Add Visibility Track button or the Object Properties dialog box. This track enables you to make the object visible or invisible. The selected track is automatically assigned the Bézier controller, but you can change it to an On/Off controller if you want that type of control. You can use function curves mode to edit the visibility track.

Adding Note Tracks

You can add note tracks to any track and use them to attach information about the track. The Add Note Track button is used to add a note track, which is marked with a yellow triangle and cannot be animated. You can add notes only in the Dope Sheet layout.

After you've added a note track in the Controller pane, use the Add Keys button to position a note key in the Key pane by clicking in the note track. This adds a small note icon. Right-clicking the note icon opens the Notes dialog box, where you can enter the notes, as shown in Figure 25-16. Each note track can include several note keys.

The Notes dialog box includes arrow controls that you can use to move between the various notes. The field to the right of the arrows displays the current note key number. The Time value displays the frame where a selected note is located, and the Lock Key option locks the note to the frame so it can't be moved or scaled.

You can use the Tracks ➪ Note Track ➪ Remove menu command to delete a selected note track.

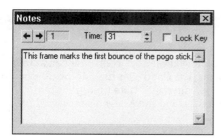

Figure 25-16: The Notes dialog box lets you enter notes and position them next to keys.

Tutorial: Animating a hyper pogo stick

As an example of working with function curves, we'll create a pogo stick that hops progressively higher.

To animate a hyper pogo stick using function curves, follow these steps:

1. Open the Hyper pogo stick.max file from the Chap 25 directory on the CD-ROM.

   This file contains a simple pogo stick model made from primitives.

2. Open the Track View – Curve Editor, and locate the pogo stick group's Position track (you can find this track under the Objects ➪ Pogo Stick ➪ Transform ➪ Position). Click the Assign Controller button to open the Assign Position Controller dialog box. Select the Bézier Position Controller, and click OK.

3. Click the Add Keys button (or press the A key), and then click six different points along any one of the curves. Notice the three different curves: one red, one blue, and one green. These colors correspond to the default coordinate axes displayed in the lower-left corner of the viewport, so red is the X-axis, green is the Y-axis, and blue is the Z-axis. Points are added on all three lines regardless of which line you click.

4. Next click the Move Keys button (or press the M key), and drag the second, fourth, and sixth points for the Z-axis (blue line) upward at increasing heights to create three peaks. Also drag each point on the X-axis (red line) upward to form a straight line of increasing slope.

   These curves define the motions of the pogo stick, which will bounce up and down along the Z-axis and gradually move to the right along the X-axis.

5. If you click the Play Animation button at this point, you might not see any motion. This is because the values are so small. You can fix this by scaling the values. Click the Scale Values button, select all the nonzero points on the X- and Z-axis curves by holding down the Ctrl key and dragging the points upward. Use the Zoom Value Extents button to resize the window, and continue to drag until the first peak is around 200. Figure 25-17 shows the results after scaling the values.

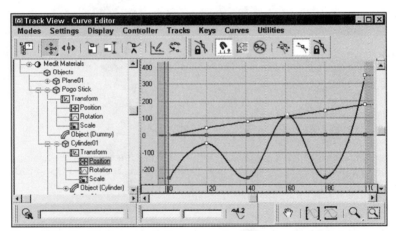

Figure 25-17: After you scale the values, the motions are visible in the viewports.

Figure 25-18 shows the pogo stick as it bounces along its way.

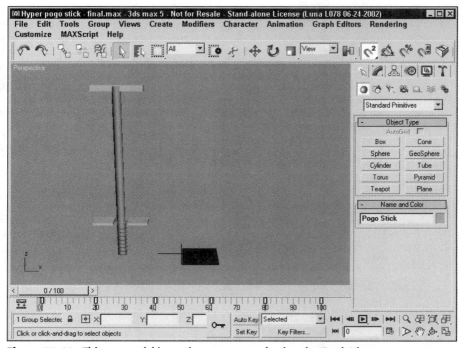

Figure 25-18: This pogo stick's motion was created using the Track View.

Synchronizing to a Sound Track

One of the default tracks for any scene is the sound track. Included in the Sound hierarchy is the metronome track. You can also set up a sound file using the Sound Options dialog box, shown in Figure 25-19. You can open this dialog box by right-clicking on the Metronome track and selecting Properties from the pop-up menu.

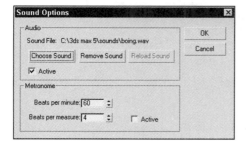

Figure 25-19: The Sound Options dialog box lets you select a sound to play during the animation.

You can make the sound track appear as a waveform curve underneath the Track Bar. This helps as you try to synchronize the sound to the movements in the viewports. To see this sound track, right-click the Track Bar and choose Configure ➪ Show Sound Track from the pop-up menu.

Using the Sound Options dialog box

You can use the Audio section of the Sound Options dialog box to load a sound or remove an existing sound. The Active option causes the sound file to play when the animation is played. The Choose Sound button can load AVI, WAV, and FLC file types. The dialog box also includes buttons to Remove Sound and Reload Sound. The Active option enables the sound file.

You can also set up a regular metronome beat with two tones. For a metronome, you can specify the beats per minute and the beats per measure. The first option sets how often the beats occur, and the second option determines how often a different tone is played. This dialog box also contains an Active option for turning the metronome on and off.

Tutorial: Adding sound to an animation

As an example of adding sound to an animation, we revisit the hyper pogo stick and synchronize its animation to a sound clip.

To synchronize an animation to a sound clip, follow these steps:

1. Open the Hyper pogo stick with sound.max file from the Chap 25 directory on the CD-ROM.

2. In the Track View window, right-click one of the sound tracks and select Properties from the pop-up menu to open the Sound Options dialog box. In this dialog box, click the Choose Sound button. Then locate the boing.wav file from the Chap 25 directory on the CD-ROM, and click OK. Make sure the Active option is selected.

   The sound file appears as a waveform in the Track View, as shown in Figure 25-20.

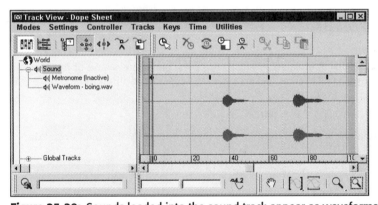

Figure 25-20: Sounds loaded into the sound track appear as waveforms.

 Note The Open Sound dialog box includes a play button that lets you play the sound before loading it.

3. Click the Move Keys button (or press the M key), and move the keys to line up with the waveforms in the sound track.

4. Click the Play Animation button, and the sound file will play with the animation.

Figure 25-21 shows the sound track under the Track Bar for this example.

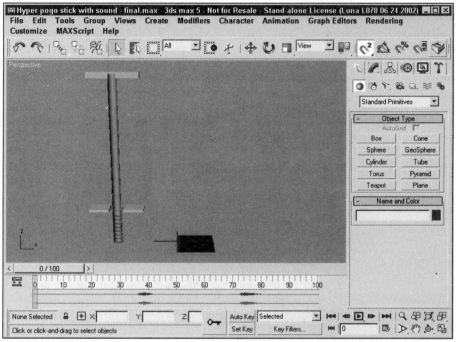

Figure 25-21: To help synchronize sound, the audio track can be made visible under the Track Bar.

Summary

Using Track View, you have access to all the keys, parameters, and objects in a scene in one convenient location. Different features are available in the different layouts. In this chapter, you've

- ✦ Learned the Track View interface elements
- ✦ Learned about the different Track View layouts including the Curve Editor, Dope Sheet, and Track Bar
- ✦ Discovered how to work with keys, times, and ranges
- ✦ Controlled and adjusted function curves
- ✦ Selected specific tracks using the Filter dialog box
- ✦ Assigned controllers
- ✦ Explored the different out-of-range types
- ✦ Added notes to a track
- ✦ Synchronized animation to a sound track

The next chapter explores the various Space Warps that you can use to add forces to the scene.

✦   ✦   ✦

Using Space Warps

Space Warps sound like a special effect from a science fiction movie, but actually they are non-renderable objects that let you affect another object in many unique ways to create special effects.

You can think of Space Warps as the unseen forces that control the movement of objects in the scene such as gravity, wind, and waves. Several Space Warps, such as Push and Motor, deal with dynamic simulations and can define forces in real-world units. Some Space Warps can deform an object's surface; others provide the same functionality as certain modifiers.

Space Warps are particularly useful when combined with particle systems. This chapter includes some examples of Space Warps that have been combined with particle systems.

Creating and Binding Space Warps

Space Warps are a way to add forces to the scene that can act on an object. Space Warps are not renderable and must be bound to an object to have an effect. A single Space Warp can be bound to several objects and a single object can be bound to several Space Warps.

In many ways, Space Warps are similar to modifiers, but modifiers typically apply to individual objects, whereas Space Warps can be applied to many objects at the same time and are applied using World space coordinates. This ability to work with multiple objects makes Space Warps the preferred way to alter particle systems.

Creating a Space Warp

Space Warps are found in the Create panel under the Space Warps category (the icon is three wavy lines). From the subcategory drop-down list, you can select from four different subcategories. Each subcategory has buttons to enable several different Space Warps. To create a Space Warp, click a button, and then click and drag in a viewport.

When a Space Warp is created, a gizmo is placed in the scene. This gizmo can be transformed as other objects can by using the standard transformation buttons. The size and position of the Space Warp gizmo often affects its results. After a Space Warp is created, it affects only the objects to which it is bound.

◆ ◆ ◆ ◆

In This Chapter

Creating and binding Space Warps to objects

Understanding the various Space Warp types

Working with Space Warps and particle systems

◆ ◆ ◆ ◆

Binding a Space Warp to an object

 A Space Warp's influence is felt only by its bound objects, so you can selectively apply gravity to only certain objects. The Bind to Space Warp button is on the main toolbar next to the Unlink button. After clicking the Bind to Space Warp button, drag from the Space Warp to the object to which you want to link it or vice versa.

All Space Warp bindings appear in the Modifier Stack. You can use the Edit Modifier Stack dialog box to copy and paste Space Warps between objects.

> **Note**
> If you look at the Modifier Stack for an object that is bound to a Space Warp, you'll see an asterisk in front of the name. This asterisk denotes that the Space Warp is applied using World coordinates.

Some Space Warps can be bound only to certain types of objects. Each Space Warp has a Supports Objects of Type rollout that lists the supported objects. If you're having trouble binding a Space Warp to an object, check this rollout to see whether the object is supported.

Understanding Space Warp Types

Just as many different types of forces exist in nature, many different Space Warp types exist. These appear in four different subcategories, based on their function. The four subcategories are Forces, Deflectors, Geometric/Deformable, and Modifier-Based.

Force Space Warps

The Forces subcategory of Space Warps is mainly used with particle systems and dynamic simulations. Space Warps in this subcategory include Motor, Vortex, Path Follow, Displace, Wind, Push, Drag, PBomb, and Gravity. Figure 26-1 shows the gizmos for these Space Warps.

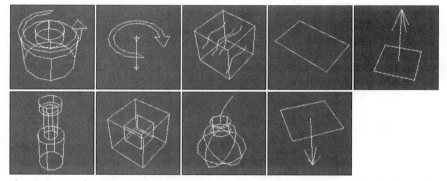

Figure 26-1: The Force Space Warps: Motor, Vortex, Path Follow, Displace, Wind, Push, Drag, PBomb, and Gravity

Motor

The Motor Space Warp applies a rotational torque to objects. This force accelerates objects radially instead of linearly. The Basic Torque value is a measurement of torque in newton-meters, foot-pounds, or inch-pounds.

The On and Off Time sets the frames where the force is applied and disabled, respectively. Many of the Space Warps have these same values.

The Feedback On option causes the force to change as the object's speed changes. When this option is off, the force stays constant. You can also set a Target Revolution units in revolutions per hour (RPH), revolutions per minute (RPM), or revolutions per second (RPS), which is the speed at which the force begins to change if the Feedback option is enabled. The Reversible option causes the force to change directions if the Target Speed is reached, and the Gain value is how quickly the force adjusts.

The motor force can also be adjusted with Periodic Variations, which cause the motor force to increase and then decrease in a regular pattern. You can define two different sets of Periodic Variation parameters: Period 1, Amplitude 1, Phase 1; and Period 2, Amplitude 2, Phase 2.

For particle systems, you can enable and set a Range value. The Motor Space Warp doesn't affect particles outside this distance. At the bottom of the Parameters rollout, you can set the size of the gizmo icon. You can find this same value for all Space Warps.

Figure 26-2 shows the Motor Space Warp twisting the particles being emitted from the Super Spray particle system in the direction of the icon's arrow.

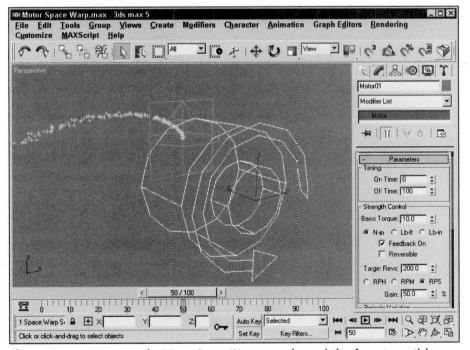

Figure 26-2: You can use the Motor Space Warp to apply a twisting force to particles and dynamic objects.

Push

The Push Space Warp accelerates objects in the direction of the Space Warp's icon from the large cylinder to the small cylinder. Many of the parameters for the Push Space Warp are similar to those for the Motor Space Warp. Using the Parameters rollout, you can specify the force Strength in units of newtons or pounds.

The Feedback On option causes the force to change as the object's speed changes, except it deals with Target Speed instead of Target Revolution like the Motor Space Warp.

The push force can also be set to include Periodic Variations that are the same as with the Motor Space Warp. Figure 26-3 shows the Push Space Warp pushing the particles being emitted from the Super Spray particle system.

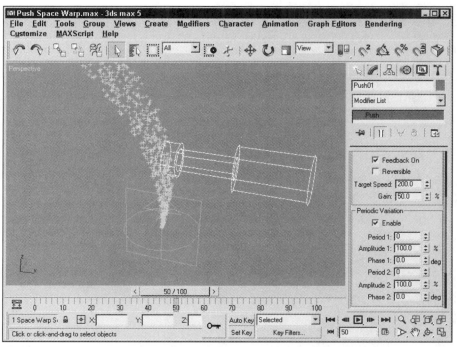

Figure 26-3: You can use the Push Space Warp to apply a controlled force to particles and dynamic objects.

Vortex

You can use the Vortex Space Warp on particle systems to make particles spin around in a spiral like going down a whirlpool. You can use the Timing settings to set the beginning and ending frames where the effect takes place.

You can also specify Taper Length and Curve values, which determine the shape of the vortex. Lower Taper Length values wind the vortex tighter, and the Taper Curve values can range between 1.0 and 4.0 and control the ratio between the spiral diameter at the top of the vortex verses the bottom of the vortex.

The Axial Drop value specifies how far each turn of the spiral is from the adjacent turn. The Damping value sets how quickly the Axial Drop value takes effect. The Orbital Speed is how fast the particles rotate away from the center. The Radial Pull value is the distance from the center of each spiral path that the particles can rotate. If the Unlimited Range option is selected, then Range and Falloff values are included for each setting. You can also specify whether the vortex spins clockwise or counterclockwise.

Figure 26-4 shows a Vortex Space Warp being bound to a particle system.

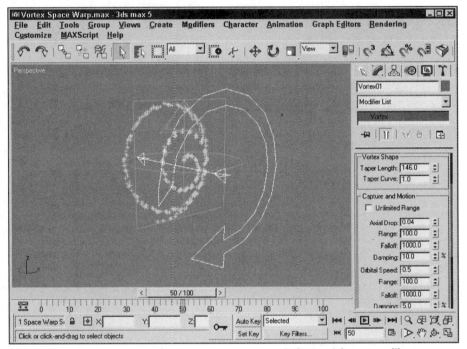

Figure 26-4: You can use the Vortex Space Warp to spiral a particle system like a whirlpool.

Drag

Drag is another common force that can be simulated with a Space Warp. The Drag Space Warp can be Linear, Spherical, or Cylindrical. This Space Warp causes particle velocity to be decreased, such as when simulating wind drag or viscosity. Use the Time On and Time Off options to set the frame where the Space Warp is in effect.

For each of the Damping shape types — Linear, Spherical, and Cylindrical, you can set the drag along each axis or in the Radial, Tangential, or Axial direction depending on the shape. If the Unlimited Range option is not selected, then the Range and Falloff values are available.

Figure 26-5 shows a Drag Space Warp surrounding a particle system.

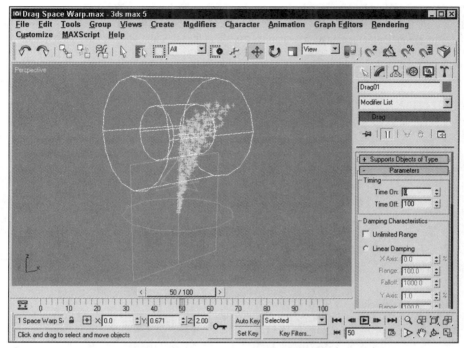

Figure 26-5: You can use the Drag Space Warp to slow the velocity of particles.

PBomb

The PBomb (particle bomb) Space Warp was designed specifically for the PArray particle system. To blow up an object with the PBomb Space Warp, create an object, make it a PArray emitter, and then bind the PBomb Space Warp to the PArray.

Cross-Reference You can find more information on the PArray particle system in Chapter 17, "Creating and Controlling Particle Systems."

Basic parameters for this Space Warp include three different blast symmetry types: Spherical, Cylindrical, and Planar. You can also set the Chaos value as a percentage.

In the Explosion Parameters section, the Start Time is the frame where the explosion takes place, and the Duration defines how long the explosion forces are applied. The Strength value is the power of the explosion.

A Range value can be set to determine the extent of the explosion. It is measured from the center of the Space Warp icon. If the Unlimited Range option is selected, the Range value is disabled. The Linear and Exponential options change how the explosion forces die out. The Range Indicator option displays the effective blast range of the PBomb.

Figure 26-6 shows a box selected as an emitter for a PArray. The PBomb is bound to the PArray and not to the box object. The Speed value for the PArray has been set to 0, and the Particle Type is set to Fragments. Notice how the PBomb's icon determines the center of the blast.

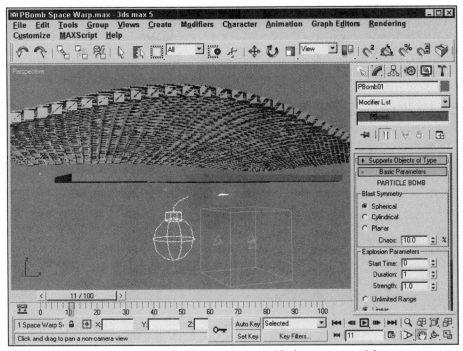

Figure 26-6: You can use the PBomb Space Warp with the PArray particle system to create explosions.

Path Follow

The Path Follow Space Warp causes particles to follow a path defined by a spline. The Basic Parameters rollout for this Space Warp includes a Pick Shape Object button for selecting the spline path to use. You can also specify a Range value or the Unlimited Range option. The Range distance is measured from the path to the particle.

Cross-Reference The Path Follow Space Warp is similar to the Path Constraint, which I discuss in Chapter 27, "Restricting Movement with Constraints."

In the Motion Timing section, the Start Frame value is the frame where the particles start following the path, the Travel Time is the number of frames required to travel the entire path, and the Last Frame is where the particles no longer follow the path. There is also a Variation value to some randomness to the movement of the particles.

The Basic Parameters rollout also includes a Particle Motion section with two options for controlling how the particles proceed down the path: Along Offset Splines and Along Parallel Splines. The first causes the particles to move along splines that are offset from the original and the second moves all particles from their initial location along parallel path splines. The Constant Speed option makes all particles move at the same speed.

Also in the Particle Motion section is the Stream Taper value. This value is the amount by which the particles move away from the path over time. Options include Converge, Diverge, or Both. Converging streams move all particles closer to the path, and diverging streams do the opposite. The Stream Swirl value is the number of spiral turns that the particles take along the path. This swirling motion can be Clockwise, Counterclockwise, or Bidirectional. The Seed value determines the randomness of the stream settings.

Figure 26-7 shows a Path Follow Space Warp bound to a Super Spray particle system. A Helix shape has been selected as the path.

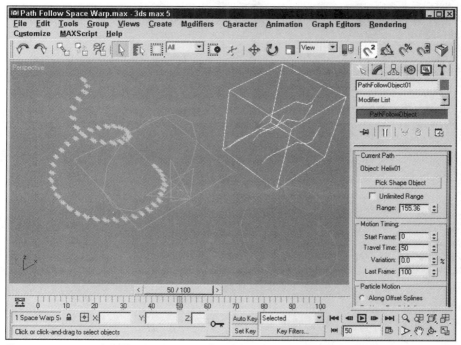

Figure 26-7: A Path Follow Space Warp bound to an emitter from the Super Spray particle system and following a Helix path.

Gravity

The Gravity Space Warp adds the effect of gravity to a scene. This causes objects to accelerate in the direction specified by the Gravity Space Warp, like the Wind Space Warp. The Parameters rollout includes Strength and Decay values. There are also options to make the gravity planar or spherical. You can turn on the Range Indicators to display a plane or sphere where the gravity is half its maximum value.

Wind

The Wind Space Warp causes objects to accelerate. The Parameters rollout includes Strength and Decay values. There are also options to make the gravity planar or spherical. The Turbulence value randomly moves the objects in different directions, and the Frequency value controls how often these random turbulent changes occur. Larger Scale values cause turbulence to affect larger areas, but smaller values are more wild and chaotic.

You can turn on the Range Indicators just like the Gravity Space Warp. Figure 26-8 shows the Wind Space Warp pushing the particles being emitted from a Super Spray particle system.

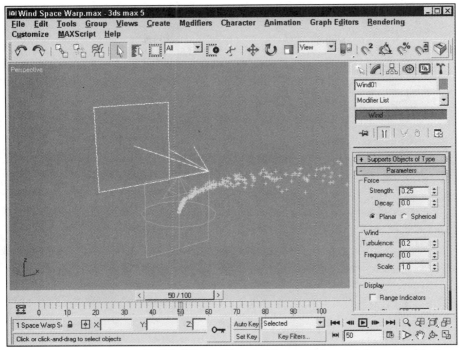

Figure 26-8: You can use the Wind Space Warp to blow particles and dynamic objects.

Displace

The Displace Space Warp is like a force field: It pushes objects and is useful when applied to a particle system. It can also work on any deformable object in addition to particle systems. The strength of the displacement can be defined with Strength and Decay values or with a grayscale bitmap.

The Strength value is the distance that the geometry is displaced and can be positive or negative. The Decay value causes the displacement to decrease as the distance increases. The Luminance Center is the grayscale point where no displacement occurs; any color darker than this center value is moved away, and any brighter areas move closer.

The Bitmap and Map buttons let you load images to use as a displacement map; the amount of displacement corresponds with the brightness of the image. There is also a Blur setting for blurring the image. You can apply these maps with different mapping options, including Planar, Cylindrical, Spherical, and Shrink Wrap. You can also adjust the Length, Width, and Height dimensions and the U, V, and W Tile values.

Cross-Reference The Displace Space Warp is similar in function to the Displace modifier. The Displace modifier is discussed in Chapter 20, "Using Material Maps."

Figure 26-9 shows two Displace Space Warps with opposite Strength values.

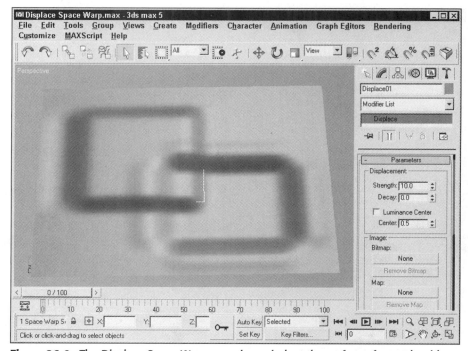

Figure 26-9: The Displace Space Warp can raise or indent the surface of a patch grid.

Deflector Space Warps

The Deflectors subcategory of Space Warps includes PDynaFlect, SDynaFlect, UDynaFlect, POmniFlect, SOmniFlect, UOmniFlect, Deflector, SDeflector, and UDeflector. You use them all with particle systems, but only the DynaFlect Space Warps can be used with dynamic objects. This category includes several different types of deflectors starting with P, S, and U. The difference between these types is their shape. P-type (planar) deflectors are box shaped, S-type (spherical) deflectors are spherical, and U-type (universal) deflectors include a Pick Object button that you can use to select any object as a deflector.

Figure 26-10 shows the icons for each of these Space Warps. All the P-type deflectors are in the first row, the S-type deflectors are in the second row, and the U-type deflectors are in the third row.

PDynaFlect, SDynaFlect, and UDynaFlect

The PDynaFlect Space Warp enables particles to affect other objects in a scene. It is planar in shape. The SDynaFlect Space Warp is similar to the PDynaFlect Space Warp, except its shape is spherical. The shape of the UDynaFlect Space Warp can be any other object within the scene. All three of these Space Warps share roughly the same parameters.

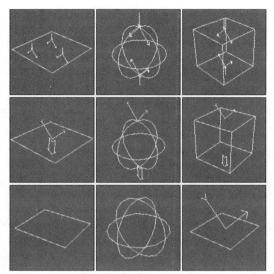

Figure 26-10: The Deflector Space Warps: POmniFlect, SOmniFlect, UOmniFlect, PDynaFlect, SDynaFlect, UDynaFlect, Deflector, SDeflector, and UDeflector

In the Particle Bounce section of the Parameters rollout, the Reflects, Bounce, Variation, and Chaos values control how particles reflect off a surface. The Reflects value determines the percentage of particles that are reflected. The Bounce value is a multiplier that defines a change in the particle's velocity after the impact: Values greater than 1 cause the particle to move faster after the impact. The Variation value causes each particle to bounce with a different value, and the Chaos value changes the randomness of the angle at which the particles leave the object. You can also set a Friction value, which causes objects to be reflected at odd angles and velocities. The Inherit Velocity value determines how much of the particle's velocity is inherited by the object being struck. This value causes the struck object to move when the particles hit it.

In the Physical Properties section, you can specify the mass of the bound particle in units of grams, kilograms (Kg), or pounds-mass (Lbm). This setting becomes important when working with dynamic systems. The UDynaFlect Space Warp includes a Pick Object button used to select the object to use as a deflector.

Figure 26-11 shows a Super Spray particle system emitting a straight line of particles at a PDynaFlect Space Warp. The PDynaFlect Space Warp is set to reflect 100 percent of the particles. The stream of particles is then reflected off an SDynaFlect Space Warp and then off a cone object that is selected as the reflecting object for the UDynaFlect Space Warp.

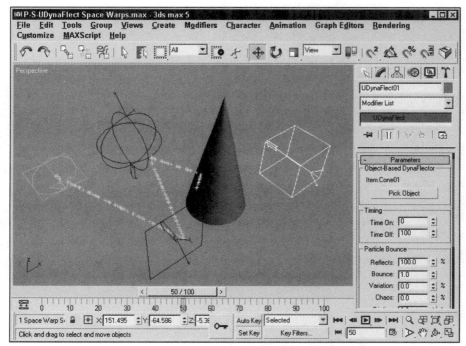

Figure 26-11: The P-, S-, and UDynaFlect Space Warps deflecting particles emitted from a Super Spray particle system

POmniFlect, SOmniFlect, and UOmniFlect

The POmniFlect Space Warp is a planar deflector that defines how particles reflect and bounce off other objects. The SOmniFlect Space Warp is just like the POmniFlect Space Warp, except it is spherical in shape. The UOmniFlect Space Warp is another deflector, but this one can assume the shape of another object using the Pick Object button in the Parameters rollout. Its Parameters rollout includes a Timing section with Time On and Time Off values and a Reflection section.

The difference between this type of Space Warps and the DynaFlect Space Warps is the addition of refraction. Particles bound to this Space Warp can be refracted through an object. The values entered in the Refraction section of the Parameters rollout change the velocity and direction of a particle. The Refracts value is the percentage of particles that are refracted. The Pass Vel (velocity) is the amount that the particle speed changes when entering the object; a value of 100 maintains the same speed. The Distortion value affects the angle of refraction; a value of 0 maintains the same angle, and a value of 100 causes the particle to move along the surface of the struck object. The Diffusion value spreads the particles throughout the struck object. You can vary each of these values by using its respective Variation value.

Note   If the Refracts value is set to 100 percent, no particles are available to be refracted.

You can also specify Friction and Inherit Velocity values. In the Spawn Effects Only section, the Spawns and Pass Velocity values control how many particle spawns are available and their velocity upon entering the struck object. Figure 26-12 shows each of these Space Warps bound to a Super Spray particle system. The Reflect percentage for each of the Space Warps is set to 50, and the remaining particles are refracted through the Space Warp's plane. Notice how the particles are also reflecting off the opposite side of the refracting object.

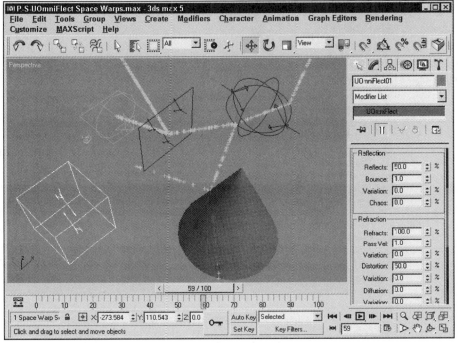

Figure 26-12: The P-, S-, and UOmniFlect Space Warps reflecting and refracting particles emitted from the Super Spray particle system

Deflector, SDeflector, and UDeflector

The Deflector Space Warp is a simplified version of the POmniFlect Space Warp. Its parameters include Bounce, Width, and Length. The SDeflector Space Warp is a simplified version of the SOmniFlect Space Warp. It includes values for Bounce, Variation, Chaos, and Inherit Velocity. The UDeflector Space Warp is a simplified version of the UOmniFlect Space Warp. It has a Pick Object button for selecting the object to act as the deflector and all the same parameters as the SDeflector Space Warp, with the addition of a Friction value.

Geometric/Deformable Space Warps

You use Geometric/Deformable Space Warps to deform the geometry of an object. Space Warps in this subcategory include FFD (Box), FFD (Cyl), Wave, Ripple, Displace, Conform, and Bomb. These Space Warps can be applied to any deformable object. Figure 26-13 shows the icons for each of these Space Warps.

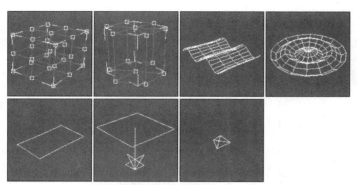

Figure 26-13: The Geometric/Deformable Space Warps: FFD (Box), FFD (Cyl), Wave, Ripple, Displace, Conform, and Bomb

FFD (Box) and FFD (Cyl)

The FFD (Box) and FFD (Cyl) Space Warps show up as a lattice of control points in the shape of a box and a cylinder; you can select and move the control points that make up the Space Warp to deform an object that is bound to the Space Warp. The object will only be deformed if the bound object is within the volume of the Space Warp.

These Space Warps have the same parameters as the modifiers with the same name found in the Modifiers ➪ Free Form Deformers menu. The difference is that the Space Warps act in World coordinates and aren't tied to a specific object. This makes it so a single FFD Space Warp can affect multiple objects.

Cross-Reference To learn about the FFD (Box) and FFD (Cyl) modifiers, see Chapter 10, "Using Modifiers."

To move the control points, select the Space Warp object, open the Modify panel, and select the Control Points subobject, which lets you alter the control points individually.

Wave and Ripple

The Wave and Ripple Space Warps create linear and radial waves in the objects to which they are bound. Parameters in the rollout help define the shape of the wave. Amplitude 1 is the wave's height along the X-axis, and Amplitude 2 is the wave's height along its Y-axis. The Wave Length value defines how long each wave is. The Phase value determines how the wave starts at its origin. The Decay value sets how quickly the wave dies out. A Decay value of 0 maintains the same amplitude for the entire wave.

The Sides (Circles) and Segments values determine the number of segments for the X- and Y-axes. The Division value changes the icon's size without altering the wave effect. Figure 26-14 shows a Wave Space Warp applied to a simple Box primitive. Notice that the Space Warp icon is smaller than the box, yet it affects the entire object.

Note Be sure to include enough segments in the bound object, or the effect won't be visible.

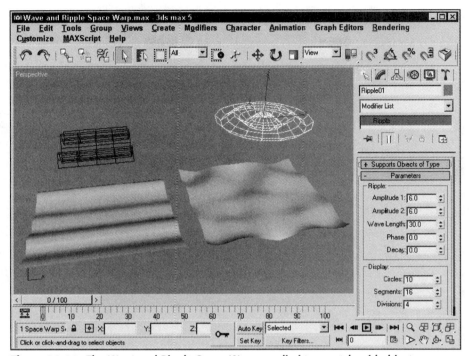

Figure 26-14: The Wave and Ripple Space Warps applied to a patch grid object

Tutorial: Creating pond ripples

For this tutorial, we'll position a patch object so it aligns with a background image and apply the Ripple Space Warp to it.

To add ripples to a pond, follow these steps:

1. Open the Pond ripple.max file from the Chap 26 directory on the CD-ROM.

   This file includes a background image or a bridge matched to a patch grid where the pond is located with a reflective material assigned to it.

2. In the Create panel, select the Space Warps category button, select the Geometric/Deformable subcategory, and then click the Ripple button. Drag in the Perspective view to create a Space Warp object. In the Parameters rollout, set the Amplitudes to 2, and the Wave Length to 30.

3. Click the Bind to Space Warp button, and drag from the patch object to the Space Warp.

Figure 26-15 shows the resulting image.

Figure 26-15: A ripple in a pond produced using the Ripple Space Warp

Conform

The Conform Space Warp pushes all object vertices until they hit another target object called the Wrap To Object, or until they've moved a preset amount. The Conform Parameters rollout includes a Pick Object button that lets you pick the Wrap To Object. The object vertices move no farther than this Wrap To Object.

You can also specify a Default Projection Distance and a Standoff Distance. The Default Projection Distance is the maximum distance that the vertices move if they don't intersect with the Wrap To Object. The Standoff Distance is the separation amount maintained between the Wrap To Object and the moved vertices. There is also an option to Use Selected Vertices that moves only a subobject selection.

Cross-Reference

The Conform Space Warp is similar in function to the Conform compound object that is covered in Chapter 16, "Building Compound Objects."

Figure 26-16 shows some text being deformed with the Conform Space Warp. A warped quad patch has been selected as the Wrap To Object.

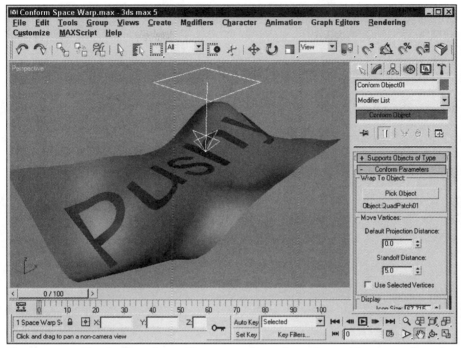

Figure 26-16: The Conform Space Warp wraps the surface of one object around another object.

Bomb

The Bomb Space Warp causes an object to explode from its individual faces. The Strength value is the power of the bomb and determines how far objects travel when exploded. The Spin value is the rate at which the individual pieces rotate. The Falloff value defines the boundaries of faces affected by the bomb. Object faces beyond this distance remain unaffected. You must select Falloff On for the Falloff value to work.

The Min and Max Fragment Size values set the minimum and maximum number of faces caused by the explosion.

The Gravity value determines the strength of gravity and can be positive or negative. Gravity always points toward the world's Z-axis. The Chaos value can range between 0 and 10 to add variety to the explosion. The Detonation value is the number of the frame where the explosion should take place, and the Seed value alters the randomness of the event. Figure 26-17 shows frame 20 of an explosion produced by the Bomb Space Warp.

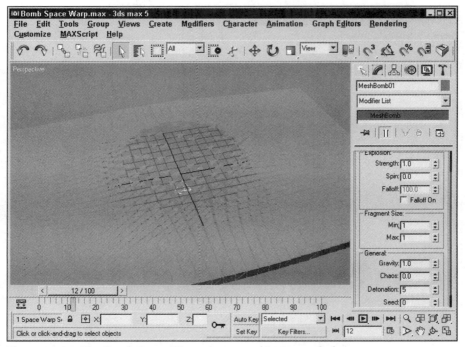

Figure 26-17: The Bomb Space Warp causes an object to explode.

Note   The Bomb Space Warp is seen over time. At frame 0, the object shows no effect.

Tutorial: Blowing a dandelion puff

You can use Space Warps with other types of objects besides particle systems. The Scatter object, for example, can quickly create many unique objects that can be controlled by a Space Warp. In this tutorial, we'll create a simple, crude dandelion puff that can blow away in the wind.

To create and blow away a dandelion puff, follow these steps:

1. Open the Dandelion puff.max file from the Chap 26 directory on the CD-ROM.

   This file includes a sphere covered with a Scatter compound object representing the seeds of a dandelion.

2. In the Create panel, click the Space Warps category, select the Geometric/Deformable subcategory, and click the Bomb button. Click in the Front view and position the Bomb icon to the left and slightly below the dandelion object. In the Bomb Parameters rollout, set the Strength to 10, the Spin to 100, and the Min and Max Fragment Size value to 24.

   This is the total number of faces included in the dandelion object.

3. Click the Bind to Space Warp button in the main toolbar, and drag from the dandelion object to the Space Warp.

Figure 26-18 shows one frame of the dandelion puff being blown away.

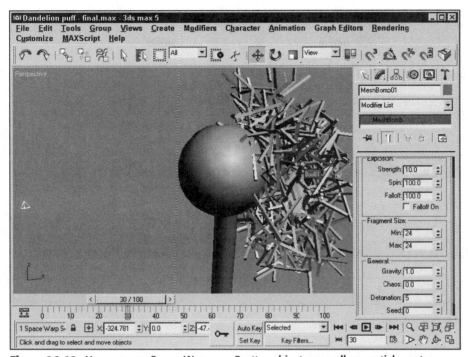

Figure 26-18: You can use Space Warps on Scatter objects as well as particle systems.

Modifier-Based Space Warps

Modifier-Based Space Warps produce the same effects as many of the standard modifiers, but because they are Space Warps, they can be applied to many objects simultaneously. Space Warps in this subcategory include Bend, Noise, Skew, Taper, Twist, and Stretch. All Modifier-Based Space Warp gizmos are simple box shapes. The parameters for all Modifier-Based Space Warps are identical to the modifiers of the same name. These Space Warps don't include a Supports Objects of Type rollout because they can be applied to all objects.

Cross-Reference For details on the Bend, Noise, Skew, Taper, Twist, and Stretch modifiers and their parameters, see Chapter 10, "Using Modifiers."

These Space Warps include a Gizmo Parameters rollout with values for the Length, Width, and Height of the gizmo. You can also specify the deformation decay. The Decay value causes the Space Warp's effect to diminish with distance from the bound object.

You can reposition the Modifier-Based Space Warp's gizmo as a separate object, but the normal modifiers require that you select the gizmo subobject in order to reposition it. Unlike modifiers, Space Warps don't have any subobjects.

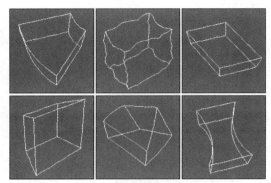

Figure 26-19: The Modifier-Based Space Warps: Bend, Noise, Skew, Taper, Twist, and Stretch

Combining Particle Systems with Space Warps

To conclude this chapter, let's look at some examples that use Space Warps along with particle systems. With all these Space Warps and their various parameters combined with particle systems, the possibilities are endless. These examples are only a small representation of what is possible.

Tutorial: Shattering glass

When glass shatters, it is very chaotic, sending pieces in every direction. For this tutorial, we'll shatter a glass mirror on a wall. The wall will keep the pieces from flying off, and most pieces will fall straight to the floor.

To shatter glass, follow these steps:

1. Open the Shattering glass.max file from the Chap 26 directory on the CD-ROM.

   This file includes a simple mirror created from patch grid objects. The file also includes a simple sphere that is animated striking the mirror.

2. In the Create panel, select the Particle Systems subcategory, and click the PArray button. Then drag in the Front viewport to create the PArray icon. In the Basic Parameters rollout, click the Pick Object button and select the first patch object. In the Viewport Display section, select the Mesh option. In the Particle Generation rollout, set the Speed and Divergence to 0. Also set the Emit Start to 30 and the Life value to 100, so it matches the last frame. In the Particle Type rollout, select the Object Fragments option, and set the Thickness to 1.0. Then in the Object Fragment Controls section, select the Number of Chunks option with a Minimum value of 30. In the Rotation and Collision rollout, set the Spin Time to 100 and the Variation to 50. These settings cause the patch to emit 30 object fragments with a slow, gradual rotation.

3. Select the Space Warps category button, and choose the Forces subcategory from the drop-down list. Click the PBomb button, and create a PBomb Space Warp in the Top view, then center it above the Mirror patch. In the Modify panel, set the Blast Symmetry option to Spherical with a Chaos value of 50 percent. Set the Start Time to 30 with a Strength value of 0.2. Then click the Bind to Space Warp button, and drag from the PBomb Space Warp to the PArray icon.

4. In the Create panel, click the Gravity button, and create a Gravity Space Warp in the Front view. Position the Gravity Space Warp so that the icon arrow is pointing down. In the Modify panel, set the Strength value to 0.1. Then bind this Space Warp to the PArray icon.

5. In the Create panel, select the Deflectors subcategory from the drop-down list, and click the PDynaFlect button. Drag this Space Warp in the Top view, and make it wide enough to be completely under the mirror object. Rotate the PDynaFlect Space Warp so that a single large arrow is pointing up at the mirror. Position it so that it lies in the same plane as the plane object that makes up the floor. In the Modify panel, set the Reflects value to 100 percent and the Bounce value to 0. Bind this Space Warp to the PArray as well; this keeps the pieces from falling through the floor. Figure 26-20 shows the mirror immediately after being struck by a ball.

Figure 26-20: A shattering mirror

Tutorial: Exploding a planet

Combining a PBomb with a PArray and a Ringwave object for a shockwave can create an attention-getting explosion. The file actually includes two Geospheres, one for the planet and the other to be used for an exploding layer of dust.

To explode a planet, follow these steps:

1. Open the Exploding Planet.max file from the Chap 26 directory on the CD-ROM.

   This file includes a couple of Geosphere objects and a Ringwave object.

2. Select Particle Systems from the subcategory drop-down list and click the PArray button. Create a PArray object in the Front viewport. Then, click the Pick Object button and select the first Geosphere. In the Viewport Display section, select the Mesh particles option. In the Particle Generation rollout, set the Speed to 10 and the Variation to 100. Then, set the Emit Start to 30 and the Display Until and Life values to 100. In the Particle Type rollout, select Object Fragments and set the Thickness to 100 and the number of Chunks to 20. In the Material Mapping and Source section, select the Picked Emitter option and then set values of 1, 2, and 3 for the Outside ID, the Edge ID, and the Backside ID. In the Rotation and Collision rollout, set the Spin Time to 50 with a Variation of 100.

3. Drag again in the Front viewport to create a second PArray. Under the Basic Parameters rollout, click the Pick Object button and select the second Geosphere. In the Particle Generation rollout, set the Speed to 10 and the Variation to 100. Then, set the Emit Start value to 25 and the Life value to 30. In the Particle Type rollout, select Object Fragments, set the Thickness to 1, and select the All Faces option. In the Material Mapping and Source section, select the Icon option. In the Rotation and Collision rollout, set the Spin Time to 20.

   This PArray will be used to create the initial dust cloud.

4. Select the Space Warps category button and choose Forces from the subcategory drop-down list. Click the PBomb button and create two PBomb objects, then click the Bind to Space Warp button on the main toolbar and drag from the first PBomb to the first PArray and from the second PBomb to the second PArray. Open the Modify panel and select each PBomb in turn, setting the Start Time for the first PBomb to 30 and the second to 25. Position both PBomb icons so they are within the Geospheres.

Tip   Make the two PBomb icons different sizes so they are easier to select.

Figure 26-21 shows the resulting planet as the explosion first starts.

Figure 26-21: Exploding a planet with a PBomb and a Ringwave

Tutorial: Making water flow down a trough

That should be enough destruction for a while. In this final example, we'll make some water particles flow down a trough. This is accomplished using the Path Follow Space Warp.

To make water flow down a trough, follow these steps:

1. Open the Water flowing down a trough.max file from the Chap 26 directory on the CD-ROM.

   This file includes a simple trough made from primitives and a spline path the water will follow.

2. Select Particle Systems from the subcategory drop-down list and click the Super Spray button. Create a Super Spray object in the Front viewport. In the Viewport Display section, select the Ticks particles option. In the Particle Generation rollout, set the Speed to 10 and the Variation to 100. Then, set the Emit Start to 0 and the Display Until and Life values to 100. In the Particle Type rollout, select MetaParticles and enable the Automatic Coarseness option.

3. Select the Space Warps category button and choose Forces from the subcategory drop-down list. Click the Path Follow button and create a Path Follow objects, then click the Bind to Space Warp button on the main toolbar and drag from the Path Follow icon to the first Super Spray icon. Open the Modify panel and select the Path Follow icon and click the Pick Shape Object button and select the path in the viewports. Set the Start Frame to 0 and the Travel Time to 100.

Figure 26-22 shows the rendered result.

Figure 26-22: Water flowing down a trough using the Path Follow Space Warp

Summary

Space Warps are useful for adding forces and effects to objects in the scene. There are several different types of Space Warps and most of them can only be applied to certain object types. In this chapter you

✦ Learned how to create Space Warps

✦ Discovered how to bind Space Warps to objects

✦ Explored in depth all the various Space Warps in several subcategories

✦ Combined some Space Warps with particle systems to shatter glass and explode a planet

If you feel that your animations are out of control, we'll next learn about constraints that you can apply to objects to better control the motion in your scene.

✦   ✦   ✦

Restricting Movement with Constraints

The trick of animating an object is to make the object go where you want it to go. Animating objects deals not only with controlling the motion of the object, but controlling its lack of motion also. Constraints are a type of animation controller that you can use to restrict the motion of an object.

Using these constraints, you can force objects to stay attached to another object or follow a path. For example, the Attachment constraint can be used to make a robot's feet stay connected to a ground plane as it moves. The purpose of these constraints is to make animating your objects easier.

Using Constraints

You can apply constraints to selected objects using the Animation ⇨ Constraints menu. The constraints contained within this menu include Attachment, Surface, Path, Position, Link, LookAt, and Orientation.

 All constraints will have the same controller icon displayed in the Motion panel or the Track View.

After you select one of the constraints from the Animation ⇨ Constraints menu, a dotted link line will extend from the current selected object to the mouse cursor. You can select a target object in any of the viewports to apply the constraint. The cursor changes to a plus sign when it is over a target object that can be selected. Selecting a constraint from the Constraints menu also opens the Motion panel where the settings of the constraint can be modified.

 You can also apply constraints using the Assign Controller button found in the Motion panel and in the Track View window.

 Cross-Reference Find out more about Controllers in Chapter 28, "Animating with Controllers," and more on the Track View window in Chapter 25, "Working with the Track View."

Working with the Constraints

Each constraint is slightly different, but learning how to use these constraints will help you control the animated objects within a scene. You can apply several constraints to a single object. All constraints that are applied to an object are displayed in a list found in the Motion panel. From this list, you can select which constraint to make active and which to delete. You can also cut and paste constraints between objects.

Attachment constraint

The Attachment constraint determines an object's position by attaching it to the face of another object. This constraint lets you attach an object to the surface of another object. For example, you could animate the launch of a rocket ship with booster rockets that are attached with the Attachment constraint. The booster rockets would move along with the ship until the time when they are jettisoned.

The pivot point of the object that the constraint is applied to is attached to the target object. At the top of the Attachment Parameters rollout is a Pick Object button for selecting the target object to attach to. You can use this button to change the target object or to select the target object if the Animation ⇨ Constraints menu wasn't used. There is also an option to align the object to the surface. The Update section enables you to manually or automatically update the attachment values.

Note   The Attachment constraint shows up in the Position track of the Assign Controller rollout as the Position List controller. To minimize the effect of other controllers, set their Weight values in the Position List rollout to 0.

The Key Info section of the Attachment Parameters rollout displays the key number and lets you move between the various keys. The Time value is the current key value. In the Face field, you can specify the exact number of the face to attach to. To set this face, click the Set Position button and drag over the target object. The A and B values represent Barycentric coordinates for defining how the object lies on the face. You can change these coordinate values by entering values or by dragging the red cross hairs in the box underneath the A and B values. The easiest way to position an object is to use the Set Position button to place the object and then to enhance its position with the A and B values. The Set Position button stays active until you click it again.

The TCB section sets the Tension, Continuity, and Bias values for the constraint. You can also set the Ease To and Ease From values.

Tutorial: Attaching a boat to the sea

One way to use the Attachment constraint is to attach characters or objects to the surface of a landscape object such as a terrain. In this example, you'll do just that by using the Attachment constraint to keep a boat object in contact with the rolling sea.

To constrain a sphere to a terrain object, follow these steps:

   1. Open the Boat on rough seas.max file from the Chap 27 directory on the CD-ROM.

   This file includes a simple terrain plane and a boat object. The Pivot Point for the boat object has been moved to the base of the boat.

2. With the boat object selected, choose Animation ⇨ Constraints ⇨ Attachment Constraint. Then in pick object mode, select the terrain object.

The boat becomes attached to the terrain object.

3. Within the Position List rollout, select the Bézier Position layer and set its Weight value to 0.

4. In the Attachment Parameters rollout, click the Set Position button and drag the object in the Perspective viewport until it is positioned on one of the terrain peaks.

Figure 27-1 shows the sphere in its resulting position on the terrain peak.

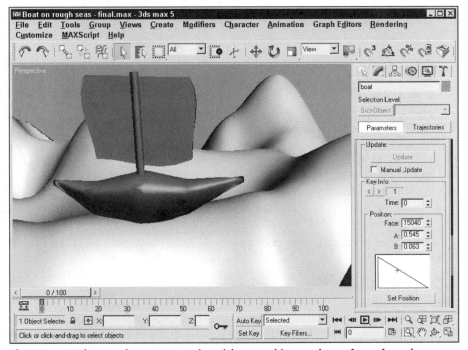

Figure 27-1: The Attachment constraint sticks one object to the surface of another.

Surface constraint

The Surface constraint moves an object so it is on the surface of another object. The object with Surface constraint applied to it will be positioned so its pivot point is on the surface of the target object. You can use this constraint only on certain objects including Spheres, Cones, Cylinders, Toruses, Quad Patches, Loft objects, and NURBS objects.

In the Surface Controller Parameters rollout is the name of the target object that was selected after the menu command. The Pick Surface button enables you to select a different surface to attach to. You can also select specific U and V Position values. Alignment options include No Alignment, Align to U, Align to V, and a Flip toggle.

Note   Don't be confused because the rollout is named Surface Controller Parameters instead of Surface Constraint Parameters. The developers at Discreet must have missed this one.

Tutorial: Rolling a tire down a hill with the Surface constraint

Moving a vehicle across a landscape can be a difficult procedure if you need to place every rotation and position key, but with the Surface constraint it becomes easy. In this tutorial, we'll use the Surface constraint to roll a tire down a hill.

To roll a tire down a hill with the Surface Constraint, follow these steps:

1. Open the Tire rolling on a hill.max file from the Chap 27 directory on the CD-ROM.

   This file includes a patch grid hill and a wheel object made from primitives.

2. Create a dummy object from the Helpers category and link the tire object to it as a child — this causes the tire to move along with the dummy object. Position the dummy object's pivot point at the bottom of the tire and at the top of the hill.

3. Select the dummy object, choose Animation ➪ Constraints ➪ Surface Constraint, and select the hill object.

4. In the Surface Controller Parameters rollout, select the Align to V and Flip options to position the dummy and tire objects at the top of the hill. Set the V Position value to 50 to move the tire down the hill.

5. Click the Auto Key button (or press the N key), drag the Time Slider to frame 100, and change the U Position to 100. Click the Animate button again to deactivate it and click the Play Animation button to see the tire move down the hill.

Figure 27-2 shows the tire as it moves down the hill. In the Top view, you can see the function curves for this motion.

Path constraint

The Path constraint lets you select a spline path for the object to follow. The object will be locked to the path and will follow it even if the spline is changed. This is one of the most useful constraints because you can control the exact motion of an object using a spline. With Max's spline features, you can control very precisely the motions of objects that are constrained with the Path constraint. A good example of this constraint is a train that is animated following a track. Using a spline to create the train tracks, the train is easily animated using the Path constraint.

When you choose the Animation ➪ Constraints ➪ Path Constraint menu command, you can select a single path for the object to follow. This path is added to a list of paths in the Path Parameters rollout.

The Path Parameters rollout also includes Add and Delete Path buttons for adding and deleting paths to and from the list. If two paths are added to the list, then the object follows the position centered between these two paths. By adjusting the Weight value for each path, you can make the object favor a specific path.

The Path Options include a % Along Path value for defining the object's position along the path. This value ranges from 0 at one end to 100 at the other end. The Follow option causes the object to be aligned with the path as it moves, and the Bank option causes the object to rotate to simulate a banking motion.

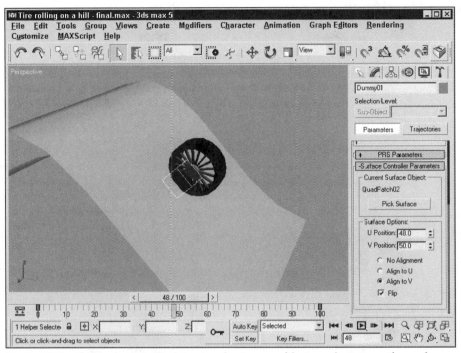

Figure 27-2: The Surface constraint can animate one object moving across the surface of another.

The Bank Amount value sets the depth of the bank, and the Smoothness value determines how smooth the bank is. The Allow Upside Down option lets the object spin completely about the axis, and the Constant Velocity option keeps the speed regular. The Loop option returns the object to its original position for the last frame of the animation setting up a looping animation sequence. The Relative option lets the object maintain its current position and does not move the object to the start of the path. From its original position, it follows the path from its relative position. At the bottom of the Path Parameters rollout, you can select the axis to use.

Tutorial: Creating a dragonfly flight path

Another way to use splines is to create animation paths. As an example we'll use a Helix spline to create an animation path. There are basically two ways to use splines for animation paths. One way is to create a spline and have an object follow it using either the Path constraint or the Path Follow Space Warp. The other way is to animate an object and then edit the Trajectory path.

In this tutorial, we'll use a simple Helix path and attach it to a Dragonfly model — the result will be a dizzy insect. The Dragonfly model was taken from the sampler CD-ROM provided by Zygote Media.

On the CD-ROM   The Dragonfly model, along with many other Zygote models, is included on the CD-ROM provided with this book.

To attach an object to a spline path, follow these steps:

1. Open the Dizzy dragonfly.max file from the Chap 27 directory on the CD-ROM.

   This file contains the Dragonfly model and a Helix spline.

2. With the dragonfly selected, choose Animation ➪ Constraints ➪ Path Constraint. Then click the Helix spline to select it as the path to follow. Select the Follow option.

3. Click the Play Animation button in the Time Controls to see the dragonfly follow the path.

Figure 27-3 shows the dragonfly in its path up the spiral.

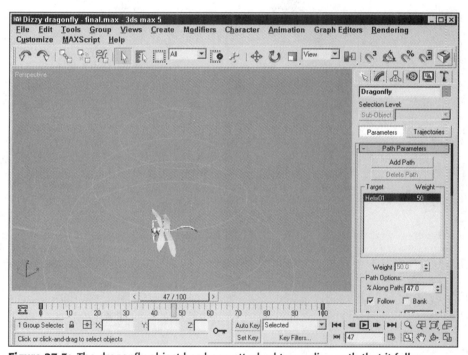

Figure 27-3: The dragonfly object has been attached to a spline path that it follows.

Position constraint

You can use the Position constraint to tie the position of an object to the weighted position of several target objects. For example, you could animate a formation of fighter jets by animating one of the jets and using Position constraints on all adjacent jets.

The Position constraint menu option lets you select a single target object, enabling you to place the pivot points of the two objects on top of one another. To add another target object, click the Add Position Target button in the Position Constraint rollout in the Motion panel. This button enables you to select another target object in the viewports; the target name will appear within the target list in the rollout.

If you select a target name in the target list, you can assign a weight to the target. The constrained object will be positioned close to the object with the higher weighted value. The Weight value provides a way to center objects between several other objects. The Keep Initial Offset option lets the object stay in its current location, but centers it relative to this position.

Figure 27-4 shows a sphere positioned between four diamond-shaped objects using the Position constraint. Notice how the weight of the left diamond object is weighted higher than the other targets, and the sphere is close to it.

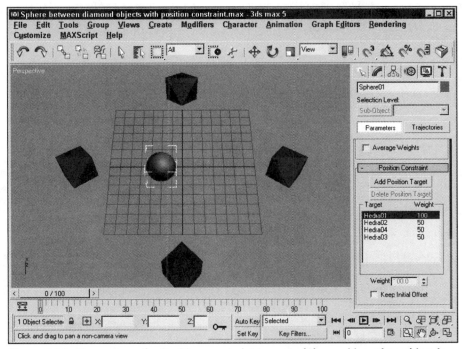

Figure 27-4: You can use the Position constraint to control the position of an object in relation to its targets.

Link constraint

The Link constraint can transfer hierarchical links between objects. This constraint can cause a child's link to be switched during an animation. Any time you animate a complex model with a dummy object, the Link constraint makes it possible to switch control from one dummy object to another during the animation sequence. This keeps the motions of the dummy objects simple.

The Link Parameters rollout includes Add Link and Delete Link buttons, a list of linked objects, and the Start Time field. To switch the link of an object, enter for the Start Time the frame where you want the link to switch, or drag the Time Slider and click the Add Link button. Then select the new parent object. The Delete key becomes active when you select a link in the list.

Note   If you create a link using the Link constraint, the object is not recognized as a child in any hierarchies.

All links are kept in a list in the Link Parameters rollout. You can add links to this list with the Add Link button or delete links with the Delete Link button. The Start Time field specifies when the selected object takes control of the link. The object listed in the list is the parent object, so the Start Time setting determines when each parent object takes control.

The Key Mode section lets you choose a No Key option. This option does not write any keyframes for the object. If you want to set keys, you can choose the Key Nodes options and set keys for the object itself (Child option) or for the entire hierarchy (Parent option). The Key Entire Hierarchy sets keys for the object and its parents (Child option) or for the object and its targets and their hierarchies (Parent option).

This constraint also includes the PRS Parameters and Key Info rollouts.

Caution   You cannot use Link constraints with inverse kinematics systems.

Tutorial: Skating a figure eight

For an animated object to switch its link from one parent to another halfway through an animation, you need to use the Link constraint. Rotating an object about a static point is easy enough — just link the object to a dummy object and rotate the dummy object. The figure-eight motion is more complex but you can do it with the Link constraint.

To move an object in a figure eight, follow these steps:

1. Open the Figure skater skating a figure eight.max file from the Chap 27 directory on the CD-ROM.

   This file includes a figure skater model imported from Poser and two dummy objects. The figure skater is linked to the first dummy object.

2. Click the Auto Key button (or press the N key), drag the Time Slider to frame 100, and rotate the first dummy object two full revolutions in the Top viewport.

3. Select the second dummy object, and rotate it two full revolutions in the opposite direction. Click the Auto Key button again to deactivate it.

4. With the figure skater selected, choose Animation ➪ Constraints ➪ Link Constraint. Then click the first dummy object (the top one in the Top viewport).

   The Link constraint is assigned to the figure skater.

5. In the Link Parameters rollout, click the Add Link button. Click the first dummy object, and set the Start Time value to 0. Then click the second dummy object, and set the Start Time to 25. Finally, click the first dummy object again, and set the Start Time to 75.

6. Click the Play Animation button (or press the / key) to see the animation play.

Tip   Another way to accomplish this same motion is to create a spline of a figure eight and use the Path constraint.

Figure 27-5 shows the skater as she makes her path around the two dummy objects.

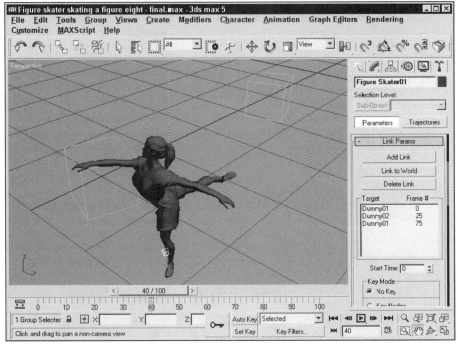

Figure 27-5: With the Link constraint, the figure skater can move in a figure eight by rotating about two different dummy objects.

LookAt constraint

The LookAt constraint won't move an object, but it rotates the object so it is always oriented toward the target object. For example, you could use the LookAt constraint to animate a character's head that is watching a flying bumblebee. It is also very useful to apply to camera objects that follow a specific object throughout the animation.

After you select a target object, a single line extends from the object and points at the target object. This line, called the Viewline, is only visible within the viewports.

The LookAt Constraint rollout, like many of the other constraints, includes a list of targets. With the Add and Delete LookAt Target buttons, you can add and remove targets from the list. If several targets are on the list, the object will be centered on a location between them. Using the Weight value, you can cause the various targets to have more of an influence over the orientation of the object. The Keep Initial Offset option prevents the object from reorienting itself when the constraint is applied. Any movement will be relative to it original position.

You can set the Viewline length, which is the distance that the Viewline extends from the object. The Viewline Length Absolute option draws the Viewline from the object to its target, ignoring the length value.

The Set Orientation button lets you change the offset orientation of the object using the Select and Rotation button on the main toolbar. If you get lost, the Reset Orientation returns the orientation to its original position. You can select which local axis points at the target object.

The Upnode is an object that defines the up direction. If the LookAt axis ever lines up with the Upnode axis, then the object will flip upside-down. To prevent this you can select which local axis is used as the LookAt axis and which axis points at the Upnode. The World is the default Upnode object, but you can select any object as the Upnode object by deselecting the World object and clicking the button to its right.

To control the Upnode, you can select the LookAt option or the Axis Alignment option, which will enable the Align to Upnode Axis option. Using this option, you can specify which axis points toward the Upnode.

Caution   The object using the LookAt constraint flips when the target point is positioned directly above or below the object's pivot point.

When you assign the LookAt constraint, the Create Key button for rotation changes to Roll. This is because the camera is locked to point at the assigned object and cannot rotate, but only roll about the axis.

You can use the LookAt constraint to let cameras follow objects as they move around a scene. It is the default transform controller for Target camera objects.

Tutorial: Watching a dragonfly fly

Earlier in this chapter, I showed you an example of a dragonfly that was attached to a spiral path. To follow the dragonfly around his path, we could clone the original path and offset it so that it is slightly behind the dragonfly and then use a Path constraint to attach a camera to this cloned path. This method would create a camera that would follow the dragonfly on its spiral path, but it wouldn't be much different from the earlier example. Instead, in this tutorial we'll use the LookAt constraint to watch the dragonfly as it circles about the spiral.

To have a camera watch the motions of an object with the LookAt constraint, follow these steps:

1. Open the Dizzy dragonfly and following camera.max file from the Chap 27 directory on the CD-ROM.

   This file is the same example that was used earlier, except I've added some cattails around the perimeter to give the scene some depth.

2. In the Create panel, click the Cameras category button and create a Free camera in any viewport. Position the camera in the center of the Helix.

3. With the camera selected, choose Animation ⇨ Constraints ⇨ LookAt Constraints. Click the dragonfly object to select it as the object to look at.

4. Move the camera up to the peak of the spiral and prepare to get really dizzy.

Figure 27-6 shows one frame of the dragonfly spinning along its path.

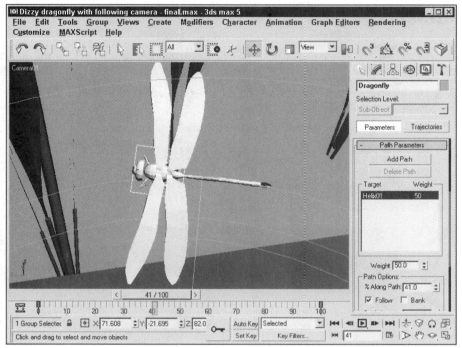

Figure 27-6: The camera in this scene follows the dragonfly on its path using the LookAt constraint.

Orientation constraint

You can use the Orientation constraint to lock the rotation of an object to another object. You can move and scale the objects independently, but the constrained object will rotate along with the target object. A good example of an animation that uses this type of constraint is a satellite that orbits the Earth. You could offset the satellite and still constrain it to the Earth's surface. Then as the Earth moves, the satellite follows.

In the Orientation Constraint rollout, you can select several orientation targets and weight them in the same manner as with the Position constraint. The target with the greatest weight value will have the most influence over the object's orientation. You can also constrain an object to the World object. The Keep Initial Offset option maintains the object's original orientation and rotates it relative to this original orientation. The Transform Rule setting determines whether the object rotates using the Local or World coordinate systems.

Summary

Using the Animation ⇨ Constraints menu, you can apply constraints to objects. This menu also lets you select a target object. You can use the various constraints to limit the motion of objects, which is helpful as you begin to animate. In this chapter, you've

✦ Learned to constrain an object to the surface of an object using the Attachment and Surface constraints

✦ Forced an object to travel along a path with the Path constraint

✦ Controlled the position and orientation of objects with weighted Position and Orientation constraints

✦ Shifted between two different controlling objects using the Link constraint

✦ Followed objects with the LookAt constraint

The next chapter explores the various controller types that are available in Max.

✦　　✦　　✦

Animating with Controllers

When you first begin animating and working with keys, it seems amazing how easy it is to have Max figure out all the frames between the start and end keys, especially if you've ever animated in 2D by drawing every frame. But soon you realize that animating with keys can be tough for complex realistic motions, and once again, Max comes to the rescue. You can use animation controllers to automate the creation of keys for certain types of motions.

Controllers store and manage the key values for all animations in Max. When you animate an object using the Auto Key button, the default controller is automatically assigned. You can change the assigned controller or alter its parameters using the Motion panel or the Track View. This chapter explains how to work with controllers and examines all the various controllers that are available. For example, you can use the Noise controller to add random motion to a flag blowing in the wind or use the Waveform controller to produce regular repeating motions such as a sine or square wave.

Understanding Controller Types

Controllers are used to set the keys for animation sequences. Every object and parameter that is animated has a controller assigned, and almost every controller has parameters that you can alter to change its functionality. Some controllers present these parameters as rollouts in the Motion panel, and others use a Properties dialog box.

In Max, there are five basic controller types that work with only a single parameter or track and one specialized controller type that manages several tracks at once (the Transform controllers). The type depends on the type of values the controller works with. The types include

  ✦ **Float controllers:** Used for all parameters with a single numeric value, such as Wind Strength and Sphere Radius

  ✦ **Point3 controllers:** Consist of color components for red, green, and blue, such as Diffuse and Background colors

  ✦ **Position controllers:** Control the position coordinates for objects, consisting of X, Y, and Z values

✦ **Rotation controllers:** Control the rotation values for objects along all three axes

✦ **Scale controllers:** Control the scale values for objects as percentages for each axis

✦ **Transform controllers:** A special controller type that applies to all transforms (position, rotation, and scale) at the same time, such as the Position, Rotation, Scale (PRS) controllers

Note   Understanding the different controller types is important. When you copy and paste controller parameters between different tracks, both tracks must have the same controller type.

Float controllers work with parameters that use float numbers, such as a sphere's Radius or a plane object's Scale Multiplier value. Float values are numbers with a decimal value, such as 2.3 or 10.99. A Float controller is assigned to any parameter that is animated. After it is assigned, you can access the function curves and keys for this controller in the Track View and in the Track Bar.

Assigning Controllers

Any object or parameter that is animated is automatically assigned a controller. The controller that is assigned is the default controller. The Animation panel in the Preference Settings dialog box lists and lets you change the default controllers. You can change this automatic default controller using the Track View window or the transformation tracks located in the Motion panel.

Automatically assigned controllers

The default controllers are automatically assigned for an object's transformation tracks when the object is created. For example, if you create a simple sphere and then open the Motion panel (which has the icon that looks like a wheel), you can find the transformation tracks in the Assign Controller rollout. The default Position controller is Position XYZ, the default Rotation controller is Euler XYZ, and the default Scale controller is the Bézier Scale controller.

The default controller depends on the type of object. For example, the Barycentric Morph controller is automatically assigned when you create a morph compound object, and the Master Point controller is automatically assigned to any vertices or control points subobjects that are animated.

Note   Because controllers are automatically assigned to animation tracks, they cannot be removed, only changed to a different controller. There isn't a function to delete controllers.

Assigning controllers with the Animation menu

The easiest way to assign a controller to an object is with the Animation menu. Located under the Animation menu are four controller submenus consisting of Transform, Position, Rotation, and Scale.

Note   Although constraints are contained within a separate menu, they control the animating of keys just like controllers.

When a controller is assigned to an object using the Animation menu, the existing controller is not removed, but the new controller is added as part of a list along with the other controllers. You can see all these controllers in the Motion panel.

For example, Figure 28-1 shows the Motion panel for a sphere object that has the default Position XYZ controller assigned to the Position track. If you choose Animation ⇨ Position Controllers ⇨ Noise, then the Position List controller is added to the Position track of which the Position XYZ and Noise controller are two available controllers.

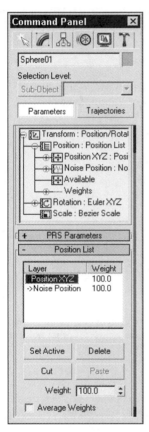

Figure 28-1: The Motion panel displays all transform controllers applied to an object.

The List controller allows you to set Weights for each of its controllers. Using the Position List rollout, you can set the active controller and delete controllers from the list. You can also Cut and Paste controllers to other tracks.

Assigning controllers in the Motion panel

The top of the Motion panel includes two buttons: Parameters and Trajectories. Clicking the Parameters button makes the Assign Controller rollout available.

To change a transformation track's controller, select the track and click the Assign Controller button positioned directly above the list. An Assign Controller dialog box opens that is specific to the track you selected.

 For more about the Trajectories button, see Chapter 24, "Animation Basics."

For example, Figure 28-2 shows the Assign Position Controller dialog box for selecting a controller for the Position track. The arrow mark (>) shows the current selected controller. At the bottom of the dialog box, the default controller type is listed. Select a new controller from the list and click OK. This new controller now is listed in the track, and the controller's rollouts appear beneath the Assign Controller rollout.

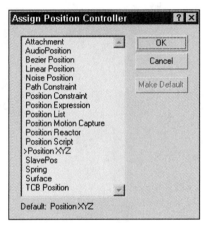

Figure 28-2: The Assign Position Controller dialog box lets you select a controller to assign.

Caution You can assign controllers to other parameters for materials and modifiers, but you can only assign controllers to the transformation tracks using the Motion panel. All other controllers are assigned using the Track View.

Assigning controllers in Track View

 You can also use the Track View to assign controllers. To do this, locate and select the track to apply a controller to, and click the Assign Controller button on the Controllers toolbar, choose the Controller ⇨ Assign (keyboard shortcut, C) menu command, or right-click on the track and select Assign Controller from the pop-up menu. An Assign Controller dialog box opens in which you can select the controller to use.

Chapter 25, "Working with the Track View," covers the details of the Track View.

You can also use the Controller toolbar to copy and paste controllers between tracks, but you can paste controllers only to similar types of tracks. When you paste controllers, the Paste dialog box lets you choose to paste the controller as a copy or as an instance. Changing an instanced controller's parameters changes the parameters for all instances. The Paste dialog box also includes an option to replace all instances. This option replaces all instances of the controller whether they are selected or not.

Setting Default Controllers

When you assign controllers using the Track View, the Assign Controller dialog box includes the option Make Default. With this option, the selected controller becomes the default for the selected track.

You can also set the global default controller for each type of track by choosing Customize ⇨ Preferences, selecting the Animation panel, and then clicking the Set Defaults button. The Set Controller Defaults dialog box opens, in which you can set the default parameter settings, such as the In and Out curves for the controller. To set the default controller, select a controller from the list and click the Set Defaults button to open a controller-specific dialog box where you can adjust the controller parameters. The Animation panel also includes a button to revert to the original settings.

Note   Changing a default controller will not change any currently assigned controllers.

Examining the Various Controllers

Now that you've learned how to assign a controller, let's take a look at the available controllers. Max includes a vast assortment of controllers, and you can add more controllers as plug-ins.

Earlier in the chapter, I mentioned six specific controller types. These types define the type of data that the controller works with. This section covers the various controllers according to the types of tracks they work with.

Note   Looking at the function curves for a controller provides a good idea of how you can control it, so many of the figures that follow show the various function curves for the different controllers.

Each of these controllers has a unique icon to represent them in the Track View. This makes them easy to identify.

Transform controllers

Multi-track transform controllers work with the Position, Rotation, and Scale tracks all at the same time. You access them by selecting the Transform track in the Motion panel and then clicking the Assign Controller button, or by choosing the Animation ⇨ Transform Controllers menu command.

Position/Rotation/Scale Transform controller

The Position/Rotation/Scale Transform controller is the default controller for all trans forms. This controller includes a Bézier controller for the Position and Scale tracks and a Euler XYZ controller for the Rotation track.

The PRS Parameters rollout, shown in Figure 28-3, lets you create and delete keys for Position, Rotation, and Scale transforms. The Position, Rotation, and Scale buttons control the fields that appear in the Key Info rollouts positioned below the PRS Parameters rollout.

Figure 28-3: The PRS Parameters rollout is the default transform controller.

Script controller

The Script controller is similar to the Expression controller, except that it can work with the MAXScript lines of code. Right-clicking a track with the Script controller assigned and selecting Properties opens the Script Controller dialog box, shown in Figure 28-4.

This dialog box includes a Script pane and a Results pane along with buttons to Save and Load scripts. After a script loads, click the Evaluate button to execute the script.

Cross-Reference   For more information on MAXScript, see Chapter 40, "Using MAXScript."

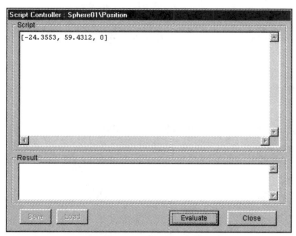

Figure 28-4: The Script Controller dialog box runs scripts to generate animation keys.

Position track controllers

Position track controller types include some of the common default controllers and can be assigned to the Position track. They typically work with three unique values representing the X-, Y-, and Z-axes. These controllers can be assigned from the Animation ⇨ Position Controllers menu. Many of the controllers found in this menu are also found in the Rotation and Scale Controllers menu.

Audio controller

The Audio controller can control an object's transform, color, or parameter value in response to the amplitude of a sound file. The Audio Controller dialog box, shown in Figure 28-5, includes Choose Sound and Remove Sound buttons for loading or removing sound files.

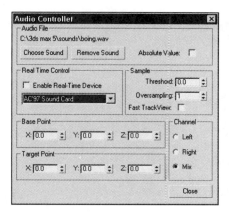

Figure 28-5: The Audio Controller dialog box lets you change values based on the amplitude of a sound file.

The Real Time Control drop-down list lets you specify a device to control the system. To control the sound input, you can specify a Sample Threshold and Oversampling rate. You can also set Base Point and Target Point values for each axis. The Channel options let you specify which channel to use: Left, Right, or Mix. Figure 28-6 shows the Audio controller assigned to the Position track.

The boing.wav file is used to affect the position of the object.

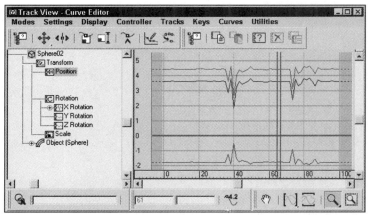

Figure 28-6: The Audio controller changes the positional value based on the amplitude of the sound file.

Bézier controller

The Bézier controller is the default controller for many parameters. It enables you to interpolate between values using an adjustable Bézier spline. By dragging its tangent vertex handles, you can control the spline's curvature. Tangent handles produce a smooth transition when they lie on the same line, or you can create an angle between them for a sharp point. Figure 28-7 shows the Bézier controller assigned to a Position track.

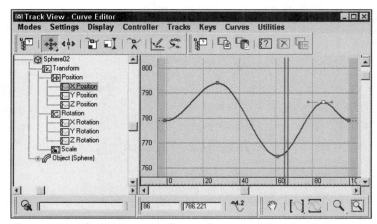

Figure 28-7: The Bézier controller produces smooth animation curves.

The Bézier controller parameters are displayed in the Motion panel under two rollouts: Key Info (Basic) and Key Info (Advanced).

At the top of the Key Info (Basic) rollout are two arrows and a field that shows the key number. The arrows let you move between the Previous and Next keys. Each vertex shown in the function curve represents a key. The Time field displays the frame number where the key is located. The Time Lock button next to the Time field can be set to prevent the key from being dragged in Track View. The value fields show the values for the selected track; the number of fields changes depending on the type of track that is selected.

At the bottom of the Key Info (Basic) rollout are two flyout buttons for specifying the In and Out curves for the key. The arrows to the sides of these buttons move between the various In/Out curve types. The curve types include Smooth, Linear, Step, Slow, Fast, Custom, and Tangent Copy.

 Cross-Reference   Chapter 25, "Working with the Track View," describes these various In/Out curve types.

The In and Out values in the Key Info (Advanced) rollout are enabled only when the Custom curve type is selected. These fields let you define the rate applied to each axis of the curve. The Lock button changes the two values by equal and opposite amounts. The Normalize Time button averages the positions of all keys. The Constant Velocity option interpolates the key between its neighboring keys to provide smoother motion.

Expression controller

 The Expression controller can define a mathematical expression that controls the track values. These expressions can use the values of other tracks and basic mathematical functions such as sines and logarithms to control animation keys.

 Cross-Reference   Chapter 29, "Using Expressions," covers the Expression controller.

Linear controller

The Linear controller interpolates between two values to create a straight line.

The Linear controller doesn't include any parameters and can be applied to time or values. Figure 28-8 shows the curves from the previous example after the Linear controller is assigned — all curves have been replaced with straight lines.

Motion Capture controller

The Motion Capture controller allows you to control an object's transforms using an external device such as a mouse, keyboard, joystick, or MIDI device. This controller works with the Motion Capture utility to capture motion data.

After you assign the Motion Capture controller to a track, right-click the track and select Properties from the pop-up menu to open the Motion Capture panel, shown in Figure 28-9. This dialog box lets you select the devices to use to control the motion of the track values. Options include Keyboard, Mouse, Joystick, and MIDI devices.

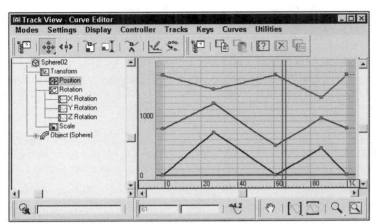

Figure 28-8: The Linear controller uses straight lines.

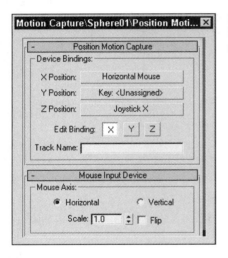

Figure 28-9: The Motion Capture controller lets you control track values using external devices.

For the Keyboard control, the Keyboard Input Device rollout appears, as shown in Figure 28-10. The Assign button lets you select a keyboard key to track. The other settings control the Envelope Graph, which defines how quickly key presses are tracked.

The Motion Capture dialog box only defines which device controls which values. The actual capturing of data is accomplished using the Motion Capture utility. Selecting the Motion Capture utility in the Utility panel displays the Motion Capture rollout, shown in Figure 28-11. This rollout includes buttons to Start, Stop, and Test the data-capturing process.

Before you can use the Start, Stop, and Test buttons, you need to select the tracks to capture from the Tracks list. The Record Range section lets you set the Preroll, In, and Out values, which are the frame numbers to include. You can also set the number of Samples Per Frame. The Reduce Keys option removes any unnecessary keys, if enabled.

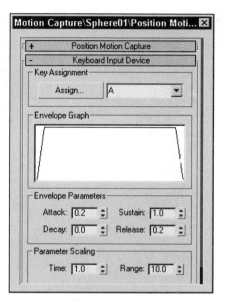

Figure 28-10: The Keyboard Input Device rollout lets you select which key press is captured.

Figure 28-11: The Motion Capture rollout includes controls for capturing motion data.

Tutorial: Drawing with a pencil with the Motion Capture controller

Some motions, such as drawing with a pencil, are natural motions for our hands, but they become very difficult when you're trying to animate using keyframes. This tutorial uses the Motion Capture controller and utility to animate the natural motion of drawing with a pencil.

To animate a pencil drawing on paper, follow these steps:

1. Open the Drawing with a pencil.max file from the Chap 28 directory on the CD-ROM.

   This file has a pencil object positioned on a piece of paper.

2. Select the pencil object, open the Motion panel, and select the Position track for the pencil object. Then click the Assign Controller button and double-click the Position Motion Capture selection.

   The Motion Capture dialog box opens.

3. Click the X Position button and double-click the Mouse Input Device selection. Then click the Y Position button and double-click the Mouse Input Device selection again. In the Mouse Input Device rollout, select the Vertical option. This sets the set the X Position to the Horizontal Mouse movement and the Y Position to the Vertical Mouse movement. Close the Motion Capture dialog box.

4. Open the Utilities panel and click the Motion Capture button. In the Motion Capture rollout, select the Position track, and get the mouse ready to move. Then click the Start button in the Record Controls section and move the mouse as if you were drawing with the mouse. The pencil object moves in the viewport along with your mouse movements.

   The Motion Capture utility creates a key for each frame. It quits capturing the motion when it reaches frame 100.

5. Click the Play Animation button (or press the / key) to see the results.

Figure 28-12 shows the scene after the Motion Capture controller has computed all the frames.

Noise controller

The Noise controller applies random variations in a track's values. In the Noise Controller dialog box, shown in Figure 28-13, the Seed value determines the randomness of the noise, and the Frequency value determines how jagged the noise is. You can also set the Strength along each axis — the > (greater than) 0 option for each axis makes the noise values remain positive.

There is also an option to enable Fractal Noise with a Roughness setting.

The Ramp in and Ramp out values determine the length of time before or until the noise can reach full value. The Characteristic Graph gives a visual look at the noise over the range. Figure 28-14 shows the Noise controller assigned to the Position track.

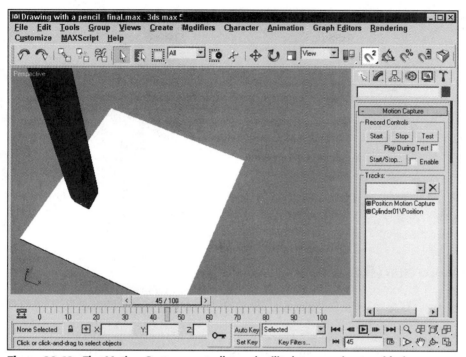

Figure 28-12: The Motion Capture controller and utility let you animate with the mouse, keyboard, joystick, or a MIDI device.

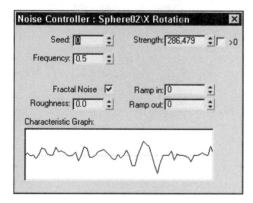

Figure 28-13: The Noise controller properties let you set the noise strength for each axis.

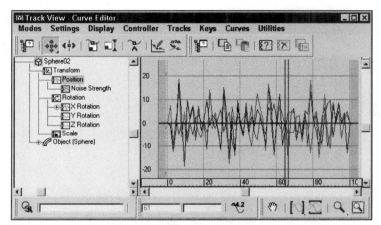

Figure 28-14: The Noise controller lets you randomly alter track values.

Quaternion (TCB) controller

The Quaternion (TCB) controller produces curved animation paths similar to the Bézier controller, except it uses the values for Tension, Continuity, and Bias to define their curvature.

The parameters for this controller are displayed in a single Key Info rollout. Like the Bézier controller rollouts, the Quaternion (TCB) controller rollout includes arrows and Key, Time, and Value fields. It also includes a graph of the TCB values; the red plus sign represents the current key's position while the rest of the graph shows the regular increments of time as black plus signs. Changing the Tension, Continuity, and Bias values in the fields below the graph changes its shape. Right-clicking the track and selecting Properties from the pop-up menu opens the TCB graph dialog box, shown in Figure 28-15.

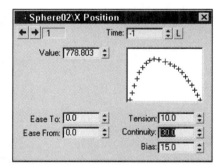

Figure 28-15: This dialog box shows and lets you control a curve defined by the Tension, Continuity, and Bias values.

The Tension value controls the amount of curvature: High Tension values produce a straight line leading into and away from the key, and low Tension values produce a round curve. The Continuity value controls how continuous, or smooth, the curve is around the key: The default value of 25 produces the smoothest curves, whereas high and low Continuity values produce sharp peaks from the top or bottom. The Bias value controls how the curve comes into and leaves the key point: High Bias values cause a bump to the right of the key, and low Bias values cause a bump to the left.

The Ease To and Ease From values control how quickly the key is approached or left.

Note   Enabling the trajectory path by clicking the Trajectory button in the Motion panel lets you see the changes to the path as they are made in the Key Info rollout.

Figure 28-16 shows three TCB curves assigned to the Position track of an object.

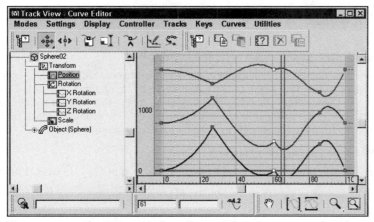

Figure 28-16: The TCB controller offers a different way to work with curves.

Reactor controller

The Reactor controller changes its values as a reaction to another controller. This con troller is different from the Attachment controller in that the motions don't need to be in the same direction. For example, you can have one object rise as another object moves to the side.

Cross-Reference   Don't confuse the Reactor controller with the Reactor utility, which computes motion based on physical dynamics. The Reactor utility is covered in Chapter 30, "Creating a Dynamic Simulation."

After the Reactor controller is assigned to a track, you can define the reactions using the Reaction Parameters dialog box, shown in Figure 28-17. Selecting and right-clicking the track with this controller assigned and selecting Properties from the pop-up menu opens this dialog box.

The React To button lets you select an object in one of the viewports. After selecting a React To object, a pop-up dialog box appears, letting you select a transform parameter. To add a reaction to the list, click the Create Reaction button. The Delete Reaction button deletes the selected reaction from the list. The Set Reaction Value button lets you specify the value for the reaction. These values are displayed in the Reaction Value field. Each reaction can have an Influence, Strength, and Falloff value.

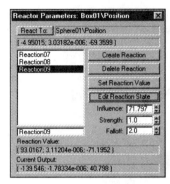

Figure 28-17: The Reactor Parameters dialog box lets you set the parameters of a reaction.

Tutorial: Rotating gears with the reactor controller

Many mechanical devices use gears, and animating these gears can be tricky because every adjacent gear will rotate in the opposite direction. Animating by linking the gears together will cause one gear to rotate around the other one. You can achieve this motion by animating the rotation of every gear individually, or you can use the Reactor controller to make the gears work like they are supposed to — which is what we'll do in this tutorial.

To rotate gears using the Reactor controller, follow these steps:

1. Open the Reactor rotating gears.max file from the Chap 28 directory on the CD-ROM.

   This file contains some gears created using the Ringwave primitive.

2. Select the first gear, click the Auto Key button (or press the N key), and drag the Time Slider to frame 100 (or press the End key). Then select the Select and Rotate button (or press the E key) and right-click it to open the Rotate Transform Type-In. Enter a value of **180** in the Z-axis field.

3. Open the Track View and locate the Rotation track for the second gear. Select this track and click the Assign Controller button. Select the Rotation Reactor option and click OK.

   The Reactor Parameters dialog box opens.

4. Drag the Time Slider back to frame 0 (or press the Home key). Click the React To button, select the first gear object, and choose Transform ➪ Rotation track from the pop-up menu.

   A reaction called Reaction01 is created in the list.

5. Drag the Time Slider to frame 100 (or press the End key), and click the Create Reaction button. This creates another reaction called Reaction02 in the list. Click the Edit Reaction State button to enable it. Then select the second gear, select and right-click the Select and Rotate button on the main toolbar, and enter **–180** in the Z-axis Offset. Click again on the Edit Reaction State button to disable it.

6. Click on the Play Animation button (or press the / key) to see the gears move together.

Figure 28-18 shows the two gears and the Reactor Parameters dialog box. The second gear rotates in the opposite direction of the first gear.

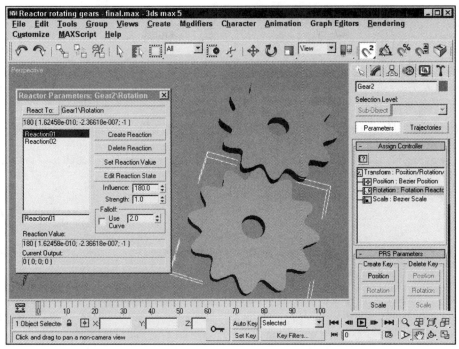

Figure 28-18: The Reactor controller animates these two opposite rotating gears.

Spring controller

The Spring controller is similar in many ways to the Flex modifier in that it adds secondary motion associated with the wiggle of a spring after a force has been applied and then removed. When the Spring controller is applied a panel with two rollouts appears. These rollouts, shown in Figure 28-19, let you control the physical properties of the spring and the forces that influence it.

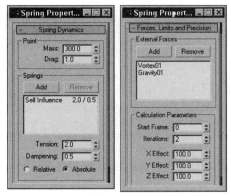

Figure 28-19: The Spring controller rollouts can add additional springs and forces.

In the Spring Dynamics rollout, you can change the Mass and Drag values. Higher mass values will result in greater secondary motion as the object is moved and the Drag value will control how quickly the bouncing motion stops. You can add multiple springs, each with its own Tension and Damping values to be applied Relative or Absolute.

The Forces, Limits and Precision rollout lets you add forces that will impact the spring motion. The Add button lets you identify these forces, which are typically Space Warps and you can limit the effect to specific axes.

Tutorial: Wagging a tail with the Spring controller

One of the best uses of the Spring controller is to gain the secondary motion associated with an existing motion. For example, if a character moves, then appendages such as a tail can easily follow if you apply a Spring controller to it.

To wag a row of spheres using the Spring controller, follow these steps:

1. Open the Spring controlled row of spheres.max file from the Chap 28 directory on the CD-ROM.

   This file contains a linked row of spheres with the head sphere animated moving back and forth.

2. Select the smallest sphere and choose the Animation ⇨ Position Controllers ⇨ Spring menu command. This will move the sphere to its parent. Choose the Select and Move button (or press the W key) and return the sphere to its original position.

3. Repeat Step 2 for the remaining spheres moving from smallest to largest.

4. Click the Play Animation button (or press the / key) to see the resulting motion.

Figure 28-20 shows a frame the final motion. Notice how the spheres aren't lined up exactly. The smallest sphere is moving the greatest distance because all the springs are adding their effect.

Position XYZ controller

The Position XYZ controller splits position transforms into three separate tracks, one for each axis. Each axis has a Bézier controller applied to it, but each component track can be assigned a different controller. The Position XYZ Parameters rollout lets you switch between the component axes. Figure 28-21 shows the Position XYZ controller assigned to a Position track with a Noise controller assigned to the X position track, the Linear controller assigned to the Y position track, and the Bézier controller assigned to the Z position track.

The Rotation tracks use a variety of controllers, many of them common to the Position track. This section lists the controllers that can be used only with the Rotation track.

Rotation and Scale track controllers

The Rotation and Scale track controller types include some of the common default controllers and can be assigned to the Rotation and Scale tracks. They typically work with three unique values representing the X-, Y-, and Z-axes. These controllers can be assigned from the Animation ⇨ Rotation (Scale) Controllers menus. Many of the controllers found in this menu are also found in the Position Controllers menu. Only the controllers unique to the Rotation and Scale tracks are covered here.

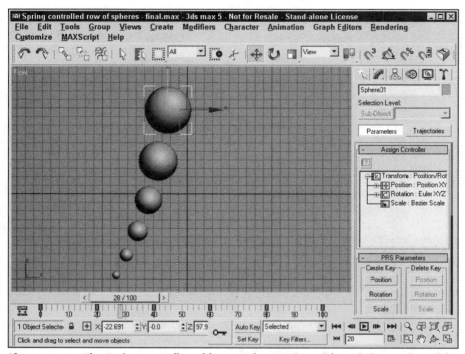

Figure 28-20: The Spring controller adds secondary motion to the existing motion of the largest sphere.

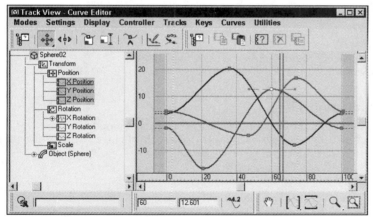

Figure 28-21: The Position XYZ controller splits each position axis into different components.

Euler XYZ Rotation controller

 The Euler XYZ Rotation controller lets you control the rotation angle along the X-, Y-, and Z-axes based on a single float value for each frame. Euler rotation is different from Max's default rotation method (which is quaternion rotation and not as smooth).

The main difference is that Euler rotation gives you access to the function curves. Using these curves, you can smoothly define the rotation motion of the object.

Note Euler XYZ Rotation values are in radians instead of degrees. Radians are much smaller values than degrees. A full revolution is 360 degrees or 2 times Pi radians, so one degree equals about 0.0174 radians.

The Euler Parameters rollout lets you choose the Axis Order, which is the order in which the axes are calculated. You can also choose which axis to work with. Figure 28-22 shows all three Rotation tracks (with the Bézier controller applied to it) for the Euler XYZ controller.

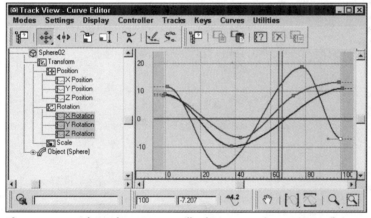

Figure 28-22: The Euler XYZ controller lets you assign separate float controllers to each axis.

Smooth Rotation controller

 The Smooth Rotation controller automatically produces a smooth rotation. This controller doesn't add any new keys but simply changes the timing of the existing keys to produce a smooth rotation. It does not have any parameters.

Scale XYZ controller

 There is one controller that you can use only in Scale tracks. The Scale XYZ controller breaks scale transforms into three separate tracks, one for each axis. This feature enables you to precisely control the scaling of an object along separate axes. It is a better alternative to using Select and Non-Uniform Scale from the main toolbar because it is independent of the object geometry.

The Scale XYZ Parameters rollout lets you select which axis to work with. This controller works the same way as the other position and rotation XYZ controllers.

Parameter controllers

Other types of controllers consist of miscellaneous collections that don't fit into the previous categories. Many of these controllers combine several controllers into one, such as the List and Block controllers. Others include separate interfaces, such as the Waveform controller for defining the controller's functions.

Most of these special-purpose controllers can only be assigned using the Track View window. The Motion panel only contains the tracks for transformations.

On/Off controller

The On/Off controller works on tracks that hold a binary value, such as the Visibility track; you can use it to turn the track on and off or to enable and disable options. In the Track View, each On section is displayed in blue, with keys alternating between on and off. No parameters exist for this controller. Figure 28-23 shows a Visibility track that has been added to a sphere object. This track was added using the Add Visibility Track button in Edit Keys mode. You can add keys with the Add Keys button. Each new key will toggle the track on and off.

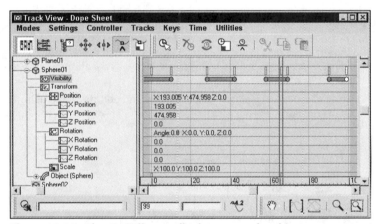

Figure 28-23: The On/Off controller lets you make objects appear and disappear.

Boolean controller

The Boolean controller, like the On/Off controller, can hold one of two states — 0 for off and 1 for on. But, unlike the On/Off controller, the Boolean controller will only change when a different state is encountered. Figure 28-24 shows the Boolean controller. Notice how several keys with the same state don't impact the controller.

The Boolean controller is new to 3ds max 5.

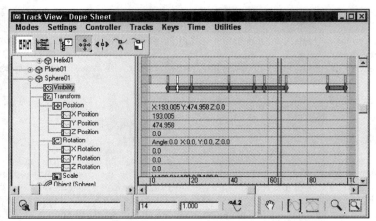

Figure 28-24: The Boolean controller lets you make objects appear and disappear.

Waveform controller

The Waveform controller can produce regular periodic waveforms, such as a sinusoidal wave. Several different waveform types can make up a complete waveform. The Waveform Controller dialog box, shown in Figure 28-25, includes a list of all the combined waveforms. To add a waveform to this list, click the Add button.

When you select a waveform in the list, you can give it a name and edit its shape using the buttons and values. Preset waveform shapes include Sine, Square, Triangle, Sawtooth, and Half Sine. You can also invert and flip these shapes.

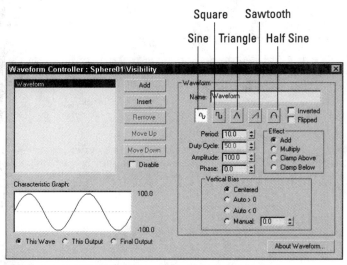

Figure 28-25: The Waveform Controller dialog box lets you produce sinusoidal motions.

The Period value defines the number of frames required to complete one full pattern. The Amplitude value sets the height of the wave, and the Phase value determines its location at the start of the cycle. The Duty Cycle value is used only for the square wave to define how long it stays enabled.

You can use the Vertical Bias options to set the values range for the waveform. Options include Centered, which sets the center of the waveform at 0; Auto > 0, which causes all values to be positive; Auto < 0, which causes all values to be negative; and Manual, which lets you set a value for the center of the waveform.

The Effect option determines how different waveforms in the list are combined. They can be added, multiplied, clamped above, or clamped below. The Add option simply adds the wave-form values together, and the Multiply option multiplies the separate values. The Clamp Above or Clamp Below option forces the values of one curve to its maximum or minimum while not exceeding the values of the other curve. The Characteristic Graph shows the selected wave-form, the output, or the final resulting curve. Figure 28-26 shows the Characteristic Graph for each Effect option when a sine wave and a square wave are combined.

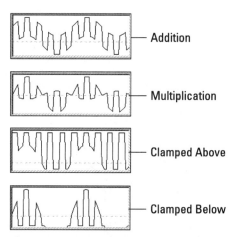

Addition

Multiplication

Clamped Above

Clamped Below

Figure 28-26: Combining sine and square waves with the Add, Multiply, Clamp Above, and Clamp Below Effect options.

Figure 28-27 shows the Waveform controller set to produce a sinusoidal curve assigned to the Radius track of a sphere object. This setting causes the size of the sphere to alternatively grow large and small.

Color RGB controller

You can use the Color RGB controller to animate colors. Color values are different from regular float values in that they include three values that represent the amounts of red, green, and blue (referred to as RGB values) that are present in the color. This data value type is known as Point3.

The Color RGB controller splits a track with color information into its component RGB tracks. You can use this controller to apply a different controller to each color component and also to animate any color swatch in Max.

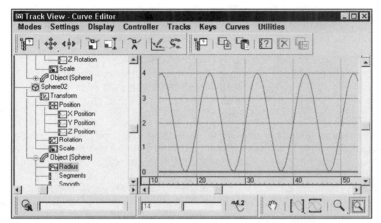

Figure 28-27: The Waveform controller lets you assign different standard mathematical curves to track values.

Figure 28-28 shows the function curves for the Color RGB controller assigned to the Diffuse Color track under the Material #1 track, including subtracks for Red, Green, and Blue. The figure shows the Bézier controller applied to the Red track, the Noise controller that is assigned to the Green track, and the Waveform controller with a triangle wave applied to the Blue track.

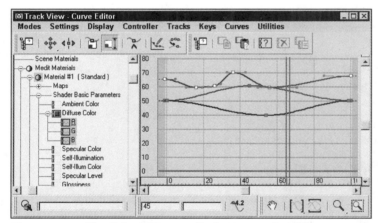

Figure 28-28: The Color RGB controller lets you assign different controllers to each color component.

Cubic Morph controller

You can assign the Cubic Morph controller to a morph compound object. You can find the track for this object under the Objects track. A subtrack of the morph object is the Morph track, which holds the morph keys.

The Cubic Morph controller uses Tension, Continuity, and Bias values to control how targets blend with one another. You can access these TCB values in the Key Info dialog box by right-clicking any morph key or by right-clicking the Morph track and selecting Properties from the pop-up menu.

Note You can also access the TCB values by right-clicking the keys in the Track Bar.

Barycentric Morph controller

The Barycentric Morph controller is automatically applied when a morph compound object is created. Keys are created for this controller based on the morph targets set in the Modify panel under the Current Targets rollout for the morph compound object. You can edit these keys using the Barycentric controller Key Info dialog box, which you can open by right-clicking a morph key in the Track View or in the Track Bar.

The main difference between the Cubic Morph controller and the Barycentric Morph controller is that the latter can have weights applied to the various morph keys.

The Barycentric Morph controller Key Info dialog box includes a list of morph targets. If a target is selected, its Percentage value sets the influence of the target. The Time value is the frame where this key is located. The TCB values and displayed curve control the Tension, Continuity, and Bias parameters for this controller. The Constrain to 100% option causes all weights to equal 100% — changing one value will change the other values proportionally if this option is selected.

List controller

You can use the List controller to apply several controllers at once. This feature enables you to produce smaller, subtler deviations, such as adding some noise to a normal Path controller.

When the List controller is applied, the default track appears as a subtrack along with another subtrack labeled Available. By selecting the Available subtrack and clicking the Assign Controller button, you can assign additional controllers to the current track.

All subtrack controllers are included in the List rollout of the Motion panel. You can also access this list by right-clicking the track and selecting Properties from the pop-up menu. The order of the list is important, because it defines which controllers are computed first.

The Set Active button lets you specify which controller you can interactively control in the viewport; the active controller is marked with an arrow, which is displayed to the left of the name. You can also cut and paste controllers from and to the list. Because you can use the same controller type multiple times, you can distinguish each one by entering a name in the Name field.

Figure 28-29 shows the List controller assigned to the Position track of a sphere. Listed are the default controller (Bézier Position) and an Available track. The Noise controller was added by selecting the Available track and clicking the Assign Controller button. Notice in the function curves how the noise is secondary to the Bézier motion.

Block controller

The Block controller combines several tracks into one block so you can handle them all together. This controller is located in the Global Tracks track. If a track is added to a Block controller, a Slave controller is placed in the track's original location.

To add a Block controller, select the Available track under the Block Control track under the Global Tracks track, and click the Assign Controller button. From the Assign Constant Controller dialog box that opens, select Master Block (Master Block is the only selection) and click OK. Right-click the Master Block track to open the Master Block Parameters dialog box, shown in Figure 28-30.

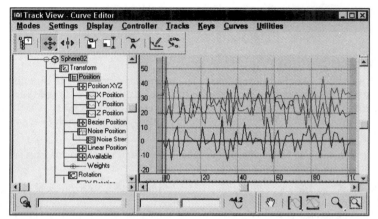

Figure 28-29: The List controller lets you assign multiple controllers to a single track.

Figure 28-30: The Master Block Parameters dialog box lists all the tracks applied to a Block controller.

In the Master Block Parameters dialog box, you can add a track to the Block controller with the Add button. All tracks added are displayed in the list on the left. You can give each track a name by using the Name field. You can also use the Add Selected button to add any selected tracks. The Replace button lets you select a new controller to replace the currently selected track. The Load and Save buttons enable you to load or save blocks as separate files.

The Add button opens the Track View Pick dialog box, shown in Figure 28-31. This dialog box displays all valid tracks in a darker color to make them easier to see, while graying out invalid tracks.

Select the tracks that you want to include and click the OK button. This Block Parameters dialog box opens, shown in Figure 28-32, in which you can name the block, specify Start and End frames, and choose a color. Click OK when you've finished with this dialog box.

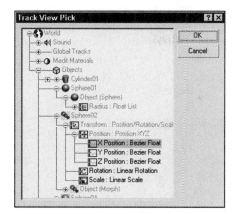

Figure 28-31: The Track View Pick dialog box lets you select the tracks you want to include in the Block controller.

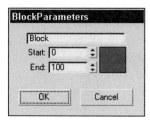

Figure 28-32: The Block Parameters dialog box lets you name a block.

Back in the Master Block Parameters dialog box, click the Load button to open a file dialog box where you can load a saved block of animation parameters. The saved block files have the .blk extension. After the parameters have loaded, the Attach Controls dialog box opens, as shown in Figure 28-33. This dialog box includes two panes. The Incoming Controls pane on the left lists all motions in the saved block. By clicking the Add button, you can add tracks from the current scene, to which you can copy the saved block motions.

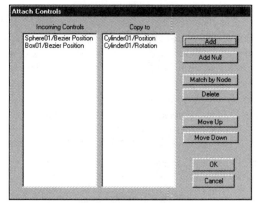

Figure 28-33: The Attach Controls dialog box lets you attach saved tracks to the Block controller.

Because the saved motions in the Incoming Controls pane will match up with the Copy To entries in the right pane, the Add Null button adds a space in place of a specific track if you don't want a motion to be copied. The Match by Node button matches tracks by means of the Track View Pick dialog box.

Figure 28-34 shows a Block controller with several motions included. The MasterBlock track also includes a Blend subtrack for defining how the various tracks interact.

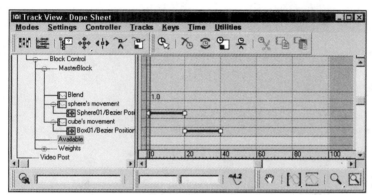

Figure 28-34: The Block controller lets you combine several tracks into a single global track.

IK controller

The IK controller works on a bones system for controlling the bone objects of an IK system. The IK controller includes many different rollouts for defining joint constraints and other parameters.

  Find out more about the IK controller in Chapter 33, "Creating and Using Inverse Kinematics."

Master Point controller

The Master Point controller controls the transforms of any point or vertex subobject selections. The Master Point controller gets added as a track to an object whose sub-objects are transformed. Subtracks under this track are listed for each subobject. The keys in the Master track are colored green.

Right-clicking a green master key opens the Master Track Key Info dialog box, shown in Figure 28-35. This dialog box shows the Key number with arrows for selecting the previous or next key, a Time field that displays current the frame number, and a list of all the vertices. Selecting a vertex from the list displays its parameters at the bottom of the dialog box.

Figure 28-36 shows the Master Point controller that was automatically assigned when a selection of vertex subobjects was moved with the Auto Key button enabled. A separate track is created for each vertex.

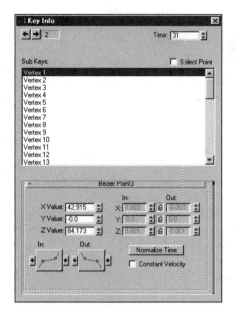

Figure 28-35: The Master Track Key Info dialog box lets you change the key values for each vertex.

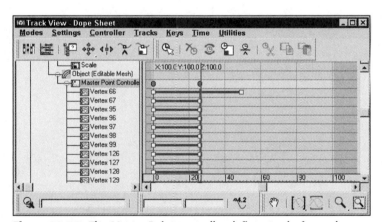

Figure 28-36: The Master Point controller defines tracks for each subobject element that is animated.

Summary

If you're an animator, you should thank your lucky stars for controllers. Controllers offer power flexibility for animating objects — and just think of all those keys that you don't have to set by hand.

In this chapter, you've

- ✦ Learned about the various controller types
- ✦ Discovered how to assign controllers using the Motion panel and the Track View

✦ Set default controllers in the Preference Settings dialog box

✦ Examined the various controllers in several different categories

✦ Seen a few examples of using controllers

In the next chapter, we'll focus on one particularly useful controller — the Expression controller. This controller enables you to animate objects by defining a mathematical expression.

✦   ✦   ✦

Using Expressions

Expressions refer to mathematical expressions or simple formulas that compute a value based on other values. These expressions can be simple, as with moving a bicycle based on the rotation of the pedals; or complex, as with computing the sinusoidal translation of a boat on the sea as a function of the waves beneath it.

You can use almost any value as a variable in an expression, from object coordinates and modifier parameters, to light and material settings. The results of the expression are computed for every frame and used to affect various parameters in the scene. You can include the number of frames and time variables in the expression to cause the animation results to repeat for the entire sequence.

Of all the controllers that are available, the Expression controller has limitless possibilities that could fill a book of its own. This short chapter covers the basics of building expressions along with several examples.

Working with Expressions in Spinners

Although much of this chapter focuses on using the expression controller, the Expression Controller Interface isn't the only place where you can play with expressions. Expressions can also be entered into spinner controls using the Numerical Expression Evaluator, shown in Figure 29-1. This simple dialog box is accessed by selecting a spinner and pressing Ctrl+N.

Cross-Reference Another common place that uses expressions is the Parameter Wiring dialog box. This dialog box is covered in Chapter 24, "Animation Basics."

To use this evaluator, just type the expression in the field and the result will be displayed in the result field. The result field is updated as you type the expression. If you make a mistake, the Result will be blanked out. The Paste button will place the result value in the spinner and the Cancel button will close the dialog box without a change.

Tip You can enter a relative value in a spinner by typing an R and a value. For example, if the Segments value of a sphere object is 32, then typing R20 will change the value to 52 and R-20 will change the value to 12.

In This Chapter

Using the Numerical Expression Evaluator

Understanding the Expression controller interface

Learning about operators, variables, and functions

Controlling object transformations

Controlling parameters

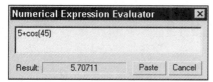

Figure 29-1: The Numerical Expression Evaluator dialog box lets you enter expressions for a spinner.

Understanding the Expression Controller Interface

The Expression controller is just one of the many controllers that are available for automating animations. This controller enables you to define how the object is transformed by means of a mathematical formula or expression, which you can apply to any of the object's tracks. It shows up in the controller list, based on the type of track that it is assigned to, as a Position Expression, Rotation Expression, Scale Expression, Float Expression, or Point3 Expression controller.

Before you can use the Expression controller on a track, you must assign it to a track. You can assign controllers using the Motion panel or the Track View. After you assign it, the Expression Controller dialog box immediately opens up or you can access this dialog box at any time by right-clicking the track and selecting Properties from the pop-up menu. For example, select an object in your scene, open the Motion panel and select the Position track. Then click on the Assign Controller button at the top of the Assign Controller rollout and select Position Expression from the list of Controllers. This causes the Expression Controller dialog box to appear.

You can use this dialog box to define variables and write expressions. The dialog box, shown in Figure 29-2, includes four separate panes, which are used to display a list of Scalar and Vector variables, build an expression, and enter a description of the expression.

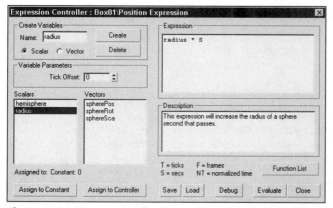

Figure 29-2: You can use the Expression controller to build expressions and define their results.

Defining variables

Variables are placeholders for different values. For example, creating a variable for a sphere's radius called "r" would simplify an expression for doubling its size from "take the sphere's radius and multiply it by two," to simply "r times 2."

To add Variables to the list panes in the Expression Controller dialog box, type a name in the Name field, select the Scalar or Vector option type, and click the Create button—the new variable appears in the Scalars or Vectors list. To delete a variable, select it from the list and click the Delete button. The Tick Offset value is the time added to the current time and can be used to delay variables.

You can assign any new variable either to a constant or to a controller. Assigning a variable to a constant does the same thing as typing the constant's value in the expression. Constant variables are simply for convenience in writing expressions. The Assign to Controller button opens the Track View Pick dialog box, shown in Figure 29-3, where you can select the specific controller track for the variable such as the position of an object.

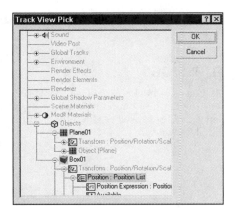

Figure 29-3: The Track View Pick dialog box displays all the tracks for the scene. Tracks that you can select are displayed in black.

Assigning a variable to a controller enables you to animate the selected object based on other objects in the scene. To do this, create a variable and assign it to an animated track of another object. For example, if you create a Vector variable named boxPos and assign it to the Position track for a box object, then within the expression you can use this variable to base the motion of the assigned object on the box's position.

Building expressions

You can type expressions directly into the Expression pane of the Expression controller dialog box. To use a named variable from one of the variable lists (Scalars or Vectors), type its name in the Expression pane. Predefined variables (presented later in the chapter) such as F and NT do not need to be defined in the variable panes. The Function List button opens a list of functions, shown in Figure 29-4, where you can view the functions that can be included in the expression. This list is for display only; you'll still need to type the function in the Expression pane.

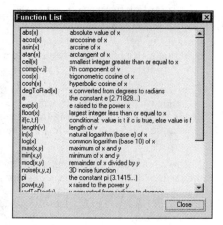

Figure 29-4: The Function List dialog box lets you view all the available functions that you can use in an expression.

Note   The Expression pane ignores any white space, so you can use line returns and spaces to make the expression easier to see and read.

Debugging and evaluating expressions

After typing an expression in the Expression pane, you can check the values of all variables at any frame by clicking the Debug button. This opens the Expression Debug window, shown in Figure 29-5. This window displays the values for all variables as well as the return value. The values are automatically updated as you move the Time Slider.

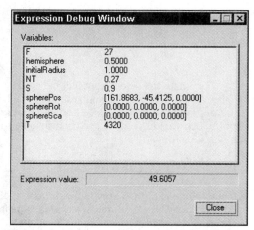

Figure 29-5: The Expression Debug window offers a way to test the expression before applying it.

The Evaluate button in the Expression Controller dialog box commits the results of the expression to the current frame segment. If there is an error in the expression, an alert dialog box warns you of the error. Replacing the controller with a different one can erase the animation resulting from an Expression controller.

Managing expressions

You can use the Save and Load button to save and recall expressions. Saved expressions are saved as files with an .XPR extension. Expression files do not save variable definitions.

Tutorial: Pulling a switch to grow a star

As a quick example, we'll start with a simple expression. By dragging a box object that acts as a switch, the radius of a star will be increased. This same functionality can be accomplished using a manipulator and wiring the parameter, but we'll show it with the Float Expression controller.

To grow a star object by moving a box object, follow these steps:

1. Open the Expanding star.max file from the Chap 29 directory on the CD-ROM. This file includes simple star and box primitives. The box primitive has been set to only move along the X-axis.

2. Select the star object and open the Track View – Dope Sheet. Locate the Radius track (found in Objects ⇨ Hedra01 ⇨ Object (Hedra) ⇨ Radius) and assign the Float Expression controller.

   The Expression Controller dialog box opens.

3. Create a new scalar variable named **initialRadius** and a new vector variable named **boxPos** by typing each name in the Name field, selecting the Scalar or Vector option, and clicking the Create button.

4. In the Scalars list, select the **initialRadius** variable and click the Assign to Constant button. Then type the value of **10** and click OK. In the Vectors variable list, select the **boxPos** variable and click the Assign to Controller button. The Track View Pick dialog box opens. Locate the box's Transform Position track (found in the Objects ⇨ Box01 ⇨ Transform ⇨ Position ⇨ X Position) and click OK.

5. In the Expression pane, erase the existing expression and type the following:

   ```
   initialRadius + abs(boxPos.x)/2
   ```

   Then click the Debug button. The Expression Debug window appears, in which you can see the variable values change as items in the scene change.

With the expression complete, you can drag the box object back and forth and watch the star object increase and decrease in size. This is a simple example, but it demonstrates what is possible.

Expression Elements

The key to making the Expression controller work is building expressions. Before you can build expressions, you need to understand the various elements that make up an expression. Expressions can consist of variables (including predefined variables), operators, and functions, so we'll start by explaining these. It is also important to understand what the expression will return and the various return types.

Predefined variables

Max includes several predefined variables that have constant values. These predefined variables are defined in Table 29-1. They are case-sensitive and must be typed exactly as they appear in the Syntax column.

Table 29-1: Predefined Variables

Variable	Syntax	Value
PI	pi	3.14159
Natural Logarithm	e	2.71828
Ticks per Second	TPS	4800
Frame Number	F	Current frame number
Normalized Time	NT	The entire time of the active number of frames
Seconds	S	The number of seconds based on the frame rate
Ticks	T	The number of ticks based on the frame rate, where 4,800 ticks equal 1 second

In addition to these predefined variables, you can choose your own variables to use. These variables cannot contain spaces, and each variable must begin with a letter. After a variable is defined, you can assign it a constant value or have it pick up its value from a controller track.

Operators

An operator is the part of an expression that tells how to deal with the variables. One example of an operator is addition — it tells you to add a value to another value. These operators can be grouped as basic operators, which include the standard math functions such as addition and multiplication; logical operators, which compare two values and return a true or false result; and vector operators, which enable mathematical functions between vectors. Tables 29-2 through 29-4 identify the operators that are in each of these groups.

Tip   Although it isn't required, scalar variables are typically lowercase and vector variables are uppercase.

Table 29-2: Basic Operators

Operator	Syntax	Example
Addition	+	i+j
Subtraction	-	i-j
Negation	-	-i
Multiplication	*	i*j
Division	/	i/j
Raise to the power	^ or **	i^j or i**j

Table 29-3: Logical Operators

Operator	Syntax	Example
Equal to	=	i=j
Less than	<	i<j
Greater than	>	i>j
Less than or equal to	<=	i<=j
Greater than or equal to	>=	i>=j
Logical Or (Returns a 1 if either value is 1)	|	i|j
Logical And (Returns a 1 if both values are 1)	&	i&j

Table 29-4: Vector Operators

Operator	Syntax	Example
Component (Refers to the x component of vector V)	.	V.x
Vector Addition	+	V+W
Vector Subtraction	-	V-W
Scalar Multiplication	*	i*V
Scalar Division	/	V/i
Dot Product	*	V*W
Cross Product	x	VxW

The order in which the operators are applied is called operator precedence. The first equations to be calculated are the expressions contained inside of parentheses. If you're in doubt about which expression gets evaluated first, place each expression in separate parentheses. For example, the expression (2 + 3) * 4 equals 20 and 2 + (3 * 4) equals 14. If the equation doesn't contain any parentheses and only simple operators, then the precedence is from left to right with multiplication and division coming before addition and subtraction.

Functions

Functions are like mini-expressions that are given a parameter and return a value. For example, the trigonometric function for sine looks like this:

```
Sin()
```

It takes an angle, which is entered within the parentheses and returns a sine value. For example, if you open the Expression Controller dialog box and enter the expression

```
Sin(45)
```

and then open the Debug window, the Expression Value will be 0.707, which is the sine value for 45 degrees.

Table 29-5 lists the functions that are used to create expressions.

Tip   You can see a full list of all the possible functions with explanations by clicking the Function List button in the Expression Controller dialog box.

Table 29-5: Expression Functions

Function	Syntax	Description
Sine	sin(i)	Computes the sine function for an angle.
Cosine	cos(i)	Computes the cosine function for an angle.
Tangent	tan(i)	Computes the tangent function for an angle.
Arc Sine	asin(i)	Computes the arc sine function for an angle.
Arc Cosine	acos(i)	Computes the arc cosine function for an angle.
Arc Tangent	atan(i)	Computes the arc tangent function for an angle.
Hyperbolic Sine	hsin(i)	Computes the hyperbolic sine function for an angle.
Hyperbolic Cosine	hcos(i)	Computes the hyperbolic cosine function for an angle.
Hyperbolic Tangent	htan(i)	Computes the hyperbolic tangent function for an angle.
Convert Radians to Degrees	radToDeg(i)	Converts an angle value from radians to degrees.
Convert Degrees to Radians	degToRad(i)	Converts an angle value from degrees to radians.
Ceiling	ceil(i)	Rounds floating values up to the next integer.
Floor	floor(i)	Rounds floating values down to the next integer.
Natural Logarithm (base e)	ln(i)	Computes the natural logarithm for a value.
Common Logarithm (base 10)	log(i)	Computes the common logarithm for a value.
Exponential Function	exp(i)	Computes the exponential for a value.
Power	pow(i,j)	Raises i to the power of j.
Square Root	sqrt(i)	Computes the square root for a value.
Absolute Value	abs(i)	Changes negative numbers to positive.
Minimum Value	min(i,j)	Returns the smaller of the two numbers.
Maximum Value	max(i,j)	Returns the larger of the two numbers.
Modulus Value	mod(i,j)	Returns the remainder of i divided by j.
Conditional If	if(i,j,k)	Tests the value of i, and if it's not zero, then j is returned, or if it is zero then k is returned.
Vector If	vif(i,V,W)	Same as the if function, but works with vectors.
Vector Length	length(V)	Computes the vector length.

Function	Syntax	Description
Vector Component	comp(V,i)	Returns the i component of vector V.
Unit Vector same direction as V.	unit(V)	Returns a vector of length 1 that points in the
Random Noise Position	noise(i,j,k)	Returns a random position.

Return types

A return type is the type of value that is expected to be returned to the track that was assigned the expression controller. For example, if you assign the Position Expression controller to the Position track of an object, then the return type will be a vector, expecting coordinate values.

Tip   In the Expression Controller dialog box, the object and track that is assigned to the controller will be displayed in the title bar.

These return types can be either a number (called a scalar), a collection of coordinates (called a vector), or a collection of color values (called a Point3). Scalars are used to control parameter values, vectors define actual coordinates in space, and the Point3 return type defines colors. Each one of these types has its own format that you need to know before you can use it in an expression.

Caution   Variables used in an expression need to match the return type. For example, if you have a Vector return type describing an object's position, it can use a scalar or vector variable, but the expression result needs to be a vector. A scalar return type (such as a sphere's Radius) cannot be multiplied by a vector; otherwise, an error appears.

Scalar return type

A scalar value is a single value typically used for an object parameter, such as a sphere's radius or the length of a Box object. This is used for tracks that have the Float Expression controller applied. Any resulting value from the expression is passed back to the assigned parameter. Scalars have no special format — only the number.

Vector return type

If a transform such as position is assigned, the Expression pane shows three values separated by commas and surrounded by brackets. These three values represent a vector, and each value is a different positional axis. You can refer to an individual axis value by placing a dot and the axis after the variable name. For example, if a vector variable named boxPosition exists, you could refer to the X-axis position component with the variable, boxPosition.x. Component values are actually scalars.

Point3 return type

Materials work with yet another return type called a Point3. This type includes three numbers separated by commas and surrounded by brackets. Each of these values, which can range between 0 and 255, represents the amount of red, green, or blue in a color.

Note   Any value that is out of range is automatically set to its nearest acceptable value. For example, if your expression returns a value of 500 for the green component, the color is shown as if green were simply 255.

Sample expressions

If you scan through your old physics and math books, you can find plenty of equations that you can use to create expressions. Following are some sample motions and their respective expressions.

For example, if the sphere object has the Float Expression controller applied to its Radius track, then a simple expression for increasing the radius from an initial radius value as the frame number increases would look like this:

```
initialRadius + F
```

You can use the trigonometric functions to produce a smooth curve from 0 to 360. Using the Sine function, you can cause the sphere's radius to increase to a maximum value of 50 and then decrease to its original radius. The expression would look like this:

```
50 * sin(360*NT)
```

To make our sphere example move in a zigzag path, we can use the mod function. This causes the position to increase slowly to a value and then reset. The expression looks like this:

```
[0, 10*mod(F,20), 10*F]
```

You can use the square root function to simulate ease in and ease out curves, causing the object to accelerate into or from a point. The expression would look like this:

```
[100*sqrt(NT*200), 10, 10]
```

Building complex expressions takes a little bit of math to accomplish, but it isn't difficult to do and the more experience you get with expressions, the easier it will become. To help get you started, Table 29-6 includes several pre-built expressions that can be entered into the Expression Controller Interface to get certain motions.

Table 29-6: Sample Expressions

Motion	Expression	Variable Description
Circular motion	[Radius1 * cos(360*S), Radius1 * sin(360*S), 0]	Where Radius1 is the radius of the orbiting path.
Elliptical motion	[Radius1 * cos(360*S), Radius2 * sin(360*S), 0]	Where Radius1 and Radius2 are the radii of the elliptical path.
Rising Circular Coil motion	[Radius1 * cos(360*S), Radius1 * sin(360*S), S*AscentSpeed]	Where Radius1 is the radius of the orbiting path and AscentSpeed is the speed that the object rises.
Back and Forth motion	[HalfDist * cos(360*S), 0, 0]	Where HalfDist is half the distance traveled.

Motion	Expression	Variable Description
Zigzag motion	[0, ZigDist*mod(F,ZagFreq), AscentSpeed*F]	Where ZigDist is the distance the object moves before returning the path, ZagFreq sets the frequency of the zigzag motion, and the AscentSpeed sets how quickly the object moves along the path.
Accelerate quickly motion	[Dist*sqrt(NT*Scale), 0, 0]	Where Dist is the distance that the object travels and Scale is how long the acceleration takes.
Y-Axis Rolling motion	BallPos.x/BallRadius	Where BallPos.x is the linear movement along the x-axis of the ball and BallRadius is the radius of the ball object.

Using Expression Controllers

You can use expressions to control the transforms of objects. You can access these transforms from the Track View or from the Motion panel. You can also use expressions to control object parameters such as a box's length or material properties such as the amount of illumination applied to a material. You can access all these parameters from the Track View.

Animating transforms with the Expression controller

After you assign a controller to a transform track, the Expression pane in the Expression Controller dialog box includes the current values of the selected object. Position transforms display the X, Y, and Z coordinates of the object; Rotation transforms display the rotation value in radians, and Scale transforms display values describing the relative scaling values for each axis.

Note

Radians are another way to measure angles. A full revolution equals 360 degrees, which equates to 2 × pi radians. The Expression dialog box includes the `degToRad` and `radToDeg` functions to convert back and forth between these two measurement systems.

Tutorial: Controlling a model plane

A lot of flight simulators are used to train pilots, but not many are designed to train pilots of model airplanes. In this tutorial, we control an airplane's motion by maneuvering a simple joystick.

To control an airplane with a joystick using the Expression controller, follow these steps:

1. Open the Joystick controlling airplane.max file from the Chap 29 directory on the CD-ROM.

   This file includes an airplane model created by Viewpoint Datalabs and two simple joystick objects created from primitives that are constrained to rotate only along a single axis.

2. With the airplane group selected, open the Motion panel, click the Parameters button, and open the Assign Controllers rollout. Select the Position track and click the **Assign Controller** button. Select the Position Expression controller from the list and click OK.

The Expression Controller dialog box opens.

3. In the Name field of the Expression Controller dialog box, type the name **joystickRot1**, and then select the Scalar type and click the Create button. Click the Assign to Controller button and, from the Track View Pick dialog box that opens, select the Local X Rotation track (which is under the Objects ⇨ Joystick01 ⇨ Transform:Position/Rotation/Scale ⇨ Rotation:Local Euler XYZ track) and click OK. Then create another scalar variable named **joystickRot2** and assign it to the Local Y Rotation track for the Joystick02 object.

4. In the Expression pane, you should see the value [150, 0, 50]. Modify the expression to read like this:

```
[50+(2*radToDeg(joystickRot2)), 0, 50+(2*radToDeg(joystickRot1))]
```

5. Now click the Debug button to see the value results. With the Expression Debug window open, click the Select and Rotate button on the main toolbar and rotate one of the joysticks to see the plane move. The values will also be updated in the Debug window. If the expression looks fine, click the Close button for the Debug window and again for the Expression Controller dialog box.

Note   Clicking the Debug button applies the expression to the objects. If you make a change to the Expression, you need to click the Debug button again.

If you apply any X-axis rotations to the joystick, the airplane automatically rises or dives. Figure 29-6 shows the airplane as it moves with the joysticks.

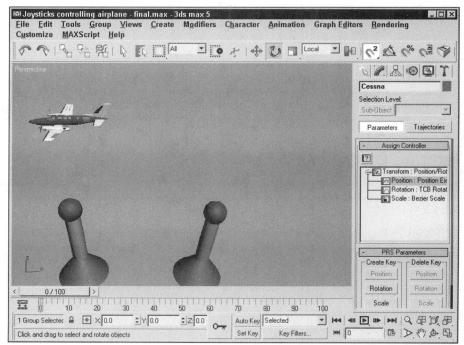

Figure 29-6: An airplane whose Z-axis position is determined by the X-axis rotation of the joystick

Animating parameters with the Float Expression controller

To assign the Float Expression controller, select an object with a parameter or a Modifier applied and open the Track View. Find the track for the parameter you want to change and click the Assign Controller button. Select the Float Controller from the list and click OK.

Note The actual controller type depends on the parameter selected. Many parameters use float expressions, but some use Transform controllers.

After you assign the Expression controller, the Expression Controller dialog box will open or you can open it by right-clicking the track and select Properties from the pop-up menu to load the dialog box. Within this dialog box, the Expression pane includes the current value of the selected parameter.

Tutorial: Inflating a balloon

The Push Modifier mimics filling a balloon with air by pushing all its vertices outward. In this tutorial, we use a balloon model created by Zygote Media to demonstrate how you can use the Float Expression controller to control the parameters of a modifier.

To inflate a balloon using the Float Expression controller, follow these steps:

1. Open the Balloon and pump.max file from the Chap 29 directory on the CD-ROM.

   This file includes a pump created from primitives and the balloon model with the Push modifier applied.

2. Next, open the Track View by choosing Graph Editors ⇨ Track View – Dope Sheet. Navigate the balloon object's tracks until you find the Push Value track (found in the Objects ⇨ b3 ⇨ Modified Object ⇨ Push ⇨ Push Value). Select the Push Value track and click the Assign Controller button. From the list of controllers, select Float Expression and click OK.

   The Expression Controller dialog box opens.

3. In the Expression pane, you should see a single scalar value of 0. Modify the expression to read like this:

   ```
   2 * NT
   ```

   Click the Debug button to see the value results. With the Expression Debug window open, drag the Time Slider and notice that the balloon inflates.

Note If you use a parameter such as Radius as part of an Expression, then the parameter will be unavailable in the Modify panel if you try to change it by hand.

Figure 29-7 shows the balloon as it's being inflated.

Animating materials with the Expression controller

You can locate the material's parameter in the Track View and assign the Expression controller to it to control material parameters. Some of these parameters are scalar values, but any material parameter set with a color swatch has a Point3 return type.

When using material parameters and color values, be sure not to combine them in expressions with vector values.

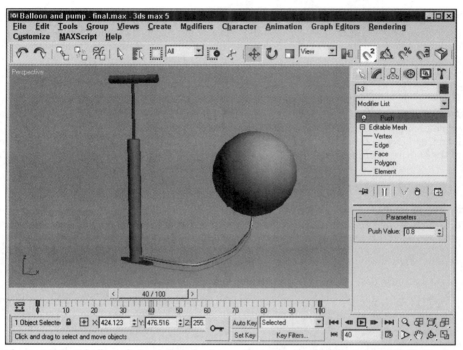

Figure 29-7: A balloon being inflated using an Expression controller to control the Push modifier

Tutorial: Controlling a stoplight

In this example, we use the if function to turn the colors of a sphere on and off to simulate a traffic light. We accomplish this task by applying the Expression controller to the Diffuse color track. The goal is to show the color green for the first third of the animation, yellow for the second third, and red for the last third.

To change the colors of spotlight sphere using the Expression controller, follow these steps:

1. Open the Stoplight.max file from the Chap 29 directory on the CD-ROM.

   This file includes a simple stoplight created using primitives. One of the spheres moves between the three light positions and has had a green material applied to it.

2. Open the Track View – Dope Sheet and locate and select the Diffuse Color track, which you can find under Objects ⇨ Sphere03 ⇨ Material #1 ⇨ Shader Basic Parameters tracks. Click the Assign Controller button and double-click the Point3 Expression selection.

   This assigns the Point3 Expression controller to the Diffuse Color track.

3. Open the Expression Controller dialog box by right-clicking the Diffuse Color track and selecting Properties from the pop-up menu.

4. In the Expression pane, enter the following:

```
[if(NT>=.33,255,0), if(NT<.66,255,0), 0]
```

Then click the Evaluate button and close the Expression Controller dialog box.

Click the Play Animation button to see the results. Figure 29-8 shows the stoplight alongside the Dope Sheet for this stoplight.

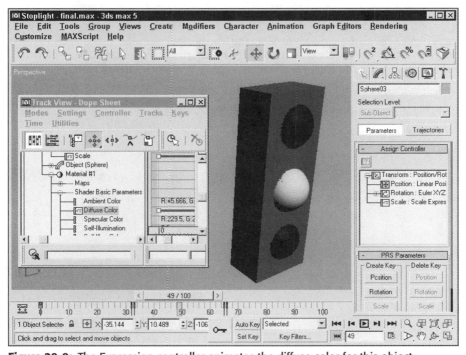

Figure 29-8: The Expression controller animates the diffuse color for this object.

Before leaving this example, let's examine the expression. The expression works with a Point3 number that includes the values of red, green, and blue. The first Point3 value represents red. Because yellow, in the RGB color system, is composed of equal parts of red and green, we want red to be visible for the last two-thirds of the time. To do this, we make the expression include the following statement:

```
if (NT >= .33, 255, 0)
```

This basically says that if the Normalized Time falls in the last two-thirds of the time, then set the red value to 255; and if it does not, then set red to 0.

The second Point3 value is green, which appears for the first third of the animation and along with red for the second third to make yellow. So the following expression needs to go where the green value would be located:

```
if (NT < .66, 255, 0)
```

This expression says that if the Normalized Time is less than two-thirds of the time, then set the green value to its maximum, and, if it isn't, then set its value to 0.

The third Point3 value is for blue. Blue doesn't appear at all in green, yellow, or red, so its value is set to 0 for the entire animation.

The completed expression for the entire animation (which you entered in Step 4 of the tutorial) looks like this:

```
[if (NT >= .33, 255, 0), if (NT < .66, 255, 0), 0]
```

Summary

This chapter covered the basics of using the Expression controller. Using mathematical formulas to control the animation of an object's transformation and parameters offers a lot of power. You can also use the values of one object to control another object.

In this chapter, you've

✦ Practiced building expressions in the Expression dialog box

✦ Learned about expressions and what they can do

✦ Reviewed the available operators, variables, and functions

✦ Tried out examples of controlling object transformations and parameters

In the next chapter, we explore the ability to animate dynamic simulations.

✦   ✦   ✦

Creating a Dynamic Simulation

If something is dynamic, it moves. Dynamic objects such as the Spring and Damper objects can be animated automatically because their positions can be computed based on certain property values.

With dynamic simulations in Max, you can animate the position and orientations of several objects in a scene automatically by setting object properties such as bounce and friction and adding forces (via Space Warps) to the scene. When you assign these properties to an object, Max can compute the effects of these properties on the motion of the object when you run the simulation.

For example, an object with a high bounce value acts like a rubber ball, and one with a lower bounce value thuds like a rock when it impacts with other objects during a dynamic simulation. Friction is a property that determines how resistant an object is to moving over another surface, such as sliding ice (lower friction) verses a sliding brick (high friction). After properties have been assigned to the objects in the simulation and Space Warps have been applied, the animation keys are determined automatically when the simulation is run.

In addition to dynamic simulations, you can use the Flex modifier to add soft-body dynamics to your scenes.

Understanding Dynamics

Dynamics is a branch of physics that deals with forces and the motions they cause, and regardless of your experience in school, physics is your friend — especially in the world of 3D. Dynamics in Max can automate the creation of animation keys by calculating the position, rotation, and collisions between objects based on physics equations.

Consider the motion of a simple yo-yo. To animate this motion with keys is fairly simple: Set rotation and position keys halfway through the animation and again at the end, and you're done.

Now think of the forces controlling the yo-yo. Gravity causes the yo-yo to accelerate toward the ground, causing the string to unwind, which makes the yo-yo spin about its axis. When it reaches the end of the string, the rotation reverses, and the yo-yo rises. Now, using Gravity and Motor Space Warps, you can simulate this motion, but setting the keys manually is probably easier for these few objects.

But before you write off dynamics, think of the motion of popcorn popping. With all the pieces involved, setting all the position and rotation keys would take a long time. For this system, using dynamics makes sense.

The Dynamics utility lets you specify objects to include in a simulation, the forces they interact with, and the objects to be involved in collisions. After the system is defined, the Dynamics utility automatically calculates the movement and collisions of these objects according to the forces involved and sets the keys for you.

Object properties determine the physical characteristics of the objects. These properties are set in the Dynamics utility and in the Material Editor and include properties such as bounce, friction, density, and volume. Using these properties you can make objects act like ice, rubber, steel, or Styrofoam.

Forces in a dynamic simulation are created using Space Warps, but not every Space Warp can be used in a dynamic simulation. You can produce additional forces using dynamic objects such as springs and dampers.

Using Dynamic Objects

In the Create panel under the Geometry category is a subcategory for creating two dynamic objects: spring and damper. These primitive objects are similar to other objects except that you can use them in dynamic simulations.

Spring

The Spring object not only looks like a simple spring but also acts with all the forces of an actual spring. In the Spring Parameters rollout, you can choose from a Free Spring or a Bound to Object Pivots spring. A free spring isn't attached to any other objects, but the Bound to Object Pivots spring lets you select Top and Bottom objects that the spring is stretched between.

The Spring Parameters rollout also includes settings that determine the spring diameter, the number of turns, and whether it winds in a clockwise or counterclockwise direction. You can create segments automatically based on the number of turns using the Automatic Segments option, or manually using the Manual Segments option. Smoothing options include All, None, Sides, and Segments. You can specify whether the spring is renderable and whether or not to automatically generate mapping coordinates.

The Wire Shape section lets you specify which type of cross section the spring will use. Parameters for the Round Wire option include Diameter and Sides. Parameters for the Rectangular Wire option include Width, Depth, Fillet, Fillet Segs (Segments), and Rotation. D-Section Wire is the same as Rectangular Wire type except that its edge corners are smoothed to form a cross section that looks like the letter *D*. For this type of wire, you can define the number of round sides. Figure 30-1 shows each of these spring types. On the left is the Round Wire spring type, in the middle is the Rectangular Wire spring type, and on the right is the D-Section Wire spring type.

The Dynamics Parameters section, not shown in either of the previous figures, includes properties for controlling the forces that the spring applies. The Relaxed Height value is the height of the spring when no forces are applied to it. The Constant k value determines the stiffness of the spring and is a measurement of the force produced by stretching the spring. This is an actual physical constant that relates to real-world springs. The measurement unit can be pounds per inch or newtons per meter. You can also specify whether the spring works in compression only, extension only, or both. Compressing a spring means pushing the ends together, and extension means pulling the ends apart from one another.

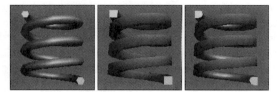

Figure 30-1: Spring objects can have three different cross sections: Round, Rectangular, or D-Section.

Springs typically move in a linear fashion: When you pull on them, they return to the same location if released. Stretching a spring beyond its limits causes nonlinear motion. By selecting the Enable Nonlinearity option, the spring is allowed to move in a nonlinear fashion if it is pulled too far from its relaxed state.

Damper

A damper is like a shock absorber—it is an object that absorbs force and transmits it at a lower level. A damper can also act as an actuator that causes regular forces. A damper object includes a base and a piston with a boot inside of a housing. You can see these damper parts in Figure 30-2. Damper objects in Max are essentially massless and cannot be used in collisions.

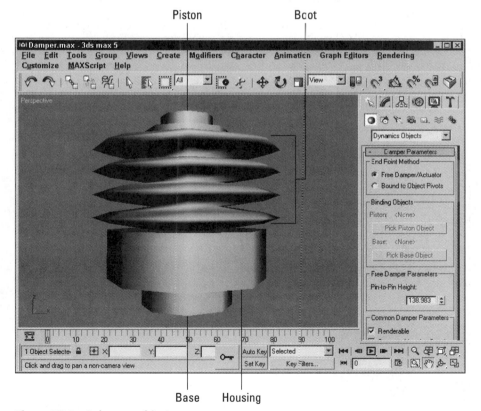

Figure 30-2: A damper object

The Damper Parameters rollout includes two End Point Method options. The first, Free Damper/Actuator, produces the forces but isn't bound to any objects. The second, Bound to Object Pivots, actually transmits forces to the bound objects. The Pick Piston Object and Pick Base Object buttons let you select the objects to bind to either end of the damper.

When Free Damper/Actuator is selected, the Pin-to-Pin Height spinner becomes active. This spinner lets you specify the height of the free damper. You can make dampers renderable and set them to automatically generate mapping coordinates.

In the Cylinder Parameters and Piston Parameters sections, you can set the diameters of the base, main, inside, and piston parts of the damper. You can also specify the heights of the base, main, and piston cylinders. For the main cylinder, you can fillet the top and bottom. There is also a Smooth Cylinder option for smoothing the base, main, and piston cylinders.

The Boot Parameters section enables you to create a boot within the main cylinder. The boot adds more dampening effect to the damper. In shock absorbers, it consists of a rubber cylinder with several folds, and a similarly shaped part is found in the dynamic damper object. The Boot Parameters section holds values for defining this part, including Minimum and Maximum Diameter, the number of Folds, and Stop Diameter and Thickness. The Stop is the end of the boot object, and the Setback value is the distance between the Stop and the end of the main cylinder. There is also an option for a Smooth Boot.

In the Dynamics Parameters section, shown in Figure 30-3, you can specify whether the object is a damper or an actuator. These options are opposite from one another. A damper absorbs force, and an actuator produces force. The Drag value is the measure of how much force the damper absorbs. It can be measured in pounds per in/sec or newtons per m/sec. Dampers can also be set to work in compression only (when end objects are pushed toward each other), extension only (when the end objects are pulled apart), or both. For an actuator, you can specify the force that it applies in pounds or newtons.

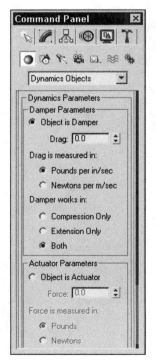

Figure 30-3: The Dynamics Parameters section of the Damper Parameters rollout defines the physical characteristics of the damper object.

Defining Dynamic Material Properties

You can use any objects in a dynamic simulation. The Material Editor can endow these objects with materials that include dynamic surface properties. These properties define how the object is animated during collisions in a dynamic simulation and can be accessed in the Material Editor by selecting the Dynamics Properties rollout, shown in Figure 30-4. The default material settings on this rollout are similar to properties for steel.

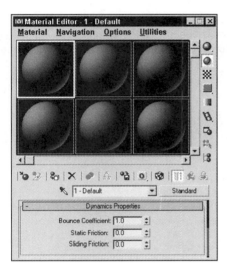

Figure 30-4: The Dynamics Properties rollout in the Material Editor lets you define physical properties.

 Cross-Reference

For more on the Material Editor, see in Chapter 18, "Exploring the Material Editor."

The Bounce Coefficient value on the Dynamics Properties rollout determines how high an object will bounce after a collision. The default of 1.0 is equal to a normally elastic collision. A ball with a value higher than 1 will continue to bounce higher with each impact.

The Static Friction value determines how difficult it is to start an object moving when it's pushed across a surface. Objects with high Static Friction values require a lot of force to move them.

The Sliding Friction value determines how difficult it is to keep an object in motion across a surface. Ice would have a low Sliding Friction value because once it starts moving, it continues easily.

Using Dynamic Space Warps

Several Space Warps are designed to work specifically with dynamic simulations. These can be used to define global effects—such as gravity—that apply to all objects in the simulation.

Space Warps that can be used in a dynamic simulation include all Space Warps in the Particles and Dynamics and the Dynamics Interface subcategories, including Gravity, Wind, Push, Motor, Pin, Bomb, PDynaFlect, SDynaFlect, and UDynaFlect.

Cross-Reference   For details on these Space Warps, see Chapter 26, "Using Space Warps."

After you add these Space Warps to a scene, you can specify their binding using the dialog boxes in the Dynamics utility rollouts shown in the next section. You don't need to bind them with the Bind to Space Warp button.

Using the Dynamics Utility

Dynamic simulations are set up and run using the Dynamics utility, which you can find in the Utilities panel. To access the Dynamics utility, open the Utilities panel and click the Dynamics button. Two rollouts open in the Utilities panel, which are shown in Figure 30-5.

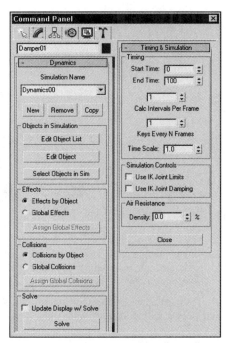

Figure 30-5: The Dynamics utility rollouts include buttons for defining which objects to include in a simulation.

Using the Dynamics rollout

The Dynamics rollout lets you create a new simulation. To do this, click the New button and enter a name in the Dynamics rollout. You can use the Remove button to delete an existing simulation from the list, and use the Copy button to create a new version of the current simulation settings.

You use the Edit Object List button to add new objects to be included in the simulation. It opens the Edit Object List dialog box, shown in Figure 30-6. This dialog box includes two panes: The one on the left holds all the objects in the scene, and the one on the right holds the objects to include or exclude in the simulation. To include an object in the simulation, select it and click the arrow pointing to the right. This moves the object name to the right pane. Similar versions of this dialog box are used to specify the objects to include in collisions and which effects to include. The Edit Object List dialog box also supports Selection Sets and the Display Subtree, Select Subtree, and Case Sensitive options. When you've selected all the objects to include, click the OK button to close the dialog box.

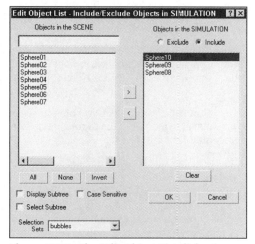

Figure 30-6: The Edit Object List dialog box lets you add objects to the simulation.

You can set object properties for each object included in the simulation. To edit these properties, click the Edit Object button in the Dynamics rollout to open the Edit Object dialog box.

The Select Objects in Sim button in the Dynamics rollout selects the objects in the viewports that are included as part of the simulation, as defined by the Edit Object List dialog box.

You can assign simulation effects in the Edit Object dialog box individually for each object, or you can select the Global Effects option in the Dynamics rollout to make all objects subject to the same effects. The Assign Global Effects button in this rollout opens the Assign Global Effects dialog box (which looks exactly like the Edit Object List dialog box), except this dialog box lists only the Space Warps included in the scene. Selecting a Space Warp and clicking the right-pointing arrow includes the selected Space Warp as a global effect. Clicking the OK button closes this dialog box.

Collisions are handled in the same way as effects—they can be assigned to react either with specific objects or globally. The Assign Global Collisions button in the Dynamics rollout opens the Assign Global Collisions dialog box (which again looks just like the Edit Object list and Assign Global Effects dialog boxes), where you can select from all the objects included in the simulation. Objects not selected are subject to the other simulation effects but pass right through other objects rather than colliding.

At the bottom of the Dynamics rollout is the Solve button, which creates the actual keys. You can also select the Update Display w/ Solve option to update the viewports as the simulation is solved.

Using the Timing & Simulation rollout

The Timing & Simulation rollout, shown previously in Figure 30-5, specifies the frame range for the dynamic simulation. The Calc Intervals Per Frame value determines how many calculations are made at each frame. This value can range from 1 to 160 — the higher the value, the more time needed to compute the solution.

The Keys Every N Frames setting determines how often keys are created. For example, a value of 2 would create a key for every other frame. You can use the Time Scale to speed or slow a simulation. A setting of 1 is normal speed, values from 0.1 up to 1 slow the animation, and values greater than 1 and up to 100 speed up the animation. You can use this setting to create a slow-motion animation of the simulation.

Inverse Kinematics systems can constrain motion through the specification of IK Joint Limits and IK Joint Damping. The Simulation Controls section includes options to enable or disable these settings.

Air resistance is a force that resists motion and is caused by an object crashing into air molecules. Air is denser the closer you are to sea level, which equates to a value of 100. In space, the air density is negligible and is represented by a value of 0.

The Close button at the bottom of the rollout closes the utility.

Editing simulation objects

In the Edit Object dialog box, shown in Figure 30-7, you can select which object to edit from the drop-down list in the upper left. This list includes all the objects in the simulation.

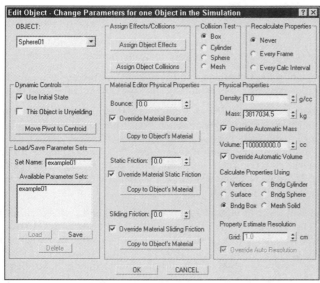

Figure 30-7: The Edit Object dialog box lets you assign simulation properties to an object.

In the Dynamic Controls section are two options: Use Initial State and This Object is Unyielding. The Use Initial State option computes the object's motion and momentum at the start time. If this option is disabled, the object is considered to be motionless at the start time and all existing keys are overwritten during the solution. The This Object is Unyielding option makes sure the object isn't moved by collisions during the solution and is the setting to use to simulate a ground plane.

The Move Pivot to Centroid button repositions the object's pivot to the object's center of mass. Moving the pivot to the center of mass speeds the simulation calculations, but it alters the positions of any linked objects that are built based on the pivot.

In the Load/Save Parameter Sets section, you can save all the parameters in the Edit Object dialog box set by giving the set a name in the Set Name field and clicking the Save button. This parameter set can then be easily loaded and applied to another object. This feature saves you from having to set all the parameters for each object individually. To load a set, select the set from the list and click the Load button.

In the Assign Effects/Collisions section, you can assign each object's different effects using the Assign Object Effects button. You can also use the Assign Object Collisions button to assign which objects to collide with. These buttons open dialog boxes that are very similar to the Assign Global Effects and Assign Global Collisions dialog boxes.

In the Material Editor Physical Properties section, you can set the same properties for Bounce, Static Friction, and Sliding Friction that can be set for materials in the Material Editor. For each of these, you also have options that enable you to override the setting in the Material Editor as well as copy the property value to the object's material.

The Collision Test section offers Box, Cylinder, Sphere, and Mesh options for use in computing the collisions between objects. The Box option calculates more quickly than the other options because it uses the object's bounding box to compute collisions, but these collisions will not be as accurate. The Mesh option determines collisions by looking at the actual object surface, but it takes the longest to calculate.

The Recalculate Properties section lets you specify how often properties are recalculated. For example, material properties (such as mass) are animatable and can change over the course of an animation—with the volume of an object, for example, increasing as the object is scaled. Recalculation options include Never, Every Frame, and Every Calc Interval. The more often these properties need to be calculated, the longer the calculation will take.

The Physical Properties section enables you to set values for density, mass, and volume. Density is the material thickness of an object, measured in grams per cubic centimeter; mass is the base weight of an object, measured in kilograms; and volume is the space that the object takes up, measured in cubic centimeters. Because these values are interrelated, the Override options enable you to modify them independent of the other values.

The Calculate Properties Using subsection enables you to compute the property values using different volumes, depending on the accuracy you need. Options include Vertices, Surface, Bndg (Bounding) Box, Bndg Cylinder, Bndg Sphere, and Mesh Solid. The bounding options enclose the objects in an easy-to-compute bounding form. The Mesh Solid option increases the computation time significantly. Selecting the Mesh Solid option enables automatic resolution, but you can override this with the Override Auto Resolution option, in which case you can set the Grid value to determine how large each cell in the mesh grid is. These cells are measured in centimeters.

Optimizing a simulation

Solving a dynamic simulation once per frame can generate an enormous number of keys, which can significantly increase the file size. Using the Track View, you can reduce the number of keys while preserving the main keys used in the simulation.

To learn more about the Track View, check out Chapter 25, "Working with the Track View."

After solving a simulation, open the Track View and select the object tracks with keys in them. Then click the Edit Keys button, select all the keys, and click the Reduce Keys button. A simple dialog box opens where you can specify the threshold value.

Tutorial: Bowling a strike

When I go bowling, I get a strike every once in a while, but in Max I can get a strike every time. (I can also secure the pins so that no one can get a strike.)

To run a dynamic simulation of a bowling lane, follow these steps:

1. Open the Bowling set.max file from the Chap 30 directory on the CD-ROM.

   This file includes a lane with ten bowling pins and a bowling ball. The lane is surrounded by POmniFlect Space Warps.

I could have used the plane object for the bowling lane, but the simulation works with the actual plane size visible in the viewport. When the simulation is solved, a warning would appear stating that the plane object has unshared edges, and the results could be unpredictable.

2. Open the Create panel, click the Space Warps category, select the Forces subcategory, click the Gravity button, and drag in the Front viewport to create a Gravity Space Warp. Position this Space Warp behind the bowling ball and point it at the bowling ball to give some thrust to the ball. In the Parameters rollout, set the Strength to 10.

3. Open the Utilities panel and click the Dynamics button to open the Dynamics rollout. Click the New button to create a new simulation. Then click the Edit Object List button, select all the objects in the left pane, move them to the right pane by clicking the arrow pointing to the right, and click OK.

4. Select the Effects by Object option in the Effects section of the rollout. Click the Edit Object button and select the Bowling ball object in the Object drop-down list in the upper-left corner. Then click the Assign Object Effects button, double-click the Gravity Space Warp to move it to the right pane, and click OK. Next select the Lane object, enable the This Object is Unyielding option, and click OK.

Because Space Warps are assigned using the Dynamics rollout, you don't need to use the Bind to Space Warp button.

5. In the Collisions section of the Dynamics rollout, select the Global Collisions option and click the Assign Global Collisions button. Click the All button to select all the objects in the left pane, and move them to the right pane by clicking the arrow pointing to the right. Then click OK.

6. In the Timing & Simulation rollout, set End Time to 40. Then select Update Display w/ Solve and click the Solve button. The simulation frames display in the viewport. When the solution is finished, click the Play Animation button to see the entire simulation.

Figure 30-8 shows a frame of the resulting simulation. Keep in mind that only the collision and simple gravity are in effect, but in reality many other forces exist. The final animation for this example shows the pins being blasted off into space.

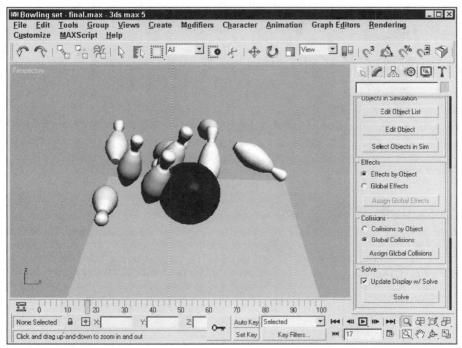

Figure 30-8: This simulation of a bowling game computed all the collisions between the bowling pins and the bowling ball.

Using the Flex Modifier

The Flex modifier can add soft body dynamic characteristics to an object. The characteristic of a *soft body* is one that moves freely under a force. Examples of soft body objects are your clothes, hair, and balloons. The opposite of soft body dynamics is *rigid body* dynamics. Think of a statue in the park. When the wind blows, it doesn't move. The statue is an example of a rigid body. On the other hand, the flag flying over the library moves all over when the wind blows. The flag is an example of a soft body.

Another way to think of soft bodies is to think of things that can flex. Objects such as a clothesline flex under very little stress, but other objects like a CD will flex only a little when you apply a significant force. The settings of the Flex modifier make it possible to represent all kinds of soft body objects.

Figure 30-9 shows many of the rollouts available for the Flex modifier.

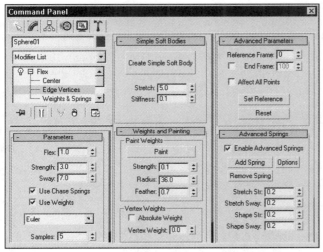

Figure 30-9: The Flex modifier rollout lets you control the flex settings.

Flex subobjects

In the Modifier Stack, the Flex modifier has three subobjects that you can access—Center, Edge Vertices, and Weights and Springs. The Center subobject is a simple box gizmo that marks the center of the flex effect. Portions of the object that are farther from the center will move a greater distance. The Edge Vertices subobjects can be selected to control the direction and falloff of the flex effect. The Weights and Springs rollout controls the Weights and Springs subobjects.

Setting flex strength

The Parameters rollout includes a Flex value, which controls the amount of bending the object does, a Strength value, which controls the rigidity of the object, and the Sway value, which controls how long the flexing object moves back and forth before coming to a stop. An antenna on a car is an example of an object that has fairly high Flex and Sway values and a low Strength value.

Chase Springs cause an object to return to its original position when the force is removed. A twig on a tree is an example of an object with Chase Springs. The Use Chase Springs option lets you disable these springs. A piece of cloth is an example of when you would want Chase Springs disabled.

Selecting Weights and Springs subobjects lets you apply weights to certain selected springs. You can disable these weights using the Use Weights option. If you disable these weights, the entire object acts together.

The Flex modifier offers three different solution methods to compute the motions of objects. These are presented in a drop-down list. The Euler solution is the simplest method, but it typically requires five samples to complete an accurate solution. The Midpoint and Runge-Kutta4 solutions are more accurate and require fewer samples, but they require more computational time. Setting the Samples value higher produces a more accurate solution.

Creating simple soft bodies

In the Simple Soft Bodies rollout, use the Create Simple Soft Body button to automatically set the springs for the selected object to act like a soft body. You can also set the amount of Stretch and Stiffness the object has. For cloth, you'll want to use a high Stretch value and a low Stiffness value, but a racquetball would have both high Stretch and Stiffness values.

Tip   You can manually set the spring settings for the object using the Advanced Springs rollout.

Painting weights

When you select the Weights and Springs subobject mode, the spring vertices are displayed on the object. The vertices are colored to reflect their weight. By default the vertices that are farthest from the object's pivot point have the lowest weight value. Vertices with the greatest weight value (closest to 1) are colored red, and spring vertices with the lowest weight value (closest to –1) are blue. Vertices in between these two values are orange and yellow. The lower-weighted vertices move the greatest distance and the higher-weighted vertices move the least.

Selecting the Weights and Springs subobject also enables the Paint button in the Weights and Springs rollout. Clicking this button puts you in Paint mode, where you can change the weight of the spring vertices by dragging a paint gizmo over the top of the object in the viewports. As you paint the spring vertices, they change color to reflect their new weight.

The Strength value sets the amount of weight applied to the vertices. This value can be negative. The Radius and Feather settings change the size and softness of the Paint brush. Figure 30-10 shows two cylinder objects with the Flex modifier applied. The cylinder on the left has the default weighted spring vertices. The vertices in the top row are blue, and those in the bottom row are orange. This causes the top end of the cylinder to sway more than the bottom end. The Paint mode was used on the right cylinder to paint all vertices in the top half of the cylinder blue with a Strength of –1. This causes the top half of the right cylinder to sway greatly compared to the lower half.

The weights applied using the Paint button are relative to the existing vertex weight. If you select the Absolute Weight option, then the Vertex Weight value is applied to the selected vertices.

Adding Forces and Deflectors

To see the effect of the Flex modifier, you need to add some motion to the scene. The flex object only flexes when it is moving. One of the easiest ways to add motion to the scene is with Space Warps.

The Forces and Deflectors rollout includes two lists — one for Forces and one for Deflectors. Below each are Add and Remove buttons. Using these buttons, you can add and remove Space Warps from the list. The Forces list can use any of the Space Warps in the Forces subcategory (except for Path Follow). The Deflector list can include any of the Space Warps in the Defectors subcategory.

Tip   When you add Space Warps to the Forces and Deflectors list for the Flex modifier, they do not need to be bound to the object.

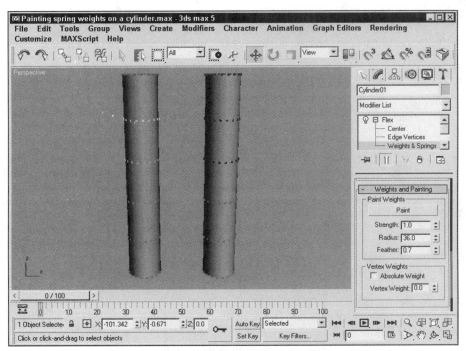

Figure 30-10: Use the Paint button to change the weight of the spring vertices.

Manually creating springs

The final two rollouts for the Flex modifier are Advanced Parameters and Advanced Springs. The Advanced Parameters rollout includes settings for controlling the Start and End frames where the Flex modifier has an effect. The Affect All Points option ignores any subobject selections and applies the modifier to the entire object. The Set Reference button updates all viewports, and the Reset button resets all the vertices' weights to their default values.

You can use the Advanced Springs rollout to manually add and configure springs to the object. Clicking on the Options button opens a dialog box where you can select the type of spring to add to the selected vertices, including Edge and Shape Springs. Edge springs are applied to vertices at the edges of an object, and Shape springs are applied between vertices. For these advanced springs, you can set the Stretch, Sway, Shape, and Shape Strength.

Tutorial: Making a waving flag

A good example of a soft body object is a flag. By making a flag wave in the wind, you can practice using the Flex modifier. In this example you'll also be applying the Flex modifier to subobjects.

To make a flag wave in the wind using the Flex modifier, follow these steps:

1. Open the Soft body flex flag.max file from the Chap 30 directory on the CD-ROM.

   This file includes a simple plane object that has been converted to an Editable Mesh.

2. With the Flag object selected, open the Modify panel and select the Vertex subobject mode in the Selection rollout. In the Front viewport, drag over all the vertices except for the left column where the flag touches the flagpole.

3. With most of the vertices selected, click on the Modifier List and select the Flex modifier (or you could choose the Modifiers ➪ Animation Modifiers ➪ Flex menu command).

4. In the Parameters rollout, set the Flex value to 3.0, the Sway value to 50, and disable the Use Weights option. In the Simple Soft Bodies rollout, click the Create Simple Soft Body button. Finally, click the Add button for the Forces list in the Forces and Deflectors rollout and select the Wind Space Warp in the Top viewport.

5. To see the final results, click the Play Animation button to see the flag wave in the viewport.

Figure 30-11 shows the flag waving.

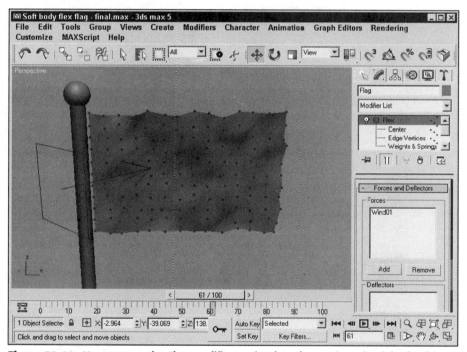

Figure 30-11: You can use the Flex modifier to simulate the motion of soft body objects like cloth.

Using the Reactor Plug-In

The Dynamics utility works well for the default Max user, but there is a better way to add physics to your scenes. The Reactor plug-in (not to be confused with the Reactor controller) is a plug-in developed by a company named Havok. Reactor is a complex piece of software with a huge assortment of features. I plan on only scratching the surface of the plug-in in this section.

New Feature Previously, reactor was only available as a separate plug-in requiring a separate purchase, but in 3ds max 5, it is included as part of the default installation.

The Reactor plug-in interface is accessed via the Utilities panel and is one of the default utilities. Clicking the reactor button opens several rollouts, as shown in Figure 30-12.

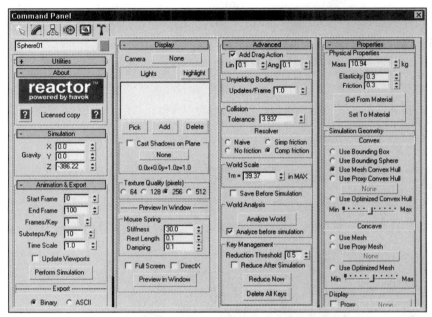

Figure 30-12: The Reactor utility rollouts offer a lot of control over objects.

If you plan on using Reactor a lot, then you'll want to access the Reactor toolbar. Using the Customize ⇨ Load Custom UI menu command, load the reactor.ui file. This gives you access to the Reactor toolbar, shown in Figure 30-13.

Figure 30-13: Use the Reactor toolbar to define physical object properties.

Table 30-1 lists and explains all these toolbar buttons.

Table 30-1: Reactor Toolbar Buttons

Toolbar Button	Name	Description
	Rigid Body Collection	Adds a rigid body collection to the simulation.
	Cloth Collection	Adds a cloth collection to the simulation.

Toolbar Button	Name	Description
	Soft Body Collection	Adds a soft body collection to the simulation.
	Rope Collection	Adds a rope collection to the simulation.
	Deforming Mesh Collection	Adds a deforming mesh collection to the simulation.
	Cloth Modifier	Applies a cloth modifier to the simulation.
	Soft Body Modifier	Applies a soft body modifier to the simulation.
	Rope Modifier	Applies a rope modifier to the simulation.
	Attach to Rigid Body Modifier	Applies the attach to rigid body modifier to the simulation.
	Constrain Solver System	Add a constraint solver to the simulation.
	Point-Nail Constraint	Add a point-nail constraint to the simulation.
	Point-Point Constraint	Add a point-point constraint to the simulation.
	Point-Path Constraint	Add a point-path constraint to the simulation.
	Spring System	Add a spring to the simulation.
	Dashpot System	Add a dashpot damper to the simulation.
	Toy Car System	Add a toy car to the simulation.
	Motor System	Add a motor to the simulation.
	Wind System	Add wind to the simulation.
	Fracture System	Add fracturing to the simulation.
	Water WSM System	Add water to the simulation.
	Plane Primitive	Add a reactor plane to the simulation.
	Show in Window	Open the simulation in a preview window.
	Perform Simulation	Execute the simulation.
	Analyze World	Analyze the simulation.
	Export World	Exports the simulation.

The toolbar provides a quick and easy way to access the various reactor elements (called collections, modifiers and systems). For example, clicking the Rope Collection button opens the Helper category in the Command Panel, selects the reactor subcategory, and selects the RPCollection button.

Using collections

One of the first steps in creating with a simulation is defining the object properties. For example, a simple sphere object in Max could represent a bowling ball, an orange, or tennis ball. Each of these objects responds very differently when being animated to drop on the floor.

In Reactor, the simulation identifies the various objects by the type of collection that it is part of. There are five different types of collections in Reactor — Rigid Bodies, Soft Bodies, Cloth, Rope, and Deformed Meshes. Rigid bodies are objects that keep their shape when pushed; soft bodies deform when pushed. Cloth and rope are intuitive, and deformable meshes are bone and skin systems.

Note   Remember that cloth, rope, and soft body objects are only as flexible as the number of segments that make up the object. For example a rope made from a spline with three vertices will only bend in the middle.

All objects that are included in the simulation need to be added to one of these collections. To include a collection in the scene, select one of the collection buttons in the toolbar (the collections also appear as buttons in the Reactor subcategory of the Create panel) and click in the active viewport to add the collection icon. The collection name appears along with a gizmo icon.

Once a collection is added to the scene, you can use its Pick button in its Properties rollout to add scene objects to the collection. The collection objects are then displayed in a list found in the Properties rollout.

Caution   Before you can add objects to the Cloth, Rope, or Soft Bodies collections, you need to apply the Cloth, Rope, or Soft Body modifiers to the object.

Setting object properties

Once objects have been added to a collection, some of the physical properties associated with the object have been established, but you'll need to set some additional properties, and these are found in the Properties rollout in the Utilities panel. For each object added to a collection, you can set its Mass, Elasticity, and Friction. The Mass properties define how heavy the object is. For example, a bowling ball would have a higher mass value than a pingpong ball. The Elasticity value defines how springy the object is; a tennis ball would be more elastic than a marble. The Friction value defines how resistant the object is to rolling or sliding along the floor. For example, a brick would have a higher friction value than an ice cube.

Tip   A rigid body with a Mass value of 0 will not move in the simulation.

If you paid attention earlier in the chapter, you'll realize that these same three physical properties can be set using a material. In the Properties rollout for Reactor there is a button labeled Get From Material that you can use to obtain the physical properties from the assigned material. You can also set the physical properties defined in the Properties rollout to the assigned material with the Set to Material button.

Note The single global property of Gravity that is offered is found in the Simulation rollout. It can be set for any axes.

Defining collision boundaries

Another common property that you can set pertains to how the object deals with collision detection. You can select the volume to use to determine when two objects collide with each other. If this sounds a bit funny because any collision volume that doesn't use the actual mesh would be inaccurate, then you need to realize that a complex simulation with lots of collisions of complex objects could take a long time to compute. If Reactor only has to compute collisions based on the object's bounding box instead of the actual mesh object, the simulation will run much more quickly and the inaccuracies wouldn't even be noticeable.

Before deciding on the collision boundary to use, you need to determine whether an object is convex or concave. A concave objects is an object that you can penetrate with a ray and only cross its mesh boundary twice. Convex objects require more than two crossings with an imaginary ray. In the Properties rollout is a button named Test Convexity that you can use to test whether an object is convex or not.

A convex objects can use a Bounding Box, a Bounding Sphere, a Convex Hull, a Proxy Convex Hull, or an Optimized Mesh as its collision boundary. A concave object can only use its Mesh, a Proxy Mesh or an Optimized Mesh as its collision boundary. All these selections are in the Properties rollout of the Reactor utility.

Calculating and previewing a simulation

There are many more controls that you can add to the simulation, but I'll show you how to execute the simulation, so you can play with what you've learned so far. To preview the simulation, click the Show in Window button on the Reactor toolbar. This opens the Havok window like the one shown in Figure 30-14. This window lets you play with your simulation. The Simulation ➪ Play/Pause menu (keyboard shortcut, P) will execute the simulation. Dragging with the left mouse button rotates the scene.

Caution The Preview window will only run if the OpenGL or the Direct3D display drivers are used. The window uses OpenGL by default or you can set it to use DirectX with the DirectX option in the Display rollout.

The fun part of the preview window is that you can interact with the objects. Right-clicking and dragging on the object moves it. If you find a position that you want to capture for Max, you can use the MAX ➪ Update Max menu command to set the starting positions of the objects in Max.

To compute the simulation, press the Perform Simulation button in the Reactor toolbar. The progress is displayed at the bottom of the Max interface. You can cancel the simulation at any time with the Esc key.

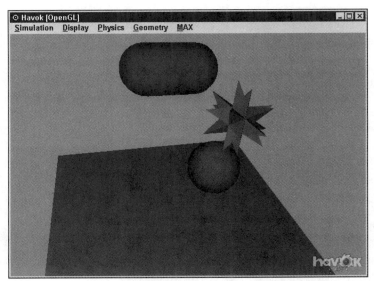

Figure 30-14: The Preview window is a fun place to play with a simulation.

Tutorial: Dropping a plate of donuts

All the great books have an element of tragedy, so consider a policeman carrying a dozen donuts on a plate who stumbles and drops the plate. Donuts everywhere, how tragic! This animation sequence would be difficult or at least time-consuming, but not with Reactor.

To use Reactor to animate a falling plate of donuts, follow these steps:

1. Open the Falling plate of donuts.max file from the Chap 30 directory on the CD-ROM.

   This file includes a simple plate of donuts created from primitives.

2. Select Customize Í Load Custom UI Scheme, select the reactor.ui file and click Open. This opens the Reactor toolbar.

3. Select the Rigid Body Collection button in the Reactor toolbar and click in the Front viewport. In the RB Collection Properties rollout, click the Pick button and select the plate object. Click the Pick button again and select the Plane object.

4. Select Edit Í Select By Í Name menu (or press the H key) to open the Select Objects dialog box and select all the Torus objects. Then click on the Soft Body Modifier button in the Reactor toolbar.

5. Then select the Soft Body Collection in the Reactor toolbar and click again in the Front viewport. In the SB Collection Properties rollout, click the Add button and select all the Torus objects again.

6. Open the Utilities panel and click on the Reactor button. Select the Plane object and in the Properties rollout, enable the Unyielding option. Select the plate object and make its Mass value 5.0. Then select each donut and make its Mass value 0.25.

7. The last step is to execute the simulation. This is done with the Perform Simulation button in the Reactor toolbar. It will take some time to compute a solution for this example. When it completes, press the Play Animation button (or press the / key) to see the results.

Figure 30-15 shows the upturned plate of donuts. Notice the Reactor toolbar, which is docked to the left of the interface.

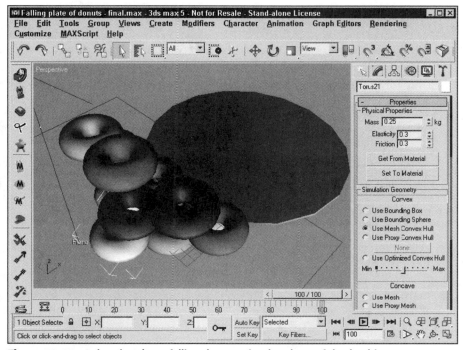

Figure 30-15: Animating these falling donuts, simulated as soft body objects, was easy with Reactor.

Constraining objects

The easiest way to constrain objects is to enable the Unyielding option in the Properties rollout. This option makes a rigid body that won't move and is a good option for the ground plane.

Another common way to constrain objects is to attach them to a rigid body. The Attach to Rigid Body modifier is helpful to use with cloth, rope, and soft body objects. After applying the modifier, you can select the rigid body to attach to in the Properties rollout. You can also use the Mesh Select object to select a specific subobject point to attach to a rigid body.

Reactor includes three other constraint options — Point to Point, Point to Path, and Point to Nail. The Point to Point constraint ties to objects to the same point, the Point to Path constraint ties an object's point to a path, and the Point to Nail constraint ties an object's point to a point in space.

Springs and dashpots can also be used to constrain objects. The Properties rollout lets you select the objects to be connected on either end of the spring.

Working with systems

In addition to collections and objects, Reactor can add several different systems to the simulation. The available systems include Spring, Dashpot, Toy Car, Motor, Wind, Fracture, and

Water. All of these systems can be added to a scene from the Reactor toolbar as Helper objects, except for Water, which is applied as a Space Warp. For each of these systems, you can set its properties in the Modify panel.

Tutorial: Working with water

One of the coolest features of Reactor is its ability to create and simulate the effects of water. Before you can use water, you must have a model that can hold water.

To use Reactor to create a body of water, follow these steps.

1. Open the Pool of water.max file from the Chap 30 directory on the CD-ROM.

    This file includes a pool to hold water created from primitives along with three spheres of different mass.

2. Select the Rigid Body Collection button in the Reactor toolbar and click in the Front viewport. In the RB Collection Properties rollout, click the Add button and select all the Box and Sphere objects.

3. In the Reactor toolbar, click on the Water WSM System button and click within the Front viewport to set the water level to fill the pool.

4. Select the left sphere in the Front viewport and open the Properties rollout in the Utilities panel. Set the Mass value to 3 kg. Select the middle sphere and set its Mass to 100 kg and then set the right sphere to 5000 kg.

5. In the Reactor toolbar, click the View in Window button, rotate the view by dragging with the left mouse button and select Simulation ⇨ Play/Pause (or press the P button) to run the simulation.

Figure 30-16 shows the simulation in the Preview window. Notice how the mass values determine whether the sphere floats or sinks.

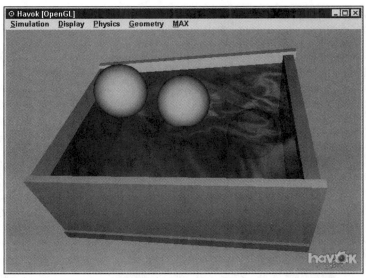

Figure 30-16: Depending on the mass property, objects sink or float.

Tutorial: Simulating falling ropes

Simulating ropes is very interesting. They typically are made from renderable splines created with the Shapes panel. In this simple example, I'll drop a row of rope objects over the top of a sphere object.

To simulate ropes falling over a sphere, follow these steps:

1. Open the Falling ropes.max file from the Chap 30 directory on the CD-ROM. This file includes several primitive objects.

2. Select the Rigid Body Collection button in the Reactor toolbar and click in the Front viewport. In the RB Collection Properties rollout, click the Pick button and select the Box and the Sphere objects.

3. Select all the line objects and click on the Rope Modifier button in the Reactor toolbar.

4. Select the Rope Collection button in the Reactor toolbar and click in the Front viewport. In the RB Collection Properties rollout, click the Add button and select all the Line objects.

5. In the Reactor toolbar, click on the Show in Window button to view the simulation in a preview window and click the P button to play the simulation.

Figure 30-17 shows the resulting preview window about midway through the simulation.

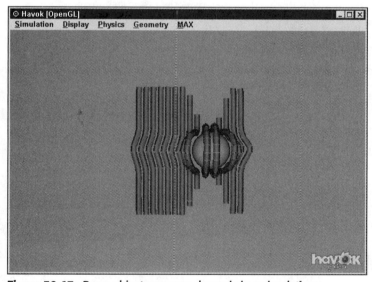

Figure 30-17: Rope objects are very dynamic in a simulation.

Troubleshooting

Reactor identifies problems before you try to preview or compute the simulation. These problems are displayed in an error window. The following are some common errors you can avoid. Use the Analyze World button to look for warnings.

✦ **Don't use the default Plane primitive.** Reactor complains if the plane object is co-planar. The problem is that without any depth, Reactor can't accurately compute collisions. Instead, just use a Box primitive or use Reactor's Plane Primitive object (found in its toolbar).

✦ **Low Mass value.** Reactor complains if the Mass value for any objects is too low. To fix this problem, just increase the Mass value for the identified object.

✦ **Interpenetrating objects:** Objects that intersect cause an error in Reactor. Just make sure that none of the objects intersect with each other.

Summary

This chapter covered the basics of animating a dynamic simulation using the Dynamics utility. In this chapter you

✦ Created and used Spring and Damper dynamic objects

✦ Defined dynamic material properties for different objects using the Material Editor

✦ Used Space Warps to add forces to dynamic simulations

✦ Learned how to use the Dynamics utility to set up dynamic simulations

✦ Optimized simulation keys using the Track View Reduce Keys button

✦ Learned about the Flex modifier

✦ Experimented with the Reactor plug-in

This chapter concludes the part of the book on animation. In the next part, we look at bones, skin, characters, and inverse kinematics.

✦   ✦   ✦

Character
Animation

Working with Bones and Skin

A linked hierarchy attaches, or links, one object to another and makes transforming the attached object by moving the one it is linked to possible. For example, the arm is a classic example of a linked hierarchy—when the shoulder rotates, so do the elbow, wrist, and fingers. Establishing linked hierarchies can make moving, positioning, and animating many objects easy.

A bones system is a unique case of a linked hierarchy that has a specific structure. You can create a structure of bones from an existing hierarchy, or you can create a bones system and attach objects to it. A key advantage of a bones system is that you can use IK Solvers to manipulate and animate the structure.

After you've created a system of bones, you can cover the bones with objects that have the Skin modifier applied. This modifier lets the covering object move and bend with the bone structure that is underneath.

Building a Bones System

In some instances, establishing a hierarchy of objects before linking objects together is easier. By building the hierarchy first, you can be sure of the links between objects. One way to build this hierarchy is to use a bones system. A bones system consists of many bone objects that are linked together. These bone objects are normally not rendered, but you can set them to be renderable, like splines. You can also assign an IK Solver to the bones system for controlling their motion.

To create a bones system, open the Create panel, click the Systems category button, and then click the Bones button. Now click in a viewport to create a root bone, then click a short distance away to create another bone, and repeat this a few more times. Each subsequent click creates another bone linked to the previous one. When you're finished adding bones, right-click to exit bone-creation mode. In this manner, you can create a long chain of bone objects all linked together.

These bones are actually linked joints. Moving one bone pulls its neighbors in the chain along with it. Bones can also be rotated, scaled, and stretched. Scaling a bones system affects the distance between the bones.

To branch the hierarchy of bones, simply click the bone where you want the branch to start while still in Bones creation mode. A new branching bone is created automatically. Click the Bones button again to create a new bone. Then continue to click to add new bones to the branch.

Figure 31-1 shows the rollouts that are available for creating bones.

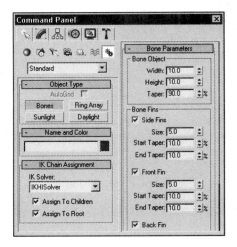

Figure 31-1: The Bone rollouts let you specify which bones get assigned an IK Controller.

Assigning an IK Solver

In the IK Chain Assignment rollout, you can select from four different IK Solvers — History Dependent, History Independent, IK Limb, and IK Spline. You can assign each of these solver types to children and to the root bone using the available options. You need to select both the Assign to Children and the Assign to Root options to assign the IK Controller to all bones in the system. If the Assign to Children option is de-selected, then the Assign to Root option is disabled.

Cross-
Reference

Chapter 33, "Creating and Using Inverse Kinematics," presents details on each of these IK Solvers.

Setting bone parameters

The Bone Parameters rollout includes parameters for setting the size of each individual bone, including its Width and Height. You can also set the percentage of Taper applied to the bone.

Fins can be displayed on the front, back, and/or sides of each bone. For each fin, you can specify its size and start and end taper values. Including fins on your bones makes correctly positioning and rotating the bone objects easier. Figure 31-2 shows a simple bones system containing two bones. The first bone has fins.

At the bottom of the Bone Parameters rollout is an option to Generate Mapping Coordinates. Bones are renderable objects, so this option lets you apply texture maps to them.

Tutorial: Making a simple puppet using bones

Starting simply, a good example is a puppet. The bones system for the puppet can be built first. If you specify the IK Solver before building the bones, then you'll be ready to animate the puppet after it is ready.

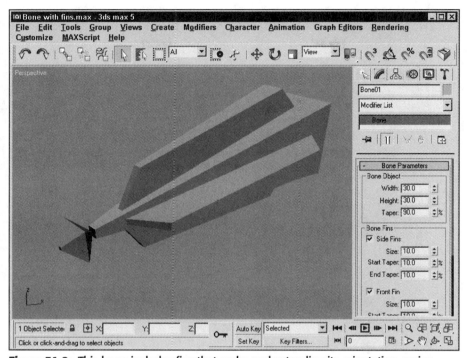

Figure 31-2: This bone includes fins that make understanding its orientation easier.

To create a simple puppet out of bones, follow these steps:

1. Open the Create panel, select the Systems category, and click the Bones button. In the IK Chain Assignment rollout, select IK Limb from the IK Solver drop-down list. To be able to see the orientation of each bone, enable the Side Fins.

2. In the Front viewport, click where you want the head bone to start and click again where the neck will be, then continue to click to form the spine, pelvis, right thigh, lower right leg, and foot bones. Then right-click to end the bones chain.

3. While still in Bones mode, click the pelvis bone in the Front viewport and drag to the left to form the left thigh bone. Continue to click to form the lower left leg and left foot bones. Right-click to end the chain.

4. Form the right arm bones by clicking the head bone and clicking consecutively to form the right upper arm, lower right arm, and hand bones. Right-click to end the chain.

5. Repeat Step 4 for the left arm.

6. Click the Select Objects button on the main toolbar to exit Bones mode and select and name each bone object so it can be easily identified later.

Figure 31-3 shows the completed bones system for the puppet. You can select the bones at the end of each chain and move it to see how the inverse kinematics solution will work.

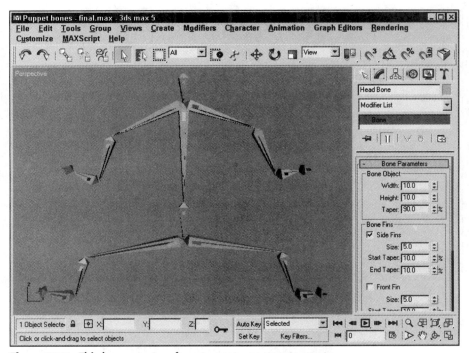

Figure 31-3: This bones system for a puppet was easy to create.

Using the Bone Tools

After you've created a bone system, you can use the Bone Tools to edit and work with the bone system. You access these tools from a panel that is opened using the Character ➪ Bone Tools menu command. Figure 31-4 shows this panel of tools that includes three separate roll-outs — Bone Editing Tools, Fin Adjustment Tools, and Object Properties.

 New Feature The Bone Tools are new to 3ds max 5.

Reordering bones

You can use the transform buttons on the main toolbar to move, rotate, and scale a bone along with all its children, but if you want to transform the parent without affecting any of the children, you'll need to open the Bone Tools panel. The Bone Edit Mode lets you move and realign a bone without affecting its children.

Clicking the Remove Bone button removes the selected bone and reconnects the bone chain by stretching the child bone. If you hold down the Shift key while removing a bone, the parent will be stretched. Clicking the Delete Bone button deletes the selected bone and adds an End bone to the last child.

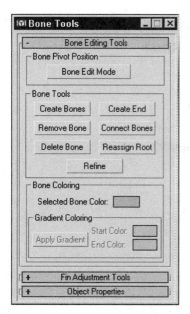

Figure 31-4: The Bone Tools palette includes several buttons for working with bone systems.

Caution Using the Delete key to delete a bone will not add an End bone and the bone chain will not work correctly with an IK Solver.

If a bone exists that isn't connected to another bone, then you can add an End bone to the bone using the Create End button. The bone chain must end with an End bone in order to be used by an IK Solver.

The Connect Bone button lets you connect the selected bone with another bone. After clicking on this button, you can drag a line from the selected bone to another bone and the two bones will be connected.

Use the Re-Root Chain button to reverse the chain and move the End bone from the parent to the last child.

Refining bones

As you start to work with a bones system that you've created, you may discover that the one long bone for the backbone of your monster is too long to allow the monster to move like you want. If this happens, you can refine individual bones using the Refine button. This button appears at the bottom of the Bone Tools section of the Bone Editing Tools rollout.

Clicking the Refine button enables you to select bones in the viewport. Every bone that you select will be broken into two bones at the location where you click. Click on the Refine button again to exit Refine mode.

Coloring bones

Bones, like any other object, are assigned a default object color and can be applied materials from the Material Editor. For each separate bone, its object color can be changed in the Modify panel or in the Bone Tools panel.

You can also apply a gradient to a bone chain using the Bone Tools palette. This option is only available if two or more bones are selected. The Start Color is applied to the chain's head and the End Color is applied to the last selected child. The colors are applied or updated when the Apply Gradient button is clicked. Figure 31-5 shows a long spiral bone chain with a white-to-black gradient applied.

 New Feature Gradient colors for bones are new in 3ds max 5.

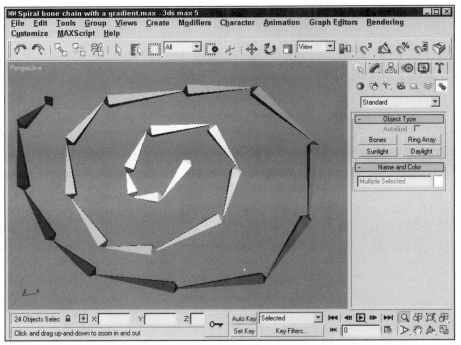

Figure 31-5: A white-to-black gradient applied to this spiral bone chain

Adjusting fins

The Fin Adjustment Tools rollout includes the same parameters as those found in the Bone Parameters rollout. You can specify the dimensions and taper of a bone and its fins. But, you can also specify that the parameters are applied using Absolute or Relative values. Relative values are based on the parameters of the bone that is above the current bone in the chain.

This rollout also includes Copy and Paste buttons that you can use to copy the bone parameters from one bone to another.

Making objects into bones

You can make any object act like a bone. To make an object into a bone, you need to open the Object Properties rollout in the Bone Tools panel. The Object Properties rollout, shown in Figure 31-6, includes a setting for Bone On/Off. If enabled, the object will act like a bone. When the Bone On/Off option is enabled, then the remaining Bone controls become available.

The Auto-Align option causes the pivot points of adjacent bones to be aligned automatically. The Freeze Length option causes a bone to keep its length as the bone system is moved. If the Freeze Length is disabled, you can specify a Stretch type. None prevents any stretching from occurring, and Scale changes the size along one axis, but Squash causes the bone to get wider as its length is decreased and thinner as it is elongated. You can also select a stretch axis and whether to Flip the axis.

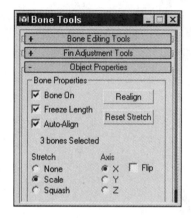

Figure 31-6: Use the Object Properties rollout to make any object act as a bone.

You can use the Realign button to realign a bone; click the Reset Stretch button to normalize the stretch value to its current value.

Tutorial: Making a linked teddy bear into a bones system

Models such as vehicles and life forms have a natural link order and often come already linked. By making a linked model into bone objects, the model will inherit the benefits of a bones system. In this tutorial, we'll import a teddy bear model created by Viewpoint Datalabs. To make the teddy bear model a bones system, follow these steps:

1. Open the Teddy bear.max file the Chap 31 directory on the CD-ROM.

   This file includes the Teddy Bear model.

2. Click the Select and Link button on the main toolbar. Drag from the left leg to the body to make the leg a child link to the body. Repeat the linking for the other leg, the arms, and the head. Link the nose to the head object.

3. With the objects all linked, choose Character ➪ Bone Tools to open the Bone Tools panel.

4. In the Object Properties rollout, select the Bone On and the Auto Align options. Select also the Squash option.

5. In the Link Display rollout of the Display panel, click the Display Links check box to see the links between the bones.

Figure 31-7 shows the bear with its bone links. Bones are created at the pivot point of each child object. To see the difference between the bones system and no bones, select the Select and Move button and try to move the head object off the bear. As a bone object, it will not move away from the body.

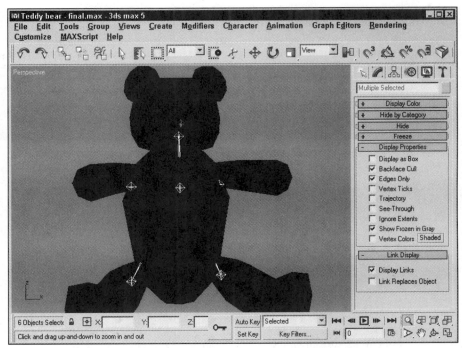

Figure 31-7: A linked teddy bear model after its objects were made into bones

Using the Skin Modifier

Unless you like working with skeletons, a bone system will typically have a skin attached to it. Any mesh can be made into a skin using the Skin modifier. With a skin attached to a bone system, you can move the bone system and the skin will follow.

Skin modifier

The Skin modifier is useful for creating skin to surround a bones system. Each object with the Skin modifier applied gets a capsule-shaped envelope attached to it. When two of these envelopes overlap, their surfaces blend together like skin around a bone joint. These envelopes can be attached to NURBS, meshes, patches, bones, or even splines.

The Parameters rollout includes an Edit Envelopes button that places you in a special mode that lets you change the envelope for each bone. Within Edit Envelopes mode, the object will be colored blue to show the areas where the envelope is within the object and red where the envelope is outside of the object. Using these visual clues, you can easily edit the envelopes to the desired effect. Once edited, you can copy and paste envelopes to other bones.

Each bone that the modifier is applied to is listed in the Parameters rollout. You can Add and Remove Bones, Add and Remove Bone Cross Sections, and control the position and size of the Envelopes. There are also settings to weight the various vertices. The Skin modifier also includes three unique deformer gizmos that can be used to control how the skin bends at the joint, bulges, and morphs over an animation sequence.

The Skin modifier is one of the keys to character animation. The ability to control a system of bones using Inverse Kinematics would not be very beneficial without the ability to cover the bones with a skin. You can apply the Skin modifier to an object or a group of objects using the Modifier List or Modifiers ⇨ Animation Modifiers ⇨ Skin.

Skin subobjects

The single subobject available for the Skin modifier is Envelope. An Envelope is an area that surrounds the bone that defines which vertices of the Skin object are to be moved with the bone. In Envelope subobject mode, you can edit the size and influence of the envelope.

Editing envelopes

The Parameters rollout includes a list of bones that are assigned to the Skin modifier. You can add and remove bones from this list using the Add Bone and Remove Bone buttons below the list. The Edit Envelope button enters a mode where you can edit the envelope of the selected bone in the list. The Edit Envelope button works the same as clicking on the Envelope subobject in the Modifier Stack.

Figure 31-8 shows a simple loft object surrounding three bone objects with a Skin modifier applied. The Add Bone button was used to include the three bones within the Skin modifier list. The first bone was selected within the list, and the Edit Envelope button was clicked, revealing the envelope for the first bone.

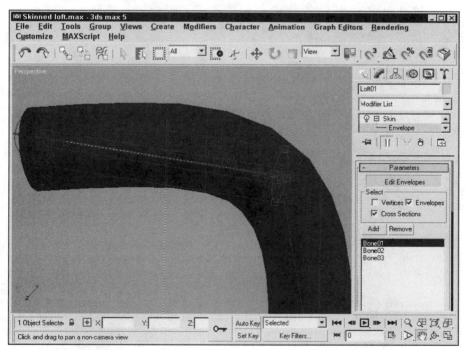

Figure 31-8: Envelopes define which Skin vertices move with the underlying bone.

For each envelope, you can add a cross section using the Add Cross Section button. This button lets you select a cross-section shape within the viewports. The Remove Cross Section button removes an added cross section from the envelope.

When the envelope is visible within the viewport, the envelope consists of two capsule-shaped areas within each other. At either end of these areas are four small square handles that can be dragged to change the cross-section radius. The cross-section area changes to pink when selected. The radius of the selected cross section is displayed in the Radius field within the Envelope Properties section of the Parameters rollout.

The viewport shades vertices on the skin surface that are included with the envelope red and vertices that aren't included within the envelope blue. These colors are visual clues that help you to see exactly which sections of the skin will move with the bones.

Figure 31-9 shows the envelope for the first bone. Notice how the size of the envelope has been increased. This was done by dragging on the cross-section handles. Also notice how the top section is shaded red, indicating that the skin will move with the bone.

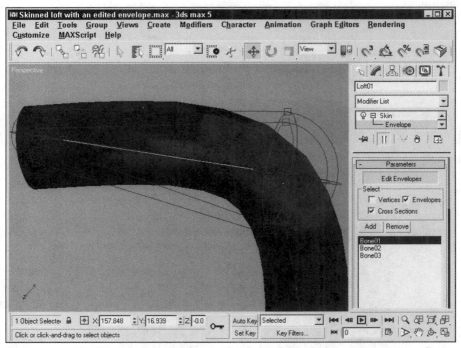

Figure 31-9: The first envelope has been edited to include all the vertices surrounding the first bone.

The Envelope Properties section of the Parameters rollout includes five icon buttons, shown in the following table. The first toggles between Absolute and Relative. All vertices that fall within the outer envelope will be fully weighted when the Absolute toggle is set, but only those within both envelopes will be fully weighted when the Relative toggle is selected.

Button	Description
A	Toggles between Absolute and Relative
/	Makes envelopes visible even when not selected
/	Sets Falloff curve
🗐	Copies envelope settings
📋	Pastes envelope settings

The second icon button enables envelopes to be visible even when not selected. This helps you see how adjacent bones overlap. The third icon button sets the Falloff curve for the envelopes. The options within this flyout are Fast Out, Slow Out, Linear, and Sinual. The last two icon buttons can be used to Copy and Paste envelope settings to other bones. The flyout options for the Paste button include Paste (to a single bone), Paste to All Bones, and Paste to Multiple Bones (which opens a selection dialog box).

When you select the Squash option in the Object Properties dialog box, you can set a Squash value, which determines the amount of squash applied to the object.

Working with weights

Working with the various envelopes and all their controls can be tricky. The Filters section can limit the controls that you can select. Filter options include Vertices, Envelopes, and Cross Sections.

The Absolute Effect field lets you specify a weight value for the selected bone or vertices. The Rigid option makes the selected vertices move only with the closest bone. The Rigid Handles causes the handles of the selected vertices to only move with the closest bone. The Normalize option requires that all the weights assigned to the selected vertices add to 1.0.

 New Feature The Weight Table is new to 3ds max 5.

The Include and Exclude Vertices buttons lets you remove the selected vertices from those being affected by the selected bone. The Select Exclude Verts button selects all excluded vertices.

Using the Weight Table

The Weight Table button opens the WeightTable interface, shown in Figure 31-10. This table displays all the vertices for the skinned object by ID in a column on the left side of the interface. All bones are listed in a row along the top. For each vertex and bone, you can set a weight.

The Edit menu includes command to Copy and Paste weights. It also includes commands to Select All, Invert, and None. A selection of vertices can be combined into a Vertex Set and named. The Vertex Sets menu lets you create and delete these sets.

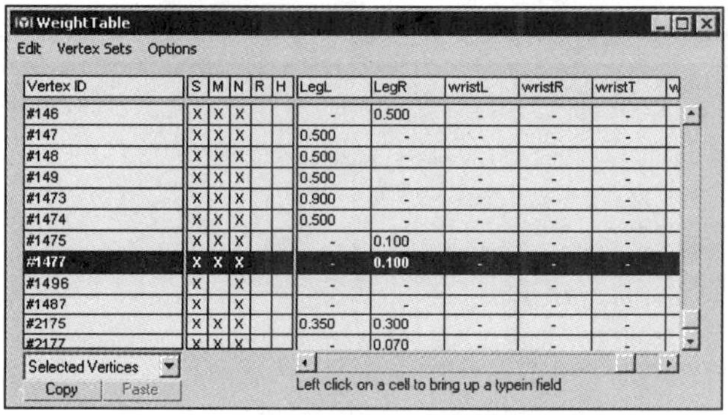

Figure 31-10: The WeightTable lets you specify weight values for each vertex and for each bone.

The Options menu lets you flip the interface so that bones are displayed in the first column and the vertex IDs are along the top row. The Update On Mouse Up option will limit the updates until the mouse is released. There are also several options for showing and hiding interface elements. The Show Affected Bones option only lists the bones that are affected. The Show Attributes option displays a column of attributes labeled S, M, N, R, and H. The Show Exclusions option makes a check box available in each cell. When checked the vertex is excluded. The Show Global option makes a drop-down list available that enables you to set an attribute for all vertices. The Show Locks (like the Show Exclusions option) makes a check box available for each cell. Enabling this check box (the left one) locks the weight so it can't change. The Set Sets UI makes two buttons for creating and deleting vertex sets available.

The S attribute is marked if a vertex is selected, the M attribute marks a vertex weight that has been modified, the N attribute marks a normalized weight, the R attribute marks rigid vertices, and an H attribute marks a vertex with rigid handles.

To set a weight, just locate the vertex for the bone and click in the cell and type the new value. If you click on a cell and drag to the left or right, the weight value changes. Weight values can be dragged between cells. Right-clicking on a cell sets its value to 0 and right-clicking with the Ctrl key held down sets its value to 1.0.

Once the vertice weights are set, you can click the Bake Selected Vertices to lock down the weight values. Changes to envelopes do not affect baked vertices.

Painting weights

Another way to assign whether vertices in the skin move with the bone is to assign weights to the vertices. Using the Paint Weights button, you can paint with a brush over the surface of the skin object. The Paint Strength value sets the value of each brush stroke. This value can be positive (up to 1.0) for vertices that will move with the bone or negative (to –1.0) for vertices that will not move the bone. The Radius and Feather settings define the size and softness of the brush.

To the right of the Paint Weights button is the Painter Options button (it actually only has three dots on it), which opens the Painter Options dialog box, shown in Figure 31-11.

New Feature   The Painter Options dialog box is new to 3ds max 5.

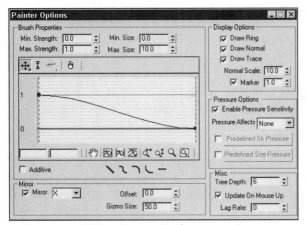

Figure 31-11: The Painter Options dialog box includes settings for controlling the size and sensitivity of the brush strokes.

The Min/Max Strength and Min/Max Size values determine the minimum and maximum weight values and paint gizmo sizes. You can define the brush falloff using the curve. This keeps the weights from making an abrupt change (muscles tend to look funny when this happens). Under the curve are several buttons for quickly defining the shape of the falloff curve including Linear, Smooth, Slow, Fast, and Flat.

The Display Options section includes options that determine the look of the painting gizmo. The Draw Ring, Normal, and Trace options make a ring; the surface normal or an arrow showing the trace direction appear. The Normal can be scaled, and the Marker option displays a small circular marker at the end of the normal.

You can enable Pressure Sensitivity for the brush gizmo. The options include None, Strength, Size, and Both. Using the graph, you can predefine Strength and Size pressure curves and then select to use them.

The Mirror option paints symmetrically on the opposite side of the gizmo across the specified axis. You can also set an Offset and the Gizmo Size. This is handy for muscles that you want to deform symmetrically. The Tree Depth, Update on Mouse Up, and Lag Rate options control how often the scene and the painted strokes are updated.

Display and Advanced settings

The Display rollout controls which features are visible within the viewports. Options include Color Vertices Weights, Draw All Envelopes, Show All Vertices, Show All Gizmos, Cross Sections on Top, and Envelopes on Top.

The Advanced Parameters rollout includes an option to Back Transform Vertices. This option avoids applying transform keys to the skin since the bones control the motion. The Rigid Vertices and Rigid Patch Handles options make the vertices so they are controlled by only one bone. This rollout also includes buttons for resetting vertices and bones. It also includes buttons for saving and loading envelopes. The envelopes are saved as files with the .env extension.

Tutorial: Applying the Skin modifier to a flamingo

The flamingo is perhaps one of the best examples of a character that needs a bone system because its legs are practically nothing but bones. Viewpoint Datalabs provided this flamingo model that we can practice with.

To apply the Skin modifier to a flamingo model, follow these steps:

1. Open the Flamingo skin.max file from the Chap 31 directory on the CD-ROM.

   This file includes a flamingo model with all its parts linked together. The leg parts have all been attached into a single object.

2. The first step is to create a bones system for the flamingo's raised leg. In the Create panel, select the Systems category and click the Bones button. Click on the flamingo where the upper leg connects to the body, click again on each joint to the foot, and right-click the complete bone system. I created five bones in the system — one to anchor the leg to the body, three for the leg, and the last one to end the bone system.

3. Use the Select and Move (W) and Select and Rotate (E) buttons on the main toolbar to align the bones within the upper leg objects. If you rotate any of the bones, select all the bones, open the Hierarchy panel, and click the Reset Transform button from the Adjust Transform rollout.

4. Select the left leg (the one that is raised) and choose Modifiers ➪ Animation Modifiers ➪ Skin to apply the Skin modifier to the leg.

5. In the Parameters rollout, click the Add Bone button. The Select Bones dialog box opens. Select the middle three bones and click the Select button. The first and last bones don't affect the model and don't need to be selected.

6. In the Parameters rollout, select the first bone in the list and click the Edit Envelopes button. Use the Zoom Region button in the Viewport Navigation button in the lower right to zoom in on the bones in the viewports. Select the cross-section handles for this bone and set the Radius values to 0.3 (near the body) and 0.2 for each end. Select the second bone in the list and set the Radius values to 0.5 and 0.6. Then select the last bone and set the Radius values to 1.0 and 2.0.

Figure 31-12 shows the resulting envelope for one of the bones.

Using deformers

Below the Advanced Parameters rollout is the Gizmos rollout. You use this rollout to apply deformers to selected skin object vertices. Three different deformers are available in the Gizmos rollout including a Joint Angle Deformer, a Bulge Angle Deformer, and a Morph Angle Deformer.

Each of these deformers is unique. They include the following features:

✦ **Joint Angle Deformer:** Deforms the vertices around the joint between two bones where the skin can bunch up and cause problems. This deformer moves vertices on both the parent and child bones.

✦ **Bulge Angle Deformer:** Moves vertices away from the bone to simulate a bulging muscle. This deformer only works on the parent bone.

✦ **Morph Angle Deformer:** Can be used on vertices for both the parent and child bones to move the vertices to a morph position.

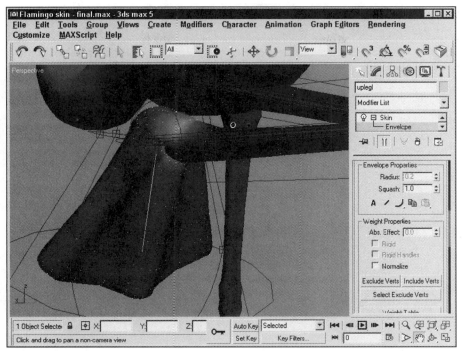

Figure 31-12: Increasing the envelope to encompass the entire leg ensures that the entire leg moves with the bones.

All deformers added to a skin object are listed in the Gizmo rollout. You can add and remove deformers to and from this list using the Add and Remove Gizmo buttons. You can also Copy and Paste the deformers to other sets of vertices. Before a deformer gizmo can be applied, you need to select vertices within the skin object. To select vertices, enable the Vertices check box of the Parameters rollout and drag over the vertices in the viewport to select the vertices.

The parameters for the deformer selected in the Gizmo rollout's list appear when the deformer is selected in the Deformer Parameters rollout. This rollout lists the Parent and Child bones for the selected vertices and the Angle between them. This rollout changes depending on the type of deformer selected.

For the Joint and Bulge Angle Deformers, the Gizmo Parameters rollout includes buttons to edit the control Lattice and to edit the deformer Key Curves. The Edit Lattice button lets you move the lattice control points in the viewports. The Edit Angle Keys Curves opens a Graph window that displays the transformation curves for the deformation.

Summary

The benefit of a bones system will become more apparent in the next chapter when we cover inverse kinematics. In this chapter, you learned how to create and work with bones systems and the skin modifier including

✦ Creating bones systems

✦ Setting bone parameters and the IK Solver

✦ Making objects into bones systems

✦ Working with the Skin modifier

This knowledge prepares you to work with characters and inverse kinematics, which I cover in the next two chapters.

✦   ✦   ✦

Working with Characters

A character is typically the main object in the scene. It is the object that moves and is the center of attention in all animation sequences. Using the character structures, you can set poses that can be reused as you animate and save animation sequences that can be reused on different characters.

Creating Characters

Imagine that you've worked for weeks to create and animate a character and you finally have it just right. Wouldn't it be nice if you could save that character out as a separate file and load it back into a different scene? Well, now you can.

New Feature   Characters are new to 3ds max 5.

Characters can be unique, portable objects in Max. These objects are created using the Character menu commands. Characters are identified with a unique icon that is the head of the entire character hierarchy. This icon is called a node. Figure 32-1 shows the character icon. The icon itself is a simple 2D disc with a simple human figure on it.

You can control the size (radius) of the character icon with the Icon Size value in the Display rollout, but increasing the icon's size has no effect on the character.

When a character is created, all the objects included in the character automatically become children objects of the Character node with the character icon acting as the parent object. Selecting the icon selects the parent object, and double-clicking on the icon selects the entire character and all of its objects.

The position of the character icon also defines the starting position of the character. Moving the character icon moves the entire character. Figure 32-2 shows the Zygote man object after it has been converted into a character. The character icon is selected and looks like a hula hoop around the character's waist.

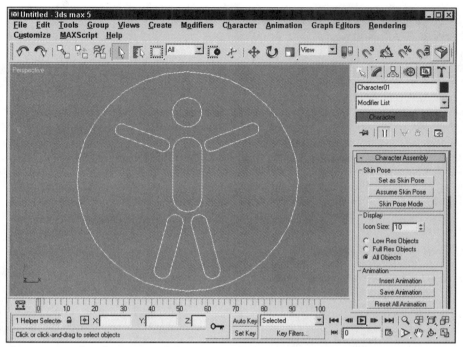

Figure 32-1: The Character node icon sits at the head of the character hierarchy.

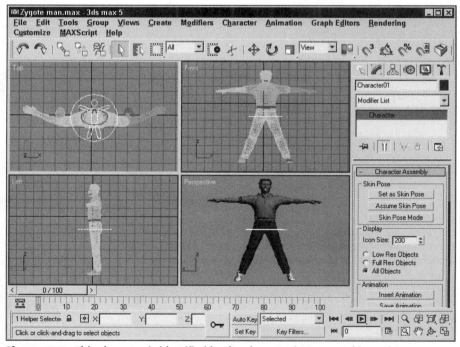

Figure 32-2: This character is identified by the character icon around its waist.

Saving and loading characters

After you have a character that you're pleased with, you can save the entire character as a separate file. Characters are saved with the .chr extension. You can use the Character ➪ Save Character menu command. The File menu commands such as Open, Save As, Merge, and Replace recognize files with the .max and the .chr extensions.

You can insert saved characters into the current scene using the Character ➪ Insert Character menu command. This command opens a File dialog box where you can specify the character to insert.

Destroying characters

Hierarchies that have been made into a character assembly can be unrecognized as a character using the Character ➪ Destroy Character menu command. This command doesn't delete the objects, but only removes the character icon and returns the objects to their default status.

Caution   If the character objects are selected when the Destroy Character menu command is used, then the character objects also will be deleted.

Working with Characters

After you create a character or insert one into a scene, you can work with the character by adding new objects to the character, saving and inserting animation, and setting poses. You find most of these commands in the Character Assembly rollout, which appears when the character icon is selected, but some are also in the Character menu.

Defining character members

While a character object is selected, all individual objects that make up the character will be listed in Character Members rollout, as shown in Figure 32-3. You use the Add and Remove buttons at the top of this rollout to add or remove objects from the current character object.

This Character Members rollout includes a check box next to each item on the list. If this check box is checked, then the item is marked to be visible during Low Res mode. The Display section of the Character Assembly rollout includes options for displaying Low Res or Full Res objects. Figure 32-4 shows a low-resolution model of the Zygote man character.

Tip   An easy way to create a low-res model is to apply the Optimize modifier to an object. This reduces the detail of the model.

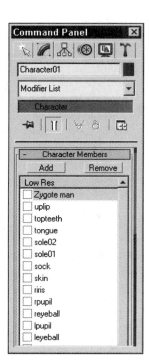

Figure 32-3: All objects that make up the character are listed in the Character Members rollout.

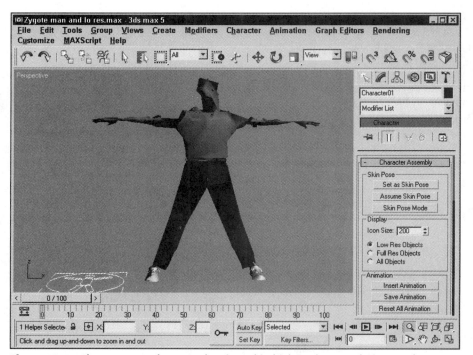

Figure 32-4: Characters can be set to be viewed in high- or low-resolution mode.

Locking and unlocking characters

Characters that are created can also be locked. A locked character hides the character icon, making it impossible to get to the character settings. To lock a character, choose Character ⇨ Lock. You can still move characters that are locked about the scene, but you cannot make any other changes to the objects in the character set.

You unlock a character with the Character ⇨ Unlock command.

Setting a skin pose

When a character is created, the character icon marks the character and its object's initial position. In addition to its initial position, you can set a skin pose. This pose defines how the character will stand. The initial pose of the character is determined by the bone structure when a skin is applied.

After the pose has changed, you can save the current pose using the Character ⇨ Set Skin Pose menu command. This saves the current pose so it can be immediately recalled using the Character ⇨ Assume Skin Pose menu command. Both of these menu commands are also available as buttons in the Character Assembly rollout.

The Skin Pose Mode button lets you make changes to the current skin pose. Figure 32-5 shows a simple frog made from primitives as the current pose is being set.

Figure 32-5: The Set and Assume Skin Pose buttons let you save and recall character poses.

Tutorial: Creating a frog character

When you begin to work with characters and inverse kinematics systems, you'll find that models with long arms and legs are easier to practice on. So for this example, I found one of the best long-legged creatures around — a frog.

To create a frog character, follow these steps:

1. Open the Frog character.max file from the Chap 32 directory on the CD-ROM. This file includes a frog model created by Zygote Media. The frog already has a bones system, and the skin modifier applied an IK setup for its legs.

2. Select the entire frog including all its bones and IK chains. Then select the Character ⇨ Create Character menu command. Set the Icon Size to 500.

3. In the Character Assembly rollout, click the Set as Skin Pose button. A simple dialog box appears asking you to confirm this action. Click Yes. This sets the current pose as the default for the frog character.

4. Click the Skin Pose Mode button. Then, select and manipulate the bones to create a new pose for the frog character.

5. Click on the Set Key button (or press the ' key). In the drop-down list about the Key Filters button, select Character01. Click the Set Keys button (or press the K key) to set the keys for the initial pose. Drag the Time Slider to Frame 30. With the Character icon selected, click the Set as Skin Pose button to assume the new pose and click the Set Keys button (or press the K key) to create the necessary keys.

6. Click the Select and Move button (or press the W key) and move the Character icon to the left. Click the Set Keys button (or press the K key) to set a key for the frog moving forward.

7. Open the Select Objects dialog box (by pressing the H key) and select all the bones. Then select Tools ⇨ Display Floater and click the Hide Selected button to hide all the bones.

8. Click on the Play Animation button (or press the / key) to see the results.

Figure 32-6 shows the frog as it jumps forward.

Saving and inserting character animations

Characters that are animated can be saved. You can insert these saved animations into a scene. You use the Save Animation button in the Animation section of the Character Assembly rollout to save an animation sequence for a character. These files are saved using the .anm extension and will include all the keys.

Animation files can also be saved as .xml files, like the one shown in Figure 32-7. XML files are a standard mark-up language for defining actions. Although XML files take longer to process than the .anm files, they offer a standard format that can be used by other animation tools.

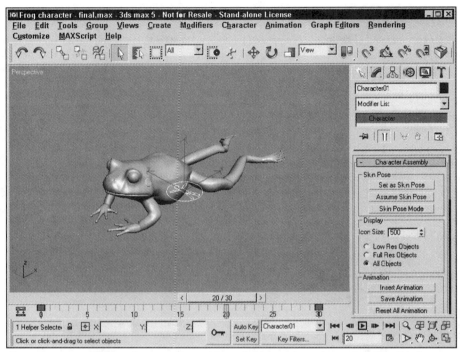

Figure 32-6: Using the character assembly and skin poses makes animating this frog easy.

Figure 32-7: Animations saved as XML documents can be viewed in a text editor.

Merging animations

After you've saved an animated sequence for a character, you can reuse it on other characters using the File ➪ Merge Animation menu command. This command opens the Merge Animation dialog box, as shown in Figure 32-8. This dialog box includes settings for specifying the animation sequence and the destination object.

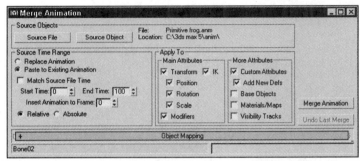

Figure 32-8: The Merge Animation dialog box lets you combine animation sequences from other characters.

The Source File and Source Object buttons open a file dialog box where you can load the animation sequence. The file dialog box for these buttons can open files with the .anm, .xml, or .max extensions. The Source Object dialog box opens a Select Objects dialog box where you can select a specific object that includes the animation sequence.

For the animation range, you can select to replace the current animation, or paste the animation sequence into the current animation. You can also select to filter the animation sequence by attributes including Transforms, Modifiers, and so on. Click the Merge Animation button to complete the merging.

If you use an animation sequence on a bone structure that is different than the source, then you can use the Object Mapping rollout, shown in Figure 32-9. This rollout lists the Source Object and the Current Objects side by side. All the bones that are animated are shown in red. You can save these mappings and load them to other objects. Mappings are saved with the .mam extension.

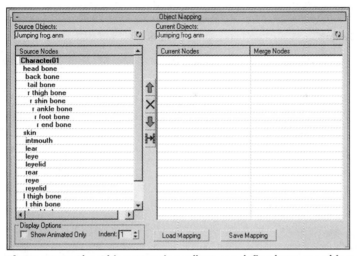

Figure 32-9: The Object Mapping rollout can define how one object maps to another.

Summary

Characters are becoming more and more important in the Max world and can be saved as separate files just like Max scene files. In this chapter, you've learned about

✦ Creating and saving characters

✦ Managing the various parts of a character

✦ Controlling various skin poses

✦ Merging animation sequences between different characters

Inverse kinematics is a powerful animation feature that is worth the time to use. In the next chapter, you'll get a chance to finally output your images and learn the basics of rendering.

✦   ✦   ✦

Creating and Using Inverse Kinematics

Kinematics is a branch of mechanics that deals with the motions of a system of objects, so inverse kinematics would be its evil twin brother that deals with the non-motion of a system of objects. Well, not exactly.

In Max, a system of objects are a bunch of objects that are linked together. After a system is built and the parameters of the links are defined, the motions of all the pieces below the parent object can be determined as the parent moves using kinematic formulas.

Inverse kinematics (IK) is similar except it determines all the motions of objects in a system when the last object in the hierarchy chain is moved. The position of the last object, such as a finger or a foot, is typically the one you're concerned with. Using IK, you can then use these solutions to animate the system of objects by moving the last object in the system.

Forward Versus Inverse Kinematics

Before you can understand Inverse Kinematics (IK), you need to realize that another type of kinematics exists — forward kinematics. Kinematic solutions only work on a kinematic chain, which you can create by linking children objects to their parents.

 Cross-Reference Chapter 8, "Grouping and Linking Objects," covers linking objects and creating kinematic chains.

Forward kinematics causes objects at the bottom of a linked structure to move along with their parents. For example, consider the linked structure of an arm, where the upper arm is connected to a forearm, which is connected to a hand, and finally to some fingers. Using forward kinematics, the lower arm, hand, and fingers all move when the upper arm is moved.

Having the linked children move with their parent is what you would expect and want, but suppose the actual object that you wanted to place is the hand. Inverse kinematics (IK) enables child objects to control their parent objects. So, using inverse kinematics, you can drag the hand to the exact position you want, and all other parts in the system will follow.

Forward kinematics in Max involves simply transforming linked hierarchies. Anytime you move, rotate, or scale a linked hierarchy, the children move with the parent, but the child object can also be transformed independent of its parent.

Creating an Inverse Kinematics System

Before you can animate an inverse kinematics system, you'll need to build and link the system, define joints by positioning pivot points, and define any joint constraints you want.

Building and linking a system

The first step in creating an inverse kinematics system is to create and link several objects together. You can create links using the Link button on the main toolbar.

With the linked system created, position the child object's pivot point at the center of the joint between it and its parent. For example, the joint between an upper and lower arm would be at the elbow, so this is where the pivot point for the lower arm should be located.

Cross-Reference Chapter 8, "Grouping and Linking Objects," covers creating linked systems and Chapter 9, "Transforming Objects," covers moving pivot points.

After you create the linked system and correctly position your pivot points, open the Hierarchy panel and click the IK button. Several rollouts open that let you control the IK system, including the Object Parameters rollout shown in Figure 33-1.

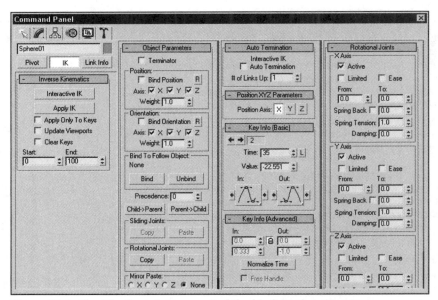

Figure 33-1: The IK rollouts let you control the binding of an IK system.

Selecting a terminator

Because child objects in an inverse kinematics system can cause their parents to move, moving a child could cause unwanted movements all the way up the system to the root object. For example, pulling on the little finger of a human model could actually move the head. To prevent this, you can select an object in the system to be a terminator.

A terminator is the last object in the IK system that is affected by the child's movement. Making the upper arm a terminator would prevent the finger's movement from affecting any objects above the arm.

To set a terminator, select an object and then enable the Terminator option in the Object Parameters rollout.

For Interactive IK mode, you can also enable the Auto Termination option included in the Auto Termination rollout. The Number of Links Up value sets the terminator a specified number of links above the current selection.

Defining joint constraints

The next step is to define the joint constraints, which you specify in the Sliding Joints and Rotational Joints rollouts. By default, each joint has six degrees of freedom, meaning that the two objects that make up the joint can each move or rotate along the X-, Y-, or Z-axes. The axis settings for all other sliding and rotational joints are identical. Defining joint constraints enables you to constrain these motions in order to prevent unnatural motions, such as an elbow bending backward. To constrain an axis, select the object that includes the pivot point for the joint and, in the appropriate rollout, locate the section for the axis that you want to restrict and de-select the Active option. If an axis's Active option is de-selected, the axis is constrained. You can also limit the motion of joints by selecting the Limited option.

When the Limited option is selected, the object can move only within the bounds set by the From and To values. The Ease option causes the motion of the object to slow as it approaches either limit. The Spring Back option lets you set a rest position for the object—the object will return to this position when pulled away. The Spring Tension sets the amount of force that the object uses to resist being moved from its rest position. The Damping value sets the friction in the joint, which is the value with which the object resists any motion.

Note   As you enter values in the From and To fields, the object will move to that value to show visually the location specified. You can also hold down the mouse on the From and To values to cause the object to move temporally to its limits. These settings are based on the current Reference Coordinate system.

Copying, pasting, and mirroring joints

Defining joint constraints can be work—work that you wouldn't want to have to duplicate if you didn't have to. The Copy and Paste buttons in the Object Parameters rollout enable you to copy Sliding Joints or Rotational Joints constraints from one IK joint to another.

To use these buttons, select an IK system and click the Copy button; then select each of the joints to be constrained in a similar manner, and click the Paste button. There is also an option to mirror the joints about an axis. It is useful for duplicating an IK system for opposite arms or legs of a human or animal model.

Binding objects

When using applied IK, you need to bind an object in the IK system to a follow object. The IK joint that is bound to the follow object will then follow the follow object around the scene. The bind controls are located in the Hierarchy panel under the Object Properties rollout. To bind an object to a follow object, click the Bind button in the Object Properties rollout and select the follow object.

In addition to binding to a follow object, IK joints can also be bound to the world for each axis by position and orientation. This causes the object to be locked in its current position so that it won't move or rotate along the axis that is selected. You can also assign a Weight value. When the IK computations determine that two objects need to move in opposite directions, the solution will favor the object with the largest Weight value.

The Unbind button eliminates the binding.

Understanding precedence

When Max computes an IK solution, the order in which the joints are solved will determine the end result. The Precedence value (located in the Object Parameters rollout) lets you set the order in which joints are solved. To set the precedence for an object, select the object and enter a value in the Precedence value setting. Max will compute the object with a higher precedence value first.

The default joint precedence for all objects is 0. This assumes that the objects farthest down the linkage will move the most. The Object Parameters rollout also includes two default precedence settings. The Child to Parent button sets the precedence value for the root object to 0 and increments the precedence of each level under the root by 10. The Parent to Child button sets the opposite precedence, with the root object having a value of 0 and the precedence value of each successive object decreasing by 10.

Tutorial: Building an extensible arm linkage

As an example of a kinematics system, we'll design a simple arm linkage composed of six struts. To the end of this linkage, we'll attach a rubber spider on a string. (This contraption will be perfect for surprising your coworkers in the office.)

To create an inverse kinematics system for an extensible arm, follow these steps:

1. Open the Extensible arm with spider.max file from the Chap 33 directory on the CD-ROM.

   This file includes a spider model on the end of a string with several strut objects. The pivot points for the positioned objects have already been moved. The spider was created by Zygote Media.

2. Click the Select and Link button on the main toolbar and link the spider to the string object by selecting the spider and dragging from the spider to the cylinder. The spider then becomes the child to the string object. Next link the string to the last strut and so on back to the first strut.

3. Next we need to define the joint constraints for the system. Open the Hierarchy panel and click the IK button. In the Object Parameters rollout, select the first strut and enable the Terminator, Bind Position, and Bind Orientation options — doing so prevents the first strut from moving anywhere. In the Sliding and Rotational Joint rollouts, deactivate all the axes except for the Rotational Z-axis. When this is done, the Active box for the Rotational Z-axis will be the only one selected. Then click the Copy buttons for both joint types in the Object Parameters rollout, select the other struts, and click both Paste buttons. This copies the joint constraints from the first strut to the other strut objects. For the string object, make all Rotational Joint axes active.

4. To test the system, select the Interactive IK button in the Inverse Kinematics rollout and select and move the spider.

All the struts will rotate together as the spider moves.

Figure 33-2 shows the struts bending to follow the spider as it is moved downward. Notice for this system how the first strut doesn't move or rotate and that all the struts can only be rotated along the Z-axis, but that the spider can move freely within the range of the string. With the Interactive IK mode disabled, any object can be moved and/or rotated and only the links will be enforced.

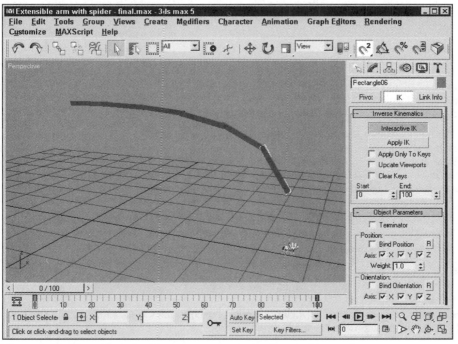

Figure 33-2: The objects in this scene are part of an inverse kinematics system.

Using the Various Inverse Kinematics Methods

After you create a linked hierarchy chain, you will need to apply an IK method to the chain before you can animate it. Max includes several different methods for animating using inverse kinematics. The traditional methods of Interactive and Applied IK are now joined with IK solvers. The Interactive and Applied IK methods are applied using the Hierarchy panel; the IK solvers can be applied to a bones system or you can use the Animation ➪ IK Solvers menu.

An IK solver is a specialized controller that computes an inverse kinematic solution. This solution is used to automatically set all the required keys needed for the animation. Max offers three different IK solvers — History Dependent (HD) IK, History-Independent (HI) IK, and the IK Limb solvers.

Interactive IK

Interactive IK is the method that lets you position a linked hierarchy of objects at different frames. Max will then interpolate all the keyframes between the various keys. This method isn't as precise, but it uses a minimum number of keys and is useful for an animation sequence involving many frames. Interactive IK interpolates positions between the two different keys, whereas Applied IK computes positions for every key. Because the motions are simple interpolations between two keys, the result may not be accurate, but the motion will be smooth.

After your IK system is established, animating using the Interactive IK method is simple. First you need to enable the Auto Key button and select the Interactive IK button in the Inverse Kinematics rollout of the Hierarchy panel. Enabling this button places you in Interactive IK mode, causing the system to move together as a hierarchy. Then reposition the system in a different frame, and Max will automatically interpolate between the two positions and create the animation keys. To exit Interactive IK mode, simply click the Interactive IK button again.

The Inverse Kinematics rollout includes several options. The Apply Only to Keys option forces Max to solve IK positions for only those frames that currently have keys. The Update Viewports option shows the animation solutions in the viewports as it progresses, and the Clear Keys option removes any existing keys as the solution is calculated. The Start and End values mark the frames to include in the solution.

IK Preference settings

The required accuracy of the IK solution can be set using the Inverse Kinematics panel in the Preference Settings dialog box, shown in Figure 33-3. You can open this dialog box by choosing Customize ➪ Preferences. For the Interactive and Applied IK methods, you can set Position and Rotation Thresholds. These Threshold values determine how close the moving object must be to the defined position for the solution to be valid.

Note   Because the Applied IK method is more accurate, you'll want to set its Threshold values lower than those of the Interactive IK method.

You can also set an Iterations limit for both methods. The Iterations value is the maximum number of times the calculations are performed. This value limits the time that Max spends looking for a valid solution. The Iterations settings control the speed and accuracy of each IK solution.

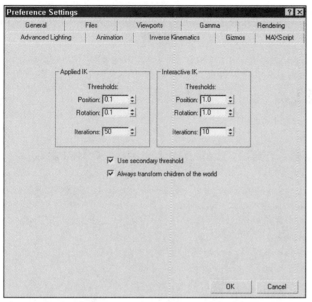

Figure 33-3: The Inverse Kinematics panel of the Preference Settings dialog box lets you set the global Threshold values.

 Note If the Iterations value is reached without a valid solution, Max will use the last calculated iteration.

The Use Secondary Threshold option provides a backup method to determine whether Max should continue to look for a valid solution. This method should be used if you want Max to bail out of a particularly difficult solution rather than to continue to try to find a solution. If you are working with very small thresholds, you will want to enable this option.

The Always Transform Children of the World option enables you to move the root object when it is selected by itself but constrains its movement when any of its children are moved.

Tutorial: Animating a simple IK propeller system

Machines are good examples of a kinematics system. In this example, you'll animate a simple gear-and-propeller system using the Applied IK method.

To animate an inverse kinematics system with a propeller, follow these steps:

1. Open the Gear and prop.max file from the Chap 33 directory on the CD-ROM.

   This file includes a simple handle and prop system.

2. The first task is to link the model. Click the Select and Link button on the main toolbar. Then drag from each child object to its parent. Connect the propeller to the shaft, the shaft to the gear, and the gear to the handle.

3. Open the Hierarchy panel and click the IK button. We'll next constrain the motions of the parts by selecting the handle object. All Sliding Joints can be deactivated, and only the Z-axis Rotational Joint needs to be activated. To do this, make sure a check mark is next to the Active option. When this is set for the handle object, click the Copy button

for both joint types, select the gear object, and click Paste to copy these constraints. Then select the shaft object, click both Paste buttons again, and repeat this process for the propeller.

4. Finally, enable the Auto Key button (or press the N key), drag the Time Slider to frame 100 (or press the End key), and click the Interactive IK button in the Inverse Kinematics rollout of the Hierarchy panel. Then select the Select and Rotate button (E) and drag in the Left viewport to rotate the handle about its Z-axis.

Figure 33-4 shows the propeller system.

Figure 33-4: The propeller rotates by turning the handle and using inverse kinematics.

Applied IK

Applied IK applies a solution over a range of frames, computing the keys for every frame. This task is accomplished by binding the IK system to an object that it follows. This method is more precise than the interactive IK method, but it creates a lot of keys. Because keys are set for every object and every transform, this solution will set a lot of keys, which will increase the size and complexity of the scene. Each frame will have its own set of keys, which could result in jerky and non-smooth results.

To animate using the Applied IK method, you need to bind one or more parts of the system to a follow object, which can be a dummy object or an object in the scene. You do so by clicking the Bind button in the Object Parameters rollout of the Hierarchy panel and selecting an object in one of the viewports. After the system has a bound follow object, select an object in the system. Open the Hierarchy panel and, in the Inverse Kinematics rollout, click the Apply

IK button. Max will then compute the keys for every frame between the Start and End frames specified in the rollout. Click the Apply IK button to start the computation process that sets all the animation keys for the range of frames indicated.

Tip If you plan on using the Applied IK method, set the Threshold values in the Inverse Kinematics panel of the Preference Settings dialog box to small values in order to ensure accurate results.

Tutorial: Animating the arm linkage using Applied IK

Now that we have built the strut linkage with the spider attached, not animating this system would be a waste. In this tutorial, we'll animate the linkage using the applied IK method.

To animate an IK system using the applied IK method, follow these steps:

1. Open the Animated IK trick spider.max file from the Chap 33 directory on the CD-ROM.

   This is the same file that we ended with in the last tutorial.

2. Open the Create panel, select the Helper category, and click the Dummy button. Then drag in the Left viewport over the top of the spider to create a dummy object.

   This dummy object will be the follow object.

3. Click the Auto Key button, drag the Time Slider to frame 100, and move the dummy object to the left in the Left viewport.

4. Select the spider object, open the Hierarchy panel, and click the Bind button in the Object Parameters rollout and select the dummy object.

5. Click the Apply IK button in the Inverse Kinematics rollout to begin the IK calculations.

   Keys will be created for every object for every frame.

6. Click the Play Animation button (or press the / key) to see the linkage move between the two positions.

Figure 33-5 shows the spider at frame 100. As expected, the linkage followed the spider's move.

History-Independent (HI) IK solver

The History-Independent (HI) IK solver looks at each keyframe independently when making its solution. You can animate linked chains with this IK solver applied by positioning the goal object; the solver will then keyframe the position of the pivot point of the last object in the chain to match the goal object.

You can apply IK solvers to any hierarchy of objects. IK solvers are applied automatically to a bones system when you create the system. You can also choose Animation ➪ IK Solvers to select an IK solver.

When you choose Animation ➪ IK Solver, a dotted line appears from the selected object. You can drag this line within a viewport and click another object within the hierarchy to be the end joint. A white line will be drawn between the beginning and ending joints. The pivot point of the end joint is the goal for the IK solver. The goal of the IK solver is marked by a blue cross. Several rollouts within the Hierarchy panel also appear. These rollouts let you set the parameters for the IK solver.

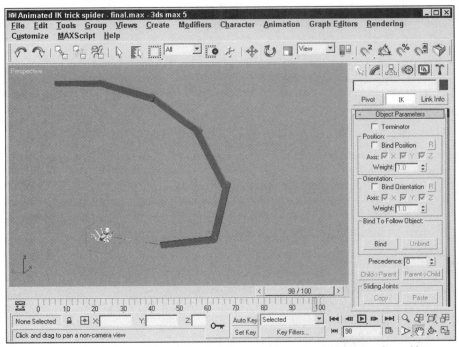

Figure 33-5: Setting keys with the Applied IK method creates a large number of keys.

The first rollout is the IK Solver rollout, shown in Figure 33-6. Using this rollout, you can select to switch between the HI IK solver and the IK Limb solver. The Enabled button lets you disable the solver. By disabling the solver, you can use forward kinematics to move the objects. To return to the IK solution, simply click the Enabled button again. The IK for FK Pose option enables IK control even if the IK solver is disabled. This lets you manipulate the hierarchy of objects using forward kinematics while still working with the IK solution. If both the IK for FK Pose and the Enabled buttons are disabled, then the goal can move without affecting the hierarchy of object.

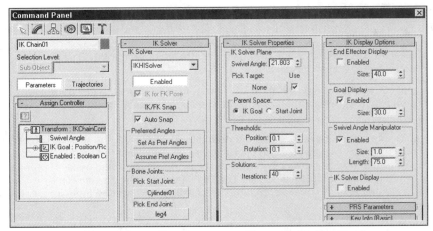

Figure 33-6: The IK Solver rollout lets you enable or disable the IK solver.

If the goal ever gets moved away from the end link, clicking the IK/FK Snap button automatically moves the goal to match the end links position. Auto Snap automatically keeps the goal and the end link together. The Set as Preferred Angle button will remember the angles for the IK system. These angles can be recalled at any time using the Assume Preferred Angle button.

When you choose Animation ➪ IK Solvers ➪ HI Solver, the start joint will be the selected object, and the end joint will be the object that you drag the dotted line to. If you want to change these objects, you can click the Pick Start Joint or Pick End Joint buttons.

Tip   The best way to select an object using the Pick Start or End Joint buttons is to open the Select by Name dialog box by pressing the H key. Using this dialog box, you can select an exact object without having to miss selecting it in a complex viewport.

Caution   If you select a child as the start joint and an object above the child as the end joint, then moving the goal will have no effect on the IK chain.

Defining a swivel angle

The IK Solver Properties rollout includes the Swivel Angle value. The swivel angle defines the plane that includes the joint objects and the line that connects the starting and ending joints. This plane is key because it defines the direction that the joint moves when bent.

The Swivel Angle value can change during an animation. Using the Pick Target button, you can also select a Target object to control the swivel angle. The Use button turns the target on and off. The Parent Space group defines whether the IK Goal or the Start Joint's parent object is used to define the plane. Having an option lets you select two different parent objects that control the swivel plane if two or more IK solvers are applied to a single IK chain.

You can also change the Swivel Angle value by using a manipulator. To view the manipulator, click the Select and Manipulate button on the main toolbar. This manipulator is a green line with a square on the end of it. Dragging this manipulator in the viewports causes the swivel angle to change.

To understand the swivel angle, consider two puppet bone systems displayed in Figure 33-7. The HI solver has been applied to the right arms of both puppets with the upper arm as the beginning joint and the hand as the end joint. The swivel angle for the left bones system is 90 degrees, and the swivel angle for the right bones system is 180. You can see the manipulators for both bone systems. The left one is pointing upward, and the right one is pointing straight out from the puppet's head. Notice how the swivel angle determines the direction the elbow joint is pointing. The left bones system's elbow is pointing up and away from the spine, and the right bones system's elbow is pointing painfully out in front of the puppet in the direction of the manipulator.

The IK Solver Properties rollout also includes Threshold values. These values determine how close the end joint and the goal must be before the solution is pronounced valid. You can set thresholds for Position and Rotation. The Iterations value sets the number of times the solution will be tried.

Tip   Setting the Iterations value to a higher number results in smoother (less jerky) results, but it increases the time required to find a solution.

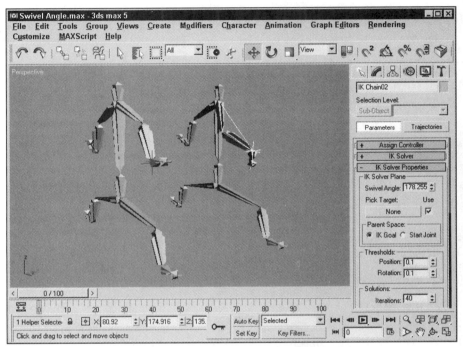

Figure 33-7: The swivel angle defines the plane along which the joint moves.

Displaying IK controls

The IK Display Options rollouts can enable, disable, and set the size of the gizmos used when working with IK solvers. Using this rollout, you can Enable the End Effector, the Goal, the Swivel Angle Manipulator, and the IK solver (which is the line connecting the start and end joints).

Tutorial: Animating a puppet with the HI IK solver

The HI solver is probably the best solver to use for animating characters. One of the tutorials in the last chapter created a simple puppet using bones. This fine fellow makes a good candidate for trying out the HI solver.

To animate a puppet with the HI IK solver, follow these steps:

1. Open the Dancing puppet.max file from the Chap 33 directory on the CD-ROM.

   This file is the same file that was created using the bones system.

2. Apply the HI solver to the arm chains by selecting the left upper arm and choosing Animation ⇨ IK Solvers ⇨ HI Solver. A dotted line appears in the viewports extending from the selected object. Move the cursor over the left hand object and click.

3. Repeat Step 2 for the right arm and both leg chains.

4. Click the Auto Key button, and drag the Time Slider to frame 20. Select the goal for the left leg IK chain, click the Select and Move button on the main toolbar (or press the W key), and move the left leg goal upward.

5. Repeat Step 4 for frames 40, 60, 80, and 100, moving the various IK chains in different directions.

6. Move the Time Slider to frame 50, and select all objects by choosing Edit ➪ Select All (Ctrl+A). Then drag all the objects upward a short distance. Drag the Time Slider to frame 100 (or press the End key), and drag all the objects back down again.

7. Click the Play Animation button (/) to see the resulting dance.

Figure 33-8 shows one frame of the dancing puppet.

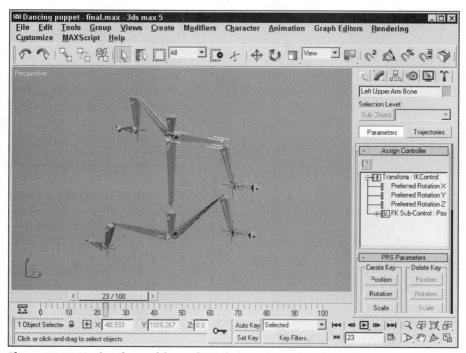

Figure 33-8: Moving the goal for each IK chain makes animating a character easy.

History-Dependent (HD) IK solver

The History-Dependent (HD) IK solver takes into account the previous keyframes as it makes a solution. This solver makes having very smooth motion possible, but the cost of time to compute the solution is increased significantly. You can also assign this IK solver to bones systems by specifying the History-Dependent solver in the IK Chain Assignment rollout or by choosing Animation ➪ IK Solvers ➪ HD Solver.

This IK solver shows up as a controller in the Motion panel. The settings are contained in a rollout named IK Controller Parameters, which will be visible in the Motion panel if you select one of the end effector gizmos. The end effector gizmo is the object that you move to control the IK chain. It is displayed as a set of crossing axes.

You can access the IK Controller Parameters rollout, shown in Figure 33-9, in the Motion panel. Any parameter changes will affect all bones in the current structure. In the Threshold section, the Position and Rotation values set how close the end effector must be to its destination before the solution is complete. In the Solutions section, the Iterations value determines the maximum number of times the solution is attempted. These Threshold and

Iteration values are the same as those in the Preference Settings dialog box, except they affect only the current linkage. The Start and End Time values set the frame range for the IK solution.

Figure 33-9: The IK Controller Parameters rollout sets the boundaries of the IK solution.

The Show Initial State option displays the initial state of the linkage and enables you to move it by dragging the end effector object. The Lock Initial State option prevents any linkage other than the end effector from moving.

The Update section enables you to set how the IK solution is updated with Precise, Fast, and Manual options. The Precise option solves for every frame, Fast solves for only the current frame, and Manual solves only when the Update button is clicked. The Display Joints options determine whether joints are Always displayed or only When Selected.

When you first create a bones system, an end effector is set to the last joint automatically. In the End Effectors section, at the bottom of the IK Controller Parameters rollout, you can set any joint to be a Positional or Rotational end effector. To make a bone an end effector, select the bone and click the Create button. If the bone already is an end effector, then the Delete button is active. You can also link the bone to another parent object outside of the linkage with the Link button. The linked object will then inherit the transformations of this new parent.

Click the Delete Joint button in the Remove IK section to delete a joint. If a bone is set to be an end effector, the Position or Rotation button will display the Key Info parameters for the selected bone.

Tutorial: Animating a spyglass with the HD IK solver

A telescoping spyglass is a good example of a kinematic system that we can use to show off the HD solver. The modeling of this example is also easy because it consists of a bunch of cylinders that gradually get smaller.

To animate a spyglass with the HD IK solver, follow these steps:

1. Open the Spyglass.max file from the Chap 33 directory on the CD-ROM.

   This file includes a simple spyglass made from primitive objects. The pieces of the spyglass are linked from the smallest section to the largest section. At the end of the spyglass is a dummy object linked to the last tube object.

2. First, you'll need to define the joint properties. Select the largest tube object, open the Hierarchy panel, and click the IK button. In the Object Properties dialog box, select the Terminator, Bind Position, and Bind Orientation options to keep this joint from moving.

3. With the largest tube section selected, make the Z-Axis option active in the Sliding Joints rollout, and disable all the axes in the Rotational Joints rollout. Then click the Copy button for both Sliding and Rotational Joints in the Object Properties rollout.

4. Select each remaining tube object individually and click the Paste buttons for both the Sliding and Rotational Joints.

   This enables the local Z-axis sliding motion for all tube objects.

5. Select the largest tube section again and choose Animation ⇨ IK Solvers ⇨ HD Solver. Then drag the dotted line to the dummy object at the end of the spyglass.

6. Select the second tube object, and for the Sliding Z-Axis select the Limited option with values from 0.0 to –80. Then click on the Copy button for the Sliding Joints in the Object Parameters rollout. Then select tubes 3 through 6 individually and click the Paste button for the Sliding Joints to apply these same limits to the other tube objects.

7. Click the Auto Key button (N), drag the Time Slider to frame 100 (End), select the Select and Move button on the main toolbar (W), and drag the dummy object away from the largest tube object.

Figure 33-10 shows the end tube segment collapsing within the spyglass.

IK Limb solver

The IK Limb solver was specifically created to work with limbs such as arms and legs. It is used on chains of three bones such as a hip, upper leg, and lower leg. Only two of the bones in the chain actually move. The goal for these three joints is located at the pivot point for the third bone.

The way this solver works is that it considers the first joint as being a spherical joint that can rotate along three different axes, like a hip or shoulder joint. The second joint can only bend in one direction, such as an elbow or knee joint.

The rollouts and controls for the IK Limb solver are exactly the same as those used for the HI solver covered earlier in this chapter.

Tutorial: Animating a flamingo's leg with the IK Limb solver

As an example of the IK Limb solver, we should probably animate a limb, and the flamingo model produced by Viewpoint Datalabs will fit the bill (although the limb bends backward). This tutorial continues the example from the last chapter in which a Skin modifier was applied to the flamingo's leg.

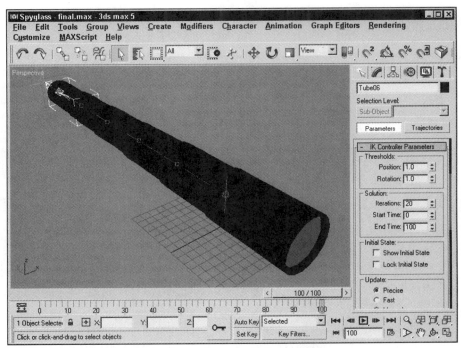

Figure 33-10: The HD IK solver is used to control the spyglass.

To animate the flamingo's leg using the IK Limb solver, follow these steps:

1. Open the Flamingo leg.max file from the Chap 33 directory on the CD-ROM.

   This file includes a flamingo model created by Viewpoint Datalabs. This file is also the result of the example in Chapter 31, "Working with Bones and Skin."

2. Click the Select by Name button on the main toolbar (or press the H key) to open the Select Objects dialog box. Double-click on the Bone02 object to select the upper leg bone object.

3. With the upper leg bone selected, choose Animation ➪ IK Solvers ➪ IK Limb Solver. A dotted line appears in the viewport. Press the H key again to open the Pick Object dialog box and double-click on the Bone04 object to select it. This bone corresponds to the foot bone, which is the end of the limb hierarchy.

4. With the IK Chain01 object selected, click the Auto Key button (or press the N key) and drag the Time Slider to frame 100 (End). With the Select and Move button (W), move the IK chain in the viewport.

   The arm chain bends as you move the third bone.

Figure 33-11 shows the flamingo's leg being moved via the IK Limb solver.

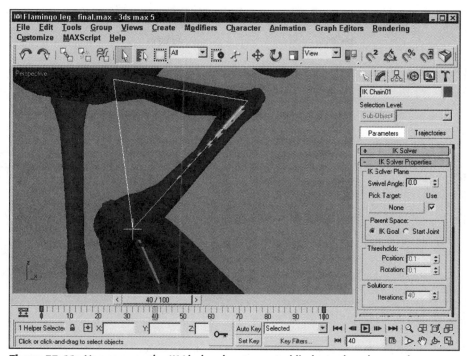

Figure 33-11: You can use the IK Limb solver to control limbs such as legs and arms.

Spline IK solver

The Limb IK solver works well for arms and legs that have a joint in their middle, but it doesn't work too well for tails. Tails are unique because they start out large and gradually are reduced in size to a point. For tails, the Spline IK solver works well.

New Feature   The Spline IK solver is new in 3ds max 5.

To use the Spline IK solver, you'll need to create a chain of bones and a spline path. By selecting the first and last bone and then selecting the spline, the bone chain will move to the spline. Each control point on the spline will have a dummy object associated with it. Moving these dummy objects you can control the position of the bones. At either end of the spline are two manipulators that you can use to twist and rotate the bones.

The easiest way to use this IK solver is to select SplineIKSolver from the drop-down list in the IK Chain Assignment rollout while you're creating the bone structure. After the bone structure is complete, the Spline IK Solver dialog box, shown in Figure 33-12, appears. With this dialog box, you can select a name for the IK chain, specify the curve type, and set the number of spline knots. The curve type options include Bézier, NURBS Point, and NURBS CV. You can also select to Create Helpers and to display several different options.

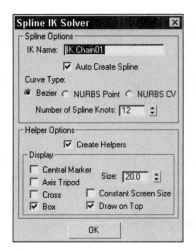

Figure 33-12: Use the Spline IK Solver dialog box to set options for the spline IK chain.

Another way to use this IK solver is with an existing bone structure. To do this, you'll need a spline curve in the scene that matches how you want the bone chain to look. Then, select the first bone where you want the solver to be applied and choose Animation ⇨ IK Solvers ⇨ Spline IK. In the viewports a dragging line appears; move the line to the last bone that you want to include and then drag a second time to the spline that you want to use.

The bone structure then assumes the shape of the spline curve. A helper object will be positioned at the location of each curve vertex. These helper objects let you refine the shape of the curve.

Tutorial: Building an IK Spline snake

The IK Spline solver is perfect for creating long, winding objects like snakes. For this example, we'll take an existing bone structure and, using the Spline IK solver, make it match a spline.

To create a bone structure for a snake that follows a spline using the IK Spline solver, follow these steps:

1. Open the Spline IK snake.max file from the Chap 33 directory on the CD-ROM.

   This file includes a simple bone chain and a spline.

2. With the first bone in the chain selected, choose Animation ⇨ IK Solvers ⇨ SplineIK Solver.

   A dragging line appears in the viewport extending from the first bone.

3. Drag and click the cursor on the last bone in the bone chain.

4. Another dragging line appears; drag and click on the spline, and the bone structure will move to match the spline's curve.

Figure 33-13 shows the bone structure for the snake. To complete and animate the snake, simply create a skin that can be bound to the bone chain.

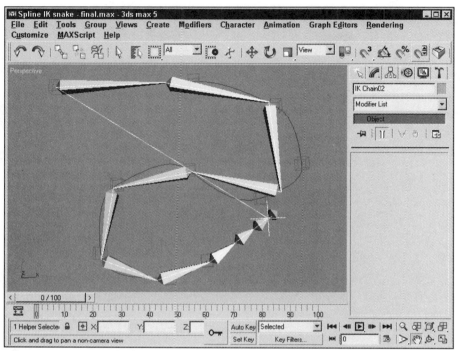

Figure 33-13: The IK Spline solver is perfect for creating objects like snakes and tails.

Summary

Inverse kinematics provides a unique way to control and animate hierarchical structures by transforming the child node. In this chapter, you've

- ✦ Learned the basic concepts behind inverse kinematics
- ✦ Explored the difference between interactive and applied IK methods
- ✦ Created and animated an inverse kinematics system
- ✦ Used the IK settings in the Preferences Settings dialog box
- ✦ Learned how to use IK solvers

Inverse kinematics is a powerful animation feature that is worth the time it itakes to use. In the next chapter, you'll get a chance to finally output your images and learn the basics of rendering.

✦   ✦   ✦

Rendering and Post-Production

Rendering Basics

After hours of long, hard work, the next step, rendering, is where the "rubber hits the road" and you get to see what you've worked so hard on. After modeling, applying materials, positioning lights and cameras, and animating your scene, you're finally ready to render the final output.

Max includes a Scanline Renderer that is optimized to speed up this process, and several settings exist that you can use to make this process even faster. Understanding the Render Scene dialog box and its functions can save you many headaches and computer cycles.

Understanding the Max Renderers

Rendering deals with outputting the objects that make up a scene at various levels of detail. Max uses several different rendering engines: one to view objects in the viewport, another to view material previews, and another to produce the final output. Each of these represents a trade-off between speed and quality. For example, the renderer used to display objects in the viewports is optimized for speed, but the renderer used to output final images leans toward quality.

Each renderer includes many different settings that you can use to speed the rendering process or improve the quality of the results. For example, you can set the objects in a viewport to different shading types, such as Smooth, Faceted, or Wireframe. You can find these settings in the Viewport Configuration dialog box and in the pop-up menu that appears when you right-click the viewport title.

 I discuss the viewport rendering options in Chapter 2, "Working with the Viewports."

The plug-in nature of Max enables you to select the renderer to use to output images. To change the default renderer, look in the Current Renderers rollout of the Render Scene dialog box (F10). You can select different renderers for the Production, Draft, and ActiveShade modes.

The Material Editor Options dialog box (O) also lets you specify which renderer is used to render material previews as shown in the sample slots. The options are the default Scanline Renderer or the renderer currently selected in the Current Renderers rollout.

The selected output renderer is used when you click the Render button in the Render Scene dialog box or from the Video Post dialog box. The Scanline Renderer generates images one horizontal line at a time, with its progress shown in the Virtual Frame Buffer and the line currently being rendered shown as a white line.

Note   Although the viewports use a renderer to display objects, this chapter focuses mainly on producing output using the Render Scene dialog box.

Previewing with ActiveShade

The ActiveShade window gives a quick semi-rendered look at the current scene. You can open it as a floater window or within a viewport using the Rendering ⇨ ActiveShade Floater or Rendering ⇨ ActiveShade Viewport. The ActiveShade window displays the effects of lights and shading as well as material maps.

Only one ActiveShade window can be opened at a time. If you try to open more than one window, a warning dialog box lets you know that opening it will close the previous window. The ActiveShade window has access to the same toolbar that is found in the Virtual Frame Buffer. The buttons on this toolbar are covered in the "Using the Virtual Frame Buffer" section later in this chapter.

Right-clicking the ActiveShade window opens a quadmenu of commands, as shown in Figure 34-1. The Render quadmenu in the upper right contains the common rendering menu options. The View quadmenu in the upper left contains the command to close the ActiveShade window.

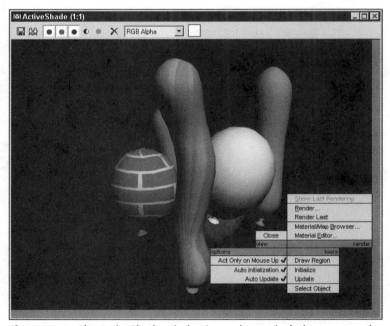

Figure 34-1: The ActiveShade window's quadmenu includes commands for updating the scene.

In the lower-left quadmenu, the Act Only on Mouse Up option will wait to update the rendered scene until the mouse is released. If disabled, the window updates immediately. Auto Initialization updates as soon as a new mapped material is applied, and the Auto Update option updates anytime a non-mapped material is applied or when the lights are altered.

The Draw Region option (keyboard shortcut, D) changes the cursor to look like a pen. Using this pen cursor, you can select a region in the ActiveShade window by dragging from corner to corner. Within a selected region, only that section will be updated. The Initialize option (keyboard shortcut, P) will reinitialize the window if the Auto Initialization option isn't enabled. The Update option is a manual update if the Auto Update option isn't selected. The Select Object option lets you pick an object in the ActiveShade window. The selected object will be bounded by brackets, and any initialization will update the mapped material on the selected object only.

Using the ActiveShade Floater

Choosing Rendering ➪ ActiveShade Floater opens the ActiveShade Floater window, as shown previously in Figure 34-1. You can zoom in on an ActiveShade window by holding down the Ctrl key and left-clicking the window. Right-clicking causes the view to zoom out. Holding down the Shift key lets you pan the ActiveShade window. You can also zoom in and out with the mouse scroll wheel (and you don't need to hold the Ctrl button). Holding down the mouse scroll wheel lets you pan the window.

Holding down the Alt key while right-clicking in the ActiveShade window changes the cursor to an eyedropper and lets you select colors. The selected color is displayed in a color swatch at the right end of the toolbar. Holding down the mouse button when clicking reveals a floating info box with details about the image size and the selected color values.

Enabling ActiveShade in a viewport

Choosing Rendering ➪ ActiveShade Viewport makes the current active viewport an ActiveShade window. You can toggle the toolbar on and off with the spacebar. Selecting the Close quadmenu option returns the viewport to its previous state.

Figure 34-2 shows the ActiveShade window in a viewport.

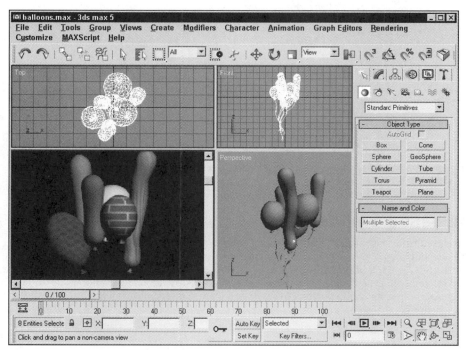

Figure 34-2: You can view the ActiveShade window in a viewport.

Render Parameters

After you're comfortable with the scene file and you're ready to render a file, you need to open the Render Scene dialog box, shown in Figure 34-3, by means of the Rendering ➪ Render menu command (F10) or by clicking the Render Scene button on the main toolbar. This dialog box has several rollouts: The first rollout is the Common Parameters rollout. Other rollouts include Render Elements, Current Renderers, Email Notifications, and a rollout for the selected renderer. The default renderer is the Scanline A-Buffer renderer.

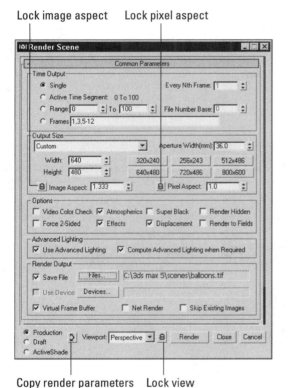

Figure 34-3: You use the Render Scene dialog box to render the final output.

Initiating a render job

At the bottom of the Render Scene dialog box are several controls that are always visible; these controls let you initiate a render job. The three render modes are Production, Draft, and ActiveShade. Each of these modes can use a different renderer with different render settings as defined using the Current Renderers rollout. The Copy Render Parameters button to the right of the render mode buttons lets you duplicate the settings from the current mode to the other mode.

The Viewport drop-down list includes all the available viewports. The one selected is the one that gets rendered when you click the Render button. The Render button starts the rendering process, and you use both the Close and Cancel buttons to exit the dialog box. You can click the Render button without changing any settings, and the default parameters will be used.

Note   When the Render Scene dialog box opens, the currently active viewport appears in the Viewport drop-down list.

When you click the Render button, the Rendering dialog box appears. This dialog box, shown in Figure 34-4, displays all the settings for the current render job and tracks its progress. The Rendering dialog box also includes Pause and Cancel buttons for halting the rendering process. If the rendering is stopped, the Rendering dialog box disappears, but the Virtual Frame Buffer stays open.

Caution   If you close the Virtual Frame Buffer window, the render job will still continue. To cancel the rendering, click the Pause or Cancel button, or press the Esc key on your keyboard.

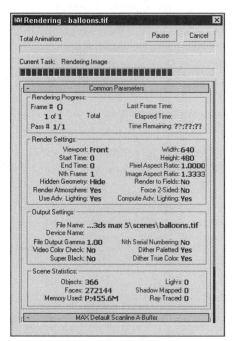

Figure 34-4: The Rendering dialog box displays the current render settings and progress of the render job.

Tip   After you've set up the render settings for an image, you can re-render an image without opening the Render Scene dialog box by clicking the Render Last button or by using the Shift+E keyboard shortcut.

Common parameters

The Common Parameters rollout in the Render Scene dialog box includes the same controls regardless of the renderer being used.

The Time Output section defines which animation frames to include in the output. The Single option renders the current frame specified by the Time Slider. The Active Time Segment option renders the complete range of frames. The Range option lets you set a unique range of frames to render by entering the beginning and ending frame numbers. The last option is Frames, where you can enter individual frames and ranges using commas and hyphens. For example, entering 1, 6, 8-12 will render frames 1, 6, and 8 through 12. There is also an Every Nth Frame value, which is active for the Active Time Segment and Range options. It renders every nth frame in the active segment. For example, entering 3 would cause every third frame to be rendered. This option is useful for sped-up animations. The File Number Base is the number to add or subtract from the current frame number for the reference numbers attached to the end of each image file. For example, a File Number Base value of 10 for a Range value of 1–10 would label the files as image0011, image0012, and so on.

The Output Size section defines the resolution of the rendered images or animation. The drop-down list includes a list of standard film and video resolutions, including various 35mm and 70mm options, Anamorphic, Panavision, IMAX, VistaVision, NTSC, PAL, and HDTV standards. There is also a Custom option for selecting your own resolution.

Aperture Width is a property of cameras that defines the relationship between the lens and the field of view. The resolutions listed in the Aperture Width drop-down list alter this value without changing the view by modifying the Lens value in the scene.

For each resolution, you can change the Width and Height values. Each resolution also has six preset buttons for setting these values.

Tip   You can set the resolutions of any of the preset buttons by right-clicking the button you want to change. The Configure Preset dialog box opens, where you can set the button's Width, Height, and Pixel Aspect values.

The Image Aspect is the ratio of the image width to its height. You can also set the Pixel Aspect ratio to correct rendering on different devices. Both of these values have lock icons to their left that lock the aspect ratio for the set resolution. Locking the aspect ratio automatically changes the Width dimension whenever the Height value is changed and vice versa. The Aperture Width, Image Aspect, and Pixel Aspect values can be set only when Custom is selected in the drop-down list.

The Options section includes the following options:

- ✦ **Video Color Check:** Enables a check for nonsafe NTSC or PAL colors. Nonsafe colors are displayed incorrectly when these formats are used.

- ✦ **Force 2-Sided:** Renders both sides of every face. This option essentially doubles the render time and should be used only if singular faces or the inside of an object are visible.

- ✦ **Atmospherics:** Renders any atmospheric effects that are set up in the Environment dialog box.

- ✦ **Effects:** Enables any Render Effects that have been set up.

- ✦ **Super Black:** Enables Super Black, which is used for video compositing. Rendered images with black backgrounds have trouble in some video formats. The Super Black option prevents these problems.

✦ **Displacement:** Enables any surface displacement caused by an applied displacement map.

✦ **Render Hidden:** Renders all objects in the scene, including hidden objects. Using this option, you can hide objects for quick viewport updates and include them in the final rendering.

✦ **Render to Fields:** Enables animations to be rendered as fields. Fields are used by video formats. Video animations include a field with every odd scan line and one field with every even scan line. These fields are composited when displayed.

The Advanced Lighting section offers options to use Advanced Lighting or Computer Advanced Lighting when Required. Advanced lighting can take a long time to compute, so these two options give you the ability to turn advanced lighting on or off.

I cover advanced lighting in more detail in Chapter 23, "Advanced Lighting and Radiosity."

The Render Output section enables you to output the image or animations to a file, a device, or the Virtual Frame Buffer. To save the output to a file, click the Files button and select a location in the Render Output File dialog box. Supported formats include AVI, BMP, Postscript (EPS), JPEG, Kodak Cineon (CIN), FLC, QuickTime (MOV), PNG, RLA, RPF, SGI's Format (RGB), Targa (TGA), and TIF. The Device button can output to a device such as a video recorder. If the Virtual Frame Buffer option is selected, then both the Files and Devices buttons are disabled. (The Virtual Frame Buffer is discussed later in this chapter.)

The Net Render option enables network rendering. The Skip Existing Images option doesn't replace any images with the same filename, a feature that you can use to continue a rendering job that has been canceled.

For more information on network rendering, see Chapter 38, "Network Rendering."

Render elements

All images are made up from several different rendering passes. For example, the first pass might place the background, the second pass might render the diffuse color of the objects, and the third might do the shadows and so forth. The Render Elements rollout will let you isolate and render individually each pass.

Using these different effects passes, you can use them to composite images or as input into different special effects packages.

The details on render elements along with render effects are covered in Chapter 36, "Using Render Elements and Render Effects."

Current renderers

The Current Renderers rollout, shown in Figure 34-5, lets you assign the renderer to use for Production, Draft, and ActiveShade render modes. Click one of the Assign buttons to select a new renderer for each mode. In the default setup, the two renderer options are the Default Scanline Renderer and the VUE File Renderer.

The VUE File Renderer is covered later in this chapter.

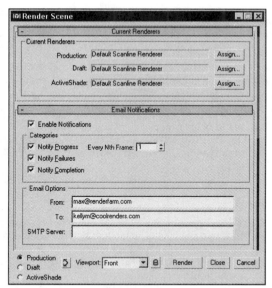

Figure 34-5: The Current Renderers and Email Notifications rollouts let you select the default renderer and configure e-mail to be sent when a rendering is complete.

E-mail notifications

The process of rendering an animation (or even a single frame) can be brief or it can take several days depending on the complexity of the scene. For complex scenes that will take a while to render, you can configure Max to send you an e-mail when your rendering is complete or if it fails.

 New Feature E-mail notifications are new to 3ds max 5.

In addition to the options, you can enter who the e-mail is from, who it is to, and an SMTP Server.

Scanline A-Buffer renderer

The Max Default Scanline A-Buffer rollout, shown in Figure 34-6, is the default renderer rollout that appears in the Render Scene dialog box. If a different renderer is loaded, then a different rollout for that renderer is displayed in the dialog box.

You can use the Options section at the top of the Scanline A-Buffer rollout to quickly disable various render options for quicker results. These options include Mapping, Shadows, Auto Reflect/Refract and Mirrors, and Force Wireframe. For the Force Wireframe option, you can define a Wire Thickness value in pixels. The Enabled SSE option will use Streaming SIMD (Single Instruction, Multiple Data) Extensions to speed up the rendering process by processing more data per instruction.

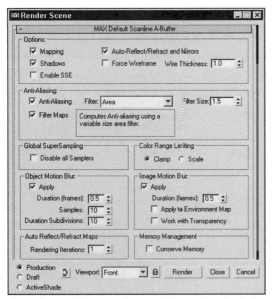

Figure 34-6: The Scanline A-Buffer rollout includes settings unique to this renderer.

Tip

Intel Pentium III and later processors include the SSE instructions and can benefit from enabling this option.

Another way to speed up rendering is to disable the Anti-Aliasing and Filter Maps features. Anti-Aliasing smoothes jagged edges that appear where colors change. The Filter Maps option enables you to disable the computationally expensive process of filtering material maps. The Filter drop-down list lets you select image filters that are applied at the pixel level during rendering. Below the drop-down list is a description of the current filter. The Filter Size value applies only to the Soften filter. Available filters include the following:

✦ **Area:** Does an anti-aliasing sweep using the designated area specified by the Filter Size value.

✦ **Blackman:** Sharpens the image with a 25-pixel area. It provides no edge enhancement.

✦ **Blend:** Somewhere between a sharp and a coarse Soften filter. It includes Filter Size and Blend values.

✦ **Catmull-Rom:** Sharpens with a 25-pixel filter and includes edge enhancement.

✦ **Cook Variable:** Can produce sharp results for small Filter Size values and blurred images for larger values.

✦ **Cubic:** Based on cubic-spline curves and produces a blurring effect.

✦ **Mitchell-Netravali:** Includes Blur and Ringing parameters.

✦ **Plate Match/MAX R2:** Matches mapped objects against background plates as used in Max R2.

✦ **Quadratic:** Based on a quadratic spline and produces blurring with a 9-pixel area.

✦ **Sharp Quadratic:** Produces sharp effects from a 9-pixel area.

✦ **Soften:** Causes mild blurring and includes a Filter Size value.

✦ **Video:** Blurs the image using a 25-pixel filter optimized for NTSC and PAL video.

Global SuperSampling is an additional anti-aliasing process that you can apply to materials. This process can take a long time to render; you can disable it using the Disable all Samplers option.

Color Range Limiting offers two methods for correcting overbrightness caused by applying filters. The Clamp method lowers any value above a relative ceiling of 1 to 1 and raises any values below 0 to 0. The Scale method scales all colors between the maximum and minimum values.

The Scanline A-Buffer rollout also offers two different types of motion blur: Object Motion Blur and Image Motion Blur. You can enable either of these using the Apply options.

Object Motion Blur is set in the Properties dialog box for each object. The renderer completes this blur by rendering the object over several frames. The movement of the camera doesn't affect this type of blur. The Duration value determines how long the object is blurred between frames. The Samples value specifies how many Duration units are sampled. The Duration Subdivision value is the number of copies rendered within each Duration segment. All these values can have a maximum setting of 16. The smoothest blurs occur when the Duration and Samples values are equal.

Image Motion Blur is also set in the Properties dialog box for each object. This type of blur is affected by the movement of the camera and is applied after the image has been rendered. You achieve this blur by smearing the image in proportion to the movement of the various objects. The Duration value determines the time length of the blur between frames. The Apply to Environment Map option lets you apply the blurring effect to the background as well as the objects. The Work with Transparency option blurs transparent objects without affecting their transparent regions. Using this option adds time to the rendering process.

Cross-Reference
You can add two additional blur effects to a scene: the Blur Render Effect, found in the Rendering Effects dialog box (covered in Chapter 36, "Using Render Elements and Render Effects") and the Scene Motion Blur effect, available through the Video Post dialog box (covered in Chapter 39, "Post-Processing with the Video Post Interface").

The Auto Reflect/Refract Maps section lets you specify a Rendering Iterations value for reflection maps within the scene. The higher the value, the more objects are included in the reflection computations, and the longer the rendering time.

The Conserve Memory option optimizes the rendering process to use the least amount of memory as possible. If you plan on using Max (or some other program) while it is rendering, you should enable this option.

Rendering Preferences

In addition to the settings available in the Render Scene dialog box, the Rendering panel in the Preference Settings dialog box includes many global rendering settings. The Preference Settings dialog box can be opened using the Customize ⇨ Preferences menu command. Figure 34-7 shows this panel.

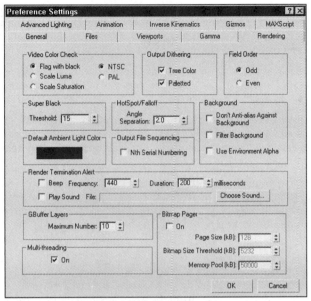

Figure 34-7: The Rendering panel in the Preference Settings dialog box lets you set global rendering settings.

The Video Color Check options specify how unsafe video colors are flagged or corrected. The Flag with black option shows the unsafe colors, and the Scale Luma and Scale Saturation options correct them by scaling either the luminance or the saturation until they are in range. You can also choose to check NTSC or PAL formats.

Caution   Be aware that the Scale options can discolor some objects.

Output Dithering options can enable or disable dithering of colors. The options include True Color for 24-bit images and Paletted for 8-bit images.

The Field Order options let you select which field is rendered first. Some video devices use even first, and others use odd first. Check your specific device to see which setting is correct.

The Super Black Threshold setting is the level below which black is displayed as Super Black.

The Angle Separation value sets the angle between the Hotspot and Falloff cones of a light. If the Hotspot angle equals the Falloff angle, then alias artifacts will appear.

The Don't Anti-alias Against Background option should be enabled if you plan on using a rendered object as part of a composite image. The Filter Background option includes the background image in the anti-aliasing calculations. The Use Environment Alpha option combines the background image's alpha channel with the scene object's alpha channel.

The Default Ambient Light Color is the darkest color for rendered shadows in the scene. Selecting a color other than black brightens the shadows.

You can set the Output File Sequencing option to list the frames in order if the Nth Serial Numbering option is enabled. If the Nth Serial Numbering option is disabled, the sequence uses the actual frame numbers.

In the Render Termination Alert section, you can elect to have a beep triggered when a rendering job is finished. The Frequency value changes the pitch of the sound, and the Duration value changes its length. You can also choose to load and play a different sound. The Choose Sound button opens a File dialog box where you can select the sound file to play.

The GBuffer Layers value is the maximum number of graphics buffers to allow during rendering. This value can range between 1 and 1000. The value you can use depends on the memory of your system.

The Multi-threading option enables the renderer to complete different rendering tasks as separate threads. Threads use the available processor cycles more efficiently by subdividing tasks. This option should be enabled, especially if you're rendering on a multiprocessor computer.

The Bitmap Pager option breaks rendered images into pages with a specified size. This keeps images from becoming so large that they become difficult to work with. Once enabled, you can specify the Page Size, the Bitmap Size Threshold, and the size in KB of the Memory Pool.

 New Feature The Bitmap Pager feature is new to 3ds max 5.

Creating VUE Files

One of the default Current Renderer options available in the Render Scene panel is the VUE File Renderer. This renderer creates VUE files. A VUE file is a text-based script for rendering a scene that you can edit using a text editor.

The contents of a VUE file include keywords followed by a list of parameters. These keywords include objects such as "light" and "camera," and commands such as "transform" and "top." Parameters can include the part name and values separated by commas. Figure 34-8 shows a sample VUE file.

```
balloons.vue - Notepad                                          _ □ ×
File   Edit   Search   Help
VERSION 202

frame 0
transform "b1" 53.8352 0 0 0 53.8352 0 0 0 53.8352 18.0705 8.8109 15.3547
transform "b2" 53.8352 0 0 0 53.8352 0 0 0 53.8352 7.192 -3.7562 10.2162
transform "b3" 53.8352 0 0 0 53.8352 0 0 0 53.8352 -15.1421 -7.7367 7.568
transform "b4" 53.8352 0 0 0 53.8352 0 0 0 53.8352 3.2247 15.9142 -3.3428
transform "b5" 53.8352 0 0 0 53.8352 0 0 0 53.8352 -4.911 -17.1343 11.2872
transform "b6" 53.8352 0 0 0 53.8352 0 0 0 53.8352 -8.3246 4.1654 10.9519
transform "string" 53.8352 0 0 0 53.8352 0 0 0 53.8352 -0.1146 -1.2278 -35.4199

frame 1
transform "b1" 53.8352 0 0 0 53.8352 0 0 0 53.8352 18.0705 8.8109 15.3547
transform "b2" 53.8352 0 0 0 53.8352 0 0 0 53.8352 7.192 -3.7562 10.2162
transform "b3" 53.8352 0 0 0 53.8352 0 0 0 53.8352 -15.1421 -7.7367 7.568
transform "b4" 53.8352 0 0 0 53.8352 0 0 0 53.8352 3.2247 15.9142 -3.3428
transform "b5" 53.8352 0 0 0 53.8352 0 0 0 53.8352 -4.911 -17.1343 11.2872
transform "b6" 53.8352 0 0 0 53.8352 0 0 0 53.8352 -8.3246 4.1654 10.9519
transform "string" 53.8352 0 0 0 53.8352 0 0 0 53.8352 -0.1146 -1.2278 -35.4199

frame 2
transform "b1" 53.8352 0 0 0 53.8352 0 0 0 53.8352 18.0705 8.8109 15.3547
transform "b2" 53.8352 0 0 0 53.8352 0 0 0 53.8352 7.192 -3.7562 10.2162
transform "b3" 53.8352 0 0 0 53.8352 0 0 0 53.8352 -15.1421 -7.7367 7.568
transform "b4" 53.8352 0 0 0 53.8352 0 0 0 53.8352 3.2247 15.9142 -3.3428
transform "b5" 53.8352 0 0 0 53.8352 0 0 0 53.8352 -4.911 -17.1343 11.2872
transform "b6" 53.8352 0 0 0 53.8352 0 0 0 53.8352 -8.3246 4.1654 10.9519
transform "string" 53.8352 0 0 0 53.8352 0 0 0 53.8352 -0.1146 -1.2278 -35.4199

frame 3
```

Figure 34-8: A sample VUE file viewed in a text editor

When the VUE File Renderer is selected, the rollout in the Render Scene dialog box includes only a single Files button for giving the VUE file a name.

Caution   Be sure to use the Files button in the VUE File Renderer rollout and not the Files button in the Common Parameters rollout. When a VUE file is rendered, the Virtual Frame Buffer opens, but no image is created.

Using the Virtual Frame Buffer

The Virtual Frame Buffer is a temporary window that holds any rendered images. Often when developing a scene, you want to test-render an image to view the shadows or transparency not visible in the viewports. The Virtual Frame Buffer, shown in Figure 34-9, enables you to view these test renderings without saving any data to the network or hard drive.

Figure 34-9: The Virtual Frame Buffer displays rendered images without saving them to a file. This scene uses a background image from Corel's Photo CD and a crocodile model created by Viewpoint Datalabs.

This buffer opens when you select the Virtual Frame Buffer option and click the Render button in the Render Scene dialog box. You can also view images from a local hard drive or a network drive in the Virtual Frame Buffer using the File ➪ View Image File menu command.

To zoom in on the buffer, hold down the Ctrl key and click the buffer. Click with the right mouse button while holding down the Ctrl key to zoom out. The Shift key enables you to pan the buffer image. You can also use the mouse wheel (if you have a scrolling mouse) to zoom and pan within the frame buffer.

Tip   You can zoom and pan the image while it is rendering.

 At the top of the frame buffer dialog box are several icon buttons. The first is the Save Bitmap button, which enables you to save the current frame buffer image.

 The Clone Virtual Frame Buffer button creates another frame buffer dialog box. Any new rendering is rendered to this new dialog box, which is useful for comparing two images.

The next four buttons enable the red, green, blue, and alpha channels. The alpha channel holds any transparency information for the image. The alpha channel is a grayscale map, with black showing the transparent areas and white showing the opaque areas. Next to the Display Alpha Channel button is the Monochrome button, which displays the image as a grayscale image.

 The Clear button erases the image from the window.

The Channel Display drop-down list lets you select the channel to display. The color swatch at the right shows the color of the currently selected pixel. You can select new pixels by right-clicking and holding on the image. This temporarily displays a small dialog box with the image dimensions and the RGB value of the pixel directly under the cursor. The color in the color swatch can then be dragged and dropped in other dialog boxes such as the Material Editor.

Using the RAM Player

Just as you can use the Virtual Frame Buffer to view and compare rendered images, the RAM Player enables you to view rendered animations in memory. With animations loaded in memory, you can selectively change the frame rates. Figure 34-10 shows the RAM Player interface, which you open by choosing Rendering ➪ RAM Player.

Figure 34-10: The RAM Player interface lets you load two different images or animations for comparison.

The button icons at the top of the RAM Player interface window, shown in the following table, enable you to load an image to two different channels named A and B. The two Open Channel buttons open a file dialog box where you can select the file to load. Notice how the image on the right side of the RAM Player is a different frame than the left side.

Button	Description
	Open Channel
	Open Last Rendered Image
	Close Channel
	Save Channel
A|B	Horizontal/Vertical Screen Split
	Double Buffer

The Open Last Rendered Image button in the RAM Player interface window provides quick access to the last rendered image. The Close Channel button clears the channel. The Save Channel button opens a file dialog box for saving the current file.

Caution   All files that load into the RAM Player are converted to 24-bit images.

The Channel A and Channel B (toggle) buttons enable either channel or both. The Horizontal/ Vertical Screen Split button switches the dividing line between the two channels to a horizontal or vertical line. When the images are aligned one on top of the other, two small triangles mark where one channel leaves off and the other begins. You can drag these triangles to alter the space for each channel.

The frame controls let you move between the frames. You can move to the first, previous, next, or last frame and play the animation forward or in reverse. The drop-down list to the right of the frame controls displays the current frame rate setting.

You can capture the color of any pixel in the image by holding down the Ctrl key while clicking the image with the right mouse button. This puts the selected color in the color swatch. The RGB value for this pixel is displayed in the blue title bar.

The Double Buffer button synchronizes the frames of the two channels.

Tip   You can use the arrow keys and Page Up and Page Down keys to move through the frames of the animation. The A and B keys are used to enable the two channels.

Render Types

From the main toolbar, the Render Type drop-down list enables you to render subsections of the scene. The default setting is View. This renders the entire view as shown in the active viewport. After you pick a selection from the list, click the Quick Render button or the Render button in the Render Scene dialog box to begin the rendering.

The Selected setting renders only the selected objects in the active viewport. The Region setting puts a frame of dotted lines with handles in the active viewport. This frame lets you define a region to render. You can resize the frame by dragging the handles. When you have defined the region, click the OK button that appears in the lower-right corner of the active viewport.

The Crop setting is similar to Region in that it uses a frame to define a region, but the Crop setting doesn't include the areas outside the defined frame. The Blowup setting takes the defined region and increases its size to fill the render window. The frame for Blowup is constrained to the aspect ratio of the final resolution.

The Box Selected setting renders the selected objects, but it presents a dialog box where you can specify the dimensions for rendering the bounding box of the selected objects. Constrain the Aspect Ratio is an additional option.

Rendering to a Texture

When working with a game engine, game designers are always looking for ways to increase the speed and detail of objects in the game. One common way to speed game calculations is to pre-render the textures used in a game and then to save these textures as a texture map. The texture map takes more memory to save, but can greatly speed the rendering time required by the game engine. This process of pre-rendering a texture is called texture baking.

 Caution   If you bake a texture into an object and then render it with the rest of the scene, then the object will get a double dose of light.

Texture baking can be accomplished in Max using the Rendering ⇨ Render to Texture menu command (or by pressing the 0 key). This opens the Render to Textures dialog box. In several ways, the Render to Textures dialog box resembles the Render Scene dialog box including the Render, Update Last, Close, and Cancel buttons found at the bottom edge of the interface.

 New Feature   The Render to Textures dialog box is new to 3ds max 5.

General Settings

In the General Settings rollout, shown in Figure 34-11, you can select to bake the Selected Objects or All Prepared Objects, which are all objects with at least one texture element. Texture elements are added using the Selected Object Settings rollout.

If the Automatic Unwrap Mapping option is enabled, then the object to be baked has the Unwrap UVW modifier applied using the Flatten mapping type. For this type, you can set the Threshold Angle (which is the difference between the normals of adjacent faces; if the angular value is greater than the Threshold Angle value, then a hard edge is created between the faces), the Spacing (which is the amount of space between different map pieces) and whether map pieces can be rotated and filled in holes of larger map pieces. The Clear Unwrappers remove any previous Unwrap UVW modifiers from the object.

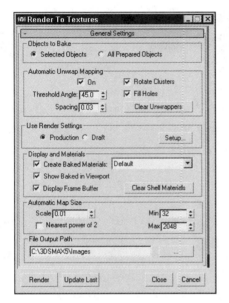

Figure 34-11: The General Settings rollout of the Render to Textures panel includes settings for all objects.

For the render pass, you can use the Production or Draft render settings. The Setup button opens the Render Scene panel, where you can change the render settings.

The Create Baked Materials option lets you select from a drop-down list the type of material to use to display the texture in the viewports. The options include Default, Standard Material – Save All, Standard Material – Complete Only, Light Map, and Metal Bump. The first three options appear in the Material Editor within a Shell material, but the Light Map and Metal Bump options are viewport shaders. If the Direct3D display driver is being used, you can access the settings for these viewport shaders at the bottom of the Material Editor.

Caution   The Direct3D viewport shaders are only available if the Direct3D display driver is being used. Chapter 4, "Customizing the Max Interface," explains how to change this display driver.

The Show Baked in Viewport displays the baked texture in the viewport, and the Display Frame Buffer option opens the Virtual Frame Buffer when the texture is rendered. This is a good check to see the resulting texture as a map. The Clear Shell Materials button removes the Shell materials for the baked objects and restores their original materials.

The size of the texture map depends on the size of the object, but you can set a Scale value for greater resolution and set a Min and Max value to keep the maps within reason. By default, maps are saved to the /images directory, but you can select a different directory if you wish.

Object Settings

The Selected Object Settings rollout, shown in Figure 34-12 can be different for different selections. The Enable option can disable the settings for the selected object. By default, the unwrap mapping uses channel 3, but you can change this channel if you wish. If a different mapping uses channel 3 and you don't change this, the new mapping will replace the old one. The Edge Padding defines the overlap in pixels of the texture.

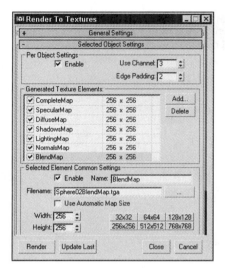

Figure 34-12: The Selected Object Settings rollout of the Render to Textures panel includes settings for specific objects.

Clicking the Add button lets you select the type of texture maps that you can render. You will want to use different maps depending on the purpose of the map, and you may want to render several at a time. The available types are CompleteMap, SpecularMap, DiffuseMap, ShadowsMap, LightingMap, NormalsMap, BlendMap, and AlphaMap. Elements that are added to the list can be disabled using the check box to its left. You can also change the map size or use the Automatic Map Size option, which will base the map size on the object size. Some map elements present of list of components to include in the map. These components will appear in another rollout.

Tutorial: Baking a hammer texture

To practice baking textures, I've reached into my toolbox and found a hammer. For this example, we'll bake a complete map of just the hammer's head. Now I need to find a game engine to run it in.

To bake a hammer texture, follow these steps:

1. Open the Hammer with baked texture.max file from the Chap 34 directory on the CD-ROM.

   This file includes a hammer model created by Zygote Media.

2. Select Rendering ➪ Render to Texture (or press the 0 key) to open the Render to Textures panel.

3. Select the hammer head object. In the Render to Textures panel, set the Threshold Angle to 75, and make sure the Display Frame Buffer option is set. In the Selected Object Settings rollout, click the Add button and double-click the CompleteMap option. Set the Map Size to 512 × 512 and click the Render button.

Figure 34-13 shows the resulting texture map. If you look in the Modify panel, you will see that Automatic Flatten UVs modifier has been applied to the object. If you look at the material applied to the object, you'll see that it consists of a Shell material.

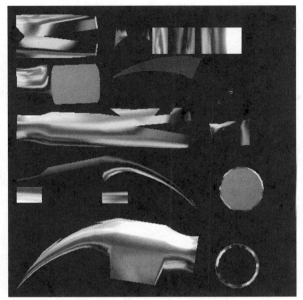

Figure 34-13: A texture map created with the Render to Textures panel

Summary

This chapter covered the basics of producing output using the Render Scene dialog box. Although rendering a scene can take a long time to complete, Max includes many settings that can speed up the process, as well as helpful tools such as the Virtual Frame Buffer and the RAM Player.

In this chapter, you've

+ Learned to work with ActiveShade window

+ Discovered how to control the various render parameters

+ Configured the global rendering preferences

+ Created VUE files

+ Learned to use the Virtual Frame Buffer and the RAM Player

+ Seen the different render types

+ Baked textures using the Render to Textures feature

The next chapter covers working with environments and atmospheric effects such as fog and fire.

✦   ✦   ✦

Working with Environments and Atmospheric Effects

◆ ◆ ◆ ◆

In This Chapter

Creating an environment

Using Atmospheric Apparatus gizmos to position atmospheric effects

Creating atmospheric effects, including Fire, Fog, and Volume Fog

◆ ◆ ◆ ◆

I n the real world, an environment of some kind surrounds all objects. The environment does a lot to set the ambiance of the scene. For example, an animation set at night in the woods would have a very different environment than one set at the horse races during the middle of the day. Max includes dialog boxes for setting the color, background images, and lighting environment; these features can help define your scene.

This chapter also covers atmospheric effects, which include the likes of clouds, fog, fire, and volume lights. These effects can only be seen when the scene is rendered.

Creating an Environment

Whether it's a beautiful landscape or just clouds drifting by, the environment behind the scene can do a lot to make the scene more believable. In this section, you learn to define an environment using the Rendering ⇨ Environment panel.

Environment maps are used as background for the scene and can also be used as images reflected off shiny objects. Environment maps are displayed only in the final rendering and not in the viewports, but you can add a background to any viewport and even set the environment map to be displayed as the viewport backdrop.

Cross-Reference
Chapter 2, "Working with the Viewports," covers adding a background image to a viewport.

But there is more to an environment than just a background. It also involves altering the global lighting, controlling exposure, and introducing atmosphere effects.

Defining the rendered environment

You create environments in the Environment panel, shown in Figure 35-1, which you can open by choosing Rendering ⇨ Environment (or by pressing the 8 key). Several settings make up an environment, including a background color or image, global lighting, exposure control, and atmospheric effects. All of these elements are available in the Environment panel.

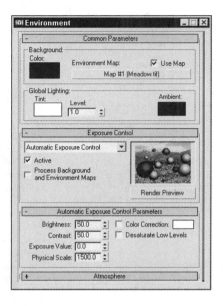

Figure 35-1: The Environment panel lets you select a background color or image, define global lighting, control exposure, and work with atmospheric effects.

Setting a background color

The first color swatch in the Environment panel lets you specify a background color. This color appears by default if no environment map is specified or if the Use Map option is disabled (and is black by default). The background color is animatable, so you can set the background color to start black and slowly fade to white.

Using a background image

To select a background image to be used as an environment map, click the Environment Map button in the Environment panel to open the Material/Map browser. If you want to load a bitmap image as the background image, double-click the Bitmap selection to open the Select Bitmap Image dialog box. Locate the bitmap to use and click OK. The bitmap name appears on the Environment Map button.

Tip

If the environment map you want to use is already displayed in one of the Material Editor sample slots, you can drag it directly from the Material Editor and drop it on the Map button in the Environment panel.

To change any of the environment map parameters (such as the mapping coordinates), you need to load the environment map into the Material Editor. You can do so by dragging the map button from the Environment panel onto one of the sample slots in the Material Editor. After releasing the material, the Instance (Copy) Map dialog box asks whether you want to create an Instance or a Copy. If you select Instance, any parameter changes you make to the material automatically update the map in the Environment panel.

Cross-Reference

For more information about the types of mapping parameters that are available, see Chapter 20, "Using Material Maps."

The background image doesn't need to be an image — you can also load animations. Supported formats include AVI, FLC, and IFL files.

Figure 35-2 shows a scene with an image of the Golden Gate Bridge loaded as the environment map. Viewpoint Datalabs created the airplane model.

Figure 35-2: The results of a background image loaded into the Environment panel.

Setting global lighting

The Tint color swatch in the Global Lighting section of the Environment panel specifies a color used to tint all lights. The Level value increases or decreases the overall lighting level for all lights in the scene. The Ambient color swatch sets the color for the ambient light in the scene, which is the darkest color that any shadows in the scene can be. You can animate all of these settings.

Tutorial: Creating a mystery with an environment map

The inspector has been called to investigate a robbery threat, but he happens to have a bad case of the flu and can't get out of bed, so he sends his apprentice to cover for him. The apprentice decides to set up a camera with a trip wire to catch the thief in the act.

The next day, after retrieving the camera, the inspector's apprentice is excited to see that a picture has been taken. It looks as if his plan has worked, but, after developing the film, the apprentice is shocked to see that someone bumped the camera and the thief got away — or did he?

To reflect an environment map, follow these steps:

1. Open the Mystery reflection.max file from the Chap 35 directory on the CD-ROM.

   This file contains a thief model. (This thief is a model imported from Poser.)

2. Choose Rendering ⇨ Environment (or press the 8 key) to open the Environment panel and then click the Environment Map button to open the Material/Map Browser. Double-click the Bitmap selection and open the interior.tif image from the Chap 35 directory on the CD-ROM (This image was taken from a Corel Photo CD.) Before closing the Environment panel, make sure the Use Map option is selected.

3. Choose Rendering ⇨ Render and click the Render button to render the image. Save it as a file named **mystery.tif**.

4. Next, open the Mystery photo.max file from the Chap 35 directory on the CD-ROM.

   This file contains a simple umbrella holder created from primitives. A raytrace material was applied to the umbrella holder to provide a good reflective surface.

5. Choose Rendering ⇨ Environment (or press the 8 key) to open the Environment panel. Click the Environment Map button to open the Material/Map Browser. Double-click the Bitmap selection to open the Select Bitmap Image File dialog box and locate and load the mystery.jpg file you created earlier.

6. Open the Material Editor and drag the environment map to the third sample slot. Select the Instance option from the Instance (Copy) Map dialog box that appears and click OK. Under the Coordinates rollout, select Cylindrical Environment from the Mapping drop-down list. Set the U Tiling value to 0.5 and the V Tiling value to 2.0.

   This positions the thief where you can see his reflection on the umbrella holder. Because the material for the Environment Map is an instance, it is automatically updated when these changes are made.

Figure 35-3 shows the resulting image with the thief reflected.

Setting exposure

The Exposure Control rollout of the Environment panel lets you control output levels and color rendering ranges. Controlling the exposure of film is a common procedure when working with film and can result in a different look for your scene. The default selection is Automatic Exposure Control.

The Active option lets you turn this feature on and off. The Process Background and Environment Maps option causes the exposure settings to affect the background and environment images. When this option is disabled, then only the scene objects will be affected by the exposure control settings. The Exposure Control rollout also includes a Render Preview button that displays the rendered scene in a tiny pane. The preview pane is small, but for most types of exposure control settings, it is enough. When you click the Render Preview button, the scene is rendered. This preview will then be automatically updated whenever a setting is changed.

New Feature   The Render Preview pane is new to 3ds max 5.

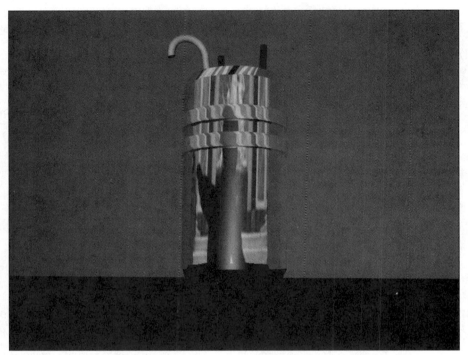

Figure 35-3: This rendered image shows an Environment Map being reflected.

Automatic, Linear, and Logarithmic Exposure Control

Selecting Automatic Exposure Control from the drop-down list automatically adjusts your rendered output to be closer to what your eyes can detect. Monitors are notoriously bad at reducing the dynamic range of the colors in your rendered image. This setting provides the needed adjustments to match the expanded dynamic range of your eyes.

When the Automatic Exposure Control option is selected, a new rollout appears in the Environment panel. This rollout includes settings for Brightness, Contrast, Exposure Value, and Physical Scale. You can also enable Color Correction and select a color and select an option to Desaturate Low Levels. The Brightness and Contrast settings can range from 0 to 100. A Contrast value of 0 displays all scene objects with the same flat gray color, and a Brightness value of 100 displays all scene objects with the same flat white color. The Exposure Value can range from –5 to 5 and determines the amount of light that is allowed in the scene.

Another exposure control option is Linear Exposure Control. Although this option presents the same settings as the Automatic Exposure Control, the differences between the minimum and maximum values are a straight line across the light spectrum.

New Feature The Linear, Logarithmic, and Pseudo Color Exposure Control options are all new to 3ds max 5.

The Logarithmic Exposure Control option replaces the Exposure Value setting with a Mid Tones setting. This setting controls the colors between the lowest and highest values. This exposure control option also includes options to Affect Indirect Only and Exterior Daylight. You should enable the Affect Indirect Only if you use only standard lights in the scene, but if your scene includes an IES Sun light, then enable the Exterior Daylight option to tone down the intensity of the light.

Cross-Reference

You should always use the Logarithmic Exposure Control setting when enabling the advanced lighting features because it works well with the low-level light. You can learn more about the advanced lighting features in Chapter 23, "Advanced Lighting and Radiosity."

Pseudo Color Exposure Control

As you work with advanced lighting solutions and with radiosity, it can be difficult to tell whether interior spaces and objects have too much light or not enough light, especially comparing objects on opposite sides of the scene. This is where the Pseudo Color Exposure Control option comes in handy.

This exposure control option projects a band of colors (or grayscale) in place of the material and object colors that represent the illumination or luminance values for the scene. With these pseudo-colors, you can quickly determine where all the lighting is consistent and where it needs to be addressed.

In the Pseudo Color Exposure Control rollout, shown in Figure 35-4, you can select to apply the colors to show Illumination or Luminance. You can also select to use a Colored or Grayscale style and to make the Scale Linear or Logarithmic. The Min and Max settings let you control the ranges of the colors, and there is also a Physical Scale setting. The color (or grayscale) band is shown across the bottom of the rollout with the values for each color underneath.

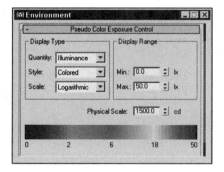

Figure 35-4: The Pseudo Color Exposure Control rollout can display illumination and luminance values as colors.

When this exposure control is used, the associated render element is automatically set in the Render Elements rollout of the Render Scene dialog box. If the scene is rendered, then the appropriate (Illumination or Luminance) render element is also rendered.

Cross-Reference

See Chapter 36, "Using Render Elements and Render Effects" for more on render elements.

Tutorial: Using the Logarithmic Exposure Control

As you start to use the new photometric lights, you'll probably find it difficult to get the settings just right. The results are oversaturation or undersaturation, but luckily the Logarithmic Exposure Control can quickly fix any problems that appear.

To adjust the effect of a photometric light using the Logarithmic Exposure Control, follow these steps:

1. Open the Array of chrome spheres.max file from the Chap 35 directory on the CD-ROM.

   This file contains lots and lots of chrome mapped spheres with advanced lighting enabled.

2. Choose Rendering ➪ Render (or press the F10 key) to open the Render Scene dialog box and click the Render button. It will take a while to render, but notice the results, shown on the left of Figure 35-5.

3. Choose Rendering ➪ Environment (or press the 8 key) to open the Environment panel. In the Exposure Control rollout, select Logarithmic Exposure Control from the drop-down list and enable the Active and Process Background and Environment Maps options. Then click the Render Preview button.

4. In the Logarithmic Exposure Control rollout, set the Brightness value to 60, the Contrast value to 100, and enable the Desaturate Low Levels option.

5. In the Render Scene dialog box, click the Render button again to see the updated rendering.

The image on the right of Figure 35-5 shows the rendered image with exposure control enabled.

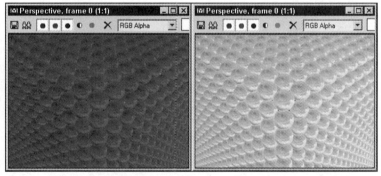

Figure 35-5: This rendered image shows an image before and after exposure control was enabled.

Creating Atmospheric Effects

The Environment panel also contains rollouts for adding atmospheric effects to your scene, but the first question is where. Atmospheric effects are placed within a container called an Atmospheric Apparatus gizmo, which tells the effect where it should be located. However, only the Fire and the Volume Fog effects need Atmospheric Apparatus gizmos. To create an

Atmospheric Apparatus gizmo, open the Create panel, click the Helper category, and select Atmospheric Apparatus from the subcategory drop-down list.

The three different Atmospheric Apparatus gizmos are BoxGizmo, SphereGizmo, and CylGizmo. Each of these has a different shape similar to the primitives.

Selecting a gizmo and opening the Modify panel reveals two different rollouts — one for defining the basic parameters such as the gizmo dimensions, and the other labeled Atmospheres & Effects, which you can use to Add or Delete an Environment Effect to the gizmo. Each gizmo parameters rollout also includes a Seed value and a New Seed button. The Seed value sets a random number used to compute the atmospheric effect, and the New Seed button automatically generates a random seed. Two gizmos with the same seed values have nearly identical results.

The Add button opens the Add Atmosphere dialog box where you can select an atmospheric effect. The selected effect is then included in a list in the Atmospheres & Effects rollout. You can delete these atmospheres by selecting them from the list and clicking the Delete button. The Setup button is active if an effect is selected in the list. It opens the Environment panel where the parameters for the effect are located. Adding Atmospheric Effects in the Modify panel is purely for convenience. They can also be added using the Environment panel.

In addition to the Modify panel, you can also add atmospheric effects to the scene using Atmosphere rollout in the Environment panel, shown in Figure 35-6. This rollout is pretty boring until you add an effect to it. You can add an effect by clicking on the Add button. This opens the Add Atmospheric Effect dialog box, which includes by default four atmospheric effects — Fire Effect, Fog, Volume Fog, and Volume Light. With plug-ins, you can increase the number of effects in this list. The effect that is selected is added to the Effects list in the Atmosphere rollout.

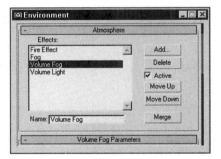

Figure 35-6: The Add Atmospheric Effect dialog box lets you select atmospheric effects.

You can delete an effect from the current Effects list in the Environment panel by selecting the effect and clicking the Delete button. The effects are applied in the order in which they are listed, so the effects at the bottom of the list are layered on top of all other effects. To the right of the Effects pane are the Move Up and Move Down buttons, used to position the effects in the list. Underneath the Effects pane is a Name field where you can type a new name for any effect in this field — this enables you to use the same effect multiple times. The Merge button opens the Merge Atmospheric Effects dialog box, where you can select a separate Max file. You can then select and load any render effects from the other file.

Using the Fire effect

To add the Fire effect to the scene, click the Add button and select the Fire Effect selection. This opens the Fire Effect Parameters rollout, shown in Figure 35-7. At the top of the Fire Effect

Parameters rollout is the Pick Gizmo button — clicking this button lets you select a gizmo in the scene. The selected gizmo appears in the drop-down list to the right. You can select multiple gizmos. To remove a gizmo from the list, select it and click the Remove Gizmo button.

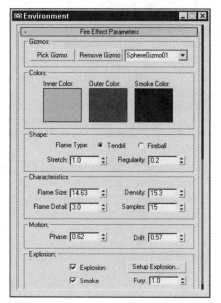

Figure 35-7: The Fire Parameters rollout lets you define the look of the effect.

Note   The Fire effect only renders in non-orthographic views such as Perspective or a camera view.

The three color swatches define the color of the fire effect and include an Inner Color, an Outer Color, and a Smoke Color. The Smoke Color is used only when the Explosion option is set. The default red and yellow colors make fairly realistic fire.

The Shape section includes two Flame Type options: Tendril and Fireball. The Tendril shape produces veins of flames, and the Fireball shape is rounder and puffier. Figure 35-8 shows four fire effects. The left two have the Tendril shape, and the two on the right are set to Fireball. The difference is in the Density and Flame Detail settings.

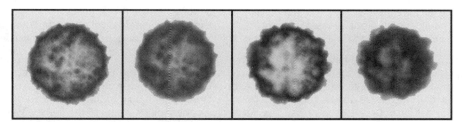

Figure 35-8: The Fire atmospheric effect can be either Tendril or Fireball shape.

The Stretch value elongates the individual flames along the gizmo's Z-axis. Figure 35-9 shows the results of using the Stretch value. The Stretch values for these gizmos are from left to right, 0.1, 1.0, 5.0, and 50.

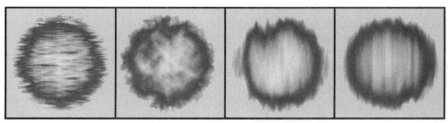

Figure 35-9: The Stretch value can elongate flames.

The Regularity value determines how much of the Atmospheric Apparatus is filled. The spherical gizmos in the previous figures were all set to 0.2, so the entire sphere shape wasn't filled. A setting of 1.0 will add a spherical look to the Fire effect, because the entire gizmo is filled. For a more random shape, use a small Regularity value.

The Flame Size value affects the overall size of each individual flame (though this is dependent on the gizmo size as well). The Flame Detail value controls the edge sharpness of each flame and can range from 1 to 10. Lower values produce fuzzy, smooth flames, but higher values result in sharper, more distinct flames.

The Density value determines the thickness of each flame in its center—higher Density values result in flames that are brighter at the center, while lower values produce thinner, wispy flames. Figure 35-10 shows the difference caused by the Density values, 10, 20, 50, and 100.

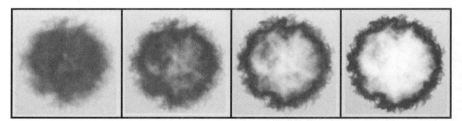

Figure 35-10: The Fire effect brightness is tied closely to the flame Density value.

The Samples value sets the rate at which the effect is sampled. Higher sample values are required for more detail, but increase the render time.

The Motion section includes options for setting the Phase and Drift of a fire effect. The Phase value determines how wildly the fire burns. For wild, out of control fire, animate the Phase value to change rapidly. For a constant, steady fire, keep the value constant throughout the frames. The Drift value sets the height of the flames. High Drift values produce high, hot-burning flames.

The Explosion section lets you make a fire into an explosion. When the Explosion check box is selected, the fire is set to explode. The Start and End Times for the explosion are set in the Setup Explosion Phase Curve dialog box that opens when the Setup Explosion button is clicked. If the Smoke option is checked, then the fire colors change to the smoke color for Phase values between 100 and 200. The Fury value varies the churning of the flames. Values greater than 1.0 cause faster churning, and values lower than 1.0 cause slower churning.

Tutorial: Creating the sun

You can use the Fire effect to create a realistic sun. The modeling part is easy—all it requires is a simple sphere—but the real effects come from the materials and the Fire effect.

To create a sun, follow these steps:

1. Open the Sun.max file from the Chap 35 directory on the CD-ROM.

   This file contains a simple sphere with a bright yellow material applied to it.

2. In the Create panel, select the Helpers category. Select the Atmospheric Apparatus subcategory. Click the SphereGizmo button and drag a sphere in the Front viewport that encompasses the "sun" sphere.

3. With the SphereGizmo still selected, open the Modify panel and click the Add button in the Atmospheres rollout. Select Fire Effect from the Add Atmospheres & Effects dialog box and click OK. Then select the Fire effect and click the Setup button.

   The Environment panel opens.

4. In the Fire Effects Parameters rollout, set the Inner Color to yellow, the Outer Color to red, and the Smoke color to black (these are the default colors). For the Flame Type, select Tendril with Stretch and Regularity values of 1. Set the Flame Size to 30, the Density to 15, the Flame Detail to 10, and the Samples to 15.

Figure 35-11 shows the resulting sun after it's been rendered.

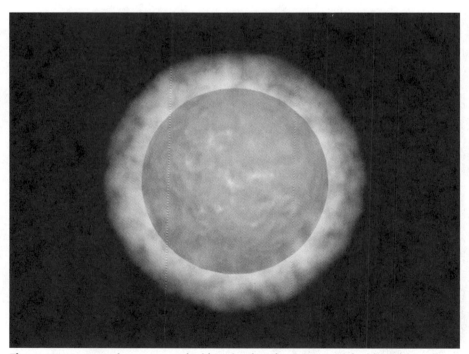

Figure 35-11: A sun image created with a simple sphere, a material with a Noise Bump map, and the Fire effect.

Tutorial: Creating clouds

Sky images are fairly easy to find, or you can just take your camera outside and capture your own. The trick comes when you are trying to weave an object in and out of clouds. Although you can do this with a Shadow/Matte mask, it would be easier if the clouds were actual 3D objects. In this tutorial, we create some simple clouds using the Fire effect.

To create some clouds for a sky backdrop, follow these steps:

1. Open the Clouds.max file from the Chap 35 directory on the CD-ROM. This file includes several hemispherical shaped atmospheric apparatus gizmos.

2. Choose Rendering ⇨ Environment (or press the 8 key) to open the Environment panel. Click the Background Color swatch and select a light blue color. In the Atmosphere section, click the Add button, select Fire Effect from the Add Atmospheric Effect list, and click OK.

3. Name the effect **Clouds**, and click each of the color swatches. Change the Inner Color to a dark gray, the Outer Color to a light gray, and the Smoke Color to white. Set the Shape to Fireball with a Stretch of 1 and a Regularity of 0.2. Set the Flame Size to 35, the Flame Detail to 3, the Density to 15, and the Samples to 15.

Tip   If you want to add some motion to the clouds, click the Animate button, drag the Time Slider to the last frame, and change the Phase value to 45 and the Drift value to 30. The clouds slowly drift through the sky. Disable the Animate button when you're finished.

4. In the Fire Effects Parameters rollout, click the Pick Gizmo button and then click on one of the gizmos in the viewports. Repeat this step until you've selected all the gizmos.

Figure 35-12 shows the resulting sky backdrop. By altering the Fire parameters, you can create different types of clouds.

Figure 35-12: You can use the Fire atmospheric effect to create clouds.

Using the Fog effect

Fog is an atmospheric effect that obscures objects or backgrounds by introducing a hazy layer — objects farther from the view are less visible. The normal Fog effect is used without an Atmospheric Apparatus gizmo and appears between the camera's environment range values. The camera's Near and Far Range settings set these values.

In the Environment panel, the Fog Parameters rollout appears when the Fog effect is added to the Effects list. This rollout, shown in Figure 35-13, includes a color swatch for setting the fog color. There is also an Environment Color Map button for loading a map. If a map is selected, the Use Map option turns it on or off. You can also select a map for the Environment Opacity, which affects the fog density.

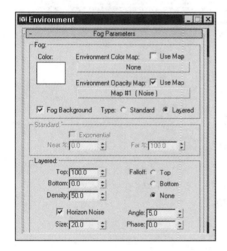

Figure 35-13: The Fog Parameters rollout lets you use either Standard fog or Layered fog.

The Fog Background option applies fog to the background image. The Type options include Standard and Layered fog. Selecting one of these fog background options enables its corresponding parameters.

The Standard parameters include an Exponential option for increasing density as a function of distance. If this option is disabled, the density is linear with distance. The Near and Far values are used to set the range densities.

Layered fog simulates layers of fog that move from dense areas to light areas. The Top and Bottom values set the limits of the fog, and the Density value sets its thickness. The Falloff option lets you set where the fog density goes to 0. The Horizon Noise option adds noise to the layer of fog at the horizon as determined by the Size, Angle, and Phase values.

Figure 35-14 shows several different fog options. The upper-left image uses the Standard option, and the upper-right image uses the Layered option with a Density of 50. The lower-left image also uses the Layered option and has a Density value of 20. The lower-right image has the Horizon Noise option enabled.

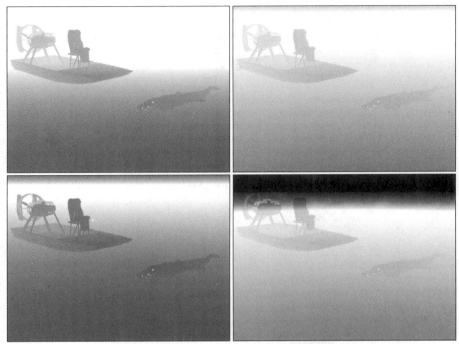

Figure 35-14: A rendered image with several different Fog effect options applied.

Using the Volume Fog effect

You can add the Volume Fog effect to a scene by clicking the Add button and selecting the Volume Fog selection. This effect is different from the Fog effect in that it gives you more control over the exact position of the fog. This position is set by an Atmospheric Apparatus gizmo. The Volume Fog Parameters rollout, shown in Figure 35-15, lets you select a gizmo to use with the Pick Gizmo button. The selected gizmo is included in the drop-down list to the right of the buttons. Multiple gizmos can be selected. The Remove Gizmo button removes the selected gizmo from the list.

Note   The Atmospheric Apparatus gizmo contains only a portion of the total Volume Fog effect. If the gizmo is moved or scaled, it displays a different cropped portion of fog.

The Soften Gizmo Edges value feathers the fog effect at each edge. This value can range from 0 to 1.

Many of the settings for Volume Fog are the same as those for the Fog effect, but Volume Fog has several settings that are unique to it. These settings help set the patchy nature of Volume Fog. Step Size determines how small the patches of fog are. The Max Steps value limits the sampling of these small steps to keep the render time in check.

The Noise section settings also help determine the randomness of Volume Fog. Noise types include Regular, Fractal, Turbulence, and Invert. The Noise Threshold limits the effect of noise. Wind settings include direction and Wind Strength. The Phase value determines how the fog moves.

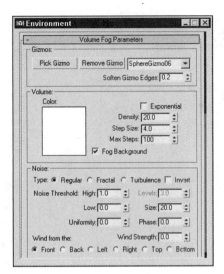

Figure 35-15: The Volume Fog Parameters rollout includes parameters for controlling the fog.

Tutorial: Creating a swamp scene

When I think of fog, I think of swamps. In this tutorial, we model a swamp scene. To use the Volume Fog effect to create the scene, follow these steps:

1. Open the Dragonfly in a foggy swamp.max file from the Chap 35 directory on the CD-ROM.

    This file includes several cattail plants and a dragonfly, created by Zygote Media, positioned on top of one of the cattails.

2. Open the Create panel and select the Helpers category. Select the Atmospheric Apparatus subcategory and click the BoxGizmo button. Drag a box that covers the lower half of the cattails.

3. Choose Rendering ➪ Environment (or press the 8 key) to open the Environment panel. Click the Add button to open the Add Atmospheric Effect dialog box and select Volume Fog. Click OK. In the Volume Fog Parameters rollout, click the Pick Gizmo button and select the BoxGizmo in a viewport.

4. Set the Density to 0.5 and the Noise Type to Turbulence. Then set the Wind Strength to 10 from the Left.

Figure 35-16 shows the finished image. Using Atmospheric Apparatus gizmos, you can position the fog in the exact place where you want it.

Using the Volume Light effect

The final choice in the effects dialog box is the Volume Light effect. This effect shares many of the same parameters as the other atmospheric effects. Although this is one of the atmospheric effects, it deals with lights and fits better in that section.

Cross-Reference   To learn about the Volume Light atmospheric effect, see Chapter 22, "Working with Lights."

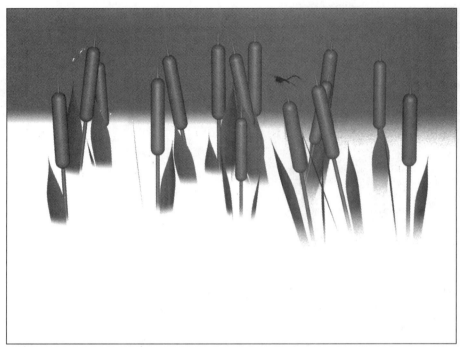

Figure 35-16: A rendered image that uses the Volume Fog effect.

Summary

Creating the right environment can add a lot of realism to any rendered scene. Using the Environment panel, you can alter the background color, load an environment map, set global lighting, and work with atmospheric effects. Atmospheric effects include Fire, Fog, Volume Fog, and Volume Light.

In this chapter, you've

- ✦ Learned to use the Environment panel to change the background color and image
- ✦ Learned how exposure controls can work
- ✦ Created Atmospheric Apparatus gizmos for positioning atmospheric effects
- ✦ Worked with atmospheric effects, including Fire, Fog, and Volume Fog

Now that we've whet your appetite for effects, you'll be pleased to know that the next chapter covers more effects, along with Render Elements.

✦   ✦   ✦

Using Render Elements and Render Effects

◆   ◆   ◆   ◆

In This Chapter

Using render elements

Adding render effects

Using the Lens Effects to add glows, rays, and streaks

Understanding the other various types of render effects

◆   ◆   ◆   ◆

You can set Max to render any part in the rendering pipeline individually. These settings are called render elements. By rendering out just the Specular layer or just the shadow, you have more control over these elements in your compositor.

Max also has a class of effects that you can interactively render to the Virtual Frame Buffer without using any post-production features such as the Video Post dialog box. These effects are called *render effects*. Render effects can save you a lot of time that would normally be spent rendering an image, touching it up, and repeating the process again and again.

This chapter presents both render elements and the various render effects and shows you how to use them.

Using Render Elements

If your production group includes a strong post-processing team that does compositing, then there will be times when you'll just want to render certain elements of the scene such as the alpha information or a specific atmospheric effect. Applying individual elements to a composite image gives you better control over the elements. For example, you could reposition or lighten a shadow without having to re-render the entire scene.

Using the Render Elements rollout of the Render Scene dialog box, shown in Figure 36-1, you can render a single effect and save it as an image.

You can select and render several render elements at the same time. The available render elements include Alpha, Atmosphere, Background, Blend, Diffuse, Ink, Paint, Reflection, Refraction, Self-Illumination, Shadow, Specular, and Z Depth.

New Feature 3ds max 5 includes several new render elements. The Ink and Paint render elements are new to version 5. Using the Exposure Control rollout of the Render Scene panel, you can enable two additional render elements—Illumination and Luminance, both of which are also new.

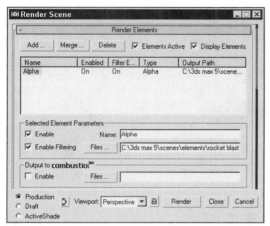

Figure 36-1: You can use the Render Elements rollout to render specific effects.

The Render Elements rollout can render several elements at once. The Add button opens the Render Elements dialog box, where you can select the elements to include. The Merge button lets you merge the elements from another Max scene, and the Delete button lets you delete elements from the list. To be included in the rendered image, the Elements Active option must be checked. The Display Elements option causes the results to be rendered separately and displayed in the Virtual Frame Buffer.

The Enable check box can turn off individual elements; Enable Filtering enables the anti-aliasing filtering as specified in the Max Default Scanline A-Buffer rollout. A separate Virtual Frame Buffer window will be opened for each render element that is enabled.

Clicking the Files button opens a file dialog box where you can give the rendered element a name. Max automatically appends an underscore and the name of the element on the end of the filename. For example, if you name the file myScene and select to render the Alpha element, the filename for this element will be myScene_alpha.

When you select the Blend and Z-Depth render elements, an additional rollout of parameters appears. You can use the Blend render element to combine several separate elements together. The Blend Element Parameters rollout includes check boxes for each render element type. The Z-Depth render element includes parameters for setting Min and Max depth values.

Figure 36-2 shows the resulting image in the Virtual Frame Buffer for the Alpha render element.

The Render Elements rollout can also output files that Discreet's Combustion product can use. These files have the .cws extension. Combustion is a compositing product that can work with individual elements to increase the highlights, change color hues, darken and blur shadows, and do many other things without having to re-render the scene.

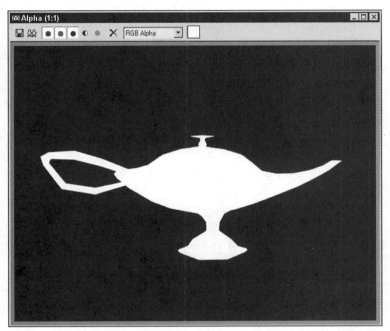

Figure 36-2: The Alpha render element shown in the Virtual Frame Buffer.

Adding Render Effects

Rendering a scene in many cases is only the start of the work to produce some final output. The post-production process is often used to add lots of different effects as you'll see when we discuss the Video Post interface. But, just because you can add it in post-production doesn't mean you have to add it in post-production. Render effects let you apply certain effects as part of the rendering process.

You can set up all render effects from the Rendering Effects panel, which you open by choosing Rendering ➪ Effects. Figure 36-3 shows this dialog box.

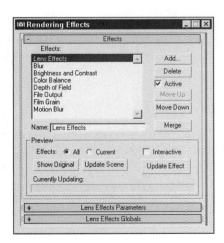

Figure 36-3: The Rendering Effects panel lets you apply interactive post-production effects to an image.

The Effects pane displays all the effects that are included in the current scene. To add a new effect, click the Add button to open the Add Effect dialog box, in which you can select from a default list of seven effects including Lens Effects, Blur, Brightness and Contrast, Color Balance, Depth of Field, File Output, Film Grain, and Motion Blur. You can delete an effect from the current list by selecting that effect and clicking the Delete button.

Below the Effects pane is a Name field. You can type a new name for any effect in this field — doing so enables you to use the same effect multiple times. The effects are applied in the order in which they are listed in the Effects pane. To the right of the Effects pane are the Move Up and Move Down buttons, which you use to reposition the effects in the list. The effects are added to the scene in the order that they are listed.

Caution   It is possible for one effect to cover another effect. Rearranging the order can help resolve this problem.

The Merge button opens the Merge Effect dialog box where you can select a separate Max file. If you select a Max file and click Open, the Merge Rendering Effects dialog box presents you with a list of render effects used in the opened Max file. You can then select and load any of these render effects into the current scene.

The Preview section holds the controls for interactively viewing the various effects. Previews are displayed in the Virtual Frame Buffer and can be set to view All the effects or only the Current one. The Show Original button displays the scene before any effects are applied, and the Update Scene button updates the rendered image if any changes have been made to the scene.

Note   If the Virtual Frame Buffer isn't open, any of these buttons opens it and renders the scene with the current settings in the Render Scene dialog box.

The Interactive option automatically updates the image whenever an effect parameter or scene object is changed. If this option is disabled, you can use the Update Effect button to manually update the image.

Caution   If the Interactive option is enabled and the Rendering Effects panel is open, the image is re-rendered in the Virtual Frame Buffer every time a change is made to the scene. This can slow down the system dramatically.

The Currently Updating bar shows the progress of the rendering update.

The remainder of the Rendering Effects panel contains global parameters and rollouts for the selected render effect. I cover these rollouts in this chapter along with their corresponding effects.

Creating Lens Effects

Of the seven available render effects, the first one of the list will be used perhaps more often than all the others combined. The Lens Effects option includes several different effects itself ranging from glows and rings to streaks and stars.

Lens Effects simulate the types of lighting effects that are possible with actual camera lenses and filters. When the Lens Effects selection is added to the Effects list and selected, several different effects become available in the Lens Effects Parameters rollout including Glow, Ring,

Ray, Auto Secondary, Manual Secondary, Star, and Streak. When one of these effects is included in a scene, rollouts and parameters for that effect are added to the panel as well.

Several of these Lens Effects can be used simultaneously. To include an effect, go to the Lens Effects Parameters rollout, select the desired effect from the list on the left, and click the arrow button pointing to the right. The pane on the right lists the included effects. Use the left-point arrow button to remove effects from the list.

Global Lens Effects Parameters

Under the Lens Effects Parameters rollout in the Rendering Effects panel is the Lens Effects Globals rollout. All effects available in Lens Effects use the two common tabbed panels in this rollout: Parameters and Scene. These two tabbed panels are shown side by side in Figure 36-4.

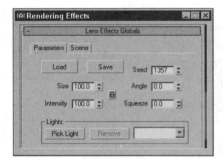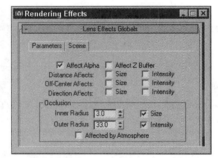

Figure 36-4: The Parameters tabbed panel of the Lens Effects Globals rollout lets you load and save parameter settings. The Scene tabbed panel lets you set the effect's Size and Intensity.

The Global Parameters tabbed panel

The Parameters panel of the Lens Effects Globals rollout includes Load and Save buttons for loading and saving parameter settings specified in the various rollouts. These settings are saved as LZV files.

The Size value determines the overall size of the effect as a percentage of the rendered image. Figure 36-5 shows the center of the Star Lens Effects with an Intensity value of 500 and Size values of 5, 10, 20, 50, and 100. The Size value increases the entire effect diameter and also the width of each radial line.

Figure 36-5: These Star Lens Effects vary in size.

The Intensity value controls the brightness and opacity of the effect. Large values are brighter and more opaque, and small values are dimmer and more transparent. The Size and Intensity values can be locked together. Intensity and Size values can range from 0 to 500. Figure 36-6 shows a glow effect with Intensity values of 50, 100, 200, 350, and 500.

Figure 36-6: Lens Effects can also vary in intensity like these glows.

The Seed value provides the randomness of the effect. Changing the Seed value changes the effect's look. The Angle value spins the effect about the camera's axis. The Squeeze value lengthens the horizontal axis for positive values and lengthens the vertical axis for negative values. Squeeze values can range from –100 to 100. Figure 36-7 shows a Ring effect with Squeeze values of –30, –15, 0, 10, and 20.

Figure 36-7: These Ring effects vary in Stretch values.

All effects are applied to light sources, and the Pick Light button lets you select a light in the viewport to apply the effect to. Each selected light is displayed in a drop-down list. You can remove any of these lights with the Remove Light button.

The Global Scene tabbed panel

The second Lens Effects Globals tabbed panel common to all effects is the Scene panel. This rollout includes an Affect Alpha option that lets the effect work with the image's alpha channel. The alpha channel holds the transparency information for the rendered objects and for effects if this option is enabled. If you plan on using the effect in a composite image, then enable this option.

Tip   Click the Display Alpha Channel button in the Virtual Frame Buffer to view the alpha channel.

The Affect Z-Buffer option stores the effect information in the Z-Buffer, which is used to determine the depth of objects from the camera's viewpoint.

The Distance Effects option alters the effect's Size and/or Intensity based on its distance from the camera. The Off-Center Effects option is similar, except it affects the effect's Size and Intensity based on its Off-Center distance. The Distance Affects options can affect the size and intensity of an effect based on the direction that a spotlight is pointing.

The Occlusion settings can be used to cause an effect to be hidden by an object that lies between the effect and the camera. The Inner Radius value defines the area that an object must block in order to hide the effect. The Outer Radius value defines where the effect begins to be occluded. You can also set the Size and Intensity options for the effect. The Affected by Atmospheres option allows effects to be occluded by atmospheric effects.

Glow

The Glow Element rollout, shown in Figure 36-8, includes parameters for controlling the look of the Glow Lens Effect. This rollout has two tabbed panels: Parameters and Options.

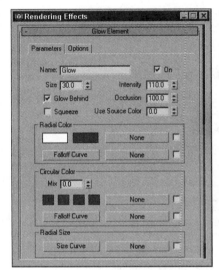 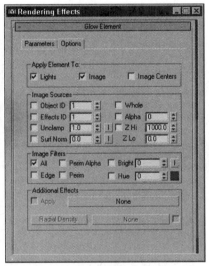

Figure 36-8: The Glow Element rollout lets you set the parameters for the Glow effect.

The Glow Element Parameters tabbed panel

In the Parameters tabbed panel of the Glow Element rollout, there is a Name field. Several glow effects can be added to a scene, and each one can have a different name. The On option can turn each glow on and off.

The Parameters panel also includes Size and Intensity values. These work with the Global settings to determine the size of the glow and can be set to any positive value. The Occlusion and Use Source Color values are percentages. The Occlusion value determines how much of the occlusion set in the Scene panel of the Lens Effects Globals rollout is to be used. If the Use Source Color is at 100 percent, then the glow color is determined by the light color; if it is set to any value below 100, then the colors specified in the Source and Circular Color sections are combined with the light's color.

There are also Glow Behind and Squeeze options. Glow Behind makes the glow effect visible behind objects. The Squeeze option enables any squeeze settings specified in the Parameters panel.

If the Use Source Color value is set to 0 percent, only the Radial Color swatches determine the glow colors. Radial colors proceed from the center of the glow circle to the outer edge. The first swatch is the inner color and the second is the outer color. The Falloff Curve button opens the Radial Falloff function curve dialog box, shown in Figure 36-9, where you can use a curve to set how quickly or slowly the colors change.

Move

Scale

Add point

Delete point

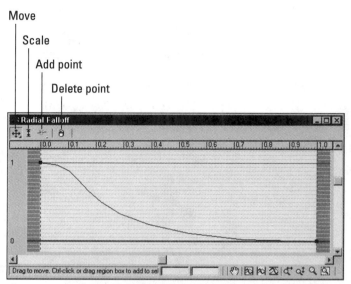

Figure 36-9: The Radial Falloff dialog box lets you control how the inner radial color changes to the outer radial color.

The Circular Color swatches specify the glow color around the glow circle starting from the top point and proceeding clockwise. The Mix value is the percentage to mix the Circular colors with the Radial Colors; a value of 0 displays only the Radial colors and a value of 100 displays only the Circular colors. You can also access the Falloff Curve dialog box for the Circular Color Falloff curve.

You can also control the Radial Size using a curve by clicking on the Size Curve button. Clicking the Size Curve button accesses the Radial Size dialog box. Figure 36-10 shows several glow effects where the radial size curve has been altered. The curves are from left to right, roughly, a descending linear curve, a v-shaped curve, a wide u-shaped curve, an m-shaped curve, and a sine curve.

Figure 36-10: These glow effects are distorted using the Radial Size function curves.

All of these colors and function curves have map buttons (initially labeled None) that enable you to load maps. Useful maps to use include Falloff, Gradient and Gradient Ramp, Noise and Swirl. You can enable a map by using the check box to its immediate right.

The Glow Element Options tabbed panel

The Options panel of the Glow Element rollout defines where to apply the glow effect. In the Apply Element To section, the first option is to apply a glow to the Lights. These lights are selected in the Lights section of the Lens Effects Globals rollout using the Pick Light button. The other two options — Image and Image Centers — apply glows using settings contained in the Options panel.

In the Image Sources section, you can apply glows to specific objects using the Object ID option and settings. Object IDs are set for objects in the Object Properties dialog box. If the corresponding Object ID is selected and enabled in the Options panel, the object is endowed with the Glow Lens Effect.

The Effects ID option and settings work in a manner similar to Object IDs, except that they are assigned to materials in the Material Editor. You can use effects IDs to make a subobject selection glow.

The Unclamp option and settings enable colors to be brighter than pure white. Pure White is a value of 1. The Unclamp value is the lowest value that glows. The Surf Norm (Surface Normal) option and value let you set object areas to glow based on the angle between the surface normal and the camera. The "I" button to the right inverts the value.

Figure 36-11 shows an array of spheres with the Surf Norm glow enabled. Because the glows multiply, a value of only 2 was applied. Notice how the spheres in the center have a stronger glow.

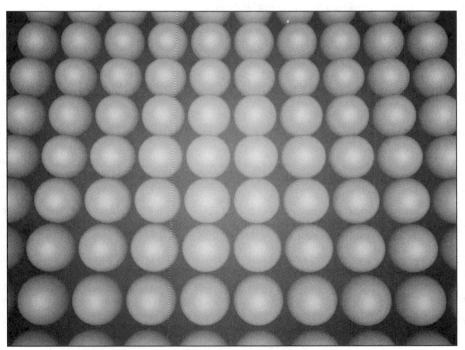

Figure 36-11: The Surf Norm option causes objects to glow, based on the angle between their surface normals and the camera.

In the Image Sources section, options enable these glows to be applied to the Whole scene, the Alpha channel, or the Z-buffer with specified Hi and Lo values.

The Image Filters section can further refine which objects to apply the glow effect to. Options include All, Edge, Perim (Perimeter) Alpha, Perim, Brightness, and Hue. The All option applies the effect to all pixels that are part of the source. The Edge, Perim Alpha, and Perim options only apply the effect to the edges, perimeter of the alpha channel, or perimeter of the source. The Brightness option includes a value and an "I" invert button. This applies the effect only to areas with a brightness greater than the specified value. The Hue option also includes a value and a color swatch for setting the hue, which receives the effect.

The Additional Effects section lets you apply a map to the Glow Lens Effect with an Apply option and a map button. You can also control the Radial Density function curve or add a map for the Radial Density.

Tutorial: Creating shocking electricity from a plug outlet

In addition to the light objects, lighting in a scene can be provided by self-illuminating an object and using a glow render effect. Self-illuminating an object is accomplished by applying a material with a Self-Illumination value greater than 0 or a color other than black. You can create glows by using the Render Effects dialog box or the Video Post dialog box.

Cross-Reference For more information on applying glows using the Video Post interface, see Chapter 39, "Post-Processing with the Video Post Interface."

Working with a faulty electrical outlet can be a shocking experience. In this tutorial, we'll create an electric arc that runs from an outlet to a plug. To create the effect of electricity, you can use a renderable spline with several vertices and apply the Noise modifier to make it dance around. You can set the light by using a self-illuminating material and a Glow render effect.

To create an electric arc that runs between an outlet and a plug, follow these steps:

1. Open the Electricity.max file from the Chap 36 directory on the CD-ROM.

   This file includes an outlet and an electric plug. There is also a spline that runs between the outline and the plug with a Noise modifier applied to it that will be our electric arc.

2. Open the Material Editor by pressing the M key and select the first sample slot. Select a yellow Diffuse color and an equally bright yellow for the Self-Illumination color. Set the Material Effects Channel to 1 by clicking the Material Effects ID button and holding it down until a pop-up array of numbers appears, and then drag to the number 1 and release the mouse. Drag this new material to the electric arc.

3. Open the Render Effects dialog box by choosing Rendering ➪ Effects. Click the Add button, select the Lens Effects option, and click OK. Then select Lens Effects from the list and double-click Glow in the Lens Effects Parameters rollout. Select Glow from the list and, in the Glow Element rollout, set the Size to 1 and the Intensity value to 50. Then open the Options panel, set the Effects ID to 1, and enable it.

Figure 36-12 shows the resulting electric arc.

Tutorial: Creating neon

You can also use the Glow render effect to create neon signs. The letters for these signs can be simple renderable splines, as this tutorial shows.

Figure 36-12: You can create electricity using a simple spline, the Noise modifier, and the Glow render effect.

To create a neon sign, follow these steps:

1. Open the Blues neon.max file from the Chap 36 directory on the CD-ROM.

   This file includes a simple sign that reads "Blues."

2. Open the Material Editor with the M key, select the first sample slot, and name it **Blue Neon**. Set its Diffuse color to blue and its Self-Illumination color to dark blue. Set the Material Effects Channel to 1, and apply the material to the sign.

3. Open the Rendering Effects panel and click the Add button. Double-click the Lens Effects option to add it to the Effects list. In the Lens Effects rollout, double-click the Glow option and select it in the list to enable its rollouts. In the Lens Effects Globals rollout, set the Size and Intensity values to 1. In the Glow Element rollout, set the Size to 10 and the Intensity to 100, and make sure the Glow Behind option is selected. For the neon color, set the Use Source Color to 100. Finally, open the Options panel and set the Effects ID to 1 and enable it.

Note   As an alternative to using the source color, you could set the Use Source Color value to 0 and set the Radial Color swatch to blue. This gives you more control over the glow color.

Figure 36-13 shows the rendered neon effect.

Figure 36-13: The glow of neon lights, easily created with render effects.

Ring

The Ring Lens Effect is also circular and includes all the same controls and settings as the Glow Lens Effect. The only additional values are the Plane and Thickness values. The Plane value positions the Ring center relative to the center of the screen, and the Thickness value determines the width of the Ring's band.

Figure 36-14 shows several Ring effects with various Thickness values: 1, 3, 6, 12, and 24.

Figure 36-14: Ring effects can vary in thickness.

Ray

The Ray Lens Effect emits bright, semitransparent rays in all directions from the source. They also use the same settings as the Glow effect, except for the Num (Number) and Sharp values. The Num value is the number of rays, and the Sharp value can range from 0 to 10 and determines how blurry the rays are.

Figure 36-15 shows the Ray effect applied to a simple omni light with increasing Num values: 6, 12, 50, 100, and 200. Notice how the rays aren't symmetrical and randomly placed.

Figure 36-15: The Ray effect extends a given number of rays out from the effect center.

Star

The Star Lens Effect radiates semitransparent bands of light at regular intervals from the center of the effect. It uses the same controls as the Glow effect, with the addition of Width, Taper, Qty (Quantity), and Sharp values. The Width sets the width of each band. The Taper value determines how quickly the width angles to a point. The Qty value is the number of bands, and the Sharp value determines how blurry the bands are.

Figure 36-16 shows several Star effects with 3, 4, 5, 6, and 12 bands.

Figure 36-16: The Star effect lets you set the number of bands emitting from the center.

Streak

The Streak Lens Effect adds a horizontal band through the center of the selected object. It is similar to the Star effect, except it has only two bands that extend in opposite directions.

Figure 36-17 shows several Streak effects angled at 45 degrees with Width values of 2, 4, 10, 15, and 20.

Figure 36-17: The Streak effect enables you to create horizontal bands.

Auto Secondary

When a camera is moved past a bright light, several small circles appear lined up in a row proceeding from the center of the light. These secondary lens flares are caused by light refracting off the lens. You can simulate this effect by using the Auto Secondary Lens Effect.

Many of the settings in the Auto Secondary Element rollout are the same as in the Glow effect rollout described previously, but there are several unique values. Figure 36-18 shows this rollout.

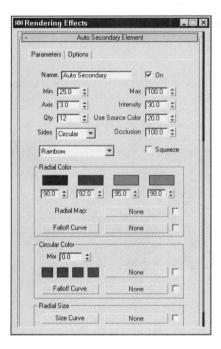

Figure 36-18: The Auto Secondary Element rollout sets the parameters for this effect.

The Min and Max values define the minimum and maximum size of the flares. The Axis is the length of the axis along which the flares are positioned. Larger values spread the flares out more than smaller values. The actual angle of the flares depends on the angle between the camera and the effect object.

The Quantity value is the number of flares to include. The Sides drop-down list lets you select a Circular flare or flares with Three to Eight sides. Below the Sides drop-down list are several preset options in another drop-down list. These include options such as Brown Ring, Blue Circle, and Green Rainbow, among others.

There are also four Radial Colors that you can use to define the flares. The color swatches from left to right define the colors from the inside out. The spinners below each color swatch indicate where the color should end.

Figure 36-19 shows the Auto Secondary effect with the Rainbow preset and the Intensity increased to 50.

Figure 36-19: The Auto Secondary Effect displays several flares extending at an angle from the center of the effect.

Manual Secondary

In addition to the Auto Secondary Lens Effect, you can add a Manual Secondary Lens Effect to add some more flares with a different size and look. This effect includes a Plane value that places the flare in front of (positive value) or behind (negative value) the flare source.

Figure 36-20 shows the same flares from the previous figure with an additional Manual Secondary effect added.

Figure 36-20: The Manual Secondary Effect can add some randomness to a flare lineup.

Tutorial: Making a genie's lamp sparkle

We all know what happens when you rub the genie's lamp, so I wonder what happens if we just make it appear to be shiny? Adding some Lens Effects to the lamp should do the trick.

To make an object bright and shiny using Lens Effects, follow these steps:

1. Open the Sparkling genie lamp.max file from the Chap 36 directory on the CD-ROM.

   This file includes a genie lamp model created by Viewpoint Datalabs.

2. Open the Create panel and click the Lights category button. Create several Omni lights and position them around the scene to provide adequate lighting. Position a single light close to the lamp's surface where you want the highlight to be located — make it near the surface and set the Multiplier value to 0.5.

3. Open the Rendering Effects panel by choosing Rendering ➪ Effects. Click the Add button and select Lens Effects. Then, in the Lens Effects Parameters rollout, select the Glow effect in the left pane and click the button pointing to the right pane.

4. In the Parameters panel, click the Pick Light button and select the light close to the surface. Set the Size around 30 and the Intensity at 100. Go to the Glow Element rollout, and in the Parameters panel set the Use Source Color to 0. Then, in the Radial Color section, click the second Radial Color swatch, and, in the Color Selector dialog box, select a color that is close to the color of the lamp and click the Close button.

5. Back up to the Lens Effects Parameters rollout, select Star, and add it to the list of effects. It automatically uses the same light specified for the Glow effect. In the Star Element rollout, set the Quantity value to 6, the Size to 200, and the Intensity to 20.

Figure 36-21 shows the resulting lamp with a nice shine.

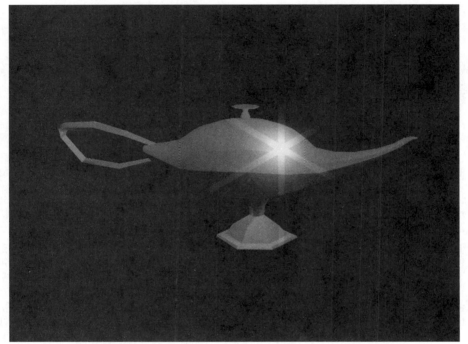

Figure 36-21: The genie's lamp has had a sparkle added to it using the Glow and Star Lens Effects.

Using Other Render Effects

Now that the big brother of the render effects is covered, let's return to the Add Effect dialog box where six other render effects are available. If these selections aren't enough, Max also enables you to add even more options to this list via plug-ins.

The CD-ROM includes a rainbow render effect plug-in developed by Furious Research.

Blur render effect

The Blur render effect displays three different blurring methods in the Blur Type panel: Uniform, Directional, and Radial. You can find these options in the Blur Type tabbed panel in the Blur Parameters rollout, shown in Figure 36-22.

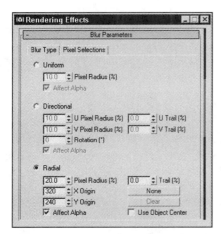

Figure 36-22: The Blur Parameters rollout lets you select a Uniform, Directional, or Radial blur type.

The Uniform blur method applies the blur evenly across the whole image. The Pixel Radius value defines the amount of the blur. The Directional blur method can be used to blur the image along a certain direction. The U Pixel Radius and U Trail values define the blur in the horizontal direction, and the V Pixel Radius and V Trail values blur in a vertical direction. The Rotation value rotates the axis of the blur.

The Radial blur method creates concentric blurred rings determined by the Radius and Trail values. When the Use Object Center option is selected, the None and Clear buttons become active. Clicking the None button lets you select an object about which you want to center the radial blur. The Clear button clears this selection.

Figure 36-23 shows a teddy bear model created by Viewpoint Datalabs. The actual rendered image shows the sharp edges of the polygons, which don't look so soft and cuddly. The Blur effect can help this by softening all the hard edges. The left image is the original bear, the middle image has a Directional blur applied, and the right image has a Radial blur applied.

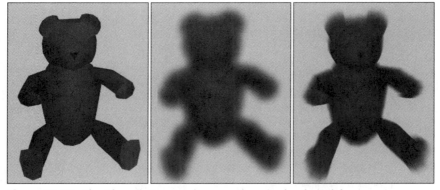

Figure 36-23: The Blur effect can soften an otherwise hard model.

The Blur Parameters rollout also includes a Pixel Selection tabbed panel, shown in Figure 36-24, that contains parameters for specifying which parts of the image get blurred. Options include the Whole Image, Non-Background, Luminance, Map Mask, Material ID, and Object ID.

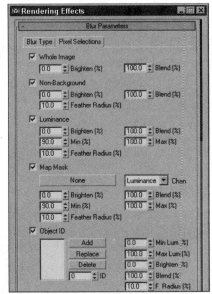
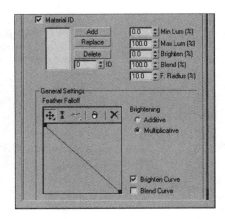

Figure 36-24: The Pixel Selections tabbed panel (shown in two parts) of the Blur Parameters rollout lets you select the parts of the image that get the Blur effect.

You can use the Feather Falloff curve at the bottom of the Blur Parameters rollout to define the Brighten and Blend curves. The buttons above this curve are for adding points, scaling, and moving them within the curve interface.

Brightness and Contrast render effect

The Brightness and Contrast render effect can alter these amounts in the image. The Brightness and Contrast Parameters rollout is a simple rollout with values for both the brightness and contrast, which can range from 0 to 1. It also contains an Ignore Background option.

Color Balance render effect

The Color Balance effect enables you to tint the image using separate Cyan/Red, Magenta/Green, and Yellow/Blue channels. To change the color balance, drag the sliders in the Color Balance Parameters rollout. Other options include Preserve Luminosity and Ignore Background. The Preserve Luminosity option tints the image while maintaining the luminosity of the image, and the Ignore Background option tints the rendered objects but not the background image.

File Output render effect

The File Output render effect enables you to save the rendered file to a File or to a Device at any point during the render effect's post-processing. Figure 36-25 shows the File Output Parameters rollout.

Using the Channel drop-down list in the Parameters section, you can save out Whole Images, as well as grayscale Luminance, Depth, and Alpha images.

Figure 36-25: The File Output Parameters rollout lets you save a rendered image before a render effect is applied.

Film Grain render effect

The Film Grain effect gives an image a grained look, which hardens the overall look of the image. You can also use this effect to match rendered objects to the grain of the background image. This helps the objects blend into the scene better.

The Grain value can range from 0 to 1. The Ignore Background option applies the grain effect to only the objects in the scene and not to the background.

Motion Blur render effect

The Motion Blur effect applies a simple image motion blur to the rendered output. The Motion Blur Parameters rollout includes settings for working with Transparency and a value for the Duration of the blur. Objects that move rapidly within the scene will be blurred.

Another way to use these effects is with the Multi-Pass Camera feature, which lets you preview the effect results in the viewport. I discuss this feature in Chapter 21, "Controlling Cameras."

Depth of Field render effect

The Depth of Field effect enhances the sense of depth by blurring objects close to or far from the camera. The Pick Cam button in the Depth of Field Parameters rollout, shown in Figure 36-26, lets you select a camera in the viewport to use for this effect. Multiple cameras can be selected, and all selected cameras are displayed in the drop-down list. There is also a Remove button for removing cameras.

In the Focal Point section, the Pick Node button lets you select an object to use as the focal point. This object is where the camera focuses. Objects far from this object are blurred. These nodes are also listed in a drop-down list. You can remove objects from the list by selecting them and clicking the Remove button. The Use Camera option uses the camera's own settings to determine the focal point.

In the Focal Parameters section, if you select the Custom option, then you can specify values for the Horizontal and Vertical Focal Loss, the Focal Range, and the Focal Limit. The Loss values indicate how much blur occurs. The Focal Range is where the image starts to blur, and the Focal Limit is where the image stops blurring.

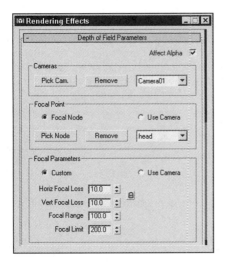

Figure 36-26: The Depth of Field Parameters rollout lets you select a camera or a Focal Point to apply the effect to.

Figure 36-27 shows a line of magnolia flowers created by Viewpoint Datalabs. For this figure, the Depth of Field effect has been applied using the Pick Node button and selecting the flower in the middle of the line. Then I set the Focal Range to 300 and the Focal Limit to 0 and locked the Focal Loss values for Horizontal and Vertical to 5.

Figure 36-27: The Depth of Field effect focuses a camera on an object in the middle and blurs objects closer or farther away.

Summary

Max's render elements enable you to pick apart the rendering details of your scene. Render effects are useful, because they enable you to create effects and update them interactively. This gives a level of control that was previously unavailable. This chapter explained how to use render elements and render effects and described the various types.

In this chapter, you've

✦ Learned how to use render elements

✦ Discovered how to apply render effects

✦ Used the Lens Effects to create glows, rays, and stars.

✦ Worked with the remaining render effects to control brightness and contrast, film grain, blurs, and more

✦   ✦   ✦

Raytracing

When computer generated 3D images started to appear, it was the raytraced images that really got the wow factor. These images were amazing in their clarity and perfect in reflecting and refracting light through the scene. Raytracing isn't new in Max, but making sense of all the raytracing features can be confusing.

Global Raytracing Settings

Raytracing is added to a scene using the Raytrace material found in the Material Editor. Applying a raytrace material to an object sets the local raytracing parameters for the object that the material is applied to, but there are other settings for determining how the raytracing is applied globally to a scene. These settings are found in the Global Raytracer Settings dialog box, shown in Figure 37-1. You access it by using the Rendering ⇨ Raytracer Settings menu command.

Controlling the raytracer

Suppose you have a scene with two mirrors that face one another. If the raytracer is allowed to track the bouncing of light rays through the scene, then it will never complete because some light rays would bounce back and forth off the mirrors and never end.

The Maximum Depth setting tells the raytracer how long to follow each ray, or you can set a Cutoff Threshold. (Lower numbers speed up render times at the expense of quality.) You can also specify a color (or select to use the background color) to use for rays that reach the Max Depth, which is useful for identifying lost rays. Lost rays are raytraced lines that don't bounce as expected and can result in a less than accurate solution.

Caution   The movement of a ray through the scene depends on the face normals. If the normals are flipped or pointing in the wrong direction, then the results will be unpredictable.

The Global Ray Antialiaser group includes a drop-down list with two options: Fast Adaptive Antialiaser and Multi-resolution Adaptive Antialiaser. These two options open separate dialog boxes, shown in Figure 37-2. The Fast Adaptive Antialiaser is quicker than its partner and offers settings for Blur and Defocus. The Multiresolution Adaptive Antialiaser takes a lot longer than the other option, but you can limit it with the Threshold and Max Rays values.

Figure 37-1: The Global Raytracer Settings dialog box includes raytracing settings that affect the entire scene.

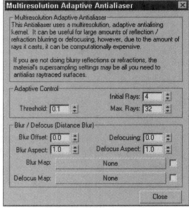

Figure 37-2: Additional anti-aliasing settings are available by clicking on the button to the right of the drop-down list.

Note If SuperSampling is enabled for a local raytracing material, then enabling a raytracing anti-aliasing option isn't needed, and vice versa unless you want to apply a blur or a defocus effect.

The Options section includes settings to Enable Raytracing, Enable Atmospherics, enable Self Reflect/Refract and Reflect/Refract Material IDs. There are also options to render the objects contained within raytraced objects, to render Atmospheric effects within raytraced objects, and to enable Color Density and Fog effects. The Show Progress Dialog and the Show Messages options let you see the progress of the raytracing engine along with any messages that the raytracing image may output. Figure 37-3 shows an example of the Message dialog box. This dialog box contains some useful information including the total number of rays traced. From this info, you can determine whether the number of rays is too many or not enough.

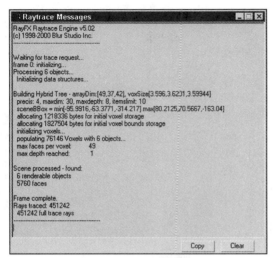

Figure 37-3: The Raytrace Message window outputs all the data from the raytracing engine.

Raytracing can take a long time, but the Acceleration Controls, shown in Figure 37-4, offer you several raytracer options that can control the speed of the process. These settings override the existing settings. Before sending rays into the scene, the scene is subdivided into a tree of nodes called a voxel tree. The complexity of this voxel tree determines the how long the raytracing solution will take. The Face Limit is the number of faces to include in a voxel node before subdividing. The Balance value defines how the scene gets subdivided. The Max Division sets the size of the voxel subdivisions and the Max Depth value limits how many times a subdivision takes place.

Figure 37-4: The Raytracing Acceleration Parameters options control the speed of the raytracing by limiting the number of faces and divisions that must be processed.

Excluding objects

One of the easiest ways to increase the speed of the raytracer is to reduce the number of objects that it has to deal with. You open the Include/Exclude dialog box for raytraced objects using the Rendering ⇨ Raytrace Global Include/Exclude menu command. From within this dialog box, shown in Figure 37-5, you can select objects to be excluded from the raytracer.

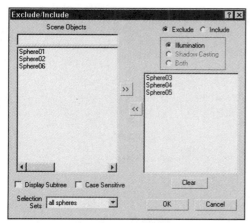

Figure 37-5: The Exclude/Include dialog box lets you select objects to be removed from the raytracer.

The Exclude/Include dialog box includes two panes. The pane on the left lists all the objects within the scene, and the one on the right lists the objects to Include or Exclude, depending on which option is selected.

Note   You use the same Exclude/Include dialog box to exclude objects from the effects of lights.

Using Raytrace Materials

Raytracing is a rendering method that calculates image colors by following imaginary light rays as they move through a scene. These rays can travel through transparent objects and reflect realistically off shiny materials. The results are stunning realistic images, but the drawback is the amount of time it takes to render using raytrace materials. Scenes with lots of lights and reflecting materials take even longer.

Raytrace materials also support special effects such as fog, color density, translucency, and fluorescence. They include the following rollouts (some of which are similar to the standard materials): Raytrace Basic Parameters, Extended Parameters, Raytracer Controls, SuperSampling, Maps, and Dynamic Properties. Figure 37-6 shows the Raytrace Basic Parameters and the Extended Parameters rollouts.

Note   Raytracing can take a long time to complete. As an alternative, you can use a Reflect/Refract map to simulate raytracing.

Raytrace Basic Parameters

The raytrace material doesn't have a shader rollout. Instead, shading is determined by a drop-down list at the top of the Raytrace Basic Parameters rollout. The options include Phong, Blinn, Metal, Oren-Nayar-Blinn, and Anisotropic. These shaders are similar to the shaders with the same names for standard materials.

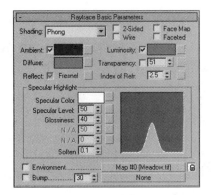 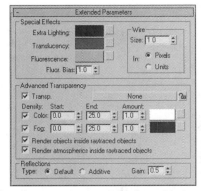

Figure 37-6: Many of the raytrace material settings are the same as those for the standard material.

The colors for a raytrace material (except for the Diffuse color) can switch between color swatches a value by enabling the check box to the left of the label. The spinners can range between 0 and 100, which equate to black and white. The Ambient color is different from that for the standard material although it is named the same. For raytrace materials, the Ambient value is the amount of ambient light that is absorbed. A setting of white is like locking a standard material's Diffuse and Ambient colors together.

The Reflect color is the color that is added to reflections. For example, if the background color is set to yellow and the Reflect color is red, then the reflections for this object will be tinted orange. This is different from the Specular highlight color, which is set in the Specular Highlight group.

The Luminosity color makes an object glow with this color, similar to the Self-Illumination color for the standard material. In fact, when the Luminosity setting is disabled, the text label changes to Self-Illumination.

The Transparency color sets the color that filters light passing through the transparent material. When the color swatch is white, the material is transparent, and when it is black, the material is opaque.

At the bottom of the Raytrace Basic Parameters rollout are two map options for Environment and Bump maps. These maps, which are also included in the Maps rollout, are here for convenience. The Environment map for raytrace materials overrides the global Environment map set in the Environment dialog box. The Environment map will only be visible if the Reflect color is enabled or its value is not 0. Figure 37-7 shows a sphere with an Environment map of a mountain meadow applied. The image is from Corel's Photo CD library.

For more information on Environment, Bump, and other maps, see Chapter 20, "Using Material Maps."

Extended Parameters rollout

The Extended Parameters rollout holds the settings for all the special material effects that are possible with the raytrace material. Only the Wire settings are the same as the standard material.

The Extra Lighting color swatch increases the effect of Ambient light. Use it to increase the ambient light for a single object or subobject area and to simulate radiosity. *Radiosity* is a rendering method that creates realistic lighting by calculating how light reflects off objects.

Figure 37-7: A sphere with an Environment map reflected off a raytrace material

Translucency lets light penetrate an object, but the objects on the other side are unclear, or semitransparent. You can use this effect to create frosted glass. Fluorescence makes materials glow like fluorescent colors under a black light. The Fluorescence Bias field, which can range between 0 and 1, controls the amount of this effect that is applied.

The Advanced Transparency group includes a shortcut for the Transparent Environment map. This map is refracted through a transparent object and is only visible if the Environment map is enabled. You can use the lock icon to the right of the Transparency map button to lock the Environment map above with this map.

Raytrace materials that are transparent can also have Color and Fog Density settings. You can use Color Density to create tinted glass — the amount of color depends on how thick the object is and the Amount setting. The Start value is where the color starts, and the End value is the distance at which the color reaches a maximum. Fog Density works the same way as Color Density and is based on object thickness. You can use this effect to create smoky glass. You also have options to render any objects or atmospheric effects contained within ray-traced objects.

The Reflections section offers a Default Reflection Type and an Additive Reflection Type. The Default type layers the reflection on top of the current Diffuse color, and the Additive type adds the reflection to the Diffuse color. The Gain value controls the brightness of the reflection and can range between 0 and 1.

Raytracer Control rollout

Raytracing can take a long time, but the Raytracer Control rollout, shown in Figure 37-8, lets you control several Raytracer options that can speed up the process. These options are all local options including Enable Raytracing, Enable Self Reflect/Refract, Raytrace Atmospherics, Reflect/Refract Material ID.

You can use this rollout to turn Raytrace Reflections or Refractions on or off. The Falloff values determine the distance at which the reflections or refractions fade to black. The Bump Map Effect increases or decreases the effect of bump maps on the reflections or refractions.

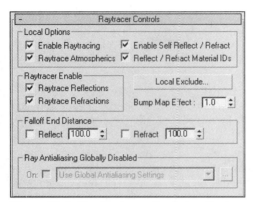

Figure 37-8: The Raytracer Controls rollout
lets you set the raytracing options.

The Raytraced Reflection and Refraction Antialiaser drop-down list includes three options: Use Global Antialiasing Settings, Fast Adaptive Antialiaser and Multi-resolution Adaptive Antialiaser. This drop-down list is only available if the Global Ray Antialiaser option found in the Global Raytracer Setting dialog box is enabled. The first selection opens the Global Raytracer Settings dialog box.

In the Raytracer Control rollout, you can also select to include or exclude objects from the effect of a local raytraced object. The Local Exclude button opens the Exclude/Include dialog box that is the same as the Global Include/Exclude dialog box.

Additional rollouts

Raytrace materials include three additional rollouts: SuperSampling, Maps, and Dynamic Properties. The Maps rollout works the same for raytrace materials as it does with standard materials, but the raytrace material includes several unique maps that aren't found in standard materials. The Dynamic Properties rollout for raytrace materials is identical to the Dynamic Properties rollout for standard materials.

Tutorial: Coming up roses

Raytrace examples often include glasses or vases because shiny, highly reflective glass surfaces show off the effects of raytracing best. Zygote Media has an object that is perfect for this task — a vase of roses. (Zygote also created the table used in this tutorial.)

To apply raytrace materials to a vase of roses, follow these steps:

1. Open the Roses on table.max file from the Chap 37 directory on the CD-ROM.

   The file includes some rose meshes in a vase on a table.

2. Open the Material Editor, select the first sample slot, and name the material Raytrace Glass. Click the Type button and double-click the raytrace material type in the Material/Map Browser. Deselect the Transparency option and set its value to 100. Set the Index of Refraction to 1.5 and raise the Specular Level to 100. Select the vase object and click the Assign Material to Selection button.

3. Select the second sample slot and name it Leaves. In the Shader Basic Parameters roll-out, select the Oren-Nayar-Blinn shader from the drop-down list. Then click the Diffuse color swatch and select a dark green color. Set the Diffuse Level, Opacity, and Roughness to 100 and the Specular Level to 10. Then select the stems and leaves and apply this material.

4. Select the third sample slot, click the Pick Material from Object tool to the left of the Name field, and then click the roses. Doing so loads the material already applied to the roses into the sample slot. Disable the Faceted option and reapply the material using the Assign Material to Selection button.

5. Select the fourth sample slot and click the square button to the right of the Diffuse color swatch to open the Material/Map Browser. Double-click the Wood map to apply this map instead of the Diffuse color and to display the map parameter rollouts. Set the Y-axis Tiling value to 20 in the Coordinates rollout. Then click the Go to Parent button and, in the Blinn Basic Parameters rollout, increase the Specular Level to 75. Name the material **Tabletop** and drag the material to the tabletop.

6. In a graphics program like Adobe Photoshop, create and save a 200 × 200 image with some repeating colored vertical stripes that can be used as wallpaper. Select the fifth sample slot and click the map button to the right of the Diffuse color. In the Material/Map Browser, double-click the Bitmap selection. A File dialog box loads, in which you can locate the wallpaper image. In the Coordinates rollout, set the U coordinate Tiling value to 100 and drag the material to the wall plane object.

Figure 37-9 shows the rendered image.

Figure 37-9: A rendered image with raytrace materials applied to the vase and table

Using a Raytrace Map

The raytrace map is an alternative to the raytrace material discussed previously and, as a map, can be used in places where the raytrace material cannot.

The raytrace map includes several similar rollouts and several unique rollouts. In the Raytracer Parameters rollout, the Local Options section lets you select to Enable Raytracing, enable Raytrace Atmospherics, Enable Self Reflect/Refract, and to use Reflect/Refract Material IDs. The Trace Mode determines how the rays are cast through the scene. Options include Auto Detect, Reflection, and Refraction. You can also use the Environment Settings or specify a color or map to use for the Background.

The Local Exclude button opens the Exclude/Include dialog box where you can select which items to include or exclude in the raytracing calculations. The Raytracing Antialiasing drop-down list is enabled using the Global Raytracing Settings dialog box.

Note   You set global raytracing options using the Rendering ⇨ Raytracer Settings menu command.

The Attenuation rollout lets you select from one of several Falloff Types. The options include Linear, Inverse Square, Exponential, and Custom Falloff. You can also set values for the Start and End distances. The Custom Falloff type lets you set a graph by adjusting Near, Far, and two Control values.

The Basic Material Extensions rollout lets you set the Reflectivity/Opacity Map and its strength. You can also set a Basic Tinting color or map. The Refractive Material Extensions rollout includes settings for specifying the Color Density (Filter color) and Fog.

Tutorial: Raytracing a wine glass

Raytracing complex scenes will require some serious processor power because each light ray that is being traced can bounce off many different objects multiple times. By applying a raytrace map to a single object, you can dramatically decrease the render time while still maintaining a quality look.

To apply a raytrace map to the glass in this scene, follow these steps:

1. Open the Table setting.max file from the Chap 37 directory on the CD-ROM.

   This file includes all the meshes used for a table setting. These models were provided courtesy of Zygote Media. The materials for everything except the wine glass are already included, assigned, and visible in the Material Editor in the first four sample slots.

2. Choose Rendering ⇨ Material Editor (or press the M key) to open the Material Editor.

3. Select the fifth sample slot, name the material **Wine Glass**, and click the map button to the right of the Diffuse color swatch to open the Material/Map Browser. In the Material/Map Browser, double-click the raytrace map.

4. In the Raytracer Parameters rollout, select the Refraction Trace Mode option and select the Black color swatch option in the Background section.

5. Drag the Wine Glass material to the wine glass object in the viewport to apply the material to the object.

Figure 37-10 shows a place setting created by Zygote Media that includes a wineglass with a raytrace map applied.

Figure 37-10: You can use the raytrace map to raytrace only select objects.

Summary

If you're looking for a rendering option that perfectly calculates reflections, refractions, and transparencies, then raytracing is what you need. Raytracing settings can be set globally and applied to selected materials using materials and maps.

In this chapter, you've

> ✦ Learned about the global raytracing settings
>
> ✦ Explored the raytrace material
>
> ✦ Worked with raytraced maps

Now that I've told you how to overload the rendering engine, the next chapter offers a way to get some help by rendering over the network.

✦   ✦   ✦

Network Rendering

Max can help you create some incredible images and animations, but that power comes at a significant price — time. Modeling scenes and animation sequences take enough time on their own, but after you're done you still have to wait for the rendering to take place, which for a final rendering at the highest detail settings can literally take days or weeks. Because the time rendering takes is directly proportional to the amount of processing power you have access to, Max lets you use network rendering to add more hardware to the equation and speed up those painfully slow jobs.

This chapter shows you how to set up Max to distribute the rendering workload across an entire network of computers, helping you finish big rendering jobs in record time.

Understanding Network Rendering

When you use network rendering to render your animation, Max divides the work among several machines connected via a network, with each machine rendering some of the frames. The increase in speed depends on how many machines you can devote to rendering frames — add just one computer and you double the rate at which you can render. Add seven or eight machines and instead of missing that important deadline by a week, you can get done early and take an extra day off.

The price of all this (besides the extra machines) is a time investment on your part. It does take a little work to get things set up properly, but it's an investment that you have to make only once. If you take the time now to make sure you do things right, you should be up and running fairly quickly and have far fewer headaches down the road.

Machines connected to handle network rendering are often referred to collectively as a *rendering farm*. The basic process during a network rendering goes like this: One machine manages the entire process and distributes the work among all the computers in the farm. Each machine signals the managing computer when it is ready to work on another frame. The manager then sends or "farms out" a new frame, which gets drawn by a computer in the rendering farm, and the finished frame gets saved in whatever format you've chosen.

Max has several additional features to make the network rendering process easier. If one of the computers in your rendering farm crashes or loses its connection with the manager, the manager reclaims the frame that was assigned to the down computer and farms it out to a different machine. You can monitor the status of any rendering job you have running, and you can even have Max e-mail you when a job is complete.

In this chapter, we step through the process of setting up network rendering on a small network I use at home. You'll find out firsthand what's involved so that setting up your own network can go smoothly.

Note   One additional caveat to using network rendering is that you have no guarantee that the frames of your animation will be rendered in order. Each participating computer renders frames as quickly as possible and saves them as bitmap files, so you cannot use network rendering to create AVI or FLC files, for example. Instead, you have to render the scene with each frame saved as a separate bitmap file, and then use Video Post or a third-party program (such as Adobe Premiere) to combine them into an animation file format such as AVI.

Network Requirements

Now that you're anxious to get things under way, let's look at what you need to set up a rendering farm:

✦ **Computers:** First, of course, you need computers. The more the merrier, but all of them need to be connected via some sort of network and need to be running TCP/IP, a very common communications protocol (we'll talk more about TCP/IP and setting it up later). As with most things related to computers, the more powerful the hardware you can get your hands on, the faster things go. All computers in your farm should meet at least the basic requirements for Max, but if they have more memory, more disk space, and faster processors, you're better off. Also, having nothing else running on the machines is preferable. Rendering is a CPU-intensive process, so any other programs you have running compete for the processor and increase the time needed to finish your rendering job.

✦ **Networking hardware:** Each computer needs some way to connect to the network. The most common way is to use a network adapter card in the computer and a cable that connects it to the rest of the network. If a computer is connected via a dial-up connection, then its networking hardware is a modem. Using network rendering on a single computer to do batch rendering is also possible, in which case only one computer is used instead of a real network. In this case, the network "hardware" isn't hardware at all — it's a piece of software that simulates a network adapter and tricks Max into thinking that it's connected to a network.

✦ **Windows 2000 or XP:** According to the Max documentation, each computer in your rendering farm must be running under Windows 2000 or Windows XP, because Max isn't stable enough when running under Windows 98. I personally have some machines that run Windows 2000 and others that run Windows 98, and I haven't had any problems to date, but it's up to you (you've been warned). The screenshots in this chapter are based on Windows 2000. Things may look slightly different in Windows 98.

Note   If your network has not been set up yet, you will probably need Windows 2000 administrative privileges on each machine.

✦ **3ds max:** Obviously you need Max to do all this, but the good news is that only one machine in your farm needs to have an authorized copy of Max installed. In order to start a network rendering job, you have to be running an authorized copy of Max; the other machines will, in effect, get their authorization via the authorized copy. (We look into this further in the next section.)

Note   No authorization whatsoever is needed on machines that are used for network rendering only. Simply install Max, and each network rendering machine gets its authorization from the computer that launched the render job.

Basically that's all you need to network render with Max. But before we move on, you should remember two important things.

First, the display capabilities of the machines in your rendering farm are irrelevant. Max uses its own rendering engine, so in network rendering, a top-of-the-line graphics adapter won't give you any better performance or quality than the cheap, factory-installed adapters that often come built into the motherboard. In fact, you can even omit the monitor on each rendering farm computer, which can really cut down on how much you have to invest to set up a good network rendering farm.

Second, if you don't have access to a bunch of computers that can be exclusively dedicated to network rendering, don't give up. Max has some great scheduling features that enable you to configure each computer so that it's available to render at certain times of the day. If you have administrative access to additional computers at work or a university lab, you can use those computers at night or on weekends, when they are generally not being used.

Setting up a Network Rendering System

Before we get into the details of setting up Max and the network itself, understanding the different parts of the network rendering system is important. Here is a list of the major players involved:

✦ **Manager:** The manager is a program (manager.exe) that acts as the network manager. It's the network manager's job to coordinate the efforts of all the other computers in your rendering farm. Only one machine on your network needs to be running the manager, and that same machine can also be used to render.

✦ **Server:** A rendering server is any computer on your network that is used to render frames of your animation. When you run the server program (server.exe), it contacts the network manager and informs it that this particular computer is available to render. The server starts up Max when the manager sends a frame to be rendered.

✦ **3ds max:** Some computer in your rendering farm must have an authorized copy of Max running, although it does not need to be the same computer that is running the manager. It is from this machine that you initiate a rendering job.

✦ **Monitor:** The Monitor (monitor.exe) is a special program that lets you monitor your rendering farm. You can use it to check the current state of jobs that are running or that have been queued. You can also use it to schedule network rendering times. The Monitor is completely independent from the actual rendering process, so you can use it on one of the machines in your rendering farm, or you can use it to remotely check the status of things by connecting over the network.

We address the task of setting up the network rendering system in three stages. The first thing you need is a functioning network, so we first go through the steps of how to get it working. Next, we look at setting up the Max software on each computer, and finally we describe how to tell Max where to find scene data it needs and where to put the finished scenes.

Setting up the network

To communicate with the different machines on the network, Max uses TCP/IP (Transmission Control Protocol/Internet Protocol), a very common network protocol. It's so common, in fact, that if your computers are already set up with some sort of network, you might already have TCP/IP installed and configured properly. If so, you are saved from several hours of work. Each machine on a network is identified by an IP address, which is a series of four numbers, each between 0 and 255, separated by periods, such as

```
192.1.17.5
```

Each computer on a network has a unique IP address as well as a unique, human-readable name. In order to use Max to do network rendering, you need to find the IP address and name of each computer used on the network.

The precise details of what constitutes a "correct" IP address are too long and boring to go into here, but for a nonpublic network, all the addresses start with 192 or 10. The second and third numbers can be anything between 0 and 255 inclusive, and the last number can be between 1 and 254 inclusive (0 and 255 have special meanings). As an example, I've chosen to set up my home network as follows:

```
Machine Name    IP Address
Greeble         10.0.0.1
Ramrod          10.0.0.2
Slazenger       10.0.0.3
Romulus         10.0.0.4
```

Notice that each address is unique and that because it's a private network, the first number in each address is 10.

Tutorial: Locating TCP/IP and gathering IP addresses

To get the computers to talk to one another, you need to make sure that each computer has the TCP/IP protocol installed, and you need to gather the IP addresses for all the machines on the network.

To see whether you already have TCP/IP installed and to find out the IP address and name of each computer, follow these steps:

1. Right-click the My Computer icon on your desktop and select Properties from the pop-up menu. The System Properties dialog box opens. Select the Network Identification panel. This panel displays the Full computer name. Write the computer name in a list of all the computers you are using to network-render. Each computer on your network needs a unique name, so if the field is blank, enter a unique name and add this computer to your list.

Caution   Remember that there are differences between Windows 2000 and Windows 98. These steps were written for Windows 2000.

2. Open the Windows Control Panel by going to the Windows taskbar and choosing Start ⇨ Settings ⇨ Control Panel.

3. Double-click the Network and Dial-up Connections icon to open the network connections window.

   This window displays a list of network connections.

4. Select and right-click the network connection identified as Local Area Connection and select Properties from the pop-up menu. The Local Area Connection Properties dialog box opens, which lists the installed protocols. At the top of the dialog box, you should see your network adapter (such as the brand and model of your Ethernet card). If it is not listed, you need to get it set up before proceeding. (Refer to the Windows 2000 Help files for more on this.) Under the network adapter is a list of installed network protocols, similar to the list in Figure 38-1. Look through the list until you find the Internet (TCP/IP) Protocol. If you find it, double-click it to bring up the TCP/IP Properties dialog box. If you don't see the TCP/IP protocol anywhere, then you have to add it yourself in order to do network rendering (see the next section for instructions).

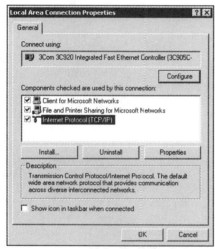

Figure 38-1: A list of the network protocols installed on this computer

In Windows 98, the protocols and network adapters are all listed together on the Configuration panel in the Network dialog box.

5. The Internet (TCP/IP) Protocol Properties dialog box has an important piece of information, called IP Address, shown in Figure 38-2. Do one of the following:

- If Obtain an IP address automatically is selected, you don't have to worry about the exact IP address of this computer, because each time the computer connects to the network, it gets an IP address from a server, and the address it gets may be different every time.

- If Specify an IP address is selected, add the IP address to your written list of computers on the network. In the IP Address panel shown in the figure, the IP address has been statically assigned, which means that this computer will always have the same IP address.

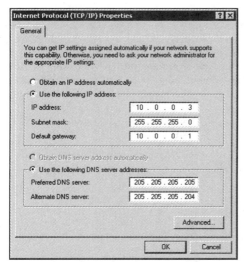

Figure 38-2: You can find the IP Address in the Internet (TCP/IP) Protocol Properties dialog box.

6. Repeat this procedure for each computer that will participate in your rendering farm. If you're lucky and all your machines have TCP/IP installed and ready to go, you can skip the next section and move on to setting up Max on your network. If not, then follow the steps for configuring TCP/IP in the next section.

Tutorial: Installing and configuring TCP/IP

If your computer doesn't already have TCP/IP installed, you have to install it in order to network-render in Max.

Caution   Be careful about changing the TCP/IP settings of computers that are on a public network or are part of a large corporate network. Incorrect settings can not only keep your computers from communicating properly but can also cause problems in many other computers on the network.

If the computers you plan on using for your rendering farm are part of a public or corporate network, seek the assistance of the network administrator. If you're in charge of the computers yourself, dig out your Windows 2000 installation CD-ROM, because you're going to need it.

To install and configure TCP/IP, follow these steps:

1. Go to the General panel on the Local Area Connection Properties dialog box if you're not still there from the previous section. To get there, click Start on the task bar, and then choose Settings ➪ Control Panel. Double-click the Network and Dial-up Connections icon to open the network connections window. Select and right-click the network connection identified as Local Area Connection and select Properties from the pop-up menu.

2. Click the Install button to open the Select Network Component Type dialog box. Select Protocol and click the Add button. From the list of protocols, select Internet (TCP/IP) Protocol, and click OK.

3. At this point Windows asks you whether you want to use DHCP. DHCP is a server that will automatically assign an IP address to you computer. If you know for sure that there is a DHCP server running, go ahead and choose Yes. If you're setting up the network yourself or you have no idea what DHCP is, choose No. If DHCP is already set up and working, it can save you a lot of time, but if not and if you're setting up the network yourself, I recommend steering away from it. You can change the settings to use DHCP at a later time if you're feeling ambitious.

4. Now Windows starts looking for the files that it needs to install, and it pops up a dialog box asking for their location. The default path it lists is probably the right one, so you can just click OK and continue. If Windows guessed wrong, or if you have the CD-ROM in a different drive, correct the path and then click OK.

5. After Windows finishes copying the files, TCP/IP will be installed but not configured. To configure the protocol, select it and click the Properties button. The Internet (TCP/IP) Protocol Properties dialog box opens, shown earlier in Figure 38-2.

6. In the General panel is a section where you choose whether you want to have an IP address assigned automatically using DHCP. If you're not using DHCP, choose Specify an IP address and enter an IP address for this machine. Refer to the beginning of this section if you need help choosing a valid IP address. (If you're a little confused about what numbers to use, you should be safe using the same numbers that I did.)

Caution   It's extremely important that you choose an IP address that is unique on the network. (Duplicate IP addresses are a great way to guarantee a nonfunctional rendering farm.)

7. Underneath the IP address section, you have to enter a subnet mask. Enter

   `255.255.255.0`

   The subnet mask is used in conjunction with the IP address to identify different networks within the entire domain of every network in the world. If you do have to change this, be sure to change it in the 3dsnet.ini files that each rendering server creates (see "Using the Network Rendering Manager" later in this chapter).

8. Now select the Obtain DNS server address automatically option unless you know the IP address of your network's DNS server.

   This setting allows you to configure the TCP/IP protocol to check your local DNS when looking up addresses.

9. Click OK in the TCP/IP Properties dialog box to close it, and then click Close on the Local Area Connection Properties dialog box to close it.

   Windows needs to shut down and restart in order for the changes to take effect. This computer now has the proper network setup for your rendering farm.

Remember to repeat these instructions for every computer that you want to use in your rendering farm. Each computer must be properly connected to the network and have TCP/IP installed and configured. This may seem like a lot of work, but fortunately it's a one-time investment.

Tutorial: Setting up Max on the networked computers

If you've made it this far, then you'll be happy to know that the worst is behind you. We've covered the most difficult parts of setting up a network rendering system; by comparison, everything else is relatively simple.

At this point, you should have a complete list of all the computers used in your network rendering system. Each computer should have a unique name and a unique IP address, and all should have TCP/IP installed and configured. You are now ready to move on to the actual Max installation for your rendering servers.

You have to set up Max on each computer in your rendering farm. Fortunately, this is as simple as a normal installation. To set up Max on each computer, follow these steps:

1. Run the setup.exe program on the Max installation CD-ROM.

Note   You don't have to have a CD-ROM drive in every computer in your rendering farm. After your computers are networked, you can map a drive from your current machine to a computer that has the Max CD-ROM in its CD-ROM drive. In Windows Explorer, choose Tools ➪ Map Network Drive and enter the path to the computer and drive with the CD-ROM. For more information on mapping drives, see the next section.

2. Move past the first few introduction screens until you get to the Setup Type screen. Choose the Compact option so that Max installs only the minimum number of files it needs to be able to render. You also need to choose a destination directory where you want Max to be installed. If possible, just accept the displayed default destination and click Next.

Tip   Installing 3ds max in the same directory on every computer can save you some maintenance headaches later on. Managing bitmap and plug-in directories is much easier if each machine has the same directory layout.

3. Continue with the rest of the installation as you would do for a normal installation of Max (although you can skip installing the online reference manuals if you want to save some disk space).

After the installation files get copied over, you'll probably have to reboot your computer for the changes to take effect.

Configuring shared directories

The last step in building your rendering farm is to tell Max where it can find the information it needs to render a scene. Max must be able to find textures and other information, and it must know where to put each frame that it renders.

Tutorial: Sharing directories

Instead of copying needed files to every machine in your rendering farm, you can share your directories across the network, which means that other computers on the network will be able to use the files in that directory.

To make a directory shared, follow these steps:

1. Open Windows Explorer by selecting Start on the Windows taskbar and then choosing Programs ➪ Accessories ➪ Windows Explorer.

2. Find the directory that you want to share, right-click it, and choose Sharing.

    The Properties dialog box opens for that directory.

3. In the Sharing panel, choose the Share this Folder option and type a name for this directory in the Share Name field if it is blank. Figure 38-3 shows the "maps" directory being set up to be shared.

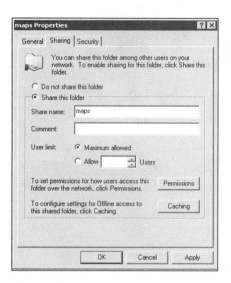

Figure 38-3: Sharing a directory so that other computers on the network can use it

Tip   Other computers will refer to the shared directory by its shared name instead of its actual name, so to keep things simple, accept the default of using the actual name for the shared name.

4. Click Permissions to open the Access Through Share Permissions dialog box. This dialog box lets you control who has access to this directory and how much access each person or group has (access could be restricted to read-only, for example). For now, make sure that the Everyone user group is listed and that this group has Full Control, as shown in Figure 38-4. If the Everyone user group is not listed, click Add, scroll down to Everyone, and double-click it. Then choose Full Control in the Type of Access pull-down menu and click OK.

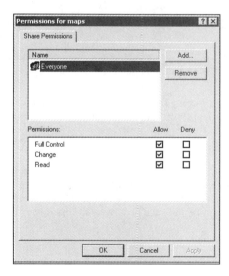

Figure 38-4: Setting share permissions for a directory. These permissions let anyone read or write to this directory.

Caution

Giving "Everyone" the Full Control access type does just what it says it does: Everyone on the entire network can read and write or erase the files in your shared directory. For now, leaving it this way until you're sure everything is configured properly is best. Later, however, restricting access to only those accounts that should have access would be a good idea.

5. Click OK in each dialog box to close them all until you're back at the Windows Explorer. If you press F5, Windows refreshes the display and your directory now has a little blue hand holding the folder. Figure 38-5 shows the "maps" directory denoted as a shared directory.

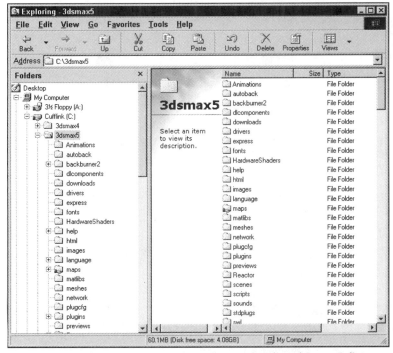

Figure 38-5: Other computers can now access the shared "maps" directory.

Other computers can access your shared directory by specifying the full name of the directory's location. In the example we've been using, the "maps" directory is on a computer named "Endor," so the full path to that directory is as follows:

```
\\endor\maps
```

You can test this by opening a Windows Explorer (like we just did in the procedure) on a different computer, choosing Tools ⇨ Map Network Drive, and entering the full path to that directory. After you've mapped a drive to a directory, Windows treats that directory as if it were an actual drive on your machine. In Figure 38-6, the N drive is mapped to point to the "maps" directory on Endor.

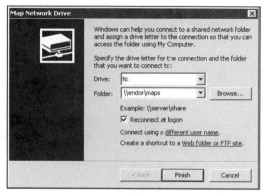

Figure 38-6: Mapping the N drive to point to \\endor\maps\

After you've mapped to a new drive, go back to the Windows Explorer and press F5 to refresh the display again. You now have a new drive for that network directory, as shown in Figure 38-7.

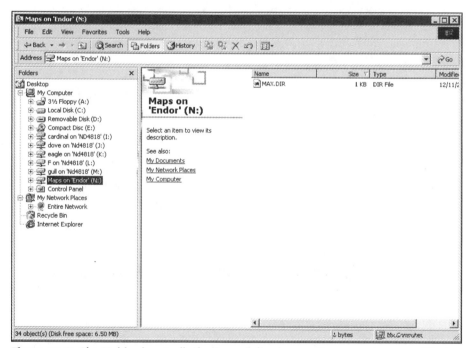

Figure 38-7: The N drive is actually the "maps" directory on the computer named Endor.

Tutorial: Choosing shared directories

Now you need to decide where to put the maps and the output files. These directories are the place from which all machines in your rendering farm read maps and images and to which they all write finished frames of your animation. The following procedure takes you through the steps for doing this using the directories I've set up on my own rendering farm.

To set up your shared directories, follow these steps:

1. First, decide which drives to use and then share them. On my network, Endor has plenty of disk space, so I used the maps and images directories that were already there from when I installed Max.

Tip   Use the maps and images directories for all the scenes that you network-render. In each directory you can create other directories to organize files for your different scenes, but putting all maps and output in the same place facilitates maintenance.

2. On each computer in your rendering farm, map a drive to your shared maps and images directories as described in the previous section. If possible, choose the same drive letters on all machines. I used the letter *N* for the maps directory on each computer.

Congratulations — you've made it through the installation and setup of your network rendering system. And no matter how long it took you, it was time well spent. The ability to network-render will easily save you more time than you invested in setting up your network.

Starting the Network Rendering System

You can finally put all your hard work into action. We're ready to start up your network rendering system.

Tutorial: Initializing the network rendering system

The very first time you start your rendering farm, you need to help Max do a little initialization.

To initialize the network rendering system, follow these steps:

1. Start the network manager on one machine in your rendering farm. This program, Manger.exe, is in the backburner2 directory. You can start the manager by selecting it and pressing Enter in Windows Explorer. After it starts up, you'll first see the BackBurner Manager General Properties dialog box. This dialog box only appears the first time you run the Manger.exe program or if you choose Edit ➪ General Settings. I cover its settings in the chapter. After setting these properties, click the OK button and the Manager window, shown in Figure 38-8, will run.

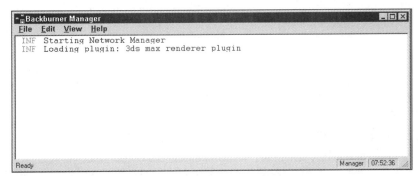

Figure 38-8: Starting the network manager

2. Now start a network server on each computer that you plan to use for rendering. To do this, find and start the Server.exe program just like you did with Manger.exe. When you start this program, the Network Server window will appear, as shown in Figure 38-9.

Figure 38-9: Starting a network server. Notice that the server found the manager successfully.

Notice that the server printed the message that it successfully registered itself with the manager using the IP address. Whenever a server starts, it automatically searches for the manager and tries to connect. The Network Manager window will also show a similar message.

If the server had trouble connecting to the manager, you need to follow these two additional steps:

1. If automatic detection of the manager fails, the server keeps trying until it times out. If it times out, or if you just get tired of waiting, choose Edit ↵ General Properties to open the Server General Properties dialog box, shown in Figure 38-10. In this dialog box, uncheck the Automatic box and type in the name or IP address of the computer that is running the network manager. In this case, the server tried but couldn't quite find the manager, so it had to be told that the manager was running on the computer whose IP address is 150.150.150.150

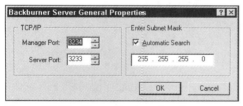

Figure 38-10: Manually choosing the manager's IP address

2. Click OK to close the Backburner Server General Properties dialog box, and then click Close to shut down the server (doing so forces the server to save the changes you've made). Restart the server the same way you did before, and now the server and manager are able to find each other.

Note

The network manager does not need to have a computer all to itself, so you can also run a network server on the same computer and use it to participate in the rendering.

Tutorial: Completing your first network rendering job

Your rendering farm is up and running and just dying to render something, so let's put those machines to work.

To start a network rendering job, follow these steps:

1. Start Max and create a simple animation scene.

   This should be as simple as possible because all we're doing here is verifying that the rendering farm is functional.

2. In Max, choose Rendering ➪ Render to bring up the Render Scene dialog box. In the Time Output section of this dialog box, be sure that Range is selected so that you really do render multiple frames instead of the default single frame. Figure 38-11 shows the Time Output Range set to render 100 frames.

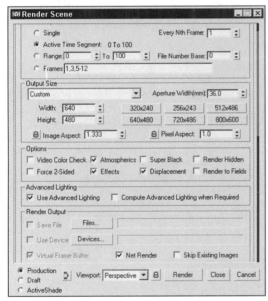

Figure 38-11: Preparing to network-render

3. In the Render Output section of the Render Scene dialog box, click Files to open the Render Output File dialog box, shown in Figure 38-12. In the Save In section, choose the output drive and directory that you created in the "Configuring shared directories" section.

4. In the File name section of the Render Output File dialog box, type in the name of the first frame. Max automatically numbers each frame for you. Choose a bitmap format from the Save as type list (remember, an animation format will not work).

5. Click Save to close the Render Output File dialog box. (Some file formats might ask you for additional information for your files; if so, just click OK to accept the default options.) Back in the Render Scene dialog box, Max displays the full path to the output directory.

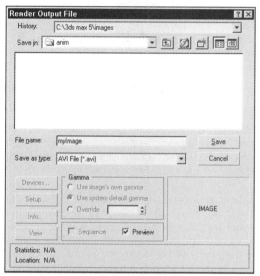

Figure 38-12: Specifying an output location. Max numbers the frames for you, so you just have to give it the filename of the first frame.

6. In the Render Output section of the Render Scene dialog box, check the Net Render box. Change any other settings you want, such as selecting a viewport, and then click Render.

A Network Job Assignment dialog box opens, like the one shown in Figure 38-13.

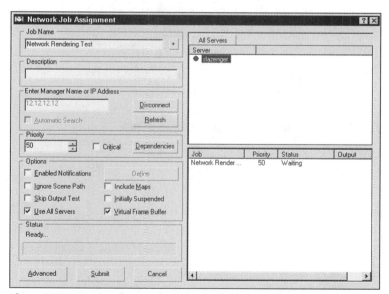

Figure 38-13: Using the Network Job Assignment dialog box to locate the manager to handle the rendering job.

7. In the Network Manager section of the Network Job Assignment dialog box, click Connect if the Automatic Search box is checked. If it isn't checked, or if your servers had trouble finding the manager in the "Initializing the Network Rendering System" section earlier in this chapter, type in the IP address of the machine that's running the manager and then click Connect.

8. Max then searches for any available rendering servers, connects with it, and adds its name to the list of available servers. Click the server name once and click Submit.

Tip   If you try to submit the same job again (after either a failed or a successful attempt at rendering), Max complains because that job already exists in the job queue. You can either remove the job using the Monitor (which I discuss later) or you can click the + button on the Network Job Assignment dialog box, and Max will add a number to the job name to make it unique.

After you've submitted your job, notices appear on the manager and the servers (like the ones shown in Figures 38-14 and 38-15) that the job has been received. Soon Max will start up on each server, and you'll see a Rendering dialog box like Figure 38-16. As you can see, this displays useful information such as what frame is being rendered and how long the job is taking. When the entire animation has been rendered, you can go to your output directory to get the bitmap files that Max generated. The render servers and the render manager keep running, ready for the next job request to come in.

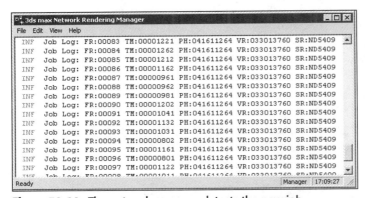

Figure 38-14: The network manager detects the new job.

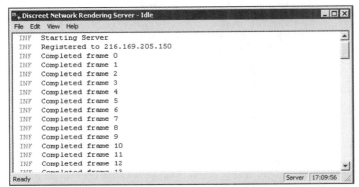

Figure 38-15: One of the network servers receives the command to start a new job.

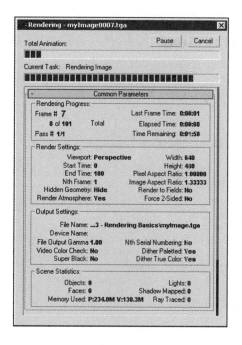

Figure 38-16: Status of the current frame being rendered

Job assignment options

The Network Job Assignment dialog box, shown in Figure 38-13, has two important sections that we didn't use for our first simple render job: Options and Notifications.

The Options section has the following settings:

✦ **Ignore Scene Path:** Use this option to force the servers to retrieve the scene file via TCP/IP. If disabled, the manager copies the scene file to the server.

✦ **Skip Output Test:** Normally Max checks all servers to see whether they can access the specified output directory. This option skips that check.

✦ **Use All Servers:** This option makes all servers listed in the Server panel fair game for rendering. To select only specific servers, disable this option and select the servers to use.

✦ **Include Maps:** Checking this box makes Max compress everything that it needs to render the scene (including the maps) into a single file and send it to each server. This option is useful if you're setting up a rendering farm over the Internet, although it does take more time and network bandwidth to send all that extra information.

✦ **Initially Suspended:** Pauses the rendering before it starts so that you can manually start it when the network is ready.

✦ **Virtual Frame Buffer:** Use this option if you want to be able to see the image on the server as it gets rendered.

The Enabled Notifications option and the Define button let you tell Max when to notify you that certain events have occurred. If you check the Enabled box, the Define button becomes active. The notifications in the Notification dialog box that opens include

✦ **Notify Failures:** Max sends you a notification on any type of failure.

✦ **Notify Progress:** Max notifies you every time it completes a certain number of frames.

✦ **Notify Completion:** Max sends you a notification when a job is complete.

✦ **Email Options:** You can specify to send an e-mail, and you can list a From, To, and SMTP Server to use.

Configuring the Network Manager and Servers

You can configure both the manager and servers using their respective General Properties dialog boxes. You open these dialog boxes by choosing Edit ⇨ General Settings.

The network manager settings

The rendering manager has some options that let you modify how it behaves. You specify these options in the Network Manager General Properties dialog box, shown in Figure 38-17. To open this dialog box, click Properties in the Manager window.

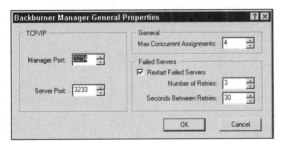

Figure 38-17: The Network Manager General Properties dialog box

This dialog box includes the following sections:

✦ **TCP/IP:** Here you can change the communications ports used by the manager and the servers. In general, leaving these alone is a good idea. If some other program is using one of these ports, however, Max won't be able to network-render, so you need to change them. If you change the Server Port number, be sure to change it to the same number on all your rendering servers. If you change the Manager Port number, you'll also need to change two files on your hard drive to match: queueman.ini (in your 3dsmax directory) and client.ini (in your 3dsmax\network directory). Both have lines for the Manager Port, and you can edit these files with any text editor or word processor.

✦ **General:** The Max Concurrent Assignments field is used to specify how many jobs the rendering manager sends out at a time. If you make this number too high, the manager might send out jobs faster than the servers can handle them. The default value here is fine for most cases.

Note The network manager can automatically attempt to restart servers that failed, giving your rendering farm much more stability.

✦ **Failed Servers:** Usually Max doesn't send more frames to a server that previously failed. If you check the Restarts Failed Servers box, Max tries to give the server another chance. The Number of Retries field tells Max how many times it should try to restart a server before giving up on the particular server for good, and the Minutes Between Retries field tells Max the number of minutes it should wait before trying to give the failing server another job.

Note The rendering manager writes the configuration settings to a file on the disk that gets read when the manager loads. If you make changes to any of the settings, shutting down the manager and starting it up again to guarantee that the changes take effect is best.

The network servers settings

As you may have guessed, the Properties button on the Network Server window serves a similar purpose as the one on the Network Manager window — it enables you to specify the behavior of the network server. Clicking this button displays the Network Server General Properties dialog box, shown in Figure 38-18.

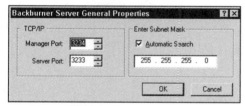

Figure 38-18: The Network Server General Properties dialog box

This dialog box has the following section:

✦ **TCP/IP:** The port numbers serve the same function as they do for the rendering manager, described in the previous section. If you change them in the manager properties, change them here. If you change them here, change them in the manager properties.

Note The Manager Name or IP Address setting lets you override automatic detection of the rendering manager and specify its exact location on the network. Generally, letting Max attempt to find the manager itself is best; if it fails, override the automatic detection by clearing the Automatic check box. If you happen to be running multiple managers on the same network, the servers connect to the first one they find. In this case, you have to manually choose the correct server.

Keep in mind that the server properties aren't shared among your servers, so if you want something to change on all your servers, you have to make that change on each machine.

Note As with the rendering manager settings, if you change anything in the Network Servers Properties dialog box, be sure to shut down the server and restart it.

Logging Errors

Both the Network Manager and Network Server windows have a Logging button that you can click to access the Logging Properties dialog box, where you can configure how log information gets handled. This dialog box, shown in Figure 38-19, looks the same for managers and servers. You can access this dialog box with the Edit ➪ Log Settings command.

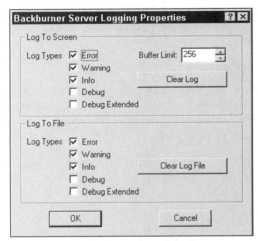

Figure 38-19: The logging options for managers and servers let you tell Max where to report what.

Max generates the following types of messages:

✦ **Error:** Anything that goes wrong and is serious enough to halt the rendering of a frame.

✦ **Warning:** A problem that Max can still work around. If a server fails, for example, a warning is generated, but Max continues the rendering job by using other servers.

✦ **Info:** A general information message, such as notification that a job has arrived or that a frame is complete.

✦ **Debug:** A lower-level message that provides information to help debug problems with the rendering farm.

✦ **Debug Extended:** The same as the Debug option with more details.

Max displays the type of message and the message itself in two locations: in the list window and in a log file (in your 3dsmax\network directory). The Logging Properties dialog box lets you choose whether each type of message gets reported to the screen, the log file, both places, or neither place. You can also use the Clear buttons to get rid of old messages.

Using the Monitor

The Monitor is a powerful utility that helps you manage your rendering farm and all the jobs in it. If you use network rendering frequently, then the Monitor will quickly become your best friend. You start it the same way you start a rendering server or manager: Go to the 3dsmax directory, find QueueManager.exe, and double-click it. Every computer that has Max installed on it also has a copy of the Monitor, so you can use it from any machine on your network. The main screen is shown in Figure 38-20.

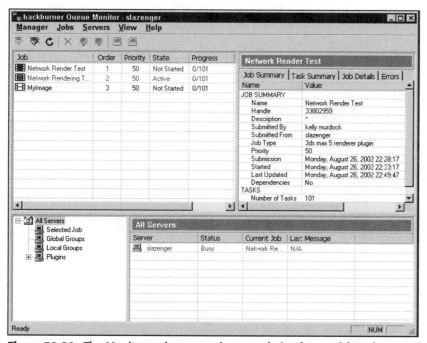

Figure 38-20: The Monitor makes managing a rendering farm quick and easy.

When the Monitor starts up, it automatically searches for the rendering manager and connects to it. (If you have more than one manager running, you have to choose which one to connect to.)

The main screen is divided into three panes. The top-left pane shows the job queue, and their Priority and Status, and the top-right pane shows information about whatever you have selected in the left pane. You can use the tabs at the top of this pane to select the information that you want to view. The information tabs include Job Summary, Frames Summary, Advanced (which shows the rendering parameters), Render Elements, and Log.

The bottom pane lists all the available servers. Next to each server in the left pane is an icon that reflects its current status. Green icons mean that the job or server is active and hard at work. Yellow means the server is idle. Red means that something has gone wrong, and gray means that a job has been inactivated or that a server is assigned to a job but is absent. When a job is complete, it can now be deleted from the queue.

Jobs

If you choose a job in the top-left pane, the top-right pane displays information about the selected job. The panels in the top-right pane are as follows:

✦ **Job Summary:** Lists some of the rendering options you chose before you submitted the job. Among other things, the example in the figure shows that the job was rendered to 640 × 480 pixels.

✦ **Frames Summary:** Lists the details of rendering each frame in the animation including the time required to render and the server used.

✦ **Advanced:** Lists advanced settings from the Render Scene dialog box and gives limited information about the scene itself.

✦ **Render Elements:** Lists the details of each render element included as part of the job.

✦ **Log File:** Displays important messages from the job log. Whereas the log file on each server lists events for a particular server, this pane lets you see all the messages relating to a particular job.

When you point at a job in the top-left pane and right-click, a small pop-up menu appears. On this menu, you can delete a job from the queue or you can choose to activate or deactivate it. If you deactivate a job, all the servers working on that job save their work in progress to disk and then move on to the next job in the queue. This feature is very useful when you have a lower-priority job that you run when no other jobs are waiting; when something more important comes along, you deactivate the job so that you can later activate it when the servers are free again.

One last useful feature for jobs is that you can reorder them by dragging a job above or below other jobs. Jobs higher on the screen will be rendered before lower ones, which enables you to "bump up" the priority of a particular job without having to deactivate other ones.

Servers

If you double-click a server, the Server Properties dialog box, shown in Figure 38-21, opens. This dialog box contains information about the selected server.

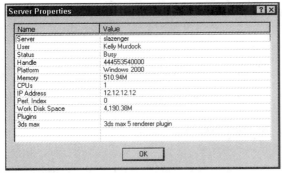

Figure 38-21: The Server Properties dialog box displays information about the server.

Many other features are available in the right-click pop-up menu. Using this pop-up menu, you can assign the server to a selected job, remove the server from its selected job, display specific server information, create a server group, or view the Week Schedule, shown in Figure 38-22. Using the Week Schedule dialog box, you can set the active rendering period for a server.

The Week Schedule dialog box lets you decide when a particular machine is available for rendering. (For example, you could have your coworker's computer automatically become available for rendering after he or she goes home for the night.)

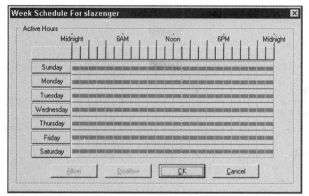

Figure 38-22: The Week Schedule dialog box can set the time during the week when a server is available for rendering.

Click and drag with your mouse over different hours to select a group of times. Alternatively, you can click a day of the week to select the entire day or click a time to select that time for every day. In the example shown in Figure 38-22, the server is scheduled to render every weekday from midnight to 5 P.M., but not in evenings or on weekends.

After you've selected a group of times, click Allow to make the server available for rendering during that time or click Disallow to prevent rendering. When you're done, click OK to close the Server Properties dialog box and return to the Monitor dialog box.

If you have several jobs going at once but suddenly need to get one done quickly, you can take servers off one job and put them on another. To remove a server, right-click its name in the left pane of the Monitor dialog box and choose Delete Server (Ctrl+Enter) from the pop-up menu. The icon next to the server turns black, indicating that it has been unassigned. To assign this server to another job, right-click the server name in the list of servers for the job you want to assign it to, and choose Assign to Selected Jobs.

Tutorial: Setting Up Batch Rendering

Network rendering provides several features that make managing many different rendering jobs easy. If you don't have a network card installed but still want to use these features (such as the Monitor), there's still hope — Max supports what is known as a loopback adapter so that you can set up a "network" on a single computer.

A loopback adapter is a piece of software that simulates a real network adapter. Data that is sent out to the adapter gets "looped back" to your own computer. And because Windows treats it as a normal network adapter, any networking programs (such as Max) don't know any better.

If you're sure you don't have a network card installed, you can add the loopback adapter by following these steps (you'll probably need your Windows 2000 CD-ROM):

1. Open the Control Panel in Windows by clicking the Windows Start button and choosing Settings ➪ Control Panel.

2. Double-click the Network and Dial-up Connections icon to open the Network and Dial-up Connections dialog box. Double-click the Local Area Network icon and click the Properties button in the Local Area Connection Status dialog box.

   The Local Area Connection Properties dialog box opens.

3. Click on the Configure button and scroll through the list of adapters until you see the MS Loopback Adapter. Select it and click OK.

4. When Windows prompts you for a frame type, click OK to accept the default.

5. After the installation files have been copied over from the CD-ROM, you need to reboot your computer for the new adapter to finish installation.

Now that you've installed the loopback adapter, you need to set up TCP/IP. Just follow the directions for setting up TCP/IP as if you were configuring it to be used as part of a real network. You have to reboot your computer one more time before you can actually use your new "network."

To use batch rendering, start a rendering manager and a rendering server on your computer and then load Max. Again, follow the same steps to submit the job as if you were rendering to a real network rendering system: Choose Net Render in the Render Scene dialog box and submit the job.

You can use the loopback adapter to submit several jobs to the rendering queue and then use the Monitor to manipulate them. That way you can still have flexible job control even if you don't have a true network rendering system.

Summary

If your goal is to spend more time modeling and less time waiting for rendering jobs to complete, then the network rendering services provided by 3ds max can help you take a step in the right direction. After the initial complexities of setting up a rendering farm are out of the way, network rendering can be a great asset in helping you reach important deadlines, and it lets you enjoy your finished work sooner. Even if you can afford to add only one or two computers to your current setup, you'll see a tremendous increase in productivity — an increase that you can't truly appreciate until you've completed a job in a fraction of the time it used to take!

In this chapter you learned how to

✦ Set up a network suitable for network rendering with Max

✦ Set up a 3ds max rendering farm

✦ Use the rendering manager and servers to carry out rendering jobs

✦ Use the Monitor to control job priority

✦ Make Max notify you when problems occur or when jobs finish

✦ Perform batch rendering even if you don't have a network

In the next chapter, we look into how to add post-production effects using the Video Post interface.

✦   ✦   ✦

Using the Video Post Interface

After you've completed your scene and rendered it, you're done right? Well, not exactly. You still have post-production to complete — that's where you work with the final rendered images to add some additional effects. This phase of production typically takes place in another package such as Discreet's Combustion or Adobe's After Effects, but Max includes an interface to add some effects.

You can use the Video Post window to composite the final rendered image with several other images and filters. These filters let you add lens effects like glows and flares, and other effects like blur and fade, to the final output. The Video Post window provides a post-processing environment within the Max interface.

Note   Many of the post-processing effects such as glows and blurs are also available as render effects, but the Video Post window is capable of much more.

Completing Post-Production with the Video Post Interface

Post-production is the work that comes after the scene is rendered. It is the time when you add effects, such as glows and highlights, as well as add transitional effects to an animation. For example, if you want to include a logo in the lower right-hand corner of your animation, you could create and render the logo and composite several rendered images into one during post-production.

Video Post interface is the post-processing interface within Max that you can use to combine the current scene with different images, effects, and image processing filters. Compositing is the process of combining several different images into a single image. Each element of the composite is included as a separate event. These events are all lined up in a queue and processed in the order in which they appear in the queue. The queue can also include looping events.

The Video Post interface, like the Render Scene dialog box (covered in Chapter 34, "Rendering Basics"), provides another way to produce final output. You can think of the Video Post process as an artistic assembly line. As the image moves down the line, each item in the queue adds an image, drops a rendered image on the stack, or applies a filter effect. This process continues until the final output event is reached.

The Video Post interface, shown in Figure 39-1, includes a toolbar, a pane of events and ranges, and a status bar. You can open it by choosing Rendering ⇨ Video Post.

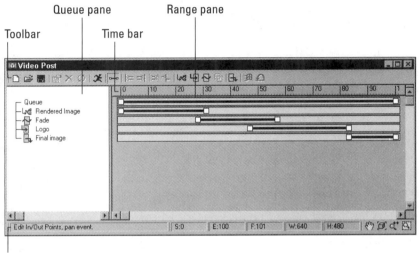

Figure 39-1: The Video Post interface lets you composite images with your final rendering.

In many ways, the Video Post interface is similar to the Track View interfaces. Each event is displayed as a track in the Queue pane to the left. To the right is the Range pane where the range for each track is displayed as lines with square boxes at each end. You can edit these ranges by dragging the squares on either end. The frame bar, above the Range pane, displays the frames for the current sequence and the status bar at the bottom of the interface includes information and view buttons.

The Video Post toolbar

At the top of the Video Post interface is a toolbar with several buttons for managing the Video Post features. Table 39-1 shows and explains these buttons.

Table 39-1: Video Post Toolbar Buttons

Toolbar Button	Name	Description
	New Sequence	Creates a new sequence.
	Open Sequence	Opens an existing sequence.
	Save Sequence	Saves the current sequence.
	Edit Current Event	Opens the Edit Current Event dialog box where you can edit events.

Toolbar Button	Name	Description
X	Delete Current Event	Removes the current event from the sequence.
(2)	Swap Events	Changes the position in the queue of two selected events.
🏃	Execute Sequence	Runs the current sequence.
■━□	Edit Range Bar	Enables you to edit the event ranges.
▤	Align Selected Left	Aligns the left ranges of the selected events.
▥	Align Selected Right	Aligns the right ranges of the selected events.
▦	Make Selected Same Size	Makes the ranges for the selected events the same size.
⊣⊢	Abut Selected	Places event ranges end-to-end.
🖾	Add Scene Event	Adds a rendered scene to the queue.
⬐	Add Image Input Event	Adds an image to the queue.
⬑	Add Image Filter Event	Adds an image filter to the queue.
▣	Add Image Layer Event	Adds a compositing plug-in to the queue.
⬓	Add Image Output Event	Sends the final composited image to a file or device.
🎞	Add External Event	Adds an external image-processing event to the queue.
⟲	Add Loop Event	Causes other events to loop.

The Video Post Queue and Range panes

Below the toolbar are the Video Post Queue and Range panes. The Queue pane is on the left; it lists all the events to be included in the post-processing sequence in the order that they are processed. You can rearrange the order of the events by dragging an event in the queue to its new location.

You can select multiple events by holding down the Ctrl key and clicking the event names, or you can select one event, hold down the Shift key, and click another event to select all events between the two.

Each event has a corresponding range that appears in the Range pane to the right. Each range is shown as a line with a square on each end. The left square marks the first frame of the event, and the right square marks the last frame of the event. You can expand or contract these ranges by dragging the square on either end of the range line.

If you click the line between two squares, you can drag the entire range. If you drag a range beyond the given number of frames, then additional frames are added.

The time bar is at the top of the Range pane. This bar shows the number of total frames included in the animation. You can also slide the time bar up or down to move it closer to a specific track by dragging it.

The Video Post status bar

The status bar includes a prompt line, several value fields, and some navigation buttons. The fields to the right of the prompt line include Start, End, Current Frames, and the Width and Height of the image. The navigation buttons include (in order from left to right) Pan, Zoom Extents, Zoom Time, and Zoom Region.

Working with Sequences

All the events that are added to the Queue pane make up a sequence. You can save these sequences and open them at a later time. The Execute Sequence button, found on the toolbar, starts the compositing process.

To save a sequence, click the Save button on the toolbar to open the Save Sequence dialog box, where you can save the queue sequence. Sequences are saved along with the Max file when the scene is saved, but they can also be saved independently of the scene. By default, these files are saved with the .VPX extension in the vpost directory.

Note   Saving a sequence as a VPX file maintains the elements of the queue, but it resets all parameter settings. Saving the file as a Max file maintains the queue order along with the parameter settings.

You can open saved sequences using the Open Sequence button on the toolbar. When a saved sequence is opened, all the current events are deleted. Clicking the New Sequence button also deletes any current events.

The Execute Sequence toolbar button opens the Execute Video Post interface, shown in Figure 39-2. The controls in this dialog box work exactly the way those in the Render Scene dialog box work.

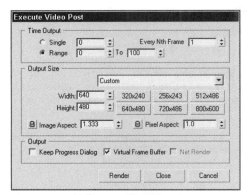

Figure 39-2: The Execute Video Post interface includes the controls for producing the queue output.

The Time Output section enables you to specify which frames to render, and the Output Size section lets you specify the size of the output. The Custom selection lets you enter Width and Height values, or you can use one of the presets in the drop-down list or one of the preset resolution buttons. This dialog box also includes controls for entering the Image and Pixel Aspect ratios.

The Output options let you select to keep the Progress dialog box open, to render to the Virtual Frame Buffer, and/or to use network rendering. When you're ready to render the queue, click the Render button.

Adding and Editing Events

The seven different event types that you can add to the queue are Image Input, Scene, Image Filter, Image Layer, Loop, External, and Image Output. If no events are selected, then adding an event positions the event at the bottom of the list. If an event is selected, the added event becomes a sub-event under the selected event.

Every event dialog box, such as the Add Input Image Event dialog box shown in Figure 39-3, includes a Label field where you can name the event. This name shows up in the queue window and is used to identify the event.

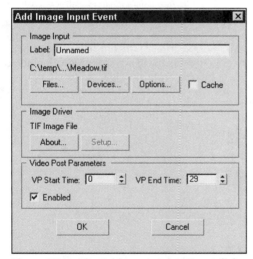

Figure 39-3: The Add Image Input Event dialog box lets you load an image to add to the queue.

Each event dialog box includes a Video Post Parameters section. This section contains VP Start Time and VP End Time values for defining precisely the length of the Video Post range. It also includes an Enabled option for enabling or disabling an event. Disabled events are grayed out in the queue.

To edit an event, you simply need to double-click its name in the Queue pane to open an Edit Event dialog box.

Adding an image input event

The Add Image Input Event dialog box lets you add a simple image to the queue. For example, you can add a background image using this dialog box rather than the Environment dialog box. To open the Add Image Input Event dialog box, click the Add Image Input Event button on the toolbar.

Tip If you don't name the image event, then the filename will appear in the Queue pane as the name for the event.

The Files button on this dialog box opens the Select Image File for Video Post Input dialog box where you can locate an image file to load from the hard disk or network. Supported image types include AVI, BMP, Kodak Cineon, FLC, GIF, IFL, IPP, JPEG, PNG, PSD, MOV, SGI Image, RLA, RPF, TGA, TIF, and YUV. The Devices button lets you access an external device such as a video recorder. The Options button becomes enabled when you load an image. It opens the Image Input Options dialog box, shown in Figure 39-4. The Cache option causes the image to be loaded into memory, which can speed up the Video Post process by not requiring the image to be loaded for every frame.

The Image Driver section of the Add Image Input Event dialog box lets you specify the settings for the image driver, such as the compression settings for an AVI file. Clicking the Setup button opens a dialog box of options available for the selected format.

The Image Input Options dialog box, shown in Figure 39-4, lets you set the alignment, size, and frames where the image appears. The Alignment section of the Image Input Options dialog box includes nine different presets for aligning the image. Preset options include top-left corner, top centered, top-right corner, left centered, centered, right centered, bottom-left corner, bottom centered, and bottom-right corner. You can also use the Coordinates option to specify in pixels the image's upper-left corner.

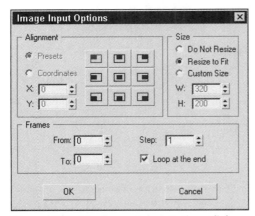

Figure 39-4: The Image Input Options dialog box lets you align and set the size of the image.

In the Size section of this dialog box, you can control the size of the image, using the Do Not Resize, Resize to Fit, or Custom Size options. The Custom Size option lets you enter Width and Height values.

The Frames section only applies to animation files. The From and To values define which frames of the animation to play. The Step value lets you play every nth frame as specified. The Loop at the End value causes the animation to loop back to the beginning when finished.

Adding scene events

A scene event is the rendered scene that you've built in Max. By clicking the Add Scene Event button on the toolbar, the Add Scene Event dialog box shown in Figure 39-5 opens. This dialog box lets you specify the scene ranges and define the render options.

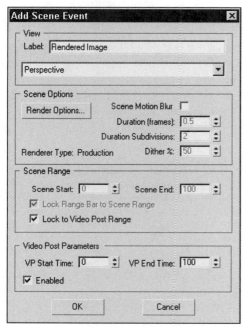

Figure 39-5: The Add Scene Event dialog box lets you specify which viewport to use to render your scene.

Below the Label field where you can name the event is a drop-down list that lets you select which viewport to use to render your scene. The active viewport is selected by default. The Render Options button opens the Render Scene panel, except the Render button has been replaced with OK and Cancel buttons because the rendering is initiated with the Execute Sequence button.

For more information about the Render Scene panel, see Chapter 34, "Rendering Basics."

The Scene Options section of the Add Scene Event dialog box also includes an option for enabling Scene Motion Blur. This motion blur type is different from the object motion blur that is set in the Object Properties dialog box. Scene motion blur is applied to the entire image and is useful for blurring objects that are moving fast. The Duration (frames) value sets how long the blur effect is computed per frame. The Duration Subdivisions value is how many computations are done for each duration. The Dither % value sets the amount of dithering to use for blurred sections.

Cross-Reference   You can find more information on object motion blur in Chapter 6, "Selecting Objects and Setting Object Properties."

In the Scene Range section, the Scene Start and Scene End values let you define the range for the rendered scene. The Lock Range Bar to Scene Range option maintains the range length as defined in the Time Slider, though you can still reposition the start of the rendered scene. The Lock to Video Post Range option sets the range equal to the Video Post range.

Adding image filter events

The Add Image Filter Event button on the toolbar opens the Add Image Filter Event dialog box, shown in Figure 39-6, where you can select from many different filter types. The available filters are included in a drop-down list under the Label field.

Below the filter drop-down list are two buttons: About and Setup. The About button gives some details about the creator of the filter. The Setup button opens a separate dialog box that controls the filter. The dialog box that appears depends on the type of filter that you selected in the drop-down list.

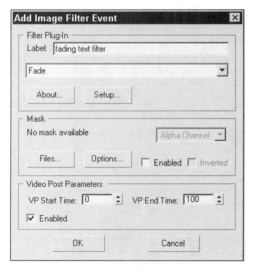

Figure 39-6: The Add Image Filter Event dialog box lets you select from many different filter types.

Several filters require a mask such as the Image Alpha filter. To open a bitmap image to use as the mask, click the Files button in the Mask section and select the file in the Select Mask Image dialog box that opens. The Options button opens the Image Input Options dialog box for aligning and sizing the mask. There is also a drop-down list for selecting the channel to use. Possible channels include Red, Green, Blue, Alpha, Luminance, Z Buffer, Material Effects, and Object. The mask can be Enabled or Inverted.

Note   Several Lens Effects filters are also included in the drop-down list. These filters use an advanced dialog box with many options, which I cover in the "Working with Lens Effect Filters" section later in the chapter.

Contrast filter

You use the Contrast filter to adjust the brightness and contrast. Selecting this filter and clicking the Setup button opens the Image Contrast Control dialog box. This simple dialog box includes values for Contrast and Brightness. Both values can be set from 0 to 1. The Absolute option computes the center gray value based on the highest color value. The Derived option uses an average value of the components of all three colors (red, green, and blue).

Fade filter

You can use the Fade filter to fade out the image over time. You can select it from the drop-down list. The Fade Image Control dialog box lets you select to fade either In or Out. The fade takes place over the length of the range set in the Range pane.

Image Alpha filter

The Image Alpha filter sets the alpha channel as specified by the mask. This filter doesn't have a setup dialog box.

Negative filter

The Negative filter inverts all the colors, as in the negative of a photograph. The Negative Filter dialog box includes a simple Blend value.

Pseudo Alpha filter

The Pseudo Alpha filter sets the alpha channel based on the pixel located in the upper-left corner of the image. This filter can make an unrendered background transparent. When this filter is selected, the Setup button is disabled, because it doesn't have a setup dialog box.

Simple Wipe filter

The Simple Wipe filter removes the image by replacing it with a black background. The length of the wipe is determined by the event's time range. The Simple Wipe Control dialog box, shown in Figure 39-7, lets you wipe from the left to the right or from the right to the left. You can also set the mode to Push, which displays the image, or to Pop, which erases it.

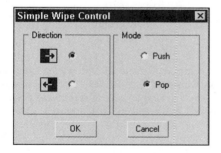

Figure 39-7: The Simple Wipe Control dialog box lets you select which direction to wipe the image.

Starfield filters

The Starfield filter creates a starfield image. By using a camera, you can motion blur the stars. The Stars Control dialog box, shown in Figure 39-8, includes a Source Camera drop-down list that you can use to select a camera.

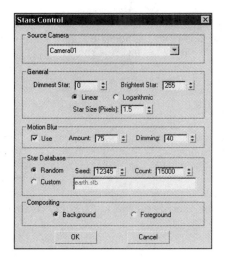

Figure 39-8: The Stars Control dialog box lets you load a custom database of stars.

The General section sets the brightness and size of the stars. You can specify brightness values for the Dimmest Star and the Brightest Star. The Linear and Logarithmic options use two different algorithms to compute the brightness values of the stars as a function of distance. The Star Size value sets the size of the stars in pixels. Size values can range from 0.001 to 100.

The Motion Blur settings let you enable motion blurring, set the blur Amount, and specify a Dimming value.

The Star Database section includes settings for defining how the stars are to appear. The Random option displays stars based on the Count value and the random Seed that determines the randomness of the star's positions. The Custom option reads a star database specified in the Database field.

Note   Max includes a starfield database named earth.stb that includes the stars as seen from Earth.

You can also specify whether the stars are composited in the background or foreground.

Tutorial: Creating space backdrops

Space backgrounds are popular backdrops, and Max includes a special Video Post filter for creating starfield backgrounds. You would typically want to use the Video Post interface to render the starfield along with any animation that you've created, but, in this tutorial, we just render a starfield for a single planet that we've created and outfitted with a planet material.

To create a starfield background, follow these steps:

1. Open the Planet with starfield background.max file from the Chap 39 directory on the CD-ROM.

   This file includes a simple space scene with a camera because the Starfield filter requires a camera.

2. Choose Rendering ⇨ Video Post to open the Video Post interface. A Scene Event must be added to the queue in order for the render job to be executed. Click the Add Scene Event button, type **planet scene** in the Label field, and click OK. This adds the event to the Queue pane.

3. Click the Add Image Filter Event button to open the Add Image Filter Event dialog box and, in the Label field, type the name **starfield bg**. Select Starfield from the drop-down list and click the Setup button to open the Stars Control dialog box. Select Camera01 as the Source Camera, set the Star Size to 3.0 and the Count to 150,000, and click OK. Click OK again to exit the Add Image Filter Event dialog box and add this event to the Queue pane.

4. Click the Execute Sequence button, select the Single output time option and an Output Size, and click the Render button.

Figure 39-9 shows the resulting space scene.

Figure 39-9: A space scene with a background, compliments of the Video Post interface.

Adding image layer events

In addition to the standard filters that can be applied to a single image, several more filters, called layer events, can be applied to two or more images or rendered scenes. The Add Layer Event button is only available on the toolbar when two image events are selected in the Queue pane. The first image (which is the selected image highest in the queue) becomes the source image, and the second image is the compositor. Both image events become sub-events under the layer event.

 Note   If the layer event is deleted, the two sub-event images remain.

The dialog box for the Add Image Layer Event is the same as the Add Image Filter Event dialog box shown earlier except that the drop-down list includes filters that work with two images.

Adobe Premiere Transition filter

When it comes to transitions, Adobe Premiere already has created so many cool transitions that it makes sense to just use theirs. In Max, you can access these filters through the Adobe Premiere Transition Filter Setup dialog box.

This dialog box includes an Add path button to tell Max where to look for filters. All available filters are displayed in the Filter Selection list. You can access the filter interface with the Custom Parameters button. The two preview windows to the right display the filter effects. You also have options to Swap Input (which switches which image is the source) and Use Stand-In (which lets you specify a sample image to preview the effect).

Simple Wipe compositor

The Simple Wipe compositor is similar to the Simple Wipe filter, except that it slides the image in or out instead of erasing it. Its setup dialog box looks just like that of the Simple Wipe Control dialog box.

Other layer filters

The remaining layer filters include simple methods for compositing images and some simple transitions. None of these other filters have a Setup dialog box.

You can use the Alpha compositor to composite two images, using the alpha channel of the foreground image. The Cross Fade Transition compositor fades one image out as it fades another image in. You can use the Pseudo Alpha compositor to combine two images if one doesn't have an alpha channel. This compositor uses the upper-left pixel to designate the transparent color for the image. The Simple Additive compositor combines two images based on the intensity of the second image.

Adding external events

The Add External Event button on the toolbar lets you use an external image-processing program to edit the image. This button is only available when an image event is selected and the image event becomes a sub-event under the external event. The Add External Event dialog box, shown in Figure 39-10, includes a Browse button for locating the external program. There is also a Command Line Options field for entering text commands for the external program. Many external programs use the clipboard to do their processing, so the Write image to clipboard and Read image from clipboard options make this possible.

Using loop events

The Add Loop Event button is enabled in the Video Post toolbar when any single event is selected. This button enables an event to be repeated a specified number of times or throughout the Video Post range. The Add Loop Event dialog box, shown in Figure 39-11, includes a value field for the Number of Times to repeat the event, along with Loop and Ping Pong options. The Loop option repeats from beginning to end until the Number of Times value is reached. The Ping Pong option alternates playing the event forward and in reverse. You can name Loop events using the Label field.

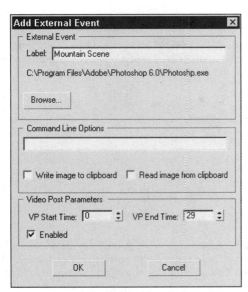

Figure 39-10: The Add External Event dialog box lets you access an external program to edit images.

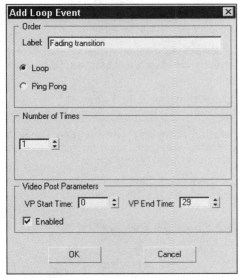

Figure 39-11: The Add Loop Event dialog box lets you play an event numerous times.

Adding an image output event

If you've added all the events you need and configured them correctly, and you click the Execute Sequence button and nothing happens, then chances are you've forgotten to add an Image Output event. This event adds the surface that all the events use to output to and should appear last in the queue.

The Add Image Output Event dialog box looks the same as the Add Image Input Event dialog box shown earlier. The output can be saved to a file or to a device, using any of the standard file types.

Note   If you don't give the output event a name, the filename automatically becomes the event name.

Working with Ranges

The Range pane in the Video Post interface is found to the right of the Queue pane. It displays the ranges for each event. These turn red when selected. The beginning and end points of the range are marked with squares. You can move these points by dragging the squares. This moves the beginning and end points for all selected events.

Note   Before you can move the ranges or drag the end points of a range, you need to select the Edit Range Bar button from the toolbar. The button is highlighted yellow when active.

When two or more events are selected, several additional buttons on the toolbar become enabled, including Swap Events, Align Selected Left, Align Selected Right, Make Selected Same Size, and Abut Selected. (Each of these buttons was shown earlier in Table 39-1.)

The Swap Events button is enabled only if two events are selected. When clicked, it changes the position of the two events. Because the order of the events is important, this can alter the final output.

The Align Selected Left and Align Selected Right buttons move the beginning or end points of every selected track until they line up with the first or last points of the top selected event.

The Make Selected Same Size button resizes any bottom events to be the same size as the top selected event. The Abut Selected button moves each selected event under the top event until its first point lines up with the last point of the selected event above it.

Figure 39-12 shows four image events that have been placed end-to-end using the Abut Selected button. Notice how the queue range spans the entire distance.

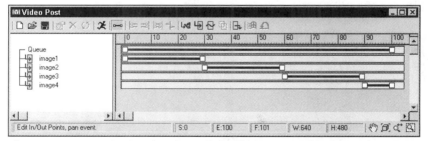

Figure 39-12: You can use the Abut Selected button to position several events end-to-end.

Working with Lens Effects Filters

The Add Image Filter Event dialog box's drop-down list has several Lens Effects filters. These filters include Lens Effects Flare, Focus, Glow, and Highlight. Each of these filters is displayed and discussed in the sections that follow, but several parameters are common to all of them.

Many lens effects parameters in the various Lens Effects setup dialog boxes can be animated. These include Size, Hue, Angle, and Intensity. These are identified in the dialog boxes by green arrow buttons to the right of the parameter fields. These buttons work the way the Animate button in the main interface works. To animate a parameter, just click the corresponding arrow button, move the Time Slider to a new frame, and change the parameter. Figure 39-13 shows how these buttons look in the Lens Effects Flare dialog box.

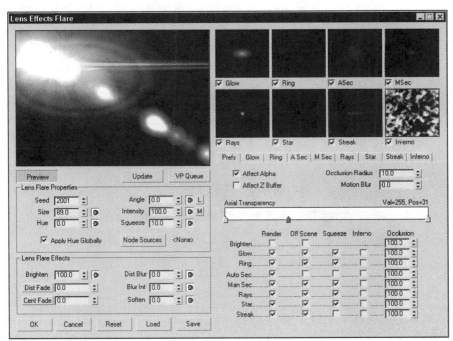

Figure 39-13: Green arrow buttons in the Lens Effects Flare dialog box identify the parameters that can be animated for this effect.

Each Lens Effects dialog box also includes a preview pane in the upper-left corner with three buttons underneath. Clicking the Preview button renders all enabled lens effects in the preview pane. The VP Queue button renders the current Video Post queue. Using the preview pane, you can get an idea of how the final output should look. With the Preview button enabled, any parameter changes in the dialog box are automatically updated in the preview pane. The Update button enables you to manually update the preview. You can right-click on the Preview pane to change its resolution for faster updates at lower resolutions.

Tip   If the VP Queue button is enabled, then a default Lens Effects image is displayed. Using this image, you can play around with the various settings while the Preview mode is enabled to gain an idea of what the various settings do.

You can save the settings in each Lens Effect dialog box as a separate file that can be recalled at any time. These saved files have a .LZF extension and can be saved and loaded with the Save and Load buttons at the bottom left of the dialog box.

Adding flares

The Lens Effects Flare dialog box includes controls for adding flares of various types to an image. This dialog box includes a main preview pane and several smaller preview panes for each individual effect. The check boxes underneath these smaller preview panes let you enable or disable these smaller panes.

Under the main preview pane are several global commands, and to their right is a series of tabbed panels that contain the settings for each individual effect type. The first panel is labeled Prefs and sets which effects are rendered (on and off scene), squeezed, which have the Inferno noise filter applied, and an Occlusion setting.

The settings for the individual flare types are included in the subsequent tabbed panels. They include Glow, Ring, A Sec, M Sec, Rays, Star, Streak, and Inferno. These tabbed panels include gradient color bars for defining the Radial Color, Radial Transparency, Circular Color, Circular Transparency, and Radial Size. Each of these tabbed panels have different settings, but Figure 39-14 shows the tabbed panels for the Glow and Ring effects.

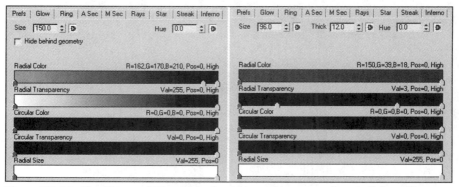

Figure 39-14: The Glow and Ring tabbed panels are representative of all the different lens effect settings.

The gradient colors found in these tabbed panels are controlled by flags that appear under the gradient band. Double-clicking a flag opens a Color Selector dialog box where you can select a new color. Dragging these flags moves the gradient color. You can add a new flag to the band by clicking under the gradient away from the existing flags. The active flag is colored green. By right-clicking on the gradient band, you can access a pop-up menu of options that let you access several options for the selected gradient color. You can even load and save gradients. Gradients are saved as files with the .DGR extension.

The right-most tabbed panel, shown in Figure 39-15, is labeled Inferno and provides a way to add noise to any of the effects. The Prefs tabbed panel includes a check box for enabling the Inferno settings for each effect. Inferno noise can be set to three different states — Gaseous, Fiery, and Electric. If your effect is looking too perfect, you can add some randomness to it with the Inferno option.

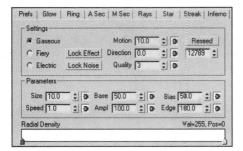

Figure 39-15: The Inferno tabbed panel includes options for enabling noise for the various flare effects.

Adding focus

The Lens Effects Focus dialog box, shown in Figure 39-16, includes options for adding Scene Blur, Radial Blur, and Focal Node effects. If the Focal Node option is selected, you can click the Select button to open the Select Focal Object dialog box in order to choose the object that sets the focal point for the scene.

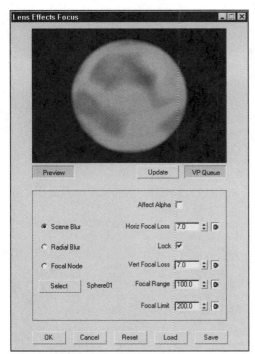

Figure 39-16: You can use the Lens Effects Focus dialog box to blur an image.

You can also set values for the Horizontal and Vertical Focal Loss or enable the Lock button to lock these two parameters together. The Focal Range and Focal Limit values determine the distance from the focal point where the blurring begins or reaches full strength. You can also set the blurring to affect the Alpha channel.

Adding glow

The Lens Effects Glow dialog box, shown in Figure 39-17, enables you to apply glows to the entire scene or to specific objects based on the Object ID or Effects ID. Other Source options include Unclamped, Surface Norm (Normals), Mask, Alpha, Z High, and Z Lo. This dialog box also enables you to Filter the glow, using options such as Edge, Perimeter Alpha, Perimeter, Bright, and Hue.

Additional tabbed panels under the preview pane let you control the Preferences, Gradients, and Inferno settings. In the Preferences tabbed panel, you can set the color of the glow to be based on the Gradient tabbed panel–defined gradients, based on Pixel or a User-defined color. You can also set the Intensity in the Preference tabbed panel.

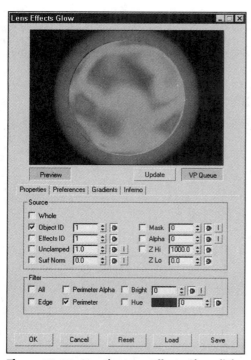

Figure 39-17: Use the Lens Effects Glow dialog box to make objects and scenes glow.

Adding highlights

The Lens Effects Highlight dialog box, shown in Figure 39-18, includes the same Properties, Preferences, and Gradient tabbed panels as the Glow dialog box, except that the effects it produces are highlights instead of glows. The Geometry tabbed panel includes options for setting the Size and Angle of the highlights and how they rotate away from the highlighted object.

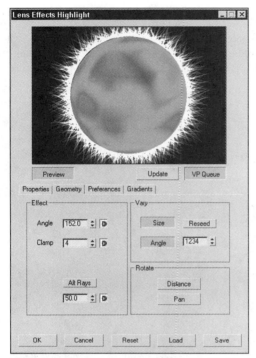

Figure 39-18: Use the Lens Effects Highlight dialog box to add highlights to scene objects.

Tutorial: Making a halo shine

When it comes to glowing objects, I think of radioactive materials, celestial object–like comets and meteors and heavenly objects like angels. In this tutorial, I'm leaning toward heaven in an attempt to create some glory. But, because I couldn't locate an angel, we'll be using a simple halo.

To add highlights to a halo using the Video Post interface, follow these steps:

1. Open the Glowing halo.max file from the Chap 39 directory on the CD-ROM.

    This file contains simple primitives to represent a head and a halo. The halo object has been set to the G-Buffer Object Channel of 1 in its Object Properties dialog box.

2. Choose Rendering ➪ Video Post to open the Video Post interface. Click on the Add Scene Event button in the toolbar.

    The Add Scene Event dialog box appears.

3. Type a name for the event in the Label text field and click OK. The event will be added to the Queue pane.

4. In the Queue pane, select the scene event and click the Add Image Filter Event button in the toolbar to open the associated dialog box. Select Lens Effects Highlight from the drop-down list and click the Setup button.

    The Lens Effects Highlight dialog box appears.

5. Click the VP Queue button followed by the Preview button to see the rendered scene. In the Properties tabbed panel, select the Object ID option and set the Object ID to 1 to match the G-Buffer channel for the halo object. In the Filter section, enable the All option. In the Preferences tabbed panel, set the Size to 3.0, Points to 4, the Color option to Pixel, and Intensity to 100. Then click OK.

6. Click the Execute Sequence button on the toolbar and then click Render in the Execute Video Post dialog box.

Figure 39-19 shows the completed halo in all its shining glory.

Figure 39-19: Using the Lens Effects Highlight dialog box, you can add shining highlights to objects like this halo.

Adding backgrounds and filters using Video Post

As an example of the Video Post interface in action, we composite a background image of a waterfall with a rendered scene of an airplane model created by Viewpoint Datalabs. We'll then add some filter effects before producing the final output image.

To composite an image with the Video Post interface, follow these steps:

1. Open the Airplane over Waterfall.max file from the Chap 39 directory on the CD-ROM.

   This file includes an airplane model. The directory also includes an image called waterfall.tif that will be used later.

2. Open the Environment dialog box by choosing Rendering ⇨ Environment, and change the background color to bright green.

   Doing so makes separating the background color from the rendered airplane easy.

3. Open the Video Post interface by choosing Rendering ➪ Video Post.

4. Add a background image to the queue by clicking the Add Image Input Event button. Click the Files button. Locate the waterfall.tif image from the CD-ROM and click OK. Then click OK again to exit the Add Image Input Event dialog box.

5. Next add the rendered image by clicking the Add Scene Event button and selecting the Perspective view. Name the event **rendered airplane**. Click the Render Options button to open the Render Scene panel. Disable the Anti-Aliasing option in the MAX Default Scanline A-Buffer rollout, and click OK. Click OK again to exit the Edit Scene Event dialog box.

6. Select both the background and rendered airplane events and click the Add Image Layer Event button. Select the Pseudo Alpha option and click OK.

   This composites the background image and the rendered image together by removing all the green background from the rendered scene.

7. Add an output event by clicking the Add Image Output Event button. Name the event **final** and click the Files button to open the Select Image File for Video Post Output dialog box, in which you can select a name and location to use for the saved output file. Click OK when finished, and then click OK again to exit the Add Image Output Event dialog box.

8. To run the processing, click the Execute Sequence button on the toolbar to open the Execute Video Post interface, select the Single output range option, click the 640 × 480 size button, and click Render.

Figure 39-20 shows the final composited image.

Figure 39-20: The airplane in this image is rendered and the background is composited.

Summary

Using the Video Post interface, you can composite several different images, filters, and effects together. All these different compositing elements are listed as events in a queue. The Video Post interface provides, along with the Render Scene dialog box, another way to create output.

In this chapter, you've

✦ Learned about the post-production process

✦ Explored the Video Post interface

✦ Worked with sequences

✦ Explored all the various filter types

✦ Learned to add and edit events and manipulate their ranges

✦ Discovered the Lens Effects filters

This concludes the rendering and post-production part of the book. The next part presents ways to extend the functionality of Max using MAXScript and plug-ins.

✦   ✦   ✦

Adding Functionality with MAXScript and Plug-Ins

Using MAXScript

The Max designers went to great lengths to make sure that you are limited only by your imagination in terms of what you can do in Max. They've packed in so many different features and so many different ways to use those features that you could use Max for years and still learn new ways of doing things.

Despite Max's wide range of capabilities, there may come a time when you wish for a new Max feature. With MAXScript, you can actually extend Max to meet your needs, customize it to work the way you want, and even have it do some of the more monotonous tasks for you.

What Is MAXScript?

In this chapter, we look at MAXScript — what it's for and why in the world you would ever want to use it. But before we get into the nitty-gritty details, let's start with a brief overview.

Simply put, MAXScript is a tool that you can use to expand the functionality of Max. You can use it to add new features or to customize how Max behaves, so that it's tailored to your needs and style. You can also use MAXScript as a sort of VCR — it can record your actions so you can play them back later, eliminating repetitive tasks.

You can use MAXScript to "talk" to Max about a scene and tell it what you want to happen, either by having Max watch what you do or by typing in a list of instructions that you want Max to execute.

The beauty of MAXScript lies in its flexibility and simplicity: It is easy to use and was designed from the ground up to be an integral part of Max. But don't let its simplicity fool you — MAXScript as a language is rich enough to let you control just about anything.

In fact, you have already used MAXScript without even knowing it. Some of the buttons and rollouts use bits of MAXScript to carry out your commands. And after you've created a new feature with MAXScript, you can integrate it into Max transparently and use it just as easily as any other Max feature.

MAXScript is a fully functional and very powerful computer language, but you don't have to be a computer programmer or even need any previous programming experience to benefit from MAXScript. In the next few sections, we look at some simple ways to use MAXScript. For now, just think of a script in Max as you would a script in a movie or play — it tells what's going to happen, who's going to do what, and when it's going to happen. With your scene acting as the stage, a script directs Max to put on a performance for you.

One final note before we dive in: MAXScript is so powerful that an entire book could be written about it and every last feature it supports, but that is not the purpose here. This chapter is organized to give you an introduction to the world of MAXScript and to teach you the basic skills you need to get some mileage out of it. What is given here is a foundation that you can build upon according to your own interests and needs.

MAXScript Tools

MAXScript is pervasive and can be found in many different places. This section looks at the MAXScript tools and how different scripts are created and used.

Let's take a look at some of the tools used in working with MAXScript. Max has several tools that make creating and using scripts as simple as possible.

The MAXScript menu

The MAXScript menu includes commands that you can use to create a new script, open and run scripts, open the MAXScript Listener window (keyboard shortcut, F11), or enable the Macro Recorder.

The New Script command opens a MAXScript editor window, a simple text editor in which you write your MAXScript. See the "MAXScript editor windows" section found later in this chapter for more on this editor window. The Open Script command opens a file dialog box that you can use to locate a MAXScript file. When opened, the script file will be opened in a MAXScript editor window, as shown in Figure 40-1. MAXScript files have an .ms or an .mcr extension. The Run Script command also opens a file dialog box where you can select a script to be executed.

Note When you use Run Script, some scripts will do something right away, whereas others will install themselves as new tools.

```
utility sphereArray "Sphere Array"
(
spinner objCount "Object count:" range:[1,100,20] type:#integer
spinner radius "Radius:" range:[1,1000,50]

button go "Go!"

on go pressed do
(
  a = selection[1]
  if a != undefined do
  (
    c = objCount.value
    r = radius.value
    for i = 1 to c do
    (
      someObj = copy a
      someObj.position.x = someObj.position.x + r
      about selection rotate someObj (random 0 359) x_axis
      about selection rotate someObj (random 0 359) y_axis
      about selection rotate someObj (random 0 359) z_axis
    )
  )
)
)
```

Figure 40-1: MAXScript is written using standard syntax using a simple text editor window.

The MAXScript Listener command opens the MAXScript Listener window. You can also open this window by pressing the F11 keyboard shortcut. The Macro Recorder command will start recording a MAXScript macro. I cover the MAXScript Listener and recording macros later in this chapter.

The MAXScript Utility rollout

You access the MaxScript Utility rollout, shown in Figure 40-2, by opening the Utilities panel in the Command Panel and clicking the MAXScript button. This opens a rollout where you can do many of the same commands as the MAXScript menu.

Figure 40-2: The MAXScript rollout on the Utilities panel is a great place to start working with MAXScript.

The MAXScript rollout also includes a Utilities drop-down list, which holds any installed scripted utilities. Each scripted utility acts as a new feature for you to use. The parameters for these utilities will be displayed in a new rollout that appears below the MAXScript rollout.

Cross-Reference   An easy way to create these utilities is with the Visual MAXScript Editor, which is covered in Chapter 41, "Using the Visual MAXScript Editor."

Tutorial: Using the SphereArray script

Here's a chance for you to play around a little and get some experience with MAXScript in the process. In the Chap 40 directory of the CD-ROM is a simple script called SphereArray.ms. It's similar to the Array command found in the Tools menu, except that SphereArray creates copies of an object and randomly positions them in a spherical pattern.

To load and use the SphereArray script, follow these steps:

1. Open the SphereArray.max file from the Chap 40 directory on the CD-ROM.

   This file contains a single box object.

2. Select the box object, open the Utilities panel in the Command Panel (the icon is a hammer), and click the MAXScript button.

The MAXScript rollout appears.

3. Click the Run Script button in the MAXScript rollout to open the Choose Editor file dialog box, locate the SphereArray.ms file from the Chap 40 directory on the CD-ROM, and click Open.

The SphereArray utility installs and appears in the Utilities drop-down list. (Because SphereArray is a scripted utility, running it only installs it.)

4. Choose SphereArray from the Utilities drop-down list. Make sure the box object is selected.

5. In the Sphere Array rollout, enter **50** in the Object Count field and **2.0** for the Radius field. Now click the Go! button to run the script.

The script adds 50 copies of your box to the scene and randomly positions them two units away from the box's position.

Figure 40-3 shows the results of the SphereArray MAXScript utility. Notice how the SphereArray script looks a lot like any other function or tool in Max.

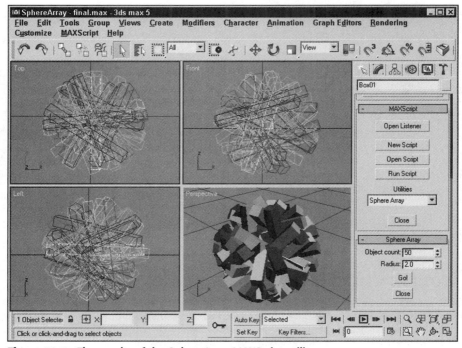

Figure 40-3: The results of the SphereArray MAXScript utility

The MAXScript Listener window

Figure 40-4 shows the MAXScript Listener window (keyboard shortcut, F11), which lets you work interactively with the part of Max that interprets MAXScript commands. The top pane of the Listener window (the pink area) lets you enter MAXScript commands; the results will be reported in the bottom pane (the white area) of the Listener window. You can also type MAXScript commands in the bottom pane, but typing them in the top pane keeps the commands separated from the results.

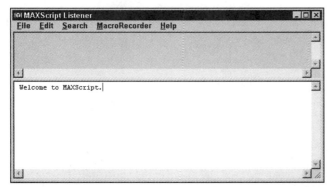

Figure 40-4: The MAXScript Listener window interprets your commands.

When you type commands into either pane and press Enter, the MAXScript interpreter evaluates the command and responds with the results. For example, if you type a simple mathematical expression such as **2+2** and press Enter, then the result of 4 will be displayed in blue on the next line. Most results appear in blue, but the results display in red for any errors that occur. For example, if you enter the command **hello there**, then a Type error result will appear in red because the MAXScript interpreter doesn't understand the command.

Caution The MAXScript interpreter is very fickle. A misspelling generates an error, but MAXScript is *case-insensitive*, which means that upper- and lowercase letters are the same as far as Max is concerned. Thus, you can type **sphere**, **Sphere**, or **SPHERE** and Max sees no difference.

The Listener window has these menus:

✦ **File:** You can use this menu to close the window (Ctrl+W), save your work (Ctrl+S), run scripts (Ctrl+R), open a script for editing (Ctrl+O), or create a new script from scratch (Ctrl+N).

✦ **Edit:** This menu is where you access all the common editing functions you'll need, such as cutting, pasting, and undoing.

✦ **Search:** You use this menu for searching through the window to find specific text (Ctrl+F), find the next instance (Ctrl+G), or replace text (Ctrl+H).

✦ **MacroRecorder:** This menu lets you set various options for the MAXScript Macro Recorder.

✦ **Help:** This menu provides access to the MAXScript Reference (F1).

Tutorial: Talking to the MAXScript interpreter

This tutorial gives you a little experience in working with the MAXScript Listener window and a chance to try some basic MAXScript commands.

To start using MAXScript, follow these steps:

1. Choose File ➪ Reset to reset Max.

2. Choose MAXScript ➪ MAXScript Listener or press F11 to open the MAXScript Listener window.

3. Click anywhere in the bottom pane of the Listener window, type the following, and press Enter:

   `sphere()`

   A sphere object with default parameters is created.

4. Next enter the following in the lower pane and press the Enter key:

   `torus radius1:50 radius2:5`

   Max creates a torus and adds it to your scene. As you specified in your MAXScript, the outer radius (radius1) is 50, and the radius of the torus itself (radius2) is 5. The output tells you that Max created a new torus at the origin of the coordinate system and gave that torus a name: Torus01.

5. Now use MAXScript to move the torus. In the Listener window, type the following:

   `$Torus01.position.x = 20`

   After you press Enter, you see the torus move along the positive X-axis. Each object in Max has certain properties or attributes that describe it, and what you've done is access one of these properties programmatically instead of by using the rollout or the mouse. In this case, you're telling Max, "Torus01 has a position property. Set the X-coordinate of that position to 20."

Note   The $ symbol identifies a named object. You can use it to refer to any named object.

6. To see a list of some of the properties specific to a torus, type the following:

   `Showproperties $Torus01`

   A list of the Torus01 properties appears in the window, as shown in Figure 40-5.

Figure 40-5 shows the MAXScript Listener window with all the associated commands and results. Figure 40-6 shows the objects completed in the Max window.

An important thing to understand from this tutorial is that you can do almost anything with MAXScript. Any property of any object that you can access via a rollout is also available via MAXScript. You could go so far as to create entire scenes using just MAXScript, although the real power comes from using MAXScript to do things for you automatically.

Tip   Max remembers the value of the last MAXScript command that it executed, and you can access that value through a special variable: ? (a question mark). For example, if you type **5 + 5** in the Listener window, Max displays the result, 10. You can then use that result in your next MAXScript command by using the question mark variable. For example, you could type **$Torus01.radius2 = ?,** and Max would internally substitute the question mark with the number 10.

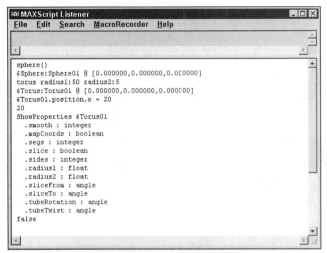

Figure 40-5: Use the MAXScript Listener window to query Max about an object's properties.

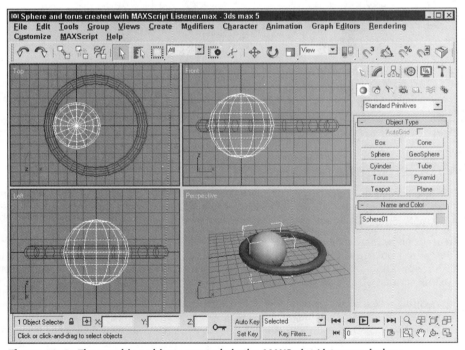

Figure 40-6: The resulting objects created via the MAXScript Listener window

At the left end of the status bar, you can access the MAXScript Mini Listener control by dragging the left edge of the status bar to the right. By right-clicking in this control, you can open a Listener Window and view all the current commands recorded by the Listener. Figure 40-7 shows this control.

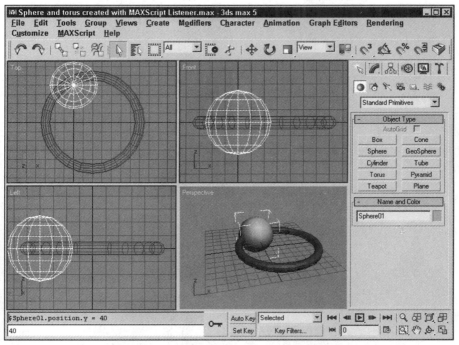

Figure 40-7: The Mini MAXScript Listener on the status bar provides quick access.

MAXScript editor windows

The MAXScript editor window enables you to open and edit any type of text file, although its most common use is for editing MAXScript files. Although you can have only one Listener window open, you can open as many editor windows as you want.

To open a new MaxScript editor window, you can choose MAXScript ⇨ New Script, choose File ⇨ New from the MAXScript Listener window, or you can click the New Script button in the MAXScript rollout in the Utility panel. You can also use MaxScript editor windows to edit existing scripts.

For creating a new script, opening both an editor window and the Listener window is usually best. Then you can try out things in the Listener window, and when the pieces of the MAXScript work, you can cut and paste them into the main editor window. Then you can return to the Listener window, work on the next new thing, and continue creating, cutting, and pasting until the script is done.

Tip You can also send text back to the Listener window for Max to evaluate. Just select some text with the cursor or mouse, and press Shift+Enter (or just Enter on the numeric keypad). Max copies the selected text to the Listener window and evaluates it for you.

The File, Search, and Help menus in the MAXScript editor window are the same as those used for the Listener window, with the exception of the Evaluate All command. This command (choose File ➪ Evaluate All to access it) is a fast way of having Max evaluate your entire script. The result is the same as if you had manually selected the entire text, copied it to the Listener window, and pressed Enter.

The Edit menu includes commands to Undo (Ctrl+Z), Cut (Ctrl+X), Copy (Ctrl+C), Paste (Ctrl+V), or Delete (Delete) text. It also includes access to the Visual MAXScript window with the New Rollout and Edit Rollout (F2) menu commands. The pop-up menu also includes a command to Select All (Ctrl+A). You can also access this menu as a pop-up menu by right-clicking in the window.

Cross-Reference   Chapter 41, "Using the Visual MAXScript Editor," covers the Visual MAXScript Editor interface.

The Macro Recorder

The MAXScript Macro Recorder is a tool that records your actions and creates a MAXScript that can be recalled to duplicate those actions. Using the Macro Recorder is not only a quick and easy way to write entire scripts, but it is also a great way to make a working version of a script that you can then refine. After the Macro Recorder has created a MAXScript from your recorded actions, you can edit the script using a MAXScript editor window to make any changes you want.

You can turn the Macro Recorder on and off either by choosing MAXScript ➪ Macro Recorder or by choosing Macro Recorder ➪ Enable in the MAXScript Listener window. The check mark next to Macro Recorder command on the MAXScript menu indicates that the Macro Recorder is turned on.

When the Macro Recorder is on, every action is converted to MAXScript and sent to the MAXScript Listener window's top pane. You can then take the MAXScript output and save it to a file or copy it to a MAXScript editor window for additional editing. The Macro Recorder continues to monitor your actions until you turn it off, which is done in the same way as turning it on.

The MacroRecorder menu in the MAXScript Listener window includes several options for customizing the macro recorder including

✦ **Enable:** This option turns the Macro Recorder on or off.

✦ **Explicit scene object names:** With this option, the Macro Recorder writes the MAXScript using the names of the objects you modify so that the script always modifies those exact same objects, regardless of what object you have selected when you run the script again. For example, if the Macro Recorder watches you move a pyramid named $Pyramid01 in your scene, then the resulting MAXScript will always and only operate on the scene object named $Pyramid01.

✦ **Selection-relative scene object names:** With this option, the Macro Recorder writes MAXScript that will operate on whatever object is currently selected. So if (when you recorded your script) you moved the pyramid named $Pyramid01, you could later select a different object and run your script, and the new object would move instead.

Note   To decide which of these options to use, ask yourself, "Do I want the script to always manipulate this particular object, or do I want the script to manipulate whatever I have selected?"

✦ **Absolute transform assignments:** This tells the Macro Recorder that any transformations you make are not relative to an object's current position or orientation. For example, if you move a sphere from (0,0,0) to (10,0,0), the Macro Recorder writes MAXScript that says, "Move the object to (10,0,0)."

✦ **Relative transforms operations:** Use this option to have the Macro Recorder apply transformations relative to an object's current state. For example, if you move a sphere from (0,0,0) to (10,0,0), the Macro Recorder says, "Move the object +10 units in the X-direction from its current location."

✦ **Explicit subobject sets:** If you choose this option and then record a script that manipulates a set of subobjects, running the script again will always manipulate those same subobjects, even if you have other subobjects selected when you run the script again.

✦ **Selection-relative subobject sets:** This tells the Macro Recorder that you want the script to operate on whatever subobjects are selected when you run the script.

✦ **Show command panel switchings:** This option tells the Macro Recorder whether or not to write MAXScript for actions that take place on the Command Panel.

✦ **Show tool selections:** If this option is selected, the Macro Recorder records MAXScript to change to different tools.

✦ **Show menu item selections:** This option tells the Macro Recorder whether or not you want it to generate MAXScript for menu items you select while recording your script.

Tutorial: Recording a simple script

In this tutorial, we'll create a simple script that squashes whatever object you have selected and turns it purple.

To create a script using the Macro Recorder, follow these steps:

1. Open the Purple pyramid.max file from the Chap 40 directory on the CD-ROM.

This file includes a simple pyramid object.

2. With the pyramid object selected, choose MAXScript ➪ MAXScript Listener (or press F11) to open the MAXScript Listener window.

3. In the Listener window, open the MacroRecorder menu and make sure that all the options are set to the relative and not the absolute object settings, thereby telling the script to work on any object that is selected instead of always modifying the same object.

4. Returning to the MacroRecorder menu, select Enable. The Macro Recorder is now on and ready to start writing MAXScript. Minimize the Macro Recorder window (or at least move it out of the way so you can see the other viewports).

5. Dock the MAXScript Listener window to the Left viewport by right-clicking the viewport name and choosing Views ➪ Extended ➪ MAXScript Listener. Now you can keep things out of the way while you work.

6. Choose Modifiers ➪ Parametric Deformers ➪ XForm to add an XForm modifier to the object.

7. Select the non-uniform scale tool and restrict it to the Y-axis. Right-click anywhere in the Front viewport to make it active (if it's not already), and then drag the Y-axis gizmo downward to squash the pyramid.

8. In the Modify panel, click the color swatch next to the object name field to open the Object Color dialog box. Pick one of the purple colors and click OK.

9. The script is done, so in the MAXScript Listener window, choose MacroRecorder ➪ Enable to turn off the Macro Recorder.

10. Now it's time to try out your first MAXScript effort. Add a sphere to your scene. Make sure it's selected before moving to the next step.

11. In the top pane of the MAXScript Listener window, select all the text (an easy way to do so is by pressing Ctrl+A), and then press Shift+Enter to tell Max to execute the MAXScript.

In Figure 40-8, you can see the script and the sphere that has been squashed and has changed color.

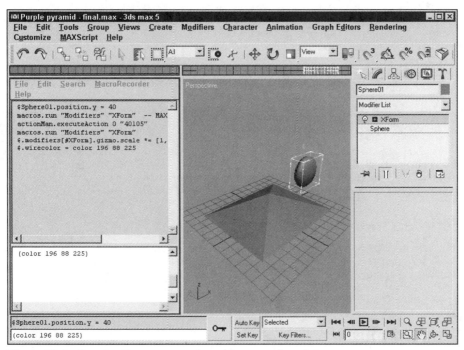

Figure 40-8: Running the new squash-and-turn-purple script

Types of Scripts

All scripts are not created equal, and Max categorizes different scripts based on how they work. For more information, the MAXScript online help provides exhaustive information on their various options.

The main thing to consider when deciding what type of script to create is the user interface. Ask yourself what the most logical user interface would be for the type of tool you're creating, and this will give you a hint as to which type of script is well suited for the task.

Macro scripts

Macro scripts are scripts created with the Macro Recorder. Any script that is associated with a toolbar button is considered a Macro script. Max organizes Macro scripts by their category, which you can change by editing the script file. To call a Macro script from another script, you can use the `macros` command. For example,

```
macros.run "objects" "sphere"
```

runs the "sphere" script in the "objects" category.

Macro scripts are generally scripts that require no other user input; you just click a button and the script works its magic.

Scripted utilities

A scripted utility is a MAXScript that has its own custom rollout in the Utilities panel, like the SphereArray example. This type of script is particularly useful when your script has parameters that the user needs to enter, such as the radius in the SphereArray script.

Cross-Reference

Scripted utilities are easy to build using the Visual MAXScript Editor covered in Chapter 41, "Using the Visual MAXScript Editor."

Scripted right-click menus

When you right-click an object in your scene, Max opens a pop-up menu of options for you to choose from, much like a quadmenu. Scripted right-click menus let you append your own menu items to the right-click menu. If you create a script that modifies some property of an object, making the script available through the right-click menu makes it easily accessible.

Scripted mouse tools

You can use scripted mouse tools to create scripts that handle mouse input in the viewports. These scripts listen for commands from the mouse, such as clicking the mouse buttons and clicking and dragging the cursor. For example, you would use this type of MAXScript if you were making a new primitive object type so that users could create the new objects just like they would a sphere or a box.

Scripted plug-ins

Scripted plug-ins are by far the most complex type of MAXScript available. They mirror the functionality of non-MAXScript plug-ins (which are written in other programming languages such as C++). You can create scripted plug-ins that make new geometry, create new shapes, control lights, act as modifiers, control texture maps and materials, and even produce special rendering effects.

Writing Your Own MAXScripts

This section presents the basics of the MAXScript language and shows you how to use the various parts of MAXScript in your own scripts. You can test any of these scripting commands using the MAXScript Listener window.

Cross-Reference Much of the discussion that follows will sound familiar if you've already read the chapter on expressions found in Chapter 29, "Using Expressions." Expressions use many of the same constructs as MAXScript.

Variables and data types

A *variable* in MAXScript is sort of like a variable in algebra. It represents some other value, and when you mention a variable in an equation you're actually talking about the value that the variable holds. You can think of variables in MAXScript as containers that you can put stuff into and take it out of later. Unlike variables in algebra, however, variables in MAXScript can "hold" other things besides numbers, as we'll soon see.

To put a value into a variable, you use the equal sign. For example, if you type

```
X = 5 * 3
```

in the MAXScript Listener window, Max evaluates the expression on the right side of the equals sign and stores the result in the variable named X. In this case, Max would multiply 5 by 3 and store the result (15) into X. You can then see what is in X by just typing **X** in the Listener window and pressing Enter. Max then displays the value stored in X, or 15.

You can name your variables whatever you want, and naming them something that helps you remember what the variable is for is a good idea. For example, if you want a variable that keeps track of how many objects you're going to manipulate, the name "objCount" would be better than something like "Z."

Note Variable names can be just about anything you want, but you must start a variable name with a letter. Also, the variable name can't have any special characters in it, like spaces, commas, or quote marks. You can, however, use the underscore character and any normal alphabetic characters.

Variables can also hold strings, which are groups of characters. For example,

```
badDay = "Monday"
```

stores the word "Monday" in the variable badDay. You can attach two strings together using the plus sign, like this:

```
grouchy = "My least favorite day is" + badDay
```

Now the variable grouchy holds the value "My least favorite day is Monday."

Try this:

```
wontWork = 5 + "cheese"
```

Max prints out an error because it's confused — you're asking it to add a number to a string. The problem is that 5 and "cheese" are two different data types. Data types are different classes of values that you can store in variables. You can almost always mix values of the same data type, but values of different types usually don't make sense together.

Note To see the data type of a variable, use the classof command. Using the previous example, you could type **classof grouchy** and Max would in turn print out String.

Another very common data type is Point3, which represents a three-dimensional point. Following are a few examples of using points, with explanatory comments:

```
Pos = [5,3,2]          -- Marks a point at (5,3,2)
Pos.x = 7              -- Change the x-coordinate to 7
                       -- Now the point is at (7,3,2)
Pos = Pos + (1,2,5)    -- Take the old value for Pos,
                       -- move it by (1,2,5) to (8,5,7)
                       -- and store the new value in Pos
```

In addition to these basic data types, each object in your scene has its own data type. For example, if you use classof on a sphere object, Max prints out Sphere. Data types for scene objects are actually complex data types or structures, which means that they are groups of other data types in a single unit. The pieces of data inside a larger object are called *members* or *properties*. Most scene objects have a member called Name, which is of type String. The Name member tells the specific name of that object. Another common property is Position, a Point3 variable that tells the object's position.

Max has a special built-in variable that represents whatever object is currently selected. This variable is $ (the dollar sign), which is used in the following tutorial.

Tutorial: Using variables

In this tutorial, you learn more about variables in MAXScript by using them to manipulate an object in your scene.

To use variables to manipulate scene objects, follow these steps:

1. Open the Teapot.max file from the Chap 40 directory on the CD-ROM.

   This file has a simple teapot object.

2. Right-click on the title for the Left viewport and choose Views ⇨ Extended ⇨ MAXScript Listener to open the MAXScript Listener window in the Left viewport.

3. Type $ and press Enter.

   Max displays information about the teapot. (Your numbers will probably be different depending on where you placed your teapot.)

4. Type in the following lines one at a time to see the property values stored as part of the teapot object:

```
$.position
$.wirecolor
$.radius
$.name
$.lid
```

5. Now type in these lines, one at a time, to set the property values of the teapot object:

```
$.lid = false
$.position.x = -20
$.segs = 20
```

Figure 40-9 shows the commands and its results in the MAXScript Listener window and also the resulting teapot object.

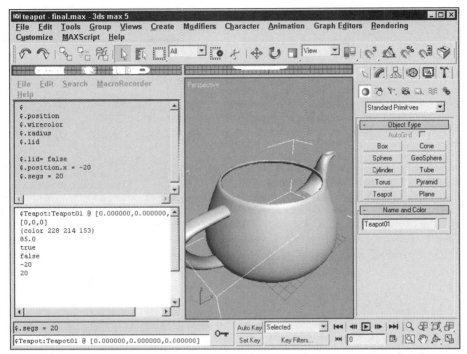

Figure 40-9: The script commands entered in the MAXScript Listener affect the objects in the viewports.

Program flow and comments

In general, when Max begins executing a script it starts with the first line of the script, processes it, and then moves on to the next line. Execution of the script continues until no more lines are in the script file. (Later we look at some MAXScript keywords that let you change the flow of script execution.)

Max lets you embed comments or notes in your script file to help explain what is happening. To insert a comment, precede it with two hyphens (--). When Max encounters the double hyphen, it skips the comment and everything else on that line and moves to the next line of the script. For example, in this line of MAXScript

```
$Torus01.pos = [0,0,0]    -- Move it back to the origin
```

Max processes the first part of the line (and moves the object to the origin) and then moves on to the next line after it reaches the comment.

Using comments in your MAXScript files is very important because after your scripts start to become complex, figuring out what is happening can get difficult. Also, when you come back a few months later to improve your script, comments will refresh your memory and help keep you from repeating the same mistakes you made the first time around.

Note   Because Max ignores anything after the double hyphen, you can use comments to temporarily remove MAXScript lines from your script. If something isn't working right, you can *comment out* the lines that you want Max to skip. Later, when you want to add them back in, you don't have to retype them. You can just remove the comment marks, and your script is back to normal.

Expressions

An *expression* is what Max uses to make decisions. An expression compares two things and draws a simple conclusion based on that comparison.

 Cross-Reference These same expressions can be used within the Expression controller. You can find details on this controller in Chapter 29, "Using Expressions."

Simple expressions

The expression

```
1 < 2
```

is a simple expression that asks the question, "Is 1 less than 2?" Expressions always ask yes/no type questions. When you type an expression in the MAXScript Listener window (or inside of a script), Max evaluates the expression and prints true if the expression is valid (like the preceding example) and false if it isn't. Try the following expressions in the Listener window, and Max will print the results as shown in Figure 40-10 (you don't have to type in the comments):

```
1 < 2            -- 1 IS less than 2, so expression is true
1 > 2            -- 1 is NOT greater than 2, so false
2 + 2 == 4       -- '==' means "is equal to". 2 + 2 is
                 -- equal to 4, so true
2 + 2 == 5       -- 4 is NOT equal to 5, so false
3 * 3 == 5 + 4   -- 9 IS equal to 9, so true

3 * 3 != 5 + 4   -- '!=' means 'not equal to'. '9 is not
                 -- equal to 9' is a false statement, so
                 -- the expression is false

a = 23           -- store 23 in variable a
b = 14 + 9       -- store 23 in variable b
a == b           -- 23 IS equal to 23, so true
```

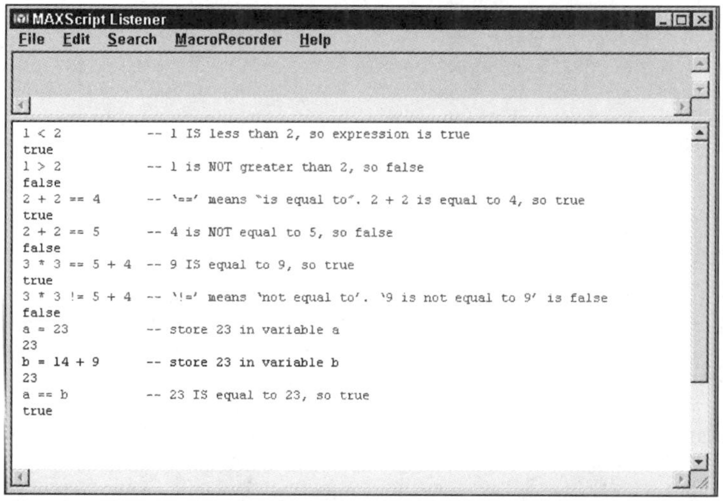

Figure 40-10: Using the MAXScript Listener to evaluate expressions

Play around with simple expressions until you're familiar with what they mean and have an intuitive feel for whether or not an expression is going to evaluate to true or false.

Complex expressions

Sometimes you need an expression to decide on more than just two pieces of data. MAXScript has the and, or, and not operators to help you do this.

The and operator combines two expressions and asks the question, "Are both expressions true?" If both are true, then the entire expression evaluates to true. But if either is false, or if they are both false, then the entire expression is false. You can use parentheses to group expressions, so an expression with the and operator might look something like this:

```
(1 < 2) and (1 < 3)      -- true because (1 < 2) is true AND
                         -- (1 < 3) is true
```

The or operator is similar to and, except that an expression with or is true if either of the expressions is true or if both are true. Here are some examples:

```
(2 > 3) or (2 > 1)       -- even though (2 > 3) is false, the
                         -- entire expression is true because
                         -- (2 > 1) is true
   (2 > 3) and (2 > 1)   -- false because both expressions are
                         -- not true
```

Try some of these complex expressions to make sure you understand how they work:

```
a = 3
b = 2
(a == b) or (a > b)      -- true because a IS greater than b
(a == b) and (b == 2)    -- false because both expressions are
                         -- not true
(a > b) or (a < b)       -- true because at least one IS true
(a != b) and (b == 3)    -- false because b is NOT equal to 3
```

The not operator negates or flips the value of an expression from true to false or vice versa. For example

```
(1 == 2)                 -- false because 1 is NOT equal to 2
not (1 == 2)             -- true. 'not' flips the false to true
```

Conditions

Conditions are one way in which you can control program flow in a script. Normally, Max processes each line, no matter what, and then quits; but with *conditions*, Max executes certain lines only if an expression is true.

For example, suppose you have a script with the following lines:

```
a = 4
If (a == 5) then
(
  b = 2
)
```

Max would not execute the line b = 2 because the expression (a == 5) evaluates to false. Conditional statements, or "if" statements, basically say, "If this expression evaluates to true, then do the stuff inside the block of parentheses. If the expression evaluates to false, skip those lines of script."

Conditional statements follow this form:

```
If <expr> then <stuff>
```

where `<expr>` is an expression to evaluate and `<stuff>` is some MAXScript to execute if the expression evaluates to true. You can also use the keyword `else` to specify what happens if the expression evaluates to false, as shown in the following example:

```
a = 4
if (a == 5) then
(
  b = 2
)
else
(
  b = 3
)
```

After this block of MAXScript, the variable `b` would have the value of 3 because the expression `(a == 5)` evaluated to false. Consequently, Max executed the MAXScript in the `else` section of the statement.

Collections and arrays

MAXScript has some very useful features to help you manipulate groups of objects. A group of objects is called a *collection*. You can think of a collection as a bag that holds a bunch of objects or variables. The things in the bag are in no particular order; they're just grouped together.

You can use collections to work with groups of a particular type of object. For example, the MAXScript

```
a = $pokey*
a.wirecolor = red
```

creates a collection that contains every object in your scene whose name starts with "Pokey" and makes every object in that collection turn red.

MAXScript has several built-in collections that you might find useful, such as cameras and lights, containing all the cameras and lights in your scene. So

```
delete lights
```

removes all the light objects from your scene (which may or may not be a good idea).

An *array* is a type of collection in which all the objects are in a fixed order, and you can access each member of the array by an index. For example

```
a = #()      -- creates an empty array to use
a[1] = 5
a[2] = 10
a[5] = 12
a
```

After the last line, Max prints out the current value for the array:

```
#(5, 10, undefined, undefined, 12)
```

Notice that Max makes the array big enough to hold however many elements we want to put in it, and that if we don't put anything in one of the positions, Max automatically puts in `undefined`, which simply means that array location has no value at all.

One last useful trick is that Max lets you use the `as` keyword to convert from a collection to an array:

```
LightArray = (lights as array)
```

Max takes the built-in collection of lights, converts it to an array, and names the array `LightArray`.

The members of an array or a collection don't all have to have the same data type, so it's completely valid to have an array with numbers, strings, and objects, like this:

```
A = #(5,"Mr. Nutty",box radius:5)
```

Note   You can use the `as` MAXScript keyword to convert between data types. For example, (5 as string) **converts the number 5 to the string "5," and** (5 as float) **converts the whole number 5 to the floating-point number 5.0.**

Loops

A *loop* is a MAXScript construct that lets you override the normal flow of execution. Instead of processing each line in your script once and then quitting, Max can use loops to do something several times.

For example,

```
j = 0
for i = 1 to 5 do
(
  j = j + i
)
```

This MAXScript uses two variables — i and j — but you can use any variables you want in your loops. The script sets the variable j to 0 and then uses the variable i to count from 1 to 5. Max repeats the code between the parentheses five times, and each time the variable i is incremented by 1. Inside the loop, Max adds the current value of i to j. Can you figure out what the value of j is at the end of the script? If you guessed 15, you're right. To see why, look at the value of each variable as the script is running:

```
When                     j    i
-----------------------------------
First line               0    0
Start of loop            0    1
After first loop         1    1
Start of second loop     1    2
After second loop        3    2
Start of third loop      3    3
After third loop         5    3
Start of fourth loop     6    4
After fourth loop        10   4
Start of fifth loop      10   5
After fifth loop         15   5
```

A loop is also useful for processing each member of an array or collection. The following MAXScript shows one way to turn every teapot in a scene blue:

```
teapots = $teapot*            -- get the collection of teapots
for singleTeapot in teapots do
(
 singleTeapot.wirecolor = blue
)
```

You can use a `for` loop to create a bunch of objects for you. Try this MAXScript:

```
for I = 1 to 10 collect
 (
 sphere radius:15
 )
```

The `collect` keyword tells Max to create a collection with the results of the MAXScript in the block of code inside the parentheses. The line

```
sphere radius:15
```

tells Max to create a sphere with radius of 15, so the entire script created 10 spheres and added them to your scene. Unfortunately, Max puts them all in the same spot, so let's move them around a bit so we can see them:

```
i = -50
For s in spheres do
(
 s.position = [i,i,i]
 i = i + 10
)
```

Study this script to make sure you understand what's going on. We use a `for` loop to process each sphere in our collection of spheres. For each one, we set its position to [i,i,i], and then we change the value of i so that the next sphere will be at a different location.

Functions

The last feature of basic MAXScript that we look at is the *function*. Functions are small chunks of MAXScript that act like program building blocks. For example, suppose you need to compute the average of a collection of numbers many times during a script you're writing. The MAXScript to do this might be

```
Total = 0
Count = 0
For n in numbers do
(
 total = total + n
 count = count + 1
)
average = total / (count as float)
```

Given a collection of numbers called `numbers`, this MAXScript will compute the average. Unfortunately, every time you need to compute the average, you have to type all that MAXScript in again. Or you might be smart and just cut and paste it in each time you need it. Still, your script is quickly becoming large and ugly, and you always have to change the script to match the name of your collection you're averaging.

A function will solve your problem. At the beginning of your script, you can define an average function like this:

```
Function average numbers =
( -- Function to average the numbers in a collection
 local Total = 0
 local Count = 0
 For n in numbers do
 (
 total = total + n
 count = count + 1
 )
 total / (count as float)

)
```

Now any time you need to average any collection of numbers in your script, you could just use this to take all the numbers in the collection called num and store their average in a variable called Ave:

```
Ave = average num       -- assuming num is a collection
```

Not only will this make your script much shorter if you need to average numbers a lot, but it makes it a lot more readable, too. It's very clear to the casual reader that you're going to average some numbers. Also, if you later realize that you wrote the average function incorrectly, you can just fix it at the top of the script. If you weren't using functions, you would have to go through your script and find every case where you averaged numbers and then fix the problem. (What a headache!)

Let's take another look at the function definition. The first line

```
Function average numbers =
```

tells Max that you're creating a new function called average. It also tells Max that to use this function, you have to pass in one piece of data, and that inside the function you'll refer to that data using a variable called numbers. It doesn't matter what the name of the actual variable was when the function was called; inside the function you can simply refer to it as numbers.

Creating functions that use multiple pieces of data is also easy. For example,

```
Function multEm a b c = (a * b * c)
```

creates a function that multiplies three numbers together. To use this function to multiply three numbers and store the result in a variable called B, you would simply enter

```
B = multEm 2 3 4
```

The next two lines

```
local Total = 0
local Count = 0
```

create two variables and set them both to 0. The local keyword tells Max that the variable belongs to this function. No part of the script outside of the function can see this variable, and if there is a variable outside the function with the same name, changing the variable inside this function won't affect that variable outside the function. That way, you never have to worry about what other variables are in use when someone calls average; even if variables are in use that are named Total or Count, they won't be affected.

The last line

```
total / (count as float)
```

uses the `Total` and `Count` values to compute the average. How does that value get sent back to whoever called the function? Max evaluates all the MAXScript inside the function and returns the result. Because the last line is the last thing to be evaluated, Max uses the result of that calculation as the result of the entire function.

Tutorial: Creating a school of fish

Let's look at an example that puts into practice some of the things you've been learning in this chapter. In this multipart tutorial, we use MAXScript to create a small school of fish that follows the dummy object around the path.

Part 1: Making the fish follow a path

In this part of the tutorial, we use MAXScript to move one of the fish along a path in the scene. To do this, follow these steps:

1. Open the Fish scene.max file from the Chap 40 directory on the CD-ROM.

   This scene consists of two fish and a dummy object that follows a path. What we need to do is use MAXScript to create a small school of fish that follows the dummy object around the path.

2. Press F11 to open the MAXScript Listener window. In the window, choose File ➪ New Script to open the MAXScript editor window, and type in the following script:

```
pathObj = $Dummy01
fishObj = $Fish1/FishBody
relPos = [0,-150,-50]    -- How close the fish is to the path

animate on
(
 for t = 1 to 100 do at time t
 (
 fishObj.position = pathObj.position + relPos
 )
)
```

3. Choose File ➪ Evaluate All or press Ctrl+E to evaluate all the MAXScript in the editor window, right-click the Camera01 viewport to activate it, and click the Play Animation button.

   The fish rigidly follows the dummy object's path. Figure 40-11 shows one frame of this animation.

Now let's explain the MAXScript entered in the previous tutorial. The first few lines create some variables that the rest of the script uses. `pathObj` tells the name of the object that the fish will follow, and `fishObj` is the name of the fish's body. (Notice that we can reference parts of the group hierarchy by using the object name, a forward slash, and then a child part.) Why bother creating a variable for the fish object? After we get this first fish working, we want to apply the same script to another fish. All we'll have to do is rename `Fish1` as `Fish2`, re-execute the script, and we're done!

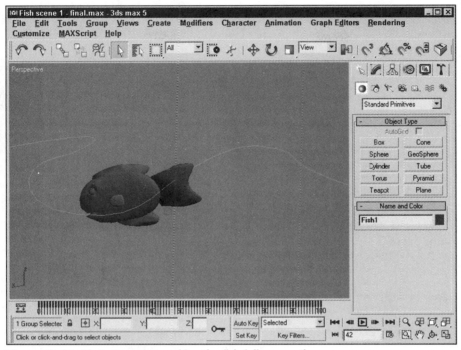

Figure 40-11: First attempt at making the fish follow a path

The script also creates a variable called relPos, which we use to refer to the relative position of the fish with respect to the dummy object. If we have several fish in the scene, we don't want them all in the exact same spot, so this is an easy way to position each one.

The next block of MAXScript is new: We're using the animate on construct. This tells Max to generate key frames for our animation. It's the same as if we had pressed Max's Animation button, run our script, and then shut Animation off. So, any MAXScript inside the animate on parentheses will create animation key frames. These parentheses define a section of the script we call a block.

Inside the animation block, we have a loop that counts from 1 to 100 (corresponding to each frame of our animation). On the end of the loop line we have at time t, which tells Max that for each time through the loop, we want all the variables to have whatever values they'll have at that time. For example, if we want the fish to follow the dummy object, we have to know the position of the object at each point in time instead of just at the beginning, so each time through the loop Max figures out where the dummy object will be for us.

Inside the loop we set the fish's object to be that of the dummy object (at that point in time) and then adjust the fish's position by relPos.

Part 2: Adding body rotation and tail animation

Let's make that fish look a little more lifelike by animating its tail and having it rotate its body to actually follow the path. Also, we'll add a little unpredictability to its motion so that when we add other fish they won't be exact copies of each other.

To improve the fish's animation, follow these steps:

1. Type in the revised version of the script (the lines that are new are in bold):

```
pathObj = $Dummy01
fishObj = $Fish1/FishBody
fishTail = $Fish1/FishBody/FishTail
relPos = [0,-150,-50]  -- How close the fish is to the path

fishTail.bend.axis = 0 -- 0 is the x-axis
zadd = 4                 -- vertical movement at each step
tailFlapOffset = (random 0 100)
tailFlapRate = 25 + (random 0 25)
animate on
(
 for t = 0 to 100 do at time t
 (
  fishObj.position = pathObj.position + relPos
  fishObj.position.z = relPos.z
  relPos.z += zadd

  -- let's say that there's a 10% chance that the fish will
  -- change directions vertically
  if ((random 1 100) > 90) then
  (
   zadd = -zadd
  )

  fishTail.bend.angle = 50 * sin (t * tailFlapRate +
  tailFlapOffset)

  oldRt = fishObj.rotation.z_rotation
  newRt = (in coordsys pathObj pathObj.rotation.z_rotation)

  if ((random 1 100) > 85) then
  (
   fishObj.rotation.z_rotation += (newRt - oldRt) *
   (random 0.5 1.5)
  )
 )
)
```

2. Save your script (File ⇨ Save) and then press Ctrl+E to evaluate the script again. This script is saved in the Chap 40 directory as FishPath2.ms. Make the Camera01 viewport active and click Play Animation. Figure 40-12 shows another frame of the animation. As you can see, the fish is heading in the right direction this time, and the tail is flapping wildly.

Okay, let's look at what changed. First, we added a variable to refer to the fish's tail, so that it will be easy to change when we add another fish. Also, we accessed the bend modifier of the tail and set its axis to 0, which corresponds to the X-axis. (You can try other values to see that it really does change the axis parameter in the rollout.)

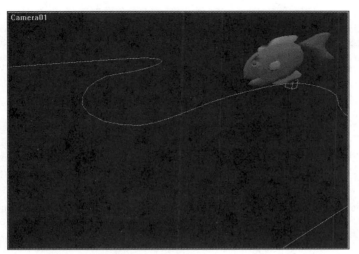

Figure 40-12: A tail-flapping fish that faces the right direction as it follows the path

Next we created some more variables. We use `zadd` to tell Max how much to move the fish in the Z direction at each step (we don't want our fish to always swim at the same level). `tailFlapOffset` and `tailFlapRate` are two variables used to control the tail flapping (I explain this when we get to the part of the script that uses them).

Inside the `for` loop notice that we've overridden the fish's Z-position and replaced it with just the relative Z-position, so that each fish will swim at its own depth and not the dummy object's depth. Then, at each step we add `zadd` to the Z-position so that the fish changes depth slowly. We have to be careful or our fish will continue to climb out of the scene or run into the ground, so at each step we also choose a random number between 1 and 100 with the function (`random 1 100`). If the random number that Max picks is greater than 90, we flip the sign of `zadd` so that the fish starts moving in the other direction. This is a fancy way of saying, "There's a 90 percent chance that the fish will continue moving in the same direction and a 10 percent chance that it will switch directions."

In the next part, we again access the tail's `bend` modifier, this time to set the bend angle. To get a nice back-and-forth motion for the tail, we use the `sin` function. In case you've forgotten all that math from when you were in school, a sine wave oscillates from 1 to –1 to 1 over and over again. By multiplying the function by 50, we get values that oscillate between 50 and –50 (pretty good values to use for our bend angle). We use `tailFlapOffset` to shift the sine wave so that the tail flapping of additional fish is out of synch slightly with this one (remember, we're trying to get at least a little realism here) and `tailFlapRate` to make each fish flap its tail at a slightly different speed.

The only thing left for us to do is to make the fish "follow" the path; that is, rotate its body so that it's facing the direction it's moving. The simplest way to do this is to use the following MAXScript (split into two lines to make it easier to read):

```
newRt = (in coordsys pathObj pathObj.rotation.z_rotation)
fishObj.rotation.z_rotation = newRt
```

The `in coordsys` construct tells Max to give us a value from the point of view of a particular coordinate system. Instead of `pathObj`, we could have asked for the Z-rotation in the world, local, screen, or parent coordinate system, too. In this case, we want to rotate the fish in the same coordinate system as the dummy object. In order to randomize the direction of the fish a little, we've made the rotation a little more complex:

```
oldRt = fishObj.rotation.z_rotation
newRt = (in coordsys pathObj pathObj.rotation.z_rotation)

if ((random 1 100) > 85) then
(
  fishObj.rotation.z_rotation += (newRt - oldRt) *
                                (random 0.5 1.5)
)
```

First, we save the old Z-rotation in `oldRt`, and then we put the new rotation in `newRt`. Once again we pick a random number to decide whether we'll do something; in this case we're saying, "There's an 85 percent chance we won't change directions at all." If our random number does fall in that other 15 percent, however, we adjust the fish's rotation a little. We take the difference between the new rotation and the old rotation and multiply it by a random number between 0.5 and 1.5, which means we'll adjust the rotation by anywhere from 50 percent to 150 percent of the difference between the two rotations. So any fish will basically follow the same path, but with a little variation here and there.

Note Max lets you use shorthand when adjusting the values of variables. Instead of saying `a = a + b`, you can just say `a += b`. Both have the same effect.

Part 3: Animating the second fish

This scene actually has two fish in it (the other one has been sitting patiently off to the side), so for the final part of this tutorial we'll get both fish involved in the animation. To animate the second fish alongside the first one, follow these steps:

1. At the top of the script, change these three lines (what changed is in bold):

```
pathObj = $Dummy01
fishObj = $Fish2/FishBody
fishTail = $Fish2/FishBody/FishTail
relPos = [50,75,0]   -- How close the fish is to the path
```

2. Choose File ➪ Evaluate All, or press Ctrl+E to run the script again, and then animate it. Figure 40-13 shows both fish swimming merrily.

This script generates key frames for the second fish because we changed the `fishObj` and `fishTail` variables to refer to the second fish. We've also moved the second fish's relative position so that the two don't run into each other.

Figure 40-13: Both fish swimming together

Summary

This chapter gave you a brief introduction to MAXScript, 3ds max's powerful, built-in scripting language. Besides describing the different types of scripts you can create, the chapter covered

✦ The basics of MAXScript

✦ Using the MAXScript tools such as the MAXScript editor and Listener windows

✦ Using the Macro Recorder to create scripts

✦ The different script types

✦ The basics of writing your own scripts

The next chapter takes scripting away from text-based commands to a visual editor. The coding will be the same, but the visual editor will make it easier to make sophisticated rollouts.

✦   ✦   ✦

Using the Visual MAXScript Editor

Building scripts can be complicated, and piecing together a roll-out for a scripted utility can be especially time-consuming and frustrating when done by hand. To help create such custom rollouts, Max includes the Visual MAXScript Editor. Using this editor, you can drag and drop rollout elements and automatically create a code skeleton for certain events.

Learning the Visual MAXScript Editor Interface

Working with textual commands can be time-consuming. In order for the script to work, you need to enter the commands exactly. This can be especially tricky when you're trying to lay out the controls for a rollout. Max includes a tool that speeds up the creation of rollouts called the Visual MAXScript Editor.

To access the Visual MAXScript window, shown in Figure 41-1, open the Utility panel in the Command Panel and click the More button. Then select the Visual MAXScript option from the list of utilities and click OK. Another way to access this window is to select Edit ⇨ New Rollout or Edit Rollout (F2) in the MAXScript editor window.

Layouts for a rollout created in the Visual MAXScript window can be saved as files with the .vms extension using the File menu. If you access the window from a MAXScript editor window, then the Save menu automatically updates the editor window.

The Editor interface

The window includes two major panes. The left pane is where the various rollout elements are assembled, and the right pane holds the Value and Event Handlers tabbed panels. The Value panel lists all the properties and their associated values for the selected element. You can change the property values by clicking on them and entering a new value. For example, if you select a Button element in the left panel, then the properties for that control are presented in the Value panel. If you click on the Caption Property, its value becomes high-lighted and you can type a new caption and the new caption will appear on the button.

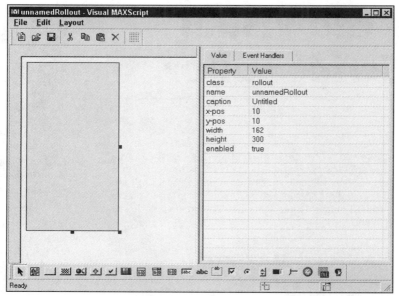

Figure 41-1: The Visual MAXScript window makes building rollouts easy.

The Event Handlers panel lists all the available events that can be associated with the selected element. Clicking the check box to the left of these events can enable the events. For a button element, you can enable the pressed event. With this event enabled, the code includes a function where you can define what happens when this event is fired.

The menus and the main toolbar

At the top of the interface are some menu options and a main toolbar. The File menu also lets you create a new layout (Ctrl+N), save (Ctrl+S) layouts to a file, and open saved layouts (Ctrl+O). The Edit menu allows you to cut (Ctrl+X), copy (Ctrl+C), and paste (Ctrl+V) form elements. You can find these same features as buttons on the top toolbar.

The Layout menu includes options for aligning elements left (Ctrl+left arrow), right (Ctrl+right arrow), top (Ctrl+up arrow), bottom (Ctrl+down arrow), vertical center (F9), and horizontal center (Shift+F9); to space elements evenly across (Alt+right arrow) or down (Alt+up arrow); make elements the same size by width, height, or both; center vertically (Ctrl+F9) or horizontally (Ctrl+Shift+F9) in the dialog box; and flip. You can use the Layout ⇨ Guide Settings menu command to specify grid snapping and spacing. Grids are enabled using the Toggle Grid/Snap button on the right end of the main toolbar.

You can also access these commands using a right-click pop-up menu when clicking on the left pane.

Toolbar elements

The toolbar along the bottom of the window contains the form elements that you can drop on the form. These buttons and elements include those shown in Table 41-1.

Table 41-1: Visual MAXScript Form Elements

Button	Element
	Bitmap: Lets you add bitmap images to a rollout.
	Button: Adds a simple button.
	Map Button: Adds a mapping button that opens the Material/Map Browser.
	Material Button: Adds a material button that also opens the Material/Map Browser.
	Pick Button: Adds a button that lets you pick an object in a viewport.
	Check Button: Adds a button that can be toggled on and off.
	Color Picker: Adds a color swatch that opens the Color Picker dialog box when clicked.
	Combo Box: Adds a list with several items.
	Drop Down List: Adds a list with one item displayed.
	List Box: Adds a list with several items displayed.
	Edit Box: Adds a text field that can be modified.
	Label: Adds a text label.
	Group Box: Adds a grouping outline to surround several controls.
	Check Box: Adds a check box control that can be toggled on or off.
	Radio Buttons: Adds a set of buttons where only one can be selected.
	Spinner: Adds an up and down set of arrows that can modify a value field.

Continued

Table 41-1 *(continued)*

Button	Element
	Progress Bar: Adds a bar that highlights from left to right as a function is completed.
	Slider: Adds a slider control that can move from a minimum to a maximum value.
	Timer: Adds a timer that counts time intervals.
	ActiveX Control: Adds a generic ActiveX control created by a separate vendor.
	Custom: Adds a custom control that can be defined as needed.

At the bottom right of the window are two text fields that display the coordinates of the current mouse cursor position and the size of the rollout. The default size of the rollout is 162 × 300, which is the size needed to fit perfectly in the Command Panel.

Laying out a Rollout

The rollout space, which appears gray in the left pane, can be selected and resized by dragging the black square handles at the edges of the form. As you change its size, its dimensions are displayed in the lower-right corner of the interface. With the rollout space correctly sized, you are ready to add elements to the space.

To add one of these elements to the form, click the element button on the toolbar and drag on the form. The element appears and is selected. The selected element is easy to identify by the black handles that surround it. Dragging on these handles resizes the element, and clicking and dragging on the center of the element repositions it within the rollout space.

The Value and Events panels are automatically updated to show the values and events for the selected element. Values such as width and x-pos are automatically updated if you drag an element or drag its handles to resize it.

Aligning and spacing elements

Although only a single element can be surrounded by black handles at a time, you can actually drag an outline in the rollout space to select multiple elements at once. With several elements selected, you can align them all to the left (Ctlr+left arrow), horizontally centered (Shift+F9), right (Ctrl+right arrow), top (Ctrl+up arrow), vertically centered (F9), or bottom (Ctrl+down arrow).

Multiple elements can also be spaced across (Alt+right arrow) or down (Alt+up arrow). To make several elements the same width, height or both, use the Layout ➪ Make Same Size menu command. The Center in Dialog menu aligns elements to the center of the dialog either vertically (Ctrl+F9) or horizontally (Ctrl+Shift+F9). The Flip command reverses the position of the selected elements.

Figure 41-2 shows a form with several aligned elements added to it.

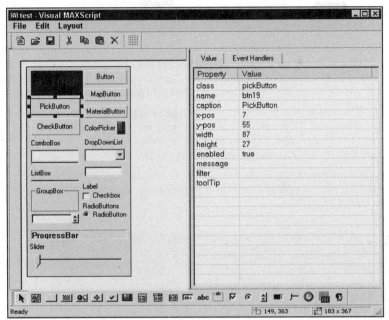

Figure 41-2: You can add control elements to the form in the Visual MAXScript window.

Tutorial: Building a custom rollout with the Visual MAXScript Editor

Now for some practice using this powerful tool. In this example, you'll use the Visual MAXScript window to layout a rollout and code the script to make it work.

To create a custom rollout using the Visual MAXScript editor, follow these steps:

1. Open the BuildCube.max file from the Chap 41 directory on the CD-ROM.

   This file includes a simple sphere object.

2. Choose MAXScript ⇨ New Script to open the MAXScript editor window. In the editor window, enter the following:

   ```
   utility buildCube "Build Cube" ( )
   ```

   This line creates a utility named buildCube. The rollout name will be Build Cube. Make sure to include a space in between the parentheses.

3. Choose Edit ⇨ New Rollout from the window menu (or press the F2 key). The Visual MAXScript window opens. The properties for this rollout are displayed in the Properties panel. Drag the lower-right black square handle to resize the rollout form.

4. Click the spinner button on the bottom toolbar and drag in the rollout form to create a spinner element. In the Properties panel, set the name to SideNum, the caption value to No. of Side Objects, select the #integer for the type, and the range to [1,100,5]. The range values set the lower, upper, and default values for the spinner. Then drag on the element handles to resize the element to fit in the form.

5. Click the spinner button again and drag in the rollout form to create another spinner element. In the Properties panel, set the name to length, the caption value to Side Length, select the #integer for the type, and set the range to [1,1000,50]. Then drag on the element handles to resize the element to fit in the form.

6. Click the button icon on the bottom toolbar and drag in the rollout form to create a button below the spinners. In the Properties panel, set the name to **createCube** and the caption value to **Create Cube**. Then drag on the element handles to resize the button so the text fits on the button. Open the Events panel and select the Pressed check box.

7. Drag over the top of both the spinners to select them both and choose Layout ➪ Align ➪ Right (or press Ctrl+right arrow) to align the spinners. Figure 41-3 shows how the rollout layout looks.

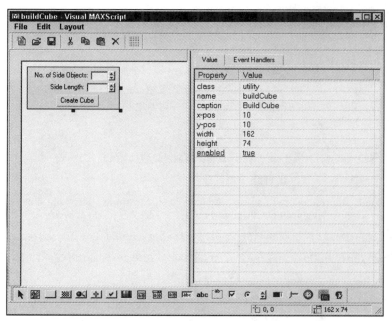

Figure 41-3: The rollout laid out in the Visual MAXScript window

8. With the layout complete, choose File ➪ Save (or press Ctrl+S) to save the layout, then close the Visual MAXScript window. The script code associated with the layout will automatically be placed in the editor window.

9. Complete the script by entering the script commands immediately after the open parenthesis that appears on the line following the `on createCube pressed do` event, as shown in Figure 41-4. See the BuildCube.ms file from the Chap 41 directory on the CD-ROM to see the entire script.

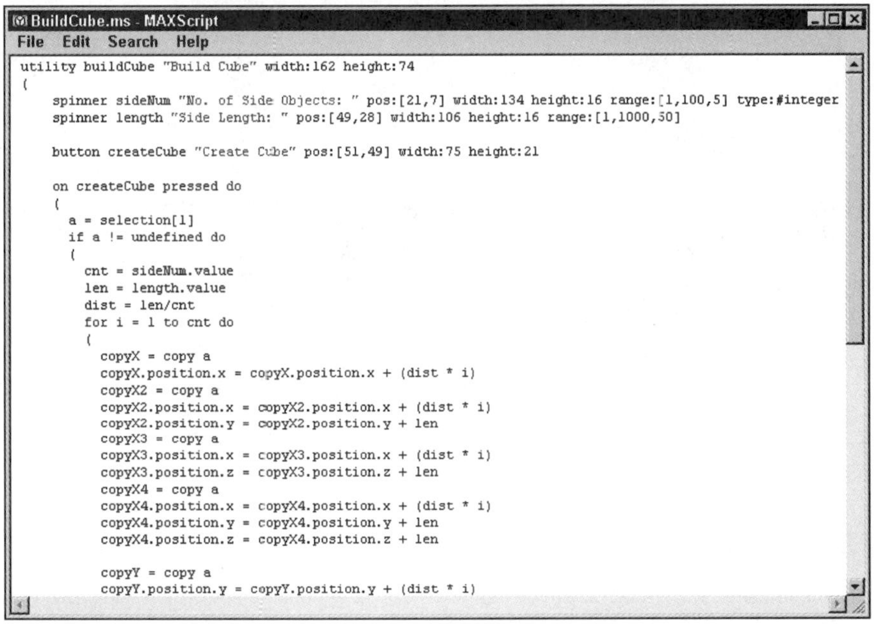

```
BuildCube.ms - MAXScript                                        _ □ ×
File  Edit  Search  Help

utility buildCube "Build Cube" width:162 height:74
(
    spinner sideNum "No. of Side Objects: " pos:[21,7] width:134 height:16 range:[1,100,5] type:#integer
    spinner length "Side Length: " pos:[49,28] width:106 height:16 range:[1,1000,30]

    button createCube "Create Cube" pos:[51,49] width:75 height:21

    on createCube pressed do
    (
      a = selection[1]
      if a != undefined do
      (
        cnt = sideNum.value
        len = length.value
        dist = len/cnt
        for i = 1 to cnt do
        (
          copyX = copy a
          copyX.position.x = copyX.position.x + (dist * i)
          copyX2 = copy a
          copyX2.position.x = copyX2.position.x + (dist * i)
          copyX2.position.y = copyX2.position.y + len
          copyX3 = copy a
          copyX3.position.x = copyX3.position.x + (dist * i)
          copyX3.position.z = copyX3.position.z + len
          copyX4 = copy a
          copyX4.position.x = copyX4.position.x + (dist * i)
          copyX4.position.y = copyX4.position.y + len
          copyX4.position.z = copyX4.position.z + len

          copyY = copy a
          copyY.position.y = copyY.position.y + (dist * i)
```

Figure 41-4: The MAXScript editor window is updated with the code from the Visual MAXScript window.

10. Open the Utilities panel and click the MAXScript button. Then click the Run Script button and select the BuildCube.ms file from the Chap 41 directory on the CD-ROM.

The utility installs and appears in the Utility drop-down list in the MAXScript rollout.

11. Select the BuildCube utility from the drop-down list in the MAXScript rollout and scroll down the Command Panel to see the Build Cube rollout. Select the sphere object and click the Create Cube button.

The script executes, and a cube of spheres is created.

Figure 41-5 shows the results of the BuildCube.ms script. You can use this script with any selected object.

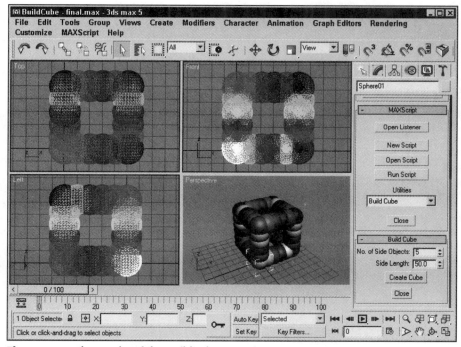

Figure 41-5: The results of the BuildCube.ms script

Summary

This chapter gave a basic introduction to creating custom rollouts for scripted utilities using the Visual MAXScript Editor. Specifically, you

✦ Explored the Visual MAXScript Editor interface

✦ Learned the features of each rollout element

✦ Discovered how to create scripted utilities with custom rollouts

Now that you're feeling more comfortable with scripts, we'll look at the pinnacle of added functionality — plug-ins.

✦　　✦　　✦

Using Third-Party Plug-Ins

A plug-in is an external program that integrates seamlessly with the Max interface to provide additional functionality. Discreet has adopted an architecture for Max that is open and enables all aspects of the program to be enhanced. Max ships with a Software Developer's Kit (SDK) that enables users to generate their own plug-ins. Many different companies currently produce plug-ins, and other users create and distribute freeware and shareware plug-ins.

It would be difficult to cover all the available plug-ins, but this chapter covers a random sampling to give you an idea of the types of plug-ins that are available and their capabilities.

The entire architecture of Max is built around plug-ins, and many of the core components of Max are implemented as plug-ins.

A key feature that allowed Max to become and remain so popular is that users can download and install plug-ins that extend Max's power and functionality. Plug-ins allow Max to adapt to the needs of each user as well as keeping up with new ideas.

Working with Plug-Ins

After you've located a plug-in that you would like to add to your system, you need to install the plug-in. Most plug-ins come with an executable setup program that automates this for you, but others will need to be installed manually, which isn't difficult.

Note   3ds max 5 was built to be backward compatible with all plug-ins for version 4. In fact, if you upgrade Max, you can simply copy your old plugins directory to the new installation, restart Max, and all your plug-ins will work.

As you begin to add plug-ins to Max, there will be times when you will want to see which plug-ins are installed and even disable certain plug-ins. Max includes tools to view which plug-ins are installed and to manage your current plug-ins.

Installing plug-ins

Most commercial plug-ins include an installation program. During the installation process, these programs ask where the Max root directory is located. From this root directory, the plug-in program files are installed in the "plugins" directory, help files are installed in the help directory, and example scenes are installed in the "scenes" directory.

Plug-in program files typically have a .dlc, .dlr, .dlo, .dlu, .dlv, or .dlm extension, depending on the type of plug-in. When Max loads, it searches the plugins directory for these files and loads them along with the program files. You install freeware plug-ins manually simply by copying the plug-in file into the plugins directory and restarting Max.

You can also place plug-ins in a different directory and load them from this directory. The Path Configuration dialog box is where you can specify additional plug-in paths.

Find out more about the Path Configuration dialog box in Chapter 4, "Customizing the Max Interface."

Most commercial plug-ins require that the plug-in be authorized after installation. You must do this before you can use the plug-in, and you can usually do it via telephone, fax, or e-mail.

To remove a plug-in, use the uninstall feature that is part of the setup process, or delete the associated program files from the plugins directory.

Plug-ins can also create a help file that explains how to work with the plug-in. These help files are installed in the /help directory where Max is installed. To view these help files, open the Additional Help dialog box by choosing Help ➪ Additional Help.

Viewing installed plug-ins

To see all the currently installed plug-ins, choose File ➪ Summary Info to open the Summary Info dialog box, and click the Plug-In Info button. This opens the Plug-In Info dialog box that lists all installed plug-ins with their details, as shown in Figure 42-1. As you can see, many plug-ins created by Discreet are installed with just the default installation.

Even if you haven't installed any plug-ins, this dialog box lists many plug-ins. These are core functions in Max that are implemented as plug-ins.

Tutorial: Manually installing the Furious Research plug-ins

Before you can install a plug-in, you need to find one to install. This first task is easy because the CD-ROM includes several custom plug-ins developed exclusively for this book.

To manually install the custom Furious Research plug-ins, follow these steps:

1. Locate the Furious Research plug-ins directory on the CD-ROM.

   This directory includes several plug-in files including BallsNStix.dlu, Brick.dlo, BrickSnap.dls, etc.

2. Select and copy all the plug-ins.

3. Locate the plugins directory where 3ds max 5 is installed and paste the plug-ins.

4. Restart Max and open the Create panel. Select the Construction subcategory from the drop-down list. There should be Brick and Gear buttons available.

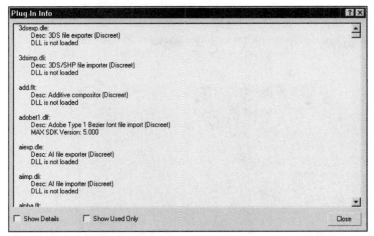

Figure 42-1: The Plug-In Info dialog box includes a list of all the currently loaded plug-ins, both internal and external.

Figure 42-2 shows a brick and gear object created using two of the new plug-ins you've manually installed.

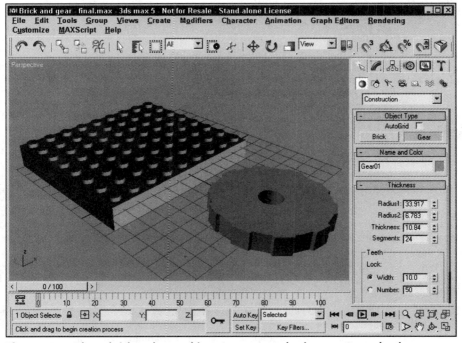

Figure 42-2: These brick and gear objects were created using a custom plug-in.

Managing plug-ins

You can manage which installed plug-ins are available using the Plug-in Manager dialog box, shown in Figure 42-3. Open this dialog box by choosing Customize ➪ Plug-in Manager.

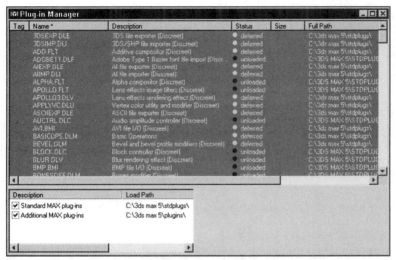

Figure 42-3: Use the Plug-in Manager dialog box to disable plug-ins.

Each column in the Plug-in Manager dialog box includes information about the plug-ins. The columns include Tag, Name, Description, Status, Size, and Full Path. You can sort the list of plug-ins alphabetically by column if you click on the column name.

Each unique directory that is specified within the Configure Paths dialog box appears in the bottom pane of the Plug-in Manager. Use the check boxes to remove all plug-ins from that directory from the list.

In the list of plug-ins, you select a specific plug-in by clicking it. You can select multiple plug-ins in the list using the Ctrl and Shift keys. A right-click pop-up menu of options lets you control the selected plug-ins. You can also tag (or mark) certain plug-ins using the Tag Selected option in the right-click pop-up menu. For tagged plug-ins, a white check mark appears in the left column.

You can also choose to load or defer selected or checked plug-ins using the right-click pop-up menu. Plug-ins with a status of loaded are currently loaded in memory and available (these plug-ins are identified with a green circle in the Status column). The deferred plug-ins are waiting in the wings and will load when needed (these plug-ins are identified with a yellow circle in the Status column). Plug-ins that are marked Unloaded (with a red circle) are not in memory.

Using the right-click pop-up menu, you can also select Load New Plug-in, which opens the Choose Plug-in File dialog box where you can select a plug-in file. The file will then be accessed from this directory and loaded into the Plug-in Manager list.

Many different types of plug-ins are used to add many different kinds of features. This section includes some tutorials that show some of the available plug-in capabilities.

Caution The following tutorials use commercial plug-ins. The respective plug-in or a demo of the plug-in must be installed in order to work with these scenes.

Tutorial: Adding rainbow rings to a planet

Some plug-ins enhance the options available in the Environment dialog box. These plug-ins can include new atmospheric effects, such as the Rainbow plug-in.

To add rainbow colored rings to a planet using the Rainbow plug-in, follow these steps:

1. Open the Planet with rainbow rings.max file from the Chap 42 directory on the CD-ROM.

   This file includes a simple sphere and a spherical atmosphere apparatus gizmo.

2. Choose Rendering ➪ Environment to open the Environment dialog box. Click the Add button, select the Rainbow option, and click OK (this option will appear if you installed the Furious Research Rainbow plug-in found on the CD-ROM).

3. Then click the Add SphereGizmo button and select the spherical gizmo. This will add the effect to the gizmo, but it won't be visible until you render.

Figure 42-4 shows a rendered image of the planet with rainbow rings.

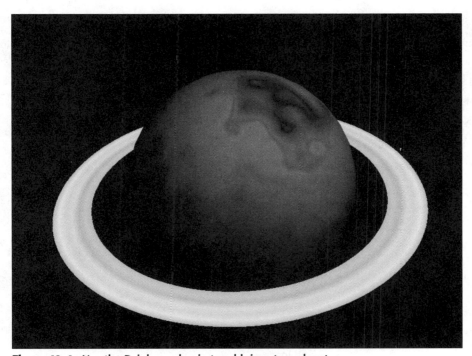

Figure 42-4: Use the Rainbow plug-in to add rings to a planet.

Locating Plug-Ins

Before you can take the advantage of plug-ins, you will need to locate, acquire, and install them. You can find plug-ins from a variety of sources — commercially, shareware, or freeware.

3ds max 5 Bible is also a source of plug-ins. You can find several exclusive plug-ins created by Furious Research on the book's CD-ROM.

The first place to look for commercial plug-ins is Digimation. It is not only a plug-in developer, but it resells many other plug-ins for other companies. You can find it online at `www.digimation.com`.

In addition to the commercially developed plug-ins, many plug-ins are available as freeware or shareware. You can find many of these plug-ins and download them via the Web.

Here are some Web sites that offer freeware or shareware plug-ins for download:

✦ **Max3D:** `http://max3d.3dluvr.com/plugins.php`

✦ **BoboLand:** `www.gfxcentral.com/bobo`

✦ **Max Underground:** `http://thebox.citydata.se/`

Plug-ins are typically not compatible between different versions of Max. For example, a plug-in written for version 2.5 will not work on version 4 or version 5 and vice versa. When downloading and purchasing plug-ins, be sure to get a version that matches your current version of Max. The exception to this bit of advice is that plug-ins for version 4 work in version 5.

Summary

By adding plug-ins, you can increase the functionality of Max far beyond its default setup. In this chapter, you've

✦ Learned what plug-ins are and how they can extend Max

✦ Learned where to find plug-ins

✦ Discovered how to install, view, and manage plug-ins

✦ Tried out the capabilities of a plug-in through a tutorial

This concludes the final part of the book; the appendixes that follow offer information on configuring a Max system and the contents of the book's CD.

Appendixes

Configuring a System for 3ds max 5

Before you can enjoy all the great features in 3ds max, you have to install the software and get your system configured properly; this appendix will help you do just that. After you're done here, you're ready to go.

Choosing an Operating System

If you're starting from scratch and have the luxury of customizing your system so that it works best with 3ds max, you can do several things that will make life easier for you. One of the big decisions you have to make is what operating system to use to run Max.

If you have the option, run 3ds max on Windows 2000 Professional or Windows XP Professional. Make sure that you have also installed the latest Service Pack (which you can download for free from Microsoft's Web page at www.microsoft.com). These operating systems are more stable than other versions of Windows, and they do a better job of managing your computer's resources (such as memory). It also enables you to run multiple copies of 3ds max at the same time on a single machine.

If either of these systems is not an option, you can also run Max on Windows 98 or Windows NT4. These systems are not as robust as Windows 2000 or XP, so you might encounter more program crashes in Max. On a Windows 98 machine, you can run only one copy of Max at a time, and network rendering is not officially supported.

Hardware Requirements

To get good performance from 3ds max, you need a fairly meaty machine. A good default system to use would be a Pentium-IV or an AMD Athlon-based computer with 1GB or more of RAM (and 2GB of swap space) and a decent-sized hard drive and monitor. If need be, you can get by with a 300 MHz Pentium II (or AMD) packing as little as 256MB of RAM (with 300MB swap space), but you may spend a lot of time watching your computer churn furiously to keep up.

Note   Max under Windows 2000 or XP can take advantage of multiprocessor machines.

One element of your system that will probably have the greatest impact on the performance of 3ds max is the graphics card. Any good graphics card has specialized hardware that will take a lot of the workload off your computer's CPU, freeing it up to do other tasks. All of Max is fairly graphics-intensive, and a little extra money in the graphics card department will go a long way toward boosting your performance.

The good news is that hardware accelerated graphics cards are becoming cheaper — you can get great cards for $200–$300. When searching for a graphics card, make sure it can support a resolution of at least 1024×768 at 16-bit color and that it comes with drivers for OpenGL 1.1 or later and/or DirectX. You'll also want a minimum of 32MB on the graphics card or 64MB for 3D graphics acceleration. You can use some of the graphics boards built to run computer games — however, be aware that some boards claim to support OpenGL but actually support only a subset of it. Before going out to make your purchase, visit the Discreet Web site (www.discreet.com) to see performance metrics for different popular graphics cards.

For the complete install, you will need 400MB of hard drive space. You can get by with less if you choose the Compact installation option. Another handy piece of hardware to have is a scrollable mouse. A scrollable mouse makes moving through menus and the Command Panel easier, plus it gives you a third button, which can be used to navigate the viewports.

Installing 3ds max 5

Installing Max is straightforward. Here's what you need to do:

1. Insert the Max CD-ROM into the CD-ROM drive, and the setup program will start up automatically. If you don't have Windows Autorun enabled, or if the setup program doesn't start, run the Setup.exe program on the CD-ROM.

2. When the setup program starts, the Choose Setup Program dialog box displays, as shown in Figure A-1. In addition to 3ds max, you can also install Apple's QuickTime software (which lets you view QuickTime animations), DirectX 8.1 for the Direct 3D display drivers, Microsoft Internet Explorer (so that you can use the online help system), or Turbo Squid (which is a plug-in allowing you to share digital content over the Web). Click the Install 3ds max 5 button to start the Max installation.

Cross-Reference   There are also two buttons for installing the License Manager and launching the Network Setup Wizard. These two options are used if you are installing Max on a network. To learn about network installation options, see Chapter 38, "Network Rendering."

3. A Welcome screen appears, advising you to shut down other applications before proceeding. Click the Next button to move on. This screen also includes a button to view the Readme file. Reading this is a good idea, because it has last-minute information that they couldn't put in the manual.

4. The next screen is the Software License Agreement. Choose your country, and read the corresponding License Agreement. After you've read the agreement, click the now-enabled "I accept" button. Click the now-enabled Next button to move on.

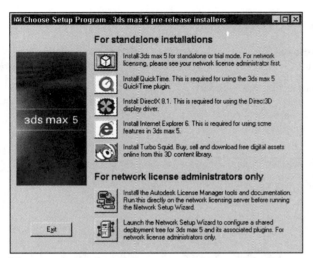

Figure A-1: The installation program lets you install more than just Max.

5. Next is the Serial Number screen. Enter the serial number and the CD-ROM key, both of which you can find on the CD-ROM's case. Then click the Next button.

6. The next screen is User Information, which asks you to input your Name and Organization. If you're using Windows 2000 or XP, this screen offers the options to install the program only for the current user or for anyone using this computer (if you have admin rights).

7. By default, Max will be installed in c:\Program Files\discreet\3dsmax5 and backburner will be installed in c:\Program Files\discreet\backburner2, but you can choose a different destination by clicking the Browse button and navigating to a different directory. When you're happy with the installation location, click the Next button to continue.

8. From the Setup Type screen, choose the type of installation you want. Which of the three choices you select depends on how you plan to use Max. If you want a minimal installation with only the components that you need, choose Compact. If you want to install the complete program including the SDK (so you can write your own plug-ins), choose Custom. In most cases, however, you can just choose Typical.

9. The next screen is the point-of-no-return, Start Copying Files screen. Click the Next button to begin the installation.

Tip

The Disk Cost button will bring up a dialog box that displays each available hard driver along with a list available and required space.

It takes a few minutes for Max to install completely. When the installation program is done, you will need to shut down your computer and restart.

Note

The hardware lock that shipped with previous editions of Max has been replaced with an easier-to-manage software lock. No special lock is needed to connect to your system's parallel port.

Authorizing the Software

After Max is installed, you need to authorize the software through Discreet. The software will continue to run for 15 days without authorization, but after 15 days it will quit working.

Figure A-2 shows the screen that first appears after you start Max after installation. Using this screen, you can launch the Authorization Wizard, buy the software, or run the software unauthorized for 15 days. The Authorization Wizard automatically appears the first time you run Max and takes you through the authorization process.

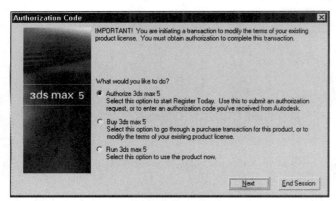

Figure A-2: The first screen to appear after installation lets you authorize your software or run it without authorization.

The first screen of the Authorization Wizard lets you get an authorization code or enter an authorization code if you have one. To obtain an authorization code, you will need to enter information such as your name, address, and company name. You can also specify whether this copy is an upgrade or not. If you're upgrading your Max version, you need to include this number. The Serial Number and Request Code will be automatically filled in using the numbers entered during the installation. You can authorize the software using a direct connection to the Web, fax, e-mail, or regular mail.

If you receive an authorization code via fax, e-mail, or mail, you can select the "Already have an authorization code" option on the first screen that appears when you run Max and click Next. A screen opens where you can enter the authorization code, and the wizard will register this number with Max and complete the registration process.

Caution   The authorization code is specific to a specific computer and will only work for that computer. If you try to install and use the authorization code on a separate computer, you'll need to obtain another authorization code.

Within Max, the Help ➪ Authorize 3ds max menu command lets you enter an authorization number to authorize the software.

Setting the Display Driver

When Max is first run, you'll see a small dialog box, shown in Figure A-3, that lets you select the display driver to use. Choosing the correct display driver is important for getting the best performance out of your computer. If you are unsure of which display driver to use (it really depends on your graphics card), choose the Software option. You can change the display driver in Max later by choosing Customize ➪ Preferences and in the Viewports panel, clicking the Choose Driver button. The Graphics Driver Setup dialog box opens. If you change the graphics driver, you will need to restart Max before the new driver is used.

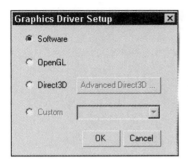

Figure A-3: Choosing the display driver to use

You can choose one of three different drivers to use in Max: Software, Direct3D, or OpenGL. There is also an option to select a custom driver.

Tip   You can also start Max with a specific display driver from the command line using the -h option. For example, 3dsmax.exe -h Direct3D will run Max using the Direct3D display drivers.

Software

The software display driver option is Max's own built-in software graphics driver called HEIDI. Because it is a software driver, it does not take advantage of any special graphics hardware that your graphics card supports, so your computer's CPU will do all the work. The nice thing about this option is that it works on any computer, even if you don't have a very good graphics card.

After you've installed Max, start it up using software drivers to make sure that everything installed correctly. From there, try out the different graphics drivers to see whether you can move up to something faster.

OpenGL

If your graphics card supports OpenGL in hardware, then this is definitely the driver to use. OpenGL works under all Windows operating systems and is typically present on high-end graphics cards. In order for Max to use OpenGL, the drivers must support OpenGL 1.1 or later. One of the features enabled with the OpenGL drivers is Virtual Viewports.

Direct3D

Direct3D uses the hardware capabilities of the graphics cards that are present and simulates anything else it needs in software. You must have DirectX 8.1 installed for these drivers to work. Simulating different features makes Direct3D run on a wide range of computers, but it can also be much slower. If your graphics card's drivers support all of Direct3D in hardware, then using this driver might give you good performance. If it switches to software mode, however, it will be much slower than HEIDI.

✦   ✦   ✦

Max Keyboard Shortcuts

The key to working efficiently with Max is learning the keyboard shortcuts. If you know the keyboard shortcuts, you can maximize the viewports using Expert Mode (Ctrl+X) and use the keyboard and mouse to access all commands.

Using Keyboard Shortcuts

Almost every separate window has its own set of keyboard shortcuts. You can use the Keyboard Shortcut Override Toggle button on the main toolbar (it looks like a keyboard key) to make the keyboard shortcuts for the other windows take precedence over the main window's shortcuts.

For example, in the main Max window, the A key toggles the Angle Snap feature on and off, but in the Track View - Curve Editor window, the A key Adds Keys. If the Curve Editor is open and the Keyboard Shortcut Override Toggle is enabled, then the Add Keys function will be performed. If the Keyboard Shortcut Override Toggle is off, then the Angle Snap will be activated.

If you want to change any of the keyboard shortcuts, the Customize User Interface dialog box includes a Keyboard panel for making changes. You can open this dialog box using the Customize ➪ Customize User Interface command.

 Cross-Reference Chapter 4, "Customizing the Max Interface," offers more details on creating custom keyboard shortcuts.

Using the Hotkey Map

In the Help menu, you can find the Hotkey Map menu command that opens an interactive window, shown in Figure B-1, that displays all the current keyboard shortcuts for the main interface.

 Note The Hotkey Map window is a Flash-enabled application and requires that the Flash plug-in is installed.

Moving the mouse cursor over the keyboard displayed in the lower-right corner of the Hotkey Map window highlights the respective section of the keyboard and displays all keyboard shortcuts associated with those keys. The icon in the upper-right corner refreshes the interface and the triangle in the lower-right corner cycles through all the keys.

 New Feature The Hotkey Map window is new to 3ds max 5.

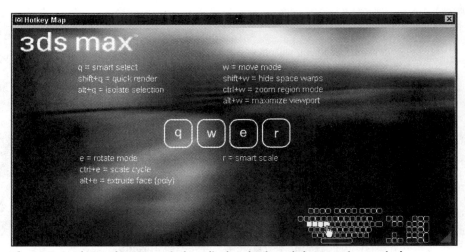

Figure B-1: The Hotkey Map window displays keyboard shortcuts interactively.

Main Interface Shortcuts

The following tables present the various shortcut keys for the main interface.

Menus	
Command	*Shortcut*
New Scene	Ctrl+N
Open File	Ctrl+O
Save File	Ctrl+S
Undo Scene Operation	Ctrl+Z
Redo Scene Operation	Ctrl+Y
Hold	Alt+Ctrl+H
Fetch	Alt+Ctrl+F
Delete Objects	Delete
Clone	Ctrl+V

Command	Shortcut
Select All	Ctrl+A
Select None	Ctrl+D
Select Invert	Ctrl+I
Select by Name	H
Transform Type-In	F12
Align	Alt+A
Spacing Tool	Shift+I
Normal Align	Alt+N
Place Highlight	Ctrl+H
Isolate Selection	Alt+Q
Undo View Change	Shift+Z
Redo View Change	Shift+Y
Viewport Background	Alt+B
Update Background Image	Alt+Shift+Ctrl+B
Match Camera To View	Ctrl+C
Redraw All Views	`
Adaptive Degradation Toggle	O
Expert Mode Toggle	Ctrl+X
Render Scene	F10
Environment	8
Advanced Lighting	9
Render to Texture	0 (zero)
Material Editor	M
Show/Hide Main Toolbar	Alt+6
Show/Hide Tab Panel	Y
Lock User Interface	Alt+0 (zero)
MAXScript Listener	F11
File Menu	Alt+F
Edit Menu	Alt+E
Tools Menu	Alt+ T
Group Menu	Alt+G
Views Menu	Alt+V
Create Menu	Alt+C

Continued

Menus *(continued)*

Command	Shortcut
Modifiers Menu	Alt+O
Character Menu	Alt+H
Animation Menu	Alt+A
Graph Editors Menu	Alt+D
Rendering Menu	Alt+R
Customize Menu	Alt+U
MAXScript Menu	Alt+M
Help Menu	Alt+H+H

Main and Floating Toolbars

Command	Shortcut
Undo	Ctrl+Z
Redo	Ctrl+Y
Select Object	Q
Select by Name	H
Rectangle, Circle, Fence, Lasso Selection Cycle	Ctrl+F, Q
Select and Move	W
Select and Rotate	E
Select and Scale	R
Scale Cycle	R, Ctrl+E
Snap Toggle	S
Angle Snap Toggle	A
Snap Percent	Shift+Ctrl+P
Snaps Cycle	Alt+S
Restrict to X	F5
Restrict to Y	F6
Restrict to Z	F7
Restrict Plane Cycle	F8
Quick Render	Shift+Q
Render Last	F9

Viewports

Command	Shortcut
Front View	F
Top View	T
Bottom View	B
Left View	L
Perspective View	P
User View	U
Camera View	C
Light View	Shift+4 ($)
Disable Viewport	D
View Pop-up Menu	V
Dynamic Resizing	drag viewport borders
Transform Gizmo Toggle	X
Transform Gizmo Size Down	-
Transform Gizmo Size Up	=
Shade Selected Subobject Faces	F2
Wireframe/Smooth+Highlights Toggle	F3
View Edged Faces	F4
Polygon Counter	7
Sound Toggle	\
Show Safeframes	Shift+F
Default Lighting	Ctrl+L
See-Through Display	Alt+X
Show/Hide Cameras	Shift+C
Show/Hide Geometry	Shift+G
Show/Hide Grids	G
Show/Hide Helpers	Shift+H
Show/Hide Lights	Shift+L
Show/Hide Particle Systems	Shift+P
Show/Hide Space Warps	Shift+W

Lower Interface Controls

Command	Shortcut
Selection Lock Toggle	Spacebar
Auto Key Mode	N
Set Key Mode	'
Set Keys	K
Play / Stop Animation	/
Backup Time One Unit	,
Forward Time One Unit	.
Go to Start Frame	Home
Go to End Frame	End

Viewport Navigation

Command	Shortcut
Zoom Mode	Alt+Z
Zoom Extents	Alt+Ctrl+Z
Zoom Extents All	Shift+Ctrl+Z
Zoom Extents Selected All	Z
Zoom Region Mode	Ctrl +W
Zoom Viewport In	[
Zoom Viewport Out	]
Pan View	Ctrl+P or drag with middle button
Interactive Pan	I (held down)
Arc Rotate	Alt+drag with middle button
Min/Max Toggle	Alt+W

Quadmenus

Command	Shortcut
Animation Quadmenu	Alt+right mouse click
Lighting/Rendering Quadmenu	Ctrl+Alt+right mouse click
Modeling Quadmenu	Ctrl+right mouse click

Command	Shortcut
Snap Quadmenu	Shift+right mouse click
Viewports Quadmenu	V
Custom 1 Quadmenu	Shift+Alt+right mouse click
Custom 2 Quadmenu	Shift+Ctrl+Alt+right mouse dick
Custom 3 Quadmenu	Shift+Ctrl+right mouse click

Virtual Viewport

Command	Shortcut
Virtual Viewport Toggle	/ (numeric keypad)
Virtual Viewport Zoom In	+ (numeric keypad)
Virtual Viewport Zoom Out	- (numeric keypad)
Virtual Viewport Pan Down	2 (numeric keypad)
Virtual Viewport Pan Left	4 (numeric keypad)
Virtual Viewport Pan Right	6 (numeric keypad)
Virtual Viewport Pan Up	8 (numeric keypad)

Note   The Virtual Viewport option is available only when the OpenGL display driver is used.

Subobjects

Command	Shortcut
Subobject mode toggle	Ctrl+B
Subobject Level Cycle	Insert
Subobject Level 1	1
Subobject Level 2	2
Subobject Level 3	3
Subobject Level 4	4
Subobject Level 5	5
Delete Subobject	Delete
Local Select Subobject by Name	Ctrl+H

Hierarchies

Command	Shortcut
Select Ancestor	Page Up
Select Child	Page Down
Select Entire Hierarchy	Double-click parent

Editable Mesh

Command	Shortcut
Vertex Subobject Mode	1
Edge Subobject Mode	2
Face Subobject Mode	3
Polygon Subobject Mode	4
Element Subobject Mode	5
Detach	Ctrl+D
Cut Mode	Alt+C
Bevel Mode	Ctrl+V, Ctrl+B
Chamfer Mode	Ctrl+C
Extrude Mode	Ctrl+E
Edge Invisible	Ctrl+I
Edge Turn	Ctrl+T
Weld Selected	Ctrl+W
Weld Target Mode	Alt+W

Editable Poly

Command	Shortcut
Vertex Subobject Mode	1
Edge Subobject Mode	2
Border Subobject Mode	3
Face Subobject Mode	4
Element Subobject Mode	5

Command	Shortcut
Object Level (disable subobject mode)	6
Repeat Last Operation	;
Grow Selection	Ctrl+Page Up
Shrink Selection	Ctrl+Page Down
Select Edge Loop	Alt+L
Select Edge Ring	Alt+R
Connect	Shift+Ctrl+E
Cut	Alt+C
Constrain to Edges	Shift+X
Quickslice Mode	Shift+Ctrl+Q
Bevel Mode	Shift+Ctrl+B
Chamfer Mode	Shift+Ctrl+C
Extrude Mode	Shift+E
Extrude Poly Face	Alt+E
Meshsmooth	Ctrl+M
Hide	Alt+H
Hide Unselected	Alt+I
Unhide All	Alt+U
Weld Mode	Shift+Ctrl+W
Cap Poly Object	Alt+P
Collapse Poly Object	Alt+Ctrl+C

NURBS

Command	Shortcut
Lock 2D Selection	Spacebar
CV Constrained Normal Move	Alt+N
CV Constrained U Move	Alt+U
CV Constrained V Move	Alt+V
Display Curves	Shift+Ctrl+C
Display Surfaces	Shift+Ctrl+S
Display Lattices	Ctrl+L

Continued

NURBS *(continued)*

Command	Shortcut
Display Shaded Lattice	Alt+L
Display Dependents	Ctrl+D
Display Toolbox	Ctrl+T
Display Trims	Shift+Ctrl+T
Select Next in U	Ctrl+Right Arrow
Select Previous in U	Ctrl+Left Arrow
Select Next in V	Ctrl+Up Arrow
Select Previous in V	Ctrl+Down Arrow
Tessellation Preset 1	Ctrl+1
Tessellation Preset 2	Ctrl+2
Tessellation Preset 3	Ctrl+3
Switch to Point Level	Alt+Shift+P
Switch to Curve Level	Alt+Shift+C
Switch to Curve CV Level	Alt+Shift+Z
Switch to Surface Level	Alt+Shift+S
Switch to Surface CV Level	Alt+Shift+V
Switch to Imports Level	Alt+Shift+I
Switch to Top Level	Alt+Shift+T
Transform Degrade	Ctrl+X

Free-Form Deformations

Command	Shortcut
Switch to Control Point Level	Alt+Shift+C
Switch to Lattice Level	Alt+Shift+L
Switch to Set Volume Level	Alt+Shift+S
Switch to Top Level	Alt+Shift+T

Edit Normals Modifier

Command	Shortcut
Object Level	Ctrl+0
Normal Level	Ctrl+1
Vertex Level	Ctrl+2
Edge Level	Ctrl+3
Face Level	Ctrl+4
Copy Normal	Ctrl+C
Paste Normal	Ctrl+V
Reset Normals	R
Specify Normals	S
Unify Normals	U
Make Explicit	E
Break Normals	B

Dialog Box Shortcuts

Use the following shortcut keys to work with the various dialog boxes. The dialog box must be selected for these shortcuts to work. It is possible for modeless dialog boxes to have the dialog box visible, but not selected.

Material Editor

Command	Shortcut
Background	B
Backlight	L
Cycle No. of Sample Slots	X
Get Material	G
Move to Sibling	Left and Right Arrow
Go to Parent	Up Arrow
Make Preview	P
Material Editor Options	O

Track View

Command	Shortcut
Edit Keys Mode	E
Function Curves Mode	F5, F
Filters	Q
Assign Controller	C
Copy Controller	Ctrl+C
Paste Controller	Ctrl+V
Make Unique	U
Add Keys	A
Move Keys	M
Snap Frames	S
Apply Ease Curve	Ctrl+E
Apply Multiplier Curve	Ctrl+M
Expand Track	T
Lock Selection	Spacebar
Nudge Keys Left	Left Arrow
Nudge Keys Right	Right Arrow
Move Highlight Down	Down Arrow
Move Highlight Up	Up Arrow
Backup Time One Unit	,
Forward Time One Unit	.
Undo Scene Operation	Ctrl+Z
Redo Scene Operation	Ctrl+A
Zoom	Z
Zoom Horizontal Extents All	Alt+X
Pan	P

Video Post

Command	Shortcut
New Sequence	Ctrl+N
Add New Event	Ctrl+A
Add Scene Event	Ctrl+S
Add Image Input Event	Ctrl+I
Add Image Filter Event	Ctrl+F
Add Image Layer Event	Ctrl+L
Add Image Output Event	Ctrl+O
Edit Current Event	Ctrl+E
Execute Sequence	Ctrl+R
Undo Scene Operation	Ctrl+Z

Unwrap UVW

Command	Shortcut
Load UVW	Alt+Shift+Ctrl+L
Edit UVWs	Ctrl+E
Unwrap Options	Ctrl+O
Update Map	Ctrl+U
Break Selected Vertices	Ctrl+B
Lock Selected Vertices	Spacebar
Filter Selected Faces	Alt+F
Get Face Selection From Stack	Alt+Shift+Ctrl+F
Get Selection From Viewport	Alt+Shift+Ctrl+P
Detach Edge Vertices	D, Ctrl+D
Planar Map Faces/Patches	Enter
Hide Selected	Ctrl+H
Freeze Selected	Ctrl+F

Continued

Unwrap UVW *(continued)*

Command	Shortcut
Snap	Ctrl+S
Mirror Horizontal	Alt+Shift+Ctrl+N
Mirror Vertical	Alt+Shift+Ctrl+M
Move Horizontal	Alt+Shift+Ctrl+J
Move Vertical	Alt+Shift+Ctrl+K
Texture Vertex Contract Selection	-
Texture Vertex Expand Selection	+
Texture Vertex Move Mode	Q
Texture Vertex Rotate Mode	Ctrl+R
Texture Vertex Weld Selected	Ctrl+W
Texture Vertex Target Weld	Ctrl+T
Pan	Ctrl+P
Zoom	Z
Zoom Extents	X
Zoom Extents Selected	Alt+Ctrl+Z
Zoom Region	Ctrl+X
Zoom Selected Elements	Alt+Shift+Ctrl+Z
Zoom to Gizmo	Shift+Spacebar

ActiveShade

Command	Shortcut
Close	Q
Draw Region	D
Render	R
Select Object	S
Toolbar Toggle	Space
Initialize	P
Update	U

Reactor Controller

Command	Shortcut
Create Reaction	Alt+Ctrl+C, C
Delete Reaction	Alt+Ctrl+D, D
Edit State Toggle	Alt+Ctrl+S, E
Set Max Influence	Ctrl+I
Set Min Influence	Alt+I
Set Reaction Value	Alt+Ctrl+V, S

Miscellaneous Shortcuts

In addition to specific shortcuts for the main interface and the dialog boxes, Max provides several general shortcuts that can be used in many different places.

General Shortcuts

Command	Shortcut
Numeric Expression Evaluator	Ctrl+N when a spinner field is selected
Cut value	Ctrl+X
Copy value	Ctrl+C
Paste value	Ctrl+V
Apply settings	Enter
Highlight next text field	Tab
Highlight previous text field	Shift+Tab
Highlight any text field	Double-click current value
Nudge selection	Arrow keys
Display quadmenus	Right-click
Display First Tab	Alt+1
Help	F1

✦   ✦   ✦

Exclusive Bible Plug-Ins

This book's CD-ROM comes with several free plug-ins for 3ds max that you can use free of charge. They are included in the Plug-ins/ Furious Research Plug-Ins directory.

This appendix describes how to install the plug-ins and gives a brief description of how to use each one.

Installing the Plug-Ins

Before you can use the plug-ins, you need to install them. The installation procedure is fairly straightforward.

To install the plug-ins from the CD-ROM, follow these steps:

1. Insert the disc into the CD-ROM drive. Locate the plug-in files in the Plug-ins/Furious Research Plug-ins directory on the CD-ROM.

2. Select all the plug-in files and copy them to the plugins directory where you've installed Max. For example, if Max is on your computer in the directory, C:/3dsmax5, then you will need to copy the plug-in files to C:/3dsmax5/plugins.

3. After the plug-in files are copied to the plugins directory, you need to restart Max before the plug-ins are available.

Using the Plug-In Manager

Another useful way to gain access to plug-ins is with the Plug-in Manager. You can open this window interface with Max and load plug-in components without having to move the plug-in files or restart Max.

To load plug-ins using the Plug-in Manager, follow these steps:

1. Choose Customize ⇨ Plug-in Manger to open the Plug-in Manager.

   The manager lists all the currently available plug-ins.

2. Right-click in the dialog box and select Load New Plug-in from the pop-up menu.

   A file dialog box opens.

3. In the file dialog box, locate the /Plug-ins/Furious Research Plug-ins directory on the CD-ROM.

4. Select the plug-in files that you want to install and click the Open button.

This will load the plug-ins and list them in the Plug-in Manager dialog box.

Caution　If you find the plug-ins in the list, the Full Path lists the path to your CD-ROM. The CD-ROM must be accessible if you want to use this plug-in. To avoid this situation, copy the plug-ins to your hard drive first.

About the Plug-Ins

This section provides a brief overview of each plug-in and gives you an idea of what you can do with it. These plug-ins work like many of the other features in Max. Reading about similar features in the related chapters will be helpful.

3D stereogram render effect

You can use this plug-in to create 3D stereographic images, such as the one shown in Figure C-1. (If you stare at it for a while and let your eyes relax somewhat, you begin to see an actual three-dimensional image come out of the page.)

Cross-Reference　If you need help using one of the following render effect plug-ins, be sure to review Chapter 36, "Using Render Elements and Render Effects," which discusses render effects in detail.

When you add this render effect to your scene you can choose whether to use random dots for the background color or whether to use a tiled image. It may take some experimentation to get the best effect if you use a bitmap to tile the background, but in general the best bitmaps to use are small ones (so that they get tiled 8 to 10 times across the page) with a fair amount of detail that isn't too distracting. If you choose to use random dots, you can configure the plug-in to use any three colors of your choice.

Figure C-1: Image generated by the 3D stereogram render effect

TV Image render effect

The TV Image render effect plug-in simulates television-quality images, as shown in Figure C-2.

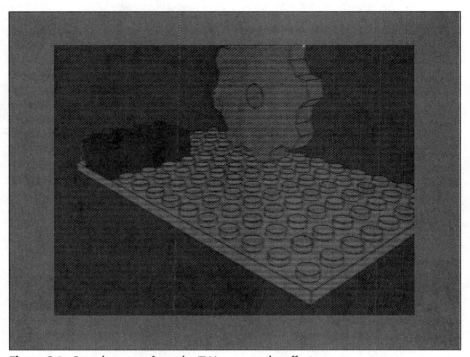

Figure C-2: Sample output from the TV Image render effect

Television images are not very sharp, and this plug-in simulates this effect as well as the interlaced lines (light and dark lines) found especially in older TVs. You can control how blurred the image is, the intensity of the interlacing, and the quantity and intensity of static using the plug-ins rollout.

Sketch render effect

You may have noticed that the objects in Figure C-2 were outline drawings instead of normal objects. You can accomplish this effect using the Sketch render effect plug-in. Instead of making your scene look more realistic, it reduces detail and color depth and outlines everything in the black lines typical of cartoons or sketches.

Cross-Reference This plug-in is similar in function to the Paint and Ink materials covered in Chapter 20, "Using Material Maps."

The rollout for this render effect includes three options for controlling the colors of your scene. By default, the plug-in won't adjust the colors at all, though you can have it render in black and white "coloring book" style or a flat shading so it looks more like a cartoon.

The Crease Angle option specifies how sharply two faces of an object can meet before the plug-in draws an actual line on their connection edge. The Roughness option lets you control how the plug-in treats irregular surfaces: A lower value means that the plug-in is less likely to sketch a line showing how the surface changes.

Gear primitive

The Gear plug-in adds a new primitive object to Max like those shown in Figure C-3. You can find this primitive (along with the new Brick primitive) in the Construction subcategory of the Create panel after they are installed. To add the primitive to a scene, click on the Gear button and drag in one of the viewports to set its radius. Drag again to set the gear thickness.

Figure C-3: The new Gear plug-in creates more realistic gears.

In the Thickness rollout, you can choose to lock the number of gear teeth so that resizing the gear also resizes the teeth, or you can lock the tooth width so that as the gear is resized, the plug-in adds or removes teeth as needed but always makes them have the same width. This feature is useful if you need to create several gears that fit together — just choose a tooth width and create as many gears as you need. Because they all share a common tooth width, they all fit together nicely.

This version of the plug-in also has a parameter that lets you adjust the taper and set the height of the gear teeth from extremely blocky to extremely pointed or anywhere in between. This gives you much more realistic-looking gears and makes two gears interlock better as well.

Brick primitive

This plug-in adds a new brick primitive to Max's set of primitives. As shown in Figure C-4, this plug-in creates interlocking building bricks (similar to Lego blocks and their various imitations).

Figure C-4: Samples of the Brick primitives

Each brick is accurately proportioned, although you can change the scale to whatever you want in this plug-in's rollout. The Flat check box lets you create thin bricks, and you can use the Detail radio boxes to choose between high and normal detail. In most cases, normal detail is sufficient, but, if you plan to be doing close-up renderings, you might want to use high detail for smoother curves.

Brick Snap plug-in

The Brick Snap plug-in is a helper plug-in that assists you in creating large objects made up of building block primitives. The plug-in provides you with snapping points on bricks that enable you to easily position two bricks so that they accurately "lock" together.

Choose Customize ➪ Grid and Snap Settings to open the Grid and Snap Settings dialog box (or right-click on any of the Snap buttons at the bottom of the Max window), and then choose Construction from the drop-down list on the Snaps tab to bring up the Brick Snap panel. From here, you can choose what parts of a building block you want to be considered snap points. After you choose which parts of the brick are to generate snap points, you need to turn snapping on before Max can actually use the snap points.

Balls and Sticks utility

The Balls and Sticks utility plug-in takes an object and converts it to a balls-and-sticks representation, as shown in Figure C-5. It's an easy way to create models of molecules, although far more interesting applications exist as well.

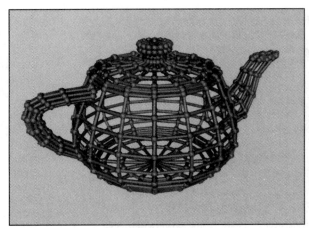

Figure C-5: The Balls and Sticks utility plug-in

The rollout for this plug-in lets you decide whether to create just balls, just sticks, or both. You also have the option to generate a stick for every edge or for visible edges only, and you can choose to have the plug-in remove the original object from the scene after converting it to balls and sticks. The other options in the rollout let you adjust the size of the balls and sticks and the level of detail for each ball or stick.

Note   This plug-in adds a sphere object for each ball and a cylinder object for each stick, which could mean adding thousands of polygons to your scene. Unless you want very high detail, using low numbers for the Ball segments and Stick sides fields in the rollout to reduce scene complexity is best.

Rainbow atmospheric effect

You can use the Rainbow atmospheric effect plug-in to create colorful rainbows. To use this effect, choose Rendering ➪ Environment to open the Environment dialog box. In this dialog box under the Atmosphere rollout, click the Add button and select Rainbow from the Add Atmospheric Effect dialog box. This will add the Parameters rollout to the Environment dialog box where you can add a SphereGizmo to the scene.

Cross-Reference   Chapter 35, "Working with Environments and Atmospheric Effects," covers atmospheric effects in more detail.

With the SphereGizmo selected, you can modify the Rainbow parameters. Under Settings in the Parameters rollout, click the color swatch to choose the base color. This is the color the plug-in uses to get Saturation and Value info (from a color's HSV definition) so you can play around with different colors. I've found that colors with medium to high saturation and low value give good effects. The plug-in ignores the hue component of the color. You can also fiddle with the alpha component and the width of the bow.

Figure C-6 shows some examples of the Rainbow plug-in.

Figure C-6: Rainbow atmospheric effect plug-in

✦   ✦   ✦

What's on the CD-ROM

Throughout the book you'll find many tutorials that help you to understand the principles being discussed. All the example files used to create these tutorials are included on the CD-ROM that came with this book. In addition to these files, you'll find sample 3D models, exclusive Max plug-ins, and several evaluation tools.

This appendix provides you with information on the contents of the CD that accompanies this book. For the latest and greatest information, please refer to the ReadMe file located at the root of the CD.

System Requirements

Make sure that your computer meets the minimum system requirements listed in this section. If your computer doesn't match up to most of these requirements, you may have a problem using the contents of the CD.

For Windows 9x, Windows 2000, Windows NT4 (with SP 4 or later), Windows Me, or Windows XP:

+ PC with a Pentium processor running at 120 Mhz or faster

+ At least 32 MB of total RAM installed on your computer; for best performance, we recommend at least 64 MB

+ A CD-ROM drive

Using the CD with Windows

To install the items from the CD to your hard drive, follow these steps:

1. Insert the CD into your computer's CD-ROM drive.

2. Click Start and choose Run from the menu.

3. Double-click the file called License.txt.

   This file contains the end-user license that you agree to by using the CD. When you are finished reading the license, close the program, most likely NotePad, that displayed the file.

4. Double-click the file called Readme.txt.

This file contains instructions about installing the software from this CD. It might be helpful to leave this text file open while you are using the CD.

5. Double-click the folder for the software you are interested in.

Be sure to read the descriptions of the programs in the next section of this appendix (much of this information also shows up in the Readme file). These descriptions give you more precise information about the programs' folder names and about finding and running the installer program.

6. Find the file called Setup.exe, or Install.exe, or something similar, and double-click on that file.

The program's installer will walk you through the process of setting up your new software.

What's on the CD

The following sections provide a summary of the software and other materials you'll find on the CD.

Author-created materials

The example files used in the tutorials throughout the book are included in the "Chapter Example Files" directory. Within this directory are separate subdirectories for each chapter. In each of the chapter directories is a zip file containing the example files for that chapter. Supplemental files such as models and images are also included in these zip files. Animated scenes include a rendered AVI file of the animation.

Plug-ins

To extend the functionality of Max, the "Plug-Ins" directory on the CD-ROM includes many full-function plug-ins. All of these plug-ins have been compiled for the latest version of 3ds max.

The "Furious Research Plug-Ins" directory contains plug-ins developed exclusively for this book. You can install these plugs-in using the Plug-In Manager or by copying them to the plug-ins directory where Max is installed.

Note   For more information on these plug-ins, see Appendix C, "Exclusive Bible Plug-Ins."

3D models

Two companies have provided sample 3D models. Many of these models were used in the tutorials, and you can find the complete set of models in the "3D Models" directory.

Table D-1 lists the model companies and the models that are included on this book's CD-ROM.

Table D-1: 3D Models

Model Company	3D Models
3D Toons Shop	Ant, Deer, Moon
Zygote Media	Basketball, Basketball Hoop, Balloons, Butterfly, Ceiling Fan, Dart, Dartboard, Dolphin, Dragonfly, Firecracker, Frog, Lamp, Fireplace, Hammer, Houseplant, Ice Cream Cone, Old Tree, Park Bench, Place Setting, Post Box, Rake, Rocket, Roses in Vase, Soda Can, Spider, Step Ladder, Sword, Table and Chairs, Turtle, TV, Umbrella, Zygote Man

Product demos

A 30-day trial version of 3ds max Version 5 has been included on the CD-ROM. You can find it in the "Product Demos" directory.

Shareware programs are fully functional, trial versions of copyrighted programs. If you like particular programs, register with their authors for a nominal fee and receive licenses, enhanced versions, and technical support. *Freeware programs* are copyrighted games, applications, and utilities that are free for personal use. Unlike shareware, these programs do not require a fee or provide technical support. *GNU software* is governed by its own license, which is included inside the folder of the GNU product. See the GNU license for more details.

Trial, demo, or evaluation versions are usually limited either by time or functionality (such as being unable to save projects). Some trial versions are very sensitive to system date changes. If you alter your computer's date, the programs will "time out" and will no longer be functional.

Troubleshooting

If you have difficulty installing or using any of the materials on the companion CD, try the following solutions:

✦ **Turn off any anti-virus software that you may have running.** Installers sometimes mimic virus activity and can make your computer incorrectly believe that it is being infected by a virus. (Be sure to turn the anti-virus software back on later.)

✦ **Close all running programs.** The more programs you're running, the less memory is available to other programs. Installers also typically update files and programs; if you keep other programs running, installation may not work properly.

✦ **Check the ReadMe:** Please refer to the ReadMe file located at the root of the CD-ROM for the latest product information at the time of publication.

If you still have trouble with the CD, please call the Customer Care phone number: (800) 762-2974. Outside the United States, call 1 (317) 572-3994. You can also contact Customer Service by e-mail at techsupdum@wiley.com. Wiley Publishing, Inc. will provide technical support only for installation and other general quality control items; for technical support on the applications themselves, consult the program's vendor or author.

✦   ✦   ✦

Index

Continued

Continued

Continued

Continued

M

Continued

Continued

Continued

Wiley Publishing, Inc.
End-User License Agreement

READ THIS. You should carefully read these terms and conditions before opening the software packet(s) included with this book "Book". This is a license agreement "Agreement" between you and Wiley Publishing, Inc. "WPI". By opening the accompanying software packet(s), you acknowledge that you have read and accept the following terms and conditions. If you do not agree and do not want to be bound by such terms and conditions, promptly return the Book and the unopened software packet(s) to the place you obtained them for a full refund.

1. **License Grant.** WPI grants to you (either an individual or entity) a nonexclusive license to use one copy of the enclosed software program(s) (collectively, the "Software" solely for your own personal or business purposes on a single computer (whether a standard computer or a workstation component of a multi-user network). The Software is in use on a computer when it is loaded into temporary memory (RAM) or installed into permanent memory (hard disk, CD-ROM, or other storage device). WPI reserves all rights not expressly granted herein.

2. **Ownership.** WPI is the owner of all right, title, and interest, including copyright, in and to the compilation of the Software recorded on the disk(s) or CD-ROM "Software Media". Copyright to the individual programs recorded on the Software Media is owned by the author or other authorized copyright owner of each program. Ownership of the Software and all proprietary rights relating thereto remain with WPI and its licensers.

3. **Restrictions On Use and Transfer.**

    (a) You may only (i) make one copy of the Software for backup or archival purposes, or (ii) transfer the Software to a single hard disk, provided that you keep the original for backup or archival purposes. You may not (i) rent or lease the Software, (ii) copy or reproduce the Software through a LAN or other network system or through any computer subscriber system or bulletin- board system, or (iii) modify, adapt, or create derivative works based on the Software.

    (b) You may not reverse engineer, decompile, or disassemble the Software. You may transfer the Software and user documentation on a permanent basis, provided that the transferee agrees to accept the terms and conditions of this Agreement and you retain no copies. If the Software is an update or has been updated, any transfer must include the most recent update and all prior versions.

4. **Restrictions on Use of Individual Programs.** You must follow the individual requirements and restrictions detailed for each individual program in the What's on the CD-ROM appendix of this Book. These limitations are also contained in the individual license agreements recorded on the Software Media. These limitations may include a requirement that after using the program for a specified period of time, the user must pay a registration fee or discontinue use. By opening the Software packet(s), you will be agreeing to abide by the licenses and restrictions for these individual programs that are detailed in the What's on the CD-ROM appendix and on the Software Media. None of the material on this Software Media or listed in this Book may ever be redistributed, in original or modified form, for commercial purposes.

5. Limited Warranty.

(a) WPI warrants that the Software and Software Media are free from defects in materials and workmanship under normal use for a period of sixty (60) days from the date of purchase of this Book. If WPI receives notification within the warranty period of defects in materials or workmanship, WPI will replace the defective Software Media.

(b) **WPI AND THE AUTHOR OF THE BOOK DISCLAIM ALL OTHER WARRANTIES, EXPRESS OR IMPLIED, INCLUDING WITHOUT LIMITATION IMPLIED WARRANTIES OF MERCHANTABILITY AND FITNESS FOR A PARTICULAR PURPOSE, WITH RESPECT TO THE SOFTWARE, THE PROGRAMS, THE SOURCE CODE CONTAINED THEREIN, AND/OR THE TECHNIQUES DESCRIBED IN THIS BOOK. WPI DOES NOT WARRANT THAT THE FUNCTIONS CONTAINED IN THE SOFTWARE WILL MEET YOUR REQUIREMENTS OR THAT THE OPERATION OF THE SOFTWARE WILL BE ERROR FREE.**

(c) This limited warranty gives you specific legal rights, and you may have other rights that vary from jurisdiction to jurisdiction.

6. Remedies.

(a) WPI's entire liability and your exclusive remedy for defects in materials and workmanship shall be limited to replacement of the Software Media, which may be returned to WPI with a copy of your receipt at the following address: Software Media Fulfillment Department, Attn.: *3ds max 5™ Bible*, Wiley Publishing, Inc., 10475 Crosspoint Blvd., Indianapolis, IN 46256, or call 1-800-762-2974. Please allow four to six weeks for delivery. This Limited Warranty is void if failure of the Software Media has resulted from accident, abuse, or misapplication. Any replacement Software Media will be warranted for the remainder of the original warranty period or thirty (30) days, whichever is longer.

(b) In no event shall WPI or the author be liable for any damages whatsoever (including without limitation damages for loss of business profits, business interruption, loss of business information, or any other pecuniary loss) arising from the use of or inability to use the Book or the Software, even if WPI has been advised of the possibility of such damages.

(c) Because some jurisdictions do not allow the exclusion or limitation of liability for consequential or incidental damages, the above limitation or exclusion may not apply to you.

7. U.S. Government Restricted Rights. Use, duplication, or disclosure of the Software for or on behalf of the United States of America, its agencies and/or instrumentalities "U.S. Government" is subject to restrictions as stated in paragraph (c)(1)(ii) of the Rights in Technical Data and Computer Software clause of DFARS 252.227-7013, or subparagraphs (c) (1) and (2) of the Commercial Computer Software - Restricted Rights clause at FAR 52.227-19, and in similar clauses in the NASA FAR supplement, as applicable.

8. General. This Agreement constitutes the entire understanding of the parties and revokes and supersedes all prior agreements, oral or written, between them and may not be modified or amended except in a writing signed by both parties hereto that specifically refers to this Agreement. This Agreement shall take precedence over any other documents that may be in conflict herewith. If any one or more provisions contained in this Agreement are held by any court or tribunal to be invalid, illegal, or otherwise unenforceable, each and every other provision shall remain in full force and effect.